THE GENTRIFICATION READER

Gentrification remains a subject of heated debate in the public realm as well as scholarly and policy circles. This reader brings together the classic writings and contemporary literature that has helped to define the field, changed the direction of how it is studied and illustrated the points of conflict and consensus that are distinctive of gentrification research.

Covering everything from the theories of gentrification through to analysis of state-led policies and community resistance to those policies, this is an unparalleled collection of influential writings on a contentious contemporary issue.

With insightful commentary from the editors, who are themselves internationally renowned experts in the field, this is essential reading for students of urban planning, geography, urban studies, sociology and housing studies.

Loretta Lees is Professor of Human Geography at King's College London, UK.

Tom Slater is Lecturer in Human Geography at the School of Geosciences, University of Edinburgh, UK.

Elvin Wyly is Associate Professor of Geography at the University of British Columbia, Canada.

The partner text to this reader is Gentrification, also by Loretta Lees, Tom Slater and Elvin Wyly.

The gentrification of urban areas has accelerated across the globe to become a central force in urban development, and it is a topic that has attracted a great deal of interest in both the academy and the popular press. Gentrification is the first comprehensive text written on the subject. International in scope, interdisciplinary in approach, and featuring a wealth of case studies, the book demonstrates how gentrification has grown from a small-scale urban process, pioneered by a liberal new middle class, to become a mass-produced 'gentrification blueprint' around the world.

The cover illustration is a collage on wood titled 'Gentrification' by New York City artist Stevenson Estimé. The collage plays off problematic stereotypes of race and class – white yuppies and black gangbangers – but it captures well a number of the contemporary features about 'gentrification', in particular it symbolises the process as 'the new urban colonialism' and the white Anglo appropriation of urban space.

The Gentrification Reader

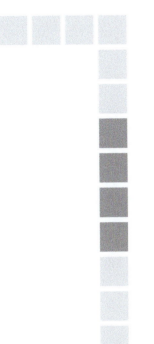

Edited by

Loretta Lees

Tom Slater

and

Elvin Wyly

Routledge
Taylor & Francis Group

LONDON AND NEW YORK

First published 2010
by Routledge
2 Park Square, Milton Park, Abingdon, Oxon, OX14 4RN

Simultaneously published in the USA and Canada
by Routledge
711 Third Avenue, New York, NY 10017

Routledge is an imprint of the Taylor & Francis Group, an informa business

Typeset in Amasis MT Light and Akzidenz Grotesk by Glyph International Ltd.

British Library Cataloguing in Publication Data
A catalogue record for this book is available from the British Library

Library of Congress Cataloging-in-Publication Data
The gentrification reader/edited by Loretta Lees, Tom Slater and Elvin Wyly.
  p. cm.
Includes bibliographical references and index.
1. Gentrification. I. Lees, Loretta. II. Slater, Tom, III. Wyly, Elvin K.
HT170.G465 2010
307.3′416–dc22   2009032198

ISBN 13: 978-0-415-54839-7 (hbk)
ISBN 13: 978-0-415-54840-3 (pbk)

Printed and bound by CPI Group (UK) Ltd, Croydon, CR0 4YY

Contents

Plate 1 **Gentrify This!! By graffiti artist Banksy, Leake Street just behind Waterloo Station, London.** Photograph by Jon Shahab.

poorest residents in the city (see also Zorbaugh's 1929, *The Gold Coast and the Slum*). But where Park and Burgess believed that the affluent would be at the forefront of moves out of the city, gentrification challenged the historical specificity of these traditional ecological models of residential location (see Lees, Slater and Wyly, 2008: xvi) in that the affluent were seen to move back to the city through a process of gentrification. The 'back to the city' myth was later shattered by gentrification researchers, who found that gentrifiers had mostly moved from elsewhere in the city and had instead chosen not to move out to the suburbs. Neil Smith's (1979) seminal paper: 'Toward a theory of gentrification: a back to the city movement by capital, not people' illustrates this well (see Chapter 9 of this Reader).

Gentrification began as a small-scale urban process, pioneered by a new liberal middle class but in which the state was involved from the beginning, to become a mass-produced, state-led process around the world, what Neil Smith calls 'a global urban strategy'. Its history, its progress from being a marginal urban process to becoming a mainstream urban process, is an interesting one given that many of the pro-gentrification policies today draw on the ideologies of pioneer gentrifiers (see Lees, 2008). Before looking a little more at that history we begin by offering a useful definition of gentrification.

DEFINING GENTRIFICATION

> Gentrification – the transformation of a working-class or vacant area of the central city into middle-class residential or commercial use.
>
> (Lees, Slater and Wyly, 2008: xv)

We have provided detailed summaries of the various definitions of gentrification in the core text that is the partner of this Reader – *Gentrification* (Lees, Slater and Wyly, 2008). We do not want to rehearse these here and, more to the point, Chapter 1 of this Reader considers definitions of gentrification. Rather we begin here with a recent descriptive summary of the process of gentrification, one that also outlines well our political stance on this process:

> Gentrification, to put it bluntly and simply, involves both the exploitation of the economic value of real estate and the treatment of local residents as objects rather than the subjects of upgrading. Even though population movement is a common feature of cities, gentrification is specifically the replacement of a less affluent group by a wealthier social group – a definition which relates gentrification to class. Whether a result of city council policies or real estate pressures, gentrification stands in contrast to earlier attempts to improve deprived neighbourhoods by addressing the built environment, the central objective of urban renewal up until the 1970s. More recently, the betterment of deprived neighbourhoods has taken a completely different form as the improvement of living conditions is no longer considered the task of the state ('to enlighten the masses'), but rather a side effect of the development and emancipation of the higher and middle classes. The state seems to have acknowledged its inability to influence the welfare of its residents directly and has left that task to the workings of the supposedly objective agency of the market. Gentrification has become a means of solving social malaise, not by providing solutions to unemployment, poverty, or broken homes, but by transferring the problem elsewhere, out of sight, and consequently also geographically marginalising the urban poor and ensuring their economic location and political irrelevance.
>
> (Berg, Kaminer, Schoonderbeek and Zonneveld, 2009 –
Houses in Transformation: Interventions in European Gentrification)

Unlike other Readers which do not offer up a favoured view of their subject, in this one we do, because the Reader is partnered with a text that is undeniably political and challenges its 'readers to think critically about the gentrification process' (Lees, Slater and Wyly, 2008: xxii) and to weigh up arguments and debates. Although we advocate 'a critical geography of gentrification, one that follows a social justice agenda and one that is focused on resisting gentrification where necessary' (p. xxiii) this does not mean that we have excluded writings that we disagree with; on the contrary, it is important to include these writings to demonstrate the academic battles (theoretical, conceptual and political) that have been fought over gentrification.

Following Clark (2005) we argue that a definition of gentrification should include the root causes of gentrification, which he sees to be 'commodification of space, polarised power relations, and a dominance of vision oversight characteristic of "the vagrant sovereign"' (p. 261; see Chapter 4 in the Reader). As we state in Lees, Slater and Wyly (2008) the term needs to be elastic enough to allow new processes of gentrification which may yet emerge to be drawn under its umbrella, for as Smith (2009: 17) says: 'it is hardly surprising that over nearly half a century the process of gentrification has transformed significantly .... the larger urban-global context is part of the story in the sense that the contemporary city is very different from that of the 1960s'. And at the same time a definition needs to be able to make political statements.

Davidson and Lees (2005) have put forward the following definition of gentrification, a definition that focused on the core elements of the process, one that is not attached to a particular landscape or context – allowing other forms of gentrification (such as rural, etc., see Chapter 32 in the Reader) currency:

1. reinvestment of capital
2. social upgrading of locale by incoming high income groups
3. landscape change
4. direct or indirect displacement of low income groups.

GENTRIFICATION – ITS HISTORIES AND TRAJECTORIES

The writings that have been selected for inclusion in this Reader are culled from nearly a half century of monographs, journal articles and edited book chapters on the process of gentrification. The time line ranges from 1964, when the British sociologist Ruth Glass was first seen to use the term 'gentrification' in a book about urban and social change in London, to recent writings on the process. This time line follows the histories and trajectories of this process as it moved from classic or first wave gentrification to second wave gentrification, to third wave or post-recession gentrification and into a fourth wave of gentrification. The time line also follows the geographical expansion of gentrification beyond the inner city to rural areas and the suburbs, and from Anglo-American cities to cities all around the world, including Less Developed World cities and ex-socialist/communist cities. Of particular relevance given the current global economic recession the time line also includes debates about the end of gentrification, especially those that surfaced during the recession of the early 1990s (see Chapter 7). These debates have some resonance for thinking about both the fate of gentrification in the current recession (see Lees, 2009) and the future of gentrification (see Lees, Slater and Wyly, 2008: Chapter 7). Smith (2009: 25) has some useful words on this:

> Yet the global economic recession that set in during 2007–2008, triggered by the home-mortgage melt-down in the US and exploding in the global debt and financial markets, will have predictable effects. Before the 1980s gentrification was effectively counter-cyclical, or at least unperturbed by economic cycles, but as it became more systemic, gentrification became highly susceptible to the cyclical movements of the wider market. A lot hinges on the economic power taken by, or allowed to, the state. The contentious 2008 bailout of Wall Street marks a denouement of a neo-liberal ideology, if not necessarily neo-liberalism per se. The state has finally revealed itself as a central puppeteer of neo-liberalism. Although not itself a gentrification measure, this and related international bailouts will have the effect – sooner or later – of enhancing the gentrification market.

One final point is worth mentioning about the histories and trajectories of gentrification. Caroline Mills (see Chapter 16 in the Reader) was already arguing that the process of gentrification had gone mainstream back in 1988:

> ... Just as blue jeans became the international uniform of the new class ... so gentrified housing became its international neighbourhood ... Ironically, as blue jeans turned into a new conformity, so does the landscape distinctiveness of the gentrified neighbourhood.
>
> (p. 186)

Yet it was not really until the late 1990s/early 2000s that gentrification was viewed in both academia and the wider world as a mainstream urban process. The result of this is that authors are only now beginning to realize that to some degree the original distinction between the marginal process of gentrification and the hegemonic process of suburbanization has begun to blur:

> Gentrification at the center and sprawl at the edge have been flipsides of the same coin. In a typically paradoxical situation, no matter how much the new, more affluent residents profess to like the 'gritty' urban character of the place, so different in their minds to the subdivision of the far suburbs, what makes the neighbourhood attractive today are less the things that are traditionally urban but those that are not. The most important of these are sharply lowered population densities, fewer poor residents, less manufacturing activity, and the things that the Lower East Side finally shares with suburbs: reliable plumbing, supermarkets with good produce, and a substantial cohort of middle-class residents.
>
> (Bruegmann, 2006: 4)

New forms of gentrification, such as new-build gentrification and super-gentrification, reveal these suburban slippages into gentrification – from the suburbanized back yards of super-gentrifiers homes in Brooklyn Heights, New York City (see Lees, 2003) to the gated developments and fearful relationship that new-build gentrifiers in Docklands, London, have to the socially mixed environment of inner London (Butler, 2007). Butler (2007: 177) argues that the aspirations of the new-build gentrifiers that he interviewed in London's Docklands echo not those of the gentrifier but those of the classic 'suburbanizer' – 'to be near but not in or of the city'. This just serves to reinforce the opening point about gentrification as a form of neo-colonialism. Future work on gentrification needs to be much more attuned to the fact that gentrification is now mainstream and to the idiosyncracies of this fact.

The Gentrification Reader and the core text *Gentrification*

This Reader is linked to the core text – *Gentrification* – which we published in 2008. The best way to describe these two books is as partners – not strictly married but designed to live side by side with each other, each enhancing and embracing the other. Although designed to be partners both of these books are also free standing.

Whereas *Gentrification* offers a comprehensive text on the forty year plus history of gentrification, outlines the main theoretical debates, and provides detailed case studies as exemplars, *The Gentrification Reader* allows the reader to consider relevant essays on gentrification that are discussed or referred to in the text book. Unlike many of the Readers that are published these days we have chosen to reprint the vast majority of the chosen readings in full. Only a handful of the forty readings are excerpts. As a result, readers do not have to go off and search for the originals to get the full journal article or book chapter, as such this is an invaluable collection for any course or research on gentrification.

Our editorial goals are to present a collection of the most original, the most important, the most cited, the most provocative, the most useful, the most informative, writings on gentrification. We have chosen classic writings that moved debates on gentrification forward, controversial writings associated with the so-called 'gentrification battleground', and writings that have forced many observers to think more deeply and indeed politically about this urban process. Given word limits we feel that we provide here as comprehensive a Reader as possible on gentrification. While word limits forced us to omit many important readings, we have referred to those contributions in various parts of the book, and in Box 1 we provide a list of monographs and edited collections on gentrification for our readers to survey. And there will always be some who will contest our choices. It is also worth pointing out that the readings here were all published in English. There are of course many writings on gentrification that have been published in French, German, Spanish and indeed in a large number of other languages too. It is very important that these non-English language accounts are heard by English speakers and vice versa, but such a task is beyond the remit of this Reader.

Along with academic geographers the Reader includes contributions by sociologists, anthropologists, urban planners, policy analysts and those who write more broadly in urban studies and housing studies. This is in recognition that gentrification is an interdisciplinary field. As such the Reader should have broad appeal across the breadth of the social sciences. This interdisciplinarity is important because it shows the reader how geographers have learnt from sociologists and vice versa, and how a very specific subject – that of gentrification – has allowed different disciplines to talk to each other and blurred these disciplinary boundaries. The spatialization (drawing on ideas about space and spatiality from geography) of sociological accounts of gentrification, as seen in Butler with Robson (2003), illustrates this well.

One thing that we strive to do in this Reader is to address some of the limitations of the core text *Gentrification*, in particular we seek to consider the issue and ideas about displacement in more detail. Displacement received much less attention than it should have in our core text (see Lees, Slater and Wyly, 2008: 217–221), we address this imbalance through Part 4 of the Reader, which focuses explicitly on displacement. In so doing we reprint Peter Marcuse's seminal work on displacement (Chapter 26), work that is of increasing relevance today, especially in the recent debates over gentrification versus reurbanization (see Rérat, Söderström and Piguet, 2010). In Chapter 7 of the Reader we also add to and update our discussion of resisting gentrification reprinting (Chapter 37) and revisiting (via Kathe Newman and Elvin Wyly, Chapter 38) Chester Hartman's 'The right to stay put' and excerpting the conclusion of a very long document by The Urban Institute (2006) – *In the face of gentrification: case studies of local efforts to mitigate displacement* (our final chapter 40). We also reprint in Chapter 7 an article that has stimulated discussion about how academics research and write about gentrification (Tom Slater's *The eviction of critical perspectives from gentrification research*, Chapter 39) indeed how some of the writing on gentrification itself has become gentrified!

Finally, it is worth noting that both the core text *Gentrification* and *The Gentrification Reader* largely (but not completely) refer to Anglo-American cases of gentrification and theories and conceptualizations based on Anglo-American experiences. The majority of the readings are by British, American and Canadian authors. One reason for this is that these three countries are where our expertise is mainly based; second, the vast majority of the gentrification literature has been published in these countries; third, all of the classic and/or most cited writings on gentrification come from these countries; fourth, it is beyond the scope of these two texts to translate literature from other languages – although we recognize that this is an important task and should be done in the future. For those of you who seek non Anglo-American writings that are published in English – we provide detailed further reading lists after each part and section. Indeed the global nature of gentrification today has meant that many edited books and journal special issues on gentrification now include work from around the globe – China, Russia, Australia, New Zealand, South Africa, Brazil, Mexico, old and new Europe, and many other places too.

THE STRUCTURE

The structure of this Reader does not simply mirror that of the core text *Gentrification* – rather it has been designed to emphasize, and add to, particular arguments and debates that we outline in that book and which we feel are the most significant since authorship on gentrification first began. Furthermore as pointed out above we have also sought to address a couple of the limitations of *Gentrification* in *The Gentrification Reader*.

The Reader contains forty readings (chapters) on gentrification; each of the seven thematic parts of the Reader includes four readings, although Part 3 on Explaining/Theorizing Gentrification has been subdivided into four sections, A through D, with four readings in each.

Each part and section of *The Gentrification Reader* has been provided with an introductory overview that situates the key arguments and contributions that the readings have made in a broad scholarly context, as well as providing background information on the ideas and the authors. Given that some 'big' names are associated with the theoretical battles that raged over gentrification – telling our readers about the authors should help them to understand where these theorists are coming from. Moreover, a little biographical detail humanizes these 'big' names – we provide this biographical detail in boxes 2–6, in which some authors also reflect on the article of theirs which we have reprinted.

The chapters in the Reader are arranged to lead the reader through old and new ideas on gentrification in a logical manner.

Parts 1 and 2 of the Reader, 'Defining Gentrification' and 'Stage Models of Gentrification' respectively, are linked to Chapter 1 of the core text *Gentrification* – on the birth of gentrification and to Chapter 5 – Towards a new stage model of gentrification (pp. 173–185). These readings demonstrate how the definition of gentrification has changed over time and the political challenges of defining this process as it moves through time and space. The writings on stage models illustrate the dynamism of this process over different periods of time, and in particular they show the initial gut feelings of some authors that this process was going against the grain of 'normal' urban filtering and that it would not last. The final reading in Part 2 by Jason Hackworth and Neil Smith shows how gentrification fought against recession and marginality and came out on top. Perhaps there are lessons to be learned here by the doom mongers who are speculating yet again on the end of gentrification in the current recession.

Part 3 of the Reader focuses on the most influential explanations and theorizations of gentrification from the literature. This has been subdivided into four sections, A to D. Section A on Production Side Explanations links directly to Chapter 2 of the core text – Producing Gentrification. Here production or supply-side arguments are made to explain the emergence of the process of gentrification. The focus is on the Marxist explanatory vehicle – the rent gap, a theory (hinged in uneven development theory) put forward by Neil Smith back in 1979. The rent gap shows how disinvestment opened up the inner city for the reinvestment of capital. Critiques and attempts to re-establish the rent gap are also included in the readings.

Section B on Consumption Side Explanations in the Reader is linked to Chapter 3 in *Gentrification* on Consumption Explanations. Here gentrifiers themselves are seen to be significant players in the production of gentrification through their consumption preferences. The politics, desires, aesthetic ideologies, and lifestyles of this new middle class of gentrifiers is the focus of the readings. This section shows how a group of middle class individuals began to identify with each other and with a series of values connected with history and heritage that gave their 'class' a 'place' in the changing urban social order.

The fact that we have used the word 'side', as in production and consumption *side* explanations, should alert the reader to the different stances or positions that authors have taken on the process of gentrification. These different stances are often allied to Marxist readings of the process versus Humanist or Postmodernist readings of the process. It was these different positions that led to what some have called the 'gentrification battleground' or the 'gentrification stalemate', a state of play demonstrated by the fact of a section titled 'The problems with production explanations' at the end of Chapter 2 (pp. 74–80) in the core text and in 'The problems with consumption explanations' at the end of Chapter 3 (pp. 121–123) in the core text. David Ley's reply to Neil Smith in Chapter 10 of the Reader illustrates this battle and stalemate. But by the early 1990s gentrification researchers were fed up with this battleground and wanted to move beyond this stalemate, for they believed that both explanations were complementary. Amongst others Lees (1994) wanted to transcend the oppositional thinking between Marxist economic analysis (on production) and postmodern cultural analysis (on consumption). She used the notion of complementarity as part of a dialectic in which she could specify the contradictions between the two, with the aim of transcending the contradictions between the two bodies of theory so as to improve our understanding of gentrification. She was clear:

> ... I do not want to choose between economic Marxism and cultural postmodernism; I want the stability of the former and the instability of the latter. I want to utilize a productive tension between the two.
>
> (p. 138)

For Lees (1994), and others, the realization that both explanations were complementary solved the problem of 'big names', whose work she respected, battling each other.

Section C reprints some of this literature that argued for explanations of gentrification to move beyond the production versus consumption stalemate and beyond singular truth claims. As Beauregard (1986: 35) argued: '... there can be no single theory of an invariant gentrification process ... different theoretical arguments must be combined in a fashion compatible with the specific instances of gentrification that we wish to explain'. Geographer Damaris Rose's 'Rethinking Gentrification: beyond the uneven development of Marxist urban theory', published in the very first volume of *Environment and Planning D: Society and Space* was one of the first articles to seek a postmodern view or anti-metanarrative stance on gentrification (see Chapter 17 in the Reader). Sociologist Sharon Zukin sought to combine production and consumption arguments and her reading here (in Chapter 18) is related to her now classic 1982 text: 'Loft Living: Culture and Capital in Urban Change'. The papers by Chris Hamnett and Eric Clark (Chapters 19 and 20 respectively) reveal the struggles that continued over the explanation of gentrification.

Section D reprints readings which show how debates over the explanation of gentrification progressed as issues not just of class, but also of gender, sexuality, and race/ethnicity, as these cleavages began to find increasing currency. A sample paper from each is included in this section of the Reader, and we finish with a more recent paper (by Cahill) that illustrates for us how the literature has moved on so that issues of class, gender, sexuality, race/ethnicity are considered not just with respect to the gentrifiers but also to the gentrified. Papers like this heed the call made in Slater, Curran and Lees (2004) to include the voices of non-gentrifiers in gentrification research.

Part 4 of the Reader focuses on one of the most negative and problematic results of gentrification – that of displacement. The readings selected here are a mix of conceptual statements about types of displacement to those that have sought to collate empirical evidence on displacement – a very difficult and often flawed task. The final reading by Freeman and Braconi (Chapter 28) led The USA Today to claim that 'Gentrification is a boost for everyone' (see Lees, Slater and Wyly, 2008: 219–220). Freeman and Braconi's conclusion that displacement as a result of gentrification was limited gave fuel to the positive spins on gentrification issued by the state in the US in order to sell their neoliberal agenda of state-led gentrification.

Part 5 of the Reader probably created the most difficult decisions with respect to which readings to include. This part on geographies of gentrification relates to Chapters 4, 5, and 6 of the core text *Gentrification*. By geographies of gentrification we mean: i) those gentrifications that are seen to have occurred outside of the central city, e.g. rural or wilderness gentrification, suburban gentrification and coastal gentrification; ii) those that focus on the spatial scales of gentrification, e.g. global gentrification, global elites, provincial gentrification, metropolitan gentrification, discussions of gentrification throughout the urban hierarchy, as Smith (2009: 19) states 'a new geo-economic competition has arisen between cities of which gentrification is a central strategy'; iii) those that focus on different types of gentrification in the city, e.g. super-gentrification, tourism gentrification, new-build gentrification, studentification; iv) those that focus on comparative work, whether comparing different neighbourhoods, different cities and/or different countries or how theories and concepts about gentrification embedded in a particular context play out in another context (e.g. the emancipatory and revanchist theses on gentrification). As you can see there is much more here than is represented by the four readings – but these should suffice to give our readers a flavour of the different debates here. It is also interesting to note here how different authors have used each others work to trigger progress in the literature on gentrification – for example Lees (2000), Chapter 29 here, drew on earlier work by David Ley (1992, 1996) for her 'geography of gentrification' and in so doing pushed the 'geography of gentrification' higher up the gentrification agenda. And drawing on Lees (2000) Slater (2004) set out to explore the emancipatory and revanchist theses on gentrification outside their immediate place-based theoretical contexts. Studying gentrification, it is important and useful to get a clear sense of where, why and how ideas and work developed.

Part 6 of the Reader relates to Chapters 5 and 6 of the core text, and is particularly important given the fact that, for the most part, gentrification around the world today is state-led through similar yet distinct policy discourses (see Lees and Ley, 2008). The different readings reprinted here look at early work that promoted gentrification as a positive process for urban change that policy makers ought to promote, to writings on the relationship between policy and gentrification. Chapters 34, 35 and 36 are critical of the import of gentrification into policy making and governmental strategies for revitalizing central cities. This work cannot be disentangled from writings on the neo-liberal city, which argue that

> If public housing and middle-class suburban housing were icons of the Keynesian managerialist city, then gentrified neighbourhoods and downtown commercial mega-projects are the icons of the neo-liberal city.
>
> (Hackworth, 2007: 78)

> ... inequitable real estate development in cities is the knife-edge of neoliberal urbanism, reflecting a wider shift toward a more individualist and market-driven political economy in cities. Gentrification, publicly funded projects for private benefit, and the demolition of affordable housing are all part of this knife edge, and all of these are occurring in very different locales.
>
> (Hackworth, 2007: 191–192)

The final part of the Reader, Part 7, reprints writings on resisting gentrification and relates to Chapter 7 (more specifically pp. 246–277) in the core text *Gentrification*. We begin with the classic text from Chester Hartman – 'The right to stay put' (see Chapter 37), then we move onto Newman and Wyly's (2006) discussion of why Hartman's text is still pertinent today and the difficulties of resisting displacement and gentrification. In chapter 39 we reprint a paper that has triggered debate recently (Slater, 2006) over the perspectives of middle class academics (many of whom are gentrifiers themselves) on gentrification, perspectives argued to be soft or pandering to neo-liberal thinking on the city. Food for thought! And finally, in Chapter 40, we finish the Reader with a chapter that summarizes some useful and successful attempts to mitigate displacement and gentrification, examples collated in a study by The Urban Institute. This final reading should make clear that resistance is not dead (contra Hackworth and Smith, 2001); however we must be clear that it is not confined to the United States and Canada either (as Chapter 40 in the Reader and the examples in Chapter 7 of Lees, Slater and Wyly, 2008, might suggest). The Transformer Houses project (Berg, Kaminer, Schoonderbeek and Zonneveld, 2009) looked all over Europe and discovered a significant number of initiatives, projects, positions and strategies that have led to interventions in gentrification. They call attention to the following:

1. Acts of protest or provocation and agitprop. The aim of these projects is to form a consciousness or at least awareness of gentrification, but the strategy deliberately uses shock and provocation.
2. Projects that address radical changes in neighbourhoods that are causing the wholesale demolition of existing houses or the eviction of unwanted residents.
3. The attempt to improve the built environment by involving locals in direct actions and encouraging local responsibility by intervening in or introducing green space.
4. Projects intended to create a local consciousness or to raise awareness of both the historical origins of the neighbourhood and the transformations presently taking place.
5. Projects which attempt to rectify or offer alternative and meaningful public space, usually as a means of forming a community, whether by inserting a social practice or by other means.

Much more detailed research needs to be done on resistance to displacement and gentrification, but reading the examples in Berg, Kaminer, Schoonderbeek and Zonneveld (2009) and Chapter 7 of the Reader is a good first step. Indeed, perhaps it is time to return to, and indeed update, texts like Pile and Keith's (1997) *Geographies of Resistance*, focusing explicitly on gentrification and displacement.

HOW TO USE THIS READER

Before reading the various writings on gentrification in this Reader we suggest that firstly you read through the partner book *Gentrification*. That book and the introductions to the different parts and sections of the Reader should make clear the main debates and issues that surround the process of gentrification. This partnership between a core text and an associated Reader gives these two books a distinct pedagogic value, providing our readers access to a guide on the debates over gentrification and access to the original source material so that students and others can see first-hand how debates have developed over time.

Since the core text and the Reader are designed to be read together we suggest that they are read in seven sittings – either using the seven chapters from the core text or the seven parts of the Reader, neither way is necessarily better given they ought to be read in conjunction with each other.

There are three ways in which the Reader and the partner core text on gentrification may be used as a basic resource for class instruction/lectures:

1. Instructors/lecturers could organize a specific course/unit/module on gentrification around the entirety of the seven parts of the Reader or the seven chapters from the core text. The Reader and the core text have been designed for this. If used for a single course we also recommend designing field trips on the topic of gentrification, showing video documentary footage of gentrification for the remains of the module, and getting students to undertake some of their own research into issues associated with gentrification – quantitative or qualitative – such activities make for a more multi-media, visual, and 'real' introduction to gentrification. Instructors should also utilize the further reading sections from both the Reader and the core text too. The further reading sections at the end of each part and section have been carefully compiled to be as up to date and expansive as possible. In effect they are a set of reading lists that can be recommended to students and other readers as they study the arguments made in the various readings.

2. But the material in the two books can also be used in a more flexible way to construct and organize the material to be used in related courses, be they generic urban geography courses or somewhat more focused courses on, for example, urban regeneration, the contemporary city, the creative class, the neo-liberal city, and so on.

These two options can be combined to provide a more basic introduction to gentrification in general first year courses, followed by semester length classes that develop in-depth analysis of particular issues and themes in the second and subsequent years of study.

After reading both the core text and this Reader students should have a good sense of why the process of gentrification emerged, how definitions of the process have changed over time, what the main theoretical battles were about, how the process has been conceptualized, who the main 'players' have been in the literature and what their particular takes on gentrification have been.

We hope that this Reader will be used rather than simply read.

OUR AUDIENCE

As with our book *Gentrification* this Reader is interdisciplinary and our target audience is wide – both undergraduate and masters students on the following courses (this is by no means an exhaustive list): geography, urban studies, sociology, anthropology, housing studies, policy studies, urban planning and political science. The Reader is also designed to be a useful resource for Ph.D students, academics, researchers, planners, policy makers, community organizers and housing activists with a particular interest in gentrification.

We want *The Gentrification Reader*, like the core text, to speak beyond disciplinary boundaries and the world of universities; as such we have approached it in an interdisciplinary manner and have concentrated on selecting readings that are accessible in style and content. The selection of readings also reinforces our goal of constituting a critical geography of gentrification, one that embraces ordinary experiences and commonsense viewpoints. The Reader should also be attractive to an international readership from around the world, given that gentrification is now the leading edge of global urbanism – its readings are as relevant in Asia, South America, Russia and Africa as they are in Europe and North America.

We hope that these readings will inspire you to study and investigate the process of gentrification further.

REFERENCES

Allen, C. (2008) *Housing Market Renewal and Social Class*. London: Routledge.

Atkinson, R. and Bridge, G. (eds) (2005) *Gentrification in a Global Context: The New Urban Colonialism*, London: Routledge.

Beauregard, R.A. (1986) 'The chaos and complexity of gentrification' in N. Smith and P. Williams (eds) *Gentrification of the City*, London: Allen and Unwin pp. 35–55.

Berg, J.-J., Kaminer, T., Schoonderbeek, M., and Zonneveld, J. (2009) *Houses in Transformation: Interventions in European Gentrification*, NAi Uitgevers/Publishers.

Blair, T. (1997) 'The will to win', ODPM, The Aylesbury Estate, 2 June, 1997 http://archive.cabinetoffice.gov.uk/seu/newsa52f.html?id=400

Bruegmann, R. (2006) *Sprawl: a compact history*, University of Chicago Press.

Butler, T. (2007) 'For gentrification?', *Environment and Planning A*, 39, 1: 162–181.

Butler, T. with Robson, G. (2003) *London Calling: The Middle Classes and the Re-making of Inner London*, Oxford: Berg.

Davidson, M. and Lees, L. (2010) 'New-Build Gentrification: its histories, trajectories, and critical geographies', *Population, Space and Place*.

Davidson, M. and Lees, L. (2005) 'New-build "gentrification" and London's riverside renaissance', *Environment and Planning A, 37*: 1165–1190.

Hackworth, J. (2007) *The Neoliberal City: governance, ideology and development in American urbanism*, London and Ithaca: Cornell University Press.

Lees, L. (2009) 'Urban renaissance in an urban recession: the end of gentrification?', *Environment and Planning A*, 41, 7: 1529–1533.

Lees, L. (2008) 'Gentrification and Social Mixing: Towards an Urban Renaissance?', *Urban Studies*, 45, 12: 2449–2470.

Lees, L. (2003) 'Super-gentrification: the case of Brooklyn Heights, New York City', *Urban Studies*, 40, 12: 2487–2509.

Lees, L. (2000) 'A reappraisal of gentrification: towards a "geography of gentrification"', *Progress in Human Geography*, 24, 3: 389–408.

Lees, L. (1994) 'Rethinking Gentrification: Beyond the Positions of Economics and Culture', *Progress in Human Geography*, 18, 2: 137–150.

Lees, L. and Ley, D. (2008) [guest editors] 'Gentrification and Public Policy', *Urban Studies*, 45, 12.

Ley, D. (1996) *The New Middle Class and the Remaking of the Central City*, Oxford: Oxford University Press.

Ley, D. (1992) 'Gentrification in recession: social change in six Canadian inner-cities', 1981–1986 *Urban Geography*, 13, 3: 230–256.

Pile, S. and Keith, M. (1997) (eds) *Geographies of Resistance*, Routledge: London.

Slater, T. (2004) 'North American gentrification? Revanchist and emancipatory perspectives explored', *Environment and Planning A*, 36, 7: 1191–1213.

Slater, T., Curran, W. and Lees, L. (2004) 'Guest editorial. Gentrification research: new directions and critical scholarship', *Environment and Planning A*, 36, 7: 1141–1150.

Stone, M. (2003) *Social Housing in the UK and US: Evolution, Issues and Prospects*, Centre for Urban and Community Research, Goldsmiths [Online] Available from: www.goldsmiths.ac.uk/cucr/publications

Wacquant, L. (2008) 'Relocating Gentrification: The Working Class, Science and the State in Recent Urban Research', *International Journal of Urban and Regional Research*, 32: 198–205.

Zorbaugh, H. (1929) *The Gold Coast and the Slum: a sociological study of Chicago's Near North Side*, Chicago: Sociological Series, University of Chicago.

Gentrification – its histories and trajectories

The writings that have been selected for inclusion in this Reader are culled from nearly a half century of monograph, journal articles and edited book chapters on the process of gentrification (see Box 1). The time line ranges from 1964, when the British sociologist Ruth Glass was first seen to use the term 'gentrification' in a book about urban and social changes in London, to recent writings.

Box 1   Monographs and Edited Collections on Gentrification

Abu-Lughod, J. (ed.) (1994) *From Urban Village to East Village: The Battle for New York's Lower East Side*, Oxford: Blackwell.

Atkinson, R. (2003) [guest editor] 'The gentry in the city: upward neighbourhood trajectories and gentrification', *Urban Studies*, 40(12).

Atkinson, R. and Bridge, G. (eds) (2005) *Gentrification in a Global Context: The New Urban Colonialism*, London: Routledge.

Avidar, P., Habik, K. and Mulder, D. (2009) *OASE 73: Gentrification*, Rotterdam, Netherlands: NAi Publishers.

Berg, J.-J., Kaminer, T., Schoonderbeek, M. and Zonneveld, J. (2009) *Houses in Transformation: Interventions in European Gentrification*, NAi Uitgevers/Publishers.

Butler, T. (1997) *Gentrification and the Middle Classes*, Aldershot: Ashgate.

Butler, T. with Robson, G. (2003) *London Calling: The Middle Classes and the Remaking of Inner London*, London: Berg.

Butler, T. and Smith, D. (2007) [guest editors] 'Extending gentrification?', *Environment and Planning A*, 39(1).

Caulfield, J. (1994) *City Form and Everyday Life: Toronto's Gentrification and Critical Social Practice*, Toronto: University of Toronto Press.

Clark, E. (1987) *The Rent Gap and Urban Change: Case Studies in Malmo, 1860–1985*, Lund: Lund University Press.

Clay, P. (1979) *Neighborhood Renewal: Middle-Class Resettlement and Incumbent Upgrading in American Neighborhoods*, Lexington, MA: D.C. Heath and Company.

DeSena, J. (2009) *The New Kid on the Block: gentrification and inequality in Brooklyn*, Lexington, MA: Lexington Books.

Freeman, L. (2006) *There Goes The 'Hood: Views of Gentrification from the Ground Up*, Philadelphia: Temple University Press.

Gale, D. E. (1984) *Neighborhood Revitalization and the Postindustrial City: A Multinational Perspective*, Lexington, MA: D.C. Heath and Company.

Glynn, S. (2009) (ed.) *Where the other half lives: lower income housing in a neoliberal world*, Pluto Press: London.

Hamnett, C. (2003) *Unequal City: London in the Global Arena*, London: Routledge.

Hartman, C., Keating, D. and LeGates, R. (1982) *Displacement: How to Fight It*, Washington DC: National Housing Law Project.

Herzfeld, M. (2009) *Evicted from Eternity: The Restructuring of Modern Rome*, Chicago: University of Chicago Press.

Holcomb, H. B. and Beauregard, R. A. (1981) *Revitalizing Cities*, Washington, D.C.: Association of American Geographers.

Imrie, R. and Raco, M. (eds) (2003) *Urban Renaissance? New Labour, Community and Urban Policy*, Bristol: The Policy Press.

Laska, S. and Spain, D. (eds) *Back to the City: Issues in Neighborhood Renovation*, New York: Pergamon.

Lees, L. and Ley, D. (2008) [guest editors] 'Gentrification and public policy', *Urban Studies*, 45(12).

Ley, D. (1996) *The New Middle Class and the Remaking of the Central City*, Oxford: Oxford University Press.

Logan, W. (1985) *The Gentrification of Inner Melbourne*, St Lucia: University of Queensland Press.

Maurrasse, D. (2006) *Listening to Harlem: Gentrification, Community and Business*, New York: Routledge.

Modan, G. (2007) *Turf Wars: Discourse, Diversity and the Politics of Place*, Malden, MA: Oxford.

Muniz, V. (1998) *Resisting Gentrification and Displacement: Voices of the Puerto Rican Women of the Barrio*, New York: Garland Publishing.

Nelson, K. (1988) *Gentrification and Distressed Cities: An Assessment of Trends in Intrametropolitan Migration*, Madison: University of Wisconsin Press.

Palen, J. and London, B. (eds) (1984) *Gentrification, Displacement and Neighborhood Revitalization*, Albany: State University of New York Press.

Pattillo, M. (2007) *Black on the Block: The Politics of Race and Class in the City*, Chicago: University of Chicago Press.

Porter, L. and Shaw, K. (eds) (2008) *Whose Urban Renaissance? An International Comparison of Urban Regeneration Strategies*, London: Routledge.

Rérat, P., Söderström, O. and Piguet, E. (2010) [guest editors] 'New forms of gentrification: issues and debates', *Population, Space and Place*.

Schill, M. and Nathan, R. (1983) *Revitalizing America's Cities: Neighborhood Reinvestment and Displacement*, Albany: State University of New York Press.

Slater, T., Curran, W. and Lees, L. (2004) [guest editors] 'Gentrification Research: new directions and critical scholarship', *Environment and Planning A*, 36(7).

Smith, N. (1996) *The New Urban Frontier: Gentrification and the Revanchist City*, London and New York: Routledge.

Smith, N. and Herod, A. (1991) *Gentrification a Comprehensive Bibliography*, Piscataway, NJ: Department of Geography, Rutgers University.

Smith, N. and Williams, P. (eds) *Gentrification of the City*, London: Allen & Unwin.

Taylor, M. (2003) *Harlem: Between Heaven and Hell*, Minneapolis: University of Minnesota Press.

Solnit, R. (2001) *Hollow City: Gentrification and the Evolution of Urban Culture*, London: Verso Books.

van Weesep, J. and Musterd, S. (eds) (1991) *Urban Housing for the Better-off: Gentrification in Europe*, Utrecht: Stedelijke Netwerken.

Zukin, S. (1982) *Loft Living: Culture and Capital in Urban Change*, Baltimore: John Hopkins University Press.

PART ONE

Defining gentrification

Plate 5 **'New Condos, New Neighborhood', West Side, Chicago.** The old site of the Henry Horner Homes completed in 1957 and then demolished between 2006 and 2008. Photograph by Elvin Wyly.

INTRODUCTION TO PART ONE

As they drew nearer to Gabriel's house, they crossed a couple of squares with which Clara was vaguely familiar, squares once thoroughly decayed, and now full of that apparatus of demolition and construction; the area attracted her strongly, in its violent seedy contrasts, its juxtaposition of the rich and poor, its rejection of suburban uniformity. Anything unfamiliar attracted her ... She looked at the peeling, cracked facades, and the newly plastered, smartly painted ones, and she thought that she would like to have lived there, among such new examples.

(From: P. Zwart, 1973, *Islington: a history and guide*, Sidgwick and Jackson: London, pp. 28)

As we can see from this description of gentrification in Islington, inner London, gentrification is complex and hides as many things as it reveals. Defining gentrification is a difficult task. As such when thinking about defining gentrification and developing definitions of gentrification it is useful to begin by thinking about what constitutes 'definition'. The following is a useful summary – a definition is:

1. A statement expressing the essential nature of something.
2. A statement of the meaning of a word or word group or a sign or symbol.
3. A product of defining.
4. The action or process of defining.
5. The action or the power of describing, explaining, or making definite and clear.

As we can see here, the act of definition is a complex process. There are questions about the meaning that we give the term through its definition – and this meaning is especially important when the word itself comes to act as a sign or symbol as the word 'gentrification' has for policy-makers, housing activists, and others, around the world. The summary above also highlights the fact that the act of definition is a process, and of course as such definitions change over time. And finally, the act of definition, of defining and describing, has a power dimension. In addition, as we made clear in our core text *Gentrification* (Lees, Slater and Wyly, 2008) the term and its definition are also ideologically and politically loaded and this relates to all the above points.

To demonstrate how definitions change let us compare how *The Dictionary of Human Geography* has defined 'gentrification' over time:

In 1994 the third edition of *The Dictionary of Human Geography* defined gentrification as:

A process of NEIGHBOURHOOD regeneration by relatively affluent incomers, who displace lower-income groups and invest substantially in improvements to homes, the quality of which has deteriorated (cf. FILTERING). Such neighbourhoods are usually accessible to the city centre and comprise substantial older dwellings – as in parts of Islington in London and Society Hill in Philadelphia.

The process of gentrification is often similar to that of INVASION AND SUCCESSION. A few gentrifiers obtain properties in a relatively run-down condition within a small area and improve them, thereby increasing the attractiveness of the area to others who would prefer such a location, so that eventually the entire area (often only a few streets) changes its socio-economic status, and property values are substantially enhanced. Real estate agents and property developers may participate in the process, as they seek to enhance the exchange value of an area and to reap substantial profits from promoting UNEVEN DEVELOPMENT at the intra-urban scale.

(pp. 216–217)

In 2000 the fourth edition of *The Dictionary of Human Geography* defined gentrification as:

The reinvestment of CAPITAL at the urban centre, which is designed to produce space for a more affluent class of people than currently occupies that space. The term, coined by Ruth Glass in 1964, has mostly been used to describe the residential aspects of this process but this is changing, as gentrification itself evolves.

Gentrification is quintessentially about urban reinvestment. In addition to residential rehabilitation and redevelopment, it now embraces commercial redevelopment and loft conversions (for residence or office) as part of a wider restructuring of urban geographical space. Gentrification proper combines this economic reinvestment with social change insofar as more affluent people – the urban 'gentry' – move into previously devalued neighbourhoods. Gentrification often involves direct or indirect displacement of poor people.

(p. 294)

And the most recent, 2009, fifth edition of *The Dictionary of Human Geography* defines gentrification as:

Middle class settlement in renovated or redeveloped properties in older, inner-city districts formerly occupied by a lower income population. The process was first named by Ruth Glass, as she observed the arrival of the 'gentry' and the accompanying social transition of several districts in central London in the early 1960s. A decade later, broader recognition of gentrification followed in large cities such as London, San Francisco, New York, Boston, Toronto and Sydney undergoing occupational transition from an industrial to a POST-INDUSTRIAL economy. But more recently gentrification has been identified more widely, in smaller urban centres, in Southern and Eastern Europe and also in some major centres in Asia and Latin America.

(pp. 273–274)

We can see here how the process moves from being defined as a relatively insubstantial urban process affecting residential neighbourhoods in 1994, to a definition that is broadened out to include commercial redevelopment and that points to gentrification as a more significant process that is part of the wider restructuring of urban geographical space in 2000, to the most recent 2009 definition which extends the definition so that gentrification is now seen as a truly global urban process affecting big and small urban centres around the world.

However, it is not just what appears in definitions but also what is hidden, ignored or sidelined. The definitions above are rooted in the city, in the urban, rural, or what Phillips calls 'other gentrifications' (see Chapter 32) are not evident!

Perhaps predictably we begin this Reader with an excerpt from Ruth Glass's (1964) *London: Aspects of Change*; it is in this excerpt that she coins the term 'gentrification'. Ruth Glass (see Box 2) was a British sociologist who used the term 'gentrification' to critique some new and distinct processes of urban change that with great foresight she predicted would become 'an embarrass de richesse' in central London (Glass, 1964: 141). The excerpt is short and to the point, Glass did not dwell on the process of 'gentrification' in *London: Aspects of Change*, yet from this brief mention came a term that has long offered some form of unity in the field. Read our discussion of why Glass used this term in Lees, Slater and Wyly (2008: 4–5) in which we point out that it was deliberately tongue in cheek, rooted in the intricacies of traditional English class structure, pointed to the emergence of a new urban gentry – and that gentry-fication referred to the replacement of an existing population by this new gentry.

In Chapter 2 we reprint the first section of Chapter 1 from Neil Smith and Peter Williams' 1986 *Gentrification of the City* – 'On definitions'. We do so not simply because this is an excellent discussion of the complexities of defining gentrification, but also because in our mind it does a great job of keeping the definition of gentrification open so as to allow it to include new types/forms of gentrification that may yet emerge. As they state, gentrification is:

> A highly dynamic process, it is not amenable to overly restrictive definitions; rather than risk constraining our understanding of this developing process by imposing definitional order, we should strive to consider the broad range of processes that contribute to this restructuring, and to understand the links between seemingly separate processes.
>
> (p. 3)

We follow on from this by reprinting Robert Beauregard's chapter from the same edited collection, 'The Chaos and Complexity of Gentrification', in which he thinks through the difficulties of defining the essential nature of gentrification as per point 1 on what a definition is. What Beauregard's chapter does is to demonstrate how defining gentrification is linked to explaining gentrification, for he wants to 'avoid a simple explanation of what is essentially a complex phenomenon' (p. 35). For Beauregard, the emphasis must be placed on contingency and complexity; he offers a theoretical analysis of 'gentrification' in an attempt to get below the surface to the hidden meanings in these theoretical explanations of gentrification. He begins by outlining the stratifications of meaning that envelop gentrification, showing that 'gentrification' has a different meaning to those who gain from the process, e.g. gentrifiers, developers, city boosters, and so on, than to those who lose from it – the indigenous groups, the displaced, and so on. He talks about the way that the term 'gentrification' is manipulated by the former groups. Importantly Beauregard links the definition of gentrification to explanations and theorizations of gentrification, showing how different theories produce different definitions. He argues that 'recognition of the complexity of processes involved furthers our sensitivity to "gentrification" as a chaotic concept. No one or even two factors are determinant' (p. 53).

In direct contrast to Beauregard, Clark (2005) refuses to resign before the complexity of gentrification, he asserts:

> I will argue for a broader definition of gentrification than is commonly found in the literature. Our overly narrow definitions render the concept genuinely chaotic by conflating contingent and necessary relations. This effectively interferes with probing underlying causes and slants our view towards particularities. I will also argue for a more inclusive geography and history of gentrification.
>
> (p. 256)

Clark holds onto 'the deeper more universal truths' about gentrification; in other words, the basic essences all types/forms of gentrification share. He sidelines the specifics and particularities of different types/forms of gentrification that create too much complexity and chaos, too much unnecessary noise that can divert us unnecessarily. His insistence on a broader definition that is more inclusive of the geography and history of gentrification is an important one. Here Clark is criticizing past definitions of gentrification for their Anglo-American bias, a bias that makes them inappropriate as a definition of gentrification in other places, such as Sweden, the country in which Clark researches and writes about gentrification (e.g. Clark, 1987). The broader history of gentrification that he seeks to include is perhaps somewhat more problematic though. For Clark, gentrification did not begin when Ruth Glass coined the term in 1964 – it has a longer history. Like Smith (1996: 34–38) before him Clark pulls the historical line of gentrification back to the mid-1800s, referring to Friedrich Engels' discussion of displacement of workers in the new industrial city and Haussmann's redevelopment of central Paris (see also Lees, Slater and Wyly, 2008: 5). Whether these earlier examples constitute gentrification is still up for debate, they certainly have little import into those discussions of gentrification that focus on the transition to post-industrial cities, a post-industrial age, and the emergence of a new middle class (see Lees, Slater and Wyly, 2008, Chapter 3). What we would concur with is Smith's (1996: 34) assertion that 'Although the emergence of gentrification proper can be traced to the postwar cities of the advanced capitalist world' these examples are 'significant precursors'. And these precursors could go back further than the mid-1800s – indeed Cybriwsky (1980) talks about a nineteenth-century print that shows the displacement of a family from a tenement in Nantes in 1685 (see Smith, 1996: 35)!

In our core text (Lees, Slater and Wyly, 2008: xxii), we follow Clark (2005) and advocate 'an elastic yet targeted definition' of gentrification. Rather than allowing the term 'gentrification' to collapse under the burden of the weights of its geography, history and particularities, we want to hold onto the label 'gentrification'. There are other advantages too, for Clark's definition allows in 'other gentrifications' like rural gentrification, suburban gentrification, new-build gentrification, and so on. These variations are important phenomena that are downplayed in the concise *Dictionary of Human Geography* definitions outlined above. Yet not everyone quite agrees. In Box 5 Damaris Rose argues instead that we need to reinvest in concept development in relation to 'gentrification' to create more order but 'not simplicity' using the vast array of case studies out there on gentrification.

The question remains – do we want a definition of gentrification that offers complexity or simplicity, chaos or order? And is that question still important?

REFERENCES AND FURTHER READING

Bondi, L. (1999) 'Between the woof and the weft: a response to Loretta Lees', *Environment and Planning D: Society and Space* 17(3): 253–255.

Clark, E. (1987) *The Rent Gap and Urban Change: Case Studies in Malmo 1860–1985*, Lund: Lund University Press.

Cybriwsky, R. (1980) 'Historical evidence of gentrification', unpublished manuscript, Department of Geography, Temple University.

Davidson, M. and Lees, L. (2005) 'New Build "Gentrification" and London's Riverside Renaissance', *Environment and Planning A* 37(7): 1165–1190.

Glass, R. (1964) 'Introduction: aspects of change' in Centre for Urban Studies (ed.) *London: Aspects of Change*, London: MacKibbon and Kee.

Lees, L., Slater, T. and Wyly, E. (2008) *Gentrification*, New York: Routledge.

Smith, D. and Butler, T. (eds) (2007) 'Extending Gentrification', Special issue of *Environment and Planning A* 39: 1.

Smith, N. (1996) *The New Urban Frontier: gentrification and the revanchist city*, New York: Routledge.

Zwart, P. (1973) *Islington: a history and guide*, London: Sidgwick and Jackson.

1
From "London: Aspects of Change" (1964)

Ruth Glass

One by one, many of the working class quarters of London have been invaded by the middle classes—upper and lower. Shabby, modest mews and cottages—two rooms up and two down—have been taken over, when their leases have expired, and have become elegant, expensive residences. Larger Victorian houses, downgraded in an earlier or recent period—which were used as lodging houses or were otherwise in multiple occupation—have been upgraded once again. Nowadays, many of these houses are being sub-divided into costly flats or 'houselets' (in terms of the new real estate snob jargon). The current social status and value of such dwellings are frequently in inverse relation to their size, and in any case enormously inflated by comparison with previous levels in their neighbourhoods. Once this process of 'gentrification' starts in a district, it goes on rapidly until all or most of the original working class occupiers are displaced, and the whole social character of the district is changed. There is very little left of the poorer enclaves of Hampstead and Chelsea: in those boroughs, the upper-middle class take-over was consolidated some time ago. The invasion has since spread to Islington, Paddington, North Kensington—even to the 'shady' parts of Notting Hill—to Battersea, and to several other districts, north and south of the river. (The East End has so far been exempt). And this is an inevitable development, in view of the demographic, economic and political pressures to which London, and especially Central London, has been subjected.

Box 2   Ruth Glass

Plate 6 Ruth Glass. Photograph from Ruth Glass' Obituary in *The Times* 9th March 1990.

Ruth Adele Glass [*née* Lazarus] (1912–1990), sociologist, was born on 30 June 1912 in Berlin, Germany. She embarked on a degree in social studies at the University of Berlin, and published a study of youth unemployment in Berlin in 1932 (reprinted in *Clichés of Urban Doom*, 1989), but following the rise of the Nazis she left Germany in 1932 before completing her degree. She studied at the University of Geneva and in Prague before arriving in London in the mid-1930s, where she resumed her sociological studies, at the London School of Economics. *Watling*, a study of a new London County Council cottage estate in Hendon, on the outskirts of London, published in 1939, established her reputation as a social scientist.

From 1940 until 1942 Ruth Glass was senior research officer at the Bureau of Applied Social Research, Columbia University, New York, and was awarded an MA degree. She returned to Britain in 1943 and became involved in town planning, as lecturer and research officer at the Association for Planning and Regional Reconstruction. From 1947 to 1948 she was a research officer for Political and Economic Planning, she returned to academic life in 1950, to University College London, which remained her academic base for the rest of her life. In 1951 Ruth Glass became director of the social research unit at University College and she founded the Centre for Urban Studies in 1951, becoming director of research in 1958, a post she retained until her death. Although she was a key figure in establishing urban sociology as an academic discipline, publishing *Urban Sociology in Great Britain* in 1955, Ruth Glass opposed the idea of research for its own sake. A Marxist all her life, she believed that the purpose of sociological research was to influence government policy and bring about social change, and to this end she involved herself in political debate. She had a passion for justice and fought hard for those she believed to be oppressed. She studied housing problems in London, editing *London, Aspects of Change* in 1964, and publishing *London's Housing Needs* (1965) and *Housing in Camden* (1969). She gave evidence to several government committees and inquiries, most notably the royal commission on local government in Greater London (1957–60). She invented the term 'gentrification', giving warnings about the squeezing of the poor out of London and the creation of upper-class ghettos.

Source: *Oxford Dictionary of National Biography* (http://www.oxforddnb.com)

2

"Alternatives to Orthodoxy: Invitation to a Debate"

From *Gentrification of the City* (1986)

Neil Smith and Peter Williams

ON DEFINITIONS

More than 20 years have passed since the term "gentrification" was first used. Originating in Britain, gentrification has become a popular concept in the United States, where its terminological debut in established dictionaries was an unheralded but nonetheless significant event. According to the *American Heritage* dictionary of 1982, gentrification is the "restoration of deteriorated urban property especially in working-class neighborhoods by the middle and upper classes." In similar vein, the *Oxford American* dictionary of two years earlier contains the following definition: "movement of middle class families into urban areas causing property values to increase and having the secondary effect of driving out poorer families."

It is remarkable how quickly this quite specific definition of a new process has become institutionalized. The explanation probably lies in the speed with which gentrification has proceeded in the urban landscape, and its high visibility in the popular press as well as academic circles. Even more remarkable is the fact that in a society and in a period when class analysis is widely held to be an historical or geographical anomaly – a holdover from the 19th century or quaintly Old World – these dictionary definitions embrace a class analysis of gentrification without the least hint of squeamishness. The temptation to dilute the phraseology must have been considerable, but perhaps the most remarkable thing of all is that with the process itself developing rapidly, these highly innovative definitions may already be outdated.

As the terminology suggests, "gentrification" connotes a process which operates in the residential housing market. It refers to the rehabilitation of working-class and derelict housing and the consequent transformation of an area into a middle-class neighborhood. Much of the early research focused on immediate empirical questions: Where is the process occurring? How widespread is it? Who are the gentrifiers (their age, race, income, life-style, occupation)? This empirical documentation marked a first phase of research into a newly emerging process. With few exceptions, the focus was on the gentrifying middle class, not the displaced working class, and on the gentrifying neighborhood, not the location and fate of displacees. Although often detached in tone, much of this early empirical work represented an uncritical celebration of the process and was at times indistinguishable from the fiscal boosterism which permeated treatments of gentrification in the popular and parochial press, especially in the United States. As such the emphasis was on effects rather than causes; the causes were generally taken for granted, but the effects were hailed by many as a timely answer to inner-city decay, and research was often orientated towards extrapolation of statistical trends and public-policy prescriptions. This empirical phase still dominates the North American literature (James 1977, Laska & Spain 1980, Schill and Nathan 1983, Gale 1984).

A second phase of research, with its origins in Britain, emerged in the late 1970s. This work emphasizes causation over effect, theoretical analysis over statistical documentation. This second phase of research tended to see gentrification not as a unique and isolated process but as integral to the broader spheres of the housing and urban land markets. Several authors attempted to explain the phenomenon in terms of public and private policies toward housing (Hamnett 1973, Williams 1976, 1978, Kendig 1979). This led, in turn, to further theoretical attempts to explain gentrification (Smith 1979a, Berry 1980b, Ley 1980) and to set it in the context of uneven development and the massive restructuring of urban space and urban land uses that is currently under way (Holcomb & Beauregard 1981, Smith 1982, Anderson *et al.* 1983). Sufficient of this work has been done to allow for the recent appearance of two comprehensive and critical reviews of theoretical work on gentrification (Hamnett 1984a, Rose 1984). [...]

If we look back at the attempted definitions of gentrification, it should be clear that we are concerned with a process much broader than merely residential rehabilitation. Even into the late 1970s, this particular definition of gentrification *vis-à-vis* redevelopment may have made some sense. But as the process has continued, it has become increasingly apparent that residential rehabilitation is only one facet (if a highly publicized and highly visible one) of a more profound economic, social, and spatial restructuring. In reality, residential gentrification is integrally linked to the redevelopment of urban waterfronts for recreational and other functions, the decline of remaining inner-city manufacturing facilities, the rise of hotel and convention complexes and central-city office developments, as well as the emergence of modern "trendy" retail and restaurant districts. Underlying all of these changes in the urban landscape are specific economic, social and political forces that are responsible for a major reshaping of advanced capitalist societies: there is a restructured industrial base, a shift to service employment and a consequent transformation of the working class, and indeed of the class structure in general; and there are shifts in state intervention and political ideology aimed at the privatization of consumption and service provision. Gentrification is a visible spatial component of this social transformation. A highly dynamic process, it is not amenable to overly restrictive definitions; rather than risk constraining our understanding of this developing process by imposing definitional order, we should strive to consider the broad range of processes that contribute to this restructuring, and to understand the links between seemingly separate processes.

REFERENCES

Anderson, J., Duncan, S. and Hudson, R. (1983) [eds] *Redundant spaces in cities and regions? Studies in industrial decline and social change*, London: Academic Press.

Berry, B. (1980b) Forces reshaping the settlement system, in H. Bryce [ed] *Cities and firms*, Lexington, Mass: Lexington Books, pp. 59–79.

Gale, D. (1984) *Gentrification, condominium conversion and revitalization*, Lexington, Mass: Lexington Books.

Hamnett, C. (1973) Improvement grants as an indicator of gentrification in inner London, *Area*, 5:4: 252–261.

Hamnett, C. (1984a) Gentrification and residential location theory: a review and assessment, in D. Herbert and R. Johnston [eds] *Geography and the urban environment, progress in research and applications*, Chichester: Wiley, pp. 282–319.

Holcomb, H. B. and Beauregard, R. A. (1981) *Revitalizing Cities*, Washington DC: Association of American Geographers.

James, F. (1977) *Private reinvestment in older housing and older neighbourhoods: recent trends and forces*, Committee on Banking, Housing and Urban Affairs, US Senate, July 7 and 8, Washington DC.

Kendig, H. (1979) *New life for old suburbs: postwar landuse and housing in the Australian inner city*, Sydney: George Allen and Unwin.

Laska, S. and Spain, D. (1980) [eds] *Back to the city: issues in neighbourhood renovation*, Elmsford, NY: Pergamon Press.

Ley, D. (1980) Liberal ideology and the postindustrial city, *Annals of the Association of American Geographers*, 70: 238–258.

Rose, D. (1984) Rethinking gentrification: beyond the uneven development of Marxist urban theory, *Environment and Planning D: Society and Space*, 2:1: 47–74.

Schill, M. and Nathan, R. (1983) *Revitalizing America's cities: neighbourhood reinvestment and displacement*, Albany: State University of New York Press.

Smith, N. (1979a) Toward a theory of gentrification: a back to the city movement by capital not people, *Journal of the American Planning Association*, 45:4: 538–548.

Smith, N. (1982) Gentrification and uneven development, *Economic Geography*, 58:2: 139–155.

Williams, P. (1976) The role of institutions in the inner London housing market: the case of Islington, *Transactions of the Institute of British Geographers*, 1: 72–82.

Williams, P. (1978) Building societies and the inner city, *Transactions of the Institute of British Geographers*, 3: 23–34.

3

"The Chaos and Complexity of Gentrification"

From *Gentrification of the City* (1986)

Robert A. Beauregard

The essence of gentrification is hidden from view. One can walk through Adams-Morgan in Washington, DC, or Queen Village in Philadelphia, through Islington in London, or the Victorian inner suburbs of Melbourne, even Over-the-Rhine in Cincinnati, and visually assess the gentrification process as expressed in rehabilitated buildings, stores and restaurants designed for the new, affluent and well dressed inhabitants. Yet the forces underlying gentrification have yet to be fully uncovered. Different layers of meaning still clothe the historical specificity of gentrification, and mask the particular confluence of societal forces and contradictions which account for its existence. Journalistic immediacy, redevelopment ideology and positivist research have obscured the essential meanings and the underlying causes.

The purpose of this chapter is to present a theoretical analysis of the process of gentrification which penetrates these various meanings, but which avoids a simple explanation of what is essentially a complex phenomenon. In fact, there can be no single theory of an invariant gentrification process. Rather, there are theoretical interpretations of how the "gentry" are created and located in the cities, how "gentrifiable" housing is produced, how those to be displaced originally came to live in inner-city neighborhoods, and finally how the various processes of gentrification unfold given the establishment of these three basic conditions. These different theoretical arguments must be combined in a fashion compatible with the specific instances of gentrification that we wish to explain. The emphasis, therefore, must be placed on contingency and complexity, set within the structural dimensions of advanced capitalism. The substantive focus of

the analysis is gentrification as it has taken place in the United States. But before addressing these issues, we should understand how our comprehension of gentrification has been distorted, and then set forth epistemological standards for the subsequent investigation.

MEANING AND EPISTEMOLOGY

Stratifications of meaning

The thinnest and outermost layer of our comprehension of the gentrification process is that of journalistic and public-relations hyperbole fostered by its "boosters:" redevelopment bodies, local newspapers, "city" magazines, mayors' offices, real-estate organizations, financial institutions, historic preservationists and neighborhood organizations comprised of middle-class homeowners. Each has an interest in increased economic activity within the city and an affinity for the middle class who function as gentrifiers. Their descriptions, analyses and advertising both present and misrepresent the phenomenon as it exists, and convey an ideology meant to foster continued gentrification.[1]

Within this layer we find the theme of the "urban pioneers" who are risking themselves and their savings to turn a deteriorated and undesirable neighborhood into a place for "good living." A new, urban life-style is touted, one which represents the consumerism and affluence of those unburdened by familial responsibilities and economic stringencies (Alpern 1979, Fleetwood 1979). These gentrifiers live in historically preserved or "high tech" domestic environments which reflect their sense of "taste."

They shop at specialty stores where unique and higher quality clothing and food convey and reinforce a sense of status. Trendy restaurants provide them with places to be seen and admired. The comforts of "civilized" living are everywhere. Urban culture is now a commodified form, leagues removed from the sense of "community" which it was once meant to convey (Williams 1977: 11–20).

This is one ideology of gentrification, part of its reality, but not representative of its essential form. The image of the city and its neighborhoods is manipulated in order to reduce the perceived risk and to encourage investment. Moreover, to believe that such description objectively captures the process of gentrification is to be deluded.

A portion of the previous chapter was devoted to unmasking this "frontier imagery of gentrification" with its pioneers, invisible natives, urban homesteading, myth of upward (through spatial) mobility and the city as a wilderness to be recaptured and tamed. Elsewhere Holcomb (1982) and Holcomb and Beauregard (1981: 52–64) have discussed the image management generally attendant on urban redevelopment schemes. The resultant hegemonic boosterism makes opposition difficult and attracts investors. More importantly, it erroneously presents gentrification as beneficial for the city as a whole. But rather than becoming implicated in the assumptions and pertinences of this ideology (Ley 1980), the point is to penetrate a way through it.

The next layer is composed of the numerous empirical assessments of gentrification, almost all of which have proceeded from a positivistic methodology which often presents empirical regularities in the guise of causal explanation.[2] These empirical investigations include both survey research (Gale 1979) and case studies (Laska & Spain 1980: 95–235), with fewer attempts to assess gentrification utilizing secondary data (Smith 1979b, Black 1980a, Spain 1980). For the most part, they focus upon changes in the built environment over time but fail to explain the dynamics that bring about these changes. The processes of gentrification are not often emphasized: Richards and Rowe (1977), London (1980), and DeGiovanni (1983), are exceptions. Moreover, the concern is almost wholly with housing redevelopment rather than with the gentrification of neighborhood commercial districts. (Aristedes 1975, Chernoff 1980, Van Gelder 1981). Lastly, the intent of most of these works is to create a Weberian "ideal-type" description of a gentrifier, a gentrifying neighborhood or a process of gentrification. Highly salient characteristics are distilled into a simplified form which lacks any sense of historical and spatial contingency.

The ostensibly prototypical gentrifier is a single-person or two-person household comprised of affluent professionals without children (Gale 1979, 1980). These "gentry" are willing to take on the risk of investing in an initially deteriorated neighborhood and the task of infusing a building with their sweat equity. Presumably, they desire to live in the city close to their jobs, where they can establish an urbane life-style and capture a financially secure position in the housing market. Their lack of demand for schools, commitment to preserving their neighborhoods, support of local retail outlets and services, and contribution to the tax base are all viewed as beneficial for the city.

The neighborhoods to be gentrified are deteriorated, and occupied by lower- and moderate-income, often elderly, households. These residential areas are located close to the central business district, and often have peculiar amenities such as views of the skyline, access to parks, or some historical significance. The housing is run-down but still structurally sound, except for the existence of abandoned and gutted buildings more popularly known as "shells." Moderate rehabilitation, for the most part, will make most housing suitable for "gentry," and facade improvements will enhance the architectural qualities and contribute to major increases in its market value.

The gentrification process involves the purchasing of buildings by affluent households or by intermediaries such as speculators or developers, the upgrading of the housing stock, governmental investment in the surrounding environment, the concomitant changeover in local retail facilities, the stabilization of the neighborhood and the enhancement of the tax base. Although residential displacement is recognized and empirically documented by researchers operating at this level, its extent and existence as a problem have been debated (Hartman 1979, Sumka 1979, LeGates & Hartman 1981).

Beneath this, and closer to the essence of gentrification, lies a third level of more theoretical analyses. Notable among these are two papers by Neil Smith. Both begin with a strong theoretical base in marxist historical materialism and attempt to unearth the underlying structural forces that have created and currently drive the process of gentrification. One of Smith's arguments (1979a) focuses upon the uneven development of metropolitan land markets. The basic theme is that disinvestment in certain areas of central cities, a disinvestment paralleling suburban investment and further exacerbated by the financial dynamics of construction and land interests (Smith 1979b), has resulted in residential areas whose capitalized ground rent is significantly below their potential ground rent. The value of the buildings themselves is considered of little moment. In the search for locations of profitable investment in metropolitan areas where suburban land has been almost fully developed, finance and real-estate capital discover these undervalued locations and undertake actions (e.g. rehabilitation, new construction, speculation) to capture the difference between the capitalized and potential ground rents. Thus it can be argued that gentrification results, in essence, from the uneven development of metropolitan land markets.

Neil Smith's second theoretical explanation (1982) is compatible with this argument, but takes place at another layer of meaning. The historically uneven development of national and international capitalism is now the starting point. The cycle of valorization and devalorization in regional land markets is now related to the "... broader rhythm and periodicity of the national and international economy" (Smith, N. 1982: 149). The inevitable falling rate of profit and the overproduction of commodities have led to a crisis of capitalism which can only be attenuated through the discovery of new investment opportunities. Following Harvey (1978), Smith maintains that such crises result in a shift of capital investment from the sphere of production to the built environment. Within that arena, the most profitable opportunities for capital accumulation are those devalorized neighborhoods where capitalized ground rent is significantly below potential ground rent. Thus the two arguments merge. The point, however, is that now gentrification is embedded more deeply in the structural dynamics of advanced capitalism in its organic totality, rather than simply in uneven development. Gentrification "operates primarily to counteract the falling rate of profit" (Smith, N. 1982: 151). This is a more incisive statement than offered previously.

However, although these theoretical explanations are commendable, since they penetrate empirical appearances and unsheath an "essence" of gentrification, they suffer from a number of problems. The "rent gap" argument provides only one of the necessary conditions for gentrification and none of the sufficient ones. Observation shows that many areas of central cities have rent gaps greatly in excess of those areas that gentrify. Thus the theory cannot easily explain why Hoboken (New Jersey) becomes gentrified, but Newark – where capitalized ground rents are extremely low and whose locational advantages relative to Manhattan and transportation facilities are on a par with Hoboken's – does not. Moreover, there is the question of how the potential ground rent is perceived, thus establishing a crucial element in determining the rent gap.

Both the "rent gap" argument and the argument focused upon the falling rate of profit suffer three additional theoretical weaknesses. One is the treatment of uneven development. Uneven development is used to explain gentrification and the rent gap, rather than the latter two phenomena being conceived as attributes of uneven development, all of which have to be explained initially by the structural tendencies of capitalism.[3] Secondly, no attempt is made to address the diverse nature of gentrification. It is collapsed into an "ideal type" concept. Lastly, the arguments are characterized by a lack of attention to the role of reproduction and consumption in gentrification. They begin and end in the economic base, the sphere of production, and do not consider how changes in these other two spheres structure, produce and even represent gentrification. Needless to say, these three weaknesses are interrelated.

Epistemological comments

From the above, albeit brief, overview of the three levels of explanation to be found in the literature, a number of epistemological issues can be identified as a means to guide any theorizing about gentrification. The objective here is to penetrate these successive layers of meaning and peer further into the core of the process. This is the first theoretical requirement: that our theory not be deluded by ideology or misrepresent empirical regularities as causal explanation. Rather, we must look beneath the phenomenal forms of gentrification, as indeed some have attempted, in order to understand both its dynamics and significance.

Secondly, "gentrification" must be recognized as a "chaotic concept" connoting many diverse if interrelated events and processes; these have been aggregated under a single (ideological) label and have been assumed to require a single causal explanation (Sayer 1982, Rose 1984). Encompassed under the rubric of gentrification are the redevelopment of historic rowhouses in Philadelphia's Society Hill initiated by an urban renewal project (Smith 1979b), the transformation of a working-class neighborhood of Victorian houses in San Francisco by gay men (Castells & Murphy 1982), the rampant speculation and displacement occurring on the Lower East Side of New York City involving multifamily structures (Gottlieb 1982), the redevelopment of abandoned housing in the Fells Point area of Baltimore, and the conversion of warehouses along the Boston waterfront to housing for the affluent. Each of these instances not only involved different types of individuals, but also proceeded differently and had varying consequences. The diversity of gentrification must be recognized, rather than conflating diverse aspects into a single phenomenon.

Thirdly, the above observations suggest that a diversity of social forces and contradictions within the social formation cohere in some fashion to bring about various types of gentrification. Moreover, it additionally suggests that gentrification is not inevitable in older, declining cities. In effect, gentrification is a conjuncture of both those structural forces necessary for its general form, and the contingent forces that make it appear at distinct points in time and in diverse ways in certain cities and not others (cf. Althusser 1977: 87–128, Beauregard 1984). Certainly the last 50 years have witnessed numerous instances where people have been displaced from cities; young and affluent households have bought property and even rehabilitated it; neighborhoods have deteriorated; governments have provided assistance to real-estate interests; and financial institutions have manipulated land markets. But only during the 1970s and 1980s did these and other forces coalesce and intensify to produce the diversity of processes referred to as gentrification.

Thus we wish to explain gentrification using both structural tendencies and historical specificities, but without extracting it theoretically from the social formation of which it is a part. More precisely, gentrification must be theorized as part of the organic totality of the social formation. This means, even more precisely, not searching for the causes of gentrification solely in the sphere of production. Rather, it is at the conjuncture of production, reproduction, and consumption, at least initially, that we must theorize (Markusen 1980, McDowell 1983, Rose 1984). Gentrification is not simply a facet of capital accumulation.

Given these various epistemological insights, the following discussion places emphasis upon those individuals commonly labeled the gentrifiers, those who serve as the proximate investors in the gentrified housing. The concern is to explain how they came to be located in central cities with reproduction and consumption needs and desires compatible with a gentrification process. After establishing their potential as gentrifiers, the next step is to explain the creation of "gentrifiable" housing and the prior placement of economically and politically vulnerable (i.e. easily displaced) individuals and families into that housing. With these three pieces of the puzzle in place, we can then explore the various processes by which they are brought together to produce gentrification itself.

THE POTENTIAL GENTRIFIERS

The explanation for gentrification begins with the presence of "gentrifiers," the necessary agents and beneficiaries of the gentrification process, and the directions taken by their reproduction and consumption. First, the demand for inexpensive, inner-city housing is not a new phenomenon, nor is the existence of politically and economically vulnerable social groups. However, the existence of affluent, professional and ostensibly "afamilial" households in central cities has become much more pronounced during these last few decades. Secondly, and more importantly, the gentrifiers are often, though seldom alone, the "agents" of the gentrification process, and thus provide the motivations and aspirations that shape it. In this way, agency is structured into our theorizing (Beauregard 1984). Lastly, without this group the whole process ceases to exist. Different types of housing stock might be rehabilitated, and diverse individuals and families displaced, but the characteristics of the gentrifiers are remarkably similar across specific instances of gentrification.

Changes in the industrial and occupational structure of the United States brought about in part by the international restructuring of capital (Bluestone & Harrison 1982: 140–90), and specifically changes in the types of economic activity which are growing and declining in the cities, have resulted in an increasingly bimodal urban labor market (Black 1980b).[4] Before World War II a strong manufacturing sector dominated central cities and provided semiskilled, medium-wage jobs with some possibility of advancement. That manufacturing sector has since declined both absolutely and relatively, and has been replaced by personal-service, administrative and professional, retail and governmental activities. In the one mode are the lower wage service jobs in the retail, office, hospitality and governmental sectors; in the other, the professional-managerial employment in the same sectors but also in corporate headquarters and business and legal services. Many lower-middle-income workers have left the city to locate nearer the manufacturing jobs now in the suburbs, and most of the unemployed poor and working poor remain in the city to engage intermittently in the growing service sector and its low-skill, low-wage employment. The professional-managerial jobs are filled with both city residents and commuters. It is within this urban, professional-managerial fraction of labor that the gentrifiers are situated.

These changes in the sphere of production are part of a long-term trend embodying the decline of the manufacturing sector and the rise of professional and managerial employment, but it is their spatial manifestation over the past two decades which is pivotal for gentrification. Of greatest importance is the absolute and relative expansion of professional and managerial jobs in the central cities. For example, professional and technical workers, managers, and administrators expanded their share of Philadelphia's labor force from 15.5 percent in 1960 to 22.6 percent in 1977. Craft and kindred workers, operatives and laborers declined from 40.1 percent during that period to 30.9 percent, whereas sales, clerical and service workers increased from 38.4 percent to 46.5 percent (City of Philadelphia 1978). More specific data on these potential gentry exist in a recent analysis of New York City's employment (Stetson 1983). Service industries increased their share of employment from 69.6 percent in 1960 to 83.8 percent in 1982. The fastest growing employment sectors from 1977 to 1982 were social services, security and commodity brokers, legal services, banking, and business services. Similar patterns are discernible in other central cities. The point is that employment opportunities for professionals and managers are becoming dominant within central cities. Admittedly, this could result in no additional professionals and managers living within these cities, since they could commute from the suburbs. It does establish, however, a necessary condition for an urban gentry to arise.

In order to explain why these professionals and managers do remain within the city and also engage in gentrification, we must move away from the sphere of production and focus upon their reproduction and consumption activities. Moreover, it is not enough to say that they desire to live in an urban environment. The issue is *why* a fraction of this group elects to remain within the city, rather than to follow the trend of suburban out-migration. What is it about an urban residence, in addition to the proximity to work, which is especially compatible with the reproduction and consumption activities of this fraction of labor?

One part of the answer involves the attitude and behavior of many professional and managerial individuals to biological reproduction. Over the last few decades there has been a trend toward the postponement of marriage and of childrearing, and, in more and more cases, decisions to remain childless, despite a more recent rise in childbearing among women in their early thirties.[5] The implications for gentrification are that these decisions create more single individual households and childless couples whose consumption needs differ from those who have traditionally migrated to the suburbs. Individual behavior concerning biological reproduction is a complex and diverse phenomenon.

One factor is the movement of women into the labor force: from 1960 to 1980 the labor-force participation rate for women increased from 37.7 to 51.5 percent (US Bureau of the Census 1982: 377). Economic necessity, the expansion in service-sector and professional-managerial jobs, feminist pressure and affirmative-action legislation have all contributed to making paid employment an available and acceptable option for many women. Certainly holding a paid job has usually been a necessity for working-class women, but economic decline has required even middle-class women to work. The desire of educated women to establish professional careers, coupled with the continued minimal childrearing participation by men, make it likely that child-bearing will be postponed or rejected. This option is facilitated by the widespread availability of birth control and the legalization of abortion in 1973. A career orientation also contributes to the postponement of marriage. A full explanation, however, requires that we consider the sphere of consumption within which both female and male professionals and managers exist.

The consumption style of this urban, professional-managerial group is partly one of conspicuous consumption, the acquisition of commodities for public display. It is facilitated by the postponement of familial responsibilities, and the accumulation of savings. Clothes, jewelry, furniture, stereo equipment, vacations, sports equipment, luxury items such as cameras and even automobiles, *inter alia*, are part of the visual and functional identity of the potential gentrifiers. In addition, more and more consumption takes place outside of the household in "public" realms: home cooking replaced by restaurants; home entertainment (with the exception of the video recorder which allows freedom from television schedules) by clubs, movies, plays, and shopping; and quiet respites at home are replaced by travel. Admittedly, these consumption habits are not dissimilar from those of other professional, middle-class individuals not in the city, but what makes them important for gentrification is their intersection with decisions on biological reproduction.

The postponement of marriage facilitates this consumption, but it also makes it necessary if people are to meet others and develop friendships. Persons without partners, outside of the milieu of college, must now join clubs and frequent places (e.g. "singles" bars) where other singles (both the never-married and the divorced) congregate in order to make close friends. Couples (married or not) need friendships beyond the workplace and may wish to congregate at "public" places. Those social opportunities, moreover, though possibly no more numerous in cities than in suburbs, are decidedly more spatially concentrated and, because of suburban zoning, tend to be more spatially integrated with residences. Clustering occurs as these individuals move proximate to "consumption items" and as entrepreneurs identify this fraction of labor as comprising conspicuous and major consumers. Both the need to consume outside of the home and the desire to make friends and meet sexual partners, either during the now-extended period of "search" before marriage or a lifetime of fluid personal relationships, encourage the identification with and migration to certain areas of the city.

At the same time, these tendencies are also and obviously important for the gentrification of commercial districts. The potential gentry represent an "up-scale" class of consumers who frequent restaurants and bars, and generally treat shopping as a social event. The objective for the entrepreneur is to capture the discretionary income of the consumer by offering an experience that is more than a functional exchange. Implicated in the purchase, be it of gourmet ice cream, a nouvelle cuisine meal, or a dance lesson, is the status of being at that shop in that neighborhood and buying that particular brand. Thus the dynamic of capital accumulation, fueled by affluence, is wedded to conspicuous consumption. Moreover, the purchase and rehabilitation of existing commercial establishments as a neighborhood begins to gentrify contribute to further residential gentrification. The two are mutually supportive.

Yet the transformation of urban, middle-class professionals into gentrifiers requires more than conspicuous consumption and postponement of marriage and childrearing. It also involves threats to their continued consumption and to their long-term economic security, threats which lead them to purchase housing in the city. This fraction of labor is not immune either to inflation or to reductions in their employment status. Both have differing but serious impacts upon the ability of this class to consume in the ways described here. Moreover, these are "educated" consumers who understand the need to engage in financial planning, whether it be through tax lawyers, voluntary savings, or investments. Even while engaging in conspicuous consumption and, at least initially, postponing major savings, they are also sensitive to the advisability of planning for the future. The maintenance of their consumption patterns in the long run cannot be left to the workings of the economy. It must be actively pursued. That becomes immediately obvious as this group begins to cluster in certain areas of the city causing a "heating up" of the housing market (and thus rising rents, condominium conversions and the like) and an increase in the price to be paid for consumption items.

As this "potential gentry" establishes an area as desirable, especially for those in similar life situations, the demand increases for housing and for restaurants, bars, movie theaters and other facilities for public but individualized consumption. Prices respond to the amount of money available, and are raised accordingly, reaching what the market will bear. Although this is not a major problem as regards most consumption items, it is as regards housing, particularly rentals. The rental market inflates, and individuals find it more and more difficult to move into these areas. For those who are already there, both "early" gentrifiers and older residents, the costs of staying in place may become onerous, and conspicuous consumption for the former is threatened. These factors encourage defensive actions to protect oneself against the vagaries of the housing market and, at the same time, to avoid the ravages of the effects of inflation on one's salary. Yet there is still the desire to live in a location with other, similar individuals and with numerous amenities of a particular quality and style. The combined search for financial security, a desirable location, access to amenities, and involvement with people of similar desires and affluence prepares these individuals to become gentrifiers. That there is a status to be gained from "home" or "apartment" ownership and a potential for high capital gains and tax benefits, not to mention the opportunity to express one's affluence and "taste" in physical surroundings, also contributes to the probability of gentrification as a solution to these problems.

Not all of the "gentry," however, will purchase a rowhouse or a condominium; some will rent luxury apartments in converted single-room-occupancy hotels or formerly working-class apartment buildings. Some of the potential gentry may be unable to amass a down payment, or wish to avoid the responsibility of home-ownership. But they should not be considered as lesser gentrifiers because of this; the conversion of apartment buildings to luxury status is also part of the gentrification process.

Still to be explained is why these potential gentry select an urban location over a suburban one, and how certain barriers to home-ownership direct them to deteriorated or lower-income residential areas. The selection of an urban location is mainly explained by the consumption and reproduction activities described earlier, and also by increasing commuting costs in metropolitan areas as rising energy costs have forced up operating costs for the automobile, and as mass transit systems have become increasingly expensive.[6] Moreover, high commuting costs and long commuting times would interfere financially and temporally with consumption activities. Reinforcing this disincentive toward suburban living is the rising cost of newly constructed housing, both in the suburbs and in urban areas. Throughout most of the postwar period, housing has been a prime investment opportunity, providing long-term financial security, precisely because of its rapid appreciation and thus high resale value, not to mention its use as collateral for other investments.[7] In fact, the average purchase price of both new and existing housing, in the suburbs as well as the cities, has risen faster than wages from 1970 to 1980.[8] Both transportation costs and housing costs, then, serve as barriers to the purchase of a suburban house.

At the same time, these individuals cannot compete in just *any* housing submarket. Both encouraging and discouraging the purchase of housing is the inflation of wages and salaries relative to housing prices. Additionally, since these potential gentrifiers tend to be relatively new to their careers, and young, they are unlikely to have extensive savings. Even though parents may contribute to a down payment, the amassing of the capital needed to purchase a well-maintained house in an already "established" and stable middle-class urban neighborhood is likely to be difficult.[9] There are thus limitations on their demands in the urban housing market.

Given the limited capital of this potential gentry, their desire to be close to their places of employment, their peculiar consumption needs, and the derivative desire to treat "housing" as both an investment item and as a statement of the image of affluence and taste which these individuals are trying to project, it is not surprising that they search for inner-city locations near central business districts, with amenities and with an architecturally interesting housing stock which has the potential to be rehabilitated and redecorated, and where housing costs are, for the moment, relatively inexpensive but prices are likely to rise. That is, the end result of these forces is the demand for a specific type of housing in specific types of residential area. That this is also recognized by developers, real-estate agents, and commercial investors reinforces the housing choices of potential gentrifiers. The point is that this is not the same as the generalized demand for inexpensive, inner-city housing. In most cities, there is a large amount of inexpensive housing, but not very much of it entices the gentrifiers. That which does not is left for lower-income groups, or is simply abandoned.

CREATION OF GENTRIFIABLE HOUSING

The next step in this theoretical penetration of the gentrification process is to explain the existence of inexpensive, inner-city housing capable of being "taken over" by "outsiders." There are two issues here: (a) the creation of gentrifiable housing, and (b) the creation of prior occupants for that housing who can easily be displaced or replaced – that is, who are unable or unwilling to resist. These are theoretically separable but interdependent processes.

The devaluation and deterioration of inner-city housing and land is a much discussed and explored phenomenon (Harvey 1973: 130–47, Smith 1979a: 543–5, 1979b, Solomon & Vandell 1982). Most importantly for the argument here, devaluation may or may not result in gentrification. Rather, the processes of residential change have the potential for numerous outcomes, ranging from gentrification to total abandonment of a neighborhood. Thus neighborhood decline is necessary but is not sufficient for gentrification to occur. Vulnerable neighborhoods may begin as areas of working-class housing, housing for the middle class, or even mixed-use (i.e. industrial, commercial, and residential) structures with a significant amount of housing interspersed.

To take the first case, there are working-class neighborhoods where housing has been well maintained for many decades, with working-class families replacing working-class families of the same or different ethnicity and race. Relative to other parts of the city, the housing may be inexpensive and thus entice the potential gentry. It is worth emphasizing that neighborhoods and housing need not be deteriorated before being gentrified. The price of housing within a given city is spatially relative. Its affordability and "acceptability" are regionally determined by prevailing wage rates, the overall cost of living, and the spatial structure of inflation in housing values. Gentrified neighborhoods of this origin seem characteristic of certain "gay" areas in San Francisco (Castells and Murphy 1982), and of traditional working-class neighborhoods comprised primarily of apartment buildings (Gottlieb 1982).

In the second case, where the residential area began not as a well maintained working-class neighborhood but as a neighborhood of middle-class homeowners, the process leading to the creation of inexpensive housing is different.[10] The devaluation of these areas is often described as one where the original middle-class residents move outward from the central city as they establish families and as their incomes rise. They are replaced by households of lower income. These replacement households may maintain the property for a time, but they soon move on the same trajectory of upward and outward mobility as those they replaced. Reproduction and consumption activities are thus central to the production of deteriorated housing. Eventually, the neighborhood is "invaded" by a group of households with a low and virtually stagnant income stream. The costs of maintenance and reinvestment in the housing exceed their financial wherewithal, and significant deterioration begins.

The result is the further in-migration of households unable to maintain their dwellings, overcrowding, the subdivision of large households into rental units in order to produce a rent roll acceptable to their owners (some of whom may be absentee landlords), and the eventual transition of home-ownership to rental tenure. The landlords may continue to invest in the property, and this process of devaluation might be averted, or at least temporarily halted. If not, disinvestment escalates as the tenants become poorer and poorer, as profits erode in the face of inflation, and as other investment opportunities compete for the landlord's capital. This leads to more rapid deterioration, actual destruction (e.g. "torching" for insurance purposes) and abandonment. The housing stock in this area is now "inexpensive."

Peculiar to even fewer cities than gentrification is "loft conversion," the creation of inexpensive housing from mixed-use districts, particularly industrial or waterfront districts with many small-scale manufacturing plants or warehouses established prior to World War II. This is the third case we shall consider. Often, these mixed-use areas are adjacent to central business districts. Cities such as New York, Philadelphia and Boston have had areas of this type abandoned, but without replacement by other industrial tenants. The buildings have remained empty, or have been rented or purchased by marginal industrial or commercial tenants who have failed to maintain them. The result has been both devaluation and deterioration. Enclosed space in these areas is thus relatively inexpensive, even though it may require significant rehabilitation before being habitable as housing. Nonetheless, the transformation of mixed-use areas and the takeover of inexpensive working-class housing are as much a part of gentrification phenomena as the more prototypical case of the redevelopment of deteriorated but once middle-class neighborhoods.

LOCATING THE GENTRIFIED

The people most likely to be gentrified (i.e. displaced) are those living in inexpensive but architecturally desirable housing near central business districts. Many are marginal to the labor market or outside it: unemployed males and working-class white, black and Hispanic youth, the elderly, "welfare" mothers, and many working-class households and underemployed individuals near the poverty line. Some are "redundant" workers, but many are part of the urban labor market.[11] They are living in these locations for a variety of reasons: the rents may be cheap, the location may hold historical and emotional significance, there may be spatial advantages in terms of private and public services needed for reproduction and consumption, or employment opportunities may be nearby. Their location may be a matter of choice; it may have stemmed from a lack of choice. Nonetheless, their existence here is a matter of the creation and location of the inner-city poor.

The explanation for the inner-city poor under capitalism is complex, involving not only the migration of black agricultural workers after World War II but also that of poor whites from rural lands (e.g. Castells 1976b). The lure of low-wage manufacturing jobs in the cities brought them there, and the subsequent diminution of such jobs left them in marginal economic straits. The opportunities for the sons and daughters of these migrants, moreover, are limited. Low-wage, unskilled manufacturing and service jobs compete with unemployment and public assistance. The link between the potential gentrifiers and the potential gentrified begins here in the labor market. The forces that have generated employment opportunities for the professional-managerial class have also diminished low-wage manufacturing jobs with opportunities for advancement, and given rise to service and clerical employment in retail establishments and offices. These latter jobs are often of low pay and with little possibility for career mobility. In the retail and hospitality sectors, for example, turnover is high and employment stability is virtually nonexistent. The restructuring of the urban labor market is thus part of the explanation for the existence of both the potential gentrifiers and the potential gentrified. The former are provided with the reasons and wherewithal to undertake gentrification; the latter are limited to certain neighborhoods within the city and are unable, because of their low economic status, to resist gentrification.

These individuals occupy housing which has the potential to be gentrified and, secondly, are themselves economically and politically powerless relative to the gentrifiers. Because they are in the low-wage sectors of the labor market, or outside it on "fixed" incomes, they have few economic resources and find themselves renting in these neighborhoods, or else barely able to maintain and hold on to houses in which they have lived for years, years that have seen their relative economic influence in the housing market erode. At the same time, their consumption potential is weak relative to other segments of the city's population, particularly the potential gentry, and thus their attractiveness to proponents of redevelopment, usually intent on creating a city of middle-class affluence, is also weak. Many of these households, additionally, are characterized by large numbers of children, or are female-headed and poor, thus requiring a greater share of local governmental services ranging from education to law enforcement. The hypothetical gap between what they demand in governmental services and what they pay in taxes and contribute to the circulation of capital through consumer expenditures combines with their inability to afford decent housing to make them relatively undesirable to local-government officials.

Thus, because these individuals and families lack economic power, and because of related disadvantages in the realms of consumption and reproduction (e.g. low purchasing power and family instability, respectively), they also lack political power. The end result is that these households are easily exploited by landlords if they are renting, unable to resist "buyouts" by the more affluent if they own their housing, and unlikely to mobilize to resist local-government encouragement of gentrification. Of course, it is not uncommon to find in gentrifying neighborhoods older homeowners and small landlords who are anxious to sell and move. However, this has not been shown to be a major proportion of those potentially gentrified, and therefore does not obviate the displacement consequences of gentrification. This group merely points up, once again, the chaotic nature of gentrification. The location of these "powerless" households in gentrifiable residential areas is not a "law" of capitalism, which inevitably produces the conditions for gentrification, nor do those potentially gentrified always succumb without a struggle (Auger 1979). Instead, the location of economically and politically weak households in certain types of neighborhood at a particular historical time combines with the inner-city location of the potential gentry, among other factors, to produce the conjuncture which is labeled gentrification.

GENTRIFICATION PROCESSES

To this point, a number of components of gentrification have been explained: the production of the potential gentry, the generation of the potentially gentrifiable neighborhoods, and the creation of the potentially gentrified. This analysis has included the possibility that any of these "productions" might not lead to gentrification. It remains to (a) identify the "facilitators" or active agents of gentrification, in addition to the potential gentry themselves, and (b) more specifically to explain why only *certain* inner-city areas with inexpensive housing opportunities occupied by the "powerless" become gentrified. Many parts of any city remain in a deteriorated condition, despite the existence within the city boundaries of potential gentry, and despite the presence of inexpensive housing occupied by the lower class.

Gentrification is partly facilitated by the federal government's inducements to home-ownership, making a housing purchase economically beneficial (Stone 1978). Basic to this policy is the tax deduction for interest payments on mortgages. There are also more recent tax deductions and credits for weatherization and energy-conservation projects (e.g. solar panels), as well as for the rehabilitation of historic structures. The purchase and rehabilitation of a house can benefit the buyer significantly, particularly in the first few years of the purchase when interest rates comprise a large proportion of mortgage payments and when rehabilitation is likely to be done. This applies, of course, to home-ownership regardless of location, though Federal Housing Administration mortgage insurance has historically favored suburban sites.

The local government often plays a more active and direct role in the gentrification process (Smith 1979b). It stands to benefit directly from the dislocation of lower-class groups which burden it through social programs, and from their replacement by middle-class consumers whose income will circulate in the local economy and whose investments will enhance the tax base. Thus one finds local governments advertising the potential for gentrification in certain of their neighborhoods; providing tax abatements for rehabilitation (e.g. the J-51 program in New York City); devoting community development funds to rehabilitation and to improving public services in these neighborhoods; using code enforcement to force landlords and homeowners to rehabilitate or to sell their properties; actively engaging in the designation of historic districts or the labeling of "neighborhoods" (e.g. the "creation" of Tribeca by the New York City Planning Commission); and diminishing public service provision elsewhere in order to encourage decline before then facilitating reinvestment (Hartman *et al.* 1981). Moreover, the local government can rezone a mixed-use district to make it easier to gentrify, or it can fail to enforce zoning statutes in a mixed-use district, thus facilitating an easier transition to residential land use.

The local government and the various tax provisions of the federal government, however, are not determinant, and their actions may not even be necessary. What is necessary, but not sufficient, is for financial and property interests to foresee the opportunities involved in the transformation of a residential area from low to middle income through investment in rehabilitation. Landlords, developers and real-estate agents, both large and small, play an important role in "steering" the potential gentry to a neighborhood, buying property and speculating (i.e. "flipping" a building by purchasing it and then selling it a short time later without adding any value to it), and displacing residents (directly or indirectly) by raising rents in order to empty a building in preparation for sale or for complete rehabilitation. In addition, rental properties are turned into condominiums or cooperatives, and even rehabilitated as rental units (Richards & Rowe 1977, Smith 1979b, Gottlieb 1982). In all these instances, property interests are exploiting those short-term investment opportunities created by other components of the gentrification process. In fact, the ways in which profits may be realized are numerous, as are the combinations of small, medium and large developers, real-estate interests and landlords who might pursue them.

Property interests, nonetheless, cannot operate without the assistance of financial entities able to lend large sums of capital (Smith 1979b). Investments in the built environment are large and usually of long duration. More importantly, the profits to be made from such investments are contingent upon low equity-to-debt ratios, which allow tax advantages, high profits and easy withdrawals (i.e. escape) from both good and bad investments. Savings and loan associations, local banks, and other financial institutions make capital available over long terms for mortgages and over shorter terms for construction and rehabilitation. Insurance companies and pension funds may also buy property and invest in neighborhoods. In the case of large buildings or complexes, new forms of creative financing (such as limited-equity partnerships) allow numerous and various fractions of capital and even labor to provide money for gentrification, and to reap the rewards from the rapid escalation in housing costs.

All of these agents, inclinations and forces must come together in specific spatial locations. These sites are often characterized by architecturally interesting housing or commercial and industrial structures "with potential:" a unique spatial amenity such as access to a waterfront, a hilltop location or a spectacular view; substandard but not structurally unsound buildings clustered relatively close together

to allow for a contagion effect to occur and for gentrifiers to "protect" themselves; proximity to the central business district (Lipton 1980) or at least good mass transportation links; and local neighborhood commercial areas with an initial attraction to the early gentrifiers but also with the potential for transformation to the types of shops, restaurants and facilities most compatible with the reproductive decisions and consumption activities of the gentry.

The actual gentrification process, though it may involve all of these actors to varying degrees, has not unfolded similarly in different cities, nor is it likely to unfold in the future. Theory must explain multiple gentrification processes.[12] The most commonly accepted version is that in which a deteriorated neighborhood is initially invaded by "pioneers." Then the process quickens as gentry, along with small real-estate interests, financial institutions and construction firms, participate in the purchase and rehabilitation of single-family dwellings (London 1980). The dynamics are different in those neighborhoods in which large-scale developers and speculators purchase multifamily housing and the area is transformed into luxury condominiums and cooperative apartments (Richards & Rowe 1977, Gottlieb 1982). One can also identify a gentrification process in which the local government takes the initiative through a major urban renewal project (e.g. Society Hill) or through homesteading programs (e.g. in Baltimore). Each of these processes (and there may be others) brings together the various actors and conditions in a different manner with varying implications for the distribution of the resultant financial and social benefits and costs.

Recognition of the complexity of processes involved furthers our sensitivity to "gentrification" as a chaotic concept. No one or even two factors are determinant. Conversely, the absence of any one factor does not mean that gentrification will not occur. Just as possible is their fusion into another form of neighborhood transformation unlike what we currently label gentrification. A sensitivity to these various possibilities is what characterizes the present theoretical analysis. It is a sensitivity both to the structural elements of advanced capitalism, which establish some of the necessary conditions for gentrification, and to the specific and contingent factors and historical timing, which must occur for gentrification to materialize. What is essential, nonetheless, is the production of that fraction of labor from which the potential gentry are drawn, the production of areas where gentrification might proceed, and the creation of a "gentrifiable" fraction of labor. That these components may exist without gentrification ensuing attests to the view of gentrification as an historical event created by the fusion of disparate forces and contradictions within a social formation which is itself characterized by both structure and contingency (Beauregard 1984).

Thus, a recognition of gentrification as both chaotic and complex has guided this work. The theoretical goal was to penetrate the layers of ideology and positivist social research which clothe gentrification, yet not to probe so deeply as to pass by its concrete manifestations. The intent was not to rediscover the essence of capitalism, but to use its structure and dynamics to explain a specific social phenomenon. Only by having gentrification clearly in view can it be scrutinized effectively.

ACKNOWLEDGEMENTS

Damaris Rose, Neil Smith and Briavel Holcomb have been most helpful in shaping my understanding of gentrification phenomena, and how to theorize about them. I would like to acknowledge their contribution.

Notes

1 It is within this layer of meaning that we find the notion that gentrification is a template for the future of urban neighborhoods, despite the obvious fact that, albeit highly visible, it is as yet a small-scale phenomenon.

2 Rose (1984) makes the point that even marxist theorists are prone to a "mix-and-match" methodology in which marxist categories are combined with positivistic empiricism to produce an eclectic and epistemologically inconsistent theoretical argument.

3 Moreover, it is not just capitalist countries that exhibit uneven development of sorts. However, this important theme cannot be discussed here.

4 International restructuring also affects the accumulation potential of different investments and thus influences gentrification. The variation in profit rates across industrial sectors, however, is always operative at the national level under capitalism and thus is not sufficient for explaining gentrification.

5 From 1970 to 1980 the following changes occurred: the percentage of married individuals fell from 62.4 to 60.8; the percentage of nonfamily, two-person households increased from 8.0 to 11.2 of all nonfamily households, a category which itself increased by 66.4 percent; and the birth rate decreased from 17.8 to 16.2 per 1 000 population (US Bureau of the Census 1981).

As for the fertility rate of women in their early thirties, the rate among women 30 to 34 years of age rose 22.5 percent from 60 births per 1000 women in 1980 to 73.5 births in 1983. In addition, "forty-four percent of the women in this age range who gave birth last year either held jobs or were seeking jobs" (Pear 1983).

6 The consumer price index for public transportation increased by 131.7 percent from 1970 to 1980, and that for private transportation by 148.4 percent. Private non-agricultural gross weekly earnings in current dollars rose by 96.2 percent (US Bureau of the Census 1981: 468).

7 This suggests that sale value, and not ground rent, is a more salient financial issue in gentrification, though primarily for the gentry and not for property or financial interests (cf. Smith 1979a). Of course, the two "values" are difficult to separate in reality.

8 Whereas the consumer price index for housing increased by 122.3 percent from 1970 to 1980, private non-agricultural gross weekly wages rose by 96.2 percent in current dollars (US Bureau of the Census 1981: 468). The median sale price of a new privately owned one-family home increased by 176.1 percent over this decade, and the sale price of an existing, privately owned single-family home by 170.4 percent (US Bureau of the Census 1982: 249).

9 Omitted from this argument, because it seems less important where gentrification has occurred, is the construction of middle-income housing on vacant land in central cities. If such land were to exist, it is difficult to predict whether it would detract from the process of gentrification.

10 This is the case most often discussed in the literature and an example of particular interest to urban sociologists of the human ecology school.

11 To the extent that they are redundant, the displacement of these marginal and working-class households may not interrupt the smooth reproduction of labor for capital. See Smith, N. (1982: 153).

12 DeGiovanni (1983) has demonstrated empirically the discontinuous nature of gentrification and its variability across gentrifying neighborhoods.

REFERENCES

Alpern, D. (1979) A city revival? *Newsweek*, 97:3: 28–35.

Althusser, L. (1977) *For Marx*, London: Verso.

Aristedes (1975) Boutique America, *American Scholar*, 44: 533–539.

Auger, D. (1979) The politics of revitalization in gentrifying neighbourhoods: the case of Boston's South End, *Journal of the American Planning Association*, 45: 515–522.

Beauregard, R. (1984) Structure, agency and urban redevelopment, in M. Smith [ed] *Capital, class and urban structure*, Beverly Hills: Sage Publications, pp. 51–72.

Black, J. (1980a) Private market housing renovation in central cities: an urban land institute survey, in S. Laska and D. Spain [eds] *Back to the city*, New York: Pergamon Press, pp. 3–12.

Black, J. (1980b) The changing economic role of central cities and suburbs, in A. Solomon [ed] *The prospective city: economic, population, energy and environmental developments*, Cambridge, Mass: MIT, pp. 80–123.

Bluestone, B. and Harrison, B. (1982) *The deindustrialization of America: plant closing, community abandonment, and the dismantling of basic industry*, New York: Basic Books.

Castells, M. (1976) The wild city, *Kapitalistate*, 4–5: 2–30.

Castells, M. and Murphy, K. (1982) Cultural identity and urban structure, in N. Fainstein and S. Fainstein [eds] *Urban policy under capitalism*, Beverly Hills: Sage Publications, pp. 237–259.

Chernoff, M. (1980) Social displacement in a renovating neighborhood's commercial district: Atlanta, in S. Laska and D. Spain [eds] *Back to the City*, New York: Pergamon Press, pp. 204–219.

City of Philadelphia (1978) *An urban strategy*, Philadelphia: City of Philadelphia.

DeGiovanni, F. (1983) Patterns of change in housing market activity in revitalizing neighbourhoods, *Journal of the American Planning Association*, 49: 22–39.

Fleetwood, B. (1979) The new elite and the urban renaissance, *New York Times* (January 14) 16–20, 22, 26, 34–35.

Gale, D. (1979) Middle class resettlement in older neighbourhoods, *Journal of the American Planning Association*, 45: 293–304.

Gale, D. (1980) Neighborhood resettlement, in S. Laska and D. Spain (eds) *Back to the city*, New York: Pergamon, pp. 95–115.

Gottlieb, M. (1982) Space invaders: land grab on the Lower East Side, *Village Voice*, 27:50 (December 14) 10–16, 50.

Hartman, C. (1979) Comment on 'neighborhood revitalization and Displacement: a review of the evidence', *Journal of American Planning Association* 45:4: 488–494.

Hartman, C., Keating, D., and LeGates, R. (1981) *Displacement: how to fight it*, Berkeley: National Housing Law Project.

Harvey, D. (1973) *Social Justice and the City*, Baltimore: John Hopkins University Press.

Harvey, D. (1978) The urban process under capitalism: a framework for analysis, *International Journal of Urban and Regional Research*, 2:1: 100–131.

Holcomb, B. (1982) Urban publicity: remaking the image of a city, *Proceedings of the Applied Geography Conferences*, 5: 161–168.

Holcomb, B. and Beauregard, R. (1981) *Revitalizing Cities*, Washington DC: Association of American Geographers.

Laska, S. and Spain, D. (1980) (eds) *Back to the city: issues in neighbourhood renovation*, Elmsford, NY: Pergamon Press.

LeGates, R. and Hartman, C. (1981) Displacement, *Clearinghouse Review*, 15: 207–49.

Ley, D. (1980) Liberal ideology and the postindustrial city, *Annals of the Association of American Geographers*, 70: 238–258.

Lipton, S. (1980) Evidence of central city revival, in S. Laska and D. Spain (eds) *Back to the City*, New York: Pergamon Press, pp. 42–60.

London, B. (1980) Gentrification as urban reinvasion: some preliminary definitional and theoretical considerations, in S. Laska and D. Spain (eds) *Back to the City*, New York: Pergamon Press, pp. 77–92.

Markusen, A. (1980) City spatial structure, women's household work, and national urban policy, *Signs* 5: 23–44.

McDowell, L. (1983) Towards an understanding of the gender division of urban space, *Society and Space*, 1:1: 59–72.

Pear, R. (1983) Sharp rise in childbearing found among US women in Early 30s, *New York Times* (June 10).

Richards, C. and Rowe, J. (1977) Restoring a city: who pays the price? *Working Papers* 4, 54–61.

Rose, D. (1984) Rethinking gentrification: beyond the uneven development of Marxist urban theory, *Society and Space* 2:1: 47–74.

Sayer, A. (1982) Explanation in economic geography: abstraction versus generalization, *Progress in Human Geography*, 6: 68–88.

Smith, N. (1979a) Toward a theory of gentrification: a back to the city movement by capital not people, *Journal of the American Planning Association*, 45:4: 538–548.

Smith, N. (1979b) Gentrification and capital: theory, practice and ideology in Society Hill, *Antipode* 11:3: 24–35.

Smith, N. (1982) Gentrification and uneven development, *Economic Geography*, 58:2: 139–155.

Soloman, A. and Vandell, K. (1982) Alternative perspectives on neighbourhood decline, *Journal of the American Planning Association*, 48: 81–98.

Spain, D. (1980) Indicators of urban revitalization: racial and socio-economic changes in central city housing, in S. Laska and D. Spain (eds) *Back to the City*, New York: Pergamon Press.

Stetson, D. (1983) US official sees New York City vulnerable as economy picks up, *New York Times* (May 10) B3.

Stone, M. (1978) Housing mortgage lending and the contradictions of capitalism, in W. Tabb and L. Sawers (eds) *Marxism and the Metropolis*, New York: OUP, 179–207.

Sumka, H. (1979) Neighborhood revitalization and displacement: a review of the evidence, *Journal of the American Planning Association*, 45:4: 480–487.

Van Gelder, L. (1981) The New World discovers Columbus, *Village Voice* (September) 23–29.

Williams, R. (1977) *Marxism and Literature*, New York: Oxford University Press.

4

"The Order and Simplicity of Gentrification – a Political Challenge"

From *Gentrification in a Global Context* (2005)

Eric Clark

As the concept of gentrification celebrates an even forty years, some of the most basic questions about the process itself remain contentious. What is gentrification? What are its root causes? There are surely no lack of answers, though these are largely stamped by disciplined convention. The purpose of this chapter is to revisit these basic questions and formulate answers that facilitate 'having gentrification clearly in view' so it can 'be scrutinized effectively' (Beauregard 1986: 54).

I will argue for a broader definition of gentrification than is commonly found in the literature. Our overly narrow definitions render the concept genuinely chaotic by conflating contingent and necessary relations. This effectively interferes with probing underlying causes and slants our view towards particularities. I will also argue for a more inclusive perspective on the geography and history of gentrification.

I will argue that the root causes of gentrification are: commodification of space, polarised power relations, and a dominance of vision over sight associated with what Wendell Berry calls 'the vagrant sovereign' (1977: 53). We are so busy pursuing superficial particular truths we lose touch with and fail to maintain these deeper more universal truths about gentrification. I will argue that we need to break with the present norm insisting upon emphasising and focusing on the chaos and complexity of gentrification. We wrongly assume that seeking to identify order and simplicity in gentrification is tantamount to reductionism and simple-mindedness, and that critical thinking requires us to stick to the lodestars of chaos and complexity. This overriding tendency in

gentrification research is not unrelated to more general trends in social science where there has been 'a remarkable turnaround in radical political sensibilities' which has seen the social construction of objects of study dominate over other discourses of understanding (Sayer 2001: 687).

A question less frequently posed is: why does gentrification lead to violent conflict in some places and not in others? Another purpose of this chapter is to suggest what the key factors are behind this difference and argue for more engagement in developing policies and practices effectively removing the bases for severe conflict. I will argue that two key factors are degree of social polarisation and practices surrounding property rights. In places characterised by a high degree of social polarisation, short on the rights of users of place and long on the rights of owners of space (i.e. where there is an abundance of vagrant sovereigns given free reins), the conflict inherent in gentrification becomes inflammatory. That is not so in places characterised by relative equality and judicially practised recognition of the rights of users of place.

I doubt any reader of this volume will have failed to notice the connection between the title of this chapter and the title of Robert Beauregard's influential chapter in *Gentrification in the City* (Smith and Williams 1986). It may appear that I aim to show just how wrong Beauregard was. Not at all. I agree with Beauregard's basic arguments and regard his seminal work among the best on gentrification.[1] My complaint is not with Beauregard but rather with how his thoughtful statement has been received and used in ways I see as misdirected.

Generally interpreted as a call to recognise and focus on the chaos and complexity of gentrification, Beauregard's genuine concern for the 'essence of gentrification', its 'essential meanings and underlying causes', its 'essential form', and the 'structural forces necessary for its general form' (1986: 35, 36, 40) has been glossed over. Indeed it would not surprise me if Beauregard would find in the literature since 1986 a need to recognise the order and simplicity of gentrification, every bit as much as its chaos and complexity.

Beauregard's 'theoretical goal was to penetrate the layers of ideology and positivist social research which clothe gentrification, yet not probe so deep as to pass by its concrete manifestations' (1986: 54). An alternative title of the present chapter indicating its purpose and direction might be 'Gentrification: probing deep'. I suggest we need more deep probing, and that this does not preclude sensitivity to the particulars and contingencies of gentrification processes in specific contexts. On the contrary, it can help us to grasp better these manifestations as opposed to resigning before their complexity.

In the end, the arguments forwarded provide a base for presenting a challenge to gentrification research. The challenge is to engage in comparative analyses with a focus on policy issues in order to foster a politics of place in which the playing field is evened, the voices of all actors involved and influenced more fully recognised and the conflicts inherent to gentrification openly negotiated.

GENTRIFICATION: AN ELASTIC YET TARGETED DEFINITION

Gentrification is a process involving a change in the population of land-users such that the new users are of a higher socio-economic status than the previous users, together with an associated change in the built environment through a reinvestment in fixed capital. The greater the difference in socio-economic status, the more noticeable the process, not least because the more powerful the new users are, the more marked will be concomitant change in the built environment. It does not matter where, and it does not matter when. Any process of change fitting this description is, to my understanding, gentrification.

There are more often than not a variety of qualifiers attached to definitions of gentrification which narrow it down to more specific contexts. 'Gentrification is an inner city process'. Why? The process occurs in other places as well, which social change in many Scandinavian fishing villages attests to. This means that any explanation for it taking place

predominantly in inner cities must be based on scrutiny of contingent relations of historically specific contexts. 'Gentrification takes place in residential areas'. Why? Are not daytime and workplace populations as relevant as night time and residential populations? What about the gentrification of waterfront warehouses and shipyards, for instance Aker Brygge in Oslo? 'Gentrification involves the rehabilitation of architecturally attractive but unmaintained buildings'. Why? In many instances, yes, but these are hardly necessary or definitive. For years I have waited for the convincing argument why renovated buildings can be sites of gentrification, but not new buildings replacing demolished buildings. With as much anticipation, I have awaited the succinct delineation between rehabilitation and clearance/new construction, wondering in which category the cleared lot with braced and girded facade will fall.

It is easy to confuse narrowness with precision, but when qualifiers are not based on relations necessary to the phenomenon, they detract from precision, the narrowness being arbitrary rather than meaningful. For some phenomena, racism for instance, a broad definition is more accurate and therefore more interesting than a narrow one, the additional qualifying abstractions of which may work in social contexts to reproduce the broader phenomenon they supposedly narrow in on. This is easy to see in the case of racism, where narrow definitions cluttered with qualifiers protect racist perspectives from scrutiny. Perhaps we should be asking ourselves, and empirically investigating, to what extent our narrow chaotic conceptions of gentrification play a role in reproducing the phenomenon we claim to zero in on.

Abstractions based on non-necessary relations lead to chaotic conceptions, and 'No amount of sophistication in research methods can compensate for such sloppy abstractions' (Sayer 2000: 19–20). There is a simple reason for these abstractions slipping into our conceptions. Causal forces are commonly found in contingent relations, analysis of which is therefore necessary for adequate explanation of a concrete process – for instance the location of a gentrifying neighbourhood. But being necessary for explaining a particular case is different from being a necessary relation basic to the wider process. Central location may be one important cause of the process in some cases, but abstracting this relation to define the process leads to a chaotic conception of the process, arbitrarily lumping together centrality with gentrification. What becomes of gentrification in rural areas? Calling it something else would involve just another form of chaotic conception based on another form of bad abstraction that arbitrarily divides gentrification, 'thereby "carving up" the object of study with little or no regard for its structure and form' (Sayer 1992: 138).

There is nothing chaotic about gentrification in inner cities and in rural areas, in neighbourhoods and in non-residential areas, through rehabilitation and through demolition/new construction. There is, however, something chaotic about conceptualising gentrification according to these aspects, since none of them stands in a necessary relation to its occurrence.

This may seem like hair-splitting, but it has consequences. The qualifiers 'inner city', 'rehabilitation' and 'residential' have been repeated enough times to become entrenched. Time and time again when inquiring about gentrification in cities I have visited the answer has been, 'No, we don't have gentrification processes here', only to find out later, after follow-up questions occasionally spurred by visual evidence, that there was gentrification going on, but not in the inner city, not through rehabilitation of buildings, and not in old residential neighbourhoods. The collective efforts of gentrification researchers have given the world a chaotic conception of a process we are supposed to know much about. How can we expect others to have more rational conceptions than the ones we generate as researchers?

This kind of chaos, not the mundane chaos associated with complexity, needs to be addressed. I agree with Atkinson (2003b: 2347) that 'the problem of gentrification is less its conceptualisation and more about the need for a project which will begin to address the systematic inequalities of urban society upon which gentrification thrives', and will address this below. I believe, however, that our infatuation with a shifting and complex understanding of gentrification and our predominantly chaotic conceptualisations of the process hinder recognition of that need and render ourselves poorly equipped to fulfil it. There is nothing quite so useful as good theory.

Another conventional truth I want to dispute concerns the time-space delineation of gentrification. There is a story about the historical origin of gentrification that reads like a mantra: once upon a time (the early 1960s to be more precise), Ruth Glass discovered the very first instance of gentrification in a London neighbourhood. She is accredited in so many words as having found and identified a *new* process whereby a *new* urban gentry transformed working-class quarters. The story conflates the origin of the concept with the origin of the phenomenon. Ruth Glass did indeed coin the term in 1964, but it is careless to turn this into an assumption that we have here the origin of the phenomenon.[2] This is untenable even with the narrowest of definitions,

yet is repeated with sufficient frequency to become believed.

With the definition forwarded above it would be a tall task to show that gentrification started in London in the early 1960s. This 'process of conquest' (N. Smith 1996: xv) goes at least as far back as the mid-1800s when Friedrich Engels observed spatially concentrated displacements of workers to make space for new 'spatial fixes' of capital in search of potential profits and land rents. And did not Haussmann's remodelling of Paris entail in some places the two kinds of change associated with gentrification? Urban history holds many examples of gentrification far earlier and far away from 1960s Islington. Holding on to the story about gentrification's origins in postwar London is grounded in convention, not critical thought.

There is a similar story about the global spread of gentrification. Confident proclamations ring out: Gentrification is now global! The problem with this is not if gentrification can be observed in places around the world, but is again the issue of time: it is *now* global. The broader, more 'rational' (less chaotic) conception of gentrification argued for here extends not only the history but also the spatial scope of the phenomenon beyond the received limitation to large postwar western Cities. This is again a matter of conflating concept with phenomenon. It is more accurate to say that the concept of gentrification is now global, diffusing as the geographic foci of gentrification research has expanded. The extent of occurrence of the phenomenon from a global historical perspective remains however largely uncharted.

If the global reach of gentrification is not new, it is certainly widened and accentuated by what Neil Smith calls 'the generalization of gentrification as a global urban strategy', based on 'the mobilization of urban real-estate markets as vehicles of capital accumulation' (2002: 437, 446). The language of this strategy is sugar coated with images of revitalisation, regeneration, renewal, reinvestment and redevelopment, while its legitimacy is anchored in the 'necessity' to become a 'global city', a 'creative city', an attractive city, in competition with other cities. The social costs of the strategy are, if at all recognised, deemed necessary and unavoidable (Asheim and Clark 2001; Lund Hansen, Andersen and Clark 2001).

THEORISING ORDER IN CONTINGENCY

A rational, non-chaotic conception of gentrification must be delineated by underlying necessary relations and causal forces as distinguished from contingent causes and relations. The root causes of gentrification are: commodification of space, polarised power relations, and a dominance of vision over sight characteristic of 'the vagrant sovereign'. Much energy has been spent in the gentrification literature distinguishing between and arguing for and against production/supply-side theory and consumption/demand-side theory. But neither side is comprehensible without the other, and all present theories of gentrification touch bottom in these basic conditions for the existence of the phenomenon.

The commodification of space opens up space for conquest, facilitating 'highest and best' land uses to supplant present uses (Blomley 2002), or as David Harvey puts it, 'forcing *the proper* allocation of capital to land' (1982: 360). Note the normative naturalising tendency – who would care to argue for lower and worse uses or improper allocations? It works in tandem with the seeking of vagrant sovereigns to realise visions through the economic exploitation of potentials, destroying the actual in the process. Polarised power relations – economic, political and judicial – are a necessary condition for the tandem dynamic to work: the more polarised, the more forceful and active the dynamic.

As a process of conquest, gentrification is related to colonialism, a relation laid bare in Neil Smith's analysis of *The New Urban Frontier* (1996). Colonialism suggests another geopolitical scale, but the underlying forces of commodified space, polarised power relations and the impulsive roamings of vagrant sovereigns connect the two processes (cf. Cindi Katz 2001 on 'vagabond capitalism'). Gentrification is colonialism at the neighbourhood scale, though the structures and mechanisms involved are by no means limited by neighbourhood boundaries, as ties to foreign direct investment and 'global city' politics makes abundantly clear.

The following passage from Wendell Berry's *The Unsettling of America* is not about gentrification, but provides nonetheless a concise formulation:

Generation after generation, those who intended to remain and prosper where they were have been dispossessed and driven out … by those who were carrying out some version of the search for El Dorado. Time after time, in place after place, these conquerors have fragmented and demolished traditional communities, the beginnings of domestic cultures. They have always said that what they destroyed was out-dated, provincial, and contemptible. And with alarming frequency they have been believed and trusted by their victims, especially when their victims were other white people.

(Berry 1977: 4)

This is as relevant in the 'new' urban post-industrial frontier as it is in the 'old' rural agricultural frontier.

The dreams and visions of vagrant sovereigns disembed and displace those of present users, a process powerfully facilitated by the operation of land markets in capitalist space economies. Potential land rents are boosted by how much vagrant sovereigns are willing to pay to realise their dreams. Actual land rents are limited by how little present users can afford in order to hang on to their dreams. Though the political economics of the rent gap mechanism and its underlying structures are vastly more complex (Clark 1987, 1995, 2004; Harvey 1982; Sheppard and Barnes 1990), this simple relation of conquest is essential to its workings.

As long as ideas of a feasible and desirable alternative to capitalism are in short supply, the possibility of capitalism within a moral society becomes the next best thing to which to turn.

(Sayer 2001: 705)

Gentrification leads to violent conflict in many cities (N. Smith 1996). In other places we can observe a 'more benign unwinding of the process' (Atkinson 2003b: 2343). I believe a comparative analysis aimed at understanding why this process turns into tumult in some places and not in others would find two key factors to be degree of social polarisation and practices surrounding property rights. In places characterised by a high degree of social polarisation, short on legally practised recognition of the rights of users of place and long on legally practised recognition of the rights of owners of space, the conflict inherent in gentrification becomes inflammatory. Not so in places characterised by relative equality and legally practised recognition of the rights of users of place. If so, this indicates a direction for political engagement aimed to curb the occurrence of gentrification and to change societal relations such that when it does occur (and it will), conditions are established for more benign ends.

This kind of comparative analysis is strikingly absent in the gentrification literature. Academia, it seems, does not encourage interest in policy issues and political engagement, rewarding instead awareness of the 'chaos and complexity' of the phenomenon. While there is no lack of critique of gentrification as a strategic policy, there is a dearth of effort to outline alternatives. This poses a considerable challenge to gentrification research.

Conflicts arise between interests associated with linear rhythms of 'consecutiveness and reproduction of the same phenomena' (users of place seeking continuity in place) and interests associated with cyclical 'rhythms of new beginnings' (owners of space, vagrant sovereigns seeking new 'rewards'), as rents flow through the circuit of built environments (Lefebvre 1996: 231). The 'essential and determinant factor is money' argued Lefebvre (1996: 225), and concluded:

> When relations of power take over relations of alliance, when the rhythms of 'the other' make impossible the rhythms of 'the self', then a total crisis explodes, with the deregulation of all compromises, arhythmy, implosion-explosion of the city ...
>
> (1996: 239)

While conflict is the necessary outcome of the forces at play, it is possible to reduce conflict and foster 'more benign unwindings'. Compromise can be regulated. Gentrification cannot be eradicated in capitalist societies, but it can be curtailed and the playing field can be changed such that when gentrification does take place it involves replacement rather than displacement, however difficult it is to draw an unambiguous line between them (Atkinson 2000b).

Gentrification underscores the importance of developing radical alternative politics of place and provides a field in which negotiations can be pursued and alternative politics honed. Where 'recognition is distorted by distribution' (Sayer 2001: 704), this needs to be addressed, partly through mechanisms of redistribution, partly through insistence on recognition in spite of warped distribution. We need a politics of place whereby political priorities are 'established out of the open but fair power-play between agonistic actors and their competing and often conflicting claims' (Amin 2004: 39). And we need to acknowledge that it is not a simple issue of defence and conservation: 'Challenges to the current construction and role of a place may sometimes be a more appropriate strategy than defence' (Massey 2004: 17).

To move successfully in this direction, we need to avoid the pitfall of simple division into conquerors and victims:

> We can understand a great deal of our history ... by thinking of ourselves as divided into conquerors and victims. In order to understand our own time and predicament and the work that is

to be done, we would do well to shift the terms and say that we are divided between exploitation and nurture. The first set of terms is too simple for the purpose because, in any given situation, it proposes to divide people into two mutually exclusive groups ... The terms exploitation and nurture, on the other hand, describe a division not only between persons, but also within persons. We are all to some extent the products of an exploitative society, and it would be foolish and self-defeating to pretend that we do not bear its stamp.

> (Berry 1977: 7)

Visiting Malmö, Neil Smith asked me to show him the battlefields of gentrification. At the time, I was at a loss to explain that there were processes of gentrification in Malmö, but no battlefields. Conflicting interests, displacement, personal tragedies, yes, but not the desperation behind battlefields. The cumulative outcome of political and legal battles in Sweden during the twentieth century set the stage for less violent ways of dealing with inherently conflictual processes of change. I believe it is fair and accurate to say this is changing, with increasing polarisation and decreasing concern for the rights of users of place. Perhaps there will in the foreseeable future be gentrification battlefields also in Sweden. That depends on our willingness to face up to the 'faces of oppression' (Young 1990; cf. Harvey 1993), to develop relations of alliance between the interests of linear and cyclical rhythms. It depends on our capacity to see the order and simplicity of gentrification, and our willingness to participate far more courageously in the political challenge it presents.

Notes

1 It is unfortunate, however, that the understanding of chaotic conceptions Beauregard conveys is inaccurate. Given the authority the chapter continues to enjoy, this has not been helpful in edifying appreciation of the problems underlying chaotic conceptions of gentrification and how a more rational conception may be tailored.

2 David Harvey, *The Economist* and others have noted that globalisation is a new and fashionable term for imperialism. Similarly, gentrification is a middle-aged term for a process for which the victims may have had words long in use. This is pure conjecture, but I would wager a pretty penny that a good urban social historian could find

some of those words with a modicum of concentrated effort. Little did Ruth Glass and whoever coined globalisation know just how successful their memes would be!

REFERENCES

Amin, A. (2004) Regions unbound: towards a new politics of place, *Geografiska Annaler B*, 86: 33–44.

Atkinson, R. (2000b) 'Professionalisation and displacement in Greater London', *Area*, 32: 287–96.

Atkinson, R. (ed.) (2003b) 'Gentrification in a new century: misunderstood saviour or vengeful wrecker? What really is the problem with gentrification?' *Urban Studies* (special issue), 40(12): 2343–50.

Asheim, B. and Clark, E. (2001) Creativity and cost in urban and regional development in the "new" economy, *European Planning Studies*, 9: 805–811.

Beauregard, R. (1986) 'The chaos and complexity of gentrification', in N. Smith and P. Williams (eds) *Gentrification of the City*, London: Unwin Hyman.

Berry, W. (1977) *The unsettling of America: culture and agriculture*, New York: Avon.

Berry, W. (1982) *The gift of good land*, New York: North Point Press.

Blomley, N. (2002) 'Mud for the land', *Public Culture*, 14: 557–82.

Clark, E. (1987) *The rent gap and urban change: case studies in Malmo 1860–1985*, Lund: Lund University Press.

Clark, E. (1995) 'The rent gap re-examined', *Urban Studies*, 32: 1489–503.

Clark, E. (2004) 'Rent rhythm in the flamenco of urban change', in Tom Mels (ed.) *Rhythms of Nature, Place and Landscape*, Aldershot: Ashgate.

Harvey, D. (1982) *The Limits to Capital*, Oxford: Blackwell.

Harvey, D. (1993) 'Social justice, postmodernism and the city', *International Journal of Urban and Regional Research*, 16: 588–601.

Katz, C. (2001) *Vagabond Capitalism and the Necessity of Social Reproduction*, Oxford: Blackwell.

Lefebvre, H. (1996) *Writings on Cities*, translated and edited by Eleonore Kofman and Elizabeth Lebas, Oxford: Blackwell.

Lund, H. A., Andersen, H. T. and Clark, E. (2001) 'Creative Copenhagen: globalization, urban governance and social change', *European Planning Studies*, 9: 851–69.

Massey, D. (2004) Geographies of responsibility, *Geografiska Annaler B*, 85: 5–18.

Sayer, A. (1992) *Method in Social Science: A Realist Approach*, London: Routledge.

Sayer, A. (2000) *Realism and Social Science*, London: Sage.

Sayer, A. (2001) 'For a critical cultural political economy', *Antipode*, 33: 687–708.

Sheppard, E. and Barnes, T. (1990) *The Capitalist Space Economy: Geographical Analysis after Ricardo, Marx and Sraffa*, London: Unwin Hyman.

Smith, N. (1996) *The New Urban Frontier: Gentrification and the Revanchist City*, London: Routledge.

Smith, N. (2002) 'New globalism, new urbanism: gentrification as global urban strategy', *Antipode*, 34(3): 428–50.

Smith, N. and Williams, P. (eds) (1986b) *Gentrification of the City*, Boston, MA: Allen & Unwin.

Young, I. M. (1990) *Justice and the Politics of Difference*, Princeton, NJ: Princeton University Press.

(a)

(b)

(c)

Plate 7 (a) Before gentrification in the Lower East Side, 1988. Photograph by Loretta Lees. (b) During gentrification in the Lower East Side, 1988. Photograph by Loretta Lees. (c) After gentrification in the Lower East Side, 1988. Photograph by Loretta Lees.

INTRODUCTION TO PART TWO

In the half-century since the term 'gentrification' was coined stage models have become persuasive and compelling for many scholars and policy elites – and for urban residents living through the everyday experiences of gentrification. Early on, the idea had almost irresistible intuitive appeal: gentrifying neighborhoods go through a series of distinct yet related stages, each one erasing more of the old working-class or poor character of place while inscribing new patterns of class privilege and wealth. While the details of vocabulary differed, most of the grammatical rules used in describing the stages were shared by long-term residents, middle-class and wealthy homebuyers, working-class community activists, university researchers, and local or federal policy makers. Most agreed that neighborhoods experiencing gentrification were undergoing a process that had a beginning, a middle, and (if not an end) a state of completion or equilibrium – the undisputed complete transformation of a poor or working-class district into something new and different. Stage models, first introduced in the outpouring of academic research on gentrification in the 1970s, proposed specific frameworks to derive generalizations from such intuitive ideas, observations, and experiences. The readings in this section document the development of stage models and their evolution over time.

Clay's (1979) work offered one of the first widely-recognized stage models. Drawing general lessons from a survey of neighborhood changes in Boston, Philadelphia, San Francisco, and Washington, DC, Clay suggested that the process could be understood in terms of four distinct stages. A first, "pioneer" stage began with the initiative of a small but active group of "risk-oblivious" people who were willing to defy conventional expectations. A second stage of slow, tentative expansion involved a small but growing number of realtors or developers who recognize the area's potential, and work to promote local investment. Some direct displacement begins, but only accelerates in a third stage when mainstream media sources take an active interest in the neighborhood's "turnaround" or "renaissance." Media interest validates the risks taken by the first wave of pioneers, and provides the seal of approval for more cautious middle-class professionals to commit to living and investing in the community. But in a fourth and final stage, these middle-class professionals face more and more competition from the established elite of the business and managerial class. The wealth of these buyers allows them to get the very best properties; their decisions provide clear signals to the entire city that a neighborhood has made it to the top of the status hierarchy.

Over the years, this simple model has been criticized and revised many times by many scholars. As many social scientists turned away from the goals of generalization towards a greater emphasis on unique circumstances and partial, situated narratives, the four-stage model began to seem rigid and unable to account for the particularities and differences among and within various neighborhoods, residents, and investors. Today, most gentrification researchers are quick to point out the limitations and problematic theoretical foundations of the simple four-stage model. Likewise, many of those living through the experiences of gentrification are able to offer rich, sophisticated analyses of context, contingency, and situated neighborhood epistemologies. Gentrifiers burned by bad timing can describe the finer details of local housing submarkets and speculative bubbles that can throw a wrench into the model's smooth progression between stages. Long-term residents and activists involved in anti-gentrification campaigns can analyze the different policies that can trigger dramatic local changes at almost any stage – and sometimes they can document hard-fought victories when the middle stages were slowed or stopped (or at least modified to minimize displacement effects for the most vulnerable residents).

All of these critiques are valuable and important. Yet they also miss the point. Even as the simplicity of the early stage models gives way to the intricate plurality of contemporary contingency, the fundamental essence – the idea that there are discernible stages, phases, or alignments of particular causes and effects related to particular trajectories – has gained even more widespread acceptance. The details of everyone's account of a particular neighborhood will differ. But nearly everyone subscribes to the same assumptions and metaphors of stages: direction, speed, motion, momentum. For many people concerned with the past, present, and future of their neighborhood, the essence of the early stage models is as relevant today as it was for residents debating the same issues 30, 40 or even 50 years ago.

In different ways, the work of Brian Berry (1985), Larry Bourne (1993), and Jason Hackworth and Neil Smith (2001) helped to transform the meanings and possibilities of stage models. In retrospect, the details of Clay's (1979) particular stages obscured the significance of the stage idea itself. Three amendments to this central concept have been most important: context, partiality, and revision.

CONTEXT

Stages of gentrification are deeply conditioned by geographical and historical context. Early stage models tended towards one of two extremes: broad, abstract generalizations about "the" process, or rich, highly localized studies of very particular cases. Berry (1985) and Bourne (1993) addressed the middle-range between these two extremes, showing how specific trajectories were shaped by metropolitan and historical context. For Berry, understanding the pace of gentrification required knowledge of regional housing market dynamics. Drawing on the housing economics literatures on filtering and submarkets, Berry showed that the sum of countless individual market transactions would only add up to gentrification in certain circumstances. The opportunities and constraints of buyers and sellers (or tenants and landlords) negotiating in any neighborhood at any stage will be shaped by the broader relations of supply and demand at the metropolitan scale. These relations will also be shaped by inter-city trends in industrial restructuring, employment change, and migration across urban systems. Berry challenged a consensus that had emerged among economists in the 1970s – that gentrification was a counter-cyclical tightening of the inner-city market during times of recession. When bad economic conditions made it difficult for the suburban new-home construction industry to provide enough new houses to meet the needs of young people forming new households, the older homes and neighborhoods of the inner city suddenly became more attractive.

Berry gathered evidence that contradicted the conventional view. Gentrification was, in fact, pro-cyclical: it was most extensive in those metropolitan areas with the fastest pace of new suburban housing construction. A proliferation of new housing units on the fringe allowed households to move into the suburbs, thereby leaving behind vacant units for other households to move into, and so on, in a cascade of "vacancy chains" that finally clustered in the oldest, lowest-quality sections of the region's housing stock. This process created widespread vacancies and even abandonment across vast inner-city "seas of decay." But in a few well-defined inner-city districts with attractive housing stock and good proximity to the downtown core, gentrification could create "islands of renewal" – but only if that downtown core had enjoyed rapid growth in office space and employment in high-paying white-collar jobs. In turn, these conditions were most pronounced in those parts of the urban system emerging as key "command and control" centers for corporate headquarters and advanced producer services industries.

Berry was not sure whether gentrification was a permanent shift or simply a temporary imbalance (see the last paragraph of his essay). Several years later, though, Larry Bourne (1993) saw enough evidence to offer a retrospective along with a clear set of predictions. After reviewing a literature that had become "voluminous, diverse, and often contradictory," Bourne presented empirical estimates showing that gentrification – compared with upgrading of elite areas and other types of neighborhood change – accounted for only a small portion of total changes in income for Toronto's inner city. Moreover, Bourne observed that many gentrified neighborhoods "have high proportions of transient student populations, singles, mobile young professionals, and the elderly," such that future mobility trends would create great uncertainty on whether and how gentrification would proceed from one stage to the next. More provocatively, Bourne suggested that all the attention to gentrification was its own kind of stage – a product of "what now appears to have been a unique period" in the last half of the twentieth century. This unique "gentrification era" involved the coincidence of several broad trends: the large "baby boom" cohort of young adults all forming new households around the same time, rising educational levels, dramatic growth in high-paying white-collar jobs, rapid appreciation of house values, sustained expansion of government spending on social services, speculative investment in real-estate development, and high levels of foreign immigration. All of these trends, except for the last one, seemed to be ending in the early 1990s, and thus Bourne predicted a "post-gentrification era."

Today, many readers are quick to criticize the specific predictions and metaphors used by Berry and Bourne. Few would predict a post-gentrification era today, even as hundreds of cities across the world are dealing with the worst housing crisis since the Great Depression of the 1930s; and in some cities, gentrification has expanded so much that one can see islands of decay (old council housing estates and public housing projects) surrounded by seas of gentrified renewal. But Berry and Bourne's specific predictions matter less than their methods and their emphasis on context: gentrification, in all of its stages, must be understood in relation to regional housing markets, national and global urban systems, and the slow but powerful forces of demography.

But another force also matters: as Jason Hackworth and Neil Smith (2001) demonstrate, government policies and political decisions reconfigured many of the factors Bourne diagnosed – turning what might have been a post-gentrification era into a much more dynamic era of turbocharged reinvestment. Once a symptom of social, economic, and geographical change, gentrification became a much more compre-hensive and coherent state strategy to remake urban space for the benefit of wealthy residents, investors, and tourists. In contrast to the early models of the stages that a gentrifying neighborhood might witness, Hackworth and Smith identified distinct stages of the political economy that shaped the context for gentri-fiers, investors, developers, and poor and working-class residents. A "first wave" prior to the early 1970s was sporadic, small-scale, and involved substantial (but often ill-fated) government support for various redevelopment schemes. After a severe recession in the 1970s, a second wave of expansion and resis-tance brought gentrification to many more cities, while political changes began to change its character. Amidst widespread cutbacks to social programs for poor people, and the accelerated loss of blue-collar jobs juxtaposed with rapid growth of high-paying downtown office jobs, gentrification began to exacerbate what Berry had earlier described as "a situation in which two labor markets, and, by extension, two soci-eties coexist, increasingly divorced from each other." Second-wave gentrification thus unleashed intense political struggles over displacement, homelessness, income inequality, and racial discrimination. Finally, Hackworth and Smith identified a third wave that began after a short recession in the early 1990s. This third wave expanded farther outward from the urban core, affecting a broader range of poor and working-class neighborhoods. It was driven by large developers, including quite a few transnational real estate firms with access to vast pools of capital from investors across the globe. And this third wave also involved much more active and coordinated interventions by government. Most federal governments in the world's wealthy countries have been "devolving" or "downloading" more responsibilities for social programs to local governments – often while slashing the funds available to pay for these obligations. Cities are thus forced to compete with one another to attract tax revenue, to reduce their expenditures on programs for poor people, and often to do both at the same time. The traditional role of city government – providing for the needs of the poor in order to protect city residents from the worst failures of private business deci-sions that worsen poverty and inequality – became much harder to sustain. Local governments abandoned policies that *reduced* social inequality, and began to pursue development and investment strategies that *worsened* inequality. Gentrification entered a distinctly more polarizing phase (see Wyly and Hammel, 1999; reprinted in Chapter 24 of the Reader).

PARTIAL, SITUATED VIEWS

The second major change in stage models involves a growing and interdisciplinary recognition of partiality and situated perspectives. To see and to experience the stages of gentrification is inescapably partial and situated. Many readers and policy-makers used the early stage models to view gentrification from the geographical and epistemological outside, in an attempt to get an objective, neutral, just-the-facts assessment of the process and its costs and benefits. But it quickly became clear that consensus and objectivity would always remain elusive. Berry's analysis of islands of renewal in seas of decay emphasized that "the most fundamental axiom of both urban geography and urban sociology is that the urban landscape is a mirror reflecting the society that maintains it," but it is also axiomatic that every society is defined by its internal relations of cooperation/conflict, unity/difference, collectivity/individuality. These relations make it impossible to describe any singular interpretation of stages of gentrification. Whether an established city resident sees Clay's "pioneer" or "mature" stage, or Hackworth and Smith's first, second, or third waves, depends on how old they are and how long they've lived in the neighborhood. Young, new arrivals may see themselves as pioneers, while older, long-term residents see the in-movers as the latest sign of gentrification accelerating into its latter, "mature" stages. Working-class renters see the rising rents of successive stages as a threat to affordability. Young gentrifiers buying homes in the neighborhood see the same trends, and find reassurance that their real-estate investment will grow over time. Elderly, working-class residents who have lived through many stages may have mixed emotions when they decide to sell: regrets of a lost sense of community are mixed with the temptations of a sales-price windfall made possible by years of gentrification and displacement. Long-term residents who endured racial discrimination and the threat of crime and violence during decades of disinvestment are happy when successive stages of gentrification bring new public services and improvements in public safety; but there is often resentment, too, because improvements arrive only when wealthy, white gentrifiers move into the neighborhood and demand attention from city officials. The unease is different, but no less significant, when the gentrifiers include many racial and ethnic minorities who have succeeded in gaining access to middle-class professional jobs.

REVISION

The third major change in stage models acknowledges the inherent dynamism of the process – and of the social and political relations it creates. Gentrification is a process and not a final state. It is always incomplete, never finished. Communities witnessing the earliest stages can be transformed fairly quickly, while neighborhoods that seem to have "completed" all stages can sometimes slide back into more unpredictable mixtures of wealth and poverty. Others in very particular locations have been re-gentrified and/or super-gentrified (see Lees, 2003). And many neighborhoods in cities around the world have been undergoing the middle stages of gentrification for 20 or 30 years. All neighborhoods are always being made, remade, and struggled over.

Gentrification intensifies these struggles, and the word itself is usually at the heart of discussion and debate. Such discussions change over time. Stage models, therefore, also serve as invitations. In almost any public discussion of gentrification, sooner or later someone will ask the obvious questions: is what we are seeing here and now a new, different stage? Is this a fundamentally different kind of gentrification? If so, what does it mean for us?

The history of stage models reminds us that we may never reach consensus on the correct answers to such questions. Sometimes, the questions we ask are more interesting and useful than the answers we might offer.

REFERENCES AND FURTHER READING

Beauregard, R.A. (1990) 'Trajectories of neighbourhood change: the case of gentrification', *Environment and Planning A* 22: 855–874.

Hackworth, J. (2002) 'Post recession gentrification in New York City', *Urban Affairs Review* 37: 815–843.

Kerstein, R. (1990) 'Stage models for gentrification: an examination', *Urban Affairs Quarterly* 25: 620–639.

Lees, L. (2003) 'Super-gentrification: the case of Brooklyn Heights, New York City', *Urban Studies* 40, 12: 2487–2509.

Lees, L. and Bondi, L. (1995) 'De-gentrification and economic recession: The case of New York City', *Urban Geography* 16, 3: 234–253.

Murphy, L. (2008) 'Thirdwave gentrification in New Zealand: the case of Auckland', *Urban Studies* 45, 12: 2521–2540.

Wyly, E. and Hammel, D. (1999) 'Islands of decay in seas of renewal: housing policy and the resurgence of gentrification', *Housing Policy Debate* 10: 711–798.

5

"The Mature Revitalized Neighborhood: Emerging Issues in Gentrification"

From *Neighborhood Renewal* (1979)

Phillip L. Clay

Timothy Pattison has examined gentrification in a Boston neighborhood and has preliminarily identified four stages through which gentrification neighborhoods go.[1] The data in this study essentially confirm Pattison's notions. The following elaborated typology of stages in the development of gentrification neighborhoods is useful for predictive purposes, as well as for explaining some of the phenomena mentioned earlier.

In stage one of gentrification a small group of risk-oblivious people move in and renovate properties for their own use. Little public attention is given to renovation at this stage, and little displacement occurs because the newcomers often take housing that is vacant or part of the normal market turnover in what is often an extremely soft market. This pioneer group accepts the risks of such a move.

Sweat equity and private capital are used almost exclusively, since conventional mortgage funds are unavailable. This first stage is well under way before it receives any public recognition, although even at this early stage the grapevine is spreading the word. The first efforts are concentrated in very small areas, often two to three blocks. The first group of newcomers usually contains a significant number of design professionals or artists who have the skill, time, and ability to undertake extensive rehabilitation. (In Boston, San Francisco, and other cities, respondents suggested it was the homosexual community who made up the population. They seek privacy and have the money and the taste to take on this challenge. One observer suggested that "Smart money will follow homosexuals in cities.")

In stage two a few more of the same type of people move in and fix up houses for their own use. Subtle promotional activities are begun, often by a few perceptive realtors. Small-scale speculators may renovate a few houses in visible locations for resale or rental. Rarely does a large speculator come in at this stage, because capital for investors and residents is still scarce. Those who come in at this stage seek units that are still relatively easy to acquire—vacant buildings owned by absentee landlords, city-owned or tax-foreclosed properties.

Some displacement occurs as vacant housing becomes scarce. Those who come in stages one and two will later be considered the old-timers in this new neighborhood.

If the neighborhood is to have its name changed, it often happens at this stage. New boundaries are identified, and the media begin to pay attention to the area. Areas undergoing gentrification today would receive some attention from public agencies, but neighborhoods that passed through this stage earlier were not noticed by planners or other city bureaucrats.

In some neighborhoods mortgage money becomes available, but the loan is more often secured by other property, given by the seller, or given for a relatively low percentage of the total investment. Renovation spreads to adjacent blocks. In this stage property is still inexpensive.

Stage three is crucial because it is at this stage that major media or official interest is directed to the neighborhood. The pioneers may continue to be important in shaping the process, but they are not the only important ones. Urban renewal may begin (the vast majority of the structures are still considered blighted), or a developer or a group of small developers may move in. Individual investors who restore or renovate housing for their own use continue to buy into the neighborhood. The trend is set for the kind of rehabilitation activity that will dominate. Physical improvements become even more visible because of their volume and because of the general improvement they make to the whole area. Prices begin to escalate rapidly.

Displacement continues, and it may increase if codes are enforced rigidly or if reassessments are made to reflect the increasing value of even the unimproved properties. Many of the better-maintained buildings become part of the middle-class market, often with only minimal improvement as landlords take advantage of the area's new prestige. This process leads to even more displacement.

The first group of gentry looks mainly for a place to live and express their life-style. The arrivals in this third stage include increasing numbers of people who see the housing as an investment in addition to being a place to live. These newer middle-class residents begin to organize their own groups or change the character of the pioneers organization.

The organized community turns outward to promote the neighborhood to other middle-class people and to make demands for public resources. It turns inward to exert peer influence on neighbors and to shape community life. Tensions between old residents and the gentry begin to emerge. Social service institutions and subsidized housing are resisted with passion. Protective or defensive actions against crime are taken. If the new residents, especially the most recent arrivals, are less tolerant of lower- or working-class behavior, these tensions may become serious. Banks begin to greenline the area, looking for spatial patterns of reinvestment and then making loans to middle-class buyers and investors within the limited area.

If the neighborhood boundaries were drawn too narrowly and if there is comparable housing stock beyond the boundary, the neighborhood expands. The popular image of the process of change at this stage is clearly gentrification and is treated as such by the media. The neighborhood is now viewed as safe for larger numbers of young middle-class professionals.

In stage four a larger number of properties are gentrified, and the middle-class continues to come. What is significant about the new residents is that more are from the business and managerial middle class than from the professional middle class.

The presence of a growing number of rental units in some communities helps broaden the income range of the middle class in the neighborhood. Single people, divorcees, and unmarried couples who want to live in the area, but do not want to buy, provide a ready market for these units.

Efforts may be made to win historic district designation or to obtain other stringent public controls to reinforce the private investment that has taken place.

Buildings that have been held for speculation appear on the market. Nonresidential buildings in the neighborhood may be turned into rental or condominium units to provide additional housing. Small, specialized retail and professional services or commercial activities begin to emerge, especially if the neighborhood is located near the downtown or a major institution. Rapid price and rent spirals are set off. Displacement now affects not only renters but some home owners as well. Additional neighborhoods in the city are being discovered to meet the increasing demand of the middle class. While some controversy emerges, especially related to displacement, relatively little is done to dampen middle-class reinvestment.

This short summary of the process is all that the present set of cases allows. But this is not the end of the story. Not all the units have been taken by the middle class, and price and demand are still high. There is room for substantial growth of the middle-class population within the present gentrification areas. A limited number of cases that go back to the late 1960s and the early 1970s do, however, provide some idea of the way that the process matures and what successive future stages might bring.

This discussion of mature renewal neighborhoods is based on observations and data from a number of cities, including Boston's South End, Philadelphia's Society Hill, San Francisco's Western Addition, and Washington's Capitol Hill. These neighborhoods started the renewal process in the late 1960s or early 1970s, and gentrification there is now advanced. Because relatively few neighborhoods have actually completed gentrification, the mature gentrified neighborhood cannot be described as confidently as the process. In the limited number of cases studied, however, the following issues seem to be emerging as important.

VALUES AND RESALE POTENTIAL

One issue relates to the increasing prices and resale values found in gentrification neighborhoods and the fears about future prices and resale values. In cities with cases of mature gentrification new neighborhoods are beginning to experience gentrification, resulting in shifts in demand and an increased supply of units available to the gentry. In Washington and San Francisco, for example, prices are rising at a feverish pace. Routine sales and resales at more than $150,000 per structure are not unusual, and few structures in these neighborhoods now sell for less than $70,000.

The price increase is fed by speculation and a high level of optimism about the neighborhood and its future. There is also the feeling that prices will be still higher in the future. The uncertainty centers on when the price spiral will end and whether some future stability in prices will be achieved. Those who buy mainly to reap substantial capital gains within three to five years cause some concern, since when they reach the limits of economic return in the area their withdrawal may put a damper on the real estate market.

Despite the joy officials feel for increasing property values, rapid price spirals in a few neighborhoods may be counterproductive to the city. Rapid price and rent spirals set off waves of speculation that exploit present and future housing consumers. The competitive position of the central city versus the suburbs for the middle class could be altered if city housing, with poor public services, costs more than suburban housing. Rapid increases in prices lead to displacement not only of low-income families but eventually of young lower middle class families as well. Finally, rapid price increases may force cities to develop measures to counter the adverse effects of reinvestment. For example, rent control or limitations on condominium conversion might be required to maintain a sufficient number of moderate-cost rental units. Although this concern has been widely expressed, none of the cities and no private interest that I studied has come forth with tools to limit the speculative activity that accounts for much of the price spiral. For the time being, consumers are still coming up with funds for this increasingly expensive housing.

A final concern is, just how much gentrification will there be in the years to come and how long the process will continue. These are extremely difficult questions to answer. Most large cities still have plenty of additional housing, and areas that would be attractive. The institutional support (banks, developers) and the political support to expand the middle class in the city are substantial. The capacity of contractors to rehabilitate is improved. State and local governments are more encouraging and supportive. All these factors point toward a continued opportunity to expand middle-class resettlements. On the other hand, location is a problem. There are only so many neighborhoods which have the locational features found to be important. There is also an inverse relationship between the number of opportunities and the requirement for reaching a threshold of middle-class dominance: The more opportunities (numbers of areas and numbers of units) that are perceived to exist, the fewer the number of neighborhoods that would be viewed as capable of reaching the threshold of middle-class dominance. This is especially true if there appear to be limits on the expansion of demand.

Gauging demand is even harder. Factors supporting the continued expansion in middle-class demand in selected city neighborhoods are:

1. The presence of a large group of young adults that will remain large until the mid 1980's;
2. The growth of nonfamily households composed of singles, divorced people, unmarried couples, and childless couples;
3. Growth in the concentration of professional jobs in the central city;
4. The rising cost of both new and existing housing in the suburbs and the relative low cost of inner city housing;
5. Growth of service and professional job opportunities in the city and the growing independence of job and residential locations from each other; and
6. A trend towards the promotion of city living.

On the other hand, the more cautious view that gentrification is limited in both time and size, and that it will not represent a significant trend in the years to come, is supported by the following factors:

1. Still serious social and environmental problems in the city;
2. Serious problems with public services, especially schools, which have yet to be addressed;
3. Increased opportunities in older suburbs where the services and ambience are better, but which are presently occupied by a late middle-age adult population with grown children; and
4. Growing tensions between middle-class gentry and long-term residents in the city, which may discourage middle-class resettlement or would at least invite caution on the part of the small-scale developer/contractors who are so necessary to the middle-class renewal process.

Even if the process continues at its present pace, middle-class resettlement will never loom as large as a statistical phenomenon as it does as a popular trend. These households presently account for less than one percent of central city households. Although the influence of such a group on the life of the city can be disproportionately large, even a doubling or tripling would not be statistically significant.

Note

1 Timothy Pattison, "The Process of Neighborhood Upgrading and Gentrification," master's thesis, Massachusetts Institute of Technology, 1977.

6

"Islands of Renewal in Seas of Decay"

From *The New Urban Reality* (1985)

Brian J. L. Berry

I recall the incredulity with which some of my urban studies colleagues at the University of Chicago greeted the first draft of my paper, "The Geography of the United States in the Year 2000," when I circulated it in 1969. I had suggested that there were clear signs that the century-long trend of population concentration was coming to an end. The society had, I thought, concocted solvents that were dissolving the glue of centrality. Urbanization, a process marked by increasing size, increasing density, and increasing heterogeneity of immigrant population clusters, was being succeeded by "counter-urbanization," a process of population deconcentration marked by decreasing size, decreasing density, and increasing homogeneity of the population selectively left behind by emigration.

The statistics that have emerged from the 1980 census bear witness to my speculations in ways that 1960–70 trends reported in the 1970 census did not: at the regional level, the more densely populated northeastern industrial heartland has declined and the Sun Belt and mountain state rimlands have grown; smaller towns and nonmetropolitan areas have expanded at the expense of metropolitan areas; and within metropolitan regions, suburbanization and exurbanization have increased and both central cities and older suburbs and industrial satellites have declined. These shifts have been facilitated by a housing industry that, despite cyclical perturbations, has consistently constructed many more housing units than the growth in numbers of households appeared to warrant, generally in new locations on the periphery of existing built-up areas, resulting in rounds of relocations that have emptied older neighborhoods.

The housing stock can be viewed as a set of gross substitutes organized into a commodity chain system.[1] Layers of new housing are attractive substitutes that draw upwardly mobile households from older housing types that, in turn, attract households from the units they occupy further down the chain. Any excess of new construction over household growth (and involuntary withdrawals from the stock caused by natural disasters, fires, redevelopment, highway programs, and the like) thus is transferred down the housing chain; "filtering" takes place as households climb the commodity chain and as older housing moves down the social scale. The final resting place of any excess supply is in the least attractive locations. If excess supplies are large, removal of the unwanted units can empty these locations of their structures, creating both a problem and an opportunity—reuse of the vacant land.

Two examples of the magnitudes involved should illustrate. In the Chicago metropolitan area, household growth between 1970 and 1980 was about 302,000, but 484,000 new housing units were built. During the decade vacancies increased by 48,000 units; however, about 135,000 housing units were withdrawn from the stock. In the Pittsburgh metropolitan area, comparable 1970–80 figures are: household growth, 69,000; new construction, 100,000; vacancy increase, 17,000; and withdrawals from stock, 14,000.[2]

In metropolitan areas as a whole, just over 6 million excess housing units were removed from the nation's housing inventory between 1960 and 1970 and some 7 million between 1970 and 1980. The rate of removal each decade was approximately 10 percent of the initial stock. Since successive waves of new housing have been added ringlike around existing built-up areas, the filtering process has always been from inner city to periphery. The excess supplies of the past two decades therefore have become all too evident in boarded-up buildings, vandalized hulks, and vacant lots in central-city neighborhoods, and as the older housing of the inner rings has been removed, the phenomenon has spread outward, producing widening seas of decay.

Yet from meager beginnings in the 1960s there is increasing evidence of the emergence of islands of renewal. In certain neighborhoods, private-market initiatives are leading to revitalization. The crude statistics of population decline mask other data that carry within them countervailing indicators. In many "declining" cities the number of households has actually increased. Metropolitan Chicago's population increased only 1.8 percent between 1970 and 1980, yet the number of households increased by 13.9 percent and housing units (occupied plus vacant) by 15.1 percent. In metropolitan Pittsburgh population declined by 5.7 percent; households increased by 9.1 percent; and housing units increased by 10.8 percent. In their respective central cities, Chicago's population declined by 10.8 percent and housing units by 2.9 percent; and Pittsburgh's population declined by 18.5 percent and housing units by 5.6 percent. But in both of these central cities the numbers and the percentages of young adults increased, particularly those engaged in the white-collar and professional occupations that have grown in downtown Chicago and have been central to Pittsburgh's two-phased "Renaissance," the transformation of a blue-collar steel city into a far-reaching headquarters city and administrative hub.

Conventional wisdom has it that these young professionals are the driving forces of "gentrification," the private-market revitalization that has produced the islands of renewal within the seas of decay. In what follows, this conventional wisdom will be assessed and additional causal elements suggested. I first review the currently available literature on the topic and then examine two derivative hypotheses about timing and location: first, the demand-shift idea associated with young professionals of the baby boom generation; and second, supply-side notions involving the pace of filtering and the magnitude of the price differentials for suburban and central-city housing. The essay concludes by linking the changes to the knowledge-and information-based postindustrial revolution that is now transforming the American economy and society.

STUDIES OF REVITALIZATION

Since the early 1970s the news media have chronicled the renewal of certain neighborhoods in U.S. central cities. The appearance of young professionals (a sort of newly arrived gentry) and of refurbished homes in deteriorated neighborhoods has provided sharp contrast to the overwhelming decline of central-city housing. Renewed interest in what was considered obsolete housing has captured the journalistic imagination and has become the hope for the eventual turnaround of central-city living environments and their residential tax bases.

Preservation of vintage housing near the traditional central business areas of American cities is, of course, a longer-term phenomenon than popularly reported. Early models predicted deterioration of central neighborhoods as upwardly mobile families moved to new housing at the developing periphery, but resistance to this tendency was soon noted. Neighborhoods in Central Boston's Back Bay and historic neighborhoods near the Common, Beacon Hill, and the Charles River were able to resist change and retain their historic values.[3] Georgetown, in Washington, D.C., exhibited early resistance to decapitalization as strong efforts were made by residents for preservation both through traditional zoning and by means of new federal legislation.[4] Such early resistance was restricted to areas occupied by the elite. Current private-market rehabilitation by young artisans or professionals is a new and significantly different force, however.

Anecdotal reporting by the media and follow-up study raise a variety of questions, including the extent of revival, the factors influencing it, neighborhood conditions during the process, and the effects on neighborhoods. Recurring themes are these: Is the phenomenon a back-to-the-city movement? Does it offer a prospect for reversing central-city decline and shoring up sagging tax bases? Is the interest in central-city housing a reflection of changing preferences in housing and life-styles, or is it due simply to a shift in relative housing prices between the suburbs and the central cities?

Extent of revival

The earliest studies of neighborhood revitalization examined the extent of revival in older New York and Philadelphia neighborhoods.[5] There were important relationships between the location of the neighborhoods and the presence of social and employment opportunities in the central core: a later study confirmed that a weak urban core precluded revival.[6]

The first cross-city studies were undertaken in the 1970s. A landmark Urban Land Institute study examined private market housing renovation in 260 central cities having populations over 50,000.[7] Forty-eight percent of the respondents said that there was some renovation taking place within their city; the total number of units being renovated was barely

48%

50,000, however, averaging 441 units per city. A National Urban Coalition study of the 30 largest central cities showed similarly modest levels of revitalization, restricted to only 100 neighborhoods overall.[8] The percentage of cities reported to be experiencing renovation increased with size and was higher in the North and South than elsewhere. Units being rehabilitated were predominantly single-family, located within areas of local or national historical importance (possibly having received historic designation), and were close to the city's central business district.[9]

An examination of the twenty largest standard metropolitan statistical areas for 1960–70 produced similar findings.[10] Certain cities with strong cores (New York, Washington, and Boston) showed extensive areas of housing improvement; in others, improvement was restricted to one or two neighborhoods near the core if the core was healthy. When the core was stagnant or deteriorating, there was little rehabilitation. Cities with the highest rates of central white-collar employment and the greatest commuting distances to new housing developments had the strongest, highest-status cores and the greatest volumes of renovation activity.

The extent of revitalization reported is not large. Renovation so far appears to have affected less than 0.5 percent of the central-city housing stock.[11] Continuing outmigration from central cities and disinvestment in housing appear to serve as brakes on private investors because the renovation that has been taking place is risk sensitive and, in most cases, limited in intensity.[12] As Sternlieb has noted; "While much has been made of the relatively few cases of middle class stabilization and/or return to the city … as yet these are relatively trivial. The decade of the 1970s … has given little promise of mass revival in the major central cities."[13]

Speculations about causes

What precipitates the decision to renovate a central-city home? Locational, aesthetic, social, and economic factors have been cited. Convenience to place of employment (usually white-collar or professional) in order to reduce commuting distance is the most often quoted reason for moving into a central-city neighborhood.[14] Families in revitalizing neighborhoods rank nearness to employment among the first three reasons for moving into the area.[15] Other factors include nearness to commercial or institutional centers and presence of other than residential rehabilitation. In New Orleans, renovation was viewed more positively than new construction.

Nonresidential upgrading occurred near 81 percent of the improved neighborhoods.[16]

Aesthetics (that is, the character of the neighborhood and style of the house) also appears to be critical in selection of a neighborhood for renovation. In virtually all areas being improved, the house is of a significant architectural style. Victorian designs are especially favored in neighborhoods that were built originally to house upper-middle-class families and have filtered yet remain basically sound. The reversal of the filtering process is in many ways due to the recognition of their earlier value and the expectation that house and neighborhood could be returned to their former state. Claims to particular historical significance have tended to reinforce the value of distinctive architecture, most dramatically in Washington, D.C.[17]

Closely related are social factors—attitudinal and life-style changes among a portion of an emerging group in demand of housing.[18] Many researchers have hypothesized that young, professional, childless couples with college educations and two incomes hold an entirely different set of preferences than was common a generation ago.[19] These persons favor lifestyles associated with aesthetics, the excitement of central-city living, and proximity to their places of professional or white-collar employment.

The shift in housing preference by this group is part of an expressed quest for a new set of social values. The appeal of an integrated neighborhood has drawn some young couples, although the level of integration appears to decline as gentrification runs its course.[20] Another attraction is nearness to adult-oriented activities and the city's cultural life.[21] The development of pro-urban values and the desire to reside in mixed ethnic and cultural environments are particularly strong stimuli.

Economic factors are vocalized least by survey respondents. However, one study of Washington, D.C., found them ranked prominently, with respondents naming the investment potential and the affordable price as the reason for selecting neighborhoods undergoing gentrification.[22] According to other studies, the baby boom population entered the housing market when new construction was low and suburban housing was relatively expensive, making the central city a sensible choice, and this opportunity for good, stylish housing at bargain prices is considered a key explanatory variable.[23] Outward shifts in housing and jobs cause a net drop in housing demand in the central city, and a comparison of housing value and potential capital growth makes central-city housing a wise investment.[24]

The potential renovator senses the increased viability of central-city housing and observes higher costs elsewhere as well as the high cost of commuting. In five major cities (Boston, Dallas, San Francisco, Atlanta, and St. Paul), due to the high cost of both new construction and existing suburban housing, the inner cities offered the home buyer more. A wide variety of convenient, reasonably priced houses in neighborhoods with high vacancy rates (for example, homes that were almost fully depreciated and outwardly uninhabitable in Boston's South End) were available for several thousand dollars.[25] Viewed in such a light, private market rehabilitation is not a chance phenomenon, but an investment decision. Movement of capital to the suburbs results in depreciation of central values and a "rent gap." When the gap is large, rehabilitation investments challenge the rates of return available elsewhere and capital returns to the city.[26]

Another factor widely hypothesized to be influential is rapidly rising commuting costs brought on by energy price increases. During the energy crisis, respondents did not want to live far from their jobs.[27] Energy costs have not been ranked significantly in many studies, however. But an alternative transportation cost rationale explaining the original movement of the affluent to the periphery and their subsequent return to the central city has been postulated.[28] It is rooted in the differential effects of price changes on income groups, not in preferences. The reversal in the location of the well-to-do is explained by a continuation, not a reversal, of the price changes that caused the flight to the periphery. Expensive transportation innovations always gave initial competitive advantages in location to the wealthy, but eventually the lower cost of that transportation allowed the poor to follow. Historically, a succession of innovations allowed the rich to maintain their superior locational advantage. But no innovation has replaced the automobile, and rich and poor now approach equal access to housing opportunity. As a result, a reversal in housing patterns is now occurring, because the rich are substituting locational for technological advantage.

Is there a back-to-the-city movement?

Much has been made of inner-city revitalization as a back-to-the-city movement. Early reporting by national and regional media developed the theme that private rehabilitation was being undertaken by families who had at one time turned their backs on

the city and were now returning, disillusioned by suburban life-styles, housing costs, and increasing costs of commuting.

This hypothesis has been tested. People moving to rehabilitated neighborhoods were questioned around the country. Their responses seem to support an alternative hypothesis, because for the most part they came from other parts of the central city. It appears to be a stay-in-the-city rather than a back-to-the-city movement.

One comparative study of Atlanta, New Orleans, New York, St. Paul, Boston, Cambridge, and Washington, D.C., showed only a minority (20 percent) of the new households coming from the suburbs. From 50 to 90 percent of new households questioned had come from somewhere else in the central city. Most were first-home buyers. A large majority of the families (60 to 90 percent) had spent their childhood in rural, small town, or suburban areas, though. They came to the city for college or employment and when ready to make an investment in housing chose the city as an environment preferable to the suburbs.[29]

In Washington, D.C., there was not so much a back-to-the-city movement as there was an investment in permanent homes by former renters.[30] Only 10 percent of new white households in the central city were returning from the suburbs, a similar percentage to that for Philadelphia, where only 14 percent of rehabilitators came from the suburbs, 72 percent came from elsewhere in the city, and 11 percent were upgrading their long-term residence.[31]

A stay-in-the-city phenomenon is thus more likely than a return from the suburbs. Newly established city families have strong reasons to stay in the city and to find investment opportunities there compatible with their needs. Established suburban dwellers, securely settled in their own housing market, employment, and social routines, have little incentive to return to the city.[32] The life-cycle change when young adults leave their parents' homes does place large numbers of youths in the city as they begin their careers or higher education, however.[33] The expansion of central-city office space and managerial and professional occupations is very attractive to young college-trained couples.[34] Centers of employment, two-wage-earner households, and the rising prices of suburban housing keep these families in the city. Surveys of central-city neighborhood attitudes report a strong satisfaction with neighborhood life among these residents. Even though residents feel the city is declining, they expect to remain.[35] Their confidence is in the neighborhood and not the city.

Stages of revitalization

According to many observers, the revitalization process changes dramatically as it progresses, producing an environment quite different from the one envisioned by the first renovating families.[36] The stages of the process are distinguished primarily by the actors involved and the extent of renovation accomplished.

STAGE ONE. A few households (either oblivious to or acceptant of the risks involved), usually singles or childless couples, purchase homes in a deteriorated neighborhood and begin renovating for their own use. These are often design professionals or artists, each one employed, who share a desire to live in a mixed ethnic neighborhood in a part of the city exhibiting popularized urban cultural values and who express their design aptitudes by restoring classic homes. Since neighborhood vacancy rates are high and the houses are often gutted shells, the cost is very low and there is little displacement of existing neighborhood residents. As a result, there is little resentment or hostility on the part of the indigenous population. Little public attention is aroused by the initial activity. The newcomers rely on private capital sources, "sweat equity" investment, and informal neighborhood organizations for support. Efforts are generally confined to a two-to-three block area.

STAGE TWO. After six months to a couple of years, knowledge of neighborhood rehabilitation spreads. Many of the same types of families are attracted, plus a new group of "risk takers"—upper-middle-income management or professional types. The price, investment potential, and neighborhood cultural, architectural, and locational characteristics are appealing, but capital still is not freely available due to continuing uncertainty. Realtors become involved in subtle promotional activities, and small-scale developers begin renovating for speculation, but in limited amounts because of a lack of institutional investment capital. The media begin to take note of the scale of rehabilitation, and the boundaries of the area expand. Vacant housing quickly disappears, and displacement begins to occur among rentals where low-income, elderly, and transient populations reside. Those who move in at stage two are not as accepting of class and cultural differences, and the indigenous population begins to express resentment as invasion threatens their stability.

STAGE THREE. There is major media and government interest in the neighborhood. Physical improvements are visible. Active governmental intervention begins. Prices escalate, developers begin larger-scale renovations, conversion of rental units to condominiums begins in force, and commercial redevelopment spreads. The area is "greenlined" by financial institutions, and investment and home improvement capital becomes more readily available. Newer groups of residents appear, including older and more affluent executives and administrators who are risk averse. They pay top prices and effectively displace most of the remaining indigenous residents. The newcomers establish their own neighborhood organizations or effectively dominate or change the character of pioneer organizations. They make demands for public resources, protection, and land use restrictions. Social service institutions and public housing or low-income housing assistance programs are resisted. *A change a lot*

The revitalizing neighborhood

What is evident from the foregoing is that there is a private-market process that is successfully running counter to the dominant forces of deconcentration and downward filtering of older housing. Residential deterioration is arrested, upgrading takes place, and the rich displace the poor.

What characteristics do revitalizing neighborhoods share in common? In the nation's thirty largest central cities, 46 percent of the structures in revitalizing areas were at least one hundred years old and another 27 percent were at least seventy-five years old.[37] The area represented the cities' most distinctive architecture, generally Victorian. Most neighborhoods were dominated by one- or two-family structures, a characteristic that was maintained through the process. Seventy-eight percent of the housing was judged to be deteriorating before investment. In about half the neighborhoods, the cost of acquisition was less than $15,000.

Changes due to rehabilitation include improvements in both buildings and public facilities. Structural improvements range from less expensive cosmetic improvements to authentic restoration or gut rehabilitation, including major structural and utilities replacement. As revitalization reaches advanced stages increasing pressure is exerted by neighborhood organizations or local government for public improvements. Demands are made and met for street and sidewalk resurfacing or replacement with paving stones, fashionable lighting, landscaping, and improved public services such as police patrols and sanitary disposal. Rehabilitators generally do not seek improvements in public education, however, since they either have few children or use private schools.[38]

The value of improved units increases rapidly. Demand for the units is brisk, and early investment and sweat equity pay off handsomely. Values in one Washington, D.C. area increased at twice the city rate.[39] There are preconditions for this success, however. The neighborhood must have definable boundaries so that there is reasonable anticipation of consolidation and stability. The housing stock must have residual strengths—a high percentage with special characteristics or potential for rehabilitation. The area must be of special historical importance or qualify for historical district designation. It must be favorably located near the central business district. There should be expectations that significant rehabilitation will take place and that government services can be improved. Influential neighborhood groups are essential. These are conditions necessary for later stages of revitalization and are seldom considered important to investment by "risk-oblivious" pioneers.[40]

What about the human characteristics of upgraded neighborhoods? The general nature of social change was outlined earlier. A detailed insight into a classic case of social interaction, confrontation, and use of organizational influence was provided in a study of the transition of Boston's South End.[41]

Before rehabilitation, residents were a racially mixed combination of settled families, singles, elderly people, and transients. Employed persons were generally blue-collar workers, clerks, and low-skilled laborers. Population densities were higher at this time than at any period later in the process.[42] In contrast, those moving in were predominantly childless, white adult households, together with many single parents in their late twenties or early thirties, professionals or managers, well educated (up to 80 percent with college degrees), affluent enough to handle self-financing, and highly motivated politically and socially.[43]

After rehabilitation was complete, about half of the neighborhood was composed of younger couples and half was of mixed age but significantly younger than the previous residents. Professional and white-collar employees assumed control of neighborhood politics and pressure group activities for public improvements.[44] The activism was short-lived, however. Once the improvements were secured, involvement by the latecomers declined. Typically, latecomers are not as neighborhood-based as the pioneers were. Their associations are based on work, and they look outside the neighborhood for recreation and consumer goods and services. Their higher-status tastes exceed what the neighborhood can provide. They prefer political issues to personalities and interest group lobbying to clubs or populist vehicles, and thus stay independent of neighborhood organizations.[45]

Positive and negative impacts

Though the extent of gentrification is not great, the available literature suggests that it has substantial impacts, both positive and negative, on the central city. Positive effects are decreases in vacancy rates, increases in property values, stability in once-declining neighborhoods, encouragement of other forms of development in or near the neighborhoods, and rekindled interest in the central city as a place to live—a real locational and economic alternative to housing in the suburbs. The positive aspects are welcomed by the city, development and business interests, and established and prospective residents, and they are lauded by the media and students of urban research.

Negative aspects, with the possible exception of displacement, are often overlooked by those interested in the benefits of rehabilitation. The costs of increased demands for service, infrastructure, and amenities and the impact on existing public services have not been studied, nor have the opportunity costs of investment capital or the problem of speculative increases in blighted property values that might be unsupportable in the long run.[46]

Of all of the problems accompanying private-market renewal, the most serious is displacement. The first to be displaced are renters. A National Urban Coalition Study found that these predominantly minority, elderly, and transient groups are always forced out casualties of owner capitalization of depreciated structures, escalating demand in a market of fixed supply, and increasing code enforcement.[47]

Accurate study of the extent of this neighborhood displacement is difficult. The cost and effort of tracing the displaced families has discouraged systematic analysis. Small samples and intuitive judgment are the basis of most conclusions. The results are as ambiguous as data on the real extent of revitalization.

Data from the Census Bureau's *Annual Housing Survey* indicate that 1 million households were displaced between 1974 and 1976, yet one study indicated the problem to be relatively small in scale, affecting 100 to 200 households per year in any city.[48] Studies of Washington, D.C., suggest that the problem grew significantly there during the 1970s, compounded by low vacancy rates due in part to suburban development moratoria that reduced housing starts. On the other hand, another study suggests that where rehabilitation occurs at a moderate pace and vacancy rates approximate the national average, the impact of displacement is modest, although the effects on affected individuals may be profound.[49]

DEMAND-SIDE DYNAMICS: THE GENTRIFICATION HYPOTHESIS

A picture begins to emerge: amidst pervasive depopulation of central cities some neighborhoods in some of these cities are beginning to attract private capital and along with it the mainly white middle class. Alliterative labels abound—rehabilitation, reinvestment, revitalization, even renaissance—but the most evocative term is the one imported from London: *gentrification.*

By conjuring the image of an aristocratic landed gentry, the gentrification label suggests that the new urban gentry are somehow different from and more exotic than normal people. An unexamined folklore has sprung up. According to the oral tradition, the urban gentry are overwhelmingly young, affluent, and nomadic. Many are artists, architects, or self-employed professionals. They include homosexuals or "swinging singles" drawn to the nightlife and the sexual marketplace of the city. Those that are married are likely to be childless two-earner couples. But this given wisdom about the new urban gentry has not been subjected to much empirical scrutiny. What literature exists on the topic tends to rely upon impressionistic and anecdotal observations, rather than on a systematic comparison of the social worlds of comparably affluent urban and suburban dwellers.

To the extent that more systematic inquiry is now being undertaken, it centers on the gentrification hypothesis: that the key role in the rehabilitation of decaying homes and the restoration of blighted neighborhoods is being played by relatively affluent childless two-worker families—"yuppies."[50]

Attributes of the new gentry

For example, one effort to model the sources of the city's upper-income renaissance concludes that upper-income residence in the city usually requires the following observable attributes:

1. Childless households. The decision to raise children implies a substantial commitment to activities focused on home and family. Individuals and couples who have not made this commitment can be expected to seek both more diversions and more social relationships outside the home than those who have. The social, cultural, and entertainment facilities of the city center can provide both things to do and opportunities for making and maintaining friendships. For individuals and couples in childless households, these facilities' marginal utility should be high and remain high even with frequent use. On the other hand, reductions in residential density are apt to provide relatively modest and rapidly declining increments to satisfaction for childless households. Exterior space where children can play safely without supervision is of obvious value where children are present, but irrelevant when children are absent from the household.

2. Unmarried adults. An interest in social relationships outside the home and in opportunities for meeting and entertaining one another should be particularly strong among unmarried adults, even when they are heads of families with children.

3. Higher educational levels. Besides the skills it develops, higher education seeks to enhance understanding and appreciation of a wide variety of cultural experiences and historical properties and neighborhoods that are most frequently found in the central city. It should therefore increase the pleasure such experiences provide and sustain it during repeated attendance or exposure that would quickly bore the uninitiated.[51]

Childlessness is a particularly important factor because childless families are relatively impervious to the turmoil in big-city school systems associated with the desegregation that has led to white flight.[52] Childlessness, in turn, flows directly from shifts in the composition and life-styles of the American population. The continued development of American society has resulted in increased economic parity for women; this enables them to have the option of roles other than those of housewife and mother. In consequence, men and women lead more independent lives and are able to exercise more options. Increasing number of couples live together without the formal ties of marriage. The direct and opportunity costs of child rearing are rising; birth control technology has improved; and abortion laws have been liberalized. Hence the birthrate is dropping. There are increasing numbers of families with two or more workers and more working wives than ever before.

The literature on residential mobility states that changes in family status—such as marriage, birth of children, or dissolution of marriage—raise the probability that a given family will change its residence; that families in different stages of the life cycle differ in their sensitivity to particular neighborhood characteristics (such as crime rates or school quality); and that families are residentially segregated on the basis of their stage in the life cycle.

In residential choice theory, a family is presumed to observe an array of neighborhoods that differ in quality of the housing structures (space, comfort); physical aspects (location, site amenities);

social character (class, ethnic, and racial composition); municipal services (quality of schools, police protection, tax rates); and housing prices. Families presumably attribute different importance to these characteristics, depending upon their stage in the life cycle, socioeconomic status, race, or ethnicity. High-income families with school-age children may place greater weight on safe streets than do low-income families without children. Or, because their wages are higher and time is more valuable, high-income families may be more willing to avoid commuting costs than low-income families.

Within the spectrum of neighborhood choices available, the reduction in fertility and the rise in female labor force participation produce a situation in which affluent, childless, two-worker families appear to be attracted to neighborhoods offering: (1) geographic clusters of housing structures capable of yielding high-quality services; (2) a variety of public amenities within safe walking distance of these areas, such as a scenic waterfront, parks, museums or art galleries, universities, distinguished architecture, and historic landmarks or neighborhoods; and (3) a range of high-quality retail facilities and services, including restaurants, theaters, and entertainment.

These neighborhoods are more often than not close to downtown and tend to have older housing, higher crime rates, worse air pollution, and schools that are perceived as worse than those in the suburbs. These factors are almost fully reflected in housing prices. For example, houses in school zones attended by low-income minorities generally command lower prices than houses located in zones attended by upper-middle-income whites. This price differential presumably reflects the competition by families with school-age children for housing in the "better" school district. Families without children have no special reason to pay a premium for living in the neighborhood with better schools and find the neighborhood with poor schools less expensive, other factors being equal. A flight of middle-class families with children from downtown neighborhoods to the suburbs thereby creates potential housing bargains for affluent families without children. This potential is realized if other relevant urban-suburban differences in neighborhood quality, such as safety and cleanliness of the streets, are reduced.[53]

Affluent, two-worker families may, of course, inherently be attracted to near-downtown residences because of the proximity to their jobs in government, communications, finance, or law. These activities are still heavily concentrated in the central business districts of many older cities despite the long-term suburbanization of employment. Indeed, analyses of centrifugal patterns of metropolitan growth through the 1960s have identified the professional-managerial group as the biggest losers: because of the high degree of centralization of their jobs in some cities, this group may face the longest commute. The situation is even more acute for two-worker professional families. Living in the peripheral suburbs, such families often spend twice as much time and money in commuting downtown as a one-worker family. Even if the secondary worker does not work downtown, a more central location provides greater access to the metropolitan labor market. Finally, peripheral residence restricts access to cultural amenities and recreational opportunities that loom large in the budgets of the more affluent.

Such observations serve to affirm one scholar's conclusion that the cities with strong upper-income neighborhoods close to downtown were, in 1960–70, dominantly those with administrative central business districts, minimal heavy industry, and long commuting distances to the suburbs.[54] Conversely, industrial cities with weak central business districts and dispersed industrial locations were unable to retain or attract the professional middle class.

Cohort effect or long-term change?

According to one line of argument, the continued decline in fertility, the prolongation of childlessness, the growth of female labor force participation, and the emergence of high-service downtown economies all bode well for the cities. Indeed, it is argued that the changes in family composition of the 1970s and 1980s may have far more impact on returning the middle class to the central city than all the urban redevelopment programs of the 1950s and 1960s.[55] A question that then arises is whether these changes will remain in the long term or simply are an effect associated with the baby boom cohort that will pass as members of that generation age.

Demographers note that even in the 1960s young people (aged 20 to 25) expressed some preference for city living.[56] Cities have long served as "staging areas"—places where young middle-class adults, while renting, could meet and marry before settling down to raise families in the suburbs. If the age-specific preferences of past decades remained the same, the maturation of the baby boom cohort would, in itself, swell the ranks of young city dwellers (though not necessarily of young central-city home buyers), but the effect would pass.

Thus one view is that reduction in urban household size represents a postponement of marriage and childbearing in the baby boom cohort, rather than a permanent shift in family patterns. The argument continues that the 1980s may see an acceleration of urban out-migration rates as the children of the baby boom years move through their own childbearing period.

In the same vein, another scholar argues that the most important influence on residential location is accessibility to the workplace, and so long as downtowns continue to lose professional and managerial jobs to the suburbs, the accessibility factor will work to the disadvantage of gentrification. He also observes that while safer neighborhoods are more important to families with children than to childless families, the difference is slight, as are the differences in preferences for neighborhood racial composition between families varying by number of children and number of workers.[57]

But others demur, arguing that the baby boom cohort is behaving differently from preceding cohorts and will continue to do so.[58] The sheer size of the cohort is said to condemn its members to perpetual relative economic disadvantage—a disadvantage that has prompted falling fertility rates, declining household size, increased female labor force participation, and a reluctance to make long-term commitments to marriage and family. This demographic determinism suggests that the tastes and preferences of the maturing baby boom generation will not change drastically, and that its members will likely remain in the city longer than those favoring the temporary nature of the cohort effect might imagine.

SUPPLY-SIDE FORCES: A NEW INTERPRETATION

The gentrification hypothesis suggests a variety of reasons why childless two-worker professional households are likely to be drawn to certain kinds of inner-city neighborhoods, while the combination of the large baby boom cohort and the rapid growth of professional employment in the last two decades indicates why this particular set of demands has grown. But why has gentrification occurred only in certain central cities? A new supply-side interpretation helps to answer this question.

The classical supply-side argument has two components. The first rests on the observation that although more households are added to the ranks of homeowners during high construction years than during low construction years,[59] rehabilitation expenditures have classically been countercyclical.[60] This observation has led to the conclusion that the forces guiding home seekers to the central city have

been greatest in periods of economic downturn and in the metropolitan housing markets where the new housing industry is weakest.

The second component is the effects of rapid increases in both building costs and housing prices in the face of increasing demand. The baby boom children graduated from high school between 1965 and 1982, so the housing market is now experiencing the full impact of that cohort. The logical resolution of the conflict between higher suburban building costs and increasing numbers of home seekers should be to increase the demand for lower-cost central-city housing or to stimulate provision of alternatives, such as factory-built (mobile) homes and condominium or cooperative ownership. This force should be greatest, according to this argument, in the housing markets with the greatest cost and demand pressures. Together, the two supply-side components lead to a prediction that gentrification is most likely in housing markets with weak new housing industries faced by both rapidly rising construction costs and housing demand and should occur countercyclically, at low points in the economic cycle.

In what follows I argue to the contrary. It is the housing markets in which the new housing industry has created the largest surpluses and in which the forces of inner-city abandonment are greatest that one finds the most extensive and sustained processes of gentrification, subject to the condition that there also be significant office growth in the central business district.

The magnitude of excess supply

The U.S. home-building industry has responded to strong housing demand in the last thirty years by constructing new homes at rates substantially greater than the rate of household growth. The amount by which new construction exceeds household growth in any housing market can be called the excess supply. Excess supplies will result either in increased vacancies or in withdrawals of older units from the housing stock as households move into the better units and the market attempts to bring demand and supply back into balance. Vacant units may also be removed from the housing stock so that in certain housing markets withdrawals from the stock may exceed excess supply by the amount by which vacancies are reduced.[61]

Nationally, some 20 million new housing units were built in the 1970s (nearly double the increase of the 1960s), so that by 1980 one in every five American households was able to reside in a home that was less than ten years old. Close to 7 million older housing units were removed from use as places of residence, although rates of displacement from housing that was condemned, demolished, or for some other reason removed from the inventory were lower than during the 1960s, when urban renewal and slum clearance programs were at a peak.[62] As a result, the availability of housing increased from 284 units per 1,000 people in 1940 to 338 in 1970 and 389 in 1980. Average household size fell from over 3.5 to 2.5 between 1940 and 1980.[63] Another result was the removal of large numbers of housing units that were no longer useful because of their absolute age and obsolescence or their configuration. If all central-city housing is taken as a group, in the brief period from 1970 to 1974, filtering made possible by excess supply produced substantial upgrading on most indices of housing quality: there was a reduction of over 25 percent in the number of units lacking some or all plumbing and in units with more than one person per room, while the number of units having no bathrooms or shared bathrooms was reduced by more than one-third.[64]

For many of the excess housing units filtered out at the unwanted end of the nation's housing chains, abandonment preceded withdrawal from the stock.[65] Technically, abandonment describes structures that are largely unoccupied and whose original use is no longer economically viable. The owners have walked away and the services that normally keep them intact are no longer being provided, property taxes are frequently unpaid, and the city may be in the process of taking title to the properties via tax foreclosure. Ultimately, most such abandoned buildings are demolished. But abandonment may also be viewed in terms of the scrappage rate familiar to businessmen: the proportion of an inventory that is removed on an annual basis. The housing scrappage rate that manifests itself in end-of-the-line abandonment approximates 1 percent of the housing stock per year, an annual loss of 600,000–800,000 units.[66]

Withdrawals from stock and contagious abandonment

When new construction is suburban and the least desirable stock is older and more central, it is easy to see how the phenomenon of inner-city abandonment—the seas of decay—can arise. As more desirable housing units are occupied and less desirable ones left behind, excess supplies of housing will show up in withdrawals from the inner-city housing stock and depopulation of the central city. This can happen in an atmosphere of general "looseness" of the housing market, when many units need

to be withdrawn from the stock to bring demand and supply into balance but vacancies still increase, or when there is a "tightening" of the market because both excess supplies and some of the existing vacancies are removed as the market readjusts toward equilibrium. In the first case, the inner city will have increasing numbers of vacant and boarded-up buildings; in the second, there will be vacant lots and empty spaces.

In the extreme case, abandonment develops a dynamic of its own, becoming a contagious process—a spreading blight that leads to the removal of far more units from the housing stock than would be warranted by smooth filtering of excess supplies to the oldest units and neighborhoods, those most in need of scrappage and replacement.[67] Contagious abandonment can lead to the removal of the good along with the bad and can rapidly transform a situation of substantial excess supply into one of significant tightness.

The conditions for gentrification

The classical supply-side argument, stated above, was that gentrification should be characteristic of housing markets where the new housing industry is weakest or faced by the greatest demand pressures. Yet if one considers the cases where significant gentrification has been recorded (for example, New York, Philadelphia, San Francisco, Boston, Washington, St. Louis, and Atlanta),[68] my research reveals that a different dynamic is taking place. Gentrification has its onset in some of the housing markets in which the housing industry is producing substantial excess supply by building far more units than the growth in the number of households requires—markets that one would expect to be among the nation's loosest. Which are being gentrified? The process appears to be limited to those housing markets in which even larger volumes of the older housing stock are being scrapped (typically as an outcome of contagious abandonment), and there is a resultant tightening of the market as the pool of vacancies is reduced.

However, the list of gentrification-eligible housing markets tightened by contagious abandonment also includes such examples as Detroit, Cleveland, and Newark, where significant gentrification has not yet occurred. This leads me to the conclusion that supply-side factors set a necessary but not a sufficient condition for gentrification to take place. There must be an additional triggering mechanism that separates the markets with the necessary combinations of excess supplies, scrappage rates, and vacancy changes into those with and those without gentrification.

The missing link has been alluded to earlier: significant central business district growth, focusing professional and white-collar jobs downtown. What separates the Cleveland, Detroit, and Newark cases from those such as Boston, Philadelphia, and Atlanta is the growth of central business district office space, averaging barely 20 percent in the cases without gentrification, but 33 percent in those with it in 1970–78 (Figure 6.1). Excessive scrappage of inner-city housing is indeed a necessary but not sufficient supply-side condition for gentrification to occur; the process has to be activated by

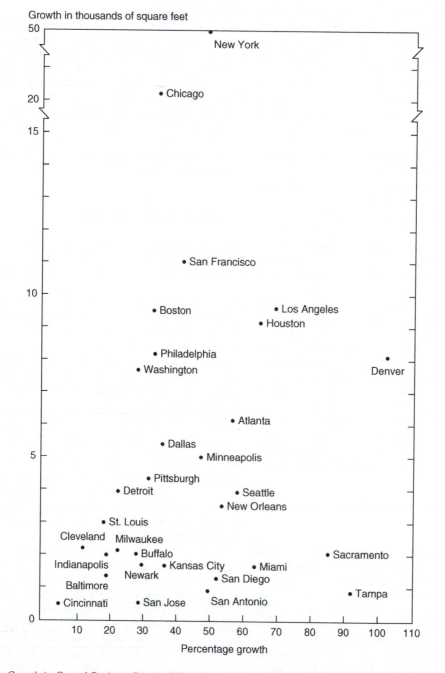

Figure 6.1 Growth in Central Business District Office Space in Thirty-one U.S. Cities, 1970–78

demand-side shifts rooted in professional job growth anchored in downtown offices and by baby boom life-style shifts.

These shifts, in turn, have their own roots in the emergence of a modern service economy after World War II and the concentration of corporate activities and key producer services in selected cities. Some of those cities—those with the necessary housing market conditions—also had gentrification. The services revolution has been charted by Thomas M. Stanbaek, Jr., and his associates.[69] The main points of their arguments are as follows.

1. Between 1948 and 1978 the share of services in U.S. employment increased from 54 percent to 67 percent. The most significant change was the rapid emergence of producer services designed to assist private-sector firms and public-sector and nonprofit institutions in carrying out administrative, developmental, and financial functions. This change brought with it a shift from blue-collar to white-collar jobs, a major expansion in the employment of women, and new characteristics relating to working conditions, terms of employment, and the distribution of earnings among workers.

2. The new jobs in corporate and producer services concentrated disproportionately in selected urban centers—what Stanback terms the nation's *nodal centers*, metropolitan areas strongly specialized and diversified in the distributive services and in corporate activities. These include four national centers—New York, Los Angeles, Chicago, and San Francisco—and nineteen regional centers, such as Boston, Philadelphia, and Atlanta. Other places affected have been a few key specialized centers characterized by the articulation of administration, research, and production in selected industrial complexes, such as Pittsburgh in steel and Rochester in scientific and office equipment.

3. The concentration of many of the growing services in the downtown areas of the nation's principal organizational and control centers, which thus focused jobs and residential choices for young white-collar and professional workers, has arisen from very traditional pulls: those of agglomeration economies that accrue to firms when they congregate. In this respect, the role of corporate headquarters, divisional offices, and other specialized service installations is of particular importance. As developmental and administrative functions have become more important, major corporate offices have increasingly been located near large banks, insurance companies, legal firms, and other producer services. In turn, they have fostered the growth of these services. These agglomeration tendencies do not simply benefit the relationship between producer services and corporate headquarters or divisional offices, however. They also attract a host of private-sector, public-sector, and nonprofit services. Specialty retail stores, fancy restaurants, theaters, universities, major hospitals, or specialized governmental services tend to locate more frequently in large places because of the larger markets to be served. In turn, corporations and their attendant producer services are drawn to these places because of the larger support system of consumer and not-for-profit services that they find there.

It is in this growing complex of modern service-sector activities that the professional and white-collar jobs supporting gentrification have emerged. To turn the supply-side argument around, the nation's key "command and control" centers provide a sufficient demand-side trigger for gentrification, provided that the necessary supply-side housing market characteristics also are present.

CONCLUSIONS

Certain neighborhoods in certain central cities are experiencing a new form of private-market revitalization—gentrification. The process is limited to urban centers of strategic national and regional importance in which the expansion of modern headquarters complexes and related producer services has led to significant new central business district growth, producing the demand-side trigger for young professional and white-collar workers. It also is limited to housing markets in which new construction substantially exceeds household growth, but in which scrappage (perhaps in the form of contagious abandonment) exceeds the excess housing supply. The result is that the markets are tightened and older central-city housing becomes an attractive option.

It is the intersection of the two sets of forces that is of interest. Central business district growth in Sun Belt urban centers lacking the necessary housing market conditions is not accompanied by gentrification. Neither is there gentrification in older urban regions where abandonment proceeds apace, but the central business district remains moribund. Both the necessary and the sufficient conditions must be satisfied for a process of gentrification to begin.

Once the process takes hold, it serves to heighten the contrast between renewal and decay. The cities that have shifted most sharply to a service employment base have at the same time experienced the most dramatic losses of their middle-income manufacturing jobs. As a result, their labor markets have become increasingly polarized between well-paying white-collar and professional employment and low-paying service jobs. The overall trend among the service industries has been toward the development of more polarized earning structures and truncated occupational systems. Most service firms tend to be structured in such a way that the two poles of their occupational system are dependent upon one another to ensure the existence and functioning of the firm, yet are rarely linked internally by ladders of upward mobility. As a result, what appears to be emerging is a situation in which two labor markets and, by extension, two societies coexist, increasingly divorced from each other.

The contrast between, yet interdependency of, the islands of renewal and seas of decay is therefore one of the manifestations of this polarization, for the most fundamental axiom of both urban geography and urban sociology is that the urban landscape is a mirror reflecting the society that maintains it.[70] To reiterate, on the demand side the services revolution contributed to the shifts in preferences and behavior of the baby boom generation that are central to the gentrification hypothesis. Yet the effect of the services revolution has been concentrated in and around the downtowns of relatively few metropolitan areas, those in which withdrawals from stock have been greater than relatively high rates of excess supply. This has led to the apparent contradictions but logical links between suburban overbuilding, contagious inner-city abandonment, decreasing vacancies and tightening markets, and gentrification.

Whether or not gentrification will become more widespread depends in turn on whether or not service-related changes in job markets continue to reinforce polarization; whether the aging baby boom generation changes preferences; whether housing markets tighten or loosen; whether polarization creates such strains that it pushes top-echelon employees and jobs to decentralize; and whether technological change in communications facilitates interaction without the need for concentration, which could lead to the dissolution of central business district agglomerations. Each of these issues must be the subject of continuing research and monitoring if society hopes to anticipate change, measure the course of its direction, and attempt to reshape it for alternative ends.

Notes

1 Lawrence D. Schall, "Commodity Chain Systems and the Housing Market," *Journal of Urban Economics*, vol. 10 (September 1981), pp. 141–63; and John B. Lansing, Charles Wade Clifton, and James N. Morgan, *New Homes and Poor People* (University of Michigan, Institute for Social Research, 1969).

2 The figures for new construction and withdrawals from stock are estimated. Comparable figures for 1960–70 in Chicago are: household growth, 285,000; new construction, 481,000; vacancy increase, 7,000; and withdrawals from stock, 189,000. For Pittsburgh, the figures are 49,000; 115,000; −2,000; and 68,000. U.S. Bureau of the Census, *Census of Population and Housing*, 1960, 1970, and 1980.

3 Walter Firey, "Sentiment and Symbolism as Ecological Variables," *American Sociological Review*, vol. 10 (1945), p. 142.

4 Eileen Zeitz, *Private Urban Renewal* (Lexington, Mass.: Lexington Books, 1979), pp. 64–65.

5 Edgar M. Hoover and Raymond Vernon, *Anatomy of a Metropolis* (Harvard University Press, 1959); and William G. Grigsby, *Housing Markets and Public Policy* (University of Pennsylvania, Institute for Urban Studies, 1963).

6 Bernard J. Frieden, *The Future of Old Neighborhoods* (MIT Press, 1964), p. 128.

7 Thomas J. Black, "Private-Market Housing Renovation in Central Cities: A ULI Survey," *Urban Land*, vol. 34 (November 1975), p. 7.

8 National Urban Coalition, *Displacement: City Neighborhoods in Transition* (Washington, D.C.: National Urban Coalition, 1978).

9 Black, "Private-Market Housing Renovation," pp. 6–7.

10 Gregory S. Lipton, "Evidence of Central City Revival," *Journal of the American Planning Association*, vol. 43 (April 1977), pp. 136–47.

11 Phillip L. Clay, *Neighborhood Renewal* (Lexington, Mass.: Lexington Books, 1979), p. 17.

12 Howard J. Sumka, "Neighborhood Revitalization and Displacement: A Review of the Evidence," *Journal of the American Planning Association*, vol. 45 (October 1979), pp. 480–87.

13 George Sternlieb, *The Maintenance of America's Housing Stock* (Rutgers University, Center for Urban Policy Research, 1980).

14 Lipton, "Evidence of Central City Revival"; Clay, *Neighborhood Renewal*; Dennis E. Gale, "Middle Class Resettlement in Older Urban Neighborhoods: The Evidence and the Implications," *Journal of the American Planning Association*, vol. 45 (July 1979), p. 297; and Deborah Auger, "The Politics of Revitalization in Gentrifying Neighborhoods: A Case of Boston's South End," *Journal of the American Planning Association*, vol. 45 (July 1979), pp. 515–22.

15 Clay, *Neighborhood Renewal*, p. 15.
16 Ibid., p. 47.
17 Gale, "Middle Class Resettlement in Older Urban Neighborhoods"; and Dennis E. Gale, "Neighborhood Resettlement in Washington, D.C.," in Shirley B. Laska and Daphne Spain, eds., *Back to the City: Issues in Neighborhood Renovation* (Pergamon, 1980), pp. 95–115.
18 Sumka, "Neighborhood Revitalization."
19 Clay, *Neighborhood Renewal*, p. 16.
20 Gale, "Middle Class Resettlement in Older Urban Neighborhoods"; and Gale, "Neighborhood Resettlement in Washington, D.C."
21 Lipton, "Evidence of Central City Revival," p. 138.
22 Gale, "Middle Class Resettlement in Older Urban Neighborhoods"; and Gale, "Neighborhood Resettlement in Washington, D.C."
23 Sumka, "Neighborhood Revitalization," p. 482; and Clay, *Neighborhood Renewal*, p. 4.
24 Anthony Downs, "Key Relationships between Urban Development and Neighborhood Change," *Journal of the American Planning Association*, vol. 45 (October 1979), pp. 462–71; and Anthony Downs, *Neighborhoods and Urban Development* (Brookings, 1981).
25 Black, "Private-Market Housing Renovation."
26 Neil Smith, "Toward a Theory of Gentrification." *Journal of the American Planning Association*, vol. 45 (October 1979), p. 545.
27 Black, "Private-Market Housing Renovation," p. 8.
28 Stephen LeBoy and Jon Soustelie, "Paradise Lost and Regained: American Cities in the 1970s" (University of California–Los Angeles, 1979).
29 Gale, "Middle Class Resettlement in Older Urban Neighborhoods"; and Gale, "Neighborhood Resettlement in Washington, D.C."
30 George Grier and Eunice Crier, *Movers to the City: New Data on the Housing Market for Washington, D.C.* (Washington Center for Metropolitan Studies, 1977).
31 Smith, "Toward a Theory of Centrification," p. 539.
32 Herbert Cans, "Why Exurbanites Won't Reurbanize Themselves," *New York Times*, February 12, 1977.
33 Larry H. Long, "Back to the Countryside and Back to the City in the Same Decade," in Laska and Spain, eds, *Back to the City*, pp. 61–76.
34 Laska and Spain, eds, *Back to the City*.
35 Ibid.
36 A four-stage process was proposed by Pattison, elaborated by Clay, and refined to three stages by Gale. See Timothy Pattison, "The Process of Neighborhood Upgrading and Centrification" (M.A. thesis, Massachusetts Institute of Technology, 1977); Clay, *Neighborhood Renewal*; Gale, "Middle Class Resettlement in Older Urban Neighborhoods"; and Gale. "Neighborhood Resettlement in Washington, D.C."
37 Clay, *Neighborhood Renewal*, p. 18.
38 Ibid., p. 63.
39 Zeitz, *Private Urban Renewal*, p. 49.
40 Black, "Private-Market Housing Renovation," p. 7; and Paul Porter, "Neighborhood Interest in a City's Recovery, "*Journal of the American Planning Association*, vol. 45 (October 1979), pp. 473–79.
41 Auger, "The Politics of Revitalization in Gentrifying Neighborhoods."
42 Zeitz, *Private Urban Renewal*, pp. 39–40.
43 Grier and Grier, *Movers to the City*; Sternlieb, *The Maintenance of America's Housing Stock*; and Black, "Private-Market Housing Renovation," p. 7.
44 Zeitz, *Private Urban Renewal*, pp. 71–72.
45 Clay, *Neighborhood Renewal*, p. 65.
46 Black, "Private-Market Housing Renovation," p. 9.
47 Cushing N. Dolbeare, "Involuntary Displacement: A Major Issue for People and Neighborhoods," report prepared for the National Commission on Neighborhoods (Government Printing Office, 1978); and National Urban Coalition, *Displacement: City Neighborhoods in Transition.*
48 Grier and Grier, *Movers to the City.*
49 Gale, "Middle Class Resettlement in Older Urban Neighborhoods"; and Gale, "Neighborhood Resettlement in Washington, D.C."
50 Martin T. Katzman, "Gentrification of Cities and the Changing Composition of American Families" (University of Texas, School of Social Sciences, 1979).
51 Clifford H. Kern, "Upper Income Renaissance in the City: Its Sources and Implications for the City's Future," *Journal of Urban Economics*, vol. 9 (January 1981), pp. 106–24.
52 Katzman, "Gentrification of Cities."
53 Ibid.
54 Lipton, "Evidence of Central City Revival."
55 Richard A. Easterlin, *Birth and Fortune: The Impact of Number on Personal Welfare* (Basic Books, 1980); and William Alonso, "The Population Factor and Urban Structure," in A. P. Solomon, ed., *The Prospective City: Economic Population, Energy, and Environmental Developments* (MIT Press, 1980), pp. 32–51.

56 Long, "Back to the Countryside and Back to the City."

57 Katzman, "Gentrification of Cities."

58 Easterlin, *Birth and Fortune.*

59 Dowell Myers, "Back-to-the-City: New Measurements in Three Cities," paper prepared for the 1980 conference of the American Planning Association.

60 Franklin J. James, "Private Reinvestment in Older Housing and Older Neighborhoods," statement before the Senate Committee on Banking, Housing and Urban Affairs, July 10, 1977; and Franklin J. James, "The Revitalization of Older Urban Housing and Neighborhoods," in Solomon, ed., *The Prospective City,* pp. 130–60.

61 In equation form, the accounting equality is that units built (U) minus household growth (H) equals excess supply (E), and excess supply in turn equals withdrawals from the stock (W) plus vacancy increase ($+V$) in the case that some of the excess remains vacant, and minus vacancy change ($-V$) in the case that there are net withdrawals from the vacancy pool:

$$U - H = E$$
$$E = W \pm V$$
$$U = H + W \pm V.$$

Tabulations of excess supplies and withdrawals from stock for the nation's "million plus" metropolitan areas for the decades 1960–70 and 1970–80 are available from the author.

62 In 1950–60, programs for the renewal of deteriorated commercial and residential areas, highway construction, and other land use clearance projects contributed to the removal of an estimated 10 million housing units from the nation's housing inventory. See the Advisory Commission on Intergovernmental Relations, *Relocation: Unequal Treatment of People and Businesses Displaced by Governments* (GPO, 1965); Martin Anderson, *The Federal Bulldozer: A Critical Analysis of Urban Renewal, 1949–1962* (MIT Press, 1964); and Cincinnati Department of Urban Development, *Family Relocation Patterns in Cincinnati* (City of Cincinnati, 1973).

63 Donald C. Dahmann, *Housing Opportunities for Black and White Households: Three Decades of Change in the Supply of Housing,* Special Demographic Analyses of the Bureau of the Census (U.S. Department of Commerce, 1981); and George E. Peterson, "Federal Tax Policy and the Shaping of the Urban Environment" (Cambridge, Mass.: National Bureau of Economic Research, 1977).

64 Dahmann, *Housing Opportunities for Black and White Households.*

65 George Sternlieb and Robert W. Burchell, *Residential Abandonment: The Tenement Landlord Revisited* (Rutgers University, Center for Urban Policy Research, 1973); Bruce Bender, "The Determinants of Housing Abandonment" (Ph.D. dissertation, University of Chicago, 1976); Michael J. Dear, "Abandoned Housing," in John S. Adams, ed., *Urban policymaking and Metropolitan Dynamics* (Ballinger, 1976), pp. 59–99; U.S. Department of Housing and Urban Development, *Residential Abandonment in Central Cities* (GPO, 1977); and U.S. General Accounting Office, *Housing Abandonment: A National Problem Needing New Approaches* (GPO, 1978).

66 Sternlieb, *The Maintenance of America's Housing Stock.*

67 Dear, "Abandoned Housing."

68 Laska and Spain, eds, *Back to the City.*

69 Thomas M. Stanback and others, *Services: The New Economy* (Totowa, N.J.: Allanheld, Osmun, 1981); and Thomas M. Stanback, Jr., and Thierry J. Noyelle, *Cities in Transition* (Totowa, N.J.: Allanheld, Osmun, 1982).

70 D. T. Herbert and R. J. Johnson, "Spatial Processes and Forms," in D. T. Herbert and R. J. Johnson, eds, *Social Areas in Cities,* vol. 1 (Wiley, 1976), p. 5.

7

"The Demise of Gentrification? A Commentary and Prospective View"

From *Urban Geography* (1993)

Larry S. Bourne

Gentrification has been a major theme in urban studies, planning, and geography for more than two decades. Indeed, it may appear to some observers that this single subject has dominated academic debate, as well as the scholarly publication record, in research on urban residential change. That literature is now voluminous, diverse, and often contradictory (Smith and Herod, 1992).[1] As a consequence, many students of the city now view the gentrification phenomenon as one of the most pervasive processes of social change operating to restructure the contemporary inner city. In the more extreme cases gentrification is seen as leading to a reversal of the traditional social status gradient in cities, ultimately resulting in an elite inner city, in effect an entire landscape recaptured by the new professional class (Bourne, 1989).

The argument of this commentary is that these kinds of generalizations, and the images and inferences that flow from them, are overdrawn and potentially misleading. Specifically, the paper attempts to encourage debate by demonstrating that the extent and impact of gentrification have been much more limited than this literature implies, that it has not been the dominant process of social and neighborhood change in even a few inner cities, and that it is largely irrelevant in most others. Further, it argues that gentrification will have even less of an imprint in the future as the contextual factors that provided the principal incentives and opportunities in the past rapidly fade in importance.

To support these generalizations, empirical evidence is drawn from an on-going research project on the changing geography of living conditions and social status in Canadian metropolitan areas and their inner cities.[2] For present purposes, however, the discussion focuses on one urban area, the inner city of the Toronto metropolitan area on one spatial scale—the neighborhood—and uses household income as a proxy for social status changes. Toronto serves as a reasonable case study, at least of the atypical, precisely because it is widely viewed as having undergone extensive gentrification, and because the literature on this city, including a recent paper in this journal (Ley, 1992), is both extensive and of very high quality (Ley, 1988; Bunting and Filion, 1988; Filion, 1991).

The discussion to follow is divided into three sections. The first briefly reviews and evaluates the definitions and applications of the gentrification process in the contemporary literature. The second offers an empirical estimation of the relative contribution of gentrification, or more precisely of gentrified neighborhoods, to aggregate income changes in Canadian inner cities; and the third section provides a set of speculative judgments on the future scale of gentrification. The latter is based on a reassessment of the contextual factors that will determine the future supply of gentrifiers and the demand for gentrified urban environments. The paper concludes with a brief discussion of the questions raised by the critique and the empirical analysis for the future condition of inner cities in a period of uncertain socioeconomic and metropolitan change.

EVALUATION PROBLEMS

Any attempt at a critical evaluation of gentrification faces two problems, one of selectivity and the other conceptual and definitional. The evidence typically advanced to demonstrate the importance of the gentrification process to the inner city has been highly selective, in terms of the measures used and the cities and neighborhoods studied (Smith and Williams, 1986). Research has tended to focus on a few global cities such as London, New York, and San Francisco, or on smaller centers such as Boston, Adelaide, Stockholm, Vancouver, and Toronto. All of these places have unique and growing service-based economies, are rich in environmental and cultural amenities, and have historic central cores as well as high levels of public investment and private wealth. Even in these kinds of cities, however, the extent of gentrification *per se*, and its impacts on the city's social geography, have often been exaggerated. For most other and less well-endowed cities the process is only of passing interest.

The other part of this evaluation problem is the lack of comparative standards against which to assess the role of gentrification. Few of the contributors to that literature have attempted to measure the importance of gentrification as a process of social and neighborhood change—either quantitatively or qualitatively—in relation to other processes affecting the inner city. Such processes would include the neighborhood effects of household and demographic change, aggregate income redistribution and wealth accumulation in elite districts (polarization), the marginalization of particular disadvantaged minority groups, the income effects of shifts in local public service provision and social assistance policies, as well as the localized impacts of changes in housing markets, tax policies, and immigration flows, to name but a few.

A second reason for the widely differing claims of the importance of gentrification in the literature on North American cities is that the concept itself is defined in widely varying ways. There is little agreement on how or where the term should be applied or the process measured, nor on how to determine its significance. How should the impact of gentrification be evaluated and at what spatial scale? Interestingly, even after two decades of research the debate on the meaning of gentrification, in theory and practice, remains intense (Berry, 1985; Beauregard, 1986; Smith, 1987; Badcock, 1991; Hamnett, 1991; Smith and Herod, 1992; Clark. 1992; Ley, 1992; Bourne, 1993).

To simplify the debate, two principal definitions of gentrification stand out in the recent literature.

The first and more *restrictive* definition refers to the invasion and succession of a neighborhood occupied by members of one social rank or class by those of another and higher class. Specifically, the transitions of interest are restricted to those that (are assumed to) involve the displacement of working class households by middle- and upper-income professional households. The second and more *inclusive* definition incorporates other forms of neighborhood change, but without the necessity of residential succession or the displacement of lower-class households. Studies based on the former definition tend to be limited to neighborhoods that were previously occupied by lower-income households, but ignore parallel income upgrading in established middle- or upper-income areas, presumably because those areas remain in the same class. Studies based on the second definition, in contrast, often do incorporate upgrading in some of the latter areas, but to do so either relax or ignore the displacement criterion. Obviously, these two definitions produce very different results empirically and thus contrasting images of the impacts of the social processes under study.

Several of the assumptions implicit in these definitional differences are worthy of further elaboration here. The restrictive definition, for example, is built on the assumption that the neighborhoods involved were previously in residential use and were internally homogeneous with respect to social status and housing conditions. They also assume that the housing stock in these neighborhoods can somehow be assigned in its entirety to one social class rather than another and that the new residents are of a distinctively different class from those in other districts. In fact, class identification often appears to be the goal of the research rather than a vehicle for understanding the diversity of social and neighborhood changes.

The inclusive definition, in contrast, allows for the classification of areas as gentrified that were previously vacant or in non-residential uses (e.g., so-called grey-field sites such as industrial, warehousing and port lands), but that were subsequently-redeveloped for middle income or luxury housing. The latter process, in my view, would be more appropriately titled redevelopment, rather than gentrification, because it involves the creation of new social spaces where none previously existed. It also produces the impression of a much more pervasive process of social transition and neighborhood change than does the restricted definition.

Neither approach is necessarily incorrect, but both can lead to erroneous interpretations. One basic problem arises when empirical results based on the use of an inclusive definition of gentrification are interpreted as if they are measuring residential succession, class change, and displacement in the specific sense implied in the restrictive conceptualization. If gentrification is argued to be significant as a process of social transition at the scale of individual neighborhoods, and as a process of displacement, then it cannot incorporate the redevelopment of grey-field sites. Conversely, if these redeveloped areas are considered part of the gentrification process then it is equally logical to include social change in other elite neighborhoods of the inner city, as this paper does, that typically are not included in the universe of gentrification.

There are other measurement problems associated with the specific variables used to define which neighborhoods are gentrified and which are not; indeed, too many to cite here. Both of the above approaches, for example, tend to use education and occupation variables as indices, which is reasonable enough, but also assume that these accurately measure social class and neighborhood composition independent of other variables, notably income, age, ethnicity, and immigration status. This assumption is often not appropriate. These and other criticisms are addressed in the following section through a single case study.

THE EMPIRICAL EVIDENCE: A CASE STUDY

To test some of these ideas, and specifically to evaluate the relative contribution of gentrification to longer-term social change in the inner city, this paper draws on the results of a project on changes in social status and wealth within the Canadian urban system over the 35-year period 1951–1986. Because of limited space, the examples reported here relate primarily to the inner city of the Toronto metropolitan area, an area that offers some of the best and the worst features of a case study (Bourne, 1991; Filion, 1991). To facilitate the time series analysis, and the use of disaggregated cross-tabulations, the study uses household income as a single index or proxy variable for social change, despite its well-known limitations, but recognizing its unique advantages for longer-time and comparative social research (Bourne, 1992). Income is used here not because it is necessarily appropriate to analyze this variable in isolation, but because it offers the only more or less consistent time series data for the entire study period. It also serves as a useful counterpoint to those studies in the gentrification literature that have avoided examining the income dimensions and consequences of neighborhood change.

Specifically, we want to know how, and why, the distribution of income has changed by source (wages and non-wage income: private and public incomes),[3] by household attributes (e.g., age, size, life cycle stage), and by neighborhood setting. This paper concentrates on the results of the neighborhood-level analysis and, it should be stressed, examines only areas of increasing social status as measured by real income growth. The analysis measures the contribution of gentrification in two ways: quantitatively, in terms of the proportion of total income growth in the inner city attributable to gentrified neighborhoods; and qualitatively, in terms of changes in the redistribution of income within those areas. The more complete geography of changes in poverty and wealth, incorporating a wider range of stable and declining neighborhoods—the latter being of most immediate policy concern—are left to another paper.

To compare changes in income, or any other social variable for that matter, over a relatively long time period requires a number of simplifying assumptions, statistical corrections, and subjective judgments. First, it should be acknowledged that income was not defined or measured in the same ways in 1986 as in earlier Canadian censuses. On balance, these measurement differences are likely to have resulted in an underestimate of the growth of incomes of higher-status households. Nor are households—as the basic units of housing demand and consumer expenditure—defined on the basis of the same criteria over the entire study period. The latter definitional changes, too many to cite here, are likely to have resulted in the identification of proportionately more households with lower income than would otherwise have been the case. Many of those households would be resident in the inner city. Nevertheless, by using standardized procedures to reduce the resulting distortions, as well as established methods of removing the effects of both inflation and the under-reporting of income, it is possible to come up with reasonable estimates of the relative geographical shifts in income within the metropolitan area over the entire study period.

THE EMPIRICAL RESULTS

This evidence, however aggregated, clearly suggests that most Canadian inner cities, despite media impressions to the contrary, widespread public and private investment, and three decades of gentrification, are still on average substantially poorer than their suburban counterparts, and becoming more so (Table 7.1). In only three census metropolitan areas (CMAs) has the overall index of inner city-to-CMA

CMA/Central city	1960	1970	1980	1985
Toronto	92.7	90.8	89.0	90.9
Montreal	88.5	86.1	80.6	79.7
Vancouver	94.1	93.8	89.8	89.7
Ottawa-Hull	100.1	100.4	95.4	93.2
Quebec	90.2	87.5	81.3	81.2
Hamilton	92.9	92.4	87.6	84.7
Halifax	101.4	103.1	97.0	96.3
Victoria	80.6	79.7	76.0	75.3

Table 7.1 Changing income distributions within selected metropolitan areas, 1960–1985[a]

[a]Average Household Income: Central City as % of CMA (CMA = 100)
Source: Census of Canada, 1961, 1971, 1981, 1986

income levels risen since the 1950s, and in each instance the increase has been modest. In Toronto, for example, the index was 93.1 in 1951, then declined to 90.8 in 1971 and to 89.0 in 1981. It then rose slightly to 90.9 in 1986. As part of this reversal some neighborhoods in the inner city now have average household incomes well above those of the CMA as a whole. Obviously, income growth and associated residential upgrading have taken place with some intensity and in a sufficient number of areas to reverse a long-standing decline in average social status for the entire inner city. But in what neighborhoods? At the same time, these gross averages conceal an immense amount of variation among individual households and neighborhoods, warranting further study.

To what sources can this modest increase in inner city income be attributed? What kinds of neighborhoods and social processes contributed most to this increase and what role have gentrified neighborhoods played? To what extent has gentrification acted to redistribute income at the intraurban scale, and particularly within the inner city?

To answer these kinds of questions empirically five different types of inner city neighborhoods of varying socioeconomic status were defined, but again excluding poorer districts and areas of extensive social housing.[4] The five types are: (1) established high status or elite districts; (2) middle-income neighborhoods; (3) redeveloped areas, most of which represent new social spaces created on derelict grey-field sites (e.g., industrial, railroad, waterfront lands) with little or no previous population; (4) areas of immigrant settlement, with their corresponding high levels of ethnic diversity and foreign-born populations; and (5) traditionally-defined gentrified neighborhoods. In many instances,

through necessity, the selection and classification of neighborhoods was based on subjective rather than statistical criteria. For each neighborhood changes were calculated in average and median household income, relative to both the inner city and the entire metropolitan area, as well as in the internal distribution of income by quintile, for each five-year census period from 1951 to 1986.[5]

The aggregate results of this analysis of the relative contribution of the five neighborhood types to total income growth in the inner city are summarized in Table 7.2. Note that the table is based only on rankings rather than actual income figures since the errors in the latter are large and tend to be compounded over time and through the aggregation procedure itself. Even so, these errors should not substantially alter the overall rankings. For illustrative purposes the real income levels in 1986 are provided in Table 7.3 for a sample of individual neighborhoods within each of the above categories.

These data, however crude, clearly suggest that gentrified neighborhoods have not been the principal contributors to overall income growth or redistribution, at least in the inner area of Toronto. In strictly quantitative terms, the largest contributors instead have been, in rank order, the incomes added by the creation of new and high-status social areas through the residential redevelopment process (largely newly-built condominiums); second, the continued accumulation of household wealth in existing elite districts; third, the parallel upgrading of incomes in middle-income areas; and fourth—but often overlooked in the gentrification literature (apparently because of problems of identifying class)—the substantial improvement of income levels in many of the city's immigrant and ethnic communities. Of the five types, the increasing incomes of gentrified neighborhoods,

Neighborhood type/process	No. of areas	Rank in income[b]	Rank in aggregate contribution
A. Upgrading of elite areas	6	1	2
B. Redevelopment—new social spaces	4	2	1
C. Upgrading of middle-class neighborhoods	11	3	3
D. Gentrified neighborhoods	6	4	5
E. Upgrading of immigrant/ethnic neighborhoods	9	5	4

Table 7.2 Rankings of neighborhoods in terms of their contribution to aggregate inner city income growth, Toronto, 1951–1986

[b] Current dollars

Inner city neighborhoods (and CT)	Household income, 1986[a]	1951 Index	1986 Index	Index change 1951–1986, %
A. Old high income:				
Rosedale (86)	122.7	160.2	285.3	78.1
Rosedale (87)	90.1	127.1	209.5	64.8
Forest Hill (130)	131.5	155.8	304.4	95.3
Forest Hill (131)	91.5	157.1	210.2	33.8
B. New condo. area:				
Waterfront (13)	123.1	–	295.7	–
C. Inner suburban:				
Bayview (264)	183.7	226.2	427.2	88.9
Don Valley (266)	118.3	186.3	275.1	47.6
D. Gentrified:				
Don Vale (67)	58.3	89.0	135.4	52.1
Don Vale (68)	43.1	90.0	100.0	11.1
E. Immigrant:				
Dundas W. (41–45)	33.5	64.1	95.1	48.4
Central city	39.1	94.5	90.9	−3.9
CMA	43.0	100.0	100.0	–

Table 7.3 Differential rates of social upgrading among elite, gentrified and immigrant neighborhoods in the inner city, Toronto, 1951–1986

[a] Average income in thousands of dollars

Source: Census of Canada, various years

at least as these are defined under the restrictive definition above, ranked fifth in terms of their contribution to overall income growth.

There are several plausible explanations for the latter result. One is clearly the limited number (six) and relatively small size of neighborhoods that qualify under the restricted definition of gentrification.

A broader definition would have resulted in the classification of several more neighborhoods as gentrified and thus a larger statistical contribution of gentrification to aggregate income growth in the inner city. Here, the effects of the arbitrary nature of such classifications, as well as the limitations of the present analysis, are clearly evident. A second reason derives from the internal social composition of gentrified neighborhoods. Although average incomes have increased dramatically in many of these neighborhoods—the income index for Don Vale, for example, rose from 89.0 of the CMA average in 1951 to 135.4 in 1986 (a relative increase of over 52 percent)—the rate of increase was still much less than that in most of the inner city's older elite neighborhoods and many middle-class districts. This increase is lower than might be expected given the extensive displacement of low-income households that is invariably associated with the gentrification process, in part because gentrification initially involves a sharp reduction in total population. It is also in part attributable to the high level of social heterogeneity (and bi-polar income distributions) that is still characteristic of most gentrified neighborhoods relative to established elite and middle-income areas. The polarized nature of these distributions in the entire central city and in the one gentrified area cited above (Don Vale) are clearly illustrated in Table 7.4. Even in the most up-scale of the gentrified neighborhoods shown here nearly 30 percent of all households were low income.

It is of course possible to criticize the above approach as too narrow and the data as too highly aggregated; or to argue that the study does not adequately measure the other varied contributions of the gentrification process to inner city upgrading (e.g., in retailing and community services), and that it explicitly does not address class-based differences in neighborhood change. These criticisms have some validity. Undoubtedly, an assessment based solely on educational and occupational indices, which, as Ley (1992) has clearly shown, produces higher indices for the inner city than does income alone; or perhaps one based on life style or political behavior, despite their ambiguity, would all give more weight to gentrification as a process of social change and thus a higher ranking to gentrified neighborhoods (Filion, 1991). Yet these indices too can be misleading. Without controlling for other variables—notably the influence of differences in age structure, ethnicity, and household status, and most emphatically household income—it is unclear what dimensions of social change (or class) are being measured. Many inner city neighborhoods that have undergone gentrification have high proportions of transient student populations, singles, mobile young professionals, and the elderly. Given the tendency of such groups to move, it is not clear what the longer-term social status of such areas will be.

Nevertheless, the evidence presented above—while incomplete—does indicate the need to discount the claims made in some of the more overzealous gentrification literature regarding the extent

District	Household income level ($)				
	Under 20,000	20,000 −29,999	30,000 −39,999	40,000 −50,000	Over 50,000
Central area	43.7	17.5	12.5	8.3	17.8
Central city	33.7	17.4	14.3	10.4	24.0
CMA (rest)	20.7	14.5	16.4	15.2	33.2
Selected inner city neighborhoods					
Gentrified area[a]	18.3	10.8	8.4	10.1	52.4
New condo area[b]	17.2	8.2	13.1	11.3	50.2
Upscale condo[c]	5.9	7.5	13.5	8.7	64.2
Mixed social housing area[d]	37.1	21.1	15.7	9.5	16.7
Old public housing area[e]	77.7	13.1	5.2	3.0	1.0

Table 7.4 Variations in income distributions, by district and neighborhood type, Toronto, 1986 (in percentages)

[a]Don Vale
[b]Harbour Square
[c]Financial District
[d]St. Lawrence
[e]Regent Park

Note: Percentages may not sum to 100 due to rounding errors

Source: Census of Canada, 1986

(in terms of the number of neighborhoods affected) and intensity (in terms of income distributions within those neighborhoods) of the process. In the Toronto example, this process has not impacted a majority of neighborhoods, has not displaced established elite districts, does not account for a large proportion of income growth, and has not created an elite inner city. It has undoubtedly redistributed population and income that might have gone elsewhere, but this is likely to have been geographically limited to the inner city and older suburbs.

It also stresses the importance for geographers of examining other processes of urban social change affecting the inner city Among these are the increasingly uneven distribution of urban incomes and opportunities, reflected in the stark contrast of continued wealth accumulation in elite districts on the one hand, and increasing poverty and marginalization—including the intensely skewed income distributions within the social housing sector—on the other hand. In the latter instances we are witnessing the localized reproduction of socially disadvantaged populations. Moreover, we also need to explore the longer-term but uneven trend to the upgrading of immigrant neighborhoods and the creation of new social spaces for the elite through inner city redevelopment and revitalization.

This conclusion is not intended to imply that gentrification has been an insignificant process. Nor does it downgrade the impacts that gentrification has had in a few selected neighborhoods, particularly with respect to dispacement. Rather, it is argued that when viewed in the context of the entire inner city, or the broader central city and older suburbs, the impact of gentrification has been much less than is often claimed, even in the favored cities. It has not been the dominant process of income growth and redistribution or of residential upgrading. The danger is that an over-emphasis on gentrification in urban geographical research has tended to obscure the much richer, more diverse, and often problematic set of social processes that are reshaping our cities.

ON THE FUTURE OF GENTRIFICATION

The third objective of this commentary is to examine the proposition that gentrification, however it has been conceptualized and measured to date, will be of less importance as a spatial expression of social change during the 1990s than it has been in the recent past. To evaluate this proposition it is necessary to reiterate the underlying conditions—in demography, the economy, educational attainment, local housing markets, choices of living arrangements, public sector activity, and capital investment—that have set the stage for the gentrification phenomenon of the last three decades. We then ask how likely are these conditions to continue in the future. Table 7.5 provides, for convenience, a brief summary of some of those factors that have been used to typify the recent "gentrification" period, and contrasts these with anticipations of trends in the same factors for the 1990s—trends that might be said to describe a "post-gentrification" era.

The evidence presented in Table 7.5, although subjective, supports the assertion that the 1990s will likely witness much less extensive gentrification, at least in the Canadian example. First, the supply of potential young gentrifiers is almost certain to be significantly smaller, given the passing of the baby-boom into middle-age, the declining rate of new household formation, and the general aging of the population. The expanding cohort of potential older gentrifiers will not be sufficient to compensate for the rapid decline in the younger cohorts. At the same time, given widespread macro-economic restructuring, corporate down-sizing and a persistent recession, we might also expect slower rates of employment growth in the service sector and associated occupations, at least through the next business cycle. Only a modest growth in real household incomes is expected until much later in this decade. Moreover, the increased level of housing consumption and diversity of choices of living arrangements characteristic of the earlier (1961–1981) period are likely to be reversed as households are squeezed by the triangular lattice of domestic responsibilities, rising living costs, and stagnant or declining real incomes.

Second, the relative supply of inner city neighborhoods and individual dwellings suitable for gentrification will decline. Most good sites and amenable settings, notably those few with distinctive environmental or historical signatures, have already been taken. The advantage of earlier price differentials, relative to the new suburban stock, has also largely vanished in those neighborhoods that have witnessed some gentrification. Although marginal gentrification will likely continue, particularly for non-traditional households, some of the elderly, and especially for female single-parent households (Rose, 1984), weaker housing markets generally will undermine the attractiveness of many older neighborhoods in the inner city for both investors and households. At the same time, alternative residential settings, especially in the older suburbs and newer exurbs are likely to become relatively more attractive because of lower land and housing prices and through gradual improvements in social services and cultural

Gentrification era	Post-gentrification era
1. Demography:	
baby boom; smaller households; fewer children; many new/younger households; increasing elderly	baby bust; fertility stable; decline in new households; more non-family households; rapidly aging population
2. Economy:	
rapid employment growth; rising real incomes; shift to service occupations; increase in dual-earners; full-time jobs	modest employment growth; stable/declining incomes; shift to services slows; dual-earners stable; part-time, flexible jobs
3. Education:	
increased educational levels; quantitative jump in higher educ.; professional degrees	increase in technical levels; emphasis on quality educ.; quasi-professional degrees
4. Living arrangements:	
diverse choices of life style; increased housing consumption; household fragmentation	more constrained choices; decreased/stable consumption; household consolidation
5. Public sector:	
rapid employment growth; major new public investments; extension of social services; state as initiator	slow or negative growth; caps on public expenditures; contracting out services public-private partnerships
6. Built environment:	
shift of capital into urban real estate; rampant speculation; escalating real prices; LBOs widespread; low vacancies	balloon has shrunk: switch of capital out of property; stable or declining prices; foreclosures common; high vacancies
7. Locational dynamics:	
downtown employment growth; congestion costs rising; institutional expansion; widening of spatial rent differential	suburban employment growth; congestion costs declining; institutional down-sizing; contraction of rent differential

Table 7.5 Contrasting factors underlying the rise and decline of inner area gentrification: the Canadian experience

facilities, as well as easier access to jobs, leisure activities, and recreational places.

The particular advantages of a central location in terms of job markets will also likely diminish with the much slower growth anticipated in private sector office development in the downtown cores of Canadian (and American) cities. The speculative real estate bubble of the 1980s has finally burst. And we might anticipate continuing constraints on employment growth in public sector activities and services. The latter, especially hospitals, research institutes, community services, and post-secondary educational facilities, have always been over-represented in the Canadian inner city and show a strong correlation with the geography of gentrification activity (Ley, 1988). At the same time, the population of severely disadvantaged households will increase, further partitioning the urban landscape into contrasting areas of plenty and areas of poverty, although less so than in many American cities (Berry, 1985; Broadway, 1989). In parallel, the continued decentralization of jobs to new suburban locations and nearby regional centers, for both highly-skilled and low-skilled service jobs, will draw more households to the urban fringe and to smaller communities nearby. Increased congestion, and especially the escalating costs and difficulties of environmental regeneration and infrastructure improvements in older districts, as well as underlying social, ethnic, and racial tensions, may well intensify the effects of the dual processes of spatial decentralization and income polarization.

As has been implied above, much of the literature on gentrification was written during what now appears to have been a unique period in post-war urban development in North America—a period that combined the baby boom, rising educational levels, a rapid growth in service employment and real income, high rates of household formation, housing stock appreciation, public sector largesse, widespread (and speculative) private investment in the built environment, and high levels of foreign immigration. This set of circumstances, except for the latter, no longer prevails.

CONCLUSION

The simple point to be made here is that these projections—although it is clearly difficult to separate the effects of the current recession from longer-term structural adjustment processes—will result in a future pool of potential gentrifiers that is smaller than that which provided much of the initial demand for central area residential locations, and a reduction in the supply of suitable venues to accommodate these demands. Does this imply the end of inner city gentrification? Or the shift to a new gentrification frontier, perhaps in the decaying older suburbs? Or does it preview the return to more traditional social geographies in the inner city? Or will variations in social housing provision, fiscal restraint, and service cutbacks become the principal architects of change in low-income neighborhoods?

The answers to these questions are ambiguous and clearly warrant further research; but the above evidence does at least suggest that the rate and impact of gentrification will be much reduced. We will need to look elsewhere for an understanding of the social processes that are likely to lead to new

social forms and different living environments within the inner city. We should instead be monitoring the recent experience of and alternative futures for a much wider range of neighborhood types—from elite through middle-income to the devastatingly poor—and for a range of ethno-cultural and life-style communities, with their associated social dynamics, in both the inner city and older suburbs. Even in those few cities that have witnessed gentrification in the past, the challenge for the future will not be the emergence of an elite inner city, but the instability, vulnerability, and in some instances rapid decline of a host of other neighborhoods.

Notes

1 This extensive bibliography contains nearly 800 entries on gentrification. A recent paper by Ley (1992) in this journal also contains an excellent synthesis of the dominant concepts and debates contained in that literature. There is no need here to replicate these bibliographies.

2 In this study several definitions of the inner city are employed (see Bourne, 1992), but for present purposes we follow the delimitations provided by the Canada Mortgage and Housing Corporation (CMHC). Essentially the inner city is that area in which the housing stock is predominantly pre-1946.

3 The income data used here refer to household income (wages, salaries, and government transfer payments to individuals, but not gifts, inheritance, or transfers in kind), as reported in the Census of Canada. We make no attempt at this point to estimate public incomes derived from the consumption of public goods and services or transfers among individuals.

4 Neighborhoods were classified on the basis of established social ecologies and delimited as single census tracts or aggregates of tracts.

5 Census of Canada data on income for 1991 will not be available until late in 1993.

LITERATURE CITED

Badcock, B., 1991, Neighbourhood change in inner Adelaide: an update. *Urban Studies*, Vol. 28(4), 553–558.

Berry, B.J.L., 1985, Islands of renewal in seas of decay. In P. Peterson, editor, *The New Urban Reality.* Washington, DC: The Brookings Institution, 69–96.

Beauregard, R., 1986, The chaos and complexity of gentrification. In N. Smith and P. Williams, editors, *Gentrification of the City*. New York: Pergamon, 3–12.

Bourne, L.S., 1990, Close together and worlds apart: an empirical analysis of the changing distribution of income within Canadian metropolitan areas, *Discussion Paper* 36, Department of Geography, University of Toronto.

——, 1991, Recycling urban systems and metropolitan areas: a geographical agenda for the 1990s. *Economic Geography*, Vol. 67(3), 185–209.

——, 1992, Population turnaround in the Canadian inner city: contextual factors and social consequences. *Canadian Journal of Urban Research*, Vol. 1(1), 69–92.

——, 1993, The myth and reality of gentrification: a commentary on emerging urban forms. *Urban Studies*, Vol. 30 (forthcoming).

Broadway, M., 1989, A comparison of patterns of deprivation between Canadian and US cities. *Social Indicators Research*, Vol. 21, 531–551.

Bunting, T. and Filion, P., editors, 1988, *The Changing Canadian Inner City*. Waterloo, Ont.: Department of Geography, University of Waterloo.

City of Toronto, 1990, *Central Area in Transition: Findings of the Residents Survey*. Toronto: City Planning and Development Department.

Clark, E., 1992, On gaps in gentrification theory. *Housing Studies*, Vol. 7(1), 16–26.

Filion, P., 1991, The gentrification-social structure dialectic: a Toronto case study. *International Journal of Urban and Regional Research*, Vol. 15(4), 553–574.

Hamnett, C., 1991, The blind men and the elephant: the explanation of gentrification. *Transactions of the Institute of British Geographers*, NS, Vol. 16, 173–189.

Ley, D., 1988, Social upgrading in six Canadian inner cities. *Canadian Geographer*, Vol. 32. 31–45.

——, 1992, Gentrification in recession: social change in six Canadian cities, 1981–86. *Urban Geography*, Vol. 13(3). 230–256.

Ram, B., Norris, M., and Skof, K., 1989, *The Inner City in Transition*. Ottawa: Statistics Canada.

Rose, D., 1984, Rethinking gentrification: beyond the uneven development of Marxist social theory. *Environment and Planning D*, Vol. 1. 47–74.

Smith, N., 1987, Of yuppies and housing: gentrification, social restructuring and the urban dream. *Environment and Planning D*, Vol. 5, 151–172.

—— and Herod, A., 1992, Gentrification: a comprehensive bibliography. *Discussion Paper, New Series #1*, Rutgers University, New Brunswick, NJ.

—— and Williams, P., editors, 1986, *Gentrification of the City*. New York: Pergamon.

Statistics Canada, 1989, *Income Distribution by Size, 1981 and 1986*. Ottawa: Ministry of Supplies and Services.

8

"The Changing State of Gentrification"

From *Tijdschrift voor Economische en Sociale Geografie* (2001)

Jason Hackworth and Neil Smith

INTRODUCTION

Late in 1998, real estate developer David Walentas was given permission by the city of New York to redevelop a portion of the northern Brooklyn waterfront next to the neighbourhood of DUMBO (Down Under the Manhattan Bridge Overpass). Walentas has been trying to gentrify DUMBO since the early 1980s, and has been seeking permission to do so for almost as long. Turning the waterfront into a commercial arcade, not unlike South Street Seaport, directly across the East River, is an important component of his bid to bring the gentry to DUMBO. Yet for most of the 1980s and early 1990s Walentas encountered nothing but resistance from City Hall and Albany (the state capital). He lacked the experience and funding, they said, to be given permission to redevelop the site (Ennen 1999). If the private market did not have enough faith to back Walentas with lending capital, why, asked public officials, should tax dollars be used to support it?

Recently, the city changed its stance towards Walentas' plan. Not only was he given the planning permission that he coveted for the waterfront, but he was also given important zoning concessions as well. This occurred despite the fact that neighbourhood residents were unified against the plan (Ennen 1999). While this case could be simply discarded as another example of the Giuliani Administration repaying campaign contributors, other (very different) examples of recently increased state involvement in gentrification imply that something larger is afoot. Several years earlier, for example, the Federal Housing Administration awarded MO Associates – a firm trying to gentrify Long Island City (LIC) – unprecedented mortgage insurance for a luxury condominium project in Queens. Not long before this, the city's department of Housing Preservation and Development (HPD) all but eliminated its anti-gentrification enforcement in the neighbourhood of Clinton. After years of *laissez-faire* politics regarding gentrification – i.e. to encourage it only if the private market has proven it viable and in some cases, even help in its resistance – local governments, state level agencies, and federal administrations are assisting gentrification more assertively than during the 1980s. In the USA, some of this shift has been formalised into urban policy, but much of this change has been played out less formally, in the form of increased local government assistance to gentrifiers, relaxed zoning, and reduced protection of affordable housing. Why is this the case? This essay explores the reasons for the return of state intervention by examining the nature of recent gentrification in three New York neighbourhoods: Clinton, Long Island City, and DUMBO (Figure 8.1). Each avoided a major bout of gentrification during the 1980s but all are presently the focus of reinvestment, largely though not exclusively because of recent state intervention. As such they represent useful case studies for exploring why – in an epoch of continual deregulation – the state is suddenly *more* involved in the process.

In order to address this question, a short history of gentrification is chronicled. Following this, explicit attention is focused on why the state's role in gentrification has increased, by drawing on the available literature and exploring the process in the aforementioned neighbourhoods.

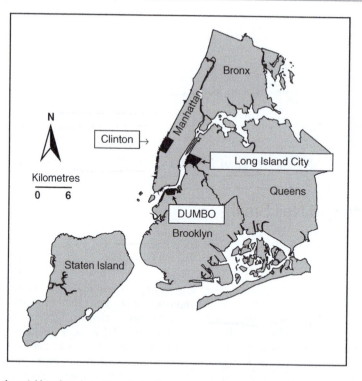

Figure 8.1 Case study neighbourhoods in New York City

WAVES OF GENTRIFICATION

While most gentrification researchers would agree with Loretta Lees (2000, p. 16) when she explains that, 'gentrification today is quite different to gentrification in the early 1970s, late 1980s, even the early 1990s', little explicit attempt has been made thus far to chronicling, much less theorising, these changes. In order to understand the changing role of the state in gentrification, it is first necessary to understand (at a minimum) the context for changes to the process as a whole.

Systematic gentrification dates back only to the 1950s but has evolved enough to assemble a periodised history of the process. Figure 8.2 is a schematic summary of this history. Each phase of gentrification in the diagram is demarcated by a particular constellation of political and economic conditions nested at larger geographical scales. Though the timeline draws heavily from the experience of gentrification in New York City it has wider applicability insofar as studies from other cities were used to assemble it. Specific dates for these phases will undoubtedly vary from place to place, but not so significantly as to diminish the influence of broader scale political economic events on the local experience of gentrification.

First-wave gentrification: sporadic and state-led – Prior to the economic recession that settled through the global economy in late 1973, gentrification was sporadic if widespread. Disinvested inner-city housing within the older north eastern cities of the USA, Western Europe and Australia became a target for reinvestment. While highly localised, these instances of gentrification were often significantly funded by the public sector (Hamnett 1973; Williams 1976; Smith 1979), as local and national governments sought to counteract the private-market economic decline of central city neighbourhoods. Governments were aggressive in helping gentrification because the prospect of inner-city investment (without state insurance of some form) was still very risky. While state involvement was often justified through the discourse of ameliorating urban decline, the effect was of course highly class specific. Conditions generally worsened for the urban working class as a result of such intervention (Smith 1996).

If the global economic recession that affected various national economies between 1973 and

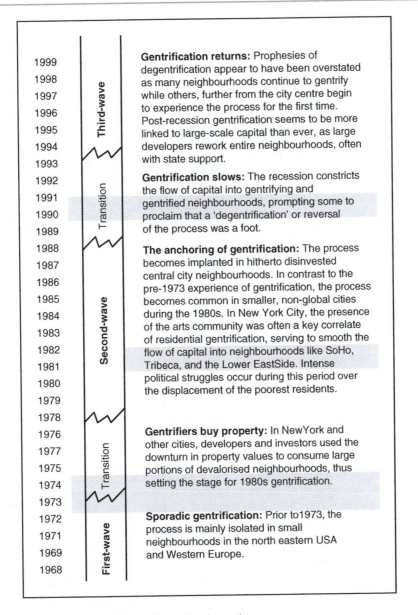

1999	**Third-wave**	**Gentrification returns:** Prophesies of degentrification appear to have been overstated as many neighbourhoods continue to gentrify while others, further from the city centre begin to experience the process for the first time. Post-recession gentrification seems to be more linked to large-scale capital than ever, as large developers rework entire neighbourhoods, often with state support.
1998		
1997		
1996		
1995		
1994		
1993		
1992	Transition	**Gentrification slows:** The recession constricts the flow of capital into gentrifying and gentrified neighbourhoods, prompting some to proclaim that a 'degentrification' or reversal of the process was a foot.
1991		
1990		
1989		
1988	**Second-wave**	**The anchoring of gentrification:** The process becomes implanted in hitherto disinvested central city neighbourhoods. In contrast to the pre-1973 experience of gentrification, the process becomes common in smaller, non-global cities during the 1980s. In New York City, the presence of the arts community was often a key correlate of residential gentrification, serving to smooth the flow of capital into neighbourhoods like SoHo, Tribeca, and the Lower EastSide. Intense political struggles occur during this period over the displacement of the poorest residents.
1987		
1986		
1985		
1984		
1983		
1982		
1981		
1980		
1979		
1978	Transition	**Gentrifiers buy property:** In NewYork and other cities, developers and investors used the downturn in property values to consume large portions of devalorised neighbourhoods, thus setting the stage for 1980s gentrification.
1976		
1977		
1975		
1974		
1973		
1972	**First-wave**	**Sporadic gentrification:** Prior to1973, the process is mainly isolated in small neighbourhoods in the north eastern USA and Western Europe.
1971		
1969		
1968		

Figure 8.2 Schematic history of gentrification (recessions in grey)

1977 also depressed national housing markets, its effects on gentrification were more ambiguous. The recession was triggered by the international oil embargo but provoked at a deeper level by various developments: falling profit rates in the productive sectors of the economy; increasing global competition and integration as Germany and Japan emerged as industrial powers; competition from the cheap labour of newly industrialising countries; and crises in the financial sector (Harvey 1989a). Despite the severity of that recession, there is little evidence that gentrification was radically circumscribed in the mid 1970s, though disinvestment intensified in certain US cities (Sternlieb & Hughes 1983). This was certainly the case in New York City where landlord abandonment and arson rose to an all-time high in the 1970s. At a more general level, the economic downturn also encouraged the shift of capital from unproductive to productive sectors, setting the stage for a reinvestment in central city office, recreation, retail and residential activities (Harvey 1985).

Second-wave gentrification: expansion and resistance – When depressed markets began to revive in the late 1970s, gentrification surged as never before. New neighbourhoods were converted into real estate 'frontiers', and cities that had not previously experienced gentrification implemented far-reaching strategies to attract this form of investment. Most local state efforts, however, focused on prodding the private market rather than directly orchestrating gentrification. Federal programmes like block grants and enterprise zones encouraged this relatively *laissez-faire* role. Despite slow economic growth between 1979 and 1983, gentrification activity remained largely unaffected (see Ley 1992 for the case of Canadian cities). In New York, sales prices in gentrifying neighbourhoods like Harlem did drop somewhat in 1982–83, apparently in response to the recession, but rebounded sharply thereafter (Schaeffer & Smith 1986). Less systematic evidence from other neighbourhoods in the city suggests that the recession was similarly mild throughout the inner city.

The second-wave, lasting almost to the end of the 1980s, was characterised by the integration of gentrification into a wider range of economic and cultural processes at the global and national scales. Nowhere was this more true than in New York, where the city's emergence as a world city, the inflation of the real estate market, and the burgeoning of an internationally recognised 'alternative' art scene in SoHo and the Lower East Side went hand-in-hand with powerful and at times ruthless gentrification (Zukin 1982, 1987; Deutsche & Ryan 1984). Although celebrated by some (Caufield 1994), gentrification was also challenged in and around places like New York's Tompkins Square Park, where homelessness, eviction and the increasing vulnerability of poor residents was directly connected to gentrification (Smith 1989, 1996). To the north, in Clinton, activists used the apparatus of local government to fight gentrification, but like the resistance in the Lower East Side, their efforts struggled to offset the overwhelming advance of the process in these neighbourhoods by the decade's end.

Third-wave gentrification: recessional pause and subsequent expansion – The stock market crash of 1987 provided the first warning signs of another imminent recession, but it was not until 1989 that inner-city residential land markets crashed along with the rest of the US economy. Unlike previous recessions in which gentrification slowed very little, during the recession of the early 1990s, gentrification came to a halt in some neighbourhoods and was severely curtailed in others. The effects of the recession certainly varied, but it was sufficiently severe to lead some critics to speculate that the 1990s were witnessing 'degentrification' (Bagli 1991). Bourne (1993), for example, predicted the 'demise of gentrification' due to an ageing of the baby boom, declining real incomes, and a relative reduction in the supply of inner-city housing. Since 1993, however, the expectation of degentrification has evaporated as reinvestment has again taken hold and a third-wave begun. In New York, all of the key inner-city housing market indicators – housing unit sale prices, rent levels, tax arrears, mortgage levels – have reversed themselves (from the recessional downturn) with the onset of the third-wave of gentrification, while growth in the suburbs has been slower to recover. The recession appears in retrospect to have been a transition period to the third-wave more than the advent of degentrification or any curtailment of inner-city reinvestment.

Post-recession gentrification – the third-wave of the process – is a purer expression of the economic conditions and processes that make reinvestment in disinvested inner-urban areas so alluring for investors (Smith & Defilippis 1999). Overall, economic forces driving gentrification seem to have eclipsed cultural factors as the scale of investment is greater and the level of corporate, as opposed to smaller-scale capital, has grown. In particular, third-wave gentrification is distinct from earlier phases in at least four ways. First, gentrification is expanding both within the inner-city neighbourhoods that it affected during earlier waves and to more remote neighbourhoods beyond the immediate core. Second, restructuring and globalisation in the real estate industry has set a context for larger developers becoming involved in gentrifying neighbourhoods (Logan 1993; Coakley 1994; Ball 1994). While such developers used to be common in the process only after the neighbourhood had been 'tamed' (Zukin 1982; Ley 1996), they are now increasingly the first to orchestrate reinvestment. Third, effective resistance to gentrification has declined as the working class is continually displaced from the inner city, and as the most militant anti-gentrification groups of the 1980s morph into housing service providers. Fourth, and of most relevance to this paper, the state is now more involved in the process than the second-wave. The remainder of this paper focuses on the possible reasons for the latter change to gentrification.

THE CHANGING STATE OF GENTRIFICATION

After a curious departure from direct involvement in gentrification during the second-wave, the state has become more interventionist in the third-wave. There are several salient aspects to this history. First, the private market expansion of gentrification in most cities has generally exhausted itself. In classic first-wave neighbourhoods, like Society Hill in Philadelphia and SoHo in New York City, the state (mostly at city and federal level) had a very direct role in organising and encouraging gentrification (Smith 1979; Zukin 1982). Inner-city reinvestment was still very risky (during the 1960s), so land assembly, tax incentives, and property condemnation were all orchestrated by the state, as were more informal attempts to convince conservative lenders and patrician families to move to such neighbourhoods (Smith 1979). After initial footholds in neighbourhoods like Society Hill and SoHo, gentrification radiated outward without such a direct need for the state because inner-city real estate investment was becoming less risky. During the 1980s, a private-market gentrification congealed into a reinvested core close to the central business district (CBD) of many cities (Hackworth 2001). But after almost two decades of this type of expansion, most of the easily gentrified (i.e. high amenity, close to the CBD) neighbourhoods have already been fully reinvested. By necessity, gentrifiers and outside investors have begun to roam into economically risky neighbourhoods – e.g. mixed-use neighbourhoods, remote locations, protected parcels like public housing – which are difficult for individual gentrifiers to make profitable without state assistance. The private-market expansion of gentrification has generally exhausted itself; state assistance (or some other form of assistance) is increasingly necessary for the process to swallow 'under-developed' parcels further from the CBD.

But the return of state intervention is more than the product of gentrification's spatial expansion. It is also encouraged by the secular tendency away from the maintenance of mass consumption – Keynesian governance. While Keynesian governance was certainly on the ebb by the mid 1970s, it would be a mistake to conclude that it had summarily expired with the election of Ronald Reagan and Margaret Thatcher. State attempts to encourage gentrification during the second-wave were still partially impeded by internal vestiges of the Keynesian state – in the USA, the Department of Housing and Urban Development (HUD) is the best example. By the late 1960s, social movements had forced the creation of the cabinet level housing agency (HUD), which, in part, restricted the private market pursuits of local government by redirecting public funding to affordable housing. As Feldman and Florida (1990) note, the effect of this change in the USA was swift and prohibitory for pro-business local states. Removing public housing – long seen as anathema to gentrification – was, for example, made practically impossible by HUD, and affordable housing construction dramatically increased between 1968 and 1973. Though the Reagan and Thatcher administrations actively assaulted such regulatory obstacles during the 1980s, their work was only partially completed by the time both left office.

The assault took the form of funding reductions for welfare and affordable housing, but more subtly it also encouraged non-Keynesian modes of *local* governance (Gaffikin & Warf 1993). The latter typically involved the encouragement of the 'entrepreneurial local state' (Harvey 1989b) through programmes that prodded the private market ('enterprise zones', for example) rather than direct subsidy. Direct intervention by the local state was, however, still constrained by agencies like HUD, which forced cities to address affordable housing issues if a gentrification plan was unveiled (Hackworth 2000). In the USA, many of these constraints were dissolved in 1994, with the swift devolution of much of the regulatory capacity (over the affordable housing sector) that was still nested in the federal state (Staeheli *et al.* 1997). HUD was disemboweled – 'reinvented' to use the euphemistic parlance used to justify it – and significantly restricted from offsetting gentrification at the local level. Their HOPE VI programme, for example, now allows municipal governments to remove public housing units for the purpose of redevelopment without one-for-one replacement (Wyly & Hammel 1999). The few remaining obstacles (within the federal state) to gentrification (which partially restricted state involvement in the second-wave) have largely been removed since the onset of the third-wave.

Paralleling heightened deregulation in the third-wave is a reduction in federal redistribution to localities. With a decline in federal redistribution during the 1990s, some of the pressures that originally encouraged the formation of the entrepreneurial local state (Molotch 1976; Harvey 1989b; Leitner 1990) have been ratcheted up even further. The imperative to generate tax dollars has, for example, become even more pressing for localities because federal funds are now more scarce. As such, many cities have embarked on a partnership with capital that exceeds even the pro-business 1980s (Smith 1999). Compounding the necessity to generate tax dollars is the need for cities to appear business friendly in order to maintain their credit rating (Gaffikin & Warf 1993, p. 78; Sassen 1996, pp. 15–16; Sinclair 1994). Ever since the well-publicised bankruptcies of several large cities in the 1970s (Tabb 1982; Lichten 1986), the lending community has become more demanding of municipalities to maintain a businesslike ledger sheet. Losing a good credit rating can be devastating for an urban regime that has leveraged the future of a given city on the redevelopment of its downtown or the gentrification of a given neighbourhood. With the decline in federal outlays to cities, the need to borrow funds for redevelopment has increased during the third-wave. In order to retain the fiscal viability necessary to keep receiving such loans, many cities have, more unabashedly than in the past, turned to the attraction and retention of the middle class to increase tax revenue (Varady & Raffel 1995).

Altogether, the state shift towards a more openly supportive role in gentrification has helped facilitate a rapid expansion of the process during the third-wave. Yet while the larger reasons for this shift are common, its local articulation is more varied.

Clinton – In Clinton, for example, the most notable shift in state involvement during the third-wave is the departure from Keynesian regulation, manifest through the Special Clinton District (SCD). The SCD was the result of community organising during the 1960s. It restricted the power of property owners to gentrify their holdings in the neighbourhood, and was enforced (somewhat effectively) by the city until the 1990s.

The genesis of the Special Clinton District is embedded in the history of the Clinton Planning Council (CPC). The CPC was established in the mid 1960s to organise against urban renewal plans that were directed at the neighbourhood. In 1968, the CPC became prominent with its opposition of the newly written New York City Master Plan, which identified Clinton as the ideal location for several large renewal projects. The Plan called for the construction of 3,000 hotel rooms, 7.5 million square metres of office space, and 25,000 new apartments in the neighbourhood (Sclar 1993). Clinton residents felt that the plan would eventually lead to their displacement and began to organise through the CPC. By 1972, this opposition to development coalesced into the 'Save Clinton Committee', which wrote an alternative 'People's Plan', and dedicated itself to the specific task of resisting the siting of a proposed convention centre in the neighbourhood (HKNA 1999; Sclar 1993). The opposition movement attracted the attention

of Congresswoman Bella Abzug who pressured city leaders to explore other neighbourhoods for the proposed centre. In response to pressure from Abzug and others, City Planning Commissioner John Zuccotti proposed special district status for Clinton, so that residents could more effectively oppose the project. In November 1973, the proposal was formalised into a one-year interim special district for Clinton (Sclar 1993). The interim district emboldened popular support for the neighbourhood's efforts so local elected officials began to warm to a more permanent designation. Shortly thereafter, Manhattan Borough President Percy Sutton took the bold step of conditioning his support of the convention centre on the establishment of a permanent district for the neighbourhood (Sclar 1993). In October 1974, the New York City Planning Commission, under increasing pressure, acquiesced, and voted to create a permanent special district for Clinton.

The goals of the permanent Special Clinton District were fairly straightforward. The District was established to protect against widespread development that might displace existing residents. The goal was to maximise the number of affordable, family-sized units within the neighbourhood to counterbalance mounting development pressure. The most restrictive clause of the district designation prohibited demolition of any structurally sound building and prohibited any alteration permit where a history of tenant harassment could be found. Harassment violations were determined by the HPD working in conjunction with the Clinton Neighborhood Preservation Office. If the proposed development took place at a site free of past tenant harassment, a certificate of non-harassment was issued by the HPD, and construction was permitted. Predominant focus was placed on a portion of the neighbourhood deemed 'the preservation area', where building heights were kept at no more than 19.8 metres (or seven stories, whichever was lower). Special variance permits could be sought for new construction, alteration, or demolition within the SCD, but only after a hearing with the city's HPD.

Yet while provisions were made for those wishing to build in the neighbourhood, most developers abhorred the District's power. It created an obstacle that many felt was excessively punitive. In 1986, BACO Fifty-Fourth Street Corporation formalised this sentiment by suing the city and the neighbourhood preservation office for establishing an unconstitutional barrier to development (HKNA 1999). BACO argued that the SCD was unconstitutional because it shackled current builders to the harassment of past owners. Tenant harassment was tied geographically to a particular plot of land rather than to a given developer so there was no way for current owners to remediate the wrongs of the past. The clause was originally created because New York developers and landlords have a long-established record of shifting properties between one another to conceal ownership, thus making it difficult, if not impossible, to trace tenant abuse (Deutsche 1996). BACO argued that, regardless of its intent, the clause was unconstitutional because landlords were unable to 'cure' the harassment of previous owners. In 1987, a federal court judge partially agreed with the company by stating that while it is entirely constitutional for the neighbourhood to define the future of development, a 'cure clause' must be added to the existing SCD that would enable developers to 'exonerate' properties from harassment committed in the past (Dunlap 1988).

More trouble for the SCD and its advocates came in 1990 when the New York State Senior Citizen Foundation (NYSF) tried to build a retirement home in Clinton. The proposal violated the 19.8-metre height limit and the anti-demolition clause of the SCD and as such, deeply divided the community between those who wanted to protect the sanctity of the SCD and those who thought that senior citizen housing was too important to limit because of District regulations (Dunlap 1988; HKNA 2000). HPD eventually made an exception for this case but because developers would now have a legal precedent to resist the SCD, city officials were forced to modify the District's regulations more generally. Later in 1990, the terms of the SCD were renegotiated by the City Planning Commission to accommodate the court order and the NYSF controversy (Sclar 1993). First, developers were given permission to 'exonerate' their properties in order to obtain a demolition or alteration permit if they agreed to devote 28% of their new structure to affordable housing units. Additionally, demolition of sound structures would be allowed if: a) the project was not eligible for subsidised rehabilitation funds; b) affordable housing was included in the overall project; and/or c) substantial preservation was required (over 20% of the residential floor area) to improve the structure (Sclar 1993). The ostensibly benign technical modifications to the SCD and the palpably less enthusiastic enforcement by the HPD (Gwertzmann 1997; Lobbia 1998) have been effective at lowering developer aversion to the neighbourhood. The local real estate press lauded the neighbourhood as one of the trendiest gentrifying districts in the city during the 1990s (Lobbia 1998; Cawley 1995; Deutsch 1996; Finotti 1995). As each of these reports have also pointed out, however, the previous ability

of the SCD to retain affordable housing has slipped away. Much of this is because the new regulations are so hard to enforce, particularly determining whether 28% of the units are affordable. Community activists have also noted that HPD under the Giuliani Administration is much quicker to deliver a requested permit than earlier administrations (Gwertzmann 1997). Paraphrasing one longtime housing activist, reporter J. Lobbia (1998) explains, 'the Department of Buildings readily gives permits to owners who, for a number of reasons, should not have them, or allows those with permits to do construction and demolition work well beyond what the permit allows' (p. 49). As housing becomes less affordable in Clinton, progressive neighbourhood activists are leaving, along with the working class residents whose housing is no longer protected (Gwertzmann 1997). As Bob Kalin, another long-time activist in the neighbourhood, explains, 'There will always be an element of poor people in this community but it will be smaller and smaller and we [activists] will end up organizing in more and more buildings where the tenants have enough money to access attorneys' (Gwertzmann 1997). Overall, the recent experience of Clinton provides a useful example of how the (few) internal (to the state) obstacles to gentrification during the second-wave have eroded to such a point as to be ineffectual during the third.

The goal of state power to resist gentrification was partially achieved with the creation of the SCD. But within the context of political deregulation, devolution of the federal state, and growth of the reinvested core, pressures to gentrify Clinton intensified and percolated through the local state to dissolve the SCD. Removing the power of the SCD was crucial for gentrification to expand in Clinton, but the impetus and backing to do so have only recently coalesced.

Long Island City – Recent state involvement with gentrification has also intensified in Long Island City, albeit in a form different than Clinton. Though local government has been trying to assist luxury residential development in LIC since the early 1980s, it is only since the onset of the third-wave that the political environment changed sufficiently for this activity to intensify without effective resistance. Banks have been squeamish about lending in Long Island City for many years, largely because it is a mixed-use neighbourhood, with many active warehouses, factories, and working-class apartment buildings. Because so much of the neighbourhood is zoned commercial, property is expensive enough to all but rule out the involvement of small-scale gentrifiers, who tend to be more dependent on traditional forms of lending capital. The state holds a crucial role in offsetting the high risk that even corporate gentrifiers face when the 'frontier' diffuses into such (relatively) remote locales.[1]

The key piece of LIC's state-facilitated gentrification is the Queens West Project – a massive plan to bring luxury residential, office and commercial space to the neighbourhood. After years of planning, the city's Economic Development Corporation (EDC) and the Port Authority of New York and New Jersey (PA) unveiled a $2.3-billion plan in the mid 1980s, which called for the construction of 6,385 residential units, 600,000 square metres of office space, a 350-room hotel, 67,500 square metres of retail space, 12,000 square metres of community facility space, and off-street parking for 5,331 cars (HPCC 1996; Port Authority 1999). The project was to be completed in three phases.

Tipped off by public officials that the waterfront area of Hunter's Point in Queens was being considered for redevelopment, William Zeckendorf Jr. and several other major developers, investment bankers and real estate brokers, began acquiring property in the neighbourhood (Moss 1990). The entry of major real estate capital into the neighbourhood, inspired a reinvestment in the housing market and emboldened City Hall to offer tax breaks to Queens West. The Koch Administration offered a 16-year tax abatement and $30 million in city money to assist the project (Moss 1990; Fainstein & Fainstein 1987). Despite such support, Queens West was still risky, but City Hall was unable or unwilling to ameliorate this risk by offering more. Other obstacles existed: community opposition to the project was beginning to coalesce by the early 1990s, and the residential portion of the project would need some form of mortgage insurance to become reality.

Local opposition became an obstacle with the formation of the Hunter's Point Community Coalition (HPCC) in 1990. The HPCC did not want the bulky project built in its neighbourhood without some guarantee that jobs and working-class residents (particularly the elderly) would be protected (HPCC 1996). Not long after the local opposition materialised, the New York State Urban Development Corporation (UDC) entered the Queens West development team (Moss 1990). The resultant behemoth (which already included the EDC and PA) was deemed 'the Queens West Development Corporation' (QWDC). The entry of the UDC substantially undermined the ability of the HPCC to resist the project and its impact. Originally established to site low-income housing complexes, the UDC has the power to override local opposition to development proposals (Gutfreund 1995). The UDC's participation

satisfied a crucial requirement for the completion of Queens West – a way to overcome neighbourhood opposition.

By 1995, the QWDC had begun making formal plans for the first phase of the project which involved a small community park and the Citylights Building – a 42-storey, 522-unit apartment building. Though the building was slated as the project 'loss leader' (apartments were to be sold at under market value), the building was still viewed as a risky prospect (Passell 1996). Convincing banks to invest luxury housing dollars into Long Island City's mixed-use landscape would require further state intervention – namely mortgage insurance. The needed support arrived in 1996 when the Federal Housing Administration (FHA) awarded the Citylights builder, Manhattan Overlook (MO) Associates, mortgage insurance for the first residential structure (Passell 1996). Though the FHA was originally established to provide home loans for working-class buyers, it backed the mortgage here even though there was an openly stated goal to make the project semi-luxurious. FHA involvement was reportedly motivated by the 'pioneer' hyperbole that the local real estate press used to frame the project (Passell 1996). Said one FHA official, 'One of the FHA's primary roles is to help the pioneers' (Passell 1996, p. 6). But given its long history of aversion to such projects, there are likely less capricious reasons for the Administration's involvement. It is perhaps more usefully framed within the gradual reorientation of such agencies away from Keynesianism.

Whatever the reason, the effect was unambiguous. After the insurance was in place, the AFL-CIO Housing Investment Trust provided the $85.6 million in mortgage capital to MO Associates and construction began (Passell 1996). Citylights was completed in 1997, and though some relatively inexpensive units were set aside, the majority of its apartments now command luxury rents (Oser 1998). Though construction of the first Queens West building has not translated into an immediate gentrification of the surrounding neighbourhood, the intense effort of government (manifest through the QWDC) to actuate this goal provides a useful window into the nature of the state-gentrification nexus in the third-wave.

The involvement of the state as profit protector in this instance is not only part of a larger return of the state to gentrification in the third-wave but also evidence that this return is not limited to the local state. As gentrification moves further from the CBD, and becomes more risky for individual investors, the state becomes more necessary to rationalise the conditions for profit. During the second-wave (when the development process for Queens West began), the federal state was not as likely to guarantee mortgages for luxury housing, primarily because of Keynesian relics in the federal state which directed attention to affordable rental housing rather than risky attempts to bring affluent living to mixed-use neighbourhoods like LIC. The Queens West case also reveals how agencies of redistribution (like FHA and UDC) are being morphed into powerful progenitors of gentrification as their regulatory capacities get removed through state restructuring.

DUMBO – Like Long Island City, DUMBO is a difficult neighbourhood to gentrify. The small loft district in northern Brooklyn is relatively isolated, zoned non-residential, and still home to competing industrial land users. As described earlier, the gentrification of DUMBO is being largely orchestrated by one real estate developer, David Walentas. But despite his power as a developer, he was until recently unable to begin implementing his plan for the neighbourhood.

Walentas first purchased property in the neighbourhood – nine turn-of-the-century industrial loft buildings at a cost of $16.5 million – in 1982 (Dunlap 1998). His plan was to transform the neighbourhood into an upscale office and residential enclave. Shortly after purchasing the buildings, Walentas was tentatively selected by the city – eager to bring some (any) productive activity to the derelict landscape – to redevelop the waterfront of DUMBO. Redeveloping it would be crucial if gentrification in DUMBO were to work, so Walentas was pleased with the nod from the city. But before he could even assemble a formal plan for the site, the city summarily removed Walentas after anti-abatement (and anti-Walentas) council member Ruth Messinger and deputy mayor Kenneth Upper publicly objected to the support (Ennen 1999). The deputy mayor justified the removal by arguing that Walentas' Two Trees Company had neither the experience nor the financing to pull off such an extravagant plan. To compound his difficulty, he also failed to procure the zoning concessions necessary to turn DUMBO into a residential enclave (Tierney 1997). Walentas had apparently failed the private-market litmus test that the local state often employed during the second-wave.

Yet while Walentas encountered difficulty in garnering support for his original plan, he did receive important support of another form. In 1986, the state of New York agreed to move its Department of Labor into one of Walentas' buildings for ten years (Ennen 1999). This provided him with the stability of a long-term renter and time to attract the necessary support from both City Hall and the lending community for his original plan. During the period 1987–97 (while the Department of Labor was present), Walentas focused on 'taming' the neighbourhood for the type of investors he was seeking. Primarily, he offered rent concessions to artists to relocate in DUMBO. By 1997, Walentas had successfully attracted three ground-floor art galleries and numerous working artists to his portion of the neighbourhood alone. DUMBO had not only been 'tamed' but it had actually become one of the city's trendiest art enclaves by the mid 1990s (Trebay 1999). A yearly arts festival and several boosterish articles by the local press (for example, Dunlap 1998; Garbarine 1998) fuelled this perception and lowered investor reluctance.

When the state's labour department left the Clocktower Building in 1997, Walentas acted quickly to convert the structure into an up-scale residential apartment complex. In March of 1998, Two Trees was able to procure a construction loan – $30 million from the Emmes Asset Management Company – after being rejected by several (more traditional) commercial institutions (Garbarine 1998). He used the loan along with $3 million of his own money to convert the structure in just under one year. Demand for Clocktower units was astonishing. By May of 1999, all but one of the building's 124 units had been sold or were under contract. Two Trees was even able to raise asking prices several times during the sales process (Ennen 1999). With demand proven, Two Trees is currently renovating several nearby loft buildings to create 1,000 more housing units.

While Walentas has done much independently to gentrify DUMBO, his effort, power, and influence would have been insufficient without the support of the local state. In addition to finally receiving the zoning concessions necessary to convert the Clocktower Building, Walentas was re-appointed as developer of the nearby waterfront just as Clocktower units were coming on the market despite community opposition. The decision by the city played no small part in fuelling and stabilising demand for the luxury units, and for the larger project of gentrifying the neighbourhood.

This case highlights yet another aspect of an interventionist state in gentrification. As large corporate developers become more involved in gentrification, the contours of the process begin to change. Such development actors are more able to hold their property until support from the lending community and state materialise. Walentas had difficulty in getting the state to support his project during the 1980s, but has found support at several levels during the third-wave. The state has made important zoning decisions and given him uncontested approval to redevelop the waterfront despite public opposition (Sengupta 1999; Finder 1999) and ambivalence from the lending community. By removing these obstacles, City Hall has removed much of the risk associated with gentrifying DUMBO, and to this extent has mirrored a larger shift towards increased state involvement in gentrification during the third-wave.

CONCLUSION

While heightened state involvement has very real consequences for localities, it is important to frame it within the broader shift that is fueling the third-wave of gentrification. This shift has translated into an expansion of reinvestment from pockets created during the first and second-waves. It has translated into larger, more corporate developers involved in the early stages of gentrification, and a palpable decline of community opposition. These changes are mutually reinforcing in complex ways and worthy of another paper in their own right.

This paper is an attempt to understand only one aspect of this larger shift – namely how, in an environment of privatisation, the state has become more direct in its encouragement of gentrification. In each of the cases described above, the state was deeply implicated during both the second and third-wave of gentrification, but it was only in the latter context that such support overwhelmed community opposition, land-use obstacles, and Keynesian relics designed to offset the process. Though work remains to be done on how the restructuring state is affecting other aspects of capitalist urbanisation, it is evident at this point that a systemic change in the way that the state relates to capital is afoot.

Note

1 Although only a kilometre (across the East River) from the most expensive neighbourhood in NYC (the Upper East Side of Manhattan), LIC is still considered 'remote' by the real estate community because it is in Queens.

ACKNOWLEDGEMENT

The support of NSF Grant #: SBR-9724988 is gratefully acknowledged.

REFERENCES

BAGLI, C. (1991), 'De-gentrification' Can Hit When Boom Goes Bust. *The New York Observer* 5 August, p. 12.

BALL, M. (1994), The 1980s Property Boom. *Environment and Planning A: Urban and Regional Research* 26, pp. 671–695.

BOURNE, L. (1993), The Demise of Gentrification? A Commentary and Prospective View. *Urban Geography* 14, pp. 95–107.

CAUFIELD, J. (1994), *City Form and Everyday Life: Toronto's Gentrification and Critical Social Practice*. Toronto: University of Toronto Press.

CAWLEY, J. (1995), New York Community Boiling Over Name Change. *The Chicago Tribune* 15 January, p. 17.

COAKLEY, J. (1994), The Integration of Property and Financial Markets. *Environment and Planning A*, pp. 697–713.

DEUTSCH, C. (1996), Worldwide Plaza and Its Neighborhood: In Hell's Kitchen, Retail is on the Front Burner. *The New York Times* 5 May, p. 5.

DEUTSCHE, R. (1996), *Evictions: Art and Spatial Politics*. Cambridge, MASS: MIT Press.

DEUTSCHE, R. & C.G. RYAN (1984), The Fine Art of Gentrification. *October* 31, pp. 91–111.

DUNLAP, D. (1988), Community Seeks End to Redevelopment Ban. *The New York Times* 10 January.

DUNLAP, D. (1998), SoHo, TriBeCa, and Now Dumbo? *The New York Times* 25 October, pp. 1, 20.

ENNEN, M. (1999), An Immodest Proposal. *Brooklyn Bridge Magazine* January, pp. 48–53.

FAINSTEIN, N. & S. FAINSTEIN (1987), Economic Restructuring and the Politics of Land Use Planning in New York City. *Journal of the American Planning Association* 53, pp. 237–248.

FELDMAN, M. & R. FLORIDA (1990), Economic Restructuring and the Changing Role of the State in U.S. Housing. *In*: W. VAN VLIET & J. VAN WEESEP, eds., *Government and Housing: Developments in Seven Countries*, pp. 31–46. Newbury Park, CA: Sage.

FINDER, A. (1999), Long View From the Waterfront: Developer Has Pursued a Brooklyn Dream for 20 Years. *New York Today* 24 June.

FINOTTI, J. (1995), Clinton: Hell's Kitchen Recipe: A Tangy Diversity. *The New York Times* 9 April, Real Estate Section.

GAFFIKIN, F & B. WARF (1993), Urban Policy and the Post-Keynesian State in the United Kingdom and

United States. *International Journal of Urban and Regional Research* 17(1), pp. 67–84.

GARBARINE, R. (1998), A Neighborhood Called Dumbo Has High Hopes. *The New York Times* 7 August, p. 8.

GUTFREUND, O. (1995), Urban Development Corporation. *In*: K. JACKSON, ed., *The Encyclopedia of New York*, pp. 1218–1219. New Haven: Yale University Press.

GWERTZMANN, M. (1997), *Keeping the 'Kitchen' In Clinton: Community Efforts to Resist Gentrification* (unpublished report, www.hellskitchen. net).

HACKWORTH, J. (2000), State Devolution, Urban Regimes, and the Production of Geographic Scale: The Case of New Brunswick, NJ. *Urban Geography* 21(5), pp. 450–458.

HACKWORTH, J. (2001), Inner City Real Estate Investment, Gentrification, and Economic Recession in New York City. *Environment and Planning A*, 33(5), pp. 863–880.

HAMNETT, C. (1973), Improvement Grants as an Indicator of Gentrification in Inner London. *Area* 5, pp. 252–261.

HARVEY, D. (1985), *The Urbanization of Capital: Studies in the History and Theory of Capitalist Urbanization*. Baltimore: The Johns Hopkins University Press.

HARVEY, D. (1989a), *The Condition of Postmodernity*. Oxford: Blackwell.

HARVEY, D. (1989b), From Managerialism to Entrepreneurialism: The Transformation of Urban Governance in Late Capitalism. *Geografiska Annaler* 71, pp. 3–17.

HKNA (1999), website: www.hellskitchen.net

HPCC (1996), *The View: Newsletter of the Hunter's Point Community Coalition* 3, p. 5.

LEES, L. (2000), A Re-appraisal of Gentrification: Towards a 'Geography of Gentrification'. *Progress in Human Geography* 24(3).

LEITNER, H. (1990), Cities in Pursuit of Economic Growth: The Local State as Entrepreneur. *Political Geography Quarterly* 9, pp. 146–170.

LEY, D. (1992), Gentrification in Recession: Social Change in Six Canadian Inner Cities: 1981–1986. *Urban Geography* 13(3), pp. 220–256.

LEY, D. (1996), *The New Middle Class and the Remaking of the Central City*. Oxford: Oxford University Press.

LICHTEN, E. (1986), *Class, Power & Austerity: The New York City Fiscal Crisis*. South Hadley, MA: Bergin & Garvey Publishers, Inc.

LOBBIA, J. (1998), Hell's Kitchen is Burning. *The Village Voice* 8 September, pp. 47–51.

LOGAN, J. (1993), Cycles and Trends in the Globalization of Real Estate. *In*: P. Knox, ed., *The Restless Urban Landscape*, pp. 33–55. Englewood Cliffs, NJ: Prentice Hall.

MOLOTCH, H. (1976), The City as Growth Machine: Toward a Political Economy of Place. *American Journal of Sociology* 82, pp. 309–330.

MOSS, M. (1990), Pinpointing Conflicts in Queen's Development: Hunter's Point Proposals Put Mayor's Pledge to Test. *Newsday* 26 April.

OSER, A. (1998), Queens West Pioneers are Getting Company. *The New York Times* 22 March, p. RE1.

PASSELL, P. (1996), Pioneers Wanted: East River Views: Innovative Financing – and $25,000 Average Prices – are Lures at First Queens West Building. *The New York Times* 6 October, Real Estate Section, pp. 1, 6.

PORT AUTHORITY (1999), website: www.panynj.gov

SASSEN, S. (1996), *Losing Control? Sovereignty in an Age of Globalization*. New York: Columbia University Press.

SCHAEFFER, R. & N. SMITH (1986), The Gentrification of Harlem? *The Annals of the Association of American Geographers* 76, pp. 347–365.

SENGUPTA, S. (1999), A Neighborhood Identity Crisis: Transformation Brings Anxiety in Brooklyn's DUMBO. *The New York Times* 9 June, pp. B1, B7.

SCLAR, E. (1993), *Analysis of the Special Clinton District: Prepared for Community Board #4* (unpublished report).

SINCLAIR, T. (1994), Passing Judgement: Credit Rating Processes as Regulatory Mechanisms of Governance in the Emerging World Order. *Review of International Political Economy* 1, pp. 133–159.

SMITH, N. (1979), Gentrification and Capital: Theory, Practice, and Ideology in Society Hill. *Antipode* 11(3), pp. 24–35.

SMITH, N. (1989), Tompkins Square: Riots, Rents, and Redskins. *Portable Lower East Side* 6, pp. 1–36.

SMITH, N. (1996), *The New Urban Frontier: Gentrification And The Revanchist City*. New York: Routledge.

SMITH, N. (1999), Which New Urbanism? New York City and the Revanchist 1990s. *In*: R. BEAUREGARD & S. BODY-GENDROT, eds., *The Urban Moment: Cosmopolitan Essays on the Late-20th Century City*, pp. 185–202. Thousand Oaks, CA: Sage.

SMITH, N. & J. DEFILIPPIS (1999), The Reassertion of Economics: 1990s Gentrification in the Lower East Side. *International Journal* of *Urban and Regional Research* 23(4), pp. 638–653.

STAEHELI, L., J. KODRAS & C. FLINT, eds. (1997), *State Devolution in America: Implications for a Diverse Society*. Thousand Oaks, CA: Sage.

STERNLIEB, G. & J. HUGHES (1983), The Uncertain Future of the Central City. *Urban Affairs Quarterly* 18(4), pp. 455–472.

TABB, W. (1982), *The Long Default: New York City and The Urban Fiscal Crisis*. New York: Monthly Review Press.

TIERNEY, J. (1997), Brooklyn Could Have Been a Contender. *The New York Times Magazine* 28 December, pp. 18–23, 37–38, 47–48.

TREBAY, G. (1998), Out of the Garret: A New Study Examines the Economic Life of Artists. *The Village Voice*, 21–27 October.

VARADY, D. & J. RAFFEL (1995), *Selling Cities: Attracting Homebuyers Through Schools and Housing Programs*. Albany: State University of New York Press.

WILLIAMS, P. (1976), The Role of Institutions in the Inner-London Housing Market: The Case of Islington. *Transactions of the Institute of British Geographers* 3, pp. 23–34.

WYLY, E. & D. HAMMEL (1999), *Islands of Decay in Seas of Renewal: Urban Policy and Resurgence of Gentrification*. CUPR Working Paper.

ZUKIN, S. (1982), *Loft Living: Culture And Capital In Urban Change*. Baltimore: Johns Hopkins University Press.

ZUKIN, S. (1987), Gentrification: Culture and Capital in the Urban Core. *American Review of Sociology* 13, pp. 129–147.

PART THREE

Explaining/
theorizing
gentrification

Plate 8 Condos coming soon: Camden, New Jersey, July, 2009. Photograph by Elvin Wyly.

SECTION A

Production-side explanations

INTRODUCTION TO SECTION A

Gentrification is a familiar and pervasive theme in today's cities. While academics, policy makers, developers, and community activists dispute its impacts and desirability, all agree that it is a significant and durable process in many cities around the world. It has become a familiar plot in feature films, stage plays, and television series. Even its most serious controversies of class and racial inequality are now routinely used in satirical humor, most recently in the blog and book, *Stuff White People Like* (Lander, 2008): "… white people love situations where they can't lose …. perhaps the safest bet a white person can make is to buy a home in an up-and-coming neighborhood."

But gentrification was not always so familiar. Thirty years ago, the process suddenly became a major point of debate because it was so unexpected, and it seemed to defy every prediction of mainstream urban theory. Every year seemed to bring more evidence of an "urban renaissance" and a wave of "urban revitalization," and so journalists and scholars worked to document the trend. Rather quickly, a new consensus began to emerge: after a long period during which middle-class households had always moved *outward* to newly-built suburbs as they moved *upward* in terms of wealth, age, and needs for space, preferences had now changed. Middle-class and even wealthy people who once opted for the suburbs were now choosing the city – and often the poor, inner-city districts abandoned by the middle classes not so long ago. The consumer preferences that had been the foundation of urban theory and policy, it seemed, had changed in a dramatic move "Back to the City" (Laska and Spain, 1980).

Production-side explanations emerged in response to the problems and limitations of this new conventional wisdom on a shift in consumer preference. The evidence on some of the "back to the city" predictions was mixed; most gentrifiers, for instance, came from other city neighborhoods, not from the suburbs. There was great uncertainty on *why* consumer preferences had changed so quickly and decisively. To be sure, many different explanations for the shift were offered: children of the "baby boom" generation rejected suburban conformity; once-neglected old homes and neighborhoods became more attractive with the growing popularity of historic preservation and heritage architecture; the cost of suburban commuting skyrocketed after the 1973 oil embargo; increased educational attainment and white-collar service jobs led working professionals to place higher values on experiencing the diversity and authenticity of the inner city; and so on. But if so many different factors were involved in shaping preferences, then how does it explain anything at all to say that gentrification is caused by a change in consumer preferences? Moreover, the overwhelming emphasis on consumer choice tended to sideline questions about displacement, inequality, and community: if the classical pattern of middle-class suburbanization caused inner-city disinvestment, decay, and abandonment, then the conventional wisdom implied that it could not possibly be a bad thing to have middle-class people choosing to return to the inner city.

This section includes five readings focusing on the most influential production-side theory addressing these critical issues. Neil Smith's 1979 article (written when he was a postgraduate student studying Baltimore, Philadelphia, and other U.S. cities; see Box 3) challenged the reliance on notions of "consumer sovereignty": we have to consider the preferences not only of gentrifiers as consumers, but also "builders, developers, landlords, mortgage lenders, government agencies, real estate agents, and tenants"; all things considered, "the needs of production – in particular the need to earn profit – are a more decisive initiative behind gentrification than consumer preference."

Why does gentrification become profitable, creating new choices for gentrifiers that were once unthinkable? Smith offers an explanation based on his reading of theories of land rent – a tradition in economics that stretches all the way back to Adam Smith, David Ricardo, Karl Marx, and other figures from classical political economy. Smith analyses how technological obsolescence and the gradual deterioration of buildings over time can create a mismatch between the economics of a particular location and the land use at that location. Smith also draws a distinction between capitalized land rent (the economic return that an owner receives from the use of their land given its current use) and potential land rent (the maximum return that could be obtained if the land were put to its optimal, "highest and best use"). In a market economy, when a neighborhood is first developed, there is usually no difference between capitalized and potential land rent: the area is built to maximize returns subject to the limitations of its location and the best technologies available at the time. Over long periods of time, however, housing units age and deteriorate, requiring more constant and expensive repairs – while newer growth areas emerge elsewhere, usually on the lower-density edge of an expanding city; thus older, centrally-located neighborhoods usually suffer disinvestment and outmigration of higher-income residents pursuing the opportunities of newer, better homes in the suburbs. The land in older inner-city neighborhoods comes to be used for ever lower-income groups, even if the broader metropolitan region enjoys rapid growth and increasing wealth. This creates a gap between the economic returns obtained from centrally-located land devoted to housing the poor and working classes, and the potential returns if the neighborhood were redeveloped for a "higher" use – such as luxury housing for the metropolitan region's highest-paid professionals employed in downtown office towers. Gentrification becomes profitable when this gap is wide enough to yield a good return after all of the costs of conversion to new land uses – rehabilitation of old run-down houses, or demolition and new construction.

Smith's rent gap framework has become one of the most influential – and one of the most controversial – foundations of the entire gentrification literature. It connects local transformations and tensions in gentrifying neighborhoods to the broader structures of uneven urban development and the inequalities of capitalism. The readings in this literature highlight three important facets of this influence and controversy. First, debate over the rent gap exposes struggles over terms and definitions. This is most apparent in Bourassa's challenge (and in a spirited response we were not able to include here, Smith, 1996a), but it also shapes some of the disagreements between Neil Smith and David Ley. For some readers, these terminological disputes are boring, and quickly "become stalled in a morass of gobbledygook," as Bourassa puts it. But we should not be surprised that there is no single, definitive, clearly-understood meaning for every term: land markets have been mysterious and fascinating for economists for centuries, and it has always been a challenge to use the right words consistently to summarize complex processes.

Second, although the concept is intuitive and logical for many readers, it is extremely difficult to measure in specific experiences of gentrification. Measurement became a major flashpoint in the exchange between Smith and Ley, written after the publication of a study by Ley that used several indicators to evaluate alternative explanations for gentrification amongst different cities across Canada. As Hammel's essay demonstrates, the difficulty in coming up with empirical tests that might resolve theoretical disagreements among Smith, Ley, Bourassa, and others, comes from two inescapable features of measurement in urban land markets. The first is that land rent is paid in different ways to different kinds of owners: for landlords capitalized land rent is received as a stream of rental payments over time; for owner-occupiers (and many speculative developers) land rent is only capitalized and received when the owner sells. The second issue involves the blending of land use and land rent. Smith's theory holds that capitalized land rent can be *influenced by* the use of the land, but that the two are conceptually distinct: the locational attractiveness of a particular parcel of land is not the same as the value of an old, run-down structure that might occupy the site. But since buildings are almost always bought and sold together with the land they occupy (although see Lees, 1994, on the English leasehold system and gentrification), it is rarely possible to separate and measure these two distinct concepts. This is one reason why Ley noted that "almost ten years after its first presentation," the rent gap theory "has still not been made empirically accountable"; shortly afterwards, however, Eric Clark (1987) published what remains the definitive, landmark historical empirical study of rent-gap dynamics, based on years of painstaking research with land-market transactions over the course of more than a century.

Third, the power and provocation of the rent-gap explanation is its challenge to common thinking: gentrification is not a natural outcome of changes in consumer preferences, but instead the result of structural features of capitalism that produce the array of things we're allowed to choose from in the first place. Gentrification, in this narrative, thrives because it has become profitable for developers, investors, government agencies, and others to produce spaces and places that become attractive options for consumer gentrifiers to choose in their pursuit of aesthetic sophistication and cultural authenticity. This perspective is important and powerful, but it is also a provocative declaration that privileges economics over culture and structure over agency. Both Smith's commentary and Ley's reply emphasize the importance and mutual interplay of production-side and consumption-side explanations of gentrification – but both authors also offered eloquent and spirited arguments on which side took priority and how it influenced the other. This exchange set the pattern for many years. Many readers over-simplified the nuanced discussion by drawing a sharp, exaggerated distinction between a Ley-inspired narrative of culture, consumption, and choice, versus a Smithian framework of economic logic, production, and structural constraint.

As we will see later in Section 3 Part C, it is important and possible to move beyond this production-consumption stalemate. But it has been a cruel irony of the cultural turn of the 1990s and 2000s that scholarly theories like the rent gap have been attacked as economically determinist at precisely the same time that public policy in nearly every country has shifted decisively toward its own kind of determinism. Consumer choice has been elevated to a doctrine. But the privatization of public services, cutbacks in social welfare assistance for low-income people, and the destruction of rental social and public housing in favor of homeownership have all narrowed the range of choices available to the poor and the working classes. Gentrification has been the leading edge, and one of the most clearly identifiable neighborhood-scale consequences, of this new form of policy-driven consumer sovereignty, and thus it remains a battleground over inequality and the right to the city.

REFERENCES AND FURTHER READING

Badcock, B. (1989) 'An Australian view of the rent gap hypothesis', *Annals of the Association of American Geographers* 79(1): 125–145.

Bourassa, S. C. (1990) 'Another Australian view of the rent gap hypothesis', *Annals of the Association of American Geographers* 80: 458–459.

Clark, E. (1987) *The Rent Gap and Urban Change: Case Studies in Malmo, 1860–1985* (Lund: Lund University Press).

Clark, E. (1988) 'The rent gap and transformation of the built environment: case studies in Malmo, 1860–1985', *Geografiska Annaler B* 70(2): 241–254.

Clark, E. (1995) 'The rent gap re-examined', *Urban Studies* 32(9): 1489–1503.

Diappi, L. and Bolchi, P. (2008) 'Smith's rent gap theory and local real estate dynamics: a multi-agent model', *Computers, Environment and Urban Systems* 32(1): 6–11.

Lander, C. (2008) *Stuff White People Like.* New York: Random House. (Original blog at http://stuffwhitepeoplelike.com).

Laska, S. and Spain, D. (eds) (1980) *Back to the City: Issues in Neighborhood Renovation.* New York: Pergamon.

Lees, L. (1994) 'Gentrification in London and New York: an Atlantic gap?', *Housing Studies* 9(2): 199–217.

O'Sullivan, D. (2002) 'Toward micro-scale spatial modeling of gentrification', *Journal of Geographical Systems* 4: 251–274.

Redfern, P. (1997) 'A new look at gentrification: 1. Gentrification and domestic technologies', *Environment and Planning A* 29: 1275–1296.

Smith, N. (1979) 'Toward a theory of gentrification: a back to the city movement by capital, not people', *Journal of the American Planning Association* 45(4): 538–548.

Smith, N. (1982) 'Gentrification and uneven development', *Economic Geography* 58(2): 139–155.

Smith, N. (1987) 'Gentrification and the rent gap', *Annals of the Association of American Geographers* 77(3): 462–478.

Smith, N. (1996a) 'Of rent gaps and radical idealism: a reply to Steven Bourassa', *Urban Studies* 33(7): 1199–1203.

Smith, N. (1996b) *The New Urban Frontier: Gentrification and the Revanchist City*, London and New York: Routledge.

Smith, N. and DeFilippis, J. (1999) 'The reassertion of economics: 1990s gentrification in the Lower East Side', *International Journal of Urban and Regional Research* 23: 638–653.

Smith, N., Duncan, B. and Reid, L. (1989) 'From disinvestment to reinvestment: tax arrears and turning points in the East Village', *Housing Studies* 4(4): 238–252.

Sykora, L. (1993) 'City in transition: the role of the rent gap in Prague's revitalization', *Tijdschrift voor Economisce en Sociale Geografie* 84(4): 281–293.

9

"Toward a Theory of Gentrification: A Back to the City Movement by Capital, not People"

From *Journal of the American Planning Association* (1979)

Neil Smith

Following a period of sustained deterioration, many American cities are experiencing the gentrification of select central city neighborhoods. Initial signs of revival during the 1950s intensified in the 1960s, and by the 1970s these had grown into a widespread gentrification movement affecting the majority of the country's older cities.[1] A recent survey by the Urban Land Institute (1976) suggests that close to half the 260 cities with over 50,000 population are experiencing rehabilitation in the inner city areas. Although nationally, gentrification accounts for only a small fraction of new housing starts compared with new construction, the process is very important in (but not restricted to) older northeastern cities.

As the process of gentrification burgeoned so did the literature about it. Most of this literature concerns the contemporary processes or its effects: the socioeconomic and cultural characteristics of inmigrants, displacement, the federal role in redevelopment, benefits to the city, and creation and destruction of community. Little attempt has been made to construct historical explanations of the process, to study causes rather than effects. Instead, explanations are very much taken for granted and fall into two categories: cultural and economic.

Cultural. Popular among revitalization theorists is the notion that young, usually professional, middle-class people have changed their lifestyle. According to Gregory Lipton, these changes have been significant enough to "decrease the relative desirability of single-family, suburban homes" (1977, p. 146). Thus, with a trend toward fewer children, postponed marriages, and a fast rising divorce rate, younger homebuyers and renters are trading in the tarnished dream of their parents for a new dream defined in urban rather than suburban terms. Other researchers emphasize the search for socially distinctive communities as sympathetic environments for individual self-expression (Winters 1978), while still others extend this into a more general argument. In contemporary "post-industrial cities," according to D. Ley, white-collar service occupations supersede blue-collar productive occupations, and this brings with it an emphasis on consumption and amenity not work. Patterns of consumption come to dictate patterns of production; "the values of consumption rather than production guide central city land use decisions" (Ley 1978, p. 11). Inner-city resurgence is an example of this new emphasis on consumption.

Economic. As the cost of newly constructed housing continues to rise and its distance from the city center to increase, the rehabilitation of inner- and central-city structures is seen to be more viable economically. Old but structurally sound properties can be purchased and rehabilitated for less than the cost of a comparable new house. In addition, many researchers stress the high economic cost of commuting—the higher cost of gasoline for private cars and rising fares on public transportation—and the economic benefits of proximity to work.

These conventional hypotheses are by no means mutually exclusive. They are often invoked jointly and share in one vital respect a common perspective—an emphasis on *consumer preference* and the constraints within which these preferences are implemented. This they share with the broader body of neoclassical residential land use theory

(Alonso 1964; Muth 1969; Mills 1972). According to the neoclassical theory, suburbanization reflects the preference for space and the increased ability to pay for it due to the reduction of transportational and other constraints. Similarly, gentrification is explained as the result of an alteration of preferences and/or a change in the constraints determining which preferences will or can be implemented. Thus in the media and the research literature alike, the process is viewed as a "back to the city movement." This applies as much to the earlier gentrification projects, such as Philadelphia's Society Hill (accomplished with substantial state assistance under urban renewal legislation), as it does to the later schemes, such as Baltimore's Federal Hill or Washington's Capitol Hill (mainly private market phenomena of the 1970s). All have become symbolic of a supposed middle- and upper-class pilgrimage back from the suburbs.[2] But as yet it remains an untested if pervasive assumption that the gentrifiers are disillusioned suburbanites. As early as 1966, Herbert Gans declared: "I have seen no study of how many suburbanites were actually brought back by urban-renewal projects" (1968, p. 287). Though this statement was made in evidence before the Ribicoff Committee on the Crisis of the Cities, Gans's challenge seems to have fallen on deaf ears. Only in the late 1970s have such studies begun to be carried out. This paper presents data from Society Hill and other revitalized neighborhoods, examines the significance of these results in terms of the consumer sovereignty theory, and attempts to deepen our theoretical understanding of the causes of gentrification.

A RETURN FROM THE SUBURBS?

Once the location of William Penn's "holy experiment," Society Hill housed Philadelphia's gentry well into the nineteenth century. With industrialization and urban growth, however, its popularity declined, and the gentry together with the rising middle class, moved west to Rittenhouse Square and to the new suburbs in the northwest and across the Schuylkill River. Society Hill deteriorated rapidly, remaining in slum condition until 1959. In that year, an urban renewal plan was implemented.

Within ten years Society Hill was transformed and—"the most historic square mile in the nation" according to Bicentennial advertising—it again housed the city's middle and upper classes. Few authentically restored houses now change hands for less than $125,000. Noting the enthusiasm with which rehabilitation was done, the novelist Nathanial Burt observed that "Remodeling old houses is, after all, one of Old Philadelphia's favorite indoor sports, and to be able to remodel and consciously serve the cause of civic revival all at once has gone to the heads of the upper classes like champagne" (1963, pp. 556–57). As this indoor sport caught on, therefore, it became Philadelphia folklore that "there was an upper class return to center city in Society Hill" (Wolf 1975, p. 325). As Burt eloquently explains:

> The renaissance of Society Hill … is just one piece in a gigantic jigsaw puzzle which has stirred Philadelphia from its hundred-year sleep, and promises to transform the city completely. This movement, of which the return to Society Hill is a significant part, is generally known as the Philadelphia Renaissance.
>
> (1963, p. 539)

By June 1962 less than a third of the families purchasing property for rehabilitation were from the suburbs[3] (Greenfield & Co. 1964, p. 192). But since the first people to rehabilitate houses began work in 1960, it was generally expected that the proportion of suburbanites would rise sharply as the area became better publicized and a Society Hill address became a coveted possession. After 1962, however, no data were officially collected. The following table presents data sampled from case files held by The Redevelopment Authority of Philadelphia; the data is for the period up to 1975 (by which time the project was essentially complete) and represents a 17 percent sample of all rehabilitated residences (Table 9.1).

It would appear from these results that only a small proportion of gentrifiers did in fact return from the suburbs; 14 percent in the case of Society Hill, compared with 72 percent who moved from elsewhere within the city boundaries. A statistical breakdown of this latter group suggests that of previous city dwellers, 37 percent came from Society Hill itself, and 19 percent came from the Rittenhouse Square district. The remainder came from several middle- and upper-class suburbs annexed by the city in the last century—Chestnut Hill, Mt. Airy, Spruce Hill. This suggests a consolidation of upper- and middle-class white residences in the city, not a return from the present day suburbs.[4] Additional data from Baltimore and Washington D.C. on the percentage of returning suburbanites support the Society Hill data (Table 9.2).

In Philadelphia and elsewhere an urban renaissance may well be taking place but it is not a significant return from the suburbs as such. This does not disprove the consumer sovereignty hypothesis but

Year	Same address	Elsewhere in the city	Suburbs	Outside SMSA	Unidentified	Total
1964	5	9	0	0	0	14
1965	3	17	7	0	0	27
1966	1	25	4	0	2	32
1969	1	9	2	0	0	12
1972	1	12	1	2	0	16
1975	0	1	0	0	0	1
Total	11	73	14	2	2	102
Percentage by origin	11	72	14	2	2	100

Table 9.1 The origin of rehabilitators in Society Hill, 1964–1975

City	Percent city dwellers	Percent suburbanites
Philadelphia		
Society Hill	72	14
Baltimore		
Homestead Properties	65.2	27
Washington D.C.		
Mount Pleasant	67	18
Capitol Hill	72	15

Table 9.2 The origin of rehabilitators in three cities

Source: Baltimore City Department of Housing and Community Development (1977), Gale (1976, 1977)

suggests some limitations and refinements. Clearly, it is possible—even likely—that younger people who moved to the city for an education and professional training have decided against moving back to the suburbs. There is a problem, however, if this is to be taken as a definitive explanation, for gentrification is not simply a North American phenomenon but is also happening in numerous cities throughout Europe (see, for example, Pitt 1977) where the extent of prior middle-class suburbanization is much less and the relation between suburb and inner city is substantially different.[5] Only Ley's (1978) more general societal hypothesis about post-industrial cities is broad enough to account for the process internationally, but the implications of accepting this view are somewhat drastic. If cultural choice and consumer preference really explain gentrification, this amounts either to the hypothesis that individual preferences change in unison not only nationally but internationally—a bleak view of human nature and cultural individuality—or that the overriding constraints are strong enough to obliterate the individuality implied in consumer preference. If the latter is the case, the concept of consumer preference is at best contradictory: a process first conceived in terms of individual consumption preference has now to be explained as resulting from cultural uni-dimensionality. The concept can be rescued as theoretically viable only if it is used to refer to collective social preference, not individual preference.

This refutation of the neoclassical approach to gentrification is only a summary critique and far from exhaustive. What it suggests, however, is a broader conceptualization of the process, for the gentrifier as consumer is only one of many actors participating in the process. To explain gentrification according to the gentrifier's actions alone, while ignoring the role of builders, developers, landlords, mortgage lenders, government agencies, real estate agents, and tenants, is excessively narrow. A broader theory of gentrification must take the role of producers as well as consumers into account, and when this is done, it appears that the needs of production—in particular the need to earn profit—are a more decisive initiative behind gentrification than consumer preference. This is not to say in some naive way that consumption is the automatic consequence of production, or that consumer preference is a totally passive effect caused by production. Such would be a producer's sovereignty theory, almost as one-sided as its neoclassical counterpart. Rather, the relationship between production and consumption is symbiotic, but it is a symbiosis in which production dominates. Consumer preference and demand for gentrified housing can be created after all, and this is precisely what happened in Society Hill.[6] Although it is of secondary importance in initiating the actual process, and therefore in explaining why gentrification occurred in the first place, consumer preference and demand are of primary importance in determining the final form and character of revitalized areas—the difference between Society Hill, say, and New York's SoHo.

The so-called urban renaissance has been stimulated more by economic than cultural forces. In the decision to rehabilitate an inner city structure, one consumer preference tends to stand out above the others—the preference for profit, or, more accurately, a sound financial investment. Whether or not gentrifiers articulate this preference, it is fundamental, for few would even consider rehabilitation if a financial loss were to be expected. A theory of gentrification must therefore explain why some neighborhoods are profitable to redevelop while others are not. What are the conditions of profitability? Consumer sovereignty explanations took for granted the availability of areas ripe for gentrification when this was precisely what had to be explained.

Before proceeding to a more detailed explanation of the process, it will be useful to step back and examine gentrification in the broader historical and structural context of capital investment and urban development. In particular, the general characteristics of investment in the built environment must be examined.

INVESTMENT IN THE BUILT ENVIRONMENT

In a capitalist economy, land and the improvements built onto it become commodities. As such they boast certain idiosyncracies of which three are particularly important for this discussion. First, private property rights confer on the owner near-monopoly control over land and improvements, monopoly control over the uses to which a certain space is put.[7] From this condition we can derive the function of ground rent. Second, land and improvements are fixed in space but their value is anything but fixed. Improvements on the land are subject to all the normal influences on their value but with one vital difference. On the one hand, the value of built improvements on a piece of land, as well as on surrounding land, influences the ground rent that landlords can demand; on the other hand, since land and buildings on it are inseparable, the price at which buildings change hands reflects the ground rent level. Meanwhile land, unlike the improvements built on it, "does not require upkeep in order to continue its potential for use" (Harvey 1973, pp. 158–59) and thereby retains its potential value. Third, while land is permanent, the improvements built on it are not, but generally have a very long turnover period in physical as well as value terms. Physical decay is

unlikely to claim the life of a building for at least twenty-five years, usually a lot longer, and it may take as long in economic (as opposed to accounting) terms for it to pay back its value. From this we can derive several things: in a well-developed capitalist economy, large initial outlays will be necessary for built environment investments; financial institutions will therefore play an important role in the urban land market (Harvey 1973, p. 159); and patterns of capital depreciation will be an important variable in determining whether and to what extent a building's sale price reflects the ground rent level. These points will be of central importance in the next section.

In a capitalist economy, profit is the gauge of success, and competition is the mechanism by which success or failure is translated into growth or collapse. All individual enterprises must strive for higher and higher profits to facilitate the accumulation of greater and greater quantities of capital in profitable pursuits. Otherwise they find themselves unable to afford more advanced production methods and therefore fall behind their competitors. Ultimately, this leads either to bankruptcy or a merger into a larger enterprise. This search for increased profits translates, at the scale of the whole economy, into the long-run economic growth; general economic stability is therefore synonymous with overall economic growth. Particularly when economic growth is hindered elsewhere in the industrial sector, the built environment becomes a target for much profitable investment, as is particularly apparent with this century's suburbanization experience. In this case, spatial expansion rather than expansion *in situ* was the response to the continual need for capital accumulation. But suburbanization illustrates well the two-sided nature of investment in the built environment, for as well as being a vehicle for capital accumulation, it can also become a barrier to further accumulation. It becomes so by dint of the characteristics noted above: near-monopoly control of space, the fixity of investments, the long turnover period. Near-monopoly control of space by landowners may prevent the sale of land for development; the fixity of investments forces new development to take place at other, often less advantageous, locations, and prevents redevelopment from occurring until invested capital has lived out its economic life; the long turnover period of capital invested in the built environment can discourage investment as long as other sectors of the economy with shorter turnover periods remain profitable. The early industrial city presented just such a barrier by the later part of the nineteenth century, eventually prompting suburban development rather than development *in situ*.

During the nineteenth century in most eastern cities, land values displayed the classical conical form—a peak at the urban center, with a declining gradient on all sides toward the periphery. This was the pattern Hoyt (1933) found in Chicago. With continued urban development the land value gradient is displaced outward and upward; land at the center grows in value while the base of the cone broadens. Land values tend to change in unison with long cycles in the economy; they increase most rapidly during periods of particularly rapid capital accumulation and decline temporarily during slumps. Since suburbanization relied on considerable capital investments in land, construction, transportation, etc., it too tended to follow this cyclical trend. Faced with the need to expand the scale of their productive activities, and unable or unwilling for a variety of reasons to expand any further where they were, industries jumped out beyond the city to the base of the land value cone where extensive spatial expansion was both possible and relatively cheap. The alternative—substantial renewal and redevelopment of the already built up area—would have been too costly for private capital to undertake, and so industrial capital was increasingly sent to the suburbs. This movement of industrial capital began in force after the severe depression of 1893–97, and was followed by a substantial migration of capital for residential construction. In the already well-established cities, the only significant exception to this migration of construction capital was in the central business district (CBD) where substantial skyscraper office development occurred in the 1920s. As will be shown, the inner city was adversely affected by this movement of capital to the suburbs where higher returns were available. A combination of neglect and concerted disinvestment by investors, due to high risk and low rates of return, initiated a long period of deterioration and a lack of new capital investment in the inner city.

Land values in the inner city fell relative to the CBD and the suburbs, and by the late 1920s Hoyt could identify for Chicago a newly formed "valley in the land-value curve between the Loop and outer residential areas" (see Figure 9.1). This valley "indicates the location of these sections where the buildings are mostly over forty years old and where the residents rank lowest in rent-paying ability" (Hoyt 1933, pp. 356–8). Throughout the decades of most sustained suburbanization, from the 1940s to the 1960s, this valley in the land value curve deepened and broadened due to a continued lack of productive capital investment. By the late 1960s the valley may have been as much as six miles wide in Chicago (McDonald and Bowman 1979). Evidence

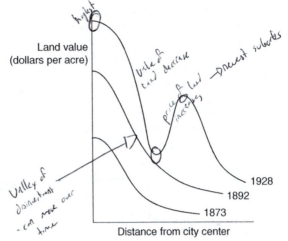

Figure 9.1 The evolution of land values in Chicago (after Hoyt 1933)

from other cities suggests that this capital depreciation and consequent broadening of the land value valley occurred throughout the country's older cities (Davis 1965; Edel and Sclar 1975), producing the slums and ghettos that were suddenly discovered as "problems" in the 1960s by the long gone suburban middle class.

A theory of gentrification will need to explain the detailed historical mechanisms of capital depreciation in the inner city and the precise way in which this depreciation produces the possibility of profitable reinvestment. The crucial nexus here is the relationship between land value and property value. As they stand, however, these concepts are insufficiently refined. Land value for Hoyt, was a composite category referring to the price of undeveloped plots and the expected future income from their use; the type of future use was simply assumed. Property value, on the other hand, is generally taken to mean the price at which a building is sold, including the value of the land. To elaborate the relationship between land value and the value of buildings in fuller detail, then, it will be necessary to disaggregate these two measures of value into four separate but related categories. These four categories (house value, sale price, capitalized ground rent, potential ground rent) remain fully or partially obscure and indistinguishable under the umbrella concepts land value and property value.

House value. Consistent with its emphasis on consumer preference, neoclassical economic theory explains prices as the result of supply and demand conditions. But if, as suggested above, the search for a high return on productive investments is the primary initiative behind gentrification, then the specific costs of production (not just the quantity of end-product—supply) will be central in the determination of prices. In opposition to neoclassical theory, therefore, it will be necessary to separate the value of a house from its price. Following the classical political economists (Smith, Ricardo), and after them Marx, this paper takes as axiomatic a labor theory of value: the value of a commodity is measured by the quantity of socially necessary labor power required to produce it. Only in the market place is value translated into price. And although the price of a house reflects its value, the two cannot mechanically be equated since price is also affected by supply and demand conditions. Thus, value considerations (the amount of socially necessary labor power) set the level about which the price fluctuates. With housing, the situation is more complex because individual houses return periodically to the market for resale. The house's value will also depend, therefore, on its rate of depreciation through use, versus its rate of appreciation through the addition of more value. The latter occurs when further labor is performed for maintenance, replacement, extensions, etc.

Sale price. A further complication with housing is that the sale price represents not only the value of the house, but an additional component for rent since the land is generally sold along with the structures it accommodates. Here it is preferable to talk of ground rent rather than land value, since the price of land does not reflect a quantity of labor power applied to it, as with the value of commodities proper.

Ground rent and capitalized ground rent. Ground rent is a claim made by landowners on users of their land; it represents a reduction from the surplus value created over and above cost-price by producers on the site. Capitalized ground rent is the actual quantity of ground rent that is appropriated by the landowner, given the present land use. In the case of rental housing where the landlord produces a service on land he or she owns, the production and ownership functions are combined and ground rent becomes even more of an intangible category though nevertheless a real presence; the landlord's capitalized ground rent returns mainly in the form of house rent paid by the tenants. In the case of owner occupancy, ground rent is capitalized when the building is sold and therefore appears as part of the sale price. Thus, sale price = house value + capitalized ground rent.

Potential ground rent. Under its present land use, a site or neighborhood is able to capitalize a certain quantity of ground rent. For reasons of location, usually, such an area may be able to capitalize higher quantities of ground rent under a different land use. Potential ground rent is the amount that could be capitalized under the land's "highest and best use." This concept is particularly important in explaining gentrification.

Using these concepts, the historical process that has made certain neighborhoods ripe for gentrification can be outlined.

CAPITAL DEPRECIATION IN THE INNER CITY

The physical deterioration and economic depreciation of inner-city neighborhoods is a strictly logical, "rational" outcome of the operation of the land and housing market. This is not to suggest it is at all natural, however, for the market itself is a social product. Far from being inevitable, neighborhood decline is

> the result of identifiable private and public investment decisions. ... While there is no Napoleon who sits in a position of control over the fate of a neighborhood, there is enough control by, and integration of, the investment and development actors of the real estate industry that their decisions go beyond a response and actually shape the market.
>
> (Bradford and Rubinowitz 1975, p. 79)

What follows is a rather schematic attempt to explain the historical decline of inner-city neighborhoods in terms of the institutions, actors, and economic forces involved. It requires the identification of a few salient processes that characterize the different stages of decline, but is not meant as a definitive description of what every neighborhood experiences. The day-today dynamics of decline are complex and, as regards the relationship between landlords and tenants in particular, have been examined in considerable detail elsewhere (Stegman 1972). This schema is, however, meant to provide a general explanatory framework within which each neighborhood's concrete experience can be understood. It is assumed from the start that the neighborhoods concerned are relatively homogeneous as regards the age and quality of housing, and, indeed, this tends to be the case with areas experiencing redevelopment.

1. **New construction and the first cycle of use.** When a neighborhood is newly built the price of housing reflects the value of the structure and improvements put in place plus the enhanced ground rent captured by the previous landowner. During the first cycle of use, the ground rent is likely to increase

as urban development continues outward, and the house value will only very slowly begin to decline if at all. The sale price therefore rises. But eventually sustained depreciation of the house value occurs and this has three sources: advances in the productiveness of labor, style obsolescence, and physical wear and tear. Advances in the productiveness of labor are chiefly due to technological innovation and changes in the organization of the work process. These advances allow a similar structure to be produced at a lower value than would otherwise have been possible. Truss frame construction and the factory fabrication of parts in general, rather than on-site construction, are only the most recent examples of such advances. Style obsolescence is secondary as a stimulus for sustained depreciation in the housing market and may occasionally induce an appreciation of value, many old styles being more sought after than the new. Physical wear and tear also affects the value of housing, but it is necessary here to distinguish between minor repairs which must be performed regularly if a house is to retain its value (e.g., painting doors and window frames, interior decorating), major repairs which are performed less regularly but require greater outlays (e.g., replacing the plumbing or electrical systems), and structural repairs without which the structure becomes unsound (e.g., replacing a roof, replacing floor boards that have dry rot). Depreciation of a property's value after one cycle of use reflects the imminent need not only for regular, minor repairs but also for a succession of more major repairs involving a substantial investment. Depreciation will induce a price decrease relative to new housing but the extent of this decrease will depend on how much the ground rent has also changed in the meantime.

2. Landlordism and homeownership. Clearly the inhabitants in many neighborhoods succeed in making major repairs and maintaining or even enhancing the value of the area's housing. These areas remain stable. Equally clearly, there are areas of owner-occupied housing which experience initial depreciation. Homeowners, aware of imminent decline unless repairs are made, are likely to sell out and seek newer homes where their investment will be safer. At this point, after a first or subsequent cycle of use, there is a tendency for the neighborhood to convert to rental tenancy unless repairs are made. And since landlords use buildings for different purposes than owner occupiers, a different pattern of maintenance will ensue. Owner occupiers in the housing market are simultaneously both consumers and investors; as investors, their primary return comes as the increment of sale price over purchase

price. The landlord, on the other hand, receives his return mainly in the form of house rent, and under certain conditions may have a lesser incentive for carrying out repairs so long as he can still command rent. This is not to say that landlords typically undermaintain properties they possess; newer apartment complexes and even older accomodations for which demand is high may be very well maintained. But as Ira Lowry has indicated, "undermaintenance is an eminently reasonable response of a landlord to a declining market" (1960, p. 367), and since the transition from owner occupancy to tenancy is generally associated with a declining market, some degree of undermaintenance can be expected.

Undermaintenance will yield surplus capital to be invested elsewhere. It may be invested in other city properties, it may follow developers' capital out to the suburbs, or it may be invested in some other sector of the economy. With sustained undermaintenance in a neighborhood, however, it may become difficult for landlords to sell their properties, particularly since the larger financial institutions will now be less forthcoming with mortgage funds; sales become fewer and more expensive to the landlord. Thus, there is even less incentive to invest in the area beyond what is necessary to retain the present revenue flow. This pattern of decline is likely to be reversed only if a shortage of higher quality accommodations occurs, allowing rents to be raised and making improved maintenance worthwhile. Otherwise, the area is likely to experience a net outflow of capital, which will be small at first since landlords still have substantial investments to protect. Under these conditions it becomes very difficult for the individual landlord or owner to struggle against this decline. House values are falling and the levels of capitalized ground rent for the area are dropping below the potential ground rent (see Figure 9.2). The individual who did not undermaintain his property would be forced to charge higher than average rent for the area with little hope of attracting tenants earning higher than average income which would capitalize the full ground rent. This is the celebrated "neighborhood effect" and operates through the rent structure.

3. Blockbusting and blow out. Some neighborhoods may not transfer to rental tenancy and they will experience relative stability or a gentler continuation of decline. If the latter occurs, it is the owner occupants who undermaintain, though usually out of financial constraints rather than market strategy. With blockbusting, this decline is intensified. Real estate agents exploit racist sentiments in white neighborhoods that are experiencing declining sale prices; they buy houses relatively cheaply,

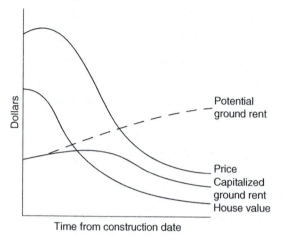

Figure 9.2 The depreciation cycle of innercity neighborhoods

and then resell at a considerable markup to black families, many of whom are desperate to own their first home. As Laurenti's research suggests, property values are usually declining before blockbusting takes place and do not begin declining simply as a result of racial changes in ownership (Laurenti 1960). Once blockbusting has taken place, however, further decline in house values is likely due to the inflated prices at which houses were sold and the consequent lack of resources for maintenance and mortgage payments suffered by incoming families. Blow out, a similar process, operates without the helping hand of real estate agents. Describing the process as it operated in the Baltimore housing market during the 1960s, Harvey et al. (1972; see also Harvey 1973, p. 173) point to the outward spread of slums from the inner city (the broadening of the land value valley) and the consequent squeezing of still healthy outer neighborhoods against secure upper middle-class residential enclaves lying further out. Thus squeezed, owner occupants in an entire neighborhood are likely to sell out, often to landlords, and flee to the suburbs.

4. Redlining. Undermaintenance gives way to more active disinvestment as capital depreciates further and the landlord's stake diminishes; house value and capitalized ground rent fall, producing further decreases in sale price. Disinvestment by landlords is accompanied by an equally "rational" disinvestment by financial institutions which cease supplying mortgage money to the area. Larger institutions offering low downpayment, low interest rate loans find they can make higher returns in the suburbs with a lower

chance of foreclosure and less risk of declining property values. Their role in the inner city is taken over initially by smaller, often local organizations specializing in higher risk financing. Redlined by larger institutions, the area may also receive loans insured by the FHA. Though meant to prevent decline, FHA loans have often been ineffectual and have even contributed to decline in places (Bradford and Rubinowitz 1975, p. 82). The loans allow properties to change hands but do little to encourage reinvestment in maintenance so the process of decline is simply lubricated. Ultimately, medium and small-scale investors also refuse to work in the area, as do mortgage insurers.

Vandalism further accelerates depreciation and becomes a problem especially when properties are temporarily vacant between tenants (Stegman 1972, p. 60). Even when occupied, however, it may be a problem, especially if a building is being under-maintained or systematically "milked." Subdivision of structures to yield more rental units is common at this stage. By subdividing, the landlord hopes to intensify the building's use (and profitability) in its last few years. But eventually landlords will disinvest totally, refusing to make repairs and paying only the necessary costs—and then often only sporadically—for the building to yield rent.

5. Abandonment. When landlords can no longer collect enough house rent to cover the necessary costs (utilities and taxes), buildings are abandoned. This is a neighborhood phenomenon, not something that strikes isolated properties in otherwise stable areas. Much abandoned housing is structurally sound and this seems paradoxical. But then buildings are abandoned not because they are unuseable, but because they cannot be used *profitably*. The final act of abandonment may be triggered (but not caused) by a variety of events, including the strict enforcement of the building code by the city housing department. Also at this stage of decline, there is a certain incentive for landlords to destroy their own property through arson and collect the substantial insurance payment.

GENTRIFICATION–THE RENT GAP

The previous section presented a summary explanation of the process commonly but misleadingly referred to as filtering. It is a common process in the housing market and affects many neighborhoods but is by no means universal. It is included here precisely because gentrification is almost always preceded by filtering, although the process need not occur fully for gentrification to ensue. Nor should this decline be thought of as inevitable. As Lowry quite correctly insists, filtering is not due simply "to the relentless passage of time" but to "human agency" (1960, p. 370). The previous section has suggested who some of these agents are, and the market forces they both react to and help create. That section also suggests that the objective mechanism underlying filtering is the depreciation and devaluation of capital invested in residential inner-city neighborhoods. This depreciation produces the objective economic conditions that make capital *revaluation* (gentrification) a rational market response. Of fundamental importance here is what I call the rent gap.

The rent gap is the disparity between the potential ground rent level and the actual ground rent capitalized under the present land use (see Figure 9.2). In the case of filtering, the rent gap is produced primarily by capital depreciation (which diminishes the proportion of the ground rent able to be capitalized) and also by continued urban development and expansion (which has historically raised the potential ground rent level in the inner city). The valley which Hoyt detected in his 1928 observation of land values can now be understood in large part as the rent gap. Only when this gap emerges can redevelopment be expected since if the present use succeeded in capitalizing all or most of the ground rent, little economic benefit could be derived from redevelopment. As filtering and neighborhood decline proceed, the rent gap widens. Gentrification occurs when the gap is wide enough that developers can purchase shells cheaply, can pay the builders' costs and profit for rehabilitation, can pay interest on mortgage and construction loans, and can then sell the end product for a sale price that leaves a satisfactory return to the developer. The entire ground rent, or a large portion of it, is now capitalized; the neighborhood has been "recycled" and begins a new cycle of use.

Once the rent gap is wide enough, gentrification may be initiated in a given neighborhood by several different actors in the land and housing market. And here we come back to the relationship between production and consumption, for the empirical evidence suggests strongly that the process is initiated not by the exercise of those individual consumer preferences much beloved of neoclassical economists, but by some form of collective social action[8] at the neighborhood level. The state, for example, initiated most if not all of the early schemes, and though it plays a lesser role today, is still important. More commonly today, with private market gentrification, one or more financial institutions will reverse a long standing redlining policy and actively target a neighborhood as a potential market for construction loans

and mortgages. All the consumer preference in the world will amount to nought unless this long absent source of funding reappears; mortgage capital is a prerequisite. Of course, this mortgage capital must be borrowed by willing consumers exercising some preference or another. But these preferences are not prerequisites since they can be socially created, as was seen above. Along with financial institutions, professional developers have acted as the collective initiative behind gentrification. A developer will purchase a substantial proportion of the properties in a neighborhood, rehabilitate them, then sell them for profit. The only significant exception to this predominance of collective action occurs in neighborhoods adjacent to already gentrified areas. There indeed, individual gentrifiers may be very important in initiating rehabilitation. Their decision to rehabilitate followed the results from the previous neighborhood, however, which implies that a sound financial investment was uppermost in their minds. And they still require mortgage capital from willing institutions.

Three kinds of developers typically operate in recycling neighborhoods: (a) professional developers who purchase property, redevelop it, and resell for profit; (b) occupier developers who buy and redevelop property and inhabit it after completion; (c) landlord developers who rent it to tenants after rehabilitation.[9] The developer's return on investment comes as part of the completed property's sale price; for the landlord developer it also comes in the form of house rent. Two separate gains comprise the return achieved through sale: capitalization of enhanced ground rent, and profit (quite distinct from builder's profit) on the investment of productive capital (see Smith 1979). Professional and landlord developers are important—contrary to the public image, they were by far the majority in Society Hill—but occupier developers are more active in rehabilitation than they are in any other sector of housing construction. Perhaps the main reason for this can be traced to the very nature of gentrification and the characteristics of investment in the built environment discussed above. Urban renewal, like rehabilitation, occurs where a rent gap has been opened up, but in the case of renewal either the dilapidated stock is unsound structurally, or the remaining structures are unsuitable for new uses. While the technical and spatial requirements for industrial and commercial buildings have altered substantially in the last hundred years, those for residences have not, and structurally sound town houses are quite useable given the right economic conditions. But since the land has already been developed and an intricate pattern of property rights laid down, it is difficult for the professional developer to assemble sufficient land and properties to make involvement worthwhile. Even landlord developers tended to be rehabilitating several properties simultaneously or in sequence. The fragmented structure of property ownership has made the occupier developer, who is generally an inefficient operator in the construction industry, into an appropriate vehicle for recycling devalued neighborhoods.

Viewed in this way, gentrification is not a chance occurrence or an inexplicable reversal of some inevitable filtering process. On the contrary, it is to be expected. The depreciation of capital in nineteenth century inner-city neighborhoods, together with continued urban growth during the first half of the twentieth century, have combined to produce conditions in which profitable reinvestment is possible. If this rent gap theory of gentrification is correct, it would be expected that rehabilitation began where the gap was greatest and the highest returns available, i.e., in neighborhoods particularly close to the city center and in neighborhoods where the sequence of declining values had pretty much run its course. Empirically, this seems to have been the case. The theory also suggests that as these first areas are recycled, other areas offering lower but still substantial returns would be sought out by developers. This would involve areas further from the city center and areas where decline was less advanced. Thus in Philadelphia, Fairmount and Queen Village are the new "hot spots" (Cybriwsky 1978; Levy 1978), and the city's triage policy for allocating block grant funds makes part of North Philadelphia a likely candidate for future redevelopment.

The state's role in earlier rehabilitation schemes is worthy of note. By assembling properties at fair market value and returning them to developers at the lower assessed price the state accomplished and bore the costs of the last stages of capital devaluation, thereby ensuring that developers could reap the high returns without which redevelopment would not occur. Today, with the state less involved in this process, developers are clearly able to absorb the costs of devaluing capital that has not yet fully depreciated. That is, they can pay a relatively high price for properties to be rehabilitated, and still make a reasonable return. It seems, then, that the state has been successful in providing the conditions that would stimulate private market revitalization.

To summarize the theory, gentrification is a structural product of the land and housing markets. Capital flows where the rate of return is highest, and the movement of capital to the suburbs along with the continual depreciation of inner-city capital, eventually produces the rent gap. When this gap grows sufficiently large, rehabilitation (or for that matter, renewal) can begin to challenge the rates of return available elsewhere, and capital flows back.

CONCLUSION

Gentrification has demonstrated that contrary to the conventional wisdom, middle- and upper-class housing is capable of intensive land use. Just how intensive is not clear, however. There is significant evidence that the once steep rent gradient (see Figure 9.1) is flattening out (Yeates 1965; Edel and Sclar 1975); and if this is the case, potential ground rent in inner-city neighborhoods may actually have decreased, presumably due to efficient transportation links to the suburbs and excessive crowding downtown. What this might mean for gentrification or for the commercial and recreational redevelopment that is also happening in some cities ought to be a topic for further research. Another topic for empirical investigation is the extent to which capital depreciation must occur in an area before gentrification can occur. This all assumes the filtering process to be the fundamental source of the rent gap, and while this is certainly so in the U.S. it may not be elsewhere. Although capital depreciation and filtering prepared the way for gentrification in Islington (Pitt 1977), in general, one would not expect it to be so prevalent in the U.K. housing market where much working class housing is produced by local government action, not the private market. In this case, rising ground rent levels due to urban expansion and development may be more important in accounting for the rent gap.

Gentrification is a back to the city movement all right, but of capital rather than people. The people taking advantage of this returning capital are still, as yet, from the city. If the city continues to attract productive capital (whether for residential or other construction) we may witness a fundamental restructuring of urban space comparable with suburbanization. Then, indeed, it would become a back to the city movement by people too—middle- and upper-class people, that is—while the working class and the poor would inherit the old declining suburbs in a cruelly ironic continuation of the filtering process. They would then be trapped in the suburbs, not the inner city. As was emphasized in the discussion of suburbanization, investment in the built environment is a major vehicle for capital accumulation. This process is cyclical and, because of the long life and fixity of such investments, new cycles of investment are often associated with crises and switches of the location of accumulation (Harvey 1978). Seen in this context, gentrification and other kinds of urban renaissance could be the leading edge (but in no way the cause) of a larger restructuring of space. According to one scenario this restructuring would be accomplished according to the needs of capital; a restructuring of middle-class culture may well accompany and influence it, but would be secondary. According to a second scenario, the needs of capital would be systematically dismantled, to be displaced by the social, economic, and cultural needs of people as the principle according to which the restructuring of space occurs.

AUTHOR'S NOTE

An earlier version of this paper was presented at the Annual Conference of the Association of American Geographers in Philadelphia, April 25th, 1979. Special thanks are due to Michele LeFaivre for her critical reading of the paper.

Notes

1 Gentrification is the process of converting working class areas into middle-class neighborhoods through the rehabilitation of the neighborhood's housing stock.
2 That the earlier projects required substantial state initiative and subsidy did not exclude them from being explained in terms of consumer preference. In Philadelphia, for example, the Greater Philadelphia Movement (GPM) was responsible for getting the state to implement Society Hill's renewal plan, and it consistently claimed that the demand to revitalize was ever-present but the cost constraints and risk were too great for private capital and individuals. It was the responsibility of the state, they argued, to use the available federal legislation to subsidize the project, thereby removing the constraints and serving a broader civic cause. On GPM's role in Society Hill, see Adde (1969, pp. 33–6). For the purposes of this paper, I am distinguishing between gentrification and urban renewal not according to whether the process is privately or publicly funded, but according to whether it is a rehabilitation process or purely new construction. As should become clear from the main argument of the paper, the distinction between public and private funding simply represents (in this context) two different mechanisms for carrying out the one essential process.
3 By suburbs I mean here the area outside the present city boundary but inside the SMSA. The older suburbs that now appear inside the city due to consequent annexations are therefore counted as sections of the city. This definition is justified here since one of the main selling points of gentrification is that it will bring additional tax revenues to the city. Clearly, annexed suburbs already pay their taxes to the city.
4 This kind of consolidation may be experienced by other cities. Several of the cities examined by Lipton (1977) display a similar consolidation.
5 For further discussion of the cross-Atlantic comparison, see Smith (1979).
6 Advertising is a primary means of creating demand. In Society Hill, the Old Philadelphia Development Corporation employed a Madison Avenue professional to sell the project (Old Philadelphia Development Corporation 1970).
7 Certainly zoning, eminent domain, and other state regulations put significant limits on the landowner's control of land, but in North America and Western Europe, these limitations are little more than cosmetic. Within these limitations, the property market continues to operate quite freely.
8 By "collective social action" I mean simply activity that is carried on jointly and simultaneously by people, not by individuals acting alone.
9 I omit speculators here for the obvious reason that they invest no productive capital. They simply buy property in the hope of selling it at a higher price to developers. Speculators do not produce any transformation in the urban structure.

REFERENCES

Adde, L. 1969. *Nine cities: anatomy of downtown renewal.* Washington D.C.: Urban Land Institute.

Alonso, W. 1964. *Location and land use.* Cambridge: Harvard University Press.

Baltimore City Department of Housing and Community Development. 1977. *Homesteading—the third year, 1976.* Baltimore: the Department.

Bradford, C. P., and Rubinowitz, L. S. 1975. The urban-suburban investment-disinvestment process: consequences for older neighborhoods. *Annals of the American Academy of Political and Social Science* 422, November: 77–86.

Burt, N. 1963. *The perennial Philadelphians.* London: Dent & Son.

Cybriwsky, R. A. 1978. Social aspects of neighborhood change. *Annals of the Association of American Geographers* 68, March: 17–33.

Davis, J. T. 1965. Middle class housing in the central city. *Economic Geography* 41, July: 238–51.

Edel, M., and Sclar, E. 1975. The distribution of real estate value changes: metropolitan Boston, 1870–1970. *Journal of Urban Economics* 2: 366–87.

Gale, D. E. 1976. The back-to-the-city movement … or is it? Occasional Paper, Department of Urban and Regional Planning, The George Washington University.

Gale, D. E. 1977. The back-to-the-city movement revisited. Occasional Paper, Department of Urban and Regional Planning, The George Washington University.

Gans, H. 1968. *People and plans.* New York: Basic Books.

Greenfield, A. M. & Co. 1964. New town houses for Washington Square East: a technical report on neighborhood conservation. Prepared for the Redevelopment Authority of Philadelphia.

Harvey, D. 1973. *Social justice and the city.* Baltimore: Johns Hopkins Press.

Harvey, D. 1978. The urban process under capitalism: a framework for analysis. *International Journal of Urban and Regional Research* 2: 101–131.

Harvey, D. et al. 1972. *The housing market and code enforcement in Baltimore.* Baltimore: City Planning Department.

Hoyt, H. 1933. *One hundred years of land values in Chicago.* Chicago: University of Chicago Press.

Laurenti, L. 1960. *Property values and race.* Berkeley: University of California Press.

Levy, P. 1978. *Queen Village: the eclipse of community.* Philadelphia: Institute for the Study of Civic Values.

Ley, D. 1978. Inner city resurgence and its societal context. Paper presented to the Association of American Geographers Annual Conference, New Orleans.

Lipton, S. G. 1977. Evidence of central city revival. *Journal of the American Institute of Planners* 43, April: 136–47.

Lowry, I. S. 1960. Filtering and housing costs: a conceptual analysis. *Land Economies* 36: 362–70.

McDonald, J. F., and Bowman, H. W. 1979. Land value functions: a reevaluation. *Journal of Urban Economics* 6: 25–41.

Mills, E. S. 1972. *Studies in the structure of the urban economy.* Baltimore: Johns Hopkins University Press.

Muth, R. 1969. *Cities and housing.* Chicago: University of Chicago Press.

Old Philadelphia Development Corporation. 1975. Statistics on Society Hill. Unpublished report.

Pitt, J. 1977. *Gentrification in Islington.* London: Barnsbury Peoples Forum.

Smith, N. 1979 (forthcoming). Gentrification and capital: theory, practice and ideology in Society Hill. *Antipode* 11.

Stegman, M. A. 1972. *Housing investment in the inner city: the dynamics of decline.* Cambridge: MIT Press.

Urban Land Institute. 1976. *New opportunities for residential development in central cities.* Report No. 25. Washington D. C.: The Institute.

Winters, C. 1978. Rejuvenation with character. Paper presented to the Association of American Geographers Annual Conference, New Orleans.

Wolf, E. 1975. *Philadelphia: portrait of an American city.* Harrisburg: Stackpole Books.

Yeates, M. H. 1965. Some factors affecting the spatial distribution of Chicago land values, 1910–1960. *Economic Geography* 41, 1: 57–70.

Box 3   Toward a Theory .....

Plate 9 Neil Smith.

It is very difficult to write a commentary on this article, not least because it has been more than 30 years since the original was penned – literally – and the process of gentrification has itself changed and developed so much. At the time gentrification was a very new process, visibly affecting a few of the world's largest and richest cities. It was notable precisely because it bucked all of the urban theory we had in the 1970s: postwar suburbanization, downtown decline and Third World rural-urban migration were the urban stories of the day, and this new phenomenon of "gentrification" seemed to deny everything we thought we knew. To be slightly autobiographical, the "we" here is a bit pretentious: I was an undergraduate when I first ran across gentrification, specifically on a year's exchange from Scotland to Philadelphia, and the empirical reality of the process in Society Hill seemed to deny everything I was learning about cities. I remember reading at the same time the economic geography of Alfred Lösch who famously (if pompously) said that if his models

did not agree with reality, then it was reality that was wrong. Well, gentrification seemed to prove that Lösch was right and that reality was somehow wrong.

Or was it? The earliest writing on gentrification in the 1960s and 1970s broadly explained the process as a result of consumer sovereignty. Consumer demand drove the shape of cities. That was the paradigm. And yet the geography of the city now suddenly reversed itself because consumers all over the world apparently in lockstep began demanding the geographical opposite. This did not seem quite plausible. The paradigm, as Thomas Kuhn (*The Structure of Scientific Revolutions*) might have put it, seemed to embody a paradigm-threatening contradiction: empirically, were the world's "consumers" really that robotic? Or was something else happening?

At the time I was deeply involved in an exploration of marxist thought and Marx in particular, and the power of capital which never figured in explanations of gentrification was very much on my mind. The "Toward a Theory" paper very much came from this context. The main challenge was integrating a sense of historical spatiality into an already existing body of social theory which, itself, seemed space-blind. Amidst the maelstrom of social change, how do places change in relation to other places with which they are connected, and how do such spatial changes themselves constitute social change? Marxist work was more useful in this exploration than any other available theory. Still, the result is a clear amalgam.

I did not guess at the time that anyone would take the paper too seriously. I thought I was doing the usual journeyman graduate student work of taking on my betters. I was confirmed in this judgment when my advisor let the paper languish for months and months on his desk, water leaking on it from the unfixed ceiling, and especially when he finally delivered the assessment that no-one would ever publish it because my efforts at theory were much too simple and definitively obvious. I had already corrected the journal's proofs.

I think and hope that the paper helped to re-orient the debate on gentrification. Much of the subsequent debate has quite reasonably settled around the question of how production-side and consumption-side arguments meld with each other, and I think this has now become an old debate. Far more interesting for me today is the extraordinary scale of gentrification in cities around the world especially in Asia – Shanghai, Mumbai, Beijing – which I think completely changes the nature of the beast. In comparison, New York looks unambitious. This is all part of the evolution of global urbanism and deserves a lot more attention than any of the older texts. If I learned anything from the original text, it was the dialectic of empirical and theoretical inquiry: without the theory I would never have understood how cities were supposed to work; but without the empirics of walking around Society Hill I would never have understood why the paradigm was wrong and needed to be changed. What are the new empirics that challenge all the existing work? We are still, inevitably, "toward a theory ...."

10A
"Commentary: Gentrification and the Rent Gap"

From *Annals of the Association of American Geographers* (1987)

Neil Smith

In less than a decade scholarly analyses of gentrification, once curious, are now commonplace as many working-class neighborhoods in cities throughout the advanced capitalist world have been transformed into middle-class reserves. Two distinct approaches have tended to dominate the literature on gentrification: first, there has been a highly empirical approach, at times verging on the empiricist, that emphasizes the collection of descriptive information about specific cases of gentrification and occasionally the comparison of results from different studies; second, and partly in response to the empirical approach, there has been a more theoretical approach concerned with explaining underlying causes of gentrification rather than describing its instances. A number of researchers have stressed the need to bridge the gap between empirical and theoretical approaches (Hamnett 1984; Rose 1984; Williams 1984; Smith and Williams 1986), and so we should applaud Ley's (1986) recent attempt to confront a series of theoretical propositions—both his own and those of others—with empirical evidence from the Canadian censuses of 1971 and 1981.

Ley hypothesizes four types of explanation for gentrification: demographic change, housing market dynamics, urban amenities, and changes in the economic base. He subjects each of these hypotheses to simple correlation procedures and principal components analysis that concludes that the "economic hypothesis" has "the strongest relationship with gentrification" (p. 529). He finds empirical evidence for rejecting widely assumed demographic explanations (such as the maturation of the baby boom

and decreased household size), and he also rejects housing market dynamics (somehow separated from economic questions) as particularly relevant for explaining gentrification. He affirms the importance of urban amenities and extrapolates from these overall results a restatement of the familiar "postindustrial city" thesis.

On examination, however, Ley's statistical exercise does more to question his hypotheses than to confirm them. Concerning the larger conclusion, severe limitations to the doctrine of postindustrial cities have already been demonstrated (Walker and Greenberg 1982) although they are unacknowledged here by Ley (but see Ley 1982). The point of this reply however is not to rehearse this larger debate but rather to question a specific section of Ley's analysis. I want to focus on the question of the rent gap, Ley's understanding of it, and its role in gentrification. In Ley's schema, the rent gap is a component of the second hypothesis, namely housing market dynamics; more precisely, the rent gap is defined as the gap between the actual *capitalized* ground rent (land value) of a plot of land given its present use and the *potential* ground rent that might be gleaned under a "higher and better" use. The latter might be brought about through the rehabilitation of existing structures on the land, complete redevelopment, or other transformations of existing uses and structures. Gentrification, briefly defined as the transformation of inner-city working-class and other neighborhoods to middle-and upper-middle-class residential, recreational, and other uses, is clearly one means by which the rent gap can be closed, wholly or partially.

Ley is adamant in dismissing the concept of a rent gap: "Evidence is entirely lacking in Canadian cities for the rent gap thesis" (p. 531). In fact, the problem lies first and foremost not with the rent gap thesis nor with Canadian cities but with Ley's comprehension and operationalization of the concepts of gentrification and rent gap. We shall examine each of these in turn.

First, Ley conceives gentrification as simply a "change in household social status" quite "independent of the housing stock involved" (p. 526). Thus he resorts to a simple index combining changes in occupation and education in inner-city census tracts as the sole indicator of gentrification. This measure is so coarse that it would actually identify many areas of suburban expansion as instances of gentrification par excellence, were its application not geographically restricted to the inner city. In fact census tracts experiencing increases in education and employment status may do so for a host of reasons quite unconnected with gentrification, and conversely tracts that are experiencing rapid gentrification may not register exceptional increases in these indicators. To give just one concrete example, in recent research on Harlem and the Lower East Side, educational and occupational measures were discarded as indicators of gentrification because there seemed to be an erratic correlation with rehabilitation, redevelopment, and the immigration of "higher-status" groups (Schaffer and Smith 1986).

The crucial point about gentrification is that it involves not only a social change but also, at the neighborhood scale, a physical change in the housing stock and an economic change in the land and housing markets. It is this combination of social, physical, and economic change that distinguishes gentrification as an identifiable process or set of processes. Upper-middle-class immigrants to a run-down neighborhood do not move into slums; they fix them up or they move into buildings already fixed up or newly built, and this inevitably involves substantial capital investment in gentrifying neighborhoods along with social change.

The most obvious result of the conceptual reductionism in Ley's analysis is that it encourages a self-fulfilling hypothesis. With economic and physical changes in the housing stock defined away, the poor correlation of these variables with gentrification is hardly surprising. Ley may only be interested in the social aspects of gentrification, but unless the full extent and breadth of the process is conceded at least in the beginning, it is difficult to retain confidence in the meaningfulness of the results.

By definition, indicators are always only approximations to the meaning of a concept, but in the case of gentrification we can get more accurate approximations. Ley is correct that there are theoretical problems attendant on using income, especially if income is seen as a surrogate for class, but these are hardly less severe than occupation and education level. In their comprehensive review of the gentrification literature, LeGates and Hartman (1981) have consistently found marked income differentials between gentrifiers and the displaced. To capture changes in the housing market, some measure of house prices and/or rental levels is also important (Marcuse 1986). The combination of income and rent indicators is a much more satisfactory one in fact. Census tracts with significant increases in both measures are clearly targets of gentrification (Schaffer and Smith 1986). Use of both measures enables us to screen out speculation since the economic rise in the housing market is paralleled by exceptional social changes indicated by higher-than-average income increases. Similarly, with parallel changes in the housing market, significant income increases are unlikely to result simply from the in situ enrichment of the existing population.

The second major problem lies in Ley's conceptualization of the rent gap. The problem here is similar but more drastic. In its original formulation, to which Ley refers, the rent gap was defined as "the disparity between the potential ground rent level and the actual ground rent capitalized under the present land use" (Smith 1979, 545). If we leave aside the crucial distinction between value and price, two aspects of this definition are particularly important. First, it refers to the value of *land* separate from any structures or improvements built on it. The value of land is appropriated in economic transactions as ground rent; hence the notion of the "rent" gap. House value is conceptually separate from land value, even if the actual selling price of a structure usually incorporates the value of the building and the land in a single dollar figure. The second important feature of the definition is that the rent gap refers to an economic gap between actual and potential land values in a given location; it is also a historical gap in that it results from a complex pattern of investment and disinvestment in the built environment and can be closed through gentrification (among other processes).

Ley's conceptual definition of the rent gap is severely distorted from the start. He redefines it as a feature of "housing market dynamics" with no direct reference to the land market, and he divorces it from the broader economic processes (investment and disinvestment in specific places and sectors of the built environment) in which the rent gap is embedded and out of which it develops. As a result, the indicator Ley actually attempts to correlate with his gentrification index has at best an accidental conceptual and empirical resemblance to the rent gap. Thus he defines two ratios, purportedly a price gap and a rent gap respectively: (1) the ratio of inner-city to metropolitan-wide house values in 1971, and (2) the ratio of inner-city to metropolitan-wide rental costs in 1971. The clumsiness of this translation from concept to operational variable is astonishing: nothing remains of the concept. First, these ratios refer not to land values at all, but to house/apartment rents, and sale prices. Second, instead of a gap between actual and potential ground rent, these ratios measure the gap between inner-city and metropolitan housing costs, a geographical gap of some interest, to be sure, but no proxy for the rent gap at given locations. The metropolitan gradient is emphatically not the rent gap. In short, this indicator does not refer to rent, nor does it even postulate an economic gap in the central city. Both ingredients are missing in a two-ingredient recipe. Ley is untroubled by the emptiness of his bowl, however, merely assuring us that the postulated ratios do represent "one valid measure of the rent gap" (p. 533) and that the "definition of the rent gap adopted does seem consistent" with the original formulation (p. 527).

The whole point of the rent gap theory is not that gentrification occurs in some deterministic fashion where housing costs are lowest, as Ley is proposing, but that it is most likely to occur in areas experiencing a sufficiently large gap between actual and potential land values. This is a fundamental distinction. Areas such as the central and inner city where the rent gap may be greatest may also experience very high land values and housing costs despite disinvestment from the built environment and the consequent rent gap. Thus instead of testing whether a rent gap was a condition for gentrification, Ley has tested the hypothesis that a relative increase in educational and occupational status is geographically correlated with inner cities where housing costs are higher than average. He is strangely surprised to find that in fact higher-status residents are clustering in areas with relatively higher housing costs.

Attempts to operationalize the rent gap theory have to be taken seriously. They will require extensive and complex data collection and manipulation rather than simple statistical exercises and the rigorous conceptual distinction between land values and house values. This is the central problem and a foreboding one, namely to acquire or create a historical series of data that traces changes in the value of land parcels separate from the structures on them.

Assessed values for tax purposes arc much too rough and arbitrary to be useful. Thus it is no accident that part of the original formulation of the rent gap thesis derived from the empirical work of the late Homer Hoyt (1933), who compiled a remarkable data set on land values in Chicago. Testing the rent gap thesis today will require an equally historical approach and a comparable sensitivity to the constitution of place. Not all neighborhoods experiencing the rent gap may experience gentrification or redevelopment; some economic opportunities remain unexploited and specific local conditions may discourage the process. Areas with the deepest rent gap may not be the first to experience the process; despite the perception of large rent gaps in some black neighborhoods, for example, the process has often been relatively slow because of a mixture of fear and racism among both individual whites and the institutions of the land and housing markets.

In testing the rent gap theory, data will be more readily available in some localities and nations than in others. And it is by no means clear in advance how the theory will fare. But only after this work will we be able to test whether there is or has been evidence of the rent gap in Canada. Ley's conceptualization of the rent gap is too clumsy for the question of differential national experiences even to be asked. In fact, it would not be surprising if the rent gap were less extreme in many Canadian cities than in the U.S. where the state is less involved in the land and housing markets and where racial and ethnic differences would seem to be more deeply rooted and more pervasive as markers of social territory. Without the data this is speculative, but Australia may represent the other extreme. There it has been suggested that though it certainly existed, the rent gap was never too deep and may now largely have been filled in through gentrification and the related restructuring of the cities (Horvarth and Engels 1985).

Whatever the shortcomings of the analysis, Ley is surely correct about one thing: there is "no single dominant explanation" of gentrification in Canada or elsewhere (p. 527). If the early literature tended narrowly to emphasize either consumption-side or production-side explanations (such as the rent gap), it should now be evident that the relationship between consumption and production is crucial to explaining gentrification. The restructuring of the city, of which gentrification is only a part, involves a social and economic, spatial and political transformation. Our understanding of these changes will be served best by trying to forge the links between the different aspects of change. The multifaceted changes in women's roles in society and the growing recognition of the role of women in gentrification may provide a fulcrum over which these contrasting aspects of change can be balanced (Rose 1984; Stimpson et al. 1981).

REFERENCES

Hamnett, Chris. 1984. Gentrification and residential location theory: A review and assessment. In *Geography and the urban environment, progress in research and application*, ed. D. Herbert and R. Johnston, pp. 283–319. Chichester: John Wiley.

Horvarth, Ron, and Engels, Benno. 1985. The residential restructuring of inner Sydney. In *Living in cities*, ed. I. Burnley and J. Forrest, pp. 143–59. Sydney: George Allen and Unwin.

Hoyt, Homer. 1933. *One hundred years of land values in Chicago*. Chicago: University of Chicago Press.

LeGates, Richard, and Hartman, Chester. 1981. Gentrification-related displacement. *Clearinghouse Review* 15(3):207–49.

Ley, David. 1982. Of tribes and idols. A reply to Greenberg and Walker, *Antipode* 14(1):38–43.
——. 1986. Alternative explanations for inner-city gentrification: A Canadian assessment. *Annals of the Association of American Geographers* 76:521–35.

Marcuse, Peter. 1986. Abandonment, gentrification and displacement: The linkages in New York City. In Smith and Williams 1986, pp. 153–77.

Rose, Damaris. 1984. Rethinking gentrification: Beyond the uneven development of Marxist urban theory. *Society and Space* 2:47–74.

Schaffer, Richard, and Smith, Neil. 1986. The gentrification of Harlem? *Annals of the Association of American Geographers* 76:347–65.

Smith, Neil. 1979. Toward a theory of gentrification: A back to the city movement by capital not people. *Journal of the American Planning Association* 45:538–48.

Smith, Neil, and Williams, Peter. eds. 1986. *Gentrification of the city*. London: George Allen and Unwin.

Stimpson, Catherine; Dixler, E.; Nelson, M.; Yatrakis, K., eds. 1981. *Women and the city*. Chicago: University of Chicago Press.

Walker, Richard, and Greenberg, Douglas. 1982. Post-industrialism and political reform: A critique. *Antipode* 14(1):17–32.

Williams, Peter. 1984. Economic processes and urban changes: An analysis of contemporary patterns of residential restructuring. *Australian Geographical Studies* 22:39–57.

10B
"Reply: The Rent Gap Revisited"

From *Annals of the Association of American Geographers* (1987)

David Ley

Professor Smith has one substantial argument in his commentary, a defense of his rent gap thesis of gentrification. Before I discuss this, however, it is necessary to deal briefly with several assertions, which indicate a none-too-careful reading of my article.

(1) The commentary objects to the use of education and occupation as indicators of gentrification, instead of income and rent levels. Occupation and education are challenged because they might equally show status increases in the suburbs. It is not clear what a study of inner-city gentrification would be looking for in the suburbs, but the important point here of course is that income or rent data share precisely the same weakness (or strength?). Moreover, all three measures of social status are highly correlated anyway. As reported in my paper, validity tests across 462 inner-city tracts show a high correlation of 0.77 between monthly rents and a social status index derived from occupation and education, and a correlation of 0.63 between income and the index (Ley 1986, Note 10). No theoretical justification is given in the commentary for discarding education and occupation and favoring income and rent. This is an arbitrary fiat, representing a minority voice in a larger literature that uses any and all of the three indicators of social status.

My own use of education and occupation rather than income or rent was predicated on three grounds. First, there is some empirical data in Canada indicating that income differentials are not as sensitive as education and occupational distinctions in separating out social classes in the city (Ley and Mercer 1980); for example, empty nesters who may have a relatively low income (but considerable equity) are a major group buying into condominiums in gentrifying districts. Second, in a gentrifying neighborhood use of rents alone may be tracing a residual population and missing recent arrivals who are home owners or apartment owners. Third, there is an important theoretical argument around the role of education as the cultural capital of the "new class" of professional and administrative workers (Gouldner 1979). The paper's interest in social class change targeted education and occupation as relevant indicators. For other purposes income or rent might be appropriate. But there is no ground for being exclusive and dismissing any indicators out of hand.

(2) Smith charges that I reject demographic and housing market explanations of gentrification. This is a misrepresentation of the results, which report that demographic variables have "modest correlations with the gentrification index in the predicted direction," while the housing squeeze argument "receives some support." Were the observations a sample (rather than a population) so that significance tests would be appropriate, the published results show that 6 of the 10 demographic variables would hover between the 0.05 and 0.1 significance thresholds: 4 of the 11 housing market variables would fall in this range. This encourages the conclusion that while the nature of the urban economy and levels of urban amenity show the highest correlations with the gentrification index, "All four of these explanations have some utility in accounting for inner-city gentrification in urban Canada between 1971 and 1981" (p. 531). The structure of intercorrelations around the housing and demographic variables leading to this outcome is explored further in the conclusion. None of these qualifications appear in the bald assertions of Smith's commentary.

(3) Remarkably, Smith alleges that "economic ... changes in the housing stock (are) defined away."

But 6 of the 11 variables in the housing market hypothesis measure the cost or the changing cost of housing. These are independent variables in the analysis. We could not test the housing market hypothesis by simultaneously allowing them to be dependent variables as well!

(4) Smith introduces the red herring of postindustrial society for criticism. This widely used concept is summarily dismissed without attention being paid to either a broader literature or the precise definition that is laid out (Note 7), a definition which does not, for example, sever the service sector from its relations with resource extraction and manufacturing. Indeed as I noted in the paper, a complementary research project on producer services is examining precisely these relationships (Ley and Hutton 1987).

The discussion of the rent gap thesis occupied only a small portion of my paper, but understandably as the author of the thesis, Professor Smith is anxious to defend it, particularly as his theoretical framework has not fared well in recent reviews (Hamnett 1984; Rose 1984; Williams 1984). The thesis has been presented in several papers as a purely theoretical concept; almost ten years after its first presentation it has still not been made empirically accountable. I attempted to operationalize the concept, while observing the difficulty of such a mapping, from a close reading of relevant papers. Smith takes exception to this mapping, but has no empirical results of his own to report.

Smith raises two criticisms in the commentary. The first is that land values are not adequately approximated by rental or house value data. Indeed, the indicators are not ideal, but ideal measures are rarely available, and no measures at all appear in the publications of the rent gap theorists. Rents and housing values are correlated ($r = 0.66$ across 462 inner-city tracts in six large Canadian cities) so the issue becomes one of the relationship between housing values (land plus improvements) and land values alone within an already built-up area. But within the built environment land value is never independent of an existing use. Thus Smith refers to "the actual capitalized ground rent (land value) of a plot of land *given its present use*" (my emphasis). In an earlier paper the variable map of ground rent was also seen as the *result* of the differential pattern of land use plus the status of residential groups (Smith 1982). Land value (capitalized ground rent), then, is defined by him relative to an existing use and users; land and improvement (its use and users) are both empirically and conceptually fused. Professor Smith cannot have it both ways; to argue in the commentary that ground rents must be separated from uses and users is a logical contradiction that also disembodies the

ground rent concept, which in his earlier paper he described as only the mediator or translator of forces emanating from variable uses and users.

A second issue is the nature of the rent gap, defined as the difference between the actual capitalized ground rent under an existing use and the potential ground rent under an alternative use. The issue in question here is whether the relationship between inner-city and suburban land values is a satisfactory measure of the rent gap. The basis for using this measure was a definition of the rent gap (proposed by Smith himself and thus cited in my paper) that drew attention to the metropolitan land value surface: "The [inner-city] valley which Hoyt detected in his 1928 observation of [Chicago] land values can now be understood in large part as the rent gap. Only when this gap emerges can redevelopment be expected. ... Gentrification occurs when the gap is wide enough. ..... If this rent gap theory of gentrification is correct, it would be expected that rehabilitation began where the gap was greatest and the highest returns available" (Smith 1979, 545–46). In this statement the rent gap is associated with the metropolitan land value gradient and the position of inner-city vis-à-vis suburban land values. Elsewhere we read of the "locational seesaw" of capital switching, "the dual process of suburban development and inner-city development. The underdevelopment of the previously developed inner city ... brought about the rent gap, and this, in turn laid the foundation for a locational switch of capital invested in the built environment" back to the inner city (Smith 1982, 150). The argument concludes that "Uneven development at the urban scale therefore brought ... gentrification ... the gentrification and redevelopment of the inner city represents a linear continuation of the forces and relations that led to suburbanization" (Smith 1982, 150). The thesis of uneven development treats the inner city and the suburbs as part of a systemic whole, where the shape of the urban land value gradient at one period will prime locational switching in investment in the next time period. The rent gap in the inner city, then, is defined relative to capitalized ground rent in the suburbs. This is the relationship operationalized in my paper.

There is a third point to be made here. Part of the boldness of the rent gap thesis is that it conceived of a "devalorization cycle" in the inner city, a downward sequence of deterioration and decline. This of course is the meaning of the inner-city "valley" of land values cited in the previous paragraph, a pattern of disinvestment accompanying obsolescence and decay. When devalorization had proceeded far enough and the rent gap (the inner-city valley) was wide enough, capital switching would return investment to the inner city. When would capital switching occur? There is a clear message in the literature that this devalorization cycle would be far advanced before gentrification would proceed, for "As filtering and neighborhood decline proceed, the rent gap widens" (Smith 1979, 545). Gentrification then would be expected in old and deteriorated neighborhoods close to downtown, advanced in the devalorization cycle so that "the sequence of declining values had pretty much run its course" (Smith 1979, 546). In Smith's study areas of Society Hill and Harlem, on a number of blocks this cycle had reached its final stages, abandonment. This association of gentrification with deterioration and even abandonment is unambiguous and has been noted by, among others, Hamnett (1984) and Rose (1984, 50), who, paraphrasing the rent gap thesis writes that eventually the devalorization cycle "leads to residential abandonment", which in turn creates the "rent gap" and thus the preconditions for new investment of productive capital in a "higher and better use" (Smith 1982). Williams sees the same association: "[Smith] develops his account around the suburbanization of development resulting in the abandonment of the inner city and the creation of a rent gap" (Williams 1984, 47).

This argument required the devalorization cycle to be far advanced, which would also drive down the price of land, "for devalorization leads to physical decline, which in turn lowers the market price of the land on which the dilapidated buildings stand" (Smith 1982, 149). This statement confirms not only that the devalorization of land values is associated with the condition of land uses in the rent gap thesis (as shown earlier), but also that devalorization is transmitted to actual prices and rents. As is implied by the fact of dereliction and abandonment in Society Hill and Harlem, prices had become very low indeed. As the devalorization cycle proceeds, it is accompanied by disinvestment for "landlords cannot collect enough house rent to cover the necessary costs" (Smith 1979, 545). The cost of housing and rents decline. From the logic of this argument it follows that gentrification is likely to occur where housing costs in the inner city are depreciated, precisely the condition I operationalized in assessing the rent gap argument.

But on the commentary Smith takes an altogether different tack. It is no longer necessary, it seems, for the devalorization cycle to be far advanced for gentrification to follow, but only that there be a significant *relative* gap between present and potential ground rent capitalized from a site. Compare the earlier "it would be expected that rehabilitation began where the gap was greatest" (Smith 1979, 546) "with the

deepest rent gap may not be the first to experience the process ... the process (there) has often been relatively slow" in the commentary. This is a shift of some significance, for it is possible now for the devalorization cycle to be intercepted at an *early* stage in the life of a neighborhood (even prior to serious deterioration and disinvestment) by gentrification. In this instance there may be no significant physical decline nor an inner-city valley of land values, though in earlier papers both were presented as part and parcel of the rent gap. I do not challenge this premise at all: indeed, my findings indicate precisely that increasing social status (gentrification) has occurred in neighborhoods between 1971 and 1981 that already enjoyed above-average rents and housing values in 1971 (which is not the same as the misrepresentation of these results in the commentary). In short these districts were far removed from an advanced stage of the devalorization cycle. What I would challenge is that this eventuality was implicit (let alone explicit) in the rent gap thesis. There is of course nothing wrong with changing one's mind, but it is a dubious practice to make the claim retroactive and assert that this is what was intended all along.

There is a final issue here. Even in its earlier form, commentators pointed out that the rent gap thesis did not offer a set of original insights: "Traditional land economists pointed this out long ago" (Hamnett 1984, 309). But as reformulated in the commentary, the distinctiveness of the position vanishes. The devalorization cycle and the mystique around the rent gap now become unnecessary baggage. All that is now required for gentrification to occur is the potential for profit. This bears striking similarity to neoclassical accounts of developer behavior and as such it is a claim that can be assessed using conventional indicators.

In conclusion let me reiterate that the rent gap thesis comprised a minor part of my analysis of gentrification in Canadian cities. Discussion of the rent gap has been labored here only because it comprises the substance of the commentary. Moreover, only those issues pertaining to the rent gap raised in the commentary have been engaged. While the results of my study stand, this is not to say that a more powerful empirical analysis could not improve upon them, though the design of such an analysis would not be easy, for my own data retrieval problems were considerable enough (and compare London, Lee, and Lipton 1986). But empirical study cannot be devalued, for without it theoretical discourse is placed in a realm beyond accountability. For some years the necessity to unite theories around production and consumption in understanding gentrification and, more generally, the making of the built environment has been apparent. Thus Professor Smith's concluding paragraph to the same effect is most welcome. While critical to strive for, such an integration will not be easily accomplished, and it will require a more careful reading of the literature, together with a less adversarial patrolling of one's own territory than appears in this commentary. Nonetheless Smith's attempt to theorize the gentrification literature has been an important contribution, and the promised synthesis that moves ahead from the "production-side" explanation of the rent gap is awaited with interest.

REFERENCES

Gouldner, A. 1979. *The future of intellectuals and the rise of the new class.* New York: Seabury Press.

Hamnett, C. 1984. Gentrification and residential location theory: A review and assessment. *Geography and the urban environment*, vol. 6, ed. D. Herbert and R. Johnston, pp. 283–319. Chichester: John Wiley.

Ley, D. 1986. Alternative explanations for inner-city gentrification: A Canadian assessment. *Annals of the Association of American Geographers* 76:521–35.

Ley, D., and Hutton, T. 1987. Vancouver's corporate complex and producer services sector: Linkages and divergence within a provincial staple economy. *Regional Studies* 21: in press.

Ley, D., and Mercer, J. 1980. Locational conflict and the politics of consumption. *Economic Geography* 56:89–109.

London, B.; Lee, B.; and Lipton, S.G. 1986. The determinants of gentrification in the United States: A city-level analysis. *Urban Affairs Quarterly* 21:369–87.

Rose, D. 1984. Rethinking gentrification: Beyond the uneven development of Marxist urban theory. *Society and Space* 2:47–74.

Smith, N. 1979. Toward a theory of gentrification: A back to the city movement by capital not people. *Journal of the American Planning Association* 45:538–48.

——. 1982. Gentrification and uneven development. *Economic Geography* 58:139–55.

Williams, P. 1984. Economic processes and urban change: An analysis of contemporary patterns of residential restructuring. *Australian Geographical Studies* 22:39–57.

11
"The Rent Gap Debunked"

From *Urban Studies* (1993)

Steven C. Bourassa

1. INTRODUCTION

Neil Smith's rent gap theory of gentrification has received a substantial amount of critical attention since it appeared in the pages of the *Journal of the American Planning Association* in 1979. Hamnett and others have subjected many aspects of the theory to detailed criticism, yet the rent gap persists in the literature of urban geography and as an apparently meaningful and useful concept (Hamnett, 1984, 1991; Beauregard, 1986). In recent years, several geographers have even attempted to determine empirically whether the rent gap exists. Ley's study of Canadian cities, published in 1986, has been followed by Clark's (1987, 1988) work on Malmö, Sweden, Kary's (1988) on Toronto, Canada, and Badcock's (1989, 1990) on Adelaide, Australia.

One crucial problem has not received adequate attention in the published commentary and empirical research on the rent gap hypothesis. This is that the concept of a rent gap depends on a distinction between *actual* and *potential* land rent that does not contribute to the explanation of changes in land use. (An analogous problem has led to confusion in the debate about the economic effects of taxes on land—see Tideman, 1982; Bourassa, 1992b.) In spite of widespread criticism of the rent gap theory, the recent attempts to measure differences between actual and potential rents reveal that there is still considerable confusion surrounding these ideas. The purpose of this paper is to dispel some of that confusion by subjecting the basic concepts of actual and potential rent to critical scrutiny. In support of this criticism of the rent gap theory, it will be shown that contrary to Clark's (1987) assertions, a careful review of the land economics literature reveals

no legitimate theoretical roots for the actual versus potential distinction. The concept of rent that is relevant to changes in land use is land rent as an opportunity cost, which is a function of the potential use of a site rather than its actual or current use. Furthermore, it will be shown that the difficulties with rent gap theory translate directly into the methodological problems that have been encountered by those researchers who have attempted to measure it.

This paper will begin with a brief sketch of the rent gap theory, an outline of basic terminology, and a discussion of some terminological problems evident in Smith's exposition of the theory. The next section of the paper will discuss the fundamental difficulties with the rent gap concept and will conclude with a critique of attempts to find theoretical antecedents for the rent gap. The third section will highlight the difficulties in testing the rent gap theory that are evident in the empirical applications by Ley, Clark, Kary and Badcock. The paper concludes with a discussion of alternatives to the rent gap.

2. THE RENT GAP THEORY

A Brief Outline of the Theory

Part of the attraction of the rent gap theory is its elegance, although this is unfortunately achieved at the expense of an over-simplified understanding of the process of gentrification (Hamnett, 1991). But, given the theory's simplicity, it can be outlined fairly quickly. Smith defined the rent gap as "the disparity between the potential ground rent level and the actual ground rent capitalized under the present land use" (Smith, 1979b, p. 545). The existence of a significant rent gap makes inner-city reinvestment attractive due to the potential for earning substantial increments in land rent and value.

Moreover, it is argued that rent gaps form due to an intrinsic tendency for capitalist urban development to be cyclical. Initial investment in an area is later followed by disinvestment as investors see more profitable opportunities elsewhere—in this case, suburban locations. Disinvestment eventually leads to a substantial disparity between the value or rent of land in its current use and its potential value if redeveloped or, in the case of gentrification, reused for a different purpose. This rent gap provides the incentive for investment to return to the inner city. Thus gentrification is essentially "a back to the city movement by capital, not people", to quote the sub-title of Smith's influential paper. Smith continues to endorse the rent gap concept in his most recent theoretical work on gentrification (Smith, 1986, 1987a, 1987b).

The discussion that follows focuses on the concepts of rent that underlie the rent gap hypothesis, and their significance for explanation of urban change. This paper is not concerned with the assertion that urban development in capitalist economies tends to involve a cyclical process of investment, disinvestment and reinvestment; however, it must be remarked that this process does not seem inevitable, as many neighbourhoods never experience disinvestment (Wong, 1988), although perhaps this observation depends on the definition of disinvestment. In any case, this is a topic for another paper. This paper is concerned instead to eliminate some imprecision in the basic concepts of rent employed to analyse processes of urban development. Such imprecision can cloud understanding or divert researchers to pursue misguided aims.

Basic terminology

It is important to define some basic concepts so that the following discussion does not become stalled in a morass of gobbledygook. There are essentially two broad categories of rent relevant to the present discussion.[1] One is the *accounting* sense, which refers to the actual cash flows from a leaseholder to a landowner. The other is the *economic* sense that is defined in terms of the opportunity cost of the rents that could be obtained from the most intensive feasible alternative use of a site. The distinction between accounting and economic rent parallels that between accounting and economic profit. While the accounting concepts are concerned with only explicit costs, the economic ones also involve implicit opportunity cost—a distinction often explained in introductory economics textbooks, such as Dolan (1983). Generally, Smith uses *actual rent* to mean the accounting cash flow and *potential rent* to mean the economic opportunity cost. The present paper will adopt a more or less standard usage of *contract rent* to refer to the cash flow and *land rent* to refer to the opportunity cost. These terms are set out in Table 11.1 so that they may be referred to readily. Table 11.1 also includes some of the terms used by Marx, Marshall and Gaffney in their discussions of rent, which will be considered later.

It should be noted that the authors listed in Table 11.1 sometimes use other terms to mean the same things; the terms listed are those employed most commonly. For example, Smith sometimes uses *capitalised ground rent* as a synonym for *actual rent*, and Marshall uses *annual site value* as a synonym for *ground rent*. Gaffney uses *land rent* and *ground rent* interchangeably, and it is undoubtedly true that in common usage either of these terms may also refer to the accounting cash flow between a leasholder and a landowner. And, just to confuse matters a bit further, Marx occasionally uses *actual rent*—e.g. in his review of Ricardo's theory of rent (Marx, 1988–91, vol. 31)—but it is clearly meant to be the equivalent of *ground rent*.

Some terminological problems

One immediately obvious problem with Smith's exposition of the rent gap theory is that he misuses terms that have well-established meanings in the land economics literature (Marxian as well as neoclassical). These terminological mistakes are relatively minor in comparison to the basic problem of the rent gap hypothesis. They merit discussion here only because they suggest that Smith's formulation of the rent gap notion was at least somewhat naïve

Usage	Sense	
	Accounting	Economic
Present paper	Contract rent	Land rent
Smith	Actual rent	Potential rent
Marx	—	Ground rent
Marshall	—	Ground rent
Gaffney	Contract rent	Land or ground rent

Table 11.1 Rent terminology

Source: See references cited in text

and that the basic concepts underlying the rent gap need careful critical scrutiny.

One terminological error is Smith's substitution of the term *ground rent* for *land value*.[2] He does this to emphasise the fact that land value cannot be construed to be the result of labour power, unlike the value of other commodities, but this seems a rather crude attempt to follow Marxian doctrine and his usage only confuses matters (although Marx himself used the term *ground rent*, he certainly did not consider it to be synonymous with *land value*). The confusion stems from the fact that *rent* implies a periodic, or recurring, payment, while *value* is a once-only payment. Land value is therefore typically defined as the present value of an expected stream of future land rents. Smith makes the error of substituting the one concept directly for the other while also neglecting the systematic relationship between them.

A second confusion is in Smith's use of the term *capitalised ground rent*. To most students of land economics, including both Marx and the neoclassical economists, this is the same as land value. The process of converting an expected stream of future rents into a present value is known as capitalisation. But Smith (1979b, p. 543) employs the term in a most unusual sense to refer to "the actual quantity of ground rent that is appropriated by the landowner, given the present use". Here the term is synonymous with *actual rent*. Smith's confusion on this point is well-illustrated by his use of *capitalised ground rent* later in the same paragraph in a context that clearly implies a present value (Smith, 1979b, p. 543): "In the case of owner-occupancy, ground rent is capitalized when the building is sold and therefore appears as part of the sale price. Thus the sale price = house value + capitalized ground rent."

3. THEORETICAL ISSUES

The rent gap and urban development[3]

According to Smith, for any given site there is, on the one hand, a potential rent, based on its so-called "highest and best use",[4] and there is also an actual rent, based on its existing use. The difference between these two amounts is the rent gap. Intuitively, this seems quite reasonable. But common sense is often misleading in economic matters. A more careful analysis reveals that the difference between the accounting cash flow and the economic opportunity cost (that is, the 'rent gap') has little direct relevance for the allocation of land use. This is because it is only land rent as an opportunity cost

that has any clear economic significance. The economically significant form of rent is independent of the current use of a site: it is a function of the site's highest and best use. This highest and best use is a function of uses on surrounding sites and is the use to which the site would be put if it were bare. As Gaffney (1969, p. 141) puts it, land rent is best defined as "the highest latent opportunity cost of land". This sense of land rent is equivalent to Smith's potential rent.

This is not to deny that actual rent may exist in the form of rents actually appropriated by landowners—that is, *contract rent*. But land rents are rarely appropriated as such by landowners (Tideman, 1982, p. 109): "most land is held by individuals or firms that use the land in conjunction with other inputs to yield an aggregate return that cannot be allocated unambiguously among inputs". Moreover, even if land is owned separately from other inputs, contract rent can be observed, and the rent gap can be measured accurately, it has only a very dubious theoretical significance. This is because the magnitude of the rent gap has at best imprecise implications for the location or timing of changes in land use or occupancy.

Contract rent is usually set to approximate what Smith calls potential rent. The landlord typically wants to collect at least the opportunity cost of a site, while the leaseholder is willing to pay at most that amount. When contract rent does not approximate potential rent, that implies that: (1) the site is being held speculatively in anticipation of future development or sale; (2) some kind of subsidy or other adjustment is involved; or (3) the parties to the lease miscalculated the site's potential rent. The latter is particularly likely to occur in the case of a long-term lease, or during periods of rapid, unpredictable change. In these cases contract (or actual) rent departs from land (or potential) rent, but not in any systematic way.

It will be helpful to consider some illustrations of the ambiguous implications of rent gaps for both the location and timing of development. It seems analytically useful to consider location first and then timing (although as a practical matter, decisions about location and timing are made jointly). Vacant sites and buildings in relatively high land value areas are prime locations for development and by definition have high rent gaps because there is no contract rent. Substantial rent gaps are likely to occur, for example, at the fringe of a developing city where vacant land is held in anticipation of conversion to urban uses. It is also true, however, that sites and buildings with relatively non-intensive uses compared to surrounding areas are likely candidates for development. In these cases, however, the rent gap may be relatively small. For example, most if not all of the rent paid to use a relatively old and derelict building at a high land value location will effectively be for the land (i.e. the location) rather than the building, and a true measure of actual rent may not differ much from potential rent. Some such properties may become vacant well before they are developed, while others may be converted rapidly from one use to another. Because disused sites in high land value locations have high rent gaps and sites with non-intensive uses in such locations may have low or zero rent gaps, while both types of sites may be equally likely to be developed, suggests that comparison of the magnitude of rent gaps across locations does not tell us too much about where development is likely to take place.

For a specific example of this, consider two inner-city sites, of which one is a vacant riverfront site likely to yield maximum return if developed as a luxury hotel and the second is an old loft building currently used as a warehouse but likely to yield maximum return if developed into rental housing. The rent gap on the first site is quite high relative to that on the second site, both because the first site currently yields no rent and also because the river view affords a premium in potential rent. Nevertheless, there is no reason to assume that the riverfront site will be developed prior to the loft building. This raises the question of the optimal timing of development. Although the riverfront site may promise substantial potential rent, the optimal timing of the hotel development could be many years into the future, while the best time for the apartment development could well be the present.

As an example of the ambiguous relationship between the rent gap and the timing of development, consider a site in the central business district of a large city that is held vacant in anticipation of an optimal future date for development. The site yields no actual rent while it remains vacant, yet it has a substantial potential rent. Alternatively, it might be feasible to lease the site for car parking during the period prior to development, in which case the actual rent would be greater than zero. The fact that the rent gap in the former case is greater than that in the latter has no bearing on the timing of development, which is the same in the two cases because it is solely a function of the site's potential rent in the new use.

An analogous example involving gentrification may easily be constructed. Consider the case of two identical adjacent houses in a gentrifying neighbourhood. Both are held by the same developer in anticipation of rehabilitation and resale. To minimise

costs, the developer plans to rehabilitate them simultaneously. One of the houses is vacant, while the other yields modest rents from relatively low-income tenants. While there is no actual rent in the former case, much of the rent paid in the second case could be imputed to the land. Here again, there is a large rent gap in one case and a small or non-existent gap in the other, but this difference in magnitude has no bearing on the timing of development.

Even if the rent gap were a meaningful indicator of the location or timing of development, it would not contribute anything to an explanation of why certain deteriorated and derelict areas of inner cities have become desirable residential neighbourhoods. The really interesting question for research on gentrification (and urban development generally) is not to measure differences between actual and potential rents, but rather to explain changes in potential rents over time. The rent gap simply attempts to measure in a rather crude way certain conditions associated with land-use change without explaining how those conditions came about.

Clark (1992) has attempted to defend the rent gap hypothesis in a recent paper that is in part a response to Bourassa (1990). In his paper, Clark makes much of a supposed "one and only land value" that he somehow associates with the argument that actual rent has no economic importance. He claims that this represents an overemphasis on long-term static equilibria in land markets and ignores the dynamics of urban development that form the motivation for the rent gap thesis. Clark also mentions that the land economist Gaffney places considerable emphasis on urban dynamics in his discussion of land rent. But it is not at all clear why the claim that potential rent is the only economically significant form of rent should in any way imply a neglect of urban dynamics. Indeed, the very word *potential* implies a focus on growth and change, and the concept is entirely consistent with Gaffney's idea of land rent and its role in allocating a continually changing pattern of land uses. While Gaffney (1962) mentions a distinction between contract rent and land (or 'ground') rent, he essentially discards the former as lacking any analytical interest because it is only the latter that is relevant to, among other things, the allocation of land among users and the timing of development.

Theoretical antecedents for the rent gap?

Although Smith makes no attempt to find antecedents for the rent gap in the history of economic ideas, Clark (1987, p. 86) claims to find at least indirect support for the concept in the work of Marx,

Marshall and others: "That the rent gap exists in reality and constitutes an important force of urban change is supported not only by 'common sense', but by the auxiliary hypotheses of such very different schools of thought as neoclassical economics and Marxian political economy". It will be convenient for the purposes of the present paper to focus on the ideas of Marshall and Marx since they present paradigmatic expressions of neoclassical and Marxian concepts of urban land rent.

Clark seems to find the most direct corroboration of the rent gap concept in Marshall's *Principles of Economics*, from which he quotes a long passage. It is worth reproducing this passage, in part to demonstrate how it has been misinterpreted and in part because it makes an important point about urban land rent:

> We have already seen that the ground rent which a builder is willing to pay for any site is governed by his estimate of the additional value which that site will give to the building erected on it. ...
>
> He contrives to the best of his ability that the site and the house (or other building), which he puts on it, shall be permanently appropriate the one to the other. In so far as he succeeds, the rent of the property at any future time is the sum of its annual site value and the annual value of the building ...
>
> As time goes on, the purchasing power of money may change; the class of house for which that site is suitable is likely to change; and the technique of building is certain to be improved. Consequently, the total annual value of the property at a later date consists of its annual site value, together with profits on the cost of building a house giving accommodation equally desirable at that date with the existing house. But all this is subject to the dominant condition that the general character of the house has remained appropriate to its site: if it has not, no precise statement as to the relation between total value, site value and building value can be made. If for instance a warehouse or a dwelling house of quite a different character is needed to develop the full resources of the site, the total value of the property as it stands may be less than its site value alone. For the site value cannot be developed without pulling down those buildings and erecting new.
>
> (Marshall, 1961, pp. 796–797)

Clark (1987, p. 56) follows the quotation with this statement: "The point Marshall makes here is that site value is independent of actual total value, the latter being comprised of building value and the

actually realized ground rent (which the existing building sets limits on)." But a careful reading of Marshall reveals that he does not imply that the existing use sets limits on contract rent—what Clark refers to here as "actually realized ground rent". Marshall is not saying anything about contract rent; he is merely pointing out that land value may exceed total property value if the value of the building is negative (due to demolition costs). Marshall's point is precisely that the existing building does *not* set limits on land value or rent. As Marshall says elsewhere in *Principles of Economics* (1961, p. 445): "site value ... is governed by causes which are mostly beyond the control of him who determines what buildings shall be put on it ..."

Clark includes his discussion of Smith's rent gap hypothesis in a chapter titled "Urban Applications of Marxian Land Rent Theory". It is revealing to observe that: Clark does not explain the connections between Marxian concepts of land rent and Smith's theory; and Smith himself identifies no such connections. In regard to the latter point, it should be noted that Smith mentions Marx only in passing in his influential paper on the rent gap. Moreover, Smith mentions Marx while endorsing the labour theory of value in the context of a discussion of house value, a matter that is not relevant to his fundamental distinction between actual and potential land rent. It is true that Smith's critique of the consumer sovereignty assumptions of neoclassical economics and his emphasis on the production side of the production–consumption equation are squarely within the Marxian tradition, but these aspects of the rent gap hypothesis in no way rely on any Marxian concepts of land rent. (The links between Marxian thought and Smith's theory of gentrification are made more explicit in Smith, 1979a, 1982 and 1984 and Smith and LeFaivre, 1984. However, none of these publications discusses Marx's concepts of land rent.)

Although Marx (1990, especially pt. 6) distinguishes several kinds of land rent, he does not devote attention to anything corresponding to Smith's actual rent. Marx identifies three forms of land rent—absolute, monopoly and differential—of which the last is divided into two sub-types—differential rent I and differential rent II. These components of land rent are summarised in Table 11.2. In regard to *absolute rent*, Marx argues that landlords will require rent to be paid on even the worst land under cultivation and that this is a consequence of the institution of landed property. If all land were used by owner-occupiers, then the requirement of absolute rent would no longer prevent marginal land from being cultivated. Evans (1988) has suggested

Component	Sources
Absolute rent	Transaction costs, uncertainty
Monopoly rent	Monopoly ownership of sites with scarce productive capabilities
Differential rent	
Differential rent I	Fertility, locational advantages
Differential rent II	Technological change, population growth

Table 11.2 Marx's components of land rent

Source: Evans (1988, 1991, 1992)

that transactions costs and uncertainty about the future may account for the existence of absolute rent. *Monopoly rent*, which is discussed only briefly by Marx, reflects the rent that "may arise if the product or service derived from a few sites may only be obtained from those sites and so the owner of the site has a monopoly over the provision of the product or service by virtue of his ownership of the site" (Evans, 1991, p. 7).[5] This is simply the standard concept of monopolistic profits applied to land rents.

Marx's concepts of differential rent seem at first sight potentially more relevant to the subject at hand. *Differential rent I* refers to the rent that arises from the differential fertility or locational advantage of land. This is quite similar to Ricardo's and von Thünen's concepts of land rent. In contrast, *differential rent II* is a somewhat more complicated concept. It refers to the rent that arises from the application of different amounts of capital to lands that otherwise would be equally productive. This could apply to the same land over time—as, for example, when increases in population result in a more intensive use of land and corresponding increases in land rent. Similarly, increases in land rent due to improvements in technology allowing more intensive use of land would also be in the form of differential rent II. It should be noted that Marx departs from Ricardian marginal analysis in his discussion of differential rent II, assuming that price is based on the average product. Aside from this point, which is not relevant to the present issue, Marx's concepts of differential rent are quite compatible with neoclassical concepts of land rent (Evans, 1992).

None of the elements of land rent distinguished by Marx involves an actual, as opposed to potential, form of rent. Marx does not even allude to such a distinction in his primary discussion of land rent, in volume 3 of *Capital*. Nor is there any such allusion in his other major discussion of land rent, in *Theories of Surplus Value* (see particularly the discussions of

Rodbertus's, Anderson's, Ricardo's and Adam Smith's theories of rent in Marx [1988–91, vol. 31, roughly pp. 250–399 and 457–580]). Clearly, Marx was concerned essentially with rent in its economic, rather than accounting, sense. Moreover, Clark's assertion of both neoclassical and Marxian support for the rent gap concept must be rejected because it is not supported by the evidence.

4. EMPIRICAL ATTEMPTS

It is not surprising that researchers who have attempted to test the rent gap theory have faced considerable methodological difficulties. In this regard it is revealing to note that the rent gap *per se* plays little or no role in Smith's *own* empirical studies of gentrification (Schaffer and Smith, 1986; Smith, 1989, 1992; Smith *et al.*, 1989; Smith and Schaffer, 1987). Although two of his empirical studies include discussions of the rent gap theory, no attempt is made actually to measure a rent gap. The researchers who have tried to measure rent gaps have encountered problems because, as noted previously, actual rent rarely appears as such and, even when it does, the relevant data are unlikely to be available. Potential rent is also difficult to measure, although it could be derived from property tax records, which typically give separate appraised values for land and improvements. Unfortunately, local property tax appraisals are notoriously unreliable and, among other problems, are slow to reflect changes in value. While empirical research has stumbled over these methodological hurdles, it has also suffered from interpretational problems stemming from lack of appreciation of the theoretical problems with the rent gap. Thus the following discussion addresses interpretational as well as methodological issues.

Ley's study of Canadian Metropolitan Areas

Ley's (1986) objective was to compare competing explanations of gentrification using a variety of data describing the 22 Census Metropolitan Areas (CMAs) in Canada in 1971 and 1981. Some 35 elements of data were employed in an attempt to compare four sets of competing explanations for gentrification involving demography, housing market dynamics, urban amenities, and the economic base. Two of the housing market elements were purportedly relevant to the rent gap hypothesis. These were the ratios of inner-city to CMA house values and house rental costs.

It is immediately obvious that the definition of these ratios bears little resemblance to Smith's definition of a rent gap. Ley (1986, p. 533, fn. 11) argues that they are appropriate measures of the rent gap because a low ratio represents a situation in which there is considerable incentive to reinvest in the inner city:

> The rent gap thesis argues that the more depreciated the inner-city land market, the higher the probability of reinvestment and gentrification. But this reinvestment is likely to occur only when the alternative suburban market is high priced and property is in short supply relative to the inner city.

This assumes, however, that appropriate and attractive properties are available in the inner city. It is easy to imagine a situation in which inner-city-CMA value and rent ratios are quite low yet there is little or no opportunity for profitable reinvestment in inner-city neighbourhoods. This could be due to factors such as lack of appropriate housing stock or buildings suitable for adaptive reuse or the existence of substantial negative externalities making inner-city locations unattractive for residential use. In any case, Ley's ratios are not capable of demonstrating whether there was or was not a gap between actual and potential rent.

Clark (1988, p. 245; cf. Smith, 1987a) makes substantially the same criticism of Ley's ratios:

> As interesting as these variables may be in the context of geographical patterns of housing costs, they tell us nothing about the existence or size of any rent gap. Building and land values are conflated in the ratios, which neither measure capitalized land rent nor potential land rent. The gap measured by Ley is that between inner city housing costs and metropolitan housing costs, which suggests that his test of the rent gap hypothesis is based on a misconception. He assumes the hypothesis to say that gentrification will take place where housing costs are lowest, when in fact the hypothesis states that the difference between potential land rent and capitalized land rent constitutes an economic force toward redevelopment and that redevelopment is therefore most likely to occur where this difference is greatest.

Ley, of course, recognises the difficulty in applying the rent gap concept, but his solution to that problem begs the question by measuring something altogether different.

Clark's study of Malmö, Sweden

Clark (1987, 1988) tried to measure more directly the rent gap in his study of sections of Malmö, Sweden, during the period 1860–85. To determine actual land rents, Clark used tax assessment data that distinguished between land and building values. With some adjustments, assessed land values were used as the basis for developing a series of actual land rents for each of the various study areas. A series of potential land rents was determined from bills of sale both just prior to the original development of sites and also just prior to their redevelopment. Interpolations between these values were based on general population and property value trends in the city.

The use of tax assessment data as a basis for determining actual rent is questionable in two key respects. First, given the vagaries of assessment practice, it is doubtful that assessed values correspond to reality as closely as one would like. Furthermore, as Clark notes, assessments may not accurately apportion total values between land and buildings. According to Clark (1987, p. 100): "This assumption is the one considerable weakness in the refined data ..." Unfortunately, there is also a much more serious problem with these data.

The second, and more crucial, problem is that generally accepted tax assessment procedure requires the calculation of land value on the basis of highest and best use, not current use. Thus it is quite revealing to observe that Clark's so-called actual land rents in many cases anticipate future changes in use (see, for example, Clark [1988, p. 250, fig. 5]). If observed sales prices for vacant land anticipate redevelopment more rapidly than assessed values, that only reflects the well-known lags and other inaccuracies that plague property assessment. This is all too evident in the fact that the measures of potential and actual rent in Clark's case-studies are not even the same at the time of redevelopment, which is precisely when the rent gap theory would predict they should be equal. The differences at the time of redevelopment are obviously due to the fact that assessed value continues to lag behind potential value, even when recent sale price data are available. They do not imply that assessors are trying to measure something other than potential value—that is, value in highest and best use.

In a recent paper, Clark (1992) has attempted to defend his attempt to apply the rent gap concept. Among other things, he argues that assessed values do reflect current use because they remain quite low for many decades, only to increase dramatically just prior to redevelopment. This could, however, easily be explained by poor assessment practice or, perhaps more likely, the fact that potential land values may make sudden changes rather than evolve smoothly over time. Indeed, it seems that Clark's method for interpolating potential land rents between development and redevelopment results in unrealistically smooth curves. He admits this in one of his case-studies (that of the Pontus block), where there was an obvious reason for doubting that the curve would be so smooth. Because the interpolations are based on growth in population and assessed property values for the entire city, they almost certainly mask the detailed changes in perceptions about potential land uses and values for the small areas used as case-studies. There is no reason to believe that these perceptions changed as smoothly as the interpolation procedure assumes.

Kary's study of Toronto, Canada

Kary (1988) tried to test the rent gap hypothesis by looking at relative house prices in Toronto. His methods involved an attempt to determine whether there was a "land value valley"—or, more precisely, a house price valley—in inner Toronto and also an analysis of the evolution of house prices in the Cabbagetown/Donvale area, described as a prime example of gentrification in Canada. Like Ley, Kary was unable to measure the rent gap directly and instead simply compared inner-city house prices with suburban ones, in the case of his more general study, or looked at relative house prices over time, in the case of the Cabbagetown/Donvale study. Neither of these approaches is capable of demonstrating the existence of a rent gap, because neither demonstrates that there was at any time a potential rent that differed from actual rent. Thus Clark's criticism of Ley's ratios applies with equal force to Kary's measures.

Badcock's study of Adelaide, Australia

Badcock (1989) attempted to determine whether there was a rent gap in the 30 local government areas of metropolitan Adelaide, South Australia, between 1970 and 1985. He used a measure of combined house and land value based on sales prices as a proxy for actual rent, on the assumption that actual value (rent) will be something less than total property value (rent). Potential value (rent) was measured by the actual sales prices of serviced vacant lots. Thus Badcock claimed to have identified a rent (or, more precisely, *value*) gap in Adelaide when

he showed that the values of bare parcels in the inner city exceeded the total property values of land parcels with houses. This gap contracted and closed between 1975 and 1980.

Badcock (1990, p. 460) mentions that in inner Adelaide in 1970 "the housing stock was dominated by undersized allotments and subject to an encumbrance prohibiting redevelopment where they fell below a minimum size". This suggests that combined house and land values in inner Adelaide were low relative to vacant lot values due to legal restrictions on redevelopment of the former. This does not imply anything about any differences between actual (contract) and potential (land) rent, if legal feasibility is a condition of potential use. After the restrictions were removed, the so-called rent gap disappeared. Instead of closure of a gap between actual and potential rent, this should be characterised as a change in potential rent. Feasible uses after removal of the restrictions were more intensive than the feasible uses while the redevelopment prohibitions remained in force.

5. CONCLUSION: ALTERNATIVES TO THE RENT GAP

Where does all of this leave the rent gap hypothesis? The notion of a rent gap relies on a concept of rent that depends on the current use of land. But, as Tideman (1982, p. 109) argues: "Such a definition has no special virtue from the perspective of theory and does not correspond to anything that might plausibly be observed empirically." Although the latter part of Tideman's remark may be overstated, it is true that attempts to apply the rent gap hypothesis in empirical studies of gentrification have encountered severe measurement problems. In regard to the more fundamental point, the concept of actual rent adds nothing to our understanding of gentrification because it explains nothing that was not already understood in more coherent terms. As Ley (1987, p. 468) concluded:

> The devalorization cycle and the mystique around the rent gap now become unnecessary baggage. All that is now required for gentrification to occur is the potential for profit. This bears striking similarity to neoclassical accounts of developer behavior and as such it is a claim that can be assessed using conventional indicators.

Indeed, the standard neoclassical account of land-use succession does not rely on any distinction between actual and potential rent or value. In the standard analysis, a property can be profitably developed only if:

$$V_n - C_n \geq V_c + D_c,$$

where: V_c is the market value of a site and the building currently on it, if any (the subscript c refers to *current* use); V_n is the expected market value of the same site and either a rehabilitated or a new building on it (n refers to the *new* use); D_c is the cost of demolishing the current building if there is one and if it is to be replaced by a new building ($D_c = 0$ if the current building is retained and rehabilitated); and C_n is the cost of rehabilitating the existing building or constructing the new building, *exclusive* of the cost of purchasing and—in the case of a new building replacing an existing one—clearing the site (this is based in part on Heilbrun, 1974).

It should be understood that, in this formula, land-use change does not depend on the existence of a gap between actual and potential *rent*, only between current and potential, feasible land *uses*. Because land rent and value change as soon as perceptions about the future change and do not wait for land use to change, the site values contained in V_c and V_n are identical—both are based on potential, rather than actual, use. Any difference between the two is due solely to the possible differences between the value of the current and the new (or rehabilitated) buildings or uses.[6] Obviously, the formula over-simplifies the development decision. A developer considers not only the potential profit from current development, but also how $V_n - C_n - V_c - D_c$ is likely to change over time in various locations, and the implications of that for the optimal location, timing and form of development—for example, it is possible that it would be profitable to develop a site immediately, but even more profitable to wait and develop it at a later date. Nevertheless, the site values contained in V_n and V_c are the same and do not depend on any distinction between actual and potential land rents. In both cases, site value is the present value of the expected future stream of land rents. More importantly, like the rent gap hypothesis, the formula does not go very far in explaining why gentrification does or does not actually take place. In other words, neither approach explains how neighbourhoods previously subject to disinvestment come to be perceived to have the potential for reinvestment and higher land rents. Detailed historical studies of the reasons for and impacts of changes in potential values and rents are needed to properly explain gentrification. Excellent examples of such studies may be found in Hamnett and Randolph's (1986)

study of tenure transformation in inner London and Zukin's (1982) study of loft housing in New York's SoHo.

In conclusion, it should be noted that this paper is not intended as a neoclassical critique of Marxian urban economics. Although it has been maintained that the neoclassical concept of urban land-use succession is more coherent theoretically than Smith's rent gap theory, that is not meant as an implied endorsement of neoclassical explanations of gentrification. As has been argued elsewhere (Bourassa, 1992a), neither explanations based on neoclassical residential location theory nor those based on (the at least ostensibly) Marxian rent gap theory provide a satisfactory account of gentrification. In fact, these competing explanations suffer from analogous problems. On the one hand, the Marxian theory fails to explore the origins of potential rent—that is, it does not explain how it historically becomes profitable to rehabilitate or redevelop inner-city neighbourhoods. On the other hand, the neoclassical theory, with its assumption of consumer sovereignty, fails to explore the origins of the tastes that underlie consumer demands. In each case, the theory fails to address and explain the most fundamental and interesting aspects of the phenomenon in question: namely, the sources of the changes in value that constitute gentrification.

Notes

1 Economists often prefer to speak in terms of land rent rather than land value, and discussion of the rent gap has followed that practice. The relationship between the two concepts is quite simple. If L is the market value of the land, E is the expected annual land rent, and r is the rate of return that could be earned on alternative equally-risky investment, then $L = E/r$.

2 Smith (1979b, pp. 542–543) wrote: "A further complication with housing is that the sale price represents not only the value of the house, but an additional component for rent since the land is generally sold along with the structures it accommodates. Here it is preferable to talk of ground rent rather than land value, since the price of land does not reflect a quantity of labor power applied to it, as with the value of commodities proper."

3 In the discussion that follows, the term *development* is used in the broadly inclusive sense to refer to redevelopment, which might involve rehabilitation of existing buildings, as well as development of previously undeveloped sites.

4 A recent treatment of the concept of highest and best use can be found in Dotzour *et al.* (1990). The reference to 'so-called' highest and best use is an allusion to the fact that the highest and best use from a private landowner's point of view is often not the same as that from a social point of view due to the existence of externalities and public goods. Dotzour *et al.* note that although highest and best use has traditionally been identified with the private landowner's point of view, social costs and benefits began to be incorporated into the concept in the 1970s.

5 Marx (1990, chs 38 and 45) sometimes uses the word *monopoly* loosely to refer to the general monopolistic control over land use maintained by landowners. The land rents arising from private landownership are typically in the form of differential or absolute rents; however, the term *monopoly rent* here refers to a form distinct from either of those two types. Marx (1990) refers to this distinct type of monopoly rent in his ch. 46.

6 As Hamnett and Randolph (1986) demonstrate in their case-study, it is possible that the differences in value may be due solely to a gap between the value of a property as 'tenanted investment' housing and its 'vacant possession' value to owner-occupiers. They show that in inner London there was an incentive to covert properties from rental to owner-occupancy due to a 'value gap': $V_n > V_c$. In this case, $C_n = D_c = 0$.

REFERENCES

BADCOCK, B. (1989) An Australian view of the rent gap hypothesis, *Annals of the Association of American Geographers*, 79, pp. 125–145.

BADCOCK, B. (1990) On the nonexistence of the rent gap: a reply, *Annals of the Association of American Geographers*, 80, pp. 459–461.

BEAUREGARD, R.A. (1986) The chaos and complexity of gentrification, in: N. SMITH and P. WILLIAMS (Eds) *Gentrification of the City*, pp. 35–55. Boston: Allen & Unwin.

BOURASSA, S.C. (1990) Another Australian view of the rent gap hypothesis, *Annals of the Association of American Geographers*, 80, pp. 458–459.

BOURASSA, S.C. (1992a) *Culture, aesthetics, residential location, and gentrification.* Paper presented at the *27th International Geographical Congess*, Washington, DC.

BOURASSA, S.C. (1992b) Economic effects of taxes on land: a review, *American Journal of Economics and Sociology*, 51, pp. 109–113.

CLARK, E. (1987) *The Rent Gap and Urban Change: Case Studies in Malmö 1860–1985.* Lund: Lund University Press.

CLARK, E. (1988) The rent gap and transformation of the built environment: case studies in Malmö 1860–1985, *Geografiska Annaler*, 70B, pp. 241–254.

CLARK, E. (1992) On gaps in gentrification theory, *Housing Studies*, 7, pp. 16–26.

DOLAN, E.G. (1983) *Basic Economics*, 3rd edn. Chicago: Dryden Press.

DOTZOUR, M.G., GRISSOM, T.V., LIU, C.H. and PEARSON, T. (1990) Highest and best use: the evolving paradigm, *Journal of Real Estate Research*, 5, pp. 17–32.

EVANS, A.W. (1988) *On absolute rent.* Department of Economics Discussion Papers in Urban and Regional Economics, Series C, Vol. 1, No. 36, University of Reading.

EVANS, A.W. (1991) On monopoly rent, *Land Economics*, 67, pp. 1–14.

EVANS, A.W. (1992) On differential rent and landed property, *International Journal of Urban and Regional Research*, 16, pp. 81–96.

GAFFNEY, M. (1962) Ground rent and the allocation of land among farms, in: F. MILLER (Ed). *Rent Theory, Problems, and Practices*, pp. 30–49. Missouri Agricultural Experimental Station Research Bulletin 810, University of Missouri.

GAFFNEY, M. (1969) Land rent, taxation, and public policy, *Papers of the Regional Science Association*, 23, pp. 141–153.

HAMNETT, C. (1984) Gentrification and residential location theory: a review and assessment, in: D.T. HERBERT and R.J. JOHNSTON (Eds) *Geography and the Urban Environment: Progress in Research and Applications, vol. 6*, pp. 283–319. Chichester: John Wiley & Sons.

HAMNETT, C. (1991) The blind men and the elephant: the explanation of gentrification, *Transactions of the Institute of British Geographers*, n.s. 16, pp. 173–189.

HAMNETT, C. and RANDOLPH, B. (1986) Tenurial transformation and the flat break-up market in London: the British condo experience, in: N. SMITH and P. WILLIAMS (Eds) *Gentrification of the City*, pp. 121–152. Boston: Allen & Unwin.

HEILBRUN, J. (1974) *Urban Economics and Public Policy.* New York: St Martin's Press.

KARY, K.J. (1988) The gentrification of Toronto and the rent gap theory, in: T.E. BUNTING and

P. FILION (Eds) *The Changing Canadian Inner City*, pp. 53–72. Department of Geography Publication Series No. 31, University of Waterloo, Ontario.

LEY, D. (1986) Alternative explanations for inner-city gentrification: a Canadian assessment, *Annals of the Association of American Geographers*, 76, pp. 521–535.

LEY, D. (1987) Reply: the rent gap revisited, *Annals of the Association of American Geographers*, 77, pp. 465–468.

MARSHALL, A. (1961) *Principles of Economics*, 9th var. edn, vol. 1, C.W. GUILLEBAUD (Ed.). London: Macmillan.

MARX, K. (1988–91 [1905–10]) Theories of surplus value, in: *Karl Marx/Frederick Engels: Collected Works, vols. 30–33*. London: Lawrence & Wishart.

MARX, K. (1990 [1894]) *Capital: A Critique of Political Economy, vol. 3*, D. Fernbach (Trans.). London: Penguin.

SCHAFFER, R. and SMITH, N. (1986) The gentrification of Harlem?, *Annals of the Association of American Geographers*, 76, pp. 347–365.

SMITH, N. (1979a) Gentrification and capital: practice and ideology in Society Hill, *Antipode*, 11, pp. 24–35.

SMITH, N. (1979b) Toward a theory of gentrification: a back to the city movement by capital, not people, *Journal of the American Planning Association*, 45, pp. 538–548.

SMITH, N. (1982) Gentrification and uneven development, *Economic Geography*, 58, pp. 139–155.

SMITH, N. (1984) *Uneven Development: Nature, Capital and the Production of Space*. Oxford: Basil Blackwell.

SMITH, N. (1986) Gentrification, the frontier, and the restructuring of urban space, in: N. SMITH and P. WILLIAMS (Eds) *Gentrification of the City*, pp. 15–34. Boston: Allen & Unwin.

SMITH, N. (1987a) Gentrification and the rent gap, *Annals of the Association of American Geographers*, 77, pp. 462–465.

SMITH, N. (1987b) Of yuppies and housing: gentrification, social restructuring, and the urban dream, *Environment and Planning D: Society and Space*, 5, pp. 151–172.

SMITH, N. (1989) Tompkins Square Park: riots, rents and redskins, *Portable Lower East Side*, 6, pp. 1–36.

SMITH, N. (1992) New city, new frontier, the Lower East Side as wild, wild West, in: M. SORKIN (Ed.) *Variations on a Theme Park: The New American City and the End of Public Space*, pp. 61–93. New York: Hill and Wang.

SMITH, N., DUNCAN, B. and REID, L. (1989) From disinvestment to reinvestment: tax arrears and turning points in the East Village, *Housing Studies*, 4, pp. 238–252.

SMITH, N. and HEROD, A. (1991) *Gentrification: A Comprehensive Bibliography*. Department of Geography Discussion Papers, n.s. No. 1, Rutgers University, New Brunswick.

SMITH, N. and LEFAIVRE, M. (1984) A class analysis of gentrification, in: J.J. PALEN and B. LONDON (Eds) *Gentrification, Displacement, and Neighborhood Revitalization*, pp. 43–63. Albany: State University of New York Press.

SMITH, N. and SCHAFFER, R. (1987) Harlem gentrification: a catch-22?, *New York Affairs*, 10, pp. 59–78.

TIDEMAN, T.N. (1982) A tax on land value *is* neutral, *National Tax Journal*, 35, pp. 109–111.

WONG, D.W.S. (1988) A critique and reformulation of Smith's rent gap theory of gentrification, *Proceedings of the Middle States Division of the Association of American Geographers*, 21, pp. 64–76.

ZUKIN, S. (1982) *Loft Living: Culture and Capital in Urban Change*. Baltimore: Johns Hopkins University Press.

12

"Re-establishing the Rent Gap: An Alternative View of Capitalised Land Rent"

From *Urban Studies* (1999)

Daniel J. Hammel

INTRODUCTION

The debate on the rent gap hypothesis appearing in part in the pages of this journal has resulted in two distinct and incompatible views of the hypothesis and related issues of land rent theory (Badcock, 1990; Bourassa, 1990, 1992, 1993; Clark, 1987, 1988, 1995; Smith, 1996). This paper serves as an addition to that debate. The intentions are threefold: to comment on the debate between Bourassa and Clark in an attempt to clarify several key issues; to begin to provide the basis for a different understanding of capitalised land rent than has been suggested by either author (although it is clearly more compatible with that of Clark); and to indicate how this new view of capitalised land rent is compatible with the rent gap theory.

The rent gap hypothesis has been the subject of a tremendous amount of debate mostly centring on its effectiveness in explaining gentrification. Much criticism of the hypothesis is external in nature, critiquing the rent gap through comparisons with other preferred explanations. Steven Bourassa, however, has taken a somewhat different approach in his critique by arguing that the hypothesis suffers from serious internal inconsistencies, and essentially is in conflict with previous work in land rent theory. It is this line of argument that he has developed in his debates first with Badcock and later with Clark, and it is this contention that will be addressed here.

Three arguments form the basis of this paper. First, the fundamental disagreement in the debates involves the role of land use in determining land rent

on a particular parcel. Neither Clark nor Bourassa has been completely convincing on either side of this issue. Secondly, Smith (1979) made a basic error in defining capitalised land rent and perhaps overemphasised the historical context for capitalised land rent at the expense of the geographical context. Both items have created confusion. Thirdly, a review of the rent gap hypothesis identifies support for an alternative view of capitalised land rent emphasising geographical context, particularly the role of scale, in understanding how land rent is determined. It is argued here that this alternative view helps to legitimise the concept of capitalised land rent in Marxist land rent theory. Before discussing these points, the paper first turns to a brief review of the rent gap hypothesis and the arguments of the major participants in this debate.

It should be noted that the intention is not to disparage or promote the rent gap as an explanation of gentrification. The goal is to step aside from the voluminous commentary on that issue, and to argue the rent gap's legitimacy as a theory concerned with urban land rent separate from its effectiveness as an explanation for gentrification.

BACKGROUND

The rent gap

The rent gap hypothesis is well connected to a long tradition of Marxist economic theory including much work on land rent (see, for example, Smith, 1982,

1984). The debates over the hypothesis, however, have focused upon the more basic aspects of the rent gap itself. In short, upon Smith's addition to land rent theory. Given this emphasis, this review will be confined to the specifics of the rent gap hypothesis and to its connections with larger issues in land rent theory.

The rent gap hypothesis is based upon the concepts of capitalised and potential land rent. Land rent according to Smith represents "a reduction from the surplus value over and above the cost-price by producers on the site" (Smith, 1979, p. 543). Capitalised land rent is "the actual quantity of ground rent that is appropriated by the land owner, given the present land use" (Smith, 1979, p. 543), alternatively, "sale price = house value + capitalized land rent" (Smith, 1979, p. 543). Potential land rent represents, "the amount (of rent) that could be capitalized under the land's 'highest and best use'" (Smith, 1979, p. 543). The key phrase here is "highest and best use" which will require closer analysis in the following sections. Both capitalised and potential land rents start at the same level when a parcel is developed. Over time, the improvements on the parcel may suffer from obsolescence or disinvestment and capitalised land rent may decline. Potential land rent, however, will gradually increase as the city grows and more capital is applied to land in the metropolitan area. The divergence between capitalised and potential land rent represents the rent gap and creates the possibility of significant profit through reinvestment in the parcel.

At this level, the hypothesis is quite simple. These seemingly straightforward ideas of capitalised and potential land rent, however, are the source of much controversy. In part, the issue is one of terminology—as can be seen in the exchanges between Bourassa (1993), Clark (1995) and Smith (1996)—but the terminological disagreements are minor compared to the real theoretical disagreement over land rent in general and capitalised land rent in particular.

The arguments

The debate in question began as a response to empirical work on the rent gap in Adelaide (Badcock, 1989, 1990; Bourassa, 1990). The objections Bourassa raised in his initial argument were developed more fully (Bourassa, 1992, 1993) and elicited more reaction (Clark, 1995). Recently, the author of the rent gap joined the debate (Smith, 1996). The points of each participant are summarised here, where relevant to the current arguments.

Bourassa raises a number of objections to the rent gap, but they can be grouped into three areas. First, he notes that most land yields an aggregate return in conjunction with other inputs. In practice, it is usually impossible to separate land rent from proceeds of the land's improvements. This "technical objection" (Badcock, 1990, p. 459) makes the rent gap—a land-rent-based explanation of gentrification—impractical, if not untenable. Secondly, Bourassa argues that land rent is determined independently of land use in traditional land rent theory. Thus, capitalised land rent, depressed by deterioration of the land's improvements, becomes a nonsensical proposition. Lastly, tax assessments—based as they are on the land's highest and best use—are representative of land rent or, in rent gap terms, potential land rent. Thus, the several empirical studies (Clark, 1987; Kary, 1988; Badcock, 1989) that used assessments as a measure of capitalised land rent committed a fatal error. Let us first turn to the issue of separating the inputs of land and improvements.

The difficulty in separating land rent and the value of improvements on a particular property is quite real, and a serious issue for Tideman (1982) and others (see, for example, Mills, 1981, 1982; Bentick, 1982; Wildasin, 1982) when discussing issues of land value taxation. The practical nature of the problem requires an accurate and clear assessment of land rent. Within the context of the rent gap, however, the issue is of little importance. As Clark points out, the inputs of land and improvements are easily separated analytically. In addition, this separation has been long accepted by land rent economists (Barlowe, 1978).

The relationship between land rent and land use poses a much more complex problem which forms the crux of the disagreement. Simply stated, Bourassa argues that "land value is defined in the land economics literature as the value of a site as if it had no improvements" (Bourassa, 1990, p. 458). Thus, capitalised land rent has no theoretical basis in land rent theory because it rests on the assumption that land use affects land rent.

Bourassa (1993) notes that land use can affect land rent, but only when it represents a deduction to land rent, as in the case of the demolition costs associated with a derelict building on the site in question. This general concept of land rent *is* consistent with the manner in which most economists have viewed land rent (see, for example, Barlowe, 1978, 1986; Dolan, 1980, 1983).

The issue of tax assessments and capitalised land rent is also a difficult one, and it flows directly from the previous argument about land use and land rent. Assessments are made with a property's highest and best use in mind, and highest and best use ought not to be affected by the land's current use. Thus, assessed values of land should fail to represent accurately capitalised land rent. In part, this argument can be dismissed quickly. Tax assessments often have no relationship to a parcel's highest and best use price because they are more affected by political influences than economic ones. However, there are situations where tax assessments may be quite accurate.[1] In these situations, Bourassa's critique can not be dismissed so easily and must be looked at in greater detail. Badcock (1989) begins this task in a necessarily brief reply. He managed, however, to identify a crucial point. In discussing the issue of land assessment, he noted that

> *pure* valuation theory … denies the validity of a measure of current market value under an existing use.
>
> (Badcock, 1989, p. 459; emphasis in original)

The key word in this case is "pure". In practice, however, land price is based on estimates of market prices for similar properties which implicitly consider land use. I argue that the nature of land assessment practices and the concept of highest and best use on which they are based form a crucial building block in the determination of capitalised land rents, an idea we will return to later.

Clark (1995) provides a point-by-point response to Bourassa's objections, but most importantly he adopts the position that land use significantly affects land rent. He argues that land rent will be depressed when land use is inappropriate for the site and when land is not in its highest and best use. Capitalised land rent exists because land returns less than its potential due to its use. This idea is in direct conflict with the traditional understanding of land rent advocated by Bourassa. Clark (1987), however, mounted a substantial search for theoretical precursors to the rent gap hypothesis and found several that recognise a relationship between land use and land rent.

The brief writings of Marshall (1936) on this topic have been printed in this journal previously, and their meaning is still in dispute (see Bourassa, 1993, p. 1736; and Clark, 1995, p. 1498). Marshall appears to suggest that the aggregate rent of a parcel may not always exceed its site rent by the full value of the improvements in situations where the improvements are not appropriate to the site. Bourassa suggests that Marshall is simply referring to the situation

where the 'improvements' represent a deduction to the land rent. Both interpretations have some merit, but with a close reading of the material it does appear that Marshall may have been referring to a situation akin to Smith's rent gap. Clark has noted, however, that this selection of Marshall's writing represents a minor sidelight (encompassing a footnote and part of an appendix) to a tome on economics, and is not a fully developed theoretical justification of the rent gap.

Clark (1995, p. 1498) also cites a passage from Engels (1955) which may provide a similar indication of a precedent for the rent gap. Engels engages in a brief discussion of the potentially depressing effect of an inappropriate land use on land rent. He too appears to be referring to a situation akin to the rent gap. Again, however, this is a brief passage and not a fully developed pre-1979 exposition of the concepts of capitalised and potential land rent.

Smith's (1996) critique of Bourassa's work is fundamentally different from previous critiques. As he notes, the paper

> is in no way a comprehensive critique or rebuttal then, but rather a statement of some basic and pervasive problems in Bourassa's piece.
>
> (Smith, 1996, p. 1199)

While not completely ignoring the specifics of Bourassa's critique, especially the terminological issues, Smith emphasises the fundamental differences between neoclassical and Marxist economic theory. In short, Smith claims that the rent gap is being evaluated as a neoclassical theory when it was never intended to be one.

Bourassa attempted to launch a general critique of the rent gap founded in both neoclassical and Marxist traditions. Instead, Smith argues, he developed a radical idealist critique that takes neoclassical economics one step farther by opening up the 'black box' of consumer sovereignty and attempting to explore its inner workings.

In addition, Bourassa's critique is ahistorical in that he ignores the fundamental changes in the meaning of such key phrases as value, rent and price from Adam Smith, Marx and Ricardo to the present-day 'reductionist' meanings of neoclassical economics. This is no small issue considering the significant historical detail in Clark's (1987) attempt to provide theoretical background for the hypothesis.

Nevertheless, Bourassa has raised some serious questions about the rent gap. The critique does point to some apparent inconsistencies in the rent gap theory—primarily that most land rent theorists do reject the idea that land use can affect land rent on a particular parcel. Thus, the hypothesis does run counter to traditional views of land rent despite the work that Clark has done to identify potential theoretical precursors.

Clark and Smith both note that this non-traditional stance in not necessarily wrong, nor is it always necessary to build on the theoretical traditions of the past, as long as the theory has explanatory power and internal consistency. In fact, the interrelationship of land rent and land use inherent to the rent gap is sprinkled throughout the history of land rent theory at least up until the writings of Marshall. However, the implicit nature of this thread has prevented Clark from establishing a completely coherent link from classical economics to the rent gap theory. The theory itself made the land rent–land use relationship quite explicit. Unfortunately, the support for this relationship, while present, is well hidden in the rent gap theory. It is suggested here that the rent gap does represent a theoretically consistent explanation of gentrification; that capitalised land rent can be seen as a coherent form of rent; that the origins of capitalised land rent must be considered at a minimum of two different scales; and that these scales can been seen in Smith's cycle of devalorisation and his further discussion of both potential and capitalised land rents.

CAPITALISED LAND RENT

Smith's definition

The original definition of capitalised land rent is problematic because as Clark points out it is inconsistent, and as Bourassa notes, the term capitalised has a specific meaning that serves to equate capitalised land rent with land price. Smith identifies capitalised land rent as the actual amount of land that a site is returning in its present use. He goes on to note that

the landlord's capitalized ground rent returns mainly in the form of house rent paid by the tenants.

(Smith, 1979, p. 543)

The suggestion of capitalised land rent occurring as a continuous flow either based on the present use or as a house rent payment led Bourassa to identify capitalised land rent as synonymous with contract rent, and reject its significance in understanding gentrification. Bourassa too quickly dismisses the concept of capitalised land rent. First, he confuses the term land value. To Bourassa, land value is

equivalent to its market value or price. To Smith, working in the Marxist tradition and subscribing to the labour theory of value, land value is unrelated to market price. In addition, Bourassa ignores the full meaning of capitalised land rent which can be seen less in Smith's definition of the term and more in his discussion of potential land rent and neighbourhood decline.

Smith's arguments

The difference between Smith's definition of capitalised land rent and other ideas contained in the same paper are significant enough to require further examination. Two areas are of particular interest: the cycle of valorisation and devalorisation that Smith uses to present the historical development of the rent gap; and the manner in which he conceptualises potential land rent.

Much of the 1979 paper involves what Smith refers to as "a rather schematic attempt to explain the historical decline of inner-city neighbourhoods" (Smith, 1979, p. 543). This five-stage model of decline provides a key insight into the nature of capitalised land rent. In the first stage, "new construction and the first cycle of use", Smith concentrates on the possible sources of depreciation: advances in the productiveness of labour, style obsolescence, and physical wear and tear. All of these processes act upon individual structures and may involve a series of decisions made by individual home-owners. The scale of analysis here is the individual structure which is similar to the scale at which Smith defines capitalised land rent. Owners, however, may take steps to modify the structure to slow style obsolescence or to invest in the structure to remedy the results of wear and tear. They could also decide to forgo further investment in the structure, sell it and invest in a newer house. Alternatively, owners may wish to invest in the structure, but may not have access to the necessary capital. The path a home-owner will follow, Smith takes pains to point out, is not merely an individual decision, but a decision that is structured by a number of housing market factors operating in the neighbourhood in question. Thus, at the end of the first cycle of use, the scale of analysis switches from the individual parcel to the neighbourhood.

The remaining four stages provide more detail about processes such as landlordism and under-maintenance, blow out and blockbusting, redlining and abandonment. Smith discusses all of these processes as operating at the neighbourhood scale. Redlining may be the most explicit example.

Financial institutions obstruct the flow of capital necessary to maintain the value of the structures by refusing to approve loans to a specific area because of the social and economic characteristics of that area. Redlining defines the process of decline at the neighbourhood level by literally defining neighbourhoods where decline will continue to occur.

The importance of the neighbourhood scale of analysis arises too in the discussion of the early stages of gentrification. Smith notes that the process is not brought about by individual decision-makers, but by collective action at the neighbourhood level. This statement is meant to contradict consumer sovereignty arguments, but it clearly indicates Smith's emphasis on the neighbourhood scale of analysis.

The discussion of potential land rent also provides indications of the importance of the neighbourhood scale in determining capitalised land rent. Smith made few comments about potential land rent, but they bear repeating. He notes that

> Under its present land use a site or neighborhood is able to capitalize a certain quantity of ground rent. For reasons of location usually, such an area may be able to capitalize higher quantities of ground rent under a different land use.
>
> (Smith, 1979, p. 543)

Smith confined his discussion to a particular site when defining capitalised land rent. In the discussion of potential land rent, however, he refers to *capitalised* land rent at the neighbourhood scale, and suggests that potential land rent is determined largely by location. This idea is far from new. It is curious, however, that Smith ignores the issue of location as a determinant of capitalised land rent except in a general manner (i.e. inner city versus suburban). It is possible that Smith adopted the emphasis that he did because he was interested in advocating an explicitly historical explanation of gentrification to link the process first with years of disinvestment and second with continuing development on the urban fringe. The research on gentrification at the time lacked the historical context found in the rent gap. Gentrification represented simply a new and different phenomenon to many, but to more critical scholars it also represented an inevitable outcome of decades of inner-city decline. In establishing this emphasis, however, Smith appears to have de-emphasised the geographical issues that could have helped to establish more firmly the concept of capitalised land rent.

We are left then with an understanding of capitalised land rent defined by Smith as operating at the scale of the individual parcel, but with origins at the neighbourhood scale, and a rent that may have some theoretical precursors as identified by Clark (1987). I suggest that capitalised land rent can be developed in a way that avoids the difficulties inherent in the present concept, and in a manner that is consistent with the less explicit meaning of capitalised land rent expressed in Smith's original paper.

AN ALTERNATIVE VIEW OF CAPITALISED LAND RENT

Determinants of land rent

The determinants of a property's land rent can be many and varied, and to a large extent depend upon the researcher's methodological orientation. The purpose here is not to delve into the nature of land rent as it is expressed, for example, in Marxian rent categories, but to look more closely at the determinants of variation in land rent within urban areas.

Land rent varies from one parcel to the next for several reasons, but predominantly, as Smith said, for "reasons of location". We have long understood that urban land with higher levels of accessibility will return higher rents (see, for example, Seyfried, 1963). A simple conception of urban land rent patterns suggests that land rents peak in the CBD and decline outward at a rapid pace (Hoyt, 1933; Knos, 1962). Other views of land rent patterns in the multicentred metropolis have identified a land rent peak in the CBD with other somewhat smaller peaks at other major nodes in the city (Berry *et al.*, 1963). Despite this theorised pattern, empirical work has identified land rent valleys in inner-city areas. Smith refers to Hoyt's work in Chicago in his 1979 paper on the rent gap hypothesis. Other work in Chicago (Yeates, 1965) and in Boston (Edel and Sclar, 1975) has also identified a similar pattern. Thus, Smith develops the idea that land rent and the sale price of much inner-city land is less than expected based on its location and accessibility. What creates this pattern? Location and accessibility are important factors, but they must be viewed at two different scales.

Potential land rent is determined at the metropolitan scale—that is, by the factors that work at the scale of an entire city. The amount of rent a parcel should be returning is based on its location in the metropolitan area, the size of the metropolitan area, the proximity to major thoroughfares, etc. Thus, the pattern of potential land rent is similar to the theorised pattern of land rents that is quite familiar to urban scholars, with inner-city properties having relatively high potential land rents and areas on the fringe having lower potential land rents.

Capitalised land rent is determined largely at the neighbourhood scale. The general socioeconomic characteristics of the neighbourhood, including land use, act to limit land rent. Thus, the capitalised land rent of a particular site may be less than its potential if the land use of the surrounding parcels is not of the type that will allow the full measure of potential land rent to be captured.

Land rent and scale

The processes of differentiation and equalisation that Smith lays out as a foundation for the rent gap (Smith, 1982, 1984) clearly rest on the issue of scale. The dialectical nature of these basic processes provides the possibility for an immensely rich and complex understanding of urban development, but even a simple view of them highlights the importance of scale. The concentration of high-priced white-collar occupations in the core of a select group of metropolises represents a process of differentiation at the national or even global scale. The resulting urban growth, often through suburbanisation, creates a form of equalisation by lowering capital investment in inner-city areas and increasing capital investment on the urban fringe. Inherent to these processes is the need to examine them at different scales because capital acts at different scales.

In a different context, Smith clearly identifies the issue of scale as being "vital" to understanding the economic geography of the American manufacturing belt (Smith and Dennis, 1987). We are introduced to the intriguing phrase, "the production of geographical scale" (p. 167). Smith and Dennis argue that one of the basic tasks of the "new regional geography" is to develop theory to identify the scale at which regions are defined. Without taking the comparison too far, it is this task that is at hand in understanding the rent gap. At what scale must it be analysed in order for it to be consistent and have explanatory power? I argue that the neighbourhood and metropolitan scales form a minimum level of analysis—that the geographical scale of gentrification is produced at those levels.

Examining the determinants of potential and capitalised land rent at different scales provides three advantages to the current rent gap hypothesis. First, this view of capitalised land rent avoids the theoretically difficult problem of the interplay of land use and land rent in a given parcel. Secondly, it is

in keeping with observations of land rent and land values in inner-city areas as seen in part by the way that we appraise the value of land. Thirdly, it is fully compatible with Smith's description of the rent gap hypothesis and our understanding of the gentrification process in general. Let us now turn to a more detailed discussion of each of these points.

Capitalised land rent determined at the neighbourhood scale avoids the theoretical difficulties arising from the effect of land use on land rent inherent in capitalised land rent, but it recognises that land use in general does affect land rent. It must. If land use has no effect on land rent, then we are back to the pre-classical notions of a natural value to land. Rent in its most basic form is a mediator between conflicting social forces vying to use land for various purposes, and as such it is inexorably linked with land use. Urban land rent is determined by matters of location, but also by infrastructural characteristics that are now 'inherent' to the land. Both of these factors are created by human action and use of land. They both enable and constrain the use of the land and determine its rent.

In urban areas, we have created a pattern of land use that, despite the pace of change, is often remarkably permanent. Inner-city areas have many sites with a potential for development that could return high levels of rent. That development never occurs, however, because the perception of an impoverished neighbourhood prevents large amounts of capital from being applied to the land. The surrounding uses make high levels of development infeasible, and the property continues to languish. Thus, the potential land rent of a parcel based on metropolitan-wide factors is quite high, but factors at the neighbourhood scale constrain the capitalised land rent to a lower level.

Land assessment practices also provide some indication of the role of scale in differentiating capitalised and potential land rents. A discussion of land assessments and assessment practices is particularly relevant here not only because they acknowledge the difference between the present price of many properties and their potential price, but also because assessments provide an important source of data for empirical study of the rent gap (Clark, 1987; Kary, 1988; Badcock, 1989) which Bourassa heavily criticised. Land is assessed, according to Bourassa, at its highest and best use. Thus, the data that Badcock, Clark and Kary used to estimate capitalised land rent were in fact indicative of potential land rent. As I will show, land assessments *are* made with the land's highest and best use, but this a slippery concept that is bound by issues of change over time and geographical scale.

Appraisers value land by its highest and best use only in theory. In practice, land value is based on the sales of surrounding comparable parcels (Badcock, 1990). The concept of highest and best use is basic to land appraisal, but this principle does not mean that all tax assessments represent a property's value at its highest and best use. As Luceno states,

> The role of highest and best use in the appraisal process is one of great significance ... , and is a culmination of the steps and influences in the appraisal process leading up to a foundation upon which the land, as though vacant, can be estimated, and the three approaches to value can be applied; ultimately resulting in a final value estimate.
>
> (Luceno, 1990, p. 123)

In other words, highest and best use is a *concept* on which an appraisal is made. Thus, Bourassa is correct that assessments are made on the basis of a property's highest and best use, but is incorrect in assuming that the assessed value represents the highest and best use value. In fact, a property could be assessed with several different values by the same appraiser all based on the same highest and best use. In addition, highest and best use is not the straightforward concept that it appears to be. Appraisers speak of multiple highest and best uses (AIREA, 1987, p. 290) and have used the term "potential future highest and best use" (AIREA, 1987, p. 271). Thus, highest and best use value of a property depends upon the way that the appraiser values the property which brings us back to the issue of scale and its effects upon the determinants of land rent.

Appraisers are required when possible to base a market value appraisal on the recent sale of a comparable property. Fundamental to the idea of using a comparable property is the issue of location. There are a number of points on which to compare properties, but propinquity is among the most important (AIREA, 1987). Thus, appraisers determine the highest and best use value of a property by comparison with other nearby properties. This practice sets a property in a context that is generally at the neighbourhood scale (see Stark's (1988) outline of the process, for example). The highest and best use of a property is determined by its immediate or neighbourhood context similar to capitalised land rent, and not a larger metropolitan context. Potential land rent, based on a metropolitan context, would be something of a foreign concept to most appraisers, and would not be the same as a parcel's highest and best use value.

The appraisal process recognises the limitations that the neighbourhood context may place on sale price and land rent. The process also emphasises the importance of scale in determining land price or land rent. Bourassa uses highest and best use as an abstract concept that is in many ways similar to potential land rent. In the appraisal process, highest and best use is seen in more realistic terms where the effects of localised land uses play an important role in determining a parcel's price and its land rent. In this sense, the appraisal process implicitly recognises the importance of scale in capitalised land rent.

This new view of capitalised land rent is also compatible with other aspects of the rent gap hypothesis. The compatibility is evident in two aspects of the hypothesis: the devalorisation process; and the root causes of gentrification identified in the hypothesis.

The devalorisation process outlines a general framework for understanding the neighbourhood decline that precedes gentrification. Smith identifies the process as leading to a decline in the traditional form of capitalised land rent, but the process just as easily provides a framework for understanding a decline in the alternative form of capitalised land rent I have described. Smith describes the process as working at the neighbourhood level, and this is no accident. The activities he refers to, such as the interplay between landlords and tenants, act at the neighbourhood scale. The processes may be widespread, but their influence is localised. Blockbusting, for example, has numerous repercussions, but it is unlikely significantly to affect property values outside the immediate area. The term itself refers to this localised effect. I do not suggest that the causes of devalorisation lie at the neighbourhood level, but that the process works itself out at that scale. Thus, the devalorisation process is compatible with a capitalised rent that is also determined at the neighbourhood level.

The root causes of gentrification, according to the rent gap hypothesis, are in the movement of capital to and within the domain of property investment (the second circuit). There is not room here to delve into the intricacies of capital circuits, but I will make one point. One of the more basic aspects of the rent gap hypothesis is the idea that gentrification is an inevitable result of the manner in which value is created and extracted in a capitalist land market. Key in this process is the dialectic between investment on the urban fringe and in the inner city. Capital's flight to the suburbs moves the devalorisation process forward, eventually creates the rent gap, and creates the potential for gentrification.

While this dialectic links distant neighbourhoods, there is nothing contradictory between capital circuits and the concept of a scale-based capitalised land rent. Capitalised land rent is determined by a set of neighbourhood-based factors that are in part a result of movement of capital and that also act to direct those movements.

CONCLUSION

Capitalised land rent determined at the neighbourhood scale provides an alternative manner of understanding the rent gap hypothesis without essentially altering most aspects of the hypothesis. It helps to resolve the issue of the effect of land use on land rent that is a serious point of contention in the arguments between Bourassa and Clark. It also appears to be consistent with traditional theories of land rent and newer ideas being developed to link the rent gap hypothesis to other land rent theory (Clark, 1996). Most importantly, however, it makes explicit the effect of scale on gentrification, and on our theories attempting to explain gentrification. To understand certain aspects of the gentrification process, any analysis must consider at least the two scales identified here—the metropolitan and the neighbourhood. There may be other important scales to consider. In fact, Smith's work on uneven development suggests that gentrification needs to be viewed in part at the global scale to be fully understood. I suggest, though, that analysis at the metropolitan and neighbourhood scales provides the minimum perspective necessary for understanding the foundations of the rent gap hypothesis.

Just as the issue of scale is implicit in the rent gap, it is also implicit to much gentrification research. Early models of the gentrification process describe the need for a critical mass of gentrifiers in a neighbourhood before the process can proceed 'successfully' (Gale, 1979). This need for a critical mass can be seen as a need for a gentrifying area to overcome the obstacles to gentrification at the neighbourhood scale, and bring land rent in the neighbourhood to the levels suggested by its location at the metropolitan scale. In addition, much of Clark's analysis of gentrification in Malmö refers to at least two scales at which land rents are determined. The method he used to operationalise potential land rent was based on metropolitan-scale factors, while the sources of capitalised land rent were more localised.

Scale is not new to gentrification research, and it played an implicit role in the development of the rent gap hypothesis. Thus, this new form of capitalised land rent forces us to view the determinants of land rent at these different scales and provides a firmer theoretical basis for the existence of two possibly divergent land rents in any parcel of urban land.

The rent gap remains a controversial explanation of gentrification, and this alteration in capitalised land rent may have no effect on the debates concerning the importance of the rent gap as an explanation of gentrification. It should, however, establish that the rent gap hypothesis is theoretically consistent with land rent theory, and can be evaluated on its ability to help us to understand gentrification—not on internal inconsistencies and theoretically confused foundations for its basic components.

Note

1 Clark's work in Malmö represents an example of the use of high-quality tax assessment data in an empirical investigation of the rent gap. Such data are rare, and even when they exist the investigator must take great pains to adjust or modify the data in some form to ensure that they are reliable. Clark's discussion of the data in Malmö provides an indication of the difficulty presented by tax assessments, but also of their potential as a source of data.

REFERENCES

AIREA (AMERICAN INSTITUTE OF REAL ESTATE APPRAISERS) (1987) *The Appraisal of Real Estate*, 9th edn. Chicago: National Association of Realtors.

BADCOCK, B. (1989) An Australian view of the rent gap hypothesis, *Annals of the Association of American Geographers*, 79, pp. 125–145.

BADCOCK, B. (1990) On the nonexistence of the rent gap hypothesis, *Annals of the Association of American Geographers*, 80, pp. 459–461.

BARLOWE, R. (1978) *Land Resource Economics*, 3rd edn. Englewood Cliffs, NJ: Prentice-Hall.

BARLOWE, R. (1986) *Land Resource Economics*, 4th edn. Englewood Cliffs, NJ: Prentice-Hall.

BENTICK, B. L. (1982) A tax on land value may not be neutral, *National Tax Journal*, 35, p. 113.

BERRY, B. J. L., TENNANT, R. J., GARNER, B. J. and SIMMONS, J. W. (1963) *Commercial structure and commercial blight*. Research Paper No. 85, Department of Geography, University of Chicago, Illinois.

BOURASSA, S. C. (1990) On 'An Australian view of the rent gap hypothesis' by Badcock, *Annals of the Association of American Geographers*, 80, pp. 458–459.

BOURASSA, S. C. (1992) *The Rent Gap Debunked.* Urban Research Program Working Paper 32, Australian National University, Canberra.

BOURASSA, S. C. (1993) The rent gap debunked, *Urban Studies*, 30, pp. 1731–1744.

CLARK, E. (1987) *The Rent Gap and Urban Change: Case Studies in Malmö 1860–1985.* Lund: Lund University Press.

CLARK, E. (1988) The rent gap and transformation of the built environment: case studies in Malmö 1860–1985, *Geografiska Annaler B*, 70, pp. 241–254.

CLARK, E. (1995) The rent gap re-examined, *Urban Studies*, 32, pp. 1489–1503.

CLARK, E. (1996) *Differential rents and rent gaps.* Paper presented at the *Association of American Geographers 92nd Annual Meeting*, 9–13 April, Charlotte, NC.

DOLAN, E. G. (1980) *Basic Economics*, 2nd edn. Hinsdale, IL: Dryden Press.

DOLAN, E. G. (1983) *Basic Economics*, 3rd edn. Chicago: Dryden Press.

EDEL, M. and SCLAR, E. (1975) The distribution of real estate value changes: metropolitan Boston, 1870–1970, *Journal of Urban Economics*, 2, pp. 336–387.

ENGELS, F. (1955) *The Housing Question.* Moscow: Foreign Languages Publishing House.

GALE, D. E. (1979) Middle class resettlement in older urban neighborhoods, *Journal of the American Planning Association*, 45, pp. 293–304.

HOYT, H. (1933) *One Hundred Years of Land Values in Chicago.* Chicago: University of Chicago Press.

KARY, K. J. (1988) The gentrification of Toronto and the rent gap theory, in: T. E. Bunting and P. Filion (Eds) *The Changing Canadian Inner City*, pp. 53–72. Department of Geography Publication Series No. 31, University of Waterloo, Ontario.

KNOS, D. S. (1962) *Distribution of Land Values in Topeka, Kansas.* Lawrence: The University of Kansas Press.

LUCENO, S. F. (1990) Highest and best use: its role in the real estate appraisal process, *ASA Valuation*, 35, pp. 122–128.

MARSHALL, A. (1936) *Principles of Economics*, 8th edn. London: Macmillan.

MILLS, D. E. (1981) The non-neutrality of land taxation, *National Tax Journal*, 34, pp. 125–130.

MILLS, D. E. (1982) Reply to Tideman, *National Tax Journal*, 35, p. 115.

SEYFRIED, W. R. (1963) The centrality of urban land values, *Land Economics*, 39, pp. 275–285.

SMITH, N. (1979) Towards a theory of gentrification, *Journal of the American Planning Association*, 45, pp. 538–549.

SMITH, N. (1982) Gentrification and uneven development, *Economic Geography*, 58, pp. 139–155.

SMITH, N. (1984) *Uneven Development.* Oxford: Basil Blackwell.

SMITH, N. (1996) Of rent gaps and radical idealism: a reply to Steven Bourassa, *Urban Studies*, 33, pp. 1199–1203.

SMITH, N. and DENNIS, W. (1987) The restructuring of geographical scale: coalescence and fragmentation of the northern core region. *Economic Geography*, 63, pp. 160–182.

STARK, R. (1988) A hidden treasure map: highest and best use analysis, *ASA Valuation*, 33, pp. 24–29.

TIDEMAN, T. N. (1982) A tax on land value is neutral, *National Tax Journal*, 35, pp. 109–111.

WILDASIN, D. E. (1982) More on the neutrality of land taxation, *National Tax Journal*, 35, pp. 105–107.

YEATES, M. (1965) Some factors affecting the spatial distribution of Chicago land values, *Economic Geography*, 41, pp. 55–70.

Plate 10 'A yuppie cull', Bristol. Photograph by Tom Slater.

INTRODUCTION TO SECTION B

The photograph that begins this section was taken at the construction site of an upmarket housing development in the predominantly working-class neighbourhood of Redfield in east Bristol, England. 'Yuppie', a derogatory term denoting young urban (or upwardly mobile) professional, has proven to be a remarkably adhesive anti-gentrification image, used to vilify unwelcome new arrivals in neighbourhoods whose spending power and lifestyle practices threaten community bonds, the longevity of affordable housing, and valued local amenities. It is tempting for critics of gentrification to rejoice in the appearance of graffiti like that captured in the photo from Bristol. But at least one astute commentator on urban affairs has issued a stark warning about 'yuppie' discourse:

> To attribute gentrification solely to yuppies is to eliminate quite complex processes and to shift the burden of the negative consequences of gentrification away from factions of capital (for example, developers) who often are responsible. Such a focus robs analysis of its structural and political perspective.
>
> (Beauregard, 1990, pp. 856–7)

'Start a yuppie cull', then, however graphic and striking, is not a very sensitive analysis of gentrification. In cities such as Bristol (which has significant housing affordability problems) even young upwardly mobile professionals have limited choices in the housing market. As we shall see in Part 7, a more concerted, politically sensible and effective strategy is required than simplistic slanders of yuppies if something is to be done about gentrification.

In the previous section we introduced Neil Smith's rent-gap thesis, the most influential 'production-side' explanation for gentrification, together with some of the debate that it generated. Of all the critiques of Smith's work over the years, probably the most tenacious has been his lack of attention to the role of human agency in the process; specifically, the absence of middle-class gentrifiers from his analysis. In Smith's defence, the rent gap was never intended to be an explanation that focused on the formation and practices of gentrifiers (either as a social group or as individuals). For important political reasons, Smith directed his attention towards the powerful role of the state and of the capitalist economy in shaping the fortunes of urban neighbourhoods. In addition, Smith (1996) was acutely aware of the problems of reducing middle-class gentrifiers to 'yuppies':

> the difficulty in identifying this new middle class, especially in economic terms, should give us pause before we glibly associate yuppies and gentrification.
>
> (1996, p. 104)

Yet as recently as 2007 these arguments over structure versus agency were still being voiced:

> [L]ocal cultures clearly have a continued agency in shaping the gentrification process to an extent far greater than is recognised by those who paint a picture of gentrification as broadly and blandly a process of global urban neocolonialism performed by upper professional groups ... By denying agency to the actors involved, 'supply siders' in the gentrification debate (Smith, 1979) have long laid themselves open to charges of overdetermination (Hamnett, 1991) and continue to do so.
>
> (Butler, 2007: 178)

For Butler, production-side explanations fail to take into account crucial questions of class constitution that are central to explaining gentrification, such as 'Who are the gentrifiers?', 'Where do they come from?', and 'What draws them to live in central city neighbourhoods?' Whether or not one agrees with Butler's insistence on human agency or Smith's sidelining of it, no Reader on gentrification can be complete without introducing some key consumption-side analyses that have explained gentrification as a consequence of changes in the industrial and occupational structure of advanced capitalist cities. For writers like Chris Hamnett (2003), gentrification is quite simply a product of the transformation of Western cities from manufacturing centres to centres of business services and the creative and cultural industries, where associated changes to the occupational and income structure produce a rapidly expanding middle class that has replaced the industrial working class in desirable central city areas. In sum:

> Not surprisingly in a market economy, the increase in the size and purchasing power of the middle classes has been accompanied by an intensification of demand pressure in the housing market. This has been particularly marked in inner London as it is here that many of the new middle class work, and this, combined with a desire to minimise commuting time, and greater ability to afford the cultural and social attractions of life in the central and inner city, has been associated with the growth of gentrification.
>
> (Hamnett 2003, p. 2424)

In advanced capitalist cities across the world, these changes, occurring as they did at a time of significant social and cultural upheaval (post-1968), were coupled with a middle class disposition towards central city living, and an associated rejection of suburbia.

For some time now, there has been wide agreement that class should be a central focus in the study of gentrification (Hamnett, 1991; Smith, 1992; Wyly and Hammel, 1999). The overwhelming research response over the last three decades has been to find out about the growth and behaviour of the middle-classes, and particularly why they are seeking to locate in previously disinvested neighbourhoods. For many researchers, gentrification first and foremost involves people – not just cycles of investment and fluctuations of capitalised ground rent. Over the years there has been increasing theoretical sophistication in research undertaken in many different countries that seeks to understand middle class gentrifiers – a very diverse, ambivalent group that cannot be reduced to conservative, self-interested yuppies, not least because the negative connotations of that term are at odds with the 'marginal' position of some gentrifiers (Rose, 1984), and the left-liberal politics that many gentrifiers espouse (Ley, 1994). If one thing above all was clear from the 1970s debates over a 'back to the city' movement across North America (see preface in Lees, Slater and Wyly, 2008), it was that more sophisticated theoretical treatments of the production of gentrifiers were needed if the consumption aspects of gentrification were to have explanatory merit. In this section we have selected four essays, three from urban Canada, one from urban Australia, that in our view best capture the analytic registers employed by those associated with consumption-side explanations.

Since the mid-1970s, David Ley has sought to understand gentrification in the context of the emergence of the *post-industrial city*, in a project that is particularly concerned with the cultural politics of gentrification, but not at the expense of economic change in Canadian cities (the myth that Ley somehow represents the 'culture and consumption' school is shattered by a reading of his 1996 book *The New Middle Class and the Remaking of the Central City*, where the first four chapters are dedicated to observing macro-economic shifts affecting urban Canada and its housing and labour markets). Guided by Daniel Bell's (1973) thesis on the rise of a post-industrial society, Ley set out to research the expansion of new middle class professionals in urban Canada with an apparent disposition 'to enhance the quality of life in pursuits that are not simply economistic' (1996, p. 15). His analysis focused not only on a changing occupational structure brought about by the transition from Fordism to post-Fordism; it also placed this transition within major societal upheavals that had created a middle class 'imagineering of an alternative urbanism to suburbanization' (p. 15) which could not be captured by explanations of gentrification that focused exclusively on the structural forces of production and housing market dynamics. The hallmark of Ley's career has been to foreground questions of human agency in geographical inquiry; his work on gentrification is no exception (see Box 4).

In the 1970s, many centrally-located neighbourhoods in urban Canada saw their social and economic status elevate as cities became arenas for post-1968 counter-cultural awareness, tolerance, diversity and liberation. In the 1970s, neighbourhoods such as Yorkville and The Annex in Toronto, Kitsilano and Fairview Slopes in Vancouver, and Le Plateau Mont-Royal in Montréal became hotbeds of 'hippie' youth reaction against political conservatism, modernist planning and suburban ideologies. But what were the politics of these youth once they grew up and became gentrifers? Or in Ley's terms, what happens to voting behaviour when 'hippies become yuppies'? In the article we have selected, Ley is clearly troubled by generalisations emanating from the United States about a conservative 'adversarial politics' among middle class gentrifiers. To counter this, he provided evidence from 1980s electoral returns in the three largest Canadian cities (Toronto, Montreal and Vancouver), showing that the gentrifying districts in each city in fact contained an electorate which predominantly sided with more left-liberal reform politics (prioritising a more 'open' government concerned with neighbourhood rights, minority rights, improved public services, and greater attention to heritage, environment, public open space, and cultural and leisure facilities). In all three cities under scrutiny there was 'no significant tendency overall for social upgrading in the city centre to be associated with [adversarial] conservative politics' (p. 70). Ley argues that the values of the counter-cultural youth movements of the late 1960s had diffused among the professional middle class, and these are *not* the self-interested 'yuppie' conservative values commonly attributed to gentrifiers. For Ley, collective new middle class disdain for the monotony of suburbia, for the mass organisation and repetition of post-war Fordism, and for corporate society and hierarchical authority could not be divorced from the explanation of gentrification in general, and the politics of gentrifiers in particular.

Keeping the focus on urban Canada, Jon Caulfield's article here is based on his influential research on 1970s and 1980s gentrification in Toronto. Caulfield argues that middle-class resettlement in central city neighbourhoods is first and foremost the spatial outcome of a collective rejection of the oppressive conformity of suburbia, and the city's post-war modernist development. Toronto's gentrification is portrayed favourably as a deliberate operation of middle class resistance, a practice 'eluding the domination of social and cultural structures and constituting new conditions for experience' (p. 624). In his interviews with Toronto's gentrifiers across the city, Caulfield observed that their affection for 'old city neighbourhoods' was rooted in their desire (hence the title of his piece reprinted here) to escape the mundane, banal routines that characterised suburbia:

> Old city places offer difference and freedom, privacy and fantasy, possibilities for carnival .... These are not just matters of philosophical abstraction but, in a carnival sense, ... the force that [Walter] Benjamin believed was among the most vital stimuli to resistance to domination. 'A big city is an encyclopaedia of sexual possibility,' a characterization to be grasped in its wider sense; the city is 'the place of our meeting with the other'.
>
> (p. 625)

In 1982, Peter Williams argued that the middle class might appropriately be called 'space invaders' (p. 51). Considered together, the work of both Caulfield and Ley challenges the negative connotations of this terminology. Both authors would argue very strongly that demonising gentrifiers for the negative effects of gentrification is unwarranted, 'a misplaced charge' in Ley's (2003) words. But we recognise context here and add the caveat that care must be taken not to think that all gentrifiers everywhere are tolerant liberals.

In his book-length treatment of gentrification, Ley (1996) explained how Canada's gentrifiers viewed the central city as 'a mark of distinction in the constitution of an identity separate from the constellation of place and identity shaped by the suburbs' (p. 211). But how is this social distinction marked out on the streets of gentrifying neighbourhoods? Crucially, what aesthetic strategies do gentrifiers (and those who produce space for them) employ to distinguish themselves from other social class groups? This has become known as 'the gentrification aesthetic', and as Michael Jager (1986) has pointed out, 'the aesthetics of gentrification not only illustrate the class dimension of the process but also express the dynamic constitution of social class of which gentrification is a specific part.' (p. 78) Jager's heavily cited essay was very original when it first appeared in 1986 – his focus was on the architectural and internal decorative aesthetics of gentrified Victorian buildings and neighbourboods in Melbourne. Jager argued that gentrifiers were 'buying into history', and by doing so were expressing their social distance not just from the working class ('symbolically obliterated') but the old middle-class (uninterested in historic preservation as status symbol and self-expression). Jager explained that urban conservation was a deliberate process of new middle class demarcation and distinction – yet one that, in time, led to what he called a 'gentrification kitsch', where imitation took precedence over authenticity in the necessity to compensate for market consumption and produce profit from a repackaged past. His essay remains a major reference point for recent and ongoing investigations into the gentrification aesthetic (see, for instance, Bridge 2001).

The final selection in this section is by Caroline Mills (one of David Ley's graduate students in Vancouver; the paper here was drawn from her Ph.D. thesis). Mills was concerned with interpreting the 'postmodern' gentrification aesthetic in Fairview Slopes, Vancouver (an eclectic mix of architectural styles, with historical and contemporary references and themes). Mills directed her attention towards the ways in which developers, architects and marketing agents were responsible for creating a new landscape of gentrification in Fairview Slopes, one that captured middle class tastes and values (following the City Council's 1970s rezoning of the neighbourhood as a medium density residential and commercial neighbourhood). As we outline in Lees, Slater and Wyly (2008: 141–144) Mills drew on the work of anthropologist Clifford Geertz (1973) to analyse the 'textual landscape' of gentrification in Fairview Slopes, looking at cultural 'texts' such as advertising, planning and architectural design, and details about the everyday lives of residents (drawn from interviews with them, as part of an intensive ethnography of the neighbourhood). She scrutinised the marketing of a gentrifier lifestyle, from 'Open House' displays of rooms to advertising brochures, teasing out a lifestyle language that attempted to sell the liveability and excitement of a central city neighbourhood. By interviewing both producers and consumers of this gentrified landscape, Mills was able to offer an interesting cultural twist on the Marxist economic concept of use-value:

> For an investment to be a good one, the commodity must sell; for it to sell, it must have use-value; and that use-value must be 'imaginable' – it must have cultural meaning.

(p. 180)

Mills' fine-grained case-study helps us to grasp the economic valorisation of the gentrification aesthetic. One of the most commonly noted trends in the process of gentrification is that places and people once deemed hip, authentic, trendy and subversive quickly become appropriated, manufactured and mass-produced kitsch for higher-earning groups. Culture and economics, consumption and production need to be considered together to offer insights on this and many other trends in gentrification – a theoretical fusion to which we turn in the next section.

REFERENCES AND FURTHER READING

Beauregard, R.A. (1990) 'Trajectories of neighbourhood change: the case of gentrification', *Environment and Planning A* 22: 855–874.

Bell, D. (1973) *The Coming of the Postindustrial Society*. New York: Basic Books.

Bowler, A. and McBurney, B. (1991) 'Gentrification and the avant-garde in New York's East Village: the good, the bad and the ugly', *Theory, Culture and Society* 8: 49–77.

Bridge, G. (2001) 'Estate agents as interpreters of economic and cultural capital: the gentrification premium in the Sydney housing market', *International Journal of Urban and Regional Research* 25: 87–101.

Bridge, G. (1995) 'The space for class? On class analysis in the study of gentrification', *Transactions of the Institute of British Geographers* 20(2): 236–247.

Bridge, G. (1994) 'Gentrification, class and residence: a reappraisal', *Environment and Planning D: Society and Space* 12: 31–51.

Butler, T. (2007) 'For gentrification?', *Environment and Planning A* 39(1): 162–181.

Butler, T. (1997) *Gentrification and the Middle Classes*. Aldershot: Ashgate.

Butler, T. and Hamnett, C. (1994) 'Gentrification, class and gender: some comments on Warde's gentrification as consumption', *Environment and Planning D: Society and Space* 12: 477–493.

Butler, T. with Robson, G. (2003) *London Calling: The Middle Classes and the Re-making of Inner London*. Oxford: Berg.

Caulfield, J. (1994) *City Form and Everyday Life: Toronto's Gentrification and Critical Social Practice*. Toronto: University of Toronto Press.

Deutsche, R. and Ryan, C. (1984) 'The fine art of gentrification', *October* 31: 91–111.

Hamnett, C. (2003b) 'Gentrification and the middle-class remaking of inner London, 1961–2001', *Urban Studies* 40(12): 2401–2426.

Hamnett, C. (1991) 'The blind men and the elephant: the explanation of gentrification', *Transactions of the Institute of British Geographers* 16(2): 173–189.

Ley, D. (1986) 'Alternative explanations for inner-city gentrification: a Canadian assessment', *Annals of the Association of American Geographers* 76(4): 521–535.

Ley, D. (1994) 'Gentrification and the politics of the new middle class', *Environment and Planning D: Society and Space* 12: 53–74.

Ley, D. (1996) *The New Middle Class and the Remaking of the Central City*. Oxford: Oxford University Press.

Podmore, J. (1998) '(Re)reading the 'loft living' habitus in Montreal's inner city', *International Journal of Urban and Regional Research* 22: 283–302.

Rose, D. (1984) 'Rethinking gentrification: beyond the uneven development of Marxist urban theory', *Environment and Planning D: Society and Space* 1: 47–74.

Short, J. R. (1989) 'Yuppies, yuffies and the new urban order', *Transactions of the Institute of British Geographers* 14(2): 173–188.

Smith, N. (1996) *The New Urban Frontier: Gentrification and the Revanchist City*. London and New York: Routledge.

Smith, N. (1992) 'Blind man's bluff, or Hamnett's philosophical individualism in search of gentrification?', *Transactions of the Institute of British Geographers* 17(1): 110–115.

Wang, J. and Lau, S. (2008) 'Gentrification and Shanghai's new middle class: another reflection on the cultural consumption thesis', *Cities* 26(2): 57–66.

Warde, A. (1991) 'Gentrification as consumption: issues of class and gender', *Environment and Planning D: Society and Space* 9: 223–232.

Wyly, E. and Hammel, D. (1999) 'Islands of decay in seas of renewal: housing policy and the resurgence of gentrification', *Housing Policy Debate* 10(4): 711–771.

13

"Gentrification and the Politics of the New Middle Class"

From *Environment and Planning D: Society and Space* (1994)

David Ley

INTRODUCTION

Gouldner begins his short but seminal book, *The Future of Intellectuals and the Rise of the New Class* (1979), with an observation from that most percipient of politicians, Otto von Bismarck:

> Discontent among the lower classes may produce a serious illness for which we have remedies, but discontent among the educated minority leads to a chronic disease whose diagnosis is difficult and cure protracted.
>
> (page vi)

In Bismarck's allusion to the educated minority, contemporary readers might see a prophetic reference to the new middle class of professional and managerial workers who have been the subject of such close attention by social and political theorists over the past twenty years. But if Bismarck poses a provocative thesis, he offers little aid in resolving the vexing questions raised by more recent and disinterested observers in pursuit of this most elusive of social categories. Who are the new class? How may they be specified? Other than in the most formal statistical sense, are they a class at all? If so, do they have a coherent politics? And if this condition is met, is that politics inherently, or even potentially, critical, as Bismarck apprehended it to be?

In this paper I address some of these questions by studying recent political tendencies in Canada's three largest cities. Like other authors I shall argue that little progress can be made until the new middle class is more closely specified. Such a specification

requires, of course, a distinct identity within a broader system of social stratification. But I shall suggest that the new class also has a geographical identity which is far from incidental; like other social groups the relationship between place and identity is mutually reinforcing. As we look for those members of the new class whom Bismarck might find most troubling because of their critical politics, we find them disproportionately located within large cities, and frequently associated with the resettlement by the middle class of older inner-city districts, a process which has been given the generic label of gentrification. A status as inner-city gentrifiers is far from the only geographical home of critical members of the new middle class, but sufficient numbers have gathered in certain inner cities to have created a distinctive political culture not only in their neighbourhoods of residence but also within a larger municipal realm. By viewing urban politics in Toronto, Vancouver, and Montreal over the past twenty-five years I shall examine the varying relations between the new middle class in the inner city and reform politics, in particular their endorsement of liberal and social democratic policies and candidates.

WHO AND WHERE IS THE ADVERSARIAL NEW CLASS?

Bismarck was not alone in identifying the strategic presence of the 'educated minority' in 19th-century Europe. Intimations of the presence of the professional and managerial cohorts are evident from the classical social theorists (Giddens, 1973). Marx's ruminations on the emergence of joint-stock companies as implying "the irrelevance of the capitalist", whose role now bifurcates into the separate categories of shareholder and manager, presages the development of the modern corporation with its cadre of professional managers. More directly, in the unfinished fragment offering a definition of class at the end of the third volume of *Capital*, there is a clear recognition of a middle-class 'other', resident in the English city:

> the stratification of classes does not appear in its pure form. Middle and intermediate strata even here obliterate lines of demarcation everywhere (although incomparably less in rural districts than in the cities).
>
> (1967, page 885)

Writing later and from a different theoretical as well as historical perspective, Weber set out a scheme of four social classes, including an expanding middle class of propertyless white-collar workers (including civil servants), and a privileged class enjoying access to property and education. With his particular focus on the state, Weber anticipated the growth of public bureaucracies and their attendant managers and functionaries.

Over the past twenty years the literature on the new middle class has expanded rapidly, in phase with the multiplication of the group itself. Bell's influential prospectus on postindustrial society identified "the centrality of theoretical knowledge" as its "axial institution" (1973, page 115). Equally central, therefore, was the expansion of the groups who transmitted theoretical knowledge, in professional, managerial, and technical positions. Published the same year that the postwar boom ended, Bell's prognosis was regarded as far too sanguine by critics. Authors such as Braverman (1974) and Wright and Singelmann (1982) argued instead for a shrinking growth of senior white-collar workers and proletarianisation of the work force. However accurate other aspects of Bell's wide-ranging conclusions may be,[1] there is now considerable agreement that his labour-force projections have proven at least half right. Reviewing US employment trends in the 1970s, Wright and Martin (1987) have noted that earlier expectations have not been met, that proletarianisation did not occur, and that managerial and professional expansion continued. By way of example, in her recent examination of New York City's changing labour market, Sassen (1991) has noted that the number of senior white-collar jobs has undoubtedly increased substantially over the past twenty years, accounting for some 40% of new positions in the strategic financial and business service sectors. However, simultaneously a large number of poorly paid jobs in the service sector have also been created with a diminution of unionised middle-income positions—a development which Bell did not elaborate.

A similar assessment has been made in Canada (Myles, 1988). Although there exists a dual labour market of skilled and unskilled jobs, over the 1961–81 period, aggregate data and survey results show "skilled jobs expanded at an accelerating rate", while a "significant part of this upgrading was a result of growth in new middle class professional and managerial occupations", with "no evidence that this occurred at the expense of (i.e. by deskilling) the working class" (Myles, 1988, page 337). Employment data indicate a sharpening of these trends through the 1980s. As a result of this cumulative growth, and in accord with Bell's prediction, professional, managerial, and technical occupations[2] contained 17% of jobs in Canada in 1961, but 30% in 1991. As we shall see shortly, in examining the *geography* of job shifts these trends are sharpened even further.

But numbers a class do not make. A few authors (for example, Ehrenreich and Ehrenreich, 1979) have sought to insert 'the professional–managerial class' as a unit into an historic class structure. But more authors have been impressed by the internal heterogeneity of the sector. Gouldner (1979) made a distinction between humanistic intellectuals and technical intelligentsia, and Lash and Urry (1987) between public and private sector members, a view shared in an empirical study by McAdams (1987) who found that the issue of state economic intervention threw a fundamental divide between professionals and private sector managers. Bell (1980) posited a far more complex set of cleavages, with divergent sets of cross-cutting economic, political, and cultural interests creating a mishmash of social groupings, making any appeal to a unitary new class empirically and theoretically untenable.

This fragmentation is abundantly evident in electoral behaviour. The notion of a 'service class' of professional and managerial workers in Britain is belied by contradictory political allegiances (Savage et al, 1988). Its members voted 54% in support of the Conservative Party in the 1983 General Election in Britain, 30% for the Liberal–Social Democratic Party Alliance, and 14% for the Labour Party (Thrift, 1987). The same spread exists in Canada where a poll in 1988 showed that 58% of highly paid Canadians (a rough approximation of the well-endowed service class) endorsed the Conservative Party, with 18% backing the Liberal Party, and 21% the New Democratic Party (NDP). US data similarly indicate a generally conservative (Republican) set of political loyalties to be held by the professional and managerial cadre (Brint, 1984). To this extent, it is puzzling to note the adversarial politics ascribed to the new middle class by a number of theorists (for example, Ehrenreich and Ehrenreich, 1979; Gouldner, 1979; Touraine, 1971), a view represented by Gouldner's remark that for a progressive politics, the new class "is a center for whatever human emancipation is possible in the foreseeable future" (1979, page 83), indeed, perhaps "the best card that history has presently given us to play" (page 7).

The basis of this optimism rests with the significant minority of the new class who do not support Conservative candidates, some 40% in the British and Canadian electoral data mentioned above. Where in the new class is this source of adversarial politics? Perhaps the most complete empirical answer to this question is Brint's (1984) detailed analysis of US survey data collected annually between 1974 and 1980. Brint begins by noting widely varying boundaries established by four key theorists demarcating the new class; at its most expansive, the definition of Ehrenreich and Ehrenreich (1977) incorporates the full gamut of professional, technical, and managerial specialities, whereas at its most restrictive, Kristol (1972) includes only tertiary-educated professionals in the arts, media, teaching, and academic positions as well as public sector managers in regulatory and welfare activities—a subgroup I shall identify as *the cultural new class*. Brint made two important discoveries in terms of the present argument. First, political distancing from business leaders was more restrained than expected among all four specifications of the new class. Second, the grouping which most consistently displayed dissent from business values was Kristol's cultural new class. It was, for example, the most highly committed to racial integration and government spending on social programmes, and the least oriented to high personal job incomes.

More detailed multivariate analysis teased out these relationships further by decomposing the new class sample into a more conventional set of socioeconomic attributes. As an entity the new class sample was *more* conservative than the employed population as a whole. When disaggregated, the most liberal cohort was consistently "social and cultural specialists", including academics, other social scientists, arts and culture professionals, architects, clergy, and doctors, and those lawyers and other professionals outside the private sector. Almost as important a predictor of liberal values was youthfulness, an age of under 35 years. Among the lesser factors, employment in the public sector exercised

some effect (notably in terms of antibusiness attitudes) and higher education was associated with liberal politics and support for social programmes. Interestingly, income showed weak and inconsistent associations with liberal values.

Brint's analysis is valuable in identifying a social location for adversarial politics in the cultural new class, and his findings are consistent with other US survey research of the 1970s (Ladd, 1979; Lipset, 1979). Moreover, more focused studies of specific social movements show the indisputable preeminence of cultural and social professionals in the peace movement (Parkin, 1968), in radical environmentalism (Betz, 1992; Cotgrove and Duff, 1980; Kriesi, 1988), and in cultural nationalism (Smith, 1982). Relevant to the empirical study which follows is the role of professionals involved in "the production of and/or dissemination of 'culture'" in Quebec nationalism, "providing the highest support for the Parti Québecois, for sovereignty-association, and for independence of any group in the society" (Hamilton and Pinard, 1982, page 223). Most remarkable has been the central part recently played by the cultural new class in the democratic and nationalist movements in Eastern Europe. In the former USSR, for example, "the role of 'motor' in the movements and the activities was invariably played by the intelligentsia", notably academics and artists; indeed "the progressive supporters of *perestroika* are setting their hopes on the intelligentsia" (Drobizheva, 1991, page 98).

The positioning of the new middle class has a *geographical* as well as a sociological dimension. Professional and managerial positions fall into the advanced services, and the advanced services as a group are highly urbanised (Daniels, 1991). The magnet of the metropolitan area has since 1971 been compelling for new-class job growth. In six Canadian metropolitan areas (Toronto, Montreal, Vancouver, Ottawa, Edmonton, and Halifax), jobs in management, administration, the professions, and technical fields, the so-called quaternary or advanced service sector, accounted for 46.5% of net employment growth between 1971 and 1981 (Ley, 1988). During the period 1981–86, when deindustrialisation was compounded by a deep recession, the addition of over 300 000 new quaternary positions in these same six metropolitan areas amounted to 59.3% of the net job gain, and, according to provisional data, an astonishing 99.5% of net labour-force growth from 1986 to 1991. This preponderance becomes even more remarkable if one discounts suburban contributions. With job shedding in other sectors, in the period 1976–88 the growth in the number of quaternary workers living in the City of Toronto accounted for 135% of the net gain in the resident work force and by 1988 they constituted 40% of that work force (PDD, 1990). This astonishing pace of embourgeoisement in the central cities gives a dramatic geographical form to the expansion of new-middle-class jobs reported by Myles (1988).

Moving up a further step in spatial resolution, the inner cities of the six census metropolitan areas (CMAs) reveal the processes of change in exaggerated form. In the 1971–86 period, collectively, the inner-city neighbourhoods gained 115 000 residents with professional and managerial positions, but lost through net out-migration 212 000 workers employed in other occupational categories (Ley, 1992). By 1981 there was an overconcentration of quaternary level employees living in the six inner cities relative to their metropolitan areas, and by 1986 this tendency had extended further.

This movement to the central city has often been led in space and time by the cultural new class, not only the most urbanised of the new class fractions in Canada, but also the most predisposed toward a home in the *central* city. Indeed, urban living provides an important ingredient of its identity formation (Caulfield, 1990; Mills, 1993). Among the six Canadian metropolitan areas mentioned earlier, the categories of artists, social scientists, and related occupations are consistently the most concentrated of occupational categories in central city neighbourhoods and equally underrepresented in the suburbs. The literature on gentrification has made frequent reference to stages in the cycle of middle-class settlement, which is initiated by the arrival of cultural professionals in the arts, media, teaching, and related professions (DeGiovanni, 1983). This trend has been repeatedly demonstrated in Canadian cities. In Montreal, neighbourhoods undergoing social upgrading in the 1970s such as Lower Outrement and the southern reaches of Plateau Mont-Royal contained two to three times their metropolitan share of professionals in the arts and social sciences in 1981 (Dansereau and Beaudry, 1985). In Vancouver, Kitsilano, site of the founding office of the Greenpeace Foundation (Ley, 1981), and Fairview Slopes (Mills, 1988), neighbourhoods with the highest proportion of artists and writers in the city in 1971, experienced the sharpest rates of gentrification over the subsequent fifteen years.[3] Last, a survey of residents in newly gentrifying parts of inner Toronto showed their occupations fell into two major groups, professionals in public sector social services and such cultural professions as the arts, media, and teaching (Caulfield, 1990). A number of those interviewed maintained

links with avant-garde arts circles and leftist political organisations.

Here the argument converges with an unexplored geographical dimension in Brint's US database. In an appendix he partitions the whole work force surveyed between 1974 and 1980 into six political categories, including "new politics liberals", those who share the adversarial attitudes of the cultural new class. The geography of each category is summarily tabulated by region and urban–rural status. New politics liberals revealed a strong bias towards big cities, heavily concentrated in the central cities of the twelve largest metropolitan areas; with less than 10% of the entire sample, these locations included almost one quarter of this political grouping. It is pertinent to add here that the incidence of gentrification across the US urban system shows precisely the same bias toward big cities (Black, 1980). In the next section I shall turn to a more focused examination of relations between the cultural new class, gentrification, and reform politics in urban Canada.

GENTRIFICATION AND REFORM POLITICS

We can now succinctly summarise the argument and prepare the way for the empirical study. The new middle class has experienced remarkable growth in recent decades, and its uneven geographical distribution is rapidly restructuring the employment profile of many metropolitan areas. At the same time a minority of the new class (some 15%–20% of new recruits in the six Canadian cities in the early 1980s) were selecting an inner-city residence, and contributing to the gentrification of those districts. This cohort included a significant representation of the cultural new class, a fraction which is the most expressive of liberal and social democratic political ideology. To what extent, then, can we expect to discern a relationship between gentrification and left-liberal political movements?

There are few instances in the literature where this question has been addressed directly, though several neighbourhood studies have given the impression that inner-city gentrifiers endorse reform politics. Neighbourhoods such as Society Hill or Fairmount in Philadelphia, the Mission district in San Francisco (Castells, 1983) and inner-city precincts of young urban professionals in New Orleans, and Atlanta (O'Loughlin, 1980) are more likely to support Democratic and racial minority candidates. Circumstantial evidence may be adduced from the recent successes of progressive political platforms in Boston, San Francisco, and Seattle (Clay, 1991;

DeLeon, 1991; Gordon et al, 1991)—each of these cities characterised by a service-based economy and by substantial gentrification in their central neighbourhoods over the past twenty years. Significantly, it is precisely these three cities that are independently selected by Stone as examples of the relatively rare class of progressive big-city regimes, a regime associated with "middle-class activists unattached to corporate business" (Stone et al, 1991, page 231). In Australia, gentrifying districts in Melbourne and Sydney are commonly represented by professionals who run as independents with a heritage and environmental platform, or else have entered local leadership of the Australian Labor Party (Logan, 1985; Mullins, 1982). The same process has been observed in parts of gentrifying north London, England, where middle-class newcomers have entered Labour Party politics in several boroughs. In a short review, however, Hamnett (1990) introduces a more complex reality, noting that as well as the spreading legacy of the "liberal Hampstead intelligentsia" in north London, recent middle-class settlement in west London and Docklands reveals Conservative sympathies. I shall return later to this dualistic politics of gentrifying districts.

CONFRONTING REGIME POLITICS: THE CONSTITUTION OF REFORM MOVEMENTS IN URBAN CANADA

The post-1945 period saw the consolidation of a well-defined political regime in each of Canada's three largest cities. The regime was most evident in Montreal where Jean Drapeau's electoral success in 1960 was the beginning of a continuous period of twenty-six years in office, following an initial term as mayor from 1954 to 1957 (Léonard and Léveillée, 1986; Sancton, 1983). Aided by huge majorities, he governed Montreal with charisma and conviction during the 1960s and 1970s. The electorate ceded authoritarian control to Drapeau as chief executive officer of a progrowth coalition that during the 1960s and 1970s fine-tuned the production of urban megaprojects and cultural spectacles, including Expo 67 and the 1976 Olympic Games. Not surprisingly, small businesses provided Drapeau with his largest cadre of city councillors; in the 1978 election, for example, half of Drapeau's Civic Party candidates were owners or managers of private companies (Léonard and Léveillée, 1986, page 49). Two years later a report of the Economic Council of Canada concluded that in urban land development, Montreal's laissez-faire 'market zoning' bore close resemblance to the nonzoned system of land-use allocation in Houston, TX (Sancton, 1983, page 71).

The ideology of unbridled growth boosterism and centralised control was shared by the post-1945 civic regimes in Toronto and Vancouver. The latter city was governed without interruption from 1937 to 1972 by the Non-Partisan Association (NPA), a free enterprise coalition which claimed to be neither partisan nor a party, but was in fact both. The typical NPA candidate was a small businessman with close links to the Vancouver Board of Trade; in 1969, as many as 73% of leaders of the NPA were owners or employees of private companies (Easton and Tennant, 1969). Indeed, Tennant (1980, pages 10–11) has well described the NPA as displaying "an abhorrence of overt partisan activity, an acceptance of civic rule by business people (with a corresponding repugnance towards socialist and working class groups), a desire for unlimited commercial and physical growth and development in the city, and no desire at all for citizen participation in civic decision-making".

In Toronto, a similar regime ideology was held by councillors in the 1960s, and, after the 1962 civic elections, a profile of the typical politician in metropolitan Toronto showed that person to be male, married with children, a homeowner, about fifty years old, an Anglican, active in business and community organisations, employed in a well-paying business or professional job, and, usually, a member of the Conservative Party (Higgins, 1977, page 259). Here, in exemplary form, was a member of the service class, but his politics were far from progressive. Limiting municipal expenditures and tax rates, and the application of good business methods, were his principal political objectives.

Against this coherent political regime, adversarial voices were raised in all three cities in the late 1960s.[4] The consequence of unfettered growth boosterism was a besieged quality of life, particularly in the inner city, where public and private redevelopment schemes threatened a wholesale reshaping of the urban landscape. Growing discontent with the policy of growth and the process of centralised control gave vent to opposition which was expressed in neighbourhood mobilisation, a flurry of publications for the popular market, and the staking out of new political spaces. Opposition emanated not only from poverty groups and ethnic minorities whose turfs were violated, but also from new groupings of middle-class professionals whose roving agenda embraced citywide as well as turf politics. Reform policies included closer management of growth and development, improved public services, notably housing and transportation, more open government with various degrees of neighbourhood empowerment, and greater attention to such amenity issues as heritage, public open space, and cultural and leisure facilities.

In Vancouver two oppositional civic parties were founded in 1968, The Electors Action Movement (TEAM), a party of young professionals with informal linkages to the federal Liberal Party, and the Committee of Progressive Electors (COPE), a left-wing association endorsed by organised labour and poverty organisations. In Toronto, the Liberals and the social democratic New Democrats developed substantial slates for the 1969 election for the first time, and in Montreal left-wing unionist and nationalist groups formed the Front d'Action Politique (FRAP) to contest the 1970 election. By 1972, reform groups had gained control in Toronto and Vancouver. Although no such breakthrough occurred in Montreal, a decisive advance was registered in 1974. The left-wing union and nationalist movement of 1970 developed a broader base with the addition of middle-class professionals engaged in the politics of consumption, including neighbourhood and environmental issues. Reconstituted as the Montreal Citizens' Movement (MCM), the group won a third of the council seats, presenting Mayor Drapeau's Civic Party with its first concerted opposition at city hall.

Thus in each city the uncontested regime politics of an established business hegemony were challenged during the 1972–74 period. With its genesis around 1968, the speed and effectiveness of this mobilisation are remarkable. No less surprising was the simultaneity of mobilisation in three cities, separated by some 2500 miles, and comprising three distinctive political cultures which cherish their independence. This timing can scarcely be accidental. It corresponds closely with the conventional dating of the onset of gentrification in Canadian cities. For example, an assessment of in-migrants to working-class Don Vale (or Cabbagetown), subsequently Toronto's most celebrated gentrified neighbourhood, showed a substantial increase in the social status of new arrivals beginning in 1968–69 at a time when there was also brisk activity in house sales (Spragge, 1983; Tsimikalis, 1983). One of these homebuyers was the lawyer and publisher James Lorimer, the most sustained critic of the growth coalition in city halls across Canada (for example, Lorimer, 1970, 1972). A few blocks away lived John Sewell, a community organiser who had aided working-class residents in nearby Trefann Court to resist urban renewal, and had carried this resistance to public development both into print (Sewell, 1972) and into municipal politics as a reform councillor in 1969, and later as mayor of Toronto between 1978 and 1980.

The profile of the reform councillors in all three cities shows some striking similarities with the caricature of the young urban professional who features so prominently in discussions of gentrification. In 1984, the NDP councillor for Toronto's Ward 7, including Don Vale, acknowledged that "Reform leadership consisted of first-wave gentrifiers. What they shared in common was a concern for neighbourhoods and the quality of life" (interview with Councillor David Reville, June 1984). Equally evident is the departure from the average Toronto politician portrayed in 1962. Reform groups showed a marked tendency toward professionals aged in their thirties and forties, in contrast to the ageing businessmen of the old guard. The average age of MCM candidates in 1974 was 35 years, and in 1986 39 years; despite an attempted new look, Civic Party candidates in 1986 were, on average, 47 years old (Léonard and Léveillée, 1986, page 47). Youthfulness was also a feature of TEAM candidates in Vancouver and reform candidates in Toronto during the 1970s.

Occupational shifts have occurred as well. In 1978 the MCM had no privately employed business person among its slate of fifty-five candidates, whereas more than half were professionals. Eight years later, professionals remained the dominant cohort, but managers and owners constituted at least one fifth of the candidates, an evolution I shall return to later. In Vancouver's twelve municipal elections from 1968 to 1990, over half of the left-liberal candidates for council were professionals, and, discounting fringe candidates, the tally rose to two thirds. An additional departure was the growing role of women in civic elections. Some 30% of Vancouver's reform candidates for Council between 1968 and 1990 were women, and a similar trend has occurred in the other cities. In Toronto, for example, half of the liberal and social democratic group elected in 1985 were women, and many identified themselves as professionals. Indeed, several of the social democratic parties aim for gender parity among their candidates.

The democratic implications of this transition in the profile of councillors should not be pressed too hard, for if former biases of age, gender, and occupation have been qualified, they have scarcely been corrected. Lower socioeconomic groups, including service workers and especially those not in the labour force (the retired, mothers without paid employment, etc) remain heavily underrepresented on election slates. Nor would the multicultural character of the three cities be evident from lists of candidates. In Vancouver, over 90% of left-liberal candidates since 1968 have European ethnic origins, and in over 60% the family names suggest British ancestry. The social biases which remain among political representatives invoke many of the distinctions which define the community of young urban professionals—and the community of gentrifiers.

Three further qualifiers need to be added lest the transition to reform parties appear too smooth and complete. First, the reform movement has been far from homogeneous, or indeed unified. Toronto's 1972 reform council was unable to sustain a common voice over many issues, with dissension and ad hoc groupings forming a recurrent pattern as Liberals, New Democrats, independents, and 'red Tories' found limited focus for a common agenda. In Vancouver, the liberal TEAM coalition was splintered and the party decimated within six years of its landslide victory, as career changes and defections to the left (to the NDP) and the right (to the NPA) resulted in an impoverished rump and eventual dissolution. The MCM in Montreal has also seen a recurrent cycle of strategic coalition building, followed by resignations and expulsions of party members who then sought to rebuild a vanished dream in a new guise, leading to electoral competition with the MCM from splinter groups of either liberal (in 1978 and 1982) or radical (in 1990) complexion. Higgins (1981, page 87) was surely correct in describing Canadian municipal politics in the 1970s (and 1980s) as including "the old guard, the progressives and the soft middle".

Second, no political party is a fixed entity, and the reshaping of political contexts makes any permanent definition of a reform agenda scarcely possible. Parties evolve in response to dominant factions and changing economic and social contexts; in electoral politics an abiding pressure is to seek the middle ground and electability. To purists, charges of heterodoxy or even heresy accompany the adjustments to elected office. Agendas untested in opposition become keenly exposed before the opportunities, but more often the constraints, of 'coming to power'. Since its election in 1986, the changes of emphasis in the MCM have received considerable scholarly attention[5] but these critics, who accurately identify a deflection of energy toward economic development, might note also the spectre of rapid economic decline in Montreal in the late 1980s and the context of strained ideological relations with senior governments in Quebec City and Ottawa who, with their own cashflow problems, are unable and sometimes unwilling to fund new social programmes in Montreal. There is no unproblematic trajectory toward the achievement of progressive goals in left-liberal politics.

Third, although the 1972–74 period was a threshold for reform politics in the three cities, it did not represent an epochal break with the past to which there could be no return. The description of hyperpluralism in contemporary urban politics (Savitch and Thomas, 1991; Yates, 1977) is surely an overstatement, but it does capture something of the messiness of the ebb and flow of electoral campaigns in the three cities over the past twenty-five years. In Toronto and Vancouver the heady days of 1972 quickly passed, and the old guard was reconstituted in new vestments. Whereas conservative parties frequently regained an electoral plurality, left-liberal groupings remained vocal minorities on city council, and in the 1980s sometimes won a majority position, in Vancouver in 1980, 1982, and 1984, in Montreal in 1986 and 1990, and in Toronto in 1988. There seems no prospect of a return to the regime politics which predated 1972. To what extent has gentrification contributed toward this redefinition of urban politics?

GENTRIFICATION AND REFORM POLITICS: ECOLOGICAL CORRELATES

I have already noted the historic coincidence between gentrification and the rise of reform politics, and the similarities in social profile between gentrifiers and reform politicians in the three cities. The method of historical narrative is attractive, but in a comparative study which moves between three cities, and elections over a twenty-year period, a more analytical method offers a complementary approach. My method in this section is to use some simple statistical analysis to come at the relations between gentrification and reform politics from a different perspective and to supplement this analysis with contextual material derived from interviews, fieldwork, and secondary sources.

The analysis focuses upon the civic elections in all three cities in 1982, and those of 1985 in Toronto, and 1986 in Vancouver and Montreal. These dates fall close to the census years of 1981 and 1986, providing a database for ecological correlation. Two major operational tasks are entailed: first, the definition both of the reform vote and of gentrification, and, second, the specification of standard geographical units for a correlation of these two variables.

For each election the reform vote was tallied by using Higgins's trichotomy of the old guard, the soft middle, and the progressives. Candidates were assigned to one of these three categories according to their designated party, or, for independents or ambiguous cases, according to press reports and the judgment of local experts. Among the major parties, TEAM (Vancouver), most Liberals and a few Conservatives (Toronto), and the Municipal Action Group (Montreal) were referred to the soft middle, whereas COPE, the NDP, and fringe left groups (Vancouver), the NDP and some Liberals (Toronto), and the MCM (Montreal) were assigned to the progressives. Analysis then proceeded in two parts, first by combining both the soft middle and progressives in a broader left-liberal category (referred to as reform 1), and, second, by considering the progressive groups alone (reform 2).

Gentrification was defined by using procedures validated in earlier research (Ley, 1988; 1992). A literature review identified educational attainment and professional-managerial employment as the two most sensitive indicators in identifying the entry of the middle class into the inner city. For each census tract in the administrative cities of Montreal, Toronto, and Vancouver the percentage of the population having completed at least some university education was assessed. The percentage of the work force with professional, managerial, and related occupations was also computed. By adding these two values and dividing by two, a simple index of social status was derived for each census tract for 1971, 1981, and 1986. The difference between the index values for 1971 and 1981, and again between 1981 and 1986, offered a measure of social upgrading, a surrogate for gentrification. Note that this view of gentrification highlights households (and voters) rather than the housing stock as of primary concern, in accordance with a literature which sees gentrification as a broader facet of economic and social restructuring in the city, regardless of whether renovation or redevelopment is the principal transition process in the housing stock (Hamnett, 1991; Sassen, 1991). Nonetheless, as we shall see later, where the form of the housing stock coincides with distinctive housing classes, then the renovation-redevelopment submarkets may be separated into somewhat divergent electoral subcultures.

A second task was to develop standardised geographic units for the electoral and social status variables. The task of matching polling districts against census tracts led to the specification of forty-three districts in Vancouver, fifty-four in Montreal, and 134 in Toronto, where the polling districts are more finely disaggregated. These districts provided the basis for a correlation of the reform vote against the incidence of social upgrading, that is, the change in social status between census dates.

The citywide vote for reform candidates appears in table 13.1. Results were similar in all three cities in 1982, with some 35%–40% support among the

City	Reform 1 (%)	Reform 2 (%)
1982 election		
Montreal	51.3	35.0
Toronto	58.3	42.2
Vancouver	50.1	39.7
1986 election[a]		
Montreal[b]		63.2
Toronto	54.2	39.4
Vancouver	44.1	40.1

Table 13.1 The vote for reform candidates for council in civic elections

[a] The Toronto election took place in 1985

[b] No centre party fielded candidates in 1986

Note: reform 1, left-liberals; reform 2, progressives

electorate for progressive candidates, and another 10%–15% for the soft middle. By 1986, however, differences are evident. In Montreal and Vancouver, support disappeared for the centre parties. The Municipal Action Group which had won 16% of the vote in 1982 dissolved and offered no candidates in 1986, an event which aided a massive MCM plurality, though as important was the retirement of Mayor Drapeau and the collapse of the Civic Party. In contrast the steady erosion of TEAM in Vancouver aided primarily the NPA which, more successfully than the Civic Party, was attempting to rejuvenate its image and disassociate itself from the unsophisticated free market ethos of the 1960s. Changes between the two elections were more limited in Toronto, with slight slippage occurring in the vote both for centrist and for progressive candidates.

Of more importance for present purposes was the electoral behaviour of gentrifying districts. In each city the voting profile was assessed for districts which fell into the top quartile of social upgrading for 1971–81 and for 1981–86 (Table 13.2). In nine of the eleven cases, the reform vote in the upgrading districts exceeded the level for the city as a whole. The predisposition toward reform candidates was most evident in Montreal. In 1982 there was an excess of some 10% in endorsements, and in 1986 the figure was 6%. The increments were smaller, but in the same direction, for both elections in Toronto. Only in Vancouver did the upgrading districts in 1982 fall behind the city as a whole in their preference for reform politicians, although by 1986 the trend was reversed. Indeed all three cities showed a rise in support for progressive candidates in their gentrifying districts between 1982 and 1986.

City	Reform 1 (%)	Reform 2 (%)
1982 election (1971–81 upgrading)		
Montreal	61.0	46 6
Toronto	61.5	43.0
Vancouver	48.0	35.3
1986 election[a] (1981–86 upgrading)		
Montreal[b]		69.3
Toronto	54.6	45.4
Vancouver	47.0	43.3

Table 13.2 The vote for reform candidates for council among districts in the top quartile of social upgrading

[a] The Toronto election took place in 1985

[b] No centre party fielded candidates in 1986

Note: reform 1, left – liberals; reform 2, progressives

However, although the overall profile endorsed reform politicians, a finer level of disaggregation shows a more complex range of political attitudes within the gentrifying inner city. The 1986 election in Vancouver revealed that support for progressive candidates among the top quartile of upgrading districts ranged from 69% to 19%, and in Toronto (for 1985) from 82% to 18% (and 0% in two districts without a progressive candidate running). Hamnett's (1990) observation concerning the electoral schizophrenia of the new class in the central city is well placed. An assessment of individual districts suggested that some distinctions could be drawn between upgrading districts that throws light on their divergent voting patterns. The strongest endorsement for progressive candidates came from districts closer to the city centre, in renovated, classically gentrified, neighbourhoods (including Plateau Mont-Royal in Montreal, and Don Vale in Toronto), or where innovative state-inspired housing projects with a social mix of residents had been developed in the 1970s (St Lawrence in Toronto, and False Creek in Vancouver).

Significantly, these neighbourhoods also contained that fraction of the new class with reputedly the most liberal sentiments, Brint's (1984) "new politics liberals". Dansereau and Beaudry (1985) have noted the vast overrepresentation of professionals in the arts and social sciences (the cultural new class) in the broadly defined region of Plateau Mont-Royal, the former home of Mayor Jean Doré and heartland of MCM endorsement in 1982 and 1986, with a block of districts recording over 75% support for the party. Similarly, in Toronto such gentrifying districts as the west Annex, Don Vale, and tracts

west of Spadina Avenue contained a large population of the cultural new class in tree-lined streets of older houses; each district showed levels of support of over 60% for progressive candidates in 1985. Kitsilano's old apartments and shared houses were the core of Vancouver's counterculture in the late 1960s. In 1981 the district still contained the highest concentration of the cultural new class, and held the strongest support for reform politicians among the city's gentrifying districts.

Occasionally, the less central inner suburbs shared a progressive political sentiment (as in west Montreal's professional inner suburbs of Côtes-des-Neiges and Snowdon), but more usually upgrading through infill in such established middle-class districts as Kerrisdale in Vancouver or High Park in Toronto did not reshape existing conservative attitudes. Another bastion of conservative support in the upgrading areas was some districts of high-priced condominiums near the central business district, notably the expensive, high-rise towers on Toronto's lakeshore, and the condominium apartments of Vancouver's Fairview district.

Although the upgrading tracts displayed disproportionate support for reform candidates, they were not necessarily the principal base of these parties. The ten districts with the strongest endorsement for progressive candidates in Toronto included only two members from the top quartile of upgrading districts in 1982 and 1986, and in 1982 in Vancouver the tally was only one, rising in 1986 to three. In these cities a long-established tradition of social democratic politics has been accompanied by an entrenched social base in blue-collar, nonanglophone, and lower-status districts.

The relationship between social upgrading and reform politics is described by a U-shaped curve, illustrated most fully in Vancouver with its rich tradition of unionisation and class-based politics. Progressive politicians find their primary level of support in blue-collar and/or low-income tracts in Vancouver's inner city, with a secondary peak in gentrifying districts. The base of the U is located in inner-suburban districts which may or may not have limited upgrading through infill or modest re-development, but which express little interest in reform candidates. The U is somewhat blurred in Toronto, where in municipal politics there has not always been as clear a relation between social class and party alignments as in Vancouver. As a result, both gentrifying and, less dependably, some existing affluent districts offer a relatively more important base for the reform sentiment, tending toward social democracy in a number of central gentrifying districts and liberalism in some of the inner suburbs.

Toronto provides a transitional position between Vancouver and Montreal in its identification of the social base of progressive politics in the 1980s. In Quebec as a whole, class-based politics has often been secondary to cultural politics. During the 1960s the hegemony of the Roman Catholic Church was shaken but replaced by a nationalist rather than a class-based ideology. So it is that the NDP is a marginal player in Quebec, and the politics of culture has been the abiding focus for the past thirty years. Remember the earlier observation that the most ardent advocates of the Parti Québecois are intellectuals involved in "the production and dissemination of 'culture'" (Hamilton and Pinard, 1982, page 223). This same cohort has provided a leadership cadre to the MCM. In its first campaign in 1974, and attempting to synthesise the older and newer cultural politics, the MCM ran Jacques Couture, a priest and social worker, as its mayoralty candidate. In 1982 and (successfully) in 1986 and 1990 its candidate was Jean Doré, a labour lawyer and former press secretary of René Lévesque when he was Parti Québecois premier of the province. No less than eight of the ten electoral districts with the strongest support for the MCM in 1982 were in the top quartile of social upgrading, and this proportion was seven out of ten in 1986. The MCM is quite simply the party of the new middle class (Collin and Léveillée, 1985; Léveillée and Léonard, 1987; Ley and Mills, 1986). So it was that in 1984 a leading MCM councillor described for me a typical supporter as we sat on the balcony of his row house overlooking a gentrifying street in Plateau Mont-Royal: "well-educated, 25–45 years old, a professional, probably in the public sector, but not necessarily career-oriented … has other goals instead" (interview with Councillor John Gardiner, June 1984).

The distinctive political cultures of the three cities are illuminated by a correlation analysis of the reform vote against several social status measures. First, the support for progressive candidates (reform 2) is linked with the social status of each district. Electoral behaviour in 1982 was correlated against 1981 social status scores, and the 1985–86 electoral map was correlated against the 1986 scores (Table 13.3). A substantial literature would anticipate strong *negative* correlations between social class and support for social democratic candidates, for our conventional understanding is that higher social status is usually accompanied by more conservative political preferences.

This expectation was fully met in Vancouver where strong negative correlations were found between social status and the progressive vote, consistent with the city's class-based politics

City	1982 vote versus 1981 SSS	1986[a] vote versus 1986 SSS
Vancouver (*n* = 43)	−0.70	−0.71
Toronto (*n* = 134)	0.03	−0.11
Montreal (*n* = 54)	0.48	0.21

Table 13.3 Correlations between social status and the vote for progressive candidates

[a] The Toronto election took place in 1985

Note: SSS, social status score, calculated by dividing by two the sum of the percentage of the population having completed some university education and the percentage of the population with professional, managerial, and related occupations

(Table 13.3). In Toronto, however, the relationship disappeared, with no consistent tendency for social status to be a useful predictor of the progressive vote, reflecting a political culture where class-based cleavages showed no simple association with municipal party politics. Last, in Montreal, the transition was completed with a significant *positive* correlation between social status and support for the MCM. Importantly, the positive relationship existed in both time periods, though it was stronger in 1982 than in 1986. This is noteworthy for, in general, commentators have observed a more pragmatic face to the MCM as the party approached power in 1986 and consolidated it through reelection in 1990 (Léveillée and Léonard, 1987; Roy and Weston, 1990; Ruddick, 1991). The correlation shows that in 1982, with a more progressive campaign platform, the MCM was able to capture middle-class support—and was ignored in poorer districts which continued to endorse the Civic Party. The more modest, yet still positive, correlation for 1986 is indicative that MCM support was diffusing into lower status tracts, an apparent irony if this election did indeed coincide with a tempering of its earlier objectives of redistribution and greater community participation.

Inspection of maps of the 1982 returns reveals that MCM strength was concentrated in two distinctive nodes, the professional and largely anglophone inner suburbs to the west, and the old, divided row houses of a sizeable district north of downtown anchored around Plateau Mont-Royal (Beauregard, 1984; Ley and Mills, 1986). This electoral map coincided closely with areas of social upgrading in the 1970s, through infill and limited redevelopment in the

City	1982 vote versus 1971–81 SUI		1986[a] vote versus 1981–86 SUI	
	Reform 1	Reform 2	Reform 1	Reform 2
Vancouver ($n = 43$)	−0.05	−0.15	−0.00	−0.07
Toronto ($n = 134$)	0.23	−0.02	0.07	
Montreal[b] ($n = 54$)	0.56	0.69		0.46

Table 13.4 Correlations between social upgrading and the reform vote

[a] In Toronto the election took place in 1985
[b] No centre party fielded candidates in 1986

Note: SUI social upgrading index, calculated as the difference between the social status score for the final year of the period with that for the first year of the period; reform 1, left-liberal; reform 2, progressives

inner suburbs and through renovation and, around the margins, limited redevelopment in the district around Plateau Mont-Royal. Consequently, a strong correlation existed between embourgeoisement and the reform vote (Table 13.4). This surprisingly robust relationship confirms our earlier argument about the distinctive social base of the MCM among the new class. "They *are* the gentrifiers" confided one informant close to the party when I asked about relations between the MCM and the gentrification process. Note also (Table 13.4), that support for the MCM was not only more closely aligned with social-upgrading than with social status (Table 13.3)—which we might have expected—but also that the alignment was oriented to the progressive option (reform 2) over the centre-plus-progressive option (reform 1)—which we might *not* have expected.

As we move through the other two cities the sequence observed earlier is repeated. In Toronto, correlations are generally low but positive, indicating a slight tendency for upgrading and the reform vote to be associated, but any stronger correlation is deflected by the fact that support for reform candidates is shared with working-class districts without much gentrification, and also because of divergent political attitudes in different upgrading districts. In Vancouver, this divergence is clearer still and correlations are negative, but very low, indicating that even here the prevalent class-based politics (Table 13.3) is muted by the effects of gentrification.

This analysis might be taken one step further. I have commented how in 1986 the MCM vote diffused from its new-class core into working-class and lower-middle-class districts. That process continued in 1990, by which point criticisms of the MCM's economic pragmatism had intensified among intellectuals. Three councillors were expelled from the party for their criticism of its reorientation away from

initial socialist principles. Leftist splinter groups ran independently in the election as alternatives to the MCM but were relatively unsuccessful. However, the three dissidents were returned to office, and leftist candidates garnered a substantial minority vote in the MCM strongholds of the greater Plateau Mont-Royal and the western inner suburbs. In a 1991 by-election, the Democratic Coalition, one of the leftist splinter groups, heavily defeated the MCM in Notre-Dame-de-Grace, part of its electoral heartland in the professional inner suburbs (Lustiger-Thaler, 1993). Within Montreal's political culture there is evidently a segment of the city's new class that cannot abide a vacuum on the left. We hardly need reminding that these districts are relatively overrepresented by residents drawn from the cultural new class.

GENTRIFICATION AND REFORM POLITICS: THE DIFFERENTIALS OF LOCAL POLITICAL CULTURE

The geography of the cultural new class might also provide a partial answer to the electoral differentials we have observed between the three cities. The cultural new class is relatively small, but, employed in such fields as the arts, media, and teaching, their business is the circulation of information, making members of this cohort influential beyond its numbers. One reason, for example, that gentrifying districts such as Kitsilano, Don Vale (Cabbagetown), or Plateau Mont-Royal are well known is that they have been publicised by novelists such as John Gray, Hugh Garner, and Michel Tremblay who have lived there or written about them.[6] Moreover, the geography of the cultural new class gravitates not only to the city centre, but also up the urban hierarchy to the largest metropolitan centres. Artists, for example, account for some 2.3% of the work force of metropolitan Toronto, 2.4% in Montreal, but only 1.9% (of a much smaller base) in Vancouver. Herein is a possible contributory factor to the relatively weaker role of gentrification in Vancouver than in the other cities in reshaping class politics. There is simply a smaller corpus of relevant individuals in a second-tier city to redirect the dominant political discourse.

There is a second inflection to the occupational profiles of the three cities which may well contribute to the diversity of local political cultures. A number of authors, particularly in Britain, have linked middle-class radicalism to professionals employed by the welfare state (Bonnett, 1993)—recall that Councillor Gardiner described a typical MCM supporter in Montreal as "probably in the public sector". Rose and Villeneuve (1993) have pointed out that relative to Toronto and Vancouver, Montreal includes a stronger representation of government and nonprofit sector workers. A principal residential concentration of such state employees is to be found in Plateau Mont-Royal and its adjacent districts (Rose, 1987)—precisely the region where support for the MCM exceeded 75% in the 1982 and 1986 elections, and where dissident leftist candidates found some endorsement in 1990. Gentrification in Montreal has a more distinctive public sector profile than in the other cities, providing a potential pool of recruits to a political culture more sympathetic to left-liberal candidates. Moreover, in a province where *cultural* politics has been the dominant discourse, the influential role of cultural professionals in left-liberal municipal politics to an extent not shared outside Montreal is readily understandable.

There is a third differential, which might account for the lesser importance of gentrifiers as a social base for progressive politics in Vancouver relative to Toronto and Montreal, and here I turn to the contingencies of housing submarkets. In the cities of central Canada the dominant form of gentrification has been the renovation of old brick or stone dwellings. In contrast, in Vancouver the prevalent building material is wood, and renovation is rarely cost-effective, particularly when renovators have to meet more demanding building codes, especially seismic codes, than the original builders. The result is that, compared with the larger cities, in Vancouver renovation is a less significant form of gentrification than is condominium redevelopment.

It is worth asking whether these alternative building patterns attract divergent housing classes, harbouring different political sympathies. There is some evidence that this could be the case. The stage

model of gentrification (DeGiovanni, 1983; Gale, 1980) envisages a sequence of householders occupying dwellings through a cycle of inflating house prices. As successively higher income households enter the market, the protection and enhancement of their investment assumes increasing significance, whereas the early stages of the cycle coincide with the arrival of more economically marginal gentrifiers, typically members of the cultural new class. Although the early arrivals tend to be risk oblivious in terms of their housing investment, later arrivals who pay a premium for the neighbourhood's then fashionable reputation are likely to be risk averse, preferring the new face of the neighbourhood over the old. Ethnographies have shown that, although early gentrifiers in renovated properties welcome social mix and housing stability for low-wage earners (Caulfield, 1990), this is less likely in later stages; in the fashionable townhouses and apartments of the new condominium district of the Fairview Slopes in Vancouver, interviews revealed that three quarters of middle-class residents opposed new social housing units for seniors or families in the district (Fujii, 1981; Mills, 1989). And whereas the early gentrifiers, predominantly members of the cultural new class, interviewed by Caulfield in inner-city Toronto had progressive political sympathies, those in Fairview Slopes, like those in the condominium districts in central Toronto, endorsed conservative politicians in municipal elections. Possibly, then, the tendency toward condominium redevelopment rather than renovation in inner-city Vancouver may be a separate contributor to the more modest role there of gentrification in reform politics.

CONCLUSIONS

In this paper I have sought to specify the social location of adversarial politics within the new middle class. Political liberalism is not, as we have seen, the typical politics of the new class employed in advanced services, and to locate an adversarial ethos one has to dissect this far from homogeneous category. A far more specific niche for left-liberal politics is found among the cadre of social and cultural professionals, often in public or nonprofit sectors, that I have called the cultural new class. Moreover, this cadre also displays a distinctive geography in Canada's largest urban centres. In its collective identity, geography matters, for central city living is far more than a convenience for the journey to work; it is constitutive of an urbane lifestyle.

The emergence of this life-style around 1970 in the inner districts of larger Canadian cities coincided with the articulation of reform sentiments in urban politics which challenged the postwar regime dominated by a scarcely democratic business hegemony. If this challenge was most urgent in its initial impulses, it has returned in recurrent episodes over the subsequent twenty-five years. Moreover, the profile of reform politicians matched the portrait of the young urban professional, male or female, in the gentrification literature. Ecological correlation revealed more nuanced relations between gentrification and reform politics. To confound conventional relations between social status and electoral choice, in all three cities there was no significant tendency overall for social upgrading in the city centre to be associated with conservative politics. Indeed, strongly in Montreal, and weakly in Toronto, social upgrading was correlated with left-liberal politics. These reform tendencies were pronounced in older neighbourhoods with concentrations of professionals in the cultural new class, the leading edge in the stage theory of gentrification. In contrast, districts where condominium redevelopment was the dominant form of embourgeoisement were more likely to endorse conservative politicians.

To what extent is the present profile of new-class politics in the central city an end point, and to what extent does it represent a stage in a transition to a new and more stable political regime than the electoral flux of the past twenty-five years? And will that regime be more conservative or more progressive than current administrations? The evolutionary trajectory of the stage model of gentrification would suggest continuous upfiltering and an eventual concentration of high-income service workers in the central city, with less economically secure members of the cultural new class priced out. This scenario of the executive city has plausibility. Although it was a vision substantially rejected by the reform councils in Vancouver and Toronto in the 1970s, the amenity enhancement of a liberal ideology unwittingly provided the positive externalities attractive to highly paid service workers (Ley, 1980). In an engaging thesis, Ruddick (1991) has argued more directly that in Montreal the MCM, as members of the sophisticated new class, are far more effective facilitators of the new international economy, harbinger of the executive city, than the parochial small business people of the Drapeau era. To this account, the apparently growing pragmatism of the Doré administration after 1986 falls readily into place.

Although plausible, this argument overlooks several contingencies that could check a right-wing succession. First, there are the unknowns of political events themselves, for example, the unexpected rise of the Bread Not Circus Coalition of poverty groups in Toronto, a coalition that was attributed an important role in the failure of the city's bid for the 1996 Olympics, a bid redolent with the right-wing boosterism of the world city. The disciplining effect of radical splinter groups in Montreal might also serve to remind the MCM leadership of its roots. Nor should we assume that rising incomes in the central city *necessarily* usher in conservative politicians. Brint's (1984) analysis showed weak and inconsistent associations between income and liberal political values among the US new class, whereas in larger cities it was those with a substantial *middle-class* constituency free of the control of corporate business that Stone et al (1991) looked to for signs of progressive politics. These expectations add saliency to the finding of this research that there are inconsistent correlations between social status and electoral support for municipal reform candidates in the three largest cities in Canada.

Finally, there is evidence that pragmatism may not be such an unworkable solution for the 1990s, as social democratic parties through the Western world have turned, like the MCM, to the market as the motor for economic development which makes possible the redistributive policies of the welfare state. Undoubtedly, this will not lead to a socialist utopia, but such an outcome has rarely been the objective of more than a very small group among the new class. Brint (1984, page 58) concluded that even the cultural new class, the most adversarial of the new class fractions, "were much more clearly reformist than expressly antagonistic to business".

Such gradualism seems to describe well the current politics of the cultural new class in the gentrifying inner city. If reform politicians are correct in saying that "there is something about choosing to live in central city that relates to political values", these same politicians are aware of the flux of inner-city living and often speak of earlier and later waves of gentrification, with the initial wave more idealistic and the more recent wave more protective of its investment. "There is always the prospect for conservative opposition" continued the Ward 7 NDP councillor, whose jurisdiction in Toronto included the gentrifiers of Don Vale, "and reform must be pitched to middle-class reform issues such as the environment and quality of life" (interview with Councillor Barbara Hall, April 1990). To the present, this qualified reform agenda has shown surprising longevity. In 1988 when reform candidates won the middle-class ring of central wards in Toronto, Councillor Hall's own victory in Don Vale, by then twenty years into the gentrification cycle, was decisively endorsed by 78% of the electorate.

ACKNOWLEDGEMENTS

This research was conducted with the aid of a grant from the Social Sciences and Humanities Research Council of Canada. I am grateful to Alastair Bonnett, Michael Brown, and Paul Villeneuve for critical comments on an earlier draft, and to Leigh Howell, Caroline Mills, and David Adelmann, talented research assistants.

Notes

(1) Bell's expansive thesis has attracted commentary from a number of fronts in sociological and, more recently, cultural theory, too extensive to note here. For the purposes of this paper I consider only Bell's labour-force analysis and attendant discussion of the new class (Bell, 1973, 1980).

(2) These categories correspond in different authors' schemata variously with the professional – managerial cohort, the quaternary sector, advanced service occupations, or, in its broadest designation, the new middle class.

(3) The catalytic role of artists as a prelude to gentrification is consistent with the account of evolutionary stages in a gentrification cycle proposed by a number of authors. Such a role also accords with the empirical expectations emanating from Zukin's (1989) intriguing thesis concerning the place of an artistic mode of production in the economic development and restructuring of major metropolitan areas. A fuller discussion appears in Ley (1994).

(4) The literature (particularly pedagogic, semipopular sources) is extensive on adversarial municipal politics during the past twenty-five years in Canada. For a systematic account emphasising the new-left movements of the 1960s, see Harris (1987), and the response by Caulfield (1988). For Toronto, a large literature from the early 1970s is reviewed in Magnusson (1983); see also Goldrick (1978). For Vancouver, earlier work is reviewed in Gutstein (1975); the liberal ideology of the 1970s is interpreted in Ley (1980) and the long view is provided by Tennant (1980); for neighbourhood politics, see Hasson and Ley (1994). Corresponding with the later onset of reform politics, material on the Montreal Citizens' Movement, in particular, is more recent, and copious. See Raboy (1982), Beauregard (1984), Milner (1988), several publications by Jacques Léveillée, including Léonard and Léveillée (1986) and others cited elsewhere in this paper, and current critical work including Roy and Weston (1990) and Lustiger-Thaler (1993), as well as the more theoretical discussion of Ruddick (1991). For critical social movements in Montreal, see Hamel (1991). A number of the publications in all three cities are self-consciously partisan, indeed they represent part of the process of local political mobilisation in a distinctively new class medium, the printed word.

(5) Critics include Milner (1988), Léveillée and Whelan (1990), Roy and Weston (1990), Ruddick (1991), and Lustiger-Thaler (1993).

(6) These neighbourhoods provide the setting for the novels of Gray (1984), Garner (1968, 1976), and Tremblay (1978–1989). A more systematic interpretation of this literary genre would be valuable, for it is quite extensive, even within the bounded confines of Canadian literature. There was, for example, a tribe of poets writing in (and about) Kitsilano during 1965–75. More accessible are the novels and short stories of Margaret Atwood which are sometimes set in gentrifying sections of inner Toronto, the site of Atwood's own in-town residence (for example, see Atwood, 1979). Symptomatically, Atwood has been active in endorsing progressive candidates for civic office in Toronto, notably in the 1988 election.

(7) There is evidence that these relations hold in other cities, such as Ottawa, Quebec City, and Halifax, and indeed the larger metropolitan areas of the Prairies. In a short review of the 1992 civic elections, Reid (1992–93) noted the "consolidation of reform politics in the narrow band of gentrifying neighbourhoods which now surround downtown Calgary", with similar successes among "the new middle class in the inner city" in Edmonton and Winnipeg, as well as in working-class areas. It is interesting to note also the survival of the reform issues of the late 1960s—identified by Reid as neighbourhood rights, minority rights, and the environment—into the 1990s.

REFERENCES

Atwood M, 1979 *Life Before Man* (McClelland and Stewart, Toronto)

Beauregard L, 1984, "Les élections municipales à Montréal en 1982: une étude de géographie politique" *Cahiers de Géographie du Québec* **28** 395–433

Bell D, 1973 *The Coming of Post-industrial Society* (Basic Books, New York)

Bell D, 1980, "The new class: a muddled concept", in *The Winding Passage* (Basic Books, New York) pp 144–164

Betz H G, 1992, "Postmodernism and the new middle class" *Theory, Culture and Society* **9** 93–114

Black J T, 1980, "Private-market housing renovation in central cities", in *Back to the City* Eds S Laska, D Spain (Pergamon Press, Elmsford, NY) pp 3–12

Bonnett A, 1993, "The formation of public professional radical consciousness" *Sociology* **27** forthcoming

Braverman H, 1974 *Labor and Monopoly Capital* (Monthly Review Press, New York)

Brint S, 1984, "New class and cumulative trend explanations of the liberal political attitudes of professionals" *American Journal of Sociology* **90** 30–71

Bruce-Briggs B (Ed.), 1979 *The New Class?* (Transaction Books, New Brunswick, NJ)

Castells M, 1983 *The City and the Grassroots* (Edward Arnold, Sevenoaks, Kent)

Caulfield J, 1988, "Canadian urban 'reform' and local conditions" *International Journal of Urban and Regional Research* **12** 477–484

Caulfield J, 1990 *City Form and Everyday Life: The Case of Gentrification in Toronto, Canada* unpublished PhD dissertation, Department of Urban Studies, York University, North York, Ontario

Clay P, 1991, "Boston: the incomplete transformation", in *Big City Politics in Transition* Eds H Savitch, J Thomas (Sage, Newbury Park, CA) pp 14–28

Collin J P, Léveillée J, 1985, "Le pragmatism des nouvelles classes moyennes et l'urbain" *Révue Internationale d'Action Communautaire* **13** number 53, 95–102

Cotgrove S, Duff A, 1980, "Environmentalism, middle class radicalism and politics" *Sociological Review* **28** 333–351

Daniels P (Ed.), 1991 *Services and Metropolitan Development* (Routledge, Chapman and Hall, Andover, Hants)

Dansereau F, Beaudry M, 1985, "Les mutations de l'espace habité montréalais 1971–1981" *Les Cahiers de l'ACFAS* **41** 283–308

DeGiovanni F, 1983, "Patterns of change in housing market activity in revitalizing neighbourhoods" *Journal of the American Planning Association* **49** 22–39

DeLeon R, 1991, "San Francisco: postmaterialist populism in a global city", in *Big City Politics in Transition* Eds H Savitch, J Thomas (Sage, Newbury Park, CA) pp 202–215

Drobizheva L, 1991, "The role of the intelligentsia in developing national consciousness among the peoples of the USSR under *perestroika*" *Ethnic and Racial Studies* **14** 87–99

Easton R, Tennant P, 1969, "Vancouver civic party leadership: backgrounds, attitudes and non-civic party affiliations" *BC Studies* **2** 19–29

Ehrenreich J, Ehrenreich B, 1977, "The professional–managerial class" *Radical America* **11** 7–31

Ehrenreich J, Ehrenreich B, 1979, "The professional–managerial class", in *Between Labor and Capital* Ed. P Walker (South End Press, Boston, MA) pp 5–45

Fujii G, 1981, "The revitalization of the inner city: a case study of the Fairview Slopes neighbourhood, Vancouver", unpublished MA thesis, Department of Geography, University of British Columbia, Vancouver, BC

Gale D, 1980, "Neighbourhood resettlement: Washington, D.C.", in *Back to the City* Eds S Laska, D Spain (Pergamon Press, Elmsford, NY) pp 95–115

Garner H, 1968 *Cabbagetown: A Novel* (Ryerson Press, Toronto)

Garner H, 1976 *The Intruders* (McGraw-Hill Ryerson, Toronto)

Giddens A, 1973 *The Class Structure of the Advanced Societies* (Hutchinson Education, London)

Goldrick M, 1978 "The anatomy of urban reform in Toronto" *City Magazine* **3** numbers 4–5, 29–39

Gordon M, Locke H, McCutcheon L, Stafford W, 1991, "Seattle: grassroots politics shaping the environment", in *Big City Politics in Transition* Eds H Savitch, J Thomas (Sage, Newbury Park, CA) pp 216–234

Gouldner A, 1979 *The Future of Intellectuals and the Rise of the New Class* (Seabury Press, New York)

Gray J, 1984 *Dazzled* (Irwin, Toronto)

Gutstein D, 1975 *Vancouver Ltd* (James Lorimer, Toronto)

Hamel P, 1991 *Action Collective et Démocratie Locale: Les Mouvements Urbains Montréalais* (Les Presses de l'Université de Montréal, Montréal)

Hamilton R, Pinard M, 1982, "The Quebec independence movement", in *National Separatism* Ed. C H Williams (University of British Columbia Press, Vancouver) pp 203–233

Hamnett C, 1990, "London's turning" *Marxism Today* **34** (July) 26–31

Hamnett C, 1991, "The blind men and the elephant: the explanation of gentrification" *Transactions of the Institute of British Geographers: New Series* **16** 173–189

Harris R, 1987, "A social movement in urban politics: a reinterpretation of urban reform in Canada" *International Journal of Urban and Regional Research* **11** 363–381

Hasson S, Ley D, 1994 *Neighbourhood Organisations and the Welfare State* (University of Toronto Press, Toronto)

Higgins D, 1977 *Urban Canada: Its Government and Politics* (Macmillan, Toronto)

Higgins D, 1981, "Progressive city politics and the citizen movement: a status report", in *After the Developers* Eds J Lorimer, C MacGregor (James Lorimer, Toronto) pp 84–95

Kriesi H, 1988, "New social movements and the new class in the Netherlands" *American Journal of Sociology* **94** 1078–1116

Kristol I, 1972, "About equality" *Commentary* **54** 41–47

Ladd E, 1979, "Pursuing the new class: social theory and survey data", in *The New Class?* Ed. B Bruce-Briggs (Transaction Books, New Brunswick, NJ) pp 101–122

Lash S, Urry J, 1987 *The End of Organized Capitalism* (Polity Press, Cambridge)

Léonard J F, Léveillée J, 1986 *Montréal After Drapeau* (Black Rose Books, Montreal)

Léveillée J, Léonard J F, 1987, "The Montreal Citizens' Movement comes to power" *International Journal of Urban and Regional Research* **11** 567–580

Léveillée J, Whelan R, 1990, "Montreal: the struggle to become a 'world city'", in *Leadership and Urban Regeneration* Eds D Judd, M Parkinson (Sage, Newbury Park, CA) pp 152–170

Ley D, 1980, "Liberal ideology and the postindustrial city" *Annals of the Association of American Geographers* **70** 238–258

Ley D, 1981, "Inner city revitalization in Canada: a Vancouver case study" *Canadian Geographer* **25** 124–148

Ley D, 1988, "Social upgrading in six Canadian inner cities" *Canadian Geographer* **32** 31–45

Ley D, 1992, "Gentrification in recession: social change in six Canadian inner cities, 1981–1986" *Urban Geography* **13** 230–256

Ley D, 1994 *The New Middle Class and the Remaking of the Central City* (Oxford University Press, Oxford)

Ley D, Mills C A, 1986, "Gentrification and reform politics in Montreal, 1982" *Cahiers de Géographie du Québec* **30** 419–427

Lipset S, 1979, "The new class and the professoriate", in *The New Class?* Ed. B Bruce-Briggs (Transaction Books, New Brunswick, NJ) pp 67–88

Logan W, 1985 *The Gentrification of Inner Melbourne* (University of Queensland Press, St Lucia)

Lorimer J, 1970 *The Real World of City Politics* (James Lewis and Samuel, Toronto)

Lorimer J, 1972 *A Citizen's Guide to City Politics* (James Lewis and Samuel, Toronto)

Lustiger-Thaler H, 1993, "On thin ice: urban politics in Montreal" *City Magazine* **14**(2) 15–17

McAdams J, 1987, "Testing the theory of the new class" *Sociological Quarterly* **28** 23–49

Magnusson W, 1983, "Toronto", in *City Politics in Canada* Eds W Magnusson, A Sancton (University of Toronto Press, Toronto) pp 94–139

Marx K, 1967 *Capital: A Critique of Political Economy. Volume 3* Ed. F Engels (International, New York)

Mills C A, 1988, "'Life on the upslope': the postmodern landscape of gentrification" *Environment and Planning D: Society and Space* **6** 169–189

Mills C A, 1989 *Interpreting Gentrification: Postindustrial, Postpatriarchal, Postmodern?* unpublished PhD dissertation. Department of Geography, University of British Columbia, Vancouver

Mills C A, 1993, "The myths and meanings of gentrification", in *Place/Culture/Representation* Eds J Duncan, D Ley (Routledge, Chapman and Hall, Andover, Hants) pp 149–170

Milner H, 1988, "The Montreal Citizens' Movement, then and now" *Quebec Studies* **6** 1–11

Mullins P, 1982, "The 'middle-class' and the inner city" *Journal of Australian Political Economy* **11** 44–58

Myles J, 1988, "The expanding middle: some Canadian evidence on the deskilling debate" *Canadian Review of Sociology and Anthropology* **25** 335–364

O'Loughlin J, 1980, "The election of black mayors, 1977" *Annals of the Association of American Geographers* **70** 353–370

Parkin F, 1968 *Middle Class Radicalism* (Manchester University Press, Manchester)

PDD, 1990, "Central area trends report", Planning and Development Department, City of Toronto, City Hall, Toronto M5H 2N2

Raboy M, 1982, "The future of Montreal and the MCM", in *The City and Radical Social*

Change Ed. D Roussopoulos (Black Rose Books, Montreal) pp 235–259

Reid B, 1992–93, "Civic elections 92: reform politics on the Prairies" *City Magazine* **14**(1) 5–9

Rose D, 1984, "Rethinking gentrification: beyond the uneven development of marxist urban theory" *Environment and Planning D: Society and Space* **2** 47–74

Rose D, 1987, "Un aperçu féministe sur la restructuration de l'emploi et sur la gentrification: le cas de Montréal" *Cahiers de Géographie du Québec* **31** 205–224

Rose D, Villeneuve P, 1993, "Work, labour markets and households in transition", in *The Changing Social Geography of Canadian Cities* Eds L Bourne, D Ley (McGill–Queen's University Press, Montreal) pp 153–174

Roy J H, Weston B (Eds), 1990 *Montreal: A Citizen's Guide to Politics* (Black Rose Books, Montreal)

Ruddick S, 1991, "The Montreal Citizens' Movement: the realpolitik of the 1990s?", in *Fire in the Hearth: The Radical Politics of Place in America* Eds M Davis, S Hiatt, M Kennedy, S Ruddick, M Sprinker (Verso, New York) pp 287–316

Sancton A, 1983, "Montreal", in *City Politics in Canada* Eds W Magnusson, A Sancton (University of Toronto Press, Toronto) pp 58–93

Sassen S, 1991 *The Global City: New York, London, Tokyo* (Princeton University Press, Princeton, NJ)

Savage M, Dickens P, Fielding T, 1988, "Some social and political implications of the contemporary fragmentation of the 'service class' in Britain" *International Journal of Urban and Regional Research* **12** 455–476

Savitch H V, Thomas J C (Eds), 1991 *Big City Politics in Transition* (Sage, Newbury Park, CA)

Sewell J, 1972 *Up Against City Hall* (James Lewis and Samuel, Toronto)

Smith A D, 1982, "Nationalism, ethnic separatism and the intelligentsia", in *National Separatism* Ed. C H Williams (University of British Columbia Press, Vancouver) pp 17–41

Spragge G, 1983, "Exploring a planning methodology: policies for white painted neighbourhoods" *Plan Canada* **23** (September) 36–50

Stone C, Orr M, Imbroscio D, 1991, "The reshaping of urban leadership in U.S. cities: a regime analysis", in *Urban Life in Transition* Eds M Gottdiener, C Pickvance (Sage, Newbury Park, CA) pp 222–239

Tennant P, 1980, "Vancouver civic politics, 1929–1980" *BC Studies* **46** 3–27

Thrift N, 1987, "The geography of late twentieth century class formation", in *Class and Space* Eds N Thrift, P Williams (Routledge, Chapman and Hall, Andover, Hants) pp 207–253

Touraine A, 1971 *The Post-industrial Society* (Random House, New York)

Tremblay M, 1978–1989 *Chroniques du Plateau Mont-Royal* 5 volumes (Leméac, Montreal)

Tsimikalis S, 1983, "The gentrification of Don Vale: the role of the realtor", unpublished MA thesis, Department of Environmental Studies, York University, North York, Ontario

Yates D, 1977, *The Ungovernable City* (MIT Press, Cambridge, MA)

Wright E O, Martin B, 1987, "The transformation of the American class structure, 1960–1980" *American Journal of Sociology* **93** 1–29

Wright E O, Singelmann J, 1982, "Proletarianization in the American class structure" *American Journal of Sociology* **88** (supplement) S176–S209

Zukin S, 1989 *Loft Living* (Rutgers University Press, New Brunswick, NJ)

Box 4   A Marginal Gentrifier: On Being Part of the Cultural New Class and an Anti-Displacement Organisation

Plate 11 **David Ley**.

First, a disclaimer: thinking back to what motivated an article published 15 years ago is an invitation to fanciful historic reconstruction! The 1994 paper was part of ongoing research on gentrification that had been running close to 15 years when the paper appeared. The project wound down a few years later when my book *The New Middle Class and the Remaking of the Central City* (1996) completed all I had to say on the topic at the time. The paper should not be excised from that stream of research; it represented part of a larger intellectual agenda.

But we must move further back again for that agenda was itself set by events dating from the early years of gentrification. I first noticed gentrification in the early 1970s in Philadelphia. Working with Roman Cybriwsky on neighbourhood racial change on the northern and eastern edges of the immigrant Fairmount district in North Philadelphia, we observed also evidence of middle-class housing renovation marching up from the vicinity of the Art Museum. Shortly after, in 1972, I moved to Vancouver as an impoverished young professional and into the Kitsilano neighbourhood, a handy inner city district, with affordable rentals at that time, between downtown and the university, and with the added benefit of a nearby beach and a neat main street with fading counter-culture relics, an amenity package that guaranteed subsequent gentrification. Like many other researchers of gentrification, the preference for urban culture was unselfconsciously shaping me as a gentrifier, albeit one of Damaris Rose's marginal gentrifiers, and thereby not the worst kind!

Almost immediately I was thrust into neighbourhood politics. Condominium redevelopment was beginning in Kitsilano and white-collar workers a bit older and wealthier than me were moving in. Affordable housing was being destroyed and students, the elderly and low paid service workers were being evicted. Within a few weeks I was part of an anti-displacement neighbourhood organisation, and picketing against a proposed high-rise condominium that would cause close to 100 evictions on the block behind my own apartment. Unknown to me, my picketing demeanour caught the attention of a TV cameraman, and I appeared on the 6pm news. My Head of Department saw the news story and commented the next day that I seemed to be making friends and settling in well [I still have the picket sign: 'Housing for Everyone – Not Just the Rich'].

The anti-gentrification neighbourhood organisation included young professionals, artists, some students, the elderly and low-income service workers. It took its case to City Hall and won some anti-gentrification zoning changes (which failed). It also built two social housing projects using state funds for experimental projects. When in the 1980s I travelled repeatedly across Canada researching gentrification in six cities I ran frequently into similar examples of neighbourhood activism, and spoke to city councillors who had been mobilised in such politics. The time had come for a more formal analysis of what had first taken place much more than a decade earlier.

What is the continuing contribution of the article? It points to the diversity and thus complexity of gentrification processes, both between cities and within the new middle class. It directed me in later research to look more closely at the cultural new class, one source of left-liberal politics, yet ironically the creator of cultural capital in the built environment subsequently transformed into economic capital by more conservative economic actors. The mixed methods approach, using field observation, interviews and simple quantitative analysis is a tried and trusted model. Empirically, the argument moved discussion into the politics of gentrifiers, a topic that had been previously overlooked. Theoretically, it emphasised the role of class in considering the historical agency of the new middle class, a class analysis that incorporated both market power and cultural preference. At the same time the theory is worn lightly in the paper, is accountable to empirical events, and does not compress places and identities into a pre-established mould. Tactically, it confirmed for me the significance of political action. In my judgement, these are lessons that continue to be worth learning.

14

"Class Definition and the Esthetics of Gentrification: Victoriana in Melbourne"

From *Gentrification of the City* (1986)

Michael Jager

As its name suggests, the process of gentrification is intimately concerned with social class, yet in economic, social and political terms, the class dimensions of gentrification are only beginning to be scrutinized. The architectural and internal decorative esthetics of gentrified buildings and neighborhoods have attracted only passing comment and almost no sustained attention. This lack of attention is particularly surprising in that the esthetics of gentrification not only illustrate the class dimension of the process but also express the dynamic constitution of social class of which gentrification is a specific part. Indeed the esthetics of the process are the most immediately visible aspects of its constitution; etched into the landscape in the decorative forms of gentrification is a picture of the dynamics of social class.

It is a tenet of this chapter that social class is not a static object, but a set of social relationships in continual constitution and reconstitution. Commenting on the formation of the original gentry in England, Wallerstein writes

> It is far more than a semantic issue but semantics plays its role ... It is no accident that the scholars debate furiously here, because the whole point is that this period in English history is not only a moment of economic change and great individual social mobility, but of the change of categories. Not only are we unsure how to designate the meaningful social groupings: the men of the time also were ... The whole point about "gentry" is not only that it was a class in formation but a concept in formation. It was, however, a case of new wine in old bottles.
>
> (Wallerstein 1974: 236–40)

Likewise, gentrification may also involve new class formation as well as a concept in formation.

Central to the processes of class constitution and definition is the built environment, as both a container and expression of social relations. The changing social order is both reflected in and reconstructed by the spatial order and the buildings which are part of it. There are numerous dimensions to this. The focus here is upon the interrelationships between class constitution and the conservation of a Victorian built environment; it draws upon a case study of Melbourne, Australia. Inevitably, certain of the features described will be specific to that city and to class relations in Australia, but the general question of class distinction and symbolism through the built environment is of universal importance to an understanding of gentrification and its wider meaning.

SOCIAL CLASS AND HOUSING FORM

An active process, urban conservation is the production of social differentiation; it is one mechanism through which social differences are turned into social distinctions. Slums become Victoriana, and housing becomes a cultural investment with facadal display signifying social ascension. Veblen's notion of conspicuous consumption catches the importance of social self-assertion which presides over the urban conservation struggle in Melbourne.

For Veblen's leisure class, servants had a dual function; they had to work and perform, and they also had to signify their masters' standing. Gentrified housing follows a similar social logic. On the one hand, housing has to confer social status, meaning and prestige, but on the other it has to obey the social ethic of production: it has to function economically. This unites the performance ethic and the signifying function; that is, it designates the social position and trajectory of certain class fractions in relation to others. Thus beyond the function as a status symbol (signifying and designating), housing mediates the constitution of class (demarcating and discriminating) (Baudrillard 1981).

For Veblen the leisure class occupied a strategic position, setting a prescriptive example of conspicuous consumption, and thereby providing the norms that organized and gave cohesion to the social hierarchy. Today this task of providing a model of emulation falls to sections of the "new middle classes" (Diggins 1978). "The grande bourgeoisie which shrank a great deal because of the economic process of concentration has had to give over to the petite bourgeoisie its function as the class whose life style was to be emulated" (Pappi 1981: 105). With its inherited if weakened function of vicarious consumption, then, the "new middle class" takes on a societal importance which is not commensurate with its numerical strength. Gentrification promotes neither a new Veblenesque leisure class, nor an equivalent of commensurate social significance, but it does affirm a parallel class tactic and movement. What social tastes are expressed in the gentrification of Victorian terrace housing? From which class are gentrifiers demarcating and separating themselves; which social position is being sanctioned; and toward which class model do they aspire (Baudrillard 1981)?

What permanently characterizes the middle classes, "the class which is neither nor" (Pappi 1981: 106), this "class in between" (Walker 1979), is that they must conduct a war on two fronts (Elias 1974: 302). On the one hand the middle classes must defend themselves against pressure from the dominant classes, retaining a certain independence and autonomy, and on the other hand they must continue to demarcate themselves from the lower orders. This permanent tension on two fronts is evident in the architecture of gentrification: in the external restorations of Victoriana, the middle classes express their candidature for the dominant classes; in its internal renovation work this class signifies its distance from the lower orders. Architectural form not only fixes a social position but also in part conveys and sanctions a social rise. A change in social position is symbolized through a change in housing.

The ambiguity and compromise of the new middle classes is revealed in their esthetic tastes. It is through facadal restoration work that urban conservation expresses its approximation to a former bourgeois consumption model in which prestige is based upon a "constraint of superfluousness" (Baudrillard 1981: 32). But in the case of urban conservation those consumption practices are anxiously doubled up on what may be termed a Victorian work ethic embedded in renovation work. In artistic terms this duality is expressed as that of form and function.

CLASS DEMARCATION AND DISTINCTION

"Economic power is firstly the capacity to put economic necessity at a distance" (Bourdieu 1979: 58). Leisure is the most direct expression of relief or freedom from economic constraints. This relative freedom or distance from economic necessity is signified through conspicuous waste and superfluity. It is forcefully expressed through the consumption of housing as an esthetic object, through the appropriation of history, and the "stylization of life" as Victorian gentility. Thus for Veblen one of the major signs of prestige for the leisure class is that of waste in either expenditure (conspicuous consumption) or inactivity (conspicuous leisure). Through those wasteful practices (which as Veblen points out are only wasteful from a naively utilitarian perspective), the leisure class for Veblen, and the bourgeoisie more generally, distinguishes and distances itself from the labouring classes.

Societally produced objects may express this same social logic (Baudrillard 1968). They signify prestige through a certain decorative excess, through form rather than function, and it is through that excess that "they no longer 'designate' the world, but rather the being and social rank of their possessor" (Baudrillard 1981: 32). Representational excesses and superfluity associated with facadal restorations are not only intended to realize additional economic profits, therefore, but also to affirm social rank.

What is being displayed and proclaimed through such artistic consecration is not simply possession, but successful triumphant possession. Victoriana is victorious possession. Conspicuous display of property is the basis upon which privileges are accorded and won. The distancing from industrial labor through excess and superfluity was achieved in Veblen's time through idleness as opposed to labor, consumption as opposed to production. However, where higher consumption standards and longer leisure time have been generalized, and hence can no longer signify distinction, new distinctive standards are called for.

"This cultivation of the aesthetic faculty" (Veblen 1953: 64), therefore, is increasingly associated with an attempt to appropriate history. It is not just conspicuous consumption but consumption and reproduction of past history that comes to signify social distinction. With its architectural renovation and decoration, urban conservation employs this more modern system of social signification. The new middle class does not buy simply a deteriorated house when it takes over a slum, nor does it just buy into future "equity;" it buys into the past.

The predilection of the petty bourgeoisie for antiques is legendary:

The taste for the bygone is characterized by the desire to transcend the dimension of economic success, to consecrate a social success or a privileged position in a redundant, culturalized, symbolic sign. The bygone is, among other things, social success that seeks a legitimacy, a heredity, a "noble" sanction.

(Baudrillard 1981: 43)

Both socially and territorially, this may be all the more important for newcomers; history is made the guarantee against modernity, the past becomes a means of acquiring historical legitimation. Thus in a status drive, the function value of certain objects could be overridden or directly contradicted by their symbolic value. Packard (1963: 67) cites certain symbolic goods of "uncertain utilitarian value" whose value as an avenue of social promotion was none the less assured.

The value of cultural commodities may be most fully and prestigiously realized through the consumption of time. The possession of antiques and the consumption of history express a certain power over time. History may be retrieved and reinstated, indeed must be, since legitimate culture is "only acquired with time"; putting time to work (*mise en oeuvre*) "supposes the leisure to take one's time" (Bourdieu 1979: 78). Artistic discernment and appropriation not only demonstrate a certain distance from the world of necessity and rigors of inner urban industrial living, but also testify to the discerning taste of the possessor. They confer the "cultural authority of wealth" (Diggins 1978: 146).

This approximation to a former bourgeois cultural model is most clearly expressed through the emphasis on historical artifacts in housing advertisements: "Historic Carlton home," "retaining many original features," including "superbly ornate cornices and fine surrounds, ceiling roses, register grate fire places and lace iron verandah, original door handles, finger plates, lock covers, and ebony handles." These features combine to produce a "truly magnificent example of Victoriana," "authentic Victoriana," "a Sterling recreation," "opposite a pretty English style park."

A note of anxiety – "facsimile of original Victorian wall paper" – is allayed with one of reassurance – "restored under architect supervision" and "retaining all its Olde Worlde splendor." This populist duality of tradition and modernity is more sharply expressed: "Victorian with modern additions," "country life" but "well appointed kitchen." This also introduces the element of kitsch so fundamental to urban conservation in Melbourne. "Secluded by nineteenth century gates," "lush ferneries" and "English styled gardens"; this advertising language from the *Melbourne Times* in 1982 expresses the internalization of nature and domestic decorating which has been historically important for the middle classes.

The lack of an indigenous or established aristocracy in Australia encouraged some early settlers to attain upper-class exclusiveness through the retention of English attitudes (Carroll 1982). This orientation reappears in urban conservation, although the credentials change. The Victorian bourgeoisie and gentry remain the principal referents. Urban conservation in Melbourne retreats into the past as far as possible, feasible, or appropriate. Classes, like historical eras, might disappear, but they leave their residues, remnants, relics and motifs, which may continue to operate. The feudalistic pretensions of "the new landed gentry" are made evident through housing displays, representing an investment in status.

If relatively conspicuous consumption represents one pole of the former upper-class ethos, its other pole was distinction. "What distinguishes the bourgeois is distinction itself" (König 1973: 148). In this manner distinction is to be equated with exclusiveness. However, since this can no longer simply be based on natural criteria, the discriminatory dimension of consumption practices must also be increasingly segregative in order to reproduce class differences. This calls for spatial separation. Residential zoning uses spatial distance to ensure social segregation. Urban conservation zones, historic building registers, and classification by the National Trust are not a functional necessity since the property market had already assured their existence. The necessity of public declaration is that of official recognition and sanctioning from above.

Those displays of artistic consecration and possession which seek to create an esthetic object rather than a simple material-use value indicate the class candidature of the new middle classes and define the limits to their social ascension. Failing to approximate fully to the former cultural model, that is, lacking sufficient economic capital to distance themselves fully from economic imperatives, and yet possessing sufficient cultural capital to ape that bourgeois cultural ethos, the new middle classes are forced back upon the employment of a second cultural model – that of work, investment and saving, the Victorian work ethic. The gentrifier is caught between a former gentry ethic of social representation being an end in itself, and a more traditional petty bourgeois ethic of economic valorization. The restoration of Victorian housing attempts the appropriation of a very recent history and hence the authenticity of its symbols as much as its economic profitability is in the beginning precarious. It succeeds only to the extent that it can distance itself from the immediate past – that of working-class industrial "slums." This is achieved externally by esthetic-cultural conferals, and internally by remodeling.

The effacing of an industrial past and a working-class presence, the whitewashing of a former social stain, was achieved through extensive remodeling. The return to historical purity and authenticity (of the "high" Victorian era) is realized by stripping away external additions, by sandblasting, by internal gutting. The restoration of an *anterior* history was virtually the only manner in which the recent stigma of the inner areas could be removed or redefined. It is in the fundamental drive to dislodge, and symbolically obliterate, the former working-class past that the estheticization of Victoriana took off. Esthetic choices may be constituted through opposition to those groups which are closest in both spatial and social terms.

In Melbourne the new middle class which remained in the inner areas was squeezed by modern urban reconstruction programs and the Victorian Housing Commission (VHC). Metaphorically the urban bulldozers leveling slums for VHC constructions were also the agents of social leveling, which meant social declassment for the new middle classes in the inner areas. The classification of housing as slums created a potential for social de-differentiation, standardization and social descent. Through Victoriana the new middle classes oppose aspects of central urban reconstruction programs. Cultural distinctions, local specificities, historical values, and esthetic standards, are brought to the fore.

The creation of Victoriana possessed the merit of rendering immediately perceptible both those strategies for social differentiation and distinction, and the cultural qualities and claims of the possessor. Housing rehabilitation strategies, together with other key consumption activities in the inner areas, had to be both clearly visible and relatively ostentatious; hence they are conspicuously represented. With a decline in real differences between levels of blue-collar and white-collar wages during the 1970s,

together with inflation and higher taxes, status differentials had to be all the more forcefully marked than before. The blurring of social differences in this way elicited a dramatic cultural offensive by the new middle class as a means to reinstate social differentiation.

The crucial architectural notions such as purity and authenticity are there to exonerate the social demarcating drive. This esthetic drive will in several instances (such as a momentary mobilization of urban conservation protagonists to exclude aboriginals from settling in Fitzroy) approximate to what Mary Douglas (1978: 101) has called the purity rule. Increasing social control accompanies a disembodiment of received, antagonistic forms of expression; ritualistic ceremonies cleanse and purify the past while they create and maintain the present social boundaries. Having been isolated and excluded, the lower orders resurface to be patronized as "the local people," the "local community," the "little tenants." Populist nostalgia is the inversion of ethnocentrism and racism, and compensates for social and spatial exclusion.

The stigmatization of slums and their contents accompanies the ennobling of Victoriana and its architects. The social demarcation and distinction of class involve the establishment of social boundaries for determining insiders from outsiders, and the architectural and territorial form of Victoriana is the most visible means of achieving this. Social boundaries are made territorial. Thus Victoriana is a fetish, in Marx's sense, in that the objects of culture are made to bear the burden of a more onerous social significance, and yet retain a distinct material function. This is clearest with internal renovations, where actually the authenticity of the 20th-century working-class home was as undesirable as that of the 19th-century Victorian home was unrealizable. For the economic investment in Victoriana depended upon thoroughly modern renovations, especially in the kitchen, and the provision of modern appliances. The Victorian esthetic had its limits; it legitimates but cannot be allowed to compromise the economic investment. Hence the uneasy recognition in housing advertisements themselves that this esthetic can never be fully realized; the emphasis is upon "combining period charm with modern amenities."

In part the emphasis on and demand for modern amenities reflects the Victorian work ethic, especially when the remodeling is done by the new occupiers themselves. Their work is generally a product of economic necessity, but a necessity which is quickly turned into luxury. The labor expended is the principal safety valve against an initially uncertain property acquisition, and it is the insurance policy for the maximization of investment. Yet it is also the means by which parts of the esthetic are created and by which the esthetic as a whole is domesticated into the 20th century. Inner worldly asceticism becomes public display; bare brick walls and exposed timbers come to signify cultural discernment, not the poverty of slums without plaster. Taking this to an extreme, one study (Hargreaves 1976) defines the quality of housing according to its capacity to sustain maximum remodeling.

In this way "the stigma of labour" (Diggins 1978: 144) is both removed and made other. Remnants of a past English colonial presence survive through the importance attributed to handmade bricks, preferably with convict thumbprints. The latter then become a cultural sign accompanying the presence of the gentry. Modernity for Veblen was always an ambiguous project in which residues of a barbaric past continued to surface. The strategy of the new middle classes is dual: they both appropriate and transform; even stigma can be made into a cultural artifact and sign of historical discernment.

A NEW CONSUMPTION CIRCUIT

As the industrial middle classes of the first half of the 19th century were influential in the expansion of fashion, as manifested in housing interiors (König 1973), so the new middle classes are influential in the extension of the consumption circuit, in which the historical past, new urban life-style, and culture are increasingly integrated. This is epitomized in Victoriana. Although gentrified housing *per se* is hardly significant enough today to usurp the broad social functions of Veblen's leisure class, it is true that vicarious and conspicuous consumption is increasingly related to property investment and purchase of housing.

The new middle class is assuming the responsibility for introducing new consumption models if not new modes of consumption (Lefebvre 1978: 45); in this they perform as cultural brokers and historical mediators of the National Estate. The emergence of the new middle class occurs at a particular stage of economic development, that of industrial saturation, where the function of this new class is precisely to promote the new consumption ethic. The "trendy" and the "taste-maker" emerge as new social types carrying this new societal function.

What characterizes this new consumption model is an emphasis upon esthetic-cultural themes. Leisure (Mullins 1982) and relative affluence create the opportunity for artistic consumption, and art becomes increasing integrated into the middle-class pattern of consumption as a form of investment, status symbol and means of self-expression. The difference between this consumption model and a more traditional middle-class one is marked. The latter has been described by Gusfield, in the study of a middle-class-status movement, in the following way:

> … tied to the values of the sober, industrious and steady middle class citizen … they operated with the conviction that such was indeed the case: that abstinence as an ideal was a mark of middle class membership.
>
> As the new middle class has developed cultural patterns distinctive to it and opposed to nineteenth-century values, the place of impulse gratification in work and leisure has been redefined. Self-control, reserve, industriousness, and abstemiousness are replaced as virtues by demands for relaxation, tolerance, and moderate indulgence. Not one's ability to produce but one's ability to function as an appropriate consumer is the mark of prestige.
>
> (Gusfield 1963: 85 and 146)

Ostentatious display, exhibitionism, and demonstration are essential for the spread of fashion, but operate only on some given stage. In a previous century the theatre itself was a privileged site of fashion display. "With the advent of the 'bourgeois tragedy'," according to König (1973: 58), "the middle classes became interested in the theatre and used it to display their wealth and the new fashions." Today the inner urban "scene" has become an important stage for promoting fashion and new urban life-style. The elaboration of consumption techniques is increasingly centered in the private residential and cultural domains, rather than in the public or occupational spheres. Thus the redevelopment necessitated by urban conservation involves the reworking and recycling of consumption objects at an accelerating rate. As the past becomes a commodity for contemporary consumption, the consumption circuit is extended both in time and space. This throws up a new type of cottage industry such as that of Brunswick Street in Melbourne where there is an "increasing concentration of alternative/new wave/avant garde galleries, studios, shops, coffee lounges, theatres, restaurants and the like" *(Melbourne Times*, 1983). This new cottage industry promotes domestic decoration, gastronomy and entertainment as the media for new consumption tastes. In all, the new consumption circuit depends not just on the consumption of objects but on the consumption of history as it is embodied in the objects. Urban conservation not so much conserves or preserves history but reuses and recycles it. This leads to a new and distinctive kitsch.

KITSCH: A NEW ESTHETIC

In urban conservation, esthetic merit does not inhere so much in a particular object or a particular quality, but rather in the combination of objects and qualities facilitating their designation as "architectural excellence and historical significance." To the extent that certain objects and combinations of qualities become stylized as signs of architectural excellence and historical significance, they become the basis of a new kitsch, as illustrated by the following:

Individual homes and streetscapes are classified by the National Trust … and the interior has French doors and the ubiquitous Spanish arch.

Spacious Victorian residence, renovated to perfection, placing emphasis on elegant living with magnificent French windows.

(*Melbourne Times*, 1982)

Counterposed to the kitsch of the European migrants of the 1950s and 1960s with Mediterranean colorings and motifs is the kitsch of the new middle classes. The latter is consecrated as esthetic.

With the consecration of the esthetic as kitsch, the esthetic itself becomes of secondary importance. It is not the esthetic itself but the social distinction it evokes which is achieved in the display of kitsch. In kitsch, imitation takes precedence over authenticity, and this expresses the uncomfortable combination of the economic and social functions of urban conservation – the necessity to produce profit *and* social distinction.

Kitsch may be defined by its simulation of authenticity and art, by its attempted approximation to a former consumption model, and by the need to compensate for market consumption. Victorian rehabilitations are caught between authenticity (high Victorian or authentic Victorian as distinct from modern simulations) and reproductions. The further the authentic dimension is compromised, the greater the facadal salvaging and display. As the cultural intention is compromised, the esthetic realm is reduced to facades, which both proclaim an artistic exhibitionism and an internal cover-up. Products about to disintegrate realize additional values and re-enter the consumption cycle, in a new form, for a second time. This is realized through marketing, which is as essential to cultural commodities as it is to fashion. In this way, Victoriana represents the hallmark of fashion, in which the alternation

of obsolescence and innovation constitutes a new dynamic potential. As with Marx's "fetishism of commodities," Veblen's "conspicuous consumption" is seen to serve deeper social ends, and this is epitomized in kitsch.

The combination of modernity and "history" is not conflictual, but rather complementary. For even with renovation, modernization takes the form of a neo-archaism – an attempt to return to a pre-industrial past with handmade bricks, and a refutation of mass products. Victoriana distinguishes itself from an industrial stigma just as contemporary kitsch distinguishes itself from an industrialized low culture. In this way the retrieval of history becomes an instance of modernity. This neoromanticism of urban conservation incorporates the most modern functional elements. History is not restored in urban conservation, but recovered in a distorted and partial form.

STYLIZATION OF LIFE

Struggles over art forms are at the same time struggles over the art of living (Bourdieu 1979). This approximate pun catches Weber's notion of status groups which are founded over a common style of life and whose characteristics are themselves significant determinants of life-chances. This struggle we can refer to as the "stylization of life," which we can define as the way in which the new middle class, through its social strength, can impose a manner of living, legitimated as natural, and can also exclude other ways of living (Weber 1978 edn: 387–90). The imposition of conformity in living styles is most evident in the increasing emphasis placed on cultural consumption. This is epitomized in the so-called "new urban life-style." The struggle to achieve this stylization of life is apparent in urban conservation, which represents an extension of initial anti-Victorian Housing Commission conflicts. Efforts to distance ugly and unsightly VHC towers gave way to the imposition of the refined esthetic of Victoriana. "Under modern conditions," wrote Veblen, "the struggle for existence has, in a very appreciable degree, been transformed into a struggle to keep up appearance" (Mills 1972: 255). Although social classes may not be directly defined by distinct styles of life, these may, nonetheless, be an important stake in class struggles.

The cultivation of housing and urban planning through urban conservation represents the imposition of an esthetic way of life which has successfully accorded priority to artistic intentions rather than to social functions, to symbolic forms rather than to economic necessities, and to representational excesses rather than to practical utilities. "As the tendency of distinction of the bourgeois upper class now spread to life as a whole" (König 1973: 149), so the constitution of housing as an esthetic-cultural commodity is extended to the inner urban and natural environments, which become an esthetic arena. This shift in priorities is amply demonstrated through the emphasis placed upon the beautification of the environment and the stylization of local politics, both of which, in budget and ideological allocations, place increasing weight on style and form rather than on content. Architecture and politics follow a similar movement, an estheticization of form, in which style itself is to be consumed. Expressionism in facadal displays, open days, fêtes, cultural days and festivals assume increasing importance in daily life and in local politics.

However, the fragility of small domestic capital in relation to other larger economic forces present in the inner areas ensures that the esthetic disposition will be tightly circumscribed. This also explains the continuance of strictly economic imperatives and determinants embedded in the estheticization of Victoriana. The slightly triumphant facades of Melbourne Victoriana are matched by more anxiously modeled interiors.

The consumption of objects becomes generalized in advanced industrial societies. This forces class differentiation to be based upon a refinement of consumption objects, which are not only differentiated but must be consumed in a particular way – demonstratively and distinctively. The style of consumption itself becomes crucial to the maintenance of social differentiation. The reproduction of social differences is no longer simply based on possession, but on being seen to have, perhaps simply in being stylish. "A consumption economy, one might say, finds its reality in appearances" (Bell 1976: 68). Conspicuous consumption is expressed not just through symbolic investment in housing but through more traditional middle-class consumption concerns such as dress, entertainment and restaurants, which are further key components in the new inner urban life-style. It may even extend to the "grammar of forms of life" (Habermas 1981: 33).

In a generalized consumption society, where class distinctions no longer appear so rigid and where consumption habits are not so rigidly dictated by class position, there is a constant jockeying for class position, played out in the sphere of consumption. Ostentatious consumption is no longer imposed directly by such rigorous social constraints, but if anything this enhances the role of consumption in the discrimination of one social class from another. A number of holding and salvaging operations are carried out by this or that class or subclass, and this leads to a displacement of struggles into the cultural, esthetic and consumption spheres.

The importance attached to rehabilitation cannot be explained solely by economic profits. Rehabilitation and urban conservation legislation also served to define and maintain class boundaries in various ways. Rehabilitation symbolized new-middle-class arrival and territorial possession. Urban conservation is a token of social position and an indicator of social aspirations. It marks social relationships and privileges. This explains why heated public disputes could take place over such apparent trivialities as restoration. This is also why Victoriana is so demonstrative. It provides a means of expressing social identity, of representing values, of affirming arrival, of symbolizing possession and of demonstrating presence.

If accumulating social distinctions and privileges was one means of ensuring middle-class identity, the economic valorization of housing was another. The gentry has in the past made fortunes through the acquisition of consecrated property: ecclesiastical property in the 16th and 17th centuries and historical property in the 20th. However, the extraction of value from housing is not simply or solely related to economic profit. Economic gains, working-class "displacement," are not the major dimensions of gentrification in Melbourne. The economic gains are too small, the fractions of capital too local and insignificant, being principally those of small domestic property. They are in themselves insufficient to ground a notion of housing class (Pratt 1982). Where economic capital is insufficient to secure substantial social privileges, then it may, when combined with more substantial cultural capital, perform more admirably. The constitution of historical property, both individual domestic property and a National Estate, has been the basis for the formation of a new local urban elite. Traditional middle-class mechanisms of status defense, such as the procuring of titles, National Trust classifications and historic zoning, have been accompanied by the securing of local-government posts and offices by the new gentry. The estheticization of the environment, "saving the inner areas," has been their historical mission. Housing representation and local political representation form the two principal activities of the gentry in Melbourne. Where real social advancement is blocked, a concern for display and signs of advancement may substitute for real achievements.

REFERENCES

Baudrillard, J. (1968) *Le systeme des objets*, Paris: Gallimard.

Baudrillard, J. (1981) *For a critique of the political economy of the sign*, St. Louis: Telos Press.

Bell, D. (1976) *The coming of postindustrial society*, New York: Basic Books.

Bourdieu, P. (1979) *La distinction critique social du jugement*, Paris: Minuit.

Carroll, J. (1982) *Intruders in the bush: the Australian quest for identity*, Melbourne: Oxford University Press.

Diggins, J. (1978) Barbarism and capitalism: the strange perspectives of Thorstein Veblen, *Marxist Perspectives* 1:2:138–155.

Douglas, M. (1978) *Natural symbols: explorations in cosmology*, Harmondsworth: Penguin.

Elias, N. (1974) *Le societe de cour*, Paris: Clamann-Levy.

Gusfield, J. (1963) (ed) *Symbolic crusade: status politics and the American temperance movement*, Urbana: University of Illinois Press.

Habermas, J. (1981) New social movements, *Telos* 49:33–38.

Hargreaves, K. (1976) *Fitzroy preservation study – comments on the social and economic aspects of architectural preservation*, Melbourne: Centre for Urban Research and Action.

Konig, R. (1973) *A la mode: on the social psychology of fashion*, New York: Seabury Press.

Lefebvre, H. (1978) *De l'etat, Vol. 4 Les contradictions de l'etat moderne*, Paris: Generale d'Editions.

Mills, C. (1972) *White collar: the American middle classes*, London: Oxford University Press.

Mullins, P. (1982) The 'middle class' and the inner city, *Journal of Australian Political Economy*, 11: 44–58.

Packard, V. (1963) *The status seekers: an exploration of class behavior in America*, Harmondsworth: Penguin Books.

Pappi, G. (1981) The petite bourgeoisie and the new middle class, in F. Bechhofer and B. Elliot (eds) *The petite bourgeoisie: comparative studies of the uneasy stratum*, London: Macmillan, pp. 105–120.

Pratt, G. (1982) Class analysis and urban domestic property, *International Journal of Urban and Regional Research*, 6:4:481–501.

Veblen, T. (1953) *The theory of the leisure class*, New York: Mentor.

Walker, R. (1979) (ed) *Between labor and capital: the professional-managerial class*, Boston: South End Press.

Wallerstein, I. (1974) *The modern world system I*, New York: Academic Press.

Weber, M. (1978) *Economy and Society*, Berkeley: University of California Press.

15

"'Gentrification' and Desire"

From *Canadian Review of Sociology and Anthropology* (1989)

Jon Caulfield

[F]ailure to comprehend the importance of culture ... represents a central weakness in the gentrification debate. (Williams, 1986: 68)

This paper argues that treatment of gentrification has often not dealt well with the relationship between groups who are typed as early-phase and later-phase gentrifiers and has not adequately considered the role of culture in the gentrification process. It explores the cultural dimension of early-phase gentrification and proposes that the relationship of early- and later-phase gentrifiers may be understood in the context of a model of entrepreneurial appropriation of marginal cultural practice.

I THE DIVERSITY OF 'GENTRIFIERS'

Like the elephant grasped by the blind men, gentrification is enigmatic: we have a good sense of many of its parts, but its essence is elusive. We are dealing with middle-class resettlement of old city neighborhoods – but here we are already on uncertain ground. Resettlers are not a tidy group. In Toronto, for example, they differ along a number of axes:

1/ *Visibility and tenure.* Resettlers range from owner-occupiers of dilapidated old houses to tenants of developer-built batches of new infill structures designed to *look* like elegant old houses.

2/ *Occupation and income.* They range from marginally employed creative workers (writers, musicians, actors) who earn their main income in blue-collar or service-sector jobs to high-salaried corporate managers.

3/ *Political outlook.* They range from people committed to movements of the political left (unionism,

feminism, ecologism) to those whose preferences are vigorously conservative.

4/ *Cultural affiliation.* They range from members of institutionally semi-complete subcultures (like gay or bohemian communities) to people whose everyday lives are fully mainstream.

5/ *Household composition and lifestyle.* They range from cosmopolitan one- or two-person households to strongly familistic couples with children.

There are no easy congruences among many of these variables. Gays may be lawyers or paperhangers; professors may live in shabby bungalows or up-market townhomes; feminists may or may not have children; and so on.

Almost everyone can agree that *some* of these resettlers are gentrifiers – those whose home-renovations are highly visible (Jager, 1986); those directly tied to a deindustrialized white-collar economy (Hamnett, 1984); those participating in a culture of conspicuous consumption (Ley, 1980; 1985); or those whose settlement patterns are linked to dramatic reversals of the rent gap (Smith, 1986; 1987),[1] or maybe some mix of these groups. But what about those who share none of these traits? There are two approaches to this question.

One approach is to label nearly *all* city resettlers gentrifiers and subsume differences among them in a stage-typology of gentrification, an exercise of which there are both non-structuralist and structuralist versions. Among non-structuralists, Holcomb and Beauregard (1981: 42–4) count as gentrifiers less affluent gays and other unconventional middle-class groups, and Ley (1985: 23, 123, 131–6) counts 'avant-garde artists' and others 'nonconformist in their lifestyle and politics'. These groups are said to dominate in the first phase of a three-part local process that is initiated by movement into a neighborhood of economically or culturally marginal middle-class resettlers drawn by cheap space, local color and tolerance for difference; is then continued by more mainstream middle-class in-movement oriented toward neighborhood fashionability and security of investment; and is finally concluded by a conjuncture of inflating prices, still more affluent arrivals, and emerging neighborhood elite status. Each phase is accompanied by the increasing involvement of real estate entrepreneurs, and consumer forces are crucial to the process. In contrast, the principal structuralist stage-typology has only two phases. Bohemians and artists, acting as a Trojan Horse for property interests and municipal boosters who have paved their way, move into a debilitated neighborhood; then, as real estate values – influenced by the avant-garde's presence – quickly inflate, developers and affluent in-movers supplant their unwitting colonists. In this view, demand-side forces are largely epiphenomenal; all that really matters are the workings of capital and of the local state, which is reduced to a branch-office of capital (Zukin, 1982a: 173–205; 1982b; Deutsche and Ryan, 1984).[2]

A second approach eschews stage-modeling, arguing that unqualified use of the term gentrifier to describe the diversity of old city neighborhood resettlers creates a 'chaotic concept' that 'combines the unrelated' (Sayer, 1982: 71). For London and Palen (1984: 7), use of gentrification to describe activities of people who 'may be only marginally middle class [and] hardly … "gentry"' smacks of abuse of language'. For Rose (1984: 57–8) and Beauregard (1986: 40), gentrification involves different actors working in different ways for different reasons, producing different results – we cannot really talk about *'the* gentrification process' – and Rose coins the term 'marginal gentrifier' to denote those whom stage-models class as first-phase. Smith, who wants to retain a coherent concept of gentrification, argues that marginal gentrifiers should be 'decoupled from [gentrification's] central defining characteristics' (Smith, 1987: 160).

Each of these approaches has strengths and weaknesses. The strength of stage-typologizing is its basal logic – its sense that in some important way the diverse elements of middle-class resettlement of old city neighborhoods hang together as an integral process. But in its particulars, because it seeks to describe specific patterns said to occur in specific neighborhoods, stage-typologizing poses problems. In Toronto, for example, three gentrifying districts near downtown elude the three-stage model: the Annex never had phase one; Yorkville skipped phase two; and Southeast Spadina has

seemed for more than a decade unable to shift to phase three. In each case there are exculpating circumstances: the Annex never really lost middle-class status in the first place; Yorkville is adjacent to the city's poshest retail strip; and Southeast Spadina has been entrenched by a stable working-class Chinese community. But counting these and other cases, more Toronto neighborhoods have varied from the model than have conformed; the typology describes only a fraction of actual cases with any precision.[3]

The structuralist model fares no better. In many Toronto cases (Donvale, South St. Jamestown, Dufferin Grove, Southeast Spadina, Quebec-Gothic) first-phase gentrifiers fought on the side of existing neighborhoods, often successfully, against developers whose notion of 'highest best use' was not chic renovation but wholesale demolition for highrise construction. For the property industry, *this* was the most profitable reversal of the rent gap. By encouraging municipal policies of neighborhood protection, first-phase gentrifiers did, in several cases, help pave the way for later more affluent in-movers. But this did not occur as structuralist canons prescribe; gentrification happened *in spite of* property capital's expressed and real interest.

The strength of the chaotic-concept approach, on the other hand, is its recognition that the notions gentrifier and gentrification as they are often used are not reducible to a common denominator. But the disaggregation of marginal from mainstream gentrifiers leaves disconnected pieces; the root logic of stage-typologizing – that the varied elements of middle-class city repopulation are somehow related – is lost.

The view of this paper is that, once distinct types of city resettlers and patterns of resettlement are 'decoupled' from beneath the monologic rubrics 'gentrifier' and 'gentrification,' it is necessary to ask if there is a right way in which these people and processes may be recoupled as elements in a process which is not chaotic but coherent. The solution is not to try simply to frame a more flexible typology of neighborhood phases. At best, this might offer a clearer sense of how varied groups of gentrifiers relate sequentially; it would not expose the social logic of the process. Rather, the course I want to follow is suggested by Smith (1987: 163–4) for whom 'the conundrum of gentrification turns … on explaining … why central and inner areas of the city, which for decades could not satisfy the demands of the middle class, now appear to do so handsomely'. And I believe that this question raises the issue of the culture of everyday life in urban modernity. Only by exploring old city neighborhoods in this context can we more fully grasp the relationship among different groups of old city neighborhood resettlers.

II BLACK BOX

This takes us onto ground that is not well-mapped. Often, culture is acknowledged as somehow or other part of the gentrification process, but its exact role – the role of the influence of philosophic or aesthetic values or of structures of feeling about everyday life – usually remains a black box.

Some writers find gentrification closely tied to current-day processes of class-constitution. For Smith (1986: 21; 1987: 168), this occurs in the context of a structuralist distinction between the *fact* of gentrification (a 'restructuring of space [that is part] of a larger social and economic restructuring of advanced capitalist economies') and the *forms* restructuring takes, forms that involve 'diversity as long as it is highly ordered and a glorification of the past as long as it is safely brought into the present' and that reflect 'patterns of consumption [that are] clear attempts at social differentiation'. Likewise, Jager (1986: 78–81), following a route sketched by Veblen and Baudrillard, finds the aesthetics of gentrification and the 'attempt [by gentrifiers] to appropriate [the] history' of old neighborhoods 'central to processes of class constitution'. And for Williams (1986: 68), 'the very act of living in areas "with history"' reflects the activity of middle-class groups 'seeking a clear identity'. It might be argued that this perspective is embedded in the kind of monologic notion of gentrification Rose labels chaotic, that it overlooks the diversity of old city neighborhood resettlers; and it might be replied that this objection is small beer, that these writers have something important to say about a major group of gentrifiers (members of the upwardly mobile 'postindustrial' middle class) to which the issue of conceptual chaos is peripheral. But I want to follow a different tack. In addressing a possible social function (class-constitution) of the forms of gentrification, Smith, Jager and Williams leave the forms themselves still a riddle. Why do *these* forms have this function? Why don't resettlers accomplish their purposes in architecturally modernist structures built where old neighborhoods are razed – why, instead, are these neighborhoods gentrified? Or, why bother to resettle in cities at all – why isn't class status constituted in some variant of the suburb? Smith's answer is the rent gap, but at least in the case of Toronto, middle-class resettlement of old city neighborhoods vigorously survives the rent gap. So how do an affection for 'diversity,'

the past, and certain architectural styles come into the picture?

Similar questions arise with Beauregard's (1986: 43–4) and Ley's (1985: 23–5) characterization of gentrification as conspicuous consumption in which particular 'amenity packages' (stylish restaurants, art galleries, architectural color) are demand-side stimulators of old neighborhood resettlement. Were postwar suburbs any less rooted in a culture of consumption – what else do we make of their landscape of housepride, late-model cars, convenient appliances, massive retail malls? Isn't the key question here how to account for the *new* 'canons of good taste' that Ley outlines? Are they simply matters of demand-side whims – in which case, should social science retire from the field, allowing market-research to provide our understanding of gentrification? No, we have not much help here with the dilemma of why inner areas of cities now seem to satisfy middle-class aspirations for which they were ill-suited only a generation ago.

Zukin (1982a: 174; 1982b: 256), like Smith, takes a structuralist, view: that urban spatial restructuring, of which gentrification is one aspect, is an investment strategy put in place by 'corporate-sector capital' in which 'spontaneous market forces' are largely illusory. But she does not wholly foreclose the role of individual agency: 'the heart of the city' may 'exert an irresistible social and existential appeal' for artists and, for more mainstream resettlers, may offer space for living which 'reflects real middle class needs and desires' (Zukin, 1982a: 174–5, 185). Here, though, we reach a blind alley. What *is* the city's existential appeal? What desires draw middle-class people into old neighborhoods, and what is their genealogy? Zukin's concern is a critique of capital's manipulation of desire, not desire itself, and she is silent on these questions.

Rose, too, writes about 'needs and desires' – those of marginal gentrifiers – and is quite specific about the kinds of needs she has in mind: those of moderate-income single mothers who may have 'difficulties … carrying on their particular living arrangements in conventional suburbs,' or of structurally unemployed young people who 'congregate in inner-city neighborhoods where certain kinds of self-employment and informal economic activities are an essential means of "making do"' (Rose, 1984: 63, 65). She is less clear, though, about the desires gentrifiers may feel – motivations toward old neighborhood resettlement rooted not in practical matters but cultural or (in Zukin's term) 'existential' dilemmas. How do we account for the movement into old neighborhoods of, say, middle-class people who have the means to live wherever they want – who, by any demographic measure, would two decades ago have settled in suburbs – and today choose the city? Or of educated young people who are not job-market casualties but forego mainstream employment, preferring inner-city marginality? What is coded in the word 'desire'?

These are examples of a consensus among diverse treatments of gentrification that in some way culture does matter. Beyond this, however, the picture is fuzzy. But several of these writers do leave us one vital clue – that gentrification may be 'in part a reaction to the perceived homogeneity of the suburban dream' (Smith, 1987: 168), 'a rejection of the suburbs as a place in which to earn and spend' (Williams, 1986: 69), a response 'to the perceived blandness and standardization of the suburbs' (Ley, 1985: 24), involving people 'repelled from ... suburban time-space rhythms of separate spheres of work and daily life' (Rose, 1984: 62). Other writers, too, cite feelings toward suburbs as a stimulus to old city neighborhood resettlement (Holcomb and Beauregard, 1981: 58; London and Palen, 1984: 2; Allen, 1984: 30). The kinds of issues raised here are not the relative transportation convenience of downtown or supposed variations in familism among urbanites, factors often cited in discussion of gentrification as main residential sorting mechanisms. Rather, these writers' concern – in language which, granted, is more suggestive than precise – is people's feelings about the culture of everyday urban life: a sense that in some basic way newer and older city places are different. This, I think, is the key to the black box of culture.

III DESIRES OF 'MARGINAL GENTRIFIERS'

This paper argues that among the vital seeds of gentrification is emancipatory practice[4] oriented toward particular use-values of older urban places that are felt to be diminished in current-day city-building. This emancipatory practice originates at society's margins from which its content, on the one hand, spreads by diffusion, partly sustaining its resistant character, and, on the other hand, is spread by rationalized commodification, here stripped from its seminal meaning.

This argument is not wholly new in Canadian treatment of gentrification. Ley (1980: 238–43) has made a case in some ways similar; but there are key differences. Ley's analysis of threats to 'the personal world of values and meaning' in current-day urbanism is framed in the context of a theorized dichotomy between the corrosive force of a 'rational, bureaucratic and secular world view'

and the resistant reflex of 'man's [sic] emotional, spiritual and aesthetic nature' (Ley, 1980: 242). In contrast, I will discuss specific perceived threats to values and meaning directly linked to modernist and capitalist city-building. Ley dates the genesis of avant-garde resistance to current-day city-building in bohemian movements of the 1960s. I believe it may be traced earlier. Finally, Ley treats the relationship between early- and later-phase gentrifiers as a matter of demand-side preference: 'The sensuous and aesthetic philosophy released by the counter-culture has been appropriated in various forms by the growing numbers of North America's leisure class.' (Ley, 1980: 242). I believe it is also necessary to explore the structural relationship of marginal cultural practice with processes of commodification.

The emancipatory objectives of old city neighborhood resettlement by marginal middle-class groups are clearly evoked in Castells' case study of San Francisco's gay enclave – 'not only a residential space but also a space for social interaction, for business activities of all kinds, for leisure and pleasure, for feasts and politics' (Castells, 1983: 151). San Francisco's gay community sought space that was a place: physically and 'ontologically'[5] secure space offering users aesthetic and social meaning – space of 'existential insideness' (Saunders, 1986: 280; Seamon, 1979: 148–9; Firey, 1945: 140–8; Relph 1976: 55). It sought space for everyday life of a kind Barthes terms erotic, 'where subversive forces, forces of rupture, ludic forces act and meet' and 'buried possibilities for expression and communication' may be recovered (Barthes, 1986: 96; Habermas, 1981: 36). It sought space for occasions of festival, for 'drinking, laughing and dancing in the streets' – for the 'ceremonial meeting place' that was a 'first germ of the city' – and for expressing a 'carnival sense of the world,'[6] 'turn[ing] oppression into creation, and subvert[ing] established values by emphasizing their ridiculous aspects' (Castells, 1983: 141, 162; Mumford, 1961: 10; Bakhtin, 1984: 107).

The view of this paper is that these desires are basic aspects of the settlement patterns of groups termed 'first-phase' or 'marginal gentrifiers,' patterns rooted in a belief that these qualities of life are impoverished by current-day city-building but may be found in older city places. A substantial body of social criticism sustains the view that there is deeply-felt dissatisfaction with contemporary urbanism within sectors of current-day culture and that the specifics of this dissatisfaction are reflected in the spatial objectives of San Francisco's gay community. In fact, there are two lines of critique: a humanist view stressing perceived consequences of modernist urban design, and a Marxian view stressing a perceived pervasion of urban life and landscape by exchange values.

In modernist urban design, the fabric of the historical city is conceived as a problem to be solved by cataclysmic refashioning,[7] a way of thinking that has found widespread application in twentieth-century city-building and generated angry humanist polemic. Modernist planning is said to reduce the city to the analogue of a machine, yielding 'depressing' and 'monotonous blocks of urban sameness,' a 'placeless' and 'absurd landscape we experience as … apart from us and indifferent to us,' the outcome of a 'paternalism' devoted to *technique* which, paradoxically, creates places that are 'dehumanising because they are excessively humanised' by a calculating rationality (Cox, 1968: 424; Kalman, 1985: 37, 44; Mumford, 1963: 174; Relph, 1976: 90, 127; 1981: 63–105). Modernism is said to destroy the quality of life of the historical city in its 'ruthless' disregard for workaday urban culture, violence to the city's 'organic' economic fabric and erasure of the 'honky-tonk' complexity of local urban form (Mumford, 1963: 164, 168: Jacobs, 1961:143–317; Venturi, 1966: 102).

The Marxian critique, on the other hand, is oriented toward a penetration of urban life by capital, as a form of social control and in the form of the commodity, for which modernist design acts as a kind of camouflage. The city is transformed to an abstraction, a 'collection of ghettos,' a 'space of variable flows … of capital, labour, elements of production,' dominated by 'monofunctional instrumentality … as the centre of ludic communion disappears' (Lefebvre in Martins, 1982: 171; Castells, 1983: 314; Gottdiener, 1985: 235; 1986: 301). Daily urban life becomes 'the society of the spectacle,' an outcome of a 'progressive shift within production toward the provision of consumer goods and services and an accompanying "colonization of everyday life",' a process evoked in its early form in Benjamin's characterization of Paris's nineteenth-century arcades (Debord, 1983; Clark, 1984: 9; Buck-Morss, 1981: 55; Chorney, 1987).

Clearly, this is not a systematic review of the humanist or Marxian briefs against contemporary urbanism, only a sampler of their particulars, meant to illustrate vigorous hostility felt in quarters of current-day urban society about social and cultural consequences of dominant patterns of modern city-building, consequences partly involving erosion of sense of place, of erotic sociability and of occasion for festival. Unlike the writers cited, most city people do not record their ideas and feelings according to conventions of intellectual practice; but they

may do so in other ways. For example, a number of artists have grappled with the city within the same structures of feeling as many social critics at least since Manet, whose work records trenchant scepticism about Parisian social life and landscape in the wake of Haussmann's reconstruction (Clark, 1984; Jeffrey, 1978; Whitford, 1985). Besides intellectual or cultural practice, city people may also express their feelings within the realm of their actual lives where they are able, individually or collectively, to pursue practices eluding the domination of social and cultural structures and constituting new conditions for experience. For the marginal middle class, resettlement of old city neighborhoods is among these activities.

This has not been just a recent occurrence. The process labelled marginal or first-phase gentrification is not, as some writers argue (Ley, 1980: 238–43; Zukin, 1982a: 191; London and Palen, 1984: 2), somehow generically linked to values of counter-cultural movements of the 1960s. Lower New York, for example, became a bohemian district much earlier; the San Francisco gay community's roots may be traced at least to the 1940s (Castells, 1983: 140–1); in Canada, culturally marginal inner-city niches have existed for decades. The process termed first-phase gentrification has, in fact, occurred through most of the era of modernist/capitalist city-building.

In summary, we may want to stand on its head a commonplace about 'gentrification,' that it is .partly rooted in 'longing for a … halcyon past,' for 'custom and routine in a world characterized by constant change and innovation' (Holcomb and Beauregard, 1981: 55; Rybczynski, 1986: 9). On the contrary, affection for old city places may be rooted not in longing for flight to the past but for a subjectively effective present, not in desire for routine but to *escape* routine – a routine of placeless space and monofunctional instrumentality (Lefebvre, 1971). Old city places offer difference and freedom, privacy and fantasy, possibilities for carnival, where 'the ultimate word … has not yet been spoken'; 'anything can happen – and it could happen right now' (Raban, 1974: 62–3, 201, 225; Bakhtin, 1984: 166; Berger, 1977: 62). These are not just matters of philosophic abstraction but, in a carnival sense, of 'the desire for pleasure, understood in its most material and sensual form,' the force that Benjamin believed was among the most vital stimuli to resistance to domination (Buck-Morss, 1981: 64). 'A big city is an encyclopedia of sexual possibility,' a characterization to be grasped in its widest sense; the city is 'the place of our meeting with the other' (Raban, 1974: 229; Barthes, 1986: 96).

IV DIFFUSION AND COMMODIFICATION

Often, people do not fall easily into nominal categories. Terms like 'conservative,' 'familistic,' 'white-collar' are firm at their core but softer as we move outward, and it is away from their core that a plurality of people are situated. Likewise, we understand what is meant by 'avant-garde,' 'bohemian,' 'culturally marginal,' but where is their perimeter? Many people share some avant-garde values, but not all, engage in only some aspects of bohemian lifestyle, have a foot in both mainstream and marginal cultural camps: many gays, for example, lead marginal leisure-lives but have conventional work-lives. It is across this blurry zone at the edge of the avant-garde that the emancipatory attraction of old city places spreads by diffusion to people not obviously thought of as marginal gentrifiers, people whom stage-typologists might label second-stage gentrifiers. Groups like hard-core bohemians or militant gays may, in their settlement patterns, act as a kind of 'cultural vanguard' for middle-class people who, if not unreconstructedly marginal, are at best only ambivalently mainstream (Castells, 1983: 160). Here, values underlying resettlement of old city neighborhoods – desire for place, erotic sociability, occasion for festival – may be diluted; people with some essential ties to dominant structures will have less inclination than cultural expatriates to create highly distinct places and rounds of life and may do so less vividly. (Included may be individuals who pursued cultural or economic marginality when younger but, with age, gravitate toward stability.) But the resettlement of old city neighborhoods does sustain some of its emancipatory character among these people – people who, not for reasons of exogenous style but of *desire*, find suburbs and modernist spaces unlivable.

This does not, however, account for the current popularity of old city places extending well beyond groups that might be reasonably called culturally marginal or quasi-marginal, the fashionable retrofitting of old neighborhoods for invasion by mainstream middle-class resettlers and by the affluent: the process of later-phase gentrification. Is this restructuring of the city as a 'bourgeois playground' (Smith, 1986: 32) simply a matter of spreading consumer demand for inner-city settlement forms initiated by marginal groups (Ley, 1980: 242–3) – demand in which, as it turns more mainstream, the emancipatory content of the forms becomes more diluted? No. Something quite different than just demand-side dynamics is at work. What occurs is a structural process rooted in the workings of what Crow (after Horkheimer and Adorno) calls

'the culture industry' and of the relationship of this industry with marginal groups:

> In our image-saturated present, the culture industry has demonstrated the ability to package and sell nearly every variety of desire imaginable, but because its ultimate logic is the strictly rational and utilitarian one of profit maximization, it is not able to invent the desires and sensibilities it exploits.
>
> (Crow, 1983: 252)

In this context, the avant-garde serves an essential function by 'search[ing] out areas of social practice which retain some vivid life'; 'the avant-garde is a kind of research and development arm of the culture industry'. Hence, the avant-garde's activities, 'which come into being as negotiated breathing space on the margins of controlled social life' may be, 'in the end, as productive for affirmative culture as they are for the articulation of critical consciousness' (Crow, 1983: 251, 253).

In vital respects, modern property entrepreneurs are part of the culture industry; they seek to produce, advertise and sell not just functional space but desirable places for everyday life. As much as housing, their product is lifestyle. Like the rest of the culture industry, though, they cannot invent the desires they commodify but need to extract them from living culture. Recently, confronted on one hand by the rent gap and by the 'larger economic and social restructuring of advanced capitalist economies' (Smith, 1986) and on another hand by 'insurmountable ... opposition to the slash-and-burn tactics' of modernist city-building (Zukin, 1982a: 176) – opposition that has been partly rooted among so-called 'early-phase gentrifiers' – property entrepreneurs required a new style of marketable desire. The forms of marginal urbanism, resonant with *place* and erotic sociability, already diffusing through the edges of the middle class, were appropriated, stripped of their disreputable taint of deviance, and packaged in a Disneyesque wrapping highly palatable to 'postindustrial' urbanites (and highly profitable to the entrepreneurs, though not so profitable as their initially preferred high-density forms). These are spaces of simulated insideness in the traditional social life of the city, locales of prefabricated eroticism and carnival. Here, we enter a landscape of commodity fetish: new houses designed to *look* like old houses; *cinema noir* Tex-Mex diners; boutique malls in modes of Victorian elegance and industrial kitsch. And trapped in the commodity matrix, old city neighborhoods from Halifax to Vancouver become as identical as fast-food burgers, reliable, unthreatening and place-less as any modernist space.

This view has implications for political discussion of gentrification. Here, a main point that is made is that the 'revitalization' of old city neighborhoods is, in fact, based in devitalization of less affluent communities. The Canadian data in this respect are fragmentary but do seem to point to a pattern of forced displacement, particularly of low-income tenants (Ley, 1985: 144–52; 1987:16–7; Howell, 1987: 25–9). The process is often more complex than a simple gentrification/displacement model suggests; in a number of Toronto neighborhoods – for example, Donvale – the crucial thrust toward devitalization was carried out not by middle-class resettlers but by highrise speculators following a blockbusting strategy of destabilization (Sewell, 1972: 141–62). But the end results are evident. Old housing does not trickle down, and groups on fixed incomes are squeezed into a tighter housing market (City of Toronto, 1987: 7–31). Immigrant-receptor areas are erased, and new migrants are often scattered across the suburbs, out of intimate touch with communities of integration that traditionally served as the fabric of immigrant everyday life (Social Planning Council, 1979). Cheap rooming-house districts are erased, aggravating the problem of homelessness.

Some structuralist critics of gentrification want to hold both so-called early-phase and later-phase gentrifiers equally responsible for this displacement. The former are said to be 'complicit' in the dislocation of low-income residents. Early-phase gentrifiers may think that they are only 'pushing into niches here and there,' but they what they 'really' do is 'activat[e] … a mechanism of revalorization [of] patrician terrain'; and they ought to read their Gramsci and mend their ways (Deutsche and Ryan, 1984: 102; Zukin, 1982a: 178). This view has a seductive quality of unsentimental ideological vigor. Certainly, in their search for place and for traditional city sociability, marginal gentrifiers are not acting according to prescribed revolutionary canons. But whether they are simply engaged in the class project of keeping the workers down is another question. Perhaps their settlement patterns are more accurately viewed in the context of the notion of 'critical urban movements': 'not agents of structural change but symptoms of resistance to … social domination' in a political atmosphere of powerlessness, collective practices that reject 'existing forms of closure and repression' (Castells, 1983: 329; Magnusson and Walker, 1987: 25). In this perspective, marginal resettlement of old city neighborhoods is not reducible to bourgeois politics but rather is an effort by people, together with their neighbors, to seek some control over their lives.

It is uncertain, for example, that people like Donvale's early-phase gentrifiers, who allied with working-class residents to create a local non-profit housing project, may be lumped holus-bolus with the affluent later resettlers who bitterly opposed them (Dineen, 1974). Nor is it clear that people in a community like Toronto's Island neighborhood – a middle-class/working-class/bohemian hodgepodge that fought more than a decade to block bull-dozing of its homes – can be held accountable for the fact that, with changing property fashions, their cottages, once labeled shacks, now run the risk of becoming prime waterfront property. Irony, yes; dupish complicity, no. The real agent of displacement has not been the gradual activity of 'early-phase gentrifiers,' usually happy to live side-by-side with older residents and often acting as a bulwark against eradication of old neighborhoods. Rather, it has been the emergence of concerted entrepreneurial interest in old city space oriented to consumers whose self-image and property values are threatened by survival of any traces of a neighborhood's unfashionable past. The final irony is that later-phase 'gentrification' displaces not only working-class and underclass districts but also the locales of 'marginal gentrification' (Simpson, 1981: 4–5). The avant-garde's search for place breeds, through the workings of the culture industry, its own displacement.

V CONCLUSION

In this paper I have argued that deeply embedded in the landscape of gentrification is an immanent critique of modernist/capitalist city-building and that the relationship among different groups of old city neighborhood resettlers may be best understood in the context of a model of entrepreneurial appropriation of marginal cultural practice. The argument is based partly on the view that the culture of everyday life is not reducible to ungrounded consumer preferences (as demand-side approaches to gentrification often suggest) or to an epiphenomenon of the momentum of capital (as Marxian structuralist approaches suggest). And it is based on the view that cultural forces may be vital in shaping urban landscapes, that not only economistic or 'practical' factors matter. Crucial among these cultural forces in the case of resettlement of old city neighborhoods is the desire of certain social actors to elude quotidian domination, whether by *technique* or by spectacle (or by the hegemony of heterosexualism).

Their activity constitutes emancipatory practice of a kind that mainstream social science, serenely naturalizing existing structures, and Marxian political economy, finding in existing structures a monologic totality, are not always well-situated to detect. In respect to gentrification, this difficulty has left them unable to solve – or, at times, even to recognize – the riddle of old city neighborhood resettlement's forms. In focussing on these forms, my interest is not to diminish the housing crisis of low-income groups victimized by gentrification. Rather, I have argued that the politics and dimensions of gentrification's displacement are more complex than past analysis has sometimes suggested; at stake may be not only people's homes and neighborhoods but the space of freedom and critical spirit of the city.

Notes

1 Rent gap denotes a difference between existing and potential property values that 'creates the opportunity for ... revalorization of this "underdeveloped"... space' (Smith, 1986: 24).

2 Smith, a main structuralist analyst of gentrification, has not framed a stage-typology but has cited Zukin's (1986: 31–2) and elsewhere implies a phase-model (1987: 160).

3 A fourth case, Donvale, experienced the three phases but is adjacent to the city's biggest public housing project where, according to Ley's model of Canadian gentrification (1985: 97), it simply should not be. In some cases – for example, Toronto's Massey-Ferguson lands, a former industrial site redeveloped with old-style townhouses – gentrification occurs in a single stage.

4 Emancipatory practice is activity oriented toward 'a freeing from [the] restraint' of cultural and social structures, 'resisting [their] tendencies to colonize the lifeworld' (Rioux, 1984: 2; Habermas, 1981: 35).

5 Ontological security denotes a sense of 'autonomy, familiarity and ... meaning within the private realm' (Saunders, 1986: 280).

6 A carnival sense of the world is oriented toward 'free and familiar contact among people ... in a concretely sensuous, half-real and half-play-acted form ... counterposed to the all-powerful socio-hierarchical relationships of noncarnival life' (Bakhtin, 1984: 107, 123).

7 Cf., e.g., Giedion, 1967: xxxiv–vii, 25, 518ff., 744ff., 831–56.

REFERENCES

Allen, I. 1984 'The ideology of dense neighborhood redevelopment.' Pp. 27–42 in J. Palen and B. London (eds.), Gentrification, Displacement and Neighborhood Revitalization. Albany: University of New York Press

Bakhtin, M. 1984 Problems of Dostoevsky's Poetics. Minneapolis: University of Minnesota Press

Barthes, R. 1986 'Semiology and the urban.' Pp. 87–98 in M. Gottdiener and A. Lagopoulos (eds.), The City and the Sign: An Introduction to Urban Semiotics. New York: Columbia University Press

Beauregard, R. 1986 'The chaos and complexity of gentrification.' Pp. 35–55 in N. Smith and P. Williams (eds.), Gentrification of the City. Boston: Allen and Unwin

Berger, P. 1977 'In praise of New York: a semi-secular homily.' Commentary 63(2): 59–62

Buck-Morss, S. 1981 'Walter Benjamin – Revolutionary Writer.' New Left Review 128: 50–75

Castells, M. 1983 The City and the Grassroots. Berkeley: University of California Press

Chorney, H. 1987 'Walter Benjamin: the culture of technical reproduction and the modern metropolis.' A paper presented to the annual meeting of the Canadian Political Science Association, McMaster University, Hamilton

City of Toronto Housing Department 1987 Living Room II: A City Housing Policy Review

Clark, T. 1984 The Painting of Modern Life: Paris in the Art of Manet and His Followers. Princeton: Princeton University Press

Cox, H. 1968 'The restoration of a sense of place: a theological reflection on the visual environment.' Ekistics 25: 422–4

Crow, T. 1983 'Modernism and mass culture in the visual arts.' Pp. 215–64 in B. Buchloh, S. Guilbaut and D. Solkin (eds.), Modernism and Modernity: The Vancouver Conference Papers. Halifax: Nova Scotia College of Art and Design

Debord, G. 1983 Society of the Spectacle. Detroit: Black and Red Press.

Deutsche, R., and C. Ryan 1984 'The fine art of gentrification.' October 31 (Winter): 91–111

Dineen, J. 1974 The Trouble With Co-ops. Toronto: Green Tree

Firey, W. 1945 'Sentiment and symbolism as ecological variables.' American Sociological Review 10: 140–8

Giedion, S. 1967 Space, Time and Architecture. Cambridge: Harvard University Press

Gottdiener, M. 1985 The Social Production of Urban Space. Austin: University of Texas Press

— 1986 'Recapturing the centre: a semiotic analysis of shopping malls.' Pp. 288–302 in M. Gottdiener and A. Lagopoulos (eds.), The City and the Sign: An Introduction to Urban Semiotics. New York: Columbia University Press

Habermas, J. 1981 'New social movements.' Telos 49 (Fall): 33–7

Hamnett, C. 1984 'Gentrification and residential location theory: a review and assessment.' Pp. 283–319 in D. Herbert and R. Johnston (eds.), Geography and the Urban Environment: Progress in Research and Applications (VI). New York: Wiley

Holcomb, B., and R. Beauregard 1981 Revitalizing Cities. Washington: Association of American Geographers

Howell, L. 1987 'The affordable housing crisis in Toronto'. City Magazine 9(1): 12–19

Jacobs, J. 1961 The Death and Life of Great American Cities. New York: Random House

Jager, M. 1986 'Class definition and the esthetics of gentrification: Victoriana in Melbourne.' Pp. 78–91 in N. Smith and P. Williams (eds.), Gentrification of the City. Boston: Allen and Unwin

Jeffrey, I. 1978 'Concerning images of the metropolis'. In I. Jeffrey and D. Mellor (eds.), Cityscape, 1910–1930: Urban Themes in American, German and British Art. Sheffield: Arts Council of Great Britain

Kalman, H. 1985 'Crisis on Main Street.' Pp. 31–53 in D. Holdsworth (ed.), Reviving Main Street. Toronto: University of Toronto Press

Lefebvre, H. 1971 Everyday Life in The Modern World. London: Allen Lane

Ley, D. 1980 'Liberal ideology and the postindustrial city.' Annals of the Association of American Geographers 70(2): 238–58

— 1985 Gentrification in Canadian Inner Cities: Patterns, Analysis, Impacts and Policy. Ottawa: Canada Mortgage and Housing Corporation

— 1987 'Gentrification: a ten-year review'. City Magazine 9(1): 12–19

London, B., and J. Palen 1984 'Issues and perspectives in neighbourhood renovation.' Pp. 1–26 in J. Palen and B. London (eds.), Gentrification, Displacement and Neighborhood Revitalization. Albany: University of New York Press

Magnusson, W., and R. Walker 1987 'De-centering the state: political theory and Canadian political economy.' A paper presented to the annual meeting of the Canadian Political Science Association, McMaster University, Hamilton

Martins, M. 1982 'The theory of social space in the work of Henri Lefebvre.' Pp. 160–85 in R. Forrest, J. Henderson and P. Williams (eds.), Urban Political Economy and Social Theory. Gower: Aldershot

Mumford, L. 1961 The City in History. New York: Brace and World

— 1963 The Highway and the City. New York: Harcourt, Brace and World

Raban, J. 1974 Soft City. London: Hamish Hamilton

Relph, E. 1976 Place and Placelessness. London: Pion

— 1981 Rational Landscapes and Humanistic Geography. London: Croom Helm

Rioux, M. 1984 'Remarks on emancipatory practices and industrial societies in crisis.' The Canadian Review of Sociology and Anthropology 21(1): 1–20

Rose, D. 1984 'Rethinking gentrification: beyond the uneven development of Marxist urban theory.' Environment and Planning D: Society and Space 1: 47–74

Rybezynski, W. 1986 Home: A Short History of an Idea. New York: Viking Press

Saunders, P. 1986 Social Theory and the Urban Question. London: Hutchinson

Sayer, A. 1982 'Explanation in economic geography.' Progress in Human Geography 6: 68–88

Seamon, D. 1979 A Geography of the Lifeworld. London: Croom Helm

Sewell, J. 1972 Up Against City Hall. Toronto: James Lewis and Samuel

Simpson, C. 1981 Soho: The Artist in the City. Chicago: University of Chicago Press

Smith, N. 1986 'Gentrification, the frontier, and the restructuring of urban space.' Pp. 15–34 in N. Smith and P. Williams (eds.), Gentrification of the City. Boston: Allen and Unwin

— 1987 'Of yuppies and housing: gentrification, social structuring and the urban dream.' Environment and Planning D: Society and Space 5: 151–72

Social Planning Council of Metropolitan Toronto 1979 Metro's Suburbs in Transition, Part I: Evolution and Overview

Venturi, R. 1966 Complexity and Contradiction in Architecture. New York: Museum of Modern Art

Whitford, F. 1985 'The city in painting.' Pp. 45–64 in E. Timms and D. Kelley (eds.). Unreal City: Urban Experience in Modern European Literature and Art. Manchester: Manchester University Press

Williams, P. 1986 'Class constitution through spatial reconstruction: a re-evaluation of gentrification in Australia, Britain and the United States.' Pp. 56–77 in N. Smith and P. Williams (eds.), Gentrification of the City. Boston: Allen and Unwin

Zukin, S. 1982a Loft Living: Culture and Capital in Urban Change. Baltimore: Johns Hopkins University Press
— 1982b 'Loft living as a "historic compromise" in the urban core.' International Journal of Urban and Regional Research 6: 256–67

16

"'Life on the Upslope': The Postmodern Landscape of Gentrification"

From *Environment and Planning D: Society and Space* (1988)

Caroline A. Mills

"Take a moment and reflect on the ideal lifestyle. Picture a home of impeccably good taste, superior quality and spectacular views. Imagine the amenities you find most pleasurable, the kind of neighbours you appreciate. A nurturing, creative environment. Think about immersing yourself in the pulse and vigor of a dynamic city …

The place you imagine exists, Rhapsody Citihomes. Overlooking a vibrant city–all the prestigous [sic] amenities you've sought. And deserve.

Now, in a city recognized across the country for its innovative architecture, there's Rhapsody.

At once fresh and familiar, an eclectic fusion of [sic] classical and contemporary details. A private enclave with panache, character, and style."

(Advertising brochure for Rhapsody Citihomes, Combined Equities Inc., 1986)

With grandiloquent words such as these, interested parties have been invited to contemplate purchase of a unit in one of about eighty condominium buildings constructed over the last two decades in the Fairview Slopes neighbourhood of inner Vancouver. "The system of organized magic which is modern advertising" (Williams, 1980, page 186) draws us into a fantastic world where distinctions between the self and the commodity grow fuzzy, where ancient impulses and contemporary mindsets merge. Advertising presents an entry point to interpreting the relation between the emerging postmodern landscape of Fairview Slopes and the cultural and social practices of its gentrifiers.

Three interrelated themes inform this paper. First, cultural meaning has been poorly theorised with respect to urban landscapes; its pertinence to gentrification and redevelopment is demonstrated in part by the literature on advertising and the commodity. Second, the relation between social and cultural categories must be explored; I approach this with some comments on the production, the

self-production, and the consciousness of gentrifiers as members of a new middle class. Third, there are fruitful connections to be made between the qualities of a postmodern landscape and characteristics of the social groups with which it is associated; the literature on postmodernism has sometimes linked new cultural practices with the economy, without highlighting their articulation through social relations; tracing a motif of tension and ambiguity serves to recover the social dimension in this case study.

ADVERTISING, COMMODITY, AND LANDSCAPE

In British Columbia, the land of potlatch, it seems appropriate to locate the glue for social cohesion at least partly in practices centred around the symbolic power of objects (Diggins, 1977). The world of commodity production has blossomed into a magical show (Jhally et al, 1985) where the material features of commodities are increasingly subordinated to their symbolic potential (especially their role as gate-keepers to positions in the social world). Williams nominates advertising as perhaps the official art of modern capitalist society, requiring a total analysis integrating economic, social, and cultural facts, following which "We may then ... find ... that we can understand our society itself in new ways" (1980, page 185).

Advertising is one conduit along which cultural meaning flows. From the culturally constituted world, meaning is transferred into consumer goods, the fashion and advertising systems are two strategies by which this is achieved. Then individuals draw that meaning from the goods by various rituals, including those of possession, exchange, and grooming (Csikszentmihalyi and Rochberg-Halton, 1981; McCracken, 1986). But the dynamic nature of these relationships cautions against decoupling reified symbols from the realm of action in any interpretation of city life (Francis, 1983). Continuities and discontinuities can both be distinguished in the history of our relationship to objects: continuity in that conceptions of material utility are always delimited by a cultural system of interpretation (Sahlins, 1976); discontinuity in that he drives for subsistence and prestige, pursued in primitive societies through separate dual economies, are now collapsed together in each contemplated act of consumption (Leiss, 1978). Transformations in advertising techniques express shifts in prevailing social practices. With a switch in social ethos "from salvation to self-realization" in turn-of-the-century America (where bourgeois Protestantism encountered the emerging consumer culture), advertising dropped its sober informational tone and adopted a style promoting therapeutic satisfaction through consumption (Lears, 1983). Since then, the frequency of advertisements offering 'magical' inducements (promises of self-transformation, power over nature and over other people) has risen substantially (Jhally et al, 1985).

Although the persistent thrust of twentieth-century advertising is to insinuate some identity of the commodity with properties of the culturally constituted world (McCracken, 1986), the latest phase is notable for a crumbling of the chain fastening advertising sign to cultural referent, making the link between product and satisfaction increasingly ambiguous (Jhally et al, 1985; Leiss, 1983). The state of advertising illustrates how "The 'fluid medium' of the mass market dissolves the social and cultural sediment in which symbolic forms are embedded" (Agnew, 1983, page 72). And, as the vanguard art of consumer culture, advertising promoted that dissolution, underwriting a condition "in which there were few symbols rooted in specific customs ... nor even

many signs with specific referents. ... There were only floating detached images that (like the flickering faces in the movies) promised therapeutic feelings of emotional or sensuous excitement" (Lears, 1983, page 22).

Williams claims that the structural similarity between advertising and art arises as "the result of comparable responses to the contemporary human condition" (1980, page 190). Cultural interpretation should trace related practices and resemblances across genres. This task is made all the more necessary at present, with both the penetration of commodity production and marketing by postmodernism in the arts, and, conversely, the dissemination of advertising and the media throughout social life (Jameson, 1983, page 124). Among the constitutive features of postmodernity Jameson identifies a "culture of the image"—in which depth is replaced by surfaces of textual play—plus a rupture of the chains linking image and reality, leaving a "rubble of distinct and unrelated signifiers" (1984a, page 72) and liberating meaning as symbols are recycled in different contexts (Cosgrove and Jackson, 1987). "Life becomes a ritualized choreography of signs, symbols, and expectations led by and mirrored in the media (especially advertising)" (Dear, 1986, page 380).

This poses problems for those who accept landscapes as innocent representations of deeper meanings. Like Lears's metaphor of the detached and flickering images engendered by advertising, landscapes have been likened to "a flickering text displayed on the word-processor screen whose meaning can be created, extended, altered, elaborated and finally obliterated by the merest touch of a button" (Daniels and Cosgrove, 1988, forthcoming). Characteristically postmodern, argue these writers, is the duplicity of landscape imagery. Drawing on Mitchell (1986) they suggest that the image is not a "transparent window" on the world; rather, it conceals and distorts by presenting a deceptive appearance of naturalness. Landscape images are social constructions meaningful to the social groups which develop them, but they are therefore also restricted ways of seeing the world (Cosgrove, 1984). Again, the metaphor stretches across other realms. In a discussion of commodity fetishism, Leiss notes: "commodities seem to be more and more the perfectly transparent repositories of ... meanings—the satisfaction of needs takes place in the context of an open-ended competitive emulation, where the assortment of both objects and symbols is constantly reshuffled" (1978, page 44). But the object of advertising is not only to sell products but to "sell the system", limiting the definition of real human needs according to those which can be satisfied through individual commodity consumption (Jhally et al, 1985); it thus promotes a restricted way of seeing the world.

Geertz's ethnography is one model for the scrutiny of landscape as cultural form. Geertz interrogates the dialogue of text and context, cultural practices and social life, through a method of "thick description" which aims to excavate the multiple layers of meaning that actions have to social actors (Geertz, 1973). The notion of thick description conveys a sense of depth. Yet Geertz draws back from an analogy of the interpretative enterprise as that of a cipher clerk translating established codes; no one construction of what is going on is privileged in advance, and anthropological writings themselves are described as "fictions" (that is, literally "fashioned") which add an extra layer of cultural meaning to the social drama. Daniels and Cosgrove (1988) refer to a similar effect arising from interpretations of a landscape, each of which has the effect of transforming the meaning of that landscape.

Though Geertz was concerned with interrelations between culture and society, those applying thick description have tended to downplay social consequences other than those of social cohesion. But, as historians have been warned, "the play is not the whole thing— … symbolic dramas, however interesting in their own right, can serve larger purposes of power, domination, exploitation, and resistance" (Walters, 1980, page 556). Dramas of landscape ideology are the focus of an expanding body of geographical work; for instance, Ley's (1987a) interpretation of landscapes in Vancouver which anchors seemingly free-floating ideologies to discrete social groups. An integration of Geertz's approach with the concept of cultural hegemony (Anderson, 1988; Lears, 1985) may be helpful in drawing out the "duplicity" of landscape (Daniels, forthcoming).

The notion of hegemony conveys the subtleties of cultural domination, deepening the view of who has power (Lears, 1985) to include those who define conceptions of taste and good manners (such as advertisers or architects). Cultural hegemony Is the "spontaneous philosophy" of a society, something which so saturates social consciousness that it defines the very substance and limits of common sense (Williams, 1980, pages 37–38). Its dynamic nature reflects its basis in the patterning of social life; a social group may fashion its own world view as reflective of its experience of everyday life and hence cement an "historical bloc". The issue is then how the world view of the historical bloc relates to the development of a hegemonic culture, the line between dominant and subordinate cultures being "a

permeable membrane, not an impenetrable barrier" (Lears, 1985, page 574). Williams (1980) describes that relationship in these terms: because any dominant system of values and practices is necessarily selective, there are always spaces in which alternative or oppositional cultures can take seed. *Residual* cultural forms preserve values and practices from previous social formations. *Emergent* cultural forms are continually germinating new meanings and practices; they may develop in association with the formation of a new class, or with the discovery of new sensibilities in the arts or other realms. The dominant culture can tolerate a certain plurality. But, being constantly "renewed, recreated and defended", it is also capable of incorporating potentially oppositional cultures which are thereby redefined as alternative lifestyles, permitted within the defined limits of the dominant culture.

In the following discussion of the Fairview Slopes landscape, I draw on a number of interdependent cultural 'texts', including planning and architectural design, advertising, and details of the everyday life of residents. Starting with an outline of the planning of the neighbourhood, I then extend the account outwards, by locating the case study within a set of broader conditions revolving around issues of postmodern design and of gentrification, and also by tracing down to the microscale of individuals involved in the 'production' and the 'consumption' of the landscape. The construction of a landscape and the constitution of a social group are interpreted with respect to the dynamic relations between emergent and dominant cultures.

DEVELOPMENT OF FAIRVIEW SLOPES

Fairview Slopes is a small neighbourhood of about twenty city blocks in the inner city of Vancouver. It lies on a steep hill overlooking False Creek (an ocean inlet), from which it commands dramatic views of the site of Expo 86 on the north shore of the creek (see Ley and Olds. 1988), the downtown office blocks beyond, and the encircling rim of the coastal mountains. For most of its ninety-year history the woodframe single-family houses have been home to petty bourgeois and working-class occupants, some of whom were employed in the lumber mills and factories of the formerly industrial False Creek basin (Gulstein, 1983). Over time, many houses were converted to rooming houses, occupied increasingly in the 1960s by artists, hippies, students, and transients who celebrated communal and countercultural life-styles. The area was virtually red-lined by mortgage companies.

In the last fifteen years, Fairview Slopes has cast off the raiment of a backwater. In 1973 one planning document described "the island that is the Slopes" as – "border[ing] on a rural lifestyle caught up in the urban animal of Vancouver" (Elligott and Zacharias, 1973, page 11). But now it is arrayed in more fashionable garments; to quote: " 'The Slopes' is currently this city's favorite architectural playground" (Fitzgerald, 1986, page 18), "one of the few neighbourhoods in Vancouver with an urban feel" (Gruft, 1983, page 320), amongst the "hottest of Vancouver's residential hotspots" (Gutstein, 1985, page 22) and "the right address for young upwardly mobile families these days" (Ovenell-Carter, 1986, page 25k). Fairview Slopes has the highest density of award-winning architecture of any residential area in the Vancouver region (Gibson, 1986) (Figure 16.1).

Fairview's rise to celebrity was initiated by the city council's redevelopment of the publicly owned south shore of False Creek. The transformation of the waterfront from industrial to medium-density residential and amenity uses began in the early 1970s, and the plans included a mixed zoning scheme for Fairview Slopes (put in place in 1972), which was intended to promote harmonious medium-density privately developed residential and commercial uses. This was in opposition to corporate preferences for high-density zoning. There was a tentative response from a couple of pioneer architects who held a personal stake in the neighbourhood. In 1976, zoning was revised to allow developers to earn bonus density for projects providing certain features such as view corridors and semipublic spaces. It was hoped that some older houses would be retained, though this was not enforced by widespread historic designation. As the positive externalities of False Creek became felt, and with the lure of bonus densities, larger development companies became involved.

As Ley has demonstrated (1980), a new liberal ideology of urban planning was introduced to Vancouver when an urban reform party, TEAM (The Electors Action Movement) assumed power in city hall in 1972. Although ultimately flawed by elitism because of its domination by young well-educated professionals, TEAM represented a substantial shift in planning philosophy. Reacting against the rationalism and boosterism of the hegemonic style of efficient city planning, it developed an alternative ideal of the humane city. Exemplifying that trend was the south side of False Creek, planned as "a picturesque, medium-density, human-scale landscape, with mixed residential, commercial and leisure uses, and expressive of a cross-section of local urban subcultures" (Ley, 1987a, page 42). While the incorporation of 'people places' gave the area

Figure 16.1 The false gables of an award-winning project reflect the Vancouver vernacular. Red facing brick and metal details seem to represent the industrial heritage of the area. Roof gardens offer views of downtown and the Expo site across False Creek, and, on this shore, the roofs of the False Creek residential development. On the rear facade of the development below, gable forms depict the ghosts of houses past

a satisfying sensuousness, the promotion of social mix in the housing developments made it politically progressive as well.

Though it was not to be publicly developed, the planning framework for Fairview Slopes was intended to underwrite a similar experiment in creating a new kind of 'livable' inner-city environment. It was used as a testing ground for participatory planning, with residents represented on a local planning committee. But there was also a confidence in the beneficial sway of liberal professionals, for the flexible-density scheme was to be controlled by city hall. Fairview's special status cannot have been unrelated to the life-style predilections of its public supporters, for a number were residents or business operators in the area[1].

Although the TEAM-dominated council was supposedly reform-oriented, the Development Permit Board sometimes sided with developers who had their eye on that young professional market from which TEAM itself had evolved. The discretionary bonus densities, which were to be earned by especially worthy designs, appear to have been granted almost as a matter of course (at least in the eyes of longer-term residents) (Gutstein, 1983). The promise of an exceptionally livable environment has been compromised in part by some inappropriate designs and poor standards of finishing, and by the loss of older houses. If False Creek south has been the liberals' favourite child, then Fairview Slopes has turned out to be its more troublesome sibling, illustrating the limitations of humanistic planning wthin a free-enterprise context. Heritage designation of Fairview houses, for example, might trigger damage claims against city hall, as their investment potential is compromised. Council today is unwilling to oppose such a populist ideology[2].

FAIRVIEW SLOPES AS A POSTMODERN LANDSCAPE

Both False Creek and Fairview Slopes have been described as postmodern landscapes. It is useful to collapse the distinction between architecture alone and the broader concept of the landscape shaped by human effort (encompassing streetscape, buildings, gardens, etc), and to focus in interpretation on the latter (Dear, 1986). Ley portrays landscape style as "intimately related to the historic swirl of culture, politics, economics and personality in a particular place at a particular time" (1987a, page 41). Define the mesh too tightly and the force of personality (the 'great men of architecture') shades out those broader influences. Widening the perspective to the

scale of an 'urban landscape' should correspond especially well with the postmodern objective to make buildings responsive to their context. Whereas modern buildings set themselves apart from the "fallen city fabric", postmodern buildings supposedly "celebrate their insertion into the heterogeneous fabric of the commercial strip ... thereby renouncing the high modernist claim to radical difference and innovation" (Jameson, 1984b, pages 64–65). Similarly, across the arts "... the artifact is likely to be treated less as a *work* in modernist terms—unique, symbolic, visionary—than as a *text* in a postmodernist sense—'already written', allegorical, contingent" (Foster, 1983, page x). Taking the approach to cultural analysis of tracing resemblances across genres (Williams, 1980, page 48), we should be attuned to sympathetic vibrations in architecture, landscape architecture, planning, media, and fashion events. It is, however, instructive to note variations in the play of architecture against the broader landscape. Though the architecture of False Creek and the earlier Fairview projects tends to modesty and understatement, the individual buildings harmonise well with their context, and the landscape as a whole is expressive of the humanistic face of postmodernism. The later Fairview developments display a more pointed postmodern sensibility, each so self-conscious in its play of codes and symbols, its attempt at distinction, that any sense of an integrated landscape is overwhelmed. In parallel with that newer style, the local cultural press has recently conferred on Vancouver architects a near-celebrity status (even featuring some as fashion models in one layout). Architects who made their reputations on Fairview Slopes are lauded in special articles: for example, "Cheng is too modest to take credit for giving life to a run-down neighborhood, but that is exactly what he did for Fairview Slopes" (Ovenell-Carter, 1986, page 25k). This trend reflects a virtual paradigm shift in the economic, social and political life of British Columbia (Ley, 1987a).

The Fairview landscape of the 1970s (the early phase of redevelopment) was suggestive of local culture and history, in harmony with its built and natural context; it retained a human scale, with structures clustered organically around landscaped courtyards. Ley (1987a) identifies features such as these (for the redevelopment of False Creek) with an ideology of "sensitive urban place-making" (Jencks, 1981, page 82). In contrast, structures built in the 1980s wield a symbolic vocabulary of design conventions drawn both from the vernacular and from other times and places (Figure 16.2). Local themes include colours and materials such as cedar siding, and architecturai elements such as the porch and

Figure 16.2 A triumphal arch frames the entrance to a project that is located close to the boundary with a zone of light industry. The facade, built to the lot line, might represent the stark exterior of a warehouse. Concealed within is the rustic nostalgia of an interior courtyard suggestive of Fairview's earlier reputation, where the arch form is repeated in trellis arbours

the gable. The gable appears functionally in smug neovernacular (Jencks, 1981, page 99); elsewhere it is abstracted, pared-down, and truncated; in one development, gable forms superimposed on the rear facade represent the ghosts of houses past, while the front facade comprises three original warehouses. Industrial materials and colours reflect the industrial heritage of the Creek. Local themes are played against a range of themes drawn from more distant sources. A Mediterranean motif fits both the topography and the orientation to the Creek; a terraced development advertised in "deep sea blue" and white is named "The Santorini". Two developments christened "The San Franciscan" (I and II) reinforce the popular reputation of Fairview Slopes as "San Francisco North". The dominant code of the most recent buildings draws on classical forms in facade proportions, columns, arches, and Palladian windows, Some have a flavour of Bath or Brighton, the elegant leisure resort. Others conjour up an urbane and cosmopolitan atmosphere to suggest rowhouses in Boston, Toronto, or Georgian London. Projects are named "Charleston Terrace", "Wembley Mews", "Ballentyne Square". But the dominant colours are pastel. Jencks centres postmodernism in the double coding of modern with traditional patterns, elite with popular codes, and it is in these later buildings that this is most evident. Recall that Rhapsody

Citihomes was "an eclectic fusion of classical and contemporary details".

The differences between the first and second stages of development represent two faces of post-modernism: "At its best … postmodern forms represent an architecture of everyday life. … At its worst, postmodernism caters in a trivial manner to the culture of consumption in advanced nations" (Ley, 1985, page 419). A dominant tone of debates in the architectural press is one of stern disapproval[3]. The significance of the postmodern, however, lies in the fact that "what appears on one level as the latest fad, advertising pitch and hollow spectacle is part of a slowly emerging cultural transformation in Western societies, a change in sensibility" (Huyssen, 1984, page 8). Assessments of that change pivot around the question of whether postmodernism has lost the critical edge of modernist aesthetics. Huyssen offers a map to the debate (see also Jencks, 1986). In the 1960s, he argues, post-modernism in the arts revitalised the heritage of the avant-garde in a revolt not against modernism per se, but against those versions of modernism which had been institutionalised, losing their adversarial perspective in the process. Themes of this post-modernism included a powerful sense of the future, a euphoric vision of post-industrial society, and a celebration of certain dimensions of mass culture against establishment notions of high culture. The drive for a postmodern architecture was similarly motivated by a reaction against the elitism and utopianism of modernist design, and the destruction of the city fabric. The landscape of False Creek and 1970s Fairview Slopes appears to reflect this postmodernism, as did the ideology of the liberal elite at the time when Vancouver's postindustrial future seemed most assured.

But this adversarial ethos was vulnerable to co-optation. Huyssen identifies the second phase as the unfolding of an "affirmative" postmodernism (with which would be aligned the Fairview architecture of the 1980s) that appears to have abandoned its claim to critique. Affirmative posimodernism is deeply implicated in consumption ideology, and it is the architecture of this phase which writers such as Frampton (1983, page 19) can condemn as "merely feeding the media-society with gratuitous, quietistic images", and in which "the strong affinity … for the rhetorical techniques and imagery of advertising is hardly accidental" (page 21). A few imaginative projects have recently been completed in Fairview, but most exemplify how developers are grasping to capitalise on available symbolic systems which will give their product a special allure.

Huyssen does perceive a possibility for a critical postmodernism, but in a radical redefinition of culture's relation to society, with art being no longer accorded a privileged and autonomous position as the authentic source of critique (this means a rejection of the modernist idea of the avant-garde). Postmodernism of all shades, he argues, "operates in a field of tension between tradition and innovation, conservation and renewal, mass culture and high art, in which the second terms are no longer automatically privileged over the first" (1984, page 48). The product of this tension depends on whether plurality and contextualism serve only to shatter the bases for critical discourse, or whether they hold out any hope for bringing the fragments back together in a revealing manner. The duplicity of a postmodern landscape such as the later Fairview Slopes, like that of the broader realms of commodity and advertising, is the opacity of its symbolic forms. Foster places this postmodernism in the context of "the fragmentary nature of late-capitalist urban life; we are conditioned to its delirium, even as its causes are concealed from us" (Foster, 1985, page 127). But it would be foolish to imply that postmodernism *must* function as the gilt on the cage of commodification. Prising open a space for cultural diversity, and nurturing a sensitivity to the bonding of community life to place, are elements of a modest environmental resistance against monolithic corporate culture, of which the south shore of False Creek and the early developments in Fairview Slopes are examples. Redeveloping inner-city neighbourhoods, not with massive modernist monuments but with sensually stimulating postmodernist enclaves, may mean a significant enrichment of the life-styles of their new middle-class settlers. On the other hand, we should also not forget that the costs fall on those poorer residents displaced from communities which may have been already rich in cultural diversity and sense of place. Postmodernism means a small victory for the quality of the urban environment, but one which confounds the assault on social injustice, except in cases such as False Creek where it was wedded to bold programmes of equitable housing allocation [see Ley (1986) for a discussion of the limited success of postmodernism in solving the crisis of meaning in urban landscapes, and its elitist consequences].

How does the notion of cultural hegemony contribute to interpreting the chain of events in False Creek and Fairview Slopes? Despite its future orientation, and its faith in the liberating power of new informed techniques and approaches, the worldview of 1970s Vancouver liberals hung partly on the revival of residual cultural forms. Williams's depiction has a striking correspondence with those events:

"In the subsequent default of a particular phase of a dominant culture, there is then a reaching back to those meanings and values which were created in real societies in the past, and which still seem to have some significance because they represent areas of human experience, aspiration and achievement, which the dominant culture undervalues or opposes, or even cannot recognise" (1980, page 42).

The new conjunction of values developed in a niche unoccupied by the prevailing ideology associated with rational planning and the corporate city; "Against the uniformity of the modern movement is a renewed interest in the specificity of regional and historical styles and a respect for the diversity of urban subcultures" (Ley, 1987a, page 43). The language of folk knowledge and urban villages and shared symbolic systems reestablishes lines of continuity with history. Its familiarity is the joy of living in a renovated inner-city neighbourhood, the enchantment of postmodern design which, "in its best moments reaches back across the wreckage of post-war urbanism to seize the strands of urban culture at the point they became unravelled" (ALA, 1983, page 254).

The return to history is one basis for the critique of postmodernism as neoconservative. But, by coupling the modernist patterns of the cultural dominant with the symbolic systems of residual cultures, bringing the latter into critical engagement with the former, residual patterns become endowed with a progressive quality and are knit into a new emergent form. On this point, the issue of "whose past?" is to be recovered begs consideration. The particular combination of residual themes in the False Creek and the early Fairview developments had an oppositional quality because it drew largely on motifs, such as that of the village, which are not associated with power and authority. Later Fairview designs have tended to use the vocabulary of grander styles and. in conjunction with the capture of folk symbolism by the producers of commodities for the affluent market, the edge of critique is dulled. In early 1970s Vancouver the dominion of the commodity form wavered temporarily; now it is again in the ascendent. How do we depict the later manifestations of postmodernism? Jameson (1984a) considers postmodernism to be the contemporary hegemonic norm, and this might be supported by Williams's argument that the space between oppositional and alternative (tolerated) practices is narrowing (Williams, 1980, page 41). Important here is the integration of aesthetic production into commodity production: "[T]he frantic economic urgency of producing, fresh waves of ever more novel-seeming goods … now assigns an increasingly essential structural function and position to aesthetic innovation and experimentation" (Jameson, 1984a, page 56). How trends in the differentiation of urban space constitute part of the strategy of flexible capital accumulation is one perspective currently under consideration in the literature on gentrification (Smith, 1987a; Zukin, 1982). It is equally important, however, to infuse such propositions with a sensitivity to how the meaning of innovative commodities, such as new urban landscapes, is socially constructed.

FAIRVIEW SLOPES AS A GENTRIFIED NEIGHBOURHOOD

During the 1970s the census tract encompassing False Creek and Fairview Slopes experienced the greatest increase in social status in Vancouver, measured by an index combining occupational and educational status of its residents (Ley, 1988). Yet Fairview Slopes does not fit the usual image of a gentrified neighbourhood. It is a landscape of redevelopment, and renting is probably still as common as owner-occupancy. "Gentrification" has, of course, been criticised as a "chaotic concept" (Beauregard, 1986; Hamnett, 1984; Rose, 1984), which aggregates a variety of contingently related processes under one unitary category according to commonsense definitions of the empirical object. Variations in the form of neighbourhoods deemed to be gentrified have served to shift attention to the processes underlying current urban change. Most recently, researchers have focused on theorising the 'production of gentrjfiers'—how the restructuring of economic activity has transformed the division of labour, how practices of social reproduction are implicated in that transformation, and how the pattern of housing demand is changed in response.

This perspective developed out of a reaction against the Marxist work represented by Smith's rent-gap analysis (1979; 1982). Smith claimed that gentrification occurs when the built environment undergoes devalorisation, opening up a disparity between the capitalised and potential ground rent of a plot of land. But, as originally stated, Smith's theory could only establish opportunities for inner-city reinvestment; in contrast, tracing the production of gentrifiers allows one to account for variations in the appearance of gentrification. Smith now emphasises the part played by gentrification in a strategy of capital accumulation by means of product differentiation, which makes new commodities available to the middle class. This strategy came into play in response to the extension of an "ethic of consumption" into the working class by the standardisation of commodity production, as exemplified by suburbanisation (Smith, 1987a). Yet this account still requires an active subject, a sociology and an anthropology of gentrification which would deal with variations in social relations over time and space. An approach which focuses upon the production of gentrifiers is an initial step in that direction, and there is now widespread agreement on the necessity of working together the economic and sociocultural aspects of gentrification (Ley, 1987b; Smith, 1987b).

In the present economic climate the motive of profitable investment becomes increasingly apparent in discourse on urban change. Dear (1986) notes a regrouping around a core emphasis on efficiency and function in planning. The same might be the case in architecture where architects are reminded of "the wellspring of most architecture … the activating purposes of a building is not to allude to [seventeenth or eighteenth century neoclassical architect] Mr. Soane (postmodern) nor even to house people (modern), but simply to make money" (Moore, 1980, page 48). Although this assertion seems to sit uneasily with postmodernism's opposition to the exaltation of efficiency and function, it does accord with the "crass commercialism" of which the second (affirmative) phase of post-modernism has been accused. In commercial architecture, affirmative postmodernism represents the necessity of negotiating a compromise between functionalism and frivolity; efficiency in design does not sell—functionalism is not functional to the developer. In Fairview Slopes each project attempts this balancing act. For one development (which does not appear to have sold well) the architect saw his role as exercising a modifying influence within tight budget constraints:

"I'm always sort of fighting them ... I understand budgets are tough to stick to when developers are costing things out, but I think it helps sell, perhaps fitting a double [bathroom] vanity, pulling in a sky-light ... some of the earlier [developments] are more interesting because they were done when the economy was a little more buoyant ... the most economical material is stucco. But I always try to ... encourage the owner to complement it with other materials" (interview with the author).

André Molnar, canny developer of projects which have a reputation for selling quickly, has taken a much bolder approach in his more theatrical designs; however, this strategy was the fruit of cautious observation:

"I looked at Fairview Slopes in the 1976–1977 era ... but I was terrified of pioneering the area ... there was a lot of squatting and it was a terrible neighbourhood at that time and I was frightened that my [middle class] customers wouldn't find it acceptable. Some other more courageous developers ... started to develop, and [then] I got involved".

Investment potential is clearly a consideration both for 'producers' and for some 'consumers'. Some of the earlier developments were MURBS (multiple unit residential buildings), built under a federal programme which provided tax incentives to investors in apartment buildings. In some non-MURB buildings there are also many absentee owners. Explains one architect:

"They're marketing the units as a *commodity*, which is something I think people tend to think like these days ... the most important thing they're trying to put over is that it's a good investment. ... People who 'pre-buy' these units can, if it's a well-marketed building, turn around after it's completely finished and make some profit" (interview with the author).

The profit motive encouraged individual owners to rent out their property over the period of Expo 86, during which some developers of new projects, before selling, also operated virtually a hotel service[4].

Previous disinvestment in the area by absentee owners of dilapidated housing created the opportunity for profitable reinvestment. But the balance between investment and other considerations has changed over time. Designers involved in the earlier phase of development were perhaps more concerned with the pursuit of aesthetic goals and with establishing their own reputations. Where investment is the prime consideration, there have been different perceptions of how best to tap that investment potential. For an investment to be a good one, the commodity must sell; for it to sell, it must have use-value; and that use-value must be 'imaginable' – it must have cultural meaning. The establishment of a reliable set of meanings associated with inner-city living is what Molnar was waiting for rather than being unilaterally imposed by the 'producers' of the landscape, the meaning of Fairview Slopes arose through a process of negotiation to which the changing mind-sets of its potential consumers were pivotal. Architects who were ahead of the game—not cautious businessmen like Molnar, but inspired by challenges of social and aesthetic experimentation—may have won professional recognition yet received a slow response from the buying public, and were in consequence unpopular with developers. In Fairview Slopes some developers have erred by building cheaper designs that fail to fire customers' imaginations, whereas others have been caught off-guard by the enthusiastic response to a well-designed building. Judging the spirit of the customer and balancing it against the constraints of the economic climate is an uncertain profession. The focus in the remainder of this paper is on the actors who have defined the style and spirit of inner-city living.

THE PRODUCTION OF FAIRVIEW SLOPES GENTRIFIERS

With an increase from 14% to 40% in managerial, administrative, professional, and technical occupations between 1971 and 1981, the Fairview labour force shows the effect of broader economic trends. In British Columbia these highest status categories grew by 40 000 jobs during the deep recession from 1981 to 1984, while other categories lost 90 000 positions. Spatially, new job formation is concentrated in the metropolitan core, especially in the finance/insurance/real estate, public administration and service industries (Ley and Hutton, 1987; Ley and Mills, 1988). Fairview residents tend to be employed either downtown (only about seven minutes away by car) or in the "Broadway corridor", the city's midtown focus of white-collar employment which defines the southern boundary of Fairview Slopes. Within the increasingly (spatially and occupationally) polarised labour market, the middle class of Fairview Slopes inhabit a distinct niche.

Implicated with labour-force restructuring is a reorganisation of patterns of domestic life, one feature of which is a movement of women into senior white-collar categories. In Fairview Slopes in 1981, 38% of the female labour force held managerial, administrative, professional, and technical occupations[5]. Over 40% of adults were single (never married), and 10% were divorced; 55% and 33% of households comprised one and two persons, respectively. There are few children. Many couples are of the dual-career type, both partners pursuing careers which require a high level of commitment. Markusen suggests that "gentrification is in large part a result of the breakdown of the patriarchal household" (1981, page 32), and my field research confirms that beliefs and practices centred around divided gender roles are fairly uncommon. Though the majority of households are 'young professionals', there is also a fair proportion of 'empty nesters' close to retirement, who might accept more traditional gender roles.

To locate such a group with respect to broad trends in economic and social restructuring is the first step in understanding patterns of housing demand. Locational features were uppermost in the minds of many Fairview slopes gentrifiers when they decided on a new home—for the convenience of short journeys-to-work (particularly important to two-wage earner households), and for the flexibility required by professional jobs which would be constrained within the "time-space rhythms" of the suburban commuting culture (Rose, 1984, page 62). In addition, the housing itself offers great practical advantages to busy households, with its condominium-style management and well-appointed units. One-bedroom or two-bedroom units on multilevels are suitable for young households, allowing two working people a degree of privacy (good "sulking space" according to one resident). In 'Open House' displays, second bedrooms are decked out as offices—in one, complete with personal computer. Although Fairview houses a relatively affluent population, it is successful partly because it offers, under reasonable financial terms, attractive but necessary conveniences to young 'professionals' not yet earning enough to buy a house in a central location.

However, the high rents charged (and paid) for some units suggest that, for some, flexibility is valued above the commitment of buying even a cheap unit.

Equally significant, though somewhat neglected so far in the literature on the production of gentrifiers, is the consumption style of gentrifiers. The 'life-style' reputation of Fairview Slopes is distinctive partly for its stress on consumption style—the conspicuous consumption of quality goods and experiences, what Veblen calls the "cultivation of the aesthetic faculty" (Veblen, 1953, page 64). Explains one architect: "It's the convenience to downtown, it's an attractive lifestyle that didn't involve having to mow the lawn at the weekends and a lot of repair, it was … very much a mean, self-centred sort of lifestyle, and the view and location and ambience were part of it" (interview with the author). The language of life-style is the dominant theme of the marketing literature: "We don't just sell you a townhome, we offer you an exciting new lifestyle". In 'Open House' displays kitchens are laid out with wineracks, microwave ovens, pasta makers, and gourmet cookbooks; storage space is advertised for bicycles and windsurfers. "Live next door to everything that makes Vancouver great" offers one pamphlet which lists the public market, restaurants, jogging paths, and marinas. Even work, which normally appears in advertising only as a source of stress (Kline and Leiss, 1978), features as a positive modifier to the notion of life-style: "Executive also means lifestyle"; "Cityside career living at its best". This implies a "simultaneous dedication to career and leisure pursuits" supposedly typical of "Yuppies" (Belk, 1986, page 514). Advertisements for this "friendly village of people on the way up" are rife in status symbolism, for here you buy "an address for those who like to set the standards". Thus the magic of advertising defines "the magical city" (Raban, 1974).

Probably because of the frivolous tone of such images, the literature seems unwilling to treat the consumption style of genirifiers seriously as a reflection of cultural practice. For example, while arguing for the significance of social trends to gentrification, Hamnett (1984, page 311) takes comfort in the fact that these can be interpreted as "crucial *material* changes". Rose (1.984) has made the observation that 'life-style' trends should be interpreted as the active response by people to broader conditions, for example, the lack of employment opportunities. This is vital for understanding the interplay of activities in the (waged) workplace and the home: how conditions in one 'sphere' contain the conditions of the other, and how residential decisions are part of the constant effort required to construct a seamless articulation of the two. We should expand this insight to take account of the effect of hegemonic and emergent cultures on the definition of life-style alternatives.

THE NEW CLASS AND THE POSTMODERN LANDSCAPE

The description of Fairview Slopes has touched on the characteristics both of the 'producers' (planners, developers, architects) and of the 'consumers' (residents) of the landscape. What can be said of their constitution as a social group? Ley (1986,1987a) has suggested that the "cultural new class" may be both patron and client of postmodernism. The "production of gentrifiers" approach depicts gentrifiers in terms of an expanding "professional-managerial fraction" of the urban labour force (Beauregard, 1986, page 42).

Amongst the trends associated with the transition to a 'postindustrial' social order, Bell (1973, 1980) has identified two of particular interest. First is a growth in professional occupations; four professional estates are identified (scientific and scholarly, technological, administrative, and cultural). Second is a cultural change involving the rise in an adversary culture espousing antibourgeois values. The two tendencies are commonly associated in the literature; for example, Gouldner (1979) draws attention to the participation of a "New Class" of intellectuals and technical intelligentsia in the political reform, ecology, and women's movements, where they challenge old ruling-class values. Gouldner locates the structural basis of this class in its control over cultural capital (special skills and techniques which provide their possessors with claims to income). This is drawn from the Weberian concept of skills as a basis for acquisition classes (see also Giddens, 1973). As a first level of abstraction, these representations correspond with the characteristics of many of the producers and consumers of Fairview Slopes, especially the residents who moved into the larger townhouses constructed in the early phase of redevelopment. The breakdown of adversary culture into hedonistic 'life-style' and the capture of its products by commodificalion, to which Bell alludes, seem reflective of the more recent stage of urban change.

The promise of these ideas in accounting for gentrification lies in some conjunction of cultural and social categories. But, in an essay on the new class as a muddled concept, Bell (1980) argues that the idea conflates two independent notions—the rise of a social stratum with some objective structural position, and the rise of those who share the modern temper of individualistic hedonism centred on self-fulfillment through experience. Bell concludes that the New Class is the second of these, a "mentality", similar to a Weberian status group, rather than a class. Because candidates for the New Class are spread over the four different estates, and also between a number of 'situses' (institutional locations such as the university and the economic enterprise), Bell claims it is impossible to identify what their common interests could be. Moreover, in politics, alignments on economic and cultural issues do not necessarily coincide. The problem with this argument lies with Bell's reliance on a positivist view that people's real interests are those which they subjectively conceive as their interests. This avoids the question of interest 'horizons', for it is possible to determine objectively a person's interests in terms of costs and benefits if we specify the context of action (Saunders, 1981, page 48). The short-term interests of employees in different situses may be objectively different over issues such as resource allocation. But a candidate for the common long-term interests of the New Class is available in the form of meritocracy, which is defended through the ideology of Gouldner's 'culture of critical discourse', that is, the justification of assertions according to an historically evolved set of rules of 'theoreticity' rather than on the basis of the speaker's social position or authority.

With the rise of the urban reform party in Vancouver, it was challenges to the established authority of business leaders, through recourse to an alternative set of rules to be logically implemented by trained and educated professionals, which defined the clash of ideologies. At that time, some sense of common consciousness according to the 'new liberalism' gave the New Class access through the ballot box to positions of power in local government. Williams (1980, pages 42–44) identifies one source of emergent culture as the formation and coming to consciousness of a new class; the other source is new insights and practices developed in realms which are not fully incorporated under the necessarily selective reach of dominant culture, such as in the arts and sciences. I have suggested that postmodernism has taken residual themes and forged them into the equivalent of a new emergent cultural form. In Vancouver, the conjunction of the two sources of emergent culture in the ascent of representatives of the New Class, for whom aesthetic issues were central to a new philosophy of urban living, could give it special potency. Once established as the new norm, however, the flaw of meritocracy—its elitism—became evident. Meritocracy can lead to a new system of privilege and authority, at which point the objective interests of those who have achieved positions of authority shifts to a defence of those positions. This was a fatal defect of reform policies. The built-in instability of interests and their ambiguous relationship to New Class ideology thus make for a set of social conditions which is fraught with tension. Additionally, in failing to recognise both the ingenuity of the commodity market to outmanoeuvre attacks on corporate culture, and the persistent human impulse to associate objects with social categories such as those of status, the temporarily dominant culture was vulnerable to co-optation: "The movement from counterculture to lifestyle ... [involved] a retention of form and a discarding of content. ... ['Lifestylers'] have become consumers with avengeance. And ... business has, as usual, had the last laugh" (Yagoda, 1979, page 234).

There are other approaches to theorising the middle class; Wright's (1978) analysis of "contradictory locations within class relations" is one alternative. My aim, however, is to raise the issue of class in relation to culture, and to suggest that further work on gentrification should give priority to this point. The issue is directly confronted in discussions on the New Class, and begs consideration in extensions of the literature on the production of gentrifiers. What characterises both the New Class literature and other attempts to account for the new middle class is the view that this social category is inherently ambiguous. Analysis of its significance to urban change must capture the tensions of ideology and interest which define its career. At the point of lived experience, the interpenetration of cultural practice with social consciousness is crucial. I shall draw out the implications of this for the landscape of Fairview Slopes.

As noted earlier, there have been suggestions that the study of contemporary' landscapes is confounded by the unstable fluid relations between signifier and signified, image and reality. No longer is it possible to map each symbolic component directly onto one meaning (see also Duncan and Duncan, 1988). The grammar of status symbolism in clothing fashion is totally transformed in the newspeak of radical chic; similarly, postmodern architecture is a pastiche of contradictory codes. What *is* possible, however, is to focus on those points where free-floating images do come to rest, where they are fixed into a new system which, at least temporarily, is reproducible. Because that grounding of images is performed by actors in the process of social interaction, we can trace meaning—not by digging behind each image to lay bare its significance, but rather by looking *across* to its new conjuncture with other images. And we can ask, what (say) has an interpenetration of folk and classical allusions *been made to*

do by these people at this time and in this place? To answer, we must look at the practices of its producers and consumers.

The producer of urban housing is rarely also its consumer. This opens up space for fatal misinterpretations, leading in architecture to such drastic solutions as the demolition of public housing projects. The disjunction of the two perspectives of producer and consumer is supposedly collapsed in postmodern architecture, which refuses to elevate high culture over folk culture; the ideal of the architect as a visionary figure seeking a radical break from the existing social and urban structures is abandoned. In Fairview Slopes it is also significant that both sets of actors are drawn from the same New Class, share a speech community, and operate within similar social circles (this was especially so in the 1970s). A number of producers lived in the area; other residents are uncommonly au courant with planning and architectural issues. Although their immediate interests in housing-market issues may not be aligned, producers and consumers together actively negotiate the meaning of living in Fairview Slopes. The market, then, does not dictate. In the meeting between producers and consumers over style and symbolism, the resultant meaning of place must engage the cultural codes of consumers.

Indeed, negotiation is frequently superseded by interpenetration. Producers' efforts to personalise their products, abetted by local architectural journalists, inform consumers that they share a social world. With name-dropping in marketing pamphlets, many residents are familiar with the identity of the architect of their dwelling. André Molnar, who describes his work as "the Pierre Cardin approach" (Figure 16.3), affixes his name prominently on advertising billboards which even light up at night (learning from Las Vegas?). Another developer assures consumers that he is someone like themselves; to quote from an advertisement: "Matthew Briscoe fits his own 'buyers profile'. His own discerning tastes allow him to design homes ... perfectly adapted to an upwardly mobile lifestyle." Launching a new development becomes a celebratory spectacle, complete with free chocolates, a hot air balloon, and a colour-coordinated (with the stucco) pop group playing all the 'baby boomer' classics—a sad echo of the festival of youth rebellion in the 1960s. From the point of view of the marketers, then, a combination of themes encompassing conventional messages of friendliness and joy is converted into a vehicle for something quite different—that is, selling a commodity. But, in selecting a Fairview condominium as their setting, what are the New Class gentrifiers making the landscape do for *themselves*? In

Figure 16.3 "La Galleria" has a glass dome covering a courtyard fountain, and architecture inspired "by the charm … of Florence". "Young and dynamic, André Molnar is perhaps North America's most innovative and eminent designer". The display suite included a personal computer and exercise bicycle. (Quotations from marketing pamphlet)

postmodern architecture, contradiction is preferred over simplification, tension over straightforwardness. And, as postmodern architecture is typified by ambiguity, so too are its New Class champions. One response to an ambiguous social position is to try to pin it down through some clever 'work' with objects and events which symbolise social categories. This involves associating oneself with some 'things', disassociating oneself from other 'things'—the meanings of which are constantly in flux. Features of the landscape are means for fixing social position. In a rare study on the significance of gentrification aesthetics, Jager (1986) looks at middle-class renovation of Victorian houses in Melbourne, noting how people with an ambiguous class position can jockey for position in the sphere of consumption. This buying into history not only recovers a sense of rootedness and a connection with cultural

heritage; it also serves to revive a symbolism of conspicuous consumption associated with the decorative excesses of Victoriana. Status is cemented through the work of remodelling houses; neighbourhood stigma is wiped out, as features such as bare brick walls and exposed timbers are redefined as tokens of aesthetic discernment. Moore (1982) interprets gentrification as "residential credentialism", a prime "positional good" (Hirsch, 1976) at a time when the suburbs have lost their exclusive status. In Fairview Slopes, advertisements stress that these are award-winning homes—"award yourself" is the slogan for one— which make (to quote from a pamphlet) "a statement about societal achievement". Paraphrasing Gouldner, Moore argues that "Just as blue jeans became the international uniform of the new class … so gentrified housing became its international neighbourhood" (1982, page 27). Ironically, as blue jeans turned into a new conformity, so does the landscape distinctiveness of the gentrified neighbourhood.

The 'discovery' of ever-new scarce commodities which can act as vehicles for status remains barely one step ahead of the mass market. The New Class seeks to define its otherwise ambiguous status by signalling through a particular combination of objects or experiences. But its efforts can never rest, for once new signs enter into a system of communication their exclusivity is lost. Authentic versions of taste and experience can however, be perpetually redefined, so that the external observer can distinguish no stable referent and the upwardly aspiring individual must be forever mastering new languages of taste. Hence the frantic inversion and shuffling of signs. What is one to make of this Fairview project?—original warehouses on one facade, representations of old houses on the other; from the junction of the two emerge luxury condominiums. A hint comes with the name: "The Sixth Estate". Does this refer just to its location (on Sixth Avenue), to the television documentary series ("The Fifth Estate" made by the Canadian Broadcasting Corporation), or does it also refer to a new social stratum one step beyond the familiar estates? Bringing together the previously unrelated, distorting matter-of-fact reality, is the strategy of constructing new signifiers from old. The schizophrenic postmodern landscape (Gibson, 1984) is the result, illustrated in Vancouver, for example, by the use of bedroom colours and sensuous curves on external walls. (It is interesting to speculate on what this says about users' attitudes to gender identity; one developer suggests that such buildings are especially attractive to women and gays. Is the postmodern landscape an androgynous landscape?)

The quality of postmodernism is one of crossing boundaries (Polan, 1984) and I conclude this paper by identifying some suggestive parallels across practices, starting with Gouldner's paradox that the ambivalent New Class is both emancipatory and elitist: the Flawed Universal Class. Its culture of critical discourse requires a broader vision than utilitarian profit-oriented pursuits. In Fairview Slopes this takes the guise of bohemia—romantic cottage eaves, garrett skylights and lofts, alternatives to the nuclear family, and a fine mesh of commercial and residential space. Yet the New Class is also elitist; a sense of superiority and an overindulgence in reflexive thought disposes it to a sometimes unhealthy self-consciousness. On the ground we see triumphal arches, classical pillars, and other accoutrements of 'high style'. Significantly, however, straight historical reproductions would not 'work': they would be considered in poor taste and reactionary. Similar use of status icons (such as plaster lions on suburban fences) by other groups is condemned as kitsch, yet the selective combination evolving here, the "kitsch of the new middle classes" is "consecrated as aesthetic" (Jager, 1986, page 78): hence the arbitrariness of the sign is revealed. Of course, the New Class is at an advantage when it comes to manipulating abstract symbols and ideas—that is, its occupation, that is the core of the culture of critical discourse. Being able to take a 'theoretical' attitude towards the world gives it the freedom to shuffle local with cosmopolitan themes, and this is reflected in architecture. At the same time, the New Class plays an ambiguous part as both the exploiter and the exploited. Williams's former university colleague found that his previous training in the criticism of advertisements made him an excellent advertiser, the knowing, humorous style of advertising makes claims "so ludicrously exaggerated as to include the critical response" (1980, page 181). A Fairview architect of a column-bedecked condominium offering some of the cheapest units in the area, claims that his customers are seduced by dreams of living in "grand mansions"—but surely they cannot expect onlookers to be deceived; the purchase of such a home must be contemplated with some degree of ironic detachment.

The meaning of Fairview Slopes is ultimately expressed in the super-image of the 'urban lifestyle'. Here we have, apparently, "City Living at its best", and residents enthusiastically describe their experience in these terms. There is pride in being "downtown people", condescension for "suburbia". This seems to celebrate the interpenetration of work with leisure, the rejection of 'separate spheres', the pleasure of feeling boundaries melt away. Of course,

the appealing urban landscape of Fairview and False Creek conceals as much as it reveals. But, for those in a position to take advantage of it, the blurring of real and imaginary is an agreeable condition, sustained in part by the synaesthesia of the advertising image. When a lumpish image falters, the marketer's intent can be revealed in all its crudity; if postmodern architecture has been accused of a "Magaziner Mentality" (Jacobs, 1983), consider this advertisement: "Daring use of space and multi-levels create dynamic interiors: dimension isn't a word but a sense that's heightened as rooms, stairs and ceilings rise around you. This is contemporaneousness that's not fadish [sic] but the stuff of full colour magazine layouts" (advertising brochure for Ballentyne Square, Adera Group of Companies, 1985). But where the codes are more skilfully handled, distinctions between place and identity remain obscure. An advertisement for a condominium named "Windgate Choklit Park" conveys this most effectively; here, we are told:

"Everywhere there is a flow to each city home as graceful as good conversation. ... The Windgate philosophy is unabashed creativity and flair. Architecturally untimid ... here is design to accent superabundance, as distinctive as you are, beyond commonplace, exuberantly original ... a setting to excite your own creative potential and forever escape the ordinary. Windgate Choklit Park is a celebration of life on the upslope" (advertising brochure, Windgate Choklit Park, First Pacific Development Corporation, 1985).

ACKNOWLEDGEMENT

I would like to thank David Ley, Gerry Pratt, Shelagh Lindsey, and Mike Bradshaw for their helpful comments on an earlier draft.

Notes

(1) Residents included an alderman who became the city's mayor from 1980 to 1986, who commissioned a townhouse; and the chair of the Development Permit Board, chief advocate of the innovative planning approach taken in Fairview Slopes.

(2) The ideology is clearly expressed in a newspaper column on heritage designation in Fairview Slopes: "Architecturai preservation ... is foisted on the public by bureaucrats and elitists who, dreaming of the Champs Elysees, forget the huge costs. ... Under the present

system, a man's home may not be his castle. It could be his prison. City hall will be the jailer" (McMarlin, 1986, page B5). Another columnist repudiates proposals for more "people places" around False Creek, condemning postmodern boutiques and restaurants ("fake Palladian with fake Italian names"), their customers ("They can't *all* be in the drug racket"), their conditions of employment ("aspiring Beautiful People at $4 an hour") and their operators ("slim young men of a kind I'm not, candidly, keen on"). "I want to see, for a change in ... this flaccid city, something actually being *produced*—not consumed. ... I want to see blue-collar workers ... paid $20 an hour, enough to buy detached houses on real lots and 10 raise decent families" (Lautens, 1987, page B9).

(3) For example, comments published in a debate (AIA, 1983) condemn postmodernism as "ephemeral, a throw-away, subject to the caprice of commercial culture and the exigencies of the marketplace"; "shoddy merchandise in titillating packages "neofashion for the bored, the rich, the jaded, the blind".

(4) Investment potential is a minor motif of the marketing campaigns, tempered by life-style imagery, and even by social concern in this advertisement: "Alderview is designed to appeal to residents who prefer a standard of luxury and lifestyle amenity normally considered executive level, thereby ... assuring a compatible attitude toward a lasting investment in real estate and real sensitivity to others" (advertising brochure for Alderview Court, 2412 Alder Development Corporation, 1985).

(5) Analysis of voters' self-definitions on the 1985 voters list assigns about 45% of women to these categories; however, nursing and teaching are found to be the most frequent occupations under these classifications for women (clerical occupations are the most frequent overall for women). Women outnumber men in positions such as social work and some medical occupations (for example, therapists). In other well-represented occupations, numbers of women are over half the numbers of men in consulting and accounting; they are over a third of the numbers of men identified as lawyers and in the somewhat vaguely-defined category of 'businesspersons'. Men outnumber women substantially as brokers, engineers, and physicians. Occupational segregation between men and women in Fairview Slopes remains quite considerable, but the occupational status of these women is high compared with women in most other areas of the city.

REFERENCES

Agnew J-C, 1983, "The consuming vision of Henry James", in *The Culture of Consumption: Critical Essays in American History* Eds R W Fox, T J J Lears (Pantheon Books, New York) pp 67–100

AIA, 1983, "Postmodernism: definition and debate" *Journal of the American Institute of Architects* **72** 238–301

Anderson K, 1988, "Cultural hegemony and the race definition process in Chinatown, Vancouver, 1880–1980" *Environment and Planning D: Society and Space* **6** 127–149

Beauregard R, 1986, "The chaos and complexity of gentrification", in *Gentrification of the City* Eds N Smith, P Williams (Allen and Unwin, Hemel Hempstead, Herts) pp 35–55

Belk R W, 1986, "Yuppies as arbiters of the emerging consumption style" *Advances in Consumer Research* **13** 514–519

Bell D, 1973 *The Coming of Post-industrial Society* (Basic Books, New York)

Bell D, 1980 *The Winding Passage* (Basic Books, New York)

Cosgrove D E, 1984 *Social Formation and Symbolic Landscape* (Croom Helm, Beckenham, Kent)

Cosgrove D E, Jackson P, 1987, "New directions in cultural geography" *Area* **19** 95–101

Csikszentmihalyi M, Rochberg-Halton E, 1981 *The Meaning of Things: Domestic Symbols and the Self* (Cambridge University Press, Cambridge)

Daniels S J, (forthcoming), "Marxism, culture and the duplicity of landscapes", in *New Models in Geography* Eds R Peel, N Thrift (Routledge, Chapman and Hall, Andover, Hants)

Daniels S J, Cosgrove D E, 1988, "Iconography and landscape", in *The Iconography of Landscape* Eds D E Cosgrove, S J Daniels (Cambridge University Press, Cambridge) forthcoming

Dear M J, 1986, "Postmodernism and planning" *Environment and Planning D: Society and Space* **4** 367–384

Diggins J P, 1977, "Reification and the cultural hegemony of capitalism: the perspectives of Marx and Veblen" *Social Research* **44** 354–383

Duncan J, Duncan N, 1988, "(Re)Reading the landscape" *Environment and Planning D: Society and Space* **6** 117–126

Elligott R, Zacharias J, 1973, "Report: Fairview Slopes", City of Vancouver Planning Department, 2675 Yukon St. Vancouver V5Y 3P9

Fitzgerald D, 1986, "A new slant on The Slopes" *Western Living* 16 January issue, pp 18–21 (Comac Communications, Vancouver)

Foster H, 1983, "Postmodernism: a preface", in *The Anti-aesthetic: Essays on Postmodern Culture* Ed. H Foster (Bay Press, Port Townsend, WA) pp ix–xvi

Foster H, 1985, "(Post)modern polemics", in *Recodings: Art, Spectacle, Cultural Politics* Ed. H Foster (Bay Press, Port Townsend, WA) pp 121–136

Frampton K, 1983, "Towards a critical regionalism: six points for an architecture of resistance", in *The Anti-aesthetic: Essays on Postmodern Culture* Ed. H Foster (Bay Press, Port Townsend, WA) pp 16–30

Francis R, 1983, "Symbols, images and social organization in urban sociology", in *Urban Social Research: Problems and Prospects* Eds V Pons, R Francis (Routledge and Kegan Paul, Andover, Hants) pp 115–145

Geertz C, 1973, *The Interpretation of Cultures* (Basic Books, New York)

Gibson E, 1984, "Traditions of landscape aesthetics: 1700–1985", research paper; mimeo available from Department of Geography, Simon Fraser University, Burnaby, BC

Gibson E, 1986, *Award-winning Vancouver Architecture: Inventory* Continuing Studies, Simon Fraser University, Burnaby, BC, and Architectural Institute of British Columbia

Giddens A, 1973, *The Class Structure of the Advanced Societies* (Hutchinson, London)

Gouldner AW, 1979, *The Future of Intellectuals and the Rise of the New Class* (Continuum, New York)

Gruft A, 1983, "Vancouver Architecture: the last fifteen years", in *Vancouver: Art and Artists 1931–1983* (Vancouver Art Gallery, Vancouver) pp 318–331

Gutstein D, 1983, "Peril on the Slopes" *Vancouver Magazine* 16 February issue, pp 32–35, 56–57 (Comac Communications, Vancouver)

Gutstein D, 1985, "Love to live there" *Vancouver Magazine* 18 October issue, pp 22–26, 54–58 (Comac Communications, Vancouver)

Hamnett C, 1984, "Gentrification and residential location theory: a review and assessment", in *Geography and the Urban Environment, Volume 6* Eds D T Herbert, R J Johnston (John Wiley, New York) pp 283–319

Hirsch F, 1976, *The Social Limits to Growth* (Harvard University Press, Cambridge, MA)

Huyssen A, 1984, "Mapping the postmodern" *New German Critique* **33** 5–52

Jacobs J, 1983, "Modern, post modern or what?" *The Canadian Architect* **28** 21–31

Jager M, 1986, "Class definition and the aesthetics of gentrification: Victoriana in Melbourne", in *Gentrification of the City* Eds N Smith, P Williams (Allen and Unwin, Hemel Hempstead, Herts) pp 78–91

Jameson F, 1983, "Postmodernism and consumer society", in *The Anti-aesthetic: Essays on Postmodern Culture* Ed. H Foster (Bay Press, Port Townsend, WA) pp 111–125

Jameson F, 1984a, "Postmodernism, or the cultural logic of late capitalism" New *Left Review* number 146, pp 53–92

Jameson F, 1984b, "The politics of theory; ideological positions in the postmodernism debate" *New German Critique* **33** 53–65

Jencks C, 1981, *The Language of Post-modern Architecture* 3rd edition (Rizzoli, New York)

Jencks C, 1986, *What is Post-modernism?* (St Martin's Press, New York)

Jhally S, Kline S, Leiss W, 1985, "Magic in the marketplace: an empirical test for commodity fetishism" *Canadian Journal of Political and Social Theory* **9** 1–22

Kline S, Leiss W, 1978, "Advertising, needs, and 'commodity fetishism'" *Canadian Journal of Political and Social Theory* **2** 5–30

Lautens T, 1987, "Pray, save us from this awful phrase" *The Vancouver Sun* 10 October, page **B9**

Lears T J J, 1983, "From salvation to self-realization: advertising and the therapeutic roots of the consumer culture, 1880–1930", in *The Culture of Consumption: Critical Essays in American History* Eds R W Fox, T J J Lears (Pantheon Books, New York) pp 3–38

Lears T J J, 1985, "The concept of cultural hegemony: problems and possibilities" *American Historical Review* **90** 567–593

Leiss W, 1978, "Needs, exchanges and the fetishism of objects" *Canadian Journal of Political and Social Theory* **2** 27–48

Leiss W, 1983, "The icons of the market place" *Theory, Culture and Society* **1** 10–21

Ley D, 1980, "Liberal ideology and the postindustrial city" *Annals of the Association of American Geographers* **70** 238–258

Ley D, 1985, "Cultural/humanistic geography" *Progress in Human Geography* **9** 415–423

Ley D, 1986, "Modernism, post-modernism and the struggle for place", paper presented to the seminar series The Power of Place, Syracuse University; mimeo available from Department of Geography, University of British Columbia, Vancouver, BC

Ley D, 1987a, "Styles of the times: liberal and neo-conservative landscapes in inner Vancouver, 1968–1986" *Journal of Historical Geography* **13** 40–56

Ley D, 1987b, "Reply: the rent gap revisited" *Annals of the Association of American Geographers* **77** 465–468

Ley D, 1988, "Attributes of areas undergoing social upgrading in six Canadian cities" *The Canadian Geographer* **32** (forthcoming)

Ley D, Hutton T, 1987, "Vancouver's corporate complex and producer services sector: linkages and divergence within a provincial staples economy" *Regional Studies* **21** 413–424

Ley D, Mills C A, 1988, "Labour markets, housing markets and the changing family in Canada's service economy", in *Industrial Transformation and Challenge in Australia and Canada* Eds R Haytér, P Wilde (Carleton University Press, Ottawa) in press

Ley D, Olds K, 1988, "Landscape as spectacle world's fairs and the culture of heroic consumption" *Environment and Planning D: Society and Space* **6** 191–212

McCracken G, 1986, "Culture and consumption: a theoretical account of the structure and movement of the cultural meaning of consumer goods" *Journal of Consumer Research* **13** 71–84

McMartin P, 1986, "A costly obsession" *The Vancouver Sun* 27 August, page 85

Markusen A, 1981, "City spatial structure, women's household work, and national urban policy", in *Women and the City* Eds C R Stimpson, E Dixler, M J Newlson, K B Yatrakis (University of Chicago Press, Chicago, IL) pp 20–41

Mitchell W J T, 1986, *Iconology, Image, Text, Ideology* (Chicago University Press. Chicago, IL)

Moore A C, 1980, "The retreat into architectural narcissism" *Journal of the American Institute of Architects* **69** 46–68

Moore P W, 1982, "Gentrification and the residential geography of the New Class",

research paper; mimeo available from Department of Geography, Scarborough College, University of Toronto, Ontario

Ovenell-Carter J, 1986, "The arrival of Jim Cheng" *Western Living* 16 August issue, pp 25c–25t (Comac Communications, Vancouver)

Polan D, 1984, Review of *The Anti-aesthetic: Essays on Postmodern Culture* Ed. H Foster *New German Critique* **33** 264–269

Raban J, 1974, *Soft City* (Dutton, New York)

Rose D, 1984, "Rethinking gentrification: beyond the uneven development of Marxist urban theory" *Environment and Planning D: Society and Space* **2** 47–74

Sahlins M, 1976, *Culture and Practical Reason* (University of Chicago Press, Chicago, IL)

Saunders P, 1981, *Social Theory and the Urban Question* (Hutchinson, London)

Smith N, 1979, "Toward a theory of gentrification: a back to the city movement by capital not people" *Journal of the American Planners Association* **45** 538–548

Smith N, 1982, "Gentrification and uneven development" *Economic Geography* **58** 139–155

Smith N, 1987a, "Of yuppies and housing: gentrification, social restructuring, and the urban dream" *Environment and Planning D. Society and Space* **5** 151–172

Smith N, 1987b, "Gentrification and the rent gap" *Annals of the Association of American Geographers* **77** 462–465

Veblen T, 1953, *The Theory of the Leisure Class* (New American Library, New York)

Walters R G, 1980, "Signs of the times: Clifford Geertz and Historians" *Social Research* **47** 537–556

Williams R. 1980, *Problems in Materialism and Culture* (Verso Editions and NLB, London)

Wright E O, 1978, *Class, Crisis and the State* (New Left Books, London)

Yagoda B, 1979, "Life style, then and now" *Dissent* **26** 233–234

Zukin S, 1982, *Loft Living: Culture and Capital in Urban Change* (The Johns Hopkins University Press, Baltimore, MD)

SECTION C

Moving outside of the production versus consumption stalemate

Plate 12 **HSBC poster with images of New York: John F. Kennedy International Airport, July, 2009.**
Photograph by Elvin Wyly.

INTRODUCTION TO SECTION C

Post-modern anti-essentialism invites us to free ourselves from the burdens which we long have carried – the burden of explaining a complex and multifaceted history with a limited set of categories …

(Graham, 1988: 64–65)

In the mid-1980s and into the mid-1990s as postmodernism took hold in the social sciences gentrification researchers, in geography and sociology in particular, began to move away from grand theory and to argue for the acceptance of multiple voices and explanations of gentrification.

By the end of the 1980s, most analysts working in the conservative tradition of neo-classical economics had concluded that gentrification was a small, insignificant process – and so most of these researchers stopped doing work on the topic. This left the gentrification literature dominated by scholars who (compared to neoclassical analysts) shared a critical perspective on gentrification and its inequalities. But these critical analysts were sharply divided on the importance of production versus consumption, economic versus cultural explanations (see Lees, Slater, and Wyly, 2008, Chapters 2 and 3). By the early 1990s, many researchers began to seek a path out of the production/consumption theoretical battleground. Marxist geographers, in particular, found this difficult but soon realized their fate if they did not concede:

If Marxists can acknowledge that their discourse is but one of many discourses, they can make themselves heard in the postmodern cacophony. If they continue to privilege Marxism as the only true discourse, they will very quickly silence themselves in the ears of others. For Marxism is patently not alone, or primary, in the community of discourses.

(Graham, 1988: 64)

In 1984 geographer Damaris Rose argued that gentrification was a 'chaotic concept' and that the 'processes and elements it comprises need to be thought through again' (p. 47). Rose rejected the idea of an analytical thread; for her, gentrification had to be seen as a multiplicity of forces (see Box 5). Rose wanted to retain a structural model of gentrification but to make it better able to deal with historical relationships. She also criticized Marxist work on gentrification for neglecting employment restructuring and changes in the reproduction of labour power, and importantly for its 'incorrect conflation of reproduction and consumption'. She argued that the '*production* of gentrifiers' had been neglected, and that Marxists had paid little attention to 'the processes behind the demographic and "lifestyle" profiles of gentrifiers' (p. 51):

The crucial point … is that '*gentrifiers*' are not the mere bearers of a process determined independently of them. Their constitution, as certain types of workers and as people, is as crucial an element in the production of gentrification as is the production of the dwellings they occupy.

(Rose, 1984: 56)

Rose asserted that it was important to look at the needs and desires of gentrifier groups and the labour relationships inherent in the restructuring of international capitalism in theorizing the production of gentrifiers. Rose was a key figure in feminist geographers' insistence that questions of social reproduction should be taken more seriously, rather than conflated with issues of consumption, which had the effect of 'obscuring the active work of household members in reproducing both labour power and people' (Rose, 1984, p. 54). In this way Rose extended a Marxist framework on gentrification, informing it with new work from feminism (on women in the city, reproduction and labour relationships) and postmodernism (on difference in the city and its politicization). Rose used the term 'marginal gentrifier' to refer to a very specific cohort of socially and culturally rich but economically poor female gentrifiers (see Box 5). Rose emphasized the growing importance both of single women professionals and dual-earner couples in gentrification and argued that inner cities may be better spaces than the suburbs for working out equitable divisions of domestic labour. Marginally-employed professionals, prominent among whom were women, single parents and those receiving moderate incomes, were attracted to central city neighbourhoods due to the range of support services they offered – which were unavailable in the suburbs. For example, the worry of precarious employment could be eased by networking and holding more than one job; and by minimizing space-time constraints, lone female parents could combine paid and unpaid (domestic) labour with greater ease than in suburban locations. Peter Williams (1986) added to this the influence of higher education in the central city:

> [H]aving become familiar with the apparently more solid, intimate and accessible world of the inner city, many [women] were encouraged to reject suburbia physically (just as they were rejecting it mentally) and opt for the world they now understood and preferred. For women, that decision gave them ready access to relatively well paid jobs, a supportive environment and the opportunity to imprint themselves and their newfound status upon the landscape.
>
> (p. 69)

Other work seeking a more complex and contextual explanation of gentrification followed suit. Munt's (1987) analysis of gentrification in Battersea, London, which set out to combine both economic and cultural explanatory frameworks is often cited. Munt's rationale for combining both explanatory frameworks was that Marxist and institutionalist approaches neglected demand and that individualist approaches failed to place demand in its economic and cultural context. That same year Smith (1987) published a paper in which he responded, in part, to Rose. He argued that Rose had forced the 'chaos' she spoke of onto gentrification through her conceptualization of 'marginal gentrifiers':

> the opportunity to gentrify has filtered down the economic hierarchy and across the political field, but it has hardly filtered down so far that female-headed households earning barely $10,000 per year should be considered 'gentrifiers'. To include such a household under the rubric of 'gentrification' is to force a chaos on the term which I do not think it has as commonly used.
>
> (p. 160)

Smith (1987) felt that Rose (1984) had opened up the term gentrification to too much complexity causing unnecessary conceptual chaos. Nevertheless, in this same paper he cedes to those hoping to move away from the theoretical stalemate in the gentrification literature: 'the notion that production and consumption are mutually implicated – should be at the top of our research agenda' (p. 163) and 'there is no argument but that demand can at times … alter the nature of production' (p. 163). Nevertheless, Smith is unwilling to back down more fully: 'The new patterns now unfolding do involve the construction of "consumption landscapes" in the city … but this does not imply that urban geographical change is somehow demand-led' (p. 151). Smith still insists that gentrification should be defined at its core (production, capital) and not its margins (consumption, culture) (p. 160).

Sociologist Sharon Zukin was one of the first authors to be sensitive to different explanations of gentrification: 'so must every attempt to understand the reshaping of cities incorporate a multidimensional perspective' (1982: 203). Her 1982 book *Loft Living: capital and culture in the urban core*, in many ways marked a turning point in the gentrification literature in recognizing the absence of culture in political-economic (Marxist) theorizations of gentrification. In much of Marxist analysis culture was ideology, reflecting the substructure and having no autonomy of its own. Zukin argued that gentrification illustrated a 'close connection, in late industrial capitalism, between accumulation and cultural consumption' (p. 177). Loft-living for Zukin was a historically contingent, culturally specific response to inner-city disinvestment. Yet in 1982 Zukin still struggled to allow culture an equal voice in her framework: 'The remarkable openness to non-economic factors that is now breathing fresh air into the social sciences should not divert attention from underlying structural changes' (p. 208). Five years later, drawing on her 1982 book, she published the 1987 article that we reprint here, and in this article she moves her earlier work further in the direction of culture and consumption. Note how Zukin (Box 6) points to the different disciplinary takes on gentrification – in 1987 the sociology community still did not consider space to be important in conceptualizations of gentrification.

Despite Rose (1984) and Zukin (1987) the theoretical battles continued in the gentrification literature. In 1991 Chris Hamnett argued for the integration of both the Neil Smith (production, capital, supply) and David Ley (consumption, culture and demand) camps, he wanted to see how both of these partial explanations would fit together. He used the old tale of the 'blind men and the elephant' – in the various versions of this tale a group of blind men touch an elephant to learn what it is like. Each one touches a different part, but only one part, such as the leg or the tusk of the elephant. They then compare notes on what they felt and find that they are in complete disagreement. The story is used to indicate that reality may be viewed differently depending upon one's perspective. Hamnett provides a useful review of production and consumption approaches and then argues, probably influenced by Rose: '... if gentrification theory has a centrepiece it must rest on the production of potential gentrifiers' (p. 187).

Like Hamnett, Clark (1992), reprinted here, was also frustrated with the centrepieces in gentrification writings and encouraged by attempts to move outside of this dichotomy. He was clear that 'even if competing theories are mutually exclusive due to incommensurable abstractions, they may both be true and necessary for a thorough description of that which theories are about' (p. 361). He made the following important statement: 'we have no foolproof holistic theory of, or methodology for, the study of gentrification, and it would be presumptuous to think we ever will' (1992: 358). It is useful to note here that there has been lots of discussion about the theoretical dimensions of gentrification but rather less on the methodological dimensions, and of course these are rarely separate.

Having not yet read Clark (1992), Lees (1994), a graduate student at the time, set out to rethink gentrification to move beyond the 'positions' of economics or culture. In so doing she sought to combine these two camps and to use the productive tensions (the differences and contradictions) between the two. Like Clark (1992) Lees adopted the concept of 'complementarity' for this task, because it allowed her to use concepts and methods of thought that were mutually exclusive in tandem: 'incompatible conceptions can be represented without direct conflict and the outcomes will support and compliment each other' (Lees, 1994: 140).

As the postmodern turn embedded itself in the social sciences gentrification researchers began to open their eyes to the full complexity of gentrification – and work was forced to look beyond the restrictive lenses of production and consumption and to consider different literatures to aid their explanations that were increasingly focusing on 'difference' – race/ethnicity, sexuality, rural versus urban, and so on. These developments have greatly enriched the understanding of gentrification among scholars concerned with what the process means for urban social inequality. And yet, as knowledge of the process has become more rich, contextual, situated, and sensitive to difference, a striking paradox has emerged. Analysts working in the tradition of neo-classical economics – a field that had generally ignored gentrification for many years – began to take a renewed interest in the topic (e.g., Glaeser et al. 2007; Kahn 2007; Vigdor 2002, 2007). Not all neo-classical economists are politically conservative, but the methods and logic of the field are especially vulnerable to co-optation by conservative political operatives. The field's emphasis on consumer choice, market equilibrium, and competitive efficiency tends to support a conservative interpretation of gentrification as unproblematic and benevolent: if middle-class and wealthy households change their preferences and out-bid the poor for inner-city locations, then the housing market will adjust, lowering rents elsewhere in the metropolis where the displaced poor can decide to move.

Contemporary work on gentrification, therefore, demonstrates several problematic paradoxes. Critical gentrification researchers have moved beyond the old stalemate between economic and cultural explanations, and in the process have become much more reluctant to assert clear, definitive general-izations about gentrification. Given the importance of difference, contingency, and context, most critical gentrification researchers have become more cautious and careful to offer complex, situated analyses of particular trajectories and experiences of gentrification. Meanwhile, economic analysts with no such reluctance offer simple, elegant, and generalized neoclassical explanations – creating a narrative that is consistent and convincing when juxtaposed with the 'it depends' contingency expressed by critical researchers. The neoclassical narrative fits smoothly into the expectations of policy-makers eager to pro-mote downtown redevelopment, creative-class subsidies, the destruction of public and social housing, and other pro-gentrification policies – and thus a cautious, nuanced critical literature on gentrification expands as researchers try to document the rich complexities of forms of gentrification driven partly by state policies justified on the foundation of elegant, simplistic forms of urban economic theory.

REFERENCES AND FURTHER READING

Davidson, M. (2007) 'Gentrification as global habitat: A process of class construction or corporate creation?', *Transactions of the Institute of British Geographers* 32: 490–506.

Glaeser, E.E., M.E. Kahn and J. Rappaport (2007) 'Why do the poor live in cities? The role of public transportation', *Journal of Urban Economics* 63(1): 1–24.

Graham, J. (1988) 'Postmodernism and Marxism', *Antipode* 22(1): 53–66.

Kahn, M.E. (2007) 'Gentrification trends in new transit-oriented communities: Evidence from 14 cities that expanded and built rail transit systems', *Real Estate Economics* 35(2): 155–182.

Lees, L. (1994) 'Rethinking gentrification: Beyond the positions of economics and culture', *Progress in Human Geography* 18(2): 137–150.

Ley, D. (2003) 'Artists, aestheticization, and the field of gentrification', *Urban Studies* 40(12): 2527–2544.

Hamnett, C. (1992) 'Gentrifiers or lemmings? A response to Neil Smith', *Transactions of the Institute of British Geographers* 17(1): 116–119.

Hamnett, C. (2003) 'Gentrification and the middle-class remaking of inner London, 1961–2001', *Urban Studies* 40(12): 2401–2426.

Munt, I. (1987) 'Economic restructuring, culture, and gentrification: a case study in Battersea, London', *Environment and Planning A* 19: 1175–1197.

Redfern, P. (1997) 'A new look at gentrification: 1. Gentrification and domestic technologies', *Environment and Planning A* 29: 1275–1296.

Smith, N. (1992) 'Blind man's bluff, or Hamnett's philosophical individualism in search of gentrification?', *Transactions of the Institute of British Geographers* 17(1): 110–115.

Smith, N. (1987) 'Gentrification and the rent gap', *Annals of the Association of American Geographers* 77(3): 462–478.

Vigdor, J. (2002) 'Does gentrification harm the poor?', *Brookings/Wharton Papers on Urban Affairs* 3: 133–182.

Vigdor, J. (2007) 'Is urban decay bad? Is urban revitalization bad too?', Working Paper W12955. Cambridge, MA: National Bureau of Economic Research.

Williams, P. (1986) 'Class constitution through spatial reconstruction? A re-evaluation of gentrification in Australia, Britain and the United States', in N. Smith and P. Williams (eds) *Gentrification of the City*, pp. 56–77. London: Unwin Hyman.

Zukin, S. (1982) *Loft Living: Culture and Capital in Urban Change*, Baltimore: Johns Hopkins University Press.

17

"Rethinking Gentrification: Beyond the Uneven Development of Marxist Urban Theory"

From *Environment and Planning D: Society and Space* (1984)

Damaris Rose

INTRODUCTION

The growth rate of literature on the 'gentrification' of inner-city neighbourhoods in North American cities seems to have at least matched the acceleration and spread of the phenomenon itself in the past few years. Empirical documentation of certain aspects of this process is now quite extensive, and attempts at explanations abound; these have now been the subject of several literature reviews (for example, see Holcomb and Beauregard, 1981; Jackson, 1983; London, 1980; St Martin, 1982), one edited collection, already published (Laska and Spain, 1980), and two more on the way (London and Palen, 1984; Smith and Williams, forthcoming). However, as Smith (1982, pages 139–141) has rightly pointed out, this mushrooming research field has thus far been characterised by ad hoc explanations of the process, in which various 'exogenous' and discrete factors, assumed to be causal, are merely added together to constitute an explanation. In the present paper, I take this epistemological critique further and argue for the need to critically reassess the concept of gentrification itself. Positivist epistemology in general, and neoclassical land-use theory in particular, still predominate in structuring ways of thinking about, and methods of, investigating gentrification. The 'consumer-choice' orientation of neoclassical theory, combined with its lack of interest in specifying the historical processes that shape change in the phenomena it seeks to model or measure, lead those taking this approach to either of two empirically contradictory conclusions.

On the one hand, gentrification may be seen as an inevitable and natural phenomenon for a city at a certain stage in its supposedly organic 'life cycle' (compare Marcuse, 1981), just as the urban decay it replaces has been frequently seen as natural and inevitable. It is practised by households at certain stages in their life cycle. Governmental policy statements and mass-media accounts tend to take this line. On the other hand, gentrification is seen by others taking a neoclassical approach as a temporary and small-scale aberration in what is seen as an equally natural and dominant process of outward migration of people from inner cities (Berry, 1980; Muller, 1981). Both of these conclusions have laissez-faire policy implications (Allen, 1980, page 425).

We should therefore welcome theoretical initiatives that are more critical, and attempt to relate the specific processes implied by the concept of gentrification to broader political-economic changes generated in the current phase of capitalist development. Thus a central theme of this paper will be, on the one hand, an emphasis on the need for more coherent perspectives on the structural conditions or 'necessary tendencies' (compare Sayer, 1982) that create the *possibility* of gentrification. On the other hand, and at the same time, it will stress the need for better understandings of the historical relationships between such enabling conditions and the concrete processes and contexts through which they may take effect (Sayer, 1982; 1983; Thrift, 1983). Developing these understandings must surely be a prerequisite for the development of progressive, yet attainable, alternative forms of urban revitalisation. These forms should prefigure (compare Rowbotham et al, 1979) socialist and feminist alternatives to capitalist domination of daily life and work in urban places. We should aim for social and environmental forms in urban neighbourhoods that enable us to "start as we mean to go on" (R Williams, quoted in Sayer, 1981, page 2).

This paper is an exploratory attempt at stimulating further debate on these points. Specifically, I shall address five issues. First, through a critical and fairly rigorous discussion of the procedures for theory development found in the as-yet small body of marxist work on gentrification, I shall point to some epistemological problems which this work has not yet adequately dealt with. Second, I shall critically discuss the *problématique* and empirical scope of extant marxist work on gentrification, pointing to the reasons for what I believe to be its very restricted frame of reference and terrain of study. Third, I shall raise the question of whether the concept of 'gentrification' may not be a 'chaotic conception', in the sense explained by Sayer (1982), and I shall argue for the importance of developing research that can help us to scrutinise the concept and to reconceptualise the processes it involves. Fourth, I shall try to show that, to move toward progressive strategies around gentrification issues, it is crucial to explore the relationships between gentrification, social and spatial restructuring of waged labour processes, and changes in the reproduction of labour-power and of people. The analysis which I shall begin to develop contrasts with an incorrect conflation of reproduction and consumption, which has characterised marxist writing on gentrification and which has also been implicit in positivist approaches. This will lead to a fifth and concluding section in which I shall tentatively suggest some areas in which empirical work might assist us in coming to more theoretically sound conceptions of progressive political (in the broad sense of the word) moves around the issue of neighbourhood revitalisation, in the contexts of current forms of gentrification in particular places.

TRADITIONAL AND CRITICAL APPROACHES TO THE STUDY OF GENTRIFICATION: EPISTEMOLOGICAL ISSUES

As marxist urban and regional analysis has matured over the past few years, it has increasingly turned to substantive empirical work. The earlier dominance of structuralism, with its inherent functionalism, in marxist urban theory had previously inhibited empirical research. This is now being outgrown, and it is more widely appreciated that social reproduction can never be assumed but is always historically *contingent*. Thus empirical investigation is always essential in order to discover how various aspects of the reproduction of capitalist social relations are, or are not, achieved in particular contexts (Sayer, 1983, page 110; also, see Giddens, 1979; 1981; Rose, 1980; 1981). However, to conduct such empirical work requires conceptual clarity and a greater attention to epistemological matters (Sayer, 1979; 1982). It becomes necessary to work out alternative research methodologies to those of positivism. As Thrift (1983) argues, such methodologies must do more than merely lurch uncertainly between the twin poles of 'structure' and 'agency'.

The process of developing critical approaches to the study of gentrification must therefore begin by questioning the epistemological bases of existing approaches. A recent paper by Smith (1982) is perhaps the most important, and provocative, piece of marxist writing on gentrification, and he is one of very few writers on this theme to attempt to deal with questions of epistemology and method. Unfortunately, his critique of positivist approaches is weakened by the fact that his assessment of the validity of neoclassical land-market theory is ultimately cast in positivist theory's own terms, that is, the correctness or incorrectness of its empirical predictions[1].

For a more fundamental critique, we should start by stressing that positivist theory is mainly intended to generate testable empirical predictions and transhistorical generalisations. It defines successful prediction in terms of reproducibility of results. It does not acknowledge that phenomena can have underlying causes beyond those that can be directly observed. Positivist approaches to gentrification have remained ad hoc, full of exceptions, and frequently contradictory to other people's positivist explanations, for two main reasons. First, since positivist theories are general predictive theories, there can be no empirical variations or 'inconsistencies' between one test of the theory and another without invalidating the explanation (prediction). Second, they lack coherent ways of conceptually organising their thinking. This means that, within a positivist mode of thinking, it is impossible to critically examine the concept of 'gentrification' itself. For example, is there one basic process, or are there a number of distinct causal processes, producing the 'outcome' of gentrified neighbourhoods? This is a very crucial point, which I discuss in a later section. In sum, then, positivist methodology does not enable the construction of explanations of gentrification which are historical and structural but which at the same time allow for empirical variations from place to place and from time to time. It is precisely this type of explanation that marxist approaches are now aiming at.

Marxist work on gentrification has insisted that the 'correct' place to begin theorising about this process is with the production of the commodities of gentrified dwellings (Smith, 1979; 1982; Holcomb and Beauregard, 1981, pages 22–24). I use the word 'correct' to draw attention to the fact that this type of insistence on a *single* analytical starting point in the 'sphere of production' is politically grounded. The belief that activities in this sphere are the primary motors of change within capitalist society, and thus that movements away from capitalist society must be initiated uniquely within this sphere, underlies extant marxist work on gentrification—a belief that I do not share. This does not necessarily mean that I substantially reject the content of this type of marxist analysis, but it does mean that I believe it to be incomplete, and somewhat arbitrary in its claim to be *the fundamental* starting point for theoretical and empirical work on *all* aspects of gentrification, as I go on to argue later.

Marxist approaches, quite rightly, have situated gentrification within the broader context of capital investments by financial institutions in an already existing built environment—rather than on the neoclassical 'clean slate'—and they have considered the ways in which such investments facilitate capital accumulation and thus social reproduction as a whole. Gentrification is seen as a means of increasing ground rent and thence capitalising upon the locational advantage of land that is currently 'underused' in terms of its capital accumulation potential (Smith, 1982). It has this aspect in common with central-city commercial redevelopment (Harvey, 1974; 1975; Holcomb and Beauregard, 1981; Lamarche, 1976; Roweis and Scott, 1981)[2]. Gentrification has been viewed as a means of "revitalising the profit rate" (Smith, 1982, page 151), in that the productive capital invested in the built environment is fixed, creating barriers to the expansion of that 'piece' of capital. Unless repairs or replacements are made to the housing stock, the capital invested will be 'devalorised' over time as investors extract returns (Harvey, 1975; Smith, 1982). Eventually this leads to residential abandonment, which in turn creates the 'rent gap' and thus the preconditions for new investment of productive capital in a 'higher and better use' (Smith, 1982). Combined with this is a secular shift by financial capital out of

the major industrial sectors because of falling rates of profit (Smith, 1982).

To a large extent, marxist approaches to gentrification have defined their objectives self-consciously in opposition to positivist approaches, demonstrating that gentrification is neither a natural development at a certain stage in a city's life-cycle nor an aberration. As Holcomb and Beauregard (1981, page 69) point out, it is important to recognise that the 'necessary conditions' and 'direction' for gentrification are set in motion by *purposive* and powerful actors who are both guided and constrained in their actions by the underlying logic of capital accumulation. A crucial element in the marxist approach, in contrast to positivist approaches, is that it sees that *gentrification is thus not reducible to the behaviour of individuals*[3].

However, when it comes to theorising—or providing methodological bases for empirically investigating—how, and under what circumstances, these preconditions for gentrification take concrete effect, and how 'gentrifiers' themselves are produced, marxist work so far is unevenly developed. Smith (1982, page 152), for instance, comments that:

> [T]he economic, demographic, lifestyle and energy factors cited by Berry as well as the back-to-the-city school *are relevant only after* consideration of this *basic* explanation (my emphasis).

However, this leaves us with no guidance as to how we are to consider these factors. Some crucial questions arise here. To what extent are any of these factors determinable on the basis solely of a theory of underlying structural processes? To what extent can they influence the operation of such processes in any particular situation? Or *are* they indeed merely factors to be 'added on afterwards', a scratch on the surface of the underlying logic of capital? Is the type of marxist theory sketched out above—in which the operation of the law of value is the paramount determining force—supposed to predict, on the basis of this law, that gentrification will definitely occur in an urban built environment with a specific spatially uneven investment history?

These questions point to some important problems of epistemology and method, which will not be resolved purely by an increased volume of literature in the same vein as the limited number of extant marxist contributions. We need to consider how extensive the terrain covered by critical approaches to gentrification should be, and what should be the relationship of this terrain to that identified and explored by positivist approaches. I explore these questions in the next section.

THE PROBLÉMATIQUE OF MARXIST WORK ON GENTRIFICATION: A SYMPATHETIC CRITIQUE

The first issue that arises is whether marxist theorising about gentrification should be limited to the specification of preconditions for the production of gentrified dwellings, without considering the production of the 'gentrifiers', the occupants of such dwellings. If we limit the scope of marxist inquiry in this way, we are then presumably supposed to look to the now-extensive conventional positivist literature for clues about such things as: the relative costs of new suburban housing and older inner-city housing; the precise types of neighbourhoods where gentrification will occur; the various 'stages of reinvasion' of a neighbourhood; the demographic, income, and occupational characteristics of the gentrifiers; where they work and what services they use; and, to complete the picture, who is displaced, the strength of incumbent neighbourhood organisations, and so on. We would presumably look at all these factors more critically than is done in most of the conventional literature, in that we would consider them in the societal context of a highly uneven distribution of economic and political power whose urban expression is reinforced or exacerbated by gentrification. This is the approach that Holcomb and Beauregard (1981) appear to favour. Essentially it entails an 'adding on' of the factors studied by conventional approaches to a structural analysis, *without changing* the way in which any of these factors are *conceptualised*. A similar path is implied, by default, by Smith (1982).

However, there are a number of problems with this line of approach. One of the most crucial is that it tends to reproduce the division between issues that are narrowly defined as 'economic' issues and so-called 'social' questions. This division has for too long characterised the social sciences and it strongly influences dominant conceptions about the 'proper sphere' of marxian political-economic analyses of urbanism (Mackenzie and Rose, 1983a). Fundamental 'economic' processes are, in this view, to be theorised in traditional marxist terms. Everything else, and especially 'social processes', either is theoretically derivable from the economic or is purely epiphenomenal. Either way, this means that many aspects of gentrification have been analytically and empirically neglected by marxist writers to date, especially the production of 'gentrifiers', whom we may, for the time being, loosely define as people who move into renovated housing in 'revitalising' neighbourhoods. Virtually no attention has

been paid by marxists to the processes behind the demographic and 'life-style' profiles of gentrifiers— behind the characterisations popularised by the mass media and the novels of, among others, Margaret Drabble (1977) for London and Margaret Atwood (1980) for 'renovation city' (Toronto).

Processes of change in the social and spatial organisation of labour processes, changing household and family structures, and changes in female labour-force participation rates have recently come under study by a few urban analysts seeking to conceptualise overall processes of metropolitan change (Fainstein and Fainstein, 1982: Ley, 1980; 1981; 1983; Scott, 1982; Tomaskovic-Devey and Miller, 1982). However, there is very little existing work that has considered gentrification in the context of how all of these processes interact with the processes that have led to the breakdown of the traditional patriarchal household, and the implications of these interactions for how people and labour power are reproduced— a lacuna which Markusen (1981, page 24) has briefly alluded to. Holcomb (1981) is an important, albeit preliminary, exception. Cox and Mergler (1982) discuss the relationships between gentrification, the decline of traditional ties to place-defined 'community', the decline of the nuclear family and an all-pervasive 'ideology of independence', which they see as endemic to market societies. However, their analysis subsumes the emancipation of women and its impacts on family structure, on household formation, and on women's daily lives within this 'cult of freedom', the parameters of which they see as being drawn entirely by commodity relations (Cox and Mergler, 1982, pages 62–63). This approach thus analytically reduces key achievements of the feminist movement, and the struggles that led to their realisation, to the ideology of the capitalist market; the authors thereby greatly downplay the active role of feminism as a social force in the economy and in cities[4].

Meanwhile, theoretical and empirical work by marxists has been exclusively preoccupied with those aspects of gentrification that can be directly related to the operation of the law of value in the built environment of capitalist cities. This is largely because of the separation of the 'economic' from the 'social', as noted already, and the insistence that we always, and exclusively, start from 'production relations' as conventionally defined. This has created not only an analytical gap but also an epistemological error of considerable importance. Some marxist writers seem to have assumed that, as long as they have the correct structural understandings about the production of gentrified housing, they may then take the findings and predictions of positivist analyses of demographic and 'life-style' aspects of gentrification and gentrifiers 'off the shelf', with the confidence that they will automatically know how to interpret and contextualise them correctly. As I hope to demonstrate in the next section, this is an unjustified assumption, which can only obfuscate our understanding and misinform our political practice regarding urban revitalisation. It reflects an epistemological eclecticism of the sort more characteristic of liberal urban theory (compare Fincher, 1983; Sayer, 1982).

In contrast to this approach, I would argue that we should certainly not leave the so-called social aspects of gentrification in the hands solely of positivist concepts and methods. Nor should we stake out the terrain of marxist work so narrowly. To do so is to make epistemological and methodological errors which both truncate and distort our understanding of gentrification. Though *some* 'social' factors may turn out to be purely contingent empirical phenomena, which should not therefore form part of any theory of gentrification (compare Sayer, 1982), there are, however, no a priori grounds for considering *all* 'social' aspects of gentrification to be epiphenomenal. As I have hinted at already, some of these factors may be expressions of a set of broader and interrelated processes producing gentrification. It may well be that we need a reworked theoretical orientation which would take the production of gentrified built environments as only *one* of a number of simultaneous analytical starting points.

It is also extremely important to recognise that a two-fold distortion is produced by combining structural analysis with conceptualisations borrowed from positivist approaches of those factors that cannot be explained as simple expressions of underlying structural forces. First of all, the production of gentrified neighbourhoods appears in this type of approach to be something that will inevitably happen to the inner areas of older cities whose central business districts (CBDs) are still favoured for commercial investment. Gentrification appears as the *only possible end-state* for such neighbourhoods, because of the immutable operation of the law of value in such built environments in the present phase of capitalism. For example, in his concern to trace out the 'fundamental' processes behind gentrification, Smith (1982) seems to have abandoned his earlier more subtle analyses of the processes of uneven development (Smith, 1979) in order to present a view of cycles of investment, disinvestment, and reinvestment in the urban built environment as direct concrete products of an inexorable law of spatially uneven development. In addition to the broader conceptual and methodological problems associated with attempts

to develop general laws about the spatial nature of uneven development[5], this conceptualisation makes it difficult to explore the contingencies that determine whether or not gentrification will occur in a given context at a particular time (Beauregard, 1983).

A methodology that combines structural analysis and positivist conceptualisations may be called a 'mix-and-match' approach. It produces a second type of distortion which overlays the first type noted above. This also reinforces the economic-social split. Certain types of people are seen to move into neighbourhoods that have gentrification potential or that have been renovated already by developers. They help to carry out this nascent process and they give it its specific form and variations. Yet they are viewed only in terms of their 'consumption' habits and patterns— 'consumption' here still being used in the neoclassical sense, referring to the (passive) process of using up the output of commodity production. These people exercise choice, but it is an overdetermined choice.

Missing in all of this is an adequate conceptualisation of the impacts of the major changes that have taken place in the processes through which people and labour power are reproduced and how these changes are actively reshaping urban space. These are themes that socialist-feminist urban theory has taken considerable steps forward in exploring (for example, see Hayden, 1981; McDowell, 1983; Mackenzie, 1983; and Markusen, 1981 for an up-to-date review). It seems at first sight curious that marxist work on gentrification has ignored the existence of this body of literature, even when it has tried to broach the subject of changes in reproduction (for example, Smith and LeFaivre, 1983). The latter authors make a serious attempt to discuss gentrification in relation to the roles of neighbourhoods and 'communities' (their term—and used in a spatially defined sense) in reproducing labour power. However, their analysis relies rather heavily upon the functionalist theorisations most clearly developed in the early work of Castells (1977). Communities that have a clear spatially defined basis are seen, in this view, as crucial to the reproduction of the working class. In a modification of Castells's argument, however, Smith and LeFaivre suggest that spatially based communities are now less crucial to the reproduction of the middle class.

This argument is contentious on a number of counts and begs many questions about the meaning(s) of 'community' in advanced capitalism. However, the major criticism to be made here is that Smith and LeFaivre (1984) do not relate changes in processes of social production to changes in the ways that people and labour power are reproduced.

This analysis, therefore, does not give us the tools with which to investigate the authors' interesting claim that gentrification may seriously interfere with the reproduction of key fractions of the work force and may thus pose a threat to the extended reproduction of capital[6].

Castells's seminal work (1977) has come under particularly heavy criticism from feminist quarters, because, although it gave analytical priority to the sphere of 'collective consumption', at the same time it analytically collapsed, into one category, *reproduction* and *consumption* (both collective and individual forms). This conflation has the effect of obscuring the active work of household members in reproducing both labour power and people. In reality, such unwaged noncommodified labour— which we may call 'reproductive work'—in the home and neighbourhood is a crucial part of the contingent processes whereby various aspects of social reproduction take place. Yet reproduction is generally seen to occur 'passively', through consumption, and reproductive work and workers remain invisible (Mackenzie, 1983). At best, marxist work on gentrification has seen only the commodified aspects of reproduction—life-styles packaged in the 'gentrification press'; the conspicuous consumption of cappucino and quiche, and the purchase of opportunities for meeting potential partners (compare Beauregard, 1983). More commonly, the literature has adopted the neoclassical view that the consumption practices of households are simply the means whereby the output of commodity production is absorbed; at the same time, it 'mixes and matches' by combining this conceptualisation with the marxist shorthand of 'production produces consumption'— an aphorism derived from Marx's lengthy discussion in the *Grundrisse* (Marx, 1973). This produces a type of analysis which, in my view, prevents us from asking questions about the significance of changes in reproduction that 'gentrifiers' themselves are bringing about, although not necessarily under conditions of their own choosing.

In contrast, I believe that it is essential to explore the relationships between gentrification and changes in the reproduction of labour power and people. This is not merely an academic point, but relates back to the political purposes of studying the phenomenon of 'gentrification'. These relationships have a crucial bearing on the possibilities of overcoming polarisations created within and between people and neighbourhoods by gentrification—a point to be taken up in the last section of this paper.

To move towards reconceptualisations of 'gentrification' which make it easier for us to address issues surrounding changes in reproduction, in relation to current forms of economic restructuring and future possibilities, it is necessary to make some theoretical clarifications concerning the relationships between consumption and reproduction, about which there has been much controversy and confusion in recent marxist debates. A number of feminist writers have argued that Marx's analysis overlooks the role of domestic labour within the family in performing the 'reproductive work' that enables consumption activities to actually take place. If homes, family structures, and so on are seen only as passive means or vehicles for consumption practices, this obfuscates the active role of household-based work and 'domestic workers' in affecting the way that reproduction of people and labour power occurs (Markusen, 1981, pages 23–24). Thus, implicitly, this line of analysis relegates to secondary or subordinate status in class struggle those whose primary work is reproductive work outside of capitalist wage labour (Mackenzie, 1983).

Marx's own analysis (Marx, 1976, pages 717–719) appeared to equate the reproduction of labour power with the individual consumption by the working class. This seems legitimate enough for the period of early factory capitalism, about which Marx was writing, when it was primarily unskilled workers that had to be reproduced, capable of work, and forced to sell their labour power for a wage. However, in the present-day context of advanced capitalism, the *form* of consumption is no longer irrelevant to the reproduction of labour power. The forms consumption take become key parts of the contingencies of social reproduction. This means that the actual *work* involved in reproducing people and their labour power, outside of the commodity form, does 'make a difference'. Moreover, labour power as a commodity is vested in and inseparable from people as active human subjects, whose reproduction cannot therefore take place entirely in the commodity form. Consumption practices *can* be said to subsume the reproduction of people and those aspects of the reproduction of labour power that occur in noncommodity forms, in the sense that this work of reproduction involves "bearing, educating and caring for the people who produce and consume the means of subsistence" (Mackenzie, 1981, page 5). Yet reproductive work of this kind has an active effect on the form taken by, and thence the meaning of consumption practices.

This has a number of implications for methods of analysing the significance of the 'sphere of consumption' and practices therein, particularly the significance of individual means of consumption, such as domestic property and privatised services, in the present period of recommodification of formerly public goods and services (compare Saunders, 1982). This issue is clearly very germane to any discussion of the political implications of consumption practices by gentrifiers. However, the primary point to be stressed here relates to the consumers of gentrified housing and the 'consumption location' (social and spatial) that they occupy. It is clear that the market for such housing certainly cannot be said to be produced purely by the production and promotion of the houses. Thus we come to the question of how the production of gentrifiers is to be approached theoretically.

THEORISING THE PRODUCTION OF GENTRIFIERS

The social and the spatial restructuring of labour processes are shaping and changing the ways that people and labour power are reproduced in cities. Considerable attention is now being paid in the literature of urban political economy to corporate investment decisions that are concentrating certain kinds of white-collar jobs in the centres of major metropolitan cities (Cohen, 1981; Scott, 1982; Simmie, 1983). Theoretical links are now beginning to be made between these changes and gentrification.

This restructuring is also changing the content of many of these jobs and the nature of the labour processes they entail[7]. Within the 'white-collar' economy, there is a widening division of labour, especially between high-level corporate control and decisionmaking activities, on the one hand, and routine office work, on the other. Smith (1983), taking a step further a line of argument developed by Cohen (1981), argues that, although routine office work, with the assistance of new technology—and, one should add, the human resources of fairly immobile pools of suburban female labour—is quite evidently being spatially deconcentrated, high-level control activities are likely to remain in the CBDs of major cities. This is because the jobs of high-level executives, especially those relating to financial markets, involve a considerable amount of unpredictable crisis-management and fast-paced decisionmaking, in addition to long-range corporate planning. This provides some justification for the traditional explanatory emphasis on the importance of face-to-face contacts, an argument dismissed out of hand by Muller (1981), because these short-term responses can still be accomplished more effectively within close spatial proximity to colleagues, experts, and competitors, electronic communications technology notwithstanding. Smith's (1982)

argument would seem to be supported, at least for New York City, by 1980 census data on the employment structure in the five boroughs and on percentage changes in employment since 1970 (*The New York Times*, 1983h). Whether or not these locational requirements will continue to be necessary for these executive labour processes is an open question. Nonetheless, this method of analysis, which relates locational requirements to the nature of the office work processes concerned, takes us a great deal further than conventional approaches. It is potentially useful for exploring the *production of gentrifiers*, in that it may help us to comprehend the complex relationships between the restructuring of international capitalism and how different fractions of labour may be produced within a particular city at a particular time. The needs and desires of these groups, in conjunction with other contingent factors, may become important in producing gentrification.

Some writers are beginning to relate these sets of changes to the 'life-styles' of gentrifiers, who are recognised as being substantially comprised of these new professional and executive fractions of the corporate labour force (Allen, 1980; Alonso, 1980; Beauregard, 1983; Guterbock, 1980; Ley, 1983). Yet this work has not dealt adequately with the processes through which these fractions of labour are *reproduced*, as workers and as people. It still implicitly relies on the neoclassical conception of 'life-style', which is summarised concisely in a recent article, by Salomon and Ben-Akiva (1983, page 624), on life-style and travel demand:

> Life-style is defined as the pattern of behavior which conforms to the individual's orientation toward the three major roles of: a household member, a worker, and a consumer of leisure, and which conforms to the constrained resources available.

These 'roles' are seen as analytically discrete, and the literature has lacked a theoretical basis for combining them within a concept of 'life-style'. Thus there has been a tendency to acknowledge "interdependencies between cultural, political, economic and ecological factors" (Guterbock, 1980, page 437), but in a conceptually incoherent manner. The result is a methodological eclecticism. This problem also bedevils the initially appealing social-movements approach (for example, see London, 1980).

Nevertheless, those aspects of the reproduction of labour power and of people that take place outside of the sphere of commodity production are not analytically reducible to what is happening in the wage workplace, any more than they are reducible to 'consumption practices'. This is a very important point when investigating the so-called 'alternative life-styles' often identified in inner-city neighbourhoods in what is termed the 'early stages' of gentrification. The crucial point here is that *'gentrifiers' are not the mere bearers of a process determined independently of them.* Their constitution, as certain types of workers and as people, is as crucial an element in the production of gentrification as is the production of the dwellings they occupy. They may or may not make the potential process happen in particular contingent situations. On the one hand, this means that the social processes behind gentrification are indeed produced by the present phase of capitalism. However, this happens in a far more subtle and inclusive way than can be inferred from a theoretical approach that looks only at the operation of necessary economic tendencies (for example, the law of value) to find necessary and sufficient conditions for gentrification. On the other hand, the process of gentrification, and the actions of those involved, now appear far less determinate. The reproduction of labour power cannot be reduced to an abstract tendency or need of capitalism, because it is inseparable in real terms from the reproduction of living thinking human beings; it is always a contingent phenomenon. Thus some of the so-called 'life-style trends' that are commonly subsumed within the category 'gentrification' may signify some important alternative forms and structures of reproduction which are facilitated by specific characteristics of the physical and social environment.

Marxist approaches to gentrification, therefore, now need to expand and clarify their theoretical and empirical terrain. We should reconceptualise those aspects of the process which marxist writers have tended to view in clothing designed by positivists, adding only some reductionist undergarments and structuralist accessories. In the next section I shall make a tentative and sketchy start on this task.

IS 'GENTRIFICATION' A CHAOTIC CONCEPT?

Both neoclassical and marxist approaches to gentrification have assumed that it is a coherent concept that refers to a single or unitary phenomenon. Despite disagreements about the best term to use (London, 1980; Weston, 1982), everything that is generally subsumed within the concept is usually assumed to be a part of the same phenomenon and assumed to be produced by the same causal process. Whatever the label, it is understood to refer

to the replacement of lower income residents of a neighbourhood with inhabitants of a higher income and socioeconomic standing, and different material interests than the incumbent residents, by means of the renovation and 'upgrading' of dwellings. Gentrifying neighbourhoods are those undergoing upward social mobility through this process. The process of change is thought to occur in several stages. In successive stages, waves of in-migration of people with different characteristics from the original residents, and from each other, take place. Properties change hands at least twice; the initial purchaser gets a bargain and then sells at a large capital gain to an individual or company that carries out major renovations, often with a municipal subsidy or tax abatement. Such successive transactions have been documented in a number of cities, including New York (*Village Voice*, 1982), Cape Town (Western, 1981), and Montréal (Dansereau et al, 1983: Ramacière, 1983). For example, in New York City's Lower East Side, the 'first wave' of in-movers consists of young white-collar workers, unemployed but educated young people, economically marginal self-employed young people, middle-class single parents, and so on (*Village Voice*, 1982). The end result, after property values have increased rapidly, is a new equilibrium of socioeconomic and cultural homogeneity (Holcomb and Beauregard, 1981, pages 42–44). As a descriptive model of occupancy change this is reasonable enough. It seems to fit the history of some gentrifying neighbourhoods quite well. However, there are many different routes to the gentrification of a neighbourhood, with different types of actors taking the lead in different contexts (de Giovanni, 1983). If one tries to imbue the simple-stage model with general theoretical significance, it is not only— obviously—teleological, but it may also contain what Sayer (1982) refers to as 'chaotic conceptions':

> In place of a theory of abstract elements of a situation and how they combine to compose concrete phenomena, there is an acceptance of unexamined, largely commonsense definitions of these *empirical* objects, and a generalisation of the features of these chaotic conceptions. ... [T]hese unities of diverse aspects are treated as single objects which can be used as a basis for aggregation or else added up for manipulation in statistical analyses.
>
> (Sayer, 1982, page 75)

For instance, there is some evidence to suggest that initial in-movers are often "attracted by low prices and tolerance of unconventional lifestyles" (Holcomb and Beauregard, 1981, page 42). The large gay in-migration to certain parts of San Francisco is a good example (Castells and Murphy, 1982). A crucial methodological problem, however, arises here. For in what sense can it be validly said that this is the first stage in *the* gentrification process? What conceptual grounds exist for assuming that these 'first stagers' and the 'end-stage' affluent residents have anything in common other than the fact that their household incomes are higher than those of the original residents? Presumably, some version of the notion of 'housing class' or 'property class' is also implicit in this model. Homeowners (in this instance, first and second waves of gentrifiers) are accordingly viewed as having materially different life-chances than renters (the incumbent residents of the neighbourhood), on account of the wealth-accumulative potential of homeownership in a situation of inflating property values (compare Saunders, 1978; 1979). If this notion is accepted, then there is a firm basis for the assumption that *all* in-moving homeowners have more materially in common with one another than they do with any of the incumbent renters. Yet within this 'all' is also included moderate-income gentrifiers. Among these are people who are buying their first home, choosing the inner-city mainly for reasons of relative cheapness; people whose combined employment and family responsibilities necessitate an inner-city location (see section after next); and the 'reluctant purchasers' or *'les acheteurs non volontaires'* of condominium apartments—who may be long-time residents of a building (L'Ecuyer, 1981). (I shall henceforth refer to all types of moderate-income gentrifiers as 'marginal gentrifiers'—admittedly an unbounded concept, which I use in this paper for heuristic reasons only.) The inclusion of the latter in the 'them' of 'them and us' in the conceptualisation of gentrification/displacement conflicts has important political implications, to which I shall return below.

However, there is good reason to question the validity of such a simply conceptualised material cleavage between homeowners and tenants in gentrifying neighbourhoods in North American cities from the mid-to-late 1970s to the present time. There is mounting evidence in North America to suggest widening gaps within the home-ownership tenure category within the past ten to fifteen years, in terms of initial access to and subsequent material opportunities afforded by homeownership. In the United States of America in the 1970s, housing prices increased faster than median family incomes. This led to substantial capital gains for some of

those who were already homeowners at the beginning of this period (Le Gates and Murphy, 1981, page 265). However, this inflation made access to homeownership more difficult for renters wishing to purchase their first home, because, as Rudel (1983b, page 1) points out, with reference to the USA from 1974 to 1978,

... unlike repurchasers who could apply the equity in their current home toward the purchase of another home, renters usually had to accumulate savings for rapidly increasing downpayments out of incomes which were increasing much less rapidly.

For the young moderate-income household, delaying starting a family and being a two-earner couple became the only way to raise the down payment. Recent evidence from Australia, which had a similar house price inflation, suggests that for such couples the wife's income goes primarily toward the down payment on a house: her income does not lead to a decision to purchase a house that will require two incomes to keep up the payments (Wulff, 1982). In Canada, increasing real rates of interest—in a context where mortgage interest is not tax-deductible, unlike in the USA and Britain—have been more significant than price increases in reducing access to and raising the carrying costs of homeownership for first-time purchasers. It has thus become essential for women to go out work and put the 'second income' toward sustaining mortgage payments (SPCMT, 1980, pages 117–119). Uncertainty about household incomes in future years, decreased locational mobility, and unpredictable interest rates and loan conditions may create a situation where, for many first-time buyers, the 'wealth-accumulative potential' of homeownership exists only on paper.

One of the most important results of these rapid increases in the real costs of entering the home-ownership market has thus been to create widening gaps between long-standing homeowners and first-time buyers (Le Gates and Murphy, 1981, page 265). In the USA, however, this does not appear to have led to a decline in the numbers of people switching from rental housing to homeownership, except in the West, according to a recent analysis *of Annual Housing Survey* data from 1974–1978 (Rudel, 1983b). (Comparable data sets are not available for Canada.) These facts suggest some major problems with the assumption that the category of 'all homeowners', based on a conceptualisation of common wealth-accumulation potential, is a valid one for inferring major cleavages over material life-chances and 'interests', as compared with a category of 'all tenants'. As Thorns (1981, page 215) points out, not least among these problems is

> ... the range of accumulative potential within owner-occupation itself. When capital gains are examined for specific groups of owner-occupiers it is clear that the rates of gain are highly varied and not assured.

Even within gentrifying neighbourhoods, capital gains are not certain. Houses and apartments renovated from badly deteriorated stock, that was never intended to last a century or so, do literally wear out, as the British experience with 'improvement grants' and the New York City experience of condominium conversions in some districts have shown (Benwell Community Project, 1978, pages 92–108; *The New York Times*, 1983c; 1983d). In such cases the owner may lose money, unless there is tremendous pressure on the location for a 'higher and better use' and governmental structures that enforce on redevelopers large compensation payments in addition to the market value of the house.

Yet it is many of these first-time purchasers of moderate income who are 'putting pressure' on older inner-city neighbourhoods and often displacing poorer tenants. Thus, I would venture to suggest, our understanding of the historical development of this situation, and of the conflicts it is creating, might be enhanced if we made some different types of comparisons than the usual one, of incumbent tenant versus incoming homeowning gentrifier, the one the displacee, the other the displacer. Comparing these two is actually rather like comparing apples and oranges, in the sense that their specific circumstances and needs may have been produced by different processes at different times. For example, we might more usefully compare the economic situation of people commonly identified as first-stage gentrifiers with the economic situation of people in the same type of occupation and life-cycle stage a decade or so ago—the latter would probably have been forming their households in suburbia. Compared to existing residents of a working-class neighbourhood, the new people certainly make the neighbourhood upwardly socially mobile, but, compared to their peers of ten years ago. some of these people have been considerably proletarianised, because of the restructuring of white-collar labour processes, rollbacks in public-sector wages, deteriorating working conditions, and reduced job security.

Moreover, we are used to thinking about 'upward mobility' and progression through 'the family life-cycle' in the same breath. As Christopherson (1983, page 24) astutely points out, geographical models of locational preference and change have been imbued with the dual assumptions that a household's residential locational shifts over a period of time are geared to the income of a male head of a nuclear family, that steadily increases as his children grow up and until his retirement. Upward mobility as a condition of years of employment experience and a single head of household who is male are implicitly taken as the norm in such models. Yet, for many so-called 'first-stage' gentrifiers, one or both parts of this assumption may be invalid, as they now are for many other groups in the present phase of advanced capitalism. In the first place, there are often two heads of household whose respective earning capacities may diverge at certain stages in their life-cycles. In the second place, female single parents, even if they hold professional jobs, are most unlikely to have incomes that increase as fast as the male norm, and in any case have major child-care expenses that detract from their incomes. In the third place, divorce, remarriage, complicated custody arrangements, and so on frequently create major disruptions in family life-cycles in relation to incomes and location decisions. Although some recent neoclassical work on residential mobility has endeavoured to take such developments into account, 'induced moves' caused by 'life-cycle changes' or employment changes are still seen, incorrectly, as being analytically separable from 'adjustment moves' based on neoclassical norms of, ceteris paribus, increasing consumer demand for residential space as income increases over time (Clark and Onaka, 1983).

Even more importantly, opportunities for increasing household incomes over time are being severely curtailed, independently of the factors mentioned above, for many people. The present phase of restructuring of industrial and clerical labour processes, and the associated segmentation of labour markets over space—as well as by sex and race—may limit lower income families' chances of upward mobility. This is of course exacerbated for female-headed households (compare Christopherson, 1983). The impacts of new technology on lower level workers' opportunities to move up through the ranks is still hotly disputed. Yet several analysts are arguing that a 'two-tier' work force is being created, with a gap that is very difficult to leap across (*The New York Times*, 1983b).

In addition, many young professionals, though clearly in a much improved material situation, can also no longer assume job security and steadily increasing incomes: college and university teachers, public-sector professionals on fixed-term contracts, and the growing army of professionals turned self-employed because of the recession are examples which spring to mind. All of these people may be excluded from more traditional white-collar housing markets by reason of house prices relative to their incomes. This has to be considered, not only in terms of the increasing real costs of homeownership, but also in terms of the downward social mobility of such groups relative to their parents or their peers of ten years ago. In New York, as previously mentioned, and in Toronto and Montréal, renovation is spreading from the best quality inner-city housing to stock of much lower quality in areas considered less desirable (Dansereau et al, 1981; Weston, 1982). Although evidence about this is piecemeal, it seems that, increasingly, white-collar households of much more modest incomes than the type who gave gentrification its name, predominate among those in renovated properties in such areas.

The changes referred to in this section are clearly among the major reasons for the 'explosion' of condominium conversions in older North American cities since the mid-1970s (Le Gates and Murphy, 1981, pages 267–268) (this is not, however, the only reason for the popularity of condominiums, as will be discussed later). As these writers point out, some of the most bitter gentrification/displacement conflicts that have broken out in the USA in recent years have been around this issue, especially between people in the 'tertiary' work force: young professional and managerial people displacing lower level white-collar workers and essential service workers (Le Gates and Murphy, 1981, pages 266–267). Both of these groups of people have good reasons for wanting an inner-city location. This is partly because of the social and spatial restructuring of employment, which, as previously mentioned, is reducing the mobility of lower level workers and 'marginalised' professionals alike. The continuing controversy over artists' housing in New York City is an interesting case in point. A three-year-long effort by the City's Department of Housing Preservation and Development to establish a scheme for building artists' condominiums out of dilapidated tenements in the Lower East Side, subsidised by federal funds, was defeated at the Board of Estimate in February 1983 (*The New York Times*, 1983f). This Artists' Home Ownership Plan had run into major opposition from neighbourhood groups, and artists themselves became divided over the issue. The opposition to the plan was due to the fact that it would have drawn upon scarce federal funds designated expressly for low-income groups and that, after three years, artists would have been able to sell their renovated condominiums at market

rates, thus making capital gains, reducing the stock of low-income housing, and promoting further gentrification. In April 1983, however, the program was revived; but this time the City proposed to spatially disperse the subsidised housing rather than locate it in an area "already rife with real estate speculation" (*Village Voice*, 1983).

In Montréal, there is also some evidence to suggest that middle level white-collar households (incomes in the range $20000–$25000)[8] are increasingly living in nonprofit rental housing cooperatives—a form of housing originally thought to have appeal only for those on the lowest incomes and/or living in 'unconventional' ways (St Martin, 1982). Funds available for nonprofit housing cooperatives are very limited, and the cooperatives have to become self-financing over time under current Canadian federal and Québec governmental regulations. Thus the proportions in this income category may well increase at the expense of those in lower (but not the very lowest) brackets, which will intensify the bimodal distribution of income categories in cooperatives that now exists, peaking at incomes in the range $7000–$11000 and $20000–$25000 (St Martin, 1982). Furthermore, there is strong pressure from the Canadian federal and Québec governments to 'commodify' housing cooperatives, allowing shares to be sold and capital gains to be made, much as in the New York equity cooperative model (Fincher, 1982). Were this to happen, Canadian housing cooperatives would obviously no longer be outside of the capitalist housing market, as they are at present to a very large extent [see footnote (3)].

Beyond chaotic conceptions

All of these developments mean that a growing number of moderate-income first-time homebuyers are likely to be 'competing' with lower-income tenants for old inner-city housing. Direct competition is of course limited, as separate housing submarkets are controlled by property-owners and developers who carry out the conversion of low-priced rental units into moderately priced owner-occupied units, with the assistance of financial institutions. At the same time, various forms of 'sweat equity' renovation by moderate-income homebuyers (recall that some of this is actually the labour of people working 'informally' who are local renters) seem likely to continue in large cities with a high density of white-collar employment, as long as appropriate and inexpensive old houses and apartments are available and as long as the new purchasers have the necessary resources to do the work[9]. There is no reason to assume that the growth in CBD employment will continue indefinitely and that the prices of properties renovated in the present period will inflate as meteorically as those of recent years. It may well be that many of the current wave of moderate-income buyers are unlikely to accumulate significant real wealth through homeownership.

I am suggesting, then, that the terms 'gentrification' and 'gentrifiers', as commonly used in the literature, are 'chaotic conceptions' which obscure the fact that a multiplicity of processes, rather than a single causal process, produce changes in the occupation of inner-city neighbourhoods from lower to higher income residents. Moreover, the existing concepts are also chaotic in extant marxist usage because they internally combine 'necessary tendencies' with 'contingent conditions' (for example, the law of value combined with a particular housing stock with particular occupants at a particular time). The concepts 'gentrification' and 'gentrifiers' need to be disaggregated so that we may then reconceptualise the processes that produce the changes we observe, and so that we may change, where necessary, our 'ways of seeing' some forms of 'gentrification' and some types of 'gentrifiers'.

In this section, I have gone a little way toward disaggregating 'gentrification'. I have focused on the needs of both of these broad groups (moderate-income 'gentrifiers' and lower income tenants) with respect to considerations of housing costs (relative to income), income prospects, and job security. However, we must also consider the forms of *reproduction* of people and labour-power that are enabled by various types of housing and neighbourhoods through their social and physical design and their locational aspects. These are equally crucial factors because of important changes in modes of reproduction which are historically interrelated to the restructuring of the labour-force (compare Mackenzie, 1983; Mackenzie and Rose, 1983a). These form the subject of the next section.

CHANGING HOUSEHOLD STRUCTURES, 'LIFE-STYLES', AND THE REPRODUCTION OF PEOPLE AND LABOUR POWER IN INNER-CITY NEIGHBOURHOODS

Often cited as an additional factor in the condominium conversion phenomenon is the growing number of one- and two-person households who do not conform to the norm of the nuclear family and who have 'nontraditional' or 'alternative' life-styles. They reject, and are repelled from, the North American suburban time-space rhythms

of separate spheres of work and daily life and the manner in which the latter is yet dominated by the former. One of the better known examples of this is among the gay population of San Francisco (Castells and Murphy, 1982, pages 254–255). Pilot studies of 'gentrifiers' by urban geography undergraduates at McGill University support these impressions (Ayotte and Cohen, 1983; Chamberland and Hemens, 1983; Lawrence, 1982).

Furthermore, it is now increasingly accepted that women are playing an active and important role in bringing about gentrification (Alonso, 1980; Holcomb, 1981; Ley, 1981; Markusen, 1981; Roistacher and Young, 1981; Wekerle, 1979; 1981). However, as I have argued elsewhere (Rose, 1984), the reasons for this have not yet been adequately conceptualised. In particular, there is a need to explore in detail the changing patterns of female employment and 'career ladders' in white-collar work and how these interact with changing family forms, domestic responsibilities, and life cycles to produce housing and neighbourhood consumers with specific packages of needs. Moreover, insufficient attention has been paid to differentiating between different groups of women involved in various forms of urban revitalisation, although there is a growing attention to differentiating among single parents (Klodawsky et al, 1983).

Traditional and marxist writings on the so-called nontraditional life-styles of many gentrifiers have both viewed 'life-style' changes as being conceptually separate from questions of affordability of owner-occupied housing and independent of the socioeconomic aspects of restructuring of white-collar employment (for example, see Alonso, 1980; Cox and Mergler, 1982; Le Gates and Murphy, 1981). Attempts at linkage are only made after the various 'elements' have been conceptualised separately (for example, Guterbock, 1980). But as I have suggested earlier in this paper, it is precisely such analytical separations that need to be overcome. I shall now discuss some of the changes in reproduction that appear to be occurring among 'marginal gentrifiers'. Some of the reasons why these changes in reproduction, in interaction with changes in production, may affect the residential location decisions of those concerned will be explored.

Much of what are often referred to as 'alternative life-styles'—reduced to exogenous 'fashions' by neo-classical theorists and viewed pejoratively by some Marxists—in fact symptomise attempts by educated young people, who may be unemployed, underemployed, temporarily employed (or all three simultaneously), to find creative ways of responding to new conditions of paid and unpaid work and worsening economic conditions. For reasons which need further investigation, people in such situations may tend to congregate in certain inner-city neighbourhoods where certain kinds of self-employment—based in people's homes—and 'informal' economic activities are an essential means of 'making-do'. This is frequently combined with unemployment insurance compensation or social assistance. Interestingly, 'under-the-table' private-house-renovation work is an important part of this economic activity (information obtained from Montréal contacts, who will remain confidential for obvious reasons). Such activities have attracted some attention among writers on urban social movements in Europe (Ceccarelli, 1982; Mingione, 1981), but their existence has been largely unexplored in North American contexts. The concept of *chômeur(euse) instruit(e)* (educated unemployed male/female) has been used to describe this group in Québec City (Villeneuve, 1983). They are perhaps 'gentrifiers' in terms of *genre de vie*, but are not able to purchase or even rent units with major renovations. Such developments are worthy of further research which relates them to the specific forms of restructuring taking place in particular cities.

It has been pointed out that gentrification generally results in more living space per gentrifier (Alonso, 1980), but in some cases this may not just be regular living space. Extra space may in particular be sought out by those seeking to work at home—for those on moderate incomes and/or with requirements for a lot of space for their work, this may result in relatively low housing quality. Artists' loft conversions, now famous (or infamous, depending on one's point of view) in New York City (Jackson, 1983; Zukin, 1982), but also found in Montréal and presumably in other places, may be seen as an extreme example of this.

ENVIRONMENTAL DESIGN, HOUSEHOLD ORGANISATION, AND THE PRODUCTION OF GENTRIFIERS WITH 'ALTERNATIVE LIFE-STYLES'

Though many studies have shown that gentrification is not usually a 'return to the city' by former suburbanites, it is now becoming clear that many who become gentrifiers do so substantially because of the difficulties, not only of affording housing, but also of carrying on their particular living arrangements in conventional suburbs (Rose, 1983). The types of household often noted as predominating in the early stages of neighbourhood renovation—single parents, gay couples, unrelated people living together, and so on—have grown rapidly in numbers nationally both in the USA and

in Canada in the last intercensal period. Evidence is beginning to surface that single parents are disproportionately represented among the occupants of inner-city condominium conversions in Canada (Dansereau et al, 1981, page 115; *Habitation*, 1982; Klodawsky et al. 1983). These are groups frequently still excluded from suburban communities because they do not meet the norms of the nuclear family still entrenched in zoning regulations (Hayden, 1981; Lees, 1983; Mackenzie and Rose, 1983a; 1983b; Wekerle, 1979)[10]. Exclusionary zoning, by lot size, building regulations, and household types, persists, especially in the USA[11]. In a recent case in a suburban municipality in Denver, for instance, an unmarried couple living together were deemed to be in breach of the law (*Life on Capital Hill*, 1983). Even in inner cities similar norms may prevail over the courts. A recent ruling by the New York State Court of Appeals upheld the provisions of a rental apartment lease in Greenwich Village that prohibited unmarried couples from moving in together (*The New York Times*, 1983a). If this ruling holds it will presumably be a significant 'push' factor from renting an apartment to owning a condominium.

More generally, the design—social and environmental—of even moderately priced suburban residential areas may also be a factor in 'pushing' some of the types of household seen as gentrifiers into the inner-city areas they move to. Recent research on the 'accessory-apartment' phenomenon in a moderate-income Long Island suburb suggests that, where such inexpensive in-house apartments are available, single parents take them up in numbers out of all proportion to their representation in the general population (Rudel, 1983a). Quite possibly, this type of housing is not only attractive in terms of price but also because of the opportunities for informal childcare networks in such demographically mixed neighbourhoods. But the vast majority of suburbs do not allow this type of housing (it may of course exist illegally) or other types of housing and 'social design' appropriate to the needs of single parents (Lees, 1983; SPCMT, 1979).

By contrast, many existing older inner-city neighbourhoods can provide housing with these features; duplex and triplex attached-housing[12] in 'ethnic' areas of Montréal is an example. Such neighbourhoods facilitate access to community services, enable shared use of facilities, provide an efficient and nonisolating environment for reproductive work, and enhance opportunities for women to develop locally based friendship networks and a supportive environment (Holcomb, 1981; Michelson, 1977; Rothblatt et al, 1979; Saegert and Winkel, 1981; Soper, 1981; Stamp, 1981; Women in Planning Steering Committee—Oregon Chapter, no date).

Moreover, a number of studies in the 'residential-satisfaction' literature have concluded that clustered condominium-type housing (whether in new communities, up-zoned suburbs, or older inner-city areas) may have distinct advantages for all women with children, in that they can potentially "provide more efficient and better organised housing environments and a more supportive set of community services" (Rothblatt et al, 1979, page 135; also see Genovese, 1981; Michelson, 1977; Popenoe, 1977). To say this is not to be an environmental determinist, but only—and importantly—to realise that environmental forms may impose real limits on the creation of alternative reproductive forms (Hayden, 1981; Mackenzie and Rose, 1983b). As yet, few new communities have been designed with such goals in mind, and thus existing inner-city neighbourhoods have been the foci of such efforts at developing alternatives[13]. It remains to be seen to what extent redesigning existing suburbs might change the current preferences of the groups discussed here for inner-city living.

REDIRECTING THE QUESTIONS: REDEFINING URBAN REVITALISATION IN PRACTICE

The preceding discussion leads to the conclusion that the 'attractions' of inner-city neighbourhoods for a number of groups of 'gentrifiers' may thus relate to the presence of considerable *need* among such groups and should not therefore be viewed in mere 'life-style' terms. Indeed, the very concept of 'life-style' conjures up scenarios of unbridled choice, influenced only by fashion, in popular parlance. It is not just a matter of simple unrestrained 'preference', given the nature of the available alternatives. This is one of the most important insights to be gained from rethinking the chaotic conceptions of gentrification that have dominated marxist as well as positivist thinking up until now.

Rather than analytically incorporating what I have termed 'marginal gentrifiers' within the same category as wealthy gentrifiers, it would, I believe, be more useful to explore the possibility of such groups having certain needs and desires in common with some of those they now compete with. In some cases they may be able to work together to develop housing alternatives that would provide them with the same 'ontological security' (Saunders, 1982) as homeownership, but without upward redistributions of wealth and compatible with, or even dovetailing with, the needs of low-income tenants[14]. As a caveat to this, I am not suggesting that we naively

assume that it would be easy, in a wide range of circumstances, to build such alliances. Yet it does seem important to further explore what the wants and the needs of these 'marginal gentrifiers' are for inner-city housing, above and beyond the limited alternative choices that are currently presented to them. It has been proposed, for instance, to develop 'urban homesteading' programs for New York City artists, in which they would form nonprofit rental housing cooperatives without using any public funds. Although this would not help low-income artists, it would reduce pressure on the low-income housing stock, would remove the units permanently from the speculative housing market, and would integrate artists more into the surrounding neighbourhoods (*Village Voice*, 1983). Explorations of such options should parallel, but interact with, work that focuses on the housing needs of various groups of low-income tenants (compare Klodawsky et al, 1983).

In the process of reshaping the physical fabric and social networks of inner-city neighbourhoods, it may be possible to make them supportive of alternatives to the patriarchal family and conventional divisions and organisation of domestic labour (compare Stamp, 1981). Also, on a very limited scale, such revitalising neighbourhoods may be supportive of alternative ways of making a living for some of those who have been economically marginalised by the present phase of restructuring. There are possibilities of developing collective forms of self-help (Castells, 1981), rather than the individualistic forms that are an integral part of the ideology of gentrification (Allen, 1980; Beauregard, 1983; Smith, 1983). Self-employment, the informal production of goods and services domestically or within neighbourhoods, producer cooperatives (Blair, 1982; Boyte, 1980; Mingione, 1981; Pahl, 1980; Tabb, 1983), and the democratising potential of new communications (Castells, 1983; Piercy, 1976; Williams, 1981, page 435)—all these are potentially 'prefigurative' forms of social organisation.

Nevertheless, there is no escaping the fact that those groups of people who may be developing alternative forms of reproduction of social life are in many cases displacing poorer residents with far fewer options—including many working-class single parents and minorities. It is easy to forget, for instance, the displacement of low-income single parents while lauding housing arrangements that enable a couple of middle-class single parents to cooperatively manage their multiple roles (Markusen, 1981, page 32).

As I have discussed elsewhere (Rose, 1983), in a sense, gentrification by employed women with children may be a deliberately sought out *environmental solution* to a set of problems that are inherently *social problems.* Becoming a gentrifier makes it easier to have a waged job in addition to doing most of the household work and childcare—in a social context where working hours are fixed, hours of services limited, transportation systems planned for traditional nuclear families, and traditional gender roles still prevail over the allocation of domestic responsibilities. Sometimes such women may even generate alternatives to the 'double day' and the individualised nature of so much reproductive work—but on a small spatial scale and probably with limited social 'spread effects' to those of lower incomes dealing with the same problems. Yet women with dual roles and low incomes are concentrated in inner-city neighbourhoods, on which they have traditionally relied, not only for cheap housing and transportation, but also for social support systems (Wekerle, 1981, page 197), as are young single women and newly divorced women, who may also be new to the job market as well as the housing market (Roistacher and Young, 1981, page 219). All these are particularly vulnerable to displacement induced by gentrification (Smith and LeFaivre, 1983). Thus the moderate-income woman's environmental solution to the problems created by her dual role exacerbates the problems of the low-income woman who is displaced to other neighbourhoods which are more environmentally restrictive and less socially supportive (Rose, 1983). Holcomb et al (1983) refer to the burden of increased childcare costs incurred by low-income service workers when previous informal social networks in black neighbourhoods of US cities are disrupted by displacement resulting from gentrification. Goldstein, writing about artists' housing in New York City (*Village Voice*, 1983), makes a related point that is well taken:

> ... the needs of artists for cheap housing are ignored by community activists at their peril. Since the poverty of artists is often voluntary, this particular proletariat is infinitely capable of competing with other low income groups.

The restructuring of white-collar work is tending to concentrate low-paid service workers and young unmarried clerical workers in inner-city neighbourhoods at the same time as it promotes gentrification by upper-income professionals and renovation by and for moderate-income white-collar households (Le Gates and Hartman, 1981). Corporate headquarters and financial centres still need the labour of these low-paid workers, and the people who fill these jobs need to live in low-cost housing that is conveniently located in inner-city

neighbourhoods. This is likely to remain true even though back-office data processing functions are increasingly transferred to suburban locations (Gad, 1979; 1981; *The New York Times*, 1983g). The latter article suggests that the gentrification of formerly moderate-income areas is contributing to a shortage of adequately educated part-time clerical workers. Hence restructuring actively contributes to the spatially based housing conflicts between different groups of workers, noted by Le Gates and Murphy (1981) and alluded to above. Moreover, in some US cities, corporate redevelopment and gentrification are proceeding hand in hand amidst extreme poverty and unemployment. This is likely to exacerbate low-income housing problems. A particularly graphic instance of this kind of spatially uneven development is depicted by a recent *New York Times* (1983e) report. Headlined: "In Hartford, It's The Best and Worst of Times", the story focuses on a woman aged forty-four years, unemployed for fifteen months in the inner city, who comments: "The town is flourishing. And I can't find a job, even washing dishes". De Giovanni (1983) reports a wave of speculator-led gentrification since 1977 in the same city. These problems are made more acute by the lack of opportunities for women in clerical and service jobs, in labour markets that are increasingly segregated and spatially differentiated, to increase their income over time (as discussed already).

I do not believe that this conflict between different fractions of labour, and frequently between groups of women, can be seen as matters of housing scarcity and differential access to resources only, although both of these are clearly important. This is a matter for much further research, grounded in the realities of neighbourhood politics as well as in analyses of the forms of restructuring of work processes and their implications (which I have only touched on here). Nor are we looking at a 'simple' class conflict. My perspective here differs from that of Smith and LeFaivre (1983), who appear to see gentrification and displacement in 'pure' class terms, on the basis of the fact (which I do not in principle dispute) that the "effects of this process are sharply delineated along class lines" (1983, page 16). However, the foregoing argument suggests that this conclusion may be conceptually and logically premature, and in some cases perhaps overly pessimistic.

CONCLUDING THOUGHTS

If we are trying to understand how and why gentrification is occurring, with the aim of going beyond sorrow and outrage about displacement and developing some progressive political strategies (Planners Network, 1980), then we need to analyse these processes in terms that go far beyond concepts of undifferentiated 'gentrifiers' and upwardly mobile neighbourhoods. We need, for example, to have a perspective that allows us to understand the situation of this college-educated single parent, who wrote a letter to the *Newsletter of the National Congress of Neighbourhood Women* (1983):

> I run through the daily obstacle course of taking my daughter to day care, rushing off to work, putting in my 8–9 hour day for my measly $195.00 a week, rushing back to day care to pick my daughter up and home again to our cozy studio apartment tucked in the not-too-nice area of Oakland. I come home, cook, tuck my precious into bed and, and, and. … Fall asleep by 9 PM, up at 5 AM and the race continues. But dammit—I want more! …. I want to get involved in the community and open up new possibilities and options not only for myself but for others living in this neighbourhood.

In conventional parlance, the writer of this letter would be seen as a 'first-stage gentrifier' or a 'pioneer'. But such a conceptualisation does not help us to comprehend her needs, her aspirations, and her relationship to older established residents.

I have argued here that chaotic conceptions of the problems and conflicts around 'gentrification' issues cannot lead us toward solutions. We ought not to assume in advance that all gentrifiers have the same class positions as each other and that they are 'structurally' polarised from the displaced. It may be much more useful to explore to what extent they may comprise different fractions of the labour force. At present, they may have similar locational needs for reasons that may be related to the interrelationships of their roles in social production and changes in reproduction. These relationships are not, however, reducible to structural forces and changes in the economy, and are malleable, potentially, by conscious human agency. It may well be that these groups have some needs and 'interests' in common[15]. Needs for certain types of services, decentralised childcare facilities, and housing that is taken out of the private market come to mind. This is not to paper over the conflicts that also undoubtedly exist, but merely to stress that, if we analytically lump together what I have called marginal gentrifiers with their wealthy namesakes, we are preventing any recognition of the possibility of forming alliances between the former groups and the groups likely to be displaced.

The operation of the private-housing market is the immediate vehicle which pits these two against one another, forcing them into competition or even actual conflict over the displacement issue. However, some of the polarisations between the two groups, as well as the struggles they share, originate in processes much broader than the operation of the land and housing markets. Yet attempts to overcome such polarisations do not have to be limited to the 'sphere of production'. Indeed, the 'sphere of everyday life' and the reproductive work carried on therein are at least equally crucial and logical starting points of political practice for those socialists who are also feminists (for example, see Luxton, 1980; Rowbotham et al, 1979; Sayer, 1981). For instance, a 'community' newspaper in Denver—clearly a product of the gentrification of the neighbourhood it serves—discusses a local zoning regulation preventing unmarried couples from living together, commenting:

> [This] zoning can be used against persons who are not acceptable in a neighbourhood. That could be the elderly, handicapped and gay. These people have already been discriminated against in many other areas. [Such restrictive] zoning is just one more slightly hidden weapon against those who do not 'fit in'.
>
> (*Life on Capital Hill*, 1983, page 11)

Though one might dismiss this as a piece of easily voiced liberalism by the privileged, I do not believe such comments should be so easily discarded. To assess the possibility of developing alliances and organisational forms that could move us a step closer to 'designing a city for all' (Abu-Lughod, 1982) in the smaller scale of a particular inner-city neighbourhood, detailed empirical research is needed. This would explore the interrelationships between the form of restructuring taking place in the city's economy, changes in labour processes, the production of different fractions of labour and changes in their reproduction, and the particular types of gentrification taking place there.

Realistically, we cannot put an end to all gentrification. Moreover, *some* of the changes which are usually subsumed within the concept 'gentrification' can bring into existing neighbourhoods intrusions of alternative ways of living, which would never be tolerated if they were not being introduced by 'middle-class' and 'professional' people in the first instance. Whether or not such alternatives remain limited to versions in the 1980s of bourgeois bohemianism and individualistic self-help, or whether they can diffuse and broaden and consciously and collectively be directed toward 'prefigurative' ways of living and working, is a wide open and contingent question. It is this political (with a small 'p') concern that has motivated the methodological and exploratory discussion pursued in this paper (compare Fincher, 1983).

Thus, rather than being constrained by the 'chaotic concept' of gentrification as it is now generally understood, I believe that it is now an urgent research priority to disaggregate this concept, question some of the existing categories, and start to explore the actual processes through which those groups we now subsume under the category 'gentrifiers' are produced and reproduced. Such work should eventually yield an expanded, and much more adequate, specification of the necessary tendencies and contingent conditions for gentrification (as currently defined) to take place. It is to be hoped that it will also help to generate more subtle and sensitive methods for exploring particular empirical situations where these tendencies may or may not become reality. This may help us clarify what constitute progressive types of intervention and to identify 'oppositional spaces', within the noncommodified sphere of daily life (compare Conway, 1982; Rose, 1980), where such interventions may be tried out.

ACKNOWLEDGEMENTS

Many thanks to Bob Beauregard, Michael Dear, Peter Jackson, Greg Levine, Alan Mabin, and an anonymous reviewer for their helpful comments and criticisms on earlier drafts of this paper. Additional thanks to my students in Geography 412B, Winter Term 1983, at McGill University for their enthusiasm, hard work, and support, all of which contributed to the writing of this paper.

Notes

(1) The problem with this line of critique is that to point out that the phenomenon of gentrification has confounded the predictions of land-market theorists about land values and land uses in the inner city, as Smith (1982, page 141) does, does not amount to a critique of the theoretical underpinnings of land-market models. It is quite possible to model or predict that the inner city will be inhabited by wealthy people, within a neoclassical framework. All that is needed is to replace a 'space-maximising' criterion with a 'free-time-maximising' criterion (Harvey, 1972). To do this it is not necessary to alter the underlying assumptions of consumer

sovereignty and purely exogenous changes affecting 'tastes and preferences'. Yet the ability to modify the model to correctly predict the occurrence of gentrification does not mean that the neoclassical approach is valid.

(2) The fact that capital invested in gentrification is productive of surplus value rather than relying on speculative gain for profit makes it additionally attractive for financial institutions, according to Smith (1982).

(3) Such a recognition is, of course, of major importance in relation to developing political strategies around gentrification and the displacement associated with it (Smith, 1979).

(4) Ironically, some positivist writers have been much more sensitive to the importance of feminism in its own right in this context, notably Alonso (1980). However, his analysis is marred by the type of ad hoc approach and conceptual incoherence referred to above. Dubious concepts such as 'life-style' are accorded theoretical validity, and households, including women, are still seen merely as 'consumers', whose demands and needs are analysed independently of the household's structural positions in the labour force and are seen as changing from time to time as a result of factors exogenous to the theory.

(5) In this paper, I suspend judgment on Smith's (1982, page 152) assertion about the "firm[ness of the] theoretical fundament" on which the 'uneven development' approach to gentrification has so far been based, although I do believe that it is necessary to scrutinise the claim of this particular conception of uneven development to be *the* basic explanation of gentrification. See Sayer (1982; forthcoming) for some critical comments on the 'misplaced concreteness' of some usages of uneven development theories.

(6) As Beauregard (1983a) has pointed out, those displaced by gentrification may sometimes be 'redundant' workers. On the other hand (Rose, 1983), they may be the crucial service workers and clerical support staff for the headquarters functions of the CBD of the 'corporate city'. These are empirical and contingent issues that cannot be determined on a generalisable basis through a structural analysis alone.

(7) This is a crucial point that is missed by those writers who insist on the inevitability of the demise of metropolitan CBDs as the dominant locations for corporate headquarters. Such writers analyse the spatial distribution of office activities independent of the nature of the

labour processes that comprise such activities, instead lumping together in a unitary conceptualisation *all* categories of office work. 'Spatial process' is thus seen by such theorists as a causal factor in its own right. Muller's work is a classic case of this type of spatial fetishism and chaotic conceptualisation: "dispersion has superseded concentration as *the dominant force governing* the intrametropolitan distribution of office activities" (Muller, 1981, page 146; my emphasis).

(8) Canadian dollars.

(9) The literature on gentrification in North America has tended to be dominated by the view that state involvement, in the form of some kind of subsidies to gentrifiers, is essential to the process. This is not necessarily so in all cases of gentrification [a point which Mabin (1983, personal communication) reminded me about]. However, pilot research on renovation by moderate-income gentrifiers in Montréal (Ayotte and Cohen, 1983) does suggest that they might not have carried out the renovation without City grants [which, incidentally, the City will entirely recoup in increased property taxes within eight or nine years, according to an official at the Service de Restauration (1983)].

(10) An extensive literature now exists on the problems that women, especially those who are both parents and wage earners outside the home, face in conventional suburbs. See Wekerle (1981) for a review of the literature to that date.

(11) Exclusionary zoning according to household type was ruled illegal by the Supreme Court of Canada in 1979 (Lees, 1983). In the USA, some relaxations in such zoning have been introduced, but they usually only cover existing residents of the municipality concerned and/or elderly people (Muller, 1981, page 97).

(12) 'Plexes' generally comprise two or three *superimposed* dwellings, in which each apartment (or every two apartments) has a private street-related entrance and an individual street address. (Upper-level apartments have an outside staircase to street level.) Since many plexes were originally built for owner-occupancy, their structural quality, size, and internal arrangement of space are frequently superior to those of purpose-built rental units. These attributes make plex apartments attractive to moderate-income purchasers buying in the copropriété (coownership) tenure form, as well as to people who may buy an entire plex building and then convert two of the units

into a single dwelling (Wexler, 1984, personal communication).

(13) However, there is an interesting review of new projects of Canadian architect-designed suburban housing for mixes of family types and incomes in, significantly, a recent issue of a women's magazine (see Surpin, 1983), and formal shared housing schemes, for reasons of social support for the elderly and for single parents, are being pioneered in the Greater Vancouver area and are now drawing some attention in the USA (*Urban Reader*, 1982b). Small 'grandmother houses' in families backyards are also beginning to make a reappearance in a few places in the USA, although in most municipalities zoning laws would render them illegal (*Urban Reader*, 1982b).

(14) In my view, nonprofit rental housing cooperatives broadly based along the lines of the Québec model (that is, all members coown all buildings comprising the cooperative, but do not own alienable shares of the capital value; each member is a tenant of the cooperative and pays a low to moderate rent for her/his unit; limits are placed on the income distribution of tenants) are among the most promising of feasible alternatives, in spite of the problems they have encountered (Fincher, 1982; St Martin, 1982).

(15) The notion of 'class interests' is a very problematic one. It is inherently a normative and evaluative notion, connoting someone's view of what constitutes 'correct' consciousness and/or practice, and has its origins in the political philosophy of utilitarianism (Therborn, 1980, pages 100–105). This is discussed in more detail in Rose (1984, chapter 5). [I am grateful to Mabin (1979, personal communication) for initially drawing my attention to the difficulties of defining 'interests'.]

REFERENCES

Abu-Lughod J, 1982, "Designing a city for all", in *Internal Structure of the City* (second edition) Ed. L S Bourne (Oxford University Press, New York) pp 594–602

Allen I, 1980, "The ideology of dense neighborhood redevelopment" *Urban Affairs Quarterly* **15** 409–428

Alonso W, 1980. "The population factor in urban structure" in *Internal Structure of the City* (second edition) Ed. L S Bourne (Oxford University Press, New York) pp 540–551

Atwood M, 1980 *Life Before Man* (McClelland and Stewart, Toronto)

Ayotte M, Cohen L, 1983, "A questionnaire on gentrification in Plateau Mont-Royal (Montréal)" mimeo available from the authors, c/o Department of Geography, McGill University, Montréal, Québec H3A 2K6, Canada

Beauregard R A, 1983, "Toward a theoretical penetration of gentrification"; mimeo available from the author, Department of Urban Planning, Lucy Stone Hall, Rutgers University, New Brunswick. NJ 08903, USA

Benwell Community Project, 1978 *Private Housing and the Working Class* Final Report Series no 3 (Benwell CDP Publications, Newcastle upon Tyne)

Berry B, 1980, "Inner city futures: an American dilemma revisited" *Transactions of the Institute of British Geographers* new series **5** 1–28

Blair J P, 1982, "Irregular economies" in *Cities in the 21st Century* volume 23 of *Urban Affairs Annual Reviews* Eds G Gappert, R V Knight (Sage, Beverly Hills, CA) pp 213–230

Boyte H C, 1980 *The Backyard Revolution: Understanding the New Citizen Movement* (Temple University Press, Philadelphia, PA)

Castells M, 1977 *The Urban Question: A Marxist Approach* (MIT Press, Cambridge, MA)

Castells M, 1981, review of *The Backyard Revolution: Understanding the New Citizen Movement* by H C Boyte *International Journal of Urban and Regional Research* **5** 588–590

Castells M, 1983, "Crisis, planning, and the quality of life: managing the new historical relationships between space and society" *Environment and Planning D: Society and Space* **1** 3–21

Castells M, Murphy K, 1982, "Cultural identify and urban structure: the spatial organisation of San Francisco's gay community" in *Urban Policy under Capitalism* volume 22 of *Urban Affairs Annual Reviews* Eds N I Fainstein, S S Fainstein (Sage, Beverly Hills, CA) pp 237–260

Ceccarelli P, 1982, "Politics, parties and urban movements: Western Europe" in *Urban Policy under Capitalism* volume 22 of *Urban Affairs Annual Reviews* Eds N I Fainstein, S S Fainstein (Sage, Beverly Hills, CA) pp 261–276

Chamberland D, Hemens B, 1983, "Pilot survey of the McGill Ghetto gentrifiers" mimeo available from the authors, c/o Department of Geography, McGill University, Montréal, Québec H3A 2K6, Canada

Christopherson S, 1983, "The household and class formation: determinants of residential location in Ciudad Juarez" *Environment and Planning D: Society and Space* **1** 323–338

Clark W A V, Onaka J L, 1983, "Life cycle and housing adjustment as explanations of residential mobility" *Urban Studies* **20** 47–57

Cohen R B, 1981, "The new international division of labor, multinational corporations and urban hierarchy" in *Urbanization and Urban Planning in Capitalist Society* Eds M Dear, A J Scott (Methuen, New York) pp 287–315

Conway D, 1982, "Self-help housing, the commodity nature of housing and amelioration of the housing deficit: continuing the Turner-Burgess debate" *Antipode* **14** 40–46

Cox K R, Mergler G J, 1982, "Gentrification and urban form" RR-27, Center for Real Estate Administration and Research, Ohio State University, Columbus, OH 43210, USA

Dansereau F, Godbout J, Collin J-P, L'Ecuyer D, Lessard M-J, Larouche G, Chabot L, 1981 "La transformation d'immeubles locatifs en copropriété d'occupation" rapport présenté au Gouvernement du Québec, Institut National de la Recherche Scientifique–Urbanisation, Université du Québec, 3465 rue Durocher, Montréal, Québec H2X 2C6, Canada

De Giovanni F, 1983, "Patterns of housing market activity in revitalizing neighborhoods" *Journal of American Planning Association* **49** 22–39

Drabble M, 1977 *The Realms of Gold* (Penguin Books, Harmondsworth, Middx)

Fainstein N I, Fainstein S S, 1982, "Restructuring the American city: a comparative perspective" in *Urban Policy under Capitalism* volume 22 of *Urban Affairs Annual Reviews* Eds N I Fainstein, S S Fainstein (Sage, Beverly Hills, CA) pp 161–189

Fincher R, 1982, "The commodification of Québec's progressive housing cooperatives" mimeo available from the author, Department of Geography, McMaster University, Hamilton, Ontario LS8 4L8, Canada

Fincher R, 1983, "The inconsistency of eclecticism" *Environment and Planning A* **15** 607–622

Gad G H K, 1979, "Face-to-face linkages and office decentralization potentials: a study of Toronto" in *Spatial Patterns of Office Growth and Location* Ed. P W Daniels (John Wiley, Chichester, Sussex) pp 277–323

Gad G H K, 1981, "Some characteristics of the process of office decentralization in Toronto" paper presented at the Annual Meeting of the Canadian Association of Geographers, Corner Brook, Newfoundland, 10–13 August; mimeo available from the author, Department of Geography,

Erindale College, University of Toronto, Toronto, Ontario M5S 1A1, Canada

Genovese R G, 1981, "A women's self-help network as a response to service needs in the suburbs" in *Women and the American City* Eds C R Stimpson, E Dixler, M J Nelson, K B Yatrakis (University of Chicago Press, Chicago, IL) pp 245–253

Giddens A, 1979 *Central Problems in Social Theory: Action, Structure and Contradiction in Social Analysis* (Macmillan, London)

Giddens A, 1981 *A Contemporary Critique of Historical Materialism* (University of California Press, Berkeley, CA)

Guterbock T M, 1980, "The political economy of urban revitalization: competing theories" *Urban Affairs Quarterly* **15** 429–438

Habitation 1982, "Pourquoi acheter un condominium?" **4** 5–8

Harvey D, 1972, "Society, the city and the space-economy of urbanism" Association of American Geographers Resource Paper, Washington, DC

Harvey D, 1974, "Class-monopoly rent, finance capital and the urban revolution" *Regional Studies* **8** 239–245

Harvey D, 1975, "The political economy of urbanization in advanced capitalist countries: the case of the United States" in *The Political Economy of Cities* volume 9 of *Urban Affairs Annual Reviews* Eds G Gappert, H Rose (Sage Publications, Beverly Hills, CA) pp 119–163

Hayden D, 1981, *The Grand Domestic Revolution: A History of Feminist Design for American Homes, Neighborhoods and Cities* (MIT Press, Cambridge, MA)

Holcomb B, 1981, "Women's roles in distressing and revitalising cities" *Transition* **11** 1–6

Holcomb B, Beauregard R A, 1981, "Revitalizing cities" Association of American Geographers Resource Paper, Washington, DC

Holcomb B, Green P, Page C, 1983, "Blacks and urban revitalization: winners or losers?" paper presented at the Annual Meeting of the Association of American Geographers, Denver, CO, 24–27 April; mimeo available from the author, Department of Urban Studies, Lucy Stone Hall, Rutgers University, New Brunswick, NJ 08903, USA

Jackson P, 1983, "Residential loft conversion and neighbourhood change" paper presented at the Annual Meeting of the Association of American Geographers, Denver, Co, 24–27 April; mimeo available from the author, Department of Geography, University College London, London WC1E 6BT, England

Klodawsky F, Spector A, Hendrix C, 1983, "The housing needs of single parent families in Canada" mimeo available from Ark Research Associates, 165 Hinton Avenue North, Ottawa, Ontario K2Y 0Z9

Lamarche F, 1976, "Property development and the economic foundations of the urban question" in *Urban Sociology: Critical Essays* Ed. C G Pickvance (Tavistock Publications, Andover, Hants) pp 85–118

Laska S B, Spain D (Eds), 1980 *Back to the City: Issues in Neighborhood Renovation* (Pergamon Press, New York)

Lawrence J, 1982, "An evaluation of neighbourhood revitalization: Montréal's Shaughnessy Village" mimeo available from the author, c/o Department of Geography, McGill University, Montréal, Québec H3A 2K6, Canada

L'Ecuyer D, 1981, "La conversion: revue de la littérature" rapport intérimaire soumis au Gouvernement du Québec, sous la direction de Jacques Godbout; Institut National de la Recherche Scientifique–Urbanisation, 3465 rue Durocher, Montréal, Québec H2X 2C6, Canada

Lees D, 1983, "Suburban dream … suburban nightmare? *Chatelaine* May issue, pp 49–51, 76, 80, 83–84

Le Gates R T, Hartman C, 1981, "Displacement" *Clearinghouse Review* **15** 207–249

Le Gates R T, Murphy K, 1981, "Austerity, shelter and social conflict in the United States" *International Journal of Urban and Regional Research* **5** 255–276

Ley D, 1980, "Liberal ideology and the postindustrial city" *Annals of the Association of American Geographers* **70** 238–258

Ley D, 1981, "Inner-city revitalization in Canada: a Vancouver case study" *Canadian Geographer* **XXV** 124–148

Ley D, 1983, *A Social Geography of the City* (Harper and Row, New York)

Life on Capitol Hill 1983, "Local zoning struggle affects unmarried couple" by J Carling, volume 9, issue 4, pp 8 and 11

London B, 1980, "Gentrification as urban reinvasion" in *Back to the City: Issues in Neighborhood Renovation* Eds S Laska, D Spain (Pergamon Press, New York) pp 77–92

London B, Palen J, 1984, *Gentrification, Displacement and Neighborhood Revitalization* (State University of New York Press, Albany, NY)

Luxton M, 1980 *More than a Labour of Love* (Women's Press, Toronto)

McDowell L, 1983, "Towards an understanding of the gender division of urban space" *Environment and Planning D: Society and Space* **1** 59–72

Mackenzie S, 1981, "Women and the reproduction of labour power in the industrial city: a case study" WP-23, Urban and Regional Studies, University of Sussex, Falmer, Brighton BN1 9RH, England

Mackenzie S, 1983 *Gender and Environment: Production and Reproduction in Post-war Brighton* PhD thesis, Graduate Division of Geography, University of Sussex, Falmer, Brighton BN1 9RH, England

Mackenzie S, Rose D, 1983a, "Industrial change, the domestic economy and home life" in *Redundant Spaces in Cities and Regions? Studies in Industrial Decline and Social Change* Eds J Anderson, S Duncan, R Hudson (Academic Press, London) pp 155–200

Mackenzie S, Rose D, 1983b, "Perspectives on urban restructuring: problems for feminist research" paper presented at the Annual Meeting of the Association of American Geographers, Denver, CO, 24–27 April; mimeo available from D Rose

Marcuse P, 1981, "The targeted crisis: on the ideology of the fiscal crisis and its uses" *International Journal of Urban and Regional Research* **5** 330–355

Markusen A, 1981, "City spatial structure, women's household work and national urban policy" in *Women and the American City* Eds C R Stimpson, E Dixler, M J Nelson, K B Yatrakis (University of Chicago Press, Chicago, IL) pp 20–41

Marx K, 1973 *Grundrisse* (Penguin Books, Harmondsworth, Middx)

Marx K, 1976 *Capital* volume 1 (Penguin Books, Harmondsworth, Middx)

Michelson W, 1977 *Environmental Choice, Human Behavior and Residential Satisfaction* (Oxford University Press, New York)

Michelson W, 1981, "Spatial and temporal dimensions of child care" in *Women and the American City* Eds C R Stimpson, E Dixler, M J Nelson, K B Yatrakis (University of Chicago Press, Chicago, IL) pp 239–244

Mingione E, 1981, "Perspectives on the spatial division of labour under the recent productive restructuring and informalisation of the economy" paper presented at the Conference on New Perspectives on the Urban Political Economy, Washington, DC, 22–24 May; mimeo available from the author, University of Messina, Messina, Italy

Muller P O, 1981 *Contemporary Suburban America* (Prentice-Hall, Englewood Cliffs, NJ)

Newsletter of the National Congress of Neighborhood Women 1983, letter to the Editor, February issue

Paul R, 1980, "Employment, work and the domestic division of labour" *International Journal of Urban and Regional Research* **4** 1–19

Piercy M, 1976 *Woman on the Edge of Time* (Fawcett Crest, New York)

Planners Network, 1980, "Towards a union of progressive planners" proceedings of the Planners Network Conference, Columbia University, NJ, 10 May; mimeo available from R A Beauregard, Department of Urban Planning, Rutgers University, Lucy Stone Hall, New Brunswick, NJ 08903, USA

Popenoe D, 1977 *The Suburban Environment* (University of Chicago Press, Chicago, IL)

Roistacher E A, Young J, 1981, "Working women and city structure: implications of the subtle revolution" in *Women and the American City* Eds C R Stimpson, E Dixler, M J Nelson, K B Yatrakis (University of Chicago Press, Chicago, IL) pp 217–222

Rose D, 1980, "Toward a re-evaluation of the political significance of home-ownership in Britain" in *Housing, Construction and the State* Conference of Socialist Economists, Political Economy of Housing Workshop (CSE-PEHW, London) pp 71–76

Rose D, 1981, "Home-ownership and industrial change: the struggle for a 'separate sphere'" WP-25, Urban and Regional Studies, University of Sussex, Falmer, Brighton, BN1 9RH, England

Rose D, 1983, "Women and gentrification: some research problems" paper presented at the Third Annual Women in Planning Conference, Rutgers University, New Brunswick, NJ, 22 April; mimeo available from the author

Rose D, 1984, *Home Ownership, Uneven Development and Industrial Change: The Making of a 'Separate Sphere' in Late Nineteenth Century Britain* D Phil thesis, Graduate Division of Geography, University of Sussex, Falmer, Brighton BN1 9QN, England

Rothblatt D W, Garr D J, Sprague J, 1979 *The Suburban Environment and Women* (Praeger, New York)

Rowbotham S, Segal L, Wainwright H, 1979 *Beyond the Fragments: Feminism and the Making of Socialism* (Merlin Press, London)

Roweis S T, Scott A J, 1981, "The urban land question" in *Urbanization and Urban Planning in Capitalist Society* Eds M J Dear, A J Scott (Methuen, New York) pp 123–158

Rudel T K, 1983a, "Household change, accessory apartments and the provision of low-income housing in American suburbs" mimeo available from the author, Department of Human Ecology, Cook College, Rutgers University, New Brunswick, NJ 08903, USA

Rudel T K, 1983b, "Inflation and regional change in access to home ownership in the 1970s" mimeo available from the author, Department of Human Ecology, Cook College, Rutgers University, New Brunswick, NJ 08903, USA

Saegert S, Winkel G, 1981, "The home: a critical problem for changing sex roles" in *New Space for Women* Eds G Wekerle, R Peterson, D Morley (Westview Press, Boulder, CO) pp 41–64

St Martin I, 1982, "La théorie de l'embourgeoisement et les coopératives d'habitation à Montréal" mimeo available from the author, c/o Department of Urban Planning, McGill University, Montréal, Québec H3A 2K6, Canada

Salomon I, Ben-Akiva M, 1983, "The use of the life-style concept in travel demand models" *Environment and Planning A* **15** 623–638

Saunders P, 1978, "Domestic property and social class" *International Journal of Urban and Regional Research* **2** 233–251

Saunders P, 1979 *Urban Politics: A Sociological Interpretation* (Penguin Books, Harmondsworth, Middx)

Saunders P, 1982, "Beyond housing classes: the sociological significance of private property rights in means of consumption" WP-33, Urban and Regional Studies, University of Sussex, Falmer, Brighton BN1 9RH, England

Sayer A, 1979, "Theory and empirical research in urban and regional political economy: a sympathetic critique" WP-14, Urban and Regional Studies, University of Sussex, Falmer, Brighton BN1 9RH; England

Sayer A, 1981, "What kind of marxism for feminism?" mimeo available from the author, School of Social Sciences, University of Sussex, Falmer, Brighton BN1 9QN, England

Sayer A, 1982, "Explanation in economic geography" *Progress in Human Geography* **6** 68–88

Sayer A, 1983, review of *A Contemporary Critique of Historical Materialism* by A Giddens *Environment and Planning D: Society and Space* **1** 109–114

Sayer A, forthcoming, "Theoretical problems in the analysis of technological change and regional development" in *Spatial Analysis, Industry and the Industrial Environment* volume III, Eds F E Hamilton, G J R Linge; details available from the author, School of Social Sciences, University of Sussex, Falmer, Brighton BN1 9QN, England

Scott A J, 1982, "Production system dynamics and metropolitan development" *Annals of the Association of American Geographers* **72** 185–200

Simmie J M, 1983, "Beyond the industrial city?" *Journal of the American Planning Association* **49** 59–76

Smith N, 1979, "Gentrification and capital: practice and ideology in Society Hill" *Antipode* **11** 24–35

Smith N, 1982, "Gentrification and uneven development" *Economic Geography* **58** 139–155

Smith N, 1983, "Gentrification, frontier and the restructuring of urban space" mimeo available from the author, Department of Geography, Columbia University, New York, NJ 10027, USA

Smith N, LeFaivre M, 1984, "A class analysis of gentrification" in *Gentrification, Displacement and Neighborhood Revitalization* Eds B London, J Palen (State University of New York Press, Albany, NY) in press

Smith N, Williams P, forthcoming *Gentrification, Housing and the Restructuring of Urban Space* (George Allen and Unwin, Hemel Hempstead, Herts)

Soper M, 1981, "Housing for single-parent families: a women's design" in *New Space for Women* Eds G Wekerle, R Peterson, D Morley (Westview Press, Boulder, CO) pp 319–332

SPCMT, 1979, *Metro's Suburbs in Transition. Part 1: Evolution and Overview* Social Planning Council of Metro Toronto, 185 Bloor St East, Toronto, Ontario M4W 3J3, Canada

SPCMT, 1980 *Metro's Suburbs in Transition. Part 2: Planning Agenda for the Eighties* Social Planning Council of Metro Toronto, 185 Bloor St East, Toronto, Ontario M4W 3J3, Canada

Stamp J, 1981, "Towards supportive neighborhoods: women's role in changing the segregated city" in *New Space for Women* Eds G Wekerle, R Peterson, D Morley (Westview Press, Boulder, CO) pp 189–198

Surpin M, 1983, "The adaptable environment, part 2: small is beautiful, again" *Homemakers Magazine* March issue, pp 115–130

Tabb W K, 1983, "A pro-people urban policy" mimeo available from the author, Department of Economics, Queens' College, The City University of New York, Flushing, NY 11367, USA

The New York Times 1983a, "Apartment sharers fret over lease ruling" by G Dullea; 16 May issue

The New York Times 1983b, "Computers: worker menace?" by B Nelson; 4 September issue

The New York Times 1983c, "Controlling the co-op conversion wave" letter to the Editor from J Eisland, City Councillor; 13 April issue

The New York Times 1983d, "Conversions: the reserve fund issue" by L A Daniels; 6 May issue

The New York Times 1983e, "In Hartford, it's the best and worst of times" by S R Freedman; 14 April issue

The New York Times 1983f, "A housing plan for artists loses in Board of Estimate" 11 February issue

The New York Times 1983g, "New York: the world financial market" by R A Bennett; 22 March issue

The New York Times 1983h, "US official sees New York City vulnerable as economy picks up" by D Stetson; 10 May issue

Therborn G, 1980 *The Ideology of Power and the Power of Ideology* (Verso, London)

Thorns D C, 1981, "The implications of differential rates of capital gain from owner-occupation for the formation and development of housing classes" *International Journal of Urban and Regional Research* **5** 205–217

Thrift N, 1983, "On the determination of social action in space and time" *Environment and Planning D: Society and Space* **1** 23–58

Tomaskovic-Devey D, Miller S M, 1982, "Recapitalization: the basic US urban policy of the 1980s" in *Urban Policy under Capitalism* volume 22 of *Urban Affairs Annual Reviews* Eds N I Fainstein, S S Fainstein (Sage, Beverly Hills, CA) pp 23–42

Urban Reader 1982a, "Tiny, perfect places" volume 10, issue 3/4, pp 6–7

Urban Reader 1982b, "Three's company" volume 10, issue 3/4, pp 33–34

Village Voice 1982a, "Portrait of the artist as a good use" by R Goldstein; 14 December issue, pp 10, 14, 16, and 50

Village Voice 1982b, "Space invaders: land grab on the Lower East Side" by M Gottlieb; 14 December issue, pp 20 and 22

Village Voice 1983, "AHOP vs UHAB: artists' housing, round two" by R Goldstein: 31 May issue, page 21

Wekerle G, 1979, "A woman's place is in the city" paper prepared for the Lincoln Institute of Land Policy; mimeo available from the author, Faculty of Environmental Studies, York University, Downsview, Ontario M3J 1P3, Canada

Wekerle G, 1981, "Women in the urban environment: a review essay" in *Women and the American City* Eds C R Stimpson, E Dixler, M J Nelson, K B Yatrakis (University of Chicago Press, Chicago, IL) pp 185–211

Western J, 1981 *Outcast Cape Town* (University of Minnesota Press, Minneapolis, MN)

Weston J, 1982, "Gentrification and displacement: an inner-city dilemma" *Habitat* **25** 10–19

Williams R, 1981 *Politics and Letters: Interviews with New Left Review* (Verso, London)

Women in Planning Steering Committee–Oregon Chapter, no date *Planning with Women in Mind* Region West Research Consultants, 520 SW Sixth, Suite 1107, Portland, OR 97204, USA

Wulff M G, 1982, "The two-income household: relative contribution of earners to housing costs" *Urban Studies* **19** 343–350

Zukin S, 1982 *Loft Living: Culture and Capital in Urban Change* (The Johns Hopkins University Press, Baltimore, MD)

Box 5   Retrospective on the 'Production of Gentrifiers' – Gendering the Gentrification Debate

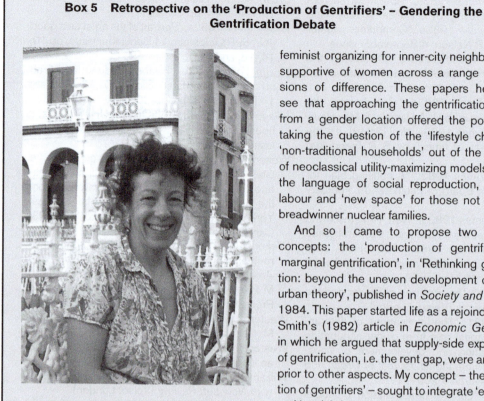

Plate 13 Damaris Rose.

In my first writing about gentrification I was trying to cast a socialist-feminist lens on what the neo-classicists were describing in terms of 'demographics and lifestyles'. Contra the arguments developed by Smith at that time (1979, 1982) I believed that the demand-side components to gentrification needed conceptualization just as much as the supply-side aspects, and that the former could not be theoretically subsumed to the latter. This thinking was much influenced by two pathbreaking articles by feminist urbanists. The first, 'City spatial structure, women's household work and national urban policy' by Ann Markusen, the first urban scholar to conceptualize high density inner-city neighbourhoods as potential sites of contestation of the hegemony of the conventional nuclear family and patriarchal gender relations as well as 'efficient' places for female gentrifiers to live. The second, a 1979 conference paper by Gerda Wekerle (eventually published in *Antipode*, 1984) called 'A woman's place is in the city', which was cautiously optimistic about

feminist organizing for inner-city neighbourhoods supportive of women across a range of dimensions of difference. These papers helped me see that approaching the gentrification debate from a gender location offered the potential for taking the question of the 'lifestyle choices' of 'non-traditional households' out of the language of neoclassical utility-maximizing models and into the language of social reproduction, domestic labour and 'new space' for those not in single-breadwinner nuclear families.

And so I came to propose two then-new concepts: the 'production of gentrifiers' and 'marginal gentrification', in 'Rethinking gentrification: beyond the uneven development of Marxist urban theory', published in *Society and Space* in 1984. This paper started life as a rejoinder to Neil Smith's (1982) article in *Economic Geography*, in which he argued that supply-side explanations of gentrification, i.e. the rent gap, were analytically prior to other aspects. My concept – the 'production of gentrifiers' – sought to integrate 'economic' and 'social-demographic' dimensions in accounts of gentrification, and also bridge the spatial scales of analysis, by considering the gender and the household composition of the 'new middle class' so as to better determine why some fractions of it, but not others, would elect to occupy 'gentrifiable' housing and neighbourhoods. I accorded especial attention to changing gender relations, seeing them as brought on by macro-societal processes and reflected in enhanced employment opportunities for educated women in advanced tertiary cities. This, in my view, led to the increased importance of women as actors in household decisions about where to live. Thus, I argued that women professionals were likely to be major actors in gentrification. If they were living alone (which they were more likely to do than male professionals) they would be more comfortable in the inner city. If they had children, gentrifying neighbourhoods would be efficient and supportive environments for combining paid work and domestic and caring work. So, I saw this approach as offering the potential to help flesh out the links that the then-emergent body of urban and regional scholarship on the 'new spatial divisions of labour', resulting from broad processes of economic restructuring, was making with the question of gentrification in cities high up in the global or national urban hierarchy. My point was that one had to take account of how the 'new urban middle class' was traversed by gender and household differences.

The concept of 'marginal gentrifiers'/ gentrification proved 'messier' and more controversial. While some construed it as a symptom of an insufficiently critical discourse, I saw it as a useful construct for better distinguishing between the temporalities and micro-geographies of gentrification, taking account of labour and housing market differences. My concept was deeply rooted in time and place, in 1983 Montréal, amid a deep and prolonged economic recession, which hit not only the industrial working-class but highly-educated young people ('*les chômeurs instruits*').

In my view, a critical or socially-progressive agenda for gentrification research in neo-liberal times should continue to explore 'who are the gentrifiers'.

First, one cannot adequately document and understand the dynamics of displacement if one only studies the experiences of the displaced or those at risk of displacement.

Second, critical perspectives on gentrification should include accounts of the production of gentrifiers that give weight to dimensions that although conjugated with social class, are not reducible to class.

Third, it is important to study the role of local states in fostering the production of gentrifiers, not least because it brings into focus the trade-offs that municipalities – trapped in mindsets of urban competitiveness at various scales – make between their 'redistributive' and 'corporate actor' responsibilities.

From: unpublished paper presented at the Annual Meeting of the Association of American Geographers, 2009 (22–28 March, Las Vegas).

18

"Gentrification: Culture and Capital in the Urban Core"

From *Annual Review of Sociology* (1987)

Sharon Zukin

INTRODUCTION

During the 1970s, throughout North America and Western Europe, new residential patterns in many old cities appeared to contradict the long-term decline of their inner core. These patterns emerged in a wave of capital reinvestment in deteriorating housing that was concentrated near central business districts (CBDs). Although some of the rehabilitation was publicly subsidized, most was financed by the private market, and a significant portion was carried out by do-it-yourself or "sweat equity" part-time workers. The progenitors of this urban "renaissance"—as magazines and newspapers termed it—had white-collar jobs. In many cases, too, they had markedly nontraditional households and styles of life. Together with a surge in service-sector employment and corresponding cultural and commercial amenities, their presence as a newly minted urban "gentry" gave the downtown a different form.

Much of the initial sociological research on gentrification concentrated on documenting its extent, tracing it as a process of neighborhood change, and speculating on its consequences in terms of both displacement of an existing population and reversal of trends toward suburbanization and urban decline. This general approach was especially characteristic of sociologists in the United States, who were still strongly influenced by positivism and the empirical tradition.

Gradually, however, the work of Marxist and left-Weberian urban sociologists and geographers broadened the study of gentrification by emphasizing an underlying dynamic of economic restructuring. The most relevant processes, in this view, were a regional and metropolitan de-industrialization and a concentration of professional and technical jobs and cultural markets in the urban core. Consequently, gentrification was subsumed under the rubrics of production and consumption rather than of demographic structure or individual choice.

Although empirical research on gentrification has repeatedly verified the extent of the phenomenon, the effort to establish a broader analytic framework is problematic. Disagreement on an underlying structure deepens the methodological schisms dividing neo-Marxist, neo-Weberian, and mainstream sociologists. Nevertheless, further research on gentrification may overcome these issues by investigating urban morphology—the shape the city takes—in terms of economic and cultural analysis. Both large and small investors are constrained by the availability of capital and the housing supply. Yet since the 1960s, the expansion of cultural patronage among middle class social strata has shown that investment in culture may augment limited means. Therefore, the accumulation strategies of large investors in central-city real estate are supported by smaller investors' patterns of cultural and social reproduction.

THE EMPIRICAL STALEMATE

From the moment an English sociologist invented the term "gentrification" to describe the residential movement of middle-class people into low-income areas of London (Glass 1964), the word evoked more than a simple change of scene. It suggested a symbolic new attachment to old buildings and a heightened sensibility to space and time. It also indicated a radical break with suburbia, a movement away from child-centered households toward the social diversity and aesthetic promiscuity of city life. In the public view, at least, gentrifiers were different from other middle-class people. Their collective residential choices, the amenities that clustered around them, and their generally high educational and occupational status were structured by—and in turn expressed—a distinctive *habitus*, a class culture and milieu in Bourdieu's (1984) sense. Thus, gentrification may be described as a process of spatial and social differentiation.

Early research denied that most gentrifiers moved "back to the city" from suburban housing (Laska & Spain 1980). Recent work confirms that they tend to come from other urban neighborhoods and large metropolitan areas (McDonald 1983, LeGates & Hartman 1986).

Yet there is much disagreement about the sources of these shifts, as well as their empirical referent. While some of the literature focuses on gentrifiers, other studies examine property that is gentrified.

In both cases, "supply-side" interpretations stress the economic and social factors that produce an attractive housing supply in the central city for middle-class individuals, and "demand-side" interpretations affirm a consumer preference, for demographic or cultural reasons, for the buildings and areas that become gentrified. Other problems are introduced by considering housing tenure—specifically, the different interests of homeowners and renters—when gentrification by both groups causes property values to rise.

Moreover, case studies that include the local political context of gentrification document the contributions of financial and political elites who seem, at first, not to be directly involved. Conflict over zoning laws, historic district designations, and property tax assessments indicates how important may be the state's role in defining the economic and social value of an urban area. Strategic shifts in government policy from 1970 to 1975 supported gentrification at the very time that rising inflation rates, fuel costs, and construction prices made rehabilitation in the center city an economically viable alternative for both homeowners and real estate developers.

At that time, local and national governments in both the United States and Western Europe shifted from supporting the demolition required by urban renewal to giving incentive grants for housing improvement. This facilitated the small-scale building rehabilitation on which gentrification depends. And though gentrification remains predominantly a privately financed action, a strong expression of local government support has generally been a precondition for the participation of lending institutions.

Little wonder, then, that British geographers call gentrification a "chaotic" concept (Rose 1984, after Sayer 1982) or that this observation has become the *cri de coeur* of some thoughtful writers (e.g. Smith & Williams 1986).

For several years, a large portion of every article on gentrification has been devoted to a literature review. Although this may suggest a welcome quality of introspection, it more likely indicates a worrisome stasis in the field.

Descriptive overview

By all accounts, a small wave of private-market capital reinvestment in deteriorating central-city housing began in the 1960s. Both early and recent studies correctly associate it with the "vitality" of an urban core (Frieden 1964, Bradbury et al 1982). But this investment shows a high degree of selectivity. There are important regional variations in its strength, and an intra-urban concentration occurs in areas of "historic" significance (Black 1975). Moreover, highly visible reinvestment and rehabilitation by upper-income residents take place alongside continuing deterioration of inner-city housing, disinvestment in the CBD, and suburbanization of most new housing construction for the private market (Clay 1979).

In no way but proximity does gentrification counteract the economic and racial polarization of most urban populations. In big cities as different as New York and San Francisco, it fails to raise median family income or to reverse a secular decrease in the number of high-status census areas; nor does gentrification always spread beyond a street or neighborhood to an entire census tract (Lipton 1977, Baldassare 1984, Marcuse 1986). At least initially, housing reinvestment may be concentrated in "pockets" or at the edges of declining districts (Schaeffer & Smith 1986, Marcuse 1986). In fact, the effects of gentrification at the "extreme micro-level" show much divergence: What appears as ethnic, racial, and economic integration at the neighborhood level may be disaggregated into traditionally segregated enclaves within the census tract, the block, and individual buildings (LeGates & Hartman 1986:195).

The gentrifiers' choice of neighborhood does not imply their social integration with existing neighbors of a different race, ethnicity, and socioeconomic status. In street encounters, they approach each other warily until familiarity with neighborhood routine ensures politeness (Anderson 1985).

New middle-class residents often expect crime to be as prevalent as "background noise" (McDonald 1983:292, Anderson 1985). For their part, existing residents may resent the superimposition of an alien culture—with different consumption patterns and an accelerated pace of change—on their community.[1]

While residents' associations sometimes mobilize to fight "developers" (Chernoff 1980, Weiler 1980), they really confront the whole set of economic and social processes that underlie "development" (Zukin 1982). This makes for an uneven social contest. In general, community mobilization cannot do battle with "the abstract logic of the private market"; and in particular, "the institutionalized procedures for responding to gentrification are weaker, more fragmented, and more costly to engage in" than those that respond to coherent public policies (Henig 1982:353–54).

Moreover, people who live in a gentrifying neighborhood have different interests. Pre-gentrification residents, as already partly noted, are likely to have consumption patterns of a lower social class, constitute a different ethnic and racial community, and an older age group (Spain 1980, Henig 1984, LeGates & Hartman 1986). When they mobilize to defend a neighborhood "as it is," they exclude the "improvements" identified with gentrification. Chief among these improvements, in the gentrifiers' view, is the restoration of historic architectural detail. Yet if existing residents join gentrifiers in associations that support the "historic" community, they may be aiding a process that causes property values to rise and leads to their own displacement. Existing homeowners, however, may have reason to do so. In economic terms, they forsake sentiment, or attachment to the community, for exchange values (Logan & Molotch 1987).

Among gentrifiers, renters have significantly lower incomes than homeowners (DeGiovanni & Paulson 1984). Thus, a cleavage develops between these groups when neighborhood associations pursue improvement strategies that cause rents to rise. Moreover, gentrifiers who buy and maintain multifamily dwellings are torn between a landlord's interest in getting higher rents and a resident's desire to keep the neighborhood unpretentious, affordable, and somewhat socially diverse (McDonald 1983).

Community organizations may mediate residents' conflicting interests in unexpected ways. In a gentrified area near downtown Brooklyn, for example, the gentrifiers' association pursued a strategy of historic preservation—to the extent of creating a "historic" neighborhood name—that permitted them to define and appropriate the area (Kasinitz 1984).

Gradually, their Puerto Rican neighbors responded by mobilizing on the basis of ethnicity. Another situation emerged in Philadelphia, when gentrifiers joined existing white ethnic residents in excluding blacks from the neighborhood (Cybriwsky 1978).[2]

When community organizations impose social and cultural homogeneity on a gentrifying neighborhood, they act as a "vanguard of the bourgeoisie" (Logan & Molotch 1987). They seem to be able to carry out their aims regardless of local government involvement or the degree to which they fabricate the area's historic past (Cybriwsky et al 1986).

While studies of gentrification agree on many of these key points, they indicate four contentious—and suggestive—areas of analysis: the use of historic preservation in constituting a new urban elite, gentrification's contribution to homelessness and displacement, the economic rationality of the gentrifier's role, and the relation between gentrification and economic transformation.

Historic preservation

It is tempting to associate contemporary gentrifiers, as part of a new middle class, with the appropriation of Victorian style (Jager 1986). Certainly the industrial bourgeoisie of the late nineteenth century bequeathed a major portion of the buildings now gentrified in North American, British, and Australian cities. But gentrifiers' tastes are conditioned by the availability and affordability of older buildings. Their aesthetic tastes may be diverted by either new construction in an older mode, like the current vogue in London of new neo-Georgian houses (Wright 1985a), or newer, perhaps Edwardian, old building styles (Williams 1984:212). Similarly, gentrification applies to a taste for restored brownstone, red brick, or gingerbread houses as well as manufacturing lofts that are converted to residential use (Zukin 1982).[3]

More significant than the impression of architectural homogeneity is the emphasis on culture in constructing new middle-class consumption patterns. By means of historic preservation, the new middle classes parlay a relatively modest investment of time and money into a quasi-bourgeois *habitus* (Williams, 1986). They are able to enjoy a solid building stock, often individualized to specific spatial requirements—notably, space that supports working at home. They also participate in the creation in their neighborhood of "a critical mass of pleasant amenity" (Logan & Molotch 1987), where shopping and housing provide serious social- and cultural experiences (Beauregard 1986).

There is some question, however, about whether historic preservation really confers or affirms more "distinction" than the modern style of most new construction. In contrast to widespread assumptions, gentrifiers have the same income level and educational background as other middle-class people who live downtown in either new or rehabilitated apartment buildings (Ford 1978). In the same ways they also resemble the middle-class residents of affluent, older suburbs (McDonald 1983).[4]

A quest for historic districts implies more, of course. It confronts the plane of modernity with the rich and varied temporality of the past—but which past, and whose? "In this new perspective [a gentrified area] is not so much a literal place as a cultural oscillation between the prosaic reality of the contemporary inner city and an imaginative reconstruction of the area's past" (Wright 1985b: 228–29).

Gentrification and displacement

In a subtle way, the ideology of historic preservation facilitates the removal of a pre-gentrification population, especially those residents whose modernization of their homes is incongruous with the spirit of authenticity in the gentrifiers' own restoration. But the pragmatic wedge of their displacement is rising rents and higher sale prices for homes in gentrifying neighborhoods.

All studies of gentrification confirm that a fairly homogeneous group of in-movers reduces residential density and replaces an existing population. The out-movers, however, are a relatively heterogeneous group (LeGates & Hartman 1986). They can be characterized as economically vulnerable though not always disadvantaged. At least through the early 1970s, white-collar workers were affected by gentrification more than blue-collar workers, with whites displaced more frequently than members of other races. After 1973, revitalization in several major US cities accelerated the displacement of blacks by whites in certain neighborhoods (Gale 1984:24). In somewhat smaller cities, also, upper-income households showed greater willingness to move into lower-class areas and racial ghettos (Henig 1984:178).

Yet to some degree, race and class may still be a barrier to gentrification. Whites and most middle-class blacks have not gentrified lower-class black areas, such as Harlem and Newark, despite a building stock and a cost structure equivalent to other areas' (Schaeffer & Smith 1986, Beauregard 1986:39).

It is generally agreed that gentrifying neighborhoods produce higher tax yields. For this reason, among others, gentrification elicits the approval of local political leaders, who correspondingly moderate their support for displacees.

In reality, the relation between gentrification and property taxes is more complex. Increases in assessed property values in gentrifying areas may not be significantly greater than in other neighborhoods; they also lag behind increases in market values (DeGiovanni 1984). Nevertheless, once assessments have been raised to reflect some rehabilitation activity, the assessed value of unimproved properties in the neighborhood also rises. So gentrifiers carry their less affluent neighbors with them on a rising tide of property tax assessments.

A more severe blow against an existing population is effected by the removal of low-price rental housing from the city's building stock (Gale 1984, Marcuse 1986). Single-room-occupancy hotels, where tenants pay by the night or week, are a vivid victim (Kasinitz 1983), but the general problem is one of *housing* rather than *household* dislocation (Gale 1984:164). As a rule, low-income residents are displaced farther from the CBD. And no matter where they move, displacees usually pay a higher rent (Kain & Apgar 1985, LeGates & Hartman 1986).

Efforts have been made to qualify these stark changes. An examination of one year's tenant outmovers from "revitalizing" areas in five US cities found the costs of displacement to be outweighed by "benefits" (Schill & Nathan 1983). Similarly, a simulation of displacement in several revitalizing low-income neighborhoods in Chicago speculated that many low-income tenants regularly move out of their neighborhood with or without gentrification; at any rate, Kain & Apgar (1985) consider that the benefits to the area and the residents who continue to live there—in improvements to capital stock—exceed the costs of displacement.

It is more worrisome to consider that spatial differentials—that is, conditions in specific neighborhoods—do not have much effect on rates of displacement (Lee & Lodge 1984). If displacement in the face of mounting rents is an important national trend, then the whole structure of housing markets and their fit with social needs should be revised.

These findings suggest that the gentrifiers' aesthetic hallmark—their investment in rehabilitation—has less of an impact on other people than does their property investment. This calls into question the relative weights of "sentiment and symbolism" (*pace* Firey 1945) and economic rationality in the gentrifiers' role.

Economic rationality

Throughout North America and Western Europe, gentrification has occurred together with a shift toward new homeownership and condominium conversion in traditionally low-rent areas of the central city. Generally these forms of housing reinvestment—rehabilitation, on the one hand, and homeownership, on the other—have to clear historical barriers posed by tenants' property rights and the taxation and credit systems (Gale 1984, Williams 1984, Hamnett & Randolph 1986). Once they do, however, they open up an avenue of speculation for both gentrifiers and real estate developers.

The small scale of gentrifiable property and the cost of rehabilitation, relative to new construction, do not attract large-scale investors. Nevertheless, the low cost of entry into this market, at least in its early years, propels significant numbers of professional, managerial, and technical employees into becoming part-time developers and landlords (Zukin 1982, McDonald 1983).

Much emphasis has been placed on the apparent lack of interest in speculation on the part of early, "risk-oblivious" gentrifiers or "urban pioneers" (Berry 1985:78–79). Yet they are hardly insensible to the rationality of a housing investment. Indeed, economic contingencies may "encourage [them to take] defensive actions to protect [themselves] against the vagaries of the housing market and, at the same time, to avoid the ravages of the effects of inflation on [their] salary" (Beauregard 1986:45). Early gentrifiers find the niche they can afford in urban housing markets.

Although respondents often fail to cite economic reasons for their involvement in gentrification (Berry 1985), some surveys have confirmed the importance to them of both investment potential and housing prices (McDonald 1983, Gale 1980:100, 1984:16). Despite this general effect, however, the decision to buy property in a gentrifiable area may reflect different material priorities.

Some gentrifiers may be most influenced by the rent gap, i.e. the difference between ground-rent levels at various locations in a metropolitan area (Smith 1979). The devalorization of capital (the decrease in the economic value of property) in the inner city offers them a fairly low-cost opportunity to get involved in its restructuring. This is especially important when a central-city location already offers some advantages. Although the rent gap introduces a mechanistic and somewhat circular argument, it does accord with real locational choices. What must be remembered is that the increases in investment and property values associated with gentrification represent only one part of a range of possible outcomes in the inner city (Beauregard 1986).

Low-income gentrifiers may have other motives for making a housing investment in gentrification. In their case, a marginal investment may ensure the conditions they require for their social reproduction (Rose 1984). Residence in a gentrified area may be especially important to single mothers, who try to stabilize their position in urban housing markets and to locate near support services by buying a low-cost, inner-city apartment.[5] Similarly, unemployed and informally employed workers, particularly in the creative and performing arts, may try to cluster in inner-city neighborhoods in order to maintain access to information, training, and markets for their work.

Thus, the economic rationality of gentrification is subject to finely tuned variations. Different forms of capital have a different relation to space and time, and the division of labor within white-collar sectors of the work force shapes both a dispersal and a concentration of middle-class residence (Smith 1986). The new middle classes' insertion into the metropolis takes place at the micro-level of both the suburb and the gentrified neighborhood. The overlay of these insertions on urban, regional, national, and international scales calls our attention to spatial switches even as they are being produced for a variety of economic and social reasons (Smith 1984, Massey 1984).

Economic restructuring

A major focus of economic shifts since the 1960s has been the recentralization of corporate investment in selected metropolitan cores (Fainstein & Fainstein 1982, Smith 1986). This process involves new uses of space and new spatial forms, as the city is restructured to suit corporate needs. While office towers sprout in underutilized or devalorized downtown districts, a new hierarchy of urban neighborhoods reflects different corporate uses. Headquarters and "back offices" no longer share space; each stratum of white-collar work generates in its proximity the amenities that suit its status, salary levels, and office rents. Manufacturing activity and blue-collar residence are displaced beyond the heart of the city (Zukin 1982).

Gentrification as a white-collar residential style reflects the agglomeration of large companies—or mainly their professional, managerial, and technical staffs and related business services—in the downtown area. Whether the crucial factor is the number of corporate headquarters in a metropolitan area (Palmer & Roussel 1986) or the presence of just a few key corporate employers (Gale 1984:155), this capital presence draws new investors and consumers. The city's population may still be polarized between rich and poor, with the poor providing personal and domestic services for the rich and working in the remaining labor-intensive manufacturing sectors (Portes & Walton 1981, Sassen-Koob 1984). But high-status gentrification, as well as other relatively affluent residential styles, reflects the expansion of high-income personnel in corporations and government and producers' services.[6]

In any city, gentrification correlates *grosso modo* with "administrative activity" (Lipton 1977) and new office construction in the CBD (Berry 1985).

Yet many analyses of gentrification persist in stressing noneconomic factors. One such factor—social solidarity—is indicated by the residential clustering of visible, highly singular social groups, such as gay householders, who constitute a plurality of residents in some gentrifying neighborhoods (McDonald 1983, Castells 1983:ch.14). Nevertheless, the creation by gays of new spatial communities in gentrifiable areas—in contrast to the older spatial division between special entertainment districts and residence submerged in heterosexual society—may be related to the participation of gay men in an expanding service economy (Fitzgerald 1986).

Most mainstream analysts still consider economic restructuring secondary to demographic, i.e. generational, life-style and life-cycle factors that have created consumer demand for new residential styles. In this view, gentrification is the mark of the zeitgeist borne by the baby-boom generation. In the spirit of synthesis, however, a recent examination of gentrification emphasizes both economic restructuring and demographic factors, without giving priority to either (London et al 1986).[7]

Proponents of demographic explanations of gentrification are not persuaded that economic restructuring constitutes a necessary and a sufficient cause. In fact, if values had not changed to accept smaller families, two-earner households, and single parents, most of the gentrifying population would lack either the means or the motivation for city living. Yet gentrifiers' residential choices are ultimately conditioned by material factors. These include the expansion of middle-class social strata because of an increase in white-collar jobs, especially in regional, national, and international business services; a secular withdrawal of investment capital from urban manufacturing, thus freeing industrial sites for redevelopment; and a recentralization of corporate activity in selected CBDs and suburban towns.

Nevertheless, the struggle to reconcile economic and demographic analysis raises the question, whether the concept of gentrification is really significant, and if so, on which level of analysis. Without conceptual agreement, empirical studies of gentrification have reached a stalemate.

METHODOLOGICAL SCHISMS

Conceptual divergence is reflected in serious disagreements on methodology. A preference for materialism on the one hand or positivism on the other leads to dichotomous views of gentrification. It is described in terms of either structural causality or individual choice (i.e. structure vs agency), cultural style or economic necessity (choice vs need), or consequences that carry greater or lesser costs (displacement vs revitalization).

The broadest analyses of gentrification (hence, those with the most interesting theoretical implications) are influenced in some way by economic paradigms. Two of these refine the Marxist emphasis on production by also considering social reproduction and consumption. A third reformulates the neoclassical model based on supply and demand.

Production/reproduction

From the outset, the Marxist epistemological critique of gentrification has targeted positivism in general and neoclassical land-use theory in particular. "Positivist approaches to gentrification," in this view, "have remained ad hoc, full of exceptions, and frequently contradictory to other people's positivist explanations" (Rose 1984). Lacking uncontestable criteria for either outcomes or causes, the concept of gentrification, as mainstream analysts use it, suffers from disorganization. Moreover, as Damaris Rose insists, what we observe as the unified phenomenon of gentrification may really result from several causes (1984).

Rose also takes issue with the dominant Marxist approach. Accepting its emphasis on structural causes and economic necessity, she nonetheless criticizes its tendency to stress a single causal factor: the production of gentrified dwellings as commodities. Besides the rent gap, the falling rate of profit, or corporate investment, all else is relegated to a residual category, "a scratch on the surface of underlying capital."

In place of a single resource-maximizing strategy that historically results in gentrification, Rose credits a number of different strategies. And in lieu of production, Rose stresses the importance of social reproduction. Thus, she accords a central role in gentrification processes to marginally employed but highly educated individuals who seek a central-city *and* low-cost residence for social or ecological reasons. Moreover, by considering social reproduction as a separate factor, Rose avoids conflating reproduction and consumption, as both positivists and Marxists tend to do.

Production/consumption

Rose's critique has influenced other Marxists to the extent that they now seek to give full weight to consumption, though not necessarily to "reproduction" (Smith & Williams 1986). Meanwhile, they continue to study processes of production and devalorization: the first, in order to identify potential gentrifiers, and the second, in order to understand how certain housing becomes gentrifiable.

A major focus of Marxist analysis is the social location of gentrifiers. Because most of them are in the new middle classes, with professional, technical, or managerial jobs, they are identified with corporate reinvestment in the CBD and the growth of local, regional, and national services. This situation has two related effects. On the one hand, whether gentrification is considered an investment for capital accumulation or an investment in social reproduction, it helps promote capital's long wave of expansion. On the other hand, ideological support for gentrification helps legitimize corporate expansion throughout the central city.

As Neil Smith (1986) points out, the ideology of gentrification often describes it as a process of *spatial* expansion—notably, as settlement on an urban "frontier." But the changes in the use of downtown space that result from corporate investment really illustrate *capital* expansion. In our time, capital expansion has no new territory left to explore, so it redevelops, or internally redifferentiates, urban space. Just as the frontier thesis in US history legitimized an economic push through "uncivilized" lands, so the urban frontier thesis legitimizes the corporate reclamation of the inner city from racial ghettos and marginal business uses.

Yet no structural process can disregard institutional constraints. Downtown reinvestment must take account of urban real estate markets, forms and degrees of government intervention, and local politics and social forces. In the United States, social support for gentrification also reflects a response to racial conflict and fiscal crisis (Williams 1986). In that sense, too, gentrification is compatible with a broad movement away from collective consumption.

In fact, much US urban redevelopment during the two decades following World War II could be called "demand-led urbanization" (Harvey 1985b). Although this differs from a process that might be "consumption led," it calls attention to shifting patterns of consumption, their basis in the public or private sector, and their material representation in urban forms.

Economic restructuring changes the basis of consumption for different social classes and also shapes their social and spatial differentiation. Consequently, in contrast to the ghettoization of large areas of the central city, gentrification represents a filtering *up* of housing. Conversely, in contrast to corporate redevelopment of the CBD, gentrification of downtown neighborhoods represents a filtering *down* of investment opportunity (Smith, forthcoming).

Supply/demand

In an attempt to infuse some of these distinctions into the neoclassical model, Brian J. L. Berry has devised a new supply-side interpretation of gentrification (Berry 1985). In Berry's view, the necessary but not sufficient conditions for gentrification are the "contagious abandonment" of large inner-city areas and a dynamic suburban housing market in new construction. Further, the catalyst of gentrification is significant corporate redevelopment of the CBD, especially office construction that locates professional and white-collar jobs downtown. "To turn the supply-side argument around, the nation's key 'command and control' centers provide a sufficient demand-side trigger for gentrification, provided that the necessary supply-side housing market characteristics also are present" (p. 95).

Berry's "new" interpretation adopts several of the neo-Marxist and neo-Weberian key assumptions: corporate centralization in a small number of urban cores (cf Cohen 1981), widespread devalorization and underutilization of inner-city property, a resulting rent gap between the inner city and the periphery, and new consumption patterns that follow the expansion of white-collar jobs. While this corrects Berry's earlier tendency to see housing in terms of rational choice (cf Gale 1984:158), it offers a descriptive rather than an analytic model.

Berry's model does highlight the historical contingency of gentrification, a point on which most Marxist analyses also agree. Moreover, it emphasizes the simultaneity of continued growth in the suburbs, and both abandonment and redevelopment of the inner core. Berry's "islands of renewal in seas of decay" are the metaphorical equivalent of the Marxists' "polarization of urban populations."

SYNTHESIS: CULTURE AND CAPITAL

By upsetting expectations about unrelieved deterioration of the central city, gentrification was initially received as a revelation. But recent analysis by sociologists and geographers emphasizes several constraints. The area transformed in gentrification's penumbra is limited by strategies for capital accumulation on the part of dominant social and economic institutions, and the related strategies of "consumption sectors" (Saunders 1984) that support the internal redifferentiation of urban space.

The emphasis on capital investment calls into question gentrifiers' identification with, and mobilization for, historic preservation. Clearly, they share with others in society a generalized appreciation of the material and aesthetic qualities that old buildings and old neighborhoods evoke. Further, their support of historic preservation and contemporary urban restorations recalls the patrician sponsorship of art and architecture in US cities in the late nineteenth century, as well as urban professionals' advocacy of "City Beautiful" programs for rebuilding cities at that time (Boyer 1983). But affluent gentrifiers' cultural appropriations do not lack economic rationality. Cultural validation helps valorize their housing investment, and activism on behalf of historic property eases the transition, for some of them, into semiprofessional and part-time real estate development.

Indeed, political mobilization for the legal status of a historic landmark designation typically unifies people with different aesthetic and material interests. While historic preservation enables some of them to satisfy civic pride, others profit by producing goods and services for a "preservationist" mode of consumption.

Yet cultural consumption also offers other dividends. Culturally validated neighborhoods automatically provide new middle classes with the collective identity and social credentials for which they strive (cf Logan & Molotch 1987). Moreover, the ideology of gentrification legitimizes their social reproduction, often despite the claims of an existing population. This is especially important when appeals are made to public opinion and municipal authorities to decide between the claims of different residential and commercial groups.

With some paradoxical results, support for gentrification also channels support to producers of cultural goods and services who seek housing in central-city areas. In the short run, proximity to markets for their services eases their insertion into the urban economy. In the long run, however, their contribution to the downtown's cultural capital may raise housing prices so high that they no longer can afford to live there.

In general, the presence of cultural markets both validates and valorizes business investment in major corporate cities. While the cultural constitution of new urban middle classes has ironically been termed an "Artistic Mode of Production" (Zukin 1982), a study by the National Endowment for the Arts found that cities with the highest percentage of artists in the labor force also had the highest rates of downtown gentrification and condominium conversion (Gale 1984:155).

Gentrification thus appears as a multidimensional cultural practice that is rooted on both sides of the methodological schisms that we have reviewed. As a form of homeownership, gentrified dwellings are both a means of accumulation and a means of social reproduction for part of the highly educated middle class. Moreover, as a reference to specific building types in the center of the city, gentrification connotes both a mode of high-status cultural consumption and the colonization of an expanding terrain by economic institutions associated with the service sector.

In the long run, economic institutions establish the conditions to which gentrifiers respond. Secular trends of disinvestment in urban manufacturing destroy the viability of industrial areas and blue-collar neighborhoods. The recent resurgence of investment in American cities by major lending institutions reflects, on the one hand, their reduction of foreign loans and, on the other, their participation in an expanding service economy. The office construction that they finance eventually provides jobs for potential gentrifiers, but it is not matched by an interest in building new housing most of these people can afford.

To some extent, also, gentrifiers' locational preferences reflect their withdrawal from a transportation and distribution infrastructure that they perceive as being archaic. Many of them prefer walking or bicycling to work instead of making a long journey to the city by car or train. Similarly, they abandon suburban shopping centers for the smaller scale of shops and the range of goods and services available in the city.

Property values rise in middle-class residential areas, reflecting increased competition for a milieu that unifies proximity to professional, managerial, and "creative" jobs; opportunities for specialized high-status consumption; and the combination of population density and individualized facilities that can support independent, quasi-bourgeois social reproduction by people who are not really rich. Thus, gentrifiers are caught between the expansion of middle-class styles of life and a market situation that makes it harder to realize such lifestyles without compromise.

Microlevel studies of gentrified neighborhoods cannot address these issues. But there are at least three alternate ways to frame a study of gentrification that would integrate cultural and economic analysis. First, the synergy between gentrification and deindustrialization suggests a comparative study of housing and labor markets in metropolitan areas. Second, the long-term plans of local financial, political, and social elites—including their investment projects and their own residential quarters—focus attention on "downtown" interests, whether they momentarily support urban renewal, gentrification, or new private-market construction (cf Ballain et al 1982, Fainstein et al 1986, Hartman 1984). And third, the morphology of urban areas—both their changing form and the way this form inserts itself into the city as a whole—shows how the spatial and built environment concretizes, transmits, and transforms the city's constituent social interests (cf Zunz 1970, Harvey 1985a, Pred 1985).

These proposals may shock traditional urban sociologists, as well as those whose reading in the field ended with the Chicago School. To them it may seem as though urban sociology has been engulfed by political economy, and the study of cities subordinated to economic processes and social class (Zukin 1980).

In fact, a number of sociologists have recently refocused the discipline's attention on economic institutions (Zukin & DiMaggio 1986). Moreover, there is a growing movement in sociology to incorporate the analysis of space and time (Giddens 1985). These interests should infuse more rigor into urban sociologists' efforts to describe the "postindustrial city," which, like "gentrification," really refers to existing patterns of social, spatial, and economic restructuring of the central city.

Notes

1 An early view of the implicit and explicit conflicts in this sort of neighborhood improvement is Lyford's (1966) study of Manhattan's Upper West Side. As various factors, including community resistance to dislocation and resulting investor uncertainty, prolonged the process of "revitaltzation" and reduced the public sector's role, urban renewal in the area was succeeded by gentrification.

2 Nevertheless, such strategies do not inevitably result in gentrification. In the Brooklyn community described by Krase (1982), white middle-class gentrifiers mobilized for historic preservation, yet by the time the study was published, the neighborhood was known again as a black ghetto. Also see Williams (1985).

3 McDonald (1983), however, claims that gentrifiers' choices may be specific to certain neighborhoods. In Boston—a city where older central-city housing is in short supply—his survey of new South End residents found that 39% had looked for housing only in that area. Yet again, the large number of multifamily dwellings in the South End that gentrifiers use for rental income suggests an economic choice.

4 McDonald's (1983) survey, however, shows a larger standard deviation in gentrifiers' household income, especially among single-person households.

5 Using a broader sample, however, a 1978 survey by the US Department of Housing and Urban Development found that women may be satisfied by suburban services (Fava 1985).

6 Like gentrification, the expansion of jobs in producers' services has no effect on metropolitan median income; neither reduces metropolitan income inequality (Nelson & Lorence 1985).

7 Using quantitative analysis and survey methods, this study offers a smorgasbord of findings. Gentrification is correlated positively with the size of the baby-boom cohort and the proportion of professional to other jobs. It is correlated negatively with young children and the percentage of the labor force employed in manufacturing. Historical preservation, culture, and corporate presence are also important (London et al 1986).

LITERATURE CITED

Anderson, E. 1985. Race and neighborhood transition. See Peterson 1985, pp. 99–128

Baldassare, M. 1984. Evidence for neighborhood revitalization: Manhattan. See Palen & London 1984, pp. 90–102

Ballain, R., Bobroff, J. Courant, G., Darris, G. et al 1982. *Evolution des Quartiers Anciens.* Paris: Plan Construction, Bilan Thématique

Beauregard, R. A. 1986. The chaos and complexity of gentrification. See Smith & Williams 1986, pp. 35–55

Berry, B. J. L. 1985. Islands of renewal in seas of decay. See Peterson 1985, pp. 69–96

Black, T. J. 1975. Private-market housing renovation in central cities: An Urban Land Institute Survey. *Urb. Land* 34 (November): 3–9

Bourdieu, P. 1984. *Distinction: A Social Critique of the Judgement of Taste*, tr. R. Nice. Cambridge, Mass: Harvard Univ. Press

Boyer, M. C. 1983. *Dreaming the Rational City: The Myth of American City Planning*. Cambridge, Mass: MIT Press

Bradbury, K. L., Downs, A., Small, K. A. 1982. *Urban Decline and the Future of American Cities*. Washington, DC: Brookings

Castells, M. 1983. *The City and the Grassroots*. Berkeley, Calif: Univ. Calif. Press

Chernoff, M. 1980. Social displacement in a renovating neighborhood's commercial district: Atlanta. See Laska & Spain 1980, pp. 204–19

Clay, P. L. 1979. *Neighborhood Renewal*. Lexington, Mass: Lexington

Cohen, R. B. 1981. The new international division of labor, multinational corporations and urban hierarchy. In *Urbanization and Urban Planning in Capitalist Society*, ed. M. Dear, A. J. Scott, pp. 287–315. London/New York: Methuen

Cybriwsky, R. A. 1978. Social aspects of neighborhood change. *Ann. Assoc. Am. Geogr.* 68:17–33

Cybriwsky, R. A., Ley, D., Western, J. 1986. The political and social construction of revitalized neighborhoods: Society Hill, Philadelphia, and False Creek, Vancouver. See Smith & Williams 1986, pp. 92–120

DeGiovanni, F. 1984. An examination of selected consequences of revitalization in six U.S. cities. See Palen & London 1984, pp. 67–89

DeGiovanni, F., Paulson, N. 1984. Housing diversity in revitalizing neighborhoods. *Urb. Aff. Q.* 20(2):211–32

Fainstein, N. I., Fainstein, S. S. 1982. Restructuring the American city: A comparative perspective. In *Urban Policy Under Capitalism*, ed. N. I. Fainstein, S. S. Fainstein, pp. 161–89. Vol. 22, Sage Urb. Aff. Ann. Rev. Beverly Hills, Calif: Sage

Fainstein, S. S., Fainstein, N. I., Hill, R. C., Judd, D. R., Smith, M. P. 1986. *Restructuring the City*. New York: Longman. Rev. ed.

Fava, S. F. 1985. Residential preferences in the suburban era: A new look? *Soc. Fore.* 18(2): 109–17

Firey, W. 1945. Sentiment and symbolism as ecological variables. *Am. Sociol. Rev.* 10(2): 140–48

Fitzgerald, F. 1986. A reporter at large (San Francisco–Pt. I). *The New Yorker*, July 21, pp. 34–70

Ford, K. 1978. *Housing Policy and the Urban Middle Class*. New Brunswick, NJ: Cent. Urb. Policy Res.

Frieden, B. 1964. *The Future of Old Neighborhoods*. Cambridge, Mass: MIT Press

Gale, D. E. 1980. Neighborhood resettlement: Washington, D.C. See Laska & Spain, 1980, pp. 95–115

Gale, D. E. 1984. *Neighborhood Revitalization and the Postindustrial City: A Multinational Perspective*. Lexington, Mass: Lexington

Giddens, A. 1985. Time, space and regionalisation. See Gregory & Urry 1985, pp. 265–95

Glass, R. 1964. Introduction. In *London: Aspects of Change*, ed. Centre for Urban Studies, pp. xiii–xlii. London: MacGibbon and Kee.

Gregory, D., Urry, J. 1985. *Social Relations and Spatial Structures*. New York: St. Martin's

Hamnett, C., Randolph, B. 1986. Tenurial transformation and the flat break-up market in London: The British condo experience. See Smith & Williams 1986, pp. 121–52

Hartman, C. 1984. *The Transformation of San Francisco*. Totowa, NJ: Rowman & Allanheld

Harvey, D. 1985a. *Consciousness and the Urban Experience*. Baltimore: Johns Hopkins Univ. Press

Harvey, D. 1985b. *The Urbanization of Capital*. Baltimore; Johns Hopkins Univ. Press

Henig, J. R. 1982. Neighborhood response to gentrification: Conditions of mobilization. *Urb. Aff. Q.* 17(3):343–58

Henig, J. R. 1984. Gentrification and displacement of the elderly: An empirical analysis. See Palen & London 1984, pp. 170–84

Jager, M. 1986. Class definition and the esthetics of gentrification: Victoriana in Melbourne. See Smith & Williams 1986, pp. 78–91

Kain, J. F., Apgar, W. C. Jr. 1985. *Housing and Neighborhood Dynamics: A Simulation Study*. Cambridge, Mass: Harvard Univ. Press

Kasinitz, P. 1983. Gentrification and homelessness: The single room occupant and the inner city revival. *Urb. Soc. Change Rev.* 17(1):9–14

Kasinitz, P. 1984. *Neighborhood change and conflicts over definitions: The "gentrification" of "Boerum Hill."* Presented at 54th Ann. Meet. East. Sociol. Assoc, Boston

Krase, J. 1982. *Self and Community in the City*. Washington, DC; Univ. Press

Laska, S. B., Spain, D. 1980. *Back to the City: Issues in Neighborhood Renovation*. New York: Pergamon

Lee, B. A., Lodge, D. C. 1984. Spatial differentials in residential displacement. *Urb. Stud.* 21(3):219–32

LeGates, R. T., Hartman, C. 1986. The anatomy of displacement in the United States. See Smith & Williams 1986, pp. 178–200

Lipton, S. G. 1977. Evidence of central-city revival. *J. Am. Plan. Assoc.* 43 (April): 136–47

Logan, J., Molotch, H. 1987. *Urban Fortunes*. Berkeley, Calif: Univ. Calif. Press. In press

London, B., Lee, B. A., Lipton, S. G. 1986. The determinants of gentrification in the United States: A city-level analysis. *Urb. Aff. Q.* 21(3): 369–87

Lyford, J. P. 1966. *The Airtight Cage: A Study of New York's West Side.* New York: Harper & Row

Marcuse, P. 1986. Abandonment, gentrification, and displacement: The linkages in New York City. See Smith & Williams 1986, pp. 153–77

Massey, D. 1984. *Spatial Divisions of Labor: Social Structures and the Geography of Production.* New York: Methuen

McDonald, S. C. 1983. *Human and market dynamics in the gentrification of a Boston neighborhood.* PhD thesis. Harvard Univ., Cambridge, Mass.

Nelson, J. I., Lorence, J. 1985. Employment in service activities and inequality in metropolitan areas. *Urb. Aff. Q.* 21(1):106–25

Palen, J. J., London, B. 1984. *Gentrification, Displacement and Neighborhood Revitalization.* Albany, NY: State Univ. NY Press

Palmer, D., Roussel, A. 1986. *Corporate headquarter presence and business service activity in U.S. central cities.* Presented at 81st Ann. Meet. Am. Sociol. Assoc., New York

Peterson, P. E. 1985. *The New Urban Reality.* Washington, DC: Brookings Inst.

Portes, A., Walton, J. 1981. *Labor, Class, and the International System.* New York: Academic

Pred, A. 1985. The social becomes the spatial, the spatial becomes the social: Enclosures, social change and the becoming of places in the Swedish province of Skane. See Gregory & Urry 1985, pp. 337–65

Rose, D. 1984. Rethinking gentrification: Beyond the uneven development of marxist urban theory. *Soc. Space* 1:47–74

Sassen-Koob, S. 1984. The new labor demand in global cities. In *Cities in Transformation: Class, Capital, and the State,* ed. M. P. Smith, pp. 139–71. Vol. 26, Sage Urb. Aff. Ann. Rev. Beverly Hills, Calif: Sage

Saunders, P. 1984. Beyond housing classes: The sociological significance of private property rights in means of consumption. *Int. J. Urb. Reg. Res.* 8(2):202–27

Sayer, A. 1982. Explanation in economic geography: Abstraction versus generalization, *Progr. Hum. Geog,* 6 (March):68–88

Schaeffer, R., Smith, N. 1986. *The gentrification of Harlem?* Ann. Assoc. Am. Geogr. 76:347–65

Schill, M. H., Nathan, R. P. 1983. *Revitalizing America's Cities: Neighborhood, Reinvestment and Displacement.* Albany, NY: State Univ. NY Press

Smith, N. 1979. Gentrification and capital: Theory, practice and ideology in Society Hill. *Antipode* 11(3):24–35

Smith, N. 1984. *Uneven Development.* Oxford: Basil Blackwell

Smith, N. 1987. Of yuppies and housing: Gentrification, social restructuring, and the urban dream. *Soc. Space.* In press

Smith, N. 1986. Gentrification, the frontier, and the restructuring of urban space. See Smith & Williams 1986, pp. 15–34

Smith, N., Williams, P. 1986. *Gentrification of the City.* Boston: Allen & Unwin

Spain, D. 1980. Indicators of urban revitalization: Racial and socioeconomic changes in central-city housing. See Laska & Spain 1980, pp. 27–41

Weiler, C. 1980. The neighborhood's role in optimizing reinvestment: Philadelphia. See Laska & Spain 1980, pp. 220–35

Williams, B. 1985, Owning places and buying time: Class, culture, and stalled gentrification. *Urb. Life* 14(3):251–73

Williams, P. 1984. Gentrification in Britain and Europe. See Palen & London 1984, pp. 205–34

Williams, P. 1986. Class constitution through spatial reconstruction? A re-evaluation of gentrification in Australia, Britain, and the United States. See Smith & Williams 1986, pp. 56–77

Wright, P. 1985a. Ideal homes: A return to the classical past. *New Socialist,* October, pp. 16–21

Wright, P. 1985b. *On Living in an Old Country: The National Past in Contemporary Britain.* London: Verso

Zukin, S. 1980. A decade of the new urban sociology. *Theory Soc.* 9(4):575–601

Zukin, S. 1982. *Loft Living: Culture and Capital in Urban Change.* Baltimore: Johns Hopkins Univ. Press

Zukin, S., DiMaggio, P. 1986. *Structures of Capital: The Social Organization of Economic Institutions.* Submitted for publication

Zunz, O. 1970. Etude d'un processus d'urbanisation: Le quartier du Gros-Caillou à Paris. *Annales, E.S.C.* 25:1024–65

Box 6   Culture and Capital: The Sequel

Plate 14 **Sharon Zukin**. Photograph by Richard Rosen.

Rereading my article about gentrification after more than 20 years, I am glad to see that the issues I outlined and the framework in which I set them out stand up to a critical view. Declining neighborhoods in the centers of cities are still being revitalized by architectural restorations, art galleries, and cocktail bars; people are living and doing creative work in former industrial lofts; tenements and warehouses that have been saved from demolition shelter affluent middle classes and bohemian hipsters: gentrification, in short, has survived the dot-com boom, subprime mortgage crisis, and economic recession to represent a powerful ideal of urban life. My contribution to all this was to emphasize the joining of cultural and economic sources of gentrification. Neither capital nor culture alone can account for the nearly universal social and spatial transformations gentrifiers have wrought.

My background for writing this article came from my study of gentrification by default in SoHo and other loft districts of lower Manhattan during the 1970s. *Loft Living* (1982) drew attention to the importance of cultural producers—in this case, mainly visual artists—in opening up derelict districts to cultural consumers. Praised by the media and exhibiting their work in storefront galleries and

performance spaces, artists created a model of the good urban life in an "interesting" way that attracted a broad middle class. Whether we look at it in terms of lifestyle or the rise of a creative class, the artistic mode of production gave old loft districts a new identity that real estate developers and public officials liked. The "authentic" city which artists and other loft dwellers created inspired gentrification's material infrastructure (old brick buildings, cast iron façades, public markets) and its aesthetic (hipster casual, flea market chic); it also gradually legitimized both historic preservation of heritage sites and new luxury construction. From the outset, though, industrial decline made loft space and working class homes vulnerable to new investment, and high corporate salaries followed by global capital flows provided the means for able and willing investors.

"Gentrification: Culture and Capital in the Urban Core" was written for the *Annual Review of Sociology* published in the United States. This gave the article definite limitations. Until recently, U.S. sociologists did not welcome an analysis of space, believing this was a topic best left to geographers. Neither were they open to urban political economists who talked about capital rather than people. Because the Annual Review where the article was published has a long lead time, requiring me to write the piece about two years before it would meet readers' gaze, the article was limited to events that had ended by 1985. But patterns and processes that I saw at that time are even clearer today. Gentrifiers' consumption patterns, translated into boutiques, cafés, and bars by new retail entrepreneurs, clash with those of longtime residents, and act as both a visible sign of safe capital investment and a force of cultural displacement. New retail establishments and trendy restaurants create a perfect storm of commercial gentrification that is just as influential as its residential twin. Tastes of different social groups come into contention over the cultural space of a neighborhood, the aesthetic of its shopping streets, and the socializing that goes on in and around its homes; the group whose idea of authenticity manages to win takes control of the space. Resistance, as I wrote then, is necessary but largely futile.

These ideas continued to shape the questions I asked in *The Cultures of Cities* (1995) and most recently *Naked City* (2009). This book focuses on the pursuit and even the production of authenticity as a force in urban redevelopment today. During the past 30 years, the city has promoted two conflicting ideas of authenticity – that of the "urban village" of low-income, marginalized social groups and that of the "corporate city" of business and political elites. Though at first we think that the urban village represents an image of the past, we realize that it has really been established as the template of gentrification. The old buildings have been saved, but not the people who were living in them when gentrifiers came. This has reurbanized the city, but at great social and psychic cost.

19

"The Blind Men and the Elephant: The Explanation of Gentrification"

From *Transactions of the Institute of British Geographers* (1991)

Chris Hamnett

INTRODUCTION

The gentrification phenomenon, and the debate over its significance, processes, explanation and effects have occupied a remarkably large amount of space in the scholarly journals over the last 10 years (see Hamnett, 1984; Smith and Williams, 1986 for recent bibliographies). In the *Annals* alone, there have been articles by Ley (1980; 1986; 1987), Schaffer and Smith (1986), Smith (1987b) and Badcock (1989).

Gentrification has now been identified in a large number of cities in North America, Europe and Australia, but despite its expansion during the 1970s and 1980s, it is still a relatively small scale and very geographically-concentrated phenomenon compared to post-war suburbanization and inner city decline. Berry (1985) dismissively refers to it as *Islands of renewal in seas of decay*. It is therefore important to ask why so much attention has been devoted to the subject. At least five possible explanations can be identified. These are outlined in ascending order of importance. First, and somewhat instrumentally, it can be suggested that gentrification has provided a convenient subject for a new generation of urban geographers and sociologists on the lookout for novel and potentially interesting city-specific research topics. Hence the large number of one-off, locally based case-studies.

A second, and more convincing explanation is that gentrification has posed a major challenge to the traditional theories of residential location and urban social structure (Hamnett, 1984). Neighbourhood change was viewed by Hoyt and Burgess as a one-way process where 'the wealthy seldom reverse their steps and move backwards into the obsolete housing which they are giving up' (Hoyt, 1939, p. 118). Gentrification undermines the dominant assumption that filtering is a uni-directional downwards process in which lower income groups move into progressively deteriorated housing, and it challenges the explicit assumption underlying Alonso's 'structural' theory of the urban land market that the preference for space and low densities are far more important than accessibility to the central city. Finally, gentrification undermines existing 'stage theories' or evolutionary models of urban residential change which see middle class suburbanization as the final stage of a progression from the pre-industrial to the industrial city. Ley (1981) has commented that as a result of:

> the revitalization process of the past decade, sections of the post-industrial inner city have begun a transformation from the homes of labouring classes toward a zone of privilege reminiscent of the inner-most residential ring in Sjoberg's model of the pre-industrial city. If present trends continue, the social geography of the nineteenth-century industrial city may even appear to urban scholars of the future as a temporary interlude to a more historically persistent pattern of higher-status segregation adjacent to the downtown core.
>
> (Ley, 1981, p. 145)

The third reason for the emergence of gentrification as a central research issue lies in the policy and political debates regarding gentrification-related displacement. Whereas gentrification has been seen by some as the saviour of the inner cities, heralding a halt to decades of white middle class flight and residential abandonment and offering an increased tax base (Sumka, 1979; Sternlieb and Hughes, 1983) others regard it as a threat to inner city working class areas (Ley, 1981; Hartman, 1979; Marcuse, 1986; LeGates and Hartman, 1986) and a prelude to the wholesale conversion of parts of the inner city into a bourgeois playground (Schaeffer and Smith, 1986).

A fourth, and related explanation, is that gentrification can be seen to constitute one of the major 'leading edges' of contemporary metropolitan restructuring. Just as suburbanization and inner city decline comprised the leading edges of urban restructuring in the 1950s and 1960s, so gentrification is argued to represent one of the leading edges of urban restructuring in the 1970s and 1980s. By slowing or reversing inner city middle class population loss and housing decay, gentrification represents a partial reversal of previous trends. From this perspective, gentrification, like suburbanization before it, highlights the importance of capital switching between different sectors of the economy and different parts of the city (Smith, 1979; Harvey, 1978; 1980; Badcock, 1989; King, 1989a; 1989b; 1989c). This argument is developed by Smith and Williams (1986) who suggest, among other things, that gentrification has to be seen as part of the changing international spatial division of labour, and the emergence of global cities with control and command functions as part of a new urban heirarchy dominated by flows of finance capital. This is leading to a restructuring of both the urban heirarchy and of intra-urban space. Schaeffer and Smith (1986) thus reject the claims of 'minimalists' such as Berry who see gentrification as a small scale process. They argue that: 'we are witnessing not a curious anomaly but a trenchant restructuring of urban space' (Schaeffer and Smith, 1986, p. 362).

The fifth, and arguably, the most important explanation for the prominence of gentrification in contemporary urban geographical literature, is that it represents one of key theoretical and ideological battlegrounds in urban geography, and indeed in human geography as a whole, between the liberal humanists who stress the key role of choice, culture, consumption and consumer demand, and the structural Marxists who stress the role of capital, class, production and supply. Gentrification is one of the main arenas of conflict between the proponents of culture, preference and human agency, and the proponents of the imperatives of capital and profitability. Indeed, two of the major combatants, David Ley and Neil Smith have been closely engaged in

wider debates about epistemology and explanation in human geography as a whole (see Duncan and Ley, 1982 and Smith, 1982; 1987c).

To the extent that this interpretation is correct, gentrification is a frontier (Smith, 1986) not just physically, economically, socially and culturally, but also theoretically, ideologically and politically. It comprises a contested boundary zone between radically different theories and explanations. And it is arguably this aspect of gentrification, above all others, which has kept the gentrification debate at the forefront of urban geographical literature for over a decade. The gentrification debate is one played for high theoretical and ideological stakes. Not surprisingly, it has also been fiercely contested, with the proponents of production and profitability sniping at the advocates of consumption and choice and vice versa. As Schaeffer and Smith (1986) clearly stated:

> the debate over causes has come to center on the issue of production based vs. consumption based explanations. ... Each of the different positions in this debate ... involves a larger theoretical commitment concerning the way in which urban space is continually patterned and repatterned.
> (Schaeffer and Smith, 1986, p. 350)

And Rose (1984) notes in her sympathetic critique of Marxist analyses of gentrification that:

> Marxist work on gentrification has insisted that the 'correct' place to begin theorising about this process is with the production of the commodities of gentrified dwellings. I use the word 'correct' to draw attention to the fact that this type of insistence on a single analytical starting point in the 'sphere of production' is politically grounded ... activities in this sphere are ... (seen as) ... the primary motors of change within capitalist society. ... To a large extent, Marxist approaches to gentrification have defined their objectives self-consciously in opposition to positivist approaches. ... A crucial element in the Marxist approach, in contrast, to positivist approaches, is that it sees that gentrification is ... not reducible to the behaviour of individuals.
> (Rose, 1984, pp. 49–50)

It is this aspect of gentrification, that of intellectual battleground between competing and radically opposed theoretical perspectives, that I intend to focus on in this article. Although several alternative explanatory emphases have been identified (Hamnett, 1984; Ley, 1986; Smith, 1986), notably those of changes in demography, life-style and urban amenity; land and housing market dynamics and in urban economic activity and employment structures, in essence they collapse into two main competing sets of explanations. The first, primarily associated with the work of Smith has stressed the production of urban space, the operation of the housing and land market, the role of capital and collective social actors such as developers and mortgage finance institutions on the supply of gentrifiable property. The second, which Smith has termed the consumption side argument, focuses on the production of gentrifiers and their associated cultural, consumption and reproductive orientations (Ley, 1980; 1981; Mullins, 1982; Moore, 1982; Rose, 1984; Williams, 1984; Beauregard, 1986).

This paper argues that both of the two principal theoretical perspectives on gentrification are partial abstractions from the totality of the phenomenon, and have focused on different aspects to the neglect of other, equally crucial elements. Like Aesop's fable of the blind men and the elephant, each of the major theories has perceived only part of the elephant of gentrification. The two theoretical perspectives are complementary rather than competing. This has subsequently been slowly appreciated, and the initial exclusionary tendencies have been watered down to some extent. The gradual emergence of an integrated theory of gentrification (Hamnett, 1984; Beauregard, 1986) has arisen from the realization that production and consumption are both crucial to a comprehensive explanation.

In arguing this thesis, only limited attention is paid to the debates over the role of the state in gentrification and to the gender dimensions of the process (Rose, 1984; 1989) but it is contended that, while important, these are essentially secondary to the central issue of production versus consumption. Although Cybriwsky et al. (1986) and Smith (1989) argue that the role of the state is important for an understanding of gentrification in certain areas, there is considerable debate over the relative importance to be given to individual actors and their motivations and to the structural role of the state. In some respects therefore, the debate over the role of the state in gentrification reflects and embodies the wider gentrification debate between the proponents of structure and agency (Gregory, 1981).

The paper is divided into nine sections. The first section defines gentrification and outlines the criteria for explanation. The second and third sections outline and assess Ley's approach. The fourth and fifth sections outline and assess Smith's initial 'rent gap' thesis. The sixth section stresses the importance of the 'production of gentrifiers' and their locational preferences, the seventh section examines Smith's reformulations and his attempt to incorporate consumption into his theoretical framework, and the eighth outlines the elements of an integrated theory. The final section summarizes and concludes the argument.

GENTRIFICATION: A DEFINITION AND CRITERIA FOR EXPLANATION

As a preliminary to the outline and analysis of the competing arguments, we first need to define gentrification, and establish the criteria for a comprehensive explanation, against which various theories can be assessed and evaluated. Hamnett (1984, p. 284) defined gentrification as:

Simultaneously a physical, economic, social and cultural phenomenon. Gentrification commonly involves the invasion by middle-class or higher-income groups of previously working-class neighbourhoods or multi-occupied 'twilight areas' and the replacement or displacement of many of the original occupants. It involves the physical renovation or rehabilitation of what was frequently a highly deteriorated housing stock and its upgrading to meet the requirements of its new owners. In the process, housing in the areas affected, both renovated and unrenovated, undergoes a significant price appreciation. Such a process of neighbourhood transition commonly involves a degree of tenure transformation from renting to owning.

Smith (1987b, p. 463) stated:

The crucial point about gentrification is that it involves not only a social change but also, at the neighbourhood scale, a physical change in the housing stock and an economic change in the land and housing market. It is this combination of social, physical, and economic change that distinguishes gentrification as an identifiable process/set of processes.

It is clear from these definitions that gentrification involves both a change in the social composition of an area and its residents, and a change in the nature of the housing stock (tenure, price, condition etc.) and an adequate explanation of gentrification will have to cover both aspects of the process; the housing and the residents. Moving from these definitions to the specification of the criteria for explanation of gentrification, I suggest that any comprehensive explanation of gentrification must explain four key aspects of the process. First, why gentrification is particularly concentrated in a small number of large cities such as Paris, London, New York, San Francisco, Toronto, Sydney and Melbourne (of why it is more limited in older industrial cities). Secondly, why gentrification occurs in some areas of housing and not others, and the characteristics of the areas involved. Thirdly, it must explain which groups become gentrifiers and why, and fourthly, it must explain the timing of gentrification. In other words, a comprehensive explanation must address the questions of where, which areas, who, when and why.

I shall argue in the remainder of this paper that each of the major explanations addresses or answers some of these questions, but not others. Indeed, it can be argued that while each is of considerable explanatory value, they are incapable, in isolation, of answering all these questions by virtue of their focus and range. Therefore they constitute partial explanations of limited validity. As Smith (1979) is in part a response to previous work by Ley (1978) and others, Ley's work will be considered first.

CULTURE AND CONSUMPTION IN THE POST-INDUSTRIAL CITY

In 1980 David Ley published 'Liberal ideology and the post-industrial city'. In this paper he set out what can be seen in retrospect to be a key theoretical statement regarding the origins and causes of gentrification although its focus was on the rise of the Electors Action Movement in Vancouver and their policy of limiting real estate and freeway development and creating a livable city. In what later proved to be a red rag to Marxist analysts, Ley argued that:

A new ideology of urban development was in the making. Urban strategy seemed to be passing from an emphasis on growth to a concern with the quality of life; the new liberalism was to be recognised less by its production schedules than by its consumption styles.

(Ley, 1980, p. 239)

Ley also argued that: 'an understanding of the emerging urban landscape requires a prior grasp of wide-ranging processes of change in society itself' (Ley, 1980, p. 240). In an attempt to identify these, Ley drew on the work of Daniel Bell on post-industrial society and Habermas on advanced capitalism. He accepted they were unlikely theoretical bedfellows, but argued there was: 'a deeper complementarity in their positions. Both see a decisive

transition between nineteenth and late twentieth century society, between the industrial period (early capitalism) and post-industrialism (late capitalism). … (p. 240).

Ley's thesis involved three key propositions focusing respectively on economics, politics and culture. As we shall see later, the order is important. First, at the level of the economy, the declining role of unskilled labour in the production process and the growing importance of technology in the factory, in the office and in administration is a major break with the nineteenth century. This has been associated with a major transformation of the labour force, with a decline in blue collar workers and a growth of white collar workers, particularly in the professional, managerial, administrative and technical occupations. Ley linked this to the shift from a goods producing to a service-producing society, and to the decline of manufacturing industry and the rise of office work.

The second proposition was that post-industrial society is distinguished from industrial society by the active role of government. As a consequence of this, Ley argued that 'decision making and allocation of resources is now referred to the political arena and not only to the market place. … The politicization of varied interest groups is challenging the formerly firm hold of the business lobby on political decision making' (Ley, 1980, p. 241). Thirdly, Ley argued that at the sociocultural level there has been a re-assertion of the role of individuality and a growth of a more sensuous and aesthetic philosophy among the growing numbers of the North American service class, particularly on the West coast. He concluded that:

we may see from this framework the appearance of a theoretically significant group of actors … (who) form a theoretical counterpoint to nineteenth century notions of capital and labor … a class in emergence. … With a secure economic base, they represent the present day counterparts of Veblen's leisure class, displaying the canons of good taste, intent upon the aesthetic. Their lifestyle is … consumption and status orientated in pursuit of self-actualization.

(Ley, 1980, pp. 242–3)

Ley's reference to 'a class in emergence' is important and he noted that as the post-industrial thesis was developed by sociologists it was not locationally specific. But he argued that 'these traits are not uniformly distributed; there is a geography of the post-industrial society … it might fit circumstances more closely in San Francisco or London than in

Cleveland or Glasgow' (Ley, 1980, pp. 242–3). This is a key point which has an important bearing on the question of where gentrification is found and Ley proceeded to apply the thesis to Vancouver, looking at changes in industrial, occupational and demographic structures and in the lifestyles and inner city housing market which had occurred. Ley did not explicitly refer to the term gentrification in this paper, but in 1981 he made a clear link between the growth of the tertiary and quaternary sectors, the growth of professional and managerial occupations, changes in the structure of housing demand in Vancouver and gentrification. As he put it:

> it is possible to follow the *transmission* of large scale adjustments in the economy to the pattern of job creation in Vancouver, with trends favouring white collar job growth in the central business district. *These contextual factors lie* behind the demographic changes in the metropolitan area and the housing demand pressures which accompanied them.
>
> (Ley, 1981, p. 128 emphases added)

But these housing demand pressures are locationally specific. Discussing the growing number of small, young, high income households and their impact on the inner city housing market, Ley argued that cultural factors are important: 'The neighbourhoods themselves include a measure of life-style, ethnic and architectural diversity, valued attributes of middle-class movers to the central city ... these desiderata of the culture of consumption should not be underestimated in interpreting the revitalization of the inner city' (Ley, 1981, p. 128).

Ley had less to say on the structure and operation of urban land and housing market and the supply and production of gentrifiable properties and areas and, where he does, it is more focused on the demand aspects of the equation. Ley noted the role of the real estate industry, but he accorded it a secondary or reinforcing role in the gentrification process. Referring to the revitalization of the inner city area of Kitsilano, he states that: 'There is little doubt that the activity of the real estate industry *added* to the instability of the local housing market, *quickening* the transition process and fuelling inflationary land values, through speculation and by *increasing* the expectations of homeowners to receive windfall prices for their homes' (Ley, 1981, p. 138, emphases added).

The causal primacy is quite clear. Ley sees property activity as stimulated by the market power of the growing white collar labour force, which is a product of changes in economic and employment structure.

He has reiterated this view in a more recent (1986) paper. As he put it:

> job growth (in) the white-collar complex of downtown head offices, producer services, and indirectly, (in) public institutions and agencies in ... nodal centres ... leads to the 'production' of professionals, managers and other quaternary employees working downtown, who then provide the demand base for housing re-investment in the inner city ... this population, as it gives political and economic expression to its own predeliction to urban amenity, will restructure the built environment and accelerate the gentrification process.
>
> (Ley, 1986, p. 532)

AN ASSESSMENT OF LEY'S THEORY OF POST-INDUSTRIAL URBANISM

There is much in Ley's thesis that Marxist analysts would strongly challenge, not least the political emphasis he accords to a new elite of tastemakers and opinion formers, the importance of culture and consumption, his acceptance of the idea of post-industrialism (Walker and Greenberg, 1982), and his seeming relegation of the production of the built environment and nineteenth-century notions of labour and capital to a secondary role in urban affairs. But Ley was not advocating an autonomous theory of consumption-determined urban development and change, or a straightforward consumer preference theory of gentrification as some of his critics have argued, and nor does his work rest just on Bell's concept of the post-industrial city. On the contrary, the importance he accords to culture and consumption in the post-industrial city are clearly rooted in the deeper changes in the structure of production, the changing division of labour, and the rise of a locationally concentrated service class.

While Ley argues that this class played a key role in politics and culture, he also identified it as a product of the changes in the division of labour and the spatially uneven nature of these changes. He thus linked together changes in the organization of production and the economy, politics and culture, into an approach to gentrification and urban change based on the production of gentrifiers and their cultural characteristics and requirements. Without this, he would have been guilty of advocating a non-materialist consumption-based, theory of gentrification as his critics have suggested. But, in my view, they have misinterpreted his stress on culture and consumption as a narrow demand and preference-based approach when, in fact, it is based on changes in the social and spatial division of labour and on the supply of potential gentrifiers. These changes underpin the development of a new culture and the residential and political demands that follow from it.

Looking at Ley's early work in general, it can be argued that its strength lies in its focus on the changes in the social and spatial divisions of labour, and the concentration in a limited number of 'post-industrial, service-dominated cities, of a professional and managerial elite. He accords a considerable stress to the role of changes in culture and consumption and the residential requirements or demands of the new elite, but he locates this in the context of changes in the nature and structure of economic organization. Ley's thesis is strongest in the explanation it offers of the type of city in which gentrification is likely to occur, and the characteristics of the gentrifiers. It also implicitly deals with the timing of gentrification through its analysis of the growth of the service economy in the 1970s and 1980s. Where it is weaker is in its explanation of the areas in which gentrification occurs, which Ley sees largely as a product of demand for inner city locations and the amenity and cultural facilities they offer to the gentrifiers. The supply of potential gentrifiable houses is assumed to follow on from the demands and market power of potential gentrifiers to outbid other users. But Ley's stress on the market power of the new elite suggests that he sees the power to outbid other users as a major determinant of the urban landscape; perhaps as important as the new elite's culture of consumption.

THE SUPPLY-SIDE ANALYSIS: GENTRIFICATION AND THE 'RENT-GAP'

Ley's approach to the explanation of gentrification stressed the production of gentrifiers and their cultural and consumption requirements as its key element. The supply of gentrifiable properties and the operation of the urban land and housing markets were accorded a secondary role. Smith (1979) completely reversed this explanatory emphasis, arguing that the 'consumer preference' arguments were taken for granted and contradictory. In his view, the actions of producers as well as consumers need to be taken into account in explaining the gentrification phenomenon. As he put it: 'To explain gentrification according to the gentrifier's actions alone, while ignoring the role of builders, developers, landlords, mortgage lenders, government agencies, real estate agents and tenants is excessively narrow. A broader theory of gentrification must take the role of producers as well as consumers into account' (Smith, 1979, p. 540).

Smith is entirely correct in this respect, and this is something that Ley largely failed to do. But what Smith then proceeded to do was to argue for producer dominance:

> it appears that the needs of production – in particular the need to earn profit – are a more decisive initiative behind gentrification than consumer preference. This is not to say in some naïve way that consumption is the automatic consequence of production, or that consumer preference is a totally passive effect caused by production. Such would be a producer's sovereignty theory, almost as one-sided as its neo-classical counterpart. Rather, *the relationship between production and consumption is symbiotic, but it is a symbiosis in which production dominates.* Although it is of secondary importance in initiating the actual process, and therefore in explaining why gentrification occurred in the first place, consumer preference and demand are of primary importance in determining the final form and character of revitalized areas.
>
> (Smith, 1979, p. 540 emphases added)

Smith concluded that:

> The so-called urban renaissance has been stimulated more by economic than cultural forces. In the decision to rehabilitate inner city structure, one consumer preference tends to stand out above the others – the preference for profit, or, more accurately a sound financial investment. Whether or not gentrifiers articulate this preference, it is fundamental, for few would even consider rehabilitation if a financial loss were to be expected. A theory of gentrification must therefore explain why some neighbourhoods are profitable to redevelop while others are not? What are the conditions of profitability? Consumer sovereignty explanations took for granted the availability of areas ripe for gentrification when this was precisely what had to be explained.
>
> (Smith, 1979, pp. 540–1)

Smith then proceeded to lay out his theory of the rent gap. This is by now very well known, and I do not intend to detail his argument in full. Suffice to say that it locates gentrification within long-term shifts of investment and disinvestment in the built environment, and focuses on the relationship between land and property value, particularly on the way in which disinvestment produces the possibility of capital reinvestment. Smith argues that in the nineteenth century, most cities had a classical land value gradient, highest at the centre and falling gradually towards the periphery. But, as the suburbanization of industry and population proceeded from the turn of the century onwards, land values in the inner city fell relative to the CBD and the suburbs and a 'valley' in the land value gradient opened up which intensified during the decades of sustained suburbanization in 1940s, 50s and 60s. This devalorization of the inner city provided the basis for subsequent profitable reinvestment.

The key for Smith, is the relationship between land value and property value. When depreciation of the existing structures has proceeded far enough, the point is reached where the capitalized ground rent of site or neighbourhood is less than its potential ground rent in its 'highest and best use'. This is the rent gap, and according to Smith, gentrification or redevelopment, can occur when the gap is wide enough to ensure a profit.

> Once the rent gap is wide enough, gentrification *may* be initiated in a given neighbourhood by several different actors in the land and housing market. And here we come back to the relationship between production and consumption, for the empirical evidence suggests strongly that the process is initiated not by the exercise of those individual consumer preferences much beloved of neoclassical economists, but by some form of collective social action at the neighbourhood level.
>
> (Smith, 1979, p. 545 emphasis added)

Smith's opposition to any explanation of gentrification based on individual consumer preferences is clear cut, and referring to the importance of mortgage funding in this process, he argues that:

> All the consumer preference in the world will come to nought unless this long absent source of funding reappears; mortgage capital is a prerequisite. Of course, this mortage capital must be borrowed by willing consumers exercising some preference or another. But these preferences are not prerequisites since they can be socially created.
>
> (Smith, 1979, pp. 545–6)

Smith summarizes his thesis as follows:

> gentrification is a structural product of the land and housing markets. Capital flows where the rate of return is highest, and the movement of capital to the suburbs along with the continual depreciation of inner city capital, eventually produces

the rent gap. When this gap grows sufficiently large, rehabilitation (or for that matter, renewal) can begin to challenge the rates of return available elsewhere and capital flows back.
>
> (Smith, 1979, p. 546)

Hence, the subtitle of Smith's paper: 'A back to the city movement by capital, not people'.

AN ASSESSMENT OF SMITH'S RENT GAP THEORY OF GENTRIFICATION

This is an elegant argument, and Smith was quite correct to attempt to shift the emphasis away from the early consumer preference and demand arguments towards a consideration of the supply of gentrifiable property and the role of mortgage finance and profitability. But it is now clear that, despite the importance of his rent gap thesis for an understanding of the uneven pattern of investment, disinvestment and reinvestment in the built environment, his rejection of alternative explanatory approaches; particularly the role of the new class, and its consumption and cultural characteristics, and his unwillingness to accord individual actors any significant role rendered his initial approach of only limited value for the explanation of gentrification. In Smith's thesis, individual gentrifiers are merely the passive handmaidens of capital's requirements.

The logical place to start is with Smith's rejection of consumer demand theory and Ley's post-industrial thesis. Smith acknowledged that only Ley's post-industrial thesis is broad enough to account for gentrification internationally, but he rejected it as being contradictory. If individual preferences change in unison, they cannot be individual preferences or the overriding constraints are strong enough to force them into the same mould. There is some truth in the second argument. Consumer preferences do not emerge out of thin air. They are partly socially created, manipulated and shaped, and they are necessarily made on the basis of the available options and constraints and not always in the circumstances of an individual's own choosing. Where Smith is wrong is in arguing that, for the concept of individual preference to be valid, individuals in different countries must make different choices. If similar groups in different countries are facing similar options at the same time, it is scarcely surprising that there may be similar outcomes. But this does not mean that individuals are totally determined in their choices as Smith (1979, p. 540) seems to imply, or that all 'preferences are ... socially created'.

Smith's solution is to redefine preference in terms of 'collective social preference', but this does not explain where collective social preferences come from. All it does is to displace the problem of explaining the origins of preference up the scale to a more ideologically acceptable, if theoretically mysterious level. It should also be stressed that only a minority of people decide to live in the inner city and become gentrifiers. Many more decide to move out to the suburbs. There remains, therefore, the problem of explaining why some people do one thing, and some do another. This cannot be explained in terms of capital flows, disinvestment and reinvestment. Although the gentrification process does involve capital flows, it also involves people, and this is the Achilles heel of Smith's supply side thesis.

Not only does Smith relegate consumer preference and demand to a subsidary role in favour of the production of residential space, he argues that the focus of a theory of gentrification must be one of the reasons why some neighbourhoods are profitable to redevelop while others are not. Smith is correct that consumer sovereignty/demand-led explanations took for granted the availability of areas ripe for gentrification. But, as we shall see, Smith fell into an almost identical trap by taking for granted the existence of a pool of gentrifiers and the conditions of demand. He assumed that if the conditions of profitability were favourable that gentrification (or, for that matter, renewal) would take place and that the potential gentrifiers were on hand to play a role in the revalorization process. Only later did he attempt to rectify this lacuna, itself a product of his tendency to assume that demand was of secondary importance to supply in the explanation of gentrification.

Smith is correct in arguing for the centrality of mortgage finance in urban residential restructuring as Harvey (1974), Williams (1976; 1978), Boddy (1976), Dingemans (1979), Wolfe *et al.* (1980), Hamnett and Randolph (1986; 1987) have also shown. But although absence of mortgage finance renders gentrification impossible on all but a small scale, its presence does not, of itself, create gentrification. Mortgage finance is a necessary but not a sufficient condition of large-scale gentrification. Nor is it adequate for Smith to argue that although 'mortgage capital must be borrowed by willing consumers exercising some preference or another ... preferences can be socially created' (Smith 1979, p. 546). This is correct, but Smith implies that all preferences are socially created which is nonsensical. Nor is it empirically correct (see Moore, 1982) to argue that: 'the process is not initiated by the exercise of individual consumer preferences ... but by some form of collective social action at the neighbourhood level' (p. 545). Smith's tendency to

consistently dismiss the role of individual gentrifiers in favour of collective social actors is clearly seen where he identifies three types of developers who typically operate in gentrifying neighbourhoods. They are:

> (a) professional developers who purchase property, redevelop it and resell for profit; (b) occupier developers who buy and redevelop property and inhabit it after completion; (c) landlord developers who rent it to tenants after rehabilitation. ... The fragmented structure of ... ownership has made the occupier developer, who is generally an inefficient operator in the construction industry into an appropriate vehicle for recycling devalued neighbourhoods.
>
> (Smith, 1979, p. 546)

What Smith is arguing is that, contrary to all his other assertions on the central importance of producer interests, and the secondary role of consumer choice, is that the individual households are themselves one of the most important and indeed, appropriate forces in the production of gentrified neighbourhoods. Only by classifying them as developers is he able to circumvent this awkward intrusion of individual renovation for consumption into his producer-dominated thesis. To the extent that individual producers/consumers play a key role in the gentrification process (and this is certainly true in London), Smith's distinction between production and consumption is an artificial one and he fails to explain where the individual developer gentrifiers come from, or why some individuals become gentrifiers, while others do not. In Smith's analysis individuals seem to gentrify because of the value gap, irrespective of their characteristics, tastes and demands, but as Rose (1984) perceptively points out:

> gentrifiers are not the mere bearers of a process determined independently of them. Their constitution, as certain types of workers, and as people, is as crucial an element in the production of gentrification as is the production of the dwellings they occupy. They may or may not make the potential process happen in particular contingent situations.
>
> (Rose, 1984, p. 56)

Rose's statement is a powerful indictment of the economistic and deterministic character of the rent gap theory of gentrification with its overriding stress on the production of gentrifiable areas. It cannot be too strongly emphasized that gentrification does not occur independently of individual gentrifiers.

Although the rent gap may be necessary for gentrification to occur, it is not sufficient. It does not necessitate that gentrification will take place. Indeed, rent gap theory says nothing about why gentrification should take place rather than some other form of renewal or redevelopment. The rent gap theory of gentrification is thus substantially under-determined. Gentrification is not 'to be expected' where the rent gap exists; it is a contingent phenomenon. Gentrification could occur but so could renewal, deterioration or abandonment.

And given that the gap between potential and actual ground rents is predicated on the existence of potential ground rent, Smith says very little about the processes by which such potential ground rents come into existence. It is possible, for example, that in gentrifying areas, the potential ground rent is, in part, a result of demand from potential gentrifiers (Moore, 1982). As Munt (1987) argues: 'As gentrifiers can afford numerous inner-city residential locations, it follows that the size of the rent gap in particular locations depends on their attractiveness, and hence on demand, which is absent from Marxist gentrification theory' (p. 1177). Ley goes further to argue that the rent gap is not even a necessary element of gentrification. In his view, all that is necessary is the potential for profit and the ability of gentrifiers to outbid existing or potential users for desirable inner city sites. Ley also argues that most developers are risk averse and will not risk entering an area until demand is proven. 'From the developers point of view, demand is the bottom line. In short capital follows demand, though this is not to say that local markets cannot be manipulated, e.g., blockbusting or that demand is produced by broader economic contexts' (1990, personal communication).

These problems with the rent gap thesis have been documented in two recent empirical studies. Clark (1988) found clear evidence of a rent gap in his pioneering analysis of the evolution of land and property values in Malmo, Sweden, but he argued that it was theoretically explicable either in terms of Marshall's neo-classical formulation or in terms of Smith's Marxist one, and that the rent gap was in no sense a determinant of gentrification or a complete explanation for it. In fact redevelopment rather than gentrification occurred in all cases in Malmo. Clark thus rejected the idea of:

> some predetermined development with the 'needs of capital' as prime mover and the rent-gap as time-set triggering mechanism. The action of agents with economic or political interests, and of individuals interested in their own housing, are

essential to the particular histories which unfold in a place.

> (Clark, 1986, p. 244)

Badcock (1989) in his study of Adelaide, South Australia, found convincing evidence that a sizeable rent gap had developed by 1970 in the City and in some of the surrounding Victorian residential suburbs and that substantial gentrification had subsequently occurred which filled in the rent gap. But he also concluded that 'the processes responsible for this rent gap are nowhere near as straightforward as Smith would have it' (Badcock, 1989, p. 132). He argued that gentrification was the third best response of capital to existing conditions in Adelaide, and was, in some ways a sub-optimal investment strategy (p. 133). In other words, gentrification was not an inevitable outcome of the rent gap.

It is clear from these two studies that the existence of a rent gap is not a sufficient condition for gentrification to occur. On the contrary, the existence of a rent gap can lead to a variety of different results including redevelopment or further decline. More generally, it appears that Smith's theory is of value insofar as it explains the existence of areas within cities where gentrification may take place. It says nothing about why gentrification tends to occur in some cities rather than others, or about the characteristics and origins of the gentrifiers themselves, and why they gentrified rather than suburbanized. As an analysis of the cycles of investment and disinvestment in the built environment it remains a major contribution, but its role in explaining other aspects of gentrification is limited.

The principal reason why Smith's theory was unable to address these other questions was that, given its focus on the production of the built environment, it was 'limited to the specification of preconditions for the production of gentrified dwellings without considering the production of 'gentrifiers', the occupants of such dwellings' (Rose, 1984, p. 51). Because Smith focused his explanation on the production of the rent gap, and conflated and dismissed as 'preferences', changes in occupational structure, demographic and reproductive behaviour, he ignored key material changes influencing the production of gentrifiers, and equated materialist explanations with the rent gap.

THE PRODUCTION OF GENTRIFIERS AND THEIR LOCATIONAL CHOICES

In the early 1980s, Ley's thesis regarding the role of changes in the social and spatial division of labour and in occupational structure and the rise of a 'new middle class' and the links to gentrification was paralleled in different ways by several other workers who made theoretical links between changes in the social and spatial restructuring of labour processes, corporate organization and what Rose (1984) termed the production of gentrifiers. One such link was made by Mullins (1982) who argued that dramatic changes had taken place in the Australian inner city. The decline of inner city manufacturing and the skilled working class resident population had been accompanied by the emergence of corporate centres for monopoly capitalism and middle class office workers. Mullins linked this to gentrification, arguing that 'whereas the working class of an earlier form of inner city lived there because of employment reasons centred on manufacturing industry, "educated labour" is coming to reside in the inner city (for) unique consumption reasons' (p. 45–6). But, as Mullins noted: 'the development of office employment cannot wholly explain the residential increase of inner city educated labour simply because the bulk of these workers … reside in the suburbs and commute. … Other processes must have been involved in this residential development' (Mullins, 1982, p. 53). A similar link was also made by Moore (1982, p. 1) who argued that 'gentrification represents the process whereby an important fraction of the new class is establishing a residential identity concomitant with its social identity, with the overall context of the central city becoming more and more a white collar city'.

Mullins pointed to the key role of production and consumption of particular leisure-oriented arts services within the inner city, which are produced and consumed by a limited number of educated workers. This explanation for gentrification, which is linked to the production of gentrifiers and to their cultural requirements is similar to Ley's thesis, and identifies a specific reason for the locational concentration of the new class in the inner cities: their cultural needs and the concentration of cultural facilities. The locational question is of crucial importance. What Mullins realized was that the growth of a new middle class or service class is necessary, but not sufficient to explain gentrification. A sufficient explanation must also account for why some of this group reside in the inner city rather than elsewhere (see also Moore, 1982).

The argument regarding the key role of the production of potential gentrifiers was developed by Rose (1984) who argued that:

theoretical and empirical work by Marxists has been exclusively preoccupied with those aspects of gentrification which can be directly related to the operation of the law of value in the built environment of capitalist cities. … This has created not only an analytical gap but also an epistemological error of considerable importance.
(Rose, 1984, p. 52)

She argues that it is essential to move beyond this very limited conception to explore the links between gentrification and changes in the social and spatial restructuring of labour processes and the reproduction of labour power and people, which have been largely ignored by economistic approaches which see social processes as either derivable from the economic or epiphenomenal. Beauregard (1986) has similarly argued that the rent gap alone is a totally inadequate explanation of gentrification. 'The explanation for gentrification begins with the presence of "gentrifiers", the necessary agents and beneficiaries of the gentrification process, and the directions taken by their reproduction and consumption' (Beauregard, 1986, p. 41).

His argument involved three key components. First, that the demand for inexpensive, inner-city housing is not a new phenomenon and cannot simply be explained by the rent gap. Secondly, that *the gentrifiers are often, though seldom alone, the "agents" of the gentrification process, and thus provide the motivations and aspirations that shape it*, and thirdly, that without this group the process ceases to exist. Different types of housing might be rehabilitated, but as characteristics of gentrifiers are broadly similar across a variety of different areas, 'gentrification is defined by the presence of gentrifiers' (Beauregard, 1986, p. 41 emphases added).

This is an argument radically at odds with that put forward by Smith. The causal primacy is exactly the reverse. Whereas Smith assumed the existence of potential gentrifiers, and saw the production of appropriate areas as the key to the process, Beauregard identifies gentrifiers as the key to explaining the process. Gentrification without gentrifiers does not exist. Like Ley and Mullins, Beauregard points to the crucial role played by the changes in industrial and occupational structure, and suggests that it is within the 'urban professional and managerial fraction of labor that gentrifiers are situated'. And like Rose (1984), Mullins (1982), Moore (1982) and Williams (1984), Beauregard argues that:

In order to explain why these professionals and managers … remain within the city and also engage in gentrification we must move away from the sphere of production and focus upon their reproduction and consumption activities. … What is it about an urban residence, in addition to proximity to work, which is especially compatible with the reproduction and consumption activities of this fraction of labour?

(1986, p. 43)

Beauregard concludes by arguing that:

the rent gap argument provides only one of the necessary conditions for gentrification and none of the sufficient ones. ... Many areas of central cities have rent gaps greatly in excess of those areas that gentrify. Thus the theory cannot easily explain why Hoboken ... becomes gentrified, but Newark ... does not.

(1986, p. 39 emphases added)

This is a crucial point which greatly weakens Smith's claims. To sum up, it is clear that the existence of a pool of new middle class potential gentrifiers is a necessary pre-requisite for gentrification to take place. So is the existence of a stock of potentially gentrifiable areas and houses. But neither of these are sufficient for gentrification to occur. That requires a fragment of the expanded professional and managerial group who wish to live in the inner areas, and a concentration of appropriate facilities and environments. Without these prerequisites, it is highly unlikely that gentrification will occur notwithstanding the actions of developers and the availability of mortgage finance.

SMITH'S ATTEMPT TO INTEGRATE CONSUMPTION INTO GENTRIFICATION

In 1986 Smith attempted to locate the rent gap thesis within a wider analysis of gentrification which included the de-industrialization of capitalist economies and the growth of white collar employment, and changes in demography and consumption patterns. This appeared to herald a significant widening of his approach, and Smith noted that 'although previous attempts at explanation have tended to fasten on one or the other trend, they may not in fact be mutually exclusive' (p. 21). This is an important concession, but Smith's view regrettably remained firmly production based, viewing demographic and cultural processes as epiphenomenon or surface froth. As he revealingly put it:

changes in demographic patterns and life-style preferences are not completely irrelevant, but ... the importance of demographic and life-style

issues seems to be chiefly in the determination of the surface form taken by much of the urban restructuring rather than explaining the fact of urban transformation. Given the movement of capital into the urban core, and the emphasis on executive, professional, administrative and managerial functions, as well as other support activities, the demographic and lifestyle changes ... help to explain why we have proliferating quiche bars rather than Howard Johnstons, trendy clothes boutiques and gourmet food shops rather than corner stores'.

(Smith, 1986, p. 31)

This view represents the total marginalization of 'consumption' to influencing the colour and design of the icing on the cake of urban restructuring and gentrification. It ignores the arguments put forward by Moore, Beauregard and Ley regarding the importance of culture and consumption in explaining why the new class gentrify the inner city rather than move out to the suburbs. While Smith accepts that it is important to explain the role of changes in the structure of production and the changing spatial division of labour in producing professional and managerial workers in the inner city, he fails to address the reason why a fraction of this group should locate in the inner city. And when he discusses the role of gentrifiers he resolutely dismisses any idea that they might play a crucial role in the process:

as with the original frontier, the mythology has it that gentrification is a process led by individual pioneers and homesteaders whose sweat equity, daring and vision are paving the way for those among us who are more timid. But ... it is apparent that where urban pioneers venture, the banks, real estate companies the state or other collective economic actors have generally gone before.

(Smith, 1986, pp. 18–19)

But this is not borne out by evidence from London and New York (Zukin, 1987) which indicates that individual pioneers do play a key initial role even if they may be often overtaken by the banks, real estate agents and developers. Munt (1987) argued that in Battersea, London, 'a gradual process of infiltration by gentrifiers ... preceeded any large scale development' (p. 1177). Contrary to Smith, there is a strong case that where the collective economic actors venture, urban pioneers have often gone before (Goetze, 1979).

In 1987 in a major paper entitled 'Of yuppies and housing: gentrification, social restructuring and the urban dream', Smith attempted to tackle the social restructuring and consumption arguments head on. Looking first at the evidence for the existence of a 'new middle class', Smith accepted that there has been an undeniable occupational transformation, with 'professional, managerial and upper level administrative personnel in expanding sectors heavily represented among gentrifiers' (Smith, 1987a, p. 154), but he argued that this does not prove the existence of a new middle class in Marxist terms (i.e. in relation to ownership and control of the means of production). This is correct, but as the social restructuring thesis is primarily concerned with occupation change and not the theoretical validity of Marxist class categories, this is largely irrelevant and Smith appears to accept the existence of a new 'class' in empirical terms if not in terms of Marxist class theory. As he puts it:

> There is no doubt that employment structure has changed dramatically and that a profound social restructuring is taking place ... and that it is altering ... the class configuration of society. Equally, this social restructuring is heavily implicated in the gentrification process.
>
> (Smith, 1987a, p. 161)

But while Smith accepted the 'overarching importance' of the new work on social restructuring for explaining gentrification he argued that:

> they also bring certain intrinsic dangers with them. *If gentrification is to be explained first and foremost as the result of the emergence of a new social group ... then it becomes difficult to avoid at least a tacit subscription to some sort of consumer preference model, no matter how watered down.* How else does this new social group bring about gentrification except by demanding specific kinds and locations of housing in the market.
>
> (Smith, 1987a, p. 163 emphases added)

Smith's fears are very clear, and they shape his attempt to resolve his problem of accepting the existence of a new social group without giving them a key role in the gentrification process. His 'solution' is ingeneous and highlights what is perhaps the key problem in the explanation of gentrification: namely its spatial manifestation. He states:

> There is no argument but that demand can at times – and especially those times when demand changes dramatically – alter the nature of production. *But the conundrum of gentrification does not turn on explaining where middle class demand comes from. Rather, it turns on explaining the essentially*

geographical question of why central and inner areas of cities, which for decades could not satisfy the demands of the middle class, now appear to do so handsomely. If, indeed, demand structures have changed, we need to explain why these changed demands have led to a *spatial* re-emphasis on the central and inner city.

(Smith, 1987a, pp. 163–4 emphases added)

Smith's argument is a fascinating one. Having accepted that demand can play a role in altering the nature of production, he then avoids the consequences of this admission by arguing that the conundrum of gentrification does not turn on where demand comes from, but on why it takes the locational form it does. This question is fundamental for the explanation of gentrification. But it is only half the issue. The conundrum of gentrification turns on *both* the explanation of where middle class demand comes from *and* on its manifestation in the central and inner cities. Smith however identifies the second question as the key one. He argues that:

> There can be little doubt that a continued and even accelerated centralization of administrative, executive, professional, managerial and some service activities may make a central domicile more desirable for a substantial sector of the middle class. But do these arguments really amount to an explanation of the geographical reversal of the location habits by a proportion of middle-class men and women? ... the argument that social restructuring is the primary impetus behind gentrification is substantially underdetermined.
>
> (Smith, 1987a, p. 164)

Smith is correct in arguing that social restructuring alone is not an adequate explanation of gentrification. But, as we have seen, the proponents of the social restructuring thesis do not argue that it is. On the contrary, they all point to the crucial role of the specific cultural and consumption requirements of a fragment of the new class, and argue that they are met by an inner city location. There is a causal link between the production of a new professional and managerial labour force, the cultural and consumption characteristics of part of that group, and the creation of potential gentrifiers. There are two steps to the argument, not one, but Smith only acknowledges the first and dismisses the second. Not surprisingly, Smith concludes that:

> *I would defend the rent-gap analysis ... not as in itself a definitive or complete explanation but as the necessary centerpiece to any theory of gentrification.*

It is the historical patterns of capital investment and disinvestment in the central and inner city cities that establishes the opportunity (not the necessity) for this spatial reversal in the first place.

(Smith, 1987a, p. 165 emphases added)

This statement represents a substantial retreat from Smith's initial position, and presupposes what Badcock (1989, p. 126) has termed 'a considerable relaxation of the theory's original assumptions'. Smith now seems to view the rent gap as a key which translates more general processes, i.e. the production of gentrifiers into a spatial reversal. But Smith's argument that the rent gap is the necessary centrepiece to any theory of gentrification is too large a claim. As Smith points out, the rent gap establishes the opportunity, not the necessity, for a spatial reversal to occur. The rent gap may provide the means, but it does not provide a motive for gentrification. For this, we need to look into what is, for Smith, the heart of darkness: locational preferences, lifestyles and consumption.

Given that Smith finds any emphasis on individual life styles and consumption unacceptable; in 1987 he outlined a way of trying to integrate production-side and consumption-side arguments vis-á-vis gentrification in terms of a historical analysis of societal restructuring. This entailed rejection of Ley's ideas about post-industrialism as a 'shallow empirical abstraction … incapable of sustaining theoretical scrutiny' (Smith, 1987a, p. 166) while reinterpreting the substance of the consumption society argument in terms of the 'regulationist' analysis of Aglietta. It is argued that as the intensive regime of accumulation began to fray at the edges in the 1970s and 1980s, there has been a switch towards a new (post-Fordist) regime of accumulation associated not with mass production and consumption, but with differentiated production and consumption. In this new regime of accumulation, the accent is on product-differentiation and niche markets. Gentrification is explained in these terms as a result of the desire of gentrifiers to differentiate themselves from other social groups. As Smith notes:

It is this question of cultural differentiation in a mass market which is most relevant to gentrification. Gentrification is a redifferentiation of the cultural social and economic landscape … gentrification and the mode of consumption it engenders are an integral part of class constitution; they are part of the means employed by new middle class individuals to distinguish themselves

from the … bourgeoise above and the working class below.

(Smith, 1987, pp. 167–8)

What Smith has done is to reinterpret, in terms of regulationist theory, Ley's work on post-industrial consumption. But Smith's interpretation of consumption and its role in gentrification is clearly very different from that suggested by Ley and others. By stressing the importance of consumption within the framework of capital accumulation he attempted to circumvent the theoretical dangers inherent in giving individual gentrifiers a key role in the gentrification process. But such differences aside, the fact that Smith had to undertake this reinterpretation is indicative of the limitations of the rent gap theory of gentrification and Smith's fundamental unwillingness to concede that individuals have any significant role in shaping their environment. Yet the closest Smith can bring himself to go is to accept the role of collective social actors and the functional requirements of differentiated consumption in new mode of regulation. It is not that Smith refuses to grant individual agency dominance – this is not the argument – but that he seems to refuse to accept it even exists at anything other than a superficial level. His opposition to any form of agency explanation reveals him as a structuralist for whom individual agency is reduced to the role of flickering shadows cast by the light of capital's fire.

TOWARDS AN INTEGRATED THEORY OF GENTRIFICATION

It has been argued that both the social restructuring thesis associated with Ley and the rent gap thesis advanced by Smith are partial attempts to explain gentrification. Ley's approach focused on changes in the social and spatial divison of labour, changes in occupational structure, the creation of cultural and environmental demands and their transmission into the housing market via the greater purchasing power of the new class. He largely took for granted the existence of potential areas suitable for gentrification and saw the process primarily in terms of housing market demand. Smith on the other hand focused on the production of gentrifiable housing through the mechanism of the rent gap. He took for granted the existence of a supply of potential gentrifiers and ignored the question of why a segment of the new class opted to locate in the inner city. Mullins, Moore, Beauregard and Rose argued that an understanding of the production of gentrifiers and their social and cultural characteristics was of crucial importance for an understanding of gentri-fication. They developed Ley's thesis considerably and argued that gentrifiers are central to the gentri-fication process. Without them, the process cannot occur at all. But gentrification is not simply a prod-uct of changes in the social and spatial division of labour, crucial though this has been. A specific locational orientation towards the inner city or spe-cific housing areas within it, is also necessary and a supply of gentrifiable areas and housing defined not just in terms of the existence of a rent gap, but also in terms of relative desirability or attrac-tiveness to the potential gentrifiers (Munt, 1987, pp. 1195–6).

There are four requirements for gentrification to occur on a significant scale. The first three are concerned, respectively, with the supply of suitable areas for gentrification, the supply of potential gen-trifiers, and the existence of attractive central and inner city environments. They comprise the neces-sary supply side elements of the equation. The final requirement involves a cultural preference for inner city residence by a certain segment of the service class. It is therefore possible to conceive of a range of possible outcomes depending on the combina-tion of these four elements. The range of outcomes are shown in Table 19.1. The important point to emerge from the schema is that gentrification only occurs under one combination of circumstances. None of the other combinations lead to gentrifica-tion, although Ley would argue that it could occur without a rent gap as long as the new class have the purchasing power to displace or replace other land users.

	Rent gap exists	No rent gap exists
No potential gentrifiers	No gentrification	No gentrification
Supply of potential gentrifiers exists		
No inner city demand	No gentrification	No gentrification
Inner city preference by a section of the 'new class'	Gentrification	Gentrification?

Table 19.1 Conditions for gentrification schema

But this is merely a classification of circum-stances. It does not, of itself, provide a basis of a theory of gentrification. And, as we have seen, the key question for such a theory is its starting point. It is inadequate to argue that gentrification is the result of a combination of circumstances with-out attempting to assign some theoretical priority to those circumstances. I have no doubt that, as Beauregard has argued, that 'the explanation for gen-trification begins with the presence of gentrifiers' and that 'gentrification is defined by the presence of gentrifiers' (Beauregard, 1986). But this does not mean that culture and consumption are assigned first place in the explanation of gentrification. As Ley, Mullins and others have pointed out, the appropriate place to start is with the changes in the structure of production and the social and spatial divisions of labour which have led to de-industrialization of advanced capitalist economies and the growth of the service sector. This, in turn, has been associ-ated with the rapid expansion of the professional and managerial service class, and the concentration of key financial, legal and other functions in a relatively small number of major cities such as London and New York and Paris and a number of other major cities such as Vancouver, Toronto, Sydney and San Francisco. It is in these cities that gentrification has been most marked.

The explanation for gentrification must therefore begin with the processes responsible for the produc-tion and concentration of key factions of the service class in a number of major cities. These processes have produced the pool of potential gentrifiers, and the primary emphasis must be on the explanation of the expansion of this key group. This is *not* a con-sumption based explanation. It is firmly based in the changes in the structure of production and the social and spatial division of labour in advanced capitalist countries. It is then necessary to explain why gentri-fication occurs in some of these cities. As we have seen, two conditions are necessary. First, it is neces-sary to have a supply of potentially gentrifiable inner city property. This is where rent gap theory comes in, explaining why a supply of devalued inner city prop-erty exists as a result of prior suburbanization and decentralization. The potential value of this prop-erty is greater than its current value. But, as we have seen, the existence of a rent gap does not necessar-ily lead to gentrification. Without the existence of a pool of potential gentrifiers and available mortgage finance, gentrification will not occur however great the rent gap and however great the desire of develop-ers to make it happen. And where appropriate inner city housing stock does not exist in sufficient quan-tity, as for example in cities such as Dallas, Phoenix and other new southern and western US cities, gentrification may be very limited, however large the new service class. In older north-eastern American cities such as Baltimore, Philadelphia and Washington D.C., on the other hand, there is an abundant supply of nineteenth century row housing, much of it devalued and run-down and home to working class and minority populations. In such cities gentrification has proceeded apace.

Secondly, there has to be some effective demand for inner city property from potential gentrifiers. This may result from financial inability to afford a suburban home or, as is more commonly argued, it may stem from a preference to live in the inner city close to central city jobs and social and cultural facilities. This, in turn, depends on both the growth of service class job opportunities downtown, and on demographic and lifestyle changes which have seen large numbers of women enter the labour force and growing numbers of both single households and dual career childless couples. For these groups, with a high disposable income, inner city locations offer proximity to employment and to restaurants, arts and other facilities. Not surprisingly, a significant proportion of them appear to have opted for inner city residence in those cities where city centre social and cultural facilities exist. Without this effective demand, based in large part on a positive orientation towards central and inner city living, gentrification is unlikely to occur however large the army of potential gentrifiers and however large the rent gap.

We are therefore faced by three sets of conditions all of which are necessary, and none of which are sufficient. But it is clear that the existence of a potential pool of gentrifiers is logically and theoretically prior to the housing preferences and lifestyles of a subgroup of the service class. And, while the existence of a supply of appropriate inner-city houses is necessary for gentrification to occur, the existence of a rent gap will not, of itself, produce gentrification. It is thus difficult to accept Smith's view that the rent gap is 'the necessary centerpiece to any theory of gentrification'. Necessary it may be, but if gentrification theory has a centrepiece it must rest on the conditions for the production of potential gentrifiers.

CONCLUSIONS

I have attempted to show that the debate over the explanation of gentrification has been broadly shaped by the conflict between those who have argued that the key to the problem lies in global changes in the structure of production and the social and spatial division of labour, and in the concentration in specific cities of a section of the 'new middle class' or 'service' class with a particular demographic composition, and cultural and consumption orientation. On the other hand Smith has consistently argued for the key role of investment and disinvestment in the built environment and for an approach based on the primacy of profitability. This conflict has manifested itself in a variety of ways. In a conflict between so-called 'supply' and 'demand' explanations, choice and culture versus capital and so on. Yet, I have argued many of these dualisms and polarities have been more apparent than real and what Smith would label the 'choice, consumption and culture' side of the debate has, in fact, always had one foot very firmly planted in the realities of changes in the material base of production and its cultural manifestations.

In some ways, the conflict has been between two interpretations of production. The one looking at changes in the social and spatial division of labour and the production of gentrifiers, and the other looking at the production of the built environment. But, until recently, Smith has consistently interpreted the former approach in terms of individual consumption, culture and choice, and has generally rejected what it had to offer. And this, as we have seen, has been considerable. Smith has recently accepted that it is important to integrate production and consumption, but this integration has still been in terms of a framework which either ascribes primacy to questions of production or re-interprets consumption in a collective non-problematic way. Smith's conception of individual action is a limited and circumscribed one. He accepts that collective social actors can make gentrification, but not a multiplicity of individual actors. If the criticism of Ley's position has been more limited, it is partly because he has said less and been far less assertive in his claims for theoretical primacy. It is also clear that his initial recognition of the key role of a new group of potential gentrifiers with their specific cultural and locational requirements was broadly correct. His sins have been of omission rather than commission. The supply of dwellings and the role of developer/speculators in the process have gone largely unexamined by Ley. They are seen as being largely derived from the demands from the new class.

Smith's claim, that gentrification is a structural product of the land and housing markets alone, can now be seen to have been misplaced as Smith now partially accepts. This is not to say that the rent gap thesis was wrong. The point is rather that the rent gap explains, at best, half the problem, and probably less. The existence of relatively cheap and devalued housing is a necessary, but far from sufficient element of an explanation. Equally, explanation of the production of potential gentrifiers, their culture, consumption and reproduction is necessary but insufficient. A comprehensive and integrated explanation of gentrification must necessarily involve the explanation of where gentrifiers come from and why they gentrify, how the areas and properties to be gentrified are produced and how the two are linked. And there is a strong case that, notwithstanding the role of institutional and collective social actors such as real estate agents, developers and mortgage lenders, the key actors in the gentrification process have been individual gentrifiers themselves. It is necessary to accept that individual agency is important in the explanation of gentrification and to seek to integrate production and consumption not in terms of structural causes or individual effects, but in terms of structures and individual agency.

Because Smith developed rent gap theory, he has been vigorous in its defence, making tactical retreats and concessions where necessary, but essentially seeking to ensure its continuing centrality in the explanation of gentrification. But while Smith has accepted that changes in the social and spatial division of labour and the concentration of professional and managerial employment in the downtown are of considerable importance, and has attempted to integrate the consumption patterns of gentrifiers into his theory, he has done this in such a way that it becomes a functional requirement of late capitalism, rather than a recognition of the role of individual preference and agency. But Smith's interventions in the gentrification debate have not been counterproductive. On the contrary, only by challenging the so-called choice and preference theories and his advocacy of a logical, coherent alternative, has the debate over explanations advanced as far as it has. Precisely because Ley and Smith pioneered radically different theories and interpretations of gentrification, it has been possible to advance our understanding of the process by seeing how the two partial explanations fit together. If their work has been shown to be limited in certain key respects and they have had to amend their explanations, this is the price paid by theoretical pioneers. Neither may have recognized the elephant of gentrification at first, but they each identified a key part of its anatomy, and other researchers have subsequently been able to piece together a more integrated explanation. As Clark (1988) concluded:

We should stop asking the one-dimensional question: 'Which theory of gentrification is true, the rent-gap theory, the post-industrial

restructuration theory, the consumer demand for amenities theory, or the institutionalist theory?', and start asking 'If it is so that there is empirical support for all these theories, can we arrive at an understanding of the ways in which they stand in a logical relation of *complementarity*?'

(p. 247 emphasis in original)

ACKNOWLEDGEMENTS

This paper was written while the author was a visiting research fellow at the Urban Research Unit, Research School of Social Sciences, The Australian National University, Canberra. Versions were given at the Institute of British Geographers Conference, University of Glasgow, January 1990 and at the workshop on European Gentrification, Department of Geography, University of Utrecht, January 1990. I am grateful for comments on the draft paper from Blair Badcock, University of Adelaide, Steve Borassa, Urban Research Unit, ANU, Tim Butler, Polytechnic of East London, David Ley and Neil Smith. The usual disclaimers apply.

REFERENCES

BADCOCK, B. (1989) 'An Australian view of the rent gap hypothesis', *Ann. Ass. Am. Geogr.* 79: 125–45

BEAUREGARD, R. A. (1984) 'Structure, agency, and urban redevelopment', in SMITH, M. P. (ed.) *Cities in transformation*, vol. 26, Urban Affairs Annual Reviews (Sage, London) pp. 51–72

BEAUREGARD, R. A. (1986) 'The chaos and complexity of gentrification', in SMITH, N. and WILLIAMS, P. (eds) *The gentrification of the city* (Allen and Unwin, London) pp. 35–55

BERRY, B. J. L. (1985) 'Islands of renewal in seas of decay', in Pederson, P. (ed.) *The new urban reality* (The Brookings Institute, Washington, D.C.)

BODDY, M. (1976) 'The structure of mortgage finance: building societies and the British social formation', *Trans. Inst. Br. Geogr.* N.S. 1: 58–71

CLARK, E. (1988) 'The rent gap and transformation of the built environment: case studies in Malmo 1860–1985', *Geografiska Annaler* 70B: 241–54

CYBRIWSKY, R. A., LEY, D. and WESTERN, J. (1986) 'The politics and social construction of revitalized neighbourhoods: Society Hill, Philadelphia and False Creek, Vancouver', in

SMITH, N. and WILLIAMS, P. (eds) *Gentrification of the City* (Allen & Unwin, London) pp. 92–120

DINGEMANS, D. J. (1978) 'Redlining and mortgage lending in Sacramento, Ca.', *Ana. Ass. Am. Geogr.* 69: 225–39

DUNCAN, J. and LEY, D. (1982) Structural marxism and human geography: a critical assessment, *Ann. Ass. Am. Geogr.* 72: 30–59

GOETZE, R. (1979) *Understanding neighbourhood change* (Ballinger, Coalbridge, Mass.)

GREGORY, D. (1981) 'Human agency and human geography', *Trans. Inst. Br. Geogr.* N.S. 6: 1–18

HAMNETT, C. (1984) 'Gentrification and residential location theory: a review and assessment', in HERBERT, D. T. and JOHNSTON, R. J. (eds) *Geography and the urban environment. Progress in research and applications*, vol. 6 (John Wiley, London) pp. 283–319

HAMNETT, C. and RANDOLPH, W. (1986) 'Landlord disinvestment and housing market transformation: the flat break-up market in London', in WILLIAMS, P. and SMITH, N. (eds) *Gentrification of the city* (George Allen and Unwin, London) pp. 121–52

HAMNETT, C. and RANDOLPH, W. (1987) *Cities, housing and profits* (Hutchinson, London)

HARTMAN, C. (1979) 'Comment on neighbourhood revitalization and displacement: a review of the evidence', *J. Am. Plan. Ass.* 45: 488–94

HARVEY, D. (1974) Class monopoly rent, finance capital and the urban revolution, *Reg. Stud.* 8: 239–55

HARVEY, D. (1978) 'The urban process under capitalism: a framework for analysis', *Int. J. Urb. Reg. Res.* 2: 101–31

HOYT, H. (1939) *The structure and growth of residential neighbourhoods in American cities* (Federal Housing Administration, Washington D.C.)

KING, R. J. (1989c) 'Capital switching and the role of ground rent: 3. Switching, between circuits, switching between submarkets, and social change', *Environ. Plann. A* 21: 853–80

LEGATES, R. T. and HARTMAN, C. (1986) 'The anatomy of displacement in the United States', in SMITH, N. and WILLIAMS, P. (eds) *The gentrification of the city* (Allen and Unwin, London), pp. 178–203

LEY, D. (1978) 'Inner city resurgence units societal context', *mimeo*, paper presented to the AAG Annual Conference, New Orleans

LEY, D. (1980) 'Liberal ideology and post-industrial city', *Ann. Ass. Am. Geogr.* 70: 238–58

LEY, D. (1981) 'Inner city revitalization in Canada: a Vancouver case study', *Canadian Geogr.* 25: 124–48

LEY, D. (1986) Alternative explanations for inner city gentrification: A Canadian assessment, *Ann. Ass. Am. Geogr.* 76: 521–35

LEY, D. (1987) Reply: the rent gap revisited, *Ann. Ass. Am. Geogr.* 77: 465–68

MARCUSE, P. (1986) 'Abandonment, gentrification and displacement: the linkages in New York City', in SMITH, N. and WILLIAMS, P. (eds) *The gentrification of the city* (Allen and Unwin, London) pp. 153–177

MOORE, P. W. (1982) 'Gentrification and the residential geography of the New Class, *mimeo*, Scarborough College, Univ. of Toronto

MULLINS, P. (1982) 'The 'middle-class' and the inner city', *J. Australian Polit. Econ.* 11, 44–58

MUNT, I. (1987) 'Economic restructuring, culture and gentrification: a case study of Battersea, London', *Environ. Plann. A* 19: 1175–97

ROSE, D. (1984) 'Rethinking gentrification: beyond the uneven development of marxist urban theory', *Society and Space* 2: 47–74

ROSE, D. (1989) 'A feminist perspective on employment restructuring and gentrification: the case of Montreal', in WOLCH, J. and DEAR, M. (eds) *The power of geography: how territory shapes social life* (Unwin Hyman, London) pp. 118–38

SCHAFFER, R. and SMITH, N. (1986) 'The gentrification of Harlem?', *Ann. Ass. Am. Geogr.* 76: 347–65

SMITH, A. (1989) 'Gentrification and the spatial constitution of the State: the restructuring of London's Docklands', *Antipode* 21: 232–60

SMITH, N. (1979) 'Toward a theory of gentrification: a back to the city movement by capital, not people', *J. Am. Plan. Ass.* 45: 538–48

SMITH, N. (1982) 'Gentrification and uneven development', *Econ. Geogr.* 58:139–55

SMITH, N. (1986) 'Gentrification, the frontier, and the restructuring of urban space', in SMITH, N. and WILLIAMS, P. (eds) *Gentrification of the city* (Allen and Unwin, London) pp. 15–34

SMITH, N. (1987a) 'Of yuppies and housing: gentrification, social restructuring and the urban dream', *Society and Space* 5: 151–72

SMITH, N. (1987b) 'Gentrification and the rent gap', *Ann. Ass. Am. Geogr.* 77: 462–78

SMITH, N. (1987c) 'Dangers of the empirical turn', *Antipode* 19: 59–68

SMITH, N. and WILLIAMS, P. (eds) (1986) *Gentrification of the city* (Allen and Unwin, London)

STERNLIEB, G. and HUGHES, J. W. (1983) 'The uncertain future of the central city', *Urban Affairs Quart.* 18: 455–72

SUMKA, H. (1979) 'Neighbourhood revitalization and displacement; a review of the evidence', *J. Am. Plan. Ass.* 45: 480–7

WALKER, R. and GREENBERG, D. (1982) 'Post-industrialism and political reform in the city: a critique'. *Antipode* 14: 17–32

WILLIAMS, P. (1978) 'Building societies and the inner city', *Trans. Inst. Br. Geogr.* 3: 23–34

WILLIAMS, P. (1984) 'Economic processes and urban change: an analysis of contemporary patterns of residential restructuring', *Austr. Geogr. Stud.* 22: 39–57

WOLFE, J., DROVER, G. and SKELTON, I. (1980) 'Inner city real estate activity in Montreal: institutional characteristics of decline', *Canadian Geogr.* 24: 348–67

ZUKIN, S. (1982) *Loft living: culture and capital in urban change* (Johns Hopkins University Press, Baltimore)

ZUKIN, S. (1987) 'Gentrification: culture and capital in the urban core', *Am. Rev. Sociology* 13: 129–47

20
"On Blindness, Centrepieces and Complementarity in Gentrification Theory"

From *Transactions of the Institute of British Geographers* (1992)

Eric Clark

... the notion of complementarity suggests itself in our position as conscious beings and recalls forcefully ... that we ourselves are both actors and spectators in the drama of existence.

(Bohr 1948, p. 318)

The recent article by Chris Hamnett in this journal on 'The blind men and the elephant: the explanation of gentrification' (Hamnett 1991) and the ensuing discussion with Neil Smith (Smith 1992; Hamnett 1992) left at least this reader with a mixture of disappointment over blindness, frustration over centrepieces and encouragement over the common interest to consider the notion of complementarity in approaches to gentrification. That we are in a sense blind men groping around and feeling different parts of the gentrification elephant is to a certain extent unavoidable – we have no foolproof holistic theory of or methodology for the study of gentrification, and it would be presumptuous to think we ever will. We specialize to some degree in a division of labour which bears various forms of fruit. But if there is one thing Aesop's fable can teach us, it is the importance of communication, which not only requires the tedious task of concisely formulating our thoughts, our research findings and our interpretations of them, but also entails the challenge of listening – without reflexive categorization.

The focus of my concern here is, as the title suggests, firstly what I perceive as disturbing instances of blindness which I hope some communication can alleviate; secondly, the problem of centrepieces as exemplified in the Hamnett-Smith debate; and thirdly the need for careful consideration of the notion of complementarity, both in general and specifically in the context of gentrification theories.

BLINDNESS

There are two instances of blindness addressed in this section. The first is a rather simple case of misunderstanding and/or carelessness which, though disturbing (coming as it does from a leading representative of comprehensive knowledge on gentrification theory), is probably of little concern to anyone but myself. The second instance however is one which has been propagated by Smith, Hamnett, Ley and others since the concept of rent gap saw the light of day – I refer to the blindness evident in the understanding of rent gaps as somehow divorced from the aspect of demand. This instance should be of concern to others than myself, and if my argument below (which feels embarrassingly obvious) has any validity, we may be able to progress beyond the arbitrarily restricted and unnecessarily inadequate conception of rent gap which has characterized thought on gentrification during the eighties.

Based on my empirical study of rent gaps in connection with urban renewal in Malmö (Clark 1987; 1988) I supposedly argued 'that the rent gap was in no sense a determinant of gentrification' (Hamnett 1991, p. 181). Upon reading this I ask myself if perhaps the study should also have been printed in Braille. For the record, I made no such argument. I argued that the presence of rent gaps is a determinant of gentrification, and that the sense in which 'determinant' should be understood in this context is non-mechanistic. Hamnett found something here he sympathized with – rejection of the 'needs of capital' as prime mover and the rent gap as a simple mechanism triggering gentrification – and apparently did not bother to read the rest! Early discussion on the role of rent gaps in gentrification suffered from eager critics interpreting the rent gap notion in overly mechanistic fashion, but I thought we had progressed beyond that already.

Then Hamnett emphasizes the previous point by explaining that in 'fact redevelopment rather than gentrification occurred in all cases in Malmö' (ibid.). Indeed, the study areas were limited to blocks that were redeveloped and in which the land use was residential both before and after redevelopment. This is a matter of sampling criteria, not research results! The findings suggested that rent gaps were essential to the redevelopment process, and that gentrification took place in connection with redevelopment. Contrary to Hamnett's assumption, redevelopment does not exclude gentrification – redevelopment is one form in which gentrification takes place. As long as we cannot reach such fundamental understandings, we gentrification researchers will probably continue to be like the blind men in the fable – studying gentrification in accordance with our idiosyncratic preconceived notions.

In all probability, no other reader noticed this case of temporary blindness or carelessness. Sloppy thinking is of course something we must beware of, but in this case it is an uninteresting detail, a bagatelle. More interesting is the question if there is not an epidemic of blindness in the discussion on rent gap explanation of gentrification.

I refer to the prevalent understanding of the rent gap concept as being unrelated to demand. It is, after all, a central concept in the 'structural Marxist' explanation of gentrification which, *as we all know* (we do, don't we? of course we do!) is lop-sided, stressing 'the role of capital, class production and supply' (Hamnett 1991, p. 174). On the other side of the fence we have the liberal humanist camp, in Hamnett's article represented by David Ley, which emphasizes 'the key role of choice, culture, consumption and demand' (ibid.). This is the self-evident point of departure in Hamnett's article and one which would probably pass among most gentrification researchers as a fitting description of the 80's and the present situation. While it is a praiseworthy ambition to critically reassess both sides of the divide in order to find points of congruence and points where incongruence is unlikely to be overcome, Hamnett's effort fails to fully recognize a much neglected link – the demand base of rent gap explanation.

If we pause a moment, stop throwing rocks from behind barricades, and contemplate the rent gap concept long enough to consider what it consists of, rather than reflexively assigning certain 'well-known' characteristics to it, many may be surprised at what we find. Those who see the 'supply side' emphasis of rent gap explanation as its major strength or weakness may want to brace themselves. The *potential land rent* of a site has its foundation in latent *demand* for 'higher and better uses' of the site. The *capitalized land rent* of a site on the other hand is founded on *demand* for the present use of the site. The latent *demand* remains latent as long as existing buildings on the site and the present use of the site secure a reasonable capitalized land rent as compared to the potential land rent which latent *demand* could make possible. Speculation (sensitive as it is to the unrealized *preferences* behind latent *demand*) on forthcoming land use change (e.g. from working-class housing to middle or upper-class housing) manifests itself in dramatic increases in capitalized land rent (increased property prices unrelated to building value) and eventually rent gap closure (capitalized land rent reaching the level of potential land rent). Gentrification is the outcome of a struggle over urban space, a struggle in which effective demand is generally considered a legitimate form of wielding power.

Without latent demand, we cannot even begin to conceptualize potential land rent. Likewise with effective demand and capitalized land rent. True, there are builders, developers, landlords, mortgage lenders, government agencies and real estate agents involved on the production and supply side, and their actions and profit motives are essential to the process of rent gap expansion and closure. But to continue to place rent gap explanation of gentrification squarely outside the cosy conceptual box of consumption and demand side explanation is to propagate a dichotomy which serves no useful purpose other than maintaining barricades and the comfort of identity they provide.

The insight that rent gaps are essentially based on demand puts Hamnett's 'Conditions for gentrification schema' (Table 19.1, page 246) in a new light, revealing problems with some of its categories and allowing clearer interpretation of others. Rent gap closure hinges on the active expression of demand for 'higher and better uses' of a site. If this demand comes from 'gentrifiers' (either directly by 'pioneers' or 'occupier developers', or indirectly – counted on by developers) or from even higher and better uses such as office or retail space is nothing which can be determined by the rent gap notion *per se*. This explains how a rent gap can lead to something other than gentrification (left column of Table 19.1): the demand behind rent gap closure (realization of potential land rent) simply comes from other quarters than a section of the 'new class'. It also explains why the assumption underlying the lower left cell of the table – that the two conditions 'rent gap exists' and 'inner city preference by potential gentrifiers' *will* lead to gentrification – is not entirely accurate. It is possible that stronger competition for the sites in question stymie potential gentrifiers from actually securing their preferences. An implicit assumption of the schema seems to be that 'potential gentrifiers' are in the driver's seat. But in some situations, the end result of 'rent gap exists' and 'inner city preference by potential gentrifiers' may instead be office development, as in Stockholm during the 1960's and 70's (Clark and Gullberg 1991).

Furthermore, consideration of rent gaps as based on demand can answer the question in the lower right cell of the table. The only way inner city preference by potential gentrifiers can coincide with 'no rent gap exists' is if in a particular context there is no inner city land where demand for the present use corresponds to a lower capitalized land rent than the land rent which could be realized by tapping these preferences of potential gentrifiers. In such a case, no gentrification takes place because the preferences of potential gentrifiers can find no place for their expression as demand. If on the other hand such preferences do find places where they can be exerted/tapped, they then constitute the basis of rent gaps and, in the absence of stronger demand for other uses, lead to gentrification. But then we have a case for the lower left cell of the table – 'rent gap exists'. Clearly, the lower right cell of the table must be: No gentrification. For if the demand of potential gentrifiers is stronger than the demand for existing use – a prerequisite for gentrification to take place – then the category 'no rent gap exists' cannot apply.

In short, there is no contradiction inherent to the combination of 'inner city preference by potential gentrifiers' and 'no rent gap exists'. Dallas and Phoenix, mentioned by Hamnett, are perhaps examples of this combination. But there is an inherent contradiction in the notion that gentrification may take place where no rent gap exists, simply because gentrification cannot occur without the demand of potential gentrifiers (potential land rent) being stronger than the demand of present residents (capitalized land rent).

The view that demand is excluded from the conception of rent gap is one which we will have to leave behind us if we are to move in the direction of integration espoused by Hamnett.

CENTREPIECES

How is such blindness perpetuated? Simplifying perhaps to an extent bordering on psychological reductionism, one answer which the Hamnett-Smith discussion nevertheless provides reason to entertain is that infatuation with centrepieces (one's own of course) is not conducive to openness of mind, not only towards others' centrepieces, but towards one's own as well. Centrepieces bind our gaze and make us blind to the centrepiece's surroundings. Elephants, could they speak, would probably be hesitant to say which of their parts they consider to be the centrepiece of their existence.

In spite of the admirable purpose of integrating the Ley and Smith camps and some valuable steps in this direction, Hamnett's article and the following discussion with Smith falls into the recognizable pattern of advancing a new centrepiece or reasserting an old one. We are asked to shift our gaze from Smith's rent gap centrepiece to a new centrepiece, 'the conditions for the production of potential gentrifiers' (Hamnett 1991, p. 187). And again, we are asked to 'accept class restructuring as the centrepiece of any theory of gentrification' (Hamnett 1992, p. 117).

Rather than blind men unable to understand each other's findings, perhaps a more apt metaphor for this type of discussion is the children's game 'king of the mountain'. In spite of its aim to integrate, Hamnett's article unfortunately tends to perpetuate this game. I hope Hamnett's effort in the direction of elucidating relations of complementarity between explanations of gentrification will incite further efforts. But I fail to see how we can progress along this path if we continue to talk in terms of (replacing) centrepieces.

COMPLEMENTARITY

Most encouraging in Hamnett's and Smith's discourse is the common interest in addressing the issue of complementarity in theories of gentrification. It is in this context important to reach clarity concerning what is meant by relation of complementarity, in order to avoid confusion. Problems of misunderstanding may result from using the concept in an unreflected everyday sense of the word, assuming that we of course all know what complementarity means. What I had in mind when I wrote the appeal quoted by Hamnett was the sense of the word expounded by Niels Bohr. The only geographer to my knowledge who has written on Bohr's concept of complementarity is Gunnar Olsson (1980), unfortunately without much apparent impact on his colleagues.

Very briefly, the notion of complementarity says that even if competing theories are mutually exclusive due to incommensurable abstractions, they may both be true and necessary for a thorough description of that which the theories are about. In McKay's words, we are faced with complementary description when 'accounts of the same happening … make different assertions, in terms of different concepts whose preconditions of use are mutually exclusive' (1958, p. 118). Concerning the particle/wave paradox, Bohr wrote that it is a matter of 'complementary aspects in the sense that they account for equally important features of the light phenomena which can never be brought into contradiction with one another, since their closer analysis in mechanical terms demand mutually exclusive experimental arrangements. At the same time, this very situation forces us to renounce on a complete causal account of the light phenomena' (1958, p. 5).

What Bohr brings our attention to is the realization that the only way an observer (including equipment) can be uninvolved is by observing nothing at all. As soon as observation tools are set up on the workbench, the system chosen to put under observation and the measuring instruments for doing the job form one inseparable whole (Holton 1970). To avoid any misunderstanding that this is a problem of mechanical disturbances of the object under study by the instruments and apparatus employed, Bohr explicitly warns that one must distinguish between mechanical disturbances and influences on the very conditions of observation. It is the latter which is the centre of focus in a discussion on the relation of theory to fact – of the instruments and apparatus employed to the observations they yield. The phrase 'instruments and apparatus employed' should not be interpreted literally. As Richards points out, 'The most important of our instruments … are our *concepts*' (1976, p. 112).

Space does not allow for a more thorough presentation of Bohr's notion of complementarity in this context, but I would warn against the hasty conclusion that this is just an easy way out of conflicting thought. One could argue that the easy way out is to cling to the comfort of a one-eyed view held up as the centrepiece of truth (see Koch 1981 for a provocative statement of this position). Progress in thought cannot be obtained without bringing incommensurabilities to the forefront of theoretical analysis. Only in this way, by distilling and juxtaposing the quintessence of different descriptions and explanations, is it possible to determine if 'the traditional path of persistently trying to dissolve them

into each other, or to conquer one by means of the other' stands a reasonable chance of success, or if it is better to accept as a tentative platform for understanding that both provide 'equally valid but complementary pictures' (Holton 1988, p. 4).

The notion of complementarity does not ask us to accept anything and everything with no concern for truth value. It does however ask that we pay attention to the circumstances under which evidence is obtained, and to recognize that accounts of the same phenomenon which make different assertions in terms of different concepts whose preconditions of use are mutually exclusive 'cannot be comprehended within a single picture, but must be regarded as complementary in the sense that only the totality of the phenomena exhausts the possible information about the objects' (Bohr 1958, p. 40). Several explanations may be considered to possess truth value, even though their standpoints of description are founded on less than entirely compatible abstractions.

CONCLUSION

How can Bohr's concept of complementarity inform our continued efforts to research the anatomy of gentrification? Each description and explanation must of course be continuously subjected to critical examination in its own terms and in the light of alternative explanations. Even if some of this examination is done in the specialized manner of neglecting aspects other than the one in focus (critique of an explanation which questions its truth value 'internally' is no less valuable than critique which merely points out neglect of entirely different aspects), we should be careful not to read in claims of monism where there are none. Clarification of the essence of an explanation may to some extent require one-eyed penetration of one aspect, and need not necessitate continuous consideration of other aspects. How are descriptions and explanations of gentrification sensitive to gender aspects to be developed if they are assaulted from the outset for neglecting this and that aspect? Only by refining explanations can they be fruitfully contrasted with alternative accounts in efforts to integrate them or clarify in what ways they are complementary.

Attempts to draw connections between different aspects of gentrification call for ambidexterity in dealing with concepts which may defy reduction to a single model. Sometimes these connections can be made through an integration which practically dissolves any previously perceived mutual exclusion. For instance, rent gap and value gap explanations render themselves to highly harmonious integration (Clark 1991). Commensurability is more descriptive of their relation than is complementarity.[1] Other times integration will not be so neat. Addressing gender aspects of gentrification, for instance, requires an altogether different perspective from that of land rent theory, and though we may speak of integration, it is clear that the same degree of integration as between rent gap and value gap considerations cannot be expected. If (how) they stand in a relation of complementarity is a question which falls outside the scope of this article. To this we may add the post-industrial city perspective, cultural aspects and more. But we should not fool ourselves with appearances of certainty and systematicity in 'integration': 'clarity does not reside in simplification and reduction to a single, directly comprehensible model, but in the exhaustive overlay of different descriptions that incorporate apparently contradictory notions' (Holton 1988, p. 102).

One fundamental characteristic of descriptions in such an overlay is that they will be based on different perceptions with regard to agency and structure. This conflict of truths shines through in the Hamnett-Smith discussion as well as earlier debate on gentrification. The concept of complementarity reminds us that we are both actors and spectators, also in the process of gentrification.

Note

1 A note of self-critique – in Clark (1991) I used the concept complementarity in the everyday sense of the word, as suitable addition contributing towards completeness. As defined here, one could argue that rent gap explanation and value gap explanation are not complementary. They are rather highly meshed and compatible, fitting consistently into a single coherent view. The preconditions of definition, observation and of use of concepts in each are not mutually exclusive. I find some comfort then in Bohr's words, immediately following the introductory quote: 'to such an utterance applies ... the recognition that our task can only be to aim at communicating experiences and views to others by means of language, in which the practical use of every word stands in a complementary relation to attempts of its strict definition' (1948, p. 318).

REFERENCES

BOHR, N. (1948) 'On the notions of causality and complementarity', *Dialectica* 2: 312–19

BOHR, N. (1958) *Atomic physics and human knowledge* (John Wiley & Sons, New York)

CLARK, E. (1987) *The rent gap and urban change: case studies in Malmö 1860–1985* (Lund University Press, Lund)

CLARK, E. (1988) 'The rent gap and transformation of the built environment: case studies in Malmö 1860–1985', *Geografiska Annaler* 70B: 241–54

CLARK, E. (1992) 'On gaps in gentrification theory', *Housing Stud.* 7: 16–26

CLARK, E. and GULLBERG, A. (1991) 'Long swings, rent gaps and structures of building provision – the postwar transformation of Stockholm's inner city', *Int. J. Urb. Reg. Res.* 15: 492–504

HAMNETT, C. (1991) 'The blind men and the elephant: the explanation of gentrification', *Trans. Inst. Br. Geogr.* N.S. 16: 173–89

HAMNETT, C. (1992) 'Gentrifiers or lemmings? A response to Neil Smith', *Trans. Inst. Br. Geogr.* N.S. 17: 116–19

HOLTON, G. (1970) 'The roots of complementarity', *Daedalus* 99: 1015–55

HOLTON, G. (1988) *Thematic origins of scientific thought* (Harvard University Press, Cambridge, Mass.)

KOCH, S. (1981) 'The nature and limits of psychological knowledge: lessons of a century qua "science"', *Amer. Psychologist* 36: 257–69

McKAY, D. (1958) 'Complementarity', *Proc. Aristotelian Soc.* 32: 105–22

OLSSON, G. (1980) *Birds in egg/Eggs in bird* (Pion, London)

RICHARDS, I. (1976) *Complementarities: Uncollected essays* (RUSSO, J. P. ed) (Carcanet, Manchester)

SMITH, N. (1992) 'Blind man's bluff, or, Hamnett's philosophical individualism in search of gentrification', *Trans. Inst. Br. Geogr.* N.S. 17: 110–15

SECTION D

Gentrification and gender, sexuality, race/ethnicity

of the patriarchal household" was too simple an explanation; instead, she called for an approach that considers how gentrification contributes to reworkings of gender divisions across different structures of patriarchy. Finally, at the time Bondi felt that the overheated tensions between production and consumption explanations (see Section C) were best addressed by research that explored the gender ideologies of estate agents, developers, architects, lending agencies and so on (the production side), as well as direct consumers of housing (the consumption side), including those negatively affected by the process.

SEXUALITY

[A] place that welcomes the gay community welcomes all kinds of people ... [G]ays can be said to be the 'canaries of the Creative Age.' For these reasons, openness to the gay community is a good indicator of the low entry barriers to human capital that are so important to spurring creativity and generating high-tech growth.

(Florida, 2003, p. 256)

The presence of a sizeable gay population in economically thriving urban neighbourhoods has recently become a high-profile urban policy issue in North America, attributable to the significant influence of Richard Florida's (2003) creative class thesis in policy circles (the above quotation captures the link he makes between gays and 'creative' cities). Florida in fact puts a positive twist on a body of scholarship that has explored the role of sexuality in the process of gentrification (a term that Florida tends to avoid!). Probably the most famous study is Manuel Castells' (1983) account of the formation of the gay community in The Castro neighbourhood of San Francisco. Castells pointed out that it was the spatial concentration of gays which made it possible for the gay liberation movement in that city (and elsewhere) to gain momentum. This spatial concentration was instrumental to gentrification, because of a demographic cohort described by Castells as follows:

many were single men, did not have to sustain a family, were young, and connected to a relatively prosperous service economy ... [which] made it easier for them to find a house in a tight housing market.

(p. 160)

Mickey Lauria and Larry Knopp, whose landmark article we have included in this Section, amplify this point:

[B]eing a gay male in this society is economically advantageous. Males make more money than their female counterparts in every sector of the economy, and gay males tend to have fewer dependents than straight men. This means that many gay men are in an excellent position to become gentrifiers.

(p. 161)

Demographics aside, however, what is particularly striking about studies of sexuality and gentrification is that contradictory, ambivalent spaces are formed as a consequence. As Lauria and Knopp point out, gay space is vital to an oppressed group seeking liberation, but gay gentrification can oppress other marginal groups via displacement. So, while gay gentrification might be explained, in Lauria and Knopp's (1985) words, by "the need to escape to an oasis of tolerance ... an opportunity to combat oppression by creating neighbourhoods over which they [gays] have maximum control" (p. 161), it can lead to another form of oppression – the displacement of low-income minorities and/or the working class in adjacent neighbourhoods. As is usually the case with gentrification, surface appearances (beautiful Victorian buildings and famous gay neighbourhoods, now often tourist attractions) mask underlying injustices and tensions.

RACE/ETHNICITY

The stereotypical image most people have of gentrifiers in the US is of white 'yuppies' moving into low-income neighbourhoods with dense concentrations of ethnic minorities, as our cover image shows well.

SECTION D

Gentrification and gender, sexuality, race/ethnicity

Plate 15 (a) **Harlem.** Photograph by Elvin Wyly. (b) **SoHa, gentrifying South of Harlem.** Photograph by Elvin Wyly.

INTRODUCTION TO SECTION D

That gentrification is fundamentally a process of class transformation is almost beyond question. In a literature characterised by political/analytical disagreement and theoretical tension, the centrality of class to the process is a rare point of common ground. This is not to say, however, that class is the only axis of difference towards which researchers have focused their attention. Since the early 1980s, coinciding somewhat with the advent of both postmodernism and the cultural turn in the social sciences, considerable analytical energy has been expended towards the intersections of fine-grained class positions with other dimensions of difference, such as gender, sexuality, and race/ethnicity. In this section, we have selected four important readings that demonstrate how the neighbourhood expression of class inequality – gentrification – creates urban arenas where space is reconfigured and contested along intersecting axes of social difference: gender, sexuality, and race/ethnicity.

GENDER

In the early 1980s it was recognised that, through increasing participation in the labour force, women were playing an active and important role in bringing about gentrification (Holcomb and Beauregard, 1981). It was Ann Markusen (1981) who explained this most clearly:

> [G]entrification is in large part a result of the breakdown of the patriarchal household. Households of gay people, singles, and professional couples with central business district jobs increasingly find central locations attractive. … Gentrification. … corresponds to the two-income (or more) professional household that requires both a relatively central urban location to minimize journey-to-work costs of several wage earners and a location that enhances efficiency in household production (stores are nearer) and in the substitution of market-produced commodities (laundries, restaurants, child care) for household production.
>
> (p. 32)

Markusen's observations led to a path-breaking article published in 1984 by Damaris Rose, which we introduced in the previous section.

As the literature on gender and gentrification grew, it became characterised by research that treated gender as an individual attribute and class as a social relation in the context of the gentrifying household. For Liz Bondi, in her important 1991 article we have selected here, this dichotomy was unhelpful, especially as gender should also be understood as a social relation. She also pointed out that even those few studies that did treat gender as a social relation tended to prioritise economic factors without considering how "changes in the sexual division of labour in the workplace, the community and the home …. are negotiated through cultural constructions of femininity and masculinity" (p. 195) – and how gender positions are expressed and forged through gentrification. Recognising that "women are involved in or affected by gentrification in different ways" (p. 192), Bondi made a powerful argument for considering the relationship between class and gender (not letting the former sideline the latter) when interpreting gentrification. Marginal middle-class women have profoundly different experiences of gentrification than working-class women. In addition, Bondi felt that Markusen's earlier view that gentrification is a "result of the breakdown of the patriarchal household" was too simple an explanation; instead, she called for an approach that considers how gentrification contributes to reworkings of gender divisions across different structures of patriarchy. Finally, at the time Bondi felt that the overheated tensions between production and consumption explanations (see Section C) were best addressed by research that explored the gender ideologies of estate agents, developers, architects, lending agencies and so on (the production side), as well as direct consumers of housing (the consumption side), including those negatively affected by the process.

SEXUALITY

[A] place that welcomes the gay community welcomes all kinds of people ... [G]ays can be said to be the 'canaries of the Creative Age.' For these reasons, openness to the gay community is a good indicator of the low entry barriers to human capital that are so important to spurring creativity and generating high-tech growth.

(Florida, 2003, p. 256)

The presence of a sizeable gay population in economically thriving urban neighbourhoods has recently become a high-profile urban policy issue in North America, attributable to the significant influence of Richard Florida's (2003) creative class thesis in policy circles (the above quotation captures the link he makes between gays and 'creative' cities). Florida in fact puts a positive twist on a body of scholarship that has explored the role of sexuality in the process of gentrification (a term that Florida tends to avoid!). Probably the most famous study is Manuel Castells' (1983) account of the formation of the gay community in The Castro neighbourhood of San Francisco. Castells pointed out that it was the spatial concentration of gays which made it possible for the gay liberation movement in that city (and elsewhere) to gain momentum. This spatial concentration was instrumental to gentrification, because of a demographic cohort described by Castells as follows:

many were single men, did not have to sustain a family, were young, and connected to a relatively prosperous service economy ... [which] made it easier for them to find a house in a tight housing market.

(p. 160)

Mickey Lauria and Larry Knopp, whose landmark article we have included in this Section, amplify this point:

[B]eing a gay male in this society is economically advantageous. Males make more money than their female counterparts in every sector of the economy, and gay males tend to have fewer dependents than straight men. This means that many gay men are in an excellent position to become gentrifiers.

(p. 161)

Demographics aside, however, what is particularly striking about studies of sexuality and gentrification is that contradictory, ambivalent spaces are formed as a consequence. As Lauria and Knopp point out, gay space is vital to an oppressed group seeking liberation, but gay gentrification can oppress other marginal groups via displacement. So, while gay gentrification might be explained, in Lauria and Knopp's (1985) words, by "the need to escape to an oasis of tolerance ... an opportunity to combat oppression by creating neighbourhoods over which they [gays] have maximum control" (p. 161), it can lead to another form of oppression – the displacement of low-income minorities and/or the working class in adjacent neighbourhoods. As is usually the case with gentrification, surface appearances (beautiful Victorian buildings and famous gay neighbourhoods, now often tourist attractions) mask underlying injustices and tensions.

RACE/ETHNICITY

The stereotypical image most people have of gentrifiers in the US is of white 'yuppies' moving into low-income neighbourhoods with dense concentrations of ethnic minorities, as our cover image shows well.

This perspective though is partial as it neglects the phenomenon of black gentrification. The rise of the black middle class has also created a large cohort of households with almost precisely the same educational, occupational, and income characteristics as white gentrifiers. In recent years, some of the most striking scholarship on gentrification has looked at the complex entanglements of race and class in changing urban settings. Harlem in New York City is doubtless the most famous African-American neighbourhood in the United States. So devastated was Harlem by post-WWII disinvestment that a ripple of astonishment was felt when Richard Schaffer and Neil Smith (1986) pointed to it as a candidate for gentrification, albeit with a question mark. A key finding was as follows:

> At present it is clear that despite prominent press reports featuring individual white gentrifiers in Harlem ... the vast majority of people involved in rehabilitation and redevelopment in Central Harlem are black.
>
> (p. 358)

Monique Taylor, a graduate student when Schaffer and Smith's article was published, decided to research the emerging black middle-class in Harlem from 1987 to 1992, and found that gentrifiers were "strongly motivated by a desire to participate in the rituals that define daily life in this (in)famous and historically black community" (p. 102). Taylor found black gentrifiers confronting what she called a "dilemma of difference" during their transition from outsider to insider in a place where their class position and lifestyle was so distinct from other lower income blacks, but also when constructing a black identity distinct from the white world of the workplace (this is also memorably depicted in a Spike Lee film, *Jungle Fever*). Economic factors are not ignored in this study, but for Taylor, black gentrification was also "a strategy of cultural survival rooted in the search for the positive meaning and support that the black community might provide" (p. 109). Homeowners in Harlem were seen to be bridging the dual worlds of race and class that they were defined by – the difference of race defined their marginal status in the workplace, but the difference of class defined their "outsiderness" in Harlem. The black middle class paved the way for accelerated gentrification by the wealthier, white middle-class that followed, making the words of Schaffer and Smith (1986) very prescient:

> The inescapable conclusion is that unless Harlem defies all the empirical trends, the process might well begin as black gentrification, but any wholesale rehabilitation of Central Harlem would necessarily involve a considerable influx of middle- and upper-class whites.
>
> (p. 359)

The final article we have included in this section, by Caitlin Cahill, is an impressive recent attempt to explore the interplay of race, class and gender (and age) in the infamous Lower East Side of New York City. Drawn from a participatory action research project with six young working-class, non-white women (aged 16–22) who grew up in that neighbourhood, Cahill's article is anchored by the hitherto unexplored question: "What does it mean to grow up in a neighbourhood as it is transformed physically, culturally, economically, and socially?" (p. 204). Particularly striking about this study is not just the empowerment of marginal young women of colour via the research process; it is also Cahill's observations that (a) displacement can be cultural (what it means to witness the transformation of one's neighbourhood) as well as residential, and (b) that people can be subject to systematic disinvestment, not just places. Cahill's conclusion that the women are ambivalent about their neighbourhood might seem surprising, but all their lives they have had to "negotiate" local grit (disinvestment) and local glamour (reinvestment); they are torn between "sticking it out" or "leaving", both of which could be interpreted as sell out or success. Cahill's article is a lesson for understanding how a class-based process involves more than just class politics.

REFERENCES AND FURTHER READING

Bondi, L. (1999) 'Gender, class and gentrification: enriching the debate', *Environment and Planning D: Society and Space* 17(3): 261–282.

Bostic, R. and Martin, R. (2003) 'Black homeowners as a gentrifying force? Neighborhood dynamics in the context of minority home-ownership', *Urban Studies* 40(12): 2427–2449.

Castells, M. (1983) *The City and the Grassroots: A Cross-Cultural Theory of Urban Social Movements*, Berkeley: University of California Press.

Florida, R. (2003) *The Rise of the Creative Class*, New York: Basic Books.

Freeman, L. (2006) *There Goes the Hood: Views of Gentrification from the Ground Up*, Philadelphia: Temple University Press.

Holcomb, H.B. and Beauregard, R.A. (1981) *Revitalizing Cities*, Washington, D.C.: Association of American Geographers.

Knopp, L. (1997) 'Gentrification and gay neighborhood formation in New Orleans: a case study', in A. Gluckman and B. Reed (eds) *Homo Economics: Capitalism, Community, Lesbian and Gay Life* pp. 45–63. London and New York: Routledge.

Markusen, A. (1981) 'City spatial structure, women's household work and national urban policy', *Signs: Journal of Women in Culture and Society* 5(3): 23–44.

Rose, D. (1989) 'A feminist perspective of employment restructuring and gentrification: the case of Montreal' in J. Wolch and M. Dear (eds) *The Power of Geography: How Territory Shapes Social Life* pp. 118–138. Boston: Unwin Hyman.

Rose, D. (1984) 'Rethinking gentrification: beyond the uneven development of Marxist urban theory', *Environment and Planning D: Society and Space* 1: 47–74.

Rothenberg, T. (1995) '"And she told two friends": lesbians creating urban social space', in D. Bell and G. Valentine (eds) *Mapping Desire: Geographies of Sexualities* pp. 165–181. London: Routledge.

Taylor, M. (2003) *Harlem: Between Heaven and Hell*, Minneapolis: University of Minnesota Press.

Shaw, W. (2000) 'Ways of whiteness: Harlemising Sydney's aboriginal Redfern', *Australian Geographical Studies* 38(3): 291–305.

Schaffer, R. and Smith, N. (1986) 'The gentrification of Harlem?', *Annals of the Association of American Geographers* 76: 347–365.

21

"Gender Divisions and Gentrification: A Critique"

From *Transactions of the Institute of British Geographers* (1991)

Liz Bondi

In the wide-ranging debate on gentrification, changes in the role of women have received increasingly frequent mention as possible explanatory factors. For example, Beauregard (1986, p. 43) draws attention to the importance of 'a trend toward the postponement of marriage and childbearing', while Markusen (1981, p. 32) cites 'the success of both gays and women in the professional and managerial classes in gaining access to decent-paying jobs'. These references might be symptomatic of the success of feminist geographers in establishing the importance of gender issues, but, as Smith (1987, p. 156) notes, the association between women and gentrification 'has remained a general affirmation with little documentation of actual trends'. Moreover, little attempt has been made to locate the role of women in gentrification within broader discussions of gender relations, although it is clearly assumed that changes in the position of women, both in the family and in the paid labour force, have been influential. This article addresses this lacuna and examines how the question of the relationship between gender and gentrification might be conceptualized. The intention is to scrutinize the theoretical bases of existing studies and thereby to open up possibilities for future research more sensitive to gender issues.

Gentrification, in its varied forms, provides graphic illustrations of the connections between production and consumption, between structure and agency, and between economy and culture. Consequently, the phenomenon has provided fertile ground for attempts to engage with, transform, and move beyond these deep-seated conceptual dichotomies. But, I argue in this article that a refusal to consider the centrality and complexity of gender repeatedly undermines these efforts. In the first section I examine empirical evidence about women and gentrification, which clearly traverses the dichotomy between production and consumption. However, locating this evidence theoretically, in section two I argue that most studies treat gender in a way that conflates structure and agency and that sets up an unhelpful dichotomy between gender as an individual attribute and class as a social relation. Further, as I show in section three, those few studies that treat gender as a social relation implicitly prioritize economy over culture, while studies concerned with the interplay between culture and economy fail to question cultural assumptions about gender. In conclusion I call for an approach that explores how women and men negotiate definitions of themselves through the processes of gentrification, in the context of complex and multi-faceted power structures and social practices.

WOMEN AND GENTRIFICATION

Gentrification illustrates the importance of both processes of production and profit-making on the one hand, and processes of consumption and 'lifestyle choice' on the other. Further, although sometimes described as signalling an 'urban renaissance', or as 'urban revitalization', gentrification is better regarded as double-edged: neighbourhoods that become subject to gentrification are not necessarily 'de-vitalized and culturally moribund'; rather gentrification often destroys what were previously 'very vital working-class communities' (Smith, 1982, p. 139). Thus, profit-making for some is impoverishment for others; the 'lifestyle choices' of some deny those of others.

References to the role of women in gentrification point principally to their prominence as members of groups fuelling demand for gentrified housing. However, discussions of marginalization and urban poverty suggest that women are also prominent among those vulnerable to displacement as a result of gentrification. Two sets of processes, relating to economic change and demographic change, and linking issues of production and consumption, are often cited to explain the presence of women on both sides of the gentrification process.

Economic change

It is widely suggested that gentrification has been stimulated by the increased participation of women (especially married women) in the labour force (Rose, 1984; Ley, 1986; Smith, 1987; Short, 1989). Of particular significance is the increasing success of middle-class women in obtaining well-paid, career jobs: women drawn from particular social groups are claimed to be swelling the ranks of the 'yuppies' (Wekerle, 1984; Short, 1989). Although overall occupational segregation remains marked and the wages gap shows little sign of closing (Beechey, 1986; Walby, 1989), improvements in the position of women within segments of some local labour markets do appear to be creating more relatively affluent households, whether consisting of single women, married or cohabiting couples. This in turn has stimulated demand for expensive private housing, as changes in the structure of employment generate changes in patterns of consumption. Some empirical evidence is provided by Smith (1987) in the context of commercially-led gentrification of neighbourhoods in New York, while Rose (1984) suggests that a more marginal and less profitable form of gentrification is being stimulated by first-time buyers on moderate incomes, employed in city centres, typically in service sector industries. This group, which includes lone women and households headed by women, takes advantage of relatively cheap property and upgrades it themselves. Supporting evidence is provided for Montreal (Rose and Le Bourdais, 1986; Rose, 1989; see also Ley, 1986).

This economic account is often linked to a claim that women prefer central residential locations to suburban living, a preference sometimes claimed of all women, and sometimes only of the well-off and childless or those in non-traditional households

(Holcomb, 1984; Wekerle, 1985; Rose, 1989). Some, albeit rather mixed, empirical evidence is available from attitudinal surveys (for example Saegert, 1981; Wekerle, 1984; Fava, 1985). However, the question remains as to why women's preferences should so recently have gained expression. Implicit in such accounts is an hypothesis to the effect that the increasing participation of women in career-oriented labour markets is giving women greater economic leverage and, therefore, greater influence in decision-making within households.

In terms of the impact of gentrification, women also appear to be prominent among the economically weakest sectors of the urban population who are most vulnerable to displacement. Certainly, the increase in female participation rates since the 1950s has been associated principally with a move into low paid, insecure jobs (Beechey, 1986). At the same time, the labour market itself has become more polarized so that the growing affluence among women entering professional and managerial occupations is counterbalanced by the growing impoverishment of women at the opposite end of the labour market (Pahl, 1988). Thus, gentrification highlights the potential for conflict between the consumption choices of the former and the consumption opportunities of the latter.

Demographic change

Changes in the position of women in the labour market are closely related to changes in the position of women in the family and again illustrate the interconnections between processes of production and consumption. Demographic accounts of the role of women in gentrification take two basic forms. First, it is suggested that gentrification is the result of an increase in the number of households in many Western societies, which is accounted for, in a large part, by an increase in the number of women living alone. Important factors here include the increasing number and independence of the elderly, among whom women predominate; the increased rate of divorce; and the rising average age of marriage. Thus, there are increasing numbers of households consisting of women who are elderly and widowed, divorced, or young and not (yet) married. The last category has itself been enlarged by the arrival at adulthood (or, more precisely, at house-purchasing age) of the post-war baby-boom generation. These trends contribute to an increase in the total demand for housing units and the potential profitability of the housing market. A number of case studies have reported a high proportion of young, single women moving into gentrifying areas (Rose, 1984; Smith, 1987; Mills, 1988). Women living alone, especially the elderly, and lone parent households headed by divorced women are also likely to be numerous among those liable to displacement (Holcomb, 1986; Morrow Jones, 1986; Walker, 1987; Winchester and White, 1988).

The second form of demographic explanation emphasizes the changing character of family units, in particular the postponement of childbearing, decreased completed family size and closer spacing of children (Martin and Roberts, 1984). Most marked among women of higher social class (Werner, 1985), these trends combine with changes in women's employment to create more small, affluent households capable of paying high prices for sought-after housing. Moreover, these households benefit more from the reduction in commuting costs associated with inner-urban residential locations than do those with only one adult working in the city centre. In some areas, a similar demand is generated by dual-career gay households (Markusen, 1981; Lauria and Knopp, 1985). Conversely, marital breakdown and lone parenthood combine with a weak labour market position to fuel the feminization of poverty and the prominence of women among those liable to displacement (Millar and Glendinning, 1987; McLanahan *et al.*, 1989; Winchester, 1990). Overall, drawing together the fragmentary evidence now available, it is apparent that women's experience of gentrification is deeply divided and that the associated social polarization may be even more marked among women than men. It is also evident that in different cities and different parts of cities, women are involved in or affected by gentrification in different ways.

GENDER CATEGORIES AND CLASS RELATIONS

The preceding section provides an apparently straightforward account of the presence of women among the beneficiaries and the victims of gentrification. It highlights the interconnections between production and consumption, and can be used to demonstrate the inherently divisive character of gentrification. However, appeals to both economic and demographic factors are embedded in theorizations of gentrification that continue to be contentious and problematic.

The debate between accounts of gentrification that focus on factors relating to housing supply, and those in which factors relating to the demand for gentrified housing are stressed, is often characterized

in terms of a dichotomy between structuralism and voluntarism (Rose, 1984; Smith and Williams, 1986; Munt, 1987). Recent studies have attempted to transcend the structure – agency dichotomy by interpreting gentrification as 'class constitution', that is, as a process through which changes in the structure of capitalism, in class relations, and in class identities, are inscribed on the built environment. In this section I show how references to the role of women are subsumed within a class framework, and how the neglect of gender as a social relation confounds attempts to resolve the tension between structuralism and voluntarism.

Crompton (1986, p. 133) has argued that many women with husbands in service class jobs are effectively 'incorporated into their husbands' work via the "two-person career"', in which domestic and other unpaid labour provided by the wife is crucial to the husband's advancement. This represents an extreme form of the asymmetrical household, and is typically associated with suburban, nuclear family living (McDowell, 1983; Mackenzie and Rose, 1983). The gentrification literature emphasizes a very different pattern, in which part of the lifestyle choice concerns changes in the position of women in both the labour market and the family that lead to a more symmetrical household form (Rose, 1984; Beauregard, 1986). Occupational position is accorded a key role in these accounts: it is suggested that women are themselves gaining entry to new middle-class (especially professional) occupations, and are increasing their scope for career progression by postponing childbearing, by having smaller families and by making extensive use of their ability to pay for childcare (Lowe and Gregson, 1989). This implies that women are prominent among gentrifiers because they are moving into new class positions in their own right, rather than merely as wives within households headed by men in the appropriate occupations. It can also be argued that women are prominent among the victims of gentrification because changes in both urban labour markets and the family are resulting in many other women moving into very different class (or underclass) positions, again in their own right, rather than because of the position of their menfolk.

This interpetation is problematical for two reasons. First, it ignores the difficulties of positioning women within existing definitions of class, and the related problem of how the occupational positions of individuals within households interact in the determination of class positions and class identities (Heath and Britten, 1984; Murgatroyd, 1984; Crompton and Mann, 1986; Walby, 1986; Abbott and Sapsford, 1987; Wright, 1989).

Secondly, despite references to women, it ignores gender in the sense of a socially constructed form of differentiation: gender is treated as an individual attribute in contrast to conceptualizations of class as relational (Christopherson, 1989; Johnson, 1989). Whereas the former difficulty calls into question conceptualizations of class (see Bondi, 1990), the latter calls into question the theoretical primacy of class.

To elaborate, as a process of class constitution, gentrification entails the differentiation of a new, urban middle-class from other elements of the middle-class engaged in suburban or ex-urban residential strategies (Thrift, 1987; Mills, 1988), from the previous inhabitants of the urban environments that are colonized (Jager, 1986; Williams, 1986), as well as from contemporary working-class or underclass neighbours (Smith, 1987). Whatever emphasis is placed on the cultural construction of class identity, as opposed to economic relations, these studies rely upon relational conceptualizations of class: class constitution can only be understood in terms of relative positions and must articulate in some way, however attenuated, with the social relations of late twentieth-century capitalism.

In contrast, the designations 'woman' and 'man' are used to describe apparently unchanging attributes of individuals who are being inserted in new ways within a dynamic, relational class structure. The roles of people who are women and men may change, but there is little sense that what gender difference means, or the structure of gender relations, might be changing. Thus, whereas class is constituted through the mediation of structure and agency, gender is treated as fixed, as something that attaches to class agents to render them 'concrete' rather than 'abstract' (cf. Acker, 1989). This has contradictory implications. On the one hand being a woman or a man appears to be unambiguously determined (whether by biology or socialization) and therefore immune from the creative action of human agents. Warde (1989, p. 7) describes one aspect of this process as 'the extended gooseberry bush theory of biological reproduction – that is people discover children under gooseberry bushes at unpredictable intervals and, when they do, are obliged to become women and rear them'.

On the other hand, being a woman or a man becomes a behavioural attribute through which choices that influence the processes of class constitution are classified. In this sense gender is treated as superstructural rather than structural, operating only to 'enliven' the structure of class relations (Johnson, 1989). Consequently 'women' and 'men' become static categories immune from both structural forces and human agency.

The treatment of gender as an individual attribute goes some way to explaining the 'chaotic' character of gentrification: that the diverse consumption practices of the new urban middle-class continue to elude coherent theorization may be a consequence of this habit of treating gender as a category rather than as a dynamic social phenomenon. By subsuming gender entirely within class processes, one potential source of differentiation is obscured, and by denying gender as a site for the mediation of structure and agency, the debate between demand-side and supply-side accounts is confounded. Moreover, treating gender as an individual attribute limits it to a binary opposition, thereby masking an important source of diversity associated with the complex and varied processes of gentrification.

GENDER, ECONOMY AND CULTURE

I have argued for a shift of focus from the role of women to consideration of gender as a social relation. Clearly, gentrification does not express a straightforward reworking of gender differentiation since women's (and men's) experience of gentrification is deeply divided by class. But neither can it be interpreted as a straightforward reworking of class differentiation since class experience is clearly divided by gender. The notion of class constitution suggests that people are never the passive bearers of class interests, but that class identities are subject to constant negotiation and renegotiation through social practices that express the mediation between structure and agency. That masculinity is deeply embedded in the creation of working-class identity has been graphically illustrated by Willis (1978), and historical analyses point to gender inequality as well as particular versions of masculinity and femininity as 'core ingredient[s] of class formation and consciousness' (Hart, 1989, p. 21; see also Davidoff and Hall, 1987; Phillips, 1987). Thus, gender constitution is inextricably bound up with class constitution.

This section is concerned with the elaboration of such a perspective in the context of gentrification. First, I argue that where gender has been accorded centrality, a more nuanced notion of gender identities is still required. Secondly, I suggest that although studies of gentrification as cultural production pay insufficient attention to gender, they open up possibilities for exploring contemporary changes in the representation and negotiation of gender identities.

Gentrification as gender constitution

That gentrification might entail a process of gender constitution as well as class constitution has been raised by a few commentators. Smith (1987, p. 164) hints at this possibility when he points to the need

> to explain why the gradual quantitative increase in the proportion of women working and women in higher income brackets translates into substantial spatial change of domicile. After all, married women were in the official work force before World War 2, albeit in smaller numbers, and some of these were in relatively well-paying professional positions, yet no gentrification process seems to have blunted the suburban flight of the time. How could such a comparatively quick spatial reversal be explained by more gradual social changes alone?

However, Smith's (1987, p. 165) continued insistence on the rent-gap as 'the necessary centrepiece of any theory of gentrification' serves as a foil against opening up questions of gender practices: he prioritizes abstract economic processes over the cultural conditions of their operation.

Elsewhere, feminist geographers have demonstrated a close connection between the restructuring of urban space and changing definitions of gender identity and gender difference. For example, the separation of home and workplace, precipitated by the advent of factory production, became a key factor in the subsequent emergence of a distinctively female domestic realm (McDowell, 1983; Mackenzie and Rose, 1983; Davidoff and Hall, 1987). Mackenzie (1988) has developed these insights in the context of Canadian urban development to suggest that periods in which concern about urban living is prominent coincide with, and are causally related to, the rise of feminism as a popular movement. Thus, in both the late nineteenth century and the late twentieth century changing patterns of production and reproduction have caused women and men to adjust their uses of space and time such that 'the process of gender constitution and the process of constituting urban environments are inextricably linked' (Mackenzie, 1988, p. 27). Echoing Harvey's (1982) notion of a 'restless landscape', in which the built environment inscribes a resolution to one crisis of accumulation only to become an obstacle inhibiting the efficiency of further capital accumulation, Mackenzie argues that each spatial solution to the 'woman question' becomes a legacy that generates new tensions in the organization of production and reproduction. In the contemporary period, this tension is evident in a lack of 'fit' between urban structure and gender divisions of labour. Urban planning, with its historical and continuing commitment to a strict separation of residential and non-residential land-uses militates against the efforts of women to combine raising a family with paid employment (Lewis and Foord, 1984; Tivers, 1985). Thus, ideas about gender difference embodied in the built environment are increasingly in conflict with the gender practices of its inhabitants.

That gentrification might be a response to this conflict is considered by Warde (1989, p. 7–8) who argues that gentrification 'can more easily be seen as [a way] in which women reorient their behaviour to domestic and labour market pressures than as class solutions to the problems of everyday life'. He suggests that different forms of gentrification express strategies adopted by career-oriented, middle-class women at different stages of the life-cycle, associating commercially-led gentrification with highly affluent, dual-career households containing childless women, and the investment of 'sweat equity' to upgrade single properties with family households, including a high proportion headed by lone women. This account draws on evidence of changes in the position of women in the family and the labour force to suggest that there are different ways of being women, different versions of femininity (and masculinity), not merely different class positions for women, and that these should be understood in terms of patriarchal gender relations rather than class constitution. However, this account is flawed by an implicit separation between employment as a site of class relations and the household as a site of gender relations (see Walby, 1989). Thus, gender appears to be negotiated around consumption while production remains the domain of class. Similarly, Markusen's (1981, p. 32) claim that 'gentrification is in a large part a result of the breakdown of the patriarchal household' is less potent than sometimes suggested: as Connell (1987) and Walby (1989) observe, the erosion of male authority within households does not necessarily herald a profound shift in power relations between women and men.

Rose (1989) employs a more wide-ranging concept of gender, stressing in particular the importance of gender relations in the restructuring of employment, and illustrating Johnson's (1989, p. 682) claim that 'class relations and our experiences of them are *predicated* on gender differentiation and inequality'. Her study also draws attention to the significance of gender within property relations (also see Madigan *et al.*, 1991) and to non-commodified elements of the reproduction of the workforce (including most childcare). She suggests that

> the residential preferences of some types of non-traditional households for inner-city neighborhoods may in part be explained by the following factors: these milieux enable a diversification of ways of carrying out reproductive work; they offer a concentration of supportive services; and they often have a 'tolerant' ambience.
>
> (Rose, 1989, p. 131)

However, although Rose footnotes her first-hand experience of living in a gentrifying neighbourhood, the gender practices to which she refers remain something of a 'black box'. Her analysis treats gender relations as primarily economic: gentrification is attributed to changes in the sexual division of labour in the workplace, the community and the home. But how such changes are negotiated through cultural constructions of femininity and masculinity is not examined.

Gentrification as cultural production

Smith (1990, p. 20) asserts that 'an understanding of gentrification begins and ends in the real estate market', but no longer claims that the real estate market is itself to be explained simply in terms of a rent-gap (Smith, 1979). Instead he draws out the interconnections between profit-making and cultural production. Although theorized in different ways, some formulations more idealist (e.g. Ley, 1987; Mills, 1988; Caulfield, 1989), others more materialist (e.g. Smith, 1987; 1990; Zukin, 1988), this inherently problematic nexus of culture and economy is a recurrent theme in recent contributions to the gentrification debate. It is in part through an insistence on culture as a domain in which class conflict is worked through, made sense of, but never resolved, that these analyses avoid reducing the built environment to a direct expression of social relations. But, even where gender is considered as a social relation, its cultural construction is ignored. Thus, while Smith (1987), Mills (1988) and Rose (1989) suggest that gentrification signals a relaxation of the conventional binary opposition between masculine and feminine, the cultural production of alternatives remains undocumented.

In practice, representations of masculinity and femininity are implicit in many accounts of the cultural meanings of gentrification. For example the reworking of a frontier mythology of the nineteenth century American west in the gentrification of New York's Lower East Side explored by Smith (1986; 1990), casts the urban pioneer as a hero whose heterosexual masculinity can scarcely be in doubt. While Smith is concerned with the way this imagery legitimates and sharpens class conflict, Caulfield (1989) points towards a psychoanalytic reading of this urban frontier rather more sympathetic to the gentrifiers. However, a Freudian, masculine subjectivity stalks his appeal to the desires of gentrifiers and to the city as 'the place of our encounter with the other' (Caulfield, 1989, p. 625, citing Barthes, 1986, p. 96): sexuality lies at its core and the lack of reference to the city as a place of sexual threat rather than erotic possibility implies a masculine speaking position. By implication, that which is encountered, whether viewed as an urban wilderness or as an eroticized 'other', is feminine. The highly polarized representations of masculinity and femininity embedded within these accounts (active/passive; known/unknown; self/other; civilized/untamed) sit uneasily with claims that gentrification entails a 'loosening of ... sexual apartheid' (Smith, 1987).

Feminist interventions in geography have generally been at pains to counter inaccurate stereotypes of women, with which such representations are associated, with accounts of the reality of women's lives. But, dispelling mythical and oppressive images does not mean living without any representations of women. Rather, as Williamson (1987, p. 25) argues, the aim of feminism is not

> to 'get rid of symbols'. It takes only the most elementary understanding of social communications to realize that you couldn't 'throw away' symbols even if you wanted to, and the whole direction of recent feminist thought has been increasingly to intervene and try to change symbols, to engage in struggle within the symbolic, and precisely to understand how our bodies and our images are used in a network of social meanings.

From this perspective, the problem of accounts such as those of Smith and Caulfield is, first, that alternative readings of the imagery and symbolism they discuss have been silenced, and, secondly, that how women and men involved in gentrification variously draw on, deal with, resist and contest the gender codings implicit in these meaning systems is ignored. And this is crucial to understand how people make sense of the processes of urban change in which they participate.

CONCLUSION

That women number among both the agents and the 'victims' of gentrification is not in doubt. However, in this article I have argued that the full import of existing empirical evidence has not been realized because of the inadequate conceptual frameworks within which they have been interpreted. To conclude, I draw out three issues for future research.

First, while gender has too frequently been marginalized by a preoccupation with class, my intention is not to advocate a re-ordering of explanatory concepts. Rather, the relationship between class and gender, and to this 'race' and ethnicity should be added, must be explored. This means developing interpretations of gentrification sensitive to what Ramazanoglu (1989) describes as 'the contradictions of oppression', highlighted, for example, by women's deeply divided experiences of contemporary urban change. Such interpretations would draw out the rich, dynamic complexity of familiar social categories. They would necessarily be specific to specific places: gentrification takes different forms in different cities and within single cities, and it has not proved possible to identify general over-arching processes. While comparative studies might assist in specifying the conditions under which particular processes dominate, local case studies that examine more closely not only which individuals are involved but how their class, gender, 'racial' and ethnic positions are expressed and forged though gentrification are also needed.

Secondly, gentrification has provoked intense interest partly because it makes visible the creation and constitution of distinctive social groups. In this context I have argued that gender, like class, should be understood as a social relation, rather than as an individual attribute, and that gender is not confined to a limited set of social practices but permeates all spheres of human life. Consequently, instead of asking whether gentrification signals a shift in the power relations between women and men, it is more appropriate to consider how gentrification contributes to reworkings of gender divisions across what Walby (1989) terms different 'structures of patriarchy'. This means investigating gentrification contextually and historically in relation to different facets of gender divisions, adding new dimensions to local narratives concerned with class relations and sometimes with 'race', racism and ethnicity.

Thirdly, I have criticized studies that equate gender relations with gender divisions of labour, suggesting instead that there is a profound tension between what women and men do, and what femininities and masculinities mean. This points to the importance of examining how ideas about class and gender, again, to which 'race' and ethnicity should be added, are negotiated through the social practices of gentrification. And this entails exploring the gender ideologies of all those involved in gentrification, including estate agents, developers, architects, lending agencies and so on, as well as direct consumers of housing, including those negatively affected by gentrification.

The linkages between urban change and the constitution of gender remain weakly elaborated for the contemporary period. With the benefit of hindsight dominant versions of femininity and masculinity may be identified, and their relationship to the organization of production and reproduction explained. In the present such patterning is harder to detect; indeed there may be more chaos than order. However, the present provides unique opportunities to investigate how women and men interpret themselves (ourselves) and their (our) environments.

ACKNOWLEDGEMENTS

Thanks to Neil Smith and to an anonymous referee for their comments on a previous incarnation of this article. Thanks to Jan Penrose for her comments on later drafts.

REFERENCES

ABBOTT, P. and SAPSFORD, R. (1987) *Women and social class* (Tavistock, London)

ACKER, J. (1989) 'Making gender visible', in WALLACE, R. (ed.) *Feminism and sociological theory* (Sage, California)

BARTHES, R. (1986) 'Semiology and the urban', in GOTTDIENER, M. and LAGOPOULOS, A. Ph. (eds) *The city and the sign* (Columbia University Press, New York)

BEAUREGARD, R. A. (1986) 'The chaos and complexity of gentrification' in SMITH, N. and WILLIAMS, P. (eds) *Gentrification of the city* (Allen and Unwin, Boston)

BEECHEY, V. (1986) 'Women's employment in contemporary Britain' in BEECHEY, V. and WHITELEGG, E. (eds) *Women in Britain today* (Open University Press, Milton Keynes)

BONDI, L. (1990) 'Women, gender relations and the "inner city"', in KEITH, M. and ROGERS, A. (eds) *Policy, theory and practice in the inner city* (Mansell, London)

CAULFIELD, J. (1989) '"Gentrification" and desire', *Canadian Rev. Socio. Anthro.* 26: 617–32

CHRISTOPHERSON, S. (1989) 'On being outside "the project"', *Antipode* 21: 83–9

CONNELL, R. W. (1987) *Gender and power* (Polity, Cambridge)

CROMPTOR, R. (1986) 'Women and the "service class"' in CROMPTOR, R. and MANN, M. (eds) *Gender and stratification* (Polity, Cambridge)

CROMPTOR, R. and MANN, M. (eds) (1986) *Gender and stratification* (Polity, Cambridge)

DAVIDOFF, L. and HALL, J. (1987) *Family fortunes* (Hutchinson, London)

FAVA, S. F. (1985) 'Residential preferences in the suburban era: a new look?', *Sociological Focus* 18: 109–17

HART, N. (1989) 'Gender and the rise and fall of class politics', *New Left Review* 175: 19–47

HARVEY, D. (1982) *The limits to capital* (Blackwell, Oxford)

HEATH, A. and BRITTEN, N. (1984) 'Women's jobs do make a difference', *Sociology* 18: 475–90

HOLCOMB, B. (1984) 'Women in the rebuilt urban environment: the United States experience', *Built Environment* 10: 18–24

HOLCOMB, B. (1986) 'Geography and urban women', *Urb. Geogr.* 7: 448–56

JAGER, M. (1986) 'Class definition and the esthetics of gentrification: Victoriana in Melbourne', in SMITH, N. and WILLIAMS, P. (eds) *Gentrification of the city* (Allen and Unwin, Boston)

JOHNSON, L. C. (1989) 'Weaving workplaces: sex, race and ethnicity in the Australian textile', *Environ. Plann. A* 21: 681–4

LAURIA, M. and KNOPP, L. (1985) 'Toward an analysis of the role of gay communities in the urban renaissance', *Urb. Geogr.* 6: 152–69

LEWIS, J. and FOORD, J. (1984) 'New towns and new gender relations in old industrial regions: women's employment in Peterlee and East Kilbride', *Built Environment* 10: 42–52

LEY, D. (1986) 'Alternative explanations for inner city gentrification: a Canadian assessment', *Ann. Ass. Am. Geogr.* 76: 521–35

LEY, D. (1987) 'Styles of the times: liberal and neo-conservative landscapes in inner Vancouver, 1968–1986', *J. Historical Geogr.* 13: 40–56

LOWE, M. and GREGSON, N. (1989) 'Nannies, cooks, cleaners, au pairs ... new issues for feminist geography?', *Area* 21: 415–17

McDOWELL, L. (1983) 'Towards an understanding of the gender division of urban space', *Environ. Plann. D: Society and Space* 1: 59–72

MACKENZIE, S. (1988) 'Building women, building cities: toward gender sensitive theory in the environmental disciplines', in ANDREW, C. and MILROY, B. M. *Life Spaces* (University of British Columbia Press, Vancouver)

MACKENZIE, S. and ROSE, D. (1983) 'Industrial change, the domestic economy and home life' in ANDERSON, J., DUNCAN, S. and HUDSON, R. (eds) *Redundant spaces in cities and regions* (Academic Press, London)

McLANAHAN, S. S., SORENSON, A. and WATSON, D. (1989) 'Sex differences in poverty, 1950–1980', *Signs* 15: 102–22

MADIGAN, R., MUNRO, M. and SMITH, S. (1991) 'Gender and the meaning of the home', *Int. J. Urb. Reg. Res.* (in press)

MARKUSEN, A. (1981) 'City spatial structure, women's household work, and national urban policy', in STIMPSON, C. R., DIXLER, E., NELSON, M. J. and YATRAKIS, K. B. (eds) *Women and the American City* (University of Chicago Press, Chicago)

MARTIN, J. and ROBERTS, C. (1984) *Women and employment: a lifetime perspective* (HMSO, London)

MILLAR, J. and GLENDINNING, C. (1987) 'Invisible women, invisible poverty', in GLENDINNING, C. and MILLAR, J. (eds) *Women and poverty in Britain* (Wheatsheaf, Brighton)

MILLS, C. (1988) '"Life on the upslope": the postmodern landscape of gentrification', *Environ. Plann. D: Society and Space* 6: 169–89

MORROW JONES, H. (1986) 'The geography of housing: elderly and female households', *Urb. Geogr.* 7: 263–9

MUNT, I. (1987) 'Economic restructuring, culture, and gentrification: a case study in Battersea, London', *Environ. Plann. A* 19: 1175–97

MURGATROYD, L. (1984) 'Women, men and the social grading of occupations', *Br. J. Sociology* 35: 473–97

PAHL, R. E. (1988) 'Some remarks on informal work, social polarization and the social structure', *Int. J. Urb. Reg. Res.* 12: 247–67

PHILLIPS, A. (1987) *Divided loyalties. Dilemmas of sex and class* (Virago, London)

RAMAZANOGLU, C. (1989) *Feminism and the contradictions of oppression* (Routledge, London)

ROSE, D. (1984) 'Rethinking gentrification: beyond the uneven development of marxist urban theory', *Environ. Plann. D* 1: 47–74

ROSE, D. (1989) 'A feminist perspective of employment restructuring and gentrification: the case of Montreal', in WOLCH, J. and DEAR, M. (eds) *The power of geography* (Unwin Hyman, Boston)

ROSE, D. and Le BOURDAIS, C. (1986) 'The changing conditions of female single parenthood in Montreal's inner city and suburban neighbourhoods', *Urb. Resources* 3: 45–52

SAEGERT, S. (1981) 'Masculine cities and feminine suburbs: polarized ideas and contradictory realities', in STIMPSON, C. R., DIXLER, E., NELSON, M. J. and YATRAKIS, K. B. (eds) *Women and the American City* (University of Chicago Press, Chicago)

SHORT, J. R. (1989) 'Yuppies, yuffies and the new urban order', *Trans. Inst. Br. Geogr.* 14: 173–88

SMITH, N. (1979) 'Toward a theory of gentrification: a back to the city movement by capital not people', *J. Am. Planners Assoc.* 45: 538–48

SMITH, N. (1982) 'Gentrification and uneven development', *Econ. Geogr.* 58: 139–55

SMITH, N. (1986) 'Gentrification, the frontier, and the restructuring of urban space', in SMITH, N. and WILLIAMS, P. (eds) *Gentrification of the City* (Allen and Unwin, Boston)

SMITH, N. (1987) 'Of yuppies and housing: gentrification, social restructuring, and the urban dream', *Environ. Plann. D: Society and Space* 5: 151–72

SMITH, N. (1990) 'New city as new frontier: the Lower East Side as Wild West', in SORKIN, M. (ed.) *Variations on a theme (park)* (Hill and Wang, New York)

SMITH, N. and WILLIAMS, P. (eds) (1986) *Gentrification of the city* (Allen and Unwin, Boston)

THRIFT, N. (1987) 'The geography of late twentieth-century class formation', in THRIFT, N. and WILLIAMS, P. (eds) *Class and space* (Routledge and Kegan Paul, London)

TIVERS, J. (1985) *Women attached* (Croom Helm, Beckenham)

WALBY, S. (1986) *Patriachy at work* (Polity, Cambridge)

WALBY, S. (1989) *Theorizing patriarchy* (Blackwell, Oxford)

WALKER, A. (1987) 'The poor relation: poverty among old women', in GLENDINNING, C. and MILLAR, J. (eds) *Women and poverty in Britain* (Wheatsheaf, Brighton)

WARDE, A. (1989) 'Gentrification as consumption: issues of class and gender', paper presented at the Seventh Urban Change and Conflict Conference, Bristol, September 1989

WEKERLE, G. R. (1984) 'A woman's place is in the city', *Antipode* 16: 11–19

WEKERLE, G. R. (1985) 'From refuge to service center: neighborhoods that support women', *Sociological Focus* 18: 79–95

WERNER, B. (1985) 'Fertility trends in social classes: 1970–83', *Population Trends* 41: 5–13

WILLIAMS, P. (1986) 'Class constitution through spatial reconstruction? A re-evaluation of gentrification in Australia, Britain and the United States' in SMITH, N. and WILLIAMS, P. (eds) *Gentrification of the City* (Allen and Unwin, Boston)

WILLIAMSON, J. (1987) *Consuming passions* (Marion Boyars, London)

WILLIS, P. (1978) *Learning to labour* (Saxon House, Farnborough)

WINCHESTER, H. P. M. (1990) 'Women and children last: the poverty and marginalization of one-parent families', *Trans. Inst. Br. Geogr.* 15: 70–86

WINCHESTER, H. P. M. and WHITE, P. E. (1988) 'The location of marginalised groups in the inner city', *Environ. Plann. D: Society and Space* 6: 37–54

WRIGHT, E. O. (1989) 'Women in the class structure', *Politics and Society* 17: 35–66

ZUKIN, S. (1988) *Loft living* (Century Hutchinson, London)

22

"Toward an Analysis of the Role of Gay Communities in the Urban Renaissance"[1]

From *Urban Geography* (1985)

Mickey Lauria and Lawrence Knopp

INTRODUCTION

"Urban renaissance" is a "chaotic" term.[2] It refers to several distinct processes and connotes a cultural as well as material rejuvenation of cities which is necessarily "good." Among the processes to which it often refers are urban redevelopment (i.e., site clearance and physical redevelopment), gentrification, the concentration of corporate-managerial activities in cities and the expansion of central-city office space, and the increased appreciation and thus development of cultural amenities in cities. This paper concerns itself with urban redevelopment and gentrification, and in particular with the social change, in terms of class, which these processes usually engender (see Smith and LeFaivre, 1984, for a class analysis of gentrification). Thus, for our purposes, it is necessary to modify the definition of urban redevelopment to include the notion of change in social class. Accordingly, we collapse urban redevelopment and gentrification into one term, the "urban renaissance," for the purposes of elucidating the role of one set of actors, gay (male) communities, in both processes. Although we recognize that the processes are distinct, it is our contention that the roles played by certain actors are quite similar in both instances.

The role of the "gay factor" is much neglected in the literature on the "urban renaissance." Its importance in both urban redevelopment and gentrification is often mentioned (Ketteringham, 1979, 1983; Pattison, 1983; Castells and Murphy, 1982; Castells, 1983; Gale, 1980; Rose, 1984; Weightman, 1981; Winters, 1979), but little work takes as its mission the determination of exactly what this role

is. There are probably several reasons for this. No doubt one is that a certain squeamishness regarding sexual issues persists among many of those studying these processes, as evidenced by the often veiled and reluctant references to the significance of gay communities (see, for example, Hodge, 1980, p. 188; Allen, 1980, p. 410). Another is that any such explanation will necessarily be quite complex. Unless one reduces its significance to an element of "demand," or denies it altogether, the role of gay communities in the "urban renaissance" can only be determined after addressing a host of issues related to the structure/agency debate in social theory. Is sexual orientation socially constructed or genetically imprinted? Is a gay cultural identity a product of history or a trans-historical fact? What is the relationship between cultural identity, which appears to be related to so much "urban renaissance" activity (Cybriwsky, 1978; Winters, 1979; Castells and Murphy, 1982) and the structural context in which it takes place? We believe that resolutions of these questions in favor entirely of either "structure" or "agency" have resulted in inadequate explanations of the "urban renaissance."

It is our contention that the role of gay communities in the "urban renaissance" is important not only because gays have been shown to figure prominently in it, but also because the determination of this role focuses attention on the need for a process theory which bridges the structure/agency debate. Very little work exists which attempts to relate so-called "social factors," such as cultural identity, to more general economic or political-economic conditions resulting in the "urban renaissance." "Voluntarist" approaches, whether "positivist" or "hermeneutic," have tended to be purely descriptive (compare Levine, 1979, and Ketteringham, 1979, 1983). Others have failed to adequately consider the structural context (e.g., Cybriwsky, 1978; Levy and Cybriwsky, 1980; Ley and Mercer, 1980; Ley, 1981). Structuralist approaches, especially political-economic ones, have done a much better job, but are still incomplete (see Rose, 1984, for a review of these attempts). Most simply treat "social factors" as epiphenomenal (e.g., Smith, 1979, 1982). One of the better (indeed one of the only) attempts to analyze the role of gay communities in the urban renaissance is the work of Castells and Murphy (1982) and Castells (1983), but these analyses were not explicitly directed toward the development of a *theory* of the role of gay communities in the "urban renaissance."

This paper develops a "social constructionist" approach to the role of gay male communities in the "urban renaissance." We assume a structural context defined by the political-economic and market analyses of Smith (1979) and Lauria (1982). The paper begins with an explanation of the relevance of the structure/agency debate to our subject, and of our contention that a process theory is the way to overcome this dualism. It is argued that such an approach necessitates the use of organizational and case-study analyses. We then discuss the social construction of the "gay identity." This is important because the nature of gay oppression in contemporary society is different from the oppression of homosexual *behavior* in past societies. We argue that it is a historically specific form of oppression which has led to particular spatial responses on the part of gay communities which take the form of involvement in the "urban renaissance." In particular, we argue that the concentration in, and transformation, of space by gays, especially within the context of rapid commodification of space (and, to a lesser extent, of sex), is a source of power. Finally, the paper provides a framework for research that uses a "social constructionist" approach, which will involve a focus on organizations and necessitates the use of case-study analysis.

STRUCTURE AND AGENCY: THE NEED FOR AN ORGANIZATIONAL FOCUS

Structural determinism and voluntarism are buzzwords for complex theories about the causal relations in society. The question they try to answer is: How is reality (institutional experience) created? Structuralism posits that evolving structural social relations (economic and political) define human roles and thus so constrain human agency that they are the prime causal relations in society. For example, the wage-labor/capital relation sets up class distinctions and socioeconomic status, and thus many individual behavioral characteristics. Voluntarism posits that both determined human agency (class structured) and chaotic human agency (incidental), through competition and/or cooperation, create observed reality and are thus the prime causal relations in society.

Structuralist theory can be seen as a reaction to positivist methodology, the great man theories of history, and pluralist theories of politics—in other words, an epistemology of "what you see is what you get." Although some human agency proponents crudely argue the opposite, it is easy for structuralists to demonstrate the evolution of structures and constraints and thus to account for change (see Sayer, 1976). Thus the problem for structuralist theorists is to account for the effect of conscious human agency.[3] On the other hand, the sophisticated human agency proponents recognize that culture, ideology, and one's life experience and history shape one's consciousness and thus activities and that these effects are based on one's structural position in society. So, in essence, there is truth in both positions. Thus the question becomes how do we get from one to the other or how do we account for them both?

An abstract structuralist would argue that theoretical development occurs at the structural level, explaining constraints and opportunities, while specific history or human agency describes the specific form (see Thrift, 1983 for a more detailed account of the debate surrounding this issue). This, in itself, is not a bad argument. The only problem is understanding how the specific form is created. Thus we have the calls for "middle-level theories" that make specific connections between broad structural constraints and specific forms based on some degree of human agency. Clark and Dear (1984) made a heroic attempt at developing a middle-level theory. They failed because they used a typology or classification scheme to associate state form, function, and apparatus. These calls and attempts are fundamentally misguided; what is needed is a process theory. In other words, what kind of process mediates structural constraints and human agency?

Unlike Flynn (1979, p. 747) who attempted to rescue structural explanations by arguing that they do not preclude an organizational focus and, in fact, need to be augmented by one, we contend that one also needs to adopt a social constructionist approach to the creation of everyday life so as to provide the mechanism for this structure/agency mediation. In using the term social constructionist we mean to depict a general approach, first coherently put forward by Berger and Luckmann (1966), in which people, through the dialectical processes of externalization, objectivation, and internalization, both create and are constrained by society. In that structurationists (Giddens, 1981; Bourdieu, 1977; Bhaskar, 1979), interactionists (Layder, 1979, 1981; Bleitrach and Chenu, 1981), sociological interventionists (Touraine, 1981), and organizational dialecticians (Benson, 1977; Clegg, 1981; Zeitz, 1980; Thompson, 1980; Ranson, Hinings and Greenwood, 1980; Morgan, 1980; Lourenco and Glidewell, 1975) have adopted this general approach and developed sophisticated abstract conceptualizations of how this mediation process operates, we welcome their insights. The differences between these theorists are in the specifics of the mediating concepts that describe the process of social construction, not in the actual practices. Since we are primarily concerned with practices, we will not replicate the differences here. The interested reader should consult Thrift (1983, pp. 28–32) for a cursory discussion of these mediating concepts and Gane (1980) for a discussion of the conspicuous lack of an analysis of the "concrete" in Gidden's work. We suggest, along with Layder (1979) and the organizational dialecticians mentioned above, that organizations[4] provide the arena in which practices are situated and thus provide an avenue for analyzing the mediation between structure and agency while maintaining a focus on concrete practices.

Generally our approach necessitates the recognition and interpretation of the multiplicity of causality between the larger societal system (structures), the organizational morphology (institutional arrangement in society), and the specific social relations within an organization (practices). In this view, social reality in general and organizational structure in particular are regarded not as fixed and permanent but rather as constantly being produced, reproduced, or rearranged. Thus any such reproduction of the social structure is constrained by the existing social structure:

> The construction of social arrangements is not a wholly rational-purposeful process …. Social arrangements are created from the basically concrete, mundane tasks confronting people in their everyday life. Relationships are formed, roles are constructed, institutions are built from the encounters and confrontations of people in their daily round of life. Their production of social structure is itself guided and constrained by the context.
>
> (Benson, 1977, p. 3)

In terms of individual organizations, the organizational substructure (its informal structure which is the pattern of personal interactions concerning ideas, interests, and power) is constrained by the existing and emerging social relations of society at large and its existing organizational morphology (the organization's formal structure). At the same time, the internal social relations of the organization are either reproducing or rearranging its organizational morphology.

It is both our social construction approach and organizational focus that necessitate the use of case-study methodology. This is so because intensive data are necessary to reconstruct practices and unravel a particular construction and reproduction of organizational relations. Given the current hegemony of statistical inference in the social sciences, case-study analysis has been discarded a priori for being "unscientific" because it is statistically fallacious to generalize from small samples. This rejection belies a sophisticated understanding of social science methodology; the real problem is in convincing critical scholars of (1) the validity of an analyst's interpretation of a specific event and (2) the applicability of that interpretation to other relevant cases. Recently, psychologists and educational scholars have developed a set of rules for drawing inferences and generalizing from case studies (Edgar and Billingsley, 1974; Edgington, 1967; Cronbach, 1975; Kratochwill, 1978; Herson and Barlow, 1976; Yin, 1981; Campbell, 1975). Kennedy (1979) adopted methods used by clinicians and judges to make suggestions for logically analyzing the representativeness of a single case and thus providing the basis for generalization. Yin (1981) has been concerned both with refuting typical misconceptions that have led many social scientists to avoid or disregard case-study research designs and with explicating a systematic method for comparing or aggregating findings from multiple case studies. These analysts are developing a rigorous set of rules for judging the validity of a particular analyst's interpretation of a case study and for determining its applicability to other cases that is comparable to that used in statistical analysis.

At this point, it is important to clarify that this organizational focus and case-study method does not preclude, but rather assumes, a market approach to the "urban renaissance." The external and internal relations of organizations are in part determined by the urban "redevelopment/rehabilitation market." Thus our approach and subsequent analysis assumes the importance of the insights of the market-oriented approach developed by Smith (1979) and Lauria (1982). Briefly, Smith (1979, 1982) has developed what many have termed a structuralist model of urban redevelopment and gentrification. The kernel of his argument is that gentrification occurs in those areas where the difference between the actual rent and the potential rent (at its "highest and best use") accruing to a parcel of land (the rent gap) is large enough to justify the costs of redevelopment and provide a competitive rate of profit. Lauria's organizational model of urban redevelopment (1982) not only demonstrates that, because of the role of community development organizations,[5] selective urban redevelopment occurs in areas where the rent gap has not reached the critical threshold, but also that the success of these organizations is dependent on both their external and internal relations.[6] While Higgins (1982, p. 117) recognized the significance of Indian organizations in redevelopment/rehabilitation areas, he asserted that not only do these organizations provide services where traditional actors have deemed them unprofitable, but they also provide an important cultural identity. This point is well taken and thus it is to the development of a gay cultural identity that we now turn.

SOCIAL CONSTRUCTION OF A GAY IDENTITY

There is considerable debate in the gay studies literature as to whether there is a panhistorical "gay aesthetic" or only a historically-contingent sexuality which is socially constructed (cf. Altman, 1982; D'Emilio, 1983; Boswell, 1980). While throughout history some individuals may have been aware of a preference for same-sex emotional and sexual relationships, the particular form which this self-perception took, the kinds of issues with which such individuals grappled, and the degree to which these people were constrained by, or defined in terms of, their sexual preferences is something which was determined by society. As a separate category, in terms of which people's personalities were defined, "homosexuality" emerged most fully in 19th-century western Europe (Adam, 1978, 1982; Foucault, 1980). Prior to this period, homosexual behavior was conceived of as a personal transgression not unlike adultery. To be sure it was frowned upon, but there was no separate category of persons labeled as "homosexuals" to which a host of characteristic personality traits was attributed.

Adherents to this social constructionist school of thought have tended to make connections between the emergence of a "gay" identity and the rise of industrial capitalism (Adam, 1978, 1982; Altman, 1982; D'Emilio, 1983; Rupp, 1984). It has been argued that capitalism based itself on an efficient and uncompensated form of social reproduction—the nuclear family,[7] which is defined here as a relatively autonomous social unit consisting of an adult male, an adult female, and their offspring (Altman, 1982; D'Emilio, 1983; Rupp, 1984). While variants of the nuclear form probably existed even under feudalism, numerous authors have shown that the socialization of production under capitalism, and especially the specialization of labor under industrial capitalism, resulted in a corresponding specialization of roles within the family, such that the structure of family *relations* was dramatically altered (Zaretsky, 1976; Smelsor, 1959; Thompson, 1963; Aries, 1960; Mackenzie and Rose, 1983; Stone, 1977; Engels, 1845). Since women were uncompensated laborers in the reproductive sphere, women and men alike had to be indoctrinated into an ideology of female inferiority. This ideology penetrated into the most private corners of people's lives, defining sexual behavior itself in terms of whether or not it reproduced the asymmetrical relations of power and worth between men and women (Kleinberg, 1982). Hence the plethora of derogatory terms, for example, for sexually active women, most of which have no equals in a male context.

Inherent in this form of social organization was a need for the repression of homosexual tendencies (see Davis, 1971). Two reasons for this have been posited. First, such tendencies conflicted with an explicitly heterosexual ideology which socialized women into a subordinate role (Adam, 1982; Kleinberg, 1982). Second, in a society in which children were an economic liability, heterosexual urges were also repressed in order to delay procreation (Fernbach, 1976). Women in particular were taught to repress their sexuality and to guard their bodies against male intrusions, while men were caught between the twin poles of sexual repression and a masculine identity defined specifically in terms of the sexual domination of women. In this context, the possibility of a homosexual "outlet" posed a significant threat to the existing social structure, particularly if it became a popular alternative.

As a result, most individuals in society (especially males) developed what has been called a "compulsive" sexuality (Fernbach, 1976), by which is meant a sexuality characterized by a preoccupation with the "getting" of sex. Usually this was (and is) heterosexual in its objects, but occasionally the complex system of socialization required to create individuals capable of managing these demands failed, and a compulsive homosexuality was created. "Homosexuals" thus created became the objects of hatred and derision on the part of less well-socialized and thus insecure "heterosexuals."

While it is not clear that the logic of capitalism requires the extreme repression of homosexuality (why, for instance, could not men dominate women and still enjoy each other?), it is quite clear that this is the form which social relations did take under early capitalism.

SPATIAL RESPONSES TO GAY OPPRESSION

The creation and oppression of a gay minority in the West is a direct consequence of a sexist social structure. The extent and virulence of this oppression are well documented and need not be recounted here. However, the ways in which gay people have responded to this oppression are important. Ethnographies have shown that even before the creation of formal institutions such as bars, gays selected particular semipublic places for the purposes of finding and conducting sexual liaisons (Humphreys, 1975; Kus, 1980; Lee, 1979). This is because anonymity, which is so important to "closeted" gays, is most easily maintained in these settings. It is also because, in the absence of formal institutions like bars, the only places to meet potential partners are public (e.g., parks).

Although such places are found in both urban and rural areas (Kus, 1980), it is in cities that these places are most numerous, and it is in cities that the first well-developed gay institutions emerged (D'Emilio, 1981; Katz, 1976). By the early 1920s, there were well-established gay male "cruising grounds" in most major American cities. In addition to the obvious reason for this concentration, e.g., the presence of a "critical mass" of gay people due to larger total populations (see Fischer, 1975, for a discussion of subcultural formation in urban areas), there is another reason to expect such a development: Only in cities is there the possibility of extensive social institutions which bear little direct relation to the family or neighborhood (Altman, 1982). Specialization and interdependence between different areas of the city require the creation of more complex and impersonal institutions, such as public transportation, waiting rooms, parks, playgrounds, public restrooms, swimming pools, bars, baths, and shopping areas. In such a context, it is more feasible for a self-conscious and complex subculture to develop, for anonymity is taken for granted in much of the city. City dwellers come to expect that a certain amount of interaction with "alien" groups will have to be tolerated. Hence cities have always constituted a social context

which was somewhat more amenable to "living gay" than other places in society. They became places where gays could, to some degree, escape from the constant pressures of an intolerant heterosexual society.

At this point, it is necessary to make explicit an important distinction between gay male and lesbian oppression. Because the onus has been on men to control society and dominate women, heterosexual ideology has always made demands on men which are different from those made on women. Men have been expected to reproduce male social dominance in the bedroom. They have had to repress feelings of sexual inadequacy or ambivalence and to objectify women. Women have been encouraged to sublimate their own sexual needs to those of men and to constantly entertain notions of sexual inadequacy. As a consequence, any signs of doubt about sexual identity have tended to be more threatening to society when coming from men than from women. Men are expected to be more sure of themselves. Only when women reject men completely do they pose an equal threat. Hence women have always been given somewhat more latitude to explore relationships of depth with one another than have men. Physicality and affection between them has been accepted. Even lesbian sexuality has been accepted under certain conditions, as when it is "performed" for men by women who conform to societal standards of beauty.

Thus, gay males, whose sexual and emotional expressiveness has been repressed in a different fashion than lesbians, may perceive a greater need for territory (Johnston, 1979). This helps explain the more visible concentrations of gay males in cities, and is in contrast to the innate male territorial imperative posited by Castells (1983) in his accounting for an alleged lack of lesbian territories comparable to those of gay males in San Francisco.

The creation and defense of gay territory is intimately connected to the social construction of the gay identity (Bluestein, 1985). Murray (1979) has shown that such an area in Toronto resembles an ethnic community in every institutional respect, and Levine (1979) showed that such areas in several cities constitute "ghettos." No such developments would be possible in the absence of a social definition of certain persons as "different" by virtue of their sexual practices. While we are sensitive to Johnston's (1979) argument that such territories constitute cultural prisons as much as they do zones of freedom, the creation of gay territories is a critical link in our analysis of the role of gay communities in the "urban renaissance." Gay territories will be presented as the bases of gay political and economic power and the loci of gay community services.

With respect to political power, this territoriality affords access to the state apparatus. Its realization, however, has been contingent upon certain developments which undermine the connection between sex and procreation. The most important of these are the spread of birth control and the attendant expansion in the commodification of sex (Slater, 1976). As we have seen, one purpose of sexual repression has been the delaying of procreation. We have also seen that homosexual repression accompanies sexual repression in general, therefore decreasing any threats to the existing social order.

Sexual orientation has simply become less relevant to the reproduction of labor power. It is still an important component of heterosexual culture, and so the potential for homosexual repression will always exist to some degree within a society based on the current relations within the nuclear family. But the continuing breakdown of this nuclear family decreases the potential repression.

One consequence of this is that formal sanctions against homosexuality (i.e., those enforced by the state) are being relaxed. In the 1960s, England and several U.S. states decriminalized homosexual acts between consenting adults. Indeed, several Western European governments and local governments in many U.S. urban areas have instigated protective legislation guaranteeing equal rights for the gay minority (Berzon and Leighton, 1979; Altman, 1982). Thus, in advanced capitalist societies, gays are looking increasingly to the local state apparatus as a potential ally in their struggle to protect themselves against the more hostile popular culture. The spatial concentration of gays in neighborhoods has been used very effectively to maximize gay political clout (Pederson, 1984). Openly gay candidates have been elected to mayoral positions, city councils, and state legislatures in San Francisco, West Hollywood, Minneapolis, Boston, Laguna Beach, and Key West. "Straight" mayors, councilors, and even statewide candidates have actively courted gay votes in virtually every major city in the country, and many have credited gays with contributing substantially to their victories (e.g., Pena of Denver, Whitmire of Houston, Royer of Seattle, Barry of Washington, D.C., Goode of Philadelphia, Washington of Chicago, Fraser of Minneapolis, and Flynn of Boston).

Gays have done more with space than simply use if as a base for political power. They continually transform and use it in such a way as to reflect gay cultural values and serve the special needs of individual gays vis-a-vis society at large. This has resulted in contradictory tensions within the gay community. In the context of a rapid commodification of space (see Saunders' 1981 discussion

of Lefebvre), the optimal strategy for gays with respect to the development of political and economic power is to participate in the revalorization of physical structures in a neighborhood—in other words, to emphasize exchange-value. But from the point of view of serving the human needs of individual gays, this may not coincide with the development of use-values. Although the contradiction between use-value and exchange-value in gay communities is only beginning to manifest itself, it is clear that the development of political power through spatial concentration and the production of exchange-values within gay territories has occurred within the context of a keen awareness of the need for the provision of needed use-values (see discussions of the formation of gay tavern guilds in D'Emilio, 1981, 1983; Castells, 1983). While we believe that this contradiction will increasingly pose problems for the gay community, it is our view that it is of little consequence with regard to the development of a theory of the role which gay communities have played in the "urban renaissance" thus far. (It is, however, at the heart of much of the animosity which exists between lesbians and gay men—see Faderman, 1981, pp. 377–391; Johnston, 1973; Altman, 1982, pp. 131–132.)

GAYS AND THE URBAN RENAISSANCE

Gentrification and urban redevelopment are in part means of closing the gap between what a piece of urban land is currently producing, in terms of profit, and what it is potentially capable of producing (Smith, 1979; Lauria, 1982; Rose, 1984). At the same time, the changing national and global economies have resulted in the social and spatial restructuring of labor processes. As foreign economies have developed to the point where their profit-making potentials as loci for industrial investment are competitive with the U.S. domestic economy, investment in industry has been encouraged to move (Bluestone and Harrison, 1982). This has enabled industry to demand wage cuts, tax breaks, and subsidies from local state apparatuses in return for agreeing not to relocate (Goodman, 1979). Much production has been farmed out to suburbs and more recently rural communities, where workers are more isolated and less organizable, and the local state apparatus more cooperative (Gordon, 1978). Much heavy industry is slowly leaving the country altogether, expanding the "reserve army" of unemployed in the process. New investment is going into high tech industries, service-sector expansion, and, most importantly, the improvement of corporate-managerial processes

(Bluestone and Harrison, 1982). The latter two investment trends have employed larger proportions of low-wage and/or part-time labor, much of it female, than did previous investments (Bluestone and Harrison, 1982). Not insignificantly, the locus of corporate-managerial and service-sector investment has tended overwhelmingly to be in the CBDs of larger cities.

Thus, the transfer of production to suburbs and small communities has been replaced by service-sector and clerical-support jobs, many of which are performed by unorganized female and other low-wage labor. The expansion of these jobs in CBDs has, for gays, constituted a significant economic pull-factor which complements the attraction of cities as centers of gay life. Many of these jobs have traditionally been performed by women (e.g., secretaries, librarians, bank tellers, food servers). Among the male minority in such jobs, a disproportionate number has always been gay (Harry and DeVall, 1978; Karlen, 1971; Gagnon and Simon, 1973). This is partially because as oppressed people, women and gay men have something in common (Nahas and Turley, 1979; Kraus, 1983; Pliner, 1979; Kleinberg, 1979; Beyer, 1977). Furthermore, heterosexual male culture is less pervasive and oppressive in these female environments than in male ones (Nyberg and Alston, 1977); thus they are more attractive to many gay males. On the other hand, males often get the more lucrative of these service-sector jobs (e.g., waiters vs. waitresses), which can militate against woman-gay male solidarity. Still, there is generally more common ground between (straight) women and gay men than between (straight) women and straight men.[8] Furthermore, males in such jobs are also in the position frequently of having to defend their sexual identities regardless of whether or not they are gay, since according to heterosexual ideology a "real man" would not be doing "woman's work," Thus we might expect that many straight men are deterred from taking such jobs. Finally, in recent decades feminism has had a profound impact on the attitudes of straight women towards sexual and gender-related issues generally, such that they are probably even more sympathetic to the plight of gay men, as evidenced by women's higher levels of support for gay rights in elections (*Socialist Review*, 1979).

Pattison (1983) has shown that relatively low-wage gay renters seeking nothing more than a place to live are sometimes the catalysts in a central-city neighborhood's upgrading. With the landlord's permission, they engage in what Clay (1983) has identified as "incumbent upgrading." While we do not wish to assert a general stage theory for the "urban renaissance" (DeGiovanni, 1983, has shown that stage theories of gentrification are difficult to support empirically, and they are clearly not applicable in the case of urban redevelopment, which usually involves site clearance), we do wish to suggest that where gays are involved, and an area becomes a gentrified gay neighborhood, a stage process is applicable.

Specifically we argue that a "first wave" of low-wage gay residences in city centers may attract other more affluent gays to the neighborhood, especially if it is ripe for redevelopment. Castells (1983) noted that the presence of gay men in the real estate and other professions in San Francisco was a major factor facilitating that city's renaissance in the 1970s. But regardless of social or occupational class, being a gay male in this society is economically advantageous (Foltz, Raine, Gonzalez and Wright, 1984; Fernbach, 1976). Males make more money than their female counterparts in every sector of the economy, and gay males tend to have fewer dependents than straight men. This means that many gay men are in an excellent position to become gentrifiers (Hadley-Garcia, 1983). Rose (1984) has noted that even some single mothers have become gentrifiers. How much more possible is it for single gay men?

This leads to another way in which gay communities and structural conditions creating the "urban renaissance" are related. Gay males, while certainly responding to economic incentives, are at the same time responding to community and individual needs. Some of these have already been touched on in the discussion of gay oppression: the need to escape to an oasis of tolerance; the need for a sense of place and belonging; and the need to develop economic and political clout as a community. In the same way that single middle-class mothers find the inner city to have locational advantages from the points of view of day care, work location, and other support services (Rose, 1984), so middle-class gay men find it to have advantages from the points of view of work location and proximity to gay cultural institutions. But for gay men there are the added dimensions of escape and community development. Gay neighborhoods increasingly play the dual roles of (1) places to which young gay men from the hinterland escape in order to "come out," or come to terms with their sexuality (Kus, 1980) and (2) bases of community economic and political development (Castells, 1983; Shilts, 1982). Gays, in essence, have seized an opportunity to combat oppression by creating neighborhoods over which they have maximum control and which meet long-neglected needs.

THE NEED FOR FURTHER INVESTIGATION

What we have been able to provide thus far is only a partial explanation for the role of gay communities in the "urban renaissance." Given the bifurcation of analysis discussed, this is inevitable. Thus, our agenda now is to suggest ways of fleshing out an explanation.

We believe that a comparative study of several gay communities involved in residential redevelopment is the most appropriate method for investigating our particular concern. In the United States, three or four communities in as many cities would constitute a sizable sample. A neighborhood should be selected to serve as a control in each city. Given the exploratory nature of this research, the concept of control is necessarily simple in that the control neighborhood will also be gentrified and will not have a conspicuous gay presence or gay identity.

The first step in data collection will be gathering information on changing property values over time: empirically establishing the "rent-gap." Concomitantly, in order to empirically document the hypothesized role of gays in the "urban renaissance," data need to be collected on gay individuals and gay organizations in the study areas. It seems that a two-phase survey would be appropriate: one, a short form that would attempt to approximate a demographic profile of the gay community, and a second, longer form aimed specifically at establishing attitudes, behaviors, and histories. In particular, questions should be asked regarding patterns of housing consumption and living arrangements, reinvestment by gay entrepreneurs of profits within gay communities, and the histories of particular communities' developments.

Second, one would need to trace the institutional and organizational development of the urban redevelopment/rehabilitation market focusing specifically on the role of gay institutions and organizations. Following Lauria (1982, 1984), the contention that the market will structure the positions of specific organizations and institutions in the redevelopment/rehabilitation process, and thus will determine the range of their competitors, their interaction patterns, and the possibilities for rent extraction, should be examined. By analyzing the difference in the urban redevelopment/rehabilitation market in the control and gay neighborhood, the role of the "gay factor" in the "urban renaissance" can be specified.

An organizational analysis will be necessary to provide an intensive understanding of the social construction of gays' role in the urban redevelopment process. This can be accomplished through the use of both participant and "passive" observation techniques. One should become familiar with formal organizations (political, business, social service), certain social networks (e.g., "cliques"), and individuals (e.g., gay gentrifiers). In addition to verifying the findings of surveys, observation should be aimed at determining what gays perceive their communities' involvements in the "urban renaissance" to be, what they perceive the relationship between this involvement and increased community clout to be, and what the relationship between these activities and gay community development is.

Formal interviews of both gay and non-gay actors in the redevelopment process should complement these techniques. In particular, city officials, realtors, officers of financial institutions, individual gentrifiers, and representatives of community organizations in both study and control areas should be contacted. Certain individuals emerging from survey responses as good sources of information regarding the historical developments of study areas may also need to be interviewed further.

In order to carry out the suggested research agenda, one must develop a rather rigorous and explicit methodological framework. This is necessary to convince skeptical scholars of the validity or plausibility of the specific interpretations of the case studies while providing a logical basis to justify any resultant generalizations. In terms of the process of investigation, such analysis requires a rigorous interrogation of the various forms of evidence, i.e., verifying, correcting, or negating one form of evidence, for example, unstructured interviews with archival documents, census data, structured interviews, participant observation, and survey instruments (see Needleman and Needleman, 1974, for a good example of such an interrogation). One important consequence of their interrogation is that most, if not all, quantitative data should be collected and analyzed subsequent to the qualitative work that determines its import.

Third, the specific criteria to be used as a basis for generalizations need to be identified as early as possible in the investigation process. One needs to determine (1) the common attributes of the sample neighborhoods and cities, (2) the attributes of the various neighborhoods and cities that are common to some predefined population, and (3) the unique characteristics of the various neighborhoods and cities. The first and third sets of characteristics will be used to confine the generalizations to a specific sub-population, and the second is necessary to determine those generalizations that can be applied to the larger population. Finally, it is necessary to explicitly assess and explain the relative importance of these different characteristics in terms of their individual and joint effects on the specific research findings.

In terms of the presentation of the research findings from this comparative case-study approach, a researcher must be particularly careful with the rendition of the explanation provided. First, it is necessary to provide an accurate and complete presentation of all the data analyzed, paying particular attention not to exclude data that contradict or do not reinforce the final interpretation. Second, all plausible explanations or interpretations should be provided and evaluated with explicit reference to the data provided. Finally, a presentation of the single best explanation based on the above evaluation is necessary.

The final portion of this research agenda is a condensation of the results of the case-study analysis and the development of variables and subsequently a survey instrument to be administered to a larger sample along the lines of a case-survey approach (see Yin, 1981; Yin and Heald, 1975; Yin, Bingham and Heald, 1976; DiMaggio and Useem, 1979, for an illustration of this approach).

CONCLUSION

In spite of the development of highly visible gay communities in areas experiencing rapid urban redevelopment/rehabilitation, current theorizing about the "urban renaissance" has tended to deemphasize the role of cultural identity.[9] We have suggested that this may be due to the fact that structuralists have considered culture an epiphenomenon while voluntarists have viewed culture as an aggregate of personal choices in "life-styles." In order to fully appreciate the role of cultural identity, it is necessary to do more than just construct the possible effects of societal constraints on individuals, organizations, and institutions. Organizational analysis is also required to elaborate the social construction of everyday life.

The emphasis of this paper has been to provide a theoretical and methodological framework for such an analysis. We have focused on the neglected case of gay involvement in the "urban renaissance." It was contended that the social construction of the "gay identity" and spatial responses to gay oppression are critical developments in the social construction of the "urban renaissance." The beginning of a specific account of this process is offered. Finally, an enumeration of what needs to be done to more fully develop this account is provided.

Notes

1 We would like to thank Michael Curry, Bob Kus, David Reynolds, Margo Schwab, Eric Sheppard, Bob Walker, and the editors and reviewers of *Urban Geography* for their constructive comments and suggestions on an earlier version of this paper.

2 We are using the term "chaotic" in the sense of Sayer (1982) and Rose (1984) to mean lacking in coherence or referring to diverse experiences not generally lending themselves to generalization.

3 If you are a social scientist, this is not a trivial question because the ideological and political justification for the social sciences' contribution to society is their assistance in guiding change.

4 We use the term organization to mean a collectivity which has devised procedures or rules for making collective decisions, delegating authority, and defining membership criteria. See Argyris and Schon (1978, pp. 12–13) for a concise presentation of this perspective. It is important to realize that these rules need not be formal or even conscious. It should be emphasized that it is these rules that transform a collectivity into an organization or collective behavior into organizational behavior.

5 Johnson (1983), working within a different theoretical framework, also argued that more attention should be focused on the role of community organizations and neighborhood groups in the neighborhood change process.

6 In terms of these internal relations, Lauria (1986) determined that the internal social relations (organizational substructure) of a community development organization are in contradiction with and thus do not reconstruct its organizational morphology. This creates many problems in the operation of the organization. This contradiction may be resolved by altering the internal social relations leading to the bureaucratization and professionalization of the organization. This occurs through changing the nature of the board of directors (its composition) and thus the internal social relations and ultimately the goals and objectives of the organization. Using a purely structural argument, it would be difficult to account for the specifics of the transformation of such an organization: We could have only tautologically concluded that it was the organization's historical development that created its downfall. On the other hand, using purely a human agency argument, we could only posit that this transformation was simply the result of individual power struggles within the organization—based on personal motivation.

Thus, recognizing no connection between the structural processes creating those motivations.

7 There is disagreement about whether or not the nuclear family is an efficient mechanism of social reproduction. See Sennett (1970) for a clear discussion of the debate between Parsons and Aries.

8 The affinity between many straight women and gay men is nicely captured in the novels of Fran Liebowitz and Armistead Maupin.

9 For an exception to this, see Zukin (1982).

LITERATURE CITED

Adam, Barry D., 1982, Where gay people come from. *Christopher Street*, Vol. 6, 22–29.

——, 1978, *The Survival of Domination*. New York: Elsevier North-Holland, Inc.

Allen, Irving, 1980, The ideology of dense neighborhood redevelopment: cultural diversity and transcendent community experience. *Urban Affairs Quarterly*, Vol. 15, 409–428.

Altman, Dennis, 1982, *The Homosexualization of America*. Boston: Beacon Press.

Argyris, Chris and Schon, Donald A., 1978, *Organizational Learning: A Theory of Actor Perspective*. Reading, MA: Addison-Wesley.

Aries, Philippe, 1960, *Centuries of Childhood*. New York: Vintage Books.

Benson, J. Kenneth, 1977, Organizations: a dialectical view. *Administrative Science Quarterly*, Vol. 22, 1–21.

Berger, Peter L. and Luckmann, Thomas, 1966, *The Social Construction of Reality*. Baltimore: Penguin.

Berzon, Betty and Leighton, Robert, 1979, *Positively Gay*. Millbrae, CA: Celestial Arts.

Beyer, Dorianne, 1977, Interview with Gloria Steinem. *Christopher Street*, Vol. 2, 7–12.

Bhaskar, Roy, 1979, *The Possibility of Naturalism*. Hassock, Sussex: Harvester Press.

Bleitrach, Danielle and Chenu, Alain, 1981, Modes of domination and everyday life: some notes on recent research. In Michael Harloe and Elizabeth Lebas, editors, *City-Class and Capital*. London: Edward Arnold.

Bluestein, Ron, 1985, San Francisco notes. *The Advocate*, Issue 415, 37–38.

Bluestone, Barry and Harrison, Bennett, 1982, *The Deindustrialization of America*. New York: Basic Books.

Boswell, John, 1980, *Christianity, Social Tolerance, and Homosexuality*. Chicago: University of Chicago Press.

Bourdieu, Pierre, 1977, *Outline of a Theory of Practice*. New York: Cambridge University Press.

Campbell, Donald T., 1975, Degrees of freedom and the case study. *Comparative Political Studies*, Vol. 8, 178–193.

Castells, Manuel, 1983, *The City and the Grassroots*. Berkeley: University of California Press.

——, and Murphy, Karen, 1982, Cultural identity and urban structure: the spatial organization of San Francisco's gay community. In Norman Fainstein and Susan Fainstein, editors, *Urban Policy Under Capitalism*. Beverly Hills: Sage.

Clark, Gordon L. and Dear, Michael, 1984, *State Apparatus; Structures and Language of Legitimacy*. Boston: Allen and Unwin.

Clay, Phillip, 1983, Urban reinvestment: process and trends. In Phillip L. Clay and Robert M. Hollister, editors, *Neighborhood Policy and Planning*. Lexington, MA: Lexington Books.

Clegg, Stewart, 1981, Organization and control. *Administrative Science Quarterly*, Vol. 26, 545–562.

Cronbach, Lee J., 1975, Beyond the two disciplines of scientific psychology. *American Psychologist*, Vol. 30, 116–127.

Cybriwsky, Roman A., 1978, Social aspects of neighborhood change. *Annals*, Association of American Geographers, Vol. 68, 17–33.

Davis, Kingsley, 1971, Sexual behavior. In Robert K. Merton and Robert Nisbet, editors, *Contemporary Social Problems*. New York: Harcourt, Brace, Jovanovich.

DeGiovanni, Frank, 1983, Patterns of housing market activity in revitalizing neighborhoods. *Journal of the American Planning Association*, Vol. 49, 22–39.

D'Emilio, John, 1981, Gay politics, gay communities: the San Francisco experience. *Socialist Review*, Vol. 55, 77–104.

——, 1983, *Sexual Politics, Sexual Communities; The Making of a Homosexual Minority in the United States, 1940–1970*. Chicago: University of Chicago Press.

DiMaggio, Paul and Useem, Michael, 1979, Decentralized applied research: factors affecting the use of audience research by arts organizations. *Journal of Applied Behavioral Science*, Vol. 15, 79–93.

Edgar, Eugene and Billingsley, Felix, 1974, Believability when N = 1. *Psychological Record*, Vol. 24, 147–160.

Edgington, Eugene S., 1967, Statistical inference from N = 1 experiments. *Journal of Psychology*, Vol. 65, 195–199.

Engels, Friedrich, 1845, *The Condition of the Working Class in England*. W.O. Henderson and W.H. Chaloner, editors and translators, 1958. Oxford: A.T. Broome and Son.

Faderman, Lillian, 1981, *Surpassing the Love of Men*. New York: William Morrow and Co.

Fernbach, David, 1976, Toward a marxist theory of gay liberation. *Socialist Revolution*, Vol. 6, 29–41.

Fischer, Claude, 1975, Toward a subcultural theory of urbanism. *American Journal of Sociology*, Vol. 80, 1319–1341.

Flynn, Rob, 1979, Urban managers in local government planning. *Sociological Review*, Vol. 27, 743–753.

Foltz, Kim, Raine, George, Gonzalez, David L. and Wright, Lynda, 1984, The profit of being gay. *Newsweek*, Vol. 1–4, 84, 89.

Foucault, Michel, 1980, *The History of Sexuality, Vol. 1*. New York: Vintage Books.

Gagnon, John and Simon, William, 1973, *Sexual Conduct*. Chicago: Aldine.

Gale, Dennis E., 1980, Neighborhood resettlement: Washington, D.C. In Shirley B. Laska and Daphne Spain, editors, *Back to the City: Issues in Neighborhood Renovation*. New York: Pergamon Press.

Gane, Mike, 1980, Anthony Giddens and the crisis of social theory. *Economy and Society*, Vol. 12, 368–399.

Giddens, Anthony, 1979, *Central Problems in Social Theory*. Berkeley: University of California Press.

——, 1981, *A Contemporary Critique of Historical Materialism*. Berkeley: University of California Press.

Goodman, Robert, 1979, *The Last Entrepreneurs: America's Regional Wars for Jobs and Dollars*. Boston: South End Press.

Gordon, David, 1978, Capitalist development and the history of American cities. In William K. Tabb and Larry Sawers, editors, *Marxism and the Metropolis*. New York: Oxford University Press.

Hadley-Garcia, George, 1983, The greening of gay money. *Christopher Street*, Vol. 7, 30–35.

Harry, Joseph and DeVall, William, 1978, *The Social Organization of Gay Males*. New York: Praeger.

Herson, Michel and Barlow, David H., 1976, *Single Case Experimental Designs*. New York: Academic Press.

Higgins, Bryan R., 1982, Urban indians: patterns and transformation. *Journal of Cultural Geography*, Vol. 2, 110–118.

Hodge, David C., 1980, Inner-city revitalization as a challenge to diversity?: Seattle. In Shirley B. Laska and Daphne Spain, editors, *Back to the City: Issues in Neighborhood Renovation*. New York: Pergamon Press.

Humphreys, Laud, 1975, *Tearoom Trade: Impersonal Sex in Public Places*. Hawthorn, NY: Aldine Publishing.

Johnson, James H., Jr., 1983, The role of community action in neighborhood revitalization. *Urban Geography*, Vol. 4, 16–39.

Johnston, Gordon, 1979, *Which Way Out of the Men's Room*? South Brunswick, NJ: A.S. Barnes and Co., Inc.

Johnston, Jill, 1973, *Lesbian Nation: The Feminist Solution*. New York: Simon and Schuster.

Karlen, Arno, 1971, *Sexuality and Homosexuality: A New View*. New York: W.W. Horton and Co.

Katz, Jonathan, 1976, *Gay American History*. New York: Thomas Crowell.

Kennedy, Mary M., 1979, Generalizing from single case studies. *Evaluation Quarterly*, Vol. 3, 661–678.

Ketteringham, William, 1979, *Gay public space and the urban landscape: a preliminary assessment*. Paper delivered to the Association of Pacific Coast Geographers Annual Conference.

——, 1983, *The broadway corridor: gay businesses as agents of revitalization in Long Beach, California*. Paper delivered to the Association of American Geographers Annual Conference.

Kleinberg, Seymour, 1979, Alienated affections: friendships between gay men and straight women. *Christopher Street*, Vol. 4, 26–40.

——, 1982, It is 1690 and you have been accused of sodomy. *Christopher Street*, Vol. 6, 46–53.

Kratochwill, Thomas R., editor, 1978, *Single Subject Research: Strategies for Evaluating Change*. New York: Academic Press.

Kraus, Krandal, 1983, Gay men make the best friends. *Christopher Street*, Vol. 6, 22.

Kus, Robert J., 1980, *Gay freedom: an ethnography of coming out*. Ph.D. dissertation, Department of Sociology, University of Montana.

Lauria, Mickey, 1982, Selective urban redevelopment: a political economic perspective. *Urban Geography*, Vol. 3, 224–239.

——, 1984, The implications of marxian rent theory for community controlled redevelopment strategies. *Journal of Planning Education and Research*, Vol. 4, 16–24.

——, 1986, The internal transformation of community controlled implementation organizations. *Administration and Society*.

Layder, Derek, 1979, Problems in accounting for the individual in marxist-rationalist theoretical discourse. *British Journal of Sociology*, Vol. 30, 149–163.

——, 1981, *Structure, Interaction and Social Theory*. Boston: Routledge and Kegan Paul.

Lee, John A., 1979, The gay connection. *Urban Life*, Vol. 8, 175–198.

Levine, Martin, 1979, Gay ghetto. *Journal of Homosexuality*, Vol. 4, 363–377.

Levy, Paul R. and Cybriwsky, Roman A., 1980, The hidden dimensions of culture and class: Philadelphia. In Shirley B. Laska and Daphne Spain, editors, *Back to the City: Issues in Neighborhood Renovation*. New York: Pergamon Press.

Ley, David, 1981, The inner city revitalization in Canada: a Vancouver case study. *Canadian Geographer*, Vol. 25, 124–148.

——, and Mercer, John, 1980, Locational conflict and the politics of consumption. *Economic Geography*, Vol. 56, 89–109.

Lourenco, Susan V. and Glidewell, John C., 1975, A dialectical analysis of organizational conflict. *Administrative Science Quarterly*, Vol. 20, 489–508.

Mackenzie, Suzanne and Rose, Damaris C., 1983, Industrial change, the domestic economy and home life. In James Anderson, Simon Duncan and R. Hudson, editors, *Redundant Spaces in Cities and Regions*. London: Academic Press.

Morgan, Gareth, 1980, Paradigms, metaphores and puzzle, solving in organization theory. *Administrative Science Quarterly*, Vol. 25, 605–623.

Murray, Stephan, 1979, The institutional elaboration of a quasi-ethnic community. *International Review of Modern Sociology*, Vol. 9, 165–177.

Nahas, Rebecca and Turley, Myra, 1979, *The New Couple: Women and Gay Men*. New York: Seaview Books.

Needleman, Martin L. and Needleman, Carolyn E., 1974, *Guerillas in the Bureaucracy*. New York: John Wiley and Sons.

Nyberg, Kenneth and Alston, Jon, 1977, Analysis of public attitudes toward homosexual behavior. *Journal of Homosexuality*, Vol. 2, 99–108.

Pattison, Timothy, 1983, The stages of gentrification: the case of bay village. In Phillip L. Clay and Robert M. Hollister, editors, *Neighborhood Policy and Planning*. Lexington, MA: Lexington Books.

Pederson, Daniel, 1984, A gay city on the hill. *Newsweek*, Vol. 4, 46.

Pliner, Roberta, 1979, Fag-Hags, friends or fellow travelers? *Christopher Street*, Vol. 4, 16–25.

Ranson, Stewart, Hinings, Bob and Greenwood, Royston, 1980, The structuring of organizational structures. *Administrative Science Quarterly*, Vol. 25, 1–17.

Rose, Damaris, 1984, Rethinking gentrification: beyond the uneven development of marxist urban theory. *Environment and Planning D: Society and Space*, Vol. 1, 47–74.

Rupp, Leila J., 1984, Sexual Politics, Sexual Communities: the Making of a Homosexual Minority in the United States, 1940–1970, by John D'Emilio, Gay/Lesbian Almanac: A New Documentary by Jonathan Ned Katz: Book Review. *Signs*, Vol. 9, 712–715.

Saunders, Peter, 1981, *Social Theory and the Urban Question*. New York: Holmes and Meier Publishers, Inc.

Sayer, Andrew, 1976, A critique of urban modeling: from regional science to urban and regional political economy. *Progress in Planning*, Vol. 6, 187–254.

——, 1982, Explanation in economic geography. *Progress in Human Geography*, Vol. 6, 68–88.

Sennett, Richard, 1970, *Families Against the City*. Cambridge, MA: Harvard University Press.

Shilts, Randy, 1982, *The Mayor of Castro Street: The Life and Times of Harvey Milk*. New York: St. Martin's Press.

Slater, Phillip, 1976, *The Pursuit of Loneliness*. Boston: Beacon Press.

Smelsor, Neil J., 1959, *Social Change in the Industrial Revolution: An Application of Theory to the British Cotton Industry*. Chicago: University of Chicago Press.

Smith, Neil, 1979, Toward a theory of gentrification: a back to the city movement by capital not people. *Journal of the American Planning Association*, Vol. 45, 538–548.

——, 1982, Gentrification and uneven development, *Economic Geography*, Vol. 58, 139–155.

——, and LeFaivre, Michele, 1984, A class analysis of gentrification. In J. John Palen and Bruce London, editors, *Gentrification, Displacement and Neighborhood Revitalization*. Albany, NY: State University of New York Press.

Socialist Review, 1979, Sexuality and the state: the defeat of the Briggs initiative and beyond, Vol. 9, 55–72.

Stone, Lawrence, 1977, *The Family, Sex and Marriage in England, 1500–1800*. New York: Harper and Row.

Thompson, Edward P., 1963, *The Making of the English Working Class*. New York: Pantheon Books.

Thompson, Kenneth, 1980, Organizations as constructors of social reality (1). In Kenneth Thompson and Graeme Salaman, editors, *Control and Ideology in Organizations*. Cambridge, MA: MIT Press.

Thrift, N.J., 1983, On the determination of social action in space and time. *Environment and Planning, D: Society and Space*, Vol. 1, 23–57.

Touraine, Alan, 1981, *The Voice and the Eye: An Analysis of Social Movements*. New York: Cambridge University Press.

Weightman, Barbara, 1981, Commentary: towards a geography of the gay community. *Journal of Cultural Geography*, Vol. 1, 106–112.

Winters, Christopher, 1979, The social identity of evolving neighborhoods. *Landscape*, Vol. 23, 8–14.

Yin, Robert K., 1981, The case study crisis: some answers. *Administrative Science Quarterly*, Vol. 26, 58–65.

——, Bingham, Eveleen and Heald, Karen A., 1976, The difference that quality makes: the case of literature reviews. *Sociological Methods and Research*, Vol. 5, 139–156.

—— and Heald, Karen A., 1975, Using the case survey method to analyze political studies. *Administrative Science Quarterly*, Vol. 20, 371–381.

Zaretsky, Eli, 1976, *Capitalism, the Family and Personal Life*. New York: Harper Colophon Books.

Zeitz, Gerald, 1980, Interorganizational dialectics. *Administrative Science Quarterly*, Vol. 25, 72–88.

Zukin, Sharon, 1982, *Loft Living: Culture and Capital in Urban Change*. Baltimore: Johns Hopkins University Press.

23

"Can You Go Home Again? Black Gentrification and the Dilemma of Difference"

From *Berkeley Journal of Sociology* (1992)

Monique M. Taylor

INTRODUCTION

In the 1970's, gentrification was identified in central city areas throughout the United States as an economic revitalization and restructuring of urban space (Smith and Williams 1986). While the rehabilitation of housing in rundown neighborhoods by a young, affluent population was heralded as a reversal of the trend that had carried middle-income families away from the city, gentrification was not without complications.

The young, upwardly mobile, and mostly white population associated with the process of gentrification has been alternately praised and cursed for its role in recasting poor communities. While the arrival of a gentry in failing inner-city areas raised hopes of improved social services, better police protection and a stimulus to the local economy, gentrification also raised fears fueled by competition over space.

Stores such as Benetton clothing and David's Cookies and an overabundance of boutiques and ice cream shops have become the divisive symbols of change in gentrifying neighborhoods across the United States. Lifestyle differences between new "yuppie" residents and their poorer neighbors created conflicts around uses of public and private space. Interactions between old and new, black and white, young and old in gentrifying neighborhoods and communities have been fraught with tensions as residents negotiated sometimes shared and often differing visions of community life (see Anderson 1990, Williams 1987, Godfrey 1988).

In Harlem, evidence of gentrification has been traced to the mid-1970's (Bailey 1984, Schaffer and Smith 1986, Foderaro 1987). Gentrification became a highly charged issue in the largely poor, predominantly minority community of Harlemites threatened by rising rents, higher taxes and fears of displacement by the young, affluent whites generally associated with the process.

The fears were only partly justified, however. Yes, gentrification has come to Harlem in the form of middle-class professionals with an appreciation for real estate bargains. But this new gentry in Harlem is also black and strongly motivated by a desire to participate in the rituals that define daily life in this (in)famous and historically black community.

For the most part, businesses and services in Harlem still cater to the black residents who form the vast majority of its inhabitants. In Harlem the sights and sounds of this famous black ghetto—stores and street vendors hawking a variety of red, black and green merchandise; black mannequins smiling out from store windows; barber shops and hair salons advertising specials on fades and braids; rap, hip-hop and reggae music resounding in the streets—imbue the community with a distinctiveness signaled by African American culture.

Middle-class blacks seem to be drawn to Harlem in an effort to connect to these and other symbols of blackness that define the existing community. While its physical boundaries contain much of what is culturally unique about Harlem, its symbolic significance extends beyond these boundaries.[1] In part the importance of Harlem as a racial community and as a symbol of blackness enables middle-class black professionals to articulate a distinctly racial identity.

But as this group comes to Harlem seeking to bolster a racial identity, class distinctions often set them apart from their neighbors as they attempt to structure their lives as middle-class homeowners in a largely poor community. Thus, the move to Harlem which enables middle-class blacks to assert an identity as blacks vis-à-vis the white world raises an interesting dilemma: how do they cope, once inside Harlem, with the transition from outsider to insider in a community where their newness, class position and lifestyle potentially set them apart?

THEORY AND METHOD

In this paper I employ a framework that explores the cultural dimensions of gentrification in Harlem. The quest for participation in a racial community by black gentry in Harlem can be explored within three theoretical constructs posited by anthropologist Victor Turner. Turner's (1967, 1974, 1977) concepts of marginality, structure and anti-structure—or communitas—allow me to analyze the search for community and identity and the dilemma posed by differences of race and class that are an underlying fact of black gentrification in Harlem.

Turner's concepts of structure and anti-structure capture the dynamic tension between race and class that this group of middle-class blacks seeks to resolve. As successful members of the middle class, Harlem's black gentry occupy a structural position in American society defined by their class position.[2] Structure's complement—communitas or social anti-structure—arises, according to Turner, for those who find themselves as members of both ascribed (in my case, race) and achieved (such as middle-class status) groups.

In this instance, as middle-class blacks who feel marginalized in the white world, Harlem's black gentry look to the "so called inferior group"—their racial group—for communitas.[3] Communitas, or social anti-structure, Turner argues, is most evident in periods when societies are in liminal transition between different social structures.

More clearly, communitas suggests a "Communion of fellowship" (Turner 1974:45) that emerges to bond people during transitional stages in history. The post-Civil Rights era—representative of America's transition to a new pattern of black/white relations—can be seen as an example of a liminal transition in the history of U.S. race relations.

But how does one operationalize the highly theoretical concept of "communitas?" Racial communitas, I argue, is created and experienced through participation in the public and social life of the community. By participating in the shared public rituals of the community—political activism, Harlem's stoop culture, community festivals and block parties, and public exchanges such as waves and hellos—black gentry, as outsiders, make a transition that redefines them as Harlem insiders.

The "data" in this paper are a combination of in-depth interviews with eleven middle-class black professionals who have moved to Harlem since 1975 and field observation conducted in Harlem from 1988–1991.[4] At a time when political and economic change would seem to obviate such a need, Harlem's black gentry are engaged in a quest for identity and belonging they believe is to be found in the black community.[5]

The atypical nature of the return by middle-class blacks to an inner-city black community goes against the general trend of suburbanization and decreasing patterns of segregation for middle-class blacks that many sociologists have stressed since the late 1960's. Thus, the choice that this group of black professionals has made to come "home to Harlem" reveals a quest for racial communitas that seems to defy and yet occurs within the context of one of the central gains of the Civil Rights Era—increasing integration in American society.

THE MORE THINGS CHANGE ... RACISM AND DIFFERENCE IN POST-CIVIL RIGHTS AMERICA

In interviews with Harlem's black gentry it was not uncommon to hear stories about negative experiences on the job and with white neighbors before making the move to Harlem. Some have endured slights as subtle as whispered comments. Others have weathered more severe attacks—racial slurs and, for one family, the fire-bombing of its new home.

Many expressed a feeling that in their own lives they continue to confront a color line that perhaps is more subtle than that in pre-civil rights America, yet still reinforces a pattern of distinct relations between blacks and whites. Evidence of the symbols and rituals of America's culture of racism that marginalize blacks in the white world are prevalent.

Yolanda Jackson, a city housing official, cited frustrations over racist encounters with her former neighbors as a primary reason for coming to Harlem. Jackson shared a story about a party she once held in her Upper East Side apartment for a Senegalese film maker. As she and her guests, including the Senegalese film maker, were having cocktails on the balcony, neighbors on a higher balcony began shouting racial slurs. To add to her embarrassment, another neighbor in the building then called the police to register a noise complaint against her.

Though she laughed as she retold the story, Jackson talked about that episode as one of a handful of painful racist encounters with neighbors in that building—such as the time one of her neighbors mistook her for a maid in the building's laundry room. There and at her job, Jackson says, she was always aware of a boundary—made clear through neighbors' and co-workers' words or indifference—that defined her as an outsider in the white world:

Well it's like it's always this attitude that you feel and sometimes is articulated in the things that people say or how they respond to you [that] you don't belong there.

On the one hand, Jackson's job in an integrated setting and her family residence on Manhattan's Upper East Side are evidence of the dissolution of a formal boundary that once restricted black-white contact. But in the integrated environments that bring blacks and whites together, some whites, through their words and actions, erect a boundary making it clear to Jackson and others that "you don't belong."

Kenyatta Davis works in downtown Manhattan in publishing, an elite industry she argued is dominated by whites:

I consider working with whites and working in the corporate environment as working in a foreign environment and I treat it as such. You know, when I enter their milieu I'm going to another country and I behave accordingly. Meaning that I try to understand them as much as possible and speak in a language that they can understand as much as possible without giving up myself. And I try to teach them about who I am. It's stressful, you know, what I have to deal with on a daily basis. They don't expect to see black people in that environment. It takes a lot out of me.

A distinction between two worlds—one black, the other white—is clear in Davis's comments. Positioning herself as an outsider, Davis defines the white environment of work as "their milieu." She likens her entry into that world to travel in a foreign environment. Her behavior and language are tailored to the culture of that milieu. And as Davis admits, in an environment where it is made clear you do not belong, day-to-day survival can be stressful.

George Carver, a magazine publisher, spoke of the "glass ceiling" that keeps many black executives out of high positions in the corporate world.

Despite the fact that he is now a successful businessman, Carver recalled years of frustration on the job throughout the fifties and sixties that shaped his political attitudes about race.

Even today, Carver lamented, many people do not view him in terms of his successes. Instead, they see him simply as a black man:

No matter what levels I strive to achieve and no matter my success, I'm subject to being mistaken for the elevator operator if I live, you know, on the East side of Manhattan. And that happens. I check into hotels, the best hotels, wherever I go around the country and somebody might mistake me for the elevator operator. It doesn't matter that I've got a briefcase in my hand and I'm wearing a $700 suit. I'm black. They don't see details. They just see color when they look at us.

Clearly, there is a level of status this man feels is not conferred upon him in the white world. Even for the executive, symbols of a structural/class position—an expensive suit, a briefcase—can't erase the differences imposed by race. Color imposes an identity that class does not diminish. Through white eyes, as Carver suggests, the class and status distinctions between elevator operator/executive are not discerned.

Indeed, interviews with Harlem's black gentry suggest that racism is, if not the most important, certainly a central reason for being pushed into the Harlem community. As a group they appear to be responding to a tension that arises as they increasingly cross once-restrictive boundaries that kept them out of certain neighborhoods and workplaces. Their increased contact with whites has given rise to encounters with racism and heightened their racial self-awareness.

The alienation many talk about must be attributed, in part, to the homeostatic principle that Orlando Patterson suggests gives rise to a resurgence of racism.[6] "It comes as no surprise," writes Patterson,

that just as the black working and middle classes began to make some headway under the impact of affirmative action laws, there was an upsurge of direct racism, reflected most crudely in the upsurge of KKK and other neofascist groups as well as the increased number of overt racist attacks but more subtly, and far more dangerously, in the powerful cultural signals given by the Reagan presidency that racist intolerance is once again acceptable.

(Patterson 1990:484)

Assimilation and integration are the source of contradictory feelings and frustrations that changes in race relations pose for those who have gained success in a social system that has become less restrictive for black mobility. The homeostatic principle suggests that structural changes reflected in the political and economic realms foster a hostile cultural reaction that reinforces racism. The irony that Harlem's black gentry hit on in these interviews is that in a new era of race relations and even by playing by the middle-class rules that determine success—mobility through education and career—their contacts with white America reinforce their marginality as blacks. Persistent racial slights and slurs make clear a boundary erected by a white world that they are unable to cross.

LIFE IN THE BLACK COMMUNITY

In an essay titled "Harlem, Ou Le Cancer de l'Amerique," Chester Mimes (1963:78) declared Harlem to be "like a cancer on the body of a nation," and concluded that "the most important thing to many Harlem Negroes is how to escape from it." We can read Himes's Harlem as a symbol of the black community in general. For many black Americans, success and mobility have been equated with achieving distance from the physical confines of the black community. In fact, years of flight by the black middle class from the Harlems of America has in part contributed to the deterioration of inner city minority communities.

Why then does Harlem represent hope, haven and community today for a group of middle class black professionals who certainly have other choices about where to live? In the following comment, Fay Johnson, a health care professional who has lived in Harlem for ten years, captured the duality of race and class that characterizes middle class professionals today and helps us understand the desire to live in the black community:

You know we're educated in the finest schools, we work in corporate America, we can fall out of this house in our Armani clothes and our Ferragamo shoes and we can speak correctly—you know rounded vowels. As black middle class people we have advantages and we can function in the white world. But we are bi-cultural in this society. Many of my generation have always been the minority. We have blazed the trail just like our parents did before us and we are the token. We are sort of a transition generation. We are very close to the civil rights

struggle of the 60s and we were raised by parents who went through the struggles of the 40s and so our mission is clear. We do race work everyday and that is clear. But when we socialize and when we relax we do that in a segregated setting where there are very few white folks. Essentially we go out into the world and we exercise our intellectual and political acumen in an integrated setting and we come back and relax and let our hair down and complain and take refuge in the black community.

Again, we see that the symbols of class—designer shoes clothing and language—are signs that the black middle class have a position in the white world. But an awareness of (racial) difference pushes many to seek out alternative spaces where they can relax among their own. Life in the black community, many argue, provides a sense of belonging not found at work or in other communities—suburban neighborhoods, downtown Manhattan—they once called home. Johnson's comment also suggests that the movement between black and white worlds occurs for a racially aware and politically active "transition generation."

In addition, many see in Harlem a chance to strengthen their self-awareness and bolster the psyche as they daily confront a world not completely accepting of them. Fred Washington argued that Harlem was important to him because:

It's a grounding, it's an anchor. When you're out there getting your tail kicked by people who don't care who you are enough to even call you by the right name, or mistake who you are when you walk into a restaurant or a building, even the one you live in, that's important. That's very important, you know.

What we can see then in the move to Harlem is a strategy of cultural survival rooted in the search for the positive meaning and support that the black community might provide.

When Reggie Smith, a television journalist, returned from a long-term assignment in Kenya he wanted to buy a home and he wanted to live in the city. So why Harlem? Smith had a preference for a black neighborhood, he explained, like the one in Chicago where he had grown up. This preference was reinforced when he experienced a "violent reaction from racism" in Chicago:

In Chicago we bought a house in a white area that was fire-bombed before we moved into it. Because I travel so much, I was worried about leaving my wife and kids alone. I made a decision to live in a black community, no matter the ills.

For some, like Smith and his family, the racism confronted is overt. The fire-bombing of one's home, for example, heightens feelings of exclusion from mainstream America. You can afford a house in a white area—but you still do not belong. For others, more subtle slights and a general lack of respect reinforce this alienation and bolster the need to participate in shared rituals of life in the black community.

June Wilson, another newcomer to Harlem, described her former job in Chicago where she worked in a mainly white environment. Wilson explained that seeking a haven from her predominantly white workplace made the draw of living in a black community and working toward its improvement worth the trouble:

> I [know this] is not such a positive thing to say [but] I worked in an environment where I didn't see many people that looked like me. So it was important for me to set up house in an area where I would be the most comfortable. That meant being around black people and being around black people who were race-minded.

Wilson's comment captures a sentiment expressed by other black gentry in Harlem. Several interviewees talked about the pressures of racism in their own lives and described what could be called living in two worlds—one white, one black. For many, there is a constant struggle to prove oneself in the white world—particularly in the workplace.

The boundaries of Harlem as a black community hold the promise of being in a place where they will find pride and respect as blacks. And by using the boundaries of Harlem to construct a world where they feel they do belong, the frustrations of life in two worlds can be diminished.

Yolanda Jackson, for example, turns to the boundaries that define the black world for support and affirmation. Creating a home in the black community, Jackson explained, helps her balance the two worlds—black and white—she operates in:

> I have always worked in predominantly white situations and socially at times I'm in mixed situations and almost predominantly white situations. It balances out though. I live in a black community and I work in primarily a white world. So, I have the balance.

Kimberly Anderson-Biggs works in downtown Manhattan for a major newspaper. That she sees having a home in the black community as a resolution of the tension associated with life in conflicting worlds is clear in the distinction she makes between work/downtown/white and home/uptown/black:

> I have real strong feelings—I really wanted to live around black people. I really did. I really get tired of going downtown and having white folks act like I don't belong down there. I get that all day long. I don't want to hear that shit when I get home. When I get home, I want people to wave at me when I come up the street. And that's what I get [living in Harlem].

Anderson-Biggs's comment suggests that a home in white and black neighborhoods offers entirely different rewards. The feeling that she gets from whites on the job—that she doesn't belong in their world—is not one she wants to follow her home to a white neighborhood. She looks on Harlem as a community that is her world. Here she does belong and when people wave, for example, they signal that welcome.

As the comments of Malcolm Balderidge reveal, the professional lives of many middle-class blacks often draw them into exclusively white worlds both on the job and, for those who live in integrated communities, at home. The desire to live in a black community is in part driven by the sense that integration in one part of life needn't mean 100 percent integration:

> I want[ed] to live here because I got tired of living in a very middle class white community, not because I'm against white folks or anything like that, because I'm not. But I got tired of having to always prove myself.

For Balderidge, the suspicious and often frightened looks of uncomfortable whites in the elevator late at night in his previous residence on the Upper West Side of Manhattan were part of what he termed "racial harassment" he received from his neighbors. Thus Balderidge decided to explore the purchase of a co-op in Harlem. For him, getting "back to the community" was one way to ease one of the tensions he experienced living in a white environment.

Balderidge's statement about the constant need to prove himself in the white world is similar to the remarks of others, who also describe the feeling of not belonging. Middle-class blacks cognizant of a subtle and sometimes overt color line that signals difference and distances them from white colleagues and peers actively engage in their own assertion of a boundary between black and white as a means of claiming an identity based on race.

Malcolm Balderidge argued that his own cultural awareness, and a lack of acceptance of it by many whites, made him more comfortable living in the black community. "I was not willing to change," he said, "and become a more proper looking African American, you know, cut my hair and not be so energetic. You see what I'm saying?" he asked touching his dreadlocks:

Since I wasn't willing to become a Negro like that, then I decided I would leave. You know, I thought it would be best for my own psychological and mental make-up to live in an African American community where they don't ask me those kind of questions, where they don't feel threatened, you know.

Others like Balderidge actively seek a connection to the black community in order to assert a racial identity and solidify a boundary based on racial identity. Given the fact that race continues to define the way many of these black professionals are defined by others and the way they think about themselves, Harlem offers the chance to bring together their class and racial identity in their use of Harlem as a home.

George Carver defines his move to Harlem as a way for him not only to remember his heritage but also to receive the respect his success accords him:

My career path has been white corporate America. And I need to come back to Harlem, if you will, to feel a part of the community.

Within the black community Carver is able to enjoy a sense of self that is defined in terms of both race and class. For Carver, a resident of one of Harlem's middle class enclaves—Hamilton Terrace—territorial stratification within the black community defines his world in terms of *both* race and class. Harlem as a racially defined community in Manhattan and Hamilton Terrace, as a middle class enclave within the community, function as a space and a space within that space in which the dual identities of being middle class and black are brought together for Carver.

The return by the middle class to the Harlem community is telling of the fact that those who have "made it" also have needs for a community and culture that are based on racial identity. In their comments, black gentry in Harlem talk about the need to belong, the desire not to have to always prove oneself, and the importance of keeping the focus on racial problems in America.

The feeling is that home should be a place where one is relaxed and respected. Harlem provides that home. Fred Washington argued that Harlem:

clearly has special significance, but only for one reason. To blacks it is the home of the renaissance. It is the cultural center of blacks throughout the world. In fact [that is] why I wanted to come here. I am very much aware of my cultural heritage. That was a draw. I wanted to be in a community where its roots have a black beginning.

Washington's claim that the "roots" of this community are the reason he is here suggests the existence of Harlem as a positive symbol of black community and culture. And, Washington continued:

Harlem is the cultural capital of the black world. There's no other place that can claim it. Do we need that symbolism? You bet we do. Because as a race we're grasping. We need that stability. We need that emotional anchor. That's what's been stripped away from us for four or five hundred years.

As an alternative—or oppositional—space, Harlem with its well understood racial boundaries provides a place of belonging. Harlem's black gentry cite belonging to the black community as one way to combat the hostility that as middle class blacks they confront in the larger white society. Harlem represents a line beyond which, in the arena of a racial community, one finds pride, validation, appreciation and respect. Harlem is a place in which racial communitas may be experienced.

CLASS DIFFERENCES IN THE BLACK COMMUNITY

But while life in Harlem presents the opportunity for black gentry to seek out a "communion of fellowship" based on race, we also must ask how class differences operate in what many believe can be both an economically diverse and harmonious racial community. Ironically, the pressures of the color line they seek to escape by moving to the black community are transformed into a "class line" of difference they must confront once in Harlem.

Those who have settled on high on the well-to-do streets of Hamilton Heights, for instance, do not confront these class differences so directly. The relatively quiet, tree-lined streets of well-preserved homes remind one of the suburban amenities that usually draw people out of the city. Harlem's middle-class enclaves are a stark contrast to the image and reality of much of life in other areas of the community.

Others who have moved closer to "the trenches," as one woman described her neighborhood, reside in the valley, or Central Harlem. Here, pockets of nice homes, streets and neighborhoods are mixed in, and among, the burned-out and abandoned buildings, empty lots and other symbols of urban poverty that contribute to the image of Harlem as a wasteland.

But the very term used to describe the actors in this process—gentry—suggests the return of an urban aristocracy to decaying inner city areas and neighborhoods that have been host to this phenomenon. The symbols of class that characterize Harlem's black gentry—both hill and valley residents—as middle-class homeowners in a largely poor community are apparent in their daily living and lifestyle choices.

Tasha Rogers, who moved to Harlem with her family five years ago when she was in high school, was cognizant of such difference:

As to being gentry, yeah I feel different from the neighbors and I don't know whether its a matter of education or if it's a class thing. We're professionals a lot of people around here are not professionals. I mean, I get funny looks when I'm walking the dog. So I know people notice us.

Malcolm Balderidge, a writer and college professor, lives in an old apartment building that recalls the architectural grandeur of Harlem's past. Balderidge resides within a fortress-like building that commands the corner of 113th Street and Afrika Boulevard. The pungent aroma of marijuana surrounds a small group conducting a thriving drug trade on the dusty, litter-strewn park at the corner. But through the building's gated courtyard, planted with roses and small trees, the world on the street is left behind.

The elevator in Brahmin Court carries one up into the large high-ceilinged rooms of a sunny ten-room apartment. Painted canvases splashed with warm oranges, greens, blues and reds color the room. Antique furniture and polished hardwood floors grace the warm and comfortable home that Balderidge and his wife have created for themselves in Harlem.

Balderidge described what are very middle-class sensibilities in discussing what he and others have striven for in their new community:

People like myself who have moved into the neighborhood want to see things happen. First of all, for selfish reasons. They are just like any other property owner. You know, they want to see the value of their property go up. You know, we're buying these apartments and on an economic level you want to see it go up rather than go down. I mean, that's just basic stuff. People who had the good sense to invest, they want to see their stuff go up. They want to see some nice things around there. So they're willing to work for that, you see.

Often, Balderidge and other newcomers worked in opposition to the older long-time residents as they sought to overturn the "status quo" that had led to the deterioration of Brahmin Court. Now, the lock on the building's gate, the roses in the courtyard and the absence of the smell of urine and feces in the elevators and stairwells are changes that the new residents claim responsibility for.

Kimberly Anderson-Biggs and Jeff Biggs appear to be "typical" gentrifiers at first glance. They are a young couple, both successful journalists for prominent New York publications, who moved to Harlem in 1985. We meet one Sunday at Johnson's—a family restaurant on 145th Street and one of the institutions of old Harlem. Over the din of clattering dishes, waitresses bustling about and the maitre d' greeting young and old church goers dressed in their Sunday best, we talk about gentrification in Harlem and how they each define their position as newcomers within the community.

Jeff Biggs was born in Harlem and lived on 145th street until the age of five when he and his family moved to a New Jersey suburb. Because he left at such a young age, Biggs did not consider himself a Harlemite/insider. Instead he thought gentrifier was an apt description of his new position in the community:

We have more money and better jobs than most of the people who live in our block. We moved in, they think we are very strange. Most of our neighbors couldn't really, like, figure out that we were there for real.

At first, their neighbors looked on these two residents, with their money and jobs, as an oddity on the block. Because of real estate speculation in Harlem many brownstones that have been purchased remain unoccupied as the owners wait out changes in the area or turn over properties for a profit. Anderson-Biggs and her husband, however, moved in when they purchased their brownstone and say that they are here to stay.

Kimberly Anderson-Biggs, a native of Chicago, grew up in the projects and this, she felt, made her no stranger to the black community. Unlike her husband, she felt that black participation in the gentrification of Harlem was a potentially loaded issue. She urged caution in applying the term. Though the two did not agree on the terms and definitions of gentrification, it became clear that they did recognize the ways they were different from many of their neighbors.

"Oh, yes. It was a little weird," Anderson-Biggs said, describing their early days in the community:

> We went out every day. We dressed up. I mean, we weren't working class people. Not that people on my block don't work. Most of the folks on my block work. But we were buppies, you know. He leaves the house in suits, I leave the house in suits, we both carry briefcases, we're both journalists, you know. So, we're bopping out of the house in the morning. One morning we walked out of the house, kissed each other goodbye, walked in opposite directions, and our neighbors were dumbfounded.

The visible characteristics of the young urban professional—suits and briefcases—simply make people like Kimberly Anderson-Biggs and Jeff Biggs a new and rare sight in their neighborhood.

Anderson-Biggs told me that at first, "there was a fair amount of resentment about it." In addition to the fact that she and her husband stood out, they had a different approach to their personal property and were not as communal toward the space as were many of their neighbors:

> [Jeff] wouldn't let people sit on the stoop anymore, you know. They used to hang out on the stoop and eat dinner and throw chicken bones down in the stairwell and stuff, and we'd make them leave, you know.

Despite the desire and intention to become an integral part of community life, class differences do mark these newcomers as outsiders. As Anderson-Biggs and her husband make adjustments to their life in Harlem, lifestyle differences between themselves and their neighbors are at times annoyances they confront:

> It's a pain to live in Harlem when you lead a life different from the life of your neighbors. When the people don't have to be at work in the morning, they can stay up all night. When you have to get up in the morning, you don't want to hear that shit [radios and talk in the streets at night]. You really don't.

Kenyatta Davis raised many of these same issues as she talked about her early days in her Harlem neighborhood:

> When I start to talk to people on my block they know that I am not your average resident, you know. They know that I have a "gifted job" and I work downtown. I know when we initially moved in we had to go through a little thing with the block, just in terms of establishing space and making clear to people that you can't eat and smoke and drink on our stoops. You know, we like you, it's cool. But you cannot eat on our stoop. And one of the things that I don't like about the white household that's on our block is that they let people abuse their stoop. And I don't know if it's they're fearful. I don't know if it's a missionary attitude. I don't know what it is. But I think that it sets a bad example, especially in light of the fact that we don't allow that, you know.

While home ownership and other symbols of class such, as expensive cars, the search for the *New York Times* and style of dress may set this black gentry apart, many argue that the "house proud"[7] attitude and middle-class lifestyle they bring to the community should be an asset in the redevelopment of Harlem.

To talk about their arrival as a positive force that broadens the economic base of the community positions the black gentry as a necessary group in the community. This reasoning is one way to grapple with class differences in a way that does not seem divisive. Getting beyond differences of class is necessary for this group to reach toward the ideal of constructing/asserting an identity based on race.

THE CONSTRUCTION OF COMMUNITAS

Despite their commitments, there is no shortage of problems associated with inner city life that make living in Harlem difficult for middle-class blacks. Yolanda Jackson listed the crack problem on her block, disregard for many of the things she has done in attempts to improve the neighborhood such as planting trees on her street, and once being confronted by a man armed with a machine gun as she climbed the steps of her brownstone.

But Jackson was firm in her resolve to stand by the choice she had made to move into this community and work at making it a more liveable place for herself and others. Jackson's vision of Harlem as a decent place to live was predicated on the notion that people like herself—middle-class black professionals—are a necessary part of the fabric of the community:

> I think that the black middle class has been negligent in its responsibility to this community. In some other communities the middle class didn't move out so the community stayed stable. There was always a mix. There were always poor people living next door to a doctor, a lawyer, a teacher or whatever. And these people were the role models. All the role models moved out in the late 60's and in the early 70's. More middle class people have to make the commitment to come back into the community and live in a community. And it doesn't mean that you have to live in a community of all middle class people. I just think that middle class blacks, professional blacks, have abandoned their community.

A political responsibility to the idea of racial community is a fundamental feature of the identity that Jackson and other black gentry in Harlem project.

The ways in which black gentry in Harlem work toward (re)constructing an economically diverse Harlem can be seen through their participation in the public culture of the community. Thus, the search for communitas in a community defined by shared ethnicity can be seen as an effort to bridge the tensions of race and class in post-Civil Rights America.

In the following comment, Reggie Smith shows concern for the role middle-class blacks should play in their own communities. "I meet blacks every day who don't want to come to Harlem," Smith confided:

> I think it's a matter of coming back to the community, investing in the community. The return of the middle class signals leadership. We're seeing pockets of neighborhoods turned around. People in these neighborhoods are retrained and reintroduced to community spirit. People with ability have to come back—it's a brain drain for the community. There has to be a positive force.

According to Freddye Crosby it does no good for middle-class blacks to move into Harlem and then distance themselves from the community. "I don't wear the middle class banner like it's a badge that you get in the girl scouts," she argued. Instead, Crosby suggested, middle-class blacks should use whatever status or power they have available to them to the benefit of the community:

> It can become important [if] I have an advantage when it comes to going in and trying to effect some change within the community. Whether it's

getting a company to donate products to a welfare hotel, whether it's trying to get a meeting with someone in city hall or whatever else, I think I owe that to the community. If you have juice anywhere you should use it. You know, you should use your influence. You need to treat it like it's money and it's valuable. And so you should use your influence where it counts the most, spend it in the best way possible, make it count.

The new black middle class in Harlem illustrates one way that successful blacks strive to achieve a balance between race and class in their lives. Often it is on the level of active political involvement that that line between insider and outsider is erased. "I think you can learn not to be an outsider," Kimberly Anderson-Biggs explained:

> If people really understand that you're committed, then you don't feel like an outsider. That's why I got involved in community [politics]. I'm on a task force on AIDS and homelessness. I sort of got in by accident, because I got into a fight about them building an AIDS hospital, an AIDS nursing home across the street from our house, which you know, sounds like self-interest, and in a lot of ways was self-interest, But we already had six other facilities in a two-block area and I said, "Yo, this is enough". Marginal neighborhoods like this cannot take that kind of proliferation. [We don't need] a 200 bed hospital and a shelter all in the same neighborhood. We need supermarkets and housing [so] middle class people can come and stabilize. We have great police service, we have great sanitation service, in part because of our activism. I'm a part of the traditional block association. We're in every 20th Precinct community council meeting. The police captain in the 20th Precinct knows me by name, by sight. He drives through our block to check on how things are. You have to work for that to happen.

Often their community participation reflects the values and consciousness about race work and social responsibility that make Harlem's black gentry aware of and concerned about the community of their "brothers" around them. By organizing neighbors and confronting the police, for example, Harlem's black gentry contribute to an ideology of control and empowerment within the community.

Yolanda Jackson, for instance, says that she "got very active, very early" on the block:

> When I got on the block there was a very serious angel dust problem and it was just really getting

on my nerves. The block association had been kind of laying dormant, so I reorganized it and got people organized to go to the police precinct and demand that they clean the mess up off of our block. And it was effective.

While Jackson claims the angel dust problem on her block got on *her* nerves, the individual action she took—to reorganize an existing but dormant block association—mobilized her neighborhood and as a group they confronted the police. This signalled to her neighbors that she was someone who cared, as well as someone who could make things happen.

Crosby's social service and volunteer work in Harlem also define her attempts at actively working toward improving life in the community:

I'm involved with other things like Copeland's Christmas Fund for Kids which is a group that was started by Mr. Copeland of Copeland's Restaurant which helps young folks. We devote the whole day of Christmas to kids in the area who are disadvantaged, whether it's welfare hotels or women in the battered women's shelters or homeless men. I work with a men's shelter. [I have also been] working with the Urban Shelter which is a battered women's shelter. A lot of the things I work with, they find their way under the same banner. So I get involved in that way.

Many like Corsby argue that their presence as successful blacks in the community is another important reason for being in Harlem. As role models, middle-class black gentry join Harlem's long-term middle class as a visible group of successful blacks in the community.

To George Carver, the fact that neighborhood kids see him—a man who has "made it"—daily has an important function in terms of the mentoring he provides by living in the community:

As far as being a role model, in spite of myself, I am. It turns out I like it. I'm very sensitive to that. The fact that my name's in this magazine, the fact that I've made the pages of major publications and black media gives me outreach to communities, black communities, all over the country. I get letters from kids in Omaha, Nebraska, Anchorage, Alaska, black kids okay? But when I come here, they can see me on an everyday basis. I walk down the street delighted that kids come across, come off the stoop, and walk me to my door. Not because I'm some hero, but I'm showing them that I'm accessible. Most blacks you'll

find get too important for that, too snobby. So, I don't have to brag about what I do or who I am. Hut kids in the block know that I'm the one that gave so and so the Hot Car Racer set for his birthday, or whatever. Or, you know, see them playing and give them 10 bucks to go buy popsicles. It's little things like that. They just see me as that guy who's friendly. You know?

For others, shopping above 110th Street, using recreational facilities, attending Harlem churches and frequenting restaurants and museums are also ways to participate in the community life of Harlem. In this case, private actions such as shopping and praying, take place in the public domain.

For Yolanda Jackson, doing business in Harlem keeps money in the community and provides jobs:

I try to do as much business [in Harlem] as possible. My dry cleaners is up here. I go to restaurants up here. There are African restaurants and Caribbean restaurants. There's a variety of things so that whatever your taste is you can just about find it in Harlem. I patronize as many things as possible. You know in doing my house most of the work that's been done has been done by black contractors, plasterers, electricians. I make it a point of trying to really keep the money in the community in that way. Every way I can, I do.

And for Jackson, the move to Harlem also has meant a reconnection with spiritual roots:

Once I bought my house I went back to church and moved back to some of my spiritual roots. I'm really enjoying being a part of Canaan Baptist Church. It's a socially responsible church and it's done so much in the Harlem community. I got involved with the church and I've gotten involved in projects at Harlem Hospital [and other] institutions within the community.

Kenyatta Davis feels that her connection to Harlem is solidified as a result of using community facilities and participating in community events such as neighborhood festivals and block parties:

I do [feel connected] in large part because I not only live here, I'm a member of the Y[WCA] so I use their services. I mean, rather than go to New York Health and Racquet Club, I'd go to the Y. I'd work out [there] and it's a hip place to meet and network with people who are also in the community. I study dance at another community center, the Hansberry Recreation Center. I participate in the neighborhood festivals. I'm not a big churchgoer, but I go to church periodically. Just [for the] political energy that's here. I'm involved in any rallies and that kind of thing that's come up, so I do feel very much part of the center. There's the Schomberg Center. I participate in a lot of activities there.

These bonds that newer residents are able to forge with the existing community provide an informal network of support that in many ways are representative of life in a small-town community. On a day-to-day basis, Harlem functions for many as a world of communal spirit and kinship. For many of Harlem's black gentry this is one thing that has drawn them to life in the black community.

Particularly during the busy days of summer when children, parents and grandparents, friends and neighbors fill the streets in conversation and play, it is customary to look out for others in the community. A mother's watchful eye looks out for a neighbor's child, not just her own. A gathering of men at the corner are an unofficial protective service watchful of women traveling alone from the subway after work. Older women, especially, peel back their curtains and note a stranger on your stoop—the time he was there, did he ring the bell or did he idly stand upon the stoop?—eager to report a person or an event out of sorts with the usual routine.

Yolanda Jackson talked about this kind of concern her neighbors showed for her. From the old ladies who pay attention to the community's comings and goings to the men at the corner who protect and maintain the order of their own "territory" in the streets, Harlem's new gentry feel that they too are drawn into this protective fold:

They watched out for me. At 6 o'clock in the morning these little old ladies would call me up and say "there's a parking space," you know its alternate side of the street parking. "You better get up and move your car and move to the other side of the street while you got a space." That could get on my nerves but they looked out for me. If they saw someone tinkering around my car they ran them away or walking up on my stoop and they knew I wasn't home they would tell them to get off the stoop, I wasn't at home, leave. Then they would tell me that. They would describe who came up on the stoop or whatever so it's like they watched out for me and I watched out for them. I mean even down to the winos or the alcoholics. If I were walking home late and didn't drive my car or whatever, they would say "we've told you about coming home late like this by yourself." One time a guy was behind me. I don't know if he was going to snatch my purse or whatever but I turned around and I saw him and when he saw me when I turned around quickly he ran off. So I walked up further and the alcoholics, you know, the drunks, said "You didn't have to worry. We saw 'at mufucker. He wadn't gun do nuthin to you. We had him scoped. You didn't have to worry about dat. But we keep telling you about walking in this neighborhood this late. We might not always be out here." Those kind of bonds were developed with the people who lived on the block and some of these people had lived on the block for twenty and thirty years.

Among my interview subjects residence in Harlem varied from ten years to one year. And yet, most everyone could relate instances that speak of the ways in which they had been taken into this protective fold. The emotional ties that the Harlem community provides when it functions on such a localized level offer another sense of the kinship and community that its black residents share.

Many of the rituals of public life that define the community become important ways to express an interactive commitment that goes beyond individualistic concerns for home and property. As part of the shared cultural life of Harlem, conversation, language and interactions on the street also become essential to the way one's position in the community is defined.

Through an act as simple as sitting on one's front stoop in the summertime with a cool drink, and asking after "so-and-so" or nodding a friendly "how do" to passers-by, one participates in the interactions that define the shared life of the community. As a ritual that takes place in the open space of one's street, public behavior signifies one aspect of a communal spirit in the black community.

Kimberly Anderson-Biggs talked fondly about how this stoop culture she remembered from growing up indeed brings her together with others in her neighborhood:

It feels like home. It's the kind of neighborhood I grew up in. I like being on the street where I know everybody, you know. I like coming up the block and having people stop and say hi. I like knowing who is home from college and who is just out of the hospital and, you know, just life living in a neighborhood that's your own neighborhood. I feel safer when I know the people I live around, and in Harlem, I do. I mean, I just have a real obsession for the way that black folks live. We're loud, playing our radios and fix[ing] our cars. We drink beer. We carry on. I mean, I sort of like it. It's stupid, I know. It's not rational at all, but I have a real fondness for it.

And, Anderson-Biggs talked about how initial perceptions neighbors had about she and her husband—two buppies who didn't fit in—changed as the two participated in the sharing of hellos and information that take place within this culture of the stoop:

> They realize that we're on the street. One night we were sitting on the stoop—see every summer, as soon as it gets warm, I take the radio, I take a glass of ice tea and I sit down on the stoop to keep other people off the stoop and remind them that we still live there, because they haven't seen us all winter. And it's also part of the neighborhood culture. People sit on stoops. That's part of black culture, anyway. So, we come out and sit on the stoop. First of all, it says to them, well, at least they sit on the stoop. We bring the radio out, we play BGO, the jazz station, because we like jazz. It also says okay, so, they're different from us, but they still sit on the stoop. It's a part of the tradition of the community.

Freddye Crosby stressed the personal need for the bonds of community that the public rituals in Harlem's shared spaces offer her:

> I'd like to see myself or at least describe myself as a part of a move to bring Harlem back to life. I think my intent is a little bit more than just buying a property and living downtown and not knowing [people]. I mean, I talk to the folks around here. I walk down the streets, I have conversations with the little folks in the bodegas and, you know, [at] the block parties I talk to the ladies. I like that because it gives me a real sense of what kind of community I'm in and it makes me feel like I'm back at home.

While Crosby sees herself as an important part of the community, she plays down the differences that might set her apart—such as gentrification in the form of speculation and/or unoccupied brownstones. Instead, her focus on the contacts, conversations, and interactions she has with workers and neighbors on her street is the image she projects of her place in the life of the community. Such rituals of neighborliness are an important dimension in the bond that unites the community and provides communitas for black gentry.

CONCLUSION

This paper has explored the dilemma of difference that confronts a group of middle-class blacks seeking community and identity as they alternate between downtown (white) and uptown (black) worlds of Manhattan in their personal and professional lives. The difference of race that defines their marginal status downtown is ironically transformed into differences of class that mark their outsiderness in a community they are drawn to seeking "bonds of fellowship" based on race.

As successful black professionals, many of the values of middle-class America that these individuals seem to embody—the importance of education, value of property ownership, the work ethic, initiative and self-reliance—are the values that define them as members of a structural group—the middle class—in American society. But continuing experiences of racism and exclusion reinforce their marginality and appear to solidify racial identification and a commitment to the black community.

It is by coming "home to Harlem," that Harlem's black gentry are able to create a community that serves their needs for racial pride and awareness that are unmet in the increasingly integrated arenas of post-Civil Rights America. As homeowners in Harlem they attempt to bridge the dual worlds of race and class they are defined by.

Active attempts at fostering community solidarity and empowerment through their attendance at town meetings, membership on task forces and political committees allow black gentry to take part in the political life of the community. And through many of the shared rituals of kinship and community that take place on the streets, blocks, and in neighborhoods throughout Harlem, the bonds of fellowship that embody a racial communitas are further cemented.

It is possible to see in black gentrification in Harlem individual acts which contribute to a sense of belonging in a larger collectivity defined by race. The story of black middle class participation in the gentrification of Harlem offers a glimpse into the complexities of class, racial identity and difference in post-Civil Rights America.

Notes

1 During the Harlem Renaissance Harlem was created and experienced as cultural space distinctive from white Manhattan and America. Therefore, I argue that today Harlem stands as a symbolic community available to a number of groups and

individuals who draw on its various meanings in the articulation of cultural, economic and political identities.

2 Turner defines structure as "the patterned arrangements of role-sets—the actions and relationships that flow from social status—and status-sets—the various positions occupied by an individual consciously recognized and regularly operative in a given society."

3 "Marginals," writes Turner, are those who "are simultaneously members (by ascription, optation, self-definition, or achievement) of two or more groups whose social definitions and cultural norms are distinct from, and often opposed to, one another. What is interesting about such marginals is that they often look to their group of origin, the so called inferior group, for communitas, and to the more prestigious group in which they mainly live and in which they aspire to higher status as their structural reference group."

4 The names of interview subjects have been changed and some details slightly altered to preserve privacy and protect anonymity.

5 Recent scholarship and debate in American race relations revolve around the intersection between race and class as well as the progress of assimilation and integration for black Americans. In *The Declining Significance of Race* William Julius Wilson argues that a "preoccupation with race and racial conflict obscures fundamental problems that derive from the intersection of class with race." Wilson concludes that "economic divisions now exist among blacks, divisions which show every sign of deepening and which have profound implications for the significance of race in the American experience." Within the sociological community reaction to Wilson's "declining significance of race" thesis was swift (see Newby 1978, Willie 1978 and 1979, Lynn and Berry 1979, Marrett 1980, Pettigrew 1980, Oliver 1982). Critics argued that the title of Wilson's work was deceptive and pointed out that the focus was on the increasing significance of class. One response to Wilson's work came from sociologist Charles Willie who posited a counterhypothesis—that there is an inclining significance of race, "especially for middle class blacks who, because of school desegregation and affirmative action and other integration programs, are coming into direct contact with whites for extended interaction." This counterhypothesis is central to my exploration of middle-class black gentry in Harlem.

6 In his essay "Toward A Study of Black America," Orlando Patterson argues that the homeostatic principle—the maintenance of relatively stable conditions by internal processes that counteract any departure from the norm—is a means of gauging persistence, despite change, in patterns of race relations. In his argument, Patterson recalls Ransom and Sutch's application of this principle: "Jim Crow had arisen as a form of racial oppression to replace an economic system that had earlier stifled black initiative, ensured black poverty, and demoralized black leaders." In effect changes in the structural relationship that altered an earlier pattern of race relations gave rise to a cultural arrangement that maintained the separation and oppression of blacks.

7 Kenyatta Davis explained house proud this way: I care enough to develop the space that I'm in. So it's one less abandoned building, it's one less building that's going to rot, one more person spending dollars here and just being a living example to other black people who are less fortunate that things can be better.

REFERENCES

Anderson, Elijah
    1990 *Streetwise: Race, Class and Change in an Urban Community.* Chicago: University of Chicago Press.

Bailey, Bruce
    1984 "Gentrification Vultures Poised To Swoop on Harlem," *Heights and Valleys* 8(1).

Foderaro, Lisa
    1987 "Harlem's Hedge Against Gentrification," *The New York Times* (August 16).

Godfrey, Brian
    1988 *Neighborhoods in Transition.* Berkeley: University of California Press.

Himes, Chester
    1963 "Harlem Ou le Cancer de l'Amerique," *Presence Africaine* 45(1) Trimestre.

Lynn, Mary and Benjamin Berry, eds.
    1979 *The Black Middle Class.* Saratoga Springs: Skidmore College Press.

Marrett, Cora Bagley
    1980 "The Precariousness of Social Class in Black America," *Contemporary Sociology* 9.

Newby, Robert
    1978 "Review of the Declining Significance of Race," *School Review* 87.

Oliver, Melvin
    1982 "The Enduring Significance of Race," *Journal of Ethnic Studies* 7(4).

Omi, Michael and Howard Winant
  1986 *Racial Formation in the United States.*
        New York: Routledge & Kegan Paul.
Patterson, Orlando
  1990 "Toward a Study of Black America,"
        Dissent (Fall).
Pettigrew, Thomas
  1980 "The   Changing–Not   Declining–
        Significance of Race," *Contemporary
        Sociology* 9 (January).
Richard Schaffer and Neil Smith
  1986 "The Gentrification of Harlem?", *Annals
        of the Association of American Geogra-
        phers* 76(3).
Smith, Neil and Peter Williams, eds.
  1986 *Gentrification of the Cily.* Boston: Unwin
        and Allen.
Turner, Victor
  1977 *The Ritual Process: Structure and Anti-
        Structure.* Ithaca: Cornell University Press.

  1974 *Dramas, Fields and Metaphors: Sym-
        bolic Action in Human Society.* Ithaca:
        Cornell University Press.
  1967 *Die Forest of Symbols: Aspects of
        Ndembu Ritual.* Ithaca: Cornell Univer-
        sity Press.
Williams, Brett
  1987 *Upscaling Downtown: Stalled Gentri-
        fication in a Washington D.C. Neigh-
        borhood.*   Ithaca: Cornell University
        Press.
Willie, Charles, ed.
  1979 *Caste and Class Controversy.* Bayside,
        New York: General Hall.
  1978 "The Inclining Significance of Race,"
        Society 15.
Wilson, William Julius
  1980 *I'he Declining Significance of Race.*
        Chicago: University of Chicago Press.

24

"Negotiating Grit and Glamour: Young Women of Color and the Gentrification of the Lower East Side"

From *City & Society* (2007)

Caitlin Cahill

NEGOTIATING GRIT AND GLAMOUR: YOUNG WOMEN OF COLOR AND GENTRIFICATION

What I think of when thinking of my neighbor-hood is Latin music and hip hop playing in the street. In the summer people hang out on the corner and in the park and what seems to be thousands of children running around playing in the street. Sprinklers on, with the smell of BBQ in the distance. The icy man yelling icy's coco and cherry, the ice cream truck music playing in the distance.

Jasmine[1]
Fed Up Honey

Jasmine's description of her neighborhood brings to mind depictions of dynamic working class urban neighborhoods like the Lower East Side. On hot summer days everyone is out on the street; music blasting, ice cream cones melting, older folks watching from park benches. It is an almost nostalgic image of public life whose loss is bemoaned by urban critics, who express concern about the lack of diversity, the erosion of public space, and the widening gap between rich and poor in contemporary cities, already a reality in regenerated neighborhoods and theme park downtowns (Mitchell 2003; Smith 2002; Sorkin 1992). This loss is also expressed by young women growing up in the gentrifiying Lower East Side neighborhood of New York City. Their affection for their old neighborhood has grown as they witness its changes, as it becomes an unfamiliar place.

Focusing on how young working class women of color make sense of processes of disinvestment and gentrification, this paper will fill "the ethnographic void" (Lees 2003), offering inside perspectives on urban restructuring rarely found in the gentrification literature (Alicea 2001; Muñiz 1998). My analysis will consider how young women negotiate contradictory subjectivities revealing how the personal is political (Cahill 2007a) and "how the intimate and global intertwine" (Pratt and Rosner 2006:15).

What does it mean to witness your neighborhood change while you are still in it? Jasmine explains:

For some reason I liked it better when no one knew our neighborhood. Now that people are trying to make a name for us we have to live up to the grittyness of the ghetto life on one side and the glamour of the club, café and boutique life on the other side.

In the context of neoliberal economic restructuring, gentrification plays a key role in cities (Smith 2002; Newman and Ashton 2004; Hackworth and Smith 2001). If gentrification is the "new urban form of globalization" (Smith 2002), a closer look at the experiences of young women may provide an understanding of how global processes take shape on the ground. My analysis adopts a dynamic inter-pretative framework to account for the disorientation between feeling "stuck in place" (Katz 2002) and flows of capital (Sassen 1998; Cox 1997; Castells 1989) associated with processes of globalization. Here this is articulated in the tension between grit and glamour. Foregrounding the anger and pain of young women marginalized and marooned by global capital (Katz 2004), I analyze the emotional geographies of abstract processes of globalization in concrete everyday lives (Mountz and Hyndman 2006). I situate the young women's experiences in a shifting topography which is global and local, and mutually constitutive. Gibson-Graham argues that one can scratch anything global and find locality-grounded practices in communities (2002: 31–2). My examination of young women of color's place-based politics and their experiences of gentrification and disinvestment on the Lower East Side provides an understanding of how the neoliberal restructuring of neighborhoods takes place at the local scale, and how it is accommodated and resisted.

Rewriting the everyday experiences of young women into global analyses foregrounds an embodied and situated geopolitics (Dowler and Sharp 2001; Nagar et al. 2002). Bridging the material and the psychological, I argue that how young women define their relationships to their neighborhood is intimately connected with how they understand their selves. I address the socio-spatial constitution of young women's identities as they interpret their experiences growing up in the Lower East Side where they have to "live up to the grittyness of the ghetto life" and "the glamour of the club, café and boutique life." Negotiating contradictory subject positions, the young women grapple with tensions between giving back to their community—what Carol Gilligan identifies as an "ethic of care" (1982)—and wanting to escape its problems, the young women reconfigure their subjectivities in personal narratives that reveal pain, critical insight, and concerns for their community. In conclusion, I consider what we can learn about the contradictions of globalization from young women's ambivalent relationships with neighborhood change.

First, I discuss young women's experience of growing up in a neighborhood in transition, focusing in particular on articulations of disinvestment. Next, I consider how they interpret processes of gentrification through the lens of whiteness, placing emphasis upon race and class. I illustrate the feelings of loss young working class women of color express as their neighborhood changes, and traces of their history and culture are erased. What does it mean to grow up in a neighborhood as it is transformed physically, culturally, economically, and socially? Few researchers have looked at what it means to grow up in a gentrifying/still disinvested neighborhood (Cahill 2000; Sharff 1998). This study aims to fill in this gap. My research also contributes to the feminist geopolitical project of bridging the interdependent scales

of the global and the body to "repopulate" globalization and gentrification discourses (Mountz and Hyndman 2006; Dowler and Sharp 2001). I want to "disrupt grand narratives of global relations by focusing on the specific, the quotidian" (Pratt and Rosner 2006:15) to demonstrate how our subjectivities are inextricably connected with processes of global urban restructuring.

THE "MAKES ME MAD" PARTICIPATORY ACTION RESEARCH PROJECT

Theories and practice of participatory action research (PAR) are particularly relevant to the study of young women's interpretations of gentrification. Building upon long-standing traditions of asset-based development and grassroots activism (Kretzmann and McKnight 1996), PAR reflects an ethical commitment to building capacity and doing research that will be useful to the community (Freire 1997; Martín-Baró 1994; Lewin 1951). The epistemological framework of PAR projects engages a bottom-up analysis, involving those most affected by the research issues, and challenging social inequalities as they are understood by those subjected to them. As a white young woman who also grew up on the Lower East Side (twenty years earlier), the decision to engage in a participatory research project represents a conscious positionality and ethical commitment to foregrounding the perspectives of young working class women of color. PAR privileges "the understanding that people—especially those who have experienced historic oppression—hold deep knowledge about their lives and experiences, and should help shape the questions, [and] frame the interpretations" of research (Torre and Fine 2006: 458).

This paper draws upon a participatory action research project developed in 2002 with six young women (aged 16–22) who grew up on the Lower East Side. This diverse research group of women, the "Fed Up Honeys," reflected neighborhood demographics, self-identifying as African-American, Puerto Rican, Dominican, Chinese, and Black-Latina. The young women were paid a stipend for their participation and trained in social research methods. I facilitated the participatory action research project and collaborated with them in developing the project. First, we investigated the neighborhood, using methods like mapping, photography, focus groups, field research, and reflective writing (for more details see Cahill et al. in press; Cahill 2007b). The young researchers were involved in all stages of the research process, from framing the questions, to collecting and analyzing the data, and developing research products. In the process of investigating the contradictions of their everyday lives, the young women came to understand their individual experiences as shared, social, and also political.

Collectively the team developed a project entitled "Makes Me Mad: Stereotypes of young urban womyn of color" which considered the relationship between gentrification, disinvestment, public (mis)representations, and young women's self-understanding. The project was developed based on personal concerns of the young women. It was a project by and for young women of color and represents a perspective on gentrification missing in the literature. The Fed Up Honeys first identified stereotypes of young women of color such as "burden to society" or "likely to be teen moms" and then worked to untangle the connections between representations that serve to "fix" young women of color in the "ghetto" or "inner city" and the gentrification of their community. One concern that emerged from our project was that as working class neighborhoods are "cleaned up" (that is gentrified), stereotypical profiles of poor communities of color as "lazy and on welfare" serve to justify their displacement. The struggle over representation is not only about the violence of stereotypes, but also about the right to remain in one's home community (Rios-Moore et al. 2004; Cahill 2006).

The research process was personally transformative for each of us. Since we wanted to make a meaningful contribution with our research, beyond an "armchair revolution" (Freire 1997), action was a critical concern. Therefore, we developed different ways of reaching out to our community, and others, to speak back to stereotypes and present our results. This included a stereotype sticker campaign; two websites: www.fed-up-honeys.org and http://www.fed-up-honeys.org/cn/ (one targets a Chinese audience); and a report distributed to youth organizations and community centers (Rios-Moore et al. 2004). The Fed Up Honey team presented at academic conferences and co-authored book chapters (Cahill et al. in press; Cahill et al. 2004). In this paper, I draw on our collective writings and transcripts from our taped discussions.

THE LOWER EAST SIDE

Centrally located in New York City's downtown Manhattan, the gentrification of the Lower East Side has proceeded in fits and starts over the past twenty years (Mele 2000; Smith 1996; Abu-Lughod 1994). The neighborhood's complex overlapping histories of waves of immigration, massive abandonment,

reinvestment, and new developments are reflected in its place-identities as the Lower East Side, Alphabet City, Loisaida, The East Village, and Da Sixth Boro. In 1988, at the time of the Tompkins Square "riots," a historic event in the gentrification literature (Mitchell 2003; Smith 1996), the young women researchers were still children. By the time they went to high school in the 1990s, Avenue A was almost completely gentrified and commercial establishments on Avenue B staked out the "new urban frontier" (Smith 1996). By 2002 much of the Lower East Side was gentrified, yet the area where most of the researchers lived, and that was the focus of our work, was still undergoing dramatic changes. This area, below 14th Street, east of Avenue B, and above the Williamsburg Bridge, has in recent years largely been inhabited by Latino residents, hence its identification as Loisaida (Nuyorican for the Lower East Side). Not coincidentally, this is also the area of the neighborhood that experienced the most disinvestment and neglect in the 1970s and 80s. Only in the last ten years processes of gentrification visibly started there.

"THE SYSTEM"

> I am proud of my neighborhood in front of people never letting someone disrespect us (unless they live there too). But also am angry for the problems we have in our neighborhood. Many things bother me about where I've grown up, about the people, about the outcome of the people I grew up with.

The young women researchers were not sentimental about their neighborhood. Growing up on the Lower East Side means to personally experience negotiations of disinvestment. Their neighborhood was identified as a ghetto, slum, or more colloquially as "LES" (Lower East Side), "Lowa" or "Da 6th Boro." Associated with growing up in the LES is a street smart awareness and sense of pride at having "survived it." This experience is not, however, monolithic. The LES was also identified positively as "home" and a significant context for memories and relationships. In their discussions about growing up on the Lower East Side, the Fed Up Honeys expressed a nuanced and deeply personal understanding of disinvestment and neighborhood change. By disinvestment I am referring to a structural context of social and economic transformations that are articulated by the young women as a part of a convergence of deepening inequalities that are understood in racial terms. The geography of gentrification that unfolded parallel to experiences of social/economic disinvestment was discussed by the young women as part of a broader context of racial discrimination and social inequities ranging from slavery to police brutality, the scarcity of jobs, cut-backs in social services, shortage of affordable housing, to the lack of financial security and support.

Identified as "the system" or "the matrix," reflecting the structural perspective the researchers developed in their collective analyses, the young women engaged a structural racism framework to explain "the ongoing disadvantages associated with being a person of color", "related to the ongoing advantages with being white (Aspen Institute 2004; MacIntosh 1989) and grounded within a particular geopolitical context. Reversing the gaze, the women developed an analysis of whiteness as they struggled to explain and negotiate processes of gentrification, as Janderie writes:

> While engaged in a deep discussion about what has become of the Lower East Side … suddenly I hear one of girls say the word gentrification. I had never heard the word before in my life, so naturally I asked "what's that mean?" She explains to me that these yuppie ass, money having, culture seeking, white people are buying us poor people out of our neighborhood in part because they want a taste of our culture rich environment and the more of them who come in, the more of us are forced to leave because we can longer afford to live here.

Constructed as a threat of social and spatial exclusion, "the more of them who come in, the more of us are forced to leave," whiteness is the face of gentrification. In contrast with its often presumed invisibility, here whiteness is marked and conspicuous. As Jasmine wrote in her journal: "Racial differences in the neighborhood: white vs. everyone else." From within the neighborhood it was difficult to make sense of changes taking place over their lifetime. Another researcher wrote in her journal: "It's like unknown people crossing over your territory and taking it for all its worth. They (who remain faceless) come in and destroy what many have tried to build up." Gentrification is viewed as an invasion or "civilian occupation" where real estate is deployed as a tactic in the contest over space (Segal and Weizman 2003). The faceless gentrifiers are described as those who claim space "for all its worth." In their discussions of gentrification, constructions of whiteness reflect concerns of the young women about

neighborhood changes (Omi and Winant 2002), as Annissa expresses:

> You would think that after 9/11 people would be getting the fuck out of the Lower East Side, and instead I see more and more people coming in. I mean the people—I live in the projects, at Baruch projects—and I see white people going for a run down Baruch drive. Unheard of ten years ago. They go for walks in the projects. There is a certain, like complete oblivion that they have that's just like—like that frickin movie 'Living in oblivion.' It's like, duh walking around, totally unaware, like doo de doo de. It's like they feel like they have a right. But they don't really have a right, you know. I guess they do. But so do we.

Just the presence of white people in her neighborhood is menacing. Anxieties about neighborhood change are projected onto white bodies that represent not only the vanguard of gentrification, but the women's potential exclusion (This is similar to what Pamela Wridt's identifies as "place panics," 2004). Whiteness is constructed as a sign of not belonging, coupled with a taken for granted privilege to cross borders into unfamiliar territories. This brings to mind euphemistic representations of gentrifiers as urban pioneers of the wild wild west (Smith 1996), or what Kristin Koptiuch identified as "third-worlding at home" (1991). Third-worlding is "a name, a representation, not a place" refers to "the effects of a process of exploitative incorporation and hegemonic domination—and its fierce contestation by subjugated peoples—that used to take place at a safe, reassuring distance" (ibid:85).

The parallels with colonialism are evident. Black Panthers identified the ghetto as an "internal colony" to draw attention to its similarities with imperialist practices around the world (Singh 2000). The geopolitical significance of an internal colony is especially pertinent for the Lower East Side's "colonial citizens," Puerto Ricans and Dominicans whose diasporic experience has been marked by involuntary resettlement, rupture, conditions of poverty, and border-crossing (Aponte-Parés 1995). White newcomers are often ignorant about the changing status of the neighborhood and its disinvested history, and may not be conscious of the impact of their presence and related displacements. Long time residents, on the other hand, are very aware of the changes and how the neighborhood is under surveillance through an increased police presence, and quality of life laws which target men in their community. The entitlement of the border-crossers is especially striking in contrast to the hyper-awareness expressed by young people of color in their own neighborhood, not to mention in unfamiliar neighborhoods. Their lack of concern signals an entitlement which endangers their "rights to stay put" in their own neighborhood (Newman and Wyly 2006).

But why are white people moving into our neighborhood? One perspective is articulated in Janderie's comments above about, "culture seeking, white people [...] want a taste of our culture rich environment." "The lack of culture" is deployed as an explanation for the imperialism associated with whiteness. From this perspective, gentrifiers want to appropriate or participate in Latino or African American culture because they need to fill a cultural void or experience a sense of community (Ramos-Zayas 2001:79). The predominance of popular Black youth culture, in music, fashion, and language in mainstream culture reaffirms this observation, coupled with the perception that white people are taking everything "but the burden" (Tate 2003a). The researchers articulate the paradox Greg Tate identifies as being "seen as the most loathed and the most alluring of creatures, the most co-optable and erasable of cultures" (Tate 2003b:14). Thus gentrification signifies an appropriation of their culture and history and simultaneously its erasure.

The progressive whitening of their community reflects changing demographics in their neighborhood, yet, there have always been white people living on the Lower East Side. The difference is that now other white, that is wealthier people, are moving into parts of the neighborhood that have been identified with working class communities of color, "slumming it" (Mele 2000). While the borderlines between the areas were never so clear, older working class Jewish and Eastern European residents and their younger Puerto Rican, African-American, and Dominican neighbors carved out distinct, yet separate, urban enclaves. In addition, the constructions of whiteness associated with the gentrifiers are not applied to the older white working class residents who are identified instead by their ethnicity. Ramos-Zayas (2001) describes this as "shades of whiteness," which reveals an implicit understanding of class-based differences.

When grappling with the complex linkages between neighborhood restructuring, racial hierarchies, and representations, the young women articulate contradictory taxonomies of whiteness which both challenge and reproduce stereotypical constructions. Sometimes guilty of stereotyping "the other" in reductive characterizations of "cultural void," unchecked ambition, and greed, they risk reaffirming the very binaries that affix young

working class women to the "ghetto." At times, the researchers conflate class and race in their correlations of whiteness with privilege. This reproduces a normative whiteness and reifies the false dichotomy that all white people are wealthy and people of color poor or working class. But if the researchers essentialize whiteness they do so strategically. If the researchers' representations of whiteness as power and privilege sometimes reproduce stereotypes, they also challenge and interrogate this relationship. Rather than pretending to represent an accurate portrayal of white culture, their representation of gentrification as whiteness is an interpretation politically situated within the geographies of inequality evident in the neighborhood.

Drawing connections between gentrification and white privilege makes sense based not only on the researchers' observations of the shifting neighborhood demographics, but also within the broader context of their experiences of structural disparities elsewhere, such as school or work. Indeed, the Fed Up Honeys articulate what Bobo et al. (1997) identify as "laissez-faire racism," the slippery relationship between global capitalism and structural discrimination, based on their intimate experience negotiating new forms of spatial and social segregation. The disinvested/gentrifying Lower East Side reflects the dichotomy of privilege versus disadvantage, and the disconnect between global and local scales. In this sense, the structural and social inequities experienced by young women at the local scale (try to) keep them stuck in place. In contrast, (white) privilege is articulated as power which is mobile and "jumps scales" (Smith 1993): the neighborhood, the city, and the nation (Pulido 2000).

Framing the disinvestment and gentrification of their neighborhood through the lens of whiteness, the young women articulate a racialized interpretation of globalization that is embodied and grounded in their everyday experiences. Flipping the script, the researchers redefine Du Bois's "problem of the color line"—or in this case the frontier of gentrification—as white privilege. Thus, they collectively reject stereotypes which blame young working class women of color for social inequities and produce a positive collective identification as young women of color (Cahill 2006).

DISINVESTING IN YOUNG PEOPLE AND THEIR COMMUNITY

As part of their research the young women considered how material conditions of structural poverty have informed different settings of their everyday lives. In the "Makes Me Mad" report they categorized "community building needs from a young womyn's perspective" in the areas of health, education, employment, housing, and finance (Rios-Moore et al. 2004). For example, the researchers consider the relationship between housing, school and underemployment for young people. They describe how a lack of employment options coupled with increasing housing costs leads to over-crowded homes where the rent is cobbled together by extended families, including school-aged girls who work after school and on the weekends. They suggest that these pressures increase tensions in apartments, and are not ideal environments for studying. Here the researchers draw connections between education and the housing market. In another example they consider the under-servicing of urban youth in education. They critique the low quality of public education, the lack of basic programs for literacy, attendance, and enrichment, and the under-funding of schools, public libraries and related programs. Taken as a whole they paint a detailed portrait of disinvestment in their daily lives to shed light on the background, struggles, "challenges that young womyn face", and "the aspects of life that make this more complicated" (Rios-Moore et al. 2004:5). In the process, they underline how stereotypes of young women of color as uneducated, ambitionless, and lazy are produced within their particular disinvested context, as Annissa suggests:

> Despite the perception that the projects are full of drug addicts, criminals, and welfare recipients, I have known my home to be full of kind, hard-working, struggling, giving and intelligent people. We have our share of people who have lost their way, but for each one there is a story. That is one aspect of my neighborhood and community that I would like to relay to a visitor or newcomer to my home, which is that like any other place that people decide to create a life in, there are countless stories that belie whatever appearance the Lower East Side gives off.

Drawing attention to the cycle of systemic denial, the young women are well aware of how their community and its residents are often misconstrued by outsiders, and the deleterious effects this has had on the neighborhood through the under-funding of programs and financial redlining.

Disinvestment is not only associated with violence in terms of the higher crime rates associated with impoverished neighborhoods, but is also experienced as violence against poor and working class communities of color (Solis 2003). The violence perpetrated within underprivileged communities is well documented in the media. But poor and minority neighborhoods are also subject to violence, particularly those on the cusp of gentrification. Social and spatial boundaries are patrolled by stepped up police forces who discipline young men of color constructed as dangerous and criminal (Lipman 2003; Parenti 1999; Fine et al. 2002). For young working class women of color, the violence against and between the men and women in their communities is a critical concern, as is the increase in police brutality and the growing prison industrial complex. These issues were expressed by the young women in the context of growing up in a "bad neighborhood" which is also related to stereotypical representations of communities of color. Violence was articulated by the women as part of neighborhood life which took the shape of physical acts of violence and hostility between residents. Raising the rhetorical question "why aren't we more considerate in a poor community?" one researcher addressed the trickle down effects of disinvestment which alienate people from each other in a context characterized by socio-economic disenfranchisement.

The violence of poverty was also articulated by the young women as a personal injustice, "the whole spirit of what we don't have affects our inner being." They express what Crosby et al. identify as a sense of "relative deprivation" (Crosby et al. 1986 cited in Fine et al. 2004), an inconsistency between what the young women believe they deserve and what they receive, coupled with an awareness that others have what you do not. For women growing up in a gentrifying neighborhood the sense of relative deprivation is heightened when the "other" lives in the new condo across the street. Faced with what you do not have, feelings of deficiency are even more tangible, whether it is the shortage of youth programs, lack of attention, representations of deficit, poor quality of housing, failing public education system, or lack of choice and opportunity. The experience of privation contributes to a sense of not being worthy of public investment. Annissa reflects:

> For those of who don't know the history we just see the results of the disinvestment. We just see the results of the degradation and all we feel is that crater and that we're just sinking deeper and deeper into it. And feel incredibly helpless and at the same time. You know, like pissed off, and not that you can't use your pissed offness in anyway.

Cumulative experiences of systematic material denial inform young women's feelings of shame, anger, and a lack of confidence in their capacity to affect change. This is reinforced by representations of young women as "at risk", of young women of color as "likely to become teen moms," "lazy and on welfare," or "high school drop outs." These stereotypes contribute to feelings of being out of control and living in a hostile territory. The revanchist rhetoric (Smith 1996) is a reminder of young women's precarious social status and operates as a threat of social and spatial exclusion. Gendered racialized representations reference historical caricatures of the "tangle of pathology" and the underclass that blame young women of color for the poverty of their community (Moynihan 1965; Briggs 2002; Kelly 1997). Neoliberal discourses of personal responsibility and corresponding stereotypes are not coincidental, but constitutive of global economic restructuring (Harris 2004). In this regard, the disinvesting of space is about material resources, but also about the regulation of young women's agency (Cahill 2006; Wilson 2004). The violence of disinvestment is most insidious when young women internalize the deprivation. In the Makes Me Mad report, the researchers argue that "too often young women take responsibility for failing institutions that underserve and undereducate them, leading to a personal sense of failure" (Rios-Moore et al, 2004:9). While taking responsibility is certainly laudable, feeling that the disinvested material conditions of their neighborhood are their fault, contributes to a sense of shame and inadequacy. Disinvestment creates a downward spiral that one young researcher, Annissa, calls "the cycle":

> Like, when kids have nowhere to go they're left with the option of staying home and doing nothing ... peer pressures for sex and drugs kick in. And they're forced to make the decisions on their own and sometimes they make the wrong ones. This is when they fall into the stereotype of the pregnant teen—the unemployed pot smoking drop out. All they need is attention! Or a challenge every now and then. The cycle of not having enough.

In their discussions about growing up on the LES, the young women spoke about their experiences of socio-economic disinvestment and how this informed their sense of self. One frequently mentioned issue was the lack of support and dearth of places to go for young people, particularly for young women. One researcher lamented "I am an interesting young woman who bores herself to delirium. Because there's nothing to do. I'm bored. [...] It's like that I'm interesting is going to waste because I have

nothing to do with it." Employing the language of waste, she uses the metaphor of urban decay. Just as her neighborhood is disinvested, so is she. Echoing this perspective, another researcher suggests that young women (that is young working class women of color) are not "getting attention—and what I mean by that is that they're not thought of [...] they're just not considered. There's no space made. They're not considered for anything at all. They're not prepared for life. They're just there," expressing a profound sense of neglect and disregard. Almost invisible, young women are not taken into account. Just as "there's no space made," the young women are "just there." While stereotypical representations of the teenage mom are hypervisible in the public sphere (Cahill 2006), the needs and desires of these young women are invisible. Instead they are figuratively and literally stuck in place or without a place, metaphors which contrast with the mobility associated with success in the global economy. In the Lower East Side, this is made even more obvious by the newcomers who breeze in and out of the community while the young women struggle to leave the neighborhood and access opportunities (education, jobs) and for the right to stay put (Newman and Wyly 2006).

DISPLACEMENTS

> Displacement has been acknowledged but seen as an unfortunate corollary of processes that are revitalizing city centres, attracting private investment and securing the physical fabric of architecturally valuable neighbourhoods. This leads us to the question of whether these benefits are justified given the social costs involved.
>
> (Atkinson 2003:2345)

The pressure of displacement is not an abstract threat but experienced in material ways: slips under the door offering a buy out in public housing, family members relocating temporarily never to return home, personal experiences of being harassed by landlords, doubling up of families in tiny apartments, and seeing friends displaced. Narratives of deceit, betrayal and loss characterize the "war stories" of displacement, offering an inside perspective on the social costs of gentrification (Alicea 2001; Muñiz 1998).

One common tale accounts how some residents "voluntarily" move out due to unprecedented rent increases or landlord harassment. For example, less than six months after Janderie learned the word gentrification in our research project, her family's rent had increased yet again and they had no choice but to leave. They moved to a neighborhood in Queens where they knew no one. Now "a bus, a train […] from everything and everyone we have ever known. Had we been able to find a decent affordable apartment in the Lower East Side we could have stayed 'home'." Though not evicted or displaced, this is not a pattern of "normal housing succession" as Freeman and Braconi suggest, but instead a "replacement" (2004:51). In this case, poor and working class folks move into other disinvested neighborhoods where they do not know anyone, and might even experience the same cycle all over (Newman and Wyly 2006; Marcuse 1986). This repeats Frederick Engels' insight from over 150 years ago that the bourgeoisie do not have any real solution to the so called housing problem, but only shift poor people elsewhere (Engels 1975:71 cited in Smith 1993). This calls into question whether gentrification really does deconcentrate poverty. Some scholars argue that the opposite is true as working class residents are forced into less desirable areas, the "inner suburbs", in effect "diffusing and defusing their political power" (LeGates and Hartman 1986:194). Newman and Wyly (2006:26) argue that gentrification processes impact those who are displaced, and the ability of working class residents to move into neighborhoods with abundant affordable housing options. In addition to displacement and relocation within the city, a new trend reverses the Great Migration north of African-American communities in the 1950s (Stack 1996). Now, "everybody moves down south […] it's like a little train," Ruby explained, who moved to Georgia two years after the project started, to take advantage of more affordable schooling and housing options. Others may move back to Puerto Rico or the Dominican Republic in a reverse migration or shift between two places trying to find work and a place to settle following in the footsteps of previous generations (Aponte-Parés 1995).

One familiar tactic to avoid displacement is for families to double or even triple up in small apartments in order to stay in their neighborhoods. As opposed to the unconvincing interpretation that long time residents stay in their gentrifying neighborhoods to benefit from the "improvements" affluent residents bring to the neighborhood (Freeman and Braconi 2004), my research and others suggest that poor and working class communities stay put for a variety of reasons (Newman and Wyly 2006; Marcuse 2005; Fullilove 2004). Significantly, there is an overall lack of affordable housing in New York City. Poor residents pay an average of 61 percent of their incomes on rent (Freeman and Braconi 2004) to stay in neighborhoods where they developed connections with

people and places. This suggests that gentrification needs to be understood as a comprehensive process of neighborhood change which cannot only be understood in terms of real estate values. Place attachment and the loss of rich networks of social capital, for example, offer another frame to understand the process from residents' perspectives. The threat of displacement (or replacement) associated with gentrification is expressed as a personal and collective loss of control as expressed by young women researchers:

Ruby: And I'm not—but it's sad—it's like we can never have our own place without someone else coming in and taking over. Now they want to take over and before they were kicking us out of the houses. So we moved into public buildings—

Carmen: She doesn't want to call them projects, she's like "public buildings."

Ruby: Public buildings. But now they trying to kick us out of the public or private or whatever building it is. To where though?

Annissa: We never had a place of our own. To begin with it wasn't our own. We don't own it, we never own anything.

Ruby: That's what I'm saying. We could never have a place of our own because of something that will always happen.

Always being pushed around and having to relocate is destabilizing and articulated as a lack of agency. "They" have the power to kick us out and "we can never have our own place." Having a place of one's own is equated with security and stability. Property ownership is identified with feelings of belonging and being in control. This coincides with President Bush's rhetoric of the "ownership society" that builds on (older) liberal discourses about property ownership as a prerequisite to citizenship, as he introduced it in his 2004 campaign: "I believe our country can and must become an ownership society. When you own something, you care about it. When you own something, you have a vital stake in the future of your country" (The Ownership Society 2004). Problematically, the concept of the ownership society suggests that those who do not own are marginalized and threatened with spatial and social exclusion as witnessed in the young women's experiences of gentrification and disinvestment. As a new buzzword that dresses privilege up in new clothes, the rhetoric of the ownership society validates the privatization of the public sphere simultaneously producing disenfranchisement. Analyzed in the framework of structural racism, Bush's ownership society is an implicit raced and classed demarcation between the "haves" and the "have nots." Here the young women articulate a subjectivity informed by discourses of the ownership society, expressing a desire for inclusion (Fine 2004). At the same time, this reveals feelings of shame, anxiety and a sense of bitter resignation: "we don't own it, we never own it" and "we could never have a place of our own." Ruby and Annissa know what they are talking about. For long term residents of the LES, particularly those who live in the areas identified with communities of color, the possibility of acquiring property was constrained by their own poverty and the financial redlining of their community. Now as the neighborhood is green-lined, ownership is constrained by an inflated market which outprices everyone but the wealthy. Not surprisingly, much of the recent real estate investment in the Lower East Side is from outside the community, indeed from abroad, which reflects trends in global urban restructuring and capital.

CULTURAL DISPLACEMENTS

To focus only on those who have to leave the neighborhood loses sight of another dimension of gentrification: cultural displacement. This perspective is missing from the gentrification literature (but see Alicea 2001; Muñiz 1998). The study of cultural displacement involves considerations of what it means to witness the transformation of one's neighborhood. This was the young women's primary shared experience when over the years they watched their neighborhood change. Janderie exclaims:

> Oh! My! God! That's what was happening to me! The trendy bars, the raised rent ... the white people! There weren't this many white people in the ghetto before, then again it's starting to look less like a ghetto and more like confusion. Cute Italian and Japanese restaurants in one corner and a broke-down project building on the next. Everyday I walked down the same three blocks and I found something else that hadn't been there before, like the annoying little boutique that sold hand-crafted figurines. And even more annoying was the tea shop that seemed to never have a customer inside. All I could think to myself was "can't wait to see how my neighborhood looks in 10 years".

Janderie's antipathy towards neighborhood change is evident in her sarcasm, "can't wait to see how my neighborhood looks in ten years." Theories of place attachment and place identity (Altman and Low 1992; Proshansky et al. 1983) suggest that the relationship to one's environmental surroundings contribute to the "formation, maintenance, and preservation of the identity of a person, group or culture" (Altman and Low 1992:10). What then, does the cultural transformation of one's community mean for self and group identifications? Place attachment describes a sense of ongoing security and the significance of place for social connections. This is especially true for places where one is immersed for a long time and where one might learn new social roles, such as when growing up.

Whose neighborhood is this anyway? In terms of cultural transformations, the semantic differences between displacement and replacement are moot. The effect is the same. Atkinson asserts that "an action at the household level appears unsuited to an analysis of strategic neighborhood dominance," (2003:2346), yet this loses sight of the empirical evidence of the wholesale transformation of the neighborhood, and the experience of it as expressed by long-time residents (Alicea 2001). The neighborhood context is being taken over and changed beyond recognition. Displacement is experienced in this regard as a process of effacement at the neighborhood scale, where the signs personal and cultural heritages are erased. What does it mean when the salon where one's mother had her hair done every two weeks closes down? Or for the Charas Community Center that was sold at city auction for private development without the community's permission? One misses the annual block parties which have ceased as many old time residents have left. Now there are only a few Puerto Rican flags which used to be a dominant symbol of the Loisaida community. What happened to the abundance of murals and graffiti walls depicting community's concerns? Such as the R.I.P memorial walls in honor of community members who have passed, or murals commemorating Puerto Rican and African-American history? For example, the mural depicting Bimbo Rivas on Avenue B, once hailed as the poet of the Loisaida, is gone; the building has been destroyed and replaced with a new condo.

In short, gentrification is experienced as a loss of self, community and culture. The threat of erasing of "my grandmother's house," "my history," and "my neighborhood" is accompanied by feelings of anxiety and anger. "I don't belong here": this anger expresses a sense of not feeling welcome in one's own community. From this perspective, Jasmine's exclamation "They are killing the neighborhood!" referring to the new upscale restaurants on Clinton Street, is understandable. In the place of their not so distant childhood memories are new businesses that symbolize gentrification and their displacement. Psychologist Mindy Fullilove's definition of "root shock" is relevant to understanding the young women's potential trauma and diminished sense of agency. Root shock is "a profound emotional upheaval that destroys the working model of the world that [...] undermines trust, increases anxiety about letting loved ones out of one's sight, destabilizes relationships, destroys social, emotional and financial resources" and increases health risks (2004:14). Although Fullilove's conceptualization of root shock refers to the aftermath of urban renewal where entire communities were displaced overnight, it captures the young women's psychological experiences of being culturally dislocated from their community while still living there. However, unlike urban renewal, gentrification is a slow process. At first almost imperceptible, slowly the neighborhood changes as indicated in new storefronts that cater to a new clientele and replace familiar bodegas, mom and pop shops, and neighborhood landmarks. This painstaking process has ramifications from a political standpoint. The young women's ambivalence towards their neighborhood speaks of their confusion, political apathy, and diminished sense of agency in the face of global urban restructuring. This has profound implications for organizing and social change initiatives.

AMBIVALENCE

I complain so much about how the white people are coming and making everything "trendy" but on the other hand, I like being trendy and I want to be able to one day mingle with that crowd but I hate the fact that they are forcing us out. Why can't it be that we all come together to form a culture rich yet trendy neighborhood? Why does it have to be one or other?

Identifying both desire and displacement with the white trendy body, Janderie raises the complex question: Where does she fit in? Janderie's analysis bridges critique and desire, as she reveals her personal struggles negotiating the material conditions of disinvestment and her desires for upward mobility and personal fulfillment. She conveys the predicament of negotiating a space of "betweenness" (Nelson 1999; Katz 1994). As one researcher articulates: "Like, I keep thinking about Foucault—like that whole idea of, like, how can you think

outside of the box if the box created you? And I think that they (the young women) are living examples that you can think outside and still be in it. Like, to be split." It was in this space of betweenness that the young researchers articulated the push and pull of being simultaneously inside and outside the box. This inability to rest comfortably in a particular subject position reflects the struggle to discursively make sense of their experience. Du Bois (1989) calls this "double consciousness." Anzaldúa goes further in her conceptualization of "mestiza consciousness:"

> cradled in one culture, sandwiched between two cultures, straddling all three cultures and their value systems, la mestiza undergoes a struggle of the flesh, a struggle of borders, an inner war [...] the coming together of two self-consistent but habitually incompatible frames of references causes *un choque*, a cultural collision.
>
> (1999:100)

Given their challenging experiences growing up on the Lower East Side, it is understandable that the young women's relationships with their neighborhood are ambivalent. The cumulative experience of socio-economic disinvestment and associated negative outcomes, can transform civic engagement into alienation. At the same time, the young women express a yearning for spaces to connect, aspirations to transform their own personal situations, coupled with a deep commitment to their families, and a desire to give back to their communities. The tensions between these radically different perspectives stake out the contours of their positions. On the one hand, there is the escape narrative which equates leaving the neighborhood with success. The other is characterized by a commitment to stick it out and an ethic of care (Gilligan 1982). Somewhere in between the young women reconfigure their subjectivities revealing the compromises of self-invention, the struggle to make sense of oneself within the stunted discourses available, and critical perspectives on their changing community.

The first story is well known. It is the classic success story where one leaves the old neighborhood for the good life. For young women from the working class LES, dreams of becoming rich and famous involve leaving the neighborhood. From this perspective, leaving equals success and staying equals failure and thus the neighborhood symbolizes failure. Paradoxically, this definition of success is defined in similar terms to selling out. Selling out is described by one researcher as the "worst thing you can do."

It means moving out of the "hood, leaving your people" behind. Like the term "acting white," which equates blackness with failure and whiteness with success, selling out is a rhetorical move reinforcing the binaries of black/white, lazy/ambitious. Selling out and acting white function to maintain the social order by threatening exile and the potential of not belonging anywhere.

Navigating the contradictory subject positions involved in selling out can feel like a catch 22. Even though "the worst thing you can do" is leave the community, in fact success is represented and understood as just that: leaving. The embodied geopolitics of progress conflate social and spatial mobility, which within the context of globalization makes sense. But, interestingly, in the gentrifying LES leaving for the good life may be as simple as moving to the condo next door. This is captured in an inflected version of selling out, "brand new," which refers to someone who acts "like they don't know where they're from or who they are," someone who might act like they are new to the neighborhood, a linguistically more appropriate metaphor in the gentrifying context where long time residents largely do not own property and technically can not "sell out." The contradictions of leaving are at once obvious and confusing when imagined in one's own neighborhood. Especially within a neoliberal context where staying put in one's neighborhood may be equated with success. The lines of demarcation between structural disadvantage (being stuck in place) and privilege are now identified along the lines of public and private, which are racially coded. The public is defined as the institutions regulated by the state like schools, hospitals, public housing developments, or parks. The private is defined by its exclusivity. Privatization may take the shape of the upscale restaurants catering to a minority, or the newer housing developments inhabited by new, wealthier (and whiter) residents. The zigzagging frontlines of globalization produce a shifting geography that the young women must negotiate gingerly.

The other end of the spectrum is more optimistic about the possibility of social change, and involves a commitment to stay in the neighborhood in order to transform it. This is associated with the discourse of responsibility prevalent in communities of color to uplift the community and give back to it once one attains success (Boyd 2005; Patillo-McCoy 1999). Jasmine describes this position:

Once your settled and grounded go back to either your community […] and educate the people who

are there on what's going on. You know it's one thing to just go in, and you know, "let me tell you this and this is going on. Okay bye." That's one thing. Another thing is to stay there and help them, make a movement about it, you know. So I think that's what could be done to change the whole system.

Here, staying in the neighborhood is associated with progress. Jasmine articulates this as integral to the community, and as a long-term process, "to change the whole system." Building community thus might be associated with an ethic of care, in which primacy is placed upon attachment and sustaining relationships within a feminist framework of identity development (Day 2000; Gilligan 1982). On the one hand, framing one's relationship to the neighborhood within the context of caring for others resonated for most of the young women who had been socialized to take care of others and who had many caregiving responsibilities in their everyday lives. On the other hand, the discourse of caring for one's community concerned some who were not interested in playing that role when they never had time to care for themselves as it was. If the escape narratives involved leaving the stereotypes behind, staying in the community involved challenging them head-on and continuing to deal with the frustrations of disinvestment and gentrification. It means having to fight to stay in the home community. But for some of the young women, to get involved in community change was asking too much, to actually give back to a context which already had negative associations, as one researcher explains:

That's why we have to teach people, like little kids, their history before the neighborhood screws them over because then their not going to want to know about the neighborhood. Because then they're going to be like why the knife keeps stabbing me? […] Young women do not feel invested in their community or connected to it if they don't have the positive aspects of their community, their lives and their personal strengths reinforced to them.

The two ends of the spectrum—the escape narrative and the commitment to stick it out—represent different approaches to negotiating complicated subject positions, individually the researchers shifted back and forth, most of the time identifying a position in between. Perhaps, the distance between the positions is not so great. This location is an emotional, cultural, psychological, political, social and geographical crossroad located in the LES. It reflects Anzaldúa's borderland, a location "created by the emotional residue of an unnatural boundary" (1999:25):

This my home
this thin edge of
barbwire.

(ibid)

It is painful. Standing on the shifting terrain of neighborhood change, the young women face the problem of trying to negotiate structural and individual interpretations of their everyday experiences. Collectively, after much discussion, dissent, and debate, and in the process of the Makes Me Mad project, they created an opening for working through the contradictions of the grit and glamour of their neighborhood and navigating the divide.

Connecting the dots between their individual experiences in schools, housing, jobs, and the neighborhood, the Fed Up Honeys developed what Cindi Katz identifies as a "topography for feminist political engagement," and "grounded but translocal politics," that highlight the contours of differently situated experiences (Katz 2001:1231). Through a collaborative process of comparing each others' personal experiences the women developed a shared social analysis attempting to bridge the differences between the two polar positions. In the Makes Me Mad report, the Fed Up Honeys take this analysis further, offering a holistic and action-oriented vision of community-controlled development and self-representation (Rios-Moore et al. 2004). Their proposal for "Community building needs from a young womyn's perspective" is in stark contrast to their current experiences of gentrification and socio-economic disinvestment:

The ultimate and most beneficial means to an end of the negative effects of such a stark lack of resources is a community that is self-sufficient and self-concerned. It is a priority to have young womyn who can feel connected and have a desire to contribute and be involved in their community ... (our) research has identified several important ways to build a stronger and more positive community, one that is able to stand in the face of the stereotypes that its children have been pegged with.

(Ibid:7; emphasis in the original)

Here the young women advocate community participation in the development of their neighborhood,

and specifically their own involvement. In the conclusion of the report they included a list of "community building needs," arguing for their concerns to be taken into account. Their language echoes the discourses of political autonomy and self-determination associated with the Black Power and radical Puerto Rican nationalist movements who assert a positive affirmation of racial identities and to end economic dependence (Pulido 2006; Aponte-Parés 1998). Calling for their participation, the researchers reaffirm for other young women of color, and young people in general, that they are transformative subjects and not passive victims of global economic restructuring (Nagar et al. 2002). Thus, the Fed Up Honeys challenge dominant constructions of young women of color and of working class poor communities.

One of the most important findings of the Makes Me Mad project was that power lies in controlling how one is defined. While young men are surveilled in public spaces, young women of color are pathologized in representations of risk in the public sphere to justify their socio-spatial displacement and disinvestment (Cahill 2006). As Lipman (in press) suggests, gendered and racialized stereotypes of young working class women of color function as "the ideological lynchpin in packaging dispossession as neighborhood reclamation." In the Makes Me Mad project, the Fed Up Honeys speak back to deficit constructions of young women and offer an interpretative framework affirming the rights to self-represent and to stay put (Newman and Wyly 2006) as mutually constitutive. The young women developed an analysis which is rooted in both challenging stereotypes and caring for one's community. This outlines possibilities of a place-based politics of identity as a form of resistance to the homogenization and "white washing" of gentrification.

Acknowledgements. It has been a complete privilege to work so closely with the Fed Up Honeys research team over many years. Thank you, as always, for your humor, insight, and encouragement. I am grateful to Cindi Katz, Michelle Fine and Roger Hart for their mentorship and ongoing support. Thanks to Jen Tilton for her generous close reading of an earlier draft of this paper. I very much appreciate the editorial guidance of Suzanne Scheld and Petra Kuppinger. I am also grateful for the critical feedback of the four reviewers whose comments were very helpful in revision. This research was supported by a fellowship from the American Association of University Women and a CUNY Writing Fellowship at Medgar Evers College.

Note

1 Names have been changed to protect the identities of the young women involved.

REFERENCES CITED

Abu-Lughod, Janet L.
  1994 From Urban Village to East Village: The Battle for New York's Lower East Side. Cambridge: Blackwell.
Alicea, Marcia
  2001 Cuando nosotros viviamos ...: Stories of displacement and settlement in Puerto Rican Chicago. Centro Journal 13(2):167–195.
Altman, Irwin and Setha Low
  1992 Place Attachment. New York: Plenum Press.
Anzaldúa, Gloria
  1999 Borderlands La Frontera: The New Mestiza. 2nd ed. San Francisco: Aunt Lute Books.
Aponte-Parés, Luis
  1998 Lessons from El Barrio – The East Harlem Real Great Society/Urban Planning Studio: A Puerto Rican Chapter in the fight for urban self-determination. New Political Science 20(4):399–420.
  1995 What Yellow and White and Has Land all around it? Appropriating Place in Puerto Rican Barrios. Centro Journal of the Center for Puerto Rican Studies 7(1):8–19.
Aspen Institute Roundtable on Community Change
  2004 Structural Racism and Youth Development: Issues, Challenges, and Implications. Washington, DC: The Aspen Institute.
Atkinson, Rowland
  2003 Introduction: Misunderstood Saviour or Vengeful Wrecker? The Many Meanings and Problems of Gentrification. Urban Studies 40(12):2343–2350.
Bobo, Lawrence, James R. Kluegel, and Ryan A. Smith
  1997 Laissez-Faire Racism: The Crystallization of a 'Kinder, Gentler' Anti-Black Ideology. In Racial Attitudes in the 1990s: Continuity and Change. Steven A. Tuch and Jack K. Martin, eds. Pp. 15–44. Greenwood, CT: Praeger.
Boyd, Christopher
  2005 The Downside of Racial Uplift: The Meaning of Gentrification in an African-American Neighborhood. City & Society 17(2):265–288.
Briggs, Laura
  2002 La Vida, Moynihan, and other Libels: Migration, Social Science, and the Making of the Puerto Rican Welfare Queen. Centro 14(1):75–101.
Cahill, Caitlin, Erica Arenas, Jennifer Contreras, Na Jiang, Indra Rios-Moore, and Tiffany Threatts
  2004 Speaking Back: Voices of Young Urban Womyn of Color Using Participatory Action Research to Challenge and Complicate Representations of Young Women. In All about the Girl: Power, Culture and Identity, Anita Harris, ed. Pp. 233–244. New York: Routledge.
Cahill, Caitlin
  2007a The Personal is Political: Developing New Subjectivities in a Participatory Action Research Process. Gender, Place, and Culture 14(3):267–292.
  2007b Doing Research with Young People: Participatory Research and the Rituals of Collective Work. Children's Geographies 5(3):297–312.
  2006 'At risk'? The Fed Up Honeys Represent the Gentrification of the Lower East Side. Women Studies Quarterly 34 (1–2):334–363.
  2000 Street Literacy: Urban Teenagers' Strategies for Negotiating their Neighborhood. Journal of Youth Studies 3(3): 251–277.
Castells, Manuel
  1989 The Informational City. London: Blackwell.
Cox, Kevin
  1997 The Spaces of Globalization. New York: Guilford Press.
Crosby, Faye, Peter Muehrer, and George Loewenstein
  1986 Relative Deprivation and Explanation: Models and Concepts. In Relative Deprivation and Assertive Action: The Ontario Symposium, J. Olson, M. Zanna and P. Hernan, eds. Pp. 214–237. Hillside, NJ: Erlbaum.
Day, Kristen
  2000 The Ethic of Care and Women's Experiences of Public Space. Journal of Environmental Psychology 20:103–124.
Dowler, Lorraine and Joanne Sharp
  2001 A Feminist Geopolitics? Space and Polity 5(3):165–176.

Du Bois, William E. B.
1989 The Souls of Black Folk. New York: Bantam Books.

Engels, Frederick
1975 The Housing Question. Moscow: Progress Publishers.

Fine, Michelle
2004 Response to Housing Responsibility and Structural Injustice by Iris Marion Young. Unpublished manuscript.

Fine, Michelle, April Burns, Yasser A. Payne, and María E. Torre
2004 Civic Lessons: The Color and Class of Betrayal. Teachers College Record 106(11):2193–2223.

Fine, Michelle, Nicholas Freudenberg, Yasser Payne, Tiffany Perkins, Kersha Smith, and Katya Wanzer
2002 "Anything Can Happen with Police Around": Urban Youth Evaluate Strategies of Surveillance in Public Spaces. Journal of Social Issues 59(1):141–158.

Freeman, Lance and Frank Braconi
2004 Gentrification and Displacement in New York City. Journal of the American Planning Association 70(1):39–52.

Freire, Paolo
1997 Pedagogy of the Oppressed. Harmondsworth: Penguin Books.

Fullilove, Mindy T.
2004 Root Shock: How Tearing up Cities Hurts America and What We Can Do About It. New York: A One World/Ballantine Book.

Gibson-Graham, J. K.
2002 Beyond Global vs. Local: Economic Politics and the Binary Frame. In Geographies of Power: Placing Scale. Andrew Herod and Melissa Wright, eds. Pp. 25–60. Oxford: Blackwell.

Gilligan, Carol
1982 In a Different Voice: Psychological Theory and Women's Development. Cambridge, MA: Harvard University Press.

Glass, Ruth
1964 Aspects of Change. London: Centre for Urban Studies and MacGibbon and Kee.

Hackworth, Jason and Neil Smith
2001 The Changing State of Gentrification. Tijdschirft voor Economische en Sociale Geografie 92(4):464–477.

Harris, Anita
2004 Future Girl: Young Women in the Twenty-First Century. London: Taylor and Francis.

Katz, Cindi
2004 Growing Up Global: Economic Restructuring and Children's Everyday Lives. Minneapolis: University of Minnesota Press.

2002 Stuck in Place: Children and the Globalization of Social Reproduction. In Geographies of Global Change: Remapping the World. 2nd Edition. R. J. Johnston, P. J. Taylor, and M. J. Watts, eds. Pp. 248–259. New York: Blackwell.

2001 On the Grounds of Globalization: A Topography for Feminist Political Engagement. Signs 26(4):1213–1234.

1994 Playing the Field: Questions of Fieldwork in Geography. Professional Geographer 46:67–72.

Kelly, Robin D. G.
1997 Yo' Mama's Disfunktional! Fighting the Cultural Wars in Urban America. Boston: Beacon Press.

Koptiuch, Kristen
1991 Third-Worlding at Home. Social Text 28:87–99.

Kretzmann, John and John K. McKnight
1996 Assets-Based Community Development. National Civic Review 85(4).

Lees, Loretta
2003 Urban Geogaphy: 'New' Urban Geography and the Ethnographic Void. Progress in Human Geography 27(1):107–113.

LeGates, Richard and Craig Hartman
1986 The Anatomy of Displacement in the US. In Gentrification and the City. Neil Smith and Peter Williams, eds. Pp. 178–200. Boston: Allen and Unwin.

Lewin, Kurt
1951 Field Theory in Social Science: Selected Theoretical Papers. New York: Harper.

Lipman, Pauline
In press, Commentary. Revolutionizing Education: Youth Participatory Action Research in Motion. In Julio Cammarota and Michelle Fine, eds. New York: Routledge.

2003 Chicago School Policy: Regulating Black and Latino Youth in the Global City. Race, Ethnicity and Education 6(4):331–355.

MacIntosh, Peggy
1989 White Privilege: Unpacking the Invisible Knapsack. Peace and Freedom 10–12.

Marcuse, Peter
2005 On the Presentation of Research about Gentrification. Department of Urban Planning. Columbia University, New York.
1986 Abandonment, Gentrification, and Displacement: The Linkages in New York City. *In* Gentrification and the City. Neil Smith and Peter Williams, eds. Pp. 153–177. Boston: Allen and Unwin.

Martin-Baro, Ignacio
1994 Writings for a Liberation Psychology. Cambridge MA: Harvard University Press.

Mele, Christopher
2000 Selling the Lower East Side: Culture, Real Estate, and Resistance in New York, 1880–2000. Minnesota: University of Minnesota Press.

Mitchell, Don
2003 The Right to the City: Social Justice and the Fight for Public Space. New York: The Guilford Press.

Mountz, Alison and Jennifer Hyndman
2006 Feminist Approaches to the Global Intimate. Women Studies Quarterly 34(1–2):446–463.

Moynihan, Daniel
1965 The Negro Family: The Case for National Action. Washington, DC: Office of Policy Planning and Research, United States Department of Labor.

Muñiz, Victoria
1998 Resisting Gentrification and Displacement: Voices of Puerto Rican Women of the Barrio. New York: Garland Publishing, Inc.

Nagar, Richa, Victoria Lawson, Linda McDowell, and Susan Hanson
2002 Locating Globalization: Feminist (Re)Readings of the Subjects and Spaces of Globalization. Economic Geography 78(3):257–284.

Nelson, Lise
1999 Bodies (and Spaces) Do Matter: The Limits of Performativity. Gender, Place and Culture 6(4):331–353.

Newman, Kathe and Philip Ashton
2004 Neoliberal Urban Policy and New Paths of Neighborhood Change in the American City. Environment and Planning A 36(7):1151–1172.

Newman, Kathe and Elvin Wyly
2006 The Right to Stay Put, Revisited: Gentrification and Resistance to Displacement in New York City. Urban Studies 34(1):23–57.

Omi, Michael and Howard Winant
2002 Racial Formation. *In* Race Critical Theories: Text and Context. Philomena Essed and David T. Goldberg, eds. Pp.123–145. Malden, MA: Blackwell Publishers.

Parenti, Christopher
1999 Lockdown America: Police and Prisons in the Age of Crisis. London: Verso.

Pattillo-McCoy, Mary
1999 Black Picket Fences: Privilege and Peril Among the Black Middle Class. Chicago: University of Chicago.

Pratt, Geraldine and Victoria Rosner, eds.
2006 The Global and the Intimate. Women Studies Quarterly 34(1–2).

Pratt, Mary L.
1999 Apocalypse in the Andes: Contact Zones and the Struggles for Interpretive Power. Américas 51(4):38–47.
1992 Imperial Eyes: Travel Writing and Transculturation. New York: Routledge.

Proshansky, Harold M., Abbe K. Fabian, and Robert Kaminoff
1983 Place-Identity: Physical World Socialization of the Self. Journal of Environmental Psychology 3(1):57–83.

Pulido, Laura
2006 Black, Brown, Yellow, and Left: Radical Activism in Los Angeles. Berkeley: University of California Press.
2000 Rethinking Environmental Racism: White Privilege and Urban Development in Southern California. Annals of the Association of American Geographers 90(1): 12–40.

Ramos-Zayas, Ana Y.
2001 All this is Turning White Now: Latino Constructions of "White Culture" and Whiteness in Chicago. Centro Journal 13(2):73–95.

Rios-Moore, Indra, Erica Arenas, Jennifer Contreras, Na Jiang, Tiffany Threatts, Shamara Allen and Caitlin Cahill
2004 Makes Me Mad: Stereotypes of Young Urban Womyn of Color. New York: Center for Human Environments, Graduate School and University Center, City University of New York.

Sassen, Saskia
1998 Globalization and its Discontents. New York: New Press.

Segal, Rafi and Eyal Weizman
  2003 Civilian Occupation: The Politics of Israeli Architecture. New York: Verso.
Sharff, Jagna W.
  1998 King Kong on Fourth Street: Families and the Violence of Poverty on the Lower East Side. Boulder: Westview Press.
Singh, Nikhil Pal
  2000 Toward an Effective Antiracism. *In* Dispatches from the Ebony Tower. Manning Marable, ed. Pp. 31–51. New York: Columbia University Press.
Smith, Neil
  2002 New Globalism, New Urbanism: Gentrification as Global Urban Strategy. Antipode 34(3):427–450.
  1996 The New Urban Frontier Gentrification and the Revanchist City. New York: Routledge.
  1993 Homeless/Global: Scaling places. In Mapping the Futures: Local Culture, Global Change. Jon Bird, Barry Curtis, Tim Putnam, George Robertson and Lisa Tickner, eds. Pp. 87–119. London: Routledge.
Solis, Jocelyn
  2003 Re-Thinking Illegality as a Violence Against, Not by Mexican Immigrants, Children, and Youth. Journal of Social Issues 59(1):15–31.
Sorkin, Michael, ed.
  1992 Variations on a Theme Park. New York: Noonday Press.
Stack, Carol
  1996 Call to Home: African Americans Reclaim the Rural South. New York: Basic Books.

Tate, Greg, ed.
  2003a Everything But the Burden: What White People are Taking from Black Culture. New York: Harlem Books.
Tate, Greg
  2003b Nigs R Us, or How Blackfolk Became Fetish Objects. *In* Everything But the Burden: What White People are Taking from Black Culture. Greg Tate, ed. New York: Harlem Books.
The Ownership Society
  2004 The Ownership Society. Online NewsHour December 15, 2004. (http://www.pbs.org/newshour/bb/economy/july-deco4/ownership_12.15.html. Accessed January 12, 2005.
Torre, Maria E. and Michelle Fine
  2006 Participatory Action Research (PAR) by Youth. *In* Youth Activism: An International Encyclopedia. Lonnie Sherrod, ed. Pp. 456–462. Westport, CT: Greenwood Publishing Group.
Wilson, David
  2004 Towards a Contingent Urban Neoliberalism. Urban Geography 25(8):771–783.
Wridt, Pamela
  2004 Childhoods in Place and Placeless Childhoods: An Historical Geography of Childhood in Yorkville and East Harlem, 1940s and 2000. PhD Dissertation in Environmental Psychology, City University of New York, Graduate Center.

Plate 16 **Gentrifying Mumbai, India.** Photograph by Andrew Harris.

INTRODUCTION TO PART FOUR

Nearly every field of study has, at its core, a fundamental essence that defines the very existence and survival of the field. For the study of gentrification, the issue of displacement constitutes this fundamental essence. Displacement, the forced disenfranchisement of poor and working class people from the spaces and places to which they have legitimate social and historical claims, is what constitutes and defines gentrification, with its remaking of space for the middle classes and the elite.

Concerns about the injustices of displacement have always been deeply politicized. In general, displacement highlights a fairly simple, straightforward dichotomy. For conservatives who favor minimal government interference with private-market innovation and competition, displacement is a regrettable but small, unavoidable consequence of the long-term, never-ending adjustment process of urban housing markets. Housing will remain most affordable, in this perspective, when the supply of housing services responds to the unregulated, efficient competition amongst the buyers and sellers of housing services: well-intentioned efforts to prevent displacement with rules like rent control will only worsen things over the long run by reducing developers' incentives to create more rental housing. For analysts and activists on the Left, by contrast, displacement is a systemic indicator – along with other injustices like homelessness – of the commodification of a basic human need. Housing, home, and community, in this perspective, should not be treated solely as goods and services to be traded according to the rules of profit and wealth accumulation – but should be recognized as essential rights to ensure individual and societal well-being.

In general, analysts who are critical about the inequalities and injustices of gentrification cite displacement as a serious, widespread, egregious, and systematic consequence of the process (Achtenberg and Marcuse, 1983; Hartman, 1982; Marcuse, 1985; Smith, 1996; Newman and Wyly, 2006; Slater, 2006). In contrast, analysts who regard gentrification as a minor byproduct of urban change, or as a worthy, benevolent goal of urban development or public policy, usually cite evidence that displacement is relatively rare, or not often caused directly by displacement (Byrne, 2003; Freeman 2004; McKinnish et al. 2008; Vigdor, 2002).

There is one major exception, however, to this Left/Right alignment. Displacement driven by government intervention in housing and land markets often leads analysts to take somewhat unexpected positions. On the Left, many analysts who documented the injustices of private-market displacement in the 1970s and 1980s now downplay the scope and significance of the problem when it is caused by increasingly popular government policies on regeneration, reurbanization, income mixing, and "creative class" development. In the U.K. and Europe, this shift is apparent in a recent revival of an old debate from the 1970s and 1980s – is "new build" gentrification a problem (or even gentrification) if new luxury developments do not directly displace working-class residents from working-class housing? (Boddy, 2007; compare with Davidson, 2008, and Slater, 2006; also Davidson and Lees, 2010 in Rérat, Söderström and Piguet, 2010). In the U.S., the shift is illustrated by many liberals' conclusion that concentrated urban poverty justifies the displacement of residents from troubled housing projects and the development of "mixed income" communities (Crump, 2002; DeFilippis and Wyly, 2008; Goetz, 2003).

On the Right, conservatives who have no objection to the displacement that happens through the innumerable, unregulated actions of private landlords raise fierce objections when government policies are involved. One of the most influential analyses of displacement appeared in a free-market conservative treatise that appeared in the same year as Ruth Glass's celebrated essay:

> During the last 15 years, notices similar to the following one have been received by hundreds of thousands of families and individuals living in cities throughout the United States.
>
> "The building in which you now live is located in an area which has been taken by the Boston Redevelopment Authority according to law as part of the Government Center Project. The buildings will be demolished after the families have been relocated and the land will be sold to developers for public and commercial uses, according to the Land Assembly and Redevelopment Plan presently being prepared."
>
> The wording varies from city to city, but the meaning is clear: the house or apartment you live in is going to be taken by the government and destroyed. The government will then sell the cleared land to someone else for private development. Please move.
>
> (Anderson, 1964, p. 1)

This is the introduction to *The Federal Bulldozer*, a devastating and incisive attack on the federal "urban renewal" programs launched by the U.S. government in 1949. While liberals, progressives, and radicals quickly saw the failures and injustices of urban renewal, what made *The Federal Bulldozer* so famous was its explicitly political attack on urban renewal from the Right. Martin Anderson was a young, rising-star economist, who in later years served as economics advisor to Richard Nixon, Ronald Reagan, and many other prominent Republicans. Anderson viewed government-driven urban renewal, "guided by the visible hand of the urban experts," as a stark failure compared to "the accomplishments of the plans of private individuals, guided by the invisible hand of the free market place" (Anderson, 1964, p. 228). Nevertheless, most of Anderson's analysis relied on precisely the same concerns for distributive and procedural justice voiced by those on the Left:

> The over-all results ... indicate that it is a regressive program, rather than progressive. It benefits high-income groups and hurts low-income groups. ... [It] has actually aggravated the housing shortage for low-income groups.
>
> (Anderson, 1964, pp. 228–229)

How pervasive and widespread is displacement? Over the years, analysts have offered a wide range of estimates of the scope, severity, and significance of the problem. Anderson's attack on U.S. urban renewal policies that began in 1949 estimated that "By March of 1963 over 609,000 people had been forced to pack their belongings and leave their homes ... If the program continues to expand, it will not be long before the number of people affected reaches into the millions" (Anderson, 1964, p. 8). Displacement caused by urban renewal, however, was dwarfed by the scale of private-market displacement. By the end of the 1970s, between 600,000 and 850,000 households across the U.S. – equivalent to 1.7 to 2.7 million people including children – were forced to move *each year* because of private activities of various kinds (data cited in Achtenberg and Marcuse, 1983, p. 206). More recent estimates from the American Housing Survey (AHS) yield roughly comparable figures. In 2007, 12.68 million renter households across the United States reported moving during the previous year. When asked to cite one or more reasons for leaving their previous unit, 452,000 cited reasons related to private displacement; 77,000 provided reasons related to government displacement; 865,000 wanted lower rent or maintenance costs; and 81,000 were evicted (U.S. Bureau of the Census, 2008, p. 228). All of these figures include displacement from all kinds of neighborhoods, but they do not measure the specific linkages between *gentrification* and displacement. Measuring these linkages proves especially difficult, as illustrated in various ways by each of the readings presented in this section.

Rowland Atkinson (2000, p. 163) famously described the challenge of documenting the effects of gentrification on displacement as "measuring the invisible." Three methodological problems are important. First, the process erases the traces of its own existence at the local scale. At the national scale, it is financially and politically feasible for government agencies to undertake large, random-sample surveys (such as the AHS in the United States) asking recent movers why they left their previous residence. But it becomes prohibitively expensive and politically contentious for any unit of government to undertake such surveys in ways that identify the highly localized contours of displacement in specific poor neighborhoods undergoing gentrification. Moreover, it is nearly impossible for independent researchers to design small, targeted studies of displacement effects in gentrifying neighborhoods: poor and working-class people displaced by gentrification have disappeared from precisely those places where researchers go to look for them. Accurate measurements of displacement are impossible with after-the-fact surveys conducted in the *origins* of displacement; instead, the researcher must find households in the *destinations* where people are forced to move. Since those displaced from a single gentrifying neighborhood may wind up in a wide variety of places – nearby poor neighborhoods, more distant low-cost suburbs, or even distant cities or regions – the only definitive way to measure gentrification-induced displacement is to track down individual households who have moved out of neighborhoods over time as gentrification proceeds, and to ask them detailed questions about their reasons for moving. This is extremely expensive and time-consuming.

A second measurement problem occurs when social reality conflicts with the 'reality' of most social statistics. Nearly all surveys and other government statistics for residential areas are based on the unit of the household – people in families (or unrelated roommates) who live in the same housing unit. Even when surveys provide information on the reasons for residential relocation, the question is usually asked only for the 'householder' – the one person deemed responsible for the apartment lease, for example. When poor renters displaced from gentrifying neighborhoods move in with friends or relatives, they disappear from even the most detailed surveys that might otherwise be used to measure the displacement process.

Third, displacement is easy to overlook amidst the dynamic mobility of all neighborhoods. Households and individuals move frequently, for a wide variety of reasons – and often for multiple reasons at the same time (a young couple getting married are most likely to cite family considerations as their reason for moving out of their old apartments, for instance, but they will also consider the location of their jobs when they search among potential new places to live). Conservatives who dismiss concerns about gentrification-induced displacement point out that poor neighborhoods typically have very high rates of turnover, with a large proportion of renters moving regardless of the conditions of disinvestment or reinvestment. Indeed, the national estimates for the U.S. cited above confirm that displacement is involved in a small number of moves: only about one in nine renters who moved in the year before 2007 cited any reason related to displacement. This does not mean that displacement is insignificant – the process affected some 1.47 million households in the U.S. that year. But identifying these displaced households in particular gentrifying neighborhoods, among everyone moving and changing household circumstances for all sorts of other reasons, is almost as difficult as identifying individual raindrops in a thunderstorm.

In recent years, as gentrification has become an increasingly transnational urban process bound up with all of the complexities of globalized uneven development, displacement has also been recognized as a globalizing process. Clearly displacement has been a severe and widespread process in cities of the Global South long before the appearance of anything resembling gentrification. Moreover, displacement in the Global South has often been most devastating in rural areas. According to one estimate, development and infrastructure projects in India between 1951 and 1990 displaced at least 14.5 million persons, with the vast majority receiving no compensation or resettlement assistance whatsoever (Sharma, 2003, p. 908). Conservative estimates place the total number of people displaced by China's enormous Three Gorges Dam project at more than 1.1 million (Heming and Rees 2000, p. 444). But as worldwide population growth is being rapidly urbanized in the Global South, so are conflicts over the use rights to urban land as a place to live, versus the exchange values of speculative real-estate development and accumulation. The Centre on Housing Rights and Evictions (2003, p. 12), in a survey of documentary sources from 60 countries in 2001 to 2002, estimated forced evictions at nearly 7 million people; preparations for Beijing's 2008 staging of the Olympic Games displaced at least 1.25 million (COHRE, 2007).

As theories and narratives of gentrification become more global and cosmopolitan, therefore, so do critical analyses of displacement and resistance. Comparative research on these processes is extremely difficult, but there are important examples (Harris, 2008; Roy, 2005). Roy (2005) offers a careful diagnosis of the contradictory implications of efforts to strengthen property rights (a familiar refrain among neoliberal policy elites from the Global North) on vulnerable residents of urban slums in the Global South: while formal land title offers the promise and possibility of security and protection from eviction, the shift from informal squatting to formal, legally-recognized tenure almost always requires a regularity that itself threatens the poor – through the "unrelenting" demands of regular, periodic payments for rent, utilities, etc. In a comparative analysis of gentrification and displacement in London and Mumbai, Harris (2008) teases out the implications of learning from the experiences of both places, and the way the experience of gentrification in each place helps to define that in the other:

> ... in considering how gentrification has become 'generalized' across cities in *both* the global North and South, it is important to recognize how convergence processes have operated in a two-way direction. Rather than exporting Eurocentric understandings of gentrification, there is a need to learn from the new sharp-edged forms and processes of socio-spatial upgrading in previously 'peripheral' cities. ... The 'social tectonics' invoked by Butler and Robson (2003) in their study of gentrifiers in London become, in the phrase of Mike Davis (2004, p. 23), the 'brutal tectonics of neo-liberal globalization' in Mumbai. The 'spectre of displacement' that Freeman (2007) raises in relation to gentrification pressures in New York is reconfigured through the spectral narratives that dominate the 'nervous system' of Mumbai's housing, where more people live in shacks or on pavements than the entire population of Greater London. ...
>
> (Harris, 2008, p. 2423)

In this section, we include four influential readings that reflect not only the extent of disagreement over the scale of displacement in different contexts, but also *the politics of evidence* on displacement. A solid grasp of the literature on displacement is crucial for any student of gentrification – this is an important (sometimes public) debate where the stakes are very high, not just politically, but analytically, theoretically, methodologically.

The context and subtext to federal government policy executive Howard Sumka's 1979 review of the evidence on displacement in the United States is post-WWII disinvestment, "white flight" and decline in central cities, which in his words "left behind a decaying core increasingly populated by low-income and minority families" (p. 480). Sumka recognized that the "spontaneous neighborhood revitalization" (note the typical neoclassical naturalizing discourses on urban processes, and note also that the word 'gentrification' does not appear in his article) in central cities across the country – welcomed by almost anyone in policy circles at the time – was generating a well documented downside: the displacement of low-income residents unable to compete in an inflated housing market. Sumka set out to examine all the available evidence on displacement to see if it really was a problem of significant magnitude, and thus a significant policy concern. As is typical of policy elites even today, Sumka has little time for qualitative inquiry – every attempted qualitative survey of displacement is viewed with disdain for being biased and unrepresentative – and even quantitative studies are treated with skepticism due to the difficulty of tracing households over time. His conclusion is telling: "the work that has been done can be characterized fairly as impressionistic and generally devoid of carefully constructed research designs." (p. 486) Whilst he does recognize the seriousness of forced relocation for "some" households, he concludes that no federal policies are needed to stem displacement, as we don't have "reliable" evidence on it, and such policies "may slow or erase the trickle of middle-class movement back to the central city", thus threatening the restoration of "fiscal balance" (ibid.) It is striking that Sumka in fact advocates revitalization (gentrification) despite his own admission that there is no reliable statistical evidence to confirm that displacement is *not* a significant problem – a perspective adopted 30 years later by Chris Hamnett (2008) in an article in *The Guardian* newspaper.

As any analyst who has spent time with those who have lost their place will explain, displacement happens in several distinct ways. In the midst of a dramatic expansion of gentrification in the 1970s and 1980s that created complex landscapes of housing abandonment alongside pockets of upscale reinvestment in New York City, urban scholar, lawyer, and planner Peter Marcuse identified four separate categories of displacement, elaborated in the article we have reprinted here: *direct last-resident displacement*; *direct chain displacement*; *exclusionary displacement*; and *displacement pressure*. We leave our readers in Marcuse's hands for the full explanation of each, but the last two categories have recently received some empirical attention (and validation) in studies of the housing market in London and Berlin (Davidson, 2008; Davidson and Lees, 2010; Bernt and Holm, 2009). Marcuse's work has lasting critical relevance at a time when consumer sovereignty accounts of gentrification and abandonment have become urban policy (see the introduction to Part Six of this book). These accounts hold that gentrification is explained by rising demand for housing, abandonment by falling demand. As Marcuse showed, these "dual market" housing demand arguments (gentrification in one market, abandonment in the other) are immediately derailed by the simple geographical fact that the two phenomena often occur around the corner from each other! Crucially, gentrification and abandonment were not explained as the result of individual household preferences, but rather as disturbing outcomes of the private and public institutional factors behind any preferences; quite simply, the state of the housing market and of public policy.

Rowland Atkinson set out to measure and reveal the potential "hidden costs" of gentrification, based on returns from the UK Census in three inner London boroughs (Kensington, Camden and Hammersmith) from 1981 to 1991. Whilst recognizing the problems of measurement, he argues that the growth of owner-occupation is explained by a worrying loss of rental accommodation; and that the loss of working-class groups and of the elderly from gentrified areas is suggestive of large-scale displacement. These findings were amplified by his conversations with staff in tenants' rights projects (the purpose of which is to protect tenants from harassment and illegal eviction) in gentrified areas. Considered as a whole, the interview quotations in Atkinson's article provide a clear illustration of not just how displacement happens, but also the effects of displacement on some of the most vulnerable of London's residents – the mentally unwell, low-income families, the elderly, ethnic minorities. Tim Butler's (2007) recent contention that gentrification research in London "needs to decouple itself from its original associations ... with working-class displacement" is, after a read of Atkinson's article, problematic.

The final article in this section is one that reignited the debate on displacement not just in New York City (the locus of the research) but within and beyond the United States. Lance Freeman and Frank Braconi were troubled by the scarcity and inconclusiveness of solid quantitative evidence on displacement, and set out to provide something more robust to feed into public policy calculations on gentrification. They drew on the triennial New York City Housing and Vacancy Survey, which contains useful data on residential mobility, to address this hypothesis: "If gentrification increases displacement, all other things being equal, we should observe higher mobility rates among disadvantaged households residing in gentrifying neighbourhoods than among those residing elsewhere in the city" [...]. There is a palpable element of surprise in the tone of the article when the authors report that lower-income households in seven gentrifying neighbourhoods across the city were "19% less likely to move than poor households residing elsewhere" [...]. Even when controlling for rent inflation, they still find a lower probability of moving among poor households in the gentrifying neighbourhoods. Puzzled by this finding (which, they felt, shattered conventional wisdom in many circles), the authors speculate that lower mobility is explained by disadvantaged residents "appreciating" gentrification and finding ways to stay put, for it "brings better retail and public services, safer streets, more job opportunities, and improvements to the built environment" [...]. Although they do offer a few minor cautions and caveats towards the end of the article, Freeman and Braconi nonetheless conclude with these words:

> Insofar as gentrification ... does not appear to cause the widespread dislocation of the disadvantaged that some observers have claimed ... municipal governments may become more inclined to pursue policies explicitly geared to promoting it.
>
> (p. 51)

In Part 7 we include an article by Kathe Newman and Elvin Wyly that offered a spirited analytical and methodological response to Freeman and Braconi's work, and the inevitable media and policy fanfare which followed its publication. We leave readers of this book now to immerse themselves in the dilemma of displacement, with two hopes: first, that considerations of measurement and interpretation must be placed within the broad thereotical context we have already introduced in earlier chapters; and second, that the 'noise' in the available data (that blocks conclusive evidence on the amount of people displaced) never silences the voices of those who have suffered the devastating experience of being forced from a home, a community, a support network, a place.

REFERENCES AND FURTHER READING

Achtenberg, E.P. and Marcuse, P. (1983) 'Towards the decommodification of housing: A political analysis and a progressive program', in Chester Hartman (ed.) *America's Housing Crisis: What is to be Done?* pp. 202–231. Boston and London: Institute for Policy Studies/Routledge and Kegan Paul.

Anderson, M. (1964) *The Federal Bulldozer: A Critical Analysis of Urban Renewal, 1949–1962.* Cambridge, MA: M.I.T. Press.

Atkinson, R. (2000) 'Measuring gentrification and displacement in Greater London', *Urban Studies* 37: 149–166.

Bernt, M. and Holm, A. (2009) 'Is it, or is it not? The conceptualization of gentrification and displacement and its political implications in the case of Berlin-Prenzlauer Berg', *CITY* 13(2): 312–324.

Boddy, M. (2007) 'Designer neighbourhoods: new-build residential development in nonmetropolitan UK cities – the case of Bristol', *Environment and Planning A* 39(1): 86–105.

Butler, T. (2007) 'For gentrification?', *Environment and Planning A* 39: 162–181.

Byrne, J. P. (2003) 'Two cheers for gentrification', *Howard Law Journal* 46(3): 405–432.

Centre on Housing Rights and Evictions (2003) *Forced Evictions: Violations of Human Rights, Global Survey No. 9.* Geneva: Centre on Housing Rights and Evictions.

Centre on Housing Rights and Evictions (2007) Beijing Muncipality and the Beijing Olympic Organising Committee of the Olympic Games Named Housing Rights Violator for Widespread Evictions and Displacements. Press Release, December 5. Geneva: Centre on Housing Rights and Evictions.

Crump, J. (2002) 'Deconcentration by demolition: Public housing, poverty, and urban policy', *Environment and Planning D: Society and Space* 20, 581–596.

Curran, W. (2007) 'From the frying pan to the oven: gentrification and the experience of industrial displacement in Williamsburg, Brooklyn', *Urban Studies* 44: 1427–1440.

Curran, W. and Hanson, S. (2005) 'Getting globalized: Urban policy and industrial displacement in Williamsburg, Brooklyn', *Urban Geography* 26(6): 461–482.

Davidson, M. and Lees, L. (2010 forthcoming) 'New-build gentrification: its histories, trajectories, and critical geographies', *Population, Space and Place*.

Davidson, M. (2008) 'Spoiled mixture: Where does state-led "positive" gentrification end?', *Urban Studies* 45(12): 2385–2406.

DeFilippis, J. and Wyly, E. (2008) 'Running to stand still: Through the looking class with federally subsidized housing in New York City', *Urban Affairs Review* 43(6): 777–816.

Freeman, L. (2005) 'Displacement or succession? Residential mobility in gentrifying neighborhoods', *Urban Affairs Review* 40(4): 463–491.

Freeman, L. and Braconi, F. (2002) 'Gentrification and displacement', *The Urban Prospect: Housing, Planning and Economic Development in New York* 8(1): 1–4.

Goetz, E. (2003) *Clearing the Way: Deconcentrating the Poor in Urban America.* Washington, DC: Urban Institute Press.

Harris, A. (2008) 'From London to Mumbai and Back Again: Gentrification and Public Policy in Comparative Perspective', *Urban Studies* 45(12): 2407–2428.

Hartman, C., Keating, D. and LeGates, R. (1982) *Displacement: How to Fight It*, Washington, DC: National Housing Law Project.

Heming, L. and Rees, P. (2000) 'Population displacement in the Three Gorges Reservoir Area of the Yangtze River, Central China: Relocation policies and migrant views', *International Journal of Population Geography* 6: 439–462.

Herzfeld, M. (2009) *Evicted from Eternity: The Restructuring of Modern Rome.* University of Chicago Press.

Lyons, M. (1996) 'Gentrification, socio-economic change and the geography of displacement', *Journal of Urban Affairs* 18: 39–62.

Marcuse, P. (1985) 'Gentrification, abandonment, and displacement: Connections, causes, and policy responses in New York City', *Journal of Urban and Contemporary Law* 28: 195–240.

McKinnish, T., Walsh, R. and White, K. (2008) 'Who gentrifies low-income neighborhoods?' National Bureau of Economic Research Working Paper No. W14036.

Newman, K. and Wyly, E. (2006) 'The right to stay put, revisited: gentrification and resistance to displacement in New York City', *Urban Studies* 43(1): 23–57.

Palen, J. and London, B. (eds) (1984) *Gentrification, Displacement and Neighbourhood Revitalization*, Albany, NY: State University of New York Press.

Rérat, P., Söderström, O. and Piguet, E. (2010 forthcoming) [guest editors] 'New forms of gentrification: issues and debates', *Population, Space and Place*.

Roy, A. (2005) 'Urban informality: Toward an epistemology of planning', *Journal of the American Planning Association* 71(2): 147–158.

Sharma, R.N. (2003) 'Involuntary displacement: A few encounters', *Economic and Political Weekly* 38(9): 907–912.

Slater, T. (2006) 'The eviction of critical perspectives from gentrification research', *International Journal of Urban and Regional Research* 30: 737–757.

Slater, T. (2009) 'Missing Marcuse: on gentrification and displacement', *City* 13(2): 293–311.

Smith, N. (1996) *The New Urban Frontier: Gentrification and the Revanchist City*. London and New York: Routledge.

Stegman, M.A. (1982) *The Dynamics of Rental Housing in New York City*. New Brunswick, NJ: Center for Urban Policy Research, Rutgers University.

Sumka, H. (1979) 'Neighborhood revitalization and displacement: a review of the evidence', *Journal of the American Planning Association* 45: 480–487.

U.S. Bureau of the Census (2008) *American Housing Survey for the United States: 2007*. Current Housing Reports, H150/07. Washington, DC: U.S. Department of Commerce.

Van Criekengen, M. (2008) 'Towards a geography of displacement: moving out of Brussel's gentrifying neighbourhoods', *Journal of Housing and the Built Environment*, 23(3): 199–213.

Vigdor, J. (2002) 'Does gentrification harm the poor?', *Brookings-Wharton Papers on Urban Affairs* pp. 134–173.

25

"Neighborhood Revitalization and Displacement: A Review of the Evidence"

From *Journal of The American Planning Association* (1979)

Howard J. Sumka

In the past twenty-five years, few issues have presented so great a challenge to urban policy makers as the decline of the nation's central cities. During this period, large numbers of middle- and upper-income families chose to live in suburban communities. In large part, these trends reflect household preferences for the amenities of suburban life and the relatively low cost of land on the suburban perimeter. For many families the suburban dream was realized because of favorable mortgage terms offered by Federal Housing Administration and Veterans Administration programs. Similarly, the transportation cost associated with locating in suburban communities was greatly reduced by the construction of interstate highways under the National Defence Highway Act of 1954. Great new swaths of freeways through and around central cities carried suburban commuters to and from jobs in the urban core.

At the same time, suburban communities restricted entry to a relatively homogeneous class of "acceptable" neighbors through a variety of exclusionary techniques. These practices included restrictive zoning or building codes and concerted efforts to discourage, and in some cases to prohibit, the construction of subsidized housing under various federal housing programs. Augmented by outright racial discrimination, these restrictions helped to broaden the rift between the central city and its suburbs. As a result, the typical metropolitan area has become characterized by serious disparities in the distribution of public needs and resources among independent political jurisdictions.

Despite evidence that these trends are continuing, there are signs that considerable neighborhood revitalization is occurring in cities across the country. While one cannot conclude yet that this foreshadows a reversal of urban decline, a new sense of activity seems to be animating numerous neighborhoods in a variety of city types. To the extent that such activity is widespread, it offers some hope that cities may be beginning to attract and hold middle- and upper-income households which, in turn, may help to achieve such long-standing urban goals as improving the housing stock, increasing the tax base, attracting jobs and commercial activity, and improving the quality of services.

The potential for widespread revitalization, however, raises questions regarding who will bear the associated costs. Numerous observers of the urban scene argue that revitalization activity has caused the involuntary dislocation of lower-income residents from their neighborhoods. The result, it is claimed, is that the people who are least able to control their own destinies, those who have fewest choices, are being victimized by a phenomenon which benefits the middle classes.

Urban displacement has thus captured the attention of the popular press and prompted calls for new policies to help lower-income families remain in the revitalizing neighborhoods. A front-page article in the *New York Times* (Reinhold 1977, p. 1) sharply contrasted the situation of a young professional couple who had purchased a home to rehabilitate in the Adams-Morgan neighborhood of Washington with the plight of a poor black woman and her young daughter, soon to be evicted from an $85 per-month apartment in the same neighborhood. Less than a month later, a *Times* editorial urged that federal and local programs be redirected toward minimizing the unanticipated side effects of the "miracle of revival in older city neighborhoods" (*New York Times* 1977). In the *Boston Globe*, an op-ed column highlighting price pressures in the North End expressed the fear that the neighborhood "will one day be Italian in flavor only" (Hartnett 1977). A follow-up editorial argued that to discourage reinvestment would be counterproductive, but that some federal assistance to help stabilize housing costs for low-income North Enders would be appropriate. It also noted that the acceptance of federal assistance would require residents to open their neighborhood to the "poor of other races" who had heretofore been excluded (*Boston Globe* 1977). One of the strongest anti-revitalization pieces (Travis 1978) cast the image of hordes of middle-class whites converging on minority neighborhoods to reclaim "the prime land in the central areas of many of the nation's oldest cities." In contrast, the *Washington Star* (1978) acknowledged that "nothing is without its cost," but stated that the revitalization trend should be viewed at least as much as a "promise" as it is a "threat."

Although displacement has received much attention, remarkably little systematic knowledge exists about its magnitude or its effects on dislocated populations. Metropolitan-specific data on these questions are sparse, and national data are almost nonexistent. We have largely impressionistic views that are based on case studies of individual neighborhoods and affected by the biases of particular observers. This paper reviews this body of evidence with the intent of placing some perspective on the growing national debate and of assessing precisely what is and is not known about the displacement phenomenon.[1]

TRENDS IN URBAN POPULATION MOVEMENT AND NEIGHBORHOOD REVITALIZATION

Extent of revitalization

Despite the increasing evidence of reinvestment activity in cities throughout the country, national and metropolitan-specific data indicate that the central city outmigration of 1950–1969 has continued through the first half of this decade. During the five-year period ending in 1975, net migration flows resulted in the loss of seven million people from central cities, with nearly six million of them moving to the suburbs and the remainder to nonmetropolitan areas (U.S. Department of Housing and Urban Development 1978). Central cities, which contained

nearly 39 percent of the U.S. population in 1950, housed less than 32 percent in 1970 and less than 30 percent in 1975 (Sternlieb and Hughes 1977). Central city decline is particularly evident in the northeast and north central regions, which are victims of the recent Sunbelt development phenomenon (Sternlieb and Hughes 1977).

A recent detailed analysis of the intrametropolitan mobility in eleven large SMSA's presents further evidence that inner city reinvestment has failed to produce a significant back-to-the-city movement (Nelson 1978). Although there is some evidence of increased central city inmigration among whites, especially among cohorts aged 20–34, "the conclusion that central cities are becoming more attractive to whites is not supported by ... other measures" (Nelson 1978, p. 19). With the exception of Los Angeles, the net migration flow of whites continues to be from the central city to the suburbs. At the same time, the number of blacks migrating to central cities has been declining. Further, blacks moving to the suburbs from the central city tend to be upper-income, suggesting that this movement was more "a matter of choice rather than a result of displacement ..." (Nelson, 1978, p. 28). Given the apparent tendency for both blacks and whites to be moving out of the central city, "abandonment and lack of demand for central city housing units would appear to be a more pressing problem than displacement in the near future" (Nelson 1978, p. 28).

These analyses pointedly suggest that the spontaneous revitalization of central cities is not yet imminent and that the problems of disinvestment and local fiscal imbalance are likely to persist through the near future.[2] In important ways, however, they do not directly address the displacement issue. A statistically obvious back-to-the-city movement is not a necessary precondition for the existence of displacement. Because of the geographical segmentation of urban housing markets, population trends that cannot be deciphered statistically at the city level may have severe impacts on specific central city neighborhoods. Whether the movement is of returnees to the city or of households who elect to stay in the city rather than move to the suburbs, a trend that is small relative to the city population may in fact be substantial relative to the size of one or more particularly attractive neighborhoods.

Indeed, a growing body of evidence suggests that neighborhood renovation is occurring with increasing frequency across the country. A 1975 survey of local housing and planning officials conducted by the Urban Land Institute (ULI) documented such activity in nearly half the central cities with populations over 50,000 (Black 1975). While that study was not designed to produce statistically reliable estimates of the extent of rehabilitation, it estimated that the total number of units undergoing renovation may be as high as 50,000 dwellings. A similar survey of forty-four cities by the National Urban Coalition (1978) found widespread evidence of housing rehabilitation, regardless of city size or geographic location. Among the thirty largest central cities, Clay (1978) found evidence of revitalization in more than 100 neighborhoods.

Despite the important insights provided by these surveys, they suffer from potential problems of unrepresentativeness. Each of these studies relied on a similar mail survey technique. Local officials were asked to supply information on the extent of private renovation in their cities, including the number, type and location of houses being rehabilitated and the characteristics of the renovators. The ULI survey was mailed to 260 cities with populations of 50,000 or more. The overall response rate of 55 percent ranged from 30 percent in the smaller cities to about 96 percent in the cities of more than 250,000 people. The Urban Coalition survey had a higher response rate, primarily because it was directed only to those cities where the coalition has local affiliates, associates, or other contacts.

More importantly, these survey techniques provide no assurance that the responses are consistent or reliable. The extent of rehabilitation reported by various respondents likely ranged from off-the-cuff estimates to hard data taken from systematic searches of building permit or other files. Apart from an effort to ascertain the characteristics of the pre- and post-rehabilitation occupants of the units, no attempt was made to determine the displacement effects of the renovation.

A systematic study of national statistics by Franklin James (1977) uncovered more conclusive evidence of heightened renovation activity in central cities. His findings were based on changes in house values and rents, in homeownership rates, and in home-improvement expenditures by central city residents. Gregory Lipton (1977) measured inner-city revival in terms of the socioeconomic status of census tracts. The extent of revitalization in a city was indicated by the number of tracts within two miles of the Central Business District (CBD) in which the average income or educational level was above that for the entire SMSA. Among the twenty largest metropolitan areas, three (New York, Washington, and Boston) showed definite improvement from 1960 to 1970. Inner-city decline or stagnation was indicated in seven areas. While Lipton's work did not focus on displacement per se, two important conclusions were reached. First revitalization is most

evident in cities where a large portion of the employment base is in administrative or other white-collar jobs and where the CBD is far from outlying suburban areas. Second, a detailed analysis of San Francisco indicated that tracts contain a great deal of internal diversity; often they are the homes of both the very wealthy and of the poor who live in subsidized housing.

In addition to these multicity studies, a growing volume of anecdotal evidence and impressionistic accounts testify to increased renovation activity across the country. While these case studies are noncomparable and provide no basis for quantitative generalizations, the totality of the evidence indicates clearly that something is occurring in many urban areas and, therefore, that the potential for displacement is widespread.

CAUSE AND LOCATION OF REVITALIZATION ACTIVITY

Some insights into the causes of spontaneous regeneration are provided by recent studies that have documented the characteristics of neighborhood inmovers. The overwhelming consensus is that the parents of revitalization are the children of the postwar baby boom, who entered the housing market at a time when the volume of new construction was low and the price of suburban housing very high (James 1977; Goetze et al. 1977). Not suprisingly, then, the revitalization of inner-city neighborhoods is the result of macro trends in housing market economics and in demographic and lifestyle changes. Newcomers tend to be relatively affluent professionals between ages 25 and 44 who live in childless households (Black 1975; Gale 1976; and Pattison 1977). In general, they can be classified according to the stage of revitalization at which they entered the neighborhood. Early entrants tend to be "risk oblivious," they are followed by the "risk takers" and, finally, by the "risk averse" (Pattison 1977, p. 170). This suggests the possibility that the revitalization movement may persist only until these classes of homebuyers have been depleted.

Unfortunately, the literature provides little basis for predicting the locus of rehabilitation and thereby anticipating where displacement may occur. In the past, neighborhood research has concentrated on neighborhood decline, which is the result of normal market process (Hoover and Vernon 1962; Public Affairs Counseling 1975). As the housing stock aged and transportation and communications technology expanded metropolitan boundaries, upper-income households moved farther out of the city, leaving behind older, sometimes obsolete housing for lower-income migrants to the city. The spontaneous regeneration of these neighborhoods was, with a few notable exceptions, unheard of. As a result, virtually no theoretical or empirical research has attempted to explain systematically the revitalization process.

Renovation activity is apparently underway in a wide range of neighborhood and city types (Rogg 1977). In general, it appears to be more likely to occur in larger cities and in older cities in the northeast and the south (Black 1975, p. 6). Neighborhoods which have some intrinsic attractiveness—based on their proximity to downtown or other major focal points of activity or on the inherent value of the housing stock, no matter how deteriorated—are the prime candidates for renovation (Shur in U.S. Senate 1977; National Urban Coalition 1978, p. 16).

Based primarily on a case study of Washington's Capitol Hill, James identified three more or less distinct geographic segments in revitalizing areas—the neighborhood core, the inner ring, and the outer ring (James 1977, p. 125). The core area of Capitol Hill was almost completely revitalized between 1960 and 1970; by the end of that decade, restoration activity had spread to the inner ring around the core. In the outer ring area of Capitol Hill, neighborhood rehabilitation had not yet begun by 1975. This suggests that revitalization tends to concentrate in well-defined areas and to spread outward, rather than to occur in a scatter-shot fashion.[3]

NEIGHBORHOOD DISPLACEMENT: THE EMPIRICAL EVIDENCE

Displacement is the most difficult aspect of revitalization to examine systematically. Although there have been some more or less careful studies of the extent, location, and process of revitalization per se, the literature is virtually devoid of comparably insightful studies of displacement.[4] Yet, with an understanding of the process and dynamics of neighborhood revitalization, it may be possible to predict fairly accurately the areas where displacement is likely to be a future problem. The extent of revitalization and the geographic area it embraces can provide an indication of the potential seriousness of the displacement problem.[5] Equally important, however, is an understanding of the pattern of property transactions and price movements within revitalizing areas.

Although the process is likely to vary from one community to another, certain consistent patterns have been observed in many areas. The most dramatic evidence of displacement occurs when real estate speculators begin acquiring rental properties in areas they believe will soon become attractive to middle-to upper-income households. Speculative activity leads to the rapid turnover of recently obtained properties. A study of property transactions in Washington documented that 20 percent of the properties sold over a two-year period were sold more than once. Of these multiple sales, the great majority occurred within ten months of each other (cited in Goldfield and Hedeman 1978).

As speculators move into an area, the first to be affected are resident renters. Although actual renovation may not occur for several years, developers and speculators have no incentive to retain current tenants, even on an interim basis. Using New York City as an example, Schur (in U.S. Senate 1977, p. 49) argues that this occurs for a variety of reasons: current rents are too low even to cover operating and maintenance costs; the existence of housing code violations creates the possibility of legal action or rent strikes; and it is easier to dispose of the property if it is vacant.

Then as neighborhood revitalization proceeds, owner-occupants are likely to be affected. While no systematic research can be cited regarding the displacement of homeowners, two mechanisms are likely to operate. Presented with seemingly good offers, owners may sell too eagerly and rapidly, thinking that the neighborhood is still in decline. By not realizing the true value of their property, these homeowners may find it difficult to purchase housing other than in areas similar to their old neighborhoods. Secondly, as the neighborhood becomes more attractive to middle- and upper-income households, the surge in property values will correspondingly drive up tax assessments. This may serve to drive out owner-occupants whose incomes cannot cover the increased costs. Low-income elderly homeowners are particularly susceptible to being forced out for this reason. It should be noted, however, that the property tax burden of elderly homeowners is pervasive and has received considerable attention. Many states have enacted so-called "circuit breaker" or "homestead exemption" laws which substantially reduce the property tax liability of these families. Although not designed to avoid displacement per se, their application reduces one problem of elderly homeowners in neighborhoods undergoing revitalization.[6]

Empirical evidence of displacement

Empirical studies of neighborhood revitalization raise more questions about displacement than they answer; at best they suggest hypotheses for further research. As noted earlier, the empirical research to date has focused primarily on revitalization, not its secondary effects. Second, the analysis of displacement raises difficult conceptual and measurement issues that no one has addressed systematically. Finally, the implementation of a displacement study is costly, time-consuming, and fraught with pitfalls, primarily because of the difficulty of tracing and locating movers.

However, relying on data from the Annual Housing Survey, Cousar (1978) estimated that during the 1974–1976 period, over a half-million households per year were displaced, about two-thirds being metropolitan households. To place this figure in perspective, it should be noted that the number of displacement moves did not exceed 4 percent of all moves in any of the years included in the study. More significantly, the data are subject to serious potential biases of an indeterminable direction. For example, moves due to rent increases are excluded, although in some cases such increases may be the result of revitalization activity. On the other hand, evictions, which were categorized as displacement moves, may be the result of factors totally unrelated to revitalization.

A recent study by Grier and Grier (1978) offers some evidence that, in numerical terms at least, displacement due to spontaneous revitalization may be a smaller problem than is commonly believed. Although their reconnaissance of selected cities was not based on scientific sampling techniques, they estimated a "reasonable upper-bound" to the extent of reinvestment displacement. Their figures indicate that, in most large cities, fewer than one or two hundred households per year are likely to be affected. Even in Washington and San Francisco, where reinvestment activity is widespread, the number of displaced households was estimated to be relatively small.

Although the Urban Coalition study was specifically designed to examine the problem of displacement, its reliance on the opinions and perceptions of "informed" observers makes its conclusions difficult to evaluate. One is unable, for example, to attach significance to the statement that "80 percent of the neighborhoods reporting elderly residents indicated a decline in their number after rehabilitation" (National Urban Coalition, 1978, p. 7).

The city of Portland, Oregon, concerned about the tightness of its housing market and the difficulty lower-income families had locating housing, commissioned two studies of residential mobility. The first, designed before displacement was perceived as a major concern, examined the broader issues of household mobility between and within the city and the surrounding suburbs. A displacement analysis constructed ex post was able to provide only limited insights into the problem (Lycan 1978).

The data indicated that slightly under 10 percent of the movers originally surveyed had moved involuntarily. Approximately 3 percent cited demolition or poor maintenance as the reason—more likely signals of disinvestment rather than revitalization. Another 2.3 percent could no longer afford the rent, but whether this was due to rent or income changes was not specified. Finally, 3.2 percent had moved either because the house was sold or the owner decided to move into it. Without additional elaboration, even these moves cannot be attributed unequivocably to revitalization. All told, it was estimated that 1.7 percent of Portland's households move involuntarily each year due to factors as disparate as disinvestment, revitalization, and idiosyncratic market factors.

In an effort to gain better insights into the displacement problem, the second Portland study focused on neighborhoods where some reinvestment was occurring (McGrath and Ohman 1978). For the purposes of the study, displacement was defined as the eviction of tenants due to the conversion of a renter-occupied unit to owner occupancy. While this definition obviously excludes much displacement that does not result in a tenure change, it is not a totally unreasonable first approximation.

Efforts were made to interview a sample of new owners of properties sold during 1977. Under the strained assumptions of the study, it was estimated that 13.5 percent of the recent movers had been displaced. No attempt was made to contact the prior renters to ascertain why they had moved. The only effort made to determine the characteristics of the previous renters involved asking the current owners. Only twelve respondents were willing to venture guesses as to the income and occupational status of the "displaced" households, and this information is so suspect it is not worth reporting here.[7]

As yet, no reliable mobility data have been collected from surveys of outmovers from revitalizing areas. Two sources of data which do exist, however, suggest that the prospect of moving out of revitalizing areas may appeal to neighborhood residents. Although 74 percent of those responding to a survey of three neighborhoods in Washington indicated that they "feel a part of (the) neighborhood," two-thirds stated that they would move out of the neighborhood "if it were possible" (Washington Urban League 1976, p. 41). Similarly, in his study of Bay Village and West Cambridge in Boston, Pattison (1977, p. 137) reports that most residents saw revitalization as an opportunity to fulfill a long-term goal of moving to the suburbs.

One should hasten to add, however, that this information can hardly be taken as indicative of the sentiments of all inner-city residents. The Boston data are not representative even of the neighborhoods that were studied. Pattison's methodology consisted of interviewing households whose names were obtained from various "leads." These respondents were then asked to suggest the names of other residents who would be amenable to interviews. As a result, respondents tended to be people who were active in the local neighborhood association, which suggests serious bias in the results.

Depending on the extent that residents view revitalization in such positive terms, however, the measurement of displacement will be even more difficult. Very little is known about the characteristics of displacees beyond the obvious point that those who suffer most from displacement are lower-income households. A study of Capitol Hill in Washington found that of sixty-five identified displacees, thirty were families with three or more children and most were black. The remainder included a large portion of elderly families (James 1977, pp. 258–60).

One must be particularly careful about these data, however; the Capitol Hill statistics are based on records maintained by Friendship House, a neighborhood service organization. These households are not likely to be representative of all the families who have left Capitol Hill during renovation. Rather, they indicate the types of families most severely affected by displacement and who seek some form of assistance in relocating.

More systematic information on displacees is available from a recent study of persons who moved from apartment buildings undergoing condominium conversion in Washington (Development Economics Group 1976). Although conversion is only one manifestation of neighborhood reinvestment, it is a fairly common response to the increasing operating costs of rental housing and to the expanding demand for central-city housing among middle- and upper-income families. Among the outmover households interviewed in this study, 45 percent were elderly, 82 percent contained one or two persons, and more than two-thirds had incomes (in 1975) of less than $15,000. Slightly over half of the households responded that they chose to move rather than purchase their apartments because it would have been too expensive to stay. Another 20 percent were not interested in becoming condominium owners. As the study documented, the cost concerns were justified; for three typical household types (elderly; small, middle-aged; and small, young) monthly housing expenses would have doubled following conversion from rental to owner status.

Combined with the basic problem of defining precisely who has been displaced, the difficulty of tracing mover households makes follow-up studies of those displaced both tedious and costly. Yet this aspect of displacement is crucial to understand, for only by carefully documenting the postmove circumstances of displacees can one fully understand the dimensions of the problem. For individual households, it is important to be able to compare housing, neighborhood, and accessibility characteristics of the residents' new and former locations. From the broader perspective of the overall impact of neighborhood regeneration, follow-up studies are required to estimate the redistribution of costs and benefits among the central city and suburban jurisdictions due to regeneration and displacement. The 1976 study of the Development Economics Group of condominium conversions provides the only systematic analysis of displacees.

Although the households affected by condominium conversions are not typical of all households threatened by displacement, it is instructive that these families fared fairly well in their search for replacement housing. By and large they were able to locate homes of similar cost and size in areas near those they left. Nearly 90 percent of the families remained in the city, and more than three-quarters of this group relocated in the same or an adjacent neighborhood.[8] More than two-thirds were able to find a new home within one month of beginning their search.

Beyond this work, only scattered evidence is available from a few case studies. These data are not based on carefully designed sampling plans, nor do they contain sufficient detail about the housing circumstances of those displaced to allow for any strong inferences to be drawn. What they do provide is a basis for generating hypotheses around which to design more comprehensive and reliable research.

Two general patterns are implied by these case studies. First, displaced persons tend to move very short distances. For example, displacees from the Adams-Morgan area of Washington often locate in the immediate environs. Those who have left the area have not severed their social ties to the neighborhood, often returning for religious or social gatherings on weekends and evenings (Smith 1977). Similarly, half of the sixty-five families tracked by Friendship House on Capitol Hill relocated to other apartments within the neighborhood, while another 40 percent moved to other row-house neighborhoods within the city (James 1977, p. 260). The Urban Coalition report supports these impressions, based not only on its study of Capitol Hill, but also on information from St. Louis.

The second, and related, point is that dislocated families often move more than once as the boundaries of the revitalizing area expand. The Adams-Morgan study documented that some families had moved as many as three times since they were first dislocated (Smith 1977). Likewise, one would expect that the families who have elected to remain in Capitol Hill will, in the not too distant future, be forced to move again (James 1977).

Some observers suggest further that those displaced by current private market revitalization are the same families who, in the past were former displacees from the urban renewal areas which were redeveloped with public funds in the last two decades (Weiler, in the U.S. Senate 1977; Myers and Binder 1977).

Contrary evidence is provided by Pattison's study of the Bay Village area in Boston. There, many homeowners realized sufficient capital gains from the sale of their properties to fulfill a long-standing goal of moving to the suburbs. Others were able to retain their properties and convert them to rentals that generated income sufficient to allow them to move to the suburbs (Pattison 1977, p. 138).

SUMMARY

The major conclusion from this survey of studies of displacement in revitalizing areas is that very little reliable information exists. The work that has been done can be characterized fairly as impressionistic and generally devoid of carefully constructed research designs. More importantly, a large portion of the work has been done in Washington, D.C., a city that is probably an extreme case. This is true for a number of reasons. First, Washington's revitalization movement has been spearheaded by young professional households. In no other city in the country is such a large proportion of the work force engaged in white-collar employment. Second, Washington has one of the lowest housing vacancy rates in the country. Despite a consistent twenty-year trend of declining population in the district, the rental vacancy rate is critically low. This suggests that many housing units are being absorbed by small families, and that dwelling unit merging may be an important aspect of the revitalization process. In part, the vacancy rate also reflects the slow-down in suburban housing construction caused by Virginia and Maryland suburban development moratoria of recent years. No hard information exists to indicate whether displacement is equally severe

in other housing markets where vacancy rates are higher and where suburban growth has proceeded more rapidly. This does not discount the seriousness of the displacement problem in Washington but merely cautions that it may represent a distorted microcosm of what is happening across the country.

Given the current state of knowledge about displacement, calls for a broad and far-reaching national policy appear to be premature. To be sure, families who are displaced likely suffer serious problems in locating new housing and adjusting to unfamiliar environments. As a matter of equity, no single class of households should be made to bear the full brunt of the costs of urban revitalization to the extent that it is occurring. Forced relocation is, therefore, an important concern of local planners and program administrators, whether the ultimate source is private or public action.

Nonetheless, there are numerous broader issues to consider.[9] Indiscriminate policies to stem displacement may slow or erase the trickle of middle-class movement back to the central city. Keeping in mind that these families may help restore some fiscal balance to urban economies, all the poor residents of the city would suffer. Ultimately, what is required is a careful analysis of the magnitude of displacement along with a consideration of the benefits of revitalization. Until we have such information, amelioration of the displacement problem should appropriately be left to local officials familiar with local problems. The role of the federal government should be restricted to making available program resources that local governments can apply sensitively to mitigate the problem without stifling the potential of inner-city revitalization.

Author's note

The author would like to thank Biliana Cincin-Sain for her assistance in compiling and reviewing the literature and Judy Dollenmayer for her editorial assistance. The views, conclusions, and recommendations in this paper are those of the author. They do not necessarily reflect the official views and policies, expressed or implied, of the Department of Housing and Urban Development or of the United States Government.

Notes

1 This paper is limited to a review of the available information on displacement in neighborhoods experiencing private market revitalization.

Displacement may also result from other causes, including disinvestment and abandonment of the housing stock as well as public actions (Grier and Grier 1978). Similarly, the body of literature emerging from the relocation problems associated with urban renewal and other direct government actions in the late 1950s and 1960s is not discussed. No attempt is made to recommend policies for neighborhoods where displacement is already an obvious problem. Discussions of policy and program options may be found in Kollias (1977) and Weiler (1978). Stephens (1978) reviews the antidisplacement strategies of local government and community groups in Washington, D.C.

2 The dimensions of disinvestment are suggested by the estimate from Annual Housing Survey data that 242,000 central city dwelling units were removed from the inventory annually during 1973–1976. Of these, 194,000 were occupied (Dolbeare 1978, p. 18).

3 This is consistent with the general theory of neighborhood externalities, which so far has been applied primarily to negative effects (Davis and Whinston 1961).

4 Even defining "displacement" causes some problems. Grier and Grier (1978) and Dolbeare (1978, p. 5) define displacement as an involuntary move precipitated by environmental changes over which the family has no control. Although conceptually adequate, the definition is not sufficiently operational for authorative research.

5 Clay (1978) distinguishes between "incumbent upgrading" and "gentrification." It is the latter that involves widespread changes in the neighborhood's residents and, consequently, may create a displacement problem.

6 Myers (1978) discusses the particular problems and needs of the elderly in the revitalization context.

7 McGrath and Ohman (1978) also tried to interview absentee owners who had recently purchased property in the neighborhood. The response rate was so low that no results were reported.

8 As a cautionary note, it should be pointed out that there may be some bias in these results, given the relative ease of locating those who made the shortest move.

9 Sumka and Cincin-Sain (1979) provide a conceptual framework for viewing the revitalization and displacement phenomena in cost-benefit terms. They also outline a research strategy for addressing the as yet unanswered questions regarding these issues.

REFERENCES

Black, Thomas. 1975. Private market housing renovation in central cities: a U.L.I. Survey. *Urban Land* November: 3–9.

Boston Globe. 1977. Pressures on the North End. June 11:6.

Clay, Phillip L. 1978. *Neighborhood revitalization: the recent experience in large American cities* Cambridge: Massachusetts Institute of Technology.

Cousar, Gloria J. 1978. Bulletin on HUD estimates of national displacement, and pertinent program information. Presentation at National Urban League Conference, August 5.

Davis, Otto A., and Whinston, Andrew B. 1961. The economics of urban renewal. *Law and Contemporary Problems* 26, Winter: 105–117.

Development Economics Group. 1976. *Condominiums in the District of Columbia*. Report to the Office of Housing and Community Development, Government of the District of Columbia.

Dolbeare, Cushing N. 1978. *Involuntary displacement: a major issue for people and neighborhoods*. Washington, D.C.: National Commission on Neighborhoods.

Gale, Dennis E. 1976. The back-to-the-city movement ... or is it?: a survey of recent homeowners in the Mount Pleasant Neighborhood of Washington, D.C., Washington, D.C.: George Washington University, Department of Urban and Regional Planning.

———. 1977. The back-to-the-city movement revisited: a survey of recent homebuyers in the Capitol Hill neighborhood of Washington, D.C., Washington, D.C.: George Washington University, Department of Urban and Regional Planning.

Goetze, Rolf; Colton, Kent W.; and O'Donnell, Vincent F. 1977. Neighborhood dynamics: a fresh approach to urban housing and development policy. Prepared for HUD, Office of Policy Development and Research. Cambridge: Public Systems Evaluation, Inc.

Goldfield, David, and Hedeman, Phyllis E. 1978. Neighborhood redevelopment and displacement in Washington, D.C.: Unpublished manuscript.

Grier, George, and Grier, Eunice. 1978. Urban displacement: a reconnaissance. Memo report prepared for the U.S. Department of Housing and Urban Development.

Hartnett, Ken. 1977. Tracking the return of the gentry: the bad side of central-city chic. *Boston Globe* May 28: 7.

Hoover, Edgar, and Vernon, Raymond. 1962. *Anatomy of a metropolis*. Garden City, N.Y.: Anchor Books, Doubleday and Company, Inc.

James, Franklin J. 1977. *Back to the city: an appraisal of housing reinvestment and population change in urban America*. Washington, D.C.: The Urban Institute.

Kollias, Karen. 1977. Internal memorandum. Office of neighborhoods, Voluntary Associations and Consumer Protection, U.S. Department of Housing and Urban Development.

Lipton, Gregory. 1977. Evidence of central city revival. *Journal of the American Institute of Planners* April: 136–147.

Lycan, Richard. 1978. Displacement of residents of Portland due to urban reinvestment. Report prepared for the Office of Planning and Development. Portland, Oregon: Center for Population Research and Census, Portland State University.

McGrath, Lindsey, and Ohman, Chris. 1978. Residential displacement: Portland 1977. Report to the Office of Planning and Development, Policy Development and Research Section. Portland, Oregon: March.

Myers, Phyllis. 1978. *Neighborhood conservation and the elderly*. Washington, D.C.: The Conservation Foundation.

Myers, Phyllis, and Binder, Gordon. 1977. *Neighborhood conservation: lessons from three cities, an issue report*. Washington, D.C.: The Conservation Foundation.

National Urban Coalition. 1978. *Displacement: city neighborhoods in transition*.

Nelson, Kathryn P. 1978. Movement of blacks and whites between central cities and suburbs in eleven metropolitan areas, 1955–1975. Annual Housing Survey working papers, report no. 2. Office of Economic Affairs, U.S. Department of Housing and Urban Development.

New York Times. 1977. When city revival drives out the poor. July 1: A–22.

Pattison, Tim. 1977. *The process of neighborhood upgrading and gentrification*. Master's Thesis. Massachusetts Institute of Technology, Department of City Planning.

Public Affairs Counseling. 1975. *The dynamics of neighborhood change*. San Francisco: U.S. Department of Housing and Urban Development, Office of Policy Development and Research.

Reinhold, Robert. 1977. Middle-class return displaces some urban poor. *New York Times* June 5: 1.

Rogg, Nathaniel H. 1977. *Urban housing rehabilitation in the United States*. Washington: United States League of Savings Associations.

Smith, Frank. 1977. *Rip-off and reinvestment: a report on speculation in Washington, D.C.* Washington, D.C.: Public Resource Center.

Stephens, Mildrilyn L. 1978. Strategies to deter real estate speculation and neighborhood displacement in the District of Columbia. Chapel Hill, North Carolina: Department of City and Regional Planning, University of North Carolina.

Sternlieb, George, and Hughes, James W. 1977. New regional and metropolitan realities of America, *Journal of the American Institute of Planners* 43, July: 227–240.

Sumka, Howard J., and Cincin-Sain, Biliana. 1979. Displacement in revitalizing neighborhoods: a review and research strategy. *Occasional papers in housing and community affairs*. Volume 2. Washington, D.C.: Office of Policy Development and Research, U.S. Department of Housing and Urban Development.

Travis, Dempsey, J. 1978. How whites are taking back black neighborhoods. *Ebony* September.

U.S. Department of Housing and Urban Development. 1978. *A new partnership to conserve America's communities: a national urban policy*.

U.S. House of Representatives, Committee on Banking, Currency, and Housing. 1976. Hearings. The rebirth of the American city. September 20–October 1.

U.S. Senate, Committee on Banking, Housing, and Urban Affairs. 1977. Hearings. Neighborhood diversity, problems of dislocation and diversity in communities undergoing neighborhood revitalization activity. 95th congress, 1st session, July 7 and 8.

Washington Star. 1978. Renovation as threat. August 18.

Washington Urban League. 1976. *SOS 1976: speakout for survival*. June.

Weiler, Conrad. 1978. Reinvestment displacement: HUD's Role in a new housing issue. Paper prepared for the Office of Community Planning and Development, U.S. Department of Housing and Urban Development.

26
"Abandonment, Gentrification, and Displacement: The Linkages in New York City"

From *Gentrification of the City* (1986)

Peter Marcuse

Abandonment and gentrification seem polar opposites. Abandonment seems to result from drastically insufficient demand, gentrification from high and increasing demand; abandonment from a precipitous decline in property values, gentrification from a rapid increase. Yet in New York City (and not only there) the two processes seem to be going on simultaneously. How can gentrification and abandonment take place at the same time, often practically side by side? This chapter will try to answer this question, and in doing so will focus on the relationship of each to the problem of displacement.

The policy relevance of the issue should be clear. Existing policy in the United States is premised on three assumptions (see, for example, US House of Representatives 1977):

(a) Abandonment is painful but inevitable. Public policy cannot reverse it; at best it can confine it to certain neighborhoods. Therefore a policy of planned shrinkage, of triage, is necessary, abandoning certain neighborhoods completely in order to try to save others.

(b) Gentrification improves the quality of housing, contributes to the tax base, and revitalizes important sections of the city. The displacement it causes (if any) is trivial. Therefore a policy of encouraging gentrification, through tax benefits, zone changes, or whatever other means are available, should be pursued.

(c) Gentrification is in fact the only realistic cure for abandonment. Especially in a time of fiscal stress, the public sector cannot hope to counter abandonment (see (a) above). Only full use of

private-sector resources can do so. Thus the gentrification of abandoned neighborhoods is particularly desirable.

This chapter takes strong issue with each of these assumptions, and consequently with the policy prescriptions based on them. In summary, the argument runs as follows. Abandonment drives some (higher-income) households out of the city, others to gentrifying areas close to downtown, still others (lower-income) to adjacent areas, where pressures on housing and rents are increased. Gentrification attracts higher-income households from other areas in the city, reducing demand elsewhere and increasing tendencies to abandonment, and displaces lower-income people, likewise increasing pressures on housing and rents. Both abandonment and gentrification are directly linked to changes in the economy of the city, which have dramatically increased the economic polarization of the population. A vicious circle is created in which the poor are continuously under pressure of displacement and the well-to-do continuously seek to wall themselves in within gentrified neighborhoods. Far from being a cure for abandonment, gentrification worsens it. Both gentrification and abandonment have caused a high level of displacement in New York City. Public policies have contributed to this result, but are also capable of countering it. Whether they will or not hinges significantly on political developments.

The meaning and definition of gentrification have been established earlier in this volume. However, less attention has been paid to abandonment. Abandonment of a unit occurs when its owner loses any economic interest in the continued ownership of the property beyond the immediate future, and is willing to surrender title to it without compensation. Physical condition is a good, but not sufficient, indicator of abandonment: some units that appear physically abandoned may instead be on hold pending re-use ("warehousing"), and others that have actually been abandoned by their owners may still be maintained in tolerable condition by their tenants. The distinction between economic and physical abandonment is an important one for analytical purposes.[1]

Abandonment of an entire neighborhood occurs when public and/or private parties act on the assumption that long-term investment in the neighborhood, whether in maintenance and improvements or in new construction, is not warranted. It is only a matter of time before residents of an abandoned unit or an abandoned neighborhood are displaced.

Abandonment and gentrification are both reflections of a single long-term process, resulting from the changing economy of the central city. This process has two aspects: the shift from manufacturing to services, from reliance on mid-level skills to automation and de-skilling, on the one hand, which renders redundant large parts of the workforce and reduces lower-income rent-paying ability; and the increasing professionalization and concentration of management and technical functions, on the other, which creates additional higher-income demand for housing. These processes have spatial consequences: blue-collar workers (and potential blue-collar workers) are no longer needed in such numbers downtown; professional and technical workers are in ever-increasing demand there. Housing adjacent to central business districts reflects these changes. The pull exerted on one group by the changing economy of the central business district (CBD) fits in with the push against another. For the gentrifiers, all roads lead to downtown. For the poor, all roads lead to abandonment.

Thus the increasing polarization of the economy is reflected in the increasing polarization of neighborhoods: at the one end, abandonment, at the other end, gentrification.

The residential restructuring brought about by changing economic patterns is reinforced by the restructuring of business locations. The expansion of business and commercial uses in downtown requires changes in land use, both downtown and in its immediate environs. Residential must give way to business, and in the residential areas that remain (or are built) higher income is demanded and lower income is not. Property values downtown must be protected

from discordant land uses and discordant elements of the population. The real-estate industry, particularly its more speculative members, both follows and accentuates these patterns.

The poor end up displaced by each of these developments. They are displaced where business wants to move in, because the land is too valuable to house them further. They are displaced where gentrification takes place, because the buildings and the neighborhoods are too good (read: too expensive) for them. They are displaced where abandonment takes place, because the buildings and the neighborhoods are not good enough to provide decent housing for them.

The next section of this chapter takes up, on a citywide scale, the extent of displacement from abandonment and from gentrification in New York City. Because data on gentrification are harder to come by than data on abandonment, and their interpretation is more controversial, the following section looks in some detail at three clearly gentrifying and two possibly gentrifying neighborhoods. The final section summarizes the major conclusions, considers the likely future course of events, and discusses some policy implications.

THE CITY-WIDE EXTENT OF DISPLACEMENT FROM ABANDONMENT AND GENTRIFICATION

Conceptual issues and measurement

Displacement may be defined in terms either of households or of housing units, in individual or in neighborhood terms, and as a consequence of physical or economic changes. The most widely accepted definition is that of George and Eunice Grier (1978). The Griers' definition clearly covers physical causes, as when lack of heat forces tenants to move, as well as economic causes such as rent increases. Although these two sets of causes often overlap substantially, it is useful to distinguish between them analytically. Thus we refer to "economic displacement" and "physical displacement." In this study we are going to examine the displacement of individual households, and it is important to make another conceptual distinction here. If one looks simply at the housing units involved, and counts the last residents in that unit, then one gets a measure of "last-resident displacement." Yet it is possible that prior households occupying the same building were also displaced, and so it is necessary to make a count of what might be called "chain displacement." Both must be considered in an attempt to estimate displacement, and would be covered by the Griers' definition.

Further, however, there is a normal movement of households in any housing market, within any neighborhood. When a particular housing unit is voluntarily vacated by one household and then gentrified (or abandoned), so that another similar household cannot move in, and the total number of units available to such a household has thereby been reduced, we may also speak of displacement: "exclusionary displacement."

Exclusionary displacement is not included within the Griers' definition. A formal definition would run as follows:

Exclusionary displacement from gentrification occurs when any household is not permitted to move into a dwelling, by a change in conditions which affects that dwelling or its immediate surroundings, which

(a) is beyond the household's reasonable ability to control or prevent;
(b) occurs despite the household's being able to meet all previously imposed conditions of occupancy;
(c) differs significantly and in a spatially concentrated fashion from changes in the housing market as a whole; and
(d) makes occupancy by that household impossible, hazardous, or unaffordable.

The before-and-after measure often used in estimating displacement, the difference in housing availability over a given time period, implicitly includes exclusionary displacement. Such a before-and-after measure is generally based on a count of housing units in a given neighborhood, their occupants, and their characteristics, in comparison to the larger area of which the neighborhood is a part. It includes exclusionary displacement, but it does not include chain displacement, since it is based on a count of units, not households.[3]

Finally, displacement affects many more than those actually displaced at any given moment. When a family sees its neighborhood changing dramatically, when all their friends are leaving, when stores are going out of business and new stores for other clientele are taking their places (or none at all are replacing them), when changes in public facilities, transportation patterns, support services, are all clearly making the area less and less livable, then the pressure of displacement is already severe, and its actuality only a matter of time. Families under such circumstances may even move as soon as they can,

rather than wait for the inevitable; they are displaced nonetheless. This can be true for displacement from both gentrification and abandonment. We thus speak of the "pressure of displacement" as affecting households beyond those actually currently displaced. It is certainly a significant part of the displacement problem. Pressure of displacement can be distinguished from subjective fear of a remote possibility of displacement by looking not only at the perception but also the reality of what is happening in a neighborhood: subjective concern plus prices rising over the city average, for instance, might be taken as a crude benchmark.

The full impact of displacement must include consideration of all four factors: direct last-resident displacement, direct chain displacement, exclusionary displacement, and displacement pressure. No one set of figures will provide a measure of all four. The first two are best approached through demographic or mobility figures, the third through housing-unit figures, the fourth through a combination of these. Adding figures from the two different sources can produce double counting; excluding any source can produce under-counting. The following discussion tries to steer a middle course between these twin dangers, attempting to err on the conservative side; the resulting counts, however, are often, at this stage, unsatisfactory. But it is worth having conceptual clarity on definitions and concepts, and orders of magnitude as to figures, even if precise measurement is as yet unattainable.

Displacement from abandonment

The best evidence on the extent of abandonment (and thus the displacement arising from it) comes from New York City's triennial Housing and Vacancy Surveys, conducted for the City by the US Bureau of the Census.[3] It provides the basis for a housing-unit-based estimate of the extent of direct last-resident displacement (but not of chain or exclusionary displacement). The key figures are shown in Table 26.1.

"Losses" include all units that were in the housing inventory in 1970 but subsequently (up to 1981) removed from it. "Abandonment losses" (our term) include all units likely, from the Census survey, to have been abandoned in the period covered. Some minor adjustments must be made to take into account "losses" that appear to be abandonment but are really preparatory to re-use, and to add other real losses that do not appear in the Census survey. The resultant average figure for the 11 years covered is 31 000 units abandoned per year, or a total of 341 000 units. However, as a result of chain

demolished	154 722
condemned	21 186
burned-out, boarded-up, exposed to the elements	99 189
Abandonment losses	275 097
conversions to non residential use	22 149
mergers with another residential unit	23 754
Other losses	45 903
Total losses	321 000

Table 26.1 Losses from the housing inventory, 1970–81

displacement and pressure of displacement, more households are displaced from abandonment than the number of housing units that are abandoned. Households whose individual unit may still be in a minimally adequate state of repair, and whose landlord is even still attempting to maintain the building on the market, may nevertheless be forced to move because of the external consequences of neighborhood abandonment. The danger of fire may be increased from empty buildings next door, the level of street crime, drug traffic, and vandalism may increase to an intolerable level, community facilities and support networks may be eroded, public services neglected, beyond the point where a decent life can be maintained.

The importance of these neighborhood abandonment factors in causing displacement can be gauged by looking at the extent to which abandonment is spatially concentrated. To give just one example: the Bronx had, in 1970, 17.5 percent of the City's households, Queens 24 percent. Yet the Bronx had 44 percent of the City's demolished buildings over the following 11 years, Queens only 3.6 percent (US Bureau of the Census 1970: Vol. 34, Table 33). Thus an analysis of reasons given by "recent movers" for leaving their existing accommodations (presented in Ch. 9) shows "neighborhood condition" as a strong motivation for moving.

The pattern in areas of neighborhood abandonment is of rapid turnover of units throughout the neighborhood, both among units currently being abandoned and among those that have not yet reached this stage. Generally, the greater the choice of housing available to a household, the more likely it is to leave before being physically forced out by lack of heat or some other crisis condition. Thus there will be displacement of slightly higher-income households from units not yet abandoned, simultaneous with displacement of lower-income households from units at the very last stage of abandonment.

Figure 26.1 shows the effects vividly. Of the five boroughs in New York City, the Bronx was most affected by abandonment. There, households at the top as well as at the bottom of the income distribution left the borough in substantial numbers during the three-year period shown. This is not explicable by population change in general: the number of renter households in the city as a whole actually went up slightly, from 1 930 000 to 1 933 887 (Stegman 1982: 73).

Although all these figures suggest that chain displacement, either from neighborhood abandonment or from earlier stages of individual abandonment, is likely to be very substantial, there is no way, with presently available data, to measure it authoritatively. It may not be unreasonable to estimate that the figure would be at least equal to that resulting from direct abandonment.

Thus the best estimate of total displacement from abandonment for New York City might well be a minimum of 31 000 but a more likely figure is 60 000 households, or 150 000 persons per year.[4]

Displacement from gentrification

Displacement from gentrification is harder to measure. Changes in absolute numbers of high- or low-income households in the city are inadequate because gentrification results more from movement *within* the city than from outside it. Mobility figures provide too little information on the cause of moves. Other figures are limited to physical displacement, and do not reflect economic displacement, or vice versa. Exclusionary displacement can be deduced from demographic figures, but must rely on rather broad assumptions about what would have happened without gentrification. Also, quantification of the pressure of displacement must be able to distinguish between the various causes of price increases more precisely than available data now permit. Nevertheless, a preliminary estimate can be made.

As to direct physical displacement, some indicators are available. Since before 1970, substantial tax benefits (both an exemption of tax on the increased value and an abatement equal to the allowable cost of the rehabilitation itself) are available to those who rehabilitate multi-family buildings under the J-51 program. Virtually all qualifying rehabilitation actually uses the program. There are no controls on the initial rent charged after rehabilitation; thus there is generally a significant turn from lower- to higher-income occupancy. The number of units affected in the 10-year period before 1980 was 376 940, or

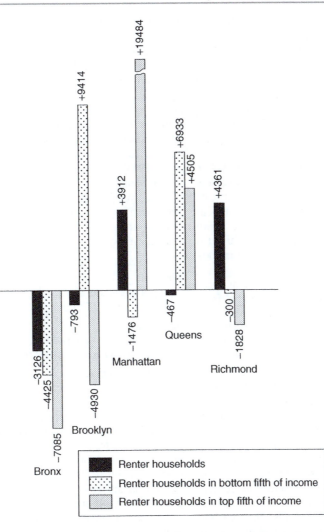

Figure 26.1 Gain or loss of renter households in bottom and top income quintiles, by borough, New York City, 1977 and 1980 (after Stegman, 1982)

about 38 000 units a year. Analysis of their location bears out the assumption that most such units are generally part of the gentrification process: over one-third were in Manhattan, and the concentration in areas of known gentrification is great: one-third of the units between 70th and 86th Streets on the West Side, for instance, used J-51 during this period (City of New York Department of City Planning 1983: 25). But some J-51-assisted units do not result in direct displacement: many subsidized units, for instance, are included in the count of those assisted by J-51. A modification downward of the 38 000 figure should thus be made. On the other hand, some rehabilitated units are not eligible for J-51; these would have to be added to the 38 000 figure.

The loss of SRO units (units in Single Room Occupancy buildings) provides a floor for the estimate of displacement, since it is generally conceded that the upgrading of SRO units results in displacement of their former residents, however displacement is defined. The number of such units has gone from 127 000 in 1970 to 20 309 in 1981, or an average of 9700 units lost each year. Those displaced from them were generally poor (85 percent with incomes under $3000 in 1979),[5] and the rehabilitation was overwhelmingly undertaken with J-51 benefits. The results were in almost every case housing for higher-income groups. A minimum of 9700 units, and perhaps as high as 38 000 households, may be estimated to have been directly displaced by the physical change in housing units in New York City each year.

As to economic displacement from gentrification, it is virtually impossible to distinguish between direct displacement, exclusionary displacement and the pressure of displacement. Economic displacement is perhaps best measured by the figures dealing with changes in gross rents. Between 1978 and 1981, at a time when the number of units renting for less than $200 decreased by 110 363, 24 096 units increased their rent from below $400 to $400–499, and a further 18 704 increased their rent from below to above $500. Clearly not all of these 42 800 units experienced rent increases as a result of gentrification or even household moves, and so this figure is on the high side for direct and exclusionary displacement. It may be less inflated once we include pressure of displacement.

Looking beyond units that remain in rental occupancy, economic displacement also results from cooperative and condominium conversions. The number of conversions in 1983 under non-eviction plans alone was 18 967 of which 6168 ended up priced at $100 000 or more. Conversions under eviction plans run at about 70 percent of the level of those under non-eviction plans (City of New York Department of City Planning 1983: 27); these are even more likely to result in direct displacement. Some of these units continue to be occupied by their former tenants, but the typical pattern is of a substantial increase in real occupancy costs after conversion. Thus there is exclusionary as well as direct displacement. Limiting ourselves to conversions resulting in units selling for over $100 000, probably 10 485 households, i.e. 6168+70% of 6168, are subject to direct or exclusionary displacement each year. This figure is in addition to the number of those economically displaced from units remaining rentals, but it does overlap with the number of those physically displaced.

Forced displacement is the most extreme form of displacement. Much of the displacement caused by gentrification appears impersonal; "market trends" cause increased prices, and an individual landlord only seems to be doing what all other landlords are doing when he raises rents, rehabilitates for a higher-income clientele, and watches as one tenant leaves and another (better able to afford the new rent) comes in. The tenant is forced to leave, just as much as if the landlord had personally visited him or her and said "Leave, or else!", with a club in his hand. But the force is of the market, not of the club. In some instances, however, the club or its equivalent is used directly. Harassment of undesired (lower-income)

tenants is hardly rare in New York. Cutting off heat or utilities, failing to make repairs, letting garbage accumulate till the stench is overpowering, leaving lights out in the hall, leaving front doors open or broken, and window-glass broken and unrepaired, steps splintered, hallways cluttered – even setting fires – are all techniques for which cases are documented in court hearings and administrative records. Over 1300 charges of harassment a year were officially reported in New York, according to the recent study by Elliott *et al.* (1983). This no doubt understates the figure for actual harassment.

The available figures that may provide the basis for estimating household displacement from gentrification, then, include the following (all figures are annual averages):

physical	
upgrading under J-51	38 000
elimination of SRO units	9 700
economic	
rent increases to <$400	42 800
co-op conversions <$100 000	10 485
harassment charges	1 300

These figures overlap, so they may not simply be summed. It seems safe to conclude that displacement from gentrification (including direct and exclusionary displacement) is probably somewhere between 10 000 and 40 000 households a year. Without including those subject to the pressure of displacement, it is probably closer to the lower figure; if they are included, the number is probably closer to the higher figure.

These figures need to be increased by another factor. All indications are that the pace of gentrification has accelerated in the last three years, that is, since the time of the 1980 Census on which the foregoing estimates are based. At the same time, it is relatively clear that the pace of gentrification slowed during the middle years of the 1970s, as economic conditions worsened (see DeGiovanni 1983: 35). Thus any figures based only on changes from 1970 to 1980 will tend to understate the problem, as will any projections into the future based on 1980 figures only.

Thus total displacement, according to our estimates, includes between 31 000 and 60 000 households displaced from abandonment, plus between 10 000 and 40 000 households displaced from gentrification, or between 41 000 and 100 000 households displaced from the two causes together, in New York

City, on the average, over the last decade. Assuming an average household size of 2.5 persons, this would mean between 102 500 and 250 000 persons not living in neighborhoods that would otherwise be home to them each year, because of the consequences of the spatial restructuring of the city.[6]

NEIGHBORHOOD ASPECTS OF GENTRIFICATION AND DISPLACEMENT

Gentrification is not a process that works uniformly throughout the city: quite the contrary. It is the essence of gentrification that gentrifying areas and declining areas (abandoning areas, in cities such as New York) are spatially linked to a process of urban restructuring. This is one of the reasons why it is so difficult to measure the resulting displacement from aggregate figures for the city as a whole. If the scale of the analysis is too large, changes cancel each other out. But they can be seen, and more accurately measured, at the neighborhood level. As an introduction to the neighborhood analysis that follows, however, one important point must be made about the larger picture.

The reason for gentrification in New York City is not that there is a net increase in high-rent-paying ability in the city as a whole. On a number of key indicators, there is in fact a decline: the total population has shrunk from 7 894 862 to 7 071 639 (all figures compare 1970 with 1980); the proportion of non-Hispanics has fallen from 61.6 percent to 51 percent; the proportion of high-income families (over $25 000 in 1970, over $50 000 in 1980, almost exactly the adjustment for inflation) has gone down from 6 percent to 5.4 percent; the number of those having a college education has declined from 813 563 to 776 557. The gentrification that is taking place results not from a massive influx of additional well-to-do to the city, but rather from a spatial reshuffling of a relatively constant or even declining number. Detailed analysis will show the pattern.

The pattern at the neighborhood level

This section examines five neighborhoods in New York City in which gentrification has been of major concern: the Upper West Side near Lincoln Centre, Manhattan Valley to the north of the West Side, Clinton just to the south of 59th Street on the West Side, the Lower East Side, and Lower East Harlem (see Figure 26.2). All of these areas are in

Manhattan; they thus do not include any areas of "family gentrification."[7]

The five areas are very different, both from each other and even internally; one of the surprising findings from the study is the fine level at which change needs to be examined to obtain a clear picture of what is going on. To understand the internal dynamics, each neighborhood was divided, for purposes of analysis, into two areas: the one more "abandoned" and less gentrified (the "A" area), the other more gentrified and less abandoned (the "B" area).

Tables 26.2 and 26.3 present key indicators of change for the most significant census tracts in each neighborhood. In each table the most important figures are the percentages in the right-hand columns. These represent the percentage change in each indicator, for a given census tract, over and above the citywide average.[8] Table 26.2 shows changes in the percentage of those with a college education. One can identify tracts undergoing gentrification by the extent to which their increase in college-educated population exceeded the city average for the period in question. Based on all of the work done in the study, changes in education level seem the most reliable single indicator of gentrification.[9]

"Pockets" and "borders" of gentrification may be identified from the analysis. Pockets are areas surrounded by dissimilar development; borders those lying between dissimilar areas. In the Upper West Side, formerly a pocket, the process of gentrification has proceeded the furthest, and abandonment is nowhere in evidence.[10] In the "B" portions of Clinton and Manhattan Valley, both of which have evolved as pockets with the growth of Mid-town, Lincoln Center, the Convention Center, and to the north with the influence of Columbia University, gentrification is proceeding apace; their "A" areas are not yet as gentrified. In Lower East Harlem and the Lower East Side, both of which are "borders" between very disparate areas, there are signs of gentrification in the "B" areas (very little in Lower East Harlem, much more on the Lower East Side), but none at all in the "A" areas (the data are from 1980, and recent developments have accentuated the trends).

The pattern becomes even clearer from Table 26.3. It shows the change in high-rent-paying households between 1970 and 1980 for the same census tracts. Rents have caught up with and are now increasing more quickly than the increase in educational level in the most gentrified area, the Upper West Side. In Clinton, rent increases lagged behind increases in educational levels; there were still some

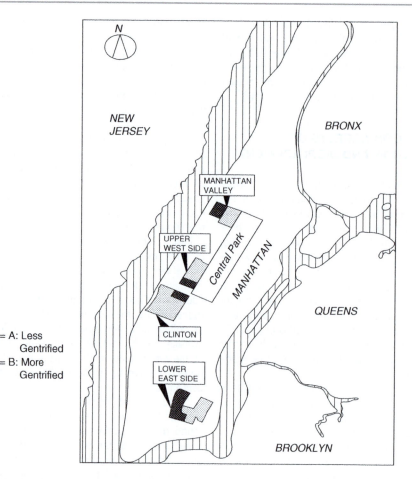

Figure 26.2 Neighborhood study areas in Manhattan

bargains to be had in 1980, but the shape of the future is clear from the change in educational level. The same is true, to a lesser degree, in Manhattan Valley, where the development is not as far along. But the process is underway throughout all three of these pockets of gentrification.

The pattern is different for the two border areas, East Harlem and the Lower East Side. Here we still see a sharp division *within* the area, in which gentrification is clear in the "A" areas, but *both* the education *and* the rent indicators are still below the citywide average change. Here the extent of future gentrification must remain (at least as of the time of the 1980 Census) an open question.

The overall pattern extrapolated from these tables, then, has three components: a substantially unchanged total demand for high-rent units (see "New York City, all" figures in both tables); stronger and clearer movement toward gentrification

in "pocket" areas than in "border" areas; and inmigration of population with higher education preceding rent increases, which follow and rise sharply as gentrification reaches maturity.

A limited analysis of changes in market prices was undertaken in each of our neighborhoods,[11] and it supports the expectations derived from the rental data. There are sharp price increases in gentrifying areas, virtually no activity in abandoning ones. Figure 26.3 summarizes the data. The annualized (uncompounded) rate of increase in price is shown on the vertical axis; the length of time between sales on the horizontal. Although the correlation is not absolute, and the sample is very small indeed, the findings are suggestive as to the role of speculation in the gentrification process.

Real-estate speculation is a strong accompaniment of gentrification. The behavior of speculators, and of the real-estate market generally, is perhaps

Area	Census tract	1970 total population	1970 college graduates	1980 college graduates	Percentage change compared with New York City	
					"A" areas	"B" areas
Clinton	121	5 790	455	2 079		+28.52
	127	8 622	352	916	+7.01	
	139	9 617	1 632	2 822		+12.84
Upper West Side	149	2 102	728	2 593		+89.20
	153	8 177	2 198	3 545	+16.94	
Manhattan Valley	189	16 021	913	824	+1.03	
	195	8 823	1 731	2 495		+9.13
East Harlem	170	9 840	321	252	−0.23	
	160.02	3 239	655	945		+9.42
Lower East Side	22.01	8 147	512	341	−1.63	
	36.02	3 437	327	385		+2.06
	38	10 456	1 137	2 271		+11.32
New York City, all		7 894 862	813 563	776 557		−0.0047

Table 26.2 Index of population change: college graduates

Area	Census tract	1970 total household	1970 tenants paying $250+	1980 tenants paying $500+	Percentage change compared with New York City	
					"A" areas	"B" areas
Clinton	121	3 327	142	291		−4.43
	127	3 998	37	8	−0.78	
	139	5 963	765	1 109		+5.72
Upper West Side	149	1 125	261	2 319		+182.98
	153	4 900	311	2 281	+30.77	
Manhattan Valley	189	5 236	128	47	−1.60	
	195	3 993	106	287		+4.58
East Harlem	170	3 735	17	0	−0.51	
	160.02	1 345	99	268		+12.52
Lower East Side	22.01	2 882	0	0	−0.05	
	36.02	1 120	0	12		+1.02
	38	5 356	22	58		+0.62
New York City, all		2 836 872	113 776	115 083		−0.0005

Table 26.3 Index of housing change: tenants paying higher rents

the single most sensitive indicator of what type of change is or is not going on in a neighborhood. Buyers and sellers in the real-estate market try to guess what will happen in the future; their actions reflect their predictions. When their interest is only short term, housing is purchased for profitable resale rather than to provide dwelling units, their actions are generally referred to as speculation. There is no reason to believe that a restraint on speculation would do more than to slow the rate of gentrification, but that slowing effect might be significant.

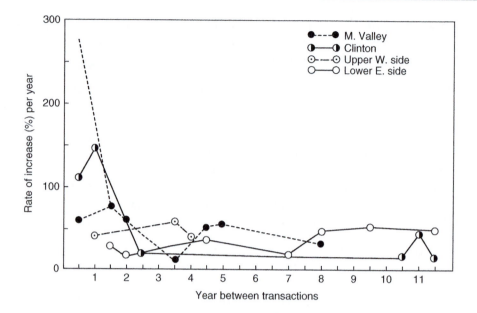

Figure 26.3

The consequences of neighborhood-level changes

Conclusions can be drawn from neighborhood-level data about three aspects of gentrification: its relation to social and economic polarization, to displacement, and to abandonment.

Gentrification contributes to increasing residential polarization of the city by income, by education, by household composition, and by race. We have already seen the striking variation even within gentrifying neighborhoods classified as "border" areas. The extent of the increasing polarization can be seen even more dramatically at the borough level. Manhattan is of course the most gentrifying borough, the Bronx the least gentrifying and the most abandoned. Between 1970 and 1980, Manhattan increased its number of college-educated residents by 22.9 percent; in the city as a whole it went down 4.5 percent, and in the Bronx it went down 36.1 percent. Per capita income went up 105.2 percent in Manhattan, compared with an increase of 96.5 percent for the city and only 81.5 percent for the Bronx. Median contract rent went up 139 percent, compared with 113.6 percent for the city and 124.1 percent for the Bronx.

The same polarization can be seen graphically in Figure 26.1, discussed earlier. Manhattan gained rich and lost poor households between 1969 and 1981; the Bronx lost both rich and poor households, and

lost many more rich than poor (rich and poor being defined as top and bottom income quintiles). The rich are concentrating in Manhattan, and they are leaving all the other boroughs except Queens, where higher-income families can find better access to larger units. The same process of restructuring is also happening to a lesser extent within each borough.

The direct measurement of displacement from these changes is difficult from census data. The calculations for sample tracts are, however, suggestive. In tract 152, for instance, on the Upper West Side, with a high level of gentrification according to any indicator, the high-income population increased by 4.7 percent (5.3 percent more than the city-wide figure), and the low-income population went down by 1.9 percent (10.7 percent lower than the citywide figure). That the increase in high-income residents *caused* the decrease in low-income residents of course cannot be conclusively established from such a simple correlation, nor can the question of whether the departure of the former residents was involuntary, but it defies common sense and daily experience to believe otherwise.

The same type of analysis can be performed for displacement using race rather than income as the indicator. Here we tested a slightly more complex hypothesis (derived from Spain 1981) that gentrification would cause not only a replacement of blacks by whites in tracts of high gentrification, but also a relocation of those displaced blacks into adjacent

	1970 percentage white	1980 percentage white	Percentage change	Percentage change, white, in comparison with New York City
New York City	77.6	60.8	−15.8	—
Lower East Side				
gentrified tract 38	88.1	76.0	−12.1	+3.7
adjacent tract 36.02	77.4	51.0	−26.4	−10.6
tract 36.01	77.7	42.1	−35.6	−19.8
Clinton				
gentrified tract 139	78.4	72.7	−5.7	+10.1
tract 135	72.1	47.0	−25.1	−9.3
adjacent tract 127	67.8	47.5	−20.3	−4.5

Table 26.4 Gentrification and racial change

tracts. Table 26.4 presents the results from three tracts on the Lower East side and three tracts in Clinton. Using citywide change as the benchmark, the percentage change of whites in the tract of higher gentrification increased, and in the adjacent tracts it decreased. The Spain hypothesis seems to be borne out.

Where there is the most substantial abandonment in certain "border" areas, the figures do not show evidence of gentrification, as of 1980. This is true for the "B" parts of the Lower East Side and of East Harlem, for example. The indicators of non-gentrification are shown in Tables 26.2 and 26.3, and are corroborated by figures on race and ethnic change, income and population change, tax arrears, market prices, and losses from the stock. Where the border between gentrification and abandonment actually lies may indeed change; that there is a border is hard to deny.

Gentrification can thus exist side by side with abandonment; each contributes to the other, as their populations move (or are forced to move) in reverse directions, and both contribute to displacement. The process of gentrification operates intensively within very sharply defined boundaries, and can affect negatively the population on both sides of that boundary.

Evidence from other scattered sources supports the conclusions. If not by its newer name, gentrification has nevertheless been anticipated for the Lower East Side since after World War I (Grebler 1952), yet each prediction of imminent change proved wrong. The same is true, if only for more recent periods and to a lesser extent, of East Harlem and Manhattan Valley. Predictions of a turnaround date back 50 years, but have yet to be fulfilled in the terms in which they were cast.

These conclusions are relevant to the question of gentrification as a private market "cure" for abandonment. Leaving apart the point that gentrification benefits an entirely different category of persons than those injured by abandonment, the question is this: how likely is it that gentrification will reverse the trend toward abandonment in affected areas in the immediate future? The data presented here suggest, at least for the areas considered, that the answer is "Not very likely." When and if gentrification comes to areas previously abandoned, it either comes far too late to have any impact on those earlier affected by the abandonment, or it in fact aggravates the displacement caused by abandonment by stimulating a new source of displacement.

Thus the high levels of concern by many residents and housing groups about gentrification in or close to areas of abandonment are justified on three grounds. First, gentrification itself causes displacement. Second, given the lack of city policy dealing with gentrification, there is no certainty where it will occur. The extent of gentrification is of course limited, but no one knows with certainty where it will take place, and therefore many more areas fear it than will face it. Third, gentrification is being put forward, however erroneously, as the answer to abandonment and blight, as a rationale for public inaction. The rejection of gentrification in these neigbborhood is thus an integral part of a program calling for public action to combat abandonment.

We have, in this section, looked at a substantial amount of neighborhood-level data; in the preceding section, the dimensions of the problem at the citywide level were examined. It is now time to return to the more general level, summarize our findings, and examine some of the policy implications.

PRESENT AND FUTURE HOUSING PATTERNS IN NEW YORK CITY

A summary picture of changes in housing in New York City would include the following components:

(a) *There is very substantial abandonment in New York City, displacing (directly, indirectly, or through chain effects) between 77 500 and 150 000 persons a year.* It has a clear spatial pattern: it takes place primarily in a secondary ring between the primary ring of increasingly upper-income housing around the central business district and the outlying suburban-type housing ring at the city's outskirts. These are the major areas of abandonment. Abandonment also takes place in individual areas close to the central business district, where, for historical reasons (working-class occupancy and building stock), the primary ring of upper-income housing did not develop.

(b) *There is very substantial gentrification in New York City, displacing (directly, indirectly, or through chain effects) between 25 000 and 100 000 persons a year in the current period.* Gentrification takes place primarily in areas immediately adjacent to the central business district and the primary ring of upper-income housing around it, radiating to the "border areas" of gentrification. Gentrification also takes place in pockets of housing occupied by poorer households within or on the fringes of the central business district, or in pockets of mixed use (loft areas, for instance) in similar locations. Although not considered here, gentrification may also take place in areas of particular environmental or housing quality convenient to the central business district (such as Brooklyn Heights or Park Slope in New York), and such areas may be more suitable for families than border or pocket areas.

(c) *Gentrification and abandonment are intimately related and mutually reinforcing.* Each directly contributes to displacement, and each aggravates the other. Abandonment aggravates gentrification by pushing out households, some of whom move and gentrify. Gentrification aggravates abandonment by siphoning off people and resources, public and private, and by inflationary pressures in the remaining intermediate areas where higher prices and declining incomes in turn produce abandonment. Each aggravates the problems of finding substitute housing for those displaced, by removing whole areas of the city from realistic consideration and inflating prices even further in others.

(d) *Gentrification and abandonment have a strong spatial relationship to each other.* Gentrification may, after some time, follow abandonment, either at borders between the two or in pockets of abandonment. Generally, however, gentrification and abandonment take place in different parts of the city: in areas of major abandonment, there will not be gentrification, and in areas of major gentrification (or where it is realistically anticipated) there will be no abandonment.

What of the future? All of the factors involved in the restructuring of the city are continuing ones: the shift of the economy from manufacturing to services, the concentration of control and management, the multiplying international linkages of business, the proportionately increasing need for managerial, professional, and technical personnel, and the decreasing need for unskilled manufacturing and service workers, the increasing polarization of the population economically, the expanded needs of business for downtown commercial and office space, the tendency of government and of the real-estate industry to follow and aggravate the results of these processes at the residential and neighborhood level. If these are the factors that produce both gentrification and abandonment, then there is no reason to expect a change of direction in the housing market.

The pace of gentrification and abandonment will, however, vary. Frank DeGiovanni, in his careful study of gentrification in multiple cities, found that "nationwide macroeconomic changes" (DeGiovanni 1983: 33) seemed decisive in determining the extent of activity at any given point. If our theoretical explanation of gentrification/abandonment is correct, then "macroeconomic changes" would *not be* synonymous with "prosperity" or "recession".[12] Rather, prosperity at the upper end of the economic spectrum and depression at the lower end are the key factors. These are only ambiguously captured by measures of national economic growth, which implicitly assume that both ends of the economic spectrum will prosper or suffer together. The historical facts are to the contrary. Indeed, we are witnessing today a period of high corporate profits and high unemployment: exactly the combination that theory would lead us to believe would most exacerbate displacement.

At the same time, the willingness of the government to comply with the wishes and preferences of those most decisive in the private market has never been greater. Public expenditures in major areas of abandonment are being reduced, and such expenditures in major areas of gentrification are being increased. The closing of hospitals, fire stations, schools, and police stations, and the generally and rapidly declining conditions of public services such as garbage pickup, accelerate abandonment. The use of Urban Development Action Grant funds for midtown hotel development, the financing of the Convention Center, and the various tax incentive programs, are all typical of actions fostering gentrification.[13] Public abandonment of some neighborhoods, following private disinvestment (redlining), and public investment in other neighborhoods, following strong private interest, both serve substantially to aggravate displacement.

By exactly the same token, however, public policy could reduce, indeed eliminate, displacement. Government plays a major role in land-use questions, and the courts have increasingly come to recognize the power (and indeed the obligation) to regulate land use for the public welfare.[14] If the objective is to improve the conditions of those with the most serious housing problems, the basic concepts are not difficult to lay out. They would run as follows.

The polarization, both of the economy and of the housing and neighborhood conditions that flow from it, must be reduced. The economic policies required for this purpose are beyond the scope of this chapter. The housing policies required are, however, relatively clear. Neighborhoods in danger of either abandonment or gentrification must be given control of their own destinies. Resources must be made available to them adequate for that purpose. Public policies dealing with housing (including the control of private actions, particularly speculative ones) must have as their clear objective the elimination of displacement in all its forms, whether by abandonment or by gentrification. Such policies have citywide implications and must be implemented citywide. The specific programs by which this could be accomplished have been presented in detail elsewhere.[15] The problem is not the lack of these ideas.

At the same time, some approaches that will *not* reduce displacement or improve housing for those most in need can be identified. Most importantly, gentrification does *not* provide the "cure" for abandonment. In the first place, gentrification will in fact only succeed abandonment in a limited number of neighborhoods (only pockets and perhaps some borders, but certainly not in centers of abandonment) by any operation of the private market. And, if it did, the cure would be as bad as the disease, because gentrification is as inherently linked with the displacement of lower-income holds as is abandonment itself. Public resources invested in such fashion as to "upgrade" a neighborhood (gentrify it),

by introducing higher-income or status groups into an area, will not help those of "lower" status already there; on the contrary.[16]

The large question is not *whether* abandonment can be avoided, gentrification controlled, displacement eliminated, or even *how* these things can be done, but rather whether there is the desire to do them. That is a question that can only be answered in the political arena.

Notes

1 For a fuller formal definition, see Marcuse (1981).
2 The adjustment procedure to include chain displacement is too complex to lay out here, but essentially it involves starting with Stegman's (1982) estimate, which covers apparent physical abandonment, and adjusting to include economic abandonment.
3 It differs from other census results in its unusual attention to vacant units, and the detail of its data on the nature of such vacancies. The purpose of the triennial surveys is to determine the "vacancy rate" for rental units, needed under state enabling legislation to determine whether or not there is a "housing emergency," defined as a situation in which the "vacancy rate" is less than 5 percent. The most recent survey (for 1981) is contained in the report by Michael Stegman (1982); the preceding one, for 1978, is by this writer (Marcuse 1979). Both contain detailed discussions of reliability and interpretation. The 1978 report also contains a general discussion of the process of housing decline and its relation to vacancies and abandonment (Marcuse 1979: 128–34).
4 This is based on the city average of 2.5 persons per household, but probably a conservative assumption here, since abandonment tends to displace poorer, and thus normally larger, households (Stegman 1982: 2,241).
5 Mayor's Office on SRO Housing; New York State Department of Social Services.
6 These figures are generally consistent with the few other detailed local studies that exist, which generally cover only direct displacement. In Seattle, a study estimated the figure at 1.4 percent of the population; in Denver, another study estimated 1.1 percent; in Portland, a study estimated 1.4 percent, with 40 percent of these from gentrification (see Ch. 9). If comparable percentages were applied to New York City, the estimate would be 39 200 displaced, 15 680 from gentrification. This is not far from the figures in the

text above. The figures might be expected to be somewhat higher in New York City, an extreme example of most urban phenomena.

7 Patterns of gentrification vary significantly by household type, even though they have a common etiology. The conventional pattern involves young couples or singles as the first gentrifying agents, households with young children moving in only later. This is plausible, given the difference in community facilities needed by the two groups, and particularly the importance of schools for young children. There are, however, a few neighborhoods where venturesome parents move in and gentrify, because prices are more favorable for their larger space needs and schools seem tolerable. In New York City such areas of "family gentrification" exist primarily in Brooklyn and perhaps Queens, but not, to this writer's knowledge, in Manhattan, with the possible exception of Hamilton Heights.

8 This methodology is similar to that used by Daphne Spain, of the Bureau of the Census's Center for Demographic Studies, and by Karl Taeuber in his studies of residential segregation (e.g. Taeuber 1982).

9 The study examined a substantial number of other potential indicators of gentrification. Two other indicators seem reasonably reliable (as well as theoretically plausible): changes in income, and race or ethnic origin. They are included in Figure 26.2.

10 Tract 149, near Lincoln Center, had major new construction; all other tracts were substantially built up in 1970. The changes they have experienced in the past decade meet the formal definition of gentrification.

11 The full data are reported in Marcuse (1984). See also Porras (1983).

12 At least not to the extent that these terms are defined using indicators of gross national product, growth rates, personal income, or other measures undifferentiated by group or class.

13 See the regular accounts in *City Limits: Community Housing News*, published monthly in New York City.

14 See the landmark Mt. Laurel II decision of the New Jersey Supreme Court (Southern Burlington County NAACP, 1983).

15 Major suggestions include the proposals for inclusionary zoning and a housing trust fund put forward by the Center for Metropolitan Action at Queens College, CUNY, and the Pratt Institute for Community and Environmental Development in Brooklyn; the proposals put forward by the present author in a report to the Community Service Society of New York; the initiatives of the Association for Neighborhood and Housing Development; and the plans of a number of thoughtful community groups in East Harlem, the Lower East Side, Brooklyn, the South Bronx, Clinton, and elsewhere. See Pratt Institute (1983).

16 The recent effort to use city-owned buildings in the Lower East Side for "artists' housing," heavily subsidized by the City, is an apparent example of such a policy; artists were certainly perceived by the community, and perhaps intended by many in city government, to be the opening wedge in introducing a new higher-status demographic group into a community suffering for years from abandonment, but potentially well located for gentrification.

REFERENCES

City of New York Department of City Planning (1983) *City fiscal year 1984 community development program*, New York: City of New York.

DeGiovanni, F. (1983) 'Patterns of change in housing market activity in revitalizing neighborhoods', *Journal of the American Planning Association*, 49: 22–39.

Elliott, N. et al. (1983) *An evaluation and redesign of New York City's anti-harassment programs*, New School for Social Research: New York.

Grebler, L. (1952) *Housing market behaviour in a declining area*, Columbia University Press: New York.

Grier, G. and Grier, E. (1978) 'Urban displacement: a reconnaissance', US Department of Housing and Urban Development: Washington, DC.

Marcuse, P. (1984) *Report on study of displacement in New York City, with conclusions and recommendations*, Community Service Sector: New York.

Marcuse, P. (1981) *Housing abandonment: does rent control make a difference?*, Conference on alternative state and local policies: Washington, DC.

Marcuse, P. (1979) *Rental housing in the City of New York, supply and conditions, 1975–1978*, Department of Housing Preservation and Development: New York.

Porras, S. (1983) *Lower East Side housing market dynamics: policy implications*, MA thesis Division of Urban Planning Columbia University.

Pratt Institute Center for Metropolitan Action (1983) *Inclusionary zoning and housing trust fund: a proposal*, Pratt Institute: New York.

Spain, D. (1981) 'A gentrification scorecard', *American Demographics*, 3: 14–19.

Stegman, M. (1982) *The dynamics of rental housing in New York City*, Center for Urban Policy Research, Rutgers University: Piscataway, NJ.

Taeuber, K. (1982) *Research issues concerning trends in residential segregation, CDE working paper 83–93*, Center for Demography and Ecology, University of Wisconsin: Madison.

US House of Representatives, subcommittee of the city (1977) *How cities can grow old gracefully*, Printing office: Washington, DC.

27

"The Hidden Costs of Gentrification: Displacement in Central London"

From *Journal of Housing and the Built Environment* (2000)

Rowland Atkinson

1. INTRODUCTION

This paper is about the social changes that have been going on in central London in recent years. The focus is on the increasing numbers of professionals moving to the central boroughs of London. Boroughs are the main administrative units of local government in London. These political entities are similar to local authorities in non-metropolitan areas of Britain. London's population of seven million is divided into thirty-three boroughs, including the City of London.

Gentrification has commonly been referred to as "the rehabilitation of working-class and derelict housing and the consequent transformation of an area into a middle class neighbourhood" (Smith and Williams, 1986, p. 1). Gentrification-induced displacement may occur when pressures on the housing market from affluent groups create inflated rents and prices which can push out the low paid or unpaid over time. In a more subtle way, influxes of these groups may alter the social characteristics and services of an area so that residents' social networks are distended while the cost of living may increase as service provision caters for higher income groups.

Here we look at the potential costs that this social upgrading of an area may impose on poorer groups living in those areas. A tendency to see only the positive sides to this process has become a dominant part of the discourse on forecasting how our cities will change and on the desirability of encouraging affluent households to move into central city areas. Given recent moves to assess the prospects for an 'urban renaissance' (Urban Task Force, 1999b) and an emphasis on the possible boon that new 'urban pioneers' may bring, it is perhaps timely that we turn our attention to the unintended consequences that such groups may have on neighbourhood outcomes.

This paper attempts to synthesise past research efforts, to draw on disparate data sources (including census and interview material), and to revitalise the debate with data that provides some evidence of a more understated view of the boon which such pioneers may represent. The connection between gentrification (Glass, 1964) and the displacement of indigenous residents has barely been made in the British and European context (though see Power, 1973; Green, 1979). However, a literature on displacement, predominantly from North America, would suggest that such problems have indeed occurred in gentrified areas.

This paper details background census and Longitudinal Study (LS) data which indicates the broad socio-economic and demographic changes occurring in the study areas before using the accounts of tenant's right's workers and estate agents in the study areas to help describe the wider costs to residents imposed by strong upward socio-economic changes in such areas. The paper concludes with comments about how the costs of gentrification may be ameliorated.

2. EVIDENCE OF DISPLACEMENT FROM NORTH AMERICA AND BRITAIN

While work has been done on gentrification in general (Smith and Williams, 1986; Van Weesep and Musterd, 1991; Smith, 1995) and its manifestation in London in particular (Hamnett and Williams, 1979; Munt, 1987; Warde, 1991; Bridge, 1993; Butler, 1996), there has been little research conducted in Britain into its ability to displace households. A lack of attention to the issue of displacement may reflect our attachment to the exchange value of houses above that of their use value. In fact, so embedded is the logic of property relations in everyday life, that Blomley has described these relations in terms of their ontological status (Blomley, 1997).

Perhaps the main reason that displacement research has not been replicated in the European context lies in the methodological problems associated with such work. This empirical gap has often been attributed to the complexity of tracking those displaced (Hamnett and Williams, 1979). As has been noted (LeGates and Hartman, 1986; Cohen and Mowbray, 1993) tracking people over space, such as the street homeless and displacees, is highly difficult. Further, the connection of housing with wider social processes makes it difficult to discern the causal mechanism by which displacement is instigated (Badcock and Cloher, 1979).

Given the virtual impossibility of finding a sample of displacees to interview, the research turned to the accounts of Tenant's Rights Workers of Central London. An advert was placed in the 'Big Issue' magazine which homeless people sell. This yielded two responses, both of which were unsuitable. Because of these problems, three tenant's rights projects were selected, which were located in areas identified using census data, to look at areas which had rapidly been gentrified during the 1981 to 1991 period. This was done using the proxy measure of increases in the resident professional and managerial population. To get a fuller impression of the changes in the areas studied, 'lifestyle' and property supplements were regularly read and the gentrified areas were visited to validate their choice as places suitable for examining the process of displacement in closer detail.

It is difficult to judge which factors, such as a lack of money, job loss, or landlord harassment, are fundamental in understanding displacement processes. It is likely that in individual cases the reasons may be complex. However, it may be possible to observe a relationship between neighbourhood change in the form of professionalisation and the exiting of various groups from that area by those with fewer resources. Structures of rent and sale values may create a strong pressure to leave and an exclusion, or diversion, from access to a neighbourhood.

Displacement is marked out by its near invisibility; where it has happened no indicators remain. However, various data sources have been used to estimate its size. Looking at twelve neighbourhoods undergoing revitalisation in six cities in North America, DeGiovanni (1984) used tenure conversion, from renting to owning, as an indicator for displacement. However, it was acknowledged that this was "a rough indicator of only one source of displacement", though likely to produce an underestimate. In a comprehensive survey of the literature, Hartman (1979a) documented the destination and living circumstances of displacees moving to more expensive and overcrowded accommodation, with more than 80% having to pay more for worse accommodation.

Writers like Lee and Hodge (1984) distinguish between liberal and conservative definitions of displacement. They have shown how such ideologies affect our perception of the magnitude of the process. From a conservative perspective, only more extreme forms of harassment and eviction are considered to be a displacement pressure. To the more liberal mind, displacement is a process that might include the pricing out of residents and the changing of shops and services. Complicating things further, it may be that groups labelled as displacees by social scientists may not class themselves as such. Rent increases may seem inevitable and displaces may be fatalistic about the way that the market operates. As Harvey (1967) comments: "What tenants have to suffer at the hands of private landlords has always been treated as a private matter with which they are expected to deal on their own and as best they can, no matter what their age or capabilities" (p. 11).

In other research, Sumka (1979) considered that of the two million people being annually displaced in the US, 86% of the moves were due to market displacement from gentrification and that the displacees were mostly urban white working-class households. This figure was strongly contested as an underestimate by Hartman (1979a). Further figures are available from Hartman (1979b), who described how the District of Columbia Rental Accommodations Office estimated that a 'mind-boggling' seventh of the entire city's population would be displaced over the next four years from gentrification activity. Marcuse (1986) has estimated that 150,000 people were displaced annually from abandonment and 38,000 from gentrification in New York.

Writers such as O'Malley (1977) have documented that street clearance and urban improvement alone in nineteenth century London evicted 100,000 people from Central London between 1830 and 1880 (O'Malley, 1977, p. 10). More recently, Jew (1994) reported that annually 9% of tenants (144,000 people) would be illegally evicted or harassed from their homes. The 1986/87 London Housing Survey (see LPAC, 1990, p. 21) estimated that 17,000 dwellings were lost annually from private renting in the mid-1980s. In interviews, recent owner-occupiers in those properties were asked who they had bought their property from. Of these, it was estimated that 3,000 were existing tenants, while three times as many (12,000) had bought from developers or builders, indicating a high rate of population turnover on the conversion of tenure.

In a study, sponsored by the then Department of the Environment, carried out in twelve inner London boroughs, a survey was used to find out what was happening to people living in housing rehabilitated using a grant disbursed by local authorities (McCarthy, 1974). Grant-aided improvements did not benefit the original residents, with 68% of applications being preceded by households leaving the accommodation. The main reason for such moves was landlord harassment (43%), and McCarthy described the process as a 'social sieve'.

Leckie (1995) has estimated that 144,000 people are forcefully evicted each year in Britain. He estimates that a further 60,000 or more will be evicted per year in the future, though clearly only a small proportion of this figure might relate to gentrification-induced displacement. In an OPCS-commissioned study (Pickering and Rauta, 1992), the figure of 1 in 10 tenants being harassed each year was given (based on a question which asked if the tenant had been made in any way uncomfortable by their landlord). In addition, 2% of all tenants in the survey had experienced landlords who had tried to evict them in 'other ways'. In the 1996/7 Survey of English Housing, 11% of renters in London had moved to their current location because their landlord told them to move out.

More recent work by Lyons (1996) finds that local migration is associated with low-status households, while longer range migration may be associated with those of higher status, indicating a greater degree of choice for such movers. This research suggests that displacee moves are predominantly made to locations nearby but to property which is in a worse condition. They often move to a friend or relative's accommodation, which may help to account for much of the subsequent overcrowding experienced by displacees and the increased amount of hidden household formation.

3. GENTRIFICATION AND DISPLACEMENT IN LONDON, 1981–1991

Here we detail the selection of the areas studied, along with background census and LS data which demonstrates the existence of possible displacement effects in areas that were gentrified. It is interesting to look at the background statistical data for the area of inner London and the three local authority or borough areas within which the tenant's rights projects were located. Taking three simple and separable measures of gentrification – namely increases in the numbers of professionally employed and managerial workers, degree holders, and owner-occupiers – we see the following increases for inner London in Table 27.1.

From the review of the displacement literature, the following groups were selected: working class, private renters, elderly (65 plus), and unskilled workers. For inner London, the mean percentage point

	Inner London	Kensington	Camden	Hammersmith
Gentrifiers				
Owner-occupiers	11.2	8.1	9.8	12.3
Professionals	8.3	9.3	7.4	11.6
Degree holders	7.4	8.6	8.4	10.4
Displacees				
Working class	−13.9	−14.6	−12.7	−15.3
Private renters	−4.9	−8.0	−7.0	−8.9
Elderly	−2.3	−1.1	−2.4	−3.8
Unskilled	−1.84	−0.2	−1.1	−2.6

Table 27.1 Percentage point changes for gentrifier and potential displacee groups between 1981 and 1991
Source: OPCS, 1981 and 1991 Censuses

	Residents in households (%)						Professional residents (over 16 years)	
	Owner-occupied		Private rented*		Local authority**			
	1981	1991	1981	1991	1981	1991	1981	1991
Inner London	29.8	43.9	23.4	20.6	46.7	35.3	24.6	32
Camden	25.9	37.8	31.6	23.9	38.1	38.1	35.1	42.6
Hammersmith	33.9	48	34.5	24.6	31.5	27.2	28.4	40
Kensington	37.4	47.7	45.9	35.6	16.5	16.5	38.9	48.2

Table 27.2 Household tenure in the study areas
Source: OPCS, 1981 and 1991 Census data
* Not including renting from a business
** Not including housing association dwellings

Displacee group	(1) Net migration for gentrified areas	(2) Percentage loss to gentrified areas	(3) Total migration flow for London
Unskilled	−1,800	−78%	19,100
Inactive	−26,100	−46%	38,500
Working class	−19,300	−38%	121,700
Elderly	−23,200	−18%	20,000

Table 27.3 Net flows and percentage gain or loss for gentrified areas in Greater London between 1981 and 1991
Source: ONS Longitudinal Study

changes in wards over the period can be seen in the first column of Table 27.1, while the other columns indicate the percentage point change for each of the boroughs in which qualitative work was engaged in.

While we do not know if the people in 1991 in these areas were the same as those in 1981, the negative changes for the displacee categories would indicate that processes of replacement or displacement had been occurring, though we can only speculate on the relative proportions of such flows. In the case study boroughs – Hammersmith, Kensington, and Camden – Table 27.1 shows some degree of variability in the experience of the average changes in the 1981–1991 period. The centrality of these areas in the city core of Greater London makes them of theoretical interest, since we might suppose that changes in this area would be more dramatic than for London as a whole. What we see in these areas is pronounced losses of working class groups and private renters. There is a relatively similar level of increases in the three gentrification proxy variables, which might indicate some overlap in these categories.

Table 27.2 provides background data illustrating the professional and tenurial structure of the inner area of London and the case study authority areas. This table illustrates the continuing and relatively unusual tenure structure of London compared to the rest of Britain. It shows a stronger rental sector than many other areas but a greater decline in this tenure than for local authority dwellings. We can also see that the relatively significant social changes were accompanied by similarly significant tenurial changes. The growth in owner-occupation, only partly explained by right to buy sales, greatly exceeded both the rest of London and national trends over the same period. The dramatic growth of owner-occupation is predominantly explained by the loss of rental accommodation. We can see an attendant increase in professional residents associated with the growth in owner-occupation.

Atkinson (2000a) shows that losses for potential displacee groups in gentrified wards were far greater than in wards in the rest of the metropolitan area. Table 27.3 uses that data to show changes over the decade in wards gentrified (measured as above-average increases in the numbers of professionals over the period in any ward). The first column shows the net change for areas which experienced above-average levels of professionalisation. Column 2 shows the percentage loss to the social group over the decade and column 3 indicates the amount of movement in the rest of the London area for the same period.

The gentrified areas covered approximately a sixteenth of the London area. Yet for many of the potential displacee groups, we see a rate of out-migration in the gentrified areas almost equal to that of London as a whole. For example, we see that the numbers of elderly leaving the gentrified areas (23,200) were actually greater than that for moves made by that group in the capital as a whole (20,000). Even if one were to suppose that migration based on retirement was a factor, this could not be used to explain the extent of the process in areas which had been gentrified. These results suggest that displacement as well as replacement was an active process over the period.

4. NEIGHBOURHOOD CHANGE AND DISPLACEMENT IN CENTRAL LONDON

This section presents the results of interviews with a range of actors in the three central London boroughs. Interviews took place over a three-month period and involved staff in three of the tenant's rights projects. The remit of these organisations is the protection of private tenant's rights and they were set up to protect tenants from harassment and illegal eviction as well as to provide advice and support regarding entitlement to benefits and help. While such a group may be considered to have a vested interest in portraying gentrification as an anti-social force, the validation of the material here with external data and inter-group confirmation lends weight to the accuracy of the accounts.

The projects were selected because they existed in areas which have been extensively gentrified and deal with a population who are the most likely candidates for displacement, namely private renters. The work of the projects is predicated on the illegal practices of landlords in the area. All of the projects reported a caseload which was stretching their capacities. Most of the work comes from representing victims of eviction who are unable to pay for their defence by solicitors. Thus, referrals to the projects come from citizen's advice bureaux and the local authority, which provided core funding for their work. While small in number, the geographical remit of the projects was wide (i.e. the entire borough), giving access to a comprehensive picture of changes and problems in the area.

The testimonies of the project workers are presented below, along with supporting data.

That material should be considered in tandem with the census evidence already developed. There is a danger of conflating data on evictions with data on displacement. We have tried to avoid this wherever possible, but it should be borne in mind that eviction was viewed as an indicator of gentrification in these areas.

Who were the displacees? The elderly were considered to be disproportionately represented among displacees by all of the project workers. The reason for this was twofold. First, physical frailty made it difficult to resist actions by landlords to have them removed. Second, this group was more profoundly affected by social changes around them. The loss of friends or kinship networks was cited as a reason for the decision to move from an area, to move where family have moved or, finally, to find someplace cheaper. These findings are consistent with research carried out by Henig (1984), who found that such groups were least able to cope with the pressures of a gentrified neighbourhood, with its radically altered kin and friendship networks. Involuntary movement from a place called 'home' was likened to grieving (see also Chan, 1986). Perhaps this should not be surprising, as Hartman argues:

> displacement means moving from a supportive, long-term environment to an alien area where substantially higher costs are involved for a more crowded, inferior dwelling.
>
> (1979b, p. 23)

Many secure tenants are found in this older age range. This often created problems when the landlord was trying to get the rent increased to a market level. Secure tenants are those who rent privately since, or before, the 1977 Protection from Eviction Act was set up. This group is therefore often comprised of older tenants. They have greater protection from rent increases, as all proposed increases in rent can be referred to the Rent Officer. When asked whether there had been harassment of secure tenants in order to get them to sign assured shorthold contracts (mentioned in Burrows and Hunter, 1990), it appeared that harassment had been more often used to get rid of tenants than to persuade them to change the conditions of their tenancy.

Table 27.4 helps to illustrate the lack of statutory activity that deals with problems of harassment in London as a whole. Here we see a stark contrast between police involvement in eviction action and the story of harassment revealed by the Tenant's Rights workers; no landlord was accused under

	Protection from eviction offences		Protection from eviction clear-ups		Persons accused of protection from eviction offences	
	1998/1999	April–Dec 1999	1998/1999	April–Dec 1999	1998/1999	April–Dec 1999
Hammersmith	3	0	2	0	0	0
Camden	1	3	0	0	0	0
Kensington	2	2	0	0	0	0
Total	6	5	2	0	0	0
Metropolitan Police Service total	54	32	9	4	1	1

Table 27.4 Protection from eviction offences, clear-ups and case results
Source: Metropolitan Police Service, Performance Information Bureau

the 1977 Protection from Eviction Act in any of the case study authorities. This disparity is explained, in part, by a lack of reporting behaviour by victims of eviction, who are often unsure of their rights. Writers such as Burrows and Hunter (1990) have also suggested that the police are often unsure of what to do in eviction cases or may take the side of the landlord. These figures stand in sharp contrast with general levels of eviction. Those levels are now higher than they were in the 1970s, especially in view of the large number of repossessions applied for. For example, in the first quarter of 1996, private landlords nationally entered 29,235 court actions for possession, while mortgage lenders entered 23,993.

Further evidence of these processes comes in the form of Rent Assessment Committees, set up under the Rent Act of 1965 to arbitrate on decisions made by Rent Officers deemed to be unfair by landlords or tenants. Their existence has not been seen to be effective, given that they have consistently favoured landlords in their decisions. In London, nearly 90% of rulings favour the landlord. Since deregulation, they have been accused of bias in order to promote the growth of the rented sector by succumbing to landlords' desires to obtain greater revenues. Rental assessments are strongly affected by surrounding locational attributes. If the area has been gentrified and its attendant services have also changed, landlords often used these developments to make the case that the area is now much more desirable and that a greater return is in order. Tenants are often deterred from court challenges because of the cost and because they often fear retaliatory evictions, ironically, if they win the case.

The Home Office Research and Statistics Department indicates that prosecutions under the Protection from Eviction Act (1977) were 84 out of

222 cases in 1993 for the whole of England and Wales. This might be considered a low figure when reports indicate that something like one in 10 tenants faces some form of harassment (Rauta and Pickering, 1992). Fines for such offences are often derisory (75% of fines were under £300 in 1993, Bedsit Briefing, April/May, 1996).

In all of the areas studied, houses in multiple occupation (HMOs) were prevalent. These units are often associated with some of the worst living conditions, yet they provide a relatively affordable form of living. Retention of these units is often viewed by boroughs as being an important issue because of the groups they cater for. However, boroughs differ markedly on discretionary policies toward HMOs. People living in this sector have often been displaced when units have been converted into owner-occupation or where units are combined into bigger dwelling spaces (London Research Centre, 1994).

Many of the case workers in the projects suggested that people with mental health problems suffered if displaced. The policy of care in the community meant that many people needing help had been left to cope in highly competitive housing markets. In particular, people with alcohol problems, HIV, or psychiatric disorders were identified by the project workers as having particular problems in relation to the housing market and have few social services to turn to.

Families on low incomes may also be trapped. Housing benefit will not be paid to them because they receive some income, yet they struggle to keep their head above water in a market where rents stretch their ability to cope to the limit. One project worker said that she had advised very low paid families to give up work in order to get help with the rent.

Another project worker summed up the position as affecting:

Single people, or couples without children who wouldn't be eligible to get local authority housing are being displaced even if they are moving into local authority housing. Even if they are on income support or on a very low income the benefit is not enough to cover their rents so the displacement now is people who would have been able to afford property because of benefit levels but now can't – it's the high rents that are displacing people but benefit rule changes are adding to that.

(Case worker, Tenant's Rights Project, Hammersmith)

The burden of displacement appeared to fall on single people in particular. It is often hard for single people to afford accommodation. This often manifests itself in the high number of flat shares and lodgers in these areas. Two of the project workers suggested that the interaction between benefit changes and rental rates was creating increased vulnerability, since lower benefit levels would mean that a tenant's capacity to resist being 'priced out' was reduced. The introduction of the single room rent, intended for housing benefit claimants who are single and under 25, means that they are tied to the average cost of shared accommodation in the area as determined by the rent officer. This further squeezes the availability of accommodation for such groups. For example, research by Kemp and Rugg (1998) found that in an inner London borough, a typical one-room rent was £65 while the single room rent level was only £45.

Ethnic minority groups were also cited as having suffered substantial displacement in certain areas. Where ethnic minorities lived in areas that had become desirable, project workers described how substantial displacement of the indigenous community, often Afro-Caribbean, Asians, and Irish, had occurred. This is a combination of the historical location of such groups in previously 'filtered' areas and their gentrification more recently. However, we should be guarded in accepting such evidence uncritically, given that census data indicates a propensity for areas being gentrified by professionals and managers to be apparent 'attractors' for such groups (Atkinson, 2000b).

In Kensington, processes of gentrification created a continued upward movement in the status of those being displaced and those acting as gentrifiers. This process was described by one project worker in terms of the 'Sloanes' (upper class young people)

of yesteryear being displaced by the stockbrokers of today due to the upward spiral of social change in that area. Just such a phenomenon is alluded to by O'Malley, reporting on work in Kensington in the late 1960s, who described how "higher income tenants who had displaced the low income families were now faced with a [local authority] plan to displace them with even higher income tenants or flat buyers" (1970, p. 104).

This suggests that gentrification is not new in the area. It is echoed by Lyons' (1996) point that gentrified areas experience outflows by successively higher status households. Such processes have also been confirmed by Dangschat (1991) in his continuum of gentrification waves from 'pioneer' to 'ultra' gentrifiers in Hamburg. In general, the characterisation of displacees given by the project workers was one of vulnerability; through physical or mental frailty, a lack of social and financial resources, and faced with a lack of affordable housing.

5. HOW DOES DISPLACEMENT OCCUR?

We have noted that displacement was most often achieved through rental and price increases, though other, more insidious, methods were also used by landlords. Tenants were sometimes encouraged to move out through inducements (cash sums for vacating the premises), harassment, violence and intimidation, while eviction and rent rises also led to displacement. One Kensington project worker described how a large number of prosecutions 'disappeared' because landlords offered often large sums of money to move away, as she put it "if you're poor enough you are going to take it". Many tenants being 'bought out' were elderly; according to an internal report from Camden, 33% of elderly regulated tenants were facing harassment or inducements to leave. An explicit link was made between gentrification and being made homeless. As one project worker suggested, "gentrification is what is making people homeless. If you are going to move a certain person into the area the only way you are going to do that is by moving someone else out." (Case worker, Tenant's Rights Project, Kensington).

For many landlords, there is no longer any need for harassment or eviction because of the landlord's ability to terminate assured shorthold tenancy agreements after the initial six-month period. However, harassment was prevalent for elderly tenants, often because it was this group that had protected tenancies. While threats often lay behind the offer of payments to leave, more direct action by landlords was not rare in the effort to get rid of unwanted tenants as a means to get better-paying tenants or to sell. The process was described in the following terms:

> some of the people who were got out were evicted; they were got out by fairly unpleasant and in most cases illegal methods. There were a lot of people displaced from that period [late eighties]. More recently it has been more an income-related thing, it's been "we don't need to resort to illegal methods all we do is basically keep upping the rent" until they can't afford it.
> (Case worker, Tenant's Rights Project, Kensington)

Where violence and threats had been used, stronger legal remedies were available to prevent harassment than where rent increases occurred. Softer forms of displacement, such as price increases, are often not viewed as displacement. They are largely seen as acceptable or tolerable forms of exclusion in the wider community. Indeed, they appeal to a market logic of property relations to which many subscribe (Blomley, 1997).

Exclusion from the case study areas has become a theme for commentators on London's housing market. This issue is reflected in recent policy concerns about the ability of essential service workers, like teachers, to live in the area they work in. Many people are diverted from entry to locations or unable to re-enter areas after being dislodged from more affordable accommodation. The children of parents in council or other protected forms of tenancy were often unable to stay in the same area after moving away from home because of high local prices and rents. Welfare benefit increasingly does not cover rents, and property agents are often not interested in those on state benefits.

In one notable case, displacement was induced to achieve greater charitable returns for a trust. The estate, gentrified to maximise rental and sales returns, was used for charitable purposes; "charitable purposes paid for by driving people off the estate" (Project worker, Case 1). In another example, a religious charitable body was linked to the displacement of tenants in order to maximise rental returns. On the Kings Road, they evicted artists from dwellings in order to sell the property. There have been other examples whereby charities have had their tenancies left un-renewed so that higher-paying tenants could enter.

It is not only in the private sector that such oddities may occur. An examination of the previous status of properties on short-term leases to housing associations and local authorities for use as temporary accommodation revealed that:

> there was concern that the development of such schemes – whose prime purpose was to house homeless people – could be directly causing homelessness by giving landlords a (financial) incentive to evict existing tenants whose rents were controlled.
> (London Research Centre, 1990, p. 25)

Displacement research has often suffered from a lack of information about where people end up. In asking the project workers about this, there was some consensus on a number of exit routes. There was widespread recognition that a significant number of displacees were made homeless. However, the main exit route was to buy or continue renting. Inevitably, this meant that displacees would be forced to move out of the area, since it would be too expensive to remain. For some, it was a case of wherever was cheapest, often renting with others or going to family and friends if they lived in London. For the elderly, the subsequent location was often to areas beyond London:

> the traditional thing – of moving to the seaside or to the country. Some of them, yes, outer ring [of London], as far as poorer displacees go I am more concerned about them, I suspect some of them end up on the street, literally. There are two issues, if they were pre-1989 renters they won't have a deposit and even if they do the levels of rents are terrifying.
> (Case worker, Tenant's Rights Project, Hammersmith)

The implications of neighbourhood-wide changes may influence such decisions. In Camden, benefit data showed that the number of claimants in hotels was 600 less between January 1996 and December 1997. This was attributed to a number of factors, including a growth in tourism. As for future rates, it was envisaged that the reduction in the availability of bed and breakfast accommodation and the loss of HMOs would increase levels of displacement, as fewer places are available at affordable rates. Guidance to prospective residents on the Borough of Camden's website advises that:

> Unless you have a great deal of money finding a place to live in London is going to be difficult. Obtaining social housing is not an option for the majority of people. Camden is one of the most expensive and desirable areas of London. There

is a great deal of competition for all types of accommodation. Landlords can choose their tenants from a pool of high earning professionals … If you are to succeed in finding accommodation you will have to look beyond Camden and beyond Central London in areas where prices are cheaper and the competition for private flats is not so great.

6. THE WIDER EFFECTS OF GENTRIFICATION

Contradictory evidence on the effect of gentrification on social networks exists. While the project workers saw widespread problems, Bridge (1993) has argued that the impact of gentrification on friendship networks in Sands End, Hammersmith was minimal. However, such an analysis is only possible where gentrification is not total or extensive. The impact of middle-class residents can also have a perverse effect on areas where:

> What is actually provided is poorer because obviously the richer the community becomes the less necessary it is to have public transport, the less necessary it is to have facilities like good libraries, leisure facilities that are subsidised by a local authority, the less pressure there is on the local authority to provide services.
>
> (Case worker, Tenant's Rights Project, Kensington)

This contradiction was especially apparent in both Camden and Kensington. There, the need for various public services was eroded by changes in consumption patterns in reaction to changes in the profile of local residents. This also acts as a self-serving legitimation for the loss of such public services, since the local authority argued that such services were not needed.

In an apparent mirroring of the process of abandonment and low demand in poor neighbourhoods, it was observed by all of the project workers that, for many residents, gentrification cumulatively eroded both their ability and their desire to remain in that location as social, physical, economic, and environmental changes took place unrelated to the patterns of their own lifestyles and the resources on which they lived. In Kensington:

> people are being offered money they can't refuse, and they are also probably moving out because as the gentrification snowball rolls down the hill so it becomes less desirable for them to stay there,

it's no longer their sort of people … There has also been the development of hundreds of poor quality hotels, part of that has been created by the need for homeless persons accommodation and most of them double as brothels.

> (Case worker, Tenant's Rights Project, Kensington)

Increasing crime levels were related by the project workers to the breakdown of close-knit communities from the impact of the turnover of residents. This seemed to be most strongly felt in South Kensington and could be related to absent owners in that area. Certainly empty property and the transitory nature of many residents left little social fabric, which was then associated with increases in crime and anti-social behaviour. A crack-cocaine problem and related street crime, already visible in the north of the borough, were making an unwelcome entrance to the area.

A trend identified in both Camden and Hammersmith was the increasing number of people from multiple-occupied properties who had mental health problems. While hospital closures and care in the community played a part, there was obviously more going on:

> so many people that you met in multi-occupied properties, pretty much left on their own … not having to conform an awful lot; lots of those people have mental health problems – that accommodation doesn't exist anymore, so they are the kind of people who are driven out. Where do those people go?
>
> (Case worker, Tenant's Rights Project, Hammersmith)

Shops and services were also affected. A new service infrastructure had sprung up around the wealthy new residents. Bars replaced pubs and delicatessens replaced grocers, increasing the cost of living or distending the scope of shopping trips. Such changes are often perceived as improving an area, yet they belie the reality that social problems have not been resolved. Instead, problem people have been moved on. The sense of separation from the boom going on around them meant that many remaining tenants expressed attitudes of resentment (see also: Rotherhithe Community Planning Centre, 1986) and racism toward wealthy British in-migrants and those from overseas. In the East End of London, similar sentiments toward lower-status in-migrants were redirected by the 'mug a yuppie' campaign of Class War, an extreme political left-wing group, as a transferral of racist aggression (Wright, 1992).

Other groups, like the 'Roughlers', a now defunct gathering of drinkers and self-proclaimed yuppie-haters on the Portobello Road in Kensington, indicate that the visible signs of a front-line have been replaced by a more insidious geography of privilege and antipathy that is more difficult to locate. The landlord of the pub where the Roughlers met described how they 'retreated' from pub to pub as the area grew ever more popular with yuppies who 'took over' the pubs.

Interviews with estate agents in north Kensington showed that the cultural infrastructure of the area and the proximity of the underground tube line were critical factors in location decisions by City workers who had moved to the area en masse. One property agent described the changes in the neighbourhood as "economic migration as it should be". Of the ten agents contacted, seven described the social change in the area in terms of negative consequences for poorly paid and unpaid residents, even though it provided a boom for their business. The embeddedness of owner-occupation as a discourse which privileges ownership over other forms is critical here, as Smith cited: "'What I want to know,' argued one recent immigrant to the neighbourhood, 'is by what authority do these people have roots? If you don't own, you don't have roots. What have they planted, their feet in the ground?" (Smith, 1996, p. 138).

As gentrification proceeds, levels of resistance to it are cumulatively lessened. Perceived levels of need were lowered, while the distance of needy residents to services set up by local authority and voluntary groups was increased. In Hammersmith, it was argued that "if the poor disappear the rationale for the group's existence similarly disappears" (Case worker, Tenant's Rights Project, Hammersmith). These problems also weakened:

people's involvement in local government, people's interest in community issues, it therefore has a knock on effect on voluntary groups, with some of the community organisations that are based in the borough – and as those weaken so the people being displaced have fewer places to go to try and resist being displaced, it's a snowball; I can't see any way it's going to stop unless we stop spiralling rents and house prices.

(Case worker A, Tenant's Rights Project, Camden)

Middle-class groupings were viewed as being closer to the local political process and knew how to 'work' it better than lower-class groupings. Political change was both complementary to the gentrification process and was also influenced by gentrifiers.

In addition to local authorities, other groups, like the Hampstead Heath Society and the Camden Amenities Forum, were considered to be very influential in development control. As a Camden project worker pointed out, "in Camden you've got council estates falling behind, private sector harassment at record levels and yet people take the council to court over their parking restrictions" (Case worker B, Tenant's Rights Project, Hammersmith).

The reasons for this lie partly in the degree of articulation of affluent groups. But they also arise because the council has less autonomy over such groups. With self-funded groups, like the Hampstead Heath Society, there is a relatively high level of independence so that political marginalisation is made more difficult. This echoes Hartman's comment that "It is not clear that the 'new urbanites' will provide so great a boon for fiscal solvency; their demands for – and ability to extract from city government – urban services and amenities may offset any additional property tax revenues" (1979b, p. 26).

The role of the local authority and a political will in general to stand back or become involved is critical in the way that gentrification proceeds. O'Malley describes how the then stockbroker chief executive, in 1968, prophesied the changes to come: "Kensington is bound to become a middle class community … the lower income people are bound to be excluded" (1977, p. 19). More recently, Hamnett and Randolph comment that "affordable private renting in central London today is no longer a possible option. Those who cannot buy here have in effect been displaced to alternative locations beyond the centre … or to alternative tenures" (Hamnett and Randolph, 1984, p. 276).

However, we should question the inevitability or a portrayed 'natural' quality of such changes as the ideology of a laissez-faire stance on neighbourhood change. Policy resolutions have been made to prevent the damaging effects of gentrification. Preventing the quick purchase and resale of property is one remedy. In the late 1970s, in Santa Cruz, California, voters passed an initiative imposing heavy taxes on the vendor of dwellings sold within four years. The levy was imposed on a sliding scale inversely related to the number of years the property was held prior to sale (Hartman, 1979b) ranging from 18% to 25%.

Such proposals may not be unrealistic, given that a similar 'sunshine tax' was recently proposed in Cornwall, South West England, due to continuing retirement to the area by wealthy migrants. Perhaps discretionary control of such policies is unlikely to be successful, given famous examples of authorities like Westminster, which have pursued gentrification as a means of securing political survival and to boost local revenue. Leckie (1995) has suggested that formal arbitration schemes for those forcefully evicted should be set up. The assessments for compensation would be based on the cost to the displacee of relocation and travel costs after displacement.

7. CONCLUSIONS

Gentrification has been construed as both destroyer and saviour in the regeneration of run-down areas, yet it is clear that it is not simply one or the other. There are both positive and negative aspects to gentrification. Its effects are mediated to vulnerable social groups by socio-legal (Leckie, 1995), welfare (Hamnett, 1996), and local democratic processes (Bourne, 1993) found in the fieldwork reported here and varying widely due to context and the political affiliation of observers. As Bourne argues, gentrification:

> has improved housing quality and social service levels, altered the political dynamic and augmented the local tax base of the central city (in part through a redistribution of investment) [but] it has contributed to a reduction in the low-rent housing stock and displaced hundreds of residents, some of whom (notably tenants) have suffered as a consequence.
>
> (Bourne, 1993, p. 185)

In some respects, public housing estates share burdens similar to those borne by poorer groups in gentrified areas. In attempting to ameliorate such burdens, we should be aware that neighbourhood change is constant, though its direction is a malleable outcome which can be and is being shaped by policy interventions. Research on tenure diversification indicates that gradual social movements are much less damaging and may bring positive social changes to run-down and public-rented areas (Atkinson and Kintrea, 1998). Where diversity and interconnections do exist, such initiatives have been seen to be positive (Jupp, 1999).

The re-emergence of central London as a middle-class city as it was in the late nineteenth century does not represent the kind of diversity or affordability that will ensure the sustainability either of that area or the surrounding neighbourhoods, which act as buffers for those excluded from central city property markets. While gentrification may often be based on the replacement of indigenous communities during 'natural' turnover, such changes are further reaching and may also be based on displacement. Recent discontent over the lack of momentum in Lord Roger's Urban Taskforce by the Government suggests a need to continue to consider the health and diversity of communities in areas like London.

REFERENCES

Atkinson, R. and Kintrea, K. (1998) Reconnecting Excluded Communities: The Neighbourhood Impacts of Owner Occupation, Scottish Homes, Edinburgh.

Atkinson, R. (2000a) Measuring Gentrification and Displacement in Greater London, Urban Studies, 37, 149–165.

Atkinson, R. (2000b) Professionalisation and Displacement in Greater London, Area, 32, 287–295.

Badcock, B. and Cloher, D. (1980) The Contribution of Housing Displacement to the Decline of the Boarding and Lodging Population in Adelaide, 1947–1977, Transactions of the Institute of British Geographers, NS 5, 151–169.

Blomley, N. (1997) The Properties of Space: History, Geography, and Gentrification, Urban Geography, 18, 286–295.

Bourne, L.S. (1993) The Myth and Reality of Gentrification: A Commentary on Emerging Urban Forms, Urban Studies, 30, 183–189.

Bridge, G. (1993) People, Places and Networks, SAUS Publications, University of Bristol.

Burrows, L. and Hunter, N. (1990) Forced Out!, Shelter, London.

Chan, K.B. (1986) Ethnic Urban Space, Urban Displacement and Forced Relocation: The Case of Chinatown in Montreal, Canadian Ethnic Studies, 18, 65–78.

Cohen, E., Mowbray, C., Bybee, D., Yeich, S., Ribisl, K. and Freddolino, P. (1993) Tracking and Follow-Up Methods for Research on Homelessness, Evaluation Review, 17, 331–352.

Dangschat, J. (1991) Gentrification in Hamburg, In: Urban Housing for the Better-Off: Gentrification in Europe (Eds, Van Weesep, J. and Musterd, S.), Stedelijke Netwerken, Utrecht, pp. 63–88.

DeGiovanni, F. (1984) An Examination of Selected Consequences of Revitalization in Six US Cities, In: Gentrification, Displacement and Neighborhood Revitalization (Eds, Palen, J. and London, B.), State University of New York Press, Albany, pp. 67–69.

Glass, R. (1964) Introduction: Aspects of Change, In: London: Aspects of Change (Eds, Centre for Urban Studies), MacGibbon and Kee, London, pp. xiii–xlii.

Green, A. (1979) Rachman, Michael Joseph, London.

Hamnett, C. (1973) Improvement Grants as an Indicator of Gentrification in Inner London, Area, 5, 252–261.

Hamnett, C. (1996) Social Polarisation, Economic Restructuring and Welfare State Regimes, Urban Studies, 33, 1407–1430.

Hamnett, C. and Randolph, B. (1988) Cities, Housing and Profits: Flat Break-Up and the Decline of Private Renting, Hutchinson, London.

Hamnett, C. and Williams, P. (1979) Gentrification in London 1961–1971: An Empirical and Theoretical Analysis of Social Change, University of Birmingham, Centre for Urban and Regional Studies, Birmingham.

Hartman, C. (1979a) Comment on 'Neighbourhood Revitalization and Displacement: A Review of the Evidence', Journal of the American Planning Association, 45, 488–491.

Hartman, C. (1979b) Displacement: A Not So New Problem, Social Policy (March/April), 22–27.

Harvey, A. (1964) Tenants in Danger, Penguin, Harmondsworth.

Henig, J. (1984) Gentrification and Displacement of the Elderly: An Empirical Analysis, In: Gentrification, Displacement and Neighborhood Revitalization (Eds, Palen, J. and London, B.), State University of New York Press, Albany, NY, pp. 170–184.

Hutton, W. (1995) The State We're In, Jonathan Cape, London.

Jew, P. (1994) Law and Order in Private Rented Housing: Tackling Harassment and Illegal Eviction, Campaign for Bedsit Rights, London.

Jupp, B. (1999) Living Together: Community Life on Mixed Tenure Estates, Demos, London.

Kemp, P. and Rugg, J. (1998) The Single Room Rent: Its Impact on Young People, Centre for Housing Policy, University of York.

Leckie, S. (1995) When Push Comes to Shove: Forced Evictions and Human Rights, Habitat International Coalition, Utrecht.

Lee, B. and Hodge, D. (1984) Social Differentials in Metropolitan Residential Displacement, In: Gentrification, Displacement and Neighborhood Revitalization (Eds, Palen, J. and London, B.), State University of New York Press, Albany, pp. 140–169.

Le Gates, R. and Hartman, C. (1986) The Anatomy of Displacement in the United States, In: Gentrification of the City (Eds, Smith, N. and Williams, P.), Unwin Hyman, London, pp. 178–203.

London Research Centre (1990) Renting Revival?, London Research Centre, London.

London Research Centre (1994) Houses in Multiple Occupation in London, London Planning Advisory Council, London.

Lyons, M. (1996) Gentrification, Socioeconomic Change, and the Geography of Displacement, Journal of Urban Affairs, 18, 39–62.

Marcuse, P. (1986) Abandonment, Gentrification and Displacement: The Linkages in New York City, In: Gentrification of the City (Eds, Smith, N. and Williams, P.), Unwin Hyman, London, pp. 153–177.

McCarthy, J. (1974) Some Social Implications of Improvement Policy in London, Department of the Environment, London.

Merrett, S. (1976) Housing and Class in Britain, Russell Press Ltd., Nottingham.

Munt, I. (1987) Economic Restructuring, Culture, and Gentrification: A Case Study in Battersea, London, Environment and Planning, A 19, 1175–1197.

O'Malley, J. (1970) Community Action in Notting Hill, In: Community Action (Ed., Lapping, A.), Fabian Society, London.

Perri, G. (1997) Escaping Poverty: From Safety Nets to Networks of Opportunity, DEMOS, London.

Power, A. (1973) David and Goliath, Holloway Neighbourhood Law Centre, Barnsbury, London.

Rauta, I. and Pickering, A. (1992) Private Renting in England, 1990, HMSO, London

Rotherhithe Community Planning Centre (1986) Our Side of the River, Rotherhithe Community Planning Centre, London.

Smith, N. (1992) Blind Man's Bluff, or Hamnett's Philosophical Individualism in Search of Gentrification, Transactions of the Institute of British Geographers, NS 17, 110–115.

Smith, N. (1995) The New Urban Frontier: Gentrification and the Revanchist City, Routledge, London.

Smith, N. and Williams, P. (Eds.) (1986) Gentrification of the City, Unwin Hyman, London.

Sumka, H.J. (1979) Neighbourhood Revitalization and Displacement. A Review of the Evidence, Journal of the American Planning Association, 45, 480–487.

Urban Task Force (1999a) But Would You Live There? Shaping Attitudes to Urban Living, Department of the Environment, Transport and the Regions, London.

Urban Task Force (1999b) Toward an Urban Renaissance, Routledge, London.

Warde, A. (1991) Gentrification as Consumption: Issues of Class and Gender, Environment and Planning, D 9, 223–232.

Wright, P. (1991) A Journey Through Ruins: The Last Days of London, Radius, London.

28

"Gentrification and Displacement: New York City in the 1990s"

From *Journal of the American Planning Association* (2004)

Lance Freeman and Frank Braconi

During the past several decades, neighborhoods in a number of cities have experienced gentrification—a dramatic shift in their demographic composition toward better educated and more affluent residents. If it continues, this reurbanization of the middle and professional classes presents a historic opportunity to reverse central-city decline and to further other widely accepted societal goals. Many cities face fiscal problems because higher income households have migrated to the suburbs and disadvantaged (poor and less educated) households are concentrated in the urban core. These problems could be ameliorated if wealthier households increasingly settle within central cities, raising taxable income and property values and stimulating retail activity and sales tax proceeds (Miesowski & Mills, 1993).

If it proceeds without widespread displacement, gentrification also offers the opportunity to increase socioeconomic, racial, and ethnic integration. An increasing middle class in central-city neighborhoods, to the degree that it includes white households, could help desegregate urban areas and, eventually, their school districts (Lee et al., 1985). Moreover, the concentrated poverty that is thought to diminish the life chances of the poor might be reduced if middle-income residents settle in formerly depressed neighborhoods (Wilson, 1987).

In addition, existing residents of inner-city neighborhoods could benefit directly from gentrification if it brings new housing investment and stimulates additional retail and cultural services. Furthermore, the infusion of residents with more political influence may help the community to procure better public services. The employment prospects of low-income residents could also be enhanced if gentrification contributes to local job creation or if informal job information networks are enriched by an influx of working residents.

Despite these potential benefits, local populations and community activists often oppose the gentrification of urban neighborhoods. Although the rhetoric of resistance sometimes expresses class and racial resentments, the principal concern is usually that lower-income households are vulnerable to displacement resulting from redevelopment projects or rising rents. A common response is for activists to pressure local government for more affordable housing development, to organize community development corporations for that end, or to establish service programs that provide legal or financial assistance to renters who face eviction. In some cases, however, opponents have sought to block community improvement projects through political pressure or legal challenge (Lin, 1995; Robinson, 1995).

The degree to which government policies should actively promote gentrification in order to achieve fiscal and societal goals is a policy calculation that should consider adverse consequences such as displacement. Consequently, it is imperative that social scientists and policy analysts provide better quantitative evidence of the extent and implications of displacement and of the effectiveness of strategies intended to mitigate it.

BACKGROUND AND PRIOR RESEARCH ON DISPLACEMENT

Scholars have been drawn to the phenomenon of gentrification since it first emerged during the 1970s as a major force shaping the fate of urban neighborhoods. They first sought to document whether inner-city revitalization was actually occurring and if so, to what extent (Baldassare, 1982; Clay, 1979; James, 1977; Lipton, 1977; National Urban Coalition, 1978; Sumka, 1979). The studies were consistent in showing that although gentrification was a small part of the overall scheme of metropolitan shifts, it was indeed a reality in many older central-city communities during the 1970s. With gentrification's existence documented, theorists debated about its origins and its consequences for cities. What emerged from this debate was recognition of the importance of several factors as preconditions for gentrification, including changing demographics and lifestyle preferences, professionals clustering in cities to provide services for the gentrifiers, and a history of disinvestment that created ripe opportunities for reinvestment in certain neighborhoods (Beauregard, 1986; Hamnett, 1991; Ley, 1980; Rose, 1984; Smith, 1979).

Although it did not signal the demise of gentrification, as some observers claimed, the recession of the late 1980s and early 1990s did reverse or at least slow the process in many cities (Lees & Bondi, 1995; Smith & Defilippis, 1999). The economic boom of the 1990s, however, erased any lingering doubts that gentrification would be a long-lasting phenomenon. The boom, coupled with shifts in the housing finance industry that were favorable to low-income neighborhoods and reinvestment in federal low-income housing through the HOPE VI program, created conditions that expanded the process of gentrification in many cities (Wyly & Hammel, 1999). To be sure, gentrification still affected only a small share of all U.S. neighborhoods (Kasarda et al., 1997), but this share was prominent enough to reawaken old fears about displacement. In response, community-oriented organizations set up web sites to dampen its impacts on the poor (PolicyLink, 2003), and even popular magazines addressed the displacement perils of gentrification, referring to it is as "hood snatching" (Montgomery, 2002, pp. 34–37). Thus, in spite of all the promise for central-city rebirth associated with gentrification, for many, the assumption that it causes widespread displacement makes it a dirty word.

Prior research and its limitations

Given the fears of displacement that have long been associated with gentrification, it is not surprising that scholars have attempted to define and measure this relationship. Researchers have generally used two approaches to assess the degree of displacement resulting from gentrification: (1) studies of succession that examine how the socioeconomic characteristics of in-movers differ from those of out-movers, and (2) surveys that ask residents why they moved from their former residence.

Succession Studies. Succession studies examine whether individuals moving into a housing unit are of higher socioeconomic status than those moving out, as would be expected if gentrification were occurring. By focusing on specific locales, one can get a sense of the extent to which gentrification is occurring. Using this approach in a study of nine Midwestern cities, Henig (1980) found that the majority of the neighborhoods lost professional households, and those that experienced a net increase did not experience a concomitant decrease in blue-collar/service workers, households headed by females, or the elderly. Henig concluded that although displacement may be a problem in certain neighborhoods, it was probably not as widespread as the popular wisdom of the time perceived it to be.

Spain et al. (1980) performed a similar analysis using American Housing Survey data for 1973–1976. If gentrification is associated with the socioeconomic and demographic transformation of neighborhoods, then middle-income households, who are often White, should increasingly occupy the units vacated by lower-income households, who are often Black. The results of their analysis were consistent with an increase in gentrification during the decade. Because Spain and her colleagues did not stratify their analysis at a finer geographic level than central city/suburb, however, it is impossible to know if the white-to-black or poor-to-middle-income successions were concentrated in gentrifying neighborhoods. Moreover, succession studies can only help to define the upper boundary of displacement; they cannot be used to determine whether housing or neighborhood transitions occurred through the induced departure of low-income households or through normal housing turnover and succession, because they do not consider other reasons that households might move. Succession studies can thus verify that the process of gentrification is underway, but without additional information, they cannot demonstrate how that process occurs.

Resident Surveys. Studies based on asking respondents why they moved generally use some variation of Grier and Grier's (1978) definition of displacement:

… when any household is forced to move from its residence by conditions which affect the dwelling or its immediate surroundings, and;

1. Are beyond the household's reasonable ability to control or prevent;
2. Occur despite the household's having met all previously imposed conditions of occupancy; and
3. Make continued occupancy by that household impossible, hazardous, or unaffordable. (p. 8)

Newman and Owen (1982) used this definition, amended to exclude natural disasters. They estimated a displacement rate of approximately 5% for the entire U.S., based on data from the Panel Study of Income Dynamics.

Lee and Hodge (1984) used a somewhat more restrictive definition, limiting it to those displaced by "private action including abandonment, demolition, eviction, condominium conversion, mortgage default and the termination of a rental contract" (p. 221). They estimated a displacement rate of 3.31% for the entire U.S., based on data from the American Housing Survey.

Out-Movers Study. The biggest problem with studies that focus retrospectively on motives for moving is that they typically fail to identify the location of the respondent's former residence. Consequently, it is impossible to determine how much, if any, of the displacement observed is due to gentrification.

Schill and Nathan (1983) attempted to solve this problem by focusing on gentrifying neighborhoods and the individuals moving out of them with a narrow definition of displacement that could be directly attributable to gentrification. They then used local sources and data from the R.L. Polk Company to track down residents who had moved from each of nine neighborhoods in five mid-sized cities in the previous year.

In the sample of out-movers from gentrifying neighborhoods, Schill and Nathan determined that 23% were displaced. The principal drawback to this method was that no baseline displacement rate could be estimated. Consequently, one cannot compare displacement rates in gentrifying and nongentrifying areas. Moreover, there is no measure of the relative mobility of households in different types of neighborhoods, so a higher percentage of moves from gentrifying areas may be displacements while the aggregate number of displacements from those neighborhoods may be the same or lower.

Comparison Study. In order to determine whether gentrification causes an increased number of disadvantaged households to be displaced, there must be a basis of comparison to neighborhoods in which gentrification is not occurring. In a recent study of the effects of gentrification on the

disadvantaged in Boston, Vigdor (2001) attempted to do just that by evaluating the mobility rates of both the poor and the less-educated households in gentrifying and nongentrifying areas. Using the American Housing Survey, which after 1985 divides the Boston metropolitan area into 36 geographic zones, Vigdor evaluated exits from housing units between 1985 and 1989. Two classifications of gentrifying zones were identified (one narrower than the other) and probit regressions were estimated. Controls were included for householder age, income, tenure, whether a unit had rent regulation, and several other household and housing characteristics.

Using his narrower classification of gentrifying zones and defining disadvantaged households as those in which the head had no post-secondary education, Vigdor found that gentrification increased the exit rate from housing units overall but decreased it for less-educated households, who were significantly more likely to remain in their housing units in gentrifying areas than those elsewhere in the metropolitan area. Although Vigdor could not determine the reasons for exits from housing units, he concluded that the results provide "compelling evidence of the importance of considering baseline exit rates in any study of residential displacement" (p. 26).

Summary. Considering the concern that residential displacement generates in gentrifying or potentially gentrifying urban neighborhoods, the research record on displacement is surprisingly inconclusive. Most of it suggests that a relatively small percentage of housing moves can be attributed to displacement, and there is little evidence that implicates neighborhood gentrification in the process. The research of Schill and Nathan (1983) does indicate that the proportion of housing exits in gentrifying areas that could be considered displacement is fairly high, but Vigdor's (2001) results indicate that overall exits of disadvantaged households from gentrifying areas are actually below those elsewhere. Although those results are not inherently contradictory, the disparity in the time and place of the two studies suggests that more research is necessary before those countervailing patterns can be considered characteristic of the gentrification process.

DISPLACEMENT IN NEW YORK CITY, 1991–1999

In this study, we focused on New York City during the 1990s. The city provides a prime laboratory to study the patterns and processes of gentrification, insofar as its size and economic vitality have produced several distinct areas of gentrification activity. Following a regional recession that bottomed out in 1993, the city experienced rapid economic growth and strong job creation for the remainder of the decade. Job creation and income growth were particularly strong in the creative and information processing sectors of the economy, including finance, insurance, and real estate; communications; higher education; and business services. Growth in those economic sectors is often considered a prerequisite for gentrification, as their businesses tend to prefer central business district locations and employ workers who have educational and other characteristics that make them predisposed to urban lifestyles and residence. A large renter population and the presence of rent regulation also permit large-sample statistical analysis of renter mobility and displacement and an evaluation of the role rent regulation may play in mitigating it.

It is well known that New York City has had some form of rent regulation in place continuously since 1943; it is less widely appreciated that the city has transitioned from the earlier, rigid form of regulation known as rent *control* to a more flexible, "second-generation" form known as rent *stabilization*. Currently, there are about 50,000 controlled rental units and 1.05 million stabilized rental units—representing about 3% and 52% of the rental stock, respectively (Lee, 2002). Under rent stabilization, permissible rent increases on 1-year and 2-year leases are determined annually by a nine-member panel composed of public, tenant, and owner representatives. Permissible rent increases for occupied units generally correspond to the rate of inflation in operating costs; vacant units are permitted to rent at higher prices according to a complex "vacancy allowance" formula. In addition, the rents of many other units are regulated through a variety of federal and state housing assistance programs.

Our study of gentrification in New York City was facilitated by the availability of the New York City Housing and Vacancy Survey (NYCHVS), a representative sample of approximately 16,000 housing units, of which about 70% are rental units. It is conducted every 3 years by the Census Bureau for New York City in accordance with the City's rent regulation guidelines. For this analysis, we used the 1991,[1] 1993, 1996, and 1999 NYCHVS longitudinal data files. Although the chief purpose of the survey is to collect data regarding New York City's vacancy rate, the NYCHVS also collects a variety of other housing, socioeconomic, and demographic data that are useful for studying gentrification.

Methodology

To discern how gentrification is related to displacement, we examined the relationship between residence in a gentrifying neighborhood and residential mobility among disadvantaged households. If gentrification increases displacement, all other things being equal, we should observe higher mobility rates among disadvantaged households residing in gentrifying neighborhoods than among those residing elsewhere in the city.

The longitudinal feature of the NYCHVS facilitates an analysis of mobility patterns. The same panel of dwelling units is generally visited for each triennial survey, with some alterations to account for additions and losses to the stock and for reweighting to account for population changes. Overall, about 90% of the observations in the 1999 survey were linked to observations of the same dwelling in previous surveys. Within that constant frame of dwelling units, the resident households may have changed, but their year of initial occupancy is provided. Those longitudinal features of the survey allowed us to identify which dwelling units had new occupants as of each survey and to recover from earlier surveys a significant amount of information about the previous occupant household. Using this procedure, we were also able to analyze exits from housing units on a neighborhood basis.

Selection criteria

Neighborhoods are defined as the 55 subborough areas coded in the NYCHVS data. These subborough areas correspond closely to New York City's Community Board Districts, the smallest unit of municipal government, which were initially drawn to represent coherent geographic, demographic, and political entities. In 1999, they consisted of approximately 46,000 households each. Although this number is much larger than what is typically considered a neighborhood in social science research, the density of New York City is unusually high, and most of these areas represent well-known sections of the city, such as the Upper East Side, Brooklyn Heights, or Flushing.

Based on our familiarity with recent trends in neighborhood change, we classified the subboroughs of Chelsea, Harlem, the Lower East Side, and Morningside Heights in Manhattan and Fort Greene, Park Slope, and Williamsburg in Brooklyn as gentrifying neighborhoods. Figure 28.1 shows the locations of these neighborhoods. Figure 28.2 illustrates how gentrifying neighborhoods changed during the 1990s

Figure 28.1 Gentrifying neighborhoods in New York City, 1999

in contrast to other New York neighborhoods: The proportion of Whites in gentrifying neighborhoods increased even as the proportion in the rest of the city declined. Moreover, average monthly rent, educational attainment, and median income were also rising faster. These changes are consistent with what would be expected for gentrifying neighborhoods—relative increases in socioeconomic status—and lend support to our designation of these neighborhoods as gentrifying.

To determine if a household subsequently moved, we first identified housing units that had a new occupant in year t. If so, we considered the occupant of that housing unit in year t–3 as having moved.[2] We then used characteristics of the occupants of the unit in year t–3 as predictors of mobility. Consequently, we observed residential mobility between 1991 and 1993, 1993 and 1996, and 1996 and 1999.

We used two indicators of disadvantage: the household's income level and the household head's educational level. A disadvantaged household had an income below the federal poverty line in the

year prior to the survey or the head lacked a college degree. While income level is more directly related to rent-paying ability, educational status is not as subject to fluctuation and thus is a more stable indicator of socioeconomic status.

Controls

To control for the possibility that disadvantaged households in gentrifying neighborhoods differ systematically in a manner that makes them less likely to move, we developed a multivariate model of residential mobility. This model is based on the life-cycle model of housing consumption, which posits that life-cycle events typically trigger consumption/needs discrepancies that lead to a decision to move (Rossi, 1980; Speare, 1974). For example, marriage is a major life-cycle event likely to trigger a move by at least one of the partners. We used this theoretical framework to guide us in the development of a logistic regression model[3] that predicts the likelihood of someone moving.

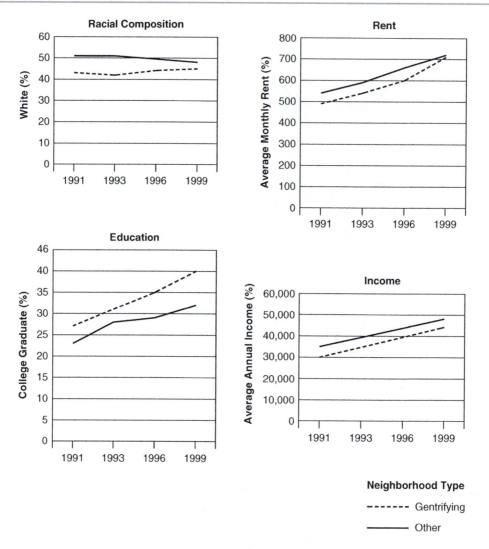

Figure 28.2 Changes in four key socioeconomic indicators, 1991–1999

Using the life-cycle framework, we controlled for age, marital status, and the presence of children in our model of residential mobility. Other demographic control variables included race, gender, income, employment status, and educational attainment. We also controlled for housing unit characteristics likely to be associated with mobility, including monthly rent, length of tenure, overcrowding, the respondent's rating of their neighborhood's physical conditions, and the number of maintenance deficiencies in their unit.

As access to both subsidized housing units and rent-regulated units occurs on a first-come, first-served basis, a model of residential mobility should also take into consideration how the rent regulation/housing subsidy status of the dwelling unit might affect a household's decision to move. Households residing in regulated or subsidized units are likely to think twice before moving, cognizant of the scarcity of other available units with mechanisms for keeping rent affordable and the high cost of housing in the unregulated private sector. With this in mind, we excluded from our analysis both residents of public housing and residents of units acquired by the City because the owners did not pay their taxes. We did control for residence in a rent-regulated unit, including those regulated under the State of New York Mitchell Llama Program[4]

Variable	Poor households		Non-college-graduate head of household	
	Gentrified neighborhoods	Other neighborhoods	Gentrified neighborhoods	Other neighborhoods
Moved	21.00%**	24.70%	21.20%***	24.00%
Monthly rent	$427.00***	$495.00	$475.00***	$550.00
Average rent increase 1991–99	25.10%***	10.40%	24.80%***	9.50%
Years in current residence	11.50***	9.40	12.30***	10.10
Rent-stabilized unit[a]	63.80%***	58.60%	59.70%***	53.60%
Rent-controlled unit[a]	9.70%***	5.00%	12.00%***	5.70%
Other regulated unit[a]	6.10%*	4.60%	6.70%***	5.20%
No. maintenance deficiencies	3.90***	3.50	3.90%***	3.50
Overcrowded unit	4.60%***	8.10%	5.30%*	6.30%
Seriously overcrowded unit	7.20%*	5.50%	5.70%***	3.80%
Native born	43.60%**	39.60%	46.30%***	43.20%
Black	26.80%	24.60%	26.30%*	24.60%
Hispanic	35.90%	37.70%	27.60%*	29.50%
Asian	14.30%***	4.80%	11.00%***	4.60%
Other	.01%	.01%	.01%	.01%
Age (years)	49.10**	47.20	49.00***	47.80
Male	34.10%***	28.40%	46.90%*	44.90%
Married	16.10%**	19.80%	26.10%***	34.50%
Has child	37.40%***	48.40%	28.10%***	36.70%
High school graduate	22.20%***	27.90%	31.50%***	36.20%
Some college	12.60%	13.50%	23.30%	24.30%
College graduate	12.10%	10.60%	–	–
Employed	17.80%	17.60%	43.60%**	46.30%
Income	$5,516.00*	$5,815.00	$23,381.00***	$24,978.00
Neighborhood Rating[b]				
Excellent	5.00%**	7.00%	6.30%***	9.30%
Good	37.50%***	44.00%	38.60%***	46.20%
Fair	37.10%***	31.00%	32.10%***	26.40%
N	760	4,527	1,179	16,489

Table 28.1 Descriptive statistics for variables used in regressions

a. Reference category: unregulated unit
b. Reference category: poor
*$p < .10$ **$p < .05$ ***$p < .01$

and under U.S. Department of Housing and Urban Development programs.[5] Our rationale for including these controls is that gentrification might increase pressure on landlords to "encourage" residents of rent-regulated units to leave and that other types of subsidized housing typically expire after a given period—say 15 or 20 years. Table 28.1 shows a full list of the variables included in the analysis and their descriptive statistics.

RESULTS OF MULTIVARIATE ANALYSES

Gentrification as independent variable

Table 28.2 presents the results of our multivariate analyses. It shows that after controlling for all of the factors described above, poor households residing in one of the seven gentrifying neighborhoods were found to be 19% less likely to move than poor

Variable	Poor households		Non-college-graduate head of household	
	Odds ratio	p value	Odds ratio	p value
Monthly rent	1.01	.01***	0.01	.01***
Residence in gentrified neighborhood	.81	.05**	.85	.01***
Years in current residence	.98	.01***	.97	.01***
Rent-stabilized unit[a]	.94	.48	.87	.01***
Rent-controlled unit[a]	1.39	.13	1.47	.01***
Other regulated unit[a]	.78	.08	.66	.01***
No. maintenance deficiencies	1.01	.32	1.01	.42
Overcrowded unit	1.37	.02**	1.17	.05*
Seriously overcrowded unit	1.17	.29	1.19	.06*
Native born	.91	.27	.96	.39
Black	.93	.46	.93	.17
Hispanic	1.03	.79	1.02	.74
Asian	.91	.56	1.11	.20
Other race	1.07	.93	.63	.23
Age	.93	.01***	.93	.01***
Age squared	1.01	.01***	1.01	.01***
Male	1.10	.27	1.14	.01***
Married	.90	.34	.86	.01***
Has child	.77	.01***	.90	.03**
High school graduate	1.17	.06*	–	–
Some college	.97	.76	–	–
College graduate	1.24	.09*	–	–
Employed	1.01	.92	1.06	.22
Annual Income	.99	.63	.99	.10*
Neighborhood Rating[b]				
Excellent	.81	.23	.82	.03**
Good	.89	.29	.83	.01***
Fair	.91	.44	.88	.08*
Year = 1993	1.45	.01***	1.52	.01***
Year = 1996	1.17	.11	1.42	.01***
Wald χ^2	191.48	.01***	783.22	.01***
Summary statistics				
% correct predictions	65%		65%	
N	4,943		16,051	

Table 28.2 Logistic regression model using gentrification as independent variable

a. Reference category: unregulated unit
b. Reference category: poor
*$p < .10$ **$p < .05$ ***$p < .01$

households residing elsewhere (see second and third columns of Table 28.2). When we controlled for the factors listed above and limited our sample to respondents who lacked a 4-year college degree, disadvantaged households residing in one of these neighborhoods were still 15% less likely to move than their counterparts residing elsewhere (see fourth and fifth columns of Table 28.2).

The results pertaining to the rent regulation variables are also suggestive. The coefficient on rent control indicates that occupants of such units exit at a much higher rate than occupants of unregulated units. This is probably because under the City's rent regulations, only apartments that have been continuously occupied since 1972 by the same tenant (or one with legal rights to succession) are "controlled." Consequently, elderly tenants, who are more apt to exit only when they retire, are institutionalized, or die, occupy controlled units disproportionately. Rent stabilization is by far the more common form of rent regulation in New York City. Our results indicate that poor tenants in such units are insignificantly less likely to exit than those in unregulated units. Rent stabilization does appear, however, to substantially reduce the odds that a less-educated household will move from their dwelling unit during any given time period. These results are consistent with conventional wisdom in New York, which holds that rent regulation is a program that primarily benefits the lower middle class rather than the very poor. In many of the city's poorest neighborhoods, regulated rents are comparable to market rents, and hence are superfluous to keeping rents affordable. We also tested in our regressions a variable interacting residence in a rent-regulated unit and in a gentrifying area and found that it was not significant. This indicates that while rent regulation tends to decrease tenant mobility, it does not do so more in gentrifying areas than in others.

Rent inflation as independent variable

Although most knowledgeable observers would concur with our designations of the seven gentrifying neighborhoods, it is possible that we have erred in our categorization. An alternative approach is simply to measure the rate of increase in neighborhood market rents, on the assumption that the market appropriately values the increasing or decreasing desirability of residential areas. After all, it is the notion that gentrification leads to increased demand in a neighborhood, and consequently to rising rents, that is thought to spur displacement.

Thus, as a further robustness check, we examined the relationship between the average rate of rent inflation among unregulated units in a neighborhood and the likelihood that a disadvantaged household in that neighborhood would move. Because of New York City's large rent-regulated housing stock, we use the rate of rent increase only for unregulated units to proxy for the degree of gentrification in a neighborhood. To the extent that gentrification causes rent inflation, and rising rents induce displacement, we would expect a positive

relationship between rent inflation and the likelihood of moving.

We found that increases in rent are indeed related to the probability of a household moving. But as was the case with the seven gentrifying neighborhoods, these increases were associated with a *lower* probability of moving rather than a higher one. Table 28.3 illustrates the results of our logistic regression analysis predicting if a household would move, using the rate of rent inflation as the independent variable.

The first and third columns show that the probability of a poor or less-educated household moving from a unit declines as the rate of rent inflation in the neighborhood increases. For poor households, a 1% increase in rent inflation is associated with a 1% decrease in the odds of moving. The same is true for households whose head lacks a college degree. Moreover, this relationship persists even when other factors associated with residential mobility are controlled for.

As a final robustness check, we tested whether rent inflation had a stronger effect on disadvantaged households in low-rent neighborhoods. These are neighborhoods where rent inflation might be especially burdensome and most associated with displacement. To test this possibility, we classified neighborhoods with rents below the citywide median in 1991 as low-rent and neighborhoods with rents above the citywide median in 1991 as high-rent, using a dummy variable. We then interacted this dummy variable with the rate of rent inflation, measured as described above. If residence in a low-rent neighborhood renders disadvantaged households especially sensitive to rent inflation, then this interaction term should be statistically significant and positive. For the sake of brevity, we do not report the results here; we only note that the interaction term was not statistically significant. This suggests that the effect of rent inflation on mobility was invariant with regard to the average rent levels in the neighborhood at the beginning of the decade. The relationship between residential mobility and gentrification thus appears robust across different measures of gentrification.

Rethinking the gentrification process

Gentrification has become one of the more controversial issues for planners and others who work in low-income communities. For reasons described in the introduction, gentrification has both boosters and detractors. The latter are motivated primarily by fears of displacement. Gentrification has typically been depicted as a process of higher socioeconomic

Variable	Poor households		Non-college-graduate head of household	
	Odds ratio	p value	Odds ratio	p value
Monthly rent	1.01	.01***	1.01	.01***
Rate of rent inflation in neighborhood	.99	.01***	.99	.01***
Years in current residence	.98	.01***	.97	.01***
Rent-stabilized unit[a]	.96	.63	.89	.01**
Rent-controlled unit[a]	1.42	.10*	1.49	.01***
Other regulated unit[a]	.81	.12	.68	.01***
No. maintenance deficiencies	1.01	.31	1.01	.40
Overcrowded unit	1.37	.02**	1.16	.06*
Seriously overcrowded unit	1.16	.30	1.19	.06*
Native born	.92	.31	.97	.44
Black	.93	.51	.93	.18
Hispanic	1.04	.74	1.02	.71
Asian	.91	.57	1.11	.20
Other race	1.08	.89	.63	.24
Age	.93	.01***	.93	.01***
Age squared	1.01	.01***	1.01	.01***
Male	1.11	.24	1.14	.01***
Married	.89	.28	.85	.01***
Has child	.77	.01***	.90	.02***
High school graduate	1.17	.06*	–	–
Some college	.97	.79	–	–
College graduate	1.25	.08*	–	–
Employed	1.01	.94	1.06	.23
Annual Income	.99	.65	.99	.08*
Neighborhood Rating[b]				
Excellent	.81	.23	.81	.02**
Good	.87	.24	.82	.01***
Fair	.90	.37	.87	.06*
Year-1993	1.45	.01***	1.52	.01***
Ycar-1996	1.16	.12	1.41	.01***
Wald χ^2	193.02	.01***	787.31	.01***
Summary statistics				
% correct predictions		64%		64%
N		4,943		16,051

Table 28.3 Logistic regression model using average rate of rent inflation as independent variable

a. Reference category: unregulated unit
b. Reference category: poor
*p < .10 **p < .05 ***p < .01

households displacing disadvantaged households. Indeed, some have defined gentrification as this type of displacement (Marcuse, 1986). The assumption behind this view is that displacement is the principal mechanism through which gentrification changes the socioeconomic character of a neighborhood. The results presented here, in conjunction with Vigdor's (2001) analysis, which produced similar findings, suggest that a rethinking of the gentrification process is in order. Insofar as many of the other reasons people change residence (marriage or divorce, change of job, want a bigger unit, want to own, etc.) would not be expected to diminish as their neighborhood gentrifies, the reduced mobility rates we find in gentrifying neighborhoods are inconsistent with a process dependent on the massive displacement of disadvantaged residents. Rather, demographic change appears to occur primarily through normal housing succession and may even be slowed by a below-normal rate of exit by existing residents.

It is possible that the lower rates of residential mobility we observed among poor and less-educated people in gentrifying neighborhoods are due entirely to a lower rate of moves *within the neighborhood*, because of a lack of affordable housing alternatives in nearby, familiar locations. However, in a separate analysis not presented here, we identified renters who had been displaced as those who had moved because (1) they wanted a less expensive residence and/or had difficulty paying their previous rent, (2) they experienced landlord harassment, or (3) their units were converted to condominiums or coops but they did not have the desire or means to stay.[6] Those displaced renters were no less likely to be found residing in gentrifying neighborhoods than in nongentrifying ones. This suggests that for residents who seek to lower their rent bills, trade-down options exist even within gentrifying neighborhoods. In any event, a claim that intraneighborhood mobility is reduced for low-income residents in gentrifying neighborhoods is fundamentally different from a claim that they will be displaced from their existing homes.

An alternative interpretation

If the lower mobility rates in gentrifying areas are not a statistical illusion, what might be causing them? The most plausible interpretation may also be the simplest: As neighborhoods gentrify, they also improve in many ways that may be appreciated as much by their disadvantaged residents as by their more affluent ones. To the extent that gentrification is associated not only with an influx of higher-income households but also with better retail and public services, safer streets, more job opportunities, and improvements in the built environment, disadvantaged households may have less reason to change residences in search of a better living environment. Indeed, the strong association between a resident's rating of their neighborhood and their propensity to remain in place is demonstrated by the results of the logistic regressions in Tables 28.2 and 28.3. Although the NYCHVS questionnaire asks respondents to rate only the *physical* condition of their neighborhood, the strong correlation between a neighborhood's physical and social conditions permits us to interpret this rating as a proxy for overall neighborhood quality. Although the coefficients are statistically significant only for the less-educated sample, mobility appears to decrease as neighborhood quality increases for both categories of disadvantaged residents.

A neighborhood can gentrify without direct displacement as long as in-movers are of a higher socioeconomic status than out-movers. Given the typical pattern of low-income renter mobility in New York City, a neighborhood could go from a 30% poverty population to 12% in as few as 10 years without any displacement whatsoever, providing that all vacated units are rented by non-poor households. Even if disadvantaged households who reside in gentrifying neighborhoods are less likely to move, these neighborhoods can still undergo demographic transformations if the households moving into vacated units are of a higher socioeconomic status than those leaving. Indeed, that appears to be the case in the gentrifying neighborhoods in New York City from 1991–1999. Table 28.4 shows that households moving into units in gentrifying neighborhoods had substantially higher incomes, higher levels of educational attainment, and lower poverty rates than the previous residents of those units. Because the NYCHVS does not allow us to determine where in-movers are coming from, we cannot be sure that all of these in-movers are indeed coming from outside of the neighborhood. While it appears that

	Average income	College graduate	Poverty rate
In-movers	$35,230*	47%*	23%*
Current residents	$26,887	23%	31%

Table 28.4 Characteristics of in-movers and current residents

*p < .01

disadvantaged households are less likely to move away if they live in a gentrifying neighborhood, they are also less likely to move into one if they do not already live there.

IMPLICATIONS FOR PLANNING

We believe our results have implications for how we understand the process of gentrification, what gentrification may mean to disadvantaged households, and how housing policy should be crafted to address concerns about gentrification. We discuss each of these below.

If our speculation that many disadvantaged households would prefer to stay in their neighborhoods as they gentrify is correct, this is all the more reason to fashion housing policy to mitigate some of the pressures of displacement. For although our results imply that the amount of displacement occurring in gentrifying areas may be no worse than in other parts of the city, this does not mean that no one is being displaced. In addition, those disadvantaged households staying in gentrifying neighborhoods may be devoting a substantial portion of their income for improved neighborhood conditions. Indeed, data from the NYCHVS shows that the average rent burden for poor households living in gentrifying neighborhoods was 61% during the study period, in contrast to a lower, although still problematic, 52% for poor households living outside of gentrifying neighborhoods.

Furthermore, disadvantaged households who wish to move into these neighborhoods may not be able to find an affordable unit, as may disadvantaged households in gentrifying neighborhoods who wish to move within their neighborhood. Moreover, if gentrification occurs on a sufficiently wide scale, it could result in a gradual shrinking of the pool of low-cost housing available in a metropolitan area. For these reasons, gentrification can still exacerbate the housing problems of the poor, even if widespread displacement is not occurring.

Ironically, two of the most maligned housing policies, rent regulation and public housing, may have a certain logic in the context of gentrification. We have already shown that rent regulation reduces housing turnover among disadvantaged renters, although no more so in gentrifying areas than elsewhere. It may be equally important in moderating the rent burdens of those who do stay in their apartments, however. Our tabulations, for example, show that between 1996 and 1999, rents for unregulated apartments in gentrifying neighborhoods of New York City

increased by an average of 43.2%. For rent-stabilized apartments, the corresponding increase was 11.4%. More research is necessary, however, to determine how rent regulations affect the rent burdens of poor families already living in gentrifying areas and how those rent burdens might change if regulations were not in place.

Public housing, often criticized for anchoring the poor to declining neighborhoods, may also have the advantage of anchoring them to gentrifying neighborhoods. The households probably least at risk of being displaced in neighborhoods like Harlem and the Lower East Side of Manhattan are those in public housing; they are insulated from rent competition with more affluent households because of public housing's income eligibility rules. Tenant-based housing assistance offers no such assurances if market rents in a neighborhood rise above fair market rent levels. Likewise, owners of Low Income Housing Tax Credit (LIHTC) developments and other types of private, assisted housing may be quicker to opt out of the program at the end of the obligatory time period if the surrounding neighborhood is undergoing gentrification. This is an important consideration that should be kept in mind, especially if gentrification becomes a more widespread phenomenon in urban areas.

CONCLUSION

Our analysis indicates that rather than speeding up the departure of low-income residents through displacement, neighborhood gentrification in New York City was actually associated with a lower propensity of disadvantaged households to move. These findings suggest that normal housing succession is the primary channel through which neighborhood change occurs. Indeed, housing turnover may actually be slowed by the reduced mobility rates of lower-income and less-educated households. The most plausible explanation for this surprising finding is that gentrification brings with it neighborhood improvements that are valued by disadvantaged households, and they consequently make greater efforts to remain in their dwelling units, even if the proportion of their income devoted to rent rises.

The results of this study and Vigdor's analysis suggest that some degree of gentrification can occur without rapid and massive displacement of disadvantaged households. Insofar as gentrification in these studies does not appear to cause the widespread dislocation of the disadvantaged that some observers have claimed and it may also help to promote important fiscal and social goals, municipal governments may become more inclined to pursue policies explicitly geared to promoting it. Before pursuing that course, however, it would be wise for planners and policymakers to gain a better understanding of whether the effects we have identified would be likely to occur under different scenarios and under what circumstances, if any, widespread displacement could be a problem.

Even though urban gentrification may provide benefits to disadvantaged populations, it may also create adverse effects that public policies should seek to mitigate. Our results indicate that rent regulation can promote residential stability for disadvantaged households, but those effects do not seem to be consistent across all subgroups of the disadvantaged population. More research is needed to evaluate the usefulness of rent regulation in reducing displacement and moderating the rent burdens of disadvantaged households in gentrifying neighborhoods. Other traditional housing assistance programs, such as public housing and Section 8 rent subsidies, also need to be re-evaluated in the context of urban gentrification, rather than in the context of urban decline.

Notes

1 The NYCHVS was conducted in 1991 instead of 1990 to avoid overlapping with the decennial census.
2 t−2 in the case of the 1991–1993 interval.
3 Because each household contributed more than one observation to the dataset (one for each year observed), it was necessary to correct our estimates for possible dependence among observations. Although our models include numerous statistical controls, observations from the same household are still unlikely to be independent, and consequently the error terms correlated as well. To address this possibility, we estimated our models using a random effects approach (Conway, 1990).
4 The Mitchell Llama Program provides housing primarily for middle-income tenants.
5 This would include units developed under Section 8 New Construction, Substantial and Moderate Rehabilitation, and other subsidized construction and rehabilitation programs.
6 We did not use this approach to link gentrification with displacement because the NYCHVS does not allow us to identify the neighborhood of origin. Thus, we can categorize some recent movers as

displaced, but we cannot say if it was due to gentrification because we do not know from which neighborhood they came.

REFERENCES

Baldassare, M. (1982). Evidence for neighborhood revitalization: Manhattan in the 1970s. *Journal of Urban Affairs, 4*, 25–37.

Beauregard, R. (1986). The chaos and complexity of gentrification. In N. Smith & P. Williams (Eds.), *Gentrification of the city* (pp. 35–55). Boston: Allen & Unwin.

Clay, P. L. (1979). *Neighborhood renewal.* Lexington, MA: Lexington Books.

Conway, M. R. (1990). A random effects model for binary data. *Biometrics, 46*, 317–328.

Grier, G., & Grier, E. E. (1978). *Urban displacement: A reconnaissance.* Washington, DC: U.S. Department of Housing and Urban Development.

Hamnett, C. (1991). The blind men and the elephant: The explanation of gentrification. *Transcripts of the Institute of British Geographers, 16*, 173–189.

Henig, J. R. (1980). Gentrification within cities: A comparative analysis. *Social Science Quarterly, 61*(3), 639–652.

James, F. J. (1977). *Back to the city: An appraisal of housing reinvestment and population change in America.* Washington, DC: Urban Institute.

Kasarda, J., Appold, S., Sweeny, S. H., & Seiff, E. (1997). Central city migration patterns: Is a turnaround on the horizon? *Housing Policy Debate, 8*(2), 307–358.

Lee, B. A., & Hodge, D. C. (1984). Spatial differentials in residential displacement. *Urban Studies, 21*, 219–231.

Lee, B. A., Spain, D., & Umberson, D. J. (1985). Neighborhood revitalization and racial change: The case of Washington, D.C. *Demography, 22*(4), 581–601.

Lee, M. W. (2002). *Housing New York City 1999.* New York: City of New York Department of Housing Preservation and Development.

Lees, L., & Bondi, L. (1995). De/Gentrification and economic recession: The case of New York City. *Urban Geography, 16*, 234–253.

Ley, D. (1980). Liberal ideology and the postindustrial city. *Annals of the American Association of Geographers, 70*, 238–258.

Lin, J. (1995). Polarized development and urban change in New York's Chinatown. *Urban Affairs Review, 30*(3), 332–354.

Lipton, G. (1977, April). Evidence of central city revival. *Journal of the American Institute of Planners, 43,* 136–147.

Marcuse, P. (1986). Abandonment, gentrification, and displacement: The linkages in New York City. In N. Smith & P. Williams (Eds.), *Gentrification of the city* (pp. 153–177). Boston: Allen & Unwin.

Meiszkowski, P., & Mills, E. (1993). The causes of metropolitan suburbanization. *Journal of Economic Perspectives, 7,* 135–147.

Montgomery, M. (2002). Ghetto red hot. *Smooth, 1*(5), 34–37.

National Urban Coalition. (1978). *Displacement: City neighborhoods in transition.* Washington, DC: Author.

Newman, S., & Owen, M. S. (1982). Residential displacement: Extent, nature, and effects. *Journal of Social Issues, 38*(3), 135–148.

PolicyLink. (n.d.). *Equitable development toolkit.* Retrieved August 4, 2003 from http://www.policylink.org/equitabledevelopment/fstest.asp

Robinson, T. (1995). Gentrification and grassroots resistance in San Francisco's Tenderloin. *Urban Affairs Review, 30*(4), 485–513.

Rose, D. (1984). Rethinking gentrification: Beyond the uneven development of Marxist urban theory. *Environment and Planning D, 2,* 47–74.

Rose, K. (2001, May/June). Beyond gentrification: Tools for equitable development. *Shelterforce.* Online. Retrieved November 17, 2003, from http://www.nhi.org/online/issues/117/Rose.html

Rossi, P. H. (1980). *Why families move.* New York: Free Press.

Schill, M. H., & Nathan, R. P. (1983). *Revitalizing America's cities: Neighborhood reinvestment and displacement.* Albany: SUNY Press.

Smith, N. (1979). Toward a theory of gentrification: A back to the city movement by capital not people. *Journal of the American Planning Association, 45,* 538–548.

Smith, N., & Defilippis, J. (1999). The reassertion of economics: 1990s gentrification in the Lower East Side. *International Journal of Urban and Regional Research, 23*(4), 638–653.

Spain, D., Reid, J., & Long, I. (1980). Housing successions among Blacks and Whites in cities and suburbs. *Current Population Reports,* Series P23, No. 101. Washington, DC: U.S. Census Bureau.

Speare, A. (1974). Residential satisfaction as an intervening variable in residential mobility. *Demography, 11*(2), 173–188.

Sumka, H. (1979). Neighborhood revitalization and displacement: A review of the evidence. *Journal of the American Planning Association, 45,* 480–487.

Vigdor, J. (2001). *Does gentrification harm the poor?* Unpublished manuscript, Duke University. Retrieved from http://www-pps.aas.duke.edu/-jvigdor/dghtp5.pdf

Wilson, W. J. (1987). *The truly disadvantaged.* Chicago: University of Chicago Press.

Wyly, E. L., & Hammel, D. J. (1999). Islands of decay in seas of renewal: Housing policy and the resurgence of gentrification. *Housing Policy Debate, 10*(4), 711–772.

PART FIVE

Geographies of gentrification

Plate 17 **Dreamers … Creative Class thinking, Chicago, 2009.** Photograph by Elvin Wyly.

INTRODUCTION TO PART FIVE

The embourgeoisement of the inner city ... is incomplete even in those neighbourhoods where it has been most prominent, but none the less it has contributed to a significant reshaping in the housing market in cities with expanding downtown employment in advanced services. This qualifier immediately leads to the important recognition that there is a geography to gentrification, that the trends remaking the inner cities of Toronto, San Francisco, or London are not shared by Winnipeg, Detroit, or Liverpool.

(David Ley, 1996, p. 8)

In Part Three, Section C we discussed the late 1980s emergence of a production versus consumption 'stalemate' with respect to explaining gentrification. Wyly and Hammel (2001) outlined just how divided the literature had become at that time:

Gentrification was used as a lens through which to view some of the richest (and most hotly disputed) dichotomies of urban research ... and thus eluded any broad consensus. By the end of the 1980s these debates seemed to exhaust themselves with no prospect of a final 'resolution' ...

(p. 215–216)

Yet one of the crucial issues that had escaped much analytical attention was the role of geographical context. Researchers had been quick to (over)draw all kinds of political and epistemological differences between Neil Smith and David Ley, yet few had apparently noticed that Smith was writing about New York City in the USA and Ley about Vancouver, Canada – two very different cities with very different political structures and historical trajectories of gentrification. It is unsurprising that their explanations for the process would be so different when taking into account the urban contexts in which they had immersed themselves. What is surprising, however, is that geographers, for so long the dominant disciplinary presence in the study of gentrification, had missed its geography. The four readings we have selected for this section are key contributions in an ongoing effort to recognise both context and scale when considering how class inequality imprints itself onto both urban and rural landscapes. This effort is significant because it has helped to invigorate the study of gentrification, moving beyond exhausted debates.

The paper by Loretta Lees was published in 2000, in retrospect probably the year that represents the high water mark of what Jason Hackworth (2002) dubbed 'post-recession gentrification'. As the first few pages of the essay explain, the pessimism of the early 1990's recession had quickly given way to a new millennium of economic recovery, another round of urban reinvestment, and rising property prices. Given its remarkable re-emergence, Lees made several arguments for fresh scholarly engagement with gentrification. The central thread of the paper was her call for 'a geography of gentrification' that would take into account context, locality, and temporality in more detail, issues that she found to be significant in her Ph.D. research comparing gentrification in London and New York City. At the time she wrote this paper, despite much analytical progress, theoretical tensions were threatening explanatory closure, but Lees argued that these tensions could be kept alive in new investigations focused on the 'geography' of the process. Perspectives on gentrification that are usually attributed to differences in theory, ideology, and methodology are equally attributable to 'geography' – the places in which the process is researched. Lees identified two contrasting discourses on gentrification in the literature – the revanchist city (primarily an American construct), and the emancipatory city (primarily a Canadian construct). In the former, gentrification is portrayed as a destructive process anchored by a state-led revenge against the working-class and the spaces they inhabit (Smith, 1996); in the latter, gentrification is portrayed as a largely positive process that brings different social groups together, presenting opportunities for interaction, tolerance and desegregation (Caulfield, 1994). Lees worked with this dualism to set out a research agenda for a 'geography of gentrification' that requires attention to the contextual specificities of the gentrification process, with particular sensitivity to the ways in which the process is configured under interlocking geographical scales. Furthermore, as Lees argued, a 'geography of gentrification' is something that has policy relevance too:

> More detailed research into the geography of gentrification … would enable us to consider the merits or dangers of cities further down the urban hierarchy taking on board the gentrification practices of cities higher up the urban hierarchy, cities with a very different geography.
>
> (p. 405)

Lees argued that the 'geography of gentrification' 'works on a number of different levels – international comparison, intranational, and citywide comparison' (p. 405). At the citywide scale, Lees noted that within a single city, gentrification of a similar time period has a quite different geography depending on its site. This is particularly evident in the work of Tim Butler and Garry Robson. In the paper we have selected here, they attempted to tease out subtle differences in the ways in which the gentrifying middle classes 'come to terms with London' in different London neighbourhoods. The impetus for their research was clearly set out:

> One criticism of existing approaches to gentrification is that they tend to see gentrification as a more or less homogenous process. … Our hypothesis is that different middle-class groups would be attracted to different areas and this would be determined by a range of factors, in addition to what they might be able to afford in particular housing markets.
>
> (p. 2146–2148)

After testing this hypothesis by interviewing gentrifiers in Telegraph Hill, Battersea and Brixton, in inner London, they found that gentrification had consolidated very different forms of middle-class identity (as a consequence of the differential deployment of social, economic and cultural capital) in each location. For example, the gentrifiers in Brixton differed significantly from their counterparts in the other two neighbourhoods – that neighbourhood context was characterised by 'tectonic' social relations, where middle-class people celebrated the demographic diversity of the area without actually interacting with neighbours not like them (local social capital was thus extremely weak, in contrast with Battersea and Telegraph Hill). They concluded with the argument that '[g]entrification … cannot in any sense be considered to be a unitary phenomenon, but needs to be examined in each case according to its own logic and outcomes' (p. 2160). Their work illustrates that there is notable differentiation in gentrification (or, more specifically, the experiences of gentrifiers) between London neighbourhoods which are not separated by much physical distance – a major finding that moves away from earlier research which took a broader, quantitative view and thus tended to refer to 'London's gentrification' (e.g., Williams, 1976; Hamnett and Randolph, 1984; Munt, 1987).

Butler and Robson's analysis is centred on the local scale. This is not to say, however, that interpreting the geography of gentrification is best done at the micro-scale. As Matthew Rofe demonstrates in the article that follows, widening the geography can teach us much about the motivations and aspirations of key agents in the process. Critical segments of local labour markets in large cities are now connected umbilically to a world urban system: local clusters of transnational corporate services and headquarters not only generate demand for local gentrified residential space, but also serve to weave this local demand into transnational circuits of labour migration amongst itinerant professionals on short-term assignments or freelance employment contracts. Based on his research in Sydney and Newcastle, Australia, Rofe argues that we are seeing the emergence of a distinct gentrifying class, in which the construction of identity is increasingly commodified and tied to specific neighbourhoods in the competitive real estate markets at the top of the world urban hierarchy (e.g. Glebe in Sydney). This commodification, he argues, erodes the symbolic significance of local gentrification processes:

> In order to maintain a distinctive identity, numerous gentrifiers are projecting their identity from the scale of the local onto the scale of the global. In doing so, these individuals actively position themselves as a global elite community.
>
> (p. 2511)

Perhaps the crucial interview quote in Rofe's paper is from an individual who feels that Glebe is a 'global suburb', offering 'the same type of lifestyle' that can be found in New York, London or Los Angeles (p. 2521). In effect, Rofe marries the gentrification literature to the world cities literature, mixing in the political geography of membership by arguing that gentrifying landscapes 'constitute a territory from which some gentrifiers construct an imagined sense of global community development' (p. 2524). It should be noted, however, that Rofe's geography of gentrification works both ways: Butler and Lees (2006) have demonstrated how elite gentrifiers in Barnsbury, London, project their global identity onto the local, resulting in a reconstitution of elite space at the neighbourhood level. In addition Bridge (2007) has argued that whilst a new middle class is reproduced in certain global cities, the diversity of aesthetic trajectories and the localisms of cosmopolitan knowledge suggest that the case for a global gentrifier class or urban new middle class is a weak one. At the global scale he sees, as much more pervasive, a quite conventional set of middle class strategies of middle class reproduction.

The final article in this section, by Martin Phillips, has a rather different view of what a 'geography of gentrification' might look like. Phillips has been at the forefront of efforts to understand gentrification in rural settings:

> Although gentrification has been the subject of widespread attention and heated debate, one of the most striking features of the debate has been its urbanity, and how this urbanity has proceeded virtually without comment.
>
> (2002, p. 284)

One might expect very different geographies of gentrification between urban and rural contexts, but Phillips documents a crucial parallel between rural and urban gentrification – both reflect distancing from suburban space and suburbia, or the existence of 'a normative geography of urbanity, rurality and suburbia' (p. 25). Phillips draws on primary and secondary research in Norfolk, England, to demonstrate that many of the arguments raised with respect to urban space 'are complementary, if not necessarily fully commensurable, with a series of rural studies'. He argues that the devaluation and subsequent reinvestment of labour, commodities and financial capital in areas of the countryside is another context that is central to understanding the complete geographical imprint of gentrification.

But as well as looking at the 'other' spaces (the spatial dimensions) of gentrification, Darren Smith's work on 'studentification' (see Smith, 2002) has shown how important it is to focus on temporality too, especially as it is related to the life courses of individuals (see Smith and Holt, 2007, on college/university students as 'apprentice gentrifiers'; see also Bridge, 2003). There is much more to investigate within this spatial-temporal nexus.

Neil Smith (2002) has argued that gentrification has become 'generalised' into a global urban strategy. When considering the spread of gentrification from San Francisco to Sydney, to Shanghai to Sao Paolo, it is difficult to disagree, and in the last few years the banner headline of Smith's argument has become something of a new conventional wisdom. But the subtleties of Smith's analysis – and of the arguments presented in the readings included in this section – require more careful consideration. Geographies of gentrification are about much more than a casual acknowledgment of contingency ('it depends ...') or a recognition of transnational networks. To be sure, geographies of gentrification refer to the varied and contextual impacts of general processes, and the distinct local conditions that mediate the relations between economic and cultural processes that shape gentrification. But other geographies also matter. Authors like us, and readers like you, learn concepts and develop theories in ways that are inherently place-based: inevitably, we draw on places we know as we study things, and this creates 'geographical biographies' of concepts like the new middle class, the rent gap, social tectonics, the revanchist city, and so on. At the same time, even the most large-scale concepts like neoliberalism and globalization have very specific geographies that should not be blurred into a vague, diffuse sense of everywhere-and-nowhere (Tickell and Peck, 2003; Harvey, 2006). Even gentrifiers who see themselves as cosmopolitan and 'global' place a high value on extremely localized experiences – particular cities, neighbourhoods, and often individual streets, intersections, shops and restaurants that have meaning in their lives. Similarly, policy elites who promote gentrification as a strategy to make their city globally competitive learn about these strategies from very specific – and always place-based – experiences, stories, or advisors. Even when an investor relies on the latest internet-driven technologies that promise to bring the 'end of geography' to learn about development opportunities in a city on the other side of the globe, geography still matters: local, regional, national, and transnational processes shape the way a particular place gentrifies, how potential gentrifiers respond to a developer's marketing strategy, and how local and more distant activists mount challenges and fight for a right to the city. Just as neoliberalism and globalization are unfolding – and are constituted – in different ways in various places, so too is gentrification.

REFERENCES AND FURTHER READING

Bridge, G. (2003) 'Time-space trajectories in provincial gentrification', *Urban Studies* 40(12): 2545–2556.

Bridge, G. (2007) 'A global gentrifier class?', *Environment and Planning A* 39(1): 32–46.

Butler, T. and Lees, L. (2006) 'Super-gentrification in Barnsbury, London: globalisation and gentrifying global elites at the neighbourhood level', *Transactions of the Institute of British Geographers* 31: 467–487.

Carpenter, J. and Lees, L. (1995) 'Gentrification in New York, London and Paris: An international comparison', *International Journal of Urban and Regional Research* 19(2): 286–303. Reprinted 2002 in Pacione, M. (ed) *The City: Critical Concepts in the Social Sciences, Vol. 2: Land-use, structure and change in the Western city*, pp. 544–566. London and New York: Routledge.

Caulfield, J. (1994) *City Form and Everyday Life: Toronto's Gentrification and Critical Social Practice*, Toronto: University of Toronto Press.

Clark, E. (1994) 'Toward a Copenhagen interpretation of gentrification', *Urban Studies* 31(7): 1033–1042.

Darling, E. (2005) 'The city in the country: wilderness gentrification and the rent-gap', *Environment and Planning A* 37(6): 1015–1032.

Donaldson, R. (2009) 'The making of a tourism-gentrified town: Greyton, South Africa', *Geography* 94(2): 88–99.

Dutton, P. (2003) 'Leeds calling: the influence of London on the gentrification of regional cities', *Urban Studies* 40(12): 2557–2572.

Fox Gotham, K. (2005) 'Tourism gentrification: the case of New Orleans' Vieux Carre (French Quarter), *Urban Studies* 42(7): 1099–1121.

Freeman, C. and Cheyne, C. (2008) 'Coasts for sale: gentrification in New Zealand', *Planning Theory and Practice* 9(1): 33–56.

Gale, D.E. (1984) *Neighborhood Revitalization and the Postindustrial City: A Multinational Perspective*, Lexington, MA: D.C. Heath and Company.

Ghose, R. (2004) 'Big sky or big sprawl? Rural gentrification and the changing cultural landscape of Missoula, Montana', *Urban Geography* 25(6): 528–549.

Hackworth, J. (2002) 'Post recession gentrification in New York City', *Urban Affairs Review* 37: 815–843.

Hamnett, C. and Randolph, B. (1984) 'The role of landlord disinvestment in housing market transformation: an analysis of the flat break-up market in Central London', *Transactions of the Institute of British Geographers* 9: 259–279.

Harvey, D. (2006) *Spaces of Global Capitalism: Towards a Theory of Uneven Geographical Development*, London: Verso.

Lees, L. (1994) 'Gentrification in London and New York: An Atlantic Gap?', *Housing Studies* 9(2): 199–217.

Lees, L. (2003) 'Super-gentrification: the case of Brooklyn Heights, New York City', *Urban Studies* 12: 2487–2510.

Ley, D. (1996) *The New Middle Class and the Remaking of the Central City*, Oxford: Oxford University Press.

Ley, D. (1992) 'Gentrification in recession: social change in six Canadian inner-cities', 1981–1986, *Urban Geography* 13(3): 230–256.

MacLeod, G. (2002) 'From urban entrepreneurialism to a "revanchist city"? On the spatial injustices of Glasgow's renaissance', *Antipode* 34(3): 602–624.

Munt, I. (1987) 'Economic restructuring, culture, and gentrification: a case study in Battersea, London', *Environment and Planning A* 19: 1175–1197.

Niedt, C. (2006) 'Gentrification and the grassroots: Popular support in the revanchist suburb', *Journal of Urban Affairs* 28(2): 99–120.

Phillips, M. (1993) 'Rural gentrification and the processes of class colonization', *Journal of Rural Studies* 9: 123–140.

Phillips, M. (2002) 'The production, symbolisation and socialisation of gentrification: a case study of a Berkshire village', *Transactions of the Institute of British Geographers* 27(3): 282–308.

Slater, T. (2004) 'North American gentrification? Revanchist and emancipatory perspectives explored', *Environment and Planning A* 36(7): 1191–1213.

Smith, D. (2002) 'Patterns and processes of "studentification" in Leeds', *Regional Review* 11: 17–19.

Smith, D. (2002) 'Extending the temporal and spatial limits of gentrification: a research agenda for population geographers', *International Journal of Population Geography* 8(6): 385–394.

Smith, D. (2002) 'Rural gatekeepers and "greentrified" pennine rurality: opening and closing the access gates', *Social and Cultural Geography* 3(4): 447–463.

Smith, D. and Phillips, D. (2001) 'Socio-cultural representations of greentrified Pennine rurality', *Journal of Rural Studies* 17: 457–469.

Smith, N. (1996) *The New Urban Frontier: Gentrification and the Revanchist City*, London and New York: Routledge.

Smith, D. and Holt, L. (2007) 'Studentification and 'apprentice' gentrification within Britain's provincial towns and cities: extending the meaning of gentrification', *Environment and Planning A* 39(1): 142–161.

Smith, N. (2002) 'New globalism, new urbanism: gentrification as global urban strategy', *Antipode* 34(3): 427–450.

Smith, N., Caris, P. and Wyly, E. (2001) 'The Camden syndrome: the menace of suburban decline. Residential disinvestment and its discontents in Camden County, New Jersey', *Urban Affairs Review* 36(4): 497–531.

Sykora, L. (2005) 'Gentrification in post-communist cities', in R. Atkinson and G. Bridge (eds) *Gentrification in a Global Context: The New Urban Colonialism*, pp. 90–105. London: Routledge.

Tickell, A. and Peck, J. (2003) 'Making global rules: globalisation or neoliberalisation?', in J. Peck and H. Yeung (eds) *Remaking the Global Economy*, pp. 163–181. London: Sage.

van Weesep, J. and Musterd, S. (eds) *Urban Housing for the Better-off: Gentrification in Europe*, Utrecht: Stedelijke Netwerken.

Wyly, E. and Hammel, D. (2004) 'Gentrification, segregation, and discrimination in the American urban system', *Environment and Planning A* 36(7): 1215–1241.

Williams, P. (1976) 'The role of institutions in the inner London housing market: the case of Islington', *Transactions of the Institute of British Geographers* 1: 72–82.

Wyly, E. and Hammel, D. (2001) 'Gentrification, housing policy, the new context of urban redevelopment', in K. Fox Gotham (ed.) *Research in Urban Sociology, Vol. 6: Critical Perspectives on Urban Redevelopment*, pp. 211–276. London: Elsevier.

29

"A Reappraisal of Gentrification: Towards a 'Geography of Gentrification'"

From *Progress in Human Geography* (2000)

Loretta Lees

I LOOKING AT GENTRIFICATION AGAIN?

> Maybe the loss of momentum around gentrification reflects its inability to open up new insights, and maybe it is time to allow it to disintegrate under the weight of these burdens.
>
> (Bondi, 1999b: 255)

Back in the early 1990s there was some speculation, both in the media (Lueck, 1991; Wright, 1992) and in the academic literature (Bourne, 1993), that the process of gentrification had run out of steam. Britain, and in particular the London area, was saddled with massive negative equity as the value of real estate plummeted leaving borrowers stuck with mortgage liabilities far in excess of the market value of their holdings. Investment in North American cities, especially in the north east and southern California, was also hard hit by recession. Waves of corporate downsizing cut a wide swath through the professional and new middle classes whose residential preferences and investment decisions had facilitated gentrification. At the same time, however, other authors were more sceptical about the emergence of a 'post-gentrification era' (Badcock, 1993; 1995; Lees and Bondi, 1995). As Neil Smith (1996: 46) correctly insisted 'it would be a mistake to assume, as the language of de-gentrification seems to do, that the economic crisis of the early 1990s spelt the secular end of gentrification'.

Recent evidence from a variety of cities worldwide points to the continuance of the gentrification process, to a process geographers are calling 'post-recession gentrification' and the media 'the yin and yang of gentrification':

> In the 27 years that he has lived in Prospect Heights, Mr. Bullock, 72, said he has watched his neighborhood rise and fall and now rise again, each trend dictated by the prosperity of the city and the ebb and flow of crime. Today, Prospect Heights is one of the many neighborhoods in New York that real estate agents often describe as 'up and coming', attracting middle-class professionals from Manhattan or nearby Park Slope who are in search of affordable homes and apartments in a convenient area.
>
> (Yardley, 1999)

With the stock market booming and record bonuses on Wall Street, *The New York Times* (Yardley 1998) has also reported that brownstones in the Park Slope neighbourhood of Brooklyn, New York City, are fetching prices not seen since the late 1980s, when the real estate market was last at these dizzying heights. Similarly, in London the economic upturn in the late 1990s has helped to fuel the gentrification of locations such as Clerkenwell and the East End (see Hamnett, 1999, on the late 1990s property boom in Britain). The metaphors of the 1970s and 1980s that geographers had associated with the gentrification process – 'urban rebirth', 'urban pioneers' (*The Observer*, 27 June 1999: 17) – are being headlined by the (London) media once again, as are more negative images – such as 'urban guerillas', 'scene of gentrification battles', 'class war' (*The Sunday Times*,

11 April 1999: 2). The continuance of gentrification has led to more conflict (over social exclusion) between the working-class population and the 'Starbucks Coffee Crowd' in cities such as London and New York. But it is not only in these so-called global cities that gentrification has been proceeding apace. Further down the urban hierarchy in cities such as Vancouver, Canada, Manchester, England, and Auckland, New Zealand, inner-city neighbourhoods are being redeveloped and revalorized. With the fall of the iron curtain and the economic liberalization that followed, gentrification has now also become a feature of eastern European cities such as Prague (Sykora, 1996).

If the process of gentrification itself is alive and well, academic writing on gentrification is a little less buoyant. Interest in the subject has declined somewhat since the early 1990s when the gentrification debate dominated urban geography discussions.[1] I would argue, like Redfern (1997a), that this decline is linked to the search for a synthesis between demand and supply-side explanations in the gentrification literature (for example, Hamnett, 1991; Lees, 1994a; Boyle, 1995). It is also linked to the publication of a number of books on gentrification which seem to culminate years of gentrification research by their respective authors (for example, Caufield, 1994; Ley, 1996; Smith, 1996; Butler, 1997). It is notable how all these books have tried to meet at some middle ground between demand and supply-side explanations. Given the well recognized *impasse* reached between the two explanations and the underdevelopment of the productive tensions between the two, it is time to step outside this consensus and its tensions. Like Redfern (1997a), I want to unlock this 'theoretical logjam' because important issues have been sidelined by it, issues I will now turn my attention to. In so doing I hope to convince gentrification researchers, such as Bondi (1999b) and others, that now is not the time to let gentrification research disintegrate under the burden of its consensus.

A focus on supply versus demand, mapped on top of economics versus culture and/or production versus consumption, has been one of the mainstays of the gentrification literature. Redfern (1997a: 1277–78) provides a superb examination of the 'adversarial patrolling' of these gentrification territories. As such the gentrification literature in the 1990s only touched upon issues of urban policy and urban politics. These issues are important ones that need to be dealt with in more detail. If we take a look at the British government's Urban Task Force (DETR, 1999) report *Towards an urban renaissance* we find a discursive construction of urban renaissance that interweaves urban regeneration policy with gentrification practices and environmentalism. Richard Rogers, the influential architect on the task force, has painted a 'green face' on the gentrification process – liveability and environmental sustainability are two of the buzzwords. These are issues that as yet have not been looked at by gentrification researchers; they are issues to be found in other, non-British, cities around the world – for example, see Lees and Demeritt (1998) on the discourse of gentrification and the liveable city in Vancouver, Canada. The Urban Task Force, the first audit of towns and cities in Britain for 20 years, is promoting a move 'back to the city'. As their mission statement says: 'The Urban Task Force will … recommend practical solutions to bring people back into our cities, towns and urban neighbourhoods. It will establish a new vision for urban regeneration …' (DETR, 1999). This 'new' vision is remarkably similar to visions of gentrification. For example, the task force tout the gentrified neighbourhood of Islington in London as a success story in terms of urban regeneration, a story from which they can learn lessons. Gentrification is in effect being promoted by the Urban Task Force as the blueprint for a civilized city life. Urban renaissance is being prescribed as the medicine for decaying inner cities. Interestingly, at the same time urban geographers are attempting to reverse the negative image that gentrification has been given by some academics and are now promoting urban renaissance and 'partial gentrification' (Hamnett, in progress).

The issues of urban policy and urban politics are not just relevant to a British context, they are important in the USA too. Wyly and Hammel (1999) argue that the post-recession resurgence of gentrification in the USA has become intertwined with shifts in housing finance and low-income housing assistance, increasing the role of public policy in the phenomenon, and indeed the phenomenon in policy. As I have argued in relation to the Urban Task Force, similarly Wyly and Hammel (1999) have found that gentrification has exerted a significant influence on urban and public policy in the USA. On looking at the US Department of Housing and Urban Development's (HUD) recent *The state of the cities* report (June 1999), the issues and solutions discussed are very similar to those of the British Urban Task Force – the redevelopment of brownfield sites, environmental sustainability, liveability and the decline in a sense of community. To counter the loss of middle-class families in the inner city HUD argues for increased support for the revitalization initiatives of community-based organizations (read pro-gentrification groups). Gentrification discourse and practices have permeated recent urban policy and urban politics.

The problem with the British *Towards an urban renaissance* and the American *The state of the cities* reports is that the policies advocated by them are 'one size fits all'. The policies take no account of geographical scale and contextual differences, of the 'geography of gentrification'. Both the Urban Task Force and HUD set out to plug the gap between successful cities and lagging cities – mostly small or mid-sized cities – yet the plugs they promote are taken from examples in successful larger cities such as London. These plugs may not be appropriate for smaller cities such as Manchester or Sheffield in England, or Portland, Maine, in the USA.

As well as urban policy and urban politics, the theoretical logjam has sidelined other important issues too – in particular the complex issues of race and a relatively new process I have called 'financification'. These two issues will be discussed in detail later, but it is relevant here to consider how they relate to my previous discussion of scale and the 'geography of gentrification'. The issue of race is especially relevant in so-called global cities where third-world immigration juxtaposes gentrifiers with people from radically different cultural backgrounds. Likewise, the process of 'financification' is only found in global cities such as London and New York, where the highly paid employees in the financial services industry are lubricating the revalorization of the inner city, and regentrifying neighbourhoods which were gentrified in the 1970s. These two factors – race and financial services – point to important spatial variations differentiating the process of gentrification in global cities from smaller ones further down the urban hierarchy.

This article reviews the recent literature on gentrification (specifically writings since the mid-1990s) in light of recent changes in the nature of the process, and it offers some tentative suggestions on how we might re-energize the gentrification debate.

II A THEMATIC REVIEW OF RECENT LITERATURE ON GENTRIFICATION

Rather than offering a relatively straightforward chronological review of the literature, I have selected for consideration four different, but overlapping, themes that continue to organize the gentrification literature. I begin my review by arguing that gentrification researchers have represented the gentrifying inner city in the terms of the *emancipatory city* thesis. I turn then to look at writings on the *New middle class* as the agents in this emancipation. Following

on from this, I consider the *revanchist city*. In large measure the emancipatory city and the revanchist city themes reflect the dichotomy in the literature between demand versus supply-side explanations, but they are not simply a mirror image of this. Finally, I consider the attempt that has been made to step outside the confines of these earlier debates. Redfern (1997a; 1997b) offers a *new look at gentrification*, and his diagnosis of consensus is a good one, but his solution is retrospective: it looks backwards too much and so has nothing to say about the important changes I have identified – contemporary urban policy and politics, the emergence of financifiers, the intricacies of race, and the ideology of liveability and sustainability.

1 The emancipatory city

From Marx's thesis that city life fosters the rise of new class consciousness by bringing different people together and enabling them to reflect on their common class positions, to Walter Benjamin's modernist vision of the free-wheeling *flâneur*, to Liz Wilson's (1991) postmodernist vision of *The Sphinx in the city*, the city has long been portrayed as an emancipatory or liberating space.[2] This spatial metaphor has also been operationalized in parts of the gentrification literature not as a deeply political agenda (like in Marxist and feminist geographies) but as a form of liberal agency. The emancipatory city thesis is implicit in much of the gentrification literature that focuses on the gentrifiers themselves and their forms of agency, for example, Ley (1996) and Butler (1997), but it is in Caulfield's (1994) work that the thesis is seen to be more explicit. Caulfield's (1994: xiii) complex analysis of gentrification in Toronto, Canada, focuses on the inner city as an emancipatory space and gentrification as an emancipatory social practice, which he defines as 'efforts by human beings to resist institutionalized patterns of dominance and suppressed possibility'. Caulfield's gentrifiers 'desire' (see also Caulfield, 1989) a city space where, following Barthes (1986: 96), 'subversive forces, forces of rupture, ludic forces act and meet'. Caulfield's analysis is in some ways Lefebvrian in that space is produced and reproduced as a site of social, political and economic struggle. Gentrification promises the emancipatory urbanism of May 1968 (see also Ley, 1996, and this article's subsection on the new middle class). By resettling old inner-city neighbourhoods, Caulfield argues that gentrifiers subvert the dominance of hegemonic culture and create new conditions for social activities leading the way for the developers that follow.

He shows how the contradictions of capitalist space contain the seeds (possibilities arising from the specific use-values city dwellers find in old inner-city neighbourhoods) for a new kind of space. Gentrification creates tolerance. For Caulfield, old city places offer 'difference' as seen in the diversity of gentrifiers: 'gays may be lawyers or paperhangers, professors may live in shabby bungalows or upmarket townhomes, feminists may or may not have children' (1989: 618).

Reflecting on Caulfield's thesis of the inner city as an emancipatory space, certain questions emerge: what is it about old buildings in inner-city neighbourhoods that makes people tolerant? Is there a necessary link between the new uses of these old inner-city buildings and social diversity? Caulfield argues that encounters between 'different' people in the city are enjoyable and inherently liberating. Young (1991), on the other hand, argues that the interaction of strangers is often quite disinterested, and Merry's (1981) empirical analysis of life in a neighbourhood of strangers in Philadelphia offers a much more pessimistic view of encounters with unknown and anonymous urban others. Far from being liberating, the anonymity of urban life, Merry suggests, is often viewed as threatening. Indeed, Zukin (1995) has argued that such anxieties about strangers have spurred the growth of private police forces and gated communities. The emancipatory inner city of Toronto thus appears as a rose-tinted vision as much as a description of contemporary urban experience.

The actual encounter with social difference and strangers, so often referred to as a source of emancipation in the city by many authors, needs to be evaluated in more depth. Caulfield's and others' (see Keith and Pile, 1993) celebration of social diversity and freedom of personal expression in the inner city inadvertently privileges particular subject positions, cultural practices and class fractions (see Pratt and Hanson, 1994, on the importance of a geography of placement). Although Caulfield is under no illusions about gentrifiers, his thesis obscures the fact that anti-gentrification groups, often largely composed of working-class and/or ethnic minorities, do not always share the same desires as gentrifiers. The dream of gentrifying tolerance and equality has struggled to accommodate people who do not accept the idea that all values deserve equal protection. Particularly in global cities like London and New York where gentrifiers are rubbing shoulders with people from radically different cultural backgrounds, these liberal values become problematic. Jane Jacobs (1996: 72), for example, has outlined competing visions for the rehabilitation of Spitalfields

in the East End of London – 'the co-presence of Bengali settlers, home-making gentrifiers and megascale developers activated an often conflictual politics of race and nation'. This radical cultural difference may set gentrification in cosmopolitan cities such as London or New York (and Toronto) apart from gentrification in cities further down the urban hierarchy where immigration is less significant and/or visible. What struggles over gentrification everywhere do share in common, however, is the formal equality of the exchange relationship. If in debates over gentrification and neighbourhood change the particular desires of gentrifiers win out over others, it is because they are willing and able to pay more for the privilege (one's capital in such circumstances includes economic, cultural and social resources). By abstractly celebrating formal equality under the law, the rhetoric of the emancipatory city tends to conceal the brutal inequalities of fortune and economic circumstance that are produced through the process of gentrification.

Gender, sexuality and gentrification, like the new middle class, are research themes closely tied to the social construction of the emancipatory city. In the 1970s and 1980s the gentrification literature suggested that gentrification was a process associated with 'marginal groups' such as gays, lesbians and other women attracted to the liberating space of the inner city. Whatever the precise relationships between gender, sexuality and the process of gentrification, there can be no mistaking the fact they have featured high on the agenda of an important segment of the academic research community. This work, I would suggest, probably reveals as much about the discipline of geography as it does about the gentrification process itself. Feminist, gay and lesbian geographers, not surprisingly, tend to be concerned with gender and sexuality. Yet, despite the academic interest in marginality, there has been relatively little attention to the intersections of race and gentrification (in the Castro District of San Francisco in the 1970s, as gay gentrification took off, incoming black gentrifiers suffered marginalization and racial abuse from white gentrifiers – see KQED, Inc., 1997). Indeed, this peculiar omission points to one important way in which, within the academy at least, marginality and difference (or at least some differences) are now mainstream (Lees, 1996: 453–54).

Interest in gender and gentrification can be traced back to Markusen's (1981: 32) argument that 'gentrification is in large part a result of the breakdown of the patriarchal household' and to Damaris Rose's (1984) challenge to Neil Smith's uneven development thesis. In the early 1990s authors such as

Bondi (1991) and Warde (1991) prioritized gender relative to class in their conceptual accounts of gentrification. Then in the mid-1990s researchers began to step back from the prioritization of gender. Butler and Hamnett (1994: 477) argued that gentrification was best understood in terms of the distinctive cultural practices of the new middle class, in which gender was an important part of its social and occupational formation. Smith (1996: 100) responded to the prioritization of gender arguing: '[i]t would be wrong to conclude that in women we find the premier agency behind gentrification'. More recently researchers on gentrification and gender (with many feminists amongst them) now generally accept the principal importance of class formation in understanding the relationship between gender and gentrification (see Butler, 1997; Bondi, 1999a).

Early work on gender and gentrification was conceptually based and empirically limited. This enabled researchers such as Lyons (1996), who undertook an empirical analysis of gender and gentrification in London, to pick holes in earlier authors' arguments. Lyons (1996) refuted part of Bondi's (1991) argument, especially the idea that 'gentrification has been stimulated by the increased participation of women (especially married women) in the labour force' (1991: 191). In her empirical investigation Lyons found that women's opportunities for full-time and permanent employment had been eroded more rapidly than those of men, especially at the top of the socioeconomic scale. She also found that most female gentrifiers were single and under the age of 30 and that relatively few high-status women took up owner occupation. As a result she concluded that little could be known about whether the evidence for female-led gentrification simply reflects a temporary life-cycle stage or whether it heralds a more permanent occupation of the inner city by women (see also Rose, 1996, on economic restructuring and gentrification).

Bondi's (1999a) reworking of the gentrification and gender argument through detailed empirical investigation in Edinburgh, Scotland, provides a timely analysis of the importance of the patterning of life courses in the articulation of class, gender and gentrification. Bondi's findings enrich the gentrification literature in a variety of ways. First, she finds that the association between gentrification and the professional middle class is not an exclusive one and that some gentrifiers do not pursue a class-based housing strategy. Secondly, Bondi 'lends weight' to the arguments that local specificity and indeed the temporality of gentrification are crucial to understanding how the process of gentrification is different in different places.

Bondi's recent article sheds a lot more light on the gentrification process, but it is not exhaustive. There are at least three conceptual and analytical avenues down which further investigation could prove to be informative. First, Bondi's discussion of the place-specific dimensions of class formation neglects Bridge's (1995) argument that most class constitutive effects occur outside the gentrified neighbourhood. Secondly, Bondi's usage of the term 'middle class' is a wide one; thus her ability to include people who, she argues, 'appear to be unusual among those found in studies of gentrification' (1999a: 276). There is little said about the 'new' middle class, or class fractions or practices within the middle class in general. This lack of conceptual detail allows Bondi (1999a: 277) to go so far as to argue that 'diversity among those purchasing in particular areas should prompt caution in the use of the term "gentrifiers"'. And finally, I argue more generally that a more detailed investigation of the constitution of masculinity and space would add to the gentrification and gender literature significantly. Knopp has discussed this with reference to gay gentrifiers (see later), but compare a recent article by Sommers (1998) which looks at the social construction of (straight) masculinity and its relevance to the gentrification of the Downtown Eastside neighbourhood in Vancouver, Canada.

In the literature focusing on gay gentrification, Rothenberg (1995) (looking specifically at Park Slope in New York City) argues that lesbians, like gays (see Castells, 1983), concentrate residentially and are active participants in the making of urban social space through gentrification. There is no denying that lesbians have been very visible participants in the gentrification of some neighbourhoods like Park Slope and, in Vancouver, Canada, the Commercial Drive area. There are questions, though, about how much this residential choice, as well as the other behaviours constituting gentrification, are influenced by sexuality as opposed to other dimensions of personal identity. Indeed, as Rothenberg (1995; 179) concludes: 'Park Slope functions for lesbians as it does for many of the other people who live in the neighbourhood'. The difficult challenge for researchers is to determine the complex relationship between the myriad aspects of personal identity and the constitution of a gentrified place (although as Bridge, 1995, suggests, this may not be a causal relationship). It could be fruitful to analyse the *tensions* between the constitution of, say, class and gender, class and sexuality, sexuality and gender, in the gentrification process. Equally interesting would be further research (following on from Rothenberg, 1995) on the differences between gay and lesbian gentrification. The best work on gentrification and sexuality both maintains the delicate balance between different aspects of personal identity such as class, gender and sexuality, and investigates the tensions between them. Lauria and Knopp (1985) and Knopp (1990a; 1990b) emphasized the interconnections between class, gender and sexuality in gay gentrification and pointed out some of the tensions between them. Knopp (1990b) managed to maintain a delicate balance between these different facets of personal identity in his explanation of gay gentrification, but as in the gender and gentrification literature he came back to class constitution as perhaps the most important agent. Yet, in a more recent contribution Knopp (1995: 161) footnotes his 1990b article with this comment: 'Unfortunately, I privileged class enormously in that particular piece'. This comment may be more indicative of how academics value membership in particular communities of researchers than it is of the gentrification process itself (see Lees, 1999b, on the sociology of academic knowledge production on gentrification).

2 The new middle class

In the literature on gentrification discussion of the 'new' middle class has become synonymous with discussion of the 'emancipated' gentrifier. One of the hallmarks of this new middle class has been its ability to exploit the emancipatory potential of the inner city, and indeed to create a new culturally sophisticated, urban class fraction, less conservative than the 'old' middle class. Gentrification is deemed to be a spatial manifestation of these new cultural values. This is the theme of David Ley's (1996) and Tim Butler's (1997) books on gentrification.

Ley (1996) identifies a distinctive new middle class whose culture and urbane values are rooted in the critical youth movements of the 1960s. Once they were hippies but now they are yuppies: gentrifiers in a postindustrial society. Ley's account of the history of gentrification is specific to Canada. Like Caulfield, Ley identifies the 1968 election of Liberal Prime Minister Pierre Trudeau (who embraced many of the counter-cultural values of the 1960s) as an important vehicle for gentrification in Canada. It is refreshing to read detailed and specific accounts such as these. Unlike those authors who look at gentrification as a more generalizable phenomenon, Ley (1996) appears to be more interested in the specific contextualities of gentrification, what he refers to as 'a geography of gentrification'.

Ley, like Caulfield, argues that gentrifiers move/d into the inner city because of its particular sense of place, but Ley is much more critical of this desire, both in his research subjects and in himself. The most poignant parts of Ley's book are those that appear most personal, such as his 'desire', following Kierkegaard, for transcendence beyond desire and for the integration of the religious, ethical and aesthetic realms. Ley (1996: 334–39) argues that gentrification has become increasingly unfulfilling due to a narrow focus on consumption and the aesthetic.

Butler (1997), like Caulfield and Ley, offers a personalized account embedded in his experiences of living in the inner London borough of Hackney in the early 1970s. In answering: 'is there anything distinctively different about the middle class who live in Hackney which might explain their reasons for living there?' (p. 1), Butler infuses class formation with gender and individual biographies, including the education, culture and lifestyles of his middle-class subjects. A sociologist, Butler nevertheless produces quite a geographical account of gentrification – 'space does matter' (p. 166) to his analysis. He concludes that Hackney's gentrifiers are 'different': '... there appears to be an increasing tendency towards spatial segmentation within the middle class both occupationally and residentially' (p. 161). The gentrification of Stoke Newington in Hackney, Butler suggests, is the outcome of community choice whereas the gentrification of the Docklands might be seen as the 'logic of capital' (p. 162). He elaborates:

> it does suggest that we might expect to find rather different processes at work in different places. I would therefore expect to find a rather different kind of gentrification process taking place in Docklands for example, which is based less around trying to recreate some sense of communality achieved at university in the context of counter-cultural politics ... it is suggestive that place, or more accurately that people's perception of place matters a lot ... (p. 162).

This is an insightful observation, if not entirely a novel one. Gentrification is not the same everywhere. Of course there are generalizable features, both internationally and within single cities, but there are also many important specificities that are equally important in any analysis of gentrification, and particularly in comparative research (Carpenter and Lees, 1995). In addition to these place-based differences there are also important temporal differences, as Ley's generational thesis implies. Gentrification today is quite different from gentrification in the early 1970s, late 1980s and even the early 1990s. Temporality was the focus of the stage models of gentrification back in the 1970s but, as the literature became more theoretically sophisticated, temporality seemed to all but disappear from analyses (compare Bondi, 1999a: 278). Temporality is an issue which needs further attention.

A glance at the Park Slope neighbourhood of Brooklyn suggests that researchers have some new pieces of the gentrification jigsaw to consider with regards to temporality. First, gentrifiers in Park Slope today are significantly wealthier than gentrifiers in the past. Sweat equity is not a prominent feature of the process today. Indeed, contemporary gentrifiers have to be wealthier than ever before because average prices for single-family townhouses have *doubled* since 1997 and prices for two–four family homes have increased by 15% (see Table 29.1). This rapid appreciation is linked to the dramatically increased value of the New York stock market and the financial services industry, whose profits have (re)lubricated gentrification in New York City. The relationship between gentrification and the financial services industry is an important factor distinguishing the process of gentrification in global cities like London and New York from elsewhere.

In neighbourhoods that gentrified early, such as Brooklyn Heights in New York City, many first-stage (sweat equity) gentrifiers have sold their property to new (very well-off gentrifiers), who are *regentrifying* property in the neighbourhood at this time. Here I lend support to Bondi 's (1999a) argument that we need to be much more cautious in the use of the term 'gentrifier'. For can the new people moving into Brooklyn Heights, people I call financiers or regentrifiers, be termed gentrifiers? After all, these newcomers are not displacing marginal groups, although they are renovating old housing, much of which has been little altered by first-wave gentrifiers. The so-called new middle classes, the types of people who got a foothold in neighbourhoods such as Brooklyn Heights in the 1960s and 1970s (the 1960s cohort that Ley defines), are being overtaken by financiers (a 1990s cohort) opening up new tensions within the middle classes.

Gentrification, I would argue, is a cyclical process driven largely, but not completely, by investment flows. Indeed, the gap between old gentrified property and newly gentrified property is as dramatic today in certain neighbourhoods as the difference between ungentrified and gentrified property (the rent gap) was back in the 1970s. This price differential is driving a whole new wave of high-end *super-gentrification* in favoured spots such as Brooklyn Heights in New York City, where fortunes from the financial services industry provide a lucky few with the wherewithal to undertake high-standard renovations. As Smith has commented, it is the measure of the success of the gentrification process in Brooklyn Heights that there is hardly a working class left to mount a challenge (email discussion October 1998 in the gentrification discussion group – gentrification@mailbase.ac.uk; www.gentrification.org). This kind of high-end gentrification is also a recent feature in London, in locations such as Battersea and Putney on the south bank of the Thames.

Gary Bridge's (1995) research offers a new jigsaw piece for the theses on gentrification and the new middle class. In calling for a more sustained application of class analysis to the gentrification process, Bridge extended his analysis to look at the influence of residence on class constitution. Through a detailed structural mapping, Bridge (1995: 245) found that 'most class constitutive effects occur outside the gentrified neighbourhood … or before the process has taken place …' If class constitution occurs outside the gentrified neighbourhood, what does this say about the emancipatory social practice of gentrification and the emancipatory potential of the inner city? The relationship between the constitution of place and the practice of gentrification remains vague and under-analysed and is, I suspect, much more complicated than the literature allows for (for a fresh analysis of the located politics of difference, see Fincher and Jacobs, 1998). This is one avenue that could throw up fruitful discussion in both the gentrification literature and the cultural studies/geography literature on place and identity.

	1993	1994	1995	1996	1997	Mid-1998
Single family	200 865	288 932	260 542	266 200	266 435	538 333
2–4 family	257 030	254 904	270 857	264 270	277 043	319 717
Condo	156 773	163 321	149 536	199 250	158 596	149 000
Co-operative	119 000	155 499	178 605	165 500	209 105	266 318

Table 29.1 Townhouses and apartments in Park Slope: average sale price 1993–98 (US$)
Source: *Concoran's Brooklyn Landmark*, 1998: 3.

This is also an issue that demands we study the 'geography of gentrification'.

3 The revanchist city

Neil Smith's (1996) book is the most graphic and vocal proponent of the idea of gentrification as a kind of spatialized revenge against the poor and minorities who 'stole' the inner city from the respectable classes. In contrast to the emancipatory city thesis, the revanchist city thesis considers the privileging of middle-class desires and the effects of the advancing gentrification 'frontier' on other class fractions. Reminiscent of the violent dispossessions of native peoples, the rhetoric of an urban or gentrification frontier operates, Smith argues, to conceal the underlying violence of the process. The inner city for Smith is not an emancipatory space but a combat zone in which capital, embodied by middle-class gentrifiers, battles it out, block by block, house by house, to retake the city.

Like Caulfield, Smith also dreams of equality, but beyond this the two rapidly part company. Smith's concern is not with the social practices of the middle classes *per se*, but with the effects of these practices on marginalized populations. Condemning Caulfield's notion of emancipatory social practice as 'Foucault run amok', Smith (1996: 43) exposes the inequalities associated with the gentrification process – displacement, injustice. Whilst holding on to a Marxian framework, Smith's recent book explores many issues he has been criticized for underplaying in the past. For example, he argues that both production and consumption are 'mutually implicated' in his rent gap theory. However, Smith could yet go further in considering the desires of middle-class gentrifiers (a point made some time ago by Rose, 1984: 56). By representing middle-class gentrifiers as inadvertent instruments of abstract economic forces, Smith unintentionally absolves them of any responsibility for their actions. This was something that Ley's humanism, with all its analytical weakness, always insisted upon.

Smith (1996: 101) expands on his earlier class-based analyses by considering gender constitution. However, the complex links between class and gender in the gentrification process have been developed further by Butler (1997) and Bondi (1999a). Butler (1997) offers a more nuanced class analysis, one in which fractions within the middle classes are explored, and Bondi (1999a) investigates the patterning of life courses in the articulation of class and gender practices. Yet, race/ethnicity remains strangely absent from these studies of class and gender.

In contrast, in analysing the race/class/gender terror associated with the new urban frontier, Smith (1996) also investigates the relationship between class, race and space. In the cities of the USA, which make up much of the empirical material in Smith's book, race is a pervasive issue. Race and gentrification have been the subject of earlier contributions, for example, Schaffer and Smith (1986) on the gentrification of Harlem and Smith's writings on the impact of gentrification on the Latino population in the Lower East Side. Yet, in *The new urban frontier* (Smith, 1996) race receives a new measure of attention – a further investigation into gentrification in Society Hill in the 1970s (pp. 137–39) and an updated look at the gentrification of central Harlem (pp. 140–64). In particular Smith teaches us about the 'contradictory connectedness of race and class identity resulting from gentrification' (p. 159) but, in so doing, he ends up asking as many questions as he answers (see p. 161). The issue of race and gentrification is an avenue that calls for further investigation, for detailed empirical studies of the kind that Butler (1997) and Bondi (1999a) have undertaken vis-à-vis class and gender. There is reason to believe that the relationship between race/ethnicity and gentrification in the 1990s is somewhat different from that of the 1970s. In London in the 1970s the small black population to be found in Barnsbury, in Islington, was displaced by gentrifiers with hardly a murmur. More recently, in Spitalfields, Jacobs (1996) discusses the politicization of the Bengali community and their construction of 'Banglatown' in part to curb their displacement by gentrification. In London's Docklands, the construction of an image of the authentic friendly East Ender, in an attempt to attract global investors, 'avoided a long history of racialized conflict where some white residents at least had intimidated Bangladeshi settlers in particular' (Eade and Mele, 1998: 61).

There have been many changes associated with race and gentrification. In Park Slope, Brooklyn, which attracted the black middle class as gentrifiers in the early 1990s (Lees, 1996: 464) there has been a significant 'whitening' of the population more recently. Very much against the trend in New York City public schools more generally, enrolment at local public schools reveals this 'whitening' of Park Slope's population. In the 1970s the school population was almost equally divided between white, black and Hispanic students; today 52% of the enrolment of public school 321 in the centre of Park Slope is white (Yardley, 1998: B4). The reasons for this have not been studied, but probably they would include issues such as social ecology and neighbourhood change (see Warf, 1990, on Brooklyn), black

Organizing focus or thesis	Gaps: issues not addressed
The emancipatory city	• liveability • conflict • third-world immigration
The new middle class	• race • financifiers
The revanchist city	• black gentrification • subversion/contestation by minorities

Table 29.2 A diagrammatic summary of the gaps to be found in the gentrification literature since the mid-1990s

out-migration to the south, and black gentrification in neighbouring Fort Greene and in the infamous Harlem (see Downer, 1999), as well as more familiar factors like discrimination.

To date class and gender studies of gentrification have far outweighed studies of ethnicity and race. Gentrification researchers could explore in much more detail the relationship between race, ethnicity and gentrification (compare Taylor, 1992). Like the example of black gentrification in parts of Harlem and Washington, DC, by the black middle classes, the Monster Houses in Vancouver, Canada (Ley, 1995) might be thought of as Chinese gentrification. What these examples point to are the problems with the implicit race and class oppositions organizing the gentrification literature: middle-class gentrifiers/ incomers (white) versus working-class residents/displaced (black). In the revanchist city thesis racial/ethnic minorities are more often than not represented as victims – Jacobs' (1996) study of the affirmation of Bengali identity and entrepreneurial spirit in the creation of 'Banglatown' in the Spitalfields area of London suggests otherwise. Table 29. 2 summarizes some of the gaps to be found in the gentrification writings published since the mid-1990s.

4 A new look at gentrification?

The companion articles by Redfern (1997a; 1997b) stand out from the rest of the recent gentrification literature in their profession to be 'a new look at gentrification'. Redfern (1997a) argues that gentrification studies are organized around two recognized traditions of explanation – the supply-side account of gentrification offered by Neil Smith and the demand-side explanation offered by David Ley. Starting with the question how gentrification

occurs, rather than why, Redfern tries to break 'the theoretical logjam' of gentrification studies by examining the role of domestic technologies in the process of gentrification. Gentrification, Redfern (1997b) contends, was only possible once the price of domestic conveniences had fallen enough (since the 1950s in the UK) relative to house prices to make investment in older properties worth while.

While Redfern (1997a) provides a very insightful overview and critique of the literature, his thesis about the necessary relationship between domestic technology and gentrification is unpersuasive (Lyons, 1998). Redfern makes a variety of unsubstantiated claims about gentrification, many of which reflect the empirical limitations of his case study of Islington, London. Key to his explanation of gentrification and its association with the falling price of domestic technology is the process of abandonment (1997b: 1335–36, 1347). Yet, he does not define what he means by abandonment. Relying on early work by a variety of authors, including Hamnett and Williams (1980), Redfern neglects more recent work in the gentrification literature that asserts that abandonment did not occur in London because 'England did not experience a postwar, state funded suburbanization programme which increased inner city abandonment as did the US ... Moreover a postwar housing shortage in England minimized abandonment' (Lees, 1994b: 207). Redfern also neglected to consider the importance of tenurial transformation (the transformation of property from rented to private ownership when their leaseholds expired) which made gentrification in the borough of Islington, and in London more generally, spatially and temporally uneven (see Hamnett and Randolph, 1986; Lees, 1994b). These empirical specificities are important because the transfer and transformation of urban household property were a significant factor in the gentrification process in London. Following Redfern's domestic technology-driven explanation of the process, one would expect the first cases of gentrification to have occurred in the USA, where the prices of domestic conveniences were cheaper. But they did not – they occurred in England (Glass, 1964), where tenurial transformation created a value gap into which gentrification leapt.

Redfern's thesis appears as a technological determinism that ignores the underlying social relations of the gentrification process. Focused on technology as a necessary pre-condition for gentrification, Redfern has little to say about the ongoing process now that cookers and washing machines have become widespread features of the domestic landscape. His technological determinism leads him to the strange conclusion that gentrification 'is a transient and historically unique phenomenon' (1997b: 1335). But what about the recent examples of post-recession gentrification in the UK and the USA? What about the impact of gentrification on British and American government urban policy? Like the syntheses he criticizes Redfern's thesis leaves a lot out. Moreover, the retrospective nature of his thesis does nothing to break the theoretical logjam or to explain the changes I have identified.

III TOWARDS A PROGRESSIVE RESEARCH PROGRAMME ON GENTRIFICATION

That gentrification has proven to be a resilient term despite its elusive and sometimes contradictory qualities suggests that it remains important to 'unpack' its characteristics.

(Bondi, 1999a: 279)

Since the mid-1990s writing on gentrification has been much less energetic and much less adversarial, and some real analytical progress has been made. The analysis of class and gender has become much more sophisticated (see Butler, 1997; Bondi, 1999a) and the issue of race is becoming more prominent (Jacobs, 1996; Smith, 1996; Eade and Mele, 1998). More recently, gentrification researchers have begun to question how we have conceptualized gentrification to date (Butler, 1997; Redfern, 1997a, 1997b; Bondi, 1999a; Lees, 1996; 1998; 1999a; 1999b; Hamnett, in progress), as such the gentrification literature is moving forward. It is the aim of this article to try to increase the pace of this momentum by outlining a number of important research avenues for researchers to think about and perhaps travel down.

I believe that the way to re-energize the study of gentrification is to focus on what Ley (1996) has called the 'geography of gentrification'. It is the 'geography of gentrification' that emerges as the common denominator for both the recent changes in the gentrification process and the holes in the gentrification literature I have identified. There are four (inter-related) 'new wrinkles' which research into the 'geography of gentrification' needs to address: 1) financifiers – super-gentrification; 2) third-world immigration – the global city; 3) black/ethnic minority gentrification – race and gentrification; and 4) liveability/urban policy – discourse on gentrification. I turn now to outline the significance of each of these in order to open up avenues for future research on gentrification.

In addressing the issue of *financifiers* gentrification researchers must return, as Bondi (1999a) did albeit inadvertently, to a consideration of temporality. For instance, I would suggest that the notion of urban community has changed, making studies such as Caulfield's (1994) less useful for studying the contemporary gentrification process. Gentrifiers moving into Brooklyn Heights and Park Slope today, for example, are quite different from those who moved into these two neighbourhoods in the 1970s. As a result the neighbourhoods' identities are changing. Wyly and Hammel (1999) have also found that capital flows are being redirected and focused on a few highly desirable neighbourhoods. The outcome is that the gentrifiers who starred in Caulfield's and Ley's books, those who embraced tolerance and diversity, like the hippies in 1970s Park Slope, for the most part no longer star. Today Park Slope's gentrifiers are well to-do folk from Manhattan, lawyers and financial consultants, financifiers who buy houses and apartments as city residences. They often also own property in suburban Long Island, Up-State New York or in 'the country' – Connecticut, etc. – where they spend their weekends. The whole concept of urban community is in transition, the financifiers' ties to the community, to the neighbourhood, are much weaker than those of the gentrifiers of old. The financifier has a much less deeply rooted relationship with his or her neighbourhood – as with the highly mobile capital they work with, these super-gentrifiers are more mobile too – their identity is arguably more fluid than rooted. As such, the term gentrifier may not even be appropriate for these new, well heeled renovators, these *super-gentrifiers* who have displaced sweat equity by employing their own architects, interior designers and builders. In fact there has been much debate over the last year about the definition of 'gentrification' (see the online gentrification discussion group – www.gentrification.org). A variety of questions emerge: are financifiers gentrifiers as such? Are they members of the new middle class? Are there conflicts between financifiers and the new middle class? What are the similarities and differences between this type of gentrification and earlier gentrification? And so on. Wyly and Hammel's (1999) study of post-recession gentrification in the USA echoes some of these questions, for they too urge the importance of looking at temporality. Their essay reveals the important questions on the historical continuity between current processes and previous generations of neighbourhood change that the resurgence of the gentrification process poses.

Contextuality and therein scale are also significant – for super-gentrification will likely only occur in global cities, such as London and New York, where the financial and information industries are primarily located, or perhaps in capital cities such as Edinburgh, Scotland, which has a similar employment structure to London.

Contextuality and scale are also relevant to a consideration of *third-world immigrants and the gentrification process*. Global cities, racially/ethnically segregated cities and multicultural cities higher up the urban hierarchy will feature prominently in studies of gentrification that consider the juxtaposition of people from radically different cultural backgrounds – that is third-world immigrants with gentrifiers. Jacobs' (1996) study of Spitalfields in London outlines the conflictual politics of race and nation that often result. Her study underlines the fact that 1) gentrifiers are not always liberal and tolerant; 2) gentrification is not a benign process; and 3) gentrifiers do not hold a monopoly on proactivity.

As in the case of third-world immigrants, *black and ethnic minority gentrification* has scarcely been researched either (see Schaffer and Smith, 1986; Taylor, 1992; Smith, 1996, for research into black gentrification). Black gay gentrifiers in the Castro District of San Francisco in the 1970s came up against racism. This distorts the image of gentrification as liberal tolerance. It also points to the complex intricacies within social cleavages – black, gay and middle class and white gay racist gentrifier. Blacks (and other ethnic groups such as Latinos), as seen in Smith's (1996) 'revanchist city thesis', are often portrayed as the 'victims' of the gentrification process. But blacks can also be the 'agents' of gentrification (see Taylor, 1992; Lees, 1996; Downer, 1999). Black gentrification is not without its problems. As Taylor (1992) outlines black gentrifiers (in Harlem) are confronted with a 'dilemma of difference' as they alternate between their work in white downtown and their home in black uptown, and

the class differences between themselves and less wealthy Harlem residents.

In 1986 Schaffer and Smith predicted that, because the number of wealthy households in Harlem were relatively small, continued gentrification would likely lead to white in-migration and the displacement of blacks. This prophecy seems to be coming true elsewhere – as I outlined earlier in this article – although Park Slope, Brooklyn, was a magnet for black gentrification in the early 1990s, by the end of the decade the neighbourhood had grown predominantly white. I would like to see more detailed studies of how race and ethnicity intersect with cleavages such as class, gender and sexuality in the gentrification process. The racial/ethnic issues associated with the gentrification process take on a different guise according to the communities involved. For example, Ley (1995) discusses the cultural conflicts between Hong Kong Chinese immigrants and the Anglo middle classes in gentrified Kerrisdale, inner Vancouver. Mitchell (1998) discusses the political repercussions of large-scale immigration from Hong Kong on the pre-existing Chinese community in downtown Vancouver (also compare Anderson, 1998, who tries to move beyond a cultural politics of race polarity). The issues surrounding race/ethnicity and gentrification are much more complex than black/Latino (displacee) versus white (gentrifier). As gentrification spreads outwards from the inner city towards the suburbs (Smith and DeFilippis, 1999, have recently found evidence of the operation of Smith's rent gap in the suburbs) these issues will continue to be significant.

I would also like to see a more updated and rigorous deconstruction of not only the process of gentrification but also *discourses on gentrification*. A closer look at how gentrification is represented (see Smith, 1986; Lees, 1996; Bondi, 1998a) and how knowledge on gentrification is produced and constructed (for example, Lees, 1999a; 1999b) will shed further light on this subject. Research into the sociology of academic knowledge production on gentrification will tell us as much, if not more, about the literature on gentrification as a literature review that compares authors' theoretical frameworks, conceptual ideas and empirical research. As part of a consideration of discourse and the construction of knowledge the importance of methodology has rarely been stressed in analyses of gentrification, despite the considerable interest in the differing outcomes of different theoretical frameworks (for example, Redfern, 1997a; 1997b). Different methodological frameworks obviously produce quite different accounts of gentrification. If we compare Smith (1996) and Butler's

(1997) methodologies we find one reason why their accounts are so different. I have written about this elsewhere:

> Butler's is an intersubjective exploration of the question: 'is there anything distinctively different about the middle class who live in Hackney which might explain their reasons for living there?' (page 1). To answer this question he relies on interviews with nearly 250 people. From these biographies he sets out to describe the lives of these people and to analyse (new middle) class constitution through the correlation of 'social being' and 'social consciousness' (page 4). Given his interview data it is no surprise that matters of lifestyle and subjectivity are so much more prominent in Butler's text than in Smith's, whose real-estate-value maps and stark images of local resistance to gentrification paint a picture of class struggle as black and white as his photographs. The contrast between these alternative views of gentrification has usually been explained in terms of theory, but it is also one of methodology. Butler's qualitative sources open a different window on social reality than Smith's sources do. Gentrification researchers need to think more carefully about how their research methods – as well as their theory – inflect their understandings'.
> (Lees, 1998: 2258)

I have argued that deconstructing discourse on gentrification is important – and I would add that it is nowhere more so than when we consider recent urban policy statements/initiatives by governments in both the UK and the USA. As I argued at the beginning of this article, the British Urban Task Force's report *Towards an urban renaissance* (DETR, 1999) and the US Department of Housing and Urban Development's *The state of the cities* report (1999) both interweave urban regeneration policy with gentrification practices and environmentalism. They subtly and not so subtly promote gentrification as a blueprint for a civilized city life. Gentrification in the guise of urban liveability/sustainability is constructed as the medicine for the problems endured by British and American cities. Analysis of how far gentrification has become a state-driven process and in this a consideration of the context of wider political forces is certainly worth while. As Wyly and Hammel (1999) indicate in their title, in an obvious play on Berry's (1985) maxim 'islands of renewal in seas of decay', the new urban reality may well be 'islands of decay in seas of renewal'. But this vision of a new urban reality by both British and American urban policy-makers is premised on a 'one size fits

all' remedy. In other words, the successes of gentrification strategies in global cities such as London and New York are being offered as blueprints for cities further down the urban hierarchy. I would argue that, for the most part, these strategies are unlikely to work for the Liverpools of the UK and the Lowells of the USA. For example, urban policy-makers in the declining northeastern city of Portland, Maine, USA, have adopted the types of strategies promoted both explicitly and implicitly in the two reports. These strategies have included a plan for liveability and sustainability – *Downtown vision: a celebration of urban living and a plan for the future of Portland* (City of Portland, Maine, 1991); a plan for an Arts District; the upgrading of the Old Port; the gentrification of the city's older residential neighbourhoods; the construction of a $5 million Portland Public Market; new downtown office blocks; and so on (see Knopp and Kujawa, 1993). This medicine has mostly failed to cure Portland's urban (economic) ills, but like the British Urban Task Force and American HUD, Portland's urban policy-makers still have the kind of faith that sees boarded-up buildings and empty piers and abandoned storefronts as opportunities.

Both context and temporality are sidelined in *Towards an urban renaissance* and *The state of the cities* report, as indeed they have been by urban policy-makers in Portland, Maine, too. Much remains to be learnt about the 'geography of gentrification'. Eade and Mele (1998) have begun 'to open up this Pandora's box' by comparing gentrification in the East Village of New York City with that in Spitalfields and Docklands in London. The 'geography of gentrification', I would argue, works on a number of different levels – international comparison, intranational, and citywide comparison. The differences between Caulfield's more utopian perspective on gentrification and Smith's more dystopian perspective are partly rooted in their respective research sites – the relatively liberal and benign Canadian inner city and the 'combat zone' of the visceral and dangerous US inner city. Moreover, in the literature on gentrification we can see that even within a single city gentrification of a similar time period has a quite different geography depending on its site, such that Butler (1997) produces a much less conflictual account of gentrification in London, specifically Hackney, than does Jacobs (1996), who discusses Spitalfields. More detailed research into the 'geography of gentrification' would enable us to say whether the gentrification of Detroit is the late 1990s version of the gentrification of Harlem. For Harlem was, and Detroit is, a seemingly unlikely target for gentrification (see Wyly and

Hammel, 1999, on Harlem and Detroit). It would also enable us to consider the merits or dangers of cities further down the urban hierarchy taking on board the gentrification practices of cities higher up the urban hierarchy, cities with a very different geography.

In conclusion, the gentrification literature has come a long way over the last 30 years but, as the above discussion suggests, there is still room for manœuvre, for progressive research. I caution against explanatory closure, a closure that gentrification researchers, more often than not, seem compelled to search for. It will be more productive for us to keep 'issues open and tensions alive', to follow a 'Brechtian strategy' (Harvey, 1995: 95) of keeping conclusions on gentrification open. A more detailed examination of the 'geography of gentrification' would constitute a progressive research programme and lead us to rethink the 'true' value of gentrification as a practical solution to urban decline in cities around the world.

ACKNOWLEDGEMENTS

Many thanks to my referees for their comments. These were very useful in the revision of this article. Thanks also to the online Gentrification Network, of which I am a member, for its musings have also informed this piece.

Notes

1 The topic of gentrification is far from exhausted. The study of displacement has to date been inadequate, the implication of gentrification in the process of globalization and global city formation has not been investigated in any great detail, and studies of the transnational nature of housing production are still in their infancy (see Badcock, 1995; Olds, 1998).

2 Elizabeth Wilson (1991) argues that the city has long provided emancipatory opportunities for women – for a critique, see Ravetz (1996) and Bondi (1998b).

REFERENCES

Anderson, K. 1998: Sites of difference: beyond a cultural politics of race polarity. In Fincher, R. and Jacobs, J., editors, *Cities of difference*, New York and London: Guilford Press, 201–25.

Badcock, B. 1993: Notwithstanding the exaggerated claims, residential revitalization really is changing the form of some western cities: a response to Bourne. *Urban Studies* 30, 191–95.

——1995: Building upon the foundations of gentrification: inner city housing development in Australia in the 1990s. *Urban Geography* 16, 70–90.

Barthes, R. 1986: Semiology and the urban. In Gottdiener, M. and Lagopoulos, A., editors, *The city and the sign: an introduction to urban semiotics*, New York: Columbia University Press, 87–98.

Berry, B. 1985: Islands of renewal in seas of decay. In Peterson, P., editor, *The new urban reality*, Washington, DC: The Brookings Institution, 69–96.

Bondi, L. 1991: Gender divisions and gentrification: a critique. *Transactions, Institute of British Geographers* 16, 190–98.

——1998a: Sexing the city. In Fincher, R. and Jacobs, J., editors, *Cities of difference*, New York and London: Guilford Press, 177–200.

——1998b: Gender, class and urban space. *Urban Geography* 19, 160–85.

——1999a: Gender, class and gentrification: enriching the debate. *Environment and Planning D: Society and Space* 17, 261–82.

——1999b: Between the woof and the weft: a response to Loretta Lees. *Environment and Planning D: Society and Space* 17, 253–55.

Bourne, L. 1993: The demise of gentrification? A commentary and prospective view. *Urban Geography* 14, 95–107.

Boyle, M. 1995: Still top of our agenda?: Neil Smith and the reconciliation of capital and consumer approaches to gentrification. *Scottish Geographical Magazine* 111, 119–23.

Bridge, G. 1995: The space for class: on class analysis in the study of gentrification. *Transactions, Institute of British Geographers* 20, 236–47.

Butler, T. 1997: *Gentrification and the middle classes*. Aldershot: Ashgate.

Butler, T. and **Hamnett, C.** 1994: Gentrification, class and gender: some comments on Warde's gentrification of consumption. *Environment and Planning D: Society and Space* 12, 477–93.

Carpenter, J. and **Lees, L.** 1995: Gentrification in New York, London and Paris: an international comparison. *International Journal of Urban and Regional Research* 19, 287–303.

Castells, M. 1983: The city and the grass roots. Berkeley, CA: University of California Press.

Caulfield, J. 1989: Gentrification and desire. *Canadian Review of Sociology and Anthropology* 26, 617–32.

——1994: *City form and everyday life; Toronto's gentrification and critical social practice.* Toronto: University of Toronto Press.

City of Portland, Maine 1991: *Downtown vision: a celebration of urban living and a plan for the future of Portland – Maine's center for commerce and culture.* City of Portland, ME.

Concoran's Brooklyn Landmark 1998: *Mid-year 1998 report.* New York: Concoran.

Department of the Environment, Transport and the Regions 1999: *Towards an urban renaissance: sharing the vision* (http: //www. regeneration.detr.gov.uk/urbanren/1. html).

Downer, L. 1999: Melting the ghetto: METROPOLIS: in hard-core Harlem. *The Financial Times* 26 June.

Eade, J. and **Mele, C.** 1998: Global processes and customised landscapes: the 'eastern promise' of New York and London. *Rising East: The Journal of East London Studies* 1, 52–73.

Fincher, R. and **Jacobs, J.,** editors, 1998: *Cities of difference.* New York and London: Guilford Press.

Glass, R. 1964: *London: aspects of change.* London: MacGibbon and Kee.

Hamnett, C. 1991: The blind men and the elephant: the explanation of gentrification. *Transactions, Institute of British Geographers* 16, 259–79.

——1999: *Winners and losers: home ownership in modern Britain.* London and Philadelphia, PA: UCL Press.

——in progress: In praise of the middle classes? Gentrification, suburbanization, and segregation. Unpublished manuscript available from the author, Department of Geography, King's College London, Strand, London WC2R 2LS, UK.

Hamnett, C. and **Randolph, B.** 1986: Tenurial transformation and the flat break-up market in London: the British condo experience. In Smith, N, and Williams, P., editors, *Gentrification of the city,* Boston, MA: Allen & Unwin, 121–52.

Hamnett, C. and **Williams, P.** 1980: Social change in London: a study of gentrification. *Urban Affairs Quarterly* 15, 469–87.

Harvey, D. 1995: Militant particularism and global ambition: the conceptual politics of place, space, and environment in the work of Raymond Williams. *Social Text* 42, 69–98.

Jacobs, J. 1996: *Edge of empire: postcolonialism and the city.* London and New York: Routledge.

Keith, M. and **Pile, S.,** editors, 1993: *Place and the politics of identity.* London and New York: Routledge.

Knopp, L. 1990a: Exploiting the rent gap: the theoretical significance of using illegal appraisal schemes to encourage gentrification in New Orleans. *Urban Geography* 11, 48–64.

——1990b: Some theoretical implications of gay involvement in an urban landmarket. *Political Geography Quarterly* 9, 337–52.

——1995: Sexuality and urban space: a framework for analysis. In Bell, D, and Valentine, G., editors, *Mapping desire,* London: Routledge, 149–61.

Knopp, L. and **Kujawa, R.** 1993: Ideology and urban landscapes: conceptions of the market in Portland, Maine. *Antipode* 25, 114–39.

KQED, Inc. 1997: *The Castro* (an episode of 'Neighborhoods: the hidden cities of San Francisco'). KQED: San Francisco, CA.

Lauria, M. and **Knopp, L.** 1985: Toward an analysis of the role of gay communities in the urban renaissance. *Urban Geography* 6, 152–69.

Lees, L. 1994a: Rethinking gentrification: beyond the positions of economics or culture. *Progress in Human Geography* 18, 137–50.

——1994b: Gentrification in London and New York: an Atlantic gap? *Housing Studies* 9, 199–217.

——1996: In the pursuit of difference: representations of gentrification. *Environment and Planning A* 28, 453–70.

——1998: Review of *The new urban frontier* by Neil Smith and *Gentrification and the middle classes* by Tim Butler. *Environment and Planning A* 30, 2257–60.

——1999a: Warping the cloth that academics weave: a reply to Bondi (and Rose and Smith). *Environment and Planning D: Society and Space* 17, 255–57.

——1999b: The weaving of gentrification discourse and the boundaries of the gentrification community. *Environment and Planning D: Society and Space* 17, 127–32.

Lees, L. and **Bondi, L.** 1995: De-gentrification and economic recession: the case of New York City. *Urban Geography* 16, 234–53.

Lees, L. and **Demeritt, D.** 1998: Envisioning the livable city: the interplay of 'Sin City' and 'Sim City' in Vancouver's planning discourse. *Urban Geography* 19, 332–59.

Ley, D. 1995: Between Europe and Asia: the case of the missing sequoias. *Ecumene* 2, 185–210.

——1996: *The new middle class and the remaking of the central city.* Oxford: Oxford University Press.

Lueck, T. 1991: Prices decline as gentrification ebbs: the future is uncertain in areas that bloomed too late in the 1980s. *The New York Times* 29 September, Section 10.

Lyons, M. 1996: Employment, feminisation, and gentrification in London, 1981–93. *Environment and Planning A* 28, 341–56.

——1998: Neither chaos, nor stark simplicity: a comment on a 'new look at gentrification'. *Environment and Planning A* 30, 367–70.

Markusen, A. 1981: City spatial structure, women's household, and national urban policy. In Stimpson, C., Dixler, E., Nelson, M. and Yatrakis, K., editors, *Women and the American city*, Chicago, IL: University of Chicago Press, 20–41.

Merry, S. 1981: *Urban danger: life in a neighborhood of strangers.* Philadelphia, PA: Temple University Press.

Mitchell, K. 1998: Reworking democracy: immigration and community politics in Vancouver's Chinatown. *Political Geography* 17, 729–50.

The Observer 1999: Urban rebirth: new dawn breaks on city streets, 27 June, 16–17.

Olds, K. 1998: Globalization and urban change: tales from Vancouver via Hong Kong. *Urban Geography* 19, 360–85.

Pratt, G. and **Hanson, S.** 1994: Geography and the construction of difference. *Gender, Place and Culture* 1, 5–29.

Ravetz, A. 1996: Reevaluations. 'The Sphinx in the city'. *City* 1, 155–61.

Redfern, P. 1997a: A new look at gentrification. 1. Gentrification and domestic technologies. *Environment and Planning A* 29, 1275–96.

——1997b: A new look at gentrification: 2. A model of gentrification. *Environment and Planning A* 29, 1335–54.

Rose, D. 1984: Rethinking gentrification: beyond the uneven development of Marxist urban theory. *Environment and Planning D: Society and Space* 1, 47–74.

——1996: Economic restructuring and the diversification of gentrification in the 1980s: a view from a marginal metropolis. In Caulfield, J. and Peake, L., editors, *City lives and city forms: critical research and Canadian urbanism*, Toronto: University of Toronto Press, 131–72.

Rothenberg, T. 1995: 'And she told two friends': lesbians creating urban social space. In Bell, D. and Valentine, G., editors, *Mapping Desire*, London and New York: Routledge: 165–81.

Schaffer, R. and **Smith, N.** 1986: The gentrification of Harlem? *Annals of the Association of American Geographers* 76, 347–65.

Smith, N. 1986: Gentrification, the frontier, and the restructuring of urban space. In Smith, N. and Williams, P., editors, *Gentrification of the city*, Boston, MA: Allen and Unwin, 15–34.

——1996: *The new urban frontier: gentrification and the revanchist city.* London and New York: Routledge.

Smith, N. and **DeFilippis, J.** 1999: The reassertion of economics: 1990s gentrification in the Lower East Side. *International Journal of Urban and Regional Research* 23, 638–53.

Sommers, J. 1998: Mapping men: masculinity and space in downtown Vancouver, 1950–1990. *Urban Geography* 19, 287–310.

The Sunday Times 1999: Urban guerillas, 11 April, 2.

Sykora, L. 1996: Economic and social restructuring and gentrification in Prague. *Acta Facultatis Rerum Naturalium Universitatis Comenianae (Geographica)* 37, 71–81.

Taylor, M. 1992: Can you go home again? Black gentrification and the dilemma of difference. *Berkeley Journal of Sociology* 37, 121–38.

US Department of Housing and Urban Development 1999: *The state of the cities* (http://www.huduser.org/publications/polleg/tso c99/tsoc_99.html).

Warde, A. 1991: Gentrification as consumption: issues of class and gender. *Environment and Planning D: Society and Space* 9, 223–32.

Warf, B. 1990: The reconstruction of social ecology and neighborhood change in Brooklyn. *Environment and Planning D: Society and Space* 8, 73–96.

Wilson, E. 1991: *The Sphinx in the city: urban life, the control of disorder, and women.* London: Virago Press.

Wright, P. 1992: The fall from grace and favour. *Guardian*, 6 May, 23.

Wyly, E. and **Hammel, D.** 1999: Islands of decay in seas of renewal: housing policy and the resurgence of gentrification. *Housing Policy Debate* 10, 711–71.

Yardley, J. 1998: Park slope reshaped by money: as rents and prices rise, some fear for neighborhood's soul. *The New York Times*, 14 March, B1, B4.

——1999: Perils amid lure of gentrification; slaying brings shock to a Brooklyn neighborhood. *The New York Times*, 11 March, B3.

Young, I. 1991: *Justice and the politics of difference.* Princeton, NJ: Princeton University Press.

Zukin, S. 1995: *The culture of cities.* Oxford: Blackwell.

30

"Social Capital, Gentrification and Neighbourhood Change in London: A Comparison of Three South London Neighbourhoods"

From *Urban Studies* (2001)

Tim Butler and Garry Robson

1. INTRODUCTION

The concept of social capital has, in the majority of British analyses, been focused on issues of social exclusion amongst disadvantaged groups (Maloney et al., 1999; Smith, 1998) and used to explore and account for the mechanisms of economic and social marginalisation. The emphasis has been on thinking about how partnerships between 'horizontal' local communities, associations and interest-groups might more successfully interact with the 'vertical', intermediate institutions (Coleman, 1988) of, for example, local government in order to facilitate the improved integration and economic renewal of marginalised groups. The dynamics of social capital have therefore largely been framed in terms of improving the situation of communities thought to be impoverished in respect of their social capital 'stocks'.

However, current empirical research into the middle-class gentrification of inner London (Robson and Butler, 2001) requires us to approach the issue of social capital from a very different position. Our analysis reveals that amongst those groups which have been engaged in 'remaking' various inner urban neighbourhoods—none of whom can be thought of as excluded in any sense—issues of social capital are of central importance. Each of the three case-study areas presented here is characterised

by different modes and levels of social capital resources and deployment. These are vitally important in the on-going social processes through which formerly deprived or 'undesirable' areas are transformed and made congenial to the requirements of middle-class life.

Current enthusiasm for social capital, however, may be in danger of reifying and oversimplifying a concept with important heuristic potential. But the latter can be maximised once it understood that social capital is *not* a novel sociological concept (Portes, 1998, p. 21) and if it is theoretically reintegrated into an analysis of its relations with the other key forms of economic and cultural capital. Our purpose here is to examine the dynamics of these forms of capital in the middle-class transformation of three inner London localities. In Bourdieu's (1986) model economic capital refers to monetary income and other financial resources and assets, finding its institutional expression in property rights. Cultural capital exists in various forms, expressing the embodied dispositions and resources of the *habitus*. This form of capital has two analytically distinguishable strains, incorporated, in the form of education and knowledge, and symbolic, being the capacity to define and legitimise cultural, moral and aesthetic values, standards and styles. Social capital refers to the sum of actual and potential resources that can be mobilised through membership in social networks of actors and organisations. Critically, this involves

> transforming contingent relations, such as those of neighbourhood, the workplace, or even kinship, into relationships that are at once necessary and elective, implying durable obligations subjectively felt (feelings of gratitude, respect, friendship, etc.).
> (Bourdieu, 1986, pp. 249–250)

This makes this form of capital more of a relational phenomenon than a tangible, or easily quantifiable, resource.

In this overall model of the relations of capital, understanding economic and social outcomes is achieved through analysis of the interaction between the three different forms. This we attempt in what follows, focusing on areas of inner south London and the economic and cultural resources, social networks and normative structures through which they have been gentrified—that is, at how differing sections of the middle class strive to create and maintain urban situations for the consolidation of prosperity and realise varying ideals of city living that exist within the middle classes. These are understood as core aspects of the necessity for middle-class groups to develop strategies of self-protection and

cultural reproduction in increasingly competitive circumstances. Although we are well aware that middle-class social networks tend to be extensive rather than local (Allan, 1989; Willmott, 1987), we focus here on those situated patterns of affect and reciprocity clearly associated with, though by no means inevitable in, contemporary gentrification processes.

2. THE RESEARCH

The research discussed in this article forms part of a project 'The middle class and the future of London' being undertaken for the ESRC *Cities: Competitiveness and Cohesion Programme*.[1] The research is a project into the on-going gentrification of inner London and draws on fieldwork conducted in eight areas (see Figure 30.1), three of which are sub-areas of Docklands. Of the remainder, two are in north London in Barnsbury in Islington and London Fields in Hackney. The remaining three areas, which provide the basis for this article, are all in south London: 'Telegraph Hill' at New Cross in Lewisham, Brixton in Lambeth and 'Between the Commons' at Battersea in Wandsworth.

The research project was conceived to investigate the pattern of gentrification in inner London

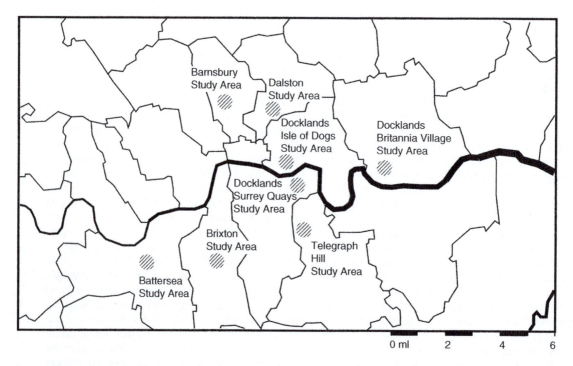

Figure 30.1 London, showing the study areas

and in particular to understand the variability of the process. One criticism of existing approaches to gentrification is that they tend to see gentrification as a more or less homogeneous process—whatever their other differences, neither Smith (1996) nor Ley (1996) appear to explore differences *within* the gentrification process. Our hypothesis is that different middle-class groups would be attracted to different areas and this would be determined by a range of factors, in addition to what they might be able to afford in particular housing markets. We believe that these divisions within the middle class are significant and reflect a broad range of cultural and 'lifestyle' factors and that they have a clear spatial manifestation (see Robson and Butler, 2001, for more on the theoretical assumptions). This determined our choice of areas. First, we made a clear distinction between what Warde (1991, p. 224) calls gentrification by 'collective action' as opposed to by 'capital'. We argued that almost exclusively in London, the latter had been confined to the Docklands area—hence our choice of three sub-areas there (see Figure 30.1). The history of gentrification in London over the past nearly 40 years has been largely one of upgrading of mainly 19th century property by individuals or small-scale developers. However, we argue that different areas appeal to and attract different sections of the middle class (Butler, 1997). This determined our selection of areas: broadly, we selected them to include areas that had been in long-term gentrification (Barnsbury, Battersea and Telegraph Hill) versus more recent areas (Brixton and London Fields—and, of course, differently, Docklands). At the same time, we looked at areas which we had identified as appealing to different social groups (broadly following Savage *et al.*'s (1992) distinction between 'corporates' and 'welfare professionals'). Telegraph Hill, London Fields and possibly Barnsbury we felt would be emblematic of the latter group, whilst Battersea would appeal to 'corporates'.[2]

Our research design called for us to complete 75 in-depth interviews with gentrifiers in each area (or 25 in each of the three Docklands sub-areas). In order to generate this number of successful interviews, we estimated that we would need to contact 750 potential interviewees; this proved largely accurate. Non-response, non-gentrifiers and geographical mobility accounted for this—we worded the letter sent to all potential respondents carefully to exclude all those who did not fit into our category. The sampling frame was drawn from the latest available electoral register, a document whose inaccuracy is well known. Despite these problems, we believe that our respondents are largely representative of the middle-class populations in each of our areas. The main characteristics of the three areas are summarised in Tables 30.1 to 30.3 ($N = 75$ in all cases).

	Telegraph Hill	Battersea	Brixton
Father's occupation			
Professional	37	38	47
Managerial	12	35	7
Brought up in London and South East	38	44	60
Education			
Privately educated	14	24	8
State grammar school educated	47	32	32
University graduate	86	85	90
Oxford/Cambridge	10	10	6

Table 30.1 Respondents' background (percentages)

	Telegraph Hill	Battersea	Brixton
Husband/wife	64	48	35
Opposite-sex partner	14	7	15
Same-sex partner	1	3	11
Multiperson	4	8	6
Single person	16	34	33
Dependent children	62	38	35
Household income >£100 000 per annum	7	15	6

Table 30.2 Respondents' household structure

Employment sector	Telegraph Hill ($N = 58$)	Battersea ($N = 61$)	Brixton ($N = 58$)
Public	40	16	38
Private	19	48	26
Self-employed	33	33	28
Voluntary	9	3	9

Table 30.3 Employment characteristics (percentages)

3. TELEGRAPH HILL

Ten minutes by train from London Bridge, this is an enclave in Lewisham in south-east London surrounded on two sides by extensive council housing, on the other two by large areas of more differentiated, mixed housing. Its readily identifiable central core is comprised of a series of four main streets. These slope up to Telegraph Hill park, which has two sections, from New Cross Road. These four main streets, and the smaller ones which cross-cut them, are of substantial, and by now mostly renovated, Victorian housing stock. The central area has a quiet, leafy and overwhelmingly calm aspect, with little or no commercial infrastructure: the only shop is a large branch of Sainsbury's situated immediately to the north of the study area across the main road. Telegraph Hill was probably 'settled' earlier than either Battersea or Brixton by its middle-class incomers. Its formerly shabby and multi-occupied aspect changed decisively at the time of its 'discovery' in the early 1980s. A process of more or less wholesale 'improvement' continued throughout that decade, peaking in the boom at its end. A comparatively static housing market and relatively low population turnover reflect its status as a stable, coherent and relatively isolated 'village' in inner-city south-east London. The far less salubrious areas of Deptford, New Cross and Peckham, for example, are close at hand. It is characterised by a notably family-based middle-class community.

A sense of urban 'vibrancy', in which individuals of many types and dispositions are thrown together in a volatile public space, is all-but-absent from daily life in the interior of Telegraph Hill. The relatively stable social boundedness of the area is mirrored in the spatial boundaries which delimit and largely define the area. Here the psychological and the social overlap in a cognitive map of the locality which serves to keep the chaotic 'there' (Peckham and Deptford) both at bay and distinct from the 'here' of a middle-class urban village. The 'hill', as it were, rises as an island of stability and 'belonging' out of a surrounding sea of chaos and diversity.

(Tina, 43) I love it here. I had a rootless childhood, and I love the very strong sense of community that the children have. It's like a village in the centre of London, it has that kind of support system. And the kids feel they belong here. I love the idea of their friendships carrying on over time … I wouldn't move away from here to anywhere else in England.

(Susan, 33) The mix of people means a lot to us, the social mix—actors, artists, people from all sorts of backgrounds. There's a lack of stereotyping, they're not all working in the City, or as solicitors. It's an intelligent group of people, on the whole.

Susan's reference to the 'social mix' is worthy of comment. It is a common response by members of a group which, in social and cultural terms, is very homogeneous, and who see diversity as the mixing of liberal, middle-class occupations. In this bounded, largely consensual and reflexive middle-class 'community', it is clear that residents are more networked and take more care in cultivating those networks with the aim of maintaining and reproducing the area's prosperity and sense of itself, than elsewhere in our study. This networking is based on a small number of key local institutions and associations: the primary school, the community centre (focus of the Telegraph Hill Association and its activities) and Telegraph Hill park, an absolutely vital public space or urban 'village green'. The local public sphere is therefore more concentrated, localised and characterised by successfully pooled and deployed social capital than in the other two areas and is far less organised around a commercial cultural infrastructure of bars, restaurants and clubs.

(Margaret, 44) The area is very mixed socially—there is a real sense of community around the school, the park, the community centre. The great thing is the extent of people's support for one another.

(Roger, 39) It has a good community feel, people brought together by the school and park and things like the annual arts festival put on by the Association.

The social mixing is seen as precisely that: people coming together through commonly shared social networks of like-minded individuals and which, in reality, is largely exclusive of non-middle-class people. The area's strong and well-deployed stock of social capital therefore arises, for the most part, from networks centred on its primary school and residents' association. The local primary school has become the dominant focus of the community: almost all of the children of our respondents were at the school, had been there or would be going there. It forms what Ball *et al.* (1995), term a cohesive and successful 'circuit of schooling'. Over the past two decades, the school has been nurtured by middle-class parents and it is the focal

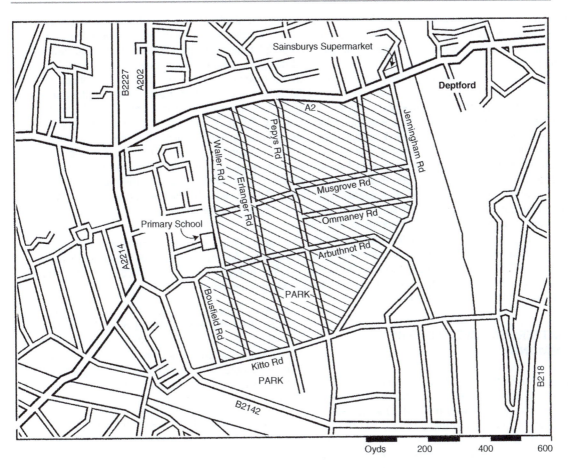

Figure 30.2 The Telegraph Hill study area

point of social interaction and friendship networks that continue long after the children have left the school. The school and its head teacher are crucial influences in designing appropriate educational strategies for each child through the various 'circuits of schooling' (state, grant maintained and private) which exist in the wider sub-regional area. Many of these initially school-based networks run other local associations.

Similarly, the strength of the Telegraph Hill Association and its success in bringing together a significant proportion of the residential community for social and cultural events (such as the Telegraph Hill festival) and council-lobbying activities (recycling facilities, road calming, educational issues affecting local schools, park improvements, etc.) appears to be in sharp contrast to the absence of any comparable force in Battersea or Brixton, where only a few specific streets have their own unfocused associations. The relation with the local authority is based

on 'personal chemistry' between local residents and officials whose values are largely shared. Although the London Borough of Lewisham houses many of London's most deprived areas and is not ideologically sympathetic to processes of gentrification and its associated forms of displacement, it is not hostile to middle-class areas like Telegraph Hill. Its officials respond well to the lobbying from fellow middle-class people such as our respondents and the effect reflects in the improvements which have been made to the local physical environment. Telegraph Hill, however, is not a priority area in this deprived local authority and it succeeds in cornering resources despite the official policy of the borough.

Although it is not without its middle-class dissidents, the Association represents an ongoing core of social activity aimed very much at maintaining and strengthening the well developed sense of localised middle-class self-awareness and cohesion. It has played an important role in supporting the development of a sense of Telegraph Hill as, at its best, a secure, comfortable and much-loved oasis of middle-class life in the heart of south-east London's urban sprawl.

Here, enlightened self-interest and community action—in a general atmosphere of well-developed civic-mindedness (Putnam, 1993)—fuse in cycles of collective social activity in which the area continually benefits from the fruits of a sustained engagement with the 'intermediate' local authority institutions through which resources can be accessed. This is almost an ideal type of horizontal-perpendicular synergy (Coleman, 1988), in which a well-educated and resourceful community with a strong affective attachment to its locality actively promotes its interests through participation in a local political structure which is unable to ignore the force and presentation of its claims. The coherence and 'success' of Telegraph Hill is the outcome of its population acting, as it were, as a 'middle class-for-itself'.

4. BATTERSEA ('BETWEEN THE COMMONS')

Under ten minutes from Victoria station, in central London, by train from Clapham Junction, this area has been transformed, over the past 20 years, out of all recognition from its formerly shabby self (as, for instance, characterised in the novel and subsequent film of down-market south London *Up The Junction*). It now has one of the busiest 'night-time economy' areas south of the River Thames. Networks of streets lying between Northcote Road and both Clapham and Wandsworth Commons—hence its estate agents' identity as 'Between the Commons'—are comprised of solid but unspectacular family houses. Its ordered, pleasant and prosperous atmosphere is palpably more 'upper' middle class than that of Telegraph Hill. A lot of people 'pretending', as one interviewee put it, 'that they're in the country'. Visually and socially, this is an area of people 'on the make' although in most cases starting from a position of relative privilege as is indicated by the data in Tables 30.1 to 30.3. A one-dimensional and rather stifling atmosphere of conformity is the concomitant of its orderliness and prosperity. Two things are strikingly apparent in the area. First, the sheer number of wine bars, restaurants and bistros strung out along Northcote Road, all apparently doing a very healthy evening trade. Secondly, a very large concentration of mothers (or nannies) pushing buggies ('nappy valley' is one of the area's sobriquets). The figures quoted above on household structure may be somewhat misleading here; there appear to be a large

number of single-person households but elsewhere our data indicate that many women have ceased to work full-time when they have had children. Many of this group also employ nannies. 'Traditional' family arrangements are very much in evidence—i.e. father at work and mother at home—and the atmosphere of the area is pronouncedly female during the day. Financial services and media are strongly represented in employment with most respondents working in central London or the City. There is, overall, a very strong sense of 'people like us' gathering together. In contradistinction to the pattern in Telegraph Hill, middle-class settlement appears to have a more instrumental tenor here

(Janice, 30) It's great for families with kids— the parks are fantastic, the schools are fantastic, nurseries, private—there's a huge choice. It's very family oriented.

(Caroline, 28) It's safe and friendly, and there's a lot of people with a shared outlook … I had nothing in common with the people in West Hampstead when I was there, but here there are more people like me, people who'll be here for 3–5 years before going somewhere else—it's a staging-post for people like me.

(Margaret, 42) It feels good and open, with a good neighbourhood feeling … it's great actually … more and more people with kids are using the area as a stepping-stone before going to the country.

This is, in a sense, an area whose 'suitability' and 'habitability' have been assiduously contrived, primarily through manipulation of markets (in education, housing and leisure) rather than associational activity. The conservative, strongly pro-market cast of the local authority has been central to this process, having had as a stated policy intention the regeneration (or 'reinvention') of the Northcote Road area. The 'synergistic' interplay of the institutions of local authority and residents is therefore of a very different character from that in Telegraph Hill. The upgrading of the area for its new population has arguably been achieved by a combination of commonality of purpose, will and high levels of resourcefulness on both sides. The local authority has been quick to meet the needs of residents through the market and has facilitated the development process; developers are regarded as partners and have transformed many of the mansion blocks which are mainly on the periphery of the study area. This has of course led to widespread displacement. The London Borough of

Figure 30.3 The Battersea study area

Wandsworth, in contrast to almost all other London boroughs, regards gentrification as a core part of its regeneration strategy. However, as elsewhere in London, the gentrification process has been largely driven by 'social action' of individual householders and small-scale developers. The difference is that in Battersea the local authority has encouraged and facilitated not only the process of residential gentrification, but also the creation of what might be termed the infrastructure of gentrification. This is nowhere better symbolised than in Northcote Road where bars, restaurants, estate agents, bathroom and kitchen shops have more or less come to dominate what is now one of the major satellite areas of consumption in south-west London.

On the whole, therefore, although with some clear life-cycle-stage differences, Battersea's residents get what they want: clean and safe streets, high-quality local amenities and successful, selective schools. The local authority fosters the process by granting licences to the 'right' kinds of leisure institutions and schools. In the case of the latter, the presence of a highly resourced clientèle in the state schools improves their performance levels and status, and Wandsworth's generalised aura of academic excellence is consolidated by a plethora of private schools and nurseries. This makes 'between the commons' one of *the* most desirable locations for young, ambitious, middle-class families in London, certainly south of the river. The emphasis here is on performance and examination success rates. It is in this 'circuit of schooling' that the instrumentalist cast of the area is most apparent—the private nurseries, nannies, prep schools and flourishing primary and secondary sectors give the place a pervasive 'hothouse' atmosphere. This part of Battersea has become a carefully cultivated 'urban village' in which young professionals can conveniently educate their children, work in the metropolitan economy and enjoy the pleasures of central London before moving on to still more desirable parts of Wandsworth or the southern Home Counties. The consequence of this instrumentalism is the absence of an affective dimension in people's relationships to the area. For all its prosperity and 'success', 'between the commons' lacks an atmosphere of depth, of attachment. This can give the place a feeling of superficial homogeneity with which residents, not tied in to its prevailing normative structure and institutions, are often uncomfortable

(Mark, 55) The council has ruined the market … the stalls used to run the whole length of the Northcote Road. … what's happened is a major disaster—the *real* dimension has been edged out.

(Malcolm, 53) It's not at all multicultural. It has simple norms, it's very easy to stand out, you know, a lot of the restaurants and bars have been taken over by the braying classes. I don't use them much now, you can't hear yourself think!

(Jane, 31) It's much more '2.4 kids' now, it has a much younger feel. The types who lived here were more varied in outlook and background, now it's the huntin', shootin' and fishin' set … the people around me in this street are very homogeneous.

These comments are in strong contrast with Telegraph Hill, where a far greater number of people articulate a much stronger sense of attachment to, and affection for, their area. These are two quite different urban villages.

It is probable that the instrumental and relatively superficial attachment to place in Battersea is a cyclical phenomenon which is facilitated not only by the ready housing market, but also by the structuring of education provision—it becomes easier for people to move on when it is convenient for them to do so. It might therefore be characterised as a middle-class community based more on high levels of economic and cultural capital, than on social capital. The high level of economic capital, at least relative to the other areas, is evidenced by the comparatively high household incomes—15 per cent of which were in excess of £100 000 a year. The relatively high number of single-person households probably means that the relative family income is underestimated. In relation to cultural capital, like our other areas, over 85 per cent had a higher education and 10 per cent had received this at Oxford or Cambridge universities. The concatenation of cultural capital with higher educational qualifications is problematic, but nevertheless follows Bourdieu's conceptualisation of the way in which middle-class families hand down educational advantage intergenerationally which is then realised in the professional labour market.

This is not to suggest, however, that social networks in Battersea are weak. This is certainly not the case, especially in relation to those that are school-based which would appear to be robust, and important in cementing the highly specific social traffic, sense of identity and norms which clearly exist in the area. These, indeed, are sufficiently stable and widely known in themselves to constitute an attraction for potential incomers. But the strength of this novel symbolic identity has been achieved more by the weight of numbers of economic and cultural capital-rich incomers. There is a sense in which the area's social capital is more latent than actualised and is stored as 'potential energy' (Paxton, 1999). The ongoing clustering of households comprises people from similar backgrounds and with commonalities of experience, interest and expectation. This provides the area with a kind of economic and cultural security which it is difficult to imagine coming under the kind of threat which might catalyse the social capital-based responses of Telegraph Hill. Crudely, people are more likely to 'eat out' than to 'join in'.

5. BRIXTON

Brixton is a busier and far more culturally and ethnically diverse area than Telegraph Hill or Battersea. Long thought of as the centre of Britain's Afro-Caribbean community, it is now more socially and culturally heterogeneous than it was in terms of both ethnicity and social class. The current boom in middle-class settlement in the area was preceded by previous waves which, however, failed to gain the momentum and solidity of contemporary processes of gentrification. The most significant of these were in the early and late 1980s. In the first period, following the civil disturbances of 1981, property prices were low enough to attract a core of adventurous 'pioneer' middle-class incomers (Butler, 1997).[3] The second, originating in the housing boom of the late 1980s, has continued since that time but accelerated dramatically in the past two or three years. Brixton's more recent status as an internationally renowned, cosmopolitan lifestyle centre—with an expanding commercial infrastructure of bars, clubs and restaurants—is clearly implicated in the more recent gentrification of the area, with many incomers attracted to its vibrancy and fashionable prestige. There is also a good deal of evidence to suggest that the growing desirability, respectability and housing-market competitiveness of Brixton is attracting an 'overspill' of middle-class incomers priced out of more solidly gentrified surrounding areas such as Clapham and Balham.

There are, strictly speaking, two residential areas involved here in our study. Each abut onto Brockwell Park; Tulse Hill to the west, Herne Hill to the east. The latter, however, is not a part of Herne Hill 'proper', but an area close to central Brixton rechristened by estate agents in recent years as 'Poet's Corner'. This small network of streets (Milton, Spenser, Shakespeare Road, etc.) has now been designated a conservation area and contains a range of highly desirable and architecturally interesting properties. The area as a whole runs parallel to Railton Road, Brixton's notorious 'front line' of the 1970s and 1980s and at the centre of the 1981 'riots'. The process of gentrification here is, given this, perhaps the most dramatic in all our areas. Streets adjacent to one of Britain's best-known symbols of urban disrepair have been settled and largely transformed over the past decade by high-income professionals reclaiming its increasingly sought after 'architectural gems'. Brixton Hill, its counterpart on the other side of Brockwell Park, is a larger area containing mostly terraced streets of housing, less spectacular but solid, desirable and more easily accessed from the centre of Brixton. It is much more socially mixed than is Poet's Corner but is, in its interior, equally calm and ordered. Both areas therefore offer residents dense but relatively peaceful environments close by one of Britain's most vibrant and volatile inner-urban areas.

It is significant that a majority of middle-class home-owners in Brixton, when asked about the appeal of the area, stressed the importance and attraction of social and cultural diversity.

(Margaret, 38) The best thing about living here is that it's an open community … There is no norm. I find that very reassuring.

(Sara, 32) It's quiet in our street, but there's lots to do nearby, you don't need a car. Practically everything you need is in Brixton, the Ritzy, restaurants, bars, fabulous things. It's a very diverse population; we don't stick out living here as two women living together … I wouldn't want to live anywhere else.

This emphasis on diversity is in sharp contrast to both Telegraph Hill and Battersea, which have tended to attract incomers seeking far less diverse social environments. In Brixton, this refers to a mix of ethnicity and class in contrast to Telegraph Hill where, although respondents used the word diverse, they were describing a range of occupations *within* the middle class rather than across social divides. But Brixton's celebration of individualism and the freedom from strong norms appears to have a downside with implications for the nature—or absence—of the social cohesion experienced by those living in the area. That is, there appears to be something of a gulf between a widely circulated rhetorical preference for multicultural experience and people's actual social networks and connections. The model of social cohesion in Brixton, where physical interaction with an extraordinarily heterogeneous social landscape is an unavoidable feature of everyday life, might be characterised as 'tectonic' (Robson and Butler, 2001). That is to say, relations between different social and ethnic groups in the area tend to

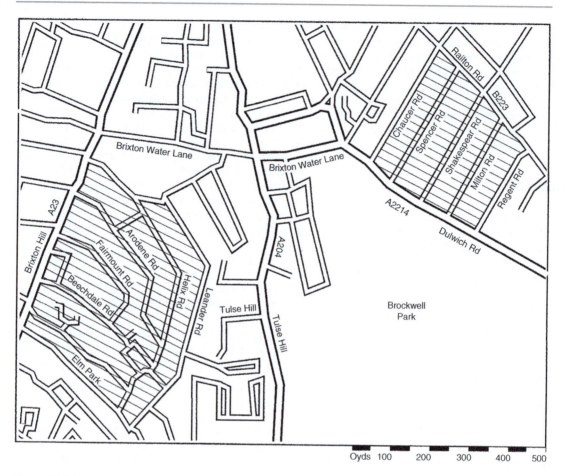

Figure 30.4 The Brixton study area

be of a parallel rather than integrative nature; people keep, by and large, to themselves.[4] The urban landscape in Brixton appears thus to serve, for most of its middle-class residents, as an ideologically charged and desirable backdrop for lives conducted at a remove from its multicultural institutions.

It is this apparent paradox of informal, voluntary segregation and the embracing of multiculturalism as an ideal of city living which gives social relations in Brixton their 'tectonic' aspect. Social groups or 'plates' overlap or run parallel to one another without much in the way of integrated experience in the area's social and cultural institutions. Crucially, however, there appears to be little cohesion among middle-class residents and little evidence of consolidating activity based on the development of social capital. A shared commitment to achieving an ordered and stable locality as an end in itself appears to be a far lower priority in Brixton than in either of the other areas. Patterns of social

interaction seem to have little coherence. They display neither the social clustering and commonalities of interest of Battersea, nor the cohesion, reflexivity and purpose of Telegraph Hill. This Brixton 'community' lacks the institutions and associational activity required for the mobilisation of middle-class social capital. The picture here is complicated by the fact that there appear to be two Brixtons in our sample which, whilst sharing most of the characteristics referred to, do have significant differences when it comes to the issue of social capital. When asked how active they were in neighbourhood associations, 16 per cent of respondents in Telegraph Hill claimed to be very active in contrast to only 5 per cent in Battersea which supports our general argument. The response rate for Brixton was between the two (10 per cent) which surprised us. However, when we investigated further we discovered that in Poets Corner it was 23 per cent and in Tulse Hill only 3 per cent. This suggests that there are in fact two middle-class Brixtons. In Poets' Corner, there is a long-standing group who have committed to Brixton and to its 'alternative' culture and multicultural institutions (such as the Ritzy cinema one of the best-known independents in the country). On the other hand, there is a much larger group who are in 'flight' from the obligations of social capital mainly living in Tulse Hill. We discuss this in greater detail in our forthcoming book on this research into middle-class London (Butler and Robson, forthcoming). However, we believe that overall the gentrification of Brixton has contributed to this 'tectonic' social structure which celebrates diversity in principle but leads to separate lives in practice: it is what we call a celebration of 'Brixton in the mind'.

Compared with the other two areas, relations with the local authority are remote and levels of trust are extremely low—open contempt for its officers and their capabilities contrasts sharply with the patterns of accommodation and synergy we have found elsewhere. Residents' associations are all but non-existent, and interest- or action-groups drawing on middle-class support or resources are difficult to identify. Crucially, the area's middle-class circuit of schooling is underdeveloped and offers a limited basis for either long-term social networks or successful cultural reproduction *in situ*. As a consequence, many families with children leave the area at or around secondary transfer stage and we found not a single middle-class family with a child in a Lambeth secondary school (Robson and Butler, 2001).

The relative absence of a stable core of families (particularly in Tulse Hill) contrasts with both our other areas, and Brixton's particularity is confirmed by the fact that such households counted for less than half our sample, with a large number of households comprised of single people. Brixton retains much of the individualist and 'creatively' diverse atmosphere with which it has long been associated, now laced heavily with an atmosphere of youthful, 'post-modern' cultural activity (O'Connor and Wynne, 1995). Herein, perhaps, lies a peculiarity that may go some way to explaining the area's under developed stocks of social capital: many residents might not regard it as especially desirable. Some of the potential—in this case constricting and anti-individualist—drawbacks of strong social capital (Portes and Landolt, 1997; Portes, 1998) are pertinent here. In Brixton, it is probable that there is a middle-class constituency that does not share assumptions about the desirability of strong, communally sustained norms and relationships organised around reciprocity. The development of social capital is thus hindered by the fragmentary and

demographically unstable nature of a middle class which appears to exist neither 'in-itself' nor 'for-itself'—although, as stated above, there is an interesting internal division in Brixton between the two areas which are the richest and poorest in social capital in the whole study—apart from Docklands where it is non-existent.

6. DISCUSSION

All three of the areas presented have been subject to on-going gentrification over the past 15–20 years, with the past 5 years being particularly intensive. The demographic shifts in Telegraph Hill and Battersea have been towards core populations of middle-class professionals sufficiently stable to have transformed the identities of their localities. Middle-class migration into Brixton, though large in scale, has been more diverse and less decisive, adding another 'tectonic' social plate to those already existing in the area.[5] Each of the three areas displays quite different patterns of capital relations, which are summarised in Table 30.4.

The strong stocks of realisable social capital evident in Telegraph Hill interact in a fundamental and symbiotic way with the formidable cultural capital contained in the area. Education is probably the most important conduit in understanding the relationship between these forms of capital. High levels of educational credentials and resources, and indeed the presence of a large number of education professionals, give it an exceptionally high profile in cultural capital terms.[6] More parents here than elsewhere are able to find solutions to the problem of secondary schooling on the basis of understanding and working the local educational system and sustaining for their children a *habitus* conducive to success in this field. This *habitus* is formed partly by the experience of schooling, but is essentially nurtured and sustained through the careful construction and implementation of educational strategies in the household. These are reinforced by the presence of like-minded households which are interconnected by strong social and personal friendship networks in which stored cultural capital is realised as neighbourhood social capital in expectations for their children and the school and non-school activities in which they engage. Although less well economically resourced than their counterparts in Battersea, it is therefore highly unlikely that their children will be disadvantaged in terms of educational outcomes. The area's primary school acts as the spatial and social focus of the networks and patterns of activity that support this successful circuit of schooling (Robson and Butler, 2001). In this

	Telegraph Hill	Brixton	Battersea
Gentrification process	Social action, synergistic	Partially realised, uneven	Market commonalities of interest
Relations of capital			
Social	Very strong	Very weak	Latent
Cultural	Very strong	Adequate	Strong
Economic	Adequate/strong	Adequate	Very strong
Other dimensions			
Circuit of education	Successful	Unsuccessful	Successful
Stability	Intergenerationally stable	Unstable, population turnover	Stable, life-cyclical

Table 30.4 Dimensions of capital formation

way, the spatial and the strategic combine to confirm the centrality of education-based cultural capital to the reproduction of this section of the middle class.

Social and cultural capital combine, furthermore, in the successful communal pursuit of improvements to the environmental and institutional infrastructure of the locality. The general upgrading of the area was realised by means of a capacity to act collectively on the basis of such expressions of cultural capital as detailed knowledge, case preparation, articulacy and social confidence—all advantages in dealings with local government officers and other key institutional personnel. The gentrification of Telegraph Hill, and its reinvention as a desirable oasis of middle-class life in an extended area otherwise devoid of promise, has been achieved by residents in command of *relatively* modest economic resources.

Contrast to this model of actualised social and cultural capital is provided by the highly successful but less 'civic' gentrification of Battersea. Here it is economic capital that predominates, enabling competitive access to an increasingly desirable and expensive stock of housing and an exclusive circuit of schooling centred on private provision. Although there is a good deal of school-gate social interaction in the area, primary schools do not fulfil quite the same function as does the primary school in Telegraph Hill. There is more emphasis, in these networks of information, on straightforwardly identifying desirable private provision than on developing strategies or campaigns. But there is also a second source of social networking evident in Battersea, where residents are often colleagues as well as neighbours as a result of the concentration of those working in the corporate and financial services sectors.[7] While this no doubt sets up conduits for the circulation of information about employment and other fiscal opportunities, our evidence suggests

that it falls short of the strong social capital network apparent in Telegraph Hill. In other words, we are claiming that social-capital-informed social networks, based on 'active mutuality', are of greater social significance than the latent forms of social capital which are expressed in the informational networks in Battersea—although, if needed, the latter can be mobilised with relative ease.

In terms of stocks of social capital, Telegraph Hill would appear to be much the stronger. This can be seen in its higher levels of voluntary co-operation and sense of geographically focused unity. In comparison, the common good in Battersea is established through market-based commonalities of interest based upon households acting atomistically. Levels of engagement, trust and reciprocity—although the latter is obviously difficult to measure in a study such as ours—are probably higher on 'the Hill'. Evidence for this might be deduced by the strength and success of the Telegraph Hill Association, the kind of voluntary residents' initiative for which there is no parallel in Battersea and which represents a textbook example of focused and directed social capital. The residents of Telegraph Hill are far more likely to contribute to and benefit from semi-formalised networks of reciprocity than their counterparts in Battersea, and it is arguable that this has an effect on the intangible but qualitatively important 'atmosphere' of the respective areas.

The social structure is more atomised in Battersea; actors are motivated instrumentally by the requirements of their households and their jobs. Although the area does have a widely understood symbolic identity, the leap towards active mutuality on the basis of enlightened self-interest appears not to have been made to any significant degree. It is the strength of the local markets in education, housing and leisure and consumption that satisfies the needs of middle-class residents. The cultural capital stored in this community being highly variable, the educational success of children and the infrastructure of social interaction can ultimately be secured through the deployment of economic capital. Although there is wide scope for commercially based social activity, the connections that derive from it operate at a lower level of interpersonal intensity than in Telegraph Hill, and support an instrumental and relatively superficial sense of place. Both this and the priority placed on solving problems through markets militate against the need or desire to develop strong social capital— but allow for it to be held in reserve, as potential. Battersea is, in short, less about formal participation and joining things than a community of interest based on loosely shared norms and expectations— the most obvious manifestation of which is probably eating out in the local restaurants. Interpersonal links are likely to be as practical as they are affective, and successful in building the conditions for the cultural reproduction of the group, grounded as this is in a core of people working and living together in a self-contained and distinctive urban niche.

The middle-class settlement of Brixton differs significantly from both of the above. It is by far the most disparate and least culturally cohesive of the three populations. No readily identifiable social 'type' predominates. Though well-resourced in terms of cultural capital and adequately in terms of economic, this group's capacity for social capital is weakened both by its lack of cohesion and by the tendency of Brixton's middle-class incomers to want to celebrate social diversity. If social cohesion is achieved in Telegraph Hill through social capital and in Battersea through market-supported commonalities of interest, Brixton appears to be the location choice of many middle-class households in flight from the normative aspects of social capital itself. As we have argued earlier, there may be a significant differentiation between the two sub-areas which would make even more dramatic the flight from social capital amongst those respondents living in Tulse Hill.

The new middle-class presence in Brixton, as in Battersea, is established and maintained through economic capital and the market. Both are social and cultural landscapes to some extent transformed by flourishing commercial and leisure infrastructures. But beyond this they have less in common. Whereas gentrification in Battersea has led to the area developing a novel and unitary symbolic identity, Brixton's younger, less family-oriented and more demographically unstable middle-class population has had to take its place in a local social structure of proximate but 'tectonic' variety—albeit from a position of relative economic security. Brixton's current *cachet* as post-modernist mecca and focus for fashionable, alternative cultural forms and lifestyles has been boosted by an influx of cultural capital-rich media professionals with very different priorities from their counterparts in our other two areas. Brixton is, in this sense, different in nature from both Telegraph Hill and Battersea. It appears not to be an area amenable to similar processes of gentrification and social capital has consequently played less of a role in establishing the conditions for middle-class life.

We have looked at the ways in which localised patterns of gentrification by differing middle-class groups are characterised by differing relations of forms of capital. This has involved examining different strategies of capital deployment in the attempt of a given group to transform the locality in which it has settled, the outcomes of which can be seen in positive changes in both the material infrastructures and symbolic values of places. Each of the three groups has played on its strengths, where it has them. Gentrification, given this, cannot in any sense be considered to be a unitary phenomenon, but needs to be examined in each case according to its own logic and outcomes. The concept of social capital, when used as an integrated part of an extended conceptual framework for the apprehension of all forms of middle-class capital relations, can thus play an important part in discriminating between differing types of social phenomena. On this basis, we would suggest that the middle-class community in Telegraph Hill be considered as a class *for* itself, in Battersea as a class *in* itself and in Brixton, where social capital is both least apparent and desired, as neither.[8]

Notes

1 ESRC grant number L13025101.

2 These decisions were based on a detailed analysis of 1991 Census data including some analysis of the Sample of Anonymised Records as well as some ethnographic observations in these and a number of areas on our short-list.

3 In 1981, there were serious disturbances in Brixton which were seen at the time as a warning-shot to the nascent Thatcher government about the risks it was running in its neo-liberal economic strategies. Lord Scarman (1982) was asked to chair a commission of inquiry into the 'riots' and their policing which received wide interest.

4 It is of course a consequence of our research design that we are unable to 'triangulate' this observation by reference to other social groups.

However, it is our strong impression that young people tend to run up against each other in ways that their parents avoid. Many of our respondents referred to how their children had been beaten up or involved in conflicts with other youth groups—particularly Afro-Caribbean.

5 The ethnic composition of Brixton has become much more complex with, for example, the arrival of refugee and other communities from central and eastern Europe and the Balkans.

6 In practice, this equates with what might elsewhere be referred to as 'human capital' which refers to the process whereby educational and other manifestations of cultural capital to which Bourdieu refers are realised in professional labour markets.

7 The feeling of claustrophobia that this can induce is summed up by one respondent (Carl, 32) who moved away from the area

The dividing line between work and leisure time is already blurred in the City, without living on top of the people you work with as well. I left Battersea because I like to make the most of my time off. I didn't like being reminded of work all the time. Northcote Road is like a branch of the City now.

8 It might, we suggest, be appropriate to see this group as epitomising the trend identified by Lash and Urry (1994) towards dislocated individuals operating in the hyperspace of informational capitalism.

REFERENCES

ALLAN, G. A. (1989) *Friendship: Developing a Sociological Perspective*. New York: Harvester Wheatsheaf.

BALL, M., BOWE, R. and GEWIRTZ, S. (1995) Circuits of schooling: a sociological exploration of parental choice of school in social class contexts, *Sociological Review*, 43, pp. 52–78.

BOURDIEU, P. (1986) The forms of capital, in: J. G. RICHARDSON (Ed.) *Handbook of Theory and Research for the Sociology of Education*, pp. 241–258. New York: Greenwood.

BUTLER, T. (1997) *Gentrification and the Middle Classes*. Aldershot: Ashgate.

BUTLER, T. and ROBSON, G. (forthcoming) *Thinking Global, Acting Local: The Middle Classes and the Remaking of Inner London*. Oxford: Berg.

COLEMAN, J. (1988) Social capital in the creation of human capital, *American Journal of Sociology*, 94, pp. 95–121.

LASH, S. and URRY, J. (1994) *Economies of Signs and Space*. London: Sage.

LEY, D. (1996) *The New Middle Class and the Remaking of the Central City*. Oxford: Oxford University Press.

MALONEY, W., SMITH, G. and STOKER, G. (1999) *Social capital and urban governance*. Working paper, *Civic Engagement, Social Capital and Cities* ESRC research project, Department of Government, Glasgow University.

O'CONNOR, J. and WYNNE, D. (1995) *City Cultures and the New Cultural Intermediaries*. ESRC Research Report. Manchester: Manchester Institute for Popular Culture.

PAXTON, P. (1999) Is social capital declining in the United States? A multiple indicator assessment, *American Journal of Sociology*, 105, pp. 88–127.

PORTES, A. (1998) Social capital: its origins and applications in modern sociology, *Annual Review of Sociology*, 24, pp. 1–24.

PORTES, A. and LANDOLT, P. (1997) The downside of social capital, *American Prospect*, 26, pp. 18–22.

PUTNAM, R. (1993) The prosperous community: social capital and public life, *American Prospect*, 13, pp. 35–42.

ROBSON, G. and BUTLER, T. (2001) Coming to terms with London: middle-class communities in a global city, *International Journal of Urban and Regional Research*, 25, pp. 70–86.

SAVAGE, M., BARLOW, J., DICKENS, P. and FIELDING, T. (1992) *Property, Bureaucracy and Culture: Middle Class Formation in Contemporary Britain*. London: Routledge.

SCARMAN, LORD (1982) *The Scarman Report: The Brixton Disorders 10–12 April 1981*. Harmondsworth: Penguin.

SMITH, G. (1998) A very social capital: measuring the vital signs of community life in Newham, *Rising East: Journal of East London Studies*, 2, pp. 40–64.

SMITH, N. (1996) *The New Urban Frontier: Gentrification and the Revanchist City*. London: Routledge.

WARDE, A. (1991) Gentrification as consumption: issues of class and gender, *Environment and Planning D*, 9, pp. 223–232.

WILLMOTT, P. (1987) *Friendship Networks and Social Support*. London: Policy Studies Institute.

31

"'I Want to be Global': Theorising the Gentrifying Class as an Emergent Elite Global Community"

From *Urban Studies* (2003)

Matthew W. Rofe

GLOBAL CULTURE? GLOBAL COMMUNITY?

On the cusp of the new millennium, the cover of the *National Geographic* magazine (1999, Vol. 196, No. 2) boldly declared the existence of a 'Global Culture'. Similarly, assertions that a global community is emerging are equally abundant (see, for example, Waters, 1995). Expounding these sentiments, the *National Geographic's* editor observed that

> As old patterns make way for new, our thinking and our ways of life become more urban, more cosmopolitan, less diverse.
>
> (Allen, 1999, p. i)

This comment epitomises much contemporary thought concerning the process of globalisation, that the world is becoming increasingly intermeshed along the trajectory of modernisation. Undeniably, globalisation embodies a significant force altering social, cultural, economic and political structures at a variety of scales. However, the perception that a single global culture or community is emerging must be treated with caution. Uncritical acceptance of such an assertion denies the social and spatial complexity of culture and its constituent communities.

It is suggested that one of the most significant consequences of globalisation has been the erosion of space as a significant determinant in social relations. It has been proposed that the technological advances underpinning globalisation have effectively eradicated space (Douglas, 1997), thereby reconfiguring formerly accepted notions of social and cultural identities (Waters, 1995). This purported reordering of socio-spatial structures has prompted Scholte (1996, p. 49) to call for the development of a "non-territorialist cartography of life". The purported erasing of space by globalisation does not necessarily imply a corresponding erasing of social and cultural differentiation. However, as spatial barriers become increasingly permeable, notions of community must likewise become increasingly fluid. Anderson's (1983) theory of community as an imaginative construct allows such fluidity. For Anderson (1983, p. 14) it is the "image of communion" that creates and sustains community bonds, rather than direct and personal interaction between community members.

Despite the proliferation of global rhetoric in popular discourse, very little academic work has been conducted into the emergence of global communities. Thus far, the most detailed theoretical accounts of an emergent global community have focused upon what Friedmann and Wolff (1982) refer to as the transnational élites. Alternatively called stateless persons (Wallerstein, 1993) and cosmopolites (Hannerz, 1992), this group is positioned as a social manifestation of the globalisation process. While compelling, this literature remains quite abstract. In applying this literature to a grounded case study, this paper seeks to examine whether the gentrifying class constitutes an emergent élite global community. Significant parallels exist between the socioeconomic profiles, lifestyle aspirations and spatial manifestations of the gentrifying class and the more theoretical notions of the transnational élite. However, this is not to assert that all gentrifiers may be defined as members of the transnational élite or vice versa. Rather, it is proposed that some members of the gentrifying class sampled displayed the required predisposition to a transnational identity.

Envisaging the emergence of a single global culture and community ignores the diversity inherent within social relations. This paper seeks to problematise the utopian belief in such a global future by teasing out the complexities inherent in community formation beyond the scale of the local. Positioning the gentrifying class as an emergent élite global community is premised upon notions of community as an imaginative construction. The spatial occurrence of the gentrifying class in a number of prominent cities around the globe lends this group a global geography. This global geography constitutes the physical-spatial foundation upon which this imaginative community is premised. Positioning the gentrifiers as an imagined global community does not diminish their perceived significance amongst their adherents and affords the opportunity to study community articulation at the scale of the global.

This research used four interrelated methods. Analysis of census data was conducted to confirm the occurrence of gentrification and to construct a statistically grounded demographic profile of the gentrifiers in each study site. Following this, a questionnaire sample of 700 randomly selected households in total was conducted, with an overall response rate of 45 per cent. The questionnaire collected information on a range of topics including demographic profiles and attitudes towards gentrification, globalisation and global community development. Questionnaire respondents were given the opportunity to participate further in the research by providing their contact details and a preferred time of contact. Respondents willing so to participate accounted for 13 per cent of the questionnaire sample. This self-selecting group were surveyed by telephone following the analysis of questionnaire data. This allowed for the clarification of ambiguities and/or the further examination of key issues arising from the questionnaire. The final phase of the research involved semi-structured interviews with both gentrifiers and real estate agents active in each study site. Those gentrifiers interviewed are indicative of a group identified in this paper as consumption gentrifiers and self-identified as members of a global élite community. In total, 10 interviews were conducted with this group. Combined, these methods provide an holistic view of the gentrifiers as an emergent élite global community and the meanings and interpretations they place upon their interaction with the local places they occupy and the global spaces upon which they imaginatively project their identity.

STUDY SITE DESCRIPTION

Two study sites, within the Australian cities of Sydney and Newcastle, were examined using a range of complementary methods. The rationale in selecting these sites was based upon the documented occurrence of the gentrification process within specific inner-city areas (see Horvath and Engels, 1985; Engels, 1999; Rofe, 2000; Bridge, 2001). Specifically, those study sites examined were the suburb of Glebe within inner Sydney and the suburbs of Newcastle East and Cooks Hill within inner Newcastle (see Figures 31.1 and 31.2). Unless otherwise stated, Newcastle East and Cooks Hill are amalgamated and hereafter referred to as Inner Newcastle.

As indicated by Figure 31.1, Glebe lies some 2 km west of Sydney's central business district. Surveyed in 1790, the area was deemed unsuitable for agriculture and lay unused until 1824 when members of Sydney's developing merchant class began establishing stately homes and estates on the colony's periphery. The harbour-side location combined with the grandeur of the homes lent Glebe an air of sophistication and prestige. However, subdivision of the area during the early 1900s for workers' cottages and terraces, combined with industrial encroachment and the depression following the First World War, resulted in a "noticeable deterioration in the [area's] housing stock" (Horvath and Engels, 1985, p. 149). Due to congested living conditions, unemployment and escalating crime rates, Glebe came to be socially stigmatised as a slum. Glebe's narrative of stigmatisation endured until after the Second World War. Changes in migrant settlement patterns, combined with changing employment structures and increasing inner-city housing demand during the 1960s, significantly reduced the stigmatised identity of many areas within inner Sydney, Glebe included (Kendig, 1984, pp. 239–241). According to Kendig (1984, p. 243), Glebe was one of the first areas of inner Sydney to experience the onset of gentrification, a trend that is continuing unabated.

Newcastle is the regional capital of the Hunter Valley, located approximately 150 km north of Sydney (see Figure 31.2). Unlike Glebe, the settlement of Newcastle was a penal colony where coal was extracted using convict labour and shipped to

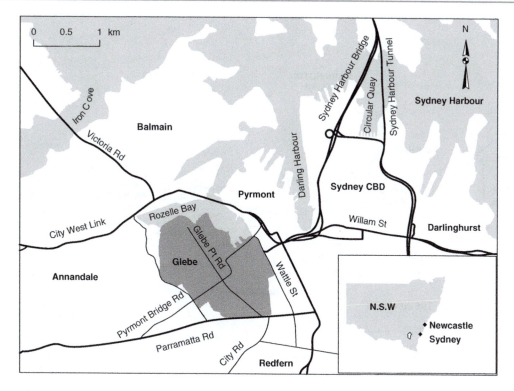

Figure 31.1 Location of the Glebe study site, NSW

Sydney. Coal mining remained a significant part of the settlement's economy following the removal of convicts in 1821 and, in 1913, the opening of the Broken Hill Proprietary (BHP) steelworks consolidated Newcastle's reputation as an industrial city. Consequently, Newcastle's identity has been epitomised by images and narratives of heavy industry and masculine endeavour (see Dunn *et al.*, 1995). However, industrial restructuring during the 1980s eroded the city's traditional employment base earning Newcastle the title of 'problem city' (Dunn *et al.*, 1995, p. 156). Combined with an earthquake which devastated parts of the city in 1989, the city lapsed into decline which until recently has stigmatised it considerably. Recently adopted entrepreneurial marketing strategies to attract investment capital (McGuirk *et al.*, 1996) have achieved considerable success as Newcastle actively reconstructs its identity as an innovative sustainable city. Since the mid 1980s, limited areas of Inner Newcastle had begun to gentrify (Rofe, 2000). The onset of gentrification was pivotal in the reorientation of Newcastle's narrative during the 1990s and has rapidly accelerated, consolidating large tracts of the inner city.

Attesting to the occurrence of gentrification within Glebe and Inner Newcastle, census data

reveals both study sites increasingly as residential zones of highly educated, professionally employed persons. Table 31.1 reveals that the proportion of persons employed in high-status, white-collar occupations (defined as persons classified as either managers and administrators or professionals) rose between 1986 and 1996 accounting for over 50 per cent of persons employed in both areas by 1996 (Glebe 57 per cent; Inner Newcastle 55 per cent). Taking into consideration those persons employed in low-status, white-collar occupations (defined as clerks, sales and personal service personnel), the proportion of persons employed within white-collar occupations accounted for over 80 per cent of persons employed in both areas (Glebe 85 per cent; Inner Newcastle 81 per cent). These figures are considerably higher than the New South Wales average (68 per cent in 1996), attesting to both Glebe and Inner Newcastle's position as increasingly élite residential areas.

Duplicating census questions concerning socio-economic profiling, questionnaire sampling revealed a continuation of this professional upgrading trend. As revealed by Table 31.2, over 60 per cent of respondents within both study sites identified as being employed in high-status, white-collar

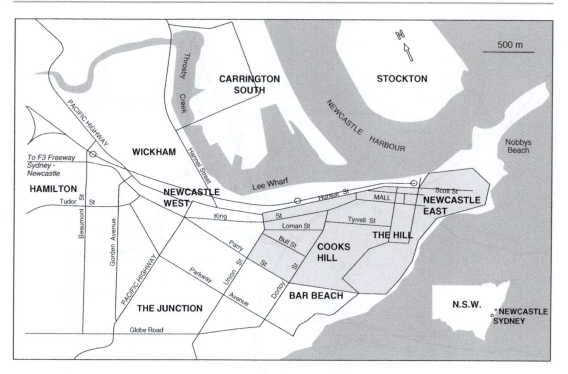

Figure 31.2 Location of the Inner Newcastle study site, NSW

Source: Rofe (2000, p. 56)

	Glebe			Inner Newcastle		
	1986	1991	1996	1986	1991	1996
Managers and administrators	8	12	10	10	11	8
Professionals	38	38	47	37	37	47
Clerks, sales and personal service personnel	27	30	28	28	29	26
Tradespersons	8	7	6	10	9	9
Plant operators, labourers and related workers	17	12	8	13	10	8
Inadequately described/not stated	2	1	1	2	4	2

Table 31.1 Occupational profile for Glebe and Inner Newcastle: 1986–96 (percentages)

Source: Australian Bureau of Statistics, Census of Population and Housing (1986, 1991, 1996)

occupations (Glebe 68 per cent; Inner Newcastle 67 per cent). Combined with persons employed in low-status, white-collar occupations, 91 per cent and 89 per cent of the Glebe and Inner Newcastle samples respectively were of white-collar employment. Professional employment is indicative of a higher education. Questionnaire sampling revealed that over 50 per cent of respondents in both sites held a degree (Glebe 53 per cent; Inner Newcastle 52 per cent), with over 20 per cent of this group in each site holding a postgraduate degree (Glebe 24 per cent; Inner Newcastle 26 per cent). The questionnaire data collected supports census trends while revealing both study sites as localised areas of professional consolidation. As anticipated, Tables 31.1 and 31.2 also indicate a decline in the proportion of blue-collar employees typical of the social transition within gentrifying areas.

	Glebe	Inner Newcastle
Managers and administrators	28	17
Professionals	40	52
Clerks, sales and personal service personnel	23	22
Tradespersons	6	5
Plant operators, labourers and related workers	2	4
Inadequately described/not stated	1	—

Table 31.2 Occupational profile of questionnaire respondents, 1998 (percentages)

Source: Glebe and Inner Newcastle questionnaire sample, 1998

GLOBALISATION AND CHANGING SOCIAL STRUCTURES

Contemporary concepts of a globalising world have proliferated since the late 1980s. Aided by advanced electronic communications technologies, it has been argued that globalisation's "eradication of space through the domestication of time" (Douglas, 1997, p. 168) has eroded the "constraints of [the] geography of social and cultural arrangements" (Waters, 1995, p. 3). Popular views of globalisation assert that this spatial erosion subverts the scales of the local and the national as significant spheres of power, privileging the scale of the global. Consequently, images and discourses of the global have come to occupy a central position in the popular imagination. Emphasising this, McHaffie (1997, p. 84) has observed that images of the global have come to represent a 'crystal ball' through which the common future of humanity can be perceived.

Exemplifying the belief in a common global future, Waters has argued that

In a globalised world there will be a single society and culture occupying the planet … Insofar as culture is unified it will be extremely abstract, expressing tolerance for diversity and individual choice. Importantly territoriality will disappear as an organizing principle for social and cultural life, it will be a society without borders.

(Waters, 1995, p. 3)

Waters' belief in an emerging world society and culture without spatial borders is not without theoretical opposition. Foremost amongst this is the assertion that globalisation embodies Western cultural imperialism as opposed to Western colonial imperialism. Huntington (2000) argues that globalisation therefore constitutes a 'clash of civilisations' between various cultural spheres. Explicit within such

conceptualisations is that globalisation is a culturally destructive force

a form of power that at once reaches into the very being of the individual and touches the … imagination of … society.

(Douglas, 1997, p. 169)

Adopting a more balanced stance, Scholte has observed that

It is *not* claimed that globalisation has touched every person, location and sphere of activity on the planet … nor that territory, place and distance have lost all their significance … and geopolitical boundaries have ceased to be important … nor that globalisation entails homogenisation and an erasure of cultural differences; nor that it heralds the birth of a world community with perpetual peace.

(Scholte, 1996, p. 47; original emphasis)

Scholte's 'nor' list is extremely provocative as it recognises that globalisation is not a spatially or a culturally uniform process. This recognition paves the way for more finely nuanced theorisations of globalisation, particularly the linkages between the spheres of the global and the local. Implicit within much globalisation theory is the creation of an artificial global–local duality. According to Smith, this duality

rests on a false opposition that equates the *local* with a … space of stasis … and the *global* as the site of dynamic change.

(Smith, 2001, p. 157; original emphasis)

In reality, these spaces are not mutually exclusive, but are intimately entwined. The linking of distant local spaces through the auspices of globalisation enables the "jumping of scales" (Smith, 2001, p. 5), creating transnational networks. In essence, then, much of what is considered to be global is in effect 'translocal'. However, the linking of spaces as 'translocal' is not a uniform process. Emphasising this, Massey (1993) considers globalisation to represent a disjunctive 'power geometry'. Like Scholte (1996), Massey (1993) asserts that globalisation's spatial reach and social impact vary significantly between different places and groups. While some places are increasingly enmeshed in empowering global networks, others are by-passed. Moreover, the social implications of globalisation vary between places and groups. As Massey observes

> Different social groups and individuals are placed in very distinct ways in relation to ... [global] flows and interconnections. This point concerns not merely the issue of who moves and who doesn't ... it is also about power in relation to the flows and movements ... some are more in charge of it than others; some initiate flows and movements, others don't; some are more on the receiving end of it than others; some are effectively imprisoned by it.
>
> (Massey, 1993, p. 61; original emphasis)

In Massey's (1993) schema, those social groups most empowered by globalisation represent pre-existing local élite groups. Utilising the technological artifices of globalisation, these local élites create 'translocal' networks linking distant spaces. However, this is not to imply that these spaces or the élites that occupy them are the harbingers of Waters' (1995) global society of tolerant diversity. Rather, these groups tend to form "occidental cultural enclaves" (Hannerz, 1992, p. 245) imbued with a sense of cosmopolitanism derived from select global networks, thereby epitomising Massey's (1993) global power geometries. These works demonstrate that recognition of the spatially fragmented and socially fragmenting nature of globalisation is vital if balanced critiques of globalisations impacts and the emergence of global élite communities are to be achieved.

Globalisation and community restructuring

Globalisation's fragmented spatial manifestation and fragmenting social influence are readily identifiable through their impacts upon existing community structures. As a process which liberates "social relations from local contexts of interaction" (Giddens,

1990, p. 21), globalisation has "made the identification of boundaries ... 'here' and 'there', 'far' and 'near' ... 'them' and 'us'—more problematic than ever" (Scholte, 1996, p. 49). The problematic identification of boundaries disembeds social existence from local spaces. Understanding the impact of this requires an examination of the traditional community literature in light of the recently emerging cybercommunity literature. Such a comparison emphasises community as a socially constructed and contested system of meaning and identity formation.

There has been much intellectual debate over what constitutes community and indeed what constitutes community membership (see, for example, Frankenberg, 1975; Eyles, 1985; Rose, 1990). Much of the early community literature expounds the need for communities to be rooted in physical territory (see, for example, Frankenberg, 1975; Eyles, 1985). As Jablonksy (1993, p. 152) asserts "community ... [is] dependent upon—indeed ... generated by—spatial forces". Similarly, Eyles (1985) believes that a sense of belonging within space is central to any definition of community. This implies that communities are entrenched in long-term social and spatial relationships within a specific physical area. The intersection of locality and longevity in community formation is perceived to give rise to a sense of social solidarity amongst community members. Rigidly associating community with a physical territory positions what Frankenberg (1975, p. 17) calls "face to face communities" as the most legitimate form of community expression. However, as globalisation expands social horizons, socially insulated, place-based communities are becoming increasingly rare.

Recent advances within electronic telecommunications technologies have reinvigorated the community debate. Spearheaded by the rapid emergence of the Internet and e-mail, a significant body of literature has developed assessing the emergence of cybercommunities (see, for example, Shields, 1996; Smith and Kollock, 2000). According to Rheingold (1993, p. 5) cybercommunities are

> social aggregations that emerge from the [Inter]Net when enough people carry on ... public discussions long enough, with sufficient human feeling, to form webs of personal relationships in cyberspace.
>
> (Rheingold, 1993, p. 5; emphasis added)

This is not to assert that cybercommunities are eliminating the significance of communities in 'real' space. Rejecting this, some theorists have attacked cybercommunities as 'simulations' (Wilbur, 1997, pp. 13–14) embodying "pale substitutes for more traditional face-to-face communities" (Smith and Kollock, 2000, p. 17). Alternatively, other theorists argue that cybercommunities may be used to augment and enhance our 'real' lives (see Wellman and Gulia, 2000).

These debates aside, cyberspace undeniably enables a technological connection between physical and often spatially remote localities. Cybercommunities then

> create a *crisis of boundaries* between the real world and the virtual, between time zones and between spaces, near and far.
>
> (Shields, 1996, p. 7; original emphasis)

The emergence of cybercommunities therefore represents a significant challenge to traditional notions of community as being anchored in specific, territorial locations.

The emergence of more flexible community forms which function beyond the strict constraints of territory engenders an appreciation of communities as constructions of the imagination. In this regard, the work of Anderson (1983) on the nation-state as an imagined community is particularly relevant. For Anderson, nations embody an imaginative construct

> because the members of even the smallest nation will never know most of their fellow-members, meet them, or hear of them, yet in the minds of each lives the *image of their communion*.
>
> (Anderson, 1983, p. 14; emphasis added)

Similarly, Rose (1990, p. 426) argues that the study "of community *as* an idea" (original emphasis) constitutes a neglected research direction. Acknowledging community as a form of "collective imagining" (Rose, 1990, p. 433) enhances the ability to conceptualise the existence of communities beyond the constraints of territory.

This is not to assert that the development of imaginative communities on a global scale is divorced from space. The relevance of space as providing a physical territory for the articulation and display of community-forming identities remains. What globalisation affords is the opportunity to communicate and even interact with similar communities beyond the local. After all, Frankenberg's (1975, p. 238) belief that "community implies having something in common" is still pertinent. Community integration beyond the local then is a selective process. While expanding social horizons enable people to interact with a wider range of cultural and social groups, it is logical that the individual will be most drawn to those community forms reflecting their

own community, with which they identify and within which they participate. The development of global communities, premised upon familiarity, may well shore-up barriers of distinction. Thus, discussion of global community development must engage with the notion of the community as a construct of the imagination.

GENTRIFIERS OR TRANSNATIONAL ÉLITE?

Theories of an emergent transnational élite stem from the global city literature. Epitomised by cities such as New York and London, global cities are considered "crucial cogs in the new global ... system" (Sassen, 1996, p. 195). Indeed, the intermeshed network of global cities constitutes a global meta-geography in its own right (see Beaverstock *et al.*, 2000). A close reading of the global city and gentrification literature reveals striking similarities between the transnational élite and the gentrifying class. In their seminal global city paper, Friedmann and Wolff (1982) proposed that increasing professional employment opportunities within the global cities, due to the acceleration of the global economy, predicated the emergence of the transnational élite. Earlier, David Ley (1980, p. 243) had proposed that the gentrifiers represented a "class in emergence" whose formation was initiated by a transition in the global city's productive capacity from an industrial to a post-industrial focus. Like Friedmann and Wolff (1982), Ley (1986, p. 532) recognised that changes in the global economy initiated shifts in the employment profile of global cities leading to the emergence of a new professional class.

Both the transnational élite and the gentrifiers are typified as being highly educated, affluent professionals employed in high-status, white-collar occupations. However, what differentiated the two groups at this stage of the literature was their proposed spatial orientation. Friedmann and Wolff (1982, p. 318) argued that "their chief characteristic ... is a willingness to serve the interests of ... global expansion, putting national interests second". Thus, the transnational élite is explicitly constructed as a nationally disembedded group whose members are globally aligned. Alternatively, Ley's (1980, p. 238) analysis emphasised gentrification as a cultural phenomenon heralding a "new ideology of livability" within the inner city. In essence, then, discussion of the transnational élite and the gentrifying class can be seen as divergent theorisations of the same group. While Friedmann and Wolff (1982) addressed the macro-scale implications of the transnational élite,

Ley (1980) was more concerned with the micro-scale manifestation of the new consumer class or gentrifiers. Essentially, both theories examined the same group, yet at different scales and through different theoretical perspectives. Positioning those gentrifiers sampled as an emergent transnational élite requires a brief discussion of their attitudes towards and aspirations to the scale of the global.

Globalisation is an undeniable facet of the respondents' lives. Reflecting this, 95 per cent of questionnaire respondents affirmed that globalisation is occurring. Moreover, the significance a global identity assumes in the lives of respondents is attested too as 74 per cent of the combined sample strongly agreed that they were global community members (see Figure 31.3). This explicit assertion provides a foundation from which to examine and tease out the complexities inherent in being both local and global simultaneously. However, this is not to assert that all members of the gentrifying class can be considered as members of the transnational élite or vice versa. Rather, it is asserted that a significant proportion of those gentrifiers sampled self-identify as being global.

Gentrifiers as transnational élite

While the literature of gentrification emphasised the gentrifiers' role as a local élite, a more esoteric theoretical path was taken in the examination of the transnational élite. According to King (1993, p. 152) the transnational élite genuinely "*believe* they live in a world culture" (original emphasis). For Hannerz (1992) and Wallerstein (1993), this belief casts the transnational élite as 'stateless persons'. The stateless person is a direct consequence of globalisation's erosion of cultural boundaries, which affords people the opportunity to escape the constraints of their local lives. This liberation, in the words of one interview respondent, provides the opportunity actively to "search and find what … [people] need to live their lives". Enthused by this liberation, this respondent continued

> No longer do you have to accept what your culture says or how your parents acted … now you can go in search of the things that interest you most, you can find where you fit into the world.

As globalisation erodes the bounded nature of space, the individual comes to be the meeting-point of a multitude of differing cultural and social values, beliefs and practices. Consequently, the stateless person may become an 'exile' within their 'home' culture (Hannerz, 1992). Feelings of an increasing distance between personal views and those of the mainstream Australian community were a recurring theme amongst respondents. Many of these lamented a growing backlash of bigotry and xenophobia perceived to arise from a fear of global integration. Despairing at this trend, one respondent believed this fear and the radical politics it spawns, generated an "excuse not to exercise [cultural] tolerance".[1] In a similar vein, another respondent believed that this "casts a racist shadow over Australia", impoverishing the nation. As exiles, many respondents felt compelled to construct communities reflecting their values and beliefs, thereby

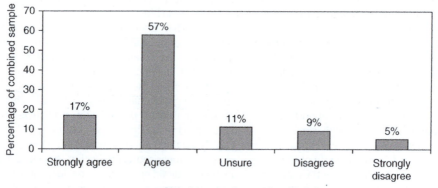

Figure 31.3 Perceived global community membership

Source: Glebe and Inner Newcastle questionnaire survey, 1998

distancing themselves further from a myopic mainstream Australian culture.

In this way, the emergence of the 'stateless person' as a global sub-culture necessitates a search for meaning and identity. This is achieved by creating an imaginative sense of belonging oriented to the scale of the global, which finds physical expression through local territory. Much has been written on gentrification as a process of identity construction through space (Ley, 1980; Jager, 1986; Mills, 1993; Rofe, 2000). Encapsulating this, Jager (1986, p. 79) considers gentrification as a spatial strategy "through which social differences are turned into social distinction". Inner-city residency for the gentrifiers constitutes a strategy of socio-spatial distinction by rejecting the values of a more suburban-oriented identity. Articulating this, one Glebe respondent proposed that

> People sort of go where they fit socially I think. When you're a professional you … you can't move to the 'burbs it's just not done. It's not what you do.

Such rhetoric casts the inner city as a cultured and vibrant place, opposing the narrow-minded nature of suburban life. Beyond this localised expression of socio-spatial distinction, sampling revealed a widespread belief that gentrifying landscapes constituted globally oriented places. In the words of one questionnaire respondent, gentrifying areas offer the "action/pulse/rhythm/opportunities" of the global at the scale of the local. Even more explicitly, one respondent stated that Australia's "global citizens" were concentrated in gentrifying areas, arguing that "global people *need* and *want* to be at the heart of the action" (emphasis added). Beyond being the local 'heart' of the global 'action', for one Glebe respondent, gentrifying areas constitute a spatial conduit through which the gentrifier-as-transnational élite gains access to other global places. In the words of this individual

> Inner Sydney, particularly Glebe, is a vibrant happening place which is going global. The people, the lifestyle, the attitudes mark Glebe as a global suburb. The same types of lifestyles can be found in NY, London or LA. People from Glebe could go to these places and feel at home, that is what being a global member is all about, being comfortable in other places due to similar lifestyles—a frame of reference.

Here, the intersection between gentrification landscapes and the transnational élites becomes explicit.

Gentrifying areas provide the conduit through which the template of a gentrification-derived transnational identity is focused and projected onto the scale of the global. As a conduit, gentrifying landscapes are therefore 'translocal' (Smith, 2001) spaces, increasingly enmeshed in global networks of flows and meaning. In short, gentrifying spaces provide a territory for the articulation of what this paper calls a global persona.

For many respondents, a global persona is indicative of their predisposition to difference. This predisposition reflects a cosmopolitan

> stance towards diversity … towards the co-existence of cultures in the individual experience. A … genuine cosmopolitanism is first of all an *orientation, a willingness to engage with* [diversity].
> (Hannerz, 1992, p. 239; emphasis added)[2]

Echoing this, one Inner Newcastle respondent characterised the most crucial aspect of a global persona as a "global state of mind". However, possessing a 'global state of mind' and being recognised as having a global persona are not necessarily congruent. To achieve this, the individual must actively construct and place on display an identity marking them as 'being global'. Reflecting the work of Bourdieu (1984, p. 236), 'being global' is a *title* of distinction, infusing the individual with a sense of cosmopolitanism.

Previous research emphasises that, as a process of identity construction, gentrification is premised upon consumption practices (Ley, 1980; Mills, 1993). The observation that "places encapsulate and communicate identity" (Mills, 1993, p. 150) resonates with the argument that for the gentrifiers "inner city residency is inherently symbolic" (Rofe, 2000, p. 65). Zukin (1991) has noted how gentrifying landscapes function as 'landscapes of power' providing spaces for the display of distinctive affluence. Consumptionscapes within both study sites embody symbolically important loci for the local gentrifying community. Characterised by the presence of cafés, restaurants, boutiques and art galleries, consumptionscapes provide a locus for the articulation and display of an affluent gentrification-derived identity. Attesting to this, an Inner Newcastle gentrifier stressed

> It's all about proximity to lifestyle, whether that be proximity to … restaurants … galleries, whatever … To me one of the prime dynamics of this whole gentrification thing is proximity to eateries … it may seem pretty simplistic to say that people are motivated by food but … that was a prime motivator for us.

Cuisine not only constructs local distinction, it is also central to the articulation of a global persona. Illustrating this, one respondent observed that in Glebe

> There are numerous restaurants, Thai, Indian, Chinese. These places are not run by Australians, they're run by people from those places, that makes them all the more global because those people have links to their homelands … The food available along Glebe Point Rd is authentic, not some cheap western copy. You see a lot of the copy restaurants around Sydney … I wouldn't eat at them. *I like to experience different cultures* not buy some fake, cheap copy (emphasis added).

In this light, 'authentic' international cuisine assumes the mantle of the 'exotic'. The ability to delineate between the fake and the authentic operates as an indicator of taste and distinction revealing the individual's sophistication in the sense of Bourdieu's (1984) notion of cultural capital. This supports May's (1996, p. 59) forthright assertion that the gentrifiers are "using their taste for exotic food as a way of distancing themselves from other social groups". However, as the pioneers of new lifestyle practices in their quest for distinction, the gentrifiers act as the arbiters of taste thereby transmitting them to the wider community. Effectively, this erodes the symbolic significance of once-fashionable consumption practices. Hence, identity is not a fixed and stable category. This is especially true for those respondents seeking to construct a global persona. As one Inner Newcastle respondent insightfully observed, a global persona "is like grains of sand in the wind, it's not fixed—things change". Consequently, identity construction is an on-going process as meanings shift and blur over time and between places.

GENTRIFYING LANDSCAPES AS COMMODIFIED TERRITORIES

As Mills (1993, p. 150) asserts "place of residence offers a map" revealing an individual's "place in society". Thus it is not surprising that, imbued as a 'landscape of power' (Zukin, 1991), the inner city has come to be commodified by property developers and real estate agents. Reflecting the work of Mills (1993), developers within both study sites are commodifying inner-city residency as an affluent niche market. Interviews with real estate agents within both study sites uncovered a deliberate and systematic strategy of luxury inscription upon Glebe and Inner Newcastle. As one prominent Inner Newcastle real estate agent commented "when it comes to the inner city living thing people are drawn to the

lifestyle". By mobilising lifestyle as a marketing ploy, real estate agents promote the inner city itself as a consumable product. Elaborating, this informant argued that the inner city had become a "highly prestigious product and that's what we sell, we sell lifestyle, we sell prestige". Concern was expressed by residents that inner-city commodification would "bring a different group of people into" the inner city. Despite possessing a significant degree of economic power, in-movers were considered to be different from Glebe and Inner Newcastle's existing residents. Such perceptions suggest the presence of a hierarchy within the gentrifying class. A fundamental basis of this hierarchy is the perceived lifestyle aspirations between what may be characterised as consumption gentrifiers and production gentrifiers. The difference between these two groups has been characterised as being related to the style of dwelling they occupy and length of residency (Rofe, 2000). Essentially, production gentrifiers

> are considered to differ from consumption gentrifiers in their motives for inner city residency. Production gentrifiers are considered to be investors in a pre-fabricated identity, rather than individuals actively constructing their own place-based identity.
>
> (Rofe, 2000, p. 63)

Stressing this point, one Glebe interview respondent stated "I take pride in the fact that … I renovated my home. I didn't buy it … I did it. I'm very proud of that". Within such a schema, a renovated dwelling becomes a physical extension of the individual, an investment in self as much as the dwelling itself. The consequence of this is that the refurbished dwelling becomes an expression of personal identity.

Individuals who purchase either an apartment or a renovated terrace are, in the opinion of the aforementioned respondent, "cheating" as they are gaining a notion of prestige "they didn't really earn". This 'instant lifestyle' is "hassle free … you don't have to invest time, [or] effort … all you have to do is pay your money". Purchasing a lifestyle as opposed to actually creating it is a fundamental difference between production and consumption gentrifiers in the minds of respondents. Much resentment stems from the perception that production gentrifiers detract from the ambience of the inner city. According to one Inner Newcastle respondent opposed to the encroachment of apartment developments in the city's East End, "those people do not belong to [their surrounding area] … they belong to that apartment building". The consequence of this detraction is an erosion of an area's perceived sense of community.

Whereas terrace-dwellers are privileged by respondents as being active in their construction of identity, apartment-dwellers are constructed as being solely interested in purchasing a pre-fabricated identity. Ultimately, the people attracted to apartment developments were seen by one Inner Newcastle respondent as having been "brainwashed by ... advertising bull***!". Impatient at the "time the trendy image would take to [construct] ... they go out and buy it"; or, even worse in another respondent's estimation, is a growing trend to "rent lifestyle". For this respondent, the ability to 'rent a lifestyle' promotes residential transience, further eroding the sense of community within inner-city areas. When asked if he considered apartment-dwellers as a form of gentrifier, this respondent indignantly replied "Certainly not! I think linking these people with gentrifiers is quite insulting; they don't have the same motivation as us. Certainly none of my friends would consider them gentrifiers".

The drawing of such a distinction is an important mechanism for group solidarity in the minds of some respondents. Resonant within this assertion is the notion that two groups are reclaiming the inner city. The first, terrace-dwellers, is characterised as comprising deep, soulful individuals concerned with preserving the ambience of the inner city. From interviews, it is possible to assert that this group constructs themselves as real or true gentrifiers. Opposing this is an emergent group of 'pretend' gentrifiers. Interview respondents characterise these individuals as apartment-dwellers, vacuous and interested in simply consuming the inner city for their own representational ends. One respondent summarised this by likening production gentrifiers to a "facsimile" of the authentic gentrifier. As a "facsimile ... they look and act very much like the real thing, but they are not". The facsimile metaphor is apt as it explicitly reveals the potential difficulty in differentiating between the authentic and the fake. In reality, both groups consume the inner city as a mechanism of lifestyle construction. However, one form of consumption is valorised over the other as authentic and desirable. Consumption gentrifiers, through their involvement in dwelling restoration, consider themselves to be a positive influence within the inner city. Opposing this, production gentrifiers are construed as being the product of a marketed lifestyle, detracting from the inner city's ambience.

The packaging and marketing of gentrifying landscapes reduce these areas and the lifestyle they embody, to what Mills (1993) refers to as the gentrification commodity. Disseminating the gentrification commodity through the wider community reduces its exclusivity and hence symbolic value as an indicator of distinction for consumption gentrifiers. Thus, lifestyle and consumption practices once imbued with notions of affluence are eroded. Emerging from this commodification process is a group here referred to as production gentrifiers. In the face of declining distinction at the scale of the local, those consumption gentrifiers sampled are imaginatively disembedding their identity from the local to that of the global. This is not to assert that these individuals are truly global, having no connection with their local environment. Despite their global reorientation, these individuals remain physically and socially connected with the local. However, in order to retain an identity rooted in notions of social distinction, the respondents are looking to the scale of the global.

Ironically, the consumption gentrifiers, through changing their focus of identity construction from the local to the global scale, are pioneering new forms of distinction. This is inevitable given their position as arbiters of taste. A commodified form of globally oriented residential identity is beginning to be marketed by property developers and real estate agents active in both inner Sydney and Newcastle. Indicative of this trend, one recently proposed luxury apartment development for Inner Newcastle has been touted as a 'mini-Paris' (Scanlon, 1999, p. 14). In time, this will require the consumption gentrifiers to develop new lifestyle practices through which to articulate social distinction.

LOCAL LIVES ... GLOBAL IMAGININGS

This paper has considered the extent to which the gentrifying class constitutes an emergent, élite global community. The notion of what constitutes community is pivotal. Community is often equated with territory, through which identity is articulated and displayed. Theorising community development beyond territory would appear contrary to the bulk of the community literature. This, however, need not be the case. While globalisation challenges traditional notions of community, community is equally a construct of the imagination (Anderson, 1983). Positioning community as an imaginative construct does not diminish its ties to localised spaces; rather, it affords the opportunity to liberate the social dimensions of community from the constraints of territory. Gentrifying landscapes constitute a territory from which some gentrifiers construct an imagined sense of global community development.

Paralleling the gentrification literature is a body of work theorising the emergence of a professional transnational élite within globalising cities. Defined as highly skilled professionals employed within globally oriented industries, a close reading of these theories reveals that the gentrifiers and the transnational élite embody the same group. Adopting different analytical scales and methods, the transnational élite literature has focused on the imagined scale of the global, the gentrification literature on the physical scale of the local. A key characteristic of both groups is a predisposition to difference as a key strategy in the articulation of a social distinction. For the gentrifiers, specific inner-city areas and consumption practices intersect forming a gentrification-oriented lifestyle. However, the gentrifiers unwittingly act as the arbiters of taste, pioneering new forms of style to the wider community.

Seeking to profit from a gentrification-oriented lifestyle, real estate agents and property developers have commodified the inner city. Interviews have revealed that two broad categories of gentrifiers have emerged from this process. These two groups are referred to as consumption and production gentrifiers. The identification of two broadly defined groups of gentrifiers offers new insights into the gentrification process. Interviews revealed concern amongst the consumption gentrifiers that the commodification of the inner city dilutes the prestige of an inner-city lifestyle. Disseminating an inner-city lifestyle through the wider community erodes its distinctive qualities for the consumption gentrifiers. In the face of declining lifestyle distinction, this group seeks new forms of lifestyle expression through which to maintain distinction. It is argued that the erosion of the distinctive local nature of gentrification has prompted members of the gentrifying class sampled to look to the scale of the global to maintain a distinctive identity. This is achieved through a range of consumption practices, which underpin the construction of a global persona. Consequently, the local comes to be equated with the ordinary and the familiar, the global with the extraordinary and the exotic.

It is the conclusion of this paper that the members of the gentrifying class sampled do indeed constitute an emerging élite global community. The local construction and subsequent global projection of a global persona mark this community as a construct of the imagination. This does not dilute the significance of this identity within the lives of its adherents. Rather, it demonstrates both the acknowledged local significance of the gentrification process and the emerging global significance of specific gentrifiers as an élite global community.

Notes

1 Numerous respondents cited the rise of Pauline Hanson's One Nation political party as indicative of a deep-seated vein of bigotry and xenophobia within the Australian community, mobilised under the guise of a concern for the perceived impact of globalisation upon a privileged Anglo-Australian way of life.

2 It must be noted that, while the cosmopolites are constructed as cultural connoisseurs, Hannerz (1992, p. 240) acknowledges that for the cosmopolites "competence with regard to alien cultures itself entails a sense of mastery, *as an aspect of the self*" (emphasis added). Thus, the construction of a cosmopolitan identity via cultural mastery may alter the very nature of the cosmopolites from cultural connoisseurs to cultural imperialists.

REFERENCES

ALLEN, W. L. (Ed.) (1999) *National Geographic, Official Journal of the National Geographic Society, Washington DC*, 196(2), p. i.

ANDERSON, B. R. (1983) *Imagined Communities: Reflections on the Origin and Spread of Nationalism*. London: Verso.

BEAVERSTOCK, J. V., SMITH, R. G. and TAYLOR, P. J. (2000) World-city network: a new metageography?, *Annals of the Association of American Geographers*, 90(1), pp. 123–134.

BOURDIEU, P. (1984) *Distinction: A Social Critique of the Judgement of Taste*. Cambridge: Cambridge University Press.

BRIDGE, G. (2001) Estate agents as interpreters of economic and cultural capital: the gentrification premium in the Sydney housing market, *International Journal of Urban and Regional Research*, 25(1), pp. 87–101.

DOUGLAS, I. R. (1997) Globalisation and the end of the state?, *New Political Economy*, 2, pp. 165–177.

DUNN, K. M., M^{c}GUIRK, P. M. and WINCHESTER, H. P. M. (1995) Place making: the social construction of Newcastle, *Australian Geographical Studies*, 33, pp. 149–167.

ENGELS, B. (1999) Property ownership, tenure, and displacement: in search of the process of gentrification, *Environment and Planning A*, 31, pp. 1473–1495.

EYLES, J. (1985) *Senses of Place*. London: Silverbrook Press.

FRANKENBERG, R. (1975) *Communities in Britain: Social Life in Town and Country*. Harmondsworth: Penguin.

FRIEDMANN, J. and WOLFF, G. (1982) World city formation: an agenda for research and action, *International Journal for Urban and Regional Research*, 6, pp. 309–344.

GIDDENS, A. (1990) *The Consequences of Modernity*. Cambridge: Polity Press.

HANNERZ, U. (1992) Cosmopolitans and locals in world culture, in: M. FEATHERSTONE (Ed.) *Global Culture: Nationalism, Globalism and Modernity*, pp. 237–251. London: Sage Publications.

HORVATH, R. and ENGELS, B. (1985) The residential restructuring of inner Sydney, in: I. BURNLEY and J. FORREST (Eds) *Living in Cities: Urbanism and Society in Metropolitan Australia*, pp. 143–159. Sydney: Allen and Unwin.

HUNTINGTON, S. P. (2000) The clash of civilizations?, in: F. J. LECHNER and J. BOLI (Eds) *The Globalization Reader*, pp. 27–33. Oxford: Blackwell.

JABLONSKY, T. (1993) *Pride in the Jungle*. Baltimore, MD: Johns Hopkins University Press.

JAGER, M. (1986) Class definition and the aesthetics of gentrification: Victoriana in Melbourne, in: N. SMITH and P. WILLIAMS (Eds) *Gentrification of the City*, pp. 78–91. Boston, MA: Allen and Unwin.

KENDIG, H. L. (1984) Gentrification in Australia, in: B. LONDON and J. PALEN (Eds) *Gentrification, Displacement and Neighbourhood Revitalisation*, pp. 235–253. Albany, NY: State University of New York Press.

KING, A. D. (1993) The global, the urban and the world, in: A. D. KING (Ed.) *Culture, Globalization and the World-System: Contemporary Conditions for the Representation of Identity*, pp. 149–154. London: Macmillan.

LEY, D. (1980) Liberal ideology and the postindustrial city, *Annals of the Association of American Geographers*, 70, pp. 238–258.

LEY, D. (1986) Alternative explanations for inner-city gentrification: a Canadian assessment, *Annals of the Association of American Geographers*, 76, pp. 521–535.

MASSEY, D. (1993) Power-geometry and a progressive sense of place, in: J. BIRD, B. CURTIS, T. PUTNAM *ET AL.* (Eds) *Mapping the Futures: Local Cultures, Global Change*, pp. 59–69. London: Routledge.

MAY, J. (1996) 'A little taste of something more exotic': the imaginative geographies of everyday life, *Geography*, 81(1), pp. 57–64.

McGUIRK, P. M., WINCHESTER, H. P. M. and DUNN, K. M. (1996) Entrepreneurial approaches to urban decline: the Honeysuckle redevelopment in Inner Newcastle, NSW, *Environment and Planning A*, 28, pp. 1815–1841.

MCHAFFIE, P. (1997) Decoding the globe: globalism, advertising and corporate practice, *Environment and Planning D*, 15, pp. 73–86.

MILLS, C. A. (1993) Myths and meanings of gentrification, in: J. DUNCAN and D. LEY (Eds) *Place/Culture/Representation*, pp. 149–169. New York: Routledge.

RHEINGOLD, H. (1993) *The Virtual Community: Homesteading on the Electronic Frontier*. Reading: Addsion-Wesley.

ROFE, M. W. (2000) Gentrification within Australia's 'problem city': Inner Newcastle as a zone of residential transition, *Australian Geographical Studies*, 38(1), pp. 54–70.

ROSE, G. (1990) Imagining Poplar in the 1920s: contested concepts of community, *Journal of Historical Geography*, 16(4), pp. 425–437.

SASSEN, S. (1996) Analytic borderlands: race, gender and representation in the new city, in: A. KING (Ed.) *Re-presenting the City: Ethnicity, Capital, and Culture in the Twenty-first Century Metropolis*, pp. 183–202. New York: Macmillan.

SCANLON, I. (1999) 'Paris' in the making, *The Newcastle Herald*, 25 August, p. 14.

SCHOLTE, J. A. (1996) Beyond the buzzword: towards a critical theory of globalization, in: E. KOFMAN and G. YOUNGS (Eds) *Globalization: Theory, Method and Practice*, pp. 43–57. New York: Pinter.

SHIELDS, R. (1996) (Ed.) *Cultures of Internet: Virtual Spaces, Real Histories, Living Bodies*. London: Sage Publications.

SMITH, M. A. and KOLLOCK, P. (Eds) (2000) *Communities in Cyberspace*. London: Routledge.

SMITH, M. P. (2001) *Transnational Urbanism: Locating Globalization*. Oxford: Blackwell.

WALLERSTEIN, I. (1993) The national and the universal: can there be such a thing as world culture?, in: A. D. KING (Ed.) *Globalization and the World System*, pp. 91–105. New York: Macmillan.

WATERS, M. (1995) *Globalization*. London: Routledge.

WELLMAN, B. and GULIA, M. (2000) Virtual communities: net surfers don't ride alone, in: M. A. SMITH and P. KOLLOCK (2000) (Eds) *Communities in Cyberspace*, pp. 167–194. London: Routledge.

WILBUR, S. P. (1997) An archeology of cyberspace: virtuality, community, identity, in: D. PORTER (Ed.) *Internet Culture*, pp. 5–22. New York: Routledge.

ZUKIN, S. (1991) *Landscapes of Power: From Detroit to Disney World*. Berkeley, CA: University of California Press.

32
"Other Geographies of Gentrification"

From *Progress in Human Geography* (2004)

Martin Phillips

I BEYOND A GEOGRAPHY OF GENTRIFICATION?

In a recent 'reappraisal' of gentrification research, Lees (2000: 405) has argued that while gentrification has been 'proceeding apace', expanding globally and down the urban hierarchy, gentrification studies have become 'a little less buoyant', seemingly beached upon a 'middle ground' of discursive calm created through the synthesis of opposing currents of argument, such as supply versus demand, culture versus economy. She adds that, while this middle ground is still riven with tensions, it may be 'time to step outside of this consensus' in order to highlight some hitherto important issues which have been sidelined. In particular, she suggests that a detailed examination of the 'geography of gentrification' would constitute 'a progressive research programme' (p. 402). In making this claim, she makes direct reference to Ley (1996) and, like him, identifies three distinct geographies of gentrification. For Lees, these geographies are described as international, intra-national and citywide; while Ley uses terms such as international, intra-metropolitan and urban neighbourhood or intra-urban. In their own work, and in reviews of other gentrification studies, Ley and Lees provide clear examples of these geographies (see not only Ley, 1996, and Lees, 2000, but also Lees, 1994a; 1994b; Lees and Berg, 1995; Carpenter and Lees, 1995), as well as stirring a range of other ingredients into gentrification studies including notions of discourse, representation and counter-cultural association.

While providing clear illustration of a 'geography of gentrification', Ley and Lees provide very little elaboration on how they, and others, might understand the phrase. For Ley this might be seen to reflect his scepticism over the value of abstract theory and preference for a 'grounded theory' which remains close to empirical observations and 'the hermeneutics of everyday communication' (Ley, 1989: 243; see also Ley, 1996: 25–26). This construction of theory and much of his discussions of the 'geography of gentrification' might be seen, however, to resonate closely with at least one highly abstract construction of theory and geography, namely Soja's (1996) 'firstspace epistemologies'. Drawing on the work of Lefebvre (1991), Soja argues that much of geography has focused on 'perceived space', which is seen as 'sensible and open, within limits, to accurate measurement and description' (Soja, 1996: 66; drawing on Lefebvre, 1991). Soja further argues that firstspace epistemologies have tended to see 'human spatiality as defined primarily by and in terms of its material configurations', and in many cases to see 'human spatiality as outcome or *product*' (p. 76). Although not making any reference in this discussion to studies of gentrification, I wish to suggest in this paper that there are many close parallels between Soja's characterization of 'firstspace epistemologies' and the geography of gentrification as outlined by Lees and Ley. I will then go on to suggest that there are also traces of other 'geographies of gentrification' in their work and in other studies of gentrification, geographies which arguably can be read as enactments of what Soja has described as 'secondspace' and 'thirdspace' epistemologies.

The geography of gentrification outlined by Lees and Ley also appears as exclusively urban in focus. Lees' discussion of intra-national gentrification, for example, very much enacts Ley's inter-metropolitan geography in that it focuses on comparisons between urban areas.[1] However, to equate the intra-national with the inter-urban excludes a number of potential geographies of gentrification, not least those of the rural. Furthermore, although Lees (1996) has sought to increase the mobility and decrease the exclusivity of conceptions of gentrification, the lowest of her three scales of analysis is described as 'citywide' (Lees, 2000: 403) and she suggests that 'all academic accounts of gentrification make use of the binary inner city-suburb' (Lees, 1996: 458). Again there is no hint here that gentrification has been found in rural spaces, nor indeed in Ley's (1996) mappings of gentrification which very much focus on comparisons between and within cities. As Smith (2002: 390) has recently argued, gentrification is widely seen as a phenomenon 'specific to a handful of inner-city areas in large metropolitan areas'. He adds, however, that it is not only 'manifest at a variety of spatial scales' but also in a range of locations, including the suburban, the rural, Central Business Districts and 'retirement hotspots' such as coastal resorts. He argues that studies of gentrification have 'failed to problematize the locations of gentrification adequately' and that there is a need to widen 'the spatial lens' of gentrification studies, although he also notes that in doing so the concept of gentrification may be extended in such a manner that 'may undermine the usefulness, and distinction, of the concept for understanding urban change' (pp. 390–92). Slightly earlier, Phillips and Smith (2001: 457–58) had indeed argued that it was 'inappropriate to simply overlay the term gentrification upon the rural terrain, despite the many overlaps between processes of revitalization in urban and rural locations', not least because 'the demand for, and perception of 'green' residential space ... stands in contrast to the 'urban' qualities which attract in-migrant counterparts in urban locations'. For Smith and Phillips rural and urban appear as culturally distinct constructions which makes the processes of revitalization and exclusion in rural and urban areas in some respects significantly different from each other.

The degree to which notions of gentrification, and geographies of gentrification, could be extended into rural spaces constitutes a second focus of this paper. It will be argued that many of the arguments advanced in urban studies have quite clear rural parallels, parallels that extend beyond processes of revitalization into the cultural constructions of space. Attention is drawn to the notion of 'complementary analysis' (Clark, 1992a; 1992b) which seeks to recognize and work with both similarities and difference. It is argued that such an approach may be of great value both in extending the spatial focus of gentrification studies into rural spaces and in exploring

first-, second- and thirdspace geographies of gentrification in both rural and urban spaces. These arguments are then briefly explored in the context of some substantive research on rural gentrification within two districts in Norfolk, England.

II SPACE EPISTEMOLOGIES AND GEOGRAPHIES OF GENTRIFICATION

1 Firstspace geographies of gentrification

At least three lines of connection can be drawn between the geography of gentrification of Ley and Lees and Soja's description of firstspace epistemologies. First, and arguably of least significance, Ley makes considerable use of quantitative measurement and statistical methods of analysis and description, albeit often in combination with qualitative research. Second, Ley discusses the geography of gentrification, at least initially, in terms of the 'spatiality of gentrification' (Ley, 1996: 120), where this is conceived in terms of the uneven incidence of gentrification and is explored both through 'the observational language of the map' and through multi-locale comparative studies. The latter, which often focus on how similar or different gentrification is in different places, also figure highly in the work of Lees (see particularly Lees, 1994a; Carpenter and Lees, 1995).

A third way that the geography of gentrification can be seen to conform to Soja's characterization of firstspace epistemologies relates to claims that both are focused on the study of outcomes. With regard to gentrification studies, Smith (2002: 387), for instance, has argued that they have been overly concerned with the 'end results' of gentrification and, as a result, have tended to concentrate on 'places that have already 'been' gentrified' and neglect 'places being gentrified' and, to extend the argument a bit further, places being made ready for gentrification. He goes on to call for a 'sensitive temporal analysis of gentrification' (p. 388), to which it might be objected that such analysis already figures highly within gentrification studies. Certainly Ley and Lees pay plenty of attention to the historical dynamics of gentrification, not least through employing 'evolutionary' (Carpenter and Lees, 1995) or 'stage-model' (Ley, 1996) perspectives on gentrification. Indeed, gentrification studies may be seen as one area where Soja's claim that there has been some shift in firstspace epistemologies towards recognizing that material spatial configurations are socially produced can be appropriately applied. Having said this, the geography of gentrification still appears quite outcome-focused in that it is often presented as a consequence of other processes: Ley (1996: 12), for instance, portrays the geography of gentrification as a consequence of processes of international scope such as postindustrialism, post-Fordism and post-modernism working in association with local conditions.

Soja notes that, while there has been some shift in firstspace analyses towards recognizing that material spatial configurations are socially produced, there has been, he argues, much less consideration given to the roles that these material geographies play in the constitution of social life. It may well be that Soja is arguably overly harsh in this assessment with respect to geography in general, but his arguments may point to a key constituent of the outcome focus of gentrification studies in that consideration of material spatiality as a causal variable has arguably not figured highly. In other words, as well as looking at the places that have been, are being and could in the future be gentrified, there is a need to consider what roles places and spaces themselves play in the constitution of gentrification.

Such a focus has not been entirely absent within gentrification studies. Zukin (1987: 131), for example, has argued that right from its coinage by Glass (1964), the term gentrification 'evoked more than a simple change of scene' but also 'suggested a new attachment to old buildings and a heightened sensibility to space and time'. She developed this line of argument further in an article on 'consumption biased socio-spatial complexes' which suggested that gentrification involves a 'specific type and *use* of space' (Zukin, 1990: 40, emphasis added). In particular, she suggests that gentrification constitutes a 'prototype' of a new 'organization of consumption' centred on areas which are '[g]eographically central, low-rise but densely constructed' and have 'housing stock that … reflects an earlier era of … commercial and industrial development' (Zukin, 1990: 40). Although these areas require some conversion to their physical infrastructure to make them desirable for modern living – 'Gentrifiers want both hot and cold running water, indoor toilets on every floor, central heating and working fireplaces' (Zukin, 1990: 41) – they have very desirable attributes, and a series of ensembles of labour, commodities and finance are invested in the area, transforming its spatial structure, which in turn come to attract subsequent rounds of investment (see Table 32.1). Significantly, even Zukin might be criticized for failing to address how particular spaces come to have the requisite characteristics for gentrification in that she begins her analysis of gentrification at the point whereby labour, commodities and finance come to be invested in refurbishing the built environment of

Types of capital and associated practices of gentrification			Phase in the circuit of capital	Type of agency gentrification
Labour/products	Physical infrastructure	Finance		
Architectural restorations	Conversion of old town houses and lofts	Investment in 'avant garde' art, restaurants	Direct capital investment	Individualized
Production of gentrification products – i.e., replicas, Victoriana, chintz	Creation of ensemble of facilities to create a downtown 'scene'	Creation of local real-estate market	Intensification of capital	Individualized but more empowered
Publication of magazines	Creation of 'landmark' districts – i.e., legally recognized area	Agencies adopt area as a tourist and retail destination; fictitious capital (credit) encourages further expansion	Symbolization of capital	National and multinational firms
Circulation of ideas and personnel	Expansion of central business district	Investment in new office construction	Diffusion and corporatization of capital	Large corporate capital

Table 32.1 Urban gentrification as a consumption space for capital circulation (based on Zukin, 1990)

an area. As such, she does not explicitly address how the spaces come to have forms which attract this investment, although this issue can be seem to have been a focus of considerable debate within gentrification relating to Smith's 'rent-gap' theorization of gentrification (see Smith, 1979; 1982; 1996; Clark and Gullberg, 1991; Clark, 1995; S'ykora, 1993) whereby places are seen to be being made ready for gentrification investment through a prior period of de-investment and devaluation. However, while Zukin (1990) does not make any explicit connections with Smith's notion of rent gaps, these would appear to be fully commensurable with her conception of a 'socio-spatial complex', and as such might be added as an initial moment of its formation (see Table 32.2).

2 Second- and thirdspace geographies of gentrification

Traces of yet other geographies may also be discerned in gentrification studies, including several of those discussed in Ley's and Lees' call for the study of 'the geography of gentrification'. Ley (1996: 82), for example, supplements his 'positivist' analysis of the geography of gentrification with references to the significance of a 'structure of feeling' relating place and identity. While much of his 'firstspace' geography of gentrification focuses on comparisons between and within cities, and associated differences in gentrification and gentrifiers, Ley goes on to effectively identify a further geography of gentrification which seems to span all locales of gentrification. This geography is a common 'structure of feeling' for the urban or more precisely perhaps, the inner city (Ley, 1996: 205):

> Whatever may be the lines of difference between gentrifiers, one thing is evident: they would be united in calling themselves urban people. The notion that the inner city acts as a temporary holding area for the new middle classes, a cheaper location to tolerate until the more desirable suburbs become affordable, is a fable that must be put to rest ... Inner-city sites ... are often selected despite cost disadvantages compared to the suburbs. But more to the point, it is the suburbs that are negatively valued; to gentrifiers they have spoiled identity ... the suburbs are too standardized, too homogenous, too bland, too conformist, too hierarchical, too conservative, too patriarchal, too straight.

Ley's urbane 'structure of feeling' involves a dualistic construction of the inner city and the suburbs, a view which is also very much in evidence in, and indeed is partly constructed from, Caulfield's slightly earlier book, *City form and everyday life* (Caulfield, 1994: 165, 190; emphasis in the original):

> Unanimity is a rare occurrence in social research, even in a targeted non probability sample of the kind pursued here. In the ... fieldwork, however, *not a single respondent interviewed* would move to a suburban locale under foreseeable circumstances ... Their suspicion is that ... suburban rounds of life are inexorably rooted in a subtext of values they describe as 'conventional' and 'traditional' ... [and the] suburbs' spatial landscape ... [is] perceived to foster homogeneity and isolation.

For both Ley and Caulfield, valuations of the inner city and denigrations of suburbia emerge as important themes in ethnographic encounters with gentrifiers and indeed may constitute a major motivation for acts of gentrification.

Lees expresses some doubts as to the temporal extensiveness of this structure of feeling, suggesting that contemporary gentrifiers in London and New York include '*financifiers*' who have little interest or sense of identity linked to inner-city neighbourhoods. There may also be spatial limitations – and an associated 'firstspace' geography – to this criticism with Lees suggesting that financifier gentrification 'will likely only occur in global cities ... or perhaps in capital cities' (Lees, 2000: 403). However, I would suggest that Ley's and Caulfield's discussions of structures of feeling and place identities transgress the bounds of Soja's 'firstspace epistemology' into some other geographies, geographies which might indeed be seen to resonate with Soja's characterization of 'secondspace' and 'thirdspace' epistemologies.

Soja (1996: 79) argues that 'secondspace epistemologies' are 'distinguishable by their explanatory concentration on conceived rather than perceived space and their implicit assumption that spatial knowledge is primarily produced through discursively devised representations of space'. He adds that secondspaces are 'made up of projections into the empirical world from conceived or imagined geographies' (p. 79). 'Thirdspace epistemologies', while recognizing the significance of firstspace and secondspace, are seen to focus attention on 'space as directly lived' (p. 67; Lefebvre, 1991: 39), and on the transformative potential of space (Soja, 1996: 68):

> Combining the real and the imagined, things and thought on equal terms, or at least not privileging one over the other a priori; these lived spaces

of representation are … the terrain for the generation of 'counterspaces', spaces of resistance to the dominant order.

Although the studies by Caulfield, Ley and Lees make no explicit reference to the work of Soja, some parallels may be posited. The dualistic urbane structure of feeling, for instance, could be characterized as a secondspace geography, involving projections into the empirical world of the inner city of a conceived or imagined geography of the inner city and suburb, particularly given that in Ley's study it is constructed by reference to a series of popular and academic literary texts, such as Whyte's (1957) *Organizational man*, Garner's (1976) *The intruders* and Atwood's (1979) *Life before man*. Ley at several points suggests that many of the authors of such texts, and indeed himself, may be writing from their own personal experiences of the gentrified inner city, and hence these studies might be seen to approach thirdspace as represented by artists and writers who might be seen to 'describe rather than decipher' (Soja, 1996: 67). Caulfield may be seen to address thirdspace more directly, not least in terms of the lived space of gentrifiers with the stated ambition of his text being to break 'the almost utter silence of 'gentrifiers' … in the substantial scholarly literature … by giving voice … to a group of middle-class in-movers' (1994: xi). Furthermore, as Lees (2000: 393) notes, the work of Ley (1996), Butler (1997) and most particularly Caulfield (1989; 1994) may be seen to embody a variant of the 'emancipatory city' thesis, whereby the city, and particularly the inner city, is seen as an 'emancipatory space' and gentrification is seen as 'an emancipatory social practice'. Caulfield, for example, suggests that gentrification may be seen as a 'critical social practice' involving, 'in part, a rupture in dominant canons of urban meaning and a cluster of social practices, carried out in the context of everyday life, orientated towards … an alternative urban future' (1994: 109).

Ley and Lees, and a number of authors (e.g., Smith, 1992; Phillips, 2002), have expressed some concerns about Caulfield's notion of gentrification as a critical practice: Lees (2000: 393), for example, suggests it 'appears as a rose-tinted vision as much as a description of contemporary urban experience'. Rather similar criticisms have been raised about Soja's notion of thirdspace – Price (1999: 343), for example, complains that Soja reduces it to 'funspace' – and I have elsewhere suggested a rather more ambiguous conception of it as embodiments of 'how people make sense, often in passive and occasionally in critical, and more generally in far from coherent or consistent ways …, of the worlds

in which they live' (Phillips, 2002: 17). Drawing on this, a thirdspace approach to gentrification could be seen to involve 'in the first instance, an examination of how people interpret, make sense of and act within the gentrified material spaces that they inhabit' (Phillips, 2002: 18–19).

3 Similarities and differences in the geographies of gentrification

While there may be value in quite directly drawing on aspects of Soja's 'trialectics of space' and the associated work of Lefebvre (see Phillips, 2002), in the present context I have simply sought to use Soja's discussions of spatial epistemologies to draw out some of the differences within a few existing studies of geographies of gentrification. If one buys into at least some of the ideas behind Soja's notion of spatial epistemologies and the associated Lefebvrian distinctions between material spatial practices, representations of space and spatial representations (see Lefebvre, 1991, Harvey, 1987, and Merrifield, 1993, for summaries), then one should expect there to be some significant differences, as well as a range of iterative interconnections, between these geographies. As outlined in Phillips (2002: 289), for Lefebvre material spaces practices, representations of space and spatial representations are 'distinctively different and yet also interconnected and intertwined'. Lees' (2002: 405) comment that there 'remains much to be learnt about the "geography of gentrification"' is an apposite one, although I would suggest that this geography may operate not only 'on a number of different levels' but also in a number of quite different ways, such that one might well argue for the study of geographies rather than geography of gentrification.

Such an argument might indeed fit in well with some earlier remarks that Lees made with regard to gentrification studies. In 1994, for example, she argued that there was a need to develop a 'dialectical approach' to gentrification studies which recognized 'complementarity' between 'Marxist economic analysis' and 'postmodern cultural analysis'. She argued that, while in the 1970s and 1980s 'geographical work on gentrification tended to follow either an economically determined or culturally determined route of investigation', from the early 1980s and into the 1990s it was increasingly recognized that 'economic and cultural analyses were both important for a sensitive investigation of gentrification', although 'ultimately, neither an economically determined nor a culturally determined framework of investigation seems to gain priority' (Lees, 1994b: 141–44). What was needed, she argued, were studies which recognized the 'complementarity' of economics and culture, where this is seen to involve recognition of both correspondence and incompatibilities.

Clark (1992a; 1992b) provides a rather more fully developed discussion of complementarity, based on notions of commensurable and incommensurable theories. The former are theories which are 'highly meshed and compatible' (Clark, 1992a: 262) in that they make use of similar and interrelatable assumptions and arguments. Incommensurable theories, on the other hand, make quite different assumptions and arguments from each other, and even when seemingly being applied to common phenomena end up focusing on quite different issues. In some cases, ways may be found to integrate seemingly incommensurable theories in that former incompatibilities may be integrated together in a way which 'dissolves' their perceived differences (Clark, 1992a: 362).[2] For instance, and to return to Lees' discussion of economic and cultural interpretations of gentrification, in the 1970s 'Marxist economic analysis' and 'postmodern cultural analyses' seemed incommensurable. However, in the 1980s attempts were made to draw these theories, and others, together in some 'integrated theory' of gentrification (see Hamnett, 1991). Lees and Clark, however, are sceptical about the degree to which such syntheses are successful, warning that they risk 'combining the uncombinable', neglecting significant differences and the tensions and contradictions such differences might create. Lees suggests, for example, that, while Zukin was one of the first people to seek to integrate the economic and the cultural, her analysis effectively reduces the cultural to the economic: 'Zukin retains a strong Marxist structuralist base. Culture is superimposed; as such, culture is made subservient to capital and only seen to be significant within accumulation activities' (Lees, 1994b: 142).

Lees' comments refer to Zukin's book *Loft living*, first published in 1982, but they may also be applicable to her discussion of socio-spatial complexes: although she argues that culture 'plays a *real*, i.e., material, role in moving … capital' (Zukin, 1990: 3), as noted earlier she starts her analysis of gentrification at the point at which various forms of capital start to become invested in an area with the desired cultural signifiers. As a result, she does not examine how these signifiers are formed, and hence her account may be seen to enact what Caulfield (1989) describes as a 'black box' approach to culture whereby various signifiers are identified as performing significant social functions such as, in Zukin's analysis, attracting investment, but there is little or no analysis of why these signifiers have this function

and how they originated. The focus, Caulfield argues, needs to be not only on the social consequences of desire but also on the formation of desire itself, a feature which, as discussed earlier, he considers in a manner akin to Soja's thirdspace epistemology.

The call for greater recognition of the dynamics of cultural formation and the roles that geography plays within them does not mean that the economic and its associated productions of material spatialities can be ignored or examined in complete isolation from second- and thirdspace perspectives. Clark and Lees do not argue for a simple return to incommensurable analyses of the 1970s and the dualistic politics of choice this created. Instead, they call for the development of 'complementary theory' whereby incommensurable theories are brought together in a manner which does not seek to dissolve differences and incompatibilities, but rather to use them in a way that different theoretical perspectives can be used to complement each other, highlighting both different aspects of a situation and the consequences of employing particular perspectives (see also Phillips, 1998a; 2002).[3] Applying this to the discussion of space epistemologies and gentrification studies, a complementary analysis will seek to recognize the distinctive and incommensurable aspects of first-, second- and thirdspace geographies of gentrification while at the same time drawing them together in a complementary manner.

III NEGLECTED GEOGRAPHIES OF GENTRIFICATION

The previous section of this paper has effectively sought to complicate or add a few further 'new wrinkles' (Lees, 2000; 402) to the call for a 'geography of gentrification' by identifying the presence of a range of different geographies in the work of people such as Lees, Caulfield and Ley, and by arguing that these geographies of gentrification may be seen as distinct although complementary. In this section, I wish to further complicate the call for a geography of gentrification by suggesting that its leading exponents have neglected at least one geography of gentrification which might be seen to register across firstspace, secondspace and thirdspace perspectives. This is the geography, or perhaps better geographies, of rural gentrification.

The notion of rural gentrification has had almost as long a history as has the term gentrification in general (Phillips, 1993). However, not only do Lees and Ley make no mention of rural gentrification but, as noted earlier, it also seems to remain beyond the spatiality of their firstspace geography of gentrification. The logic of such neglect, at least within a firstspace perspective, appears questionable given that a number of studies have identified a series of parallels between studies of rural socio-economic change and urban gentrification (see Phillips, 1993; 2002; Smith, 2002; Smith and Phillips, 2001). The parallels may well extend beyond the prominent – beyond the use of the term gentrification by both urban and rural researchers and the recognition of 'dramatic population transformations … multiple waves of in-, out- and intra-migration of relatively affluent and lower income households' (Smith, 2002: 386) – and may be so extensive as to make it hard to suggest a rationale for conceiving of gentrification as exclusively an urban phenomenon, at least within firstspace perspectives.[4] For example, the notion of post-productivism which has gradually risen to prominence in rural studies (Kneale *et al.*, 1992; Lowe *et al.*, 1993; Ward, 1993; Halfacree, 1997; Ilbery and Bowler, 1998; Wilson, 2001; Evans *et al.*, 2002; Holmes, 2002) can be seen to connect to the study of rural gentrification and also to have some similarities with the 'rent-gap' theorizations of urban gentrification discussed earlier.

Wilson (2001), for instance, notes that although the term post-productivism has come to be interpreted in a range of different ways (see also Evans *et al.*, 2002), some of its earliest advocates placed particular emphasis on the devalorization of land and building with respect to agricultural capital and its revalorization with respect to other capital networks (e.g., Kneale *et al.*, 1992; Murdoch and Marsden, 1994). Rural gentrification might hence be seen as one form of the revalorization of resources and spaces that have become seen as unproductive or marginal to agrarian capital, and indeed a variety of other rural capitals. The 'barn conversion' provides perhaps the clearest example of such processes of revalorization, but the revaluation of rural spaces and resources is not just restricted to barns but may include a whole range of other agricultural properties, including the houses of farmers and farm workers, as well as a range of other rural properties, such as schools, railway stations and churches. Furthermore, rural gentrification can be seen to involve not simply the revalorization of spaces formerly used by agrarian and other rural capitals for residential development but also, as with urban space (e.g., Beauregard, 1986; Mills, 1986; Featherstone, 1991), for retail, leisure and even industrial uses (see Phillips, 1993).

A neglect of the rural is also evident in second- and thirdspace discussions of gentrification and structures of feeling. Ley (1996: 208), for example, argues that he and Caulfield identify a common 'landscape of desire' underpinning gentrification, a landscape which is not only, as discussed earlier, conceived of in a manner which seems commensurable with Soja's description of a 'secondspace epistemology' but which also seems incommensurable with rural space in that Ley explicitly identifies it as a desire for urban living. Recognition of this secondspace geography might indeed be seen to provide a rationale for differentiating rural and urban gentrification despite their firstspace parallels, and even for possibly restricting the application of the term to urban spaces.[5]

Before jumping to endorse such a conclusion, however, it should be noted that a rather different reading of the texts of Caulfield and Ley can be suggested, namely that they actually identify a common 'landscape of despair' (Ley, 1996: 206) and that Caulfield identifies two 'landscapes of desire', only one of which is recognized by Ley.[6] While Caulfield does argue, *à propos* Ley, that inner-city areas held 'a kind of utopian quality for many respondents', he also records that for many of them 'the city is an environment that sometimes pales when measured against the imagined possibility of out-of-city living' (Caulfield, 1994: 165). For many of his respondents, inner cities and 'small town, rural environments' (p. 165) constituted landscapes of desire, both being seen as desirable alternatives to the 'landscape of despair' of suburban space. At the very least, such comments seem to suggest that secondspace geographies of gentrification may have some rural element within them, and also might also raise questions as to the degree of difference between constructions of the inner city and rural space.

As noted earlier, Ley's (1996) discussion of the inner city as a landscape of desire and the suburb as a landscape of despair draws in part on a review of a range of academic and popular texts. Support for Caulfield's creation of dual landscapes of desire and a singular landscape of despair can likewise be found in readings of academic and popular texts. In a series of works on representations of the English landscape, for example, Matless has suggested that the urban and the countryside 'remain a powerful double act in the English imagination' (Matless, 1994: 78; see also Matless, 1990; 1998), both elements of which commonly express an 'anti-suburbanism'. A 'normative geography' is enacted in which 'urbanity and rurality is asserted over an England-in-between of suburb', which become 'anti-settlements, places not fit for any purpose' (Matless, 1998: 32). In other words, there is at least one significant similarity between English constructions of urbanity and rurality; namely that they are both constructed, at least in part, in differentiation from suburban space.

Matless (1994: 78) adds that this normative geography was evident when 'talking to people living in certain Cotswold villages in 1990' in that 'the form of settlement given as not only different but antagonistic to the village was less the city than the suburb'. A strong anti-suburbanism was also very evident in interviews I have been recently conducting in relation to 'rural gentrification' (see Phillips, 2002). In some cases this anti-suburbanism exhibited a fair degree of social criticism, often centring on standardization and materialism (see Phillips, 2000: 18–19) and as such may be considered as thirdspace. On the other hand, such criticisms were often associated with regulative and exclusionary arguments, and in some cases might be seen to involve a proprietorial NIMBYism focused on 'the material and monetary value of ... properties' (Phillips, 2002: 18).

A similar ambivalent thirdspace perspective is arguably identifiable within Smith and Phillips' (2001) study of rural gentrification in the Yorkshire Pennines. They suggest, in a manner not dissimilar to the arguments of Ley (1996), that many of the values and attitudes of 1960 and 1970 'hippie culture' have been adopted, in part, by 'New Age professionals', although they suggest the latter social group might be seen as "stepping out', rather than ... 'dropping-out' from the 'rat-race' of mainstream capitalist society' (Smith and Phillips, 2001: 465). They go on to distinguish four distinct ways in which rural gentrifiers might be seen to express 'counter-cultural differences': namely, involvement in non-traditional parenting and partnering; non-conventional employment and occupational orientations; a tolerance of non-conventional social relations and attachment to community. All these features have been identified in studies of urban gentrification, including those of Caulfield and Ley, although Smith and Phillips go on to suggest that gentrifiers differ in the precise combination of counter-cultural attributes that they have and that these combinations are entwined with cultural constructions of rural space, which in turn contribute to the locational decisions of gentrifiers.

Just as Ley might be criticized for ignoring rural parallels to his thirdspace geographies of gentrification, so Phillips and Smith could be criticized for neglecting urban parallels to their arguments, with Ley, for example, suggesting that social zonation of residents may be associated with a 'spatialization of ... critical values' (Ley, 1996: 197):

from the standpoint of these values, the suburbs invoke conformity, the inner city dissent. In both sequences the arts and the artists are at the centre, simultaneously the core of adversarial values, and the most centralized in urban space. Their nemesis are the graduates of business school, more likely to be suburban in their residential choice.

Ley also suggests that there is a temporality as well as spatiality to differences in critical values, proposing an 'ideal case ... stage model' whereby a series of occupational groups of decreasing counter-cultural orientation move into a gentrifying area (Ley, 1996: 1999):

it is the artists and cultural professionals who are the first to establish a presence in the inner city, followed by the professionals in education, health care and related fields, with the natural scientists (including engineering), financial services, and managers and administrators in the private sector the last entrants to a district.

While stage models have been widely employed in urban gentrification studies since the late 1970s (see Kerstein, 1990), that of Smith and Phillips is one of the first studies to identify a temporal sequence with regard to rural gentrification, suggesting that (2001: 459):

The early stages of rehabilitation were initiated by a small influx of newcomers ... drawn ... by idyllic representations of Pennine rurality. They bought cheap, decaying properties, often in remote areas ... [D]uring the 1970s ... commercial interests became involved in the renovation and development process, producing ready-made 'rural' commodities aimed at attracting managerial and professional inhabitants. The redefined landscapes were actively promoted amongst the growing new middle classes of the surrounding metropolitan areas and beyond ... leading to escalating house prices.

Smith and Phillips hint at connections between the temporality of gentrification, on the one hand, and the formation of critical values and cultural constructions of place, on the other, although not pursuing these as systematically as does Ley. Nevertheless there are striking parallels between their study and Ley's critical value stage-model which suggest that thirdspace perspectives may be commensurable with the analysis of both rural and urban space.

Making such a claim involves reading Ley (1996) and Smith and Phillips (2001) against the grain of many of the arguments made in these studies, which in the case of the former effectively ignore the rural and in the latter posit rural and urban space as culturally incommensurable. Conversely, the critical value stage model of Ley and the similar although less formalized analysis of Smith and Phillips may be seen to posit considerable commensurability between first-, second- and thirdspace spatialities of gentrification in that differences in cultural conformity are mapped directly onto socio-cultural productions of space which in turn appear to map directly onto flows of occupational groups and also capital. Given this last connection it might indeed be appropriate to construct a composite 'stage-model' linking the work of Ley and Smith and Phillips with Zukin's capital focused stage-model of socio-spatial complexes (see Table 32.2).

Constructing such a model, even as a theoretical heuristic 'ideal type' (Ley, 1996), is, however, far from unproblematic. A series of questions have, for instance, been raised about whether such models negate difference by transforming highly salient but complex and temporally and spatially specific characteristics into simplified forms 'which lack any sense of historical and spatial contingency' (Beauregard, 1986: 37). In the present context, the model may be seen to map first-, second- and thirdspace epistemologies too readily together and neglect important incommensurabilities between their associated geographies. Having said this, as discussed earlier, recognition of incommensurabilities does not necessarily need to lead to separation of incommensurable theories but might lead to complementary theorizations which seek to recognize and work with both commensurability and incommensurability. The final section of the paper will address these claims by exploring the production of a firstspace geography of rural gentrification and some of its commensurabilities and incommensurabilities both with regard to analyses of urban gentrification and second- and thirdspace rural geographies of gentrification. The arguments will also draw on some substantive research on rural gentrification within two districts in Norfolk, England.

IV PRODUCTIONS OF GENTRIFICATION IN RURAL SPACE

As noted earlier, commensurabilities can be discerned between conceptions of urban gentrification and seemingly quite distant rural concepts and studies, such as the 'postproductivist countryside'. Not only may the origins of this concept lie in part on the processes of devalorization and revalorization central to the 'rent-gap' conception of urban gentrification and indeed to broader circuit of capital-centred accounts such as those of Zukin (1990) and Smith (1982; 1996), but recent discussions of the 'postproductivist countryside' also echo many of the areas of debate within gentrification studies.[7] Wilson (2001: 85–86), for example, suggests that conceptualization of post-productivism tended to be inconsistent, unidimensional and economistic, and pays 'insufficient attention to local action and thought', comments which have resonance with the culture-versus-economy gentrification debates discussed earlier. Similarly, Evans et al.'s (2002) discussion has echoes of Beauregard's critique of the essentialism of stage-models of gentrification when they complain that post-productivism neglects spatial differentiation and the complexities of temporal change in favour of abstract and dualistic theorization.

Postproductivism does not necessarily have to be interpreted as being an inherently temporal concept,[8] although as Evans et al. (2002) document it often has been. As such, it may fall prey to several of the perils of 'transition models' as identified by Thrift (1989), including the overemphasis on the strength of transitions via neglect of earlier parallels with contemporary change. It is certainly clear that the devaluation of rural space is not simply a feature of the 'post-productivist era', but that there have also been earlier phases of devaluation of agricultural land, such as in the agricultural depression of the 1870s and early twentieth century which saw declining investment of capital in agricultural production and land being taken out of production as a response to falling commodity prices (see Newby, 1987; Goodman and Redclift, 1991). There was also in this period a significant change in the structure of landownership with many large rural estates being broken up and much of this land being purchased by agricultural owner-occupiers. These changes, as much as more recent devalorizations, may play an important role in the formation of spaces for gentrification given that, as Spencer (1997: 78) has put it, the socio-demographic make-up of much of the British countryside may be being formed by 'events in the present' which are 'rooted in structures created in the past'.

Spencer (1995; 1997) argues that major landowners in so-called 'closed parishes' – that is, parishes where a few landowners own most of the property – often acted in the past to prevent or minimize residential growth. Even after the 1947 Town and Country Planning Act, growth in such areas has been limited, either through direct landowner control over the release of land for development and influence over local planning decisions, or more generally through the tendency of local planning policies

Types of capital and associated practices of gentrification			Phase in the circuit of capital	Type of agency gentrification	Cultural orientation
Labour/products	Physical infrastructure	Finance			
Decline of agricultural workforce	Devalorized properties	Centralization of capital ownership, productive capital investment in agriculture	Devalorization of capital	Multiple	Devalorization of long-standing hegemonic blocs
Rebuilds and restorations	Refurbishment of rustic properties	Investment in residential properties	Direct capital investment	Individualized	Gentrifiers with high degree of counter-cultural orientation
Production of gentrification products – i.e., replica products and buildings	Creation of ensemble of facilities to create a rural 'scene'	Creation of local real-estate marked investment in consumption services	Intensification of capital	Individualized but more empowered	Decreasing counter-cultural orientation
Gentrified lifestyle magazines; village publications	Demarcation of historical buildings, vernacular house styles, conservation zones	Promotion of area as desirable residential and perhaps tourist and retail destination; fictitious capital (credit) encourages further expansion	Symbolization of capital	National and multinational firms	Increasing use of commodified cultural textures
Circulation of ideas and personnel	Pressure for gentrified new-build	Professionalized agencies of rural gentrification emerge	Diffusion and corporatization of capital	Large corporate and specialist capital	Emergence of new gentrified hegemonic bloc

Table 32.2 Rural gentrification as a consumption space for capital circulation

to seek to conserve, rather than reformulate, existing distributions of population and development. Within a seemingly homogenized land-use planning system, the countryside was widely compartmentalized into 'growth centres' and areas where development was to be 'restricted', a feature which was very much the focus of one of the first studies to use the term 'rural gentrification' (Parsons, 1980).

In his study of gentrification in south Nottinghamshire and north Norfolk, Parsons (1980: 17) argued that local planning authorities in Britain have tended to exercise development control through a framework of settlement classification based on 'selected growth centres' and places in which development is discouraged, and that this framework has 'influenced the geographical impact of gentrification in rural areas' (Parsons, 1980: 17). In particular he suggests that gentrification, largely conceptualized in terms of an expanding middle-class presence, was greatest in areas where development was discouraged and least in areas selected for growth.

For Parsons, explanation of this geography of gentrification lay largely in the lack of low- to medium-cost local-authority housing in areas not selected for growth, although he does note that conservation status may attract in-migration by people concerned about house-price security (see also Cloke, 1979; 1983; Cloke and Thrift, 1987). While the demise of council-house provision following the 1980 Housing Act might be seen to undermine Parsons' principal line of argument, studies have suggested that the sale of council-housing properties was proportionally greatest in 'smaller village locations' (Milbourne, 1998: 175; see also Beazley et al., 1980) and that these sales, at least in rural Northamptonshire, were accompanied by a substantial influx of 'service-class households' (Chaney and Sherwood, 2000: 79–94). Hence, not only may the decrease in social housing be greatest in small rural settlements, but this decline may itself contribute to the gentrification of areas which, by the logic of Parsons, were already attracting affluent in-migrants.

While there is clearly scope for substantive work on the specific arguments of Parsons and Spencer, more abstractly they may be seen to signpost the firstspace geographies of uneven incidence and use of socially constructed space, and also routes towards secondspace and thirdspace geographies of rural gentrification. With reference to firstspace perspectives, there is, as Smith and Phillips (2001: 457) put it, a 'knowledge gap' not only about the uneven geography of instances of rural gentrification but also about whether particular social constructions of space play an active role in the constitution of

this geography of gentrification. The work of Spencer and Parsons may be seen, however, to suggest that rural gentrification is focused on spaces composed of small, low-density settlements in which there is relatively little new house construction, particularly within large, modernist, estates. Such settlements conform closely with the secondspace, normative geographies of the English landscape identified by people such as Matless, whereas many of the growth settlements might be seen to transgress the boundaries of a 'proper' rural settlement, becoming some settlement in between the urban, the rural and the suburb.

The emphasis on historicity also points to these areas having commensurability with Zukin's urban socio-spatial complexes of initial gentrification, although the importance of such features as geographical centrality and social density are not necessarily shared, at least to the same extent. As Smith and Phillips (2001: 458) remark, there is a need to recognize the 'cultural and social differentiation which is embedded within and between social contexts', such as the urban and the rural, and indeed within and between different urbanities and ruralities. They focus particularly on the latter, suggesting that in the Hebden Bridge area of west Yorkshire two distinct constructions of rural space were of significance to gentrifiers, namely 'remote' and 'village' rurality. In the former, desirable rurality involved (relative) isolation from modern, capitalist society and placement in a historic and natural but challenging environment, while in the latter it was constructed more by reference to notions of communal intimacy, support and safety. Such constructions of rurality have wider currency, bearing close resemblance, for instance, to aspects of both Cloke et al.'s (1995; 1998) 'move-in for self' and 'move-in and join-in' households and, even more generally, to Short's (1991: xvi) 'environmental myths' of 'wilderness' and 'countryside' which he sees as '(re)-presentations of reality which resonate across space and over time' being 'broad enough to encompass diverse experiences yet deep enough to anchor these experiences in a continuous medium of meaning'. Smith and Phillips, however, stress that these conceptions of rurality had local inflections connected to the historical production of material landscapes, with 'successive systems of agriculture and textile production of the past' being 'intimately bound up with difference now inscribed within this contemporary cultural landscape' (Smith and Phillips, 2001: 459). This emphasis on the historical materialist productions of spatialized identities is very much shared by Zukin in her notion of gentrification as a 'socio-spatial complex', although as noted earlier she initiates her analysis after the construction of a desirable material landscape.

The onset of gentrification may be seen not only to require the construction of desired material landscapes, and the associated construction of landscapes of desire and distaste, but also to involve the construction of 'channels of entry' into that space (see Beauregard, 1986). It is here that the devaluation of rural space associated with early discussions of post-productivism may be of considerable significance in understanding the geographies of rural gentrification. Changes such as the centralization of capital ownership, an increasing focus on direct productive capital investment as opposed to investment in social capital and the substitution of capital for labour in modern agriculture have all served to produce properties and areas of land which are of less value to agricultural users, and hence which may well be made available to agents of gentrification. As has been well documented by agricultural geographers, the implementation of such change has been temporally and spatially uneven, features which may further contribute to the uneven geographies of rural gentrification. Furthermore, the outcome of these changes has also been historically and geographically varied, a point which can be illustrated through Drudy's (1978) study of demographic and agricultural change in north Norfolk and the results of some recent research in the area discussed in Phillips (2001; 2004).

Drudy characterized north Norfolk as an area of prosperous agriculture and argued that the prosperity of the region's agriculture had been brought about through the substitution of capital for labour, and a resultant fall in the agricultural labour force. He argued that, while depopulation is often associated with economic marginality, itself a product of agrarian restructuring which means farmers in some regions become uncompetitive (see also Drudy and Drudy, 1979), in north Norfolk these changes, while productive of regional economic prosperity, also created rural depopulation by removing occupational opportunities in rural areas. In addition, these changes may have altered the housing situation in many villages in that the process of capital substitution may have devalorized not only the agricultural labourer but also many of the residential properties held by agricultural landowners.

One aspect of this was that with fewer agricultural workers there were fewer tenants to live in tied cottages, while at the same time many agricultural landowners were seeking sources of finance to enable the substitution of capital for labour. As a number of studies have outlined (e.g. Bettley-Smith, 1982; Bowler and Lewis, 1987), for many landowners

this combination of circumstances was resolved by selling off their rented accommodation to realize capital to invest in agriculture and/or in the purchase of more land, a practice which acted as a further stimulus to out-migration as many former tenants could not afford to purchase properties. Out-migration was further stimulated, so Drudy argued, by a loss of various services within the village, with this decline in services being initially triggered by the decline in the agricultural population of the village. Drudy (1978) conducted an analysis of population change in the period from 1951 to 1971, and suggested that there was an overall decline in the population of north Norfolk of just over 10% in this period.

Drudy's analysis of demographic change centres on the number of individuals, and some more recent work (e.g., Weekley, 1988; Spencer, 1995; 1997; Lewis, 1998) has argued that attention needs to be paid to relating household and total population levels. Lewis (1998), for instance, records a decline in the number of people and households in the neighbouring district of Breckland between 1961 and 1971, but notes that the figure was less than 1% for household losses. In the case of north Norfolk, the average level of change in the district's non-urban parishes in this period was actually an increase of population of just under 1%, while the average number of households actually grew by over 6.5%. However, as Figure 32.1 shows, these overall figures mask considerable variations between parishes, and the tendency of those with low population densities to have experienced deductions in both population numbers and households, while those with above-average population densities saw both population and household numbers increasing, with the latter increasing to a greater extent than the former. These figures suggest that in the smallest settlements the classical image of a 'landscape of depopulation' (Weekley, 1988: 127), involving unoccupied properties falling into dereliction, may have had some validity in north Norfolk in the 1960s, but in many other settlements there was continuity or growth in household occupation, albeit accompanied by decreases in household size, a decrease which in some cases spelt a decline in population numbers even though the number of households was static or increasing.

This pattern of change may be indicative of gentrification. Spencer (1997: 75), for instance, has argued that divergence between household and population trends may be seen as a product of gentrification in that net losses to an area's population may occur when 'affluent households comprising one or two persons (often middle aged

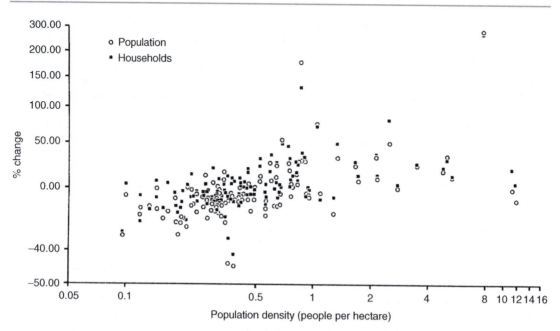

Population density (people per hectare)

Figure 32.1 Population and household change in parishes in north Norfolk, 1961–1971

Sources: Figures derived from General Register Office 1964: Census 1961 England and Wales County Report, Norfolk, London: HMSO; and Office of Population Censuses and Surveys 1973: Census 1971 England and Wales County Report, Norfolk, London: HMSO

or elderly)' move into a house previously occupied by a larger family. This depopulation through population turnover may well be triggered by the tenurial changes identified as a causal factor in rural depopulation in that many sitting tenants could not afford to purchase properties when estate landowners decided to convert them from rented properties, and as a result the properties were brought by smaller but more affluent, more 'middle class' households. Spencer (1997: 89), for instance, records that tenurial restructuring in the parish of Stoke Talmage in Oxfordshire triggered 'greater turnover within the existing dwelling stock than the parish had hitherto experienced' with the area becoming 'colonized by middle-aged gentrifiers'. Spencer concludes that 'landowner disinvestment … created a supply of potentially gentrifiable properties inhabited by relatively powerless social groups who were easily persuaded (or forced) to move away' (p. 89), a comment which has striking parallels with Beauregard's (1986: 47) view that gentrification requires not only the creation of gentrifiable housing but also 'the creation of prior occupants for that housing who can easily be displaced or replaced'. Gentrified population turnover does not necessarily have to involve depopulation, and Parsons (1979)

identifies cases in north Norfolk where 'occupied housing or former single person dwellings' came to be occupied by young families, suggesting that 'very often the size of the family was itself a motivation' for residential refurbishment (see also Phillips, 1993).

A second consequence of changes in the region's agriculture of significance to gentrification was that a series of non-residential properties also became available for purchase and conversion as many agricultural buildings became unsuited to housing the increasingly large-scale agricultural machinery. An examination of planning applications within the districts of north and south Norfolk reveals a range of agriculture and agriculture-related buildings being converted to residential use, including barns, cowsheds, dairies, stables and mills. Third, the decline in local services associated with rural depopulation also provided further buildings that might be suitable for conversion: hence the planning registers of the two districts record the conversion of buildings such as post offices and shops, public houses, tea rooms and hotels, laundries, schools, chapels, workshops and warehouses. Fourth, while disinvesting themselves from residential and agrarian properties, many landowners were simultaneously expanding their agricultural land-holdings, a practice which could significantly restrict land for new-build development (see Spencer, 1997; Phillips, 2001) and which in turn could lead to increasing house prices for existing properties.

The degree to which areas underwent such changes is clearly conditioned by a range of factors including the precise accumulation strategies adopted by particular landowners (see Spencer, 1995; 1997; and, for an urban illustration, Lees, 1994a). Furthermore, as mentioned previously, the timing of change could also vary considerably, with many of the changes identified above with the period of rural depopulation in the second half of the twentieth century occurring earlier in some localities and later in others. As in the firstspace geography of urban gentrification, this areal variation could occur at a variety of scales down to the very localized. In Phillips (2002; 2004), for instance, I contrast the village of Thornage in north Norfolk, which appears to have undergone many of the changes identified above during the period of rural depopulation, with the village of Shotesham in south Norfolk, where the closed structure of land-holding collapsed in the early twentieth century when the major estate landowner, like many other landed gentry, sold off both land and properties.

Such studies not only reinforce the arguments made earlier about the complex temporalities of gentrification but also reveal how material, symbolic and lived constructions of space may themselves impact the course of gentrification with an area. In the case of Thornage, for example, capital disinvestment occurred during the period of rural depopulation at the start of the second half of the twentieth century and was very much focused on the disposal of residential and agrarian property within the village, with agrarian land-holdings outside of the village remaining in the hands of the estate landowner. While this provided a stimulus for gentrification in this period, it subsequently restricted opportunities for residential new-build and thwarted various attempts to develop communal facilities (see Phillips, 2001). This latter feature can be seen to have made the village less attractive for people with children or those wishing to 'move-in and join-in', although it might have made it more attractive for those seeking a quiet living space.

In the case of Shotesham, its history of a highly closed property structure created a settlement which had a scale and historicity of appeal to gentrifiers (see Phillips, 2001; 2004), while the breakup of this structure in the early twentieth century, together with subsequent movements of capital within agriculture, served to release a range of spaces and properties for revalorization as gentrified residential property. Indeed, a range of gentrified recreational, retailing

and consumption sites also emerged in the area surrounding this and neighbouring gentrified villages, suggestive of an intensification of gentrification capital as outlined by Zukin (see Tables 32.1 and 32.2). As recorded earlier, Smith and Phillips (2001: 459) note the increasing involvement of commercial agencies and the production of ready-made gentrification commodities. In the case of the two Norfolk villages, local building and development companies were actively involved in attempts to both refurbish existing properties and to develop new housing, often of a style that simulated refurbished gentrified properties. In Shotesham, some of the small-scale landowners transformed themselves into property developers, and there was also evidence of small-scale 'hobby gentrifiers' who undertook the purchase and refurbishment of a series of properties, either in series or parallel, as a part-time activity (see Phillips, 1999). In the area surrounding the village, there has emerged a veritable 'gentrification industry', focused both on the refurbishment of existing buildings and furnishings, and also on the production of replica products and buildings. With the intensification came rising prices, particularly for those properties able to claim some degree of authenticity among the spiralling replication.

As well as intensification, the two villages have been subject to growing symbolization, gaining recognition as conservation areas and many of the buildings receiving designations of historical association and housing style. Much of the initiative for these designations came from the gentrifiers themselves and hence may be seen to connect to thirdspace constructions of rurality as lived space (see also Phillips, 2002). However, also driving much of this growing symbolization of gentrified rural space has been the involvement of larger units of capital and increasingly specialized and professional agencies of rural gentrification. Much of this is connected with continued pressure for further development of these gentrified areas, in many cases via large-scale new-build developments. Such developments threaten the small-scale character of the settlements prized by many gentrifiers and have been met by resistance by existing gentrifiers, other rural residents and local planning authorities. To help assuage such conflicts there appears to be an increasing use of professional agencies such as planning and design consultants, many of which are themselves locating with gentrified rural areas and very much specializing in the promotion of gentrification. As in Zukin's urban prototype (Table 32.1), it is possible to see rural gentrification as stimulating a self-reproducing circulation of ideas and personnel focused on the symbolic and material construction of gentrified forms of rural space. First-, second- and thirdspaces are, in such instances, being clearly drawn together, although this should not be seen to imply that full closure is achieved, or indeed is likely to be achieved.

V CONCLUSION

This paper has sought to explore the call to examine the 'geography of gentrification'. It began by arguing that the call has been conducted in such a way that this geography is construed as involving examination of the uneven incidence of gentrification. It is suggested that this construction of the geography of gentrification enacts what, following (Soja, 1996), might be described as a 'firstspace epistemology'. However, traces of other, first-, second- and thirdspace epistemologies are also identified within gentrification studies. It is argued that these geographies may not be fully commensurable with each other but that complementary accounts of them can potentially be constructed.

While the first main section of the paper sought to widen the scope of studies of the geography of gentrification into the study of commensurable and incommensurable geographies of gentrification, the second section of the paper sought to widen the scope of the geographies of gentrification beyond the urban. The call for an examination of the geography of gentrification has been almost exclusively urban in focus, but this paper argues that many of the arguments raised with respect to urban space are complementary, if not necessarily fully commensurable, with a series of rural studies. This argument is developed further in the third section of the paper, which has explored the notion of gentrification as a socio-spatial complex, drawing on existing studies and some of the author's own research in Norfolk. Although this examination focuses very much on the first-space geographies of rural gentrification, the significance of a normative geography of urbanity, rurality and suburbia is also highlighted. As discussed in the second section of the paper, this normative geography resonates with notions of secondspace and thirdspace, although in this paper attention is primarily focused on consideration of how this geography is implicated in the firstspace geography of rural gentrification associated with the devaluation and reinvestment of labour, commodities and financial capital in areas of the countryside. There clearly are many other geographies of gentrification to be written relating both to this case study and to the gentrification of rural and urban spaces more generally. These geographies may well contain

significant elements of commensurability, but also incommensurability, and a key but far from easy task in the study of the geographies of gentrification may well be, as Smith and Phillips (2001: 458) comment, to 'tease out' the differentiations which are embedded 'within' as well as 'between' particular spatial contexts.

ACKNOWLEDGEMENTS

This paper draws on research which was conducted through receipt of an ESRC Research Fellowship on 'The processes of rural gentrification' (ref: H53627500695) and their support, together with that of the University of Leicester, is gratefully acknowledged. Thanks are also due to the two anonymous referees for their challenging yet constructive comments on the initial paper, and also to the editor, Ron Johnson, for his succinct charting of ways to improve the paper.

Notes

1 This is not to say that no differences can be seen to exist between the intra-national and the inter-metropolitan. Lees, for instance, has on several occasions stressed the importance of national context (see Lees, 1994a; Carpenter and Lees, 1995) and her notion of an intra-national analysis can be seen as a call to conduct comparisons between cities within a national space. Ley's 'inter-metropolitan' focus at times takes a similar form, as in his analyses of six Canadian cities (Ley, 1988; 1992; 1996), but appears to relate more to the presence of comparative data within national territories rather than a theoretical claim about the role of the nation in the constitution of gentrification. Ley (1996) does posit some national variations, claiming that Australian and Canadian gentrification may be rather different from gentrification in the USA but these seem to stem from similarities and differences in the economic structure of cities in these countries rather than any 'particularities of the nation state' (p. 81). As a consequence Ley's 'inter-metropolitan' focus would be as appropriately conducted as a comparative study of cities across nations, save for the lack of 'truly comparative data' (p. 81). Despite these differences, Ley's 'inter-metropolitan' and Lees' 'intra-national' both share a focus on comparative studies between cities.

2 This is the form of integration which Hamnett (1991) was seeking to forge, and Clark (1992a) suggests that it is clearly evident with respect to rent-gap and value-gap explanations of gentrification (see also Clark, 1992b). Bridge's (1994) discussion of class and gentrification can also be seen as endeavouring to increase the commensurability of gentrification theory, although he also highlights conjunctural aspects as well.

3 As noted in Phillips (2002), although Lees (1994b: 140) argues for a recognition of 'complementarity' whereby 'synthesis and a concern for contradiction and dialectical opposites become equally important', she also calls for 'higher modes of representation which synthesize'. This later request could be interpreted as a call for the commensurable rather than complementary theory, particularly given her remark that 'complementarity … is not a profound solution' (p. 140). She suggests that the higher mode of representation is dialectics, although one might question whether dialectics necessarily involves the dissolution of incommensurability or its displacement into new registers (see Phillips 2002 on distinction between *aufheben* and *überwinden* dialectics, and their relation to commensurability and incommensurablity and a Lefebvrian 'trialectics of space').

4 This is not to say that a people will not express such a viewpoint. One of the referees for this paper, for instance, claimed that rural 'gentrification' studies were not examining 'gentrification in the "true" sense of the word' but rather should be described as studies of 'rural upgrading'. Such arguments can, however, be criticized on several counts. First, they express what I have described elsewhere (Phillips, 2002) as a 'legislative epistemology' which seeks to establish and defend definitive understandings of terms such as gentrification on the basis that this is the only strategy for creating representations of the world. As outlined in Phillips (2002), such an epistemology has been widely critiqued beyond and within gentrification studies, not least for its neglect of the indeterminancy, mobility and exclusionary aspects of theory (Lees, 1996). The claim that urban studies holds the true meaning of the term gentrification may be seen as questionable on all three grounds. First, it overlooks the considerable degree of contestation over the meaning of the term within urban studies, a contestation which has filled in the essentially very scant definition of gentrification contained in Glass (1964) with a whole host of commensurable and incommensurable concepts: as Jager (1986: 78)

put it, gentrification was 'a concept in formation' and arguably should be allowed to remain so. Second, the positing of gentrification as essentially urban ignores the evident mobility of the term, which has both long established usage in rural as well as urban studies (see Phillips, 1993) and also clear rural roots in its initial formulation, it being suggested that Glass coined the term because of the parallels she saw between change in 1960s London and the processes of social emulation identified in historical studies of rural gentry (see for example, Hamnett, 2003). Third, the differentiation of 'urban gentrification' and 'rural upgrading' may produce further unwarranted divisions in thought. The term 'upgrading' has been described by Smith (1996: 32) as 'anodyne terminology' which lacks the critical connotations associated with the word gentrification. Given the claim of Murdoch and Marsden (1994: 1) of an 'aversion to notions of class in rural studies', then the value of selecting a term with such potential impacts should be considered carefully (similar comments might also be made about the concept of 'greenification' proposed by Smith and Phillips, 2001). Furthermore, the term upgrading may also be seen to enact the 'outcome focus' identified by Smith (2002) and discussed further in the text of this paper. While many studies of 'rural gentrification' have arguably failed to proceed much beyond the identification of a 'social upgrading outcome' – generally a rise in 'middle-class incomers' and a decline in 'working class locals' (see Cloke and Thrift, 1987, for a critical review) – this should not be taken to imply that many of the processes identified with respect to urban gentrification are necessarily absent from rural areas. Indeed, as outlined in the text, a variety of studies have identified numerous rural parallels to the processes of gentrification detailed within urban studies.

5 Phillips and Smith (2001) might be seen to provide an illustration of the former position in that, as outlined earlier in the paper, they see 'urban gentrification' being stimulated by ' "urban" qualities' and rural gentrification (or 'rural greenification' as they prefer to call it) by 'the demand for, and perception of "green" residential space' (p. 457). The second, more exclusionary position, might be seen to be enacted in a further argument advanced by the referee who wished to restrict the application of the term gentrification to urban space, namely that 'gentrification' is 'about … urbanity, about … embracing the city' while 'rural upgrading' is 'about rurality' and 'about rejecting the city'.

6 A few traces of a rural landscape of desire may indeed be identified in Ley's text. He, for example, makes reference to a quote from one of Caulfield's respondents who speaks of living in a village-like neighbourhood (Ley, 1996: 208; quote from Caulfield, 1994: 170).

7 This is of course not to say that rural gentrification and post-productivism are necessarily fully commensurable concepts. Although the latter term has often been promoted as a way of recognizing ruralities beyond the agricultural, the possibilities of a '"post-agricultural" future for the countryside' (Evans et al., 2002: 328) and for recognizing 'horizontal' linkages between agriculture and other sectors of rural economy, many of its elaborations have been conducted with almost exclusive reference to agriculture (e.g., Ilbery and Bowler, 1998; Wilson, 2001; Evans et al., 2002). Evans et al. (2002) have critiqued the concept of post-productivism, arguing among other things that it is overly abstract and over-arching, and, while they advance these criticisms solely in relation to 'developing theoretically informed perspectives on agriculture', it could be argued that these arguments are equally pertinent to attempts to extend the concept to encompass elements of the non- or extra- agricultural, such as rural gentrification, particularly given long-running arguments about the distinctiveness of agricultural activity within capitalist economies and societies (e.g., Kautsky, 1989; Winter, 1984; Mann, 1990; Goodman and Redclift, 1991; Page, 1996; Goodman and Watts, 1997). Having said this, as argued in the text the origins of the post-productivist concept do lie, in part, in just such arenas and many of its claims revolve around an examination of their interconnections with the agricultural. Not only would rural gentrification appear to be commensurable with such elements of post-productivist theorizing but it might be suggested that the concept of post-productivism itself encompasses potential incommensurabilities and might be conceived as a form of complementary rather than fully commensurable theorizing.

8 Evans et al. (2002) very much stress a temporal construction of post-productivism and highlight some of the inconsistencies in the dating of a supposed transition to post-productivism. They suggest that there are close parallels between the concept of post-productivism and those of post-Fordism and postmodernism, and perhaps could usefully have made some reference to debates surrounding these two concepts over whether the 'post-' prefix implies 'a periodizing concept' as Jameson (1985: 113) argues, or

whether it has no chronological connotations, as people such as Eco (1984) have argued (see also Cloke et al., 1991; Dear, 2000; Phillips, 1998b). Likewise, while it may be that the term post-productivism is being widely interpreted as after-productivism, and hence Evans et al. (2002) usefully highlight discrepancies in the chronology of its emergence, post-productivism may be interpreted in other ways, such as unconformity to productivism or a self-aware productivism. In the present study, the term is effectively being used in the first of these two non-temporal senses, but the second sense of the term raises a series of other questions which if pursued might lead one to question Evans et al.'s (2002: 325) conclusion that post-productivism is 'a distraction from developing theoretically informed perspectives on agriculture'.

REFERENCES

Atwood, M. 1979: *Life before man.* Toronto: McClelland and Stewart.

Beauregard, R.A. 1986: The chaos and complexity of gentrification. In Smith, N. and Williams, P., editors, *Gentrification of the city*, London: Allen and Unwin, 35–55.

——1990: Trajectories of neighbourhood change: the case of gentrification. *Environment and Planning D: Society and Space* 22, 855–74.

Beazley, M., Gavin, D., Gillon, S., Raine, C. and Staunton, M. 1980: *The sale of council houses in a rural area: a case study of South Oxfordshire.* Working Paper 44, Department of Planning, Oxford Polytechnic.

Bettley-Smith, R. 1982: *Capital investment by landowners on tenanted agricultural estates, 1972–1977.* Discussion Paper no. 8. Department of Land Economy, University of Cambridge.

Bowler, I. and **Lewis, G.** 1987: The decline of private rental housing in rural areas: a case study of villages in Northamptonshire. In Lockhart, D.G. and Ilbery, B., editors, *The future of the British rural landscape*, Norwich: GeoBooks, 115–36.

Bridge, G. 1994: The space for class? On class analysis in the study of gentrification. *Transactions of the Institute of British Geographers* NS 20, 236–47.

Butler, T. 1997: *Gentrification and the middle classes.* Aldershot: Ashgate.

Cameron, S. 1992: Housing, gentrification and urban regeneration. *Urban Studies* 29, 3–14.

Carpenter, J. and **Lees, L.** 1995: Gentrification in New York, London and Paris: an international comparison. *International Journal of Urban and Regional Research* 19, 287–303.

Caulfield, J. 1989: Gentrification and desire. *Canadian Review of Social Anthropology* 26, 616–32.

——1994: *City form and everyday life: Toronto's gentrification and critical social practice.* Toronto: University of Toronto Press.

Chaney, P. and **Sherwood, K.** 2000: The resale of right to buy dwellings: a case study of migration and social change in rural England. *Journal of Rural Studies* 16, 79–94.

Clark, E. 1992a: On blindness, centrepieces and complementarity in gentrification theory. *Transactions of the Institute of British Geographers* NS 17, 358–62.

——1992b: On gaps in gentrification theory. *Housing Studies* 7, 16–26.

——1995: The rent gap re-examined. *Urban Studies* 32, 1489–503.

Clark, E. and **Gullberg, A.** 1991: Long swings, rent gaps and structures of building provision – the postwar transformation of Stockholm's inner city. *International Journal of Urban and Regional Research* 15, 492–504.

Cloke, P. 1979: *Key settlements in rural areas.* London: Methuen.

——1983: *An introduction to rural settlement planning.* London: Methuen.

Cloke, P. and **Thrift, N.** 1987: Intra-class conflict in rural areas. *Journal of Rural Studies* 4, 321–33.

Cloke, P., Phillips, M. and **Thrift, N.** 1995: The new middle classes and the social constructs of rural living. In Butler, T. and Savage, M., editors, *Social change and the middle classes*, London: UCL Press, 220–38.

——1998: Class, colonisation and lifestyle strategies in Gower. In Boyle, P. and Halfacree, K., editors, *Migration to rural areas*, London: Wiley, 166–85.

Cloke, P., Philo, C. and **Sadler, D.** 1991: *Approaching human geography.* London: Paul Chapman.

Dear, M. 2000: *The postmodern urban condition.* Oxford: Blackwell.

Drudy, P. 1978: Depopulation in a prosperous agricultural sub-region. *Regional Studies* 12, 49–60.

Drudy, P. and **Drudy, S.** 1979: Population mobility and labour supply in rural regions: North Norfolk and Galway Gaelacht. *Regional Studies* 13, 91–99.

Eco, U. 1984: *Postscript to the Name of the Rose.* San Diego: Harcourt Brace Jovanovich.

Evans, N., Morris, C. and **Winter, M.** 2002: Conceptualizing agriculture: a critique of post-productivism as the new orthodoxy. *Progress in Human Geography* 26, 313–32.

Featherstone, M. 1991: *Consumer culture and postmodernism.* London: Sage.

Garner, H. 1976: *The intruders.* Toronto: McGraw Hill Ryerson.

Glass, R. 1964: *London: aspects of change.* London: MacGibbon and Kee.

Goodman, D. and **Redclift, M.** 1991: *Refashioning nature: feed, ecology and culture.* London: Routledge.

Goodman, D. and **Watts, M.** 1997: *Globalising food: agrarian questions and global restructuring.* London: Routledge.

Halfacree, K. 1997: Contrasting roles for the post-productivist countryside: a postmodern perspective on counterurbanisation. In Cloke, P. and Little, J., editors, *Contested countryside: otherness, marginalisation and rurality*, London: Routledge, 109–22.

——1998: Neo-tribes, migration and the post-productivist countryside. In Boyle, P. and Halfacree, K., editors, *Migration into rural areas*, London: Wiley, 200–14.

Hamnett, C. 1991: The blind men and the elephant: the explanation of gentrification. *Transactions of the Institute of British Geographers* NS 16, 173–89.

——2002: Gentrification and the middle class remaking of London. European Online Seminar on Urban Transformation, Poverty, Spatial Segregation and Social Exclusion. http://www.shakti.uniurb.it/eurex/syllabus/syllabus.htm (last accessed 15 August 2003).

Harvey, D. 1987: Flexible accumulation through urbanisation: reflections of 'postmodernism' in the American city. *Antipode* 19, 260–86.

Holmes, J. 2002: Diversity and change in Australia's rangelands: a post-productivist transition with a difference. *Transactions of the Institute of British Geographers* NS 27, 362–84.

Ilbery, B. and **Bowler, I.** 1998: From agricultural productivism to post-productivism. In Ilbery, B., editor, *The geography of rural change*, Harlow: Longman, 57–84.

Jager, M. 1986: Class definition and the esthetics of gentrification: Victoriana in Melbourne. In Smith, N. and Williams, P., editors, *Gentrification of the city*, London: Unwin and Hyman, 78–81.

Jameson, F. 1985: Postmodernism and consumer society. In Foster, H., editor, *Postmodern culture*, London: Pluto Press, 111–25.

Kautsky, M. 1989: *The agrarian question*. London: Zwan.

Kerstein, R. 1990: Stage models of gentrification: an examination. *Urban Affairs Quarterly* 25, 620–39.

Kneale, K., Lowe, P. and **Marsden T.** 1992: *The conversion of agricultural buildings: an analysis of variable pressures and regulations towards the post-productivist countryside*. ESRC Countryside Change Initiative Working Paper no. 29, University of Newcastle.

Lees, L. 1994a: Gentrification in London and New York: an Atlantic gap? *Housing Studies* 9, 199–217.

——1994b: Rethinking gentrification: beyond the positions of economics or culture. *Progress in Human Geography* 18, 137–50.

——1996: In the pursuit of difference: representations of gentrification. *Environment and Planning A* 28, 453–70.

——2000: A reappraisal of gentrification: towards a 'geography of gentrification'. *Progress in Human Geography* 24, 389–408.

Lees, L. and **Berg, L.D.** 1995: Ponga, glass and concrete: a vision for urban socio-cultural geography in Aotearoa/New Zealand. *New Zealand Geographer* 51, 32–41.

Lefebvre, H. 1991: *The production of space*. Oxford: Blackwell.

Lewis, G. 1998: Rural migration and demographic change. In Ilbery, B., editor, *The geography of rural change*, Harlow: Longman, 131–60.

Ley, D. 1988: Social upgrading in six Canadian inner cities. *Canadian Geographer* 32, 31–45.

——1989: Fragmentation, coherence, and limits to theory in human geography. In Kobayashi, A. and MacKenzie, S., editors, *Remaking human geography*, London: Unwin Hyman, 227–44.

——1992: Gentrification in recession: social change in six Canadian inner cities, 1981–1986. *Urban Geography* 13, 230–56.

——1996: *The new middle class and the remaking of the central city*. Oxford: Oxford University Press.

Lowe, P., Murdoch, J., Marsden, T., Munton, R. and **Flynn, A.** 1993: Regulating the new rural spaces: the uneven development of land. *Journal of Rural Studies* 9, 205–22.

Mann, S. 1990: *Agrarian capitalism*. Durham: University of North Carolina Press.

Matless, D. 1990: Ages of English design: preservation, modernism and tales of their history, 1926–1939. *Journal of Design History* III, 203–13.

——1994: Doing the English Village, 1945–90: an essay in imaginative geography. In Cloke, P., Doel, M., Matless, D., Phillips, M. and Thrift, N., *Writing the rural: five cultural geographies*, London: Paul Chapman, 7–88.

——1998: *Landscape and Englishness*. London: Reaktion Books.

Merrifield. A. 1993: Place and space: a Lefebvrian reconciliation. *Transactions of the Instititute of British Geographers* NS 18, 516–31.

Milbourne, P. 1998: Local responses to central state restructuring of social housing provision in rural areas. *Journal of Rural Studies* 14, 167–84.

Mills, C. 1986: 'Life on the upslope': the postmodern landscape of gentrification. *Environment and Planning D: Society and Space* 6, 169–89.

Murdoch, J. and **Marsden, T.** 1994: *Reconstituting rurality: class, community and power in the development process*. London: UCL Press.

Newby, H. 1987: *Country life: a social history of rural England*. London: Wiedenfeld and Nicolson.

Page, B. 1996: Across the great divide: agriculture and industrial geography. *Economic Geography* 67, 281–315.

Parsons, D. 1979: A geographical examination of the twentieth century theory and practice of selected village development in England. Unpublished PhD thesis, University of Nottingham.

——1980: *Rural gentrification: the influence of rural settlement planning policies*. Department of Geography Research Paper no. 3, University of Sussex, Brighton.

Phillips, M. 1993: Rural gentrification and the processes of class colonisation. *Journal of Rural Studies* 9, 123–40.

——1998a: Investigations of the British rural middle classes: part 1, fragmentation, identity, morality and contestation. *Journal of Rural Studies* 14, 427–43.

——1998b: The restructuring of social imaginations in rural geography. *Journal of Rural Studies* 18, 21–153.

——1999: *The processes of rural gentrification*. Project report, ESRC Research Fellowship (H53627500695). Working Paper, Department of Geography, University of Leicester.

——2001: Making space for rural gentrification. In Hernando, F.M., editor, *2nd Anglo-Spanish Symposium of Rural Geography*, Valladolid: University of Valladolid, section 1.2, 1–21.

——2002: The production, symbolisation and socialisation of gentrification: impressions from two Berkshire villages. *Transactions of the Institute of British Geographers* NS 27, 282–308.

——2004: Differential productions of rural gentrification: illustrations from east Norfolk. *Geoforum*, in press.

Price, P. 1999: Longing for less of the same. *Annals of the Association of American Geographers* 89, 342–44.

Rose, D. 1984: Rethinking gentrification: beyond the uneven development of Marxist urban theory. *Environment and Planning D: Society and Space* 2, 47–74.

Short, J.R. 1991: *Imagined country: society, culture and environment.* London: Routledge.

Smith, D. 2002: Extending the temporal and spatial limits of gentrification: a research agenda for population geographers. *International Journal of Population Geography* 8, 385–94.

Smith, D. and **Phillips, D.** 2001: Socio-culrural representations of greentrified Pennine rurality. *Journal of Rural Studies* 17, 457–69.

Smith, N. 1979: Toward a theory of gentrification: a back to the city movement by capital not people. *Journal of the American Planners Association* 35, 538–48.

——1982: Gentrification and uneven development. *Economic Geography* 58, 139–55.

——1992: Blind man's bluff or, Hamnett's philosophical individualism in search of gentrification. *Transactions of the Institute of British Geographers* NS 17, 110–15.

——1996: *The new urban frontier: gentrification and the revanchist city.* London: Routledge.

——1999: The reassertion of economics: 1990s gentrification in the Lower East side. *International Journal of Urban and Regional Research* 23, 638–53.

Soja, E. 1996: *Thirdspace: journeys to Los Angeles and other real-and-imagined places.* Oxford: Blackwell.

Spencer, D. 1995: Counterurbanisation: the local dimension. *Geoforum* 26, 153–73.

——1997: Counterurbanisation and rural depopulation revisited: landowners, planners and the rural development process. *Journal of Rural Studies* 13, 75–92.

S'ykora, L. 1993: City in transition: the role of rent gaps in Prague's revitalization. *Tijdschrift voor Economische en Sociale Geografie* 84, 281–93.

Thrift, N. 1989: New times and new spaces? The perils of transition models. *Environment and Planning D: Society and Space* 7, 127–29.

Ward, N. 1993: The agricultural treadmill and the rural environment in the post-productivist era. *Sociologia Ruralis* 23, 348–64.

Weekley, I. 1988: Counterurbanisation and rural depopulation: a paradox. *Area* 20, 127–34.

Whyte, W. 1957: *The organizational man.* Garden City, NY: Doubleday.

Wilson, G.A. 2001 From productivism to post-productivism … and back again? Exploring the (un)changed natural and mental landscapes of European agriculture. *Transactions of the Institute of British Geographers* NS 26, 77–102.

Winter, M. 1984: Agrarian class structures and family farming. In Bradely, T. and Lowe, P., editors, *Locality and rurality: economy and society in rural regions*, Norwich: GeoBooks, 113–28.

Zukin, S. 1982: *Loft living: culture and capital in urban change.* New Brunswick: Rutgers University Press.

——1987: Gentrification: culture and capital in the urban core. *American Review of Sociology* 13, 129–47.

——1990: Socio-spatial prototypes of a new organization of consumption: the role of real cultural capital. *Sociology* 24, 37–56.

PART SIX

Gentrification and urban policy

Plate 18 **'Revitalize!' Saint Louis, Missouri, 2007.** Photograph by Elvin Wyly.

INTRODUCTION TO PART SIX

By the 1990s, gentrification had flourished for 30 years, and so had a vibrant, sophisticated academic literature on the topic (Smith and Herod, 1991). There was also a rising wave of anti-gentrification activism in many neighborhoods in many cities around the world. Yet the major efforts devoted to understanding the dynamics of production and consumption – and their interdependency – seemed to have exhausted many scholars. When Liz Bondi, a prominent feminist geographer and gentrification researcher, voiced her skepticism on the value of additional work on the topic, she was expressing a fairly widespread sense that the most important theoretical breakthroughs had already been achieved. For Bondi (1999, p. 255), efforts to push the theoretical frontier had stretched the concept too far (see Lees, Slater and Wyly, 2008: 154–155):

> … the more researchers have attempted to pin it down the more burdens the concept has had to carry. Maybe the loss of momentum around gentrification reflects its inability to open up new insights, and maybe it is time to allow it to disintegrate under the weight of these burdens.

Ironically, scholars began to turn their attention away at precisely the moment when the process was on the verge of a major acceleration – and a major transformation that linked gentrification to increasingly powerful instruments of public policy. Indeed, in a valuable but often-overlooked essay a few years earlier, Jan van Weesep (1994, p. 74) had surveyed a literature that was at once vast and yet "narrowly focused on whether or not gentrification is worth arguing about … and, above all, on its current causes." van Weesep (1994, p. 74) understood that something else was urgently needed:

> This review and interpretation of the recent literature is intended to broaden the scope again and thus to put the gentrification debate into a policy perspective. Its focus is on the effects of gentrification rather than on its causes.

Shifting the focus from cause to effect revealed a remarkably broad, deep, and significant change that was underway: more and more elected officials, bureaucrats, consultants, lobbyists, and all the other actors involved in shaping public policy, began to devise programmes to encourage gentrification. Policy has always been at least partly performative: its consequences depend just as much on what elite decision-makers believe as what is "true" in any epistemological sense. What this means is that, in terms of policy, scholarly debates on the relative importance of culture and economy, consumption and production in explaining gentrification are largely irrelevant: what matters is what those in a position to shape policy believe, and how they act on those convictions.

The new policy interest certainly had a precedent. In the 1970s in the United States policy-makers had actively tried to promote gentrification, only to see the efforts fail amidst poor economic conditions (runaway inflation and high interest rates), and to be confused when confronted with protest and resistance by advocates for poor, working-class, and racially marginalized communities. The new wave of policy interest in the 1990s, by contrast, was much more cautious in its language, promotion, and marketing – but much more ambitious in its efforts to remake inner-city space for middle-class and wealthy residents, investors, and tourists. In the United Kingdom, a new policy movement emerged to promote 'urban renaissance', the 'regeneration' and 'revitalization' of British city centres (see Imrie and Raco, 2003). In the United States, the movement began as an initiative to redirect resources into the "underserved markets" of the inner city, and to "revitalize" some of the problems caused by the ill-planned urban renewal and public housing programmes of a previous generation. By the late 1990s and continuing on through the next decade, in more countries around the world, several conditions brought a "perfect storm" that created a new relationship between policy and gentrification:

1) Population and economic activity continued to centralize into large metropolitan regions – in many cases driving a simultaneous intensification of suburbanization and recentralization – while transnational networks strengthened in trade, investment, and migration.
2) Political realignments drove a widening mismatch in the scales of social and economic policy. Economic policies on taxes, trade, and the like, became more centralized in national governments, and free-trade agreements shifted some economic decisions "up" to the scale of global institutions. Meanwhile, many responsibilities for social-welfare spending were devolved and "downloaded" to states, provinces, regions, and cities – forcing them to become much more competitive and entrepreneurial.
3) Middle-class and wealthy voters became ever more reluctant to support social welfare expenditures to benefit the poor, reinforcing an established preference among elected officials to promote tax cuts and subsidies for wealthy households, corporations, and investors.
4) Competition became more intense for cities and regions bidding for the "right" to host itinerant "mega-event" spectacles like the Olympic Games, World Expositions, and many other recurrent continental or global-scale sporting events and festivals. Redevelopment schemes associated with the Olympics have driven direct displacement on an astonishing scale: 720,000 forcibly evicted in Seoul in 1988, at least 1.25 million in Beijing in 2008, and many thousands elsewhere in other host cities (see COHRE 2007). A 2004 study by the European Culture Commission (Palmer Study) demonstrated that the title of 'European Capital of Culture' designated every year by the European Union to a city in Europe to show case its culture serves as a catalyst for the socio-economic and cultural development and transformation of the city chosen. As a result the impacts on, and the benefits for, the city in terms of its socio-economic development are now considered in determining the chosen cities. This is the case with the Olympics too, indeed, London's success in the 2012 Olympic bid was the result of its revitalization plans for East London, plans which will bolster and extend the gentrification frontier in East London. The anti-gentrification struggle has begun in East London!
5) Import/export imbalances between countries of the Global North and East Asia widened, leading central banks in Asia to buy dollar-denominated investments as a way of managing exchange rates and protecting their export market shares. The result was a flood of investment capital into the U.S. that kept interest rates low and fueled a massive binge in consumption and borrowing – especially for real estate and home mortgages (see Lees, Slater, and Wyly 2008, p. 179–180).

It would be far too simplistic to suggest that these factors created a new form of policy-driven gentrification. Each of these factors played out somewhat differently, depending on continental and national context. Nevertheless, the general trend was unmistakable: in country after country, and city after city, more and more public policies began to encourage the kind of investment, subsidy, and planning processes that have long been understood to reinforce gentrification pressures. In general, efforts to use policy to cushion the worst inequalities caused by gentrification were scaled back or abandoned, while policies that unleashed gentrification became much more popular. For a time, pro-gentrification policies were constrained by the serious potential for activism and resistance – leading to a proliferation of old and new euphemisms in place of the term 'gentrification' in an attempt to defuse criticism (e.g. urban renaissance, urban regeneration, mixed communities). By the time Richard Florida's work on the "creative class" made him a best-selling author and earned him many thousands of dollars in lecture fees, it was clear that part of the allure involved a clear, convincing new language that allowed policy makers to promote gentrification while describing their strategies in a new, popular language summarized in the "three T's" of technology, talent, and tolerance (Florida, 2003, 2005, 2008). As Jamie Peck (2005, p. 740–741) notes,

In the field of urban policy, which has hardly been cluttered with new and innovative ideas lately, creativity strategies have quickly become the policies of choice, since they license both a discursively distinctive and an ostensibly deliverable development agenda. No less significantly, though, they also work quietly with the grain of extant 'neoliberal' development agendas, framed around interurban competition, gentrification, middle-class consumption and place-marketing ...

Such policies, moreover, interact with broader causal forces driving gentrification in a two-way street that recognizes the authenticity of place while eroding its foundations. "In order to be enacted," creative-city strategies

presume and work with gentrification, conceived as a positive urban process, while making a virtue of selective and variable outcomes, unique neighborhood by unique neighborhood. And with almost breathtaking circularity, it is now being proposed that these gentrification-friendly strategies should be evaluated, not according to hackneyed metrics like job creation or poverty alleviation, but according to more relevant measures like ... increased house prices! ... As if this were not circular enough, it is increasingly common for cities to evaluate the effectiveness of their creativity strategies according to their shifting position in Florida's league tables.

(Peck, 2005, p. 764)

In this section, four readings illustrate different facets of the link between gentrification and public policy. For William Whyte, the displacement threats of gentrification pale in comparison to the effects of urban disinvestment on poor and working-class communities. "What our center cities have needed most is more people living in the center," Whyte emphasizes, and gentrification will always remain a small, niche market that will have negligible consequences for displacement. Good public policy goes hand in hand with good architectural and urban design. Many of the key principles of Whyte's case for gentrification have been echoed and elaborated in subsequent policy defenses, such as Duany (2001); Byrne (2003); Galster (2002), and Florida's (2005, 2008) creative adaptation of the ideas of Jane Jacobs.

Wyly and Hammel present an alternative view of the relation between policy and gentrification. After many years of gentrification, they suggest, private-market reinvestment in many cities has become so pervasive that it has bumped up against the last remaining legacies of the 1960s-era welfare state – the large public housing projects for the poorest of the poor. "Islands of decay" are now surrounded by "seas of renewal," in a reversal of the pattern Berry had documented years earlier. Gentrification had become a major consideration in the formulation of new policies regarding housing for the urban poor.

Neil Smith, in his 'New globalism, new urbanism,' places these trends in a much broader context – connecting the local experiences of gentrification to global urban networks. For too long, Smith argues, "global cities" have been defined by Eurocentric assumptions that privilege the "command and control functions" of producer services and headquarters functions, while ignoring the worldwide networks of urban regions bound up with "the global production of surplus value." Smith diagnosed how gentrification evolved from its role as a small housing-market niche in a relatively few large cities of the Global North, to become a key instrument of policy, growth, and competition:

Even where gentrification per se remains limited, the mobilization of urban real-estate markets as vehicles of capital accumulation is ubiquitous. ... Whereas the major territorial axis of economic competition prior to the 1970s pitted regional and national economies against each other, by the 1990s the new geographical axis of competition was pitting cities against cities in the global economy.

Gentrification specifically, and real-estate speculation more generally, were central in this newly intensified competition. Unfortunately, some of the key factors in the new gentrification policy nexus noted earlier – especially the massive expansion of mortgage debt – were fundamentally unsustainable. Smith's prescient article appeared in 2002, just as the world economy entered what is now recognized as one of the most dramatic real estate and debt bubbles in history – eventually triggering what is now understood as the most severe global recession since the Great Depression of the 1930s. Estimates of the worldwide economic losses due to the collapse now exceed US$60 trillion.

Finally, Uitermark et al. offer a nuanced and contextual analysis of state-led gentrification in part of Rotterdam. Accounts of new stages of gentrification that are based on the experience of the United States and the U.K., they argue, cannot be applied without a careful understanding of the institutional and policy complexity of the Netherlands, where governance networks between the national and the urban scale have created distinctive policies towards disadvantaged neighborhoods. To some degree, the history of Dutch public and policy concerns about the poor, and especially the poor living in state-subsidized housing, followed a trajectory similar to that in the U.S. and the U.K. But coalitions supporting state-led gentrification became much more influential in Dutch cities. Moreover, they operated according to a different logic once gentrification was defined as the required solution to the "problem neighbourhoods" where social housing had created concentrations of poverty and 'deviant' behavior.

> … social cohesion in the neighbourhood or profit margins may be important, but their first priority is to create a neighbourhood with a stable social order. … these institutional actors achieve their operational goals by sometimes acting against sound business logic (they do not invest in the areas with the best potential for profitable investment) and against the interests of neighborhood residents (the interventions are so drastic that they reduce social cohesion and force residents to relocate).

(p. 138)

Each of these readings illuminate a different facet of the link between gentrification and public policy. The mixture of relations and processes analyzed in each reflect, to some degree, the time and place in which the research quite literally took place. This mixture will change as conditions evolve: there will be a temptation to view the current economic crisis – a truly global economic realignment that has inspired widespread comparisons with the emergence of a new financial order out of the ashes of the Great Depression and the Second World War – as the demise of gentrification. But histories of gentrification, and of policies associated with gentrification, suggest that the process will survive, and may become an even more central (if sometimes carefully disguised) feature of the urban policy infrastructure.

REFERENCES AND FURTHER READING

Badyina, A. and Golubchikov, O. (2005) 'Gentrification in central Moscow – a market process or a deliberate policy? Money, power and people in housing regeneration in Ostozhenka', *Geografiska Annaler B*, 87: 113–129.

Bondi, L. (1999) 'Between the Woof and the Weft: A Response to Loretta Lees', *Environment and Planning D: Society and Space* 17(3): 253–255.

Byrne, J. P. (2003) 'Two cheers for gentrification', *Howard Law Journal* 46(3), 405–432.

Cameron, S. (2003) 'Gentrification, housing redifferentiation and urban regeneration: "Going for Growth" in Newcastle upon Tyne'. *Urban Studies* 40: 2367–2382.

Centre on Housing Rights and Evictions (2007) *Fair Play for Housing Rights: Mega-Events, Olympic Games, and Housing Rights*. Geneva: Centre on Housing Rights and Evictions.

Davidson, M. (2008) 'Spoiled mixture: Where does state-led "positive" gentrification end?' *Urban Studies* 45(12): 2385–2406.

Duany, A. (2001) 'Three cheers for gentrification.' *The American Enterprise*, April/May, 36–39.

Florida, R. (2003) *The Rise of the Creative Class*, New York: Basic Books.

Florida, R. (2005) *Cities and the Creative Class*, New York: Routledge.

Florida, R. (2008) *Who's Your City?* New York: Random House.

Galster, G. (2002) 'Gentrification as diversification: Why Detroit needs it and how it can get it.' *Journal of Law in Society* 4: 29–43.

Hamnett, C. (1979) 'Improvement grants as an indicator of gentrification in inner London', *Area* 1973, 5(4): 252–261.

Harris, A. (2008) 'From London to Mumbai and back again: gentrification and public policy in comparative perspective', *Urban Studies* 45(12): 2407–2428.

Imrie, R. and Raco, M. (eds) (2003) *Urban Renaissance? New Labour, Community and Urban Policy*, Bristol: The Policy Press.

Lees, L. (2003) 'Visions of "Urban Renaissance": the urban task force report and the urban white paper', in Imrie, R. and Raco, M. (eds) *Urban Renaissance? New Labour, community and urban policy*, pp. 61–82. Bristol: Policy Press.

Lees, L. (2008) 'Gentrification and social mixing: Towards an urban renaissance?' *Urban Studies* 45(12): 2449–2470.

Lees, L. and Ley, D. (2008) (eds) 'Gentrification and public policy', Special Issue of *Urban Studies* 45(12).

Lees, L., Slater, T. and Wyly, E. (2008) *Gentrification*, New York: Routledge.

Newman, K. and Ashton, P. (2004) 'Neoliberal urban policy and new paths of neighborhood change in the American inner city', *Environment and Planning A* 36(7): 1151–1172.

Peck, J. (2005) 'Struggling with the creative class', *International Journal of Urban and Regional Research* 29(4): 740–770.

Slater, T. (2004) 'Municipally-managed gentrification in South Parkdale, Toronto', *The Canadian Geographer* 48(3): 303–325.

Smith, N. and Herod, A. (1991) *Gentrification: A Comprehensive Bibliography*. New Brunswick, NJ: Department of Geography, Rutgers University.

Smith, N. (2002) 'New globalism, new urbanism: gentrification as global urban strategy', *Antipode* 34(3): 427–450.

Wyly, E. and Hammel, D. (2000) 'Capital's metropolis: Chicago and the transformation of American housing policy', *Geografiska Annaler B* 82(4): 181–206.

Wyly, E. and Hammel, D. (2001) 'Gentrification, housing policy, the new context of urban redevelopment', in K. Fox Gotham (ed.) *Research in Urban Sociology, Vol. 6: Critical Perspectives on Urban Redevelopment*, London: Elsevier, pp. 211–276.

van Weesep, J. (1994) 'Gentrification as a research frontier.' *Progress in Human Geography* 18(1): 74–83.

33

"The Case for Gentrification"

From *City: Rediscovering the Center* (1988)

William H. Whyte

u Stayes

What our center cities have needed most is more people living in the center. If only, the hope has been voiced, younger people would come back to the old neighborhoods and fix them up, what a boon it would be. Here and there a few heartening precedents could be spotted. When I worked on the *Fortune* series on "The Exploding Metropolis" in 1957 we were able to run a portfolio of attractive blocks in various cities. These were mostly upper-income places, however, and from the market studies we did it was hard to see any substantial shift back to the center city.

One large reason was the kind of housing offered. The kind most in demand were the row houses of Georgetown and Brooklyn Heights. These were clearly out of reach for most people but they did provide strong cues for design and marketing of new housing. They were not heeded. The federal Title I urban redevelopment projects were just getting under way, and in scale and spirit they were the diametric opposite of the old blocks. With little variation from city to city the process was the same; not only were blocks razed, but streets as well, and huge superblock projects grouped colonies of high-rise towers in abstract green space.

A terrible mistake was being made. These bleak new Utopias were not bleak because they had to be. They were the concrete manifestation—and how literally—of a deep misunderstanding of the function of the city.

By such measures as tenant satisfaction, crime rates, and maintenance it should have been evident that the high-rise towers were proving much less suitable for families with children than low-rise units. But the momentum was unstoppable. In New York City the project format became so imbedded in the rules that it was difficult to build any public housing that departed from it. And it was a photogenic format. What on the ground looked like dirty, gray concrete gleamed white against cloud-filled skies in architectural photographs. Particularly attractive were the photos of the Pruitt-Igoe project in St. Louis.

But cities—older cities especially—had a great asset: a plentiful supply of old housing. The houses were not of the quality of the redbrick Federal houses of Georgetown or Brooklyn Heights. They were ugly, many of them: brownstones, for example, the felicities of which took a lot of time to appreciate. Most of the housing was in bad shape, much of it foreclosed. But this proved a blessing. Some sites actively promoted their rehabilitation. Baltimore, for one, set up a "homesteading" program with its stock of tax-foreclosed properties; to buyers who would pledge to fix them up the city would sell the houses for a nominal sum. The result has been some very attractive neighborhoods. One, the Otterbein houses, is a very Baltimore place and with front steps as white as any in the city.

Pittsburgh is another city that has had homesteading programs. It started with a "Great House Sale," in which it put fifty-eight city-owned houses up for sale at one hundred dollars apiece to people who would rehabilitate them. Since then prices have gone up; it has been selling abandoned properties to homesteaders for three hundred dollars apiece.

By and large, however, the people who have been rehabilitating old neighborhoods have been doing it without much help from government—sometimes despite government. The federal government subsidized suburbia with FHA-guaranteed mortgages but offered no such help for rehabilitating

need more gov.t support! → b to increase

city houses. The Department of Housing and Urban Development did have some demonstration programs, including one for "new towns in town." It was, if anything, too well meant. It was thoroughly suburban in its assumptions and was so laden with antidensity, anticity provisions that it was bound to founder.

Banks and insurance companies were not much help either. Banks would withhold mortgage financing from areas being rehabilitated until the rehabilitation was largely completed and financing no longer so needed. Then they would lend. Insurance companies were often so wary of older neighborhoods that obtaining adequate fire and liability policies was extremely difficult and costly.

Cash was the big problem. When banks did offer mortgage financing there was a sizeable gap to fill. The home buyer usually had to put up about 30 percent of the purchase price in cash, and raising it took some doing. Money for the actual renovation was hard to come by too. Rates on second mortgages were astronomical and the terms too short.

Despite the difficulties, the rehabilitation movement gained force. There was common sense to it. The neighborhoods might have looked shabby with their Perma-Stone facades, broken windows, and vacant lots. But with them went an infrastructure of streets and utilities and urban services substantially intact. For a fraction of any pro rata replacement cost, the home buyer was acquiring a share of this urban base.

In the eyes of these beholders the old houses acquired a beauty that had not been so discernible before. There was, for example, a considerable shift in aesthetic judgments on the brownstones. They used to be drab, dark, and monotonous—indeed, ugly. But then, with no physical change to speak of, they changed. They became fine examples of the Italianate style, their stoops a graceful evocation of the urban rhythm. To paint over the brown, as remodelers did earlier, was sacrilege. If, as in Park Slope, the brownstones were twenty-four feet or more wide, had parquet floors and stained glass, they became objects of veneration. Even the basic eighteen-footers—the tract houses of their day—commanded respect. And rising prices. People who bought them thought they were getting a tremendous bargain. As the real estate market was subsequently to demonstrate, they were indeed.

Good news? You would think so. But many people do not think so. Invoking that dread term of urban affairs, they say it is "gentrification," and those who hailed the possibility of a middle-class revival of neighborhoods are unhappy now it has become a reality. They say that it is elitist; that it has been at the expense of the poor; that the displacement of them by middle-class people has broken up once stable neighborhoods and ethnic groups. There is not a conference on city problems that does not ring with protestations of guilt over gentrification. Shame on us for what we have done.

The gentrification charge has had an inhibiting effect on government support. Let me go back to one of the first cases. In the 1969 *Plan for New York City*, the planning commission hailed the brownstones revival with enthusiasm. "If brownstoners have done what they have done in the face of major difficulties," the plan said, "it is staggering to think of what could be done if the difficulties were removed." To that end, it proposed

■ municipal loans or mortgage guarantees for one- and two-family homes.
■ a revolving fund to bridge the gap between the price of the house and a conventional mortgage.
■ long-term loans for renovation work.
■ municipal second mortgages for twenty years at regular mortgage rates.
■ temporary tax abatement on house improvements.

The proposals were not supported. They were criticized, and by many of the civic activists that had been expected to support them. Elitism, they charged. The great reservoir of brownstones was in Brooklyn—many square miles of it—but to judge from the criticisms, the brownstone movement was something fomented by a small coterie of smart-aleck Manhattan liberals and quiche eaters. (This was before the term "yuppies" was invented.)

What displacement? And when? The gentrification charge is very misleading. Check the year-by-year changes in neighborhood households and you will find very few cases of direct displacement; that is, a renter going out the door as a homeowner comes in. Low-income renters are frequent movers; 40 percent of the renters in a city neighborhood will move. Of all moves, the Department of Housing and Urban Development has estimated, only 4 percent are caused by displacement. When there is displacement, furthermore, it comes early in the game, usually well before the home buyers arrive.

What causes it? The implicit assumption of the gentrification concept is that the chief threat to housing for the poor is the improvement of neighborhoods. The problem is the opposite. The chief threat is the deterioration of neighborhoods. The poor are not being hurt by middle-class investment. They are being hurt by disinvestment—by landlords and owners who let buildings go to rot, who walk away from

Aussie

them, who torch them. More units have been lost through abandonment in the Bronx alone than have been provided by brownstone rehabilitation in all of New York City.

The worst case of disinvestment is the federal government public housing program. The number of units constructed each year has been falling precipitously: from 68,500 in 1978 to 1,426 in 1985. The condition of units is worsening; by law the rent cannot be more than 30 percent of the family's income but local housing authorities are having trouble holding the line. Maintenance has suffered—and lately to such an extent that more units are being lost than built. Our public housing program needs an overhaul in policy and design. What it needs most, however, is a fair amount of money.

Rehabilitation programs are proceeding well and they are doing it without displacement. As part of its "Landmark Rehabilitation" program, Savannah, Georgia, is restoring 1,200 units in its Victorian district and will rent 600 of them to low-income blacks. In Kansas City the Quality Hill redevelopment is restoring what is left of a former gold coast by rehabilitating old structures and infilling with new three-story row housing. During the staged construction the project has been able to house most of the people who were on the site earlier.

Harlem might one day be an example. It has already suffered disinvestment and displacement. It is, in fact, underpopulated, having lost almost a third of its population since 1970. Much of the tenement housing is burnt out. But Harlem has great advantages. It is well served with mass transit; it has broad, tree-lined avenues and excellent access to parks. There are many cleared sites for new housing; there is a fine stock of brownstones, some blocks of which, such as Striver's Row, have been kept in excellent shape.

In the country as a whole, let it be noted, the market for rehabilitated center-city housing is a small one. Most of the data available indicate that the prime prospects are people already living in the city. Next are people who normally would go to the suburbs but who have elected to stay in the city for one reason or another. This is probably the swing sector and could be enlarged were the supply of units increased and the cost not. About a third are people who have been living in suburbia; a considerable proportion of them are empty nesters, whose children have grown up and moved away. All in all, it has been estimated, house sales in rehabilitated city neighborhoods number no more than 100,000 units a year.

These few people, however, can have a profound impact on the center city and the perception of it by others. Since the base is so small, a relatively small addition can carry a lot of leverage. In Denver, for example, another twenty-seven hundred people would double the downtown resident population. Such additions will not jam the bars and put hordes on the streets at night. Like their counterparts in suburbia, city residents are homebodies. But their presence does make a difference, and a very healthy one. In Charlotte, North Carolina, the NCNB bank sponsored a town house development that is only five blocks from the center of downtown. People walk to work from it. They also agitate for more retailing and services, more activity at night. Of such steps is a center revitalized.

Cities-within-cities, alas, are still being built. They are usually very large—often on clear tracts, such as obsolete freight yards, that give architects and developers the blank slate they would be better off for not having. The projects are sufficient unto themselves; the surrounding neighborhoods are not in the province of their planning. For urban services the projects provide bits and pieces within: a gourmet food shop, a simulation of a raffish pub. A recent example is Presidential Towers, a middle-class development in Chicago. Writing in *Inland Architect*, Catharine Ingraham hails it as ersatz city. "The idea that one can imitate the diversity of cities in isolated developments by bringing together desirable pieces of the urban fabric has taken hold of city planning. Paradoxically, the more one imitates, or extracts things from the vernacular city, the more artificial the results seem. The development stands as a bulwark against the very diversity that it capitalizes on."

But there are some good prototypes. There have been for some time, which makes the bad ones all the less understandable. Here and there, year after year, residential projects have been built that are of reasonably high density, eminently economical, of pleasing scale, and thoroughly urban. They do not date.

One of the best contemporary models is St. Francis Square in San Francisco. With its townhouse groupings, interior open spaces, and private patios, it is one of the pleasantest neighborhoods you will see anywhere. It was built for low- and middle-income people twenty-five years ago. To repeat a point: a design that is well conceived for a time and place tends to be timeless. We should not have to search hard for such lost lessons. They are all about us.

34

"Islands of Decay in Seas of Renewal: Housing Policy and the Resurgence of Gentrification"

From *Housing Policy Debate* (1999)

Elvin K. Wyly and Daniel J. Hammel

INTRODUCTION

The gentrification of Harlem?

In geographic theory and on the urban landscape, gentrification has inspired two decades of spirited debate over the extent, causes, and significance of neighborhood change in the inner city. Near the peak of theoretical debate during the 1980s, the empirical reality of Manhattan's overheated real estate market allowed Schaffer and Smith (1986) to point a lens toward an especially unlikely candidate for gentrification:

> There is little disagreement that Harlem represents a difficult target for gentrification; to the extent that it takes place, we should be more inclined to see the general process of gentrification as trenchant and long term. If it were temporary and small in scale, why would developers and incoming residents make such long-term investments here rather than in neighborhoods perceived as socially and economically less risky? (352)

Schaffer and Smith (1986) proceeded to document the early stages of gentrification with the cold statistics of demography, real estate, and city planning, as well as the words of public officials and developers trying to "circle the wagons around" before attacking the heart of disinvestment in Central Harlem.[1] Nevertheless, the early stage of the process and the scholarly debate over what it meant for urban theory

called for a question as a title: "The gentrification of Harlem?" (Schaffer and Smith 1986).

A decade later no question mark is needed. The revival of land markets in such unlikely places no longer seems to evoke surprise or skepticism, and mainstream discussion of the trajectories of inner-city neighborhoods such as Harlem are as likely to find their way into the "House and Home" section (Rozhon 1998) as the front page of the *New York Times* (Foderaro 1998). New York's especially violent confrontations in the late 1980s tainted the word "gentrification" to such a degree that it has been banished from most mainstream accounts,[2] but there is little doubt that the city's recovery has returned the process to Harlem with a vengeance. Brokers report surging house prices, thanks to a growing stream of refugee professionals priced out of the overheated neighborhoods of Chelsea and Tribeca, among them many middle-class African Americans for whom "reading the writers of the Harlem Renaissance created a lot of mythologies" (B5) added to the incentives of Manhattan's last frontier of reasonably priced spacious brownstones (Foderaro 1998). When they arrive, the entrepreneurial spirit takes hold to fill the retail and entertainment vacuum with plans for new coffeehouses and restaurants, now joined by an effort to expand national franchises with help from the Local Initiatives Support Corporation and Bankers' Trust. Work is under way on Harlem USA, a $65 million retail and entertainment complex to attract Disney and other high-profile anchors to Harlem with city, state, and federal Empowerment Zone incentives (Pataki 1998). A few blocks away,

negative association

local and federal grants for low- and moderate-income housing construction are leveraged with capital from private developers alongside plans for luxury condos and co-ops with retail space for the Gap and Starbuck's (Rozhon 1998).

If the boosterish portrayal of the *Times* and other outlets is to be accepted at face value, we are seeing nothing more than a fin-de-siècle Harlem Renaissance that returns a vibrant cultural energy to the northern reaches of Manhattan. Moreover, Harlem is in many respects an exceptional case of inner-city revival, given its historical and cultural symbolism and proximity to New York's enormous concentrations of wealth. Yet the changes here run parallel to those in scores of neighborhoods in other cities. And even after accounting for the hyperbole of many newspaper accounts, there is credible evidence that important developments are unfolding. As Schaffer and Smith (1986) put it, "[T]he fact that the process has begun at all, that gentrification is even on the agenda in Harlem, lends support to the claim that we are witnessing not a curious anomaly but a trenchant restructuring of urban space" (362). More than a decade later, in the wake of spirited debate on the emergence of a "postgentrification" era (Bourne 1993a, 1993b; Lees and Bondi 1995), evidence points to two additional shifts in the gentrification of American cities. This article attempts to document and interpret these trends and their implications for urban theory and policy.

The resurgence of gentrification

The first shift is purely empirical. Gentrification has witnessed a resurgence in the 1990s that has quickly erased any lingering suspicion that the process was only a brief historical aberration. To be sure, gentrification affects only a tiny segment of the housing market of older cities and is dwarfed by suburban expansion. Yet widespread evidence points to a revival of central land markets in the wake of the recession of the early 1990s. In Chicago, conversion or construction is under way on more than 3,500 lofts, condominiums, and luxury apartments in and around the Loop, including a $120 million gated community designed to create a "garden in the city" in an old industrial district on the banks of the Chicago River (Chanen 1998; Klages 1998). In Boston, "old money" enclaves are being invaded by still wealthier newcomers: With an influx of the new elite of high technology and financial services, recent home sales in parts of Beacon Hill have topped $4 million, prompting sociologist Alan Wolfe to conclude, "You could

call it turbo-gentrification" (Goldberg 1999, A16). A recent survey of 25 downtowns reveals an average expected growth of 75 percent in downtown population between 1998 and 2010 (Sohmer and Lang 1999).

New York certainly offers the most vivid images of renewed capital investment and intensely localized instances of class and race polarization, although its oft-trumpeted global city/dual city status perhaps makes it unique (Mollenkopf and Castells 1991; Sassen 1994; Storper 1997). The decade began with a dystopian reevaluation of the city's recent adventures:

> In some corners of the city, the experts say, gentrification may be remembered, along with junk bonds, stretch limousines, and television evangelism, as just another grand excess of the 1980s.... As the dust settles, we can see that the areas that underwent dramatic turnarounds had severe limitations. Rich people are simply not going to live next to public housing.
>
> (Lueck 1991, 1)

Indeed, New York's heavy reliance on financial services devastated both commercial and residential real estate in the late 1980s and early 1990s, lending a concrete if temporary reality to the degentrification hypothesis (Lees and Bondi 1995). In 1991, an office market saturated with vacant "see-throughs" led the Downtown Lower Manhattan Association to propose a Lower Manhattan Project to convert office buildings to residential use. As Fitch (1993) observed, the "proposal had a certain karmic logic: if the city could subsidize the creation of the office buildings in the seventies, why not subsidize their liquidation in the nineties?" (30). Initially viewed skeptically as what one developer dubbed "a 'field of dreams' market" (Garbarine 1998), Wall Street eventually gained almost 3,300 apartments from conversion, thanks to city-sponsored tax incentives. By the time the initial wave of leases began expiring in late 1998, the revival of the city's tight rental market allowed annual increases of up to 18 percent in the financial district, approaching $2,500 a month for a one-bedroom apartment (Garbarine 1998).

Despite the stock market's vacillations in the wake of global financial crises in 1998, the city's commercial and residential real estate markets point to a rebound that mirrors and sometimes exceeds the boom of the 1980s. Downtown vacancy rates in large commercial buildings fell from a staggering peak of 22.8 percent in late 1993 to 8.2 percent in the third quarter of 1998, a low not seen since 1984; midtown vacancy rates have reached

4.1 percent from a 1991 peak of 15.5 percent (Holusha 1998).[3] Residential brokers now describe the market for new co-ops as "helium-filled," in part due to the revision of the city's rent control regulations in 1997 (Hevesi 1998). Average loft prices in Manhattan are approaching $700,000, pushing a wave of loft conversions outward to the old industrial neighborhoods of Williamsburg and Greenpoint (Brooklyn), Long Island City and Astoria (Queens), and even old parts of the South Bronx (Hevesi 1999). A wave of new development projects, including a total of 2,000 apartments and two large hotels, is under way at Battery Park City (Dunlap 1999). And true to form, Donald Trump is busy constructing what he bills as the world's tallest residential tower, a 72-story skyscraper towering over the United Nations Secretariat building (Goldberger 1999).

Housing policy and the reinvention of gentrification

A second shift in gentrification during the 1990s has been more subtle, and—at least until recently—much more difficult to see in the urban landscape. Transformations in the national system of housing finance and housing policy have become closely intertwined with the market-driven revival of certain inner-city neighborhoods. While the boundary between unfettered market forces and public policy has been a blurry and contested frontier for more than half a century, we believe that recent trends have altered the context for gentrification in important ways. Equally important, three decades of gentrification have altered the context for certain facets of housing policy. As a consequence, gentrification has become mutually constituted with a nascent regime under a devolved, privatized, and "reinvented" policy framework, such that the current surge of investment into city neighborhoods carries dramatic implications for accelerated class polarization. When viewed at the level of the inner city, Berry's (1985) islands of renewal in seas of decay have been transformed into islands of decay in seas of renewal.

We elaborate this argument by drawing on a diverse set of literature as well as empirical evidence from an ongoing research project on the gentrification of large U.S. cities during the 1990s. We present our analysis in six parts. In the next two sections, we advance a working definition of gentrification and present our argument that urban policy has transformed islands of renewal in seas of decay into islands of decay within seas of renewal. We then turn to a brief discussion of our evidence, which is drawn

from three complementary sources of quantitative and qualitative data. Next, we present our empirical analysis in three sections: (a) a baseline snapshot of the resurgence of mortgage capital into gentrified neighborhoods in eight cities between 1992 and 1997, (b) a review of local public housing redevelopment plans in relation to gentrification activity, and (c) a multivariate analysis of mortgage market dynamics in gentrified areas. The analysis reveals a striking resurgence of capital investment in the wake of the recession of the early 1990s and a strong connection between housing policy and gentrification. In the final section, we offer a few concluding remarks on the implications of our findings.

ISLANDS OF RENEWAL IN SEAS OF DECAY

Research on gentrification expanded dramatically during the 1980s, spurring widespread debate on the magnitude, significance, and implications of a seemingly new process that was variously dubbed "revival," "revitalization," or "renaissance." In part, these different labels reflected more fundamental disagreement in how the process was defined by scholars and policy makers. A wide spectrum of alternatives emerged, many of them implicit. For some, it meant the inmigration of middle-class suburbanites back to the city, and the displacement of poor or working-class residents was said to be inherent in the process. For others, it was simply the visible neighborhood expression of broader societal forces—new cultural practices and consumption preferences of the professional middle class as exemplified by "yuppies,"[4] or new conditions of the circulation of capital at the urban and regional level.

In this article, we analyze gentrification as a process that is fundamentally rooted in class and inherently geographic in its manifestation. It is the class transformation of those parts of the city that suffered from systematic outmigration, disinvestment, or neglect in the midst of rapid economic growth and suburbanization—generally accepted in the United States as the period from World War II to the early 1970s. Class transformation is rooted in long-term changes in the distribution of wealth, income, and educational opportunity, as well as a more complex division of labor, but it is the intersection of these trends in the creation of new geographies that makes gentrification significant for theory and policy. The importance of the process is magnified by its concentration in those parts of the city where public policy is often required to ameliorate systemic housing market failures.

Changes in the built environment often provide a valuable guide to describe the process, but actually are incidental to the place-based class transformation itself. Gentrification may involve "lofting" or condominium conversion in a warehouse district; it may entail a slow turnover in a neighborhood of attractive Victorian houses; or it may take the form of new luxury condominium towers on an abandoned waterfront site. The consequences of this class shift, therefore, can also take different forms: When it involves "invasion-succession" displacement, the process sometimes leads to open conflicts among old and new residents. New construction or "gray-field" redevelopment avoids these conflicts but is also usually bound up with comprehensive schemes to privatize public space and exclude the city's poor from areas now reserved for affluent residents, white-collar workers, and patrons of upscale retail and entertainment facilities.

Definitions vary in the literature on gentrification, but there is even wider disagreement on the prospects for a general urban revival. In the shadow of established urban theory inherited from the Chicago School, the apparent reversal of ecological invasion and succession processes certainly carried enormous implications for our understanding of the amorphous construct of the "inner city" and its future. At one end of the continuum, a secular restructuring of the relationship between production and consumption signaled the emergence of new class structures in the postindustrial metropolis:

If present trends accelerate, the social geography of the nineteenth century industrial city may appear to urban scholars as a temporary interlude to a more historically persistent pattern of higher status segregation adjacent to the downtown core. (Ley 1981, 145)

At the other extreme, skeptics viewed gentrification as a temporary interlude, an aberration induced by the unlikely intersection of demographic and macroeconomic forces. In the most prominent and comprehensive elaboration of this view, Berry (1985) explained the emergence of islands of renewal as the outcome of metropolitan housing construction and filtering processes that produced vast seas of decay at the urban core. The necessary conditions for islands of renewal are established when removals from the inner-city housing stock outpace the creation of excess housing supply such that "the markets are tightened and older central-city housing becomes an attractive option" (Berry

1985, 95). The sufficient condition depends on the expansion of downtown office and professional employment growth associated with the concentration of advanced service functions in the nation's key command and control centers. In this framework, the continued expansion of islands of renewal is contingent on a rare constellation of urbanization trends, reflecting the "apparent contradictions but logical links between suburban overbuilding, contagious inner-city abandonment, decreasing vacancies and tightening markets, and gentrification" (Berry 1985, 96).

ISLANDS OF DECAY IN SEAS OF RENEWAL

Causes and consequences

Berry's (1985) synthesis was perhaps the most comprehensive and prominent interpretation of gentrification within the prevailing neoclassical framework for housing market analysis. Not surprisingly, this framework meshed well with the axioms and principles of the nation's skeletal urban policy infrastructure. Yet this perspective was only one of several alternatives (Berry 1985; Ley 1980, 1981, 1996; Smith 1996; Smith and Williams 1986). And despite attempts to forge a new synthesis (Lees 1994; Rose 1984), much of the contemporary literature remains balkanized along lines of debate established a generation ago. Gentrification has been used as a vehicle to investigate broader dichotomies in urban studies—production/consumption, economy/culture, agency/structure—and has become a battleground for wide-ranging disagreement over alternative causal explanations for neighborhood change. In light of this long history of spirited debate, it is hard to see how the current renaissance of research inspired by renewed gentrification activity will generate a consensus this time around.

The debate over the causes of gentrification, however, does not exhaust the range of important and relevant questions. A focus on the root causes of gentrification risks imposing a narrow, constraining view on a process that has become a durable feature of the neighborhood ecology of western cities in general and U.S. cities in particular. In this context, we concur with van Weesep (1994) who proposes a more careful scrutiny of "the effects of gentrification rather than its causes" in order to "put the gentrification debate into a policy perspective" (74).

Regardless of its underlying causes, gentrification has become an important element of contemporary urbanization processes. It has also been subsumed under broader portrayals of urban fortunes—in the popular press and in policy circles—in ways that echo the discourse of "renewal" in the 1950s and "renaissance" in the 1970s. Yet in the wake of perceived and real transformations in the economy and in the scale of regulation from the national to the local, current discourse departs from earlier discussions in important ways (Beauregard 1993). What passes for urban policy in the United States now takes place in the unvarnished language of privatization, devolution, and the "reinvention" of housing policy. Gentrification has been incorporated into this discussion in a number of ways: directly and indirectly, conceptually and empirically. Thus, understanding gentrification in the late 1990s may be less a matter of evaluating alternative causal explanations and more a task of decoding the logic, rhetoric, and ideology of public policy and its relationship to underlying urbanization processes. In this regard, we must consider the role of public policy in mediating processes of social segregation in urban housing markets.

Housing markets, public policy, and urban social segregation

The role of housing market dynamics in race- and class-based segregation is well known, and a voluminous interdisciplinary literature has documented the long-term rigidity of entrenched patterns and processes (Boger and Wegner 1996; Jackson 1985; Massey and Denton 1993). In the past decade, however, an unlikely intersection of forces has finally begun to dismantle the institutional framework responsible for the spatial concentration and isolation of low-income households. The outlines of a more complex, dynamic landscape are gradually becoming clear. To begin with, landmark legal precedents established since the late 1960s, most prominently Chicago's *Gautreaux* and New Jersey's *Mount Laurel* decisions, have laid the foundation for stepped-up efforts to "open up the suburbs" (Downs 1973) in a small trickle after withstanding decades of litigation and fierce suburban opposition. A simultaneous and countervailing policy thrust has continued the long-standing tradition of attempting to attract private market activity back to the inner city through spatially targeted mechanisms that might best be called "e-zones," depending on the nomenclature in vogue: economic development, enterprise, or empowerment.

Meanwhile, short-term responses to the well-documented spatial mismatch in urban housing and labor markets (Ihlanfeldt and Sjoquist 1998;

Kain 1992) have spawned scores of reverse commuting programs, many subsidized by partnerships between private employers and public or quasi-public transportation agencies (Hughes 1995). By the early 1990s, urban policy was fragmented among three alternative strategies for dealing with concentrated poverty: *dispersing* low-income residents to the suburbs, *redeveloping* inner-city neighborhoods to provide jobs and housing, and fostering *mobility* between urban neighborhoods and scattered suburban job sites (Hughes 1995).

This structural fragmentation, particularly the tension between dispersal and redevelopment, proved decisive in the context of two major transformations in the national housing policy framework—one a long-term shift in housing finance, the other a sudden restructuring of low-income housing assistance. Both have altered the historically complex relationship between public policy and gentrification.

Changes in housing finance

The first shift has involved an ongoing evolution in housing finance in the United States, bound up with broader economic and policy questions on household consumption, inequality, and the costs and benefits of homeownership. Through the early 1980s, most of these debates were framed against a backdrop of a housing finance system established during the 1930s and periodically revised in times of crisis. It is universally recognized that the central parameters of this regime—manifest in the endless array of legal precedents, social norms, institutional practices, and explicit business criteria for access to mortgage capital—perpetuated the sociospatial processes of redlining, white flight, and suburbanization that confronted urban geography in the 1960s and 1970s. Gentrification attracted attention for its potential to reverse this outcome of the housing finance system.

A generation later, housing finance no longer stands in opposition to gentrification, and in some circumstances it is instrumental in lubricating the process. Macroeconomic trends have certainly helped. An extremely vibrant economic expansion (in its eighth full year as of this writing), combined with low inflation and low interest rates, has reduced borrowing costs and increased competition and consolidation in the financial services sector, as total outstanding mortgage debt mushroomed from less than $1.5 trillion in 1985 to $3.6 trillion a decade later (Simmons 1998). The dramatic expansion of the secondary mortgage market, driven as a matter of policy to direct more capital to housing generally and homeownership in particular (Stegman et al. 1991), has enabled and required broader standardization of underwriting. Given the extremely low risk of residential lending in boom times and the lure of mortgage-backed securities as a hedge against other financial instruments, standardization has effectively meant liberalization across the board. Thus while conventional 30-year loans in an earlier generation required a down payment of at least 10 percent, the current benchmark demands only 5 percent, along with permissible household debt burdens that are far higher than in previous years (Listokin et al. 1998).

Meanwhile, in an era of federal retrenchment, community activism and regulatory intervention, as well as political and fiscal conservatism, have intersected in the use of homeownership as a solution to individual and neighborhood-level poverty. Mortgage lending has increasingly been seen as a domain in which the goals of public policy are readily adapted to the imperatives of profitability in a competitive industry. As part of the savings and loan bailout, Congress required the two dominant secondary-market purchasers (Fannie Mae and Freddie Mac) to increase their acquisitions of primary-market loans to minority and low-income borrowers and neighborhoods (Federal Housing Enterprises Financial Safety and Soundness Act 1992). Parallel shifts have followed at the state and local levels and in the private sector, where the language of "fair lending" has been replaced with widespread discussion of how to reach "untapped" or "underserved" markets (Carliner 1998; Fannie Mae Foundation 1997; Listokin et al. 1998; Stegman et al. 1991). The result has been a proliferation of means-tested mortgage products, some tied to borrower income and some tied to property location in a private echo of the federal urban homesteading programs of the 1970s.

All of these changes have broadened access to homeownership and strengthened certain factions of the community development movement. But these trends have also transformed the environment in which gentrification, quite literally, takes place. Lending institutions now see significant profit potential in formerly redlined areas. Indeed, as lending to minorities and low-income borrowers ballooned in the 1990s, some analysts argued that access to credit is no longer a serious impediment to homeownership; rather, the crucial question is whether borrowers are able to obtain conventional credit on favorable terms—or find themselves slotted into the subprime and Federal Housing Administration (FHA) markets (for the latest salvo in this debate, see Bradford 1998).

Changes in low-income housing policy

A second shift is tied explicitly to low-income housing policy. Always embattled by fiscal shortfalls and a narrow, powerless constituency, assisted housing was already in the midst of a gradual transition after the mid-term elections of 1994 when conservative interests in Congress coalesced around the agenda of privatization and devolution of federal policy. While this agenda altered the landscape in all domains of economic and social policy, trends moved especially rapidly in assisted housing, where the Clinton administration co-opted much of the Republican agenda under the rubric of Gore's reinvention initiative. The result was an accelerated movement from the spatial isolation of publicly owned and operated housing developments to semiprivatized and integrated redevelopment plans, along with the dispersal of vouchers and certificates.

This movement was justified on the basis of an eclectic mixture of theories, ranging from blatant architectural determinism to more sophisticated (but still largely untested) theories of income mixing (Newman 1972, 1980; Schwartz and Tajbakhsh 1997; Varady 1994). In late 1994, the Clinton administration proposed eliminating nearly all project-based housing, and in the ensuing legislative struggle over the future of the Department of Housing and Urban Development (HUD), a solution was found in a small demonstration program born of a commission's study of severely distressed public housing projects in the early 1990s (Epp 1998; National Commission on Severely Distressed Public Housing 1992; Nenno 1998). Known as HOPE VI for its lineage tracing to Jack Kemp's "Home-ownership Opportunities for People Everywhere" initiatives, the program seeks to revitalize HUD's role in assisted housing by demolishing troubled projects, redeveloping sites where feasible and in ways that reduce concentrations of low-income families, and offering tenant-based vouchers and certificates for use in the private market (Epp 1998). The program offers sizable grants to public housing authorities (PHAs) contingent on (1) innovative and creative strategies to leverage federal funds through partnerships with local governments and private developers and (2) integration of redevelopment with support services that emphasize principles of work, self-sufficiency, and personal responsibility (Epp 1998; see also HUD 1999, 17).[5]

This juncture alters the balance between dispersal and redevelopment (Hughes 1995) in a way that unhinges federal, categorical restrictions from the relationship between gentrification and low-income housing assistance at the local level. To be sure, HOPE VI is only the latest incarnation of a federal bureaucracy's interpretation of social science research in the context of a free-market ideology (Marcuse 1998). For decades, HUD has assembled a portfolio of acronyms and programs— a redevelopment effort here, a dispersal scheme there. But HOPE VI appears to be the first program to encapsulate both of these principles in a single, coordinated initiative, with an explicit emphasis on local flexibility, partnerships, and market discipline (Marcuse 1998; Quercia and Galster 1997). By the mid-1990s, local public housing authorities confronted a near-universal vilification of public housing and were suddenly presented with sweeping mandates to make radical, innovative changes to local housing assistance strategies. In many cities, however, local housing officials faced an urban land market that contrasted with earlier generations in important ways. The gentrification of the 1970s and 1980s laid the foundation for the spatial integration of subsidized and market-rate housing, but only in the boom of the late 1990s has this possibility become a reality. The new context of the inner city created by postrecession gentrification has presented local officials with redevelopment options that were not previously possible.

Hypotheses

The 1990s have brought two major transformations in the national urban policy framework: a new regime of housing finance and an emergent consensus on low-income housing assistance. Our purpose in this article is to explore how these shifts have reflected and reinforced a resurgence of private-market gentrification in American cities since the recession of the early 1990s. Figure 34.1 depicts the interrelations among these trends and suggests three central research hypotheses essential to judging the extent and implications of post-recession gentrification.

First, the vibrant economic recovery of the 1990s merits a reevaluation of the degentrification hypothesis put forward by Bourne (1993a, 1993b) and others. We believe that there is ample evidence of a resurgence of gentrification in many different cities, but to provide a rigorous test of this hypothesis, we use a crucial indicator of market activity: individuals seeking to borrow money secured by mortgages on properties in gentrified neighborhoods. If the process has indeed recovered from the depths of the recession, mortgage lending in these neighborhoods should grow at least as fast as city-wide averages.

Second, we propose that the cumulative history of gentrification has altered the context for the reinvention of low-income housing policy. While inner-city revitalization is still dwarfed by suburban expansion, when we focus on the urban core we see a diverse, dynamic landscape created by several decades of class turnover. In some cities, the process has proceeded far enough to create seas of renewal that now surround the islands of decay inscribed by the boom in public housing construction during the 1950s and 1960s. Chicago's Cabrini-Green public housing development is perhaps the most widely known example: Vibrant retail and housing market activity has steadily encroached on the projects since the 1970s, and now the place is a legendary illustration of the sharp boundaries between poverty and wealth similar to those that inspired Chicago School works such as Zorbaugh's (1929) *The Gold Coast and the Slum*. In this context, gentrification mediates the balance between alternative strategies to reinvent distressed public housing: Private-market gentrification is a necessary, although by no means sufficient, condition for market-rate development and income mixing.

Our third hypothesis focuses on the links between the national system of housing finance and gentrification. The expansion of the secondary mortgage market has proceeded in tandem with widespread standardization and a secular relaxation of borrowing constraints, alongside a simultaneous rush to tap underserved markets in the inner city. As a consequence, we argue, mortgage capital now facilitates gentrification in ways that depart radically from earlier decades.

This final hypothesis entails frustrating methodological constraints. Ideally, a comprehensive assessment of long-run changes in the role of housing finance in neighborhood change would draw on data that allow microlevel analysis of supply- and demand-side processes in specific neighborhoods, in several cities, through several business cycles. Unfortunately, data meeting these requirements became available only in 1990; before that time, the data we use to examine the role of housing finance in neighborhood change (described below) were simply not collected. It is impossible, therefore, to conduct a precise historical comparison of mortgage lending dynamics in gentrified neighborhoods. Nevertheless, our hypothesis is bolstered by the historical baseline established in a broad and interdisciplinary literature in urban research. Every shred of evidence from the literature on redlining, suburbanization, and gentrification suggests that private, unsubsidized mortgage capital has always preferred the safety and profitability of the suburbs or established middle-and

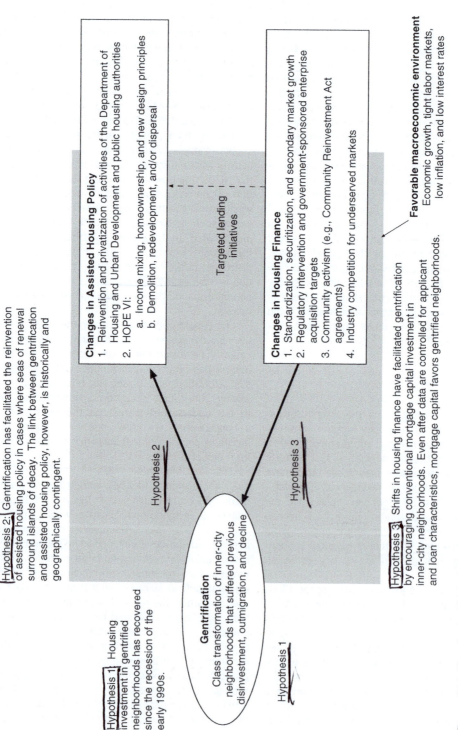

Hypothesis 2: Gentrification has facilitated the reinvention of assisted housing policy in cases where seas of renewal surround islands of decay. The link between gentrification and assisted housing policy, however, is historically and geographically contingent.

Hypothesis 1 Housing investment in gentrified neighborhoods has recovered since the recession of the early 1990s.

Changes in Assisted Housing Policy
1. Reinvention and privatization of activities of the Department of Housing and Urban Development and public housing authorities
2. HOPE VI:
   a. Income mixing, homeownership, and new design principles
   b. Demolition, redevelopment, and/or dispersal

Targeted lending initiatives

Changes in Housing Finance
1. Standardization, securitization, and secondary market growth
2. Regulatory intervention and government-sponsored enterprise acquisition targets
3. Community activism (e.g., Community Reinvestment Act agreements)
4. Industry competition for underserved markets

Favorable macroeconomic environment
Economic growth, tight labor markets, low inflation, and low interest rates

Hypothesis 2

Hypothesis 3

Gentrification
Class transformation of inner-city neighborhoods that suffered previous disinvestment, outmigration, and decline

Hypothesis 1

Hypothesis 3: Shifts in housing finance have facilitated gentrification by encouraging conventional mortgage capital investment in inner-city neighborhoods. Even after data are controlled for applicant and loan characteristics, mortgage capital favors gentrified neighborhoods.

Figure 34.1 Hypothesized Links between Housing Policy and Gentrification

upper-middle-class urban neighborhoods to the risks of the gentrifying inner city. Indeed, in the 1970s, remain on the sidelines until artists, nontraditional households, or other urban pioneers proved that a neighborhood could successfully be revitalized (or until suitable public subsidies were offered), thus leading to stage theories of gentrification (Beauregard 1990; DeGiovanni 1983; Smith and Williams 1986). If we can demonstrate that conventional mortgage capital no longer systematically avoids gentrified neighborhoods (and if this result holds up when considering variations among applicants), it provides strong evidence that standardization and secondary market flows have altered the role of housing finance in neighborhood change.

MAPPING THE RESURGENCE OF GENTRIFICATION

Gentrification is notoriously difficult to measure, and results are sensitive to the indicators chosen, the time periods under investigation, and thresholds used to distinguish among neighborhoods. To develop a coherent portrait of the process, we draw on three complementary data sources.

Gentrification database

Our first data set may best be described as an ongoing effort to "ground-truth" the familiar census reports that form the mainstay of so much urban studies research. Over the past five years, we have assembled a growing database of gentrified neighborhoods in large U.S. cities, with a long-term goal of full coverage of the 30 most populous metropolitan areas. This study involves analyzing gentrification in eight cities: Boston, Chicago, Detroit, Milwaukee, Minneapolis–St. Paul, Philadelphia, Seattle, and Washington, DC. While these do not constitute a representative sample of U.S. cities, they vary widely in economic structure, housing markets, and the extent and intensity of gentrification.

Identifying and measuring gentrification is no simple matter. Typically, analysts identify the phenomenon by selecting a handful of demographic variables from tract-level census reports and then locating neighborhoods exceeding some specified threshold (for example, Lipton 1977 and Nelson 1988). When applied without complementary qualitative or historical sources, this approach amounts to what might be called inductive empiricism and is plagued by several flaws. Class turnover is

exceedingly difficult to measure in a cross-sectional snapshot, and neighborhood change often frustrates the investigator by straddling decennial census years. Housing measures are sensitive to displacement or filtering processes that diffuse rent increases outward from tightened markets in gentrified neighborhoods (Waldorf 1991). Most important, this method invariably identifies elite and middle-class urban neighborhoods that never experienced sustained outmigration or disinvestment; in an incisive critique of the literature, Bourne (1993a, 1993b) seizes on this flaw in order to question the magnitude and relevance of gentrification for urban theory and urban policy.

In our research, we adopt an alternative approach designed to compensate for the inherent flaws of uncritical reliance on tract-level summary statistics. Our method involves three steps in each city: First, we review scholarly research, city planning documents, and local press sources to develop an initial list of gentrified neighborhoods. Second, we conduct a block-by-block field survey of tracts identified in the literature review. In this survey, we seek out visible evidence of housing reinvestment and class turnover; while not without its limitations, this approach captures the distinctive consumption norms, aesthetic sensibilities, and housing investments of the "new middle classes" responsible for a more restless urban landscape (Knox 1991). Third, we calibrate multivariate discriminant analysis models to distinguish gentrified areas from other urban neighborhoods on the basis of socioeconomic benchmarks of class turnover.[6]

As our database has grown, we have been able to use discriminant models derived from previous rounds of fieldwork to predict gentrified tracts in other cities, where we subsequently verify our hypotheses in the field. This technique allows an iterative blend of qualitative and quantitative sources to detect a phenomenon widely regarded as complex, diverse, and variable in its timing and empirical manifestation (Beauregard 1986, 1990; Bourne 1993a, 1993b).

We argue that a geographic perspective on neighborhood change requires integrating quantitative evidence with the more nuanced perspective allowed by field observation; although each addition to our database improves the sensitivity of our discriminant models, the idiosyncrasies of spatial aggregation and census classification are laid bare by site visits to suburban-style subsidized housing that suddenly boosts rents or house values averaged across tracts, or luxury apartments recently constructed at the frontier between gentrified enclaves and severe inner-city poverty. To capture these differences, we develop a neighborhood taxonomy to account for varied levels of intensity and spatial configuration of gentrification. First, we operationalize Berry's (1985) seas of decay by identifying central-city census tracts with median household income below the citywide median in 1960; this is the "inner city," most of which suffered outmigration, disinvestment, and decline during the vigorous housing boom of the early postwar period. From this set of neighborhoods we distinguish intensely gentrified core districts and fringe areas where reinvestment is comparatively modest, spatially fragmented, or in its early stages.

Figure 34.2 depicts this taxonomy for Chicago, and table 34.1 summarizes our fieldwork to date in eight cities that permit a test of our three hypotheses. In 1990, the population of core gentry neighborhoods stood at just under 300,000, while an additional 271,000 lived in fringe areas. Consequently, our islands of renewal account for just under 22 percent of the total population of the seas of decay in these eight cities. Clearly, gentrification affects only a small fraction of the central-city housing market and is dwarfed by continued metropolitan expansion. Yet the process merits attention not on the basis of its magnitude, but for the intersection of complex economic and cultural processes at the neighborhood level (Beauregard 1986, 1990, 1994).[7]

Other indicators provide further insight into long-term neighborhood change in these cities. Table 34.2 presents the results of stepwise discriminant analyses that identify variables distinguishing gentrified tracts from surrounding inner-city areas. Separate discriminant functions for core and fringe neighborhoods yield fairly robust accuracy: With a combination of income, education, occupation, and racial indicators, the models confirm approximately nine-tenths of the districts identified in our field surveys. Education is the single best discriminator, but income and income growth are also important: As a group, core gentry areas posted real growth in average family income[8] of 80 percent, contrasting sharply with the slight erosion in the remainder of the inner city. In light of the methodological problems associated with identifying a process that varies widely in its timing in different cities, these results are encouraging.[9] Nevertheless, the models yield a large number of type II errors—inner-city tracts that are mistakenly classified as gentrified. The factors behind these errors are complex and diverse, reflecting the problems of area averages and different types of public and private redevelopment activities (Hammel and Wyly 1996). These results suggest, however, that our approach provides a conservative estimate of gentrification.

Mortgage disclosure files

Our second source of evidence allows an unusually sharp image of capital flows on an annual basis. Since the early 1990s, disclosure requirements have required all but a small fraction of the nation's mortgage lending institutions to report information on the personal characteristics and action taken on individual loan applications (Federal Financial Institutions Examination Council [FFIEC] 1999; Fishbein 1992; Holloway 1998). These data have spawned an explosion in research on fair lending and redlining, but they also allow us to chart the demand for and supply of capital to one important segment of gentrifiers: middle- and upper-middle-income residents who must secure a loan to buy a house in a gentrified neighborhood. We assembled Home Mortgage Disclosure Act (HMDA) data on our eight case study metropolitan statistical areas (MSAs) for the boom period between 1992 and 1997. We use simple tabulations of these data to measure housing investment in the neighborhoods documented in our gentrification database. A multivariate model is developed and estimated with the HMDA data to test the hypothesis that conventional mortgage capital no longer systematically avoids the gentrifying inner city.

HOPE VI site profiles

Our third source of evidence is drawn from policy documents filed by local public housing officials. As part of the application process for federal grants under HOPE VI, PHAs must submit application materials that include a site profile for each public housing development slated for revitalization or demolition (Housing Research Foundation 1998). These profiles vary somewhat in length and coverage, but at a minimum they specify the PHA's plans to redevelop sites in ways that avoid the supposed ills of high-rise public housing design and prevent the reconcentration of low-income households. They also specify plans to integrate subsidized project-based assistance with scattered-site construction, rehabilitation, vouchers and certificates for use on the open market, and criteria to be used in mixed-income redevelopment of the original site. HUD encourages innovative leveraging of federal funds with Community Development Block Grant, HOME, and local financing as well as private capital (see Epp 1998; HUD 1997; U.S. Congress 1998).

We emphasize that these profiles are far from perfect: They are only capsule summaries of full applications, and our use of successful files certainly

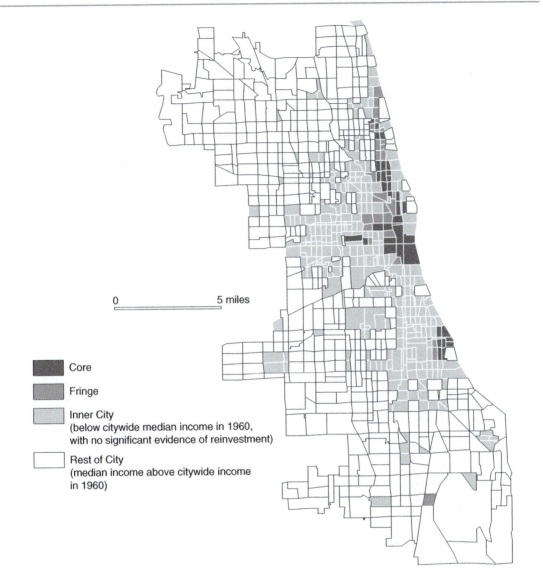

Figure 34.2 Gentrification Field Survey in Chicago

introduces some selection bias into the equation. Their utility lies in the aggregate picture that emerges when these developments are coded to our field-verified database on gentrification. We propose the underwhelming hypothesis that localized instances of gentrification have been incorporated into low-income housing assistance plans as local authorities confront the imperatives of devolution, privatization, and market discipline in attempting to meet the needs of extremely poor families while securing cross-subsidies from market-rate units (Marcuse 1998; Quercia and Galster 1997).

THE RESURGENCE OF GENTRIFICATION

We begin our empirical analysis with a simple question: Has capital investment in gentrified neighborhoods recovered after the recession of the early 1990s? To answer this question, we examine the geographic distribution of mortgage lending between 1992 and 1997 (the latest year for which data are available). Our goal is to assess the willingness of borrowers, lenders, and housing market intermediaries to accept the risks of investing in gentrified neighborhoods; thus we restrict our attention

City	Date of Baseline Fieldwork	Number of census tracts	
		Core	Fringe
Boston	March 1998	14	11
Chicago	August 1995	37	32
Detroit	July 1998	3	4
Milwaukee	August 1995	6	7
Minneapolis–St. Paul	January 1994	7	19
Philadelphia	July 1998	13	7
Seattle	July 1998	9	12
Washington, DC	July 1995	17	11
Total		106	103

Table 34.1 Summary of Gentrification Field Surveys, 1994 to 1998

Model 1		Aggregated values	
	Wilks' Lambda	Core	Rest of Inner City
1. Share of persons 25 and over with college degree, 1990	0.585	56.8	14.7
2. Ratio of average family income, 1990/1970*	0.539	1.80	0.94
3. Homeownership rate, 1990	0.526	26.7	31.9
4. Change in 1946–1960 birth cohort as share of total population, 1970–1990	0.514	3.79	−6.86
5. Poverty rate, 1990	0.506	14.7	36.3
6. White nonfamily households as share of total households, 1990	0.499	58.7	19.2
7. African-American population as share of total, 1990	0.494	17.9	60.2
8. Managerial and administrative workers as share of total workforce, 1990	0.490	21.7	9.85
9. Share of persons 25 and over with some college, 1990	0.487	15.3	14.9
Percentage of core tracts correctly classified	91 (9 type I errors)		
Percentage of inner-city tracts correctly classified	94 (44 type II errors)		

Model 2		Aggregated Values	
	Wilks' Lambda	Fringe	Rest of Inner City
1. Change in share of persons 25 and over with college degree, 1970–1990	0.730	28.0	8.75
2. 1946–1960 birth cohort as share of total population, 1990	0.680	24.9	22.0
3. Ratio of average family income, 1990/1970*	0.664	1.31	0.94
4. Share of persons 25 and over with some college, 1990	0.649	17.9	14.9
5. Non-Hispanic white population as share of total, 1990	0.638	64.1	23.9
6. Change in white nonfamily households as share of total, 1970–1990	0.634	22.2	8.54
7. Managerial and administrative workers as share of total workforce, 1990	0.630	15.4	9.85
8. Change in share of persons 25 and over with some college, 1970–1990	0.627	6.45	8.58
9. Average family income, 1990	0.619	$43,158	$27,554
Percentage of fringe tracts correctly classified	86 (14 type I errors)		
Percentage of inner-city tracts correctly classified	89 (86 type II errors)		

Table 34.2 Stepwise Discriminant Analysis of Gentrified Neighborhoods, 1970 to 1990

Source: Authors' fieldwork and analysis of data from Tobin (1993)

*Measured in constant 1990 dollars

to conventional loans that were approved and originated.[10] We also focus on comparisons between 1992 and 1997, although figures are presented as well for 1993 (when conventional, fixed 30-year interest rates briefly dipped below 7 percent).[11] We hypothesize that core and fringe gentrified areas will at least keep pace with metropolitan growth in mortgage investment. To the degree that core and fringe investment accelerates more rapidly than suburban expansion, we may conclude that gentrification has rebounded from the stalled property markets of the early 1990s. Whether growth in capital investment reflects demand- or supply-side factors, or even new housing construction, is largely irrelevant; demonstrating the resurgence of gentrification simply requires that aggregate investment grow more rapidly in these neighborhoods than in other parts of the metropolis.

As a group, these cities have attracted substantial reinvestment in the recovery of the 1990s (table 34.3). Given the risks that must be borne by home buyers, conventional loans for the purchase of single-family homes provide the most conservative test of our hypothesis. Between 1992 and 1997, total conventional home purchase lending grew by 50 percent, from $31.5 billion to $47.5 billion. Not surprisingly, the suburban ring accounts for the vast majority (more than 85 percent) of total capital flows. Yet growth rates have been disproportionately concentrated at the interior of the metropolis. Conventional home purchase lending to core gentry neighborhoods grew by 129 percent, from $358 million in 1992 to $763 million in 1997, and median loan amounts more than kept pace with suburban growth rates. This evidence alone is sufficient to cast doubt on predictions of degentrification: These neighborhoods attracted a wave of long-term investment that grew at 2.3 times the suburban rate. More significantly, reinvestment has spilled out into adjacent fringe neighborhoods, which posted growth rates 2.4 times that of the suburban ring. The rest of the inner city, which encompasses many different types of neighborhood changes since the 1960s, outpaced suburban expansion by a factor of 2.2. The remainder of the central cities lags slightly behind the suburban ring (45 percent growth rate versus 49 percent).

Considering other types of lending adds complexity to the picture but does not detract from the general trend. Gentrified neighborhoods mirror the suburbs in refinancing activity, which surged with the fall in interest rates in 1993. Median refinancing amounts in the suburbs and gentrified areas have fluctuated only slightly (9.3 percent in the most extreme case), but other central-city neighborhoods

have seen a progressive shift in the refinance market toward smaller loans. This result may stem from the growth in home equity lending to moderate-income urban homeowners. Not surprisingly, multifamily lending accounts for a larger share of investment in urban neighborhoods than in the suburbs: Multifamily lending is equivalent to less than 1 percent of single-family lending in the suburbs, compared with 6.2 percent in core gentry areas. Home improvement loans, however, account for a larger fraction of investment in the suburbs (5.0 percent of the amount devoted to single-family purchases) than in gentrified areas (1.7 percent in the core, 2.4 percent in the fringe).

It is important to recognize that these figures reflect a complex set of supply- and demand-side processes, as well as certain features of the HMDA database. Single-family home purchase loans, for example, include those for new detached homes and condominium units as well as older houses renovated by previous owners. Nevertheless, we can conclude that reinvestment in gentrified neighborhoods is not simply a product of small-scale renovation; it is dominated by home-purchase lending at the upper reaches of the central-city price range. On this crucial indicator, gentrified areas have enjoyed a resurgence of investment at a pace exceeding 2.3 times the suburban growth rate. Clearly, the dramatic resurgence of capital investment ushered in with the economic recovery of the 1990s has increasingly focused on the urban core.

Each of these cities has followed a distinctive trajectory in recent rounds of urban restructuring, and local reinvestment flows reflect these differences (see table 34.4). Measured against the growth rate of suburban investment, capital flows into core gentrified neighborhoods are most pronounced in Milwaukee, Seattle, and Washington, DC; fringe reinvestment has accelerated most briskly in Boston, Chicago, and Philadelphia. In general, fringe reinvestment has accelerated most rapidly in heavily gentrified cities, consistent with the notion of outward expansion in the wake of previous rounds of disinvestment and reinvestment. This interpretation is intuitively appealing, given the more active real estate activity in many transitional fringe neighborhoods. In Boston, Chicago, and Philadelphia, reinvestment activity has moved beyond the firmly established core of gentrification, and even the remainder of the inner city outpaces growth rates in suburban lending activity by a wide margin. Washington, DC, however, stands out as a striking exception, with growth in capital flows continuing to favor core gentrified areas as the fringe saw a net loss. We suspect that the sustained level of investment

	Total loan volume			Median loan amount		
	1992	1993	1997	1992	1993	1997
Home Purchase						
Core	358,531	467,892	763,362	135	140	138
Fringe	176,400	225,746	382,746	118	115	124
Inner city	462,329	585,928	953,599	81	86	95
Rest of city	2,797,714	3,224,993	4,066,592	92	89	92
Suburbs	27,721,245	34,731,730	41,223,003	126	128	127
Home Improvement						
Core	22,131	25,509	13,010	32	28	20
Fringe	12,817	14,218	9,180	20	18	16
Inner city	54,467	108,091	74,313	7	8	10
Rest of city	292,177	476,400	354,158	9	10	10
Suburbs	2,200,086	3,379,268	2,063,924	14	12	15
Refinancing						
Core	651,914	912,436	419,602	139	132	144
Fringe	307,428	449,144	234,483	115	113	119
Inner city	808,912	1,110,191	884,824	93	89	60
Rest of city	5,163,065	7,400,078	4,326,689	85	84	60
Suburbs	61,307,792	90,720,188	36,421,343	106	107	102
Multifamily*						
Core	62,292	64,407	47,346	458	412	344
Fringe	117,021	121,291	31,415	469	384	352
Inner city	127,718	141,980	118,515	292	263	230
Rest of city	389,846	450,321	317,616	263	252	248
Suburbs	718,211	943,626	459,526	269	251	244

Table 34.3 Aggregate Capital Investment in Selected Metropolitan Statistical Areas: Total Value of Conventional Loans Approved and Originated, 1992 to 1997

Source: FFIEC (1993, 1994, 1999)

Note: All values are expressed in thousands of constant 1997 dollars, adjusted for inflation with Metropolitan Statistical Area–level Consumer Price Index series for housing expenditures

*Multifamily loans include home purchase, home improvement, and refinancing loans on structures with four or more units

growth in these core neighborhoods reflects the steady turnover of affluent professionals associated with the city's agglomeration of government agencies, lobbying concerns, and national associations.[12] After the collapse of the early 1990s, indicators on a citywide basis point to a general resurgence of real estate activity in Washington, DC, as private employment growth is now more than compensating for public sector retrenchment. Homes sold in the first half of 1998 increased by 48 percent over the same period of 1997, after a comparable expansion of 30 percent the previous year (Monteilh and Weiss 1998).

By contrast, until a recent surge of mortgage activity in core neighborhoods, cities where gentrification affects a smaller fraction of the urban housing market have lagged behind. To be sure, this trend may reflect any number of complex forces at work in local housing and mortgage markets. For example, core neighborhoods registered a temporary peak of lending activity in Detroit, Milwaukee, and Minneapolis–St. Paul when conventional, fixed 30-year interest rates briefly dipped below 7 percent in 1993. Gentrification activity is comparatively modest in these cities, suggesting that a narrow window of affordability may have been important in attracting buyers to core neighborhoods. No such peak is apparent in any of the other cities, where lending volume has advanced consistently in the face of interest rate fluctuations. Nevertheless, capital investment

	1992	1993	1997	Growth rate, 1992–1997	Ratio to suburban Growth rate
Boston					
Core	76,452	113,675	179,786	135.2	1.58
Fringe	11,145	24,021	53,170	377.1	4.40
Inner city	21,896	24,821	54,510	148.9	1.74
Rest of city	165,605	221,338	320,314	93.4	1.09
Remainder, metro	2,762,218	3,903,628	5,129,899	85.7	—
Chicago					
Core	131,417	178,567	323,508	146.2	1.89
Fringe	53,004	80,646	159,840	201.6	2.61
Inner city	240,460	336,946	576,097	139.6	1.81
Rest of city	1,031,708	1,204,992	1,526,348	47.9	0.62
Remainder, metro	5,208,004	6,216,322	9,232,715	77.3	—
Detroit					
Core	569	990	1,150	102.3	1.09
Fringe	1,150	847	2,155	87.5	0.94
Inner city	8,112	10,202	18,125	123.4	1.32
Rest of city	40,151	51,415	116,731	190.7	2.04
Remainder, metro	3,343,691	4,396,080	6,467,229	93.4	—
Milwaukee					
Core	2,784	4,944	5,993	115.3	3.70
Fringe	9,196	15,257	12,079	31.4	1.01
Inner city	19,671	21,770	26,821	36.3	1.17
Rest of city	185,848	265,610	239,902	29.1	0.93
Remainder, metro	1,169,203	1,471,114	1,532,991	31.1	—
Minneapolis–St. Paul					
Core	11,560	16,726	15,053	30.2	0.64
Fringe	17,048	26,426	37,921	122.4	2.59
Inner city	52,695	70,436	106,011	101.2	2.14
Rest of city	173,176	232,981	343,304	98.2	2.08
Remainder, metro	2,232,363	3,480,191	3,287,196	47.3	—
Philadelphia					
Core	48,641	51,429	66,764	37.3	2.47
Fringe	2,205	4,184	4,542	106.0	7.04
Inner city	29,261	34,759	42,044	43.7	2.90
Rest of city	272,328	315,792	327,989	20.4	1.36
Remainder, metro	3,514,242	4,463,600	4,043,542	15.1	—
Seattle					
Core	42,308	47,438	106,629	152.0	3.25
Fringe	46,245	47,058	79,694	72.3	1.55
Inner city	67,585	60,981	97,196	43.8	0.94
Rest of city	719,042	712,047	953,213	32.6	0.70
Remainder, metro	2,956,994	3,019,263	4,339,095	46.7	—
Washington, DC					
Core	44,801	54,123	64,479	43.9	4.38
Fringe	36,408	27,307	33,345	−8.4	—
Inner city	22,648	26,012	32,795	44.8	4.46
Rest of city	209,857	220,818	238,791	13.8	1.37
Remainder, metro	6,534,531	7,781,532	7,190,336	10.0	—

Table 34.4 Capital Reinvestment by Neighborhood Type in Selected Metropolitan Statistical Areas: Total Value of Conventional Originations for One- to Four-Family Home Purchase Loans, 1992 to 1997

Source: FFIEC (1993–1998)

Note: All values are in thousands of constant 1997 dollars, adjusted with Metropolitan Statistical Area–level Consumer Price Index series for housing expenditures

has surged even in Milwaukee and Detroit. Between 1996 and 1997, investment increased by 133 percent in Detroit's core gentry neighborhoods and by 211 percent in fringe areas. These extraordinary rates of increase were based on extremely small absolute lending volumes, however, and so it remains to be seen whether growth will continue. By 1997, conventional home purchase lending in Milwaukee's core and fringe neighborhoods stood at only $18 million, and Detroit had only $3.3 million. Nevertheless, reinvestment does seem to be under way. By the latter half of the decade, the national economic recovery had finally reached the abandoned blocks of central Detroit, and the *Free Press* tallied up a total of $5.74 billion in new public and private development planned or under construction, including new stadia for the Tigers and the Lions, General Motors' takeover and proposed facelift of the Renaissance Center to accommodate 9,000 workers, and Chrysler's expansion plans for six plants throughout the city (Dixon and Solomon 1997).[13] By the time we conducted our fieldwork in the city in the summer of 1998, the neighborhoods immediately adjacent to downtown were undergoing a kind of resurgence that seems to happen only in Detroit: new single-family homes starting at $425,000 across the street from boarded-up houses and deteriorated streetcar retail strips and apartment buildings, all within a stone's throw of the river.

These results demonstrate that predictions of the demise of gentrification were exaggerated (Bourne 1993a, 1993b). While contextual variations are important, gentrified neighborhoods in all of these cities enjoyed a remarkable surge in capital investment in the recovery of the 1990s. As a group, gentrified neighborhoods attracted mortgage capital at a rate that grew more than twice as fast as in the suburbs. The particularly rapid acceleration of reinvestment in fringe areas provides a vivid illustration of rent gap dynamics in the inner city. Capital began to fill the vacuum left behind by a wave of disinvestment that rippled outward from the urban core as metropolitan expansion boosted potential land rents far above the levels capitalized through prevailing local land uses (Clark 1995; Hammel 1999; Smith 1979, 1996). The current wave of mortgage investment in gentrified areas, however, departs from earlier generations in important ways. Historically, the spatial allocation of mortgage credit was responsible for the *creation* or *exacerbation* of rent gaps, not their elimination. Biased lending practices, often explicitly rooted in ecological theories of neighborhood change, as well as blatant racial and ethnic discrimination, were instrumental in prompting disinvestment and selective outmigration

from older residential districts near the urban core (Bradford 1998; Jackson 1985; Smith 1979, 1996; Squires 1992).

As outlined earlier, however, this link has been altered and in some cases reversed by long-term changes in the nation's housing finance system. Two specific changes have been especially important for inner-city neighborhood change. First, a secular relaxing of borrowing constraints (Linneman and Wachter 1989), along with a dynamic erosion of the boundaries between conventional and government-backed lending and between market-rate and means-tested loans, has proceeded throughout the mortgage market. Reading the housing finance literature, especially in the applied policy arena, has become an exercise in sifting through hundreds of acronyms, trademarks, and specialized underwriting criteria. Even if one ignores the scores of state and local mortgage subsidy packages and the federally backed FHA guarantees, the dominant secondary market purchaser (Fannie Mae) offers 72 different "products" (sets of guidelines under which Fannie Mae will purchase a loan originated by a primary-market lender). Many of these are means tested by borrower income, permitting more flexible criteria in order to reach borrowers who would be excluded on standard conventional terms; but Fannie Mae also reaches HUD-designated underserved census tracts with the "FannieNeighbors®" mortgage, which removes the income limit altogether" (Fannie Mae 1996, 18).

Second, activist research and mobilization since the late 1980s has achieved substantial victories against lending institutions accused of discrimination and redlining (Schwartz 1998; Squires 1992). In a movement that has increasingly been regarded as a form of regulation from below (Fishbein 1992) compatible with the political realities of privatization and public-sector retrenchment, community groups and advocacy research institutions have mobilized to document redlining (using data made public under HMDA) and to challenge institutions involved in such practices (under the Community Reinvestment Act [CRA] of 1977). CRA provisions require regulators to evaluate the degree to which institutions offer credit to all areas from which they accept deposits, and these annual CRA ratings are considered along with public input in applications for mergers, acquisitions, and major reorganizations. CRA challenges (and the threat of such challenges) thus became increasingly common with the rapid consolidation of the financial services sector in the 1990s. The first Clinton administration, moreover, revised assessment guidelines and reporting requirements under HMDA and CRA (see Vartanian et al. 1995). The results have been dramatic: In the past 20 years, more than 300 community reinvestment agreements valued at more than $350 billion have been negotiated (Schwartz 1998).

REINVENTION AND REVITALIZATION IN THE ISLANDS OF DECAY

Shifts in housing finance have coincided with, and in some cases been linked to, policy changes in housing assistance as devolution and privatization have gathered momentum. The proliferation of affordable mortgage products and dedicated loan pools, for example, has been essential in efforts to increase homeownership in central cities at the same time that local governments seek to transform their stock of public housing in line with new federal priorities. The reinvention of assisted housing, however, takes place in the context of an inner-city landscape influenced by three decades of neighborhood change. As a consequence, gentrification has become an important factor that conditions the implementation of reforms in assisted housing.

HOPE VI, while still a small program in its early stages, provides an ideal case study of this process. The program grew out of a long history of policy formulation and experience with the management challenges faced by PHAs (Epp 1998; Lane 1995; Schill 1997), but it also incorporates key assumptions drawn from influential theories in the social sciences. In particular, the formulation and implementation of HOPE VI plans have drawn heavily on theories relating social behavior to various aspects of the urban environment. These theories focus on two spatial scales. First, at the level of the housing development itself, social behavior is linked to architectural design. Since the 1970s, Oscar Newman's (1972, 1980) work on defensible space has forged a consensus that the modernist design principles embodied in tower-in-the-park public housing projects have failed: Public housing towers are not believed to be conducive to the creation of shared public areas that foster collective monitoring and other protective behavior by residents. In response, some redevelopment plans have drawn inspiration from the work of the "new urbanist" movement in city planning, which emphasizes the creation of physical spaces that encourage pedestrian circulation and informal social interaction (Bennett and Reed 1999; Bothwell, Gindroz, and Lang 1998).

Second, at the level of the neighborhood and the inner city, social behavior has been linked to the spatial concentration of poverty. William Julius Wilson's (1987, 1996) work has been especially influential, giving rise to a wide-ranging debate on the relative importance of behavior and structural constraints in the emergence of an urban underclass (Jencks and Mayer 1990; Massey and Denton 1993). While debate on these questions persists, the consensus among policy makers is that poverty is fundamentally transformed by its spatial concentration: When neighborhood poverty rates exceed some critical threshold, contagion effects spread behavioral pathologies through peer groups, while collective socialization erodes because children no longer see adults in positive role models as educated workers and married parents (Jencks and Mayer 1990). This consensus has driven efforts to integrate poor inner-city residents into the social and economic mainstream, either by dispersing concentrations of poverty or by redeveloping neighborhoods to achieve a mixture of incomes and racial groups. HOPE VI encourages PHAs to pursue either or both of these strategies, depending on the condition of existing public housing developments, the viability of the local housing market, and the prospects for attracting private developers and tenants. Reviewing the experience of public housing officials with the Urban Revitalization Demonstration (URD) program that preceded HOPE VI, Epp (1998) summarizes the challenges this way:

> Creating a new mixed-income community might be feasible in those cities with strong housing markets and with URD sites in neighborhoods that can attract households with different incomes. Participants in the URD program have pointed out that not all sites have income-mixing potential between 60 and 80 percent of area median and that even fewer sites can attract market-rate families (with incomes greater than 95 percent of area median). (131)

This suggests the hypothesis that gentrification mediates the choice between redevelopment and dispersal of distressed public housing projects. Where the class transformation of neighborhoods tightens the housing market in the vicinity of public housing, mixed-income redevelopment is both feasible and profitable if the parcel is configured in such a way that higher-income residents do not feel threatened by the proximity of poor families. By contrast, public housing developments that are distant from areas undergoing private-market revitalization will have difficulty attracting market-rate residents. When viewed at the metropolitan level, gentrification may indeed be confined to islands of renewal in seas of decay (Berry 1985), but it has inscribed a new context for efforts to "transform public housing communities from islands of despair and poverty into a vital and integral part of larger neighborhoods" (Epp 1998, 126).

To test this hypothesis, we reviewed all of the successful HOPE VI grant applications filed by PHAs in our eight cities for fiscal years 1993 through 1998 (all were obtained from Housing Research Foundation 1998). These grants account for a total of $652.8 million promised by the federal government (not counting local government or private funding leveraged by PHAs), representing 21.2 percent of all grant amounts awarded nationally under the program in these years. Table 34.5 summarizes key elements of these redevelopment plans. Our hypothesis centers on the columns denoting (1) whether a site redevelopment plan involves moderate- or market-rate units, and (2) a development's situation in relation to local gentrification as defined in our field survey.

Dispersal, redevelopment, and gentrification

PHAs must prioritize the needs of large inventories, and the location of severely distressed developments chosen for HOPE VI applications reflects the cumulative legacy of neighborhood change as well as resident admissions criteria and management capability. Thus, it is not surprising to see a wide range of redevelopment plans, each tailored to the unique conditions of the housing complex, its surrounding neighborhood, and the city's overall housing market. Nevertheless, redevelopment plans provide qualified support for our hypothesis. Ten grants involve demolition and/or implementation with no provision for moderate- or market-rate housing on the original site; six of these developments have no nearby gentrification activity. Of the remaining four, two are in cities with relatively weak gentrification pressures (Detroit and Milwaukee), and two are in cities where private-market revitalization is more significant (Boston and Philadelphia). This suggests that nearby gentrification is not sufficient, by itself, to induce market-rate redevelopment.

Six plans involve explicit provisions for market-rate housing on the original site. Four of these are within or immediately adjacent to gentrified tracts, and in every case the plans acknowledge the effect of surrounding activity on the feasibility of attracting market-rate residents. Similarly, three of the four plans slated for moderate-income redevelopment are surrounded by core or fringe tracts. Two redevelopments, however, run counter to our hypothesis by proposing income mixing in areas distant from gentrification. In Washington, DC, one

market-rate redevelopment (Valley Green/Skytower) is at the boundary between the city and suburban Prince George's County and includes a HUD-owned Section 8 foreclosure. In Seattle, the city's largest public housing development is more than three miles from any gentrification activity. This development, Holly Park, is a 102-acre parcel strewn with 1- and 2-story wood-frame town houses constructed as temporary war worker housing in the early 1940s. Redevelopment plans call for three construction phases over a five- to six-year period, drawing on an intricate combination of funding sources and including 300 market-rate homeownership units.[14] The site lies between a corridor of working-class neighborhoods south of downtown Seattle and a ring of stable middle-class areas around Lake Washington; thus, local land market pressures are likely to support the plan.

With these notable exceptions, redevelopment plans generally confirm our hypothesis. Gentrification tightens local housing markets, enabling the integration of the publicly owned, affordable, and market-rate housing that is at the heart of HUD's reinvention. Contrasts among different cities are particularly striking. In the vibrant housing market of the Chicago metropolitan area, four of the city's five redevelopment plans include provisions for moderate-income or market-rate housing, while none of the plans in Detroit or Milwaukee involve market-rate units. Differences within cities are also important and highlight the fine-grained variation of development pressures and neighborhood conditions at the frontier between decay and reinvestment.

One of Washington, DC's revitalization plans offers a particularly ambitious agenda and a vivid illustration of the links among gentrification, physical design and portrayals of the built environment, and the transformation of low-income housing policy.

The Ellen Wilson Dwellings occupied a 5.3-acre site nestled behind the major freeway corridor that bisects Southeast Washington. The complex, which opened in 1941, consisted of 134 units in walk-up brick buildings. By the 1980s, the structures had deteriorated so much that the local housing authority declared the development uninhabitable and closed it in 1988. The project was thus the only HOPE VI site among those studied in HUD's *Historical and Baseline Assessment* (Abt Associates 1996) that was entirely vacant at the time of application. Plans for demolition and redevelopment were delayed several times in the midst of turmoil at the housing authority, but demolition finally commenced in April 1996. The complex, now redeveloped, lies immediately south of several blocks of rehabilitated rowhouses a short walk from a Metro station and

City and development	Award[a]	Fiscal year	Type[b]	Demolition	Rehabilitation	New	Mix[c]	Description	Tract	Location
Chicago										
Cabrini Homes Extension	50,000	1994	I	660	65	493	Market	Mixed with market rate units; most replacement units in surrounding community.	819	Surrounded by core and fringe tracts.
ABLA Homes/ Henry Horner/ Rockwell Gardens	400	1995	P							
Robert Taylor Homes	25,000	1996	D-R	790	125	125		No replacement units on site; site to be developed as light industrial park.	3817	Surrounded by poor tracts; more than 1 mile from nearest gentrification activity (fringe tract).
Brooks Extension	24,483	1996	D	300		200	Moderate	Mixed with moderate: half of units will be open to families earning 50 percent to 80 percent of area median income (AMI); the remaining half will be reserved for those earning less than 30 percent of AMI. Adjoining parcels to be acquired; 54 units to be built on site, 146 on adjacent parcels.	2820	In fringe tract.

Table 34.5 Profile of HOPE VI Demolition and Redevelopment Plans in Case Study Cities, 1993 to 1998

City and development	Award[a]	Fiscal year	Type[b]	Demolition	Rehabilitation	New	Mix[c]	Description	Tract	Location
Henry Horner Homes	18,435	1996	I	743		150	Moderate	Mixed with moderate: half of units will be open to families earning 50 percent to 80 percent of AMI; remaining half reserved for those earning less than 30 percent of AMI.	2804	Adjacent to fringe tract.
ABLA Homes	35,000	1998	I	2,776		2,598	Market	Site replacement includes 1,052 public units; 580 affordable rental/ownership units, and 966 market-rate rental/ownership units.	2820	In fringe tract.
Boston										
Mission Main	49,992	1993	I	807		850	Market	Plan to build 850 mixed-income condominium, ownership, and market-rate rental units, and four- to six-story public housing units.	808	Adjacent to fringe tract.
Orchard Park	30,400	1995	P, I	441		280		On-site development of 280 public housing units, 40 tax-credit rental units, 10 ownership units; 224 public units to be constructed in surrounding area.	803/ 804	Approximately 0.4 miles from core tract.
Detroit										
Parkside Homes	48,120	1994 1995	P, I	392	350	180		Plan to demolish about half of the 60 buildings, reconfigure remaining units, construct 180 town houses in adjacent neighborhoods, and acquire and rehabilitate 345 single-family homes throughout Empowerment Zone to be sold to public-eligible households.	5122	No gentrification within 2 miles.

Table 34.5—Cont'd

City and development	Award[a]	Fiscal year	Type[b]	Demolition	Rehabilitation	New	Mix[c]	Description	Tract	Location
Jeffries Homes	49,807	1994 1996	D, I	612				Construction of low-rise replacement units both on and off site.	5207	Approximately 0.5 miles from downtown core tract.
Parkside Addition/ Herman Gardens/ Gardenview	400	1995	P							
Herman Gardens	24,224	1996	D-R	1,223	274	672		Plan to increase income of current residents; 176 ownership units to be constructed for residents completing self-sufficiency program.	5454	No gentrification within 3 miles.
Milwaukee Hillside Terrace	45,689	1993 1995 1996	I[d]	119				Goal to reduce density and revitalize existing development.	141	Approximately 0.5 miles from downtown core and fringe tracts.
Parklawn	34,230	1998	I	138	380	40		Demolition of 138 public units, to be replaced by 40 new single-family lease-to-purchase homes, half on site and half off site. Remaining public units to be rehabilitated.	40	No gentrification within 5 miles.
Philadelphia Richard Allen Homes	50,000	1993	I	129	314	80		Plan to reconfigure three existing quadrants to 314 town house units and construct new five-story building with 80 units for older people.	131, 132	Approximately 0.25 miles from fringe and core tracts.

Table 34.5—Cont'd

City and development	Award[a]	Fiscal year	Type[b]	Demolition	Rehabilitation	New	Mix[c]	Description	Tract	Location
Martin Luther King	25,630	1995 1998	P, I	537		330	Moderate	Plan to build 85 new public units, 93 affordable rental units, and 152 homeownership units for "a range of incomes."	15	Bordered by core tracts on north and east.
Schuylkill Falls	26,401	1997	I	266		300	Moderate	Plan to build 330 new rental and homeownership units for a cross-section of incomes. Families with incomes up to 120 percent of AMI to have opportunity to purchase home through lease-to-own program.	207	No gentrification within 4 miles.
Seattle										
Holly Park Apartments	48,617	1993 1995 1996	P, I[d]	893		1,200	Market	Complex development with multiple financing sources; consists of three phases. Plan for 800 total rental units, 40 market-rate; 400 total ownership units, 300 at market rates.	110	No gentrification within 3 miles; between poor and middle-class tracts.
Rainier Vista/High Point	400	1995	P							
Roxbury House/Roxbury Village	17,810	1996 1998	D, I	60	151	60		Plans to rehabilitate Roxbury House, a 151-unit high-rise for older people; Roxbury Village to be demolished and replaced with 60 family townhomes.	114	No gentrification within 4 miles.

Table 34.5—Cont'd

City and development	Award[a]	Fiscal year	Type[b]	Demolition	Rehabilitation	New	Mix[c]	Description	Tract	Location
Washington, DC Ellen Wilson Dwellings	25,076	1993 1995	I[d]	134		153	Market	Construction of townhouse units to integrate development into surrounding historic district; 19 market-rate units, remaining 134 organized as co-op. Half of co-op units open to families earning 50 percent to 80 percent of AMI; provision for up to 20 units at no more than 115 percent of AMI.	70	In core gentry tract.
Sheridan Terrace Fort Dupont	400 1,995	1995 1996	P D	133				Demolition only.	99.02	No gentrification within 3 miles.
Valley Green/Skytower	20,300	1997	I	312		314	Market	Plan for 48 new public units; 100 public housing units for older people; 30 public lease-to-purchase homes; 32 market-rate rentals; and 104 for-sale homes.	97	No gentrification within 3 miles.

Table 34.5—Cont'd

Source: Authors' analysis of site profiles published by Housing Research Foundation (1998)
Note: Minneapolis and St. Paul were ineligible to apply under the initial HOPE VI criteria but received $1.8 million in fiscal year 1998 to demolish the Glenwood/Lyndale Towers
a Grant awards are expressed in thousands of dollars, not adjusted for inflation; awards are conditional federal commitments spread over several years and do not include leveraged funds from local government or private sources
b Grant type codes: P = Planning; D = Demolition; R = Revitalization; I = Implementation
c Mix: Explicit goals of redevelopment with regard to mixed-income housing on original site
d Includes amendment funds

less than a mile from the Capitol; the site, therefore, stands in a very tight local housing market at the sharp frontier of one of the most heavily gentrified parts of Washington. Moreover, the complex is part of a designated Historic District. The goals of the HOPE VI redevelopment plan, not surprisingly, include the "re-establishment of the small-scale rowhouse appearance, consistent with the historic patterns and appearance of residential development" in the surrounding Capitol Hill Historic District (Housing Research Foundation 1998).

The plan involved the demolition of all of the existing structures, reconfiguration of streets and the restoration of mews, and the construction of a community center along with 153 new town house units. Nineteen of the town houses scattered throughout the development will be sold at prevailing market rates; the remainder (corresponding to a one-for-one replacement) will be owned and operated as a co-op with oversight functions shared by the resident-owners and a private management firm. The community will be divided into three income bands: One-quarter of the units will be open to residents earning no more than 25 percent of the area median income (AMI); one-quarter will be available to those earning 25 percent to 50 percent of the AMI; and the remainder will be open to moderate-income families earning between 50 and 80 percent of the AMI. Up to 20 of the 67 units in the top income band, however, will be available to residents earning no more than 115 percent of the AMI—$72,105 for a family of four—"to enhance marketability and expand the range of household incomes in the new community" (Housing Research Foundation 1998).

The case of Chicago

It is in Chicago, however, that one finds the most compelling evidence that gentrification conditions the reinvention of assisted housing policy. At first glance this assertion might seem absurd to those familiar with the debate over Chicago's "Mixed Income New Communities Strategy" (MINCS). Lake Pare Place, arguably the nation's most prominent model of a reinvented, mixed-income public housing project, is not surrounded by gentrification, but by some of the city's poorest neighborhoods.[15] This project, however, has a complex history in which income mixing was proposed long after a site was chosen for rehabilitation. The Lakefront Properties, consisting of six 15-story towers, were vacated in 1985 in preparation for renovation, but controversy soon erupted over alternative plans for the structures. When a former developer, Vincent Lane, assumed

control of the Chicago Housing Authority (CHA) in 1988, the site was chosen as the demonstration for an ambitious strategy to transform the city's distressed public housing. When finally completed, Lake Pare Place stood out from the surrounding neighborhood as "a high-security gated community" (Vale 1998, 749) and "an enclave of superior amenity and management" (Vale 1998, 754).[16,17]

In every other effort to reinvent public housing under HOPE VI, however, the CHA has been acutely aware of the fine-grained geography of gentrification and disinvestment in the inner city. On the city's poor, mostly black South Side, the nation's largest public housing community is being redeveloped under one of Chicago's four HOPE VI implementation grants. The Robert Taylor Homes, a corridor of 28 buildings with more than 4,300 units built between 1959 and 1963, have become central in the iconography of urban decay, racial and income segregation, and the failures of public policy. The location of the Robert Taylor Homes was determined by the city's segregated racial geography in the middle of the 20th century, but over time the projects themselves became an important causal factor in the neighborhood (Hirsch 1998). Given the massive disinvestment, poverty, and outmigration from the South Side, the Taylor HOPE VI plan relinquishes any hopes of new housing construction: Five buildings have already been demolished, with residents receiving Section 8 certificates. A small number of replacement and rehabilitation units will be scattered across the Greater Mid-South area, and the original parcel will be developed as a light industrial park incorporated into the city's Empowerment Zone.

On the West and North Sides, however, HOPE VI revitalization takes place in the context of vibrant growth and expansion of what many Chicagoans have come to call the "Super Loop." The plan for the Henry Horner Homes, on the Near West Side, grew out of a legal settlement of a 1991 lawsuit charging the CHA with intentional neglect as part of an effort to eventually demolish the project and disperse its residents (Bennett 1999). The HOPE VI plan specified a net onsite reduction from 743 units to 150, to be replaced by a mixed-income community and relocation of displaced residents with vouchers and new units in adjoining West Side neighborhoods. However, Bennett (1999) reports problems in finding suitable properties near the Horner development, which is adjacent to the United Center (site of the 1996 Democratic National Convention and many other events): "In addition to its encountering skyrocketing real estate prices, the off-site developer has also met with disapproval by homeowners' groups concerned about the movement of public housing relocatees into their blocks" (Bennett 1999, 11). Similar problems are apparent at the ABLA development, which consists of four separate West Side housing complexes (Addams, Brooks, Loomis, and Abbott) nestled between the campus of the University of Illinois at Chicago and the nation's largest medical district. The revitalization plan calls for a net elimination of three-fifths of the public housing units on site: About one-fifth of new on-site units are to be "affordable," and almost two-fifths will be market-rate rental and homeowner ship units.

Finally, on the Near North Side, demolition and revitalization are well under way at Cabrini-Green, one of the nation's most notorious public housing projects which now appears to have replaced the Lakefront Properties as the CHA's banner initiative for mixed-income communities (Bennett 1998; Bennett and Reed 1999; Salama 1999; Schill 1997; Smith 1999; U.S. GAO 1998). The Cabrini-Green development consists of a mixture of low-rise units built in the early 1940s, in addition to some 31 high-rise buildings constructed in the late 1950s and early 1960s, and occupies a 70-acre site on what was once known as Chicago's "Little Hell." This part of the Near North Side has always been a polarized landscape of poverty and wealth (this was the slum studied by Zorbaugh in 1929), but in the past 30 years, the rhythms of neighborhood change have fundamentally altered the area surrounding the cluster of public housing. Gentrification swept through Lincoln Park to the north in the 1960s, and to the south, galleries and restaurants invaded an old warehouse district that was renamed River North in the 1980s.

The Cabrini-Green HOPE VI plan was stillborn in the midst of the federal takeover of the CHA,[18] but after HUD approved a revised plan in 1997, the revitalization effort has proceeded rapidly. The original HOPE VI plan called for the demolition of buildings containing a total of 660 units, with funds for 493 replacement units, most of them in surrounding neighborhoods; the revised plan calls for the demolition of 1,324 units, a net reduction of 79 percent in public units, and an ultimate neighborhood mix of 30 percent public housing, 20 percent moderate-income families, and 50 percent market-rate units (Salama 1999; U.S. GAO 1998).

In June 1996, Mayor Daley unveiled the Near North Redevelopment Initiative (NNRI), an ambitious effort to marshal an estimated $315 million in public and private investment to transform the area surrounding Cabrini-Green. Bennett and Reed (1999) have published a comprehensive analysis of the history and sociological assumptions behind the

NNRI (see also Bennett 1998; Salama 1999; Smith 1999), but for our purposes it is instructive simply to consider the metaphors used to describe a public housing complex that has become surrounded by gentrification. The CHA's revised HOPE VI plan portrays Cabrini-Green as "a pocket of isolated and concentrated poverty surrounded by wealth, and the challenge is to end years of isolation for public housing residents through integration of public housing in a vibrant revitalized Near North Side neighborhood" (CHA 1997, 1.2). The CHA's original HOPE VI application made the puzzling assertion that the social isolation of Cabrini-Green residents "is more profound than other CHA communities," presumably the Robert Taylor Homes, that are "within the poorest neighborhoods of the city" (CHA 1993, 20). And yet "Cabrini-Green, due to its location, over time became surrounded by wealthy communities that are racially diverse.... Cabrini-Green resembles an island—cut off from nearby resources by vast and insurmountable racial and social boundaries, as well as physical ones" (CHA 1993, 20). Assessing the progress of the HOPE VI revitalization, the U.S. GAO recognized that the long history of mistrust between public housing residents and the CHA is especially severe in the case of Cabrini-Green: "Both HUD and housing authority officials told us that because promises made to residents by the housing authority's former management have not been kept and because residents view the revised revitalization proposal as a land grab by the housing authority, the city, and the developers, the residents do not trust the responsible parties" (1998, 58).

MODELING THE CONTEXT AND CONTINGENCY OF RENEWAL

Thus far, our analysis has focused on two processes: the resurgence of aggregate capital investment into gentrified neighborhoods in the inner city, and the explicit linkage of public housing revitalization to the local context of gentrification. The evidence marshaled reveals a widespread, dramatic resurgence in urban land markets that has inscribed a new environment for the reformation of publicly assisted housing policy. However, housing policy has also influenced gentrification. While acknowledging the impossibility of drawing rigorous historical comparisons (because of the data limitations described earlier), we believe that there is ample evidence to conclude that shifts in housing finance have transformed gentrification in important ways (see hypothesis 3, figure 34.1). Specifically, we hypothesize that mortgage securitization and standardization have lubricated the flow of capital investment into inner-city neighborhoods once redlined as unacceptable risks.

Simple tabulations of mortgage loans (such as those presented earlier) are insufficient to test this hypothesis, because lending growth could result from changes in the applicant pool in gentrified neighborhoods. It is entirely possible, for example, that public policy has filled the vacuum left by degentrification. Targeted lending criteria, mixed-income housing initiatives, and subsidies for low- and moderate-income homeownership programs could account for a large part of the surge in private mortgage investment in the inner city. These trends might therefore signal that gentrification is becoming more of a middle- and moderate-income phenomenon.

Model specification

Assessing this argument requires that we return to the mortgage data for a multivariate analysis. To disentangle supply and demand effects, we begin with a simple model of loan denial

$$\ln\left[\frac{P_{denial}}{1-P_{denial}}\right]=b_0+b'A_i+b''R_i+b'''I_i+e_i \quad (34.1)$$

where A_i is a vector of applicant financial characteristics, R_i is a set of variables denoting applicant racial/ethnic origin, and I_i is a set of controls for institutional-level variations. This model is an "accept/reject" specification that is widely used in studies of mortgage lending discrimination (Carr and Megbolugbe 1993; Holloway 1998; Munnell et al. 1992, 1996). Typically, positive and significant coefficients for the race terms for minorities are interpreted as evidence of discriminatory practices in loan underwriting, but critics charge that this simple specification is vulnerable to omitted-variable bias. The most prominent discrimination study, conducted by the Boston Federal Reserve Bank, dealt with this problem by obtaining comprehensive loan and applicant information directly from a sample of cooperating lending institutions (Munnell et al. 1996). Because we are limited to the information in the public-release HMDA files, we adopt an alternative approach proposed by Abariotes et al. (1993) and used by Holloway (1998) to construct an instrumental variable representing the likelihood that an applicant is rejected on the basis of bad credit history.[19] Adding this instrument yields the best model of the lending decision that is possible given

the limitations of current publicly available data:

$$\ln\left[\frac{P_{denial}}{1-P_{denial}}\right]=b_0+b'A_i+b''C_i+b'''R_i$$
$$+b''''I_i+e_i \quad (34.2)$$

We are now able to test for contextual variations in mortgage market activity that persist after taking into account the varied characteristics of applicants. Consider the addition of variables to capture differences in housing and mortgage market conditions across the eight cities (*MSA*) and to test for distinctive lending decisions in core (*CORE*) and fringe (*FRINGE*) gentrified neighborhoods:

$$\ln\left[\frac{P_{denial}}{1-P_{denial}}\right]=b_0+b'A_i+b''C_i+b'''R_i$$
$$+b''''I_i+b_1MSA_i+b_2CORE_i$$
$$+b_3FRINGE_i+e_i \quad (34.3)$$

This specification essentially exploits omitted-variable bias to capture distinctive neighborhood effects in gentrified areas undergoing a resurgence in capital investment. We deliberately exclude tract-level conditions associated with property appraisal, such as housing vacancy rates, rent levels, housing values, and so on. Our purpose is to determine whether the core and fringe gentry designations are sufficient to account for these neighborhood conditions.[20] In other words, after controlling for all applicant-level characteristics, do we find that gentrified neighborhoods exhibit lending decisions that diverge from those elsewhere in the metropolis?

Finally, interaction terms allow us to test for differences in lending to potential homebuyers with varied incomes (*INC*):

$$\ln\left[\frac{P_{denial}}{1-P_{denial}}\right]=b_0+b'A_i+b''C_i+b'''R_i+b''''I_i$$
$$+b_1MSA_i+b_2CORE_i+b_3INC_i^*$$
$$CORE_i+b_4FRINGE_i+b_5INC_i^*$$
$$FRINGE_i+e_i \quad (34.4)$$

Taken together, these models allow progressively rigorous tests of the hypothesis that mortgage market activity has contributed to the resurgence of gentrification in the 1990s. We estimate models for equations 2, 3, and 4 with 1996 and 1997 loan records for conventional home-purchase loan applications; observations with missing or questionable data are excluded on the basis of generally accepted criteria used in the discrimination literature.[21] A standard set of applicant and institutional variables is defined for these models, each of which also includes the instrument derived from the bad credit model (see table 34.6).

Model results

Consider first the model restricted to applicant and institutional variables (table 34.7, Model 1). This specification fits well and conforms closely to the findings of the vast literature on lending discrimination. Denial is less likely with increasing income and loan amount, although lenders clearly must enforce ceilings on mortgage debt burdens (as evidenced by the doubling of denial odds for applicants with loan-to-income ratios over 3.0). The credit history instrument, not surprisingly, is critical in evaluating loan applications. Compared with independent mortgage companies, depositories are only one-quarter to one-half as likely to deny applications, a reflection of the high degree of specialization and segmentation in the housing finance system. Finally, racial disparities in the lending decision persist even after

we control for all other factors: African Americans are 1.12 times more likely to be denied than similarly qualified non-Hispanic whites.

Adding contextual variables and specifying tests for gentrification effects yields mixed results (see table 34.7, Models 2 and 3). Note that substantial variations are apparent across metropolitan mortgage markets, with likelihood of denial greatest in Detroit. After we control for these variations, however, gentrified neighborhoods do not register higher approval rates. Fringe areas are not significantly different from the rest of the metropolitan area, while applicants in core areas are 1.17 times *more* likely to be rejected. The enhanced model with interaction terms helps illuminate these unexpected results (see table 34.7, Model 3). The income-gentry interaction parameters are positive and significant, indicating that high-income applicants are more likely to be denied in gentrified areas than their affluent counterparts elsewhere in the metropolis. Nevertheless, after we control for the higher relative denial rates of high-income borrowers, strong gentrification effects do appear: Rejection is only 0.72 times as likely in core areas and only 0.66 times as likely in fringe neighborhoods. We emphasize

	Parameter estimate	e^B
Intercept	−3.1391**	
Applicant income (× 1,000)	−0.0075**	0.993
Loan amount (× 1,000)	−0.0056**	0.994
Female?	−0.1529**	0.858
Traditional white family[a]	−0.2514**	0.778
African American (1 = yes)	1.0463**	2.847
Hispanic (1 = yes)	0.2894**	1.336
Other race (1 = yes)	−0.1374*	0.872
Race unreported (1 = yes)	0.891**	2.438
Office of the Comptroller of the Currency	1.2157**	3.373
Federal Reserve Board	0.7674**	2.154
Federal Deposit Insurance Corporation	0.7329**	2.081
Office of Thrift Supervision	1.1196**	3.064
National Credit Union Administration	0.3231**	1.381
Number of observations	389,274	
−2 LL	101,808	
Chi-square versus null model	8,191**	
Percentage correctly classified	71.5	

Table 34.6 Logistic Regression of Application Denial for Poor Credit History, 1996 to 1997

Source: FFIEC (1997, 1998)
[a] Traditional white family is defined as a white male applicant with a white female coapplicant
*$p \leq 0.01$. **$p \leq 0.001$.

	Model 1: Applicant and institutional variables		Model 2: Metropolitan controls and gentrification		Model 3: Contingent gentrification	
	Parameter estimate	e^B	Parameter estimate	e^B	Parameter estimate	e^B
Intercept	−0.757**		−1.1021**		−1.084**	
Applicant income (× 1,000)	−0.00303**	0.997	−0.003**	0.997	−0.00342**	0.997
Loan amount (× 1,000)	−0.00626**	0.994	−0.00582**	0.994	−0.00577**	0.994
Female?	−0.1144**	0.892	−0.0904**	0.914	−0.0915**	0.913
Traditional white family[a]	−0.3229**	0.724	−0.2821**	0.754	−0.2797**	0.756
African American (1 = yes)	0.1112**	1.118	0.128**	1.137	0.1341**	1.144
Hispanic (1 = yes)	−0.0237	0.977	0.1085**	1.115	0.1083**	1.114
Other race (1 = yes)	−0.0722**	0.930	−0.0464**	0.955	−0.046*	0.955
Race unreported (1 = yes)	0.0964**	1.101	0.1544**	1.167	0.1596**	1.173
Office of the Comptroller of the Currency	−0.7976**	0.450	−0.6997**	0.497	−0.6957**	0.499
Federal Reserve Board	−0.7161**	0.489	−0.6851**	0.504	−0.6833**	0.505

Table 34.7 Logistic Regression Models, Conventional Home-Purchase Loans, 1996 to 1997

that the standard econometric criticism in this sort of situation—omitted-variable bias—only strengthens our argument. Whether reduced probability of denial stems from unmeasured applicant characteristics or from underwriting practices is irrelevant. Our purpose is simply to show that conventional home-purchase mortgage capital, a critical ingredient of neighborhood investment flows, is no longer a reluctant participant in gentrification in the 1990s. The resurgence and historical durability of gentrification, coupled with shifts in housing finance, have fostered an acceleration of lending to core and fringe neighborhoods. While mortgage capital flows may have been responsible for disinvestment and the creation of rent gaps in an earlier generation (and may still be doing so in other inner-city neighborhoods), in the boom of the late 1990s, lending now appears to be leading the reinvestment process in the established outposts of gentrification. The model results, incorporating a comprehensive array of controls, including an estimate of applicant credit history, provide strong multivariate support for our central hypothesis that shifts in housing finance have facilitated the movement of capital back into gentrified neighborhoods.

The role of gentrification in widening class polarization, however, implies that distinctive neighborhood effects should be most pronounced among high-income households. On this point our results are counterintuitive, and the higher relative denials of high-income applicants compared with their affluent peers elsewhere imply a transformation of gentrification as much as a resurgence. To examine this issue more closely we constructed conditional probability plots (see Holloway 1996, 1998) to relate predicted probability of denial to income in different neighborhoods. We constructed these plots by calculating denial odds for the traditional target market for conventional lending: non-Hispanic white males filing applications with white female coapplicants and seeking loans at twice their annual income; mean values for all of the other variables are used in the logit equation. By calculating probabilities separately by neighborhood type and varying income, we can determine contrasts in the relative advantage or disadvantage among different high-income applicants.

The results of this analysis are illuminating (see figure 34.3). The downward sloping curves confirm, not surprisingly, that denial odds fall among more affluent households. But higher-income applicants in gentrified areas seem to face a more gradual relaxation of scrutiny at higher incomes than their peers in the suburbs. Put another way, the easier

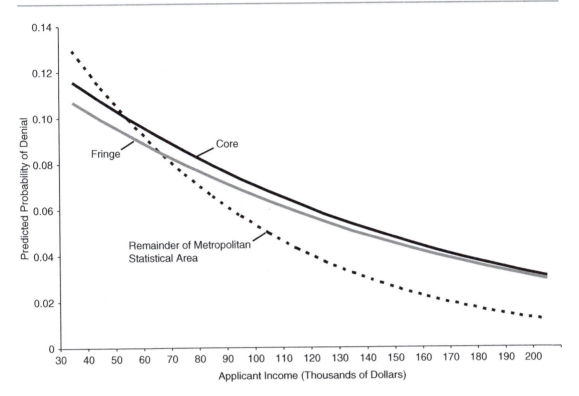

Figure 34.3 Conditional Plot of Probability of Denial by Applicant Income

access of high-income applicants remains biased toward suburban areas. Among borrowers earning more than $160,000, *ceteris paribus* odds of denial in gentrified areas are twice those in the rest of the metropolis. By contrast, probability of denial varies little across neighborhoods in the middle-income ranges (probabilities of 8 percent to 9.5 percent at the mean income of $71,600), while gentrified areas enjoy an advantage in the moderate-income range.

What kind of transformation?

At first glance, these findings might suggest that gentrification is becoming more of a middle- and moderate-income phenomenon, with concomitant theoretical implications for displacement and class polarization. For several reasons, we believe that this diagnosis is wrong. First, the technical limitations of all analyses of this type must be acknowledged: Spatial aggregation to the tract level is necessary, but certainly not ideal in light of the fine-grained scale of disinvestment and reinvestment in many inner-city areas.

Second, our models of the conventional mortgage market present only a partial picture of household and capital movement into and out of gentrified neighborhoods at a particular point in time. Mortgage disclosure records miss buyers who choose to buy homes outright, borrowers who obtain seller financing, and renters moving into luxury apartments. And these data tell us nothing about retail development, office construction, and all the other public and private investments required to transform parts of the inner city into places where the professional middle class lives, works, or plays.

Third, and most important, our results are not inconsistent with the general image of gentrifiers that emerges from two decades of research on the subject. The unexpected results for high-income applicants might be explained by a surge in young professionals with high income but few assets; these applicants exemplify the stereotypical yuppie influx at the heart of both economic and cultural theories of gentrification but represent substantial risks if they are unable to make a sizable down payment.[22] Also, the probability of denial curves may reflect an influx of buyers who are simply attempting to reach beyond their means, either on the basis of

Denial Reason Cited	Percentage of all denial codes reported					
	All applicants			Applicants with income over $100,000		
	Core	Fringe	Suburbs	Core	Fringe	Suburbs
Debt-to-income ratio	25.5	26.4	25.7	13.4	21.9	19.0
Employment history	3.5	4.0	4.9	2.9	2.9	3.6
Credit history	18.7	19.6	33.8	17.2	14.3	25.9
Collateral	12.3	12.3	5.8	18.5	18.1	8.9
Insufficient cash for down payment/closing costs	8.3	7.3	6.4	7.1	7.6	6.1
Unverifiable information	3.0	3.1	2.3	2.1	1.0	3.6
Credit application incomplete	9.5	7.0	5.6	9.7	10.5	11.1
Mortgage insurance denied	2.5	0.8	1.2	1.3	1.9	1.1
Other	16.7	19.6	14.3	27.7	21.9	20.7
Totals	100.0	100.0	100.0	100.0	100.0	100.0
Total denial rate	11.3	12.2	12.8	8.1	9.1	6.0
Percentage of denials for which credit history is primary reason	15.0	14.6	28.1	16.8	13.3	22.3
Percentage of denials for which no reason is cited	21.9	27.8	42.8	22.1	20.4	25.1

Table 34.8 Reasons for Denial of Application, Conventional Home-Purchase Loans, 1996 to 1997

Source: FFIEC (1997, 1998)

Note: Lenders may, but are not required to, report up to three reasons for loan denials. Tabulations do not include tracts in the "inner city" and "rest of city" categories as shown in tables 34.3 and 34.4. Percentages may not total 100 percent because of rounding

household finances or the perceived potential of a particular property. Several pieces of evidence support this interpretation. The mean income of approved applicants in core areas jumped significantly between 1996 and 1997 ($95,324 to $100,487, prob > T value = 0.0011), placing these borrowers far above the suburban level ($74,207 to $77,677, prob > T value = 0.0001). Moreover, from the perspective of lending institutions, rejections in gentrified areas generally paint a picture of a fairly attractive applicant pool.

Table 34.8 presents aggregated denial codes for all rejections and for denials of borrowers with incomes over $100,000. Note that poor credit history is cited as the primary reason nearly twice as often among suburbanites (26 percent) as among applicants in core (17 percent) and fringe areas (14 percent). Home buyers in gentrified districts may be seeking homes at the frontier of reinvestment where conventional lenders remain cautious and skeptical: Compared with the suburbs, twice as many denials of high-income applicants in gentrified neighborhoods cite collateral. Affluent borrowers in

fringe areas also may be stretching their household debt burdens more than their wealthy peers in core gentry neighborhoods.

Further, the large proportion of rejections for "other" reasons may be a red flag. We suspect that many of these applicants may be turned down because of the differential calculus of portfolio loans. At incomes over $100,000, borrowers who seek loans at the standard multiple rapidly bump up against the limits for mortgages that Fannie Mae will purchase (conforming limits ranged from $215,000 for a single-family home to $412,000 on a four-family house in 1997). Lenders exercise far greater individual discretion—both in terms of the borrower and the property—in portfolio lending than in conforming salable loans. Lenders may be reluctant to accept these risks at the frontiers of gentrification. But this simply provides indirect support for our hypothesis, which is that shifts in the national housing finance system—that is, the standardization of loan products and the relaxation of underwriting criteria for loans salable to Fannie Mae and other large national purchasers—has lubricated the flow of mortgage capital into gentrified areas. The ironic result is a relative advantage in the middle-income ranges, reminiscent of Holloway's (1998) finding that targeted lending initiatives in the inner city can sometimes reverse well-documented racial disparities in loan disposition.

A final possibility merits consideration. In an innovative analysis set in New Orleans, Lauria (1998) suggests that under certain circumstances, labor market and real estate cycles can be more important than "white flight" in neighborhood racial turnover. Lauria marshals evidence that many white professionals buying into New Orleans's middle-class neighborhoods in the mid-1980s had high debt loads and little equity when the regional recession hit a few years later, leading to disproportionate default and foreclosure rates. Where these loans were spatially concentrated, the result was to make more homes affordable to African Americans and thereby to accelerate racial turnover. A similar process could be at work in the resurgence of capital flows in neighborhoods defined in our study.

While data limitations preclude a rigorous, direct test of Lauria's (1998) foreclosure hypothesis,[23] we find little evidence of expanding homeownership opportunity for minorities in gentrified neighborhoods. While African Americans account for a growing share of all applicants for conventional home purchase loans in fringe tracts (from 4.5 percent in 1992 to 8.7 percent in 1997), the figure remains small, and no similar increase is apparent in core neighborhoods (6.9 percent in 1992, 6.8 percent in 1997). African Americans do account for a larger share (almost one-fifth) of applicants for FHA-insured loans, but this market segment is underrepresented in gentrified areas. In 1997, FHA-insured loans accounted for only 5.1 percent of all home purchase applications in core tracts, compared with 11.4 percent in fringe tracts and 18.1 percent in the suburbs. The FHA/conventional split remained stable in core and fringe neighborhoods between 1992 and 1997. Moreover, there is no evidence of beneficial effects in gentrified areas for African Americans applying for conventional loans. Adding interaction terms to the denial model indicates that African-American applicants in fringe tracts experience no significant difference in loan disposition compared with their counterparts in other neighborhoods (table 34.9). African Americans applying in core neighborhoods are 1.45 times more likely to be rejected than African Americans who apply elsewhere. The processes that yield distinctive place-based outcomes (enhanced loan approvals in gentrified areas) also appear to reinforce racial segregation. While Lauria's (1998) work

suggests that a regional recession can contribute to racial transition by expanding opportunities for minority homeownership, we find no evidence for this in the boom of the 1990s.

CONCLUSIONS

Evidence of postrecession gentrification is clear. Not surprisingly, those cities attracting the most intense activity during previous rounds of investment are also prominent targets in the boom of the late 1990s. Yet cities at the margins of the national revival of central-city land markets cannot be ignored. The pace of investment has accelerated rapidly in cities like Milwaukee and Detroit, and it is in these places that gentrification holds the greatest potential to restructure the urban landscape—for good or ill. The initial waves of class turnover and capital reinvestment in Detroit in the late 1990s mirror those observed more than a decade ago in Harlem.

Whether viewed through the detached lens of census tract statistics or in the field, the quickening pace of reinvestment in parts of the inner city is truly staggering. Between 1992 and 1997, gentrified neighborhoods in our eight case study cities attracted mortgage investment that grew more than 2.3 times as fast as the suburban rate. As gentrification has reshaped significant portions of the urban fabric, it has altered the environment in which policy makers seek to revitalize the concentrations of poverty inscribed by several generations of public housing policy. When viewed at the level of the metropolitan region, gentrification remains confined to islands of renewal in seas of decay, but when the lens is focused on the urban core, it is clear that public officials now view some of the nation's most distressed public housing projects as islands of decay in seas of renewal. Perhaps "[r]ich people are simply not going to live next to public housing" (Lueck 1991, 1), but policy increasingly relies on a rhetoric emphasizing the virtues of mixing poor and middle-income residents. What remains to be seen is whether dispersal, demolition, and redevelopment simply alter the geometry of class polarization without promoting social and economic mobility. There is no doubt, however, that some inner-city landscapes are enduring a restless turbulence comparable to that observed in the industrialization of the early 20th century. In the summer of 1999, several vacant towers in Chicago's Cabrini-Green complex awaited the wrecking ball, as the CHA attempts to integrate the island of poverty with the surrounding neighborhood of wealth and renewal. Little more than a block away to the Northeast, construction is

	Parameter estimate	e^B
Intercept	−1.0839**	
Applicant income (× 1,000)	−0.00342**	0.997
Loan amount (× 1,000)	−0.00576**	0.994
Female?	−0.0919**	0.912
Traditional white family[a]	−0.2804**	0.755
African American (1 = yes)	0.1271**	1.136
Hispanic (1 = yes)	0.1076**	1.114
Other race (1 = yes)	−0.0464*	0.955
Race unreported (1 = yes)	0.1588**	1.172
Office of the Comptroller of the Currency	−0.6964**	0.498
Federal Reserve Board	−0.6839**	0.505
Federal Deposit Insurance Corporation	−0.9381**	0.391
Office of Thrift Supervision	−1.1619**	0.313
National Credit Union Administration	−1.3424**	0.261
Year 1997 (1 = yes)	0.070**	1.073
Loan for owner occupancy (1 = yes)	0.1234**	1.131
Credit history instrument	8.1372**	999
(Loan/income) > 3.0? (1 = yes)	0.643**	1.902
CORE	−0.3866**	0.679
FRINGE	−0.4341**	0.648
Boston[b]	0.0661**	1.068
Detroit	0.5893**	1.803
Milwaukee	−0.4372**	0.646
Minneapolis–St. Paul	0.0449*	1.046
Philadelphia	−0.1618**	0.851
Seattle	0.3664**	1.442
Washington, DC	0.2954**	1.344
INC*CORE	0.00678**	1.007
INC*FRIN	0.0069**	1.007
African American*CORE	0.3708**	1.449
African American*FRINGE	0.0685	1.071
Number of observations	734,437	
−2 LL	506,475	
Chi − square versus null model	61,371**	
Percentage correctly classified	73.4	

Table 34.9 Logistic Regression with Race-Gentry Interaction Terms

Source: FFIEC (1997, 1998)

[a] Traditional white family is defined as a white male applicant with a white female coapplicant

[b] Chicago is the reference category for metropolitan dummies.

*$p \leq 0.01$. **$p \leq 0.001$

nearing completion on a three-story, 4,000-square-foot single-family home promoted by a yard sign as "housing for today's urban lifestyle." With a rooftop deck and a posted price just shy of $1,100,000, this home offers the prospect of a million-dollar view as Zorbaugh's *The Gold Coast and the Slum* (1929) is reinvented in line with the imperatives of devolution, privatization, and the transformation of assisted housing policy.

The resurgence of mortgage investment into gentrified neighborhoods signifies a fundamental restructuring of the process. Capital flows that once decimated the inner city have been redirected and focused on a few highly desirable neighborhoods, as attempts to reach underserved markets have fostered reinvestment elsewhere in the city. Mortgage market regulation, securitization, and standardization have reduced or eliminated many of the practices responsible for redlining, but in so doing these innovations have unleashed powerful gentrification pressures.

The links between public policy and gentrification are hardly new, but they have evolved considerably since the days of urban renewal in the 1950s and the piecemeal initiatives of the stillborn national urban policy of the 1970s. In the past decade, shifts in mortgage markets have intersected with privatization, devolution, and the reinvention of housing assistance. Contemporary gentrification, therefore, has become mutually constituted with housing policy: It has been reshaped by housing finance, while its cumulative imprint now helps mediate the tensions between dispersal, demolition, and redevelopment of distressed public housing projects. Ultimately, housing policy and market forces have created a turbulent landscape of decay and renewal that demands careful scrutiny of the implications for residents and neighborhoods in the inner city.

Authors

We are grateful to Robert E. Lang for guidance and suggestions and to the anonymous referees for helpful comments on an earlier version. Norman Glickman, Jason Hackworth, and Don Krueckeberg provided valuable feedback and criticism on several important points. Ioan Voicu provided superb research assistance. Partial financial support was provided by a University Research Grant from the College of Arts and Sciences at Illinois State University.

Notes

1 The phrase is that of a member of a city task force on the redevelopment of Harlem. See Schaffer and Smith (1986, 360), and Smith (1996, 164).

2 Processes that were routinely portrayed in the stark class terms of "gentrification" by the *New York Times* in the 1980s are now more likely to be described in terms of housing market recovery, commercial and retail revitalization, or playful neighborhood acronyms such as Brooklyn's "Dumbo" (down under the Manhattan Bridge overpass). The contemporary discourse used by the *Times* is a striking contrast to the language required to describe the open conflicts erupting in New York's Lower East Side in 1988,

when protest placards proclaimed "Gentrification is class war" and automated teller machines were spraypainted with exhortations to "Mug a yuppie" (see Jacobs 1998; Smith 1996). When the term does appear, it usually merits a spirited defense. Edward I. Koch, mayor at the time of what some residents call the "Battle of Tompkins Square" in 1988, recently declared that "gentrification has definitely returned to the East Village. And like Martha Stewart says, 'It's a good thing'" (Jacobs 1998).

3 New York's experience mirrors a national recovery in commercial real estate. Nationwide, downtown office vacancy rates have declined consistently since 1994, reaching 9.7 percent in the second quarter of 1998 (CB Richard Ellis 1998).

4 The "yuppie" neologism was coined to explain the unexpected success of Gary Hart in the 1984 Democratic primaries. After *Newsweek* famously crowned 1984 as "the year of the yuppie" (1984), the "young, upwardly mobile urban professional" was used to explain all sorts of political, economic, and cultural trends. Ehrenreich (1989) provides an excellent history of popular debate on this hybrid category that was "a mixture of age, address, and class" (196). The label rapidly evolved from status symbol to an epithet for greed, but it spawned many other neologisms—some explicitly linked to gentrification. The most recent coinages, in the summer of 1999, apply to rural gentrification of the style observed in Long Island's Hamptons several generations ago: "Hamptification" or "Hamptonization" represents the invasion of historic vacation spots such as Nantucket by "newly rich dot.com moguls roaring around in Range Rovers, bulldozing landmark properties and braying into cell phones at the farmer's market" (Cooke 1999, A19).

5 Given the focus of our analysis, this discussion greatly simplifies the emergence and evolution of HOPE VI. Epp (1998), Nenno (1998), and Salama (1999) provide valuable reviews and analyses of the program, and the U.S. General Accounting Office (GAO) (1998) provides an assessment of the progress of several developments. The program has been revised several times, and each Notice of Funding Availability issued by HUD to PHAs has emphasized slightly different priorities. The cumulative effect of these changes has strengthened the link between public housing revitalization and surrounding private market activity. Key points in the evolution of HOPE VI include eliminating the limit of 500 public housing units slated for demolition or revitalization (September 1994), suspending

the one-for-one housing replacement requirement (July 1995), expanding program eligibility to all PHAs with troubled housing (April 1996), and requiring that PHAs demolish at least one obsolete building, along with strong encouragement to establish self-sufficiency programs, strict occupancy and eviction rules, and mixed-income sites (July 1996) (see U.S. GAO 1998, 18).

6 We recognize the limitations of these methods and have sought to compensate for the most obvious problems (the time lapse between 1990 census enumerations and the dates of our field surveys) (Wyly and Hammel 1998). While visible housing reinvestment is often an important outcome of gentrification, regulatory and tax codes in some housing markets (particularly New York) create powerful incentives for affluent owners to conceal rather than display housing wealth. And as Smith and Caris (1998) have emphasized, the circulation of capital investment in the urban landscape is often masked by the more readily apparent racial and class characteristics of who moves in and who moves out of a neighborhood: "One does not generally 'see' a bank refuse a mortgage for the resale of a house, or refuse a refinancing loan to make additions or repairs to perform periodic maintenance" (2).

7 Gentrification is often dismissed on the grounds of empirical magnitude, but few other social and economic processes are held to this standard. The problem of the urban underclass, for example, has prompted wide-ranging and interdisciplinary debate because of the problems facing poor residents and because the phenomenon is a theoretical battleground between structural explanations and individual culture-of-poverty theories. But so-called underclass neighborhoods account for a small fraction of the population and land area of cities, mostly old industrial centers of the Midwest and Northeast (Kasarda 1993; Ricketts and Sawhill 1988). Core and fringe gentry areas encompassed a total of 570,408 residents of our eight cities in 1990, equivalent to 21.6 percent of the total population in the inner city as defined above. Corresponding underclass estimates for these cities are 526, 566 (using Ricketts and Sawhill's 1988 criteria) and 419,780 (with Kasarda's [1993] more restrictive Public Use Microdata Sample–based calculations). (See Kasarda 1993, appendix 1–F.)

8 Average family income is by no means an optimal indicator: Median household income is superior, as is per capita income (Smith 1996). Unfortunately, average family income is the only relevant figure available in the census database we use

(Tobin 1993). The Urban Institute constructed a customized tabulation that adjusts 1970 and 1990 census estimates to consistent 1980 tract boundaries, providing an unparalleled tool for analyzing neighborhood change, but the data set has only a selected set of variables. In previous research, we used printed census reports for 1960 through 1990, but this approach demands labor-intensive adjustments that do not substantially alter the results (see Wyly and Hammel 1998).

9 It is worth noting that gentrification preceded the widespread attention devoted to it in the 1970s, and thus our analysis does not capture the early stages. Ruth Glass (1964) coined the term to describe changes in London in the 1950s and early 1960s, and Smith (1996) identifies a number of important precursors. Of the cities included in the present study, Washington, DC, probably experienced the process earliest. Green (1963) dates the transformation of Georgetown to the 1920s: "The remodeling started then had proceeded slowly during the depths of the Depression, but about 1934 suddenly gained momentum. Impecunious New Dealers moved into the cramped restored little houses" (399). By 1970, the core gentry neighborhoods in the eight cities included here registered an average family income that stood at 144 percent of the average for the surrounding inner city.

10 The HMDA files permit analysis of four types of conventional mortgage loans: (1) purchase of single-family homes, (2) improvement of single-family dwellings, (3) refinancing of mortgages on single-family homes, and (4) loans for multifamily structures (including purchase, improvement, and refinancing). HMDA reporting requirements define single-family dwellings as those accommodating four or fewer families; all other dwellings are classified as multifamily. Condominium units are classified as single-family dwellings, even if they are located in multiple-unit buildings. See FFIEC (1999), 27.

11 We analyzed lending for all years between 1992 and 1997, but 1993 is the only significant interruption of the secular trend.

12 Using the admittedly crude census benchmark (the proportion of persons aged five and over who moved at least once in the five years before a decennial enumeration), the neighborhoods of Capitol Hill stand out for particularly high rates of turnover. In the solidly gentrified tract immediately behind the Capitol, fewer than 35 percent of the residents had lived there for more than five years; fully one-third had moved

from another metropolitan area between 1985 and 1990.

13 Not counted in this tally was a projected $1.2 billion investment associated with city-approved riverfront sites that will eventually accommodate three casinos to compete with those across the river in Windsor, Ontario. The first casino, a $220 million MGM Grand, opened on a temporary site in late July 1999 (Meredith 1999).

14 The Seattle Housing Authority's site profile for the Holly Park redevelopment is among the most detailed of those examined in this study and includes an itemized list of funding sources. The federal contribution under HOPE VI implementation grants comprises only 21 percent of the estimated costs; other sources include Tax Exempt First Mortgages (9 percent), Low-Income Housing Tax Credit equity (15 percent), Community Facilities Partners (2 percent), home sales (31 percent), Seattle Housing Authority capital funds (6 percent), State of Washington contributions (5 percent), and City of Seattle funds (9 percent). Note that the use of home sales to fund the ongoing phases of the redevelopment exceeds the federal grant contribution by a large margin, exemplifying the cross-subsidization imperatives facing housing authorities under HUD's reinvention (Quercia and Galster 1997).

15 Lake Parc Place is just over three miles south of the Loop, separated from the lakefront by the old rail corridor of the Illinois Central and Lake Shore Drive. The surrounding Oakland neighborhood has a median household income of less than one-fifth the citywide median, is more than 99 percent African American, and lost more than half its population between 1980 and 1990 (Schill 1997).

16 Vincent Lane led the CHA as director and then chair from 1988 until the federal government took over the agency in May 1995. The CHA lobbied Congress to establish a demonstration program in the National Affordable Housing Act of 1990 to permit regulatory flexibility in design, income formulas, resident screening, and rules governing contracts with private landlords (Lane 1995; Schill 1997). Two renovated towers, containing a total of 282 units, opened in 1991, with the goal of achieving a 50–50 mix of residents with very low incomes (less than 50 percent of the area median) and low incomes (between 50 and 80 percent of the area median). The remaining towers of the Lakefront Properties were demolished in 1997. The sociological and behavioral assumptions underlying MINCS have prompted praise as well as strident criticism (Bennett and

Reed 1999; Miller 1998; Nyden 1998; Rosenbaum, Stroh, and Flynn 1998; Schill 1997; Vale 1998).

17 Vale (1998) points out that MINCS has been promoted partially on the grounds that revitalized public housing will spur private market activity in the surrounding neighborhood. Vale's assessment, however, is an eerie echo of Berry's (1985) islands of renewal in seas of decay on a more localized level. Vale (1998) sees little "progress on the broader plan for reinvestment in Lake Parc Place's wider neighborhood. Lake Parc Place fronts neither lake nor park; it is squeezed between a set of railroad tracks and a devastated landscape of disinvestment. As [Rosenbaum, Stroh, and Flynn 1998] acknowledge, it is an 'island.' Its promoters rescued a piece of the public housing stock, but at great cost. Much of this money seems to have been well spent creating an enclave of superior amenity, security, and management" (754).

18 HUD rejected the CHA's original HOPE VI application in fiscal year 1993, but a provision of the 1994 appropriations act required HUD to make awards, without competition, to all PHAs that applied in 1993. HUD took over the CHA shortly after the agency had submitted a revitalization plan in early 1995, and a revised plan was not approved until September 1997 (see U.S. GAO 1998).

19 For many years, lending industry researchers have lamented the dearth of information on applicant financial characteristics in the mortgage disclosure files, which include nothing more than applicant income. For denied applications, however, lenders may (but are not required to) report up to three reasons for their decision. Options include an excessive debt-to-income ratio, unstable employment history, poor credit history, insufficient collateral, insufficient cash to meet down payment or closing costs, unverified information, incomplete application, denial of private mortgage insurance, and an unspecified "other" category. Our instrumental variable is constructed from a logit model predicting the likelihood that any one of the three denial indicators is reported for poor credit history. Given the optional nature of denial reporting, this is certainly not a perfect measure of applicant credit risk, but it represents the best possible approach, and the burgeoning attention to lending discrimination over the past decade gives lenders powerful incentives to report why they deny applications.

20 Other concerns merit the exclusion of neighborhood-level variables. On technical grounds,

using 1990 census estimates becomes more dubious with each passing year; however, the proprietary nature of commercial tract estimates (from Claritas, Inc., or other well-known vendors) precludes any scrutiny of methods used to update decennial figures. On theoretical grounds, underwriting standards are undergoing a shift in scale, possibly rendering tract-level controls irrelevant. Current secondary-market underwriting guidelines advise appraisal of the immediate vicinity (analogous to the block or block-group level) as opposed to the broader geographic assessments that historically played a role in blatant racial redlining (Jackson 1985). Then again, there is anecdotal evidence of an opposite scale shift in some inner-city lending initiatives. One mortgage bank relied on suburban comparables to assess properties in Detroit's first new private construction of single-family homes in 40 years (Listokin et al. 1998).

21 Following most discrimination studies, we exclude observations with missing values or with data quality flags in the loan application register. We also exclude observations on the basis of three additional criteria: extremely high or low applicant income (less than $10,000 or more than $500,000 annually), applicants refusing to state whether they are men or women (mostly applications taken by telephone), and applications that are incomplete, withdrawn, or approved without subsequent origination of the loan.

22 Unfortunately, it is impossible to determine down payment or loan-to-value ratios from the HMDA records.

23 Lauria's (1998) analysis includes, but does not focus on, FHA-insured loans. An ideal test of the hypothesis that foreclosures contribute to racial change would consider lender and realtor steering into FHA products; such an analysis would require identifying properties in which a lender foreclosed on a white household defaulting on a conventional loan, followed by a sale to an African-American household securing an FHA-insured loan.

REFERENCES

Abariotes, Andriana, Sarita Ahuja, Helen Feldman, Carol Johnson, Lekha Subaiya, Nathan Tiller, Julie Urban, and Samuel L. Myers. 1993. Disparities in Mortgage Lending in the Upper Midwest: Summary of Results Using 1992 Home Mortgage Disclosure Act Data. Paper presented at the Fannie Mae University Colloquium on Race, Poverty, and Housing Policy, Minneapolis.

Abt Associates, Inc. 1996. *An Historical and Baseline Assessment of HOPE VI.* Volume I. Cross-Site Report. Washington, DC: U.S. Department of Housing and Urban Development, Office of Policy Development and Research.

Beauregard, Robert. 1986. The Chaos and Complexity of Gentrification. In *The Gentrification of the City*, ed. Neil Smith and Peter Williams, 35–55. Boston: Allen and Unwin.

Beauregard, Robert. 1990. Trajectories of Neighborhood Change: The Case of Gentrification. *Environment and Planning A* 22:855–74.

Beauregard, Robert. 1993. *Voices of Decline.* Oxford: Basil Blackwell.

Beauregard, Robert. 1994. Neighborhood Circuits: From Gentrification to Urbanization. Paper presented at the Annual Meeting of the Association of American Geographers, San Francisco.

Bennett, Larry. 1998. Do We Really Wish to Live in a Communitarian City? Communitarian Thinking and the Redevelopment of Chicago's Cabrini-Green Public Housing Complex. *Journal of Urban Affairs* 20(2):99–116.

Bennett, Larry. 1999. Restructuring the Neighborhood: Public Housing Rehabilitation and Neighborhood Dynamics in Chicago. Paper presented at the Annual Meeting of the Urban Affairs Association, Louisville, KY.

Bennett, Larry, and Adolph Reed Jr. 1999. The New Face of Urban Renewal: The Near North Redevelopment Initiative and the Cabrini-Green Neighborhood. In *Without Justice for All: The New Liberalism and Our Retreat from Racial Equality*, ed. Adolph Reed Jr., 175–211. Boulder, CO: Westview Press.

Berry, Brian J. L. 1985. Islands of Renewal in Seas of Decay. In *The New Urban Reality*, ed. Paul E. Peterson, 69–96. Washington, DC: Brookings.

Boger, John C., and Judith W. Wegner, eds. 1996. *Race, Poverty, and American Cities*. Chapel Hill: University of North Carolina Press.

Bothwell, Stephanie, Raymond Gindroz, and Robert E. Lang. 1998. Restoring Community through Traditional Neighborhood Design. *Housing Policy Debate* 9(1):89–114.

Bourne, Larry S. 1993a. The Demise of Gentrification? A Commentary and Prospective View. *Urban Geography* 14(1):95–107.

Bourne, Larry S. 1993b. The Myth and Reality of Gentrification: A Commentary on Emerging Urban Forms. *Urban Studies* 30(1): 183–89.

Bradford, Calvin. 1998. *The Two Faces of FHA: A Case of Government Supported Discrimination against Minority and Racially Changing Communities*. Chicago: Chicago Area Fair Housing Alliance.

Carliner, Michael S. 1998. Development of Federal Homeownership "Policy." *Housing Policy Debate* 9(2):299–321.

Carr, James, and Isaac Megbolugbe. 1993. The Federal Reserve Bank of Boston Study on Mortgage Lending Revisited. *Journal of Housing Research* 4:277–314.

CB Richard Ellis, Inc. 1998. *Office Vacancy Index of the United States, June 30, 1998*. World Wide Web page <http://www.cbrichardellis.com/corp/vacancy/vacoff2q98.pdf> (accessed August 16, 1999).

Chanen, Jill S. 1998. New Residential District Is Born in Chicago. *New York Times*, September 6, p. RE 2.

Chicago Housing Authority. 1993. *The Urban Revitalization Demonstration Program*. Chicago.

Chicago Housing Authority. 1997. *HOPE VI Revitalization Plan: Cabrini-Green Extension*. Chicago.

Clark, Eric. 1995. The Rent Gap Re-Examined. *Urban Studies* 32(9):1489–1503.

Cooke, Patrick. 1999. Hamptonization and Its Discontents. *New York Times*, August 11, p. A19.

DiGiovanni, Frank. 1983. Patterns of Change in Housing Market Activity in Revitalizing Neighborhoods. *Journal of the American Planning Association* 49:22–39.

Dixon, Jennifer, and Deborah Solomon. 1997. Motown Rebound: Detroit Sees $5.74 Billion in New Investments. *Detroit Free Press*, April 15, p. A1.

Downs, Anthony. 1973. *Opening Up the Suburbs: An Urban Strategy for America*. New Haven, CT: Yale University Press.

Dunlap, David W. 1999. Filling in the Blanks at Battery Park City. *New York Times*, February 7, section 11, p. 1.

Ehrenreich, Barbara. 1989. *Fear of Falling: The Inner Life of the Middle Class*. New York: Harper Collins.

Epp, Gayle. 1998. Emerging Strategies for Revitalizing Public Housing Communities. In *New Directions in Urban Public Housing*, ed. David P. Varady, Wolfgang F. E. Preiser, and Francis P. Russell, 121–41. New Brunswick, NJ: Center for Urban Policy Research.

Fannie Mae. 1996. *A Guide to Homeownership*. Washington, DC.

Fannie Mae Foundation. 1997. *Annual Report, 1996*. Washington, DC.

Federal Financial Institutions Examination Council. Annual. *Home Mortgage Disclosure Act Data*. Machine-readable data files on CD–ROM. Washington, DC.

Federal Financial Institutions Examination Council. 1999. *A Guide to HMDA Reporting: Getting It Right*. Washington, DC.

Federal Housing Enterprises Financial Safety and Soundness Act. 1992. U.S.C. 4543 and 4546.

Fishbein, Allen J. 1992. The Ongoing Experiment with "Regulation from Below": Expanded Reporting Requirements under HMDA and CRA. *Housing Policy Debate* 3(2):601–36.

Fitch, Robert. 1993. *The Assassination of New York*. New York: Verso.

Foderaro, Lisa W. 1998. For Affluent Blacks, Harlem's Pull Is Strong. *New York Times*, September 18, p. A1.

Garbarine, Rachelle. 1998. Apartment Rents Going Up in Converted Downtown Buildings. *New York Times*, October 30, p. B6.

Glass, Ruth. 1964. *London: Aspects of Change*. London: McGibben and Kee.

Goldberg, Carey. 1999. Behind the Curtains of Boston's Best Neighborhood, A New Elite. *New York Times*, February 18, p. A16.

Goldberger, Paul. 1999. Zone Defense: Is Donald Trump Unstoppable? *New Yorker*, February 22 and March 1, pp. 176–81.

Green, Constance McLaughlin. 1963. *Washington: Capital City, 1879–1950*. Princeton, NJ: Princeton University Press.

Hammel, Daniel J. 1999. Gentrification and Land Rent: A Historical View of the Rent Gap in Minneapolis. *Urban Geography* 20(2): 116–45.

Hammel, Daniel J., and Elvin K. Wyly. 1996. A Model for Identifying Gentrified Areas with Census Data. *Urban Geography* 17(3): 248–68.

Hevesi, Dennis. 1998. Apartment Prices as Moving Targets. *New York Times*, July 26, section 11, p. 1.

Hevesi, Dennis. 1999. Lofty Prices Send Loft Pioneers in Search of New Frontiers. *New York Times*, February 21, section 11, p. 1.

Hirsch, Arnold R. 1998. *Making the Second Ghetto: Race and Housing in Chicago, 1940–1960*. Chicago: University of Chicago Press.

Holloway, Steven R. 1996. Job Accessibility and Male Teenage Employment: The Declining

Significance of Space? *Professional Geographer* 48(4):445–58.

Holloway, Steven R. 1998. Exploring the Neighborhood Contingency of Race Discrimination in Mortgage Lending in Columbus, Ohio. *Annals of the Association of American Geographers* 88(2):252–76.

Holusha, John. 1998. Space Is Tight, Office Markets Robust. *New York Times*, September 20, section 11, p. 1.

Housing Research Foundation. 1998. *HOPE VI Implementation and Planning Grant Awards, 1993–1998*. Washington, DC: Housing Research Foundation. World Wide Web page <http://www.housingresearch.org> (accessed September 1998).

Hughes, Mark A. 1995. A Mobility Strategy for Improving Opportunity. *Housing Policy Debate* 6(1):271–97.

Ihlanfeldt, Keith R., and David L. Sjoquist. 1998. The Spatial Mismatch Hypothesis: A Review of Recent Studies and Their Implications for Welfare Reform. *Housing Policy Debate* 8(3):849–92.

Jackson, Kenneth T. 1985. *Crabgrass Frontier: The Suburbanization of the United States*. New York: Oxford.

Jacobs, Andrew. 1998. A New Spell for Alphabet City. *New York Times*, August 9, section 14, pp. 1, 10.

Jencks, Christopher, and Susan E. Mayer. 1990. Residential Segregation, Job Proximity, and Black Job Opportunities. In *Inner-City Poverty in the United States*, ed. Lawrence E. Lynn Jr. and Michael G. McGreary, 187–222. Washington, DC: National Academy Press.

Kain, John F. 1992. The Spatial Mismatch Hypothesis: Three Decades Later. *Housing Policy Debate* 3(2):371–460.

Kasarda, John D. 1993. *Urban Underclass Database*. Machine-readable data file and technical documentation. New York: Social Science Research Council.

Klages, Karen E. 1998. Sweet Home Chicago. *Chicago Tribune Magazine*, February 22, pp. 12–16.

Knox, Paul L. 1991. The Restless Urban Landscape: Economic and Sociocultural Change and the Transformation of Metropolitan Washington, DC. *Annals of the Association of American Geographers* 81(2):181–209.

Lane, Vincent. 1995. Best Management Practices in U.S. Public Housing. *Housing Policy Debate* 6(4):867–904.

Lauria, Mickey. 1998. A New Model of Neighborhood Change: Reconsidering the Role of White Flight. *Housing Policy Debate* 9(2): 395–424.

Lees, Loretta. 1994. Rethinking Gentrification: Beyond the Positions of Economics or Culture. *Progress in Human Geography* 18(2): 137–50.

Lees, Loretta, and Liz Bondi. 1995. De-Gentrification and Economic Recession: The Case of New York City. *Urban Geography* 16(3):234–53.

Ley, David. 1980. Liberal Ideology and the Postindustrial City. *Annals of the Association of American Geographers* 70(2):238–58.

Ley, David. 1981. Inner-City Revitalization in Canada: A Vancouver Case Study. *Canadian Geographer* 25:124–48.

Ley, David. 1996. *The New Middle Class and the Remaking of the Central City*. Oxford and New York: Oxford University Press.

Linneman, Peter, and Susan Wachter. 1989. The Impacts of Borrowing Constraints on Homeownership. *AREUEA Journal* 17(4): 389–402.

Lipton, S. Gregory. 1977. Evidence of Central City Revival. *American Institute of Planners Journal* 45:136–47.

Listokin, David, Elvin Wyly, Larry Keating, Susan M. Wachter, Kristopher M. Rengert, and Barbara Listokin. 1998. *Successful Mortgage Lending Strategies for the Underserved*. Volume I. *Industry Strategies*. Volume II. *Case Studies*. Washington, DC: U.S. Department of Housing and Urban Development, Office of Policy Development and Research.

Lueck, Thomas J. 1991. Prices Decline as Gentrification Ebbs: The Future Is Uncertain in Areas That Bloomed Too Late in the 1980s. *New York Times*, September 29, section 10, p. 1.

Marcuse, Peter. 1998. Mainstreaming Public Housing: A Proposal for a Comprehensive Approach to Housing Policy. In *New Directions in Urban Public Housing*, ed. David P. Varady, Wolfgang F. E. Preiser, and Francis P. Russell, 23–44. New Brunswick, NJ: Center for Urban Policy Research.

Massey, Douglas S., and Nancy A. Denton. 1993. *American Apartheid: Segregation and the Making of the Underclass*. Cambridge, MA: Harvard University Press.

Meredith, Robyn. 1999. Detroit, Still Blighted, Puts Hopes in Casinos. *New York Times*, July 30, p. A12.

Miller, Shazia Rafiullah. 1998. Order and Democracy: Trade-Offs between Social Control and

Civil Liberties at Lake Pare Place. *Housing Policy Debate* 9(4):757–73.

Mollenkopf, John H, and Manuel Castells, eds. 1991. *Dual City: Restructuring New York.* New York: Russell Sage.

Montielh, Richard, and Michael Weiss. 1998. *The Economic Resurgence of Washington, DC: Citizens Plan for Prosperity in the 21st Century.* Washington, DC: District of Columbia Department of Housing and Community Development/Strategic Economic Development Plan for Washington, DC.

Munnell, Alicia, Lynne Browne, James McEneaney, and Geoffrey Tootell. 1992. Mortgage Lending in Boston: Interpreting HMDA Data. Working Paper 92–7. Boston: Federal Reserve Bank of Boston.

Munnell, Alicia, Geoffrey Tootell, Lynne Browne, and James McEneaney. 1996. Mortgage Lending in Boston: Interpreting HMDA Data. *American Economic Review* 86:25–53.

National Commission on Severely Distressed Public Housing. 1992. *Final Report of the National Commission on Severely Distressed Public Housing: A Report to the Congress and the Secretary of Housing and Urban Development.* Washington, DC: U.S. Government Printing Office.

Nelson, Kathryn P. 1988. *Gentrification and Distressed Cities.* Madison, WI: University of Wisconsin Press.

Nenno, Mary K. 1998. New Directions for Federally Assisted Housing: An Agenda for the Department of Housing and Urban Development. In *New Directions in Urban Public Housing,* ed. David P. Varady, Wolfgang F. E. Preiser, and Francis P. Russell, 205–225. New Brunswick, NJ: Center for Urban Policy Research.

Newman, Oscar. 1972. *Defensible Space: Crime Prevention through Urban Design.* New York: Macmillan.

Newman, Oscar. 1980. *Community of Interest.* Garden City, NY: Anchor.

Nyden, Philip. 1998. Comment on James E. Rosenbaum, Linda K. Stroh, and Cathy A. Flynn's "Lake Parc Place: A Study of Mixed-Income Housing." *Housing Policy Debate* 9(4): 741–48.

Pataki, George E. 1998. *Governor Pataki Commits $3 million to Harlem USA.* Press Release, July 27. Albany, NY: Office of the Governor.

Quercia, Roberto, and George C. Galster. 1997. The Challenges Facing Public Housing

Authorities in a Brave New World. *Housing Policy Debate* 8(3):535–69.

Ricketts, Erol, and Isabel Sawhill. 1988. Defining and Measuring the Underclass. *Journal of Policy Analysis and Management* 7:316–25.

Rose, Damaris. 1984. Rethinking Gentrification: Beyond the Uneven Development of Marxist Urban Theory. *Environment and Planning D* 2:47–74.

Rosenbaum, James E., Linda K. Stroh, and Cathy A. Flynn. 1998. Lake Pare Place: A Study of Mixed-Income Housing. *Housing Policy Debate* 9(4):703–40.

Rozhon, Tracie. 1998. Dreams, and Now Hope, among the Ruins. *New York Times,* April 16, p. F1.

Salama, Jerry J. 1999. The Redevelopment of Distressed Public Housing: Early Results from HOPE VI Projects in Atlanta, Chicago, and San Antonio. *Housing Policy Debate* 10(1): 95–142.

Sassen, Saskia. 1994. *Cities in a World Economy.* Thousand Oaks, CA: Pine Forge Press.

Schaffer, Richard, and Neil Smith. 1986. The Gentrification of Harlem? *Annals of the Association of American Geographers* 76(3):347–65.

Schill, Michael H. 1997. Chicago's Mixed Income New Communities Strategy: The Future Face of Public Housing? In *Affordable Housing and Urban Development in the United States,* ed. Willem van Vliet, 135–57. Thousand Oaks, CA: Sage.

Schwartz, Alex. 1998. From Confrontation to Collaboration? Banks, Community Groups, and the Implementation of Community Reinvestment Agreements. *Housing Policy Debate* 9(3):631–62.

Schwartz, Alex, and Kian Tajbakhsh. 1997. Mixed-Income Housing: Unanswered Questions. *Cityscape: A Journal of Policy Development and Research* 3(2):71–92.

Simmons, Patrick. 1998. *Housing Statistics of the United States.* Lanham, MD: Bernan Press.

Smith, Janet L. 1999. Cabrini-Green and the Redevelopment Imperative. Paper presented at the Annual Meeting of the Urban Affairs Association, Louisville, KY.

Smith, Neil. 1979. Toward a Theory of Gentrification: A Movement Back to the City by Capital, Not People. *Journal of the American Planning Association* 45:538–48.

Smith, Neil. 1996. *The Revanchist City.* London and New York: Routledge.

Smith, Neil, and Paul D. Caris. 1998. 'The Camden Syndrome' and the Geopolitics of Suburban

Decline: Residential Disinvestment and Its Discontents in Camden County, NJ. Unpublished working paper. Rutgers University, Department of Geography.

Smith, Neil, and Peter Williams, eds. 1986. *The Gentrification of the City*. Boston: Allen and Unwin.

Sohmer, Rebecca, and Robert E. Lang. 1999. Life at the Center: The Rise of Downtown Housing. *Housing Facts and Findings* 1(1). World Wide Web page <http://www.fanniemaefoundation. org/research/facts/sp99s3.html> (accessed August 17, 1999).

Squires, Gregory D., ed. 1992. *From Redlining to Reinvestment*. Philadelphia: Temple University Press.

Stegman, Michael, Roberto Quercia, George McCarthy, and William Rohe. 1991. Using the Panel Survey of Income Dynamics (PSID) to Evaluate the Affordability Characteristics of Alternative Mortgage Instruments and Homeownership Assistance Programs. *Journal of Housing Research* 2(2):161–211.

Storper, Michael. 1997. *The Regional World: Territorial Development in a Global Economy*. New York: Guilford.

Tobin, Mitch. 1993. *User's Guide for the Urban Institute's Under Class Data Base (UDB)*. Technical documentation and machine-readable data file on CD–ROM. Washington, DC: The Urban Institute.

U.S. Congress. 1998. *An Act Making Appropriations for the Department of Veterans Affairs and Housing and Urban Development. Fiscal Year Ending September 30, 1999*. H.R. 4194, passed in October. Washington, DC: U.S. Government Printing Office.

U.S. Department of Housing and Urban Development. 1997. The HUD 2020 Management Reform Plan. *Federal Register* 62(155): 43204–34.

U.S. Department of Housing and Urban Development. 1999. *Fiscal Year 2000 Budget Summary: Opening Doors for More Americans, Leading Communities into the New Century*. Washington, DC.

U.S. General Accounting Office. 1998. *HOPE VI: Progress and Problems in Revitalizing Distressed Public Housing*. GAO/RCED–98–187. Washington, DC.

Vale, Lawrence J. 1998. Comment on James E. Rosenbaum, Linda K. Stroh, and Cathy A. Flynn's "Lake Parc Place: A Study of Mixed-Income Housing." *Housing Policy Debate* 9(4): 749–56.

van Weesep, Jan. 1994. Gentrification as a Research Frontier. *Progress in Human Geography* 18(1):74–83.

Varady, David P. 1994. Middle Income Housing Programs in American Cities. *Urban Studies* 31(8):1345–66.

Vartanian, Thomas P., Robert H. Ledig, Alicia Babitz, William L. Browning, and James G. Pitzer. 1995. *The Fair Lending Guide*. Volumes 1 and 2. Little Falls, NJ: Glasser LegalWorks.

Waldorf, Brigitte S. 1991. A Spatial Analysis of Rent Shifts in the Chicago Rental Housing Market, 1970–1980. *Urban Geography* 12(5):450–68.

Wilson, William Julius. 1987. *The Truly Disadvantaged: The Inner City, the Underclass, and Public Policy*. Chicago: University of Chicago Press.

Wilson, William Julius. 1996. *When Work Disappears: The New World of the Urban Poor*. New York: Knopf.

Wyly, Elvin K., and Daniel J. Hammel. 1998. Modeling the Context and Contingency of Gentrification. *Journal of Urban Affairs* 20(3):303–26.

The Year of the Yuppie. 1984. *Newsweek*, December 31, cover.

Zorbaugh, Harvey W. 1929. *The Gold Coast and the Slum*. Chicago: University of Chicago Press.

35

"New Globalism, New Urbanism: Gentrification as Global Urban Strategy"

From *Antipode* (2002)

Neil Smith

Four sets of events in New York City at the end of the 1990s succinctly captured some of the central contours of the new neoliberal urbanism. The first concerns capital and the state. In the last days of 1998, New York Mayor Rudy Giuliani announced a huge "Christmas gift" to the city's most elite capitalists. Responding to "threats" that the New York Stock Exchange (NYSE) might relocate a mile across the Hudson River to New Jersey, Giuliani announced a $900 million taxpayer subsidy, ostensibly to keep the stock exchange in the city. This was only the latest and largest in a series of "geobribes" paid by the city to global corporations. The subsidy includes $400 million with which the city and state will build a new 650,000-square-foot Wall Street office for the NYSE. There was never any pretense that financial need was even an issue in this deal, since the subsidy came at a time when the stock exchange was siphoning unprecedented amounts of surplus capital from economies around the globe. Rather, city and state officials referred to the deal as a "partnership." There had, of course, been public–private partnerships previously, but this one was unprecedented in two ways. First—and most obvious—was the scale of the geobribe to private capital: topping $1 billion by 2001, the scale of this subsidy was wholly without precedent. Second, and more importantly, the local state in this instance eschewed all pretense of regulation or steerage of the private sector toward results it could not otherwise accomplish on its own. Instead, the subsidy was justified as an investment by the city and the state, as "good business practice." That the threat was in all likelihood hollow and that the NYSE would never seriously have considered leaving the city only confirms the point: rather than modulating the track taken by private investment, the local state simply fitted into the grooves already established by market logics, becoming, in effect, a junior if highly active partner to global capital. The destruction of the World Trade Center raises the very real possibility that the new stock exchange will occupy that site.

The second set of events concerns the social reproduction of the labor force. Earlier in 1998, the New York City Department of Education announced that it faced a shortage of mathematics teachers and as a result was importing forty young teachers from Austria. Even more extraordinary, in a city with more than two million native Spanish speakers, a shortage of Spanish teachers was to be filled by importing teachers from Spain. Annual international recruitment of high school teachers is now routine. At about the same time, it was announced that the New York City Police Department would take over responsibility for security in the city schools from the School Board. Taken together, these events connote a deep crisis, not just in the city's education system but in the wider system of social reproduction.

The third set of events speaks to a drastic heightening of social control. In 1997, the horrifying case of police brutality against Abner Louima, a Haitian immigrant, came to light. A year and a half later, unarmed Guinean immigrant Amadou Diallo was shot dead in a hail of forty-one police bullets in the vestibule of his apartment. Two of Louima's attackers were eventually imprisoned, but—like the majority of cops who gunned down innocent New Yorkers in the late 1990s—Diallo's killers were cleared of any criminal responsibility. The following year, in a move put on hold by Diallo's killing, the NYPD was issued with infamous "dum-dum" bullets, which are designed to do maximum bodily harm. Meanwhile, it was revealed that between 1994 and 1997, the City of New York had paid a record $96.8 million to settle burgeoning numbers of police-brutality lawsuits. Prior to the World Trade Center catastrophe, ordinary New Yorkers increasingly felt that their police force was out of control; even the president of the notorious police union expressed the fear that the city's repressive policing strategies of the late 1990s were "a blueprint for a police state and tyranny" (Cooper 1998: B5; Cooper 1999). These events were the direct result of Giuliani's imposition of "zero-tolerance tactics," but they were equally part of a larger shift in urban policy, from the liberalism that dominated much of the twentieth century toward what has elsewhere been called "the revanchist city" (Smith 1996; Swyngedouw 1997).

The fourth event—and possibly the most intriguing—concerns the changing political role of city government. Angry at the abandon with which United Nations (UN) diplomats seemed to flaunt local parking laws, and blaming them for much of Manhattan's gridlock, Giuliani threatened to begin towing illegally parked cars with diplomatic plates. Now openly derided for his policies of petty and not so petty repression, "Benito" Giuliani (as even the *New York Times* nicknamed him) was just as angry at the US State Department for seemingly capitulating to this UN vehicular malfeasance. Maybe it has come to the point, Giuliani huffed, where New York City needs to have its own foreign policy.[1] The larger point is that amidst a restructuring of the relationship between capital and the state, a burgeoning crisis of social reproduction, and heightened waves of political repression, there is also a rescaling of urban practices, cultures, and functions in the context of changing global relations and a dramatically altered fate of the nation-state.

These four events hint at much about the neoliberal urbanism that has been slouching toward birth since the 1980s. By neoliberalism, I mean something quite specific. Eighteenth-century liberalism, from John Locke to Adam Smith, pivoted on two crucial assumptions: that the free and democratic exercise of individual self-interest led to the optimal collective social good; and that the market knows best: that is, private property is the foundation of this self-interest, and free market exchange is its ideal vehicle. Twentieth-century American liberalism, from Woodrow Wilson to Franklin Roosevelt to John F. Kennedy—emphasizing social compensation for the excesses of market and private property—is not

so much a misnomer, therefore—it by no means abrogated these axioms of liberalism—but it is an outlier insofar as, in a co-optive response to the challenge of socialism, it sought to regulate their sway. The neoliberalism that carries the twentieth into the twenty-first century therefore represents a significant return to the original axioms of liberalism, albeit one galvanized by an unprecedented mobilization not just of national state power but of state power organized and exercised at different geographical scales.

Accordingly, the connections between capital and the state, social reproduction and social control have been drastically altered. And this transformation, the outlines of which we are only beginning to see, is being expressed most vividly through an altered geography of social relations—more concretely, through a rescaling of social processes and relations that creates new amalgams of scale replacing the old amalgams broadly associated with "community," "urban," "regional," "national," and "global." I focus in this paper only on neoliberal urbanism and the relationship between global and urban. I do not in any way intend to infer that other scales are less relevant in the broad scheme of things, but I do want to pick up on what seems to be a special nexus that is being forged between global and urban change. In particular, I want to make two arguments that will seem at first to be quite separate. In the first place, I want to argue that in the context of a refashioned globalism, widely (if partially) expressed via the ideological discourses of "globalization," we are also seeing a broad redefinition of the urban scale—in effect, a new urbanism—that refocuses the criteria of scale construction, in this case toward processes of production and toward the extraordinary urban growth in Asia, Latin America, and Africa. Second, focusing more on Europe and North America, I want to argue that the comparatively recent process of gentrification has been generalized as a central feature of this new urbanism. I therefore offer two threads of an argument suggesting how neoliberalism evolves new forms within the larger history of capitalist urbanization. In concluding, I hope to show that the two shifts explored here are actually interconnected.

NEW URBANISM

In her skillfully synthetic accounts (1992, 1998, 2000), Saskia Sassen offers a benchmark argument about the importance of local place in the new globalism. Place, she insists, is central to the circulation of people and capital that constitute globalization, and a focus on urban places in a globalizing world brings with it a recognition of the rapidly declining significance of the national economy, while also insisting that globalization takes place through specific social and economic complexes rooted in specific places. This builds on a familiar picture of globalization, defined in terms of the economic shift from production to finance. Global cities emerged when, in the 1970s, the global financial system expanded dramatically and foreign direct investment was dominated, not by capital invested directly in productive functions, but rather by capital moving into and between capital markets. This, in turn, pollinated a broad expansion of ancillary producer services concentrated in command and control posts in the financial economy, and those new urban forms are marked by extreme bifurcations of wealth and poverty, dramatic realignments of class relations, and dependence on new streams of immigrant labor. This, of course, is the paradigmatic global city. The balance of economic power has shifted since the 1970s "from production places, such as Detroit and Manchester, to centers of finance and highly specialized services" (Sassen 1992:325).

A welcome alternative to the blithe optimism of globalized utopias, Sassen's account is astute about the shifting contents of some urban economies. However, it is vulnerable on both empirical grounds, which indicate a far more complicated set of relationships connecting global cities and a wider range of cities that can be grouped under the label, global cities (Taylor 1999), and on theoretical grounds. In the end, Sassen's argument is a little vague about how places are, in fact, constructed. It does not go far enough. It is as if the global social economy comprises a plethora of containers—nation-states—within which float a number of smaller containers, the cities. Globalization brings about a dramatic change in the kinds of social and economic relations and activities carried on in these containers, a re-sorting of activities between different containers, and an increased porosity of the national containers, such that turbulence in the wider global sea increasingly buffets cities directly. However, with the exception of some national containers that may actually sink, the containers themselves remain rather rigidly intact in this vision, even as the relations between them are transformed. As Brenner (1998:11) puts it, Sassen's account remains "surprisingly statecentric." I want to argue here that in the context of a new globalism, we are experiencing the emergence of a new urbanism such that the containers themselves are being fundamentally recast. "The urban" is being redefined just as dramatically as the global; the old conceptual containers—our 1970s assumptions

about what "the urban" is or was—no longer hold water. The new concatenation of urban functions and activities vis-à-vis the national and the global changes not only the make-up of the city but the very definition of what constitutes—literally—the urban scale.

Cities have historically performed multiple functions ranging from the military and religious to the political and commercial, the symbolic and the cultural, depending on the history and geography of their construction and transformation. The scale of the urban is similarly expressive of particular social geographies and histories. With the development and expansion of industrial capitalism, burgeoning cities increasingly express the powerful impulse toward the centralization of capital, while the *scale* of the urban is increasingly defined in terms of the geographical limits to daily labor migration. That is, as soon as the *social* division of labor between production and reproduction become simultaneously a spatial division, and whatever other functions the city performs and activities it embodies, the social and territorial organization of the social reproduction of labor—the provision and maintenance of a working-class population—comes to play a pivotal role in the determination of the urban scale. More than anything else, the scale of the modern city is thereby calibrated by something quite mundane: the contradictory determinations of the geographical limits of the daily commute of workers between home and work (Smith 1990:136–137).

The Keynesian city of advanced capitalism, in which the state underwrote wide swaths of social reproduction, from housing to welfare to transportation infrastructure, represented the zenith of this definitive relationship between urban scale and social reproduction. This is a consistent theme that has run through the work of European and American urban theorists since the 1960s, from urban revolution (Lefebvre 1971) to urban crisis (Harvey 1973) and Castells' (1977) explicit definition of the urban in terms of collective consumption, and has been an enduring concern of feminist urban theory (Hansen and Pratt 1995; Katz 2001; Rose 1981). Equally a center of capital accumulation, the Keynesian city was in many respects the combined hiring hall and welfare hall for each national capital. Indeed the so-called urban crisis of the late 1960s and 1970s was widely interpreted as a crisis of social reproduction, having to do with the dysfunctionality of racism, class exploitation, and patriarchy and the contradictions between an urban form elicited according to criteria of accumulation and one that had to be justified in terms of the efficiency of social reproduction.

Let us now step back and look at the question of "globalization," because if we are talking about global cities presumably their definition is implicated in the processes thereof. What exactly is globalizing at the beginning of the twenty-first century? What is new about the present? Certainly it is not commodity capital that is globalizing: Adam Smith and Karl Marx both recognized a "world market." Nor, by the same token, can it be financial capital that is globalizing. Contemporary levels of global financial interchange are only now beginning to reach again the levels of the period between the 1890s and World War I. The Bretton Woods institutions established after 1944, especially the International Monetary Fund, were intended to re-stimulate and regulate global financial flows interrupted by depression and war. Viewed in this historical light, the global expansion of stock and currency markets and broad financial deregulation since the 1980s may be more a response to globalization than its cause. The globalization of cultural images in the era of computers and unprecedented migration is also very powerful, but it is difficult to sustain a claim for the novelty of cultural globalization given the extent of pre-existing cultural cross-fertilization. Long before the 1980s, all "national" cultures were more or less hybrid. This leaves us with production capital, and I think a good case can be made that to the extent that globalization heralds anything new, the new globalism can be traced back to the increasingly global—or at least international—scale of economic production. As late as the 1970s, most consumer commodities were produced in one national economy either for consumption there or for export to a different national market. By the 1990s, that model was obsolete, definitive sites of production for specific commodities became increasingly difficult to identify, and the old language of economic geography no longer made sense. In autos, electronics, garments, computers, biomedical, and many other industrial sectors ranging from high tech to low, production is now organized across national boundaries to such a degree that questions of national "import" and "export" are supplanted by questions of global trade internal to the production process. The idea of "national capital" makes little sense today, because most global trade across national boundaries is now intrafirm: it takes place *within* the production networks of single corporations.

There is little doubt that in strictly economic terms, the power of most states organized at the national scale is eroding. This in no way invokes a "zero-sum" conception of scale (Brenner 1998; MacLeod 2001), nor is it a simplistic argument that the nation-state is withering away. In the first

place, the political and cultural power of national-scale power is not necessarily eroding at all and may be hardening in many places. Second, the erosion of economic power at the national scale is highly uneven and not necessarily universal, with the US or Chinese state enjoying a quite different fate from Malaysia or Zimbabwe. For example, Mészáros (2001) has argued that the ambition of the US state seems to be its transformation into a global state, and the conduct of the brutal "war on terrorism"—in reality a war for global hegemony (Smith forthcoming)—seems to confirm this analysis. Yet the sources of increased economic porosity at the national scale are undeniable: communications and financial deregulation have expanded the geographical mobility of capital; unprecedented labor migrations have distanced local economies from automatic dependency on home grown labor; national and local states (including city governments) have responded by offering carrots to capital while applying the stick to labor and dismantling previous supports for social reproduction; and finally, class and race-based struggles have broadly receded, giving local and national governments increased leeway to abandon that sector of the population surplused by both the restructuring of the economy and the gutting of social services. The mass incarceration of working-class and minority populations, especially in the US, is the national analogue of the emerging revanchist city. Comparatively low levels of struggle were crucial in the virtual nonresponse by government to the Los Angeles uprisings after 1992, which stand in dramatic contrast to the ameliorative—if paternalistic—response after the uprisings of the 1960s.

Two mutually reinforcing shifts have consequently restructured the functions and active roles of cities. In the first place, systems of production previously territorialized at the (subnational) regional scale were increasingly cut loose from their definitive national context, resulting not just in the waves of deindustrialization in the 1970s and 1980s but in wholesale regional restructuring and destructuring as part of a reworking of established scale hierarchies. As a result, production systems have been downscaled. The territorialization of production increasingly centers on extended metropolitan centers, rather than on larger regions: the metropolitan scale again comes to dominate the regional scale, rather than the other way round. In place of the American Northeast or Midwest, the English Midlands, and the German Ruhr, for example—classic geographical fruits of modern industrial capitalism— we have São Paulo and Bangkok, Mexico City and Shanghai, Mumbai and Seoul. Whereas the traditional industrial regions were the backbone of national capitals in the nineteenth and much of the twentieth centuries, these new, huge urban economies are increasingly the platforms of *global* production. This rescaling of production toward the metropolitan scale is an expression of global change; at the same time, it lies at the heart of a new urbanism.

The corollary is also taking place, as national states have increasingly moved away from the liberal urban policies that dominated the central decades of the twentieth century in the advanced capitalist economies. In the US, President Ford's refusal to bail out New York City amidst a deep fiscal crisis (immortalized in the famous *Daily News* headline: "Ford to City: Drop Dead"), followed by the failure of President Carter's attempted urban plan in 1978, gave the first intimation of a national economy increasingly delinked from and independent of its cities. The wholesale demise of liberal urban policy followed in fits and starts, working toward Clinton's cynical slashing of the social welfare system in 1996. If the effects are often more muted and take myriad forms, the trajectory of change is similar in most of the wealthiest economies, although Italy—the transfer of some national state power to the European Union notwithstanding—may be an exception.

The point here is not that the national state is necessarily weakened or that the territoriality of political and economic power is somehow less potent. This argument—that global power today resides in a network of economic connections rather than in any particular place—is embodied in the influential treatment of *Empire* by Hardt and Negri (2000), but it is flawed by a certain necromancy with finance capital and a blindness to the contradictions of power that comes with the necessary fixing of economic activities and political control in space. Certainly, specific functions and activities previously organized at the national scale are being dispersed to other scales up and down the scale hierarchy. At the same time, however, national states are reframing themselves as purer, territorially rooted economic actors in and of the market, rather than external compliments to it. Social and economic restructuring is simultaneously the restructuring of spatial scale, insofar as the fixation of scales crystallizes the contours of social power—who is empowered and who contained, who wins and who loses—into remade physical landscapes (Brenner 1998; Smith and Dennis 1987; Swyngedouw 1996, 1997).

As various contributions to this volume suggest, neoliberal urbanism is an integral part of this wider rescaling of functions, activities, and relations. It comes with a considerable emphasis on the nexus of production and finance capital at the expense of questions of social reproduction. It is not that the organization of social reproduction no longer modulates the definition of the urban scale but rather that its power in doing so is significantly depleted. Public debates over suburban sprawl in Europe and especially the US, intense campaigns in Europe promoting urban "regeneration," and the emerging environmental justice movements all suggest not only that the crisis of social reproduction is thoroughly territorialized but, conversely, that the production of urban space has also come to embody that crisis. A connection exists between the production of the urban scale and the efficient expansion of value, and a "mis-scaled" urbanism can seriously interfere with the accumulation of capital. The crisis of daily commuting lies at the center of this crisis. I once surmised (Smith 1990:137) that where the geographical expansion of cities outstripped their ability to get people from home to work and back again, the result was not just urban chaos but a "fragmentation and disequilibrium in the universalization of abstract labour" that went to the heart of economic cohesion. While this contradiction between geographical form and economic process no doubt endures, the evidence from cities in many parts of Asia, Africa, and Latin America presents a rather different picture. The daily commute into São Paulo, for example, can begin for many at 3:30 a.m. and take in excess of four hours in each direction. In Harare, Zimbabwe, the average commuting time from black townships on the urban periphery is also four hours each way, leading to a workday in which workers are absent from home for sixteen hours and sleeping most of the rest. The economic cost of commuting for these same workers has also expanded dramatically, in part as a result of the privatization of transportation at the behest of the World Bank: commutes that consumed roughly 8% of weekly incomes in the early 1980s required between 22% and 45% by the mid 1990s (Ramsamy 2001:375–377).

Why is this happening? Many well-meaning planners indict the lack of suitable infrastructure, and that is undeniably an issue. However, if we step back one level of abstraction, there is a fundamental geographical contradiction between the dramatically increased land values that accompany the centralization of capital in the core of these metropolises and the marginal, exurban locations where workers are forced to live due to the pitiful wages on which that capital centralization is built. Yet, extraordinarily, chaotic and arduous commutes have not yet led to an economic breakdown; the impulses of economic production—and, especially, the need to have workers turn up at the workplace—have taken precedence over any constraints emanating from the conditions of social reproduction. The rigors of almost unbearable commuting have not yet compromised economic production. Instead, they have elicited a "desperate resilience" and been absorbed amidst the wider social breakdown that Katz (forthcoming) calls "disintegrating developments."

Thus, the leading edge in the combined restructuring of urban scale and function does not lie in the old cities of advanced capitalism, where the disintegration of traditional production-based regions and the increasing dislocation of social reproduction at the urban scale is certainly painful, unlikely to pass unopposed, but also partial. Rather, it lies in the large and rapidly expanding metropolises of Asia, Latin America, and parts of Africa, where the Keynesian welfare state was never significantly installed, the definitive link between the city and social reproduction was never paramount, and the fetter of old forms, structures, and landscapes is much less strong. These metropolitan economies are becoming the production hearths of a new globalism. Unlike the suburbanization of the postwar years in North America and Europe, Oceania, and Japan, the dramatic urban expansion of the early twenty-first century will be unambiguously led by the expansion of social production rather than reproduction. In this respect, at least, Lefebvre's announcement of an urban revolution redefining the city and urban struggles in terms of social reproduction—or indeed Castells' definition of the urban in terms of collective consumption—will fade into historical memory. If "capitalism shifted gears" with the advent of Keynesianism "from a 'supply-side' to a 'demand-side' urbanization," as Harvey (1985:202,209) once observed, twenty-first-century urbanism potentially reverses this shift.

This restructuring of scale and the cautious re-empowerment of the urban scale—Giuliani's ambition for a five-borough foreign policy—represents just one thread of neoliberal urbanism. It dovetails with the more culturally attuned assessment of political geographer Peter Taylor (1995:58), who argues that "[C]ities are replacing states in the construction of social identities." Cities like São Paulo and Shanghai, Lagos and Bombay, are likely to challenge the more traditional urban centers, not just in size and density of economic activity—they have already done that—but primarily as leading incubators in the global economy, progenitors of new urban form, process, and identity. No one seriously argues that the twenty-first century will see a return to a world of city-states—but it *will* see a recapture of urban political prerogative vis-à-vis regions and nation-states.

Finally, the redefinition of the scale of the urban in terms of social production rather than reproduction in no way diminishes the importance of social reproduction in the pursuit of urban life. Quite the opposite: struggles over social reproduction take on a heightened significance precisely because of the dismantling of state responsibilities. However, state abstention in this area is matched by heightened state activism in terms of social control. The transformation of New York into a "revanchist city" is not an isolated event, and the emergence of more authoritarian state forms and practices is not difficult to comprehend in the context of the rescaling of global and local geographies. According to Swyngedouw (1997:138), the substitution of market discipline for that of a hollowed-out welfare state deliberately excludes significant parts of the population, and the fear of social resistance provokes heightened state authoritarianism. At the same time, the new urban work force increasingly comprises marginal and part-time workers who are not entirely integrated into shrinking systems of state economic discipline, as well as immigrants whose cultural and political networks—part of the means of social reproduction—also provide alternative norms of social practice, alternative possibilities of resistance.

In summary, my point here is not to argue that cities like New York, London, and Tokyo lack power in the global hierarchy of urban places and high finance. The concentration of financial and other command functions in these centers is undeniable. Rather, I am trying to put that power in context and, by questioning the common assumption that the power of financial capital is necessarily paramount, to question the criteria according to which cities come to be dubbed "global." If there is any truth to the argument that so-called globalization results in the first place from the globalization of production, then our assessment of what constitutes a global city should presumably reflect that claim.

URBAN REGENERATION: GENTRIFICATION AS GLOBAL URBAN STRATEGY

Let me now shift scales and focus toward the process of gentrification. If one dimension of neoliberal urbanism in the twenty-first century is an uneven inclusion of Asian and Latin American urban experiences, especially at the forefront of a new urbanism, a second dimension concerns what might be called the generalization of gentrification as a global urban strategy. At first glance these surely seem like two quite different arguments, the one about luxury housing in the centers of global power, the other about new models of urbanism from the integrating peripheries. They certainly express contrasting experiences of a new urbanism, but that is precisely the point. Neoliberal urbanism encompasses a wide range of social, economic, and geographical shifts, and the point of these contrasting arguments is to push the issue of how varied the experience of neoliberal urbanism is and how these contrasting worlds fit together.

Most scholars' vision of gentrification remains closely tied to the process as it was defined in the 1960s by sociologist Ruth Glass. Here is her founding 1964 statement (Glass 1964:xviii), which revealed gentrification as a discrete process:

> One by one, many of the working-class quarters of London have been invaded by the middle classes—upper and lower. Shabby, modest mews and cottages—two rooms up and two down—have been taken over, when their leases have expired, and have become elegant, expensive residences. Larger Victorian houses, downgraded in an earlier or recent period—which were used as lodging houses or were otherwise in multiple occupation—have been upgraded once again … Once this process of "gentrification" starts in a district it goes on rapidly until all or most of the original working-class occupiers are displaced and the whole social character of the district is changed.

Almost poetically, Glass captured the novelty of this new process whereby a new urban "gentry" transformed working-class quarters. Consider now an updated statement thirty-five years later, again from London. The following is an excerpt from the 1999 decree for "Urban Renaissance" (DETR 1999) released by a special Urban Task Force appointed by the UK Department of the Environment, Transport and the Regions (DETR):

> The Urban Task Force will identify causes of urban decline … and practical solutions to bring people back into our cities, towns, and urban neighborhoods. It will establish a new vision for urban regeneration … [Over the next twenty-five years] 60% of new dwellings should be built on previously developed land … [W]e have lost control of our towns and cities, allowing them to become spoilt by poor design, economic dispersal, and social polarisation. The beginning of the 21st century is a moment of change [offering] the opportunity for an urban renaissance.

This language of urban renaissance is not new, of course, but it takes on far greater significance here. The scale of ambitions for urban rebuilding has expanded dramatically. Whereas state-sponsored postwar urban renewal in Western cities helped to encourage scattered private-market gentrification, that gentrification and the intensified privatization of inner-city land and housing markets since the 1980s has, in turn, provided the platform on which large-scale multifaceted urban regeneration plans, far outstripping 1960s urban renewal, are established. The current language of urban regeneration, particularly in Europe, is not one-dimensional, but it bespeaks, among other things, a generalization of gentrification in the urban landscape.

Consider some key differences in the visions presented by Glass and the DETR. Whereas, for Glass, 1960s gentrification was a marginal oddity in the Islington housing market—a quaint urban sport of the hipper professional classes unafraid to rub shoulders with the unwashed masses—by the end of the twentieth century it had become a central goal of British urban policy. Whereas the key actors in Glass's story were assumed to be middle- and upper-middle-class immigrants to a neighborhood, the agents of urban regeneration thirty-five years later are governmental, corporate, or corporate-governmental partnerships. A seemingly serendipitous, unplanned process that popped up in the postwar housing market is now, at one extreme, ambitiously and scrupulously planned. That which was utterly haphazard is increasingly systematized. In scale and diversity, the process of gentrification has evolved rapidly, to the point where the narrowly residential rehabilitation projects that were so paradigmatic of the process in the 1960s and 1970s now seem quaint, not just in the urban landscape but in the urban-theory literature.

Most importantly, perhaps, a highly local reality, first identified in a few major advanced capitalist cities such as London, New York, Paris, and Sydney, is now virtually global. Its evolution has been both vertical and lateral. On the one hand, gentrification as a process has rapidly descended the urban hierarchy; it is evident not only in the largest cities but in more unlikely centers such as the previously industrial cities of Cleveland or Glasgow, smaller cities like Malmö or Grenada, and even small market towns such as Lancaster, Pennsylvania or České Krumlov in the Czech Republic. At the same time, the process has diffused geographically as well, with reports of gentrification from Tokyo to Tenerife

(Garcia 2001), São Paulo to Puebla, Mexico (Jones and Varley 1999), Cape Town (Garside 1993) to the Caribbean (Thomas 1991), Shanghai to Seoul. In some kind of irony, even Hobart, the capital of Van Diemen's Land (Tasmania), where dispossessed British peasants turned poachers and rebels were exiled in the nineteenth century and where, in turn, the local people were annihilated, is also undergoing gentrification.

Of course, these experiences of gentrification are highly varied and unevenly distributed, much more diverse than were early European or North American instances of gentrification. They spring from quite assorted local economies and cultural ensembles and connect in many complicated ways to wider national and global political economies. The important point here is the rapidity of the evolution of an initially marginal urban process first identified in the 1960s and its ongoing transformation into a significant dimension of contemporary urbanism. Whether in its quaint form, represented by Glass's mews, or in its socially organized form in the twenty-first century, gentrification portends a displacement of working-class residents from urban centers. Indeed, the class nature of the process, transparent in Glass's version of gentrification, is assiduously hidden in the verbiage of the British Labour government. That symptomatic silence says as much about the city's changing social and cultural geography, twinned with a changing economic geography, as do its more visible and voluble signs.

In the context of North America and Europe, it is possible to identify three waves of gentrification (Hackworth 2000). The first wave, beginning in the 1950s, can be thought of as sporadic gentrification, much as Glass observed it. A second wave followed in the 1970s and 1980s as gentrification became increasingly entwined with wider processes of urban and economic restructuring. Hackworth (2000) labels this the "anchoring phase" of gentrification. A third wave emerges in the 1990s; we might think of this as gentrification generalized. Of course, this evolution of gentrification has occurred in markedly different ways in different cities and neighborhoods and according to different temporal rhythms. In Mexico City, for example, the process is nowhere as highly capitalized or widespread as in New York, remaining confined to the city's central district, in addition to Coyoacán, and the demarcation of three identifiable waves of gentrification has little if any empirical validity there. In Seoul or São Paulo, the process is geographically isolated and in its infancy. In the Caribbean, the increasing connections between gentrification and global capital generally filter through the tourist industry, giving it its own distinct flavor.

By the same token, the transformation of mile after mile of old wharf and warehouse properties along both banks of the Thames suggests that gentrification in London is more expansive than in most North American cities. Insofar as it is an expression of larger social, economic, and political relations, gentrification in any particular city will express the particularities of the place in the making of its urban space.

And yet, to differing degrees, gentrification had evolved by the 1990s into a crucial urban strategy for city governments in consort with private capital in cities around the world. Liberal urban policy, which in Europe dated back in some places to the end of the nineteenth century and in North America to the transition from the Progressive Era to Roosevelt's New Deal, was systematically defeated beginning with the political economic crises of the 1970s and the conservative national administrations that followed in the 1980s. From Reagan to Thatcher and, later, Kohl, the provisions of that liberal urban policy were systematically disempowered or dismantled at the national scale, and public policy constraints on gentrification were replaced by subsidized private-market transformation of the urban built environment. This transformation was intensified by the coterie of neoliberal leaders that followed—Clinton, Blair, Schröder—and the new phase of gentrification therefore dovetails with a larger class conquest, not only of national power but of urban policy. By the end of the twentieth century, gentrification fueled by a concerted and systematic partnership of public planning with public and private capital had moved into the vacuum left by the end of liberal urban policy. Elsewhere, where cities were not governed by liberal urban policy during much of the twentieth century, the trajectory of change has been different, yet the embrace of a broadly conceived gentrification of old centers as a competitive urban strategy in the global market leads in a similar direction. In this respect, at least, turn-of-the-century neoliberalism hints at a thread of convergence between urban experiences in the larger cities of what used to be called the First and Third Worlds.

The generalization of gentrification has various dimensions. These can be understood in terms of five interrelated characteristics: the transformed role of the state, penetration by global finance, changing levels of political opposition, geographical dispersal, and the sectoral generalization of gentrification. Let us examine each of these in turn. First, between the second and third waves of gentrification, the role of the state has changed dramatically (Hackworth and Smith 2001). In the 1990s, the relative withdrawal of the national state from subsidies to gentrification that had occurred in the 1980s was reversed with the intensification of partnerships between private capital and the local state, resulting in larger, more expensive, and more symbolic developments, from Barcelona's waterfront to Berlin's Potsdamer Platz. Urban policy no longer aspires to guide or regulate the direction of economic growth so much as to fit itself to the grooves already established by the market in search of the highest returns, either directly or in terms of tax receipts.

The new role played by global capital is also definitive of the generalization of gentrification. From London's Canary Wharf to Battery Park City— developed by the same Canadian-based firm—it is easy to point to the new influx of global capital into large mega-developments in urban centers (Fainstein 1994). Just as remarkable, however, is the extent to which global capital has percolated into much more modest, neighborhood developments. Emblematic in this regard is a new sixty-one-unit condominium building in New York's Lower East Side, two miles from Wall Street, where every apartment is wired with the latest high-speed Internet connections. This is a small development by global city standards, but it was built by nonunion immigrant labor (a stunning development in New York in the 1990s), the developer is Israeli, and the major source of financing comes from the European American Bank (Smith and DiFilippis 1999). The reach of global capital down to the local neighborhood scale is equally a hallmark of the latest phase of gentrification.

Third, there is the question of opposition to gentrification. From Amsterdam to Sydney, Berlin to Vancouver, San Francisco to Paris, gentrification's second wave was matched by the rise of myriad homeless, squatting, housing, and other antigentrification movements and organizations that were often loosely linked around overlapping issues. These rarely came together as citywide movements, but they did challenge gentrification sufficiently that, in each case, they were targeted by city politicians and police forces. Apart from anything else, the heightened levels of repression aimed at antigentrification movements in the 1980s and 1990s testified to the increasing centrality of real-estate development in the new urban economy. Cities' political regimens were changing in unison with their economic profile, and the dismantling of liberal urban policy provided as much a political opportunity as an economic one for new regimes of urban power. The emergence of the revanchist city (Smith 1996) was not just a New York phenomenon: it can be seen in the antisquatter campaigns in Amsterdam in the 1980s, attacks by Parisian police on homeless (largely immigrant) encampments, and

the importation of New York's zero-tolerance techniques by police forces around the world. In São Paulo, highly repressive tactics applied to the city's street people are rationalized in terms of the "scientific" doctrine of "zero tolerance" emanating from New York. In all of these cases, the new revanchism was explicitly justified in terms of making the city safe for gentrification. The new authoritarianism both quashes opposition and makes the streets safe for gentrification.

The fourth characteristic of this latest phase is the outward diffusion of gentrification from the urban center. This is far from a smooth or regular process, but as gentrification near the center results in higher land and housing prices, even for old, untransformed properties, districts further out become caught up in the momentum of gentrification. The pattern of diffusion is highly variable and is influenced by everything from architecture and parks to the presence of water. Above all, it is geared to the historical patterns of capital investment and disinvestment in the landscape. The more uneven the initial outward growth of capital investment and the more uneven the disinvestment in these newer landscapes, the less even will be the diffusion of gentrification. By the same token, in cities where the majority of spatial expansion has occurred in recent years and where the opportunities for sustained disinvestment have been circumscribed, the diffusion of gentrification may be similarly limited.

Finally, the sectoral generalization that typifies this most recent phase goes to the heart of what distinguishes the new gentrification. Whereas urban renewal in the 1950s, 1960s, and 1970s sought a full-scale remaking of the centers of many cities and galvanized many sectors of the urban economy in the process, it was highly regulated and economically and geographically limited by the fact that it was wholly dependent on public financing and therefore had to address issues of broad social necessity, such as social housing. In contrast, the earliest wave of gentrification that followed urban renewal proceeded with considerable independence from the public sector. Despite considerable public subsidy, the full weight of private-market finance was not applied until the third wave. What marks the latest phase of gentrification in many cities, therefore, is that a new amalgam of corporate and state powers and practices has been forged in a much more ambitious effort to gentrify the city than earlier ones.

Retaking the city for the middle classes involves a lot more than simply providing gentrified housing. Third-wave gentrification has evolved into a vehicle for transforming whole areas into new landscape complexes that pioneer a comprehensive class-inflected urban remake. These new landscape complexes now integrate housing with shopping, restaurants, cultural facilities (cf Vine 2001), open space, employment opportunities—whole new complexes of recreation, consumption, production, and pleasure, as well as residence. Just as important, gentrification as urban strategy weaves global financial markets together with large- and medium-sized real-estate developers, local merchants, and property agents with brand-name retailers, all lubricated by city and local governments for whom beneficent social outcomes are now assumed to derive from the market rather than from its regulation. Most crucially, real-estate development becomes a centerpiece of the city's *productive* economy, an end in itself, justified by appeals to jobs, taxes, and tourism. In ways that could hardly have been envisaged in the 1960s, the construction of new gentrification complexes in central cities across the world has become an increasingly unassailable capital accumulation strategy for competing urban economies. Herein lies a central connection to the larger outline of a new urbanism, and we shall return to it shortly.

The strategic appropriation and generalization of gentrification as a means of global interurban competition finds its most developed expression in the language of "urban regeneration." Consonant with the importance of the state in the new wave of urban change, it is not in the US that this process has proceeded furthest, but rather in Europe. Tony Blair's Labour administration may be the most outspoken advocate of reinventing gentrification as "urban regeneration," but gentrification is a Europe-wide movement. Denmark, for example, made regeneration official policy in 1997 with a separate National Secretariat for Urban Regeneration, and Berlin bureaucrats have come to view the entire period of rebuilding after 1991 as one of "urban regeneration," A major conference was held in Paris in December 2000 on the theme of "Convergence in Urban Regeneration and Housing Policy in Europe." The conference was attended by senior policy directors and advisors representing all governments of the European Union, together with some neighboring states aspiring to EU membership; its brochure signaled the intent to push the "debate on housing and regeneration ... beyond the narrow span of physical development to examine the institutional arrangements which have to be put into place" in order to make "urban regeneration" a reality. The mission of those attending the conference was practical and comprehensive: large-scale urban transformation will require solid links between "the providers of social housing, private investors, [and] those responsible for training or policing" as

well as between "local regeneration agencies, local authorities, and national governments." Regeneration policies are multifaceted and include various efforts that would not normally be included under the label of "gentrification," yet it also makes sense to see these initiatives—the British urban regeneration manifesto, European state policies, and the efforts to establish a Europe-wide urban regeneration strategy—as the most ambitious attempts to incorporate gentrification into the heart of transnational urban policies.

There are a number of striking aspects of these new "urban regeneration" agendas. First is a question of scale. The coordination of urban "regeneration" strategies across national boundaries is unprecedented. While various international sources certainly contributed to the rebuilding of European cities after World War II, the subsequent urban renewal programs were resolutely national in origin, funding, and scope. Today, by contrast, Europe-wide initiatives on urban regeneration are pioneering cross-national gentrification at a scale never before seen. A central concern lies with efforts to integrate housing initiatives with "other regenerative activities." Thus, as the title of the Paris conference conveys, this transition from housing-centered gentrification policy to a broad-based multisectoral "regeneration" is still in process—and, unlike the situation in the US, the question of social housing cannot be entirely excluded from the vision of regeneration. While a Europe-wide state-centered strategy of urban regeneration is by no means yet in place, therefore, for Eureaucrats, developers, and financiers throughout the continent, it is very much in sight. A crucial connection to the earlier discussion of the new urbanism becomes clear: third-wave gentrification is increasingly expressive of the rescaling of the urban vis-à-vis national and global scales.

Second is the question of geographical focus. The 1999 British regeneration manifesto, apparently watchful of the environmental consequences of continued suburban sprawl, declares that over the next twenty-five years, 60% of new housing provision should occur on "brownfield" sites—that is, on urban land that has already gone through one or more cycles of development. Clearly, this initiative will be aimed at older urban areas that have undergone sustained disinvestment, and while these can be scattered throughout metropolitan areas, it is reasonable to expect that they would be concentrated in or near urban centers. Enveloped as regeneration, gentrification is thus recast as a positive and necessary environmental strategy.

Connected is the question of "social balance" and the need, as the regeneration strategy puts it, to "bring people back into our cities" (DETR 1999). "Social balance" sounds like a good thing—who could be against social balance?—until one examines the neighborhoods targeted for "regeneration," whereupon it becomes clear that the strategy involves a major colonization by the middle and upper-middle classes. To the politician, planner, or economist, social balance in London's Brixton means bringing "back" more of the white middle classes. Advocates of "social balance" rarely, if ever, advocate that white neighborhoods should be balanced by equal numbers of people of African, Caribbean, or Asian descent. Thus, it is not "people" in general who are to be brought "back into our cities"; this appeal is not aimed at Welsh coal miners, Bavarian farm workers, or Breton fisher folk. Rather, the appeal to bring people back into the city is always a self-interested appeal that the white middle and upper-middle classes retake control of the political and cultural economies as well as the geography of the largest cities. Probing the symptomatic silence of who is to be invited back into the city begins to reveal the class politics involved.

Then there is the question of the anodyne language of "regeneration" in itself. In the first place where does this language come from? A biomedical and ecological term, "regeneration" applies to individual plants, species, or organs—a liver or a forest might regenerate—and insinuates that the strategic gentrification of the city is actually a natural process. Thus, the advocacy of regeneration strategies disguises the quintessentially social origins and goals of urban change and erases the politics of winners and losers out of which such policies emerge. Gentrification generally involves displacement, yet neither the British manifesto for "urban regeneration" nor the agenda of the Europe-wide Paris conference registers any recognition of the fate of those people displaced by the proposed reconquest of the city.

The language of regeneration sugarcoats gentrification. Precisely because the language of gentrification tells the truth about the class shift involved in "regeneration" of the city, it has become a dirty word to developers, politicians, and financiers; we find ourselves in the ironic position that in the US, where the ideology of classlessness is so prevalent, the language of gentrification is quite generalized, whereas in Europe it is suppressed. Thus even seemingly progressive planners and local councillors from Bochum to Brixton, who still think of themselves as socialists and who may be keenly aware of the dangers of displacement, have become captured by the bureaucratic promise of "regeneration"

to such an extent that the integral agenda of widespread gentrification of urban centers is largely invisible. Not only does "urban regeneration" represent the next wave of gentrification, planned and financed on an unprecedented scale, but the victory of this language in anesthetizing our critical understanding of gentrification in Europe represents a considerable ideological victory for neoliberal visions of the city.

The point here is not to force a one-to-one mapping between regeneration and gentrification strategies, or to condemn all regeneration strategies as Trojan horses for gentrification. Rather, I want to insist that gentrification is a powerful, if often camouflaged, intent within urban regeneration strategies and to mount a critical challenge to the ideological anodyne that sweeps the question of gentrification from sight even as the scale of the process becomes more threatening and the absorption of gentrification into a wider neoliberal urbanism becomes more palpable. Gentrification as global urban strategy is a consummate expression of neoliberal urbanism. It mobilizes individual property claims via a market lubricated by state donations.

CONCLUSION

In this paper, I present two rather different arguments. On the one hand, I challenge the Eurocentric assumption that global cities should be defined according to command functions rather than by their participation in the global production of surplus value. On the other hand, I want to highlight the ways in which gentrification has evolved as a competitive urban strategy within the same global economy. The post-1990s generalization of gentrification as a global urban strategy plays a pivotal role in neoliberal urbanism in two ways. First, it fills the vacuum left by the abandonment of twentieth-century liberal urban policy. Second, it serves up the central- and inner-city real-estate markets as burgeoning sectors of *productive* capital investment: the globalization of productive capital embraces gentrification. This was neither inevitable nor accidental. Rather, as cities became global, so did some of their defining features. The emerging globalization of gentrification, like that of cities themselves, represents the victory of certain economic and social interests over others, a reassertion of (neoliberal) economic assumptions over the trajectory of gentrification (Smith and DiFilippis 1999).

Even where gentrification per se remains limited, the mobilization of urban real-estate markets as vehicles of capital accumulation is ubiquitous.

A further symptom of the intense integration of the real-estate industry into the definitional core of neoliberal urbanism comes from cities such as Kuala Lumpur, Singapore, Rio de Janeiro, and Mumbai, where real-estate prices in the 1990s have multiplied many-fold. The same processes of capital central-ization that accentuate the contradiction between production and social reproduction also enhance the gentrification process, although of course this works out in very different ways in different places. In Mumbai, in particular, market deregulation and global competition in the mid-1990s led to "extrav-agantly high prices" that briefly eclipsed even those in New York, London, and Tokyo (Nijman 2000:575). The highly volatile extremes of 1996 have receded, but the upper end of the Mumbai real-estate mar-ket now forever finds itself in competition with real estate in cities across the world, a condition which has brought small-scale but very real gentrification to some neighborhoods.

Whereas the major territorial axis of economic competition prior to the 1970s pitted regional and national economies against each other, by the 1990s the new geographical axis of competition was pitting cities against cities in the global economy. This com-petition takes place not simply in terms of attracting and keeping industrial production but also in the marketing of cities as residential and tourist destina-tions. This has been explicit in British regeneration policies such as the City Challenge in the 1990s (Jones and Ward this volume), and equally explicit from New York to Atlanta to Vancouver, where anti-homeless policies have been justified in terms of an enhanced tourist industry. *Travel and Leisure* mag-azine now hosts a regular feature that appropriates the language of "emerging economies" to put a spot-light on "emerging cities." Montevideo is renowned for its "thriving café society"; Tunis "has a grandeur that calls to mind Prague and Vienna"; "Panama City is fashioning itself as the culturally savvy gateway" to the Canal Zone: "[O]nce you've settled in, get out and shop"; and "Cracow is experiencing a renais-sance" (On the Town 2000:50). Similar aspirations scripted Mayor Giuliani's intense urban boosterism following the World Trade Center catastrophe: "[G]o out and lead a normal life," he exhorted three days after September 11. "Go to restaurants, go to plays and hotels, spend money."

Lefebvre (1971) once argued that urbanism had supplanted industrialization as the motive force of capitalist expansion: industrialization might have bred systemic urbanization, but urbanization now engendered industrialization. That claim has not withstood the test of time, especially in light of the globalization of industrial production and the

expansion of East Asia that was well in tow as Lefeb-vre wrote. And yet, he seems to have anticipated something very real. In a global sense urbanization has not, of course, supplanted industrialization; all of the products that fuel urbanization are made some-where in the global economy. Nonetheless, urban real-estate development—gentrification writ large—has now become a central motive force of urban economic expansion, a pivotal sector in the new urban economies. An adequate theoretical under-standing of neoliberal urbanism will have to revisit Lefebvre's argument and differentiate its insights from its exaggerations.

ACKNOWLEDGMENTS

I am very happy to acknowledge the comments and support of Julian Brash, Eliza Darling, Jeff Derksen, and David Vine, in addition to comments by the editors and reviewers of this piece.

Note

1 This notion of city-based foreign policies with global reach was quite illiberally lifted from social democratic proposals made at a concurrent New York-based international conference orga-nized by the ex-mayor of Barcelona, Pasqual Maragal. Giuliani refused to attend, but appropri-ated their ideas anyway.

REFERENCES

Brenner N (1998) Global cities, glocal states: Global city formation and state territorial restruc-turing in contemporary Europe. *Review of International Political Economy* 5:1–37.

Castells M (1977) *The Urban Question.* London: Edward Arnold.

Cooper M (1998) Study says stricter oversight of police would save city money. *New York Times* 16 November:B1, B5.

Cooper M (1999) Vote by PBA rebukes Safir and his policy. *New York Times* 15 April:B3.

Department of the Environment, Transport and the Regions (DETR) (1999) Towards an Urban Renaissance, http://www.regeneration.detr.gov.uk/utf/renais/ (last accessed 9 February 2002).

Fainstein S (1994) *City Builders: Property, Politics, and Planning in London and New York.* Oxford: Basil Blackwell.

Garcia LM (2001) Gentrification in Tenerife. Paper presented to the ISA Group 21 Conference, Amsterdam, June.

Garside J (1993) Inner-city gentrification in South Africa: The case of Woodstock, Cape Town. *GeoJournal* 30:29–35.

Glass R (1964) *London: Aspects of Change.* London: Centre for Urban Studies and MacGibbon and Kee.

Hackworth J (2000) "The Third Wave." PhD dissertation, Department of Geography, Rutgers University.

Hackworth J and Smith N (2001) The state of gentrification. *Tijdschrift voor Economische en Sociale Geografie* 92(4):464–477.

Hanson S and Pratt G (1995) *Gender, Work, and Space.* London: Routledge.

Hardt M and Negri A (2000) *Empire.* Cambridge, MA: Harvard University Press.

Harvey D (1973) *Social Justice and the City.* London: Edward Arnold.

Harvey D (1985) *The Urbanization of Capital.* Oxford: Basil Blackwell.

Jones G and Varley A (1999) The reconquest of the historic centre: Urban conservation and gentrification in Puebla, Mexico. *Environment and Planning A* 31:1547–1566.

Katz C (2001) Vagabond capitalism and the necessity of social reproduction. *Antipode* 33:708–727.

Katz C (forthcoming) *Disintegrating Developments: Global Economic Restructuring and Children's Everyday Lives.* Minneapolis: University of Minnesota Press.

Lefebvre H (1971) *La Révolution Urbaine.* Gallimard: Paris.

MacLeod G (2001) New regionalism reconsidered: Globalization and the remaking of political economic space. *International Journal of Urban and Regional Research* 25:804–829.

Mészáros I (2001) *Socialism or Barbarism: From the "American Century" to the Crossroads.* New York: Monthly Review.

Nijman J (2000) Mumbai's real estate market in the 1990s: Deregulation, global money and casino capitalism. *Economic and Political Weekly* 12 February:575–582.

On the Town. Emerging Cities (2000) *Travel and Leisure* January 42–50.

Ramsamy E (2001) "From Projects to Policy: The World Bank and Housing in the Developing World." PhD dissertation, Department of Urban Planning, Rutgers University.

Rose D (1981) Accumulation versus reproduction in the inner city. In M Dear and A Scott (eds)

Urbanization and Urban Planning in Capitalist Society (pp 339–382). London: Methuen.

Sassen S (1992) *The Global City.* Princeton, NJ: Princeton University Press.

Sassen S (1998) *Globalization and Its Discontents,* New York: New Press.

Sassen S (2000) *Cities in the World Economy.* Thousand Oaks, CA: Pine Forge Press.

Smith N (1990) *Uneven Development: Nature, Capital, and the Production of Space.* Oxford: Basil Blackwell.

Smith N (1996) *New Urban Frontier: Gentrification and the Revanchist City.* London: Routledge.

Smith N (forthcoming) Scales of terror: The manufacturing of nationalism and the war for US globalism. In S Zukin and M Sorkin (eds) *After the World Trade Center.* New York: Routledge.

Smith N and W Dennis (1987) The restructuring of geographical scale: Coalescence and fragmentation of the northern core region. *Economic Geography* 63:160–182.

Smith N and J DiFilippis (1999) The reassertion of economics: 1990s gentrification in the Lower East Side. *International Journal of Urban and Regional Research* 23: 638–653.

Swyngedouw E (1996) Reconstructing citizenship, the rescaling of the state, and the new authoritarianism: Closing the Belgian mines. *Urban Studies* 33:1499–1521.

Swyngedouw E (1997) Neither global nor local: "Glocalization" and the politics of scale. In K Cox (ed) *Spaces of Globalization: Reasserting the Power of the Local* (pp 137–166). New York: Guilford.

Taylor P (1995) World cities and territorial states: The rise and fall of their mutuality. In P Knox and P Taylor (eds) *World Cities in a World System* (pp 48–62). Cambridge, UK: Cambridge University Press.

Taylor P (1999) So-called "world cities": The evidential structure within a literature. *Environment and Planning* 31:1901–1904.

Thomas G (1991) The gentrification of paradise: St John's, Antigua. *Urban Geography* 12: 469–487.

Vine D (2001) "Development or Displacement?: The Brooklyn Academy of Music and Gentrification in Fort Greene." Unpublished paper presented at the conference on Gotham: History of New York, CUNY Graduate Center, 7 October.

Neil Smith is Distinguished Professor of Anthropology and Geography at the Graduate Center of the City University of New York (CUNY) and Director of the Center for Place, Culture and Politics. He works on the broad connections between space, social theory and history, and his books include *New Urban Frontier: Gentrification and the Revanchist City* (New York: Routledge, 1996) and *Uneven Development: Nature, Capital and the Production of Space* (Oxford: Blackwell, 1991). He is author of more than 120 articles and book chapters and sits on numerous editorial boards. His newest book is *Mapping The American Century: Isaiah Bowman and the Prelude to Globalization* (Berkeley: University of California Press, forthcoming). He has received Honors for Distinguished Scholarship from the Association of American Geographers and has been a John Simon Guggenheim Fellow. He is also an organizer of the International Critical Geography Group.

36

"Gentrification as a Governmental Strategy: Social Control and Social Cohesion in Hoogvliet, Rotterdam"

From *Environment and Planning A* (2007)

Justus Uitermark, Jan Willem Duyvendak and Reinout Kleinhans

1 INTRODUCTION

In the Netherlands, state actors and housing associations ambitiously pursue a project of state-led gentrification in disadvantaged neighbourhoods. The state induces housing associations and seduces private developers to invest in the construction of middle-class, owner-occupied housing in disadvantaged urban neighbourhoods with many low-cost social rented dwellings. Researchers refer to this form of government intervention as 'urban restructuring' (Kleinhans, 2003; MVROM, 1997; 2000; van Kempen and Priemus, 1999). Even though Dutch housing policy is subject to constant revision, it is clear that, over the next two decades, hundreds of neighbourhoods will experience such restructuring. First of all, this means that the share of social rented housing in the neighbourhoods designated for restructuring will decline from around 62% in the year 2000 to 45% in the year 2010. National and local state agencies, together with housing associations, are responsible for urban restructuring that aims to improve the economic appeal as well as the 'liveability' of designated neighbourhoods (see Tunstall, 2003). In the discourse about this policy, a 'liveable neighbourhood' refers to a 'balanced' neighbourhood with a low level of crime and a sizeable share of middle-class households. It does not refer to a neighbourhood where government agencies develop policies to ameliorate the social conditions of the most disadvantaged groups.

Restructuring policy attempts to promote gentrification in even the most disadvantaged and peripheral boroughs of Dutch cities. As we will show, however, conventional explanations of gentrification do not fully explain the scope, scale, and form of the processes involved. In the absence of profit motives or significant consumer demand, why do Dutch state actors and housing associations promote gentrification? Our response will focus on the institutional networks that promote it and on the discourse that legitimises it. Thus, we will show how the notion of liveability emerged out of a new institutional constellation where state actors and housing associations increasingly consider gentrification as the only conceivable solution to urban problems.

We develop our theoretical framework in the next section. Then we discuss why a massive programme of urban restructuring started in 1997 and has since received support from various coalitions of political parties, both nationally and locally. We also touch on the changing discourse on urban restructuring, urban decay, and marginality in Rotterdam, a city that is very much a focal point in urban developments and policy in the Netherlands. In the following section, we focus on the neighbourhood level and show how gentrification plays out in Hoogvliet, a peripheral borough of Rotterdam. We demonstrate how different actors pursue various goals by promoting gentrification. Our empirical data draw on three independent but comparable neighbourhood studies from 1998, 2003, and 2005. The final section presents our conclusions.

2 REASONS BEHIND STATE-LED GENTRIFICATION

While gentrification research initially focused on specific forms of neighbourhood change, now it deals with such diverse issues as office development, changes in the retail environment, city marketing, and zero-tolerance policing strategies (eg Atkinson, 2003; Atkinson and Bridge, 2005; Smith, 2001; 2002; Zukin, 1995). In a review of the literature, Slater et al (2004, page 1145) argue that the term 'gentrification' now encompasses all processes related to the "production of space for—and consumption by—a more affluent and very different incoming population." This definition leads us to reconsider the image of gentrification as a process that takes place exclusively in inner cities or historic neighbourhoods, Clark (2005, page 258) suggests that gentrification "is a process involving a change in the population of land-users such that the new users are of a higher socio-economic status than the previous users, together with an associated change in the built environment through a reinvestment in fixed capital." If we adopt this definition, it becomes clear that many urban policies are attempts to promote gentrification by encouraging middle-class households to move into working-class neighbourhoods. Indeed, Smith suggests that the language of urban renaissance in British urban policy "bespeaks of the generalization of gentrification in the urban landscape" (2002, page 438). This remark applies as much, or even more so, to the Dutch context, where the restructuring policy for promoting liveability by increasing the share of middle-class households involves practically all disadvantaged urban neighbourhoods.

This transformation of gentrification from a piecemeal process in inner cities to a large-scale urban strategy forces us to reconceptualise the role of governance networks (eg Slater et al, 2004; van Weesep, 1994). With some notable exceptions, few authors have attempted a systemic explanation of why and how state agencies shape gentrification processes in different places and periods (see Slater, 2004a; 2004b; Ward, 2003). Hackworth and Smith (2001) take a step in the right direction by indicating that the role of the state depends on a number of factors. They demonstrate that, paradoxically, the state is increasingly involved in gentrification in a time of purported 'privatisation':

First, continued devolution of federal states has placed even more pressure on local states to actively pursue redevelopment and gentrification as ways of generating tax revenue. Second, the diffusion of gentrification into more remote portions of the urban landscape poses profit risks that are beyond the capacity of individual capitalists to manage. Third, the larger shift towards post Keynesian governance has unhinged the state from the project of social reproduction and as such, measures to protect the working class are more easily contested.

(page 464)

Following this line of reasoning, observers often assume that measures to generate social order which harm the interests of poor urban dwellers are ultimately attempts to reconquer the city for the middle class and to increase the profit margins of developers and the tax bases of local governments (Smith, 1996), According to this view, the state acts in the interests of capitalists and legitimates itself by stigmatising the victims of its policies (eg Smith, 1999), Many gentrification researchers even define the very process by the harm it causes among lower-class households, precluding the possibility that these households support gentrification or benefit from it (Slater et al, 2004).

This conceptual framework explains some of the gentrification processes in the Netherlands, but not the kind we want to explore. We focus on forms of gentrification involving housing associations and local governments, which are not as subordinate to market forces as the agents analysed by researchers such as Neil Smith. Though housing associations have been financially independent institutions since January 1995, they do not primarily pursue profit. They are legally bound to reinvest all their profits in housing for the target groups of social housing policies. Municipal agencies, moreover, do not have to attract middle-class households to strengthen their tax base, as in the United States, since cities receive most of their resources from the national state (Terhorst and van de Ven, 1998). In short, there must be something else that drives gentrification strategies in the Netherlands.

Explanations that focus less on capital flows might be more appropriate, although arguments that regard gentrification as the outcome of changing lifestyles and of the emergence of new groups of urban consumers (see Ley, 1996) are not persuasive. Such groups would probably be more interested in spacious suburban housing or luxury apartments in central areas. Instead, we observe that in the Dutch case state actors and housing associations promote gentrification in areas that are currently least in demand. Developers would normally not invest in areas like Hoogvliet.

For a better understanding of state-led gentrification, we need to look beyond the economic dimension (eg Smith and DeFilippis, 1999) and address governmental and institutional dimensions as well (compare Flint, 2004). As in other countries, the Dutch government and its allies strive to create social order in places where the state appears to have lost its grip on social life (Dikeç, 2006). Thus, in order to understand the form, scale, and scope of state-led gentrification (Lees, 2000), we develop a theoretical framework that emphasises the *operational goals* of government agencies and their institutional partners (see Allison, 1971; March and Olsen, 1996). With respect to these goals, we show below that neighbourhood degradation negatively affects the ability of these actors to carry out routine tasks in poor districts, which include renting out, maintaining, and selling housing and preventing civil unrest. Serving the middle classes, we suggest, is not their ultimate *goal*. Instead, gentrification is a *means* through which governmental organisations and their partners lure the middle classes into disadvantaged areas with the purpose of civilising and controlling these neighbourhoods.

Of course, changing the social composition of a neighbourhood is not the only way or even an effective way to combat incivilities. Theoretically, state agencies and their partners could also pursue such a goal by increasing social cohesion or by combating the marginalisation that arguably causes civil disorder. We will show how the first of these alternatives failed. Explaining why combating marginalisation is not considered a viable solution to neighbourhood problems would take us far beyond the discussion on gentrification. Let us say, though, that the crisis of the Fordist state produced high levels of advanced marginality (Wacquant, 1999), which in turn led to social crises in many poor neighbourhoods, including Hoogvliet. Powerful actors in these neighbourhoods, especially housing association and local governments, have been unable to solve the problems that emerged and, as a result, urban policy has turned into crisis management (Brenner, 2004; Jones and Ward, 2002).

While postwar disadvantaged neighbourhoods clearly face a social crisis, this does not necessarily mean that state-led gentrification is the appropriate response. The word 'liveability' is key to understanding this project (compare Lees, 2000, page 301). For housing associations, liveability means that neighbourhoods are orderly in the sense that they exhibit a low level of crime, vandalism, and nuisance. Basically, it refers to the ambition to create social order in neighbourhoods that are prone to degradation. We will show below why housing associations

and state agencies now consider gentrification a sine qua non for promoting liveability.

3 THE DUTCH AND ROTTERDAM CONTEXT

While many authors have emphasised that the American state has largely withdrawn from ghettos (see Wacquant, 1998; 2001), the picture in the Netherlands is quite different. Public schools, the police, and benefits and community workers are all paid, directly or indirectly, by the national government. In their race for electoral success, politicians often visit disadvantaged neighbourhoods. If disorders break out in these neighbourhoods, the national media immediately cover the developments and local as well as national politicians seek to restore order. In short, there are many interdependencies between institutional actors in disadvantaged neighbourhoods (for example, state institutions, housing associations, and civic associations) and powerful national actors (Uitermark, 2003; 2005).

The nature of these interdependencies has changed substantially during the last two decades. We can roughly discern three phases. In the first phase, until the beginning of the 1990s, the national government financially supported municipal governments in the provision of social rented housing and other services. Housing associations were basically state organisations that were used as an intermediary between the government and residents. Authorities considered social housing a right at this time and viewed a high share of social rented housing as an asset to their city. In the second phase, which began around 1990 and lasted until about 2000, authorities started seeing social housing as a problem. Economic motives played an important role in this change of perspective. Rent subsidies demanded more financial resources than the national state was ready to grant. Furthermore, the government white paper *Housing in the 1990s* (MVROM, 1989) fundamentally changed the relation between the state and housing associations. The latter no longer received state subsidies, but acquired more discretion in formulating and executing their own housing-stock policies. As private companies with a public task, housing associations are supposed to sustain themselves financially. In this context, another development took place as well. Participants in the policy discourse increasingly associated social housing with social dislocation and disorder, and associated disadvantaged neighbourhoods with 'unliveable' conditions. In the 1970s and 1980s residents had argued against large-scale demolition of social housing because this would reduce the liveability of their neighbourhoods. During these years, urban renewal policies threatened liveability. In the 1990s, however, the term's meaning changed and began to refer to the disruptions of daily life caused by antisocial or criminal behaviours of neighbourhood residents. State actors as well as housing associations adopted the term 'liveability' and argued that the concentration of social problems in urban neighbourhoods inevitably caused incivilities. By this time, everyday incivilities had become the main threat to liveability. This discursive shift signals a major change in the role of urban renewal. Whereas policy makers previously saw social provisions as solutions for social ills, by the 1990s they argued that concentration itself was the problem. Hence, they began attributing incivilities that undermine liveability to the high share of social rented housing in many disadvantaged neighbourhoods. Whereas the central state used to support local governments and housing associations with the provision of social housing, now it started to encourage local governments and housing associations to construct owner-occupied housing and to demolish social housing in order to create neighbourhoods with a balanced social composition (eg MVROM, 2000). In the third phase, which we have just entered, social housing has become a social ill in itself. Participants in the urban policy discourse now associate owner-occupation with freedom and active citizenship, and associate social housing with dependency (see especially MVROM, 2000).

The transition from one phase to the next is particularly visible in the city of Rotterdam. For a long time, this city was a social-democratic bulwark with a strong commitment to social housing. In the 1990s, however, the city adopted a policy of social mixing and selling social housing. This policy faced little resistance, because demand for social housing was in decline and because most people involved agreed that owner-occupied dwellings were beneficial for the city. In 2002 Rotterdam adopted a more assertive and even aggressive approach (cf City of Rotterdam, 2003b), largely as a result of the electoral victory of the late Pim Fortyn's 'Liveable Rotterdam' (*Leefbaar Rotterdam*) and the loss of the social-democratic party and its Green coalition partner (see Uitermark and Duyvendak, 2005). The city now actively markets itself as a good place for affluent residents and especially targets the so-called creative class (see Florida, 2005). The city has boosted both the construction of owner-occupied dwellings and the demolition of social rented housing. Each year, developers add about 3000 new owner-occupied dwellings to the total of

250 000 dwellings, while demolishers destroy about 4000 social houses (City of Rotterdam, 2003a). In language that hardly requires textual deconstruction, the government of Rotterdam declares that it aims to attract "desired households" to "problem areas" (City of Rotterdam, 2006, page 15), thereby reinforcing and politicising the connection between owner-occupied housing and liveability. This discourse no longer only involves the right-wing parties that were in office since 2002. The Labour Party that won the local elections of February 2006 supports similar policies. A document produced by top civil servants to articulate a new vision after Labour's victory explicitly argues that gentrification needs to be 'enhanced' and that large investments should be made "to improve the quality of life" by building more owner-occupied housing in order to meet the demand of the "new middle classes" (City of Rotterdam, 2006, page 15). How do these developments on the national and city level translate into local policies? How does the relation between the state as an agent of gentrification, housing associations, and residents in disadvantaged urban neighbourhoods evolve?

4 LOCAL PRACTICE: GENTRIFICATION AND SOCIAL CONTROL IN NIEUW ENGELAND, HOOGVLIET

4.1 Background: a Keynesian suburb

Until the 1950s Hoogvliet was a small village in the southwest of Rotterdam. When in the 1930s the construction of a harbour created a demand for housing, Rotterdam annexed Hoogvliet with the intention of turning the village into a working-class suburb. This plan came to fruition in the 1950s and Hoogvliet became a typical Keynesian suburb of Rotterdam, with its own borough authority.

Urban planners cooperated with companies such as Shell and worked according to modernistic architectural principles in the renewal of Hoogvliet. This resulted in the sharp division of functions, many apartment blocks, and extensive green public spaces. At the time, more than 70% of the housing stock consisted of social housing. The new borough was very stable, mostly because of a structural demand for industrial labour. However, in the course of the 1980s the economic recession hit Hoogvliet particularly hard, generating structural unemployment among poorly qualified and industrial workers. According to Heeger and van der Zon (1988), Hoogvliet exhibited a subculture of unemployed youth that celebrated lawlessness, vandalism, and so forth. As an extensive informal and illegal economy of clandestine bars, drug dealing, and other types of criminal activity emerged, the idea took hold that Hoogvliet might be turning into a 'ghetto'.

At that time, Nieuw Engeland was one of the most disadvantaged neighbourhoods in the borough of Hoogvliet. It consisted of around 1200 dwellings, of which 900 were social rented housing. Probably due to the common identity and mutual social bonds that had survived the economic recession, many residents felt strongly attached to the neighbourhood and resisted further decline and accelerating vacancy rates. They developed a plan for demolishing some of the flats and when other residents joined them established the action committee "There is no such thing as 'can't do' " (*Kenniet Bestaat Niet*). Since the Housing Association Hoogvliet (*Stichting Volkshuisvesting Hoogvliet*) favoured its plan, the action committee tried to convince the borough authorities of the necessity of demolition. It enjoyed the support of the local political party, IBP (*Initiatiefgroep Boomgaardshoek en Platen*), which had gained a strong position in the borough council. The goal of this coalition was *not* to disperse poor households or to solve disorderly conduct. During a protest action at city hall, residents indicated that they primarily wanted to improve the quality of their houses. They constructed an imitation of a Hoogvliet flat and asked the mayor to try to fit himself and his family into a living area of 16 m^2. In addition, residents wanted to do something about rising vacancy rates and they considered renovation, demolishment, and reconstruction as possible solutions to this problem.

However, at the end of the 1980s the idea of demolishing social rented housing was not popular among politicians and civil servants. They wanted to maintain a large amount of social housing and were simply not accustomed to the idea that demolishing social houses could be part of a programme for urban renewal. Moreover, other residents in the targeted demolition blocks (who were not involved in the action committee) resisted the coalition's plans.

In the end, the central city government of Rotterdam decided to demolish 400 multifamily dwellings in the Hoogvliet neighbourhood Nieuw Engeland, which was far less than the 1000 dwellings favoured by the Housing Association Hoogvliet. It opted to renovate rather than demolish the remainder of the multifamily dwellings. This was also the case with 'De Waaier', a bow-shaped block of multifamily dwellings at the northern border of Nieuw Engeland suffering from nuisance and other social problems. Another element of the compromise was the replacement of demolished housing by more expensive social housing.

After demolition in 1990, developers constructed 222 new houses, mainly single-family dwellings. Half of the residents who moved to these new dwellings in 1991 and 1992 came from within Nieuw Engeland itself. Thus, many original residents 'returned' to the same neighbourhood, while renters of the new dwellings had to meet standards for financial stability. Still, more than 75% of the relocated households from the demolished housing had left the neighbourhood.

In short, most of the households held responsible for the disorderly conduct that inspired the intervention moved out of the neighbourhood, even if this was not a stated goal of the organised residents. At the same time, the poor were not exactly "swept out through demolition" (J Smith, 1999). Not only were the new social rented houses affordable for many of them, the initial resistance of other residents in the targeted demolition blocks quickly evaporated when they could move to social housing elsewhere in Rotterdam. Since the new residents in Nieuw Engeland were generally only slightly better off than the old residents, the form of gentrification was relatively mild in this case. What were the long-term effects of gentrification? More specifically, how do residents and other stakeholders in Nieuw Engeland perceive urban renewal and the resulting social order?

4.2 Disidentification and revanchist sentiments

Our first inquiry into Hoogvliet started in 1998, about six years after the construction of 222 new dwellings. We wanted to evaluate the effects of restructuring efforts and focused on the neighbourhood of Nieuw Engeland, which had a relatively high number of problematic housing blocks. We conducted seven interviews with stakeholders in the urban restructuring process, including community workers from the Welfare Foundation Hoogvliet (*Stichting Welzijn Hoogvliet*), staff members of the borough authorities and the Housing Association Hoogvliet, the neighbourhood police officer, representatives of the residents' council (*Bewonersraad Nieuw Engeland*), and a representative of the small residents' association (BOOT) representing the interests of the small block of owner-occupied houses in Nieuw Engeland. We also conducted a small survey that we will explain below.

Our questions to the key informants concentrated on the motivations behind, and the effects of, the urban restructuring operation. All our key informants related the urban restructuring to the social conduct of former and current residents. While the stated goal had initially been to upgrade the housing stock and prevent vacancy, at this point they judged the intervention according to a very different criterion: had it succeeded in removing or keeping out undesired households? They no longer perceived housing as a provision that could be improved but rather as a mechanism for selecting certain types of residents. The chair of the association for owner-occupied housing (BOOT) argued:

The renewal is going too slow. The core of dilapidation is still there. A lot of nuisance is caused by Antilleans. The cause of decline is the influx of less-adapted people. Many of the original residents have moved because of the decline. The only durable solution is to increase the share of owner-occupied housing.

Here we clearly see sentiments that Smith (1996) would describe as 'revanchist'. In this instance, the call for gentrification derives from the idea that 'less-adapted' people cause the social problems and that bringing in middle-class households will help revitalise the neighbourhood. Other informants are equally outspoken on these issues. Two representatives of the residents' council said that the biggest problems in the neighbourhood were:

a strong influx of ethnic minorities and a high vacancy rate in the housing stock. The residents in the newly-built housing are dissatisfied and are leaving.

The residents who had originally pushed for the restructuring operation play an interesting role here. They strongly identified with the neighbourhood. Soon they experienced disillusion with the results of the intervention. Their response was to leave the area or to call for more drastic measures. One of our informants at the borough authorities concluded:

The operation has failed. A few blocks of new housing is not enough to upgrade the neighbourhood. It might have worked if De Waaier had also been demolished before the completion of the new houses.

The complex De Waaier appeared as an island of decay in a neighbourhood that was otherwise going in the right direction (compare Wyly and Hammel,

1999). As our informants from the residents' council at that time remarked:

The new housing does not work because of the rotten living environment. De Waaier is still there.

Thus, the parties responsible for the intervention (the local government and the housing association) claim that restructuring failed as a solution for the pressing social problems. Nevertheless, they believe that more intense measures along similar lines could have had the desired result: social order through exclusion and dispersion.

However, informants from the borough authorities and the Welfare Foundation Hoogvliet, and the neighbourhood police officer reported their awareness that physical measures alone could not address the social problems. These informants argued for an alternative strategy to gentrification. The police officer said that people who had moved into the newly built housing felt betrayed when they found out that social problems had not disappeared but had only been relocated. Consequently, the police officer and local community workers wanted the new residents to play a pivotal role in the neighbourhood. They tried very hard to integrate the residents of the new housing with the residents of De Waaier. Here we see the beginning of an alternative strategy to gentrification: these actors tried to promote a strategy that was meant to increase social cohesion. By bringing people into contact with each other, they hoped they would identify with each other and with the neighbourhood to increase their collective efficacy in efforts to counter incivilities. Among such efforts was the establishment of a neighbourhood management board, with residents from all parts of Nieuw Engeland, a garden association, neighbourhood parties, and so-called stairway discussions (portiekgesprekken). According to the Welfare Foundation Hoogvliet and the borough authorities, these initiatives initially raised the frequency of social contacts between residents and their identification with the neighbourhood.

In sum, two strategies prevailed at this point. On the one hand, participants attempted to change the composition of the neighbourhood and attract more-affluent households. Many tenants in less attractive social housing were considered as a nuisance to other neighbourhood residents. On the other hand, participants tried to build social cohesion among the new and the old residents. This second strategy, however, was doomed to failure since the restructuring operation created a cleavage between the residents: the social cohesion that neighbourhood activities aimed

Indicator	Better	The same	Worse	Net change
Social cohesion	4	71	25	−21
Social involvement	4	76	20	−16
Population composition	16	59	25	−9
Neighbourhood facilities	17	60	23	−6
Social atmosphere	17	62	21	−4
Neighbourhood reputation	35	42	23	+12
Liveability[a]	47	40	13	+34

Table 36.1 Perceived changes in the neighbourhood due to restructuring, according to long-term stayers ($n = 216$) in Nieuw Engeland and in percentages (1998)

[a] Defined as clean, safe, and well maintained

Note: Missing values (about 2%) are excluded from the table

to promote was undermined by the restructuring operation that was taking place at the same time.

The acceptance of demolition as a solution for social problems pitted residents of new and old housing blocks against each other. In a sense, there is a self-fulfilling prophecy at work here. Demolition of a large block of social housing initially appears more effective and concrete than a long-term strategy of social investment. As soon as demolition starts, tensions in the neighbourhood increase between those who bear the costs of forced relocation and those who (expect to) receive the benefits. This in turn produces anomie which, in the prevailing policy discourse, authorities seek to reduce through further gentrification.

At this point, our survey in Nieuw Engeland becomes relevant. We distributed and recollected written questionnaires in a door-to-door campaign. Out of a 'population' of 862 houses, we received 216 completed questionnaires (25%). Subsequently, we acquired census data for Nieuw Engeland—on variables such as age, ethnic background, and tenure—from the Centre of Research and Statistics in Rotterdam. We compared those data with the equivalent survey variables. This analysis showed that the response is a fairly representative sample of the population in Nieuw Engeland (Kleinhans et al, 2000). We also compared the response from different blocks with their share in the total housing stock. We found that the response rates from the newly constructed and the older owner-occupied housing correspond to their shares in the neighbourhood housing stock. However, the response from De Waaier is slightly underrepresented, mainly because of high vacancy rates in those blocks at the time of the survey. Here we are particularly interested in the opinions of residents who witnessed the situation before and during the restructuring efforts, and who still lived in Nieuw Engeland at the time of our survey. More than half of the 216 respondents fall within this category. Table 36.1 indicates their evaluation of the long-term results with regard to seven aspects of neighbourhood quality. The respondents could indicate whether each aspect had improved, got worse or remained the same.

As table 36.1 shows, liveability has increased substantially but social cohesion and social involvement seem to have suffered from the changes. The social ties and networks that could have supported a strategy of social investment (see above) have eroded. This in turn makes it less likely that neighbourhood residents will collectively solve their problems.

Such *disidentification* makes it likely that more-established residents will develop even stronger revanchist sentiments (see de Swaan, 1997; Elias and Scotson, 1965). To put it concretely, once mutually antagonistic sentiments and interests had formed in response to the first intervention, the residents of the new dwellings could argue for the demolishment of De Waaier so that 'all' residents could enjoy a liveable environment. In fact, the very name of De Waaier symbolised the purpose of intervention. It made sense to designate that particular complex of buildings as an isolated and desolate space within the neighbourhood once the surroundings had been improved. Many residents in Nieuw Engeland perceived residents of De Waaier as unadjusted intruders, even though many of them had lived in the area longer than the residents in new dwellings. In particular, representatives of the association of homeowners in the neighbourhood, the housing association, and the neighbourhood borough felt that the restructuring operation was not complete as long as De Waaier still existed.

As a result of this changing balance of forces, the borough authorities and housing association increasingly focused on social control and demolition of social rented housing. In line with general Dutch trends, tenant protection and maintenance of public housing became less and less of a concern (Priemus, 1995). Instead, the borough authorities argued that "large concentrations of similar housing types are undesirable from the viewpoint of controllability" (Ds+V, 1994). They announced the demolition of 620 of the remaining 1460 maisonnette dwellings in other neighbourhoods of Hoogvliet and soon afterwards developed additional plans for demolition. These plans intended to increase the share of owner-occupied and single-family dwellings in the housing stock, while decreasing the share of multifamily social rented dwellings (Woonbron-Maasoevers Hoogvliet, 1998). What had initially started as an isolated restructuring intervention had now become a substantial gentrification programme that is currently still underway. In Nieuw Engeland, authorities decided to demolish the remaining old social housing blocks in 1999 and spread the gentrification process throughout the entire borough.

4.3 The Nieuw Engeland intervention fifteen years later

For our recent interviews with eighteen stakeholders, conducted in early 2005, we went back to Nieuw Engeland to study the long-term effects of the intervention that we studied in 1998. We interviewed a similar range of actors as seven years before. We talked to representatives of the housing association, civil servants from the local borough, community workers, the local police officer, a representative from the shopkeepers association, and residents who are active in the neighbourhood as volunteers.

The most striking event that occurred in the meantime was the demolition of De Waaier. In our 2005 study, we again asked questions to professionals and current residents about the interventions that had taken place in Nieuw Engeland fifteen years ago. Now that the whole area of Hoogvliet is subject to intensive urban restructuring, we also asked respondents to compare that specific intervention to current interventions in other neighbourhoods in Hoogvliet. The civil servant responsible for the restructuring operation in Hoogvliet is quite clear in his judgment of the lessons learned from earlier urban restructuring efforts:

The Nieuw Engeland neighbourhood you researched some years ago represents a good

example of how you should not do it. The social rented blocks with lower classes have remained and so the place is still a mess. Those people have just been put back, so there is no differentiation in the composition of the neighbourhood population. In Digna Johanna [the adjacent neighbourhood] it has been done in the right way. It has a mix of owner-occupied and social rented housing. That is a vital neighbourhood … it is more cohesive.

A staff member of the housing association, now called Woonbron Hoogvliet, shares his view. She says that the housing association wants more diversity in Hoogvliet:

The residents should be more diverse in terms of income and background. A one-sided composition of the people causes problems. We do not want to make a connection between income and residential behaviour but it is better if people have more things to do during the day-activities. Owner-occupied houses offer advantages: the residents are usually more involved with the neighbourhood. That is why we mix.

Even though we only spoke to a limited number of informants, a clear pattern emerges from the results. Respondents representing the institutional actors that are part of the coalition promoting gentrification (that is, the housing association and the local borough) do not mention any disadvantages. According to their view, mixing not only addresses and prevents social disorder, it also creates an involved and cohesive community of residents. However, others only partly share this view. Respondents who are professionally responsible for social cohesion, such as community workers, as well as active residents argue that Hoogvliet has not become an integrated district since the restructuring operation started. For example, the enthusiasm for government-initiated neighbourhood events is now notoriously low. The neighbourhood police officer of Nieuw Engeland remarks:

You can organise all you like in this neighbourhood. But then you are told: the Antilleans are there, so we won't come. So then it just becomes another Antillean party. I myself go to these initiatives but there are only a few whites.

He confirms that new residents in particular are not very eager to participate in neighbourhood activities. Two community workers experience similar difficulties:

> We want to strengthen social cohesion. The neighbourhood population is very diverse: Turks, Moroccans, Surinamese, and Antilleans. The Dutch feel they are a minority and that is indeed the case. ... We invite everybody but it is just a tiny group of people that participate. ... If community workers do not take the initiative, nothing would happen here anymore.

Joint activities are clearly no solution for a lack of social cohesion. When activities do take place, they tend to exacerbate rather than resolve social tension in the neighbourhood. Rosanna (white, female) remarks that:

> Nowadays you see more groups that belong together and to which I do not belong. ... In the past, when I had a dark-skinned partner, they more or less accepted me but now it is very difficult. I have to watch very carefully what I say or else I'll get a knife in my back. I am not allowed to say anything about nuisance caused by other groups. The whites are being held down in this neighbourhood.

The quotes of the community workers and Rosanna illustrate that the perceived lack of social cohesion is strongly associated with interethnic relationships. The diversity and high share of ethnic minorities fuel the anxiety of institutional state actors and some of the residents, who fear that the remaining social housing in Hoogvliet will attract the type of people who gave the now demolished Waaier its bad reputation. As Tessa, who herself lived in De Waaier, remarks:

> Neighbourhood safety has improved. Nieuw Engeland has improved. We hardly see police cars nowadays; we used to see many. It is more quiet. But the problems are still in Hoogvliet. In Oudeland there are many former residents of De Waaier—you do not want to be there at night. There are a lot of vacant houses and demolition is still going on. It is comparable to De Waaier. The problems are relocating.

For the local borough and the housing association the only conceivable strategy to deal with the fact that problems tend to be relocated rather than solved is to intensify the restructuring process, to build even more owner-occupied housing, and to attract new middle-class residents. The housing association

Woonbron publicised this strategy in 1998 when it issued a borough-wide plan for urban restructuring (see section 4.2). Both institutional actors and homeowners in Hoogvliet support the discourse in this plan. A representative from the association of homeowners has a strong viewpoint on this matter:

> Owner-occupied housing should be radically promoted; otherwise this neighbourhood will turn into a ghetto. Already we are on the verge of becoming caught in a downward spiral. If no action is undertaken now, the white and affluent households will leave the neighbourhood en masse.

In this discourse, the homeowners, who are more active and involved than renters, appear as saviours of the neighbourhood. To test this assumption, we analysed data from a recent residents' survey (2003) in Digna Johanna and Westpunt. These neighbourhoods are adjacent to Nieuw Engeland and experienced restructuring after the intervention in Nieuw Engeland. The survey methodology is the same as the procedure described in section 4.2. Here, out of a population of 981, we received 448 completed questionnaires. The response rate (46%) is highly representative for the population in Digna Johanna and Westpunt, and for the tenure distribution (see Kleinhans, 2005). Our analysis distinguished not only between renters and homeowners, but also between long-time stayers and newcomers—who arrived in Digna Johanna and Westpunt after completion of the new dwellings. The reason is that the tenure distinction does not fully overlap the difference between long-term stayers and newcomers, because there are still social rented dwellings. Nevertheless, the restructuring raised the already existing share of owner-occupied housing. This is reflected in the higher share of homeowners among newcomers than among stayers (see table 36.3).

We measured resident involvement with three binomial indicators. First, we evaluated whether respondents actively cooperated with other residents to achieve something useful or beneficial for the neighbourhood (for example, cleaning public greens or jointly organising a street barbecue party). Secondly, we observed whether respondents are active members of resident or neighbourhood associations. And, thirdly, we measured to what extent residents supported their neighbours in practical ways. Tables 36.2 and 36.3 show the results. For each category, the tables depict only the share of respondents who answered affirmatively to the corresponding question.

Indicators	Renters ($n = 192$)	Homeowners ($n = 256$)	Total ($n = 448$)	Difference tests[a]
Tenure	42.9	57.1	100.0	
Collective action with other residents (in the past year)	6.4	8.7	7.7	Pearson $x^2 = 0.8$ (ns)
Active member of a neighbourhood association	6.8	11.7	9.6	Pearson $x^2 = 3.1$ (ns)
Has offered help to neighbours in last two months	60.0	64.7	62.7	Pearson $x^2 = 0.9$ (ns)

Table 36.2 Involvement of renters versus homeowners, in percentages (2003). The table depicts the share of respondents who answered affirmatively to the corresponding question (source: own research)

[a] ns = not significant

While table 36.2 seems to indicate that home-owners are more often involved, the differences with renters are not significant for any of the three indicators. Thus, our data do *not* provide evidence for the assumption that homeowners are more active and more involved than renters. But if restructuring measures have increased the influx of owner-occupiers, as in Digna Johanna and Nieuw Engeland, there might be a difference between newcomers and long-term stayers that weighs heavier than tenure difference. This is what we tested in table 36.3. The test results show that newcomers are not more involved than long-term stayers. In fact, long-term stayers are significantly more often active members of neighbourhood associations and report higher levels of helping neighbours than newcomers.

Of course, these data cannot provide a comprehensive picture of social cohesion in Hoogvliet. Our interview informants, however, sketch a general picture with regard to social cohesion in Hoogvliet,

showing that the result of restructuring efforts in several neighbourhoods is not a cohesive living environment, but rather a neighbourhood where people live their own lives and avoid confrontations with members of other groups.

The main reason why the housing association and borough regard homeowners as assets is not that they contribute much, but rather that they do not cause nuisance and mind their own business. The role of new owners is generally one of limited involvement.

From our perspective, previous rounds of gentrification have increased the contrasts in lifestyles in such a way that collective action becomes increasingly unlikely. Slater (2004a) and Robson and Butler (2001) report similar findings. They show that gentrification produces a situation that can be characterised as 'social tectonics', by which they mean that relations between different social and ethnic groups in an area are parallel rather than

Indicators	Longtime stayers ($n = 257$)	Newcomers ($n = 191$)	Total ($n = 448$)	Difference tests[a]
Home owners	48.2	69.1	57.1	
Renters	51.8	30.9	42.9	
Collective action with other residents (in the past year)	7.2	8.4	7.7	Pearson $x^2 = 0.2$ (ns)
Active member of a neighbourhood association	14.4	3.1	9.6	Pearson $x^2 = 16.0$**
Has offered help to neighbours in last two months	68.3	55.1	62.7	Pearson $x^2 = 7.8$*

Table 36.3 Involvement of 'original' longtime residents versus newcomers, in percentages (2003). The table depicts the share of respondents who answered affirmatively to the corresponding question (source: own research)

*$p < 0.01$; **$p < 0.001$ (two-sided); [a] ns = not significant

not much mixing

integrative. The ambition to create social cohesion gradually becomes more illusory as lifestyle differences increase. The success of urban restructuring is almost exclusively measured in terms of liveability. The housing association, local borough, and homeowner representatives consider the operation successful if people feel that they live in a clean and safe environment.

4.4 A third wave?

Recently, arguments related to social control have become somewhat less important than economic arguments for promoting gentrification. Could it be that liveability is no longer 'enough' and that Hoogvliet wants to attract owners not so much to keep the neighbourhood stable but to boost property prices? At this point, we can give only a tentative answer to this question. For our respondents, economic motives do not yet seem to play a significant role. However, it appears that local authorities, together with private developers, are currently taking the restructuring of Hoogvliet to a higher level. These developers advertise Hoogvliet as a 'green and safe place' where you can play tennis and ride horses in the direct vicinity. They also boast that Hoogvliet has the character of a village and a vibrant associational life. Whereas in previous rounds of restructuring, most renters from demolished dwellings could return to the neighbourhood, this is now increasingly difficult. As one long-term resident remarks:

> There are new projects in Nieuw Engeland. People who move into this area have to join the association of owners—you are obliged to pay for this membership. In another project that is currently under construction, you are obliged to rent parking space. Renters are being pushed aside. ... I have always said: after the restructuring nothing but carton boxes remains for the poor people. Less affluent people cannot afford this, so they move out. They just won't get it.

We observed in both rounds of interviews that restructuring is used quite effectively to disperse or dissolve disorderly behaviour. It does so, however, at the cost of deepened social cleavages and growing indifference. Already, there is a strong feeling among respondents that neighbourhood contacts and social cohesion have suffered from the operation. The current restructuring efforts tend to increase the polarisation that is at the basis of this erosion since they attract households who differ strongly in terms

of income and lifestyle from residents in the remaining social housing in Hoogvliet. New entrants into owner-occupied housing tend to dissociate themselves from their less-affluent neighbours in the social rented housing. From this perspective, we may speculate that the new wave of gentrifiers currently entering Hoogvliet is likely to call for even more gentrification.

5 CONCLUSION

In order to grasp the specifics of state-led gentrification in the Netherlands, it is necessary to study the evolution and nature of the governance networks that promote urban restructuring in disadvantaged neighbourhoods. Unlike in the United States, it is not self-evident that economic motives are primary in the Dutch context. In general, explanations for gentrification that are derived from the US case are not fully applicable in countries where local governments receive most of their funds from national governments, and where housing associations play an important role in the housing market, such as the Netherlands but also France or the United Kingdom. Because the existing gentrification literature cannot fully account for these policies of enforced social upgrading, we developed an alternative framework that stresses the need to examine institutional linkages and the discourse of the key agents behind state-led gentrification in the Netherlands. Initially, interventions in the housing stock aimed to meet demands of residents and to ensure the availability of rental houses. In the course of the 1990s, though, urban restructuring became a way to alter the social composition of neighbourhoods. At present, gentrification enjoys public legitimacy. Authorities pursue it mainly as a means to improve the 'liveability' in disadvantaged neighbourhoods.

This goal often conflicts with the interests of residents, but resistance by tenants against gentrification was relatively low in the 1990s, especially if one takes into consideration the high levels of neighbourhood activism in the Netherlands during the 1970s and 1980s. Residents themselves by and large accepted the dominant discourse that equated gentrification with neighbourhood improvement. In the case of Hoogvliet, working-class residents as well as more-affluent residents favoured housing policies that dispersed groups associated with social disorder. They perceived gentrification in the 1990s not as a 'class war' (compare Smith, 1996), but as the only conceivable way to improve conditions in the neighbourhood.

As Clark (2005) rightly suggests, we should not analyse gentrification as a simple confrontation between perpetrators and victims. Yet, this process of state-led gentrification has its price. Forced relocation, for instance, has become increasingly common. A more problematic aspect of state-led gentrification, however, is that the influx of middle-class residents does not increase social cohesion, contrary to the suggestions of its proponents. Contacts between low-income and higher-income households, and between tenants and homeowners, in restructured neighbourhoods tend to be superficial at best and outright hostile at worst—a finding anticipated by Gans (1990; compare van Beckhoven and van Kempen, 2003; Veldboer et al, 2002). Even though the influx of even more and even richer homeowners is likely to increase the mental and social distance between neighbourhood residents, the parties involved promote this strategy as the main solution to remaining urban problems. It is important to recognise that this solution reflects the interests and working methods of the main agents behind gentrification: housing associations and local government agencies, backed up by the national state. For these parties, social cohesion in the neighbourhood or profit margins may be important, but their first priority is to create a neighbourhood with a stable social order. We have shown that these institutional actors achieve their operational goals by sometimes acting against sound business logic (they do not invest in the areas with the best potential for profitable investment) and against the interests of neighbourhood residents (the interventions are so drastic that they reduce social cohesion and force residents to relocate). Attracting middle-class households, is, for the institutional actors, a legitimate and perhaps the only conceivable way to civilise the neighbourhood. While this holds true for almost all actors involved (no actors argue against restructuring per se), promoters of gentrification and gentrifiers do not identify any negative effects, while those on the receiving end (professionals in the neighbourhood and residents of social housing) express doubts about the social effects, of gentrification. However, the very process of restructuring has undermined the collective identities and identifications that could have facilitated resistance or produced alternative strategies to combat urban problems.

This tendency of both lower-class and middle-class households, and of migrants as well as indigenous Dutch, to (passively) support further gentrification has emerged in the context of a relatively novel situation: the local government of Hoogvliet now actively promotes gentrification, not only for reasons related to liveability but also to promote economic growth. Even though it is too early to argue that this is a fundamental change in policy and to speculate about its consequences for residents of social housing, there are signs that gentrification is now becoming a goal in itself. In the past, policy makers have always seen Hoogvliet as a problem area that could benefit from an influx of gentrifiers. Now their position is the reverse: they currently advertise Hoogvliet as an interesting and exciting place for potential gentrifiers. In this context, they will increasingly assume that social housing is a burden rather than a necessary provision.

ACKNOWLEDGEMENTS

We acknowledge the helpful comments of Maarten Loopmans, Fenne Pinkster, Bahar Sakizlioğlu, and Leeke Reinders. A warm thanks also goes out to Simone Best, who provided excellent research assistance.

REFERENCES

Allison G, 1971 *The Essence of Decision: Explaining the Cuban Missile Crisis* (Little, Brown, Boston, MA)

Atkinson R, 2003, "Domestication by cappuccino or a revenge on urban space? Control and empowerment in the management of public spaces" *Urban Studies* **40** 1829–1843

Atkinson R, Bridge G (Eds), 2005 *Gentrification in a Global Context* (Routledge, London)

Brenner N, 2004 *New State Spaces: Urban Governance and the Rescaling of Statehood* (Oxford University Press, Oxford)

City of Rotterdam
   2003a *Wonen in Rotterdam. Aanpak tot 2006. Koers tot 2017* [Housing in Rotterdam. Approach to 2006. Course to 2017]
   2003b *Rotterdam zet door. Op weg naar een stad in balans* [Rotterdam perseveres. Towards a city in balance]
   2006 *Bouwen aan Balans, actieprogramma Rotterdam Zet door. Evaluatie en aanbevelingen* [Building on balance, action programme Rotterdam perseveres. Evaluation and recommendations]

Clark E, 2005, "The order and simplicity of gentrification", in *Gentrification in a Global Context. The New Urban Colonialism* Eds R Atkinson, G Bridge (Routledge, London) pp 256–264

de Swaan A, 1997, "Uitdijende kringen van desidentificatie: gedachten over Rwanda" [Expanding circles of disidentification: thoughts about Rwanda] *Amsterdams Sociologisch Tijdschrift* **24** 3–23

Dikeç, 2006, "Two decades of French urban policy: from social development of neighbourhoods to the republican penal state" *Antipode* **38** 59–81

Ds+V, 1994 *Structuurschets Rondom Digna Hoogvliet* [Strategic vision around Digna Hoogvliet] Dienst Stedebouw & Volkshuisvesting, Postbus 6699, 3002 AR Rotterdam

Elias N, Scotson J L, 1965 *The Established and the Outsiders: A Sociological Enquiry into Community Problems* (Frank Cass, London)

Flint J, 2004, "Reconfiguring agency and responsibility in the governance of social housing in Scotland" *Urban Studies* **41** 151–173

Florida R, 2005 *Cities and the Creative Class* (Routledge, London)

Gans H J, 1990 *People, Plans, and Policies: Essays on Poverty, Racism, and Other National Urban Problems* (Columbia University Press, New York)

Hackworth J, Smith N, 2001, "The changing state of gentrification" *Tijdschrift voor Economische en Sociale Geografie* **92** 464–477

Heeger H, van der Zon F, 1988 *Nieuw Engeland, Hoogvliet: perspectieven voor een naoorlogs woongebied in Rijnmond* [Nieuw Engeland, Hoogvliet: perspectives for a postwar housing area in Rijnmond] (Delft University Press, Delft)

Jones M, Ward K, 2002, "Excavating the logic of British urban policy: neoliberalism as the 'crisis of crisis-management' " *Antipode* **34** 473–494

Kleinhans R J, 2003, "Displaced but still moving upwards in the housing career? Implications of forced residential relocation in the Netherlands" *Housing Studies* **18** 473–499

Kleinhans R J, 2005 *De sociale implicaties van herstructurering en herhuisvesting* [The social consequences of restructuring and residential relocation] (Delft University Press, Delft)

Kleinhans R J, Veldboer L, Duyvendak J W, 2000 *Integratie door differentiatie? Een onderzoek naar de sociale effecten van gemengd bouwen* [Integration through differentiation? Research into the social effects of residential mixing] Ministry of Housing, Planning and Environment, The Hague

Lees L, 2000, "A re-appraisal of gentrification: towards a geography of gentrification" *Progress in Human Geography* **24** 389–408

Ley D, 1996 *The New Middle Class and the Remaking of the Central City* (Oxford University Press, Oxford)

March J, Olsen J, 1996, "Institutional perspectives on political institutions" *Governance* **9** 247–264

MVROM, Ministry of Housing, Planning and Environment, The Hague

1989 *Nota Volkshuisvesting in de jaren negentig* [Housing in the 1990s]

1997 *Nota Stedelijke Vernieuwing* [Policy memorandum on urban renewal]

2000 *Mensen Wensen Wonen: Wonen in de 21ste eeuw* [What people want, where people live]

Priemus H, 1995, "How to abolish social housing? The Dutch case" *International Journal of Urban and Regional Research* **19** 145–155

Robson G, Butler T, 2001, "Coming to terms with London: middle class communities in a global city" *International Journal of Urban and Regional Research* **25** 70–86

Slater T, 2004a, "Municipally managed gentrification in South Parkdale, Toronto" *Canadian Geographer* **48** 303–325

Slater T, 2004b, "North American gentrification? Revanchist and emancipatory perspectives explored" *Environment and Planning A* **36** 1191–1213

Slater T, Curran W, Lees L, 2004, "Gentrification research: new directions and critical scholarship" *Environment and Planning A* **36** 1141–1150

Smith J, 1999, "Cleaning up public housing by sweeping out the poor" *Habitat International* **23** 49–62

Smith N, 1996 *The New Urban Frontier: Gentrification and the Revanchist City* (Routledge, London)

Smith N, 2001, "Global social cleansing: postliberal revanchism and the export of zero tolerance" *Social Justice* **28**(3) 68–74

Smith N, 2002, "New globalism, new urbanism: gentrification as a global urban strategy" *Antipode* **34** 427–451

Smith N, DeFillipis J, 1999, "The reassertion of economics: 1990s gentrification in the Lower East Side" *International Journal of Urban and Regional Research* **23** 638–653

Terhorst P, van de Ven J, 1998, "Urban policies and the polder model: two sides of the same coin" *Tijdschrift voor Economische en Sociale Geografie* **89** 467–473

Tunstall R, 2003, " 'Mixed tenure' policy in the UK: privatisation, pluralism or euphemism?" *Housing Theory and Society* **20** 153–159

Uitermark J, 2003, " 'Social mixing' and the management of disadvantaged neighbourhoods: the Dutch policy of urban restructuring revisited" *Urban Studies* **40** 531–549

Uitermark J, 2005, "The genesis and evolution of urban policy: a confrontation of regulationist and governmentality approaches" *Political Geography* **23** 137–163

Uitermark J, Duyvendak J W, 2005, "Civilizing the city: revanchist urbanism in Rotterdam (the Netherlands)", ASSR WP 05/05, Amsterdam School of Social Science Research, University of Amsterdam

van Beckhoven E, van Kempen R, 2003, "Social effects of urban restructuring: a case study in Amsterdam and Utrecht, the Netherlands" *Housing Studies* **18** 853–875

van Kempen R, Priemus H, 1999, "Undivided cities in the Netherlands: present situation and political rhetoric" *Housing Studies* **44** 641–657

van Weesep J, 1994, "Gentrification as a research frontier" *Progress in Human Geography* **18** 74–83

Veldboer L, Kleinhans R, Duyvendak J W, 2002, "The diversified neighbourhood in Western Europe and the United States: how do countries deal with the spatial distribution of economic and cultural differences?" *Journal of International Migration and Integration* **3**(1) 41–64

Wacquant L, 1998, "Negative social capital: state breakdown and social destitution in America's urban core" *Netherlands Journal of Housing and the Built Environment* **13** 25–40

Wacquant L, 1999, "Urban marginality in the coming millennium" *Urban Studies* **36** 1639–1647

Wacquant L, 2001, "Deadly symbiosis: when ghetto and prison meet and mesh" *Punishment and Society* **3** 95–134

Ward K, 2003, "Entrepreneurial urbanism, state restructuring and civilizing 'New' East Manchester" *Area* **35** 116–127

Woonbron Maasoevers Hoogvliet, 1998 *Hoogvliet aan zet. Strategisch voorraadbeleidsplan Hoogvliet* [Hoogvliet's turn. A strategic asset management plan for Hoogvliet] Woonbron, Postbus 2346, 3000 CH Rotterdam

Wyly E, Hammel D, 1999, "Islands of decay in seas of renewal: housing policy and the resurgence of gentrification" *Housing Policy Debate* **10** 711–771

Zukin S, 1995 *The Cultures of Cities* (Blackwell, Oxford)

PART SEVEN

Resisting gentrification

(a)   (b)

Plate 19 **(a) Front page press coverage of the anti-gentrification riots in Tompkins Square Park, the Lower East Side, 1988.** Image copied by Loretta Lees. **(b) The 'March for Housing' in Vancouver, April, 2009.** Photograph by Elvin Wyly.

INTRODUCTION TO PART SEVEN

Those who take other people's place should have very good reason, and the moral principle of universalization, expressed in the question of how they would feel if the positions were reversed, is an appropriate test of whether the reason is good enough.

(David Smith, *Geography and Social Justice*, 1994: 276)

When writing the final chapter of our textbook on gentrification (Lees, Slater and Wyly, 2008), we were surprised by how few academic studies there were on resistance to gentrification. The process may have produced one of the largest literatures in urban studies, but it did seem that focused analyses of anti-gentrification protests, struggles and activism had been sidelined by all the attention to (and debate over) cause and effect. But might the paucity of research on resistance be indicative of the paucity of resistance itself? In a characteristically incisive global survey of the changing nature of urban social movements over the last 40 years, Mayer (2009) outlines the institutional pressures on such movements that have led to a situation where many protests have morphed into programs. Due to the shrinkage of the local state under neoliberalization, social movement organizations reproduce and sometimes reinvent themselves by implementing local social and employment programs or community development, with the following outcome:

[T]heir mobilizing capacity has eroded, and most have buried formerly held dreams of 'the self-determined city' or even of liberated neighbourhoods, as they limit themselves to what seems feasible under the given circumstances. And local governments which contract with these community-based service delivery and development organizations have come under enormous pressure, as more and more responsibilities and risks have been downloaded to municipal administrations, while their budgets are squeezed like never before.

(p. 364–5)

As far as anti-gentrification movements are concerned, in an essay we have reprinted in Part Two of this Reader (Chapter 8), Hackworth and Smith (2001) provided a concise explanation for their decline since the early 1990s:

[E]ffective resistance to gentrification has declined as the working class is continually displaced from the inner city, and as the most militant anti-gentrification groups of the 1980s morph into housing service providers.

(p. 468)

Another factor that has been outlined in the dwindling of community opposition to gentrification is the emergence, in the last fifteen years, of a brutal new authoritarianism in urban spaces, or the neoliberal "penal state" (Wacquant, 2009), which squashes protest almost before it has a chance to make its presence felt. For example, on the morning of December 20th 2007, New Orleans City Council voted in favor of the US Department of Housing and Urban Development's (HUD) HOPE VI plan to demolish over 4500 public housing units damaged by the floodwaters that followed Hurricane Katrina in 2005, and replace them with (gentrified) "mixed-income" housing developments (see Lees, Slater and Wyly, 2008). Locked out of their homes for more than two years, many residents of these housing units (along with activists that constitute the city's Coalition to Stop the Demolition) arrived at New Orleans City Hall to insist on their Right to the City (a growing global justice movement), only to find themselves locked out of the meeting where the voting was taking place. Behind the residents stood horse-mounted police, and behind the large metal gates keeping them out of the building were many more heavily armed officers. Duncan Plaza, adjacent to City Hall, had for some time been a significant homeless encampment for many people displaced by the 2005 tragedy, and many Plaza dwellers came over to show their support for the protestors' cause. In outrage at being refused admittance, the expanding group shook and broke the gates, and the police reacted with pepper spray, stun-guns and batons, quickly beating back anyone near the entrance, including several female senior citizens. According to the police, fifteen arrests were made, nine people were injured, four of whom were taken to hospital, although unofficial statements suggest these numbers were far higher. With this sort of authoritarianism, it becomes enormously challenging to fight gentrification on the streets. (We should also note that in the US, residents are evicted from public housing if a family member has a drug conviction – so they cannot fight displacement, for they have already been displaced.)

Yet the existence of the Coalition to Stop the Demolition is an indication that it would be analytically erroneous and politically irresponsible to suggest that anti-gentrification movements are on the way out. Some types of militant movements have declined in number. Many others have changed strategy. And in nearly every community experiencing gentrification, there is an enormous but latent reservoir of hidden resistance. At times this hidden, shared sense of frustration boils over, and sometimes seemingly unrelated controversies (protests over allegations of unequal treatment by the police, fights over the form of a particular development proposal) are intensified by the underlying polarization of gentrification. Among those researching gentrification, what is perhaps required is knowledge not only of the upheaval and hardship gentrification places on low-income/working-class communities, but also of the enormous creativity and resilience of the people and groups trying to resist displacement. In an era when most institutions and many individuals are committed to the notion that unregulated markets always work best, and that gentrification is nothing more than a change in the equilibrium of urban location, it is not easy to protect affordable housing and to make the case for a right to home, shelter, and community. But this is essential work. In this chapter we have selected four pieces of writing that in their own different ways make a contribution not just to scientific understanding of resistance, but to resistance itself. All four pieces certainly problematize Sharon Zukin's argument in Box 6 of this Reader that resistance to gentrification is "necessary but futile".

For over four decades activist, planner and scholar Chester Hartman has been a key figure in the displacement debate in the United States, but more importantly a key figure in struggles against displacement. *Displacement: How to Fight It* (1982) is arguably Hartman's most lasting contribution – the key publication that emerged as part of the San Francisco-based Legal Services "Anti-Displacement Project", a national campaign to protect affordable housing occupants from the displacement pressures of profiteering reinvestment in America's cities during the 1970s. This book gained much of its political energy from a protracted struggle over "urban renewal" – the construction of San Francisco's Yerba Buena Center, a massive convention, performing arts and public space complex in the city's South of Market (SoMa) area. To create Yerba Buena, the San Francisco Redevelopment Agency displaced over 4000 poor elderly tenants from Single Room Occupancy Hotels (SROs) in SoMa, in a particularly brutal case of what Hartman (who observed much of the struggle and interviewed many displacees for a National Housing Law Project survey) appropriately called "land grab" (Hartman, 1974). Something of the experience of displacement was later captured in retrospect by Hartman, with poignant eloquence:

For many pensioners, accustomed to forty-dollar- and fifty-dollar-per-month rents, relocation was a terrifying experience. … The interviews … revealed the disruption of social networks caused by displacement. For older people in particular, personal friendships are perhaps the most important aspect of day-to-day life. Loss of familiar faces in the streets and in the hotel lobbies, of people to talk to, eat, drink, and play cards with is a severe shock. Similarly, the loss of stores, restaurants, and other commercial institutions can rob people of an important basis of stability, a place to obtain credit, to meet friends.

(Hartman, 2002, p. 66, p. 74.)

The losses were immeasurable, but the fight against the callous obliteration of a working-class quarter of San Francisco, led by a tenants' organization called Tenants and Owners in Opposition to Redevelopment

(TOOR) with the support of non-profit legal organizations, saw some impressive gains. After protracted litigation battles, half the units torn down in SoMa were replaced, and subsidized for permanent low-rent occupancy by federal and state sources and the city's hotel tax, with TOOR acting as developers and managers of much of the new housing. It was a lengthy and messy process, but those who fought Yerba Buena provided inspiring proof that something could be done about gentrification and displacement. The TOOR slogan said it all: "We Won't Move."

Hartman's most famous article that we reprint here has a title that is also a useful political slogan: *The Right To Stay Put*. It is an example of what is becoming an endangered species in urban studies – spirited policy critique with a rallying cry for urgent reform (as opposed to vague and inconsequential "policy relevance"). This is seen most clearly in Hartman's rejection of conventional cost-benefits thinking in housing policy, in favor of an understanding of displacement costs as emotional, psychological, individual and social: "Is it not reasonable to assert that such costs are a concern for public policy?" (p. 308). Hartman explains that a right to stay put is "in the public interest":

> More stable communities are likely to produce greater care of property and a lower incidence of crime. There will be fewer antisocial acts related to the anger and impotence experienced by those who are forcibly displaced. The rate at which housing costs are inflating will be reduced. Individual misery will decrease. But the underlying motivation for asserting and supporting such a right is primarily an interest in securing greater equity: more rights and benefits for those in the society who fall at the lower end of the spectrum of resources and power.
>
> (ibid.)

Perhaps the main contribution of Hartman's essay is that it now serves as a touchstone, both political and contextual, foreshadowing the insights of the nascent (Lefebvrian) "Right to the city" movement (see Harvey, 2008) and of an emerging political philosophy for a "right to place" (Imbroscio, 2004).

We follow Hartman's article with one by Kathe Newman and Elvin Wyly that revisits the right to stay put over two decades later, in the context of the media and policy reaction to some high-profile work we featured in Part Four of this book (Lance Freeman and Frank Braconi's study of displacement in New York City – Chapter 28). Despite the clear cautions and caveats in that study, Newman and Wyly document how its central argument (that displacement caused by gentrification doesn't, after all, affect that many low-income urban residents), was hugely appealing to policy elites and journalists seeking neat soundbytes and tidy statistics, especially as it supported the equally high-profile study of Vigdor (2002) in Boston produced two years earlier. The *USA Today*, for instance, covered Freeman's research under the headline: *Studies: Gentrification a Boost for Everyone*. For Newman and Wyly, such headlines were far removed from the situation in gentrifying New York City neighborhoods, both statistically and verbally. Whilst applauding Freeman and Braconi's methodological sophistication, Newman and Wyly used the same data set (the New York City Housing and Vacancy Survey) to show that the rate of displacement between 1989 and 2002 was in fact higher (between 6.6 and 9.9 percent of all local moves among rental households), and also that the data set cannot be treated as a reliable resource if we are to understand the magnitude of the problem:

> the NYCHVS does not include displaced households that left New York City, doubled up with other households, became homeless, or entered the shelter system … [it] also misses households displaced by earlier rounds of gentrification and those that will not gain access to the now-gentrified neighborhoods in the future.
>
> (Newman and Wyly, 2006: 51)

Crucially, Newman and Wyly conducted 33 field interviews with community residents, community organization staff and staff at city-wide agencies in the seven neighborhoods that Freeman and Braconi studied, and these interviews yielded fascinating insights into (a) the strategies of resistance families and community groups adopted to ensure that they did indeed 'stay put' in the face of massive gentrification, and (b) the policies that are so vital in protecting against displacement – policies that are under serious threat of extermination due to deepening neoliberalization. Newman and Wyly's argument is that gentrification is not a boost for everyone, and neither are low-income renters and those who represent their interests powerless to resist its effects. Resistance creates a policy paradox, however: the individual strategies used to cope with displacement, and the remaining public policies like rent regulations that protect some households, can hide the true quantitative magnitude of displacement pressures – making it easier for developers and policy elites to cite the erroneously small displacement numbers in their efforts to roll back rent regulations and to promote all-out gentrification.

As soon as one becomes well acquainted with the gentrification literature (no easy task given how vast and interdisciplinary it has become), it becomes clear that the sheer volume of critical scholarship can itself be treated as an act of resistance to gentrification and displacement. In the 1980s theoretical debates were anchored in a broad concern for social justice; scholars may have clashed over explanation, but a meeting point (avoided by those of a neoclassical persuasion) was social critique – people were losing their homes, cities were becoming more unequal, and the challenge was to understand, explain, and put forward alternatives. The third article in this chapter is an intervention by Tom Slater, who argues that we have witnessed a fundamental shift since the mid-1990s in the study of gentrification, captured by the title: "the eviction of critical perspectives." After taking issue with overt, glib celebrations of the process in some work emanating from the United States (which does nothing more than parrot conventional media and policy views of "revitalization"), Slater contends that British scholarship oriented towards interpreting the life and times of the gentrifying middle-classes (together with something of an infatuation with how to define 'gentrification') has erected an epistemological screen, blocking intellectual attention to the negative aspects of gentrification. He moves on to argue that we might be witnessing the 'gentrification of gentrification research' itself, via the sidelining of displacement as a primary research concern, the pointless repetition of old debates (stifling fresh critique), and the uncritical acceptance of 'social mix' policies towards disinvested neighborhoods. This article raised uncomfortable yet urgent questions about positionality, policy-oriented research and indeed the purpose of the analyst in the moral economy of gentrification (which were debated in the *International Journal of Urban and Regional Research* 2008: 32(1)). We see a crucial role for scholars in resistance to gentrification. This role is threatened by "policy relevant" publications (such as Vigdor, 2002; Byrne, 2003, Cooke, 2008) that give the false impression that gentrification is nothing more than a convenient opportunity for policy-makers to take advantage of interesting cultural transformations (cr. Cameron and Coaffee, 2005; Ross, 2006). Gentrification has a harsh and inescapable materiality: the process can be devastating for some of the people in its path.

The final selection in this section is the conclusion from a lengthy and important report written by three scholars (Diane Levy, Jennifer Comey and Sandra Padilla) based in the non-partisan *Urban Institute* in the United States. The title of the report: "In the Face of Gentrification" gives a clue to what can be found within – a set of case studies from six different cities across the US (St. Petersburg, Sacramento, Atlanta, Los Angeles, Seattle and Chicago) where displacement has not only been prevalent but also challenged in different ways. These challenges reflect an important but often-overlooked facet of policy and resistance: the coalition of interests promoting gentrification is not monolithic, and at times it can be somewhat unstable. There are many potential allies in unexpected places. Sometimes, local policy makers who would normally support the full "growth machine" agenda of development and growth raise objections, because they see the direct local consequences of unrestrained commodification, displacement, and community tension. In other cases, policy-makers responsible for social welfare decisions (on poverty, education, etc.) cite concerns over gentrification and displacement to question the priorities of policy-makers responsible for real-estate development and investment.

Recognizing that there is significant disagreement on how to define gentrification and whether displacement can be included in the definition, the authors embark on a useful mixed-methods survey of gentrification in these cities, where the process is reported to be in either early, middle or late stages.

Probably the most politically salient sentence of the entire report appears at the start of their conclusion: "Our findings begin with the fact that none of the [housing] practitioners believed it was too late to implement some type of affordable housing strategy." This is a profoundly important reminder to researchers in cities such as London, New York and San Francisco, where a commonly held view is that it is way too late in many neighborhoods to make a difference. The authors go on to outline their recommendations and strategies for "mitigating displacement" – whilst it must be said that none are exactly rocket science (and nor do they call into question the underlying structure of socio-political interests constituting capitalist urban and land economies and policies), they certainly deserve visibility and repetition. They are affordable housing production *and* retention (key to which involves anticipation of accelerating gentrification from non-profits); asset building (empowering and enabling people to meet housing needs); capturing parcels of urban land before costs become prohibitive for affordable housing development; capturing local government support (especially with regards to anti-displacement zoning regulations); enabling community involvement and organizing (especially before gentrification "takes off") and understanding that displacement is also a consequence of urban poverty (employment and education programs can make a difference). Perhaps Levy et al.'s report should be read in the spirit that resistance has to start somewhere, and read alongside the further reading below, it might lead us to the precipice of the plausibility of truly radical change.

REFERENCES AND FURTHER READING

Aardema, N. and Knoy, S.J. (2004) 'Fighting gentrification Chicago style', *Social Policy* 34(4): 1–6.

Achtenberg, E.P. and Marcuse, P. (1986) 'Toward the decommodification of housing', in R. Bratt, C. Hartman and A. Meyerson (eds) *Critical Perspectives in Housing*, Temple University Press: Philadelphia, pp. 474–483.

Addie, J. (2008) 'The rhetoric and reality of urban policy in the neoliberal city: implications for social struggle in Over-the-Rhine', Cincinnati, *Environment and Planning A* 40(11): 2674–2692.

Berg, J.-J., Kaminer, T., Schoonderbeek, M. and Zonneveld, J. (2009) *Houses in Transformation: Interventions in European Gentrification*, NAi Uitgevers/Publishers.

Blomley, N. (2004) *Unsettling the City: Urban Land and the Politics of Property*, New York: Routledge.

Bridge, G., Butler, T. and Lees, L. (eds) (forthcoming) *Mixed Communities: Gentrification by Stealth?* Bristol: Policy Press.

Byrne, J.P. (2003) 'Two cheers for gentrification', *Howard Law Journal* 46(3): 405–432.

Cameron, S. and Coaffee, J. (2005) 'Art, gentrification, and regeneration: From artist as pioneer to public arts', *European Journal of Housing Policy* 5(1): 39–58.

Cooke, P. (ed.) (2008) *Creative Cities, Cultural Clusters and Local Economic Development*, Cheltenham: Edward Elgar.

DeFilippis, J. (2004) *Unmaking Goliath: Community Control in the Face of Global Capital*, New York: Routledge.

Dulchin, B. (2003) 'Organizing against gentrification, fighting the free market: the displacement-free zone campaign', *Social Policy* 34(2): 29–34.

Haas, G., Benitez, T. and Wells, C. (2008) *We Shall Not be Moved: Posters and the Fight Against Displacement in LA's Figueroa Corridor*, PM Press.

Hackworth, J. and Smith, N. (2001) 'The changing state of gentrification', *Tijdschrift voor Economische en Sociale Geografie* 92: 464–477.

Hartman, C. (2002) *City for Sale: The Transformation of San Francisco*, Berkeley, CA: University of California Press.

Hartman, C. (1974) *Yerba Buena: Land Grab and Community Resistance in San Francisco*, San Francisco: Glide Publications.

Hartman, C., Keating, D. and LeGates, R. (1982) *Displacement: How to Fight It*, Washington DC: National Housing Law Project.

Harvey, D. (2008) 'The right to the city', *New Left Review* 53: 23–40.

Henig, J. (1982) 'Neighborhood response to gentrification – conditions of mobilization', *Urban Affairs Quarterly* 17(3): 343–358.

Hughes, D. (2000) *Wake up and Smell the Dollars! Whose Inner City is it Anyway! One Woman's Struggle Against Sexism, Classism, Racism, Gender, and the Empowerment Zone*, New York: Amber Books.

Imbroscio, D. L. (2004) 'Can we grant a right to place?', *Politics & Society* 32: 575–609.

International Journal of Urban and Regional Research (2008) Debates section, 32(1).

Lees, L. (2008) 'Gentrification and social Mixing: Towards an urban renaissance?', *Urban Studies* 45(12): 2449–2470.

Marcuse, P. (1985) 'To control gentrification: anti-displacement zoning and planning for stable residential districts', *Review of Law and Social Change* 13: 931–945.

Mayer, M. (2009) 'The "Right to the City" in the context of shifting mottos of urban social movements', *City*, 13(2–3): 362–374.

Muniz, V. (1998) *Resisting Gentrification and Displacement: Voices of the Puerto Rican Woman of the Barrio*, New York: Garland Publishing.

Peck, J. (2005) 'Struggling with the creative class', *International Journal of Urban and Regional Research* 29(4): 740–770.

Robinson, T. (1995) 'Gentrification and grassroots resistance in San Francisco's tenderloin', *Urban Affairs Review* 30(4): 483–513.

Ross, A. (2006) 'Nice work if you can get it: The mercurial career of creative industries policy', *Work Organization, Labour and Globalization* 1(1): 13–30.

Slater, T. (2008) 'A literal necessity to be replaced': a rejoinder to the gentrification debate, *International Journal of Urban and Regional Research* 32(1): 212–223 .

Slater, T. (forthcoming 2011) *Fighting Gentrification*, Oxford: Blackwell.

Slater, T., Curran, W. and Lees, L. (2004) [guest editors] 'Gentrification research: new directions and critical scholarship', special issue of *Environment and Planning A* 36(7).

Smith, D. M. (1994) *Geography and Social Justice*, Oxford: Blackwell.

Vigdor, J. (2002) 'Does gentrification harm the poor?', *Brookings-Wharton Papers on Urban Affairs*: 133–173.

Wacquant, L. (2009) *Punishing the Poor: The Neoliberal Government of Social Insecurity*, Duke University Press.

Wilson, D., Wouters, J. and Grammenos, D. (2004) 'Successful protect community discourse: spatiality and politics in Chicago's Pilsen neighbourhood', *Environment and Planning A* 36(7): 1173–1190.

37
"The Right to Stay Put"

From *Land Reform, American Style* (1984)

Chester Hartman

[handwritten: not a good experience]

Residential stability engenders a host of personal and social benefits. Long-term residence brings safety of person and property ("eyes on the street," people looking out for each other and each other's homes), helpful and satisfying social ties to neighbors and local commercial establishments, greater care for public and private space, and lower housing costs (Fried, 1973; Gans, 1962). This is not to say that mobility is to be avoided. Change of residence may be necessary and advisable to meet changing space needs and preferences, to take advantage of employment opportunities, to satisfy shifting personal consumption preferences, to escape what is perceived to be a confining social or physical environment, to secure change for change's sake, or for other reasons. The distinction between involuntary and voluntary change of residence is, however, crucial. Shifts of residence that are sought — for which people are financially and socially prepared — clearly are nondetrimental to society. But changes of residence which are foisted on people, which they did not seek out or propose, for which they may lack the social and economic coping resources — these are detrimental to the individuals and families involved, and produce social costs as well.

In theory, the economic, political, and social forces that trigger these involuntary moves may be associated with societal benefits that outweigh the costs to those forced to move (a point that will be explored in greater detail below). But, aside from those rare instances in which the person forcibly displaced winds up retrospectively grateful for what was initially perceived as a catastrophe, we can safely say that from the displacee's perspective forced displacement is most often a severely damaging experience.

Quantitatively, the problem of forced displacement is substantial and probably growing. A recent study by the Legal Services Anti-Displacement Project concludes that "2.5 million persons a year in the United States is a conservative estimate of the magnitude of displacement at the present time" (LeGates and Hartman, 1981). The proximate cause of most displacement is private-sector rather than public-sector action. This has been true for the last decade and represents a shift from the 1950s and 1960s, when government programs, particularly urban renewal and construction of the interstate highway system, were the primary displacing forces. *[handwritten: old reasons 4 displacement]*

Government still has a substantial role in the displacement process today. Some direct government-initiated displacement still occurs for a wide variety of public-works projects — highways and roads, dams, public buildings, airports. And a great deal of ostensibly private-sector displacement is supported by or the indirect result of government policies, programs, or action. Examples are private-market ripple effects caused by government investment in downtown redevelopment, public transit, or housing rehabilitation; tax policies that foster home ownership and thus encourage conversion of rental units into condominiums, or that encourage luxury renovation of historic properties; policies of federal financial-institution regulatory bodies that permit and encourage a shift from fixed- to variable-rate interest mortgages; and state and local landlord-tenant laws that permit easy evictions

(Roisman, 1981). But in the vast proportion of cases today, the direct displacing agent is in the private sector.

Forced displacement produced by the private sector may be divided roughly into that related to *revitalization* forces in the private market and that related to *disinvestment* forces in the private market.

DISPLACEMENT GENERATED BY REVITALIZATION

Home owners as well as renters (although overwhelmingly the latter) may be forced out by actions associated with increasing investment in and attractiveness of an area — what has commonly been referred to by the British term "gentrification." Older structures may be rehabilitated by new or existing owners in order to take advantage of an area's new market attractiveness, due in turn to location, inherent structural or historic qualities, taste and fad, or other factors.

Where the work is done by an investor/developer, such rehabilitation often requires removal of the current residents in order to allow the work to be done efficiently. The rehab work itself may result in higher rental costs which current residents cannot afford or do not choose to bear. A change in unit sizes following rehab — conversion of large units into smaller ones, or vice versa — may make unworkable the former fit between space and occupants. Or a desired change in the social character of the area may make the rehabber unwilling to allow former residents to continue living in the renovated unit. New owner-occupants, whether or not they undertake renovation work, will displace the existing residents of the units they wish to occupy.

Gentrification probably will lead to overall rent increases in an area, even if no or only cosmetic improvements are made in a building located there; and these increases, too, will cause existing residents to move. Property tax increases can also be expected as an area is upgraded, and these also cause rent increases, as well as increased tax bills for home owners, who then may be forced to move. Such "house-rich" but otherwise lower-income persons can reap the windfall benefits of increased property values when they sell, of course, but the social and personal disruption in their lives caused by their inability to pay sharply increased tax bills may be severe, especially since their "windfall" may have to be used to pay higher housing costs elsewhere. Gentrification also is associated with speculative buying and selling of properties, conversion of housing into office and other commercial use, and

condominium conversion, all of which are leading causes of displacement.

DISPLACEMENT GENERATED BY DISINVESTMENT

The disinvestment process sets in motion an opposite set of forces, for the most part similarly rooted in the profit considerations of those who own and control property. At the extreme, owners simply abandon, or walk away from, properties they no longer regard as profitable or potentially profitable, leaving unpaid mortgages, property taxes, and utility bills in their wake. A final touch may be "selling out to the insurance company" — that is, arson. A less extreme version of this response is under-maintenance, investing little or nothing in upkeep and repairs, in an effort to keep up profits. "Disinvestment" of this type often is followed shortly by abandonment.

Obviously, such processes cause displacement, when a building is made unfit for habitation or so dangerous and unpleasant that seeking out another place is preferable to staying. A public version of the disinvestment process is withdrawal of municipal services, such as fire stations, street cleaning and repairs, hospitals and clinics, and police protection. Sometimes the disinvestment is a result of inadequate local political power to compel the city to serve the area properly; at other times it may represent a city's conscious policy of "planned shrinkage" or "triage" to induce people to move as a way of preparing the area for some form of redevelopment without the necessity of eminent domain and formal relocation services. As with the revitalization phenomenon, owners as well as renters may be forced out, although the latter predominate. The concept of a "forced" move means not just the legally enforceable decision by someone who owns and controls the property to evict those living there as tenants; it also involves a decision by an occupant to sell or depart because external forces have made continued residence undesirable or impossible.

IS DISPLACEMENT EVER IN THE PUBLIC INTEREST?

Given the undeniable magnitude of the nation's displacement problem (U.S. Dept. of Housing and Urban Development, 1981) and the severity of its impacts on those displaced, what can be said about the competing claims of the public- and private-sector actors involved? At present, an entire legal, political, and economic structure undergirds the displacement process. Generally speaking, those who own property have the legal right, within some broad constraints, to decide how and by whom that property will be used. Those who own property obviously tend to be persons and institutions with wealth and political power. As the data below on housing tenure by income show (see Table 37.1), far fewer lower-income residents than upper-income residents live in their own homes. Lower-income home owners tend to be the elderly, who are most vulnerable to the rising costs of home ownership in revitalizing areas. They are therefore most likely to have to take their equity and run when the inevitable reassessments occur.

No national data exist on who owns the rental properties that tenants occupy, but it is unlikely that a substantial proportion of renters have incomes or wealth positions higher than their landlords'. Also, owners of rental property have in recent years been able to organize themselves into effective local and state trade associations, lobbying groups, and political action committees. These owners have exercised their influence over politicians and the political process by electing candidates, affecting legislation, and defeating local housing-reform initiatives (Hartman, 1979).

Virtually every case study of displacement (see the summaries of existing studies in Hartman, 1964; Hartman, 1971; LeGates and Hartman, 1982) arrives at a similar conclusion: those displaced are poor, with disproportionate numbers of nonwhites, elderly, and large households among them. In seeking a new place to live, the displaced tend to move as short a distance as possible, in an effort to retain existing personal, commercial, and institutional ties and because of the economically and racially biased housing-market constraints they face. What they find

Annual income	Percent home owner households	Percent tenant households
Under $7,000	45%	55%
$7,000–9,999	53%	47%
$10,000–14,999	56%	44%
$15,000–24,999	70%	30%
$25,000–49,999	86%	14%
Over $50,000	92%	8%

Table 37.1 Home ownership rates and income (1980)

Source: Census Bureau/HUD, *Annual Housing Survey for 1980*

usually costs more, has less adequate space, and is of inferior quality. Involuntary residential changes also produce a considerable amount of psychosocial stress, which in its more extreme form has been found analogous to the clinical description of grief (Fried, 1963).

Some variations from these patterns have been found in particular types of displacement — condominium conversions to date have affected mainly moderate- and middle-income whites, and the gentrification process up to this point seems to have hit fewer nonwhite neighborhoods than were affected by earlier public displacement programs. Yet the overall pattern described above has been remarkably persistent for several decades, regardless of who was displaced or displacing and for what reasons the displacement occurred.

The motivations of the displacers almost invariably are tied to their profit calculations, or at times to their own class-based residential needs and preferences. For instance, when a gentrifying family *displacing many ppl* returns from the suburbs with the resources and desire to restore an older Victorian house to its original middle-class single-family use, it may empty the house of the several low-income households currently occupying the units that the house was cut up into years back. In the less frequent instances when a government agency is doing the displacing, some version of the "public interest" may be involved. But when subjected to scrutiny, it usually emerges that the public interest to be served is class-biased toward the same interests that undertake private displacement.

The philosophical and political question then becomes: whose rights are paramount, those of the displacer or those of the displacee? Under current conditions the answer is clear. Almost any owner of residential property in the United States can force out a nonowning resident, even though on occasion some trouble and time are required. There are some *legal fact* exceptions, to be discussed below. But the "right to displace" is an overwhelming fact of life, which is why over 1 percent of the population is kicked out of their homes each year (LeGates and Hartman, 1981) and several times that number live under the very real threat that displacement is only a short time off.

In opposition to this "right to displace," I would like to put forth a "right to stay put," a kind of tenure guarantee for those who do not own their own homes. This right would allow them to stay as long as they want, so long as they meet certain fundamental obligations as tenants. While there are some legal underpinnings for such a right, which will be discussed, the fundamental arena for creating it — as with the assertion of new rights generally — is political. In the course of, or following, the political struggle to achieve such a right, the appropriate legal theories and mechanisms will be fashioned and accepted.

DEVELOPING A "RIGHT TO STAY PUT"

In establishing the concept of a "right to stay put," it is useful to itemize the many ways in which the absolute right of the owner of a piece of property to do with it as he/she sees fit already has been breached. Many of these are relatively new developments in law and public acceptance; others have a long history:

■ Zoning regulations put considerable limits on an owner's free use of property. Type, intensity, timing, and many other elements of use are controlled in the public interest, even when these regulations limit the owner's profit and freedom.

■ Housing and building codes setting minimum construction, rehabilitation, and occupancy standards must be met, even though they are quite costly for the owner. These minimum legal standards have been strengthened by court decisions and state legislation establishing a "warranty of habitability" — consumer protection that someone holding out residential property for rent guarantees it to be habitable. Breach of this warranty becomes a legal basis for withholding rent, resisting eviction, and bringing damage claims. Legalized rent withholding and court appointment of receivers to make needed repairs that landlords refuse to perform have provided tenants with self-help remedies to facilitate compliance with these codes (Blumberg and Robbins, 1976).

■ Eminent-domain laws give governments the power to appropriate land and buildings altogether for public purposes, with compensation that may not meet the owner's expectations or claims.

■ A wide variety of uses may be prohibited via restrictive covenants.

■ Uses of property that are illegal or that create a nuisance can be banned.

■ The owner's freedom to set rents and evict occupants is subject to legal limits in many localities.

■ Short-term buying and selling of housing is discouraged by antispeculation ordinances or high capital-gains taxes.

■ Conversion of residential units to nonresidential uses, removal of units from the market, and conversion of rental units to condominiums all are limited or banned in some localities.

■ Property owners who do displace occupants are required in some areas to provide home-finding assistance and monetary compensation to those they move out.

Some of these restrictions on the absolute rights of property owners relate solely to the owner and his/her use of the property: eminent-domain and nuisance laws, sales-profit limits, conversion restrictions, and use restrictions based on covenants. Others restrict the owners' rights with respect to nonowning users of the property, who thereby are invested with a set of rights. Rent and eviction controls and required relocation compensation and aids, for example, give to those who by choice or necessity do not own the place they live in a shield against self-interested or arbitrary behavior by the legal owners. The controls may properly be described as a form of property or tenure right.

We need to begin to distinguish between ownership of property that is someone's home and ownership of other kinds of property. The property someone lives in but does not own engenders a special relationship between user and property, consisting of ties built up around that residency. Breaking these ties — destroying the bonds built up through usage (often long-term usage) — produces large individual and social costs. An extreme (but by no means unheard-of) example: although a family may have lived in a rental unit for thirty years, a decision by the legal owner to end that tenancy or sell the property can often require the family to move out in thirty days, or at the end of the lease period, should there be a lease. The financial and psychological costs of such a move, as well as the difficulties of obtaining alternative accommodations, are in most cases deemed legally irrelevant.

Is it not reasonable to assert that such costs are a concern for public policy? The importance of property as residence and the realities of the housing market warrant legal protection for nonowners. Such considerations are often more socially meritorious than the legal owner's right to maximize profits, ignoring all other considerations and rights.

The arguments for the right to stay put in part derive from a concept of the public interest. (Additionally, Paul Davidoff has recently put forth the notion that a legal argument for a right not to be displaced might be fashioned based on the right to travel that the Supreme Court has found implicit in the Constitution [Davidoff, 1983].) More stable communities are likely to produce greater care of property and a lower incidence of crime. There will be fewer antisocial acts related to the' anger and impotence experienced by those who are forcibly displaced. The rate at which housing costs are inflating will be reduced. Individual misery will decrease. But the underlying motivation for asserting and supporting such a right is primarily an interest in securing greater equity: more rights and benefits for those in the society who fall at the lower end of the spectrum of resources and power.

Let us look at what this right might mean in detail, how it could be instituted, and what specific instances there have been of such a right in action. The issue breaks down differently depending on whether the persons being protected against forced displacement own or rent their homes.

Protecting home owners

The case of home owners is easier to handle (and unfortunately involves far fewer people), since it does not require intervening in the rights and expectations of another actor — the owner of the property — but merely altering those external conditions that are forcing the home owner to sell and move.

These changed external conditions usually involve one of several situations. Property-tax assessments and bills may increase beyond the household's ability to pay. Mortgage-payment costs may increase due to general inflation that in turn triggers an increase in the interest rate under the new variable-rate mortgage instruments now being widely introduced. The quality of public services may deteriorate so as to make the neighborhood less desirable or less suited to the household's needs. The owner's home may deteriorate due to inadequate resources to maintain and repair the building. Mortgage funds to undertake needed rehabilitation may be unavailable. Illegal practices or "scams" related to mortgage financing and home repairs may be perpetrated that deprive home owners of their property. Ways of protecting home owners against each of these threats are suggested below.

Property-tax increases. To handle the problem of increased property taxes in an area that is experiencing rapid gentrification, enactment of a version of some of the more progressive features of California's Proposition 13 would be a relatively simple and effective reform. That is, assessment increases could be limited — in California the cap is 2 percent annually — so long as there is no transfer of property ownership. Only when ownership is transferred can reassessment take place. The reform would effectively insulate existing home owners who wish to remain in an area from the economic forces swirling around them.

A variation of this Proposition 13 feature might be to postpone collection of increased property taxes until title is transferred, rather than having the city entirely forgo the revenue increases. This variation would perhaps better balance the public's and the home owner's interests. The city would recapture the tax based on the increased value upon sale, or it would acquire a lien on the home owner's estate upon death. Eventual repayment of the increased tax obligation thus would be required, without interfering with the owner's current status or plans. Another possibility would be some form of full or partial purchase of the home by the city in exchange for reduction, elimination, or forgiving of property-tax payments.

Mortgage-payment increases. The displacement effects of the new inflation-sensitive mortgage instruments are yet to be felt, but it is inevitable that the mortgages will turn into a major source of displacement. They have indisputably been introduced as an attempt to solve the problems of savings institutions rather than those of housing consumers. Under the traditional level-payment mortgage, the home owner was assured that for the length of the mortgage (usually twenty-five to thirty years), principal and interest payments — the central element in housing costs — were fixed and predictable. Under some of the new mortgage forms — the graduated-payment mortgage, for example — payments rise over the course of the mortgage, but at rates and to levels that are laid out in advance. Under others — the variable-rate mortgage, for instance — the rate and level of increase are not known in advance; they rise (and in theory can fall as well) according to some inflation index, usually with a built-in ceiling.

Consumers desperate to become home owners or to trade up enter into these arrangements; they hope their payment capacities will rise at least as fast as inflation. Many of these owners seem unrealistically optimistic, and some will default as their monthly payments rise. These effects are not neighborhood-specific, but society-wide. The only way to prevent this type of displacement — other than expensive "gap" subsidies to individual households — is to reverse the trend away from fixed-interest-rate mortgages. Possibilities range from consumer and political demands to retain the traditional mortgage instrument to more radical proposals to eliminate mortgage costs entirely in favor of outright housing construction and rehabilitation grants (Hartman and Stone, 1980).

Deterioration in public services. Public disinvestment in basic services, a problem that leads to displacement of owners and renters alike, is an issue that must be aggressively exposed and fought politically, as it was by a community group in the Northside section of Brooklyn, New York. This neighborhood of 12,000 people, an area the city wanted for new industrial development, began to see its sanitation, police, and health services gradually cut back during the mid-1970s. When the city announced it was closing Engine Company #212, located for 114 years in Northside, the neighborhood knew it had to act. The dense wood-frame tenements, nearby paint and chemical factories, and other combustibles made good fire services a must — to close the station was to sign the neighborhood's death warrant. The day before the scheduled closing, hundreds of neighborhood residents surrounded the firehouse and held it hostage. For sixteen months they ran it as "People's Firehouse #1," collecting information to back their claim for reopening the station, researching shortcomings in the area's fire protection system, and running community programs from the building. They also mounted a series of dramatic public protests, including a rush-hour sit-in on the Brooklyn-Queens Expressway following a destructive fire that would have been far less damaging had equipment from Engine Company #212 been able to respond.

In the end, the city finally gave in, restoring services in two stages. The various residential and commercial revitalization projects begun by the residents in People's Firehouse #1 have started to reverse the trend of decline and population loss. Recent firehouse closings in Massachusetts mandated by Proposition 2 J4 have led to establishment of parallel "people's firehouses" in four communities there, the list of which was aided by "how-to-do-it" lessons given by their Brooklyn predecessors.[1]

Redlining. Unavailability of rehabilitation loans in a given area — a practice termed "redlining" — is a problem Congress addressed when it passed the Home Mortgage Disclosure Act (HMDA) of 1975 and the Community Reinvestment Act (CRA) of 1977. In effect, the HMDA provides a data base to ascertain whether a particular lending institution in fact is redlining, while the CRA provides a tool for community groups to use in fighting this practice. The CRA adds to a lending institution's service obligation to provide credit within its service area, and permits community groups to present negative information to the federal financial regulatory bodies when lending institutions seek permission to expand, merge, acquire, or close branches.

While few instances exist of actual denial of permission to lending institutions based on their redlining practices, the few cases that do exist are sufficiently frightening to the institutions that they are willing to go to considerable lengths to avoid the possibility of highly lucrative moves being barred. Community groups have found that the main utility of the CRA has been as a threat to induce lenders to negotiate concessions (Center for Community Change, 1979, 1981; National Training and Information Center, 1979). In order to be a truly effective antidisplacement tool, the CRA needs to be strengthened, and community groups need clear antidisplacement demands to bring to the negotiating table.[2]

Criminal practices. Home owners may be displaced by shady practitioners who prey on ill-informed persons needing help with mortgage-loan management or home repairs. Often they use a device known as a "lien sale contract," under which home owners who fail to meet payments can lose their homes. Such practices are rife where owner-occupied single-family homes in stable, moderate-income neighborhoods are rapidly appreciating in value. In Los Angeles, where such scams have been notorious, they were effectively countered by a combination of good investigative reporting by the *Los Angeles Times*, subsequent prosecution by state and local agencies, establishment of home owner fraud-prevention projects by city and county governments, and passage of new state laws.

Protecting renters

As noted, the problem of tenant displacement is far more complex than that of home owner displacement, since it springs from the competing rights of owner and user of a given property. To the extent a landlord is denied the traditional perogatives and expectations of property ownership, the owner may withdraw. Fewer persons may be willing to own residential rental property. Thus the assertion of a tenure right for renters necessarily means developing alternatives to the present mode of owning and managing property.

More precisely, if tenants are to avoid displacement, they need protection from eviction, from rent increases beyond their ability to pay, and from removal of their units through demolition or conversion. Yet the concept that the landlord has a right to evict tenants for virtually any reason, with but thirty days' notice or upon termination of the lease period, still dominates relations between the vast majority of American tenants and landlords. Federal, state, and local antidiscrimination laws can on occasion alter this dominance, but discrimination is terribly hard to prove, particularly in a tight housing market where there may be many competitors for any available unit. Landlords rarely are foolish enough to announce — in the presence to witnesses — that illegal prejudices have motivated a decision to evict a tenant or reject an applicant for a vacancy. Eviction in retaliation for assertion of legal rights — particularly the right to have the housing code enforced or to otherwise ensure habitable conditions — also is barred in many jurisdictions. But again motivation is hard to prove. Given the wide range of legally acceptable reasons for eviction — including the absence of a requirement that a reason be offered at all — it is the equally rare landlord who will announce in public a motive of spiteful retaliation when presenting an eviction notice.

"Just-cause" eviction. So-called "just-cause" or "good-cause" eviction statutes may represent a fundamental change in the one-sided landlord-tenant relationship. Such statutes now apply to most federally assisted housing, to every tenant in the state of New Jersey and the District of Columbia, and to certain segments of the renter population in many other states and cities. Residents of mobile homes — usually owners of their home but renters of the lot on which the home stands, and therefore particularly vulnerable to eviction threats — are protected by "just-cause" eviction statutes in Florida, and to some extent in California. Similar protection is offered as part of rent-control laws — to prevent circumvention by means of eviction — in New York City, Los Angeles, San Francisco, San Jose, and over a dozen other municipalities in Connecticut, Massachusetts, California, Virginia, Maryland, and the Virgin Islands. In theory, "just-cause" eviction statutes reverse the tenant-landlord relationship; instead of a landlord having a right to kick a tenant out for virtually any (or no) stated reason, a set of allowable reasons for eviction is stipulated in the law. Only these reasons may be the basis for a court-ordered eviction. A tenant has a secure right of tenure so long as one or more of these conditions is not violated. If the tenant challenges the eviction notice, the burden of proof falls on the landlord to demonstrate that the cause for eviction is one permitted by the statute.

Yet in practice the range of stipulated just causes for eviction is so broad — with many lying outside the tenant's control — that no meaningful right of tenure is created. Nonpayment of rent, violating lease conditions, creating a nuisance, or destroying property — all just causes for eviction in most of these ordinances — can be avoided by most tenants. But the landlord's desire to recover possession for his/her own use or use by a close relative, or to

remodel or demolish the property, are matters over which the tenant has no control; most ordinances consider these reasons just causes for eviction.

The greater the number of just causes, the larger the loopholes. If the owner is permitted eviction to allow a relative to move in, how does one protect against the fraudulent use of this reason? The law can include penalties to deter this behavior. But once the tenant is gone, follow-up to ascertain whether the relative actually moved in is unlikely. Even if the relative does not move in, how can one distinguish a genuine change of plans from intentional, collusive misuse of the just cause?

If just-cause eviction statutes are to grant tenants effective security of tenure, they must be written so as to apply to tenant behavior only. This means depriving the property owner of the freedom to evict because he or she wants the unit for personal use or use by a relative, or because the owner wants to remodel the unit, or because the owner wants to remove the unit from the market. Such use or occupancy changes would not necessarily be barred, but they would have to take place only between tenancies, after a truly voluntary move-out of the current occupant.

These are not radical concepts. A unanimous Massachusetts Supreme Court decision recently upheld a Cambridge ordinance that gives the city discretion to grant or withhold eviction permits when the purchaser of a condominium unit wants to evict the current occupant so a new purchaser can move into the unit. The court held that the right to own property did not automatically grant the right to occupy it, that there was a legitimate public interest to be served in government regulation of evictions.[3]

If such rights can be invoked against would-be owner-occupants, obviously they can be invoked against owners whose personal interest is more remote. Controls over removal of units from the rental stock through demolition or conversion to condominiums already appear in several local rent-control ordinances, such as those of Santa Monica and Berkeley, California, and New York City. These cities regard preservation of the rental-housing stock as in the public interest, given the shortage of such housing, the threats to it from profit-seeking developers, the low rates of new construction, and the low incomes and limited choice that renters have.

Thus an important step in guaranteeing a right to stay put is to enact a "just-cause" eviction statute that permits eviction only for a very few tenant-caused reasons — that is, nonpayment of rent, persistent disorderly conduct that neighbors regard as a nuisance, willful or grossly negligent behavior that is destructive of property, or persistent breach of reasonable written rules. It should be noted that in some instances evictions, even for just cause, are now forbidden during extremely cold weather, because of the health consequences of putting families out in such weather. A recent amendment to the District of Columbia Landlord-Tenant Act stipulates that "no landlord shall evict a tenant on any day when the National Weather Service predicts at 8 a.m. that the temperature at the National Airport Weather Station will not exceed twenty degrees Fahrenheit within the next twenty-four hours."[4] Relatedly, the Secretary of Housing and Urban Development issued a telegram in February of 1977 ("Subject: Weather/Fuel Shortage Problems") to all HUD regional and area offices enunciating a policy that "no persons will be evicted from HUD-owned property unless you are certain that the persons evicted are able to move into decent, safe, sanitary and satisfactorily heated housing. Absent such assurances, no occupants will be evicted" (National Housing Law Project, 1977).

Rent controls. Control over arbitrary and inflationary rent increases is another key element of a tenant's right to stay put. In a situation where the demand for decent rental housing far exceeds the supply — the case in nearly every part of the U.S. today — the free market system works to the detriment of consumers. Unlike most other commodities, an excess of demand over supply in housing does not quickly result in increased production to meet the demand or to restore market equilibrium. The shortage and high cost of construction financing and permanent financing, the fear and reality of regulation, high land costs and restrictive land-use regulations, difficulties in managing rental property, and greater available profits from other forms of real-estate development and manipulation — these all combine to retard the market response, which at a minimum occurs over several years. If renters — a disproportionate number of whom are low-income, elderly, nonwhite, or large households — are to be protected from injurious market forces, government regulation of landlords' profit drives is mandatory. Difficulties have appeared in some rent-control ordinances: partial circumvention through black-market practices; the cost of establishing the necessary regulatory mechanisms; reduced attractiveness of owning, maintaining, and improving rental property. But these defects often result from passing weak, compromised legislation designed to minimize offense to property-owning interests, or from neglecting to fashion the needed array of mechanisms that will produce a combination of controlled rents, adequate property maintenance, and protection and expansion of the rental-housing supply.

A well-designed rent-control ordinance must:

- Keep rent increases to a level that reflects only real and unavoidable cost increases to the landlord.
- Forbid landlords from escaping controls by converting housing to uncontrolled uses (condominiums, commercial activities, new construction).
- Cover as much of the rental-housing stock as possible.
- Regulate rents for the unit regardless of continuity of a specific tenancy.
- Have adequate enforcement mechanisms.

No rent-control ordinance currently in force in the U.S. adequately meets all these criteria. (For an example of the specific provisions such an ordinance might contain, see Hartman, Keating, and LeGates, 1982). But such an ordinance, along with the strong "just-cause" eviction statute outlined above (which also does not currently exist in the United States), would go a long way towards creating truly secure tenure for those who cannot afford or do not wish to own their homes. It cannot, of course, make housing affordable for those who have extremely low incomes. Nor will the ordinance be much help to those with incomes that are not keeping up with inflation. Nor will it help with the housing costs that landlords can legitimately pass on to tenants even under a strong rent-control ordinance — for instance, increases in property taxes, utility costs where these are paid by the landlord, maintenance costs, and mortgage-interest costs where the landlord does not have a fixed-interest-rate mortgage. Rent control can at best only help keep housing affordable. It cannot create universally affordable housing.

To create truly secure tenure, a well-crafted rent-control ordinance would have to be supplemented by a program of housing subsidies to those who need them. If, even under rent control, a tenant household cannot afford the allowable rent increase, or cannot afford the rent level altogether without paying an unacceptable portion of its income, then adequate government subsidies must be forthcoming. This is a crucial element of any meaningful right to stay put.

THE RIGHT TO DECENT HOUSING

The right to stay put is but a short step from a right to be decently housed. Effective antidisplacement measures are an integral part of a comprehensive housing-reform program. A right not to be displaced implies a right to have been housed satisfactorily in the first place. The same social, political, and moral considerations that condemn the displacement of 2½ million Americans each year so that landlords and developers can make profits also apply to the tens of millions of Americans who are inadequately housed today.

Existing constitutional theories and statutes do not offer a strong basis for asserting that there is a "right to housing" (Michelman, 1970). None of our housing programs has been regarded as vesting an "entitlement" to receive benefits on the entire class of persons eligible for these benefits. (Ironically, the home owners' deduction, although not commonly regarded as a housing program *per se*, grants to all owners who itemize their deductions an entitlement to deduct from their taxable income base all mortgage- interest and property-tax payments. This set of benefits — estimated by the Congressional Budget Office to be $48 billion in fiscal 1983, $57 billion in fiscal 1984 — accrues overwhelmingly to upper-income taxpayers.) But the policies and rights — and above all, political action — outlined above can move us toward some more solid legal underpinnings. Aggressive, carefully designed litigation can advance the day when such a right will be upheld in the courts.

Recent developments around the problem of "homelessness" suggest some promising precedents. A class-action suit brought against the City and State of New York on behalf of men without shelter led to a court-ordered consent judgment in August 1981. Under the consent decree, the city guarantees to provide a shelter, with minimum standards, for any homeless man requesting it (*New York Times*, 1981). The agreement has subsequently been extended to include homeless women (*New York Times*, 1983b). The men's case relied on a provision of the New York State Constitution that made the state responsible for providing "aid, care, and support of the needy," as well as for other statutory obligations to the indigent. The government's acknowledgment of a statutory obligation to house its homeless, at least to a minimum standard, may be regarded as establishing a limited right to housing.

In addition, the District of Columbia government was recently enjoined from closing its men's shelters. The decision was based on a set of rights deriving from the city's policy on homelessness, its past practice of providing these shelters, and its failure to observe due process in arbitrarily attempting to close the shelters without sufficient notice or the opportunity of the shelter residents to challenge the proposed closing.[5]

The homelessness problem, and the nation's awareness of it, are likely to grow. Cuts in federal and state social-welfare programs, decreasing vacancy rates, skyrocketing rents and utility rates, rising unemployment, deinstitutionalization of people with mental disabilities, and the weakening of central-city welfare agencies because of fiscal pressures are likely to lead to increased homelessness (*New York Times*, 1982; *San Francisco Examiner*, 1982; *Washington Post*, 1982). The obligation of government to provide decent housing for the homeless may be extended to other populations, including those who are inadequately housed and those who can find housing only by paying proportions of their income that make impossible the provision of other household necessities.

The recent rise in organized "squatting" also warrants mention here. In Philadelphia, Tulsa, Atlanta, St. Louis, Houston, and other cities, successful campaigns have been organized to move people without adequate housing into empty, often abandoned buildings. Much of this activity has been led by ACORN (the Association of Community Organizations for Reform Now), a nationwide community-organizing group.

Such actions provide housing for those who need it, build strong popular organizations and movements, and bring to light the contradiction of having empty houses at a time when people need housing. Some of these campaigns are aimed at publicly owned properties, in particular housing that has come into HUD's possession as mortgage insurer when the owner/developer abandoned a property or defaulted; others are aimed at privately owned buildings.

While these campaigns have not housed great numbers of people, they highlight the issue of housing/ human rights vs. property rights. The response from the public and media has been extraordinarily supportive. A major "Walk-In Urban Homesteading" campaign in Philadelphia, organized by Milton Street, now a state senator, forced HUD to turn over title to 150 homes occupied by "do-it-yourself" homesteaders. While government officials railed against "violation of property rights" and "anarchy," the major Philadelphia newspapers supported the squatters. For example, a *Philadelphia Daily News* (August 8, 1977) editorial, headed "Squatters' Rights," stated:

Milton Street stems to be an expert at what no other government agency — city or federal — is very good at. And he is doing it without miles of red tape, bureaucratic forms, administrators, inspectors, lawyers and all the other things that make bureaucracy the monster it is. He is putting people who need homes into houses that have stood vacant for far too long. ... Rather than doing battle with Street, the [Mayor] Rizzo administration and HUD should get behind the man and help him.

ACORN's dozen recent squatting campaigns have received similar media support, with sympathetic "human-interest" news accounts, editorials (*St. Louis Post-Dispatch*, 1982; Brashear, 1982), and columns. Neal Peirce's column in the May 15, 1982, *Washington Post*, "'Squatter' Housing Is Sign of Times," concluded:

Oddly enough, housing squatters may be doing a big favor for Europe and North America. Though their actions are technically illegal, they are occupying only long-deserted buildings. In a colorful, compelling way they underscore the blindness of governments that fail — by defective national economic policies and by sluggish local housing bureaucracies — to provide affordable housing and protect the treasure that a nation's old housing stock represents.

This encouraging sign — that common sense and common decency about meeting people's housing needs may transcend formal, legal precepts regarding ownership of property — suggests that carefully prepared publicity and organizing campaigns can be important building blocks toward political and legal acceptance of a "right to housing."

Additionally, litigation over exclusionary zoning is moving toward establishment of a set of housing rights. In the most recent and far-reaching in this line of cases, the New Jersey Supreme Court, in its unanimous "Mt. Laurel II" decision, ordered all of the state's municipalities to take steps to insure housing opportunities for low- and moderate-income households — a decision the state's public advocate characterized as "the most dramatic opinion handed down by any court anywhere in the United States since the one-man, one-vote decision" (*New York Times*, 1983a).

We are increasingly seeing that the profit system is incompatible with the national housing goal of "a decent home and suitable living environment for every American family" that Congress first promulgated in the 1949 Housing Act and reasserted in the 1968 Housing Act. This goal is impossible if people have to pay more than they can afford to reach it or if people constantly are faced with the threat and reality of forced uprooting. For American society the displacement problem raises land reform issues of the profoundest sort.

Notes

1 A detailed account of this and other specific antidisplacement strategies actually undertaken by community groups can be found in Hartman, Keating, and LeGates (1982).

2 Further information on proposals for strengthening the HMDA and CRA can be obtained through National People's Action, 954 West Washington Blvd., Chicago, IL 60607.

3 See *Flynn* v. *City of Cambridge*, 418 N.E. 2d 335 (1981).

4 See 2, D.C. Act 4–143, new See. 501a.

5 See *Williams* v. *Barry*, 490 F. Supp. 941 (1980).

REFERENCES

Blumberg, Richard, and Robbins, Brian Quinn. 1976. "Beyond URLTA: a program for achieving real tenant goals." *Harvard Civil Rights – Civil Liberties Law Review* 11: 1–47.

Brashear, Bob. 1982. "Housing Tulsa's other 'refugees'." *Tulsa* (Oklahoma) *Tribune* (May 14).

Center for Community Change. 1981. *The Community Reinvestment Act: A Citizens' Action Guide*. Washington, DC: Center for Community Change.

Center for Community Change, Neighborhood Revitalization Project. 1979. *Neighborhood Based Reinvestment Strategies: A CRA Guidebook*. Washington, DC: Center for Community Change.

Davidoff, Paul. 1983. "Decent housing for all: an agenda." In *America's Housing Crisis: What Is To Be Done?* Edited by Chester Hartman. Boston: Routledge and Kegan Paul.

Fried, Marc. 1963. "Grieving for a lost home." In *The Urban Condition*. Edited by Leonard Duhl. New York: Basic Books.

Fried, Marc, et al. 1973. *The World of the Urban Working Class*. Cambridge, MA: Harvard University Press.

Gans, Herbert. 1962. *The Urban Villagers*. Glencoe, IL: Free Press.

Hartman, Chester. 1964. "The housing of relocated families." *Journal of the American Institute of Planners* (November): 266–86.

——. 1971. "Relocation: illusory promises and no relief." *Virginia Law Review* 57: 745–817.

——. 1979. "Landlord money defeats rent control in San Francisco." *Shelterforce* (Fall).

Hartman, Chester, Keating, Dennis, and LeGates, Richard. 1982. *Displacement: How to Fight It.* Berkeley: National Housing Law Project.

Hartman, Chester, and Stone, Michael. 1980. "A socialist housing program for the United States." In *Urban and Regional Planning in an Age of Austerity.* Edited by Pierre Clavel, John Forester and William Goldsmith. New York: Pergamon Press.

LeGates, Richard, and Hartman, Chester. 1981. "Displacement." *Clearinghouse Review* 15 (July): 207–49.

——. 1982. "Gentrification-caused displacement." *The Urban Lawyer* 14: 31–55.

Michelman, Frank I. 1970. "The advent of a right to housing: a current appraisal." *Harvard Civil Rights – Civil Liberties Law Review* 5: 207–26.

National Housing Law Project. 1977. *Law Project Bulletin.* Berkeley: National Housing Law Project VII (January–February): 1.

National Training and Information Center. 1979. *Home Mortgage Disclosure Act and Reinvestment Strategies: A Guidebook.* Chicago: National Training and Information Center.

New York Times 1981. "Pact requires city to shelter homeless men." (August 27).

——. 1982. "Increase in homeless people tests U.S. cities' will to cope." (May 3).

——. 1983a. "Jersey ruling aids housing for the poor." (January 21).

——. 1983b. "Equality in shelters." (February 9).

Peirce, Neal. 1982. "'Squatter' housing is sign of times." *Washington Post* (May 15).

Roisman, Florence Wagman. 1981. *Combatting Private Displacement.* Available from National Clearinghouse for Legal Services, 500 N. Michigan Ave., Suite 1940, Chicago, IL 60611.

San Francisco Examiner. 1982. "Hard times for new homeless." (August 29).

St. Louis Post-Dispatch. 1982. "Toward homesteading?" (April 5).

U.S. Department of Housing and Urban Development. 1981. *Residential Displacement: An Update – Report to Congress.* Washington, DC: HUD Office of Policy Development and Research.

Washington Post. 1982. "1982's homeless: Americans adrift in tents, autos." (August 14).

38

"The Right to Stay Put, Revisited: Gentrification and Resistance to Displacement in New York City"

From *Urban Studies* (2006)

Kathe Newman and Elvin K. Wyly

On 23 December 1985, Neil Smith was in bed paging through the *New York Times* when he came to the paper's most prominent and pricey advertising space, the bottom right quarter of the Opinion Page. On this day, the Real Estate Board of New York, Inc., had purchased the spot for an essay appearing under a question set in large, bold type: "Is Gentrification a Dirty Word?" The essay offered a spirited defence of a process in which "neighborhoods and lives blossom", while admitting that

> The greatest fears inspired by gentrification, of course, are that low-income residents and low-margin retailers will be displaced by more affluent residents and more profitable businesses.
>
> (reprinted in Smith, 1996, p. 31)

The Board's plea on behalf of the villainised gentry was, of course, shot through with contradictions—for instance, citing studies showing "that residential rent regulations gave apartment dwellers substantial protection against displacement" while neglecting to mention the long-standing industry campaign to liberate 'free' market forces by destroying things like rent regulation. But what Smith found most astonishing about the Board's advert was its very existence

> How did it come about that the very powerful Real Estate Board of New York, Inc.—the professional lobby for the city's largest real estate developers, a kind of chamber of commerce for promoting real estate interests—found itself in such a defensive position that it had to take out an

advertisement in the *Times* for the purpose of trying to redefine one of its major preoccupations?
>
> (Smith, 1996, p. 30)

Almost 20 years later, we found ourselves in downtown Minneapolis for a one-day symposium attended by several hundred delegates from non-profit housing service organisations from across the US. Sponsored by the Congressionally chartered Neighbourhood Reinvestment Corporation, the event was held to discuss ways to 'manage' the effects of a decade of turbulent inner-city transformation—under the catchy title "When Gentrification Comes Knocking: Navigating Social Dynamics in Changing Neighbourhoods" (Neighborhood Reinvestment Corporation, 2005). But on the morning of the symposium, hundreds of delegates opened their hotel room doors to find copies of *USA Today*, with the national section carrying a bold headline: "Studies: Gentrification a boost for everyone" (Hampson, 2005). The article showcased the surprising findings of several recent studies (Freeman, 2005; Freeman and Braconi, 2002a, 2002b, 2004; Vigdor, 2002) suggesting that gentrification does not, after all, cause very much displacement of low-income urban residents. The article devoted prominent coverage to several econometric studies of specialised housing and income datasets, including two studies by Lance Freeman, an Assistant Professor of Urban Planning at Columbia University who happened to be at the Minneapolis symposium. Freeman instantly became one of the celebrities of the event and played a key role in discussions of the consequences of gentrification and how to reconcile interpretations of 'official' statistics and other quantitative evidence, as opposed to the voices of residents, community activists and similar kinds of qualitative evidence. Meanwhile, debates at the Minneapolis symposium were echoed electronically when the *USA Today* piece made its way across several listservs, attracting commentary by (among others) prominent urban theorists Herbert Gans and Peter Marcuse, as well as the more neo-traditional neo-liberal urbanist John Norquist (President of the Congress for the New Urbanism and former Milwaukee Mayor). Freeman, an exceedingly careful and rigorous analyst, also circulated a clarification of several issues that had been distorted or ignored in the *USA Today* coverage.

Displacement, always a central axis of academic, policy and popular concerns over gentrification, is back on the agenda (Freeman and Braconi, 2004; Atkinson, 2004; Slater *et al.*, 2004; Marcuse, 2005). In this paper, we report on a mixed-methods study of gentrification, displacement and low-income renters' survival strategies in New York City between the early 1990s and 2003. We begin from the premise that one answer to Smith's poignant question involves *resistance*: the powerful Real Estate Board felt compelled to defend its interests in the face of militant mobilisation drawing inspiration from the legal and political principles established in Chester Hartman's famous essay "The Right to Stay Put" (Hartman, 1984/2002; see also Mitchell, 2003; Imbroscio, 2004). After 20 years of intense gentrification and sweeping public policy changes, many of the people who would mobilise to resist displacement have themselves been displaced. And more than two generations after Ruth Glass's original term was imported from London's Covent Garden into the American lexicon, the urban trade balance swings back a bit, with Freeman and Braconi's New York work informing debates on the UK's 'urban renaissance'. Indeed, a central theme in much of the UK scholarship on 'regeneration' policy is that displacement constitutes a critical litmus test: redevelopment, renewal, revitalisation, regeneration and reinvestment are good, but these are understood to be different from *gentrification*, which involves direct, conflict-ridden displacement. Although this distinction was thoroughly debated (and generally rejected) many years ago (Marcuse, 1986, 2005; Smith and Williams, 1986; Smith, 1996), it returned as a prominent theme in many of the papers presented at the September 2002 conference, "Upward Neighbourhood Trajectories: Gentrification in a New Century" at the University of Glasgow.[1] The distinction also influences Rowland Atkinson's (2004) comprehensive review of the international English-language evidence on gentrification in relation to the

UK 'urban renaissance' and it figures prominently in Chris Hamnett's analysis of London, where he is concerned that Atkinson's research "misleadingly conflates displacement with replacement" (Hamnett, 2003, p. 182). Secular replacement and class transformation, Hamnett concludes, take place "largely as a result of long-term industrial and occupational change, not of gentrification *per se*" (Hamnett, 2003, p. 182).

The new evidence on gentrification and displacement provided by Freeman, Braconi and Vigdor, therefore, has enormous implications—and it has rapidly jumped out of the obscure scholarly cloister to influence policy debates that have been ripped out of context from New York City and the US. The new evidence on displacement is being used to dismiss concerns about a wide range of market-oriented urban policies of privatisation, home-ownership, 'social mix' and dispersal strategies designed to break up the concentrated poverty that has been taken as the shorthand explanation for all that ails the disinvested inner city (Crump, 2002; Merrifield, 2002; Fraser *et al.*, 2003). If displacement is not a problem, many are saying, then regeneration (or whatever else the process is called) is fine too. Perhaps it will even give some poor people the benefits of a middle-class neighbourhood without requiring them to move to a middle-class community (Byrne, 2003; Duany, 2001).

In this paper, we take Freeman and Braconi's (2004, 2002a, 2002b) research as a starting-point for our analysis of gentrification, displacement and resident survival strategies in an increasingly competitive housing market. We hypothesise that national and regional housing-market dynamics create a variety of displacement pressures at the city-wide level and that these pressures are expressed in complex mixtures of direct and indirect displacement as well as succession and replacement—all intersecting in locally contingent ways at the neighbourhood scale. Understanding the full implications of displacement processes, therefore, requires that we examine variations among the case study neighbourhoods examined by Freeman and Braconi.

We undertook a mixed-method evaluation of displacement in New York City to draw on the partial and selective strengths of: extensive, quantitative measurement of secondary datasets; and, intensive, qualitative understanding of the multifaceted experiences of residents, community organisers and other individuals living and working in gentrifying neighbourhoods. First, we modify the econometric methods used by Freeman and Braconi, and we present an alternative view of displacement from the same dataset they used (the New York City

Housing and Vacancy Survey, conducted every three years in order to implement the City's rent regulation statutes). We hypothesise that displacement pressures worsened as the economy boomed and housing markets tightened in the late 1990s; we also hypothesise that, as gentrification intensified, displaced renters regardless of whether they were directly forced out of gentrifying neighbourhoods or moved for other reasons, have been forced to look farther away from the cores of housing market competition to find available affordable units. Secondly, we undertook a series of field investigations and interviews to understand the context for the quantitative results and to gain insight into the ways that individuals, organisers and neighbourhoods understand and resist displacement pressures. We conducted 33 field interviews with community residents, community organisation staff and staff at city-wide agencies in the seven gentrifying subborough areas included in Freeman and Braconi's quantitative analysis to understand better the individual displacement stories and the neighbourhood context for gentrification. Finally, the interviews provided a wealth of information about how low-income residents remain in gentrifying neighbourhoods, a critical point raised by both Freeman and Braconi (2004) and Vigdor (2002).

The rest of this paper is organised as follows. In the next section, we provide a concise review of the role of displacement in the gentrification literature and we summarise the new stream of quantitative research led by Freeman, Braconi and Vigdor. We then present our own quantitative analysis and evaluate our hypotheses on the extent and neighbourhood location of displacement pressures. We next turn to the qualitative evidence, which offers a nuanced view of gentrification and displacement from the ground up. We consider the views of residents and community activists working in gentrifying neighbourhoods, the new places that displacees are moving to and the web of public and private mechanisms that provide limited protections for those trying to resist displacement. Finally, we offer a conclusion that recognises the limited empirical reach of displacement, but emphasises its continued theoretical significance and its enormous consequences for individual families and neighbourhoods.

A GENERATION OF DEBATE ON GENTRIFICATION AND DISPLACEMENT

Gentrification is directly related to how cities experience economic transformation and policy interventions. The urban disinvestment produced by economic change and federal urban policy along with the individual desire for the suburban dream laid the groundwork for gentrification's appearance. The renewed position of cities in the global economy has fuelled gentrification's expansion. We do not consider residential displacement as a litmus test for gentrification. Neighbourhoods, especially those with considerable disinvestment and de facto forms of housing abandonment, could experience waves of gentrification for decades without extensive displacement. When we consider the negative impacts of gentrification, we can think not only of residents who are immediately displaced by gentrification processes but also of the impact of the restructuring of urban space on the ability of low-income residents to move into neighbourhoods that once provided ample supplies of affordable living arrangements.

Since gentrification came to attention in the 1960s, researchers and policy-makers have sought to resolve the sharp dividing line between equitable reinvestment and polarising displacement. LeGates and Hartman frame the issue

> In the optimistic view, gentrification will not cause social conflict and will produce neighbourhoods which are an exciting mix of different races, classes and lifestyle groups living together. The HUD *Displacement Report* takes the position that revitalization offers a 'unique opportunity' for integration (US Department of Housing and Urban Development 1979). A more pessimistic view holds that gentrification will force low-income minority groups out of desirable inner-city neighbourhoods to less desirable areas, thus reducing their quality of life and diffusing and defusing their political power.
>
> (LeGates and Hartman, 1986, p. 194)

These questions are again at the forefront of policy debates 25 years later, although the context has changed. Forty years of experience with gentrification suggests its powerful ability to revitalise communities. And in a neo-liberal policy context, gentrification appears to many as an ideal solution to long-term urban decay. The state, which in the past had been hesitant to encourage gentrification processes, has since taken a much more aggressive role by acting as a catalyst to encourage gentrification (Smith, 2002; Hackworth and Smith, 2001). In the UK, regeneration policy blurs the line between urban redevelopment and gentrification. As Atkinson notes

Increasing demolition, affordable housing problems, housing market failure and a design-led approach to promote 'liveability' and recapturing middle-class households appear as strategies linked to renewal but also to gentrification.

(Atkinson, 2004, p. 107)

Residential displacement is one of the primary dangers cited by those concerned about the exclusionary effects of market- as well as state-driven gentrification. Residents may be displaced as a result of housing demolition, ownership conversion of rental units, increased housing costs (rent, taxes), landlord harassment and evictions. Those who avoid these direct displacement pressures may benefit from neighbourhood improvements but may suffer as critical community networks and culture are displaced (Freeman and Braconi, 2004, 2002a, 2002b; Atkinson, 2000; Marcuse, 1986). Increased housing expenses associated with gentrification displace current residents as well as those who might have moved there in the future. Neighbourhoods become off-limits, forcing lower-income residents to look to lower-cost neighbourhoods for housing, producing what Marcuse (1986) calls exclusionary displacement.

Even though some cities experienced an in-migration of higher-income households in the 1970s, cities were perceived as following a downward trajectory as population decline and disinvestment continued (Beauregard, 1993). This tempered concern about residential displacement and provided an incentive for the state to encourage gentrification. If private investment was pouring into cities, then the government could withdraw public resources. But if private revitalisation was moving so swiftly that it was dislocating low-income residents, then the state could intervene by addressing the displacement issues. HUD weighed these questions in the 1970s and concluded that neither gentrification nor the displacement it produced was of sufficient scale to warrant concern (Nelson, 1988; US Department of Housing and Urban Development, 1979).

HUD's inaction stemmed in part from an inability to quantify the problem. Measuring how gentrification affects low-income residents is methodologically challenging and estimating the scope and scale of displacement and exploring what happens to people who are displaced have proved somewhat elusive. In short, it is difficult to find people who have been displaced, particularly if those people are poor. Atkinson (2000, p. 163) likens it to "measuring the invisible". By definition, displaced residents have disappeared from the very places where researchers or census-takers go to look for them.

Despite the challenges, researchers have used a variety of methods and datasets since the 1970s to make inferences about the extent of displacement. Past research has estimated the total number of people displaced nationally (Newman and Owen, 1982; LeGates and Hartman, 1986) and within particular cities (Marcuse, 1986; Schill and Nathan, 1983; Grier and Grier, 1980), has traced where people have gone and has measured how gentrification impacts displacees. These studies focused on refining methodologies in order to quantify the problem accurately. Few questioned whether gentrification produced displacement.

After the initial interest in quantifying the negative impacts of gentrification, research through much of the 1990s turned to explaining gentrification's causes and processes. Interest in displacement re-emerged towards the end of the 1990s as a new gentrification wave once again pushed these questions to the forefront. Using a longitudinal dataset, Atkinson (2000) documented substantial residential displacement in London and found that 78 per cent of the displaced were in unskilled occupations. Research in the US has produced decidedly different findings. Contrary to past research that accepted that displacement was part of the gentrification process and merely sought to estimate the impact, Freeman and Braconi (2004, 2002, 2002b) and Vigdor (2002) questioned whether low-income residents are indeed displaced and whether gentrification hurts the poor. Both of these studies assert that the literature on gentrification has failed to quantify accurately the negative impacts of gentrification. In their view, questions about how gentrification affects low-income residents remain in the absence of strong evidence.

Freeman and Braconi (2004, 2002, 2002b) used the New York City Housing and Vacancy Survey (NYCHVS), conducted by the US Bureau of the Census about every three years, to measure the number of people displaced during the 1990s, to calculate displacement rates and to measure whether low-income people in gentrifying areas are more mobile than those in non-gentrifying areas. The first part of their analysis is focused on measuring residential displacement. For their most recent study period, they found that 37 766 renters were displaced between 1996 and 1999, which equates to 5.47 per cent of all moves by renters. In the second part of their analysis, Freeman and Braconi sought to determine whether low-income residents were more likely to move out of seven sub-borough areas of New York City that they classified as gentrifying—Central Harlem, Morningside Heights, Lower East Side, Chelsea, Williamsburg, Fort Greene and Park Slope—than out of non-gentrified neighbourhoods.[2] They found that disadvantaged households in gentrifying areas were less likely to move away than similar households in non-gentrifying areas. Echoing many of the themes emphasised by Sumka (1980), Freeman and Braconi conclude that gentrification does not cause the displacement of low-income households. Instead

> the primary mechanism seems to be normal housing succession; when rental units become vacant in gentrifying neighbourhoods, they are more likely to be leased by middle-income households. Only indirectly, by gradually shrinking the pool of low-rent housing, does the reurbanisation of the middle class appear to harm the interests of the poor.
>
> (Freeman and Braconi, 2002a, p. 4)

These findings are provocative but they also raise many questions. First, can we understand displacement if we measure it only as a snapshot in time? The areas of the city selected by Freeman and Braconi cover much of Manhattan below 96th Street and brownstone Brooklyn. We might expect that few low-income residents were left in these areas after 1990 and those who remained stayed through some combination of regulatory protection and individual sacrifice or creativity. Measuring displacement in the heart of gentrified neighbourhoods in the late 1990s creates considerable selection bias: after two generations of intense gentrification, any low- and moderate-income renters who have managed to avoid displacement are likely to be those people who have found ways to adapt and survive in an increasingly competitive housing market. This is a fascinating and important finding, but it does not mean that displacement is not a problem. Secondly, Freeman and Braconi's control group (moves from non-gentrifying neighbourhoods) includes residents of some of the poorest areas of the city including all of the Bronx and parts of Brooklyn and Queens with high poverty rates. We might expect that these residents move more frequently than those in other areas of the city, producing an artificially high standard to use as a comparison for displacement rates from gentrifying neighbourhoods.[3] Peter Marcuse (2005) emphasises the critical importance of the comparison group, as well as the interpretation of mobility as entirely voluntary:

> Do they not move because there are no feasible alternatives available for them to move to, in a tight housing market? ... Do they have a 'lower propensity to move' because they are finally getting decent neighbourhood services? (an odd phrase, incidentally, quantitatively considered:

judging just by statistics, prison inmates have a 'low propensity to move').

> (Marcuse, 2005)

Thirdly, the sub-borough areas constituting their study areas are quite expansive; each includes several distinct neighbourhoods, each with its own trajectory of class transformation, housing market pressures and demographic trends. Tabulating displacement rates by sub-borough area (an unfortunate limitation of the dataset) ignores the fine-grained context and contingency of gentrification (Beauregard, 1986).

We find Freeman and Braconi's work provocative on the basis of its methodological innovations; moreover, we applaud their call for research on the adaptive strategies that low-income renters use if they wish to 'stay put' in gentrifying neighbourhoods that are becoming ever more expensive and competitive. But we dispute the widespread perceptions that displacement is not a problem and that Freeman and Braconi have finally provided the definitive verdict on the costs and benefits of gentrification.

MEASURING AND MODELLING DISPLACEMENT

Our empirical analysis begins with a quantitative evaluation of displacement in New York City and its changes over the past decade. As did Freeman and Braconi (2004, 2002a, 2002b), we rely on the New York City Housing and Vacancy Survey (US Bureau of the Census, 2003), which provides information on a longitudinal sample of approximately 18 000 housing units every 3 years. The sample frame is augmented to account for additions and alterations to the housing stock. Households in occupied units are asked a wide range of questions pertaining to demographic characteristics, employment, housing conditions and mobility. One question asks residents who recently moved into the unit to choose the primary reason (from a list of more than 30 options) for their relocation. Freeman and Braconi (2004, 2002b) examined renter households and defined as displaced those who chose any of three reasons: wanted a less expensive residence or had difficulty paying rent; moved because of landlord harassment; or, were displaced by private action (such as condo conversions, landlords taking over units for their own living space, etc.). Freeman and Braconi emphasise the many limitations of this measure: it may overestimate displacement by including households who voluntarily move in search of cheaper living arrangements, but it underestimates the problem by ignoring those who leave the city, fall into homelessness, or double-up with friends or relatives. Freeman and Braconi also provide a rationale for excluding evictions from the definition of displacement.[4]

We analysed the last five surveys—1991, 1993, 1996, 1999 and 2002—to identify all current renters who moved into their units since the previous survey.[5] We excluded those who moved from another unit in the same building, as well as those moving from anywhere outside the city: thus our analysis is centred on the dynamics of local, intraurban mobility and sets aside the question of how gentrification is affected by newcomers to the city and those forced to leave it. The Census Bureau revised the NYCHVS sample frame several times, altering the corresponding weights for individual observations. Surveys from different years, therefore, are not strictly comparable and thus we must exercise extreme caution when evaluating small changes or differences over time.[6] Nevertheless, the results provide a rare and valuable glimpse into the phenomenon (Table 38.1).

The extent of displacement

Overall, our criteria yield estimates of displacement from New York City neighbourhoods ranging between 25 023 and 46 606 households for each of the time-periods covered by the separate surveys. This translates to an annual estimate between 8341 in the 1991–93 period and a high of 11 651 per year between 1999 and 2002 (Table 38.1). Put another way, the displacement rate fluctuated between 6.2 and 9.9 per cent of all local moves among renter households in the City (Table 38.1). The vast majority of these households were forced to move by cost considerations; landlord harassment and displacement by private action are rarely cited as primary reasons for moving and these factors show no sign of worsening over time. Cost drives the overall trend, with fluctuations in unemployment, income and rental inflation combining to force households into various relocation or adjustment strategies. These constraints appear to have grown particularly severe in the recession of the early 1990s and to have moderated during the hesitant recovery between 1993 and 1996. The acceleration of economic growth in the late 1990s may have boosted employment and income, but it also seems to have unleashed greater housing cost pressures before the sudden uncertainties in the months after 11 September 2001. Displacement rates reached nearly a tenth of all movers between 1999 and 2002.

Our *numerical* estimates of displacement are somewhat lower than Freeman and Braconi's (2002a) figures (which fluctuate slightly below 10 000 households per year), possibly because we excluded renters moving between different units in the

	1989–91	1991–93	1993–96	1996–99	1999–2002	
Number of displacees[a]	31 091	25 023	31 113	43 067	46 606	(*increase*)
Number of movers	381 257	264 712	500 260	485 807	471 988	
Displacement rate	8.15	9.45	6.22	8.87	9.87	
Percentage of households moving because						
Wanted less expensive residence/had difficulty paying rent or mortgage	5.46	7.91	5.64	6.85	8.29	
Harassment by landlord	1.35	0.54	0.36	0.70	0.45	
Displaced by private action (other than eviction)	1.35	1.01	0.78	1.31	1.14	
Percentage moving for other displacement-related reasons						
Evicted	0.87	0.63	0.65	0.76	0.62	
Displaced by urban renewal, highway construction, or other public activity	0.10	0.07	0.22	0.22	0.13	

Table 38.1 Displacement rates in New York City, 1989–2002

[a]Includes only moves for reasons of housing expense, landlord harassment, and displacement by private action
Data source: US Bureau of the Census (2003)

same building. Our *rate* estimates are substantially higher (6.2–9.9 per cent versus their range of 5.1–7.1 per cent), because our denominator does not include renters who moved from outside New York City. A valid analytical case can be made for either measure, but it is possible with these data to expand the geographical scope of only part of the fraction. Those in the numerator—displaced households—disappear from view if they leave the city. If we then define the denominator to include renters arriving from elsewhere, the measure captures only half of the city's role in regional, national and global migration circuits. An expanded denominator would include the city's role as a mecca for élite professionals coming from other global cities, as well as young American Midwesterners responding to what the real estate editor of *New York Magazine* dubs the "*Friends* effect", thanks to NBC's decade-long prime-time "infomercial for New York" (Pi Roma, 2003). (Now brokers speak of the "*Sex in the City* effect", for the HBO series that lives on through reruns.) And although it might be possible to capture the effects of low-wage immigrants and refugees willing to double- or triple-up in a single housing unit to afford the rent, our analysis like Freeman and Braconi's (2004, 2002a, 2002b), relies on the *householder's* response to the displacement question. Since the NYCHVS asks only about the move of the 'reference person', it does not identify persons who were displaced from a previous home and who now live with a householder who was not displaced, or who has lived in the same unit for a number of years; in other words, the single most logical strategy that can be used by a victim of displacement (doubling-up with relatives or friends) immediately renders the family invisible from official estimates of displacement. And unfortunately, we lose sight of anyone who leaves the city. Understanding the displacement rate among these movers would be essential for an accurate quantitative measure of the effects of gentrification (see Frey, 1996; Hempstead, 2002; Ley, 2002).

Regardless of these differences, the analysis confirms that, although displacement affects a very small minority of households, it cannot be dismissed as insignificant. Ten thousand displacees a year should not be ignored, even in a city of 8 million. Moreover, the recent history of American public policy provides ample illustrations of extremely limited empirical evidence (often in the form of widely repeated anecdotes about one or a few *individuals*) justifying major investment and policy changes.[7] Citing low figures to support an argument that displacement is not a problem does have a certain comforting quantitative certainty; but the logic takes us perilously close to a tyranny of the statistical majority in which we would dismiss so many other signs of inequality on the same grounds: racial profiling, illegal employer retaliation against union organisers, employment discrimination, homelessness, racially disparate exposure to environmental toxins, biases in arrests, sentencing and incarceration, personal bankruptcy, loss of health insurance and so on. These phenomena vary widely in terms of their individual and social costs—and, viewed separately, each may victimise only a tiny proportion of the population. But they are not separate: they constitute various facets of the aggressive reassertion of class privilege that has come with the imposition of market principles in so many areas of social life. Displacement is the leading edge of the central dilemma of American property—the use values of neighbourhood and home, versus the exchange values of real estate as a vehicle for capital accumulation. Additionally, our estimates are constrained by the fact that households can choose only one reason from a long list of alternative explanations of mobility. The measure ignores a variety of scenarios in which displacement pressures are embedded in the social and economic complexity of everyday urban life.[8, 9]

Looking beyond the aggregate displacement rate, the effects of gentrification are dynamic and vary widely with context. First, displacement appears to fluctuate substantially over time in the context of rhythms of housing market competition. Although the temporal cycle of the NYCHVS is a bit coarse, it is possible to stratify results by the year in which each renter household moved into their current unit (Table 38.2).[10] This tabulation

Year renter moved into current unit	Percentage displaced from previous residence
1989	8.3
1990	8.6
1991	7.8
1992	9.3
1993	6.9
1994	6.9
1995	5.4
1996	8.2
1997	8.1
1998	8.6
1999	9.4
2000	8.0
2001	11.6
2002	9.0

Table 38.2 Displacement rates by year of occupancy

Data source: US Bureau of the Census (2003)

reveals quite pronounced spikes in the displacement rate in 1992, 1996 and 2001. Secondly, displacement varies widely with *neighbourhood* context. The NYCHVS identifies the 'sub-borough area' for each sampled housing unit, an area roughly equivalent to the community district level. Sub-borough areas, unfortunately, are coarse aggregations of several different neighbourhoods, each with fine-grained variations in social character, housing stock and histories of community change. Nevertheless, mapping displacement rates at this level does give us some limited information on where displacees are going. (Another limitation of the survey is that we have even less detailed information on where renters were displaced *from*.)

Overall, neighbourhood context does seem to matter (Figure 38.1). Between 1989 and 2002, more than 15 per cent of all renters moving into the Williamsburg/Greenpoint neighbourhood in Brooklyn were displaced from their previous homes.

At the other extreme, displacement affected only 3.7 per cent of arrivals in the Flatlands/Canarsie section of Brooklyn around Jamaica Bay. Yet these effects have shifted considerably over time. Between 1989 and 1993, displaced arrivals comprised between a tenth and a fifth of movers into the Manhattan neighbourhoods of the Lower East Side, Chelsea, Clinton, Midtown and the Upper West Side, and a broad swathe of Brooklyn and Queens from Williamsburg to Ozone Park and Howard Beach (Figure 38.2). The pattern cannot be clearly linked to localised gentrification pressures and, indeed, we see surprisingly low displacement rates for Harlem and other parts of northern Manhattan during this period. But a decade later the pattern is quite different, with shifting flows of displaced renters in various parts of central Brooklyn and all the way up to Co-op City in the north-east quadrant of the Bronx (Figure 38.3). Not surprisingly, more fine-grained stratification of the data reveals

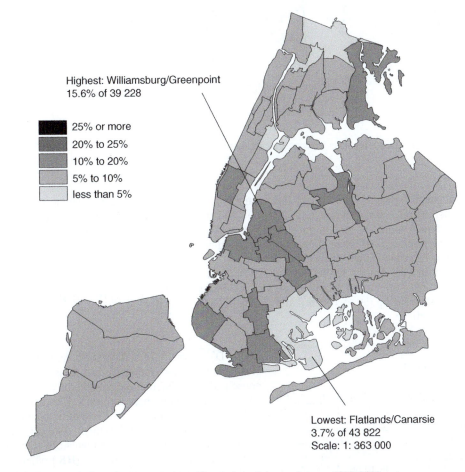

Highest: Williamsburg/Greenpoint
15.6% of 39 228

25% or more
20% to 25%
10% to 20%
5% to 10%
less than 5%

Lowest: Flatlands/Canarsie
3.7% of 43 822
Scale: 1: 363 000

Figure 38.1 Renters displaced from previous residence, by sub-borough area, 1989–2002

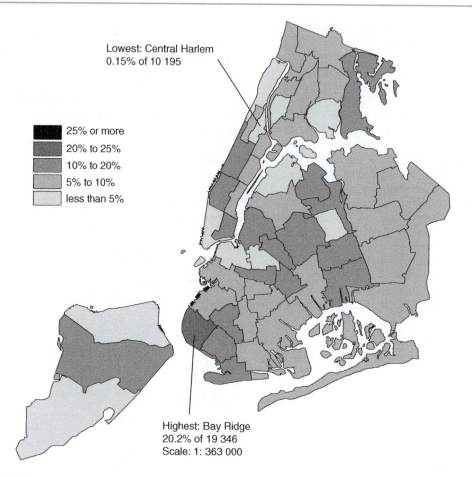

Lowest: Central Harlem
0.15% of 10 195

25% or more
20% to 25%
10% to 20%
5% to 10%
less than 5%

Highest: Bay Ridge
20.2% of 19 346
Scale: 1: 363 000

Figure 38.2 Renters displaced from previous residence, by sub-borough area, 1989–93

even greater contextual variations, although at the expense of smaller sample sizes. Between 2000 and 2002, more than a third of renters moving into Bushwick were displaced, as were a quarter of those moving into Brooklyn Heights/Fort Greene and Brownsville/Ocean Hill. Among households in poverty, displacement rates are highest among those moving into Stuyvesant Town (50 per cent) and Co-op City (40 per cent).

A model of displacement

We hypothesise that urban and metropolitan housing market dynamics create a variety of displacement pressures at the city-wide level and that these pressures are expressed in varied combinations at the neighbourhood scale. The clearest way of testing this hypothesis is to determine if all of the

variation in the maps of displacement rates can be explained in terms of characteristics of the renters. Consider a model to distinguish displacees from other renters who recently moved into their homes

$$\ln\left[\frac{P_{Displaced}}{1 - P_{Displaced}}\right] = \beta_0 + \beta_D \mathbf{D}' + \beta_R \mathbf{R}' + \beta_1 \mathbf{I} + \varepsilon$$

(38.1)

where, $\mathbf{D}'$ is a vector of demographic, human-capital and labour market characteristics; $\mathbf{R}'$ is coded for householders of different racial and ethnic identities; and $\mathbf{I}$ measures household income.[11] This approach yields a baseline view of socioeconomic characteristics associated with displacement. We can then test to determine if the housing regulatory status of the unit where the renter now lives ($\mathbf{HR}'$) differs for displacees and other movers, and we can estimate

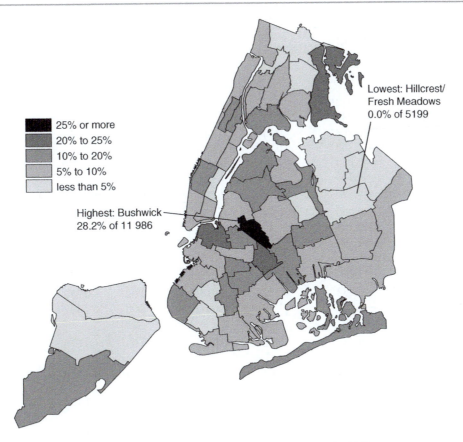

Lowest: Hillcrest/
Fresh Meadows
0.0% of 5199

25% or more
20% to 25%
10% to 20%
5% to 10%
less than 5%

Highest: Bushwick
28.2% of 11 986

Figure 38.3 Renters displaced from previous residence, by sub-borough area, 1999–2002

another specification which adds a set of housing quality and housing cost measures (**HQ′**).

$$\ln\left[\frac{P_{Displaced}}{1 - P_{Displaced}}\right] = \beta_0 + \beta_D \mathbf{D}' + \beta_R \mathbf{R}' + \beta_1 \mathbf{I}$$
$$+ \beta_{HR}\mathbf{HR}' + \beta_{HQ}\mathbf{HQ}' + \varepsilon$$
(38.2)

Finally, we can add variables to measure changes over time and contrasts among the different sub-borough areas across the city. Unless the dynamics of gentrification and displacement have changed significantly over the past decade and across neighbourhoods, adding this final set of variables will yield no significant coefficient estimates or improvements in model fit.

We defined a standard menu of variables to operationalise the socioeconomic and housing circumstances described above. Many of our measures follow those of Freeman and Braconi (2004, 2002a, 2002b), but we added controls for missing and unexpected values. We adjusted income

and rent for inflation (using the regional CPI to convert all values into 2002 dollars) and defined codes for income and rent intervals. We also created exclusive categories for poverty and the income ranges (since poverty-level incomes depend on family composition).[12] Reference categories for the variables are not explicitly defined in Table 38.3, but most of these are readily inferred from the omitted categories for each group of measures.[13] We estimated a sequence of logit models to evaluate the effects of different sets of predictors and the stability of various coefficient estimates. The models were weighted with the corresponding NYCHVS household weights, using a normalisation procedure so that the sum of the weights equals the number of observations.[14]

Model results

Consider first the baseline model (Table 38.3, Model 1). Although the likelihood ratio chi-squared

	Model 1		Model 2		Model 3	
	Coefficient estimate	e^β	Coefficient estimate	e^β	Coefficient estimate	e^β
Intercept	−2.214***		−2.285***		−2.266***	
Age younger than 25	−0.342**	0.71	−0.317*	0.73	−0.370**	0.69
Age 25–34	−0.263*	0.77	−0.242	0.79	−0.281*	0.76
Age 35–45	−0.203	0.82	−0.181	0.83	−0.212	0.81
Age 45–54	−0.003	1.00	0.018	1.02	−0.020	0.98
Age 55–64	0.100	1.11	0.114	1.12	0.102	1.11
Age unreported	−0.406	0.67	−0.395	0.67	−0.528	0.59
High school graduate	−0.060	0.94	−0.054	0.95	−0.027	0.97
Some college	0.105	1.11	0.112	1.12	0.147	1.16
College, associate, or professional degree	−0.100	0.91	−0.100	0.91	−0.050	0.95
Education unreported	−0.320	0.73	−0.302	0.74	−0.173	0.84
Worked last week	−0.082	0.92	−0.078	0.92	−0.072	0.93
Employment last week unreported	−0.004	1.00	0.002	1.00	0.147	1.16
Married-couple household	−0.083	0.92	−0.075	0.93	−0.078	0.92
Children under 18 in household	−0.194**	0.82	−0.191**	0.83	−0.218**	0.80
Female-headed household	0.146*	1.16	0.143	1.15	0.136	1.15
Household type unknown	0.749	2.11	0.761	2.14	0.753	2.12
Non-Hispanic Black	−0.315***	0.73	−0.323***	0.72	−0.418***	0.66
Hispanic	−0.226**	0.80	−0.241**	0.79	−0.313***	0.73
Asian	−0.240*	0.79	−0.238*	0.79	−0.281**	0.75
Other (includes multiracial)	−0.629	0.53	−0.627	0.53	−0.707*	0.49
Race unreported	−10.363	0.00	−10.369	0.00	−10.434	0.00
Foreign-born	0.231**	1.26	0.234***	1.26	0.221***	1.25
Born in Puerto Rico	0.043	1.04	0.035	1.04	0.029	1.03
Householder birthplace unreported	−0.701	0.50	−0.705	0.49	−0.473	0.62
Household in poverty	0.296*	1.34	0.270	1.31	0.127	1.14
Income less than $10 000	−0.370	0.69	−0.414	0.66	−0.547	0.58
Income $10 000–19 999	0.158	1.17	0.146	1.16	0.027	1.03
Income $20 000–29 999	0.160	1.17	0.150	1.16	0.039	1.04
Income $30 000–39 999	0.174	1.19	0.170	1.19	0.073	1.08
Income $40 000–59 999	0.269	1.31	0.268	1.31	0.178	1.19
Income $60 000–99 999	0.168	1.18	0.170	1.19	0.082	1.08
Household income not reported	0.304	1.35	0.307	1.36	0.203	1.22

Table 38.3 Logistic regression models of displacement, 1989–2002

	Model 1		Model 2		Model 3	
	Coefficient estimate	e^β	Coefficient estimate	e^β	Coefficient estimate	e^β
Rent controlled or pre-1947 stabilised			0.094	1.10	0.012	1.01
Rent post-1947 stabilised			0.067	1.07	0.029	1.03
Public housing or HUD-regulated			0.228*	1.26	0.001	1.00
Other regulated housing			0.018	1.02	−0.055	0.95
In Rem housing			−0.426	0.65	−0.651	0.52
Monthly gross rent less than $300					0.663**	1.94
Rent $300–$499					0.541**	1.72
Rent $500–749					0.395*	1.48
Rent $750–999					0.349	1.42
Rent $1 000–1 499					0.373*	1.45
Rent $1 500–1 999					0.303	1.35
Rent unreported					0.485	1.62
One maintenance deficiency					0.239***	1.27
Maintenance deficiencies 2–4					0.217**	1.24
Five or more deficiencies					−0.135	0.87
Maintenance deficiencies unreported					−0.066	0.94
Overcrowded (1.25–1.50 persons per room)					−0.024	0.98
Seriously overcrowded (1.50 or more)					0.257**	1.29
Persons per room not calculated					−9.914	0.00
Rates neighbourhood excellent					−0.373**	0.69
Rates neighbourhood good					−0.357***	0.70
Rates neighbourhood fair					−0.179	0.84
Rating unreported					−0.669	0.51
Likelihood ratio χ^2	77.0***		82.2***		120.7***	
χ^2 vs Model 1			5.2		43.7***	
χ^2 vs Model 2					38.5***	
Percentage correctly classified	56.4		56.9		58.7	
Number of observations	12 258		12 258		12 258	

Table 38.3—Cont'd

*Significant at p < 0.10; **p < 0.05; ***p < 0.01
Data source: US Bureau of the Census (2003)

implies a statistically significant improvement over a coin toss, the model is not much better than that. Barely more than half the observations are correctly classified and few of the coefficient estimates attain statistical significance. Indeed, many of the significant estimates are unexpected: for instance, Black, Hispanic and Asian renters are less likely to have been displaced than similarly situated non-Hispanic Whites. Displacement appears slightly more likely among the foreign-born, female-headed households, those in poverty and those in older age-groups. This socioeconomic profile bears at least some resemblance to the kind of renter discussed in many New York City debates over gentrification and displacement. Legislation introduced in the New York state legislature a few years ago, for example, proposed a trial programme to offer tax abatements to landlords to close part of the gap between rising market rents and what they currently get from long-term tenants. This was an attempt to prevent landlords "from evicting long-term, elderly, disabled, or otherwise vulnerable tenants" (Kilgannon, 2003). The proposal was devised by the Fifth Avenue Committee and press coverage in early 2003 profiled Rose Quiles, a 72-year-old woman who had suffered four strokes, barely met the rent obligation with her Social Security cheque and had lived for 20 years on the top floor of a four-storey Brooklyn walk-up that was not covered by state rent regulations (Kilgannon, 2003). Nevertheless, our baseline regression model provides only the most limited, qualified evidence on the socioeconomic profile of displaced renters. The weak predictive power of the model implies that socioeconomic characteristics predict only a small amount of variation between displacees and other movers: put another way, displacement seems to affect a small fraction of movers from a fairly wide range of socioeconomic groups. Nevertheless, some of these effects are surprising: racial and ethnic minorities, for instance, are significantly less likely to report displacement from their previous place of residence, after accounting for age, income and other controls.[15]

Adding sequential batches of variables to the models still produces mixed results (Table 38.3, Model 2). With the exception of public housing, rent regulation has no significant effect on displacement after accounting for all other factors in the model. Recall, however, that we have no information on the regulatory status of the *previous* unit from which households may have been displaced; the results simply mean that displacees are no more and no less likely to wind up in a stabilised unit after they are forced to leave their previous home. Housing cost and housing quality measures do seem to matter somewhat, significantly boosting model fit and yielding several robust coefficient estimates (Table 38.3, Model 3). Not surprisingly, those living in lower-cost units are more likely to have been displaced compared with those able to afford high-rent apartments. Renters living in sub-standard units or in seriously overcrowded homes are more likely to have been displaced; those who are highly satisfied with the housing stock in their neighbourhood are less likely to have been displaced.

Contextual effects

Although the models thus far offer predictive lacklustre power, they do provide an effective control for those socioeconomic and housing characteristics that are associated with displacement. Thus, adding variables to capture the role of context—variations over time and across different parts of the city—should have no effect if displacement is just a matter of a few imperfections in the housing market forcing a small number of households to move out. Conversely, statistically significant model improvements would confirm changes in the displacement process and the importance of variations across the city's many housing sub-markets. We add three simple contextual measures: the borough from which the household moved; the borough of the current residence; and, the year of the HVS panel. At this point, we also calculated standardised logit coefficients to put all of the measures on the same scale: these coefficients tell us which variables are most important in explaining the overall pattern of differences between displacees and other movers.[16]

The expanded model results emphasise the importance of context, even when it is measured with the crude indicators adopted here (Table 38.4). Not surprisingly, renters moving from the Bronx, Brooklyn and Queens are less likely to have been displaced compared with similar movers leaving Manhattan. Viewed another way, renters moving into Brooklyn and Queens are much more likely to have been displaced than otherwise identical renters moving into Manhattan. The odds that a new renter is a displacee are two and one half times higher in Brooklyn than in Manhattan, even after accounting for all demographic and housing circumstances. Geographical variations, even measured at a very crude scale, post the largest standardised coefficients for the entire model, meaning that they contribute the most to understanding the distinguishing features of displaced movers. There is also some evidence, although it is far from conclusive, that

	Coefficient estimate	e^β	Standardised coefficient
Intercept	−2.3575***		
Age younger than 25	−0.3938**	0.67	−12.0
Age 25–34	−0.2767*	0.76	−12.7
Age 35–45	−0.2225	0.80	−9.2
Age 45–54	−0.0276	0.97	−0.9
Age 55–64	0.1138	1.12	2.6
Age unreported	−0.5443	0.58	−2.1
High school graduate	−0.0298	0.97	−1.3
Some college	0.1355	1.15	5.1
College, associate, or professional degree	−0.0793	0.92	−3.7
Education unreported	−0.1455	0.86	−0.9
Worked last week	−0.092	0.91	−4.3
Employment last week unreported	0.1647	1.18	1.0
Married-couple household	−0.0738	0.93	−3.4
Children under 18 in household	−0.1976**	0.82	−9.3
Female-headed household	0.1531*	1.17	7.8
Household type unknown	0.8219	2.27	2.6
Non–Hispanic Black	−0.4035***	0.67	−16.2
Hispanic	−0.2442**	0.78	−10.6
Asian	−0.2887**	0.75	−8.1
Other (includes multiracial)	−0.6596	0.52	−6.0
Race unreported	−11.287	0.00	−25.0
Foreign-born	0.165**	1.18	8.5
Born in Puerto Rico	0.0668	1.07	1.6
Householder birthplace unreported	−0.516	0.60	−4.6
Household in poverty	0.137	1.15	6.0
Income less than $10 000	−0.5017	0.61	−3.6
Income $10 000–19 999	0.0206	1.02	0.6
Income $20 000–29 999	0.0553	1.06	1.9
Income $30 000–39 999	0.0513	1.05	1.7
Income $40 000–59 999	0.1737	1.19	6.7
Income $60 000–99 999	0.0699	1.07	2.5
Household income not reported	0.2581	1.29	4.4
Rent controlled or pre-1947 stabilised	0.0901	1.09	4.4
Rent post-1947 stabilised	0.0655	1.07	2.0
Public housing or HUD-regulated	0.0302	1.03	0.8
Other regulated housing	0.00848	1.01	0.1
In Rem housing	−0.5058	0.60	−8.6
Monthly gross rent less than $300	0.6225**	1.86	15.9
Rent $300–$499	0.5148*	1.67	14.3
Rent $500–$749	0.3888	1.48	18.2
Rent $750–$999	0.2847	1.33	14.2
Rent $1 000–$1 499	0.3176	1.37	13.8
Rent $1 500–$1 999	0.2281	1.26	5.1
Rent unreported	0.4793	1.61	4.4

Table 38.4 Expanded displacement models

	Coefficient estimate	e^β	Standardised coefficient
One maintenance deficiency	0.236***	1.27	10.2
Maintenance deficiencies 2–4	0.2299***	1.26	10.4
Five or more deficiencies	−0.1024	0.90	−2.1
Maintenance deficiencies unreported	−0.0566	0.94	−1.5
Overcrowded (1.25–1.50 persons per room)	−0.0326	0.97	−0.7
Seriously overcrowded (1.50 or more)	0.2384*	1.27	6.1
Persons per room not calculated	−10.516	0.00	−9.1
Rates neighbourhood excellent	−0.3317**	0.72	−10.7
Rates neighbourhood good	−0.3496**	0.70	−16.0
Rates neighbourhood fair	−0.1781	0.84	−7.5
Rating unreported	−0.686	0.50	−7.4
Previous residence in the Bronx	−0.51***	0.60	−17.6
Previous residence in Brooklyn	−0.7756***	0.46	−30.4
Previous residence in Queens	−0.268*	0.76	−10.7
Previous residence in Staten Island	−0.4228	0.66	−7.6
Current residence in the Bronx	0.0774	1.08	3.1
Current residence in Brooklyn	0.9116***	2.49	52.8
Current residence in Queens	0.4342***	1.54	20.3
Current residence in Staten Island	0.1573	1.17	3.1
1993 HVS	0.1342	1.14	5.4
1996 HVS	−0.2689**	0.76	−10.7
1999 HVS	0.1258	1.13	5.3
2002 HVS	0.2563**	1.29	10.8
Likelihood ratio χ^2	226.3***		
Percentage correctly classified	62.4		
Number of observations	12 258		

Table 38.4—Cont'd

*Significant at $p < 0.10$; **$p < 0.05$; ***$p < 0.01$
Data source: US Bureau of the Census (2003)

displacement has changed over time in ways that cannot be explained in terms of the characteristics of renters, homes and different parts of the city. Compared with the 1991 sample, recently moved renters surveyed in the 1996 panel were less likely to have been displaced (note the odds ratio of 0.76), while the situation worsened in subsequent years (to the 2002 odds ratio of 1.29).[17]

But context is clearly much more localised than the broad variations among boroughs. For renters' current residence, the NYCHVS allows us to identify the sub-borough location of the unit. Adding these measures and estimating separate models over time allows us to test a crucial hypothesis: that the accumulated pressures of gentrification and housing market competition have forced displaced renters to look farther afield for affordable homes. The

voluminous output from these sub-borough models is not presented here, but several key findings deserve mention. First, measuring context in this way greatly boosts overall model fit. On one measure, the percentage correctly classified, jumps to a bit over 71 per cent for the 1993 and 2002 models, and to the 74–76 per cent range for the other models. Secondly, the coefficient estimates point to shifting combinations of processes driving displacement over time. The pooled models imply that, after we account for income and other factors, displacement is less likely among Blacks, Hispanics and Asians (Table 38.4). The stratified models, however, indicate that this effect has been inconsistent over time: racial differences are insignificant except for 1993 (where Hispanics and Asians are less likely among displacees) and 1999 (for Blacks and Hispanics).

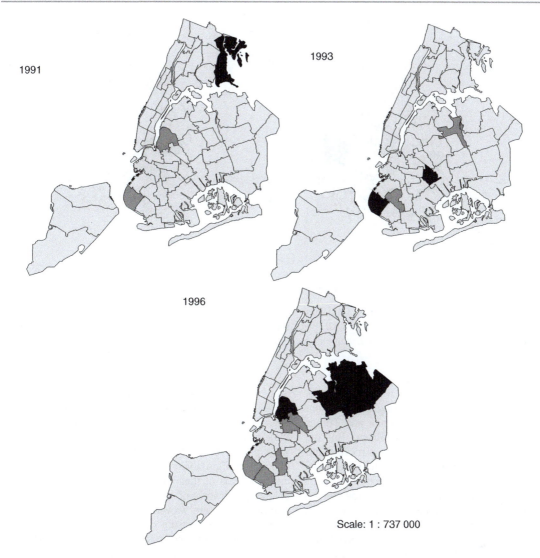

1991

1993

1996

Scale: 1 : 737 000

Figure 38.4 Neighbourhood destinations for displaced renters, 1991, 1993 and 1996

Notes: Statistically significant odds ratios (p < 0.10) from logistic regression displacement models. Medium-grey sub-borough areas have odds ratios between 2.3 and 3.9. Black sub-borough areas have odds ratios from 4.0 to 7.0

There are similar shifts in the effects for several other predictors (for instance, the clearest link between displacement and poverty or low-income status appears in 1999 and is much weaker in other years).

But a third finding stands out as most relevant to our hypothesis. Even after accounting for all other factors in the models, renters in some sub-borough areas are more likely to have been displaced from their previous homes. Figures 38.4 and 38.5 display odds ratios for sub-boroughs, comparing each with the reference category of Lower Manhattan (defined here as the four zones south of Central Park). In 1991, displacement effects were most likely among renters in Co-op City (in the northern Bronx), Williamsburg and Bay Ridge; no other parts of the city were different from lower Manhattan after accounting for the characteristics of renters and housing units. But as the 1990s proceeded, displacement effects appear in more and more parts of Brooklyn and even Queens. By 1999, broad sections of Brooklyn and Queens serve as destinations for displacees. The 2002 panel

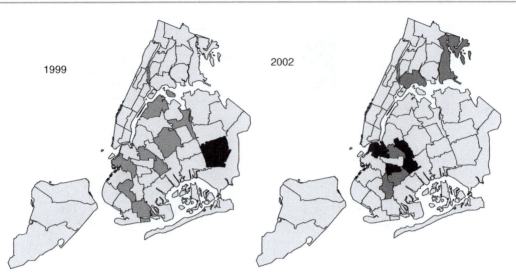

1999   2002

Figure 38.5 Neighbourhood destinations for displaced renters, 1999 and 2002

Notes: Statistically significant odds ratios (p < 0.10) from logistic regression displacement models. Medium-grey sub-borough areas have odds ratios between 2.3 and 3.9. Black sub-borough areas have odds ratios from 4.0 to 7.0. The cross-hatched area (Morningside Heights/Hamilton Heights) has an odds ratio of 0.18

seems to suggest a slight return to the spatial patterns of earlier years, with strong displacement effects in the Mott Haven, Hunts Point and Throgs Neck/Co-op City sections of the Bronx. But the effects are even stronger among renters moving into areas all the way from Fort Greene to Flatbush in Brooklyn.

Overall, the quantitative analysis provides an essential overview of the magnitude of displacement across the city and changes in the process over the past 15 years. Direct displacement is involved in a relatively small proportion of moves within the city, but it cannot be dismissed or ignored: displacement affects 6–10 per cent of all rental moves within the city each year. For those displaced renters who are able to find new accommodations in the city, and who are not forced to double-up, our multivariate models suggest that they are looking farther afield in the outer boroughs to find affordable arrangements. As gentrification swept with renewed intensity across Manhattan through the 1990s, renters forced to seek homes elsewhere moved farther into Brooklyn and increasingly into Queens and the Bronx.

Nevertheless, many poor renters do find ways of staying in gentrifying areas. In the seven neighbourhoods examined by Freeman and Braconi, there are still nearly 54 000 renter households in poverty (Table 38.5). Replacement and displacement both seem to be underway: the number of poor renters in these communities has fallen by 30 per cent since the recession of the early 1990s and rent burdens have risen considerably: by 2002, more than three-quarters of poor households in these areas were paying more than the standard 30 per cent of income affordability threshold; half were devoting two-thirds of their income to rent. And yet the unique patchwork of city, state and federal programmes that are woven together in New York City offer some measure of protection. Only 1 out of 15 poor renters living in gentrifying neighbourhoods is able to do so in the unregulated rental market (the 'other rental' category in Table 38.6). Public housing and early-20th-century rent stabilisation are critically important. This is the key paradox that explains the dangers in any casual reading of Freeman and Braconi's research. Just as the growth-machine class attacked rent regulation in the 1980s even while citing those same regulations to dismiss concerns about displacement (Smith, 1996), too many observers have seized the USA Today headline verdict on Freeman and Braconi's evidence—"Studies: gentrification a boost for everyone"—while ignoring the more subtle point that:

Ironically, two of the most maligned housing policies, rent regulation and public housing, may have a certain logic in the context of

	Monthly gross rent as percentage of household income				
	1991	1993	1996	1999	2002
Top decile	101+	101+	101+	101+	101+
Top quarter	89.4	101+	101+	101+	101+
Median	55.5	56.8	62.7	66.2	65
Bottom quarter	32.3	34.7	34.1	37.8	37.2
Bottom tenth	26.6	26.9	26.9	27.4	27.4
Total number of renters in poverty in gentrifying neighbourhoods	65 562	77 990	71 499	62 306	53 885

Table 38.5 Rent burden of poverty households in gentrifying neighbourhoods

Note: Rent-to-income ratios are topcoded at 101 per cent or more

	Percentage of poor renters living in specified housing type				
	1991	1993	1996	1999	2002
Public housing	28.8	26.1	29.9	30.1	28.9
Article 4 or 5 building	0.24	0.40	0.90	0.51	0.78
HUD-regulated	3.87	5.85	8.00	7.66	6.58
Stabilised, pre-1947	40.1	38.6	37.6	41.4	38.2
Stabilised, post-1947	2.52	3.03	2.1	2.71	6.02
Other rental	7.18	8.05	6.47	6.72	6.34
Mitchell-Lama rental	2.14	3.42	3.68	3.03	5.9
Controlled	6.28	7.21	6.03	4.52	3.73
In Rem	8.91	7.32	5.33	3.38	3.56
Total	100.0	100.0	100.0	100.0	100.0
Total number of units	65 562	77 990	71 499	62 306	53 885

Table 38.6 Rent regulation and poverty households in gentrifying neighbourhoods

gentrification ... rent regulation reduces housing turnover among disadvantaged renters. ... Public housing, often criticized for anchoring the poor to declining neighbourhoods, may also have the advantage of anchoring them to gentrifying neighbourhoods.

(Freeman and Braconi, 2004, pp. 50–51)

It is deeply troubling that public regulation of the market helps to mitigate displacement pressures and that this fact is then used to justify deregulation and privatisation, because, we are told, gentrification is a boost for everyone.

Ultimately, the quantitative analysis has its limits. Although the NYCHVS is one of the best datasets on urban housing market changes, it is ill-suited for an analysis of the full social complexity of individual and family circumstances. Renters who cannot compete in the city's red-hot real estate market and who leave for New Jersey (or elsewhere) disappear from view. Displaced individuals and families who are forced to double-up cannot be identified. And the structure of the survey (allowing only one choice on the question for the householder's reason for moving) terribly simplifies the circumstances of renters who were pushed out of their homes in the midst of other crises, such as unexpected bills that made it more difficult to meet the rent, job loss, or a divorce. Ultimately, then, our quantitative glimpse of housing market conditions across the city from 1989 to 2002 provides only a partial view of the processes of gentrification and displacement, and confirms that we need to consider the nuanced, qualitative experience of individuals struggling to remain in their homes in dynamic, gentrifying neighbourhoods.

DISPLACEMENT: A VIEW FROM THE NEIGHBOURHOODS

In the second part of our study, we conducted field research in neighbourhoods within the seven sub-borough areas identified by Freeman and Braconi as gentrifying (Fort Greene, Greenpoint/Williamsburg and Park Slope in Brooklyn and the Lower East Side, Chelsea/Clinton, Central Harlem and Morningside Heights in Manhattan). We sought to assess the catalysts for physical, demographic, political and economic change, organisational dynamics and the roles of private and public groups and leaders, neighbourhood activism, interventions to ensure that disadvantaged groups could remain in the neighbourhoods and the effect of neighbourhood changes on different disadvantaged groups. We were particularly interested in the trajectories of neighbourhood change over time from the 1970s onwards, which groups have been displaced and or are threatened with displacement, what happens to those who are displaced and public or private assistance and decisions that enable low-income residents to remain in gentrifying neighbourhoods.

Before entering the field, we conducted a literature review to understand the histories of change in the study neighbourhoods. We walked through each neighbourhood and conducted in-depth field interviews with 33 respondents in those neighbourhoods. The interviews did not seek to provide objective or statistically representative estimates of the magnitude or scale of displacement. Rather, the interviews were intended to shed light on the qualitative aspects of trends identified in secondary datasets and on the perspectives of individuals and groups living through neighbourhood changes. Interviews were conducted as narrative conversations. Interviewees were not treated simply as research subjects; rather, researchers and interviewees were understood as "equal participant(s) in the interaction" (Fontana and Frey, 2000, p. 664; Seidman, 1991). Questions focused on describing the gentrification process, neighbourhood change and its impact on low-income residents.

To identify interviewees, we drafted a preliminary list of neighbourhood and city-wide contacts identified through Internet searches, a literature review and personal contacts to start our 'snowball' sample (Marshall and Rossman, 1999). We sought out

community residents, community organisers and staff at local community-based organisations, people who come in contact with those most threatened with displacement, to understand the pressures, situations, contexts and what happens to those who are displaced. In many cases, the community resident, organiser and staff person at a local CBO was the same person. New York's political culture of tenant activism has produced many local leaders who staff the city's non-profit community organisations, often as housing organisers. These respondents, who often live in the neighbourhoods in which they work and benefit from dense family and community networks and an intimate knowledge of their communities, offer an on-the-ground look at gentrification processes and effects.

We present the findings from the field research in two parts. In the first part, we discuss the displacement pressures on residents. In the second part, we discuss the public and private interventions that enable low-income residents to remain in gentrifying neighbourhoods.

Neighbourhood gentrification in the 1990s

Interviewees from all seven study neighbourhoods described dramatic changes in their communities from the mid 1990s onwards as a tremendous surge of gentrification increased displacement pressures. Even though many of these neighbourhoods experienced some form of gentrification during earlier economic booms in the 1970s and 1980s, the transformations brought about by what Hackworth and Smith (2001) labelled post-recession gentrification or the gentrification wave that occurred in the late 1990s, were different in scale and scope. Interviewees describe an influx of new residents, gentrification processes that expanded further into not yet fully gentrified parts of the neighbourhoods, dramatic demographic changes, housing revitalisation and new construction, and commercial corridor revitalisation.

The changes in Lower Park Slope are fairly typical of the changes occurring in many of the study neighbourhoods. Lower Park Slope, home to a mixture of residents including older Italian families, Latinos and longtime and more recent White residents, experienced a massive influx of gentrification that transformed 5th Avenue, a major commercial corridor, and drove up housing prices. Residents appreciate many of the changes, but fear that the changes ultimately will displace them. A Latina former resident who became a community organiser after she was displaced from the neighbourhood described her experience

In 1999 my landlord doubled the rent in the apartment but we didn't understand why ... My rent went from $750 to $1200. So he almost doubled it. There were five other families in the building, one from Ecuador, one from Columbia ... worked in factories all of their lives, lived there for about 28 years; we were there for 8 years ... My apartment was taken over by a couple and their cat. So that's what he wanted. He always said he wanted to put trees on the block. It faced a factory, which he owned. It was part of Park Slope but not very residential, more like a commercial block. He put trees on it, fixed the gates and then sends everybody a letter saying the rent doubled. It wasn't that he wanted to make it nice for us. That's where gentrification affects people. He was making it look better and fixing it up but he was doing it with a mission to put in luxury condos for other people.

(interview, 2003)

Like Lower Park Slope, the northern part of Brooklyn's Fort Greene neighbourhood has been rapidly gentrifying since the mid 1990s, pricing out many lower-income residents who had remained there despite the earlier rounds of gentrification during the 1970s and 1980s. Myrtle Avenue, known locally as 'Murder Avenue', because of the crack cocaine issues in the 1980s, became the site of rapid gentrification in the late 1990s and early 2000s, which transformed it from a disinvested corridor to a neighbourhood asset with fashionable restaurants, dry cleaners and an ice cream shop. The transformation brought with it higher rental prices for the units above the commercial properties and helped to set off a rapid transformation of the housing stock just north of Myrtle which had until recently been one of the few remaining affordable areas.

Central Harlem received an influx of middle-class residents throughout the 1970s and 1980s but the changes during the late 1990s and early 2000s are different. Harlem's residents report a solid flow of SUVs (sports utility vehicles) of people driving through the neighbourhood scouting for homes. One resident described the housing demand: "People are coming up while you're on the street asking who owns the building. It's a daily thing". The neighbourhood also appeals to renters seeking liveable space with manageable commutes. In less than 15 minutes, residents are whisked to midtown on a 2 or A train; in 30 minutes, they can reach jobs on Wall Street.

A 20-minute cab ride gets you to LaGuardia Airport and every highway intersects with Harlem. Rents for floor-through apartments in brownstones are capturing $1 700 a month.

Many residents of gentrifying neighbourhoods like Park Slope, Fort Greene and Harlem view gentrification and the transformations it brings as a mixed blessing. A Harlem resident describes the changes on 125th Street in Central Harlem. "People love Starbucks. People who would buy 50-cent coffee now go in there and buy one for $3.00". But residents fear that their new shopping venues come with a high price tag and may help to spur the revitalisation that will ultimately displace them. One resident explained that he liked the new stores but feared displacement:

I don't want to have to take a train to go to the Magic Johnson theatre. I live on 126th. I should be able to walk to there and when I'm done, walk back.

Longtime residents are frustrated that after years of fighting to improve their neighbourhoods during periods of severe disinvestment, now that the neighbourhoods are improving, these residents will not be able to stay. A resident of the Lower East Side explained mixed feelings about gentrification:

I've never had a problem with it. I've welcomed it. But we feel a little bit cheated. We were here when no one wanted to be here. Landlords were selling buildings for $10 000 to 12 000. Now that it's gotten better, we want to be here too. We don't want to wind up moving. It is so unfair ... We made it better for our community and ourselves. We are here because we had nowhere else to go.

(interview, 2003)

This resident's explanation highlights the irony faced by many lower-income residents. For decades, community residents of inner-city neighbourhoods built organisations and fought to revitalise their communities. Now that these communities are improving, they find it increasingly difficult to remain. In the next section, we discuss displacement pressures on low-income residents.

Gentrification and low-income residents

The rapid gentrification put tremendous pressure on low-income residents. Community leaders, residents and advocates revealed that displacement from the mid 1990s onwards was a tremendous problem for many population sub-groups including the poor and working class, elderly and immigrants. While it is certainly difficult to understand what happens to residents as they move, residents and community leaders report that residents often double- or triple-up with family and friends, become homeless or move into the city shelter system, or move out of the city. None of these mobility dynamics is captured in the NYCHVS dataset, suggesting that it underestimates displacement by a significant but unmeasurable amount.

According to neighbourhood informants, many displacees are moving out of the city to upstate New York, New Jersey and Long Island. Community residents and organisers in Fort Greene and Harlem described a reverse great migration with many residents returning to communities of origin in the South. A resident explains where displacees go:

A lot of people go to the South, some to upstate New York, Schenectady; Albany historically has been very cheap and also Poughkeepsie is cheap and Orange County. A lot of people are going to where they had property, to their families in Atlanta, the Carolinas.

(interview, 2003)

Some groups, including seniors, find it particularly difficult to remain in the gentrifying city when housing prices increase while their incomes do not. An organiser from Brooklyn explains:

Most of the displacement is the result of landlords tripling rents who know that a senior's income doesn't go up. It stays the same. You know she can't pay you $1500 especially when she's lived there with you for years. They have to move in with their kids; they can't go to senior housing because there aren't any—they are booked and the waiting-lists are really long. Often they go live with family or kids which is hard because they are so independent.

(interview, 2003)

In neighbourhoods throughout Central and Northern Brooklyn, we heard about elderly women occupying apartments for decades while paying less than market rate rent. As gentrification transformed their neighbourhoods, pressure to raise their rents increased. Landlords of rent-regulated buildings that offer below-market rents to senior citizens can receive a tax abatement called SCRIE, the Senior Citizen Rent Increase Exemption, but unregulated buildings provide little protection from the increases.

There are few alternatives within the city since most senior buildings are full, with long waiting-lists. Elderly women frequently double-up or move in with family outside the city.

New immigrants face similar issues including accepting poor housing quality, overcrowding, or they leave the city to find housing. A community organiser describes the displacement choices of the people he works with:

People we just worked with went back to Mexico. They were evicted from two unregulated places. They ran out of money and went back. Some people move to Bushwick; other people are moving in with family members. A lot of times you just don't know what happens ... Quite a few of the tenants I've worked with who have been evicted, the Latino population, generally have family in the neighbourhood. One part of the generation lives in regulated housing; another lives in unregulated. They will get evicted and move in with family members who have protection from eviction.

(interview, 2003)

For those with no alternative, there is the city's shelter system. Community organisers described their frustration when efforts to find affordable housing for tenants failed and tenants turned to the shelter system. In 2003, community leaders in a Williamsburg nonprofit referred people to the shelter system for the first time since their organisation's founding in the 1970s. The number of people in New York City's shelter system suggests the severity of the city's current housing affordability crisis. In July 2003, more than 38 000 people, including 8249 families and more than 16 500 children, used the New York City shelter system, far exceeding the last peak of 28 737 reached in March 1987 (Supportive Housing Network of New York, 2003).

These interview reports are of course anecdotal. It is difficult to know with certainty whether they represent isolated incidents or widespread trends. But these findings appear in interviews with sufficient consistency and frequency to provide important evidence augmenting and filling in important gaps in our quantitative analysis.

HOW LOW-INCOME RESIDENTS STAY IN GENTRIFYING NEIGHBOURHOODS

Freeman and Braconi (2004, 2002a, 2002b) found that low-income residents in gentrifying neighbourhoods had lower mobility rates than similar residents in non-gentrifying areas. This seems counter-intuitive but raises important and unexplored questions about how low-income residents stay in gentrifying neighbourhoods. Certainly not all residents are displaced, but what enables them to stay? We address this question in the next section.

Public interventions

Of the myriad forms of assistance available, interviewees identified the city's rent regulations as the single most important form of public intervention. In 2002, 49 per cent of housing units in New York City were rent-stabilised, 3 per cent were rent-controlled and another 17 per cent were regulated by some other form of regulation, leaving 32 per cent unregulated (Previti and Schill, 2003). Changes to rent regulation legislation over the past 10 years, however, have reduced the regulated housing stock by about 105 000 units city-wide, suggesting that the role of this important safeguard has diminished over time (Chen, 2003).

Interviewees identified problems affecting the regulated stock in gentrifying neighbourhoods. Landlords illegally charge excessive rents for stabilised units, send tenants threatening notices to leave the regulated stock, stop providing services and threaten to look at immigration papers. The Rent Regulation Act of 1997 allows landlords to increase the rent of regulated apartments by between 18 and 20 per cent upon vacancy. When the rent reaches $2000, landlords can remove the unit from the regulated housing stock. In a market with soaring market rents, and the ability to reach a rent level that enables them to decontrol units, landlords have an obvious incentive to increase rents to reach the luxury decontrol cap. In Clinton, the area in Manhattan in the west 50s, landlords are reportedly using a variety of illegal tactics to capture higher rents. In one scheme, landlords rotate tenants in rent-stabilised buildings to capture the rent increase, pushing the units more quickly towards $2,000 so that they can decontrol and capture windfall profits in what one community leader describes as "the most intensely gentrified neighbourhood, right west of Midtown" (interview with community leader, 2003). For their part, tenants reportedly choose not to challenge landlords to improve housing quality or charge legal rents in rent-stabilised buildings because they are afraid that landlords will harass them. An organiser explained:

They are happy that they have some sort of apartment even though the landlord is overcharging

under rent stabilisation. In this one building, it was pretty clear that everyone in the building was overpaying at $1700. They were being overcharged but in their mentality, to have a $1700 apartment in Manhattan was great and they did not want to make waves.

(interview, 2003)

In Brooklyn, the story is similar.

The only tenants we have now who are in danger are in rent-stabilised apartments. The landlord has been harassing them for a long time to try to get them out. Landlord tries to increase the rent to $2000 or beyond and deregulate.

(interview with a community organiser, 2003)

Staff at the Pratt Area Community Council (PACC), a CDC, related the story of a tenant in a rent-stabilised apartment whose landlord constantly files frivolous cases with city and state agencies as a form of harassment (interview with a community organiser, 2003). Community organisation staff members report a sharp increase in the number of residents seeking help to cope with landlords who file personal holdover evictions, and suggest that the process is being abused to remove tenants illegally.[18] Tenants in designated SROs (single room occupancy units) are also facing displacement pressures even though they have eviction protection. Since 1983, landlords are required to get a certificate of no harassment before removing tenants in certified SROs. Technically, landlords cannot convert units without the consent letter, but community leaders report that landlords remove tenants by buying them out, converting the units illegally, or cutting off services with the intention of wearing the tenants down until they leave. A neighbourhood organiser in Fort Greene described one situation: "We worked with an SRO building … the landlord cut off heat and hot water. Now it's boarded up" (interview, 2003).

Interviewees listed assisted housing as the next most used support. Thousands of residents live in housing with some form of public subsidy, including federal public housing, housing vouchers and Section 8, or New York State's Mitchell-Lama programme. Public housing offers considerable protection against displacement for 181 000 households. Vouchers provide another critical form of support but are threatened by proposed federal cutbacks. Another 20 000 people with HIV/AIDS receive rental assistance from the city's Human Resources Administration (Supportive Housing Network of New York, 2003). Even with these supports, the supply of affordable housing is inadequate to meet needs.

> Currently 224 000 households are on the waiting-list for Section 8 rental vouchers … A typical family now spends eight years on the waiting-list for an apartment in one of the city's public housing developments.
>
> (Rose *et al.*, 2004, p. 12)

Some of these programmes, like the federal Section 8 programme and the state Mitchell-Lama programme, are time-delimited, enabling owners to opt out of the programme at the end of their contracts and many of these contracts are due to expire within the next 10 years, threatening thousands of affordable housing units (DeFillipis, 2003). Some neighbourhoods have high concentrations of Section 8 housing and could expect a severe loss in affordable units in the next few years. The Lower East Side could lose more than half of its 3064 project based Section 8 units by 2006 under rules currently in effect. Harlem could lose 77 per cent of its nearly 3900 units by 2009 (HUD Section 8 Database). Community leaders and residents are working aggressively, especially on the Lower East Side, to ensure that landlords renew contracts, but this is time- and energy-intensive and produces contracts that last for only a few years at a time, forcing tenants to do battle constantly to save their homes.

Some low-income residents benefit from the city's voluntary 80/20 inclusionary zoning programme, but community groups argue that, given the city's recent upzoning of many neighbourhoods and the expected high production rates in the private housing market, the programme should be mandatory. Upzoning enables landowners to capture windfall profits; the city should capture some of this back in the form of affordable housing units for the benefit of the entire city. Mandating inclusionary zoning in developing neighbourhoods could produce units for low-income residents, rather than simply assuming that units will trickle down by increasing supply. This is particularly an issue as the number of low-income units decreases. The waiting-lists for these programmes suggest the extent of outstanding need. Community organisation and industrial organisation leaders also argue that some zoning changes in formerly industrial areas that allow for mixed zoning including residential facilitates gentrification by allowing residential conversions which negatively impact local jobs and affordable housing (Curran, 2004; interviews, 2003).

Public interventions enable many low-income residents to remain in gentrifying neighbourhoods but they are not the only interventions. We turn next to private strategies including community organisation production and organising, the decisions of individual landlords and resident decisions.

Private strategies

For many low-income residents, staying in gentrifying neighbourhoods means accepting poor housing quality, coping with high housing cost burdens and/or sharing housing with other residents. A community leader explained the choices in Brooklyn:

> If a unit is unregulated, there is no eviction protection; there are no controls of the rent. If you can't pay it, you just leave. If you move away from the brownstone area of Fort Greene and move closer to Bed Stuy, the tenants in the unregulated housing will be families pooling their resources, Mexican immigrant families with terrible housing conditions and overcrowding. One of the ways people cope is to crowd it out. You either accept sub-standard housing or pool your resources.
>
> (interview, 2003)

Housing quality and affordability become a trade-off; residents fear that complaining about housing quality will result in displacement. An organiser explained that some low-income tenants in Fort Greene "are paying below market rate, but they are in really hazardous conditions" (interview, 2003). Some displacees, especially single parents, the elderly, immigrants and younger families, remain in the city by doubling up with family or friends. Overcrowding is a particularly serious problem in poor immigrant communities. Poles and Latinos in Williamsburg, Africans and Latinos in Harlem, Chinese on the Lower East Side and an array of immigrants in Brooklyn often live in severely overcrowded conditions merely to pay the rent.

While many low-income residents are forced to live in sub-standard housing to find affordable rents, many other low-income residents live in good-quality private rental housing and pay below market rents. Interviewees throughout many of the study communities described an informal housing market in which landlords know the tenants, in many cases for decades, and charge rent that the tenants can afford. A community leader explains how this works:

> Landlords are not always maximising their income. Many things affect the decisions of landlords. There are members of the community, there are thousands and thousands of disabled people

and older people, for example, who pay far below the market rate and have been for a long time because the landlord knows them and has a relationship with them. He makes this illogical decision and that's why the old lady comes in and has been paying $600 for the last decade. There are community values that mediate the market. Not 100 per cent but in many cases, there is a community consensus that we shouldn't evict the disabled, single person; this mediates the pressure to raise the rents. As the market rate goes up and up, that consensus breaks down. One older woman was paying $500, the market was paying $800. The landlord knew she couldn't pay it and it wasn't worth it to raise the rent; he didn't really need the money. By 2002, market rate was up to $1100. It's one thing to lose $300 a month, another thing to lose $600 a month.

(interview 2003)

The informal housing market provides housing to many otherwise vulnerable residents but it is highly unstable. These are tenuous relationships that end as landlords pass away or sell their buildings. And gentrification itself has been chipping away at the informal housing market as landlords realise the extent of their lost income and raise rents accordingly. Home-ownership is often viewed as a protection against gentrification but, as housing values increase, rising property taxes often make home-ownership impossible, especially for the elderly and other residents on fixed incomes. Since 1981, New York City's property tax structure has benefited residents who own and live in one to three family buildings. Property taxes can increase only 6 per cent a year or 20 per cent over 5 years and properties are taxed only at 8 per cent of their assessed value (Collins and Werkstell, 2003). A tax benefit created to keep homeowners in Queens and Staten Island from leaving the city now ironically provides protection to home-owners who would otherwise be displaced by rising property taxes. This no doubt provides a benefit for some low-income households, but few such households in New York are home-owners. Interestingly, the tax structure may benefit moderate-income households who bought homes in neighbourhoods as they were gentrifying.

Community organisations play an important role in ensuring the availability of affordable housing through their organising and housing production efforts. Even though many of New York's housing units are regulated, thousands of units are not regulated and there is an important geography to the regulation. Since fewer units in Brooklyn's inner-ring

brownstone neighbourhoods are regulated, community organisers have sought strategies to stem the effects of displacement. Lower Park Slope's Fifth Avenue Committee (FAC) launched an anti-displacement campaign to transform neighbourhood political culture and challenge landlords who displace residents through excessive rent increases (Slater, 2004).

Groups throughout Central and Northern Brooklyn adopted FAC's strategy. In 2001, the Pratt Area Community Council (PACC) created Brooklyn Community Action to build leadership among people who might be faced with displacement. Their initial efforts quickly expanded into Displacement Watch, a programme that "holds weekly meetings for tenants, negotiates with landlords and organises letter-writing campaigns, prayer vigils and demonstrations" (Jackson, 2002). The anti-displacement campaigns and organising efforts are designed to pressure landlords into reducing rents. A community leader explains an action:

The first case we took was for a tenant who lived on Myrtle above a popular restaurant. She had a Section 8 voucher, lived there over a decade, had a kid and was very active in the neighbourhood. A new landlord took over and served 30-day eviction notices to her and another family in the building. Through a clergy campaign and threatening boycott of his store, we got her a two-year lease. This was relatively pretty easy. The other family in the building did not work with us. She ended up going into the shelter system with her son. The landlord did not call off that eviction proceeding.

(interview with a community leader, 2003)

Hartman and Robinson (2003) note that organisations in other parts of the country have adopted similar strategies. They describe these as

useful quivers in the antidisplacement armamentarium, and even when evictions are ultimately still carried out, they serve to dramatically publicise housing problems and injustices, stressing the property rights vs. housing rights theme.

(Hartman and Robinson, 2003, p. 484)

The effect of these campaigns is uncertain. It is hard to say whether a new neighbourhood norm is created in Park Slope or whether landlords are altering their behaviour beyond individual cases.

In addition to organising, the city's community development corporations and other non-profit housing developers have produced thousands of units of affordable housing. The additional production has certainly helped to relieve the need for housing but some, including those running neighbourhood non-profits, point out the limitations. First, organisations acknowledge that these efforts are a drop in the bucket compared with the housing need. Secondly, support for higher-end housing and the need for affordable home-ownership opportunities in many neighbourhoods shift the agenda of the bigger organisations to producing affordable home-ownership, leaving few organisations producing housing for very low-income residents. The housing market boom has also made it more difficult for community organisations to purchase property for development. In the 1970s, 1980s and 1990s, groups could easily find property and often acquired it for free or for a small cost from the city. The city's Third Party Transfer programme allowed the city to transfer ownership of buildings with unpaid property taxes at risk of abandonment to other entities. Community organisations used to acquire buildings through this programme but now find themselves competing with private developers.

As Freeman and Braconi suggest, many low-income families stay in gentrifying neighbourhoods, but the interventions that enable them to do so all have serious limitations. Publicly assisted programmes are losing support and the informal private market is crumbling. Inclusionary zoning holds the most potential to capture some of the advantage of the booming real estate market.

CONCLUSION

For at least a generation, proponents of gentrification have argued that the process involves little or no displacement—and that, in any case, its benefits for cities far outweigh the costs imposed on a few unfortunate poor households (Sumka, 1980). In recent years, some proponents have gone even further to argue that the process is inherently good, even for its victims. The new urbanist architect Andres Duany cries out in the pages of the *American Enterprise Magazine* with "Three cheers for gentrification", contending that it "rebalances" concentrated poverty while offering the improved tax-base, "rub-off work ethic" and political power of the middle class: "It is the rising tide that lifts all boats" (Duany, 2001, p. 37). Georgetown Law Professor J. Peter Byrne does not shout quite as loudly in his "Two cheers for gentrification", but he still contends that "gentrification is good on balance for the poor and ethnic minorities" (Byrne, 2003, p. 406). In an era of aggressive, state-driven privatised deregulation marked by

intense rivalry among cities trying to gentrify themselves (Smith, 2002), the defiant cries on behalf of the poor, hated gentrifiers are at once ironic, amusing and politically effective. Moreover, gentrification proponents have carefully selected from the evidence provided by Freeman, Braconi and Vigdor—ignoring their careful qualifications and warnings. Freeman and Braconi (2004, p. 51) caution that "Even though gentrification may provide benefits to disadvantaged populations, it may also create adverse effects that public policies should seek to mitigate"; and Vigdor (2002, p. 171) is careful to emphasise the enormous difficulties in answering "the question of whether gentrification harms the poor". Yet these caveats and nuances are usually lost in the press coverage of the research: "Gentrification: a boost for everyone" (Hampson, 2005).

Underestimating displacement involves high costs for theoretical understanding of neighbourhood change and even higher tolls for poor and working-class residents and the tattered policies in place to give them some protection. Those who are forced to leave gentrifying neighbourhoods are torn from rich local social networks of information and cooperation (the 'social capital' much beloved by policy-makers); they are thrown into an ever more competitive housing market shaped by increasingly difficult trade-offs between affordability, overcrowding and commuting accessibility to jobs and services. All of the pressures of gentrification are deeply enmeshed with broader inequalities of class, race and ethnicity, and gender (Atkinson, 2002; Curran, 2004; Rose, 1984; Smith, 1996).

We found that between 8300 and 11 600 households per year were displaced in New York City between 1989 and 2002, slightly lower than the total number identified in earlier estimates (Freeman and Braconi, 2002a). However, our displacement rates are slightly higher, reaching between 6.6 and 9.9 per cent of all local moves among renter households. We expect that both figures underestimate actual displacement, perhaps substantially, because the NYCHVS does not include displaced households that left New York City, doubled up with other households, became homeless, or entered the shelter system—all of which were identified as widespread practices in the field interviews. The dataset also misses households displaced by earlier rounds of gentrification and those that will not gain access to the now-gentrified neighbourhoods in the future.

We concur with Freeman and Braconi's finding that not all low-income residents are displaced by gentrification. The historically specific web of housing supports that developed in New York City from the 1920s to the 1970s has played a key role in mediating the effects of current rounds of gentrification. If they were not already displaced in the massive housing market changes of the 1970s and 1980s, some low-income renters in gentrifying neighbourhoods of New York are protected, to a greater degree than residents in many other cities, from some of the direct displacement pressures that have accelerated in recent years. The pressures on land markets in these global cities are particularly intense. But for those cities where previous generations saw the creation of a few regulatory mechanisms, the current environment is mixed, precarious and set for dramatic change. As affordable housing protections are dismantled in the current wave of neo-liberal policy-making, we are likely to see the end-game of gentrification as the last remaining barriers to complete neighbourhood transformation are torn down.

For decades, New York has sought to attract new middle-class residents and federal priorities echo these strategies. But the recent gentrification wave has fundamentally altered the development context in many formerly disinvested neighbourhoods. Focused on market-based solutions, the neo-liberal state and even some community-based developers, have neglected the housing needs of poorer residents. Inclusionary zoning, housing preservation and new construction can complement the market rate and high-end affordable housing development and rehabilitation well underway in these neighbourhoods. Community organisations, residents and organisers are strenuously working to ensure that affordable housing exists, but the urgency of the need has yet to reach policy-makers at city, state or federal levels.

US cities are at a critical turning-point and New York City, as a global city with a long history of gentrification, is facing these issues earlier than many other places. It is an instructive case that suggests the benefits of housing protections for low-income residents in gentrifying communities and the potential pitfalls of weakening these supports. The goal of home-ownership and revitalisation of mixed income/mixed race neighbourhoods will not produce the beneficial changes policy-makers seek if protections for low-income residents are not also included. Community actors and policy-makers have argued that gentrification is necessary to revitalise low-income neighbourhoods. But the context for redevelopment has changed. Gentrification is not a minor phenomenon that affects a few communities; it is evidence of vast urban restructuring. The recent wave of gentrification washed through the city with a speed and a force that few, if any, predicted. Low-income residents who manage to

resist displacement may enjoy a few benefits from the changes brought by gentrification, but these bittersweet fruits are quickly rotting as the supports for low-income renters are steadily dismantled.

Notes

1 Many of the papers presented at the September 2002 conference were published in the November 2003 issue of *Urban Studies*, while several others appear in *The New Urban Colonialism* (Atkinson and Bridge, 2005).

2 The NYCHVS uses sub-borough areas, which are similar to Community Districts. Sub-borough areas are quite large and include a number of neighbourhoods with different political cultures, physical and locational characteristics and populations.

3 Hartman and Robinson (2003, p. 467) cite evidence on the higher mobility rates of lower-income renters.

4 Freeman and Braconi's displacement estimates are presented in a table in their article in *The Urban Prospect* (2002a, p. 2), and their definitions are described at length in a longer, preliminary version of their 2003 *JAPA* article that was kindly provided by Lance Freeman (Freeman and Braconi, 2002b). They exclude evictions from the definition of displacement because, they suggest, the processes associated with evictions are theoretically and practically distinct from the processes driving gentrification-induced displacement. In particular, Freeman and Braconi note that the vast majority of eviction notices are filed against tenants who fail to pay rent and that most of these court filings do not result in actual evictions:

> We have not included evictions in our estimate of displacement because both anecdote and logic suggest that nonpayment evictions are more often due to household financial crises than to incremental rent increases, even if relatively large. Short of an abrupt shock to income or to non-housing household expenditures, a rational renter would not remain in an unaffordable dwelling unit until the point where a non-payment eviction order is executed.
>
> (Freeman and Braconi, 2002a, pp. 10–11)

To maintain comparability, our analysis follows Freeman and Braconi in excluding evictions from the displacement estimates; yet it is crucial to recognise the substantial implications of this decision. Freeman and Braconi cite a total of 23 830 evictions in 1999–compared with a total estimate of 37 766 movers who were displaced over a 4-year period (1996–99) according to their more limited set of criteria. As Hartman and Robinson (2003, p. 463) emphasise, tenants threatened with eviction face a long and complicated legal process and they "may move out and give up the battle at many different stages". As a consequence, even the few official data sources on evictions that do exist may understate the full extent of forced evictions. This is particularly important in cases where renters are facing a variety of individual and household difficulties at the time when a landlord initiates the action, either through friendly pressures, various forms of harassment or formal legal process. Renters may or may not cite 'eviction' as the single most important reason for their previous move when asked in the NYCHVS if, for example, they were subtly pressured by a landlord at the time that they were going through a divorce and having increasing difficulty paying a rent that had increased steadily over the previous few years.

5 We used a three-year time window for 1991 and 1993, and a four-year window in the case of the other surveys. This maximises coverage of householders who moved between 1989 and 2002, but it does introduce the possibility of some double-counting: our dataset might, for instance, include a renter who moved into a unit in 1993 and responded to both the 1993 and 1996 NYCHVS questionnaires. Our dataset, which combines the multiple waves of the NYCHVS, cannot therefore be used to obtain unbiased estimates of overall mobility rates. But there is no reason for any systematic relationship between this possible double-counting and the incidence of displacement, so our analysis should not be affected.

6 The Census Bureau has reweighted the microdata files when new information from the decennial Census counts have become available. The Bureau produced a matched version of the 1991, 1993, 1996 and 1999 files permitting comparable analyses of certain trends in the existing housing stock for these years. But the 2002 survey (as well as the 2005 survey now underway) is weighted according to the 2000 Census count and thus cannot be taken as strictly comparable with the earlier sample factors.

7 The clearest illustrations in the US include welfare reform, in which Ronald Reagan's apocryphal (and ideologically powerful) story about a 'welfare queen' driving a Cadillac animated Congressional debates in the 1980s and resurfaced in social-scientific guise in the underclass literatures of the 1990s; the transformation of public housing, in which underfunding and severe deterioration of a small subset of a small fraction of the nation's small stock of affordable government-owned housing was used to justify sweeping changes emphasising deconcentration and market-oriented vouchers for housing 'choice'; and the selective use of measures of extremely rare (but high-impact) events, most notably violent crime and terrorism, to justify increased expenditures on policing, surveillance and 'security'–and to legitimate ever deeper cuts in investments for social welfare.

8 Consider the hypothetical case of two young people living separately with their families in Hell's Kitchen in the late 1990s, as the area began to witness significant reinvestment and rental inflation. If these people wish to move into a new place together, they may not even think of looking nearby in their suddenly popular, suddenly unaffordable neighbourhood. If they manage to find a run-down apartment on a subway line in Bushwick and they are asked in the NYCHVS why they left their previous residence, the one designated as the 'householder' will almost certainly choose 'newly married' or 'wanted to establish separate household'. But as we will see from the qualitative results later in this study, these partners were unable to establish their new household in their gentrifying neighbourhood and would certainly have strong feelings about gentrification and displacement, even if they did not meet the strict criteria used here.

9 It is also important to re-emphasise that displaced households 'disappear' from the data if they double up or leave the city. If gentrification-induced displacement follows the pattern of eviction, this bias is likely to be substantial. The number of NYCHVS renter households reporting eviction from their prior residence is only about a tenth of the figure of actual evictions reported by the Rent Guidelines Board (2000, p. 56).

10 This stratification is vulnerable to the possibility of double-counting described in note 5 and so the number of households is not shown. Since there is no reason to expect this replication to be more or less common among displacees, the *rates* should be immune to bias.

11 We considered alternative modelling approaches (such as probit analysis), and ultimately settled on the logit framework as the most

intuitive and appropriate. Logistic regression makes the assumption that the underlying response variable is qualitative (directly relevant for our needs), while probit analysis assumes an underlying quantitative response corresponding to the cumulative normal distribution function (Pampel, 2000). Both approaches yield similar results in terms of coefficient direction and significance, but logit results are more readily interpreted.

12 This means that our low-income, non-poverty categories are comprised of students, single-person households and others with limited resources who would nevertheless not be classified as poor by the Census Bureau.

13 For example, the reference category for age is persons over age 65; for education, less than a high school diploma or G.E.D.; and for employment status, did not work last week. For the rent regulation variables, the reference category is private, unregulated market rentals: public housing and HUD-regulated units include those owned and managed by the New York City Housing Authority and units in buildings receiving subsidies that require HUD to regulate rents in the building. The HUD lists used by Census Bureau staff to code the NYCHVS are organised by building rather than housing unit, so they do not identify units where renters receive Section 8 certificates or vouchers unless the entire building is federally subsidised (see US Bureau of the Census, 1999). For the race and ethnicity of the householder, those choosing multiple responses on the 2002 survey constitute only 0.65 per cent of the weighted population estimate of renters moving since the previous survey; these householders are included in the category for 'other' race.

14 The *weighting* procedure is necessary to adjust for the fact that some populations are represented better than others in the survey sample; the *normalisation* procedure is necessary because simply weighting the regression will artificially inflate the statistical significance of coefficient estimates.

15 The unexpected racial and ethnic contrasts in displacement, coupled with the lack of consistent income variations, present some intriguing possibilities. A generation of immigration and suburbanisation has transformed many facets of New York City's housing and neighbourhoods, and thus it is entirely possible that we must reconsider longstanding assumptions regarding the disparate impacts of displacement. Yet definitive conclusions are problematic

because of the invisibility of displaced renters who leave the city: all of the model coefficients for race/ethnicity and income are subject to bias if those leaving the city are different from displacees who manage to find alternative apartments in New York. Obviously, the NYCHVS cannot be used to test for or control these biases. But there is a general consensus that out-migration cannot be ignored: the city is a key national source for retirement migrants (who tend to be middle- or higher-income Whites) and the long-running 'balkanisation' debate implies that immigration accelerates the departure of unskilled native-born workers (Frey, 1996). The precise mixture of these class and racial/ethnic variations remains unclear; but Ley's (2002) recent analysis of Canadian and Australian evidence points to the importance of housing market pressures more than job competition and there are other signs corroborating the notion that some displacees may be leaving the city. Stack's (1996) ethnographic work reveals that strengthened migration streams of African Americans out of northern industrial cities have been important factors in a number of poor rural counties in the South. In an analysis of New York City in the 1980s, Hempstead (2001, 2002) found little evidence that immigration-induced labour market competition drove unskilled native-born workers out of New York; but she did find that native-born Blacks and Whites are equally likely to move out of the metropolitan area—a stark contrast to the predominance of Whites in intracity and city-to-suburb moves (Hempstead, 2001). And in a rare examination of the relationship between migration and changes in household structure, Salvo *et al.* (1990) drew on PUMS data for the 1.5 million persons in households who lived outside New York City in 1980 and who had at least one household member who migrated from the city since 1975; among their findings were distinctive patterns among native-born African Americans and Puerto-Ricans "indicative of return migration into existing married-couple households" (Salvo *et al.*, 1990, p. 316).

16 The standardised coefficients are calculated as

$$100 \times [(e^{\beta_i \sigma_i}) = 1]$$

where, β_i is the coefficient estimate for predictor variable i; σ_i is the standard deviation of variable i, and e is the base of the natural logs.

17 These findings are not conclusive and must be regarded with caution because of changes in the

Census Bureau's weighting procedures for different HVS samples. Pooling these samples and coding dummies for the years introduces a risk that the coefficient will measure two things that cannot be separated: the phenomenon of interest (in this case, systemic changes over time); and, changes in the sample design and weighting schemes between different HVS panels. This risk depends on whether changes in the sample frame had different effects on the coverage of displacees versus other renters. Stratifying the models for separate HVS panels, as done here, eliminates this risk entirely and thus provides a safer way to evaluate changes over time.

18 Landlords can file personal holdover evictions to occupy rent-stabilised units for their own use or for use by a family member.

REFERENCES

ATKINSON, R. (2000) Measuring gentrification and displacement in Greater London, *Urban Studies*, 37(1), pp. 149–165.

ATKINSON, R. (2002) *Does gentrification help or harm urban neighbourhoods? An assessment of the evidence-base in the context of the new urban agenda*. Paper 5, Center for Neighborhood Research. June (accessed on-line).

ATKINSON, R. (2004) The evidence on the impact of gentrification: new lessons for the urban renaissance?, *European Journal of Housing Policy*, 4(1), pp 107–131.

ATKINSON, R. and BRIDGE, G. (Eds) (2005) *The New Urban Colonialism: New Perspectives on the Gentry in the City*. London: Routledge.

BEAUREGARD, R. (1986) The chaos and complexity of gentrification, in: N. SMITH and P. WILLIAMS (Eds) *Gentrification of the City*. London: Unwin Hyman.

BEAUREGARD, R. (1989) The spatial transformation of postwar Philadelphia, in: R. BEAUREGARD (Ed.) *Atop the Urban Hierarchy*, pp. 197–240. Totowa, NJ: Rowman and Littlefield.

BEAUREGARD, R. (1993) *Voices of Decline*. Oxford: Blackwell.

BERRY, B. (1985) Islands of renewal in seas of decay, in: P. PETERSON (Ed.) *The New Urban Reality*. Washington, DC: The Brookings Institute.

BYRNE, J. P. (2003) Two cheers for gentrification, *Howard Law Journal*, 46(3), pp. 405–432.

CHEN, D. (2003) Bit by bit, government eases its grip on rents in New York, *New York Times*, 19 November.

COLLINS, J. A. and WERKSTELL, B. (2003) *The New York City Property Tax: An Overview in Plain English*. New York: Drum Major Institute for Public Policy. (http://www.drummajorinstitute.org/plugin/template/dmi/14/1461; accessed 24 November).

CRUMP, J. (2002) Deconcentration by demolition: public housing, poverty, and urban policy, *Environment and Planning D*, 20, pp 581–596.

CURRAN, W. (2004) Gentrification and the nature of work: exploring links in Williamsburg, Brooklyn, *Environment and Planning A*, 36(7), pp. 1141–1330.

DEFILIPPIS, J. (2003) *Keeping the doors open: HUD-subsidized housing in New York City*. Community Service Society Policy Brief (http://www.cssny.org/pubs/policybrief/policybrief13.pdf; accessed 21 January).

DUANY, A. (2001) Three cheers for gentrification, *American Enterprise Magazine*, April/May, pp. 36–39.

FONTANA, A. and FREY, J. H. (2000) The interview: from structured questions to negotiated text, in: N. DENZIN and Y. LINCOLN (Eds) *Handbook of Qualitative Research*. 2nd edn. Thousand Oaks, CA: Sage Publications.

FRASER, J., LEPOFSKY, J., KICK, E. and WILLIAMS, J. (2003). The construction of the local and the limits of contemporary community-building in the United States, *Urban Affairs Review*, 38, pp. 417–445.

FREEMAN, L. and BRACONI, F. (2004) Displacement or succession? Residential mobility in gentrifying neighborhoods, *Urban Affairs Review*, 40(4), pp. 463–491.

FREEMAN, L. and BRACONI, F. (2002a) Gentrification and displacement, *The Urban Prospect*, 8(1), pp. 1–4

FREEMAN, L. and BRACONI, F. (2002b). *Gentrification and displacement: New York City in the 1990s*. Unpublished draft manuscript.

FREEMAN, L. and BRACONI, F. (2004) Gentrification and displacement: New York City in the 1990s, *Journal of the American Planning Association*, 70(1), pp. 39–52.

FREY, W. (1996) Immigration, domestic migration, and demographic balkanization, *Population and Development Review*, 22, pp. 741–763.

FREY, W. (2004) *The new great migration: Black Americans' return to the South, 1965–2000*. Washington, DC: The Brookings Institution, Center on Urban and Metropolitan Policy.

GRIER, G. and GRIER, E. (1980) Urban displacement: a reconnaissance, in: S. BRADWAY LASKA and D. SPAIN (Eds) *Back to the City: Issues* in *Neighborhood Renovation*, pp. 252–269. New York: Pergamon Press.

HACKWORTH, J. and SMITH, N. (2001) The changing state of gentrification, *Tijdschrift voor Economische en Sociale Geografie*, 92(4), pp. 464–477.

HAMNETT, C. (2003) *Unequal City: London in the Global Arena*. London: Routledge.

HAMPSON, R. (2005) Studies: gentrification a boost for everyone, *USA Today*, 20 April, pp. 13A–14A.

HARTMAN, C. (1984/2002) Right to stay put, reprinted in: *Between Eminence and Notoriety*. New Brunswick, NJ: CUPR Press.

HARTMAN, C. and ROBINSON, D. (2003) Evictions: the hidden housing problem, *Housing Policy Debate*, 14(4), pp. 461–501.

HEMPSTEAD, K. (2001) *Immigration and native migration in New York City, 1985–1990*. Unpublished working paper (available at www.newschool.edu/icmec/lucepaper2.htm; accessed 14 August 2003).

HEMPSTEAD, K. (2002) Immigration and Net Migration in New York City 1980–90: A Small-Area Analysis, *Policy Studies Journal*, 30(1), pp. 92–107.

IMBROSCIO, D. L. (2004) Can we grant a right to place?, *Politics & Society*, 32(4), pp. 575–609.

JACKSON, N. B. (2002) "If you're thinking of living in Fort Greene. Diversity, Culture and Brown-stones, too", *New York Times*, 1 September, p. 5.

KILGANNON, C. (2003) In a test program, a landlord gets to play the good guy, *New York Times*, 28 February.

LEES, L. (2000) A reappraisal of gentrification: towards a 'geography of gentrification', *Progress in Human Geography*, 24(3), pp. 389–408.

LEGATES, R. and HARTMAN, C. (1986) The anatomy of displacement in the US, in: N. SMITH and P. WILLIAMS (Eds) *The Gentrification of the City*, pp. 178–200. Boston, MA: Allen and Unwin.

LEY, D. (2002) *Immigration and domestic migration in gateway cities: Canadian and Australian reflections on an 'American dilemma*. Center for Research on Immigration and Integration in the Metropolis, Vancouver.

MARCUSE, P. (1986) Abandonment, gentrification, and displacement: the linkages in New York City, in: N. SMITH and P. WILLIAMS (Eds) *Gentrification and the City*, pp. 153–177. London: Unwin Hyman.

MARCUSE, P. (2005) *On the presentation of research about gentrification*. Department of Urban Planning, Columbia University, New York.

MARSHALL, C. and ROSSMAN, G. (2000) *Designing Qualitative Research*. 3rd edn. Thousand Oaks, CA: Sage Publications.

MERRIFIELD, A. (2002) *Dialectical Urbanism: Social Struggles in the Capitalist City*. Monthly Review Press.

MITCHELL, D. (2003) *The Right to the City: Social Justice and the Fight for Public Space*. New York: Guilford Press.

NEIGHBORHOOD REINVESTMENT CORPORATION (2005) *When gentrification comes knocking: navigating social dynamics in changing neighborhoods*. Conference Binder CB901, Symposium on 20 April. Washington, DC: Neighborhood Reinvestment Corporation.

NELSON, K. (1988) *Gentrification and Distressed Cities: An Assessment of Trends in Intrametropolitan Migration*. Madison, WI: University of Wisconsin Press.

NEWMAN, S. J. and OWEN, M. S. (1982) *Residential displacement in the U.S.: 1970–1977*. Ann Arbor, MI: The University of Michigan, Institute for Social Research.

PAMPEL, F. C. (2000) *Logistic Regression: A Primer*. Quantitative Applications in the Social Sciences No. 132. Thousand Oaks, CA: Sage Publications.

PI ROMA, R. (2003) *Interview with Chris Bonanos, Real Estate Editor of New York Magazine*. New York Voices (available at www.thirteen.org; accessed 30 July).

PREVITI, D. and SCHILL, M. (2003) *The State of New York City's Neighborhoods, 2003*. New York City: Center for Real Estate and Urban Policy.

RENT GUIDELINES BOARD (2000) *Housing NYC: Rents, Markets, and Trends 2000*. New York City: New York City Rent Guidelines Board.

ROFE, M. (2004) From 'problem city' to 'promise city': gentrification and the revitalization of Newcastle, *Australian Geographical Studies*, 42(2), pp. 193–206.

ROSE, D. (1984) Rethinking gentrification: beyond the uneven development of Marxist urban theory, *Society and Space*, 2, pp. 24–74.

ROSE, K., LANDER, B. and FENG, K. (2004) *Increasing housing opportunity in New York City: the case for inclusionary zoning*. A Report by Policy-Link and Pratt Institute Center for Community and Environmental Development.

SALVO, J., BANKS, L. E. and MANN, E. S. (1990) Reconceptualizing migration as a household phenomenon: outmigration from New York City by race and Hispanic origin, *International Migration*, 28(3), pp. 311–325.

Schill, M. and Nathan, R. (1983) *Revitalizing America's Cities: Neighborhood Reinvestment and Displacement*. Albany: SUNY Press.

Seidman, E. (1991) *Interviewing as Qualitative Research*. New York: Teachers College Press.

Slater, T. (2004) North American gentrification? Revanchist and emancipatory perspectives explored, *Environment and Planning A*, 36(7), pp. 1191–1213.

Slater, T., Curran, W. and Lees, L. (2004). Guest editorial, *Environment and Planning A*, 36(7), pp. 1141–1150.

Smith, N. (1996) *The New Urban Frontier: Gentrification and the Revanchist City*. New York: Routledge.

Smith, N. (2002) New globalism, new urbanism: gentrification as global urban strategy, *Antipode*, 34(3), pp. 427–450.

Smith, N. and Williams, P. (Eds) (1986) *Gentrification of the City*. London: Unwin Hyman.

Stack, C. (1996) *Call to Home*. New York: Basic Books.

Sumka, H. (1980) Federal antidisplacement policy in a context of urban decline, in: S. Laska and D. Spain (Eds) *Back to the City: Issues in Neighborhood Renovation*, pp. 269–287. New York: Pergamon Press.

Supportive Housing Network of New York (2003) *Blueprint to end homelessness in New York City*. New York: Supportive Housing Network of New York.

US Bureau of the Census (1999) *Definitions of Rent Regulation Status*. Guide prepared by New York City Department of Housing Preservation and Development, Office of Housing Analysis and Research (available at: www.census.gov/hhes/www/housing/nychvs/defin99.html; accessed 27 July 2003).

US Bureau of the Census (2003) *New York City Housing and Vacancy Survey, 1989–2002* (available at: http://www.census.gov/hhes/www/nychvs.html).

US Department of Housing and Urban Development (1979) *Displacement Report*. Washington: The Department.

US Department of Housing and Urban Development (n.d.) *MultiFamily Assistance and Section 8 Contracts Database* [as of 9 October 2003] (accessed at: http://www.hud.-gov/offices/hsg/mfh/exp/mfhdiscl.cfm).

Vigdor, J. (2002) Does gentrification harm the poor?, *Brookings–Wharton Papers on Urban Affairs*, pp. 134–173.

Wallin, D., Schill, M. and Daniels, G. (2003) *State of New York City's housing and neighborhoods 2003*. Furman Center for Real Estate and Urban Policy and Robert F. Wagner Graduate School of Public Service, New York University (available at: http://www.law.nyu/edu/realestatecenter/).

Wyly, E. and Hammel, D. (1999) Islands of decay in seas of renewal: housing policy and the resurgence of gentrification, *Housing Policy Debate*, 10(4), pp. 711–781.

39

"The Eviction of Critical Perspectives from Gentrification Research"

From *International Journal of Urban and Regional Research* (2006)

Tom Slater

When President Bush insists that 'out of New Orleans is going to come that great city again', it is difficult to believe that good quality, secure and affordable social housing is what this administration has in mind. Wholesale gentrification at a scale as yet unseen in the United States is the more likely outcome. After the Bush hurricane, the poor, African-American and working class people who evacuated will not be welcomed back to New Orleans, which will in all likelihood be rebuilt as a tourist magnet with a Disneyfied BigEasyVille oozing even more manufactured authenticity than the surviving French Quarter nearby. We can look back and identify any number of individual decisions taken and not taken that made this hurricane such a social disaster. But the larger picture is more than the sum of its parts. It is not a radical conclusion that the dimensions of the Katrina disaster owe in large part not just to the actions of this or that local or federal administration but the operation of a capitalist market more broadly, especially in its neo-liberal garb.

(Neil Smith, 2005)

The city was moving in the right direction before Katrina struck. While residents felt the hangover from the historical heritage of political corruption (45 percent of residents say city government has low ethical standards), a large majority felt their leadership was moving New Orleans in the 'right direction'. On a visit to the city in August, I was struck by the large number of professional ex-pats who had been attracted back to

New Orleans because of that change of direction. Tremendous enthusiasm was being generated by the efforts of Greater New Orleans Inc., Lt. Gov. Mitch Landrieu, and others to spur the development of dynamic creative-industry clusters around the region's technology base, universities, tourism, and music and film industries … The people of New Orleans know what they want. More than just reconstructed levees, a refurbished downtown, or even rebuilt homes, they want the soul of the city back. Their insights — both angry and enthusiastic — remind us of the underlying source of resilience that really rebuilds fallen cities: the people. Let's hope that their leaders will understand this, and provide us all with a compelling model of a creative, prosperous and sustainable city.

(Richard Florida, 2006)

LATTES AND LETHARGY

One of the more memorable comments to come my way since I began researching and writing about gentrification was from a German political scientist who had spent five years living in the gentrifying neighbourhood of Prenzlauer Berg, Berlin. At a workshop in Vancouver, when I explained my research interests, he replied 'Interesting. But surely gentrification research is just an excuse to hang out in cool neighbourhoods sipping lattes?' This comment, intended in jest, is actually rather astute, for it captures precisely the popular, and increasingly scholarly, image of gentrification. The perception is no longer about rent increases, landlord harassment and working-class displacement, but rather street-level spectacles, trendy bars and cafes, i-Pods, social diversity and funky clothing outlets. As David Ley (2003: 2527) put it, gentrification is 'not a sideshow in the city, but a major component of the urban imaginary'. As the municipal rush to endorse Richard Florida's celebration and promotion of a new 'creative class' in urban centres attests (see Peck, 2005, for a swashbuckling critique), gentrification — not so much the term itself, which is mercifully still something of a 'dirty word' (Smith, 1996), but the *image* of hip, bohemian, cool, arty tribes who occupy the cafes, galleries and cycle paths of formerly disinvested neighbourhoods once lacking in 'creativity', is increasingly seen as a sign of a healthy economic present and future for cities across the globe. In keeping with the discursive strategy of the neoliberal project, which deploys carefully selected language to fend off criticism and resistance, organized around a narrative of competitive progress (Bourdieu and Wacquant, 2001; Tickell and Peck, 2003), we have apparently arrived in the age of regeneration, revitalization and renaissance in the hearts of Richard Florida's (2002) cities of technology, talent and tolerance. Lost in the alliterative maze are the critical perspectives on gentrification upon which our understandings of the process and its effects were built. This article seeks to uncover how and why critical perspectives got evicted from gentrification research, and argues that they need to be reinstated in the context of distressing evidence of continuing evictions of low-income and working-class residents from neighbourhoods, and continuing embourgoisement of central city locations resulting in severe housing affordability problems. The apparent lethargy towards addressing the negative effects of gentrification (particularly in Britain) has been pointed out in a recent editorial on the subject (Slater *et al.*, 2004), so this article takes up this issue in an attempt to throw critical light on what Peck (2005: 760) has called 'cappuccino urban politics, with plenty of froth'.

GENTRIFICATION WEB

In early 2000, frustrated by the lack of public information on gentrification available online, I wrote and designed *Gentrification Web*.[1] As a brief visit to the website reveals, I knew (and still know) nothing about effective web design, but I did know enough about gentrification to summarize decades of debate in accessible terms, and spell out what the process

is and who it affects, accompanied by some photographs I snapped in London and a few relevant links. The tone of the website is largely critical, partly because two years previously I had been evicted from my flat in gentrifying Tooting, London, because of a rent increase, but mostly because the gentrification literature which informed it is predominantly critical. After I launched the site, I received little feedback and very few emails, and wondered why I had bothered. But around six months later, my inbox began receiving several emails a week from interested browsers, which has remained the case to this day. Aside from a marketing executive from the *Seagram* corporation, former owners of the trendy *Oddbins* wine stores in the UK, who asked me for a list of gentrifying neighbourhoods in British cities so he could advise the company board where to locate future stores,[2] the people who have contacted me over the years have one thing in common — they are against gentrification because of what they have seen, heard or experienced. Neighbourhood organizations, displaced tenants and political activists from Boston to Buenos Aires to Budapest have told me stories about gentrification in their part of the world; other browsers have sent attachments documenting local struggles over gentrification through photographs, flyers and protest art. Some stories of upheaval and landlord harassment have been quite distressing to read, whilst some accounts of resistance and fighting for affordable housing have been very uplifting. With the feedback from traffic to the website it became impossible to see gentrification as anything other than a serious issue — a major disturbance in the lives of urban residents who are not homeowners, gentrifiers or hipsters. Not only has the website proved to be a useful tool in combining scholarship with political commitment — its very existence counters the latte-soaked image of gentrification articulated by journalism and policy discourse.

Yet this is an image which, at precisely the same time as these emails have been arriving, has been additionally fuelled by some recent scholarship on gentrification, which is far removed from the radical, critical politics of gentrification research of previous decades. A process directly linked not just to the injustice of community upheaval and working-class displacement but also to the erosion of affordable housing in so many cities is now seen by increasing numbers of researchers as less of a problem than it used to be, or worse, as something positive. The next section of this article provides a taster of some of the published work that contributes to the now popularly held, yet ultimately incorrect, assumption that gentrification 'isn't so bad after all'.

THE TRAGICALLY HIP?[3]

In a quite remarkable about-turn in her perspective on gentrification, Sharon Zukin recently co-authored an article focusing on the commercial activity taking place on one block in the East Village of Lower Manhattan (a neighbourhood which has seen more than its fair share of gentrification and displacement) and argued that 'far from destroying a community by commercial gentrification, East Ninth Street suggests that a retail concentration of designer stores may be a territory of innovation in the urban economy, producing both a marketable and a sociable neighbourhood node' (Zukin and Kosta, 2004: 101). Even more remarkably, Zukin appears persuaded by the arguments of Richard Florida (2002) on the aesthetic and economic benefits of bourgeois bohemia, as evidenced by passages such as 'the East Village illustrates how a cultural enclave that is stable, diverse and broad-minded can attract the "creative class"' (Zukin and Kosta, 2004: 102) and 'far from criticizing new consumer culture as evidence of gentrification, we think it is good to encourage consumption spaces that provide complementary kinds of distinction' (2004: 102). The entire article treats East Ninth Street as a block utterly independent from the rest of the neighbourhood and all its history of class struggle and political turbulence: 'the block does not exactly conform to this wild history' (2004: 106). This is a conclusion drawn from unsubstantiated comments of storeowners on the block, some with a hazy grasp of history,[4] and from an observational research project that feels more like a series of shopping excursions. In its theoretical redundancy,[5] rather tedious street-level detail[6] and obvious affection for Eileen Fisher's clothing store,[7] this article is particularly disappointing, not least because it comes from the pen of an eminent urban sociologist whose landmark book *Loft living* (1982) had the dual impact of first, critically exposing the 'artistic mode of production'[8] behind rampant gentrification and industrial displacement in New York's SoHo district, and second, convincing gentrification researchers that culture and capital could be understood as complementary forces in driving the reinvestment and resultant middle-class conquest of urban neighbourhoods. On the basis of this article, opponents of gentrification, it seems, may have seen the defection to the creative class of one of their best and most critical voices.

Up until the late 1980s, very few, if any, scholarly articles celebrating gentrification existed. The academic literature was characterized by increasing theoretical sophistication as researchers tried to understand the causes of the process, and this was often in response to the clear injustice of the displacement of working-class residents, and the far from innocent role of both public and private institutions (see Wyly and Hammel, 2001, for an excellent discussion). Celebrations of gentrification were confined to media and popular discourse, especially surrounding the yuppie-boom years of the 1980s, and most memorably on the pages of the *New York Times*, when the Real Estate Board of New York felt it needed to defend the process in the face of major resistance by taking out an advert trumpeting how 'neighbourhoods and lives blossom' under gentrification (see Smith, 1996: 31; Newman and Wyly, 2006: 23–4). The gentrifiers themselves were seldom a topic of investigation; when they were, influential statements on class constitution vis-à-vis gentrification were published that never entertained the prospect of gentrification being the true *saviour* of central-city neighbourhoods, even if these statements were guided by contrasting political ideologies and theoretical frameworks (e.g. Rose, 1984 for a socialist feminist perspective; Smith, 1987a for a Marxist perspective; and Ley, 1980 for a liberal humanist perspective).

In 1989, a very different assessment was offered by the Canadian sociologist Jon Caulfield, in an article entitled 'Gentrification and desire' (Caulfield, 1989). In a deliberate riposte to the dominance of Marxist/structuralist interpretations of gentrification, he argued that 1970s and 1980s gentrification in Toronto was a collective middle-class rejection of the oppressive conformity of suburbia, modernist planning and market principles — all part of what became known (and now often romanticized) as the 'reform era' of Canadian urban politics. Gentrification was pitched as a 'critical social practice' (see Caulfield, 1994) — a concerted effort by Toronto's expanding middle-class intelligentsia to create an 'alternative urban future' to the city's post-war modernist development. Heavily influenced by Walter Benjamin, Roland Barthes, Jonathan Raban and Marcel Rioux, he argued the following:

> Old city places offer difference and freedom, privacy and fantasy, possibilities for carnival … These are not just matters of philosophical abstraction but, in a carnival sense … the force that Benjamin believed was among the most vital stimuli to resistance to domination. 'A big city is an encyclopaedia of sexual possibility,' a characterization to be grasped in its wider sense; the city is 'the place of our meeting with the other'.
>
> (Caulfield, 1989: 625)

Caulfield concluded his article by commending Toronto's middle-class gentrifiers for attempting to 'meet with the other' in their resistance to faceless suburbia: 'resettlement of old city neighbourhoods is not reducible to bourgeois politics but rather is an effort by people, together with their neighbors, to seek some control over their lives' (1989: 627). In his important book on Toronto's gentrification, Caulfield (1994: 201–11) does acknowledge that these early gentrifiers became increasingly concerned about what was happening to their neighbourhoods (and working-class neighbours) as gentrification accelerated and matured, but his closing argument that early gentrification in Toronto amounted to a Castells-like urban social movement (*ibid*.: 228–9) played a key role in producing the *emancipatory discourse* on gentrification in Canada that has been documented elsewhere (Slater 2002; 2004a; 2005). In its focus on the desiderata for middle-class residence in 'old city' places, this discourse tends to sugarcoat the process with a sort of romantic glaze that has the (often unintended) consequence of steering the understanding of gentrification away from the negative effects it produces.

This romanticism has been taken to an extreme form in two pieces of recent writing on gentrification in American cities, one by an architect/journalist, another by a legal scholar, with more or less the same title — 'Three cheers for gentrification' and 'Two cheers for gentrification', respectively. In the former, Andres Duany promoted gentrification as follows:

> For every San Francisco and Manhattan where real estate has become uniformly too expensive, there are many more cities like Detroit, Trenton, Syracuse, Milwaukee, Houston, and Philadelphia that could use all the gentrification they can get.
>
> (2001: 36)

The emancipatory discourse was then taken to new levels in the following sentence:

> Gentrification rebalances a concentration of poverty by providing the tax base, rub-off work ethic, and political effectiveness of a middle-class, and in the process improves the quality of life for all a community's residents. It is the rising tide that lifts all boats.
>
> (*ibid*.: 36)

The conclusion, in particular, shows the dismissive, almost vitriolic way in which Duany treated critics of gentrification:

> So what is the fuss over gentrification about? Many times it's just the squawking of old neighbourhood bosses who can't bear the self-reliance of the incoming middle-class, and can't accept the dilution of their political base. But theirs is a swan song. Middle-class Americans arc choosing to live in many inner-city neighbourhoods because these places possess urbane attributes not found in newer residential areas, and this flow cannot be regulated away ... And finally, people should not be prevented from profiling on the natural appreciation of their neighbourhoods. Not in America.
>
> (*ibid*.: 39)

A couple of years later, Peter Byrne, an American legal scholar, provided a more comprehensive, scholarly round of applause for gentrification, contending that the process is 'good on balance for the poor and ethnic minorities' (Byrne, 2003: 406). Byrne argued that gentrification benefits low-income residents economically, by 'expanding more employment opportunities in providing locally the goods and services that more affluent residents can afford' (*ibid*.: 419), politically, by creating 'urban political fora in which affluent and poor citizens must deal with each other's priorities in a democratic process' (*ibid*.: 421), and socially, as 'new more affluent residents will rub shoulders with poorer existing residents on the streets, in shops, and within local institutions, such as public schools' (*ibid*.: 422). In his conclusion, Byrne, a self-confessed gentrifier living in Washington DC, provides a telling illustration of bourgeois emancipatory romanticism vis-à-vis gentrification:

> On a recent Saturday, I attended a multi-family yard sale at the nearby Townhomes on Capitol Hill with my wife and teenage daughter. The member co-op that manages the project had organized the sale as a 'community day.' We strolled along the sidewalks chatting with the residents about how they enjoyed living there and examining their modest wares. We bought a number paperbacks, many of which were by black authors. My daughter bought a remarkable pink suitcase, rather beat up, which perfectly met her sense of cool. My wife, being who she is, reorganized several residents' display of goods to show them off to better effect, to the delight of the sellers. I bought and devoured a fried fish sandwich that Mrs. Jones was selling from her apartment. Such a modest event hardly makes news and certainly does not cancel the injustices of our metropolitan areas. No public officials attended nor made claims for what it promised for the future. Yet it was a time of neighbourly

intercourse, money circulation and mutual learning. If multiplied many times, it promises a better future for our communities.

(*ibid.*: 431)

Together, paperbacks, pink suitcases and fried fish sandwiches blend into a startlingly upbeat and perhaps tragically hip representation of a neighbourhood which has been documented by others as having severe housing affordability problems — in fact, as Wyly and Hammel (2001: 240) point out, it is 'one of the most intensely gentrified neighbourhoods in the country', so much so that the adjacent Ellen Wilson Dwellings public housing complex was subjected to HOPE VI demolition and then gentrification in the form of 'a complete [mixed-income] redevelopment of the site with 153 townhouse units designed to resemble mews typical of the historic district of which the complex is part' (*ibid.*: 240). No doubt Byrne would be delighted.

Two striking recent research trends in the gentrification literature, particularly in British contexts, have shifted attention away from the negative effects of the process. The first, and perhaps most prevalent, is research which investigates the constitution and practices of middle-class gentrifiers.[9] The basis for this work was a feeling that the only way to gain a complete understanding of the causes of gentrification is to trace the movements and aspirations of the gentry. For some time now, there has been wide agreement that class should be the undercurrent in the study of gentrification (Hamnett, 1991; Smith, 1992; Wyly and Hammel, 1999), and the research response has been to find out about the behaviour of the *middle* classes, particularly why they are seeking to locate in previously disinvested neighbourhoods. In Britain, and especially London, the middle-class dilemma of having to live in a certain 'catchment area' to send your child to a rare 'good school' (a parental strategy of social reproduction deployed to ensure that children will also be middle class) has been captured by work explaining how gentrification is anchored around the intersection of housing and education markets (e.g. Butler and Robson, 2003; Hamnett, 2003). Absent from this work is any careful qualitative consideration of working-class people and how the gentrification-education connection affects them. It seems that there is something of an obsession with the formation of middle-class metropolitan 'habituses', using Bourdieu's *Distinction* as a theoretical guide, and if the working class are mentioned at all, it is usually in the form of how the middle classes feel about 'others', or neighbours not like them. These feelings are often rather depressing, as evidenced by Tim

Butler's investigation of gentrification in Barnsbury, London:

Gentrification in Barnsbury (and probably London) is therefore apparently playing a rather dangerous game. It values the presence of others — that much has been seen from the quotations from respondents — but chooses not to interact with them. They are, as it were, much valued as a kind of social wallpaper, but no more.

(Butler, 2003: 2484)

Yet Butler quickly moves away from portraying gentrification as a dangerous game, and offers this interpretation in the final sentences of his paper:

This is an inseparable element of the metropolitan habitus — of feelings, attitudes and beliefs — which transforms the inner city into the natural habitat for a section of the new (urban-seeking) middle classes. At the same time, the imperatives of everyday life (work and consumption) and intergenerational social reproduction (schooling and socialisation) give rise to a group of embattled settlers. Thus, a group that has transformed an inner-city working-class district into one of the iconic sites of middle-class living nevertheless still often attributes 'authenticity' to a largely nonexistent native working class. Gentrification has not so much displaced the working class as simply blanked out those who are not like themselves: they do not socialise with them, eat with them or send their children to school with them.

(2003: 2484)

Might it be an equally dangerous game, first, to portray the inner city as a 'natural habitat' for the new middle classes; second, to portray this same group as 'embattled settlers' when the structural constraints on their own lifestyle preferences is a far less worrying problem than being priced out of a city altogether, as has happened to so many worse-off Londoners in the last 20 years; and third, to argue from a study which did not set out to study displacement in London that gentrification 'has not so much displaced the working class'? On that last point, it is worth noting that a decade earlier, Loretta Lees published a paper on the same neighbourhood and pointed out this:

Creeping [vacancy] decontrol enabled the 'winkling' of tenants and the sale of buildings to developers and/or individuals who would then gentrify the property. 'Winkling' refers to the process of tenants being forced to leave their

homes by bribery and harassment. In Barnsbury when vacant possession value became
higher than tenanted investment value 'winkling'
occurred and the vacated property was sold.
When one of Knight's [an unscrupulous Barnsbury landlord] tenants reported him to the rent
tribunal, he turned off the electricity, locked her
out, threw out her belongings, bolted the door,
libelled her and threatened to shoot her.

(Lees, 1994: 208)

My purpose here is *not* to criticize research (or
researchers) that seeks to understand the urban
experiences of more advantaged social groups, and
certainly not to demonize gentrifiers, whose identities are multiple and whose ambivalent politics often
contradict assumptions of a group intent on booting
out extant low-income groups from their neighbourhoods (Ley, 2004), but rather to point out that there
is next to nothing published on the experiences of
non-gentrifying groups living in the neighbourhoods
into which the much-researched cosmopolitan middle classes are arriving en masse. A dozen years ago
now Jan van Weesep argued that we need to focus
on the effects — not the causes — of gentrification, and that one way to do this is through the lens
of urban policy, or in his words, 'to put the gentrification debate into policy perspective' (van Weesep,
1994: 74). His call drew numerous responses, and it
could be argued that he changed the course of the
gentrification debate, as exemplified by the emphasis
on the role of policy in so much recent and current
research.[10] One wonders what might have been the
outcome if van Weesep had said that we need 'to put
the gentrification debate into working-class perspective'. Instead, academic inquiry into gentrification
has looked at either the role of urban policy in har-
nessing the aspirations of middle-class professionals,
or provided a closer view of the issues that they are
confronting when choosing where to live. It is as if
the middle classes are the only characters occupying
the stage of the gentrification, with the working-class
backstage, both perennial understudies and perenni-
ally understudied. This is particularly disappointing,
for middle-class gentrifiers are, of course, only one
part of a much larger story (Slater *et al.*, 2004).

The second research trend serving as a screen
that obfuscates the reality of working-class upheaval
and displacement via gentrification is the infatuation with how to define the process, and whether we
should remain faithful to Ruth Glass's (1964) coinage.
While Peter Marcuse (1999) is right to argue that
how gentrification is evaluated depends a great deal
on how it is defined, it is baffling to see entire articles
deliberating the definition of the term (e.g. Redfern,

2003), given the extraordinary depth and progression
of so much gentrification scholarship since 1964.
Hackworth and Smith (2001) helpfully set out the
ways in which gentrification has mutated since the
1960s, using New York City as an analytical lens, but
thankfully stopped short of ruminating at length over
what gentrification actually *is*. Hackworth (2002: 815)
later succinctly defined gentrification as 'the production of space for progressively more affluent users',
the justification being:

in light of several decades of research and debate
that shows that the concept is usefully applied to
non-residential urban change and that there is frequently a substantial time lag between when the
subordinate class group gives way to more affluent users. That is, the displacement or replacement is often neither direct nor immediate, but the
process remains 'gentrification' because the space
is being transformed for more affluent users.

(*ibid.*: 839)

As well as trying to capture recent changes to the
gentrification process that were impossible to predict
in 1964, Hackworth is tuned in to another part of the
Ruth Glass definition which, it seems, many authors
cannot find — the critical emphasis on class transformation. This strikes me as the central problem
in the work of Martin Boddy and Christine Lambert
(Boddy and Lambert, 2002; see also Boddy, forthcoming), insisting that the 'new-build' developments
in central Bristol and elsewhere (and the mixed-use
consumption landscapes that accompany them) are
not gentrification:

We would question whether the sort of new
housing development and conversion described in
Bristol and other second tier UK cities, or indeed
the development of London's Docklands can, in
fact, still be characterised as 'gentrification' …
'[G]entrification', as originally coined, referred primarily to a rather different type of 'new middle
class', buying up older, often 'historic' individual
housing units and renovating and restoring them
for their own use — and in the process driving up property values and driving out former,
typically lower income working class residents …
We would conclude that to describe these processes as gentrification is stretching the term and
what it set out to describe too far.

(Boddy and Lambert. 2002: 20)

In reaction, it is worth reminding ourselves that we
are *over forty years* beyond Ruth Glass' coinage! So
much has happened to city economies (especially

labour and housing markets), cultures and land-scapes since then that it makes no sense to focus on this narrow version of the process anymore, and to insist that gentrification must remain faithful to the fine empirical details of her geographically and historically contingent definition. Furthermore, in Boddy and Lambert's work there is no sense that they have considered what *is* still relevant from Glass' classic statement — the political importance of capturing a process of class transformation. In Bristol, it is hard to get beyond the bare fact that the new developments described are appearing both in reaction to and to stimulate further demand from a specific class of resident — the middle-class consumer. The middle classes are the *gentri*- part of the word, and they are moving into new-build residential developments — built on formerly working-class industrial space — which are off limits to the working classes. Furthermore, as Davidson and Lees (2005: 1186) have explained in a study of new-build developments of London, such developments 'have acted like beachheads from which the tentacles of gentrification have slowly stretched into the adjacent neighbourhoods'.

The trendy developments taking place adjacent to the waterfront in Bristol's city centre have also been the focus of some more policy-oriented (and funded) research (Tallon and Bromley, 2004; Bromley *et al.*, 2005). In contrast to some highly critical work on the gentrifying intentions behind the British government's 'urban renaissance' strategy (Smith, 2002; Lees, 2003a), these authors argue that what we are seeing is actually an emerging *residentialization*,[11] not gentrification. The basis for this argument is drawn from a household survey where respondents emphasized the 'mundane' attractions of city living such as the convenience of being close to points of employment and consumption, with middle-class 'lifestyle concerns' less prevalent. The authors conclude as follows:

> Armed with a knowledge of the different appeals of city centre living, policy should continue to promote further housing and residential development and social mix in the city centre, creating further opportunities for public and private developers to invest in the city centre and for more people to move to the area.
>
> (Tallon and Bromley, 2004; 785)

In a later paper, environmental arguments are brought in to bolster this conclusion:

> Residential development can contribute to sustainability through the recycling of derelict tend

and buildings, This can reduce demand for peripheral development and assist the development of more compact cities ... All these points emphasise the contributions of city centre regeneration to sustainability and the importance of encouraging housing in a location which can appear high-cost in the short-term.
>
> (Bromley *et al.*, 2005: 2423)

Particularly telling here is how these authors account for 'residentialization' — a 'response to the new spaces and opportunities created by deindustrialisation, decentralisation and suburbanisation' (*ibid.*: 2423). These are precisely the same conditions — systematic disinvestment in inner-city locations — that many theorists explain as fundamental to the gentrification process (e.g. Smith, 1986; Beauregard, 1990; Wyly and Hammel, 1999; Curran, 2004). The Bristol study under discussion thus exemplifies something captured by Smith:

> Precisely because the language of gentrification tells the truth about the class shift involved in the 'regeneration' of the city, it has become a dirty word to developers, politicians and financiers; we find ourselves in the ironic position that in the US, where the ideology of classlessness is so prevalent, the language of gentrification is quite generalized, whereas in Europe it is suppressed.
>
> (Smith, 2002: 445)

How did we arrive at a time when gentrification, in the country where it was first observed and coined, has now become a dirty word to some academics in their published research?

THREE REASONS FOR THE EVICTION OF CRITICAL PERSPECTIVES

It is possible to identify not one but *three* key reasons why discussions of rent increases, affordable housing crises, class conflict, displacement, and community upheavals have morphed into, *inter alia*, 'cheering' gentrification, middle-class 'natural habitats' and 'residentialization'. There may indeed be more reasons, but the following are particularly noticeable from a close reading of the literature.

The resilience of theoretical and ideological squabbles

Ley's conceptualisation of the rent-gap is too clumsy for the question of differential national experiences [of gentrification] even to be asked ... Whatever the shortcomings of his analysis ... it should now be evident that the relationship between consumption and production is crucial to explaining gentrification.

(Smith, 1987b: 464)

For some years the necessity to unite theories around production and consumption in under-standing gentrification ... has been apparent ... While critical to strive for, such an integration will not be easily accomplished, and it will require a more careful reading of the literature, together with less adversarial patrolling of one's own terri-tory than appears in this [Smith's] commentary.

(Ley, 1987: 468)

With boisterous exchanges like those above, it is not difficult to see how these two leading experts on gentrification are often portrayed as exact opposites, utterly divided on the explanation of gentrification, and guided by completely contrasting conceptual frameworks, methodologies and ideologies. Further-more, the influence and volume of their work was such that both Neil Smith and David Ley became treated by almost every researcher as the de facto representatives of the 'economic' and 'cultural' expla-nations of the process, respectively, something which many writers insist on re-emphasizing time and time again. But if we take a closer look at these quota-tions, published in 1987, we can see that both ana-lysts were committed to searching for an explanation of gentrification that took into account both eco-nomic (production) and cultural (consumption) fac-tors. Indeed, their books on gentrification, published in the same year (1996) are not nearly as one-sided in the explanation of gentrification as many newcom-ers to the topic might think. To argue that David Ley ignored economic transformation in Canadian cities in his work is nothing short of preposterous, and the same can be said for any writing which gives the impression that Neil Smith ignored the cul-tural aspects of gentrification in the Lower East Side during his research there in the late 1980s. As Atkin-son (2003: 2344) explained, 'the implied economic and cultural imperatives central to each theory have often been interpreted as a sign of mutual exclu-sivity, although this is perhaps something of an "overdistinction"'. In short, while their explanations of gentrification did differ significantly, the *divisions* between these two scholars became, in the hands of other writers, the most overdrawn contest in the history of urban studies, and they become misrep-resented on numerous occasions, with the serious effect of making gentrification a subject where many

researchers ended up taking sides and 'throwing rocks from behind barricades' (Clark, 1992: 359), rather than finding ways to work with and through competing explanations and theoretical tensions.

A survey of more recent scholarship on post-recession gentrification shows that gentrification discourse is to some extent *still* locked within the zeitgeist of the 1980s, rehashing the tiresome debates of old — precisely the reason why Bondi (1999b) suggested we let gentrification research 'disintegrate'. Take for example a recent paper by Chris Hamnett, where the recent calls to move away from this exhausted debate appear to have gone unnoticed:

The argument made here is that the basis of an effective explanation has to rest on the demand side as much or more than the supply side of the equation ... Smith's objection to demand-led explanations is that they are overly individualis-tic, place too much stress on shifts in consumer choice and preference, and fail to provide an adequate explanation of underlying changes in the land and property markets. He also argues that they are insufficiently materialist in their the-oretical approach in that they fail to deal with underlying economic changes. But demand-based arguments are not just based on consumer taste and preference ... [T]hey locate the basis of gentrification demand in the shifts in industrial, occupational and earnings structures linked to the shift from industrial to post-industrial cities.

(Hamnett, 2003: 2403)

In addition, Hamnett, just as he did in an influen-tial essay published twenty years earlier (Hamnett, 1984), actually spends two pages criticizing Smith's rent-gap thesis (with precisely the same criticisms!). Badcock (2001: 1561) also joined in, claiming that it is: 'impossible to escape the structuralist and functionalist overtones of the rent-gap hypothesis'.

This debate was very important in the 1970s and 1980s as we tried to understand and explain gentrification, but by the twenty-first century few gentrification researchers needed to be reminded of what is excluded by the rent-gap thesis! One commentator has recently attempted to take the gentrification debate in a different direction, but reading between the rather opaque lines, it actually steers us back into the same territory:

What needs rethinking on both sides of gentrifica-tion debate is the implicit assumption that gentri-fiers gentrify because they have to, in some form or another. This paper seeks to argue that they gentrify because they can. Clearly, on the supply side, this argument is made by emphasising the new-found ability lo improve a property, although this is far from being a sufficient condition. On the demand side, the insistence that gentrifiers gentrify because they have to is manifested in the position that gentrification represents some form of class constitution in itself, or that, alternatively, it represents the expression of some new form of class constitution.

(Redfern, 2003: 2352)

The problem with re-hashing these old debates is not just epistemological, that it just precludes widespread agreement that gentrification is a *multi-faceted* process of class transformation that is best explained from a holistic point of departure; it is also *political*, in that critical perspectives get lost within, or are absent entirely from, the squabbling about whether Smith or Ley has got it right in a certain gentrification context. So much time and ink has been spent in disagreement over what is causing the process that one wonders whether labour could have been better spent, first, accepting something pitched by Eric Clark:

Attempts to draw connections between different aspects of gentrification call for ambidexterity in dealing with concepts which may defy reduction to a single model. Sometimes these connections can be made through an integration which practically dissolves any previously perceived mutual exclusion.

(Clark, 1992: 362)

and, second, moving on to acknowledge that gentrification is an expression of urban inequality and has serious effects, and that academics have a role to play in exposing these effects and perhaps even challenging them (Hartman *et al.*, 1982).

Displacement gets displaced

Displacement from home and neighbourhood can be a shattering experience. At worst it leads to homelessness, at best it impairs a sense of community. Public policy should, by general agreement, minimize displacement. Yet a variety of public policies, particularly those concerned with gentrification, seem to foster it.

(Marcuse, 1985a: 931)

Until very recently, studies of gentrification-induced displacement, part of the original definition of the process and the subject of so much sophisticated

inquiry in the late 1970s and 1980s, had all but disappeared. Many of the articles in early collections on gentrification such as Laska and Spain (1980), Schill and Nathan (1983), Palen and London (1984) and Smith and Williams (1986) were concerned with displacement and, indeed, much greater attention was paid to the effects of gentrification on the working class than to the characteristics of the new middle class that was moving in. Although there was not necessarily agreement on the severity and extent of the problem (Sumka, 1979), displacement was undoubtedly a major theme. Even scholars (wrongly) associated with a less critical take on the process were very concerned about displacement:

The magnitude of dislocation is unknown … though the scale of renovation, demolition, deconversion, and condominium conversion noted … implies that tens of thousands of households have been involuntarily displaced through various forms of gentrification over the past twenty-five years in Toronto, Montreal, Vancouver, and Ottawa alone.

(Ley, 1996: 70)

Displacement is and always will be vital to an understanding of gentrification, in terms of retaining definitional coherence and of retaining a critical perspective on the process.

The reason why displacement itself got displaced from the gentrification literature was methodological. In 2001, I remember being told by a community organizer in Park Slope, Brooklyn, that the best way I could help with local efforts to resist gentrification was to 'come up with some numbers to show us how many people have been and are being displaced'. He was not impressed when I explained what a massive undertaking this is, if indeed it was possible at all. Atkinson (2000) has called measuring displacement 'measuring the invisible', whereas Newman and Wyly sum up the quantification problem as follows:

In short, it is difficult to find people who have been displaced, particularly if those people are poor … By definition, displaced residents have disappeared from the very places where researchers and census-takers go to look for them.

(Newman and Wyly, 2006: 27)

In the 1990s especially, these considerable barriers to a research agenda did not steer researchers in the way of a qualitative agenda to address displacement, but rather steered them away from displacement altogether. In the neoliberal context of public policy being constructed on a 'reliable' (i.e. quantitative) evidence base, no numbers on displacement meant no policy to address it. It was almost as if displacement didn't exist. This is in fact the conclusion of Chris Hamnett (2003: 2454) in his paper on London's rampant gentrification from 1961 to 2001; in the absence of data on the displaced, he reasserts his thesis that London's labour force has 'professionalized':

> The transformation which has taken place in the occupational class structure of London has been associated with the gradual replacement of one class by another, rather than large-scale direct displacement.

Yet isn't it precisely a sign of the astonishing scale of gentrification and displacement in London that there isn't much of a working class left in the occupational class structure of that city? Labour force data support an interesting story Hamnett has been telling for over a decade now, but in the absence of any numbers on displacement it appears that he is blanking out the working class in the same manner as Butler's interviewees in Barnsbury.

The lack of attention to displacement has recently changed — dramatically — with the work of Lance Freeman and Frank Braconi (2002; 2004), who are increasingly seen by the media and, worryingly, policymakers, as putting forward the 'definitive verdict' on gentrification and displacement (see Newman and Wyly, 2006: 29) — the verdict being that displacement is negligible and gentrification therefore isn't so bad after all. Their work has been summarized at length elsewhere (Newman and Wyly, 2005; 2006), but briefly. Freeman and Braconi examined the triennial *New York City housing and vacancy survey* (which contains questions pertaining to demographic characteristics, employment, housing conditions and mobility), and found that between 1996 and 1999, lower-income and lesser-educated households were 19% less likely to move in the seven gentrifying neighbourhoods studied than those elsewhere, and concluded that displacement was therefore limited. They suggested that such households stay put because they appreciate the public service improvements taking place in these neighbourhoods and thus find ways to remain in their homes even in the face of higher rent burdens. This was the main reason that the *USA Today*, on 20 April 2005, decided to feature their work with the spurious headline: 'Gentrification: a boost for everyone'. The media coverage completely ignored the fact that Freeman and Braconi (2002: 4) cautioned that 'only indirectly, by gradually shrinking the pool of low-rent housing, does the reurbanization

of the middle class appear to harm the interests of the poor', and that Freeman more recently wrote this:

> The chief drawback [of gentrification] has been the inflation of housing prices on gentrifying neighbourhoods ... Households that would have formerly been able to find housing in gentrifying neighbourhoods must now search elsewhere ... Moreover, although displacement may be relatively rare in gentrifying neighbourhoods, it is perhaps such a traumatic experience to nonetheless engender widespread concern.
>
> (Freeman, 2005: 488)

On the point of shrinking the pool of low-rent housing, it is important to return to Peter Marcuse's identification of 'exclusionary displacement' under gentrification, referring to households unable to access property because it has been gentrified:

> When one household vacates a unit voluntarily and that unit is then gentrified ... so that another similar household is prevented from moving in, the number of units available to the second household in that housing market is reduced. The second household, therefore, is excluded from living where it would otherwise have lived.
>
> (Marcuse, 1985b: 206)

As Marcuse (2005) has recently pointed out, the Freeman/Braconi work only touches on this crucial question: are people not moving not because they like the gentrification around them, *but rather because there are no feasible alternatives available to them in a tight/tightening housing market* (i.e. that so much of the city has gentrified that people are trapped)? This is the carefully considered conclusion of an excellent recent paper on the gentrification of Brussels by Mathieu van Criekingen:

> Evidence highlighted in Brussels strongly suggests that poorly-resourced households are less likely to move away from marginal gentrifying districts because they are 'trapped' in the lowest segment of the private rental housing market, with very few alternatives outside deprived neighbourhoods, even in those areas experiencing marginal gentrification.
>
> (van Criekingen, 2006: 30)

On the point of traumatic experiences of displacement, these have been documented recently in New York City by Curran (2004), Slater (2004a) and particularly Newman and Wyly (2006), who as well as conducting interviews with displaced tenants, used the same data set as Freeman and Braconi to demonstrate that displacement is not 'relatively rare' but occurs at a significantly higher rate than they implied. This points to the absolute necessity of mixing methods in the study of displacement:

> The difficulties of directly quantifying the amount of displacement and replacement and other 'noise' in the data are hard to overcome. It may be that further research at a finer spatial scale using a more qualitative approach could usefully supplement this work.
>
> (Atkinson, 2000: 163)

In a huge literature on gentrification, there are almost no qualitative accounts of displacement. Doing something about this is vital if critical perspectives are to be reinstated.

Neoliberal urban policy and 'social mix'

The current era of neoliberal urban policy, together with a drive towards homeownership, privatization and the break-up of 'concentrated poverty' (Crump, 2002), has seen the global, state-led process of gentrification via the promotion of social or tenure 'mixing' (or 'social diversity' or 'social balance') in formerly disinvested neighbourhoods populated by working-class and/or low-income tenants (Hackworth and Smith, 2001; Smith, 2002; Slater, 2004b; 2005; plus many articles in Atkinson and Bridge, 2005). But social mixing may not necessarily be a neoliberal enterprise — in a striking recent study, Rose (2004: 280) acknowledges that gentrification is 'a particularly "slippery" area of social mix discourse' and demonstrates the impact of recent municipal policies to encourage the movement of middle-income residents into Montreal's inner-city neighbourhoods. Much of this is facilitated by new housing construction, 'instant gentrification' as Rose calls it, yet there has also been a municipal drive to provide social housing in the vicinity of middle-income developments. As she points out, unlike in Toronto (Slater, 2004b), 'the Montreal policies and programs can scarcely be cast in terms of a neoliberal agenda' (Rose, 2004: 288); there are geographical variances in policy-led gentrification in Canada (Ley, 1996). By interviewing professionals who moved into small-scale 'infill' condominiums (constructed by private developers on land often purchased from the city) in Montreal between 1995 and 1998, Rose harvested the views of gentrifiers on municipally encouraged 'social mix'. Interestingly, the majority of these 50 interviewees expressed either tolerant or egalitarian sentiments with respect to the prospect of adjacent social housing; as one interviewee remarked:

> At a certain point, I think you shouldn't live in a closed circle where everybody has the same [middle-class] social standing, where everything is rose-coloured. That's not the way it is … The attraction of a city in general is that it's where things happen. And, everyone has the right to be there and to express themselves [translation].
>
> (interviewee 479 quoted in Rose, 2004: 299–300)

While Rose is undoubtedly correct to divorce social mix from neoliberal ideas and sentiments in the Montreal case, unlike some other researchers (Florida, 2002; Bromley *et al.*, 2005) she does stop short of pushing social mix as a remedy for urban disinvestment and decay, which is *precisely* the intention of neoliberal urban policies elsewhere.

In a powerful study of Vancouver's tortured Downtown Eastside, Nick Blomley has commented on just how 'morally persuasive' the concept of social mix can be in the face of addressing long-term disinvestment and poverty:

> Programs of renewal often seek to encourage home ownership, given its supposed effects on economic self-reliance, entrepreneurship, and community pride. Gentrification, on this account, is to be encouraged, because it will mean the replacement of a marginal anticommunity (nonproperty owning, transitory, and problematized) by an active, responsible, and improving population of homeowners.
>
> (Blomley, 2004: 89)

Blomley's work helps us to think more in terms of who has to move on to make room for a social mix:

> The problem with 'social mix' however is that it promises equality in the face of hierarchy. First, as often noted, it is socially one-sided. If social mix is good, argue local activists, then why not make it possible for the poor to live in rich neighbourhoods? … Second, the empirical evidence suggests that it often fails to improve the social and economic conditions for renters. Interaction between owner-occupiers and renters in 'mixed' neighbourhoods seems to be limited. More importantly, it can lead to social segregation and isolation.
>
> (*ibid.*: 99)

As Smith (2002) has noted, creating a social mix invariably involves the movement of the middle class into working-class areas, not vice versa, working on the assumption that a socially mixed community will be a socially 'balanced' one, characterized by positive interaction between the classes. Such planning and policy optimism, however, rarely translates into a happy situation in gentrifying neighbourhoods, not least South Parkdale, Toronto, where a deliberate policy of social mixing initiated in 1999 exacerbated homeowner NIMBYism, led to rent increases and tenant displacement (Slater, 2004b). Gentrification disguised as 'social mix' serves as an excellent example of how the rhetoric and reality of gentrification has been replaced by a different discursive, theoretical and policy language that consistently deflects criticism and resistance. In the UK, social mix (particularly tenure mix) has been at the forefront of 'neighbourhood renewal' and 'urban regeneration' policies for nearly a decade now, but with one or two well-known exceptions (Smith, 2002; Lees, 2003a) there is still not much of a critical literature that sniffs around for gentrification amidst the policy discourse. If we listen to one influential analyst, we are still under a linguistic anaesthetic:

Not only does 'urban regeneration' represent the next wave of gentrification, planned and financed on an unprecedented scale, but the victory of this language in anaesthetizing our critical understanding of gentrification in Europe represents a considerable ideological victory for neoliberal visions of the city.

(Smith, 2002: 446)

At a time when cities 'have become the incubators for many of the major political and ideological strategies through which the dominance of neoliberalism is being maintained' (Brenner and Theodore, 2002: 375–6), and at a time when so many urban researchers are charting and challenging neoliberalism, it is surprising that there are fewer critical takes on policy-led gentrification in Europe than ever before. It is difficult to isolate why this is the case, but the very nature of policy research, usually funded by policy institutions, may be a significant factor. Loic Wacquant has captured this well:

In the United States, it is 'policy research' that plays the lead role as a cover and shield against critical thought by acting in the manner of a 'buffer' isolating the political field from any research that is independent and radical in its conception as in its implications for public policy. All researchers who want to address state officials are obliged to pass through this mongrel field, this 'decontamination chamber,' and agree to submit

to severe censorship by reformulating their work according to technocratic categories that ensure that this work will have neither purchase nor any effect on reality (over the entrance gates of public policy schools is written in invisible letters: 'thou shall not ask thy own questions'). In point of fact, American politicians never invoke social research except when it supports the direction they want to go in anyway for reasons of political expediency; in all other cases, they trample it shamelessly.

(Wacquant 2004: 99)

This also applies to the case of policy research in Britain, where uncomfortable findings and academic criticisms of policy are often watered down by those who fund such research. Furthermore, when the language of gentrification is used in a research proposal, it is very difficult to secure research funding from an urban policy outlet to assess the implications of an urban policy designed to entice middle-class residents into working-class neighbourhoods! A dirty word has its limits.

ADDRESSING AN ENDURING DILEMMA

I would love to see a world after gentrification, and a world after all the economic and political exploitation that makes gentrification possible.

(Smith, 1996: xx)

Gentrification cannot be eradicated in capitalist societies, but it can be curtailed.

(Clark, 2005: 263)

It can therefore be argued that gentrification has been too limited in Danish urban renewal.

(Skifter-Anderson, 1998: 127)

Only a manic optimist could look upon Kilburn High Road and not feel suicidal: it's going to take a *lot* of gentrifying.

(Dyckhoff, 2006: 76)

In a systematic review of 114 published studies on gentrification, Atkinson found that:

On the issue of neighbourhood impacts it can be seen that the majority of research evidence on gentrification points to its detrimental effects … [R]esearch which has sought to understand its impacts has predominantly found problems and social costs. This suggests a displacement and moving around of social problems rather than a net gain either through local taxes, improved physical environment or a reduction in the demand for sprawling urban development.

(Atkinson, 2002: 20–1)

This suggests that we have a serious social problem affecting central cities, which must be seen in a negative light. Yet Atkinson's conclusion steers us away from the critical attention his review findings might warrant:

> [T]he wider and positive ramifications of gentrification have been under-explored … a move away from a black and white portrayal of the process as simply good or bad will inevitably be an improvement.
>
> (*ibid.*: 21)

It is a puzzling conclusion, to suggest that in the absence of many positive accounts of gentrification we must now go and find the positives! Yet on the basis of some recent work on the subject discussed in this paper, it seems that some researchers are attempting to do just that. It is a sign of the times that in the latest edited book on the subject, a very useful resource on the global diffusion of the process, the editorial introduction summarizes some recent work and lists a number of 'positive neighbourhood impacts' of gentrification (Atkinson and Bridge, 2005: 5), alongside the negatives. It was not so easy to find a list of positives[12] when people first began researching gentrification.

Gentrification is not, as one might be encouraged to think from reading recent scholarship, the saviour of our cities. The term was coined with critical intent to describe the disturbing effects of the middle classes arriving in working-class neighbourhoods and was researched in that critical spirit for many years. It has since been appropriated by those intent on finding and recommending quick-fix 'solutions' to complex urban problems, and in extreme cases depoliticized and called something else. In two Chicago neighbourhoods, Brown-Saracino (2004: 153) refers to a process of 'social preservation', defined as 'the culturally motivated choice of certain highly educated people to live in the central city or small town in order to live in authentic community embodied by the sustained presence of old-timers'. Despite the efforts of the highly educated to protect the 'old-timers' from displacement, one has to question whose interests it serves to avoid using the term gentrification when it so clearly captures what has been happening extensively in the neighbourhoods of 'capital's metropolis' (Wyly and Hammel, 2000). Surely it is a sign of the scale and continuing threat of gentrification in

Chicago that 'social preservationists' now want to protect the perceived authenticity that real estate corporations and media marketed to them?

The eviction of critical perspectives is very serious for those whose lives are affected by reinvestment designed for the middle-class colonization of urban neighbourhoods. Qualitative evidence establishes beyond dispute that gentrification initiates a disruption of community and a crisis of affordable housing for working-class people — how could it be anything other than a crisis, given the widening inequalities produced by the system of uneven capital flows upon which gentrification flourishes? Furthermore, and in contrast to what journalists informed by researchers somewhat less critical of the process like to put forward, gentrification is neither the opposite of nor the remedy for urban 'decay':

> Gentrification is no miracle cure, but nor is it a disease. As Larry Bourne tells me, in diplomatic fashion, 'it certainly seems better than the alternative' of constant, pervasive, apocalyptic decay. As a process and an end result, it's the best we've got.
>
> (Whyte, 2005)

Perhaps a key victory for opponents of gentrification would be to find ways to communicate more effectively that *either* unliveable disinvestment and decay *or* reinvestment and displacement is actually a *false choice* for low-income communities (DeFilippis, 2004: 89), and that progress begins when gentrification is accepted as a problem and not as a solution to urban poverty and blight. As community organizations such as Brooklyn's Fifth Avenue Committee have shown (see Slater, 2004a), it is possible to enlist the support of residents of gentrifying neighbourhoods and use research findings to find ways to work outside, wherever possible, the ball and chain of market transactions and insist on the human and moral right that is adequate and affordable housing. And finally, the task for academics interested in resisting gentrification and reinstating a largely critical perspective is best described as follows:

> Critical thought must, with zeal and rigor, take apart the false commonplaces, reveal the subterfuges, unmask the lies, and point out the logical and practical contradictions of the discourse of King Market and triumphant capitalism, which is spreading everywhere by the force of its own self-evidence, in the wake of the brutal collapse of the bipolar structure of the world since 1989 and the suffocation of the socialist project (and its adulteration by supposedly leftwing governments

de facto converted to neoliberal ideology). Critical thought must tirelessly pose the question of the social costs and benefits of the policies of economic deregulation and social dismantling which are now presented as the assured road to eternal prosperity and supreme happiness under the aegis of 'individual responsibility' — which is another name for collective irresponsibility and mercantile egoism ... [T]he primary historical mission of critical thought ... [is] to perpetually question the obviousness and the very frames of civic debate so as to give ourselves a chance to think the world, rather than being thought by it, to take apart and understand its mechanisms, and thus to reappropriate it intellectually and materially.

(Wacquant, 2004: 101)

Notes

I learned a lot from the comments of three referees – thank you for your confidence. The trouble-making in this paper is all my own, but for their ongoing support and encouragement, I thank Neil Brenner, Winifred Curran, Mark Davidson, James DeFilippis, Dan Hammel, David Hulchanski, David Ley, Gordon MacLeod, Kathe Newman, Damaris Rose, Mathieu Van Criekingen and Alan Walks. Finally, I am indebted to Elvin Wyly and Loretta Lees, whose contributions to my understanding of urban issues and especially qentrification have been immense and inspiring.

1 http://members.lycos.co.uk/gentrification. This reference to my website should not be treated as a form of advertising; I discuss it to point out the overwhelmingly critical reactions to gentrification that I have learned about since I launched the site.

2 I refused, though I must confess to being tempted to ask for a year's supply of wine in return.

3 The Tragically Hip is the name of a well known Canadian rock band from Kingston, Ontario – but it's an equally suitable name for a band of scholars promoting gentrification (even if this promotion is sometimes unintentional).

4 For example, one interviewee 'discusses racial diversity and mentions that Charlie Parker, the jazz musician, lived in the East Village for years with his white wife; he speculates that they felt comfortable here. At this point in the early 1980s, despite low-key racial integration, fears about disorder, and low rents, an astute observer could feel a new wave of change' (Zukin and Kosta, 2004: 108). These sentences would be fine, were it not for the fact that Charlie Parker died in 1955!

5 Both the title of the paper and the mention of 'distinction' suggest that Zukin was guided by Pierre Bourdieu in making these arguments, but his significant theoretical framework for the interpretation of middle-class constitution and practices is never fully explored nor deployed. There are in fact subsections entitled 'The anatomy of the block' and 'The synergies of diversity', which seem more of a nod to the rhetoric of Richard Florida.

6 'Because many of the stores stay open until 7 or 8 at night, seven days a week, there are always men and women strolling the block. This evening time is almost a rush hour, with some residents returning home from work and visitors who have come to eat or drink in the East Village pausing to do a little window-shopping. The Ukrainian restaurant, moreover, is open 24 hours a day, and since it spills around the corner, it adds to the block's vitality. The other restaurant, Ninth Street Café, is located in the middle of the block. It attracts a large number of young people, who wait outside for a table for brunch on the weekend. Especially in summer, when Ukrainia's sidewalk tables are crowded and the stores leave their doors open, there is an attractive, sociable, and ultimately safe feeling to the block – all of which is accomplished without a uniform design code or the visible presence of security guards' (Zukin and Kosta, 2004: 106).

7 'Like The Gap, which underwent a full-fledged corporate makeover in the 1980s, these small shops installed large plate-glass windows, used bright lighting, and painted the walls white; their clean lines and illumination accentuated the subtle colors [at Eileen Fisher]' (Zukin and Kosta, 2004: 109).

8 A cultural consumption strategy for the urban middle classes, rooted in public-private historic preservation, setting in motion a capital accumulation strategy.

9 For example, see Caulfield (1994), Podmore (1998), Bondi (1999a), Bridge (2001; 2003), Butler and Robson (2001; 2003), Robson and Butler (2001), Hamnett (2003), Karsten (2003), Rofe (2003).

10 For example, Smith and DeFilippis (1999), Wyly and Hammel (1999; 2001), Badcock (2001). Hackworth and Smith (2001), Hackworth (2002), Lees (2003a; 2003b), Slater (2004b), plus many of the papers in the special issue of *Urban Studies* (2003).

11 'The introduction of more housing and therefore more residents within the city centre can
be defined as a process of *residentialisation*,
whereby housing replaces other land uses.
The integration of residentialisation within city
centre regeneration policy was seen as enhancing the vitality and viability of city centres'
(Bromley *et al.*, 2005: 2408)

12 As I see it, and in homage to the German political
scientist I discussed at the start of this article,
the only positive to gentrification is being able
to find a good cup of coffee when conducting
fieldwork.

REFERENCES

Atkinson, R. (2000) Measuring gentrification and
displacement in Greater London. *Urban Studies*
37.1, 149–65.

Atkinson, R. (2002) Does gentrification help or harm
urban neighbourhoods? An assessment of the
evidence-base in the context of the new urban
agenda [WWW document]. Centre for Neighbourhood Research Paper 5, URL http://www.
bristol.ac.uk/sps/cnrpapersword/cnr5pap.doc
[accessed on 8 February 2006].

Atkinson, R. (2003) Introduction: misunderstood saviour or vengeful wrecker? The many
meanings and problems of gentrification. *Urban
Studies* 40.12, 2343–50.

Atkinson, R. and G. Bridge (eds.) (2005) *Gentrification in a global context: the new urban
colonialism*. Routledge, London.

Badcock, B. (2001) Thirty years on: gentrification and class changeover in Adelaide's
inner suburbs, 1966–96. *Urban Studies* 38,
1559–72.

Beauregard, R. (1990) Trajectories of neighbourhood change: the case of gentrification.
Environment and Planning A 22, 855–74.

Bromley, N. (2004) *Unsettling the city: urban
land and the politics of property*. Routledge,
New York.

Boddy, M. (forthcoming) Designer neighbourhoods: new-build residential development in
non-metropolitan UK cities – the case of Bristol.
Environment and Planning A.

Boddy, M. and C. Lambert (2002) Transforming the city: post-recession gentrification and
re-urbanisation. Paper presented to Upward
Neighbourhood Trajectories conference. University of Glasgow, 27 September 2002.

Bondi, L. (1999a) Gender, class, and gentrification: enriching the debate. *Environment*

and Planning D: Society and Space 17,
261–82.

Bondi, L. (1999b) Between the woof and the
weft: a response to Loretta Lees. *Environment and Planning D: Society and Space* 17,
253–60.

Bourdieu, P. and L. Wacquant (2001) Neoliberal
newspeak: notes on the new planetary vulgate.
Radical Philosophy 105, 2–5.

Brenner, N. and N. Theodore (2002) Cities and the
geographies of 'actually existing neoliberalism'.
Antipode 34, 349–79.

Bridge, G. (2001) Bourdieu, rational action
and the time–space strategy of gentrification.
*Transactions of the Institute of British Geogra-
phers* NS 26, 205–16.

Bridge, G. (2003) Time–space trajectories in
provincial gentrification. *Urban Studies* 40.12,
2545–56.

Bromley, R., A. Tallon and C. Thomas (2005) City-
centre regeneration through residential development: contributing to sustainability. *Urban
Studies* 42.13, 2407–29.

Brown-Saracino, J. (2004) Social preservationists
and the quest for authentic community. *City and
Community* 3.2, 135–56.

Butler, T. (2003) Living in the bubble: gentrification
and its 'others' in London. *Urban Studies* 40.12,
2469–86.

Butler, T. and G. Robson (2001) Social capital, gentrification and neighbourhood change in
London: a comparison of three south London
neighbourhoods. *Urban Studies* 38, 2145–62.

Butler, T. and G. Robson (2003) Plotting the middle-
classes: gentrification and circuits of education
in London. *Housing Studies* 18.1, 5–28.

Byrne, J.P. (2003) Two cheers for gentrification.
Howard Law Journal 46.3, 405–32.

Caulfield, J. (1989) Gentrification and desire.
*Canadian Review of Sociology and Anthropol-
ogy* 26.4, 617–32.

Caulfield, J. (1994) *City form and everyday
life: Toronto's gentrification and critical social
practice*. University of Toronto Press, Toronto.

Clark, E. (1992) On blindness, centrepieces
and complementarity in gentrification theory.
*Transactions of the Institute of British Geogra-
phers* NS 17, 358–62.

Clark, E. (2005) The order and simplicity of gentrification: a political challenge. In R. Atkinson
and G. Bridge (eds.), *Gentrification in a global
context: the new urban colonialism*. Routledge,
London.

Crump, J. (2002) Deconcentration by demolition:
public housing, poverty, and urban policy.

Environment and Planning D: Society and Space 20.5, 581–96.

Curran, W. (2004) Gentrification and the nature of work: exploring the links in Williamsburg, Brooklyn. *Environment and Planning A* 36.7, 1243–58.

Davidson, M. and L. Lees (2005) New-build gentrification and London's riverside renaissance. *Environment and Planning A* 37.7, 1165–90.

DeFilippis, J. (2004) *Unmaking Goliath: community control in the face of global capital*. Routledge, New York.

Duany, A. (2001) Three cheers for gentrification. *American Enterprise Magazine* April/May, 36–9.

Dyckhoff, T. (2006) Let's move to … Kilburn, north-west London. *The Guardian Weekend* 4 February, 76–7.

Florida, R. (2002) *The rise of the creative class*. Basic Books, New York.

Florida, R. (2006) The keys to the city. *The Philadelphia Inquirer* 22 January.

Freeman, L. (2005) Displacement or succession? Residential mobility in gentrifying neighbourhoods. *Urban Affairs Review* 40.4, 463–91.

Freeman, L. and F. Braconi (2002) Gentrification and displacement. *The Urban Prospect* 8.1, 1–4.

Freeman, L. and F. Braconi (2004) Gentrification and displacement: New York City in the 1990s. *Journal of the American Planning Association* 70.1, 39–52.

Glass, R. *et al.* (1964) Introduction. In University of London, Centre for Urban Studies (ed.), *London: aspects of change*. MacGibbon and Kee, London.

Hackworth, J. (2002) Post-recession gentrification in New York City. *Urban Affairs Review* 37, 815–43.

Hackworth, J. and N. Smith (2001) The changing state of gentrification. *Tijdschrift voor Economische en Sociale Geografie* 92, 464–77.

Hamnett, C. (1984) Gentrification and residential location theory: a review and assessment. In D. Herbert and R.J. Johnston (eds.), *Geography and the urban environment: progress in research and applications*. Wiley and Sons, New York.

Hamnett, C. (1991) The blind men and the elephant: the explanation of gentrification. *Transactions of the Institute of British Geographers* NS 16, 173–89.

Hamnett, C. (2003) Gentrification and the middle-class remaking of inner London, 1961–2001. *Urban Studies* 40.12, 2401–26.

Hartman, C., D. Keating and R. LeGates (1982) *Displacement: how to fight it*. National Housing Law Project, Washington DC.

Karsten, L. (2003) Family gentrifiers: challenging the city as a place simultaneously to build a career and to raise children. *Urban Studies* 40, 2573–85.

Laska, S. and D. Spain (eds.) (1980) *Back to the city: issues in neighborhood renovation*. Pergamon. New York.

Lees, L. (1994) Gentrification in London and New York: an Atlantic gap? *Housing Studies* 9.2, 199–217.

Lees, L. (2003a) Visions of 'urban renaissance': the Urban Task Force Report and the Urban White Paper. In R. Imrie and M. Raco (eds.), *Urban renaissance? New Labour, community and urban policy*. Policy Press, Bristol.

Lees, L. (2003b) Policy (re)turns: gentrification research and urban policy – urban policy and gentrification research. *Environment and Planning A* 35, 571–4.

Ley, D. (1980) Liberal ideology and the post-industrial city. *Annals of the Association of American Geographers* 70, 238–58.

Ley, D. (1987) The rent-gap revisited. *Annals of the Association of American Geographers* 77, 465–8.

Ley, D. (1996) *The new middle class and the remaking of the central city*. Oxford University Press, Oxford.

Ley, D. (2003) Artists, aestheticisation and the field of gentrification. *Urban Studies* 40.12, 2527–44.

Ley, D. (2004) Transnational spaces and everyday lives. *Transactions of the Institute of British Geographers* 29.2, 151–64.

Marcuse, P. (1985a) To control gentrification: anti-displacement zoning and planning for stable residential districts. *Review of Law and Social Change* 13, 931–45.

Marcuse, P. (1985b) Gentrification, abandonment and displacement: connections, causes and policy responses in New York City. *Journal of Urban and Contemporary Law* 28, 195–240.

Marcuse, P. (1999) Comment on Elvin K. Wyly and Daniel J. Hammel's 'Islands of decay in seas of renewal; housing policy and the resurgence of gentrification'. *Housing Policy Debate* 10, 789–97.

Marcuse, P. (2005) *On the presentation of research about gentrification*. Department of Urban Planning, Columbia University, New York.

Newman, K. and E. Wyly (2005) Gentrification and resistance in New York City [WWW document]. *Shelterforce Magazine Online*,

Issue 142 (July/August). URL http://www. nhi.org/online/issues/142/gentrification.html [accessed on 23 August 2006]

Newman, K. and E. Wyly (2006) The right to stay put, revisited: gentrification and resistance to displacement in New York City. *Urban Studies* 43.1, 23–57.

Palen, J. and B. London (eds.) (1984) *Gentrification, displacement and neighbourhood revitalization.* SUNY Press, Albany, NY.

Peck, J. (2005) Struggling with the creative class. *International Journal of Urban and Regional Research* 29.4, 740–70.

Podmore, J. (1998) (Re)reading the 'loft living' habitus in Montreal's inner city. *International Journal of Urban and Regional Research* 22, 283–302.

Redfern, P. (2003) What makes gentrification 'gentrification'? *Urban Studies* 40.12, 2351–66.

Robson, G. and T. Butler (2001) Coming to terms with London: middle-class communities in a global city. *International Journal of Urban and Regional Research* 25, 70–86.

Rofe, M. (2003) 'I want to be global': theorising the gentrifying class as an emergent elite global community. *Urban Studies* 40, 2511–26.

Rose, D. (1984) Rethinking gentrification: beyond the uneven development of Marxist urban theory. *Environment and Planning D: Society and Space* 1, 47–74.

Rose, D. (2004) Discourses and experiences of social mix in gentrifying neighbourhoods: a Montreal case study. *Canadian Journal of Urban Research* 13.2, 278–316.

Schill, M. and R. Nathan (1983) *Revitalizing America's cities: neighborhood reinvestment and displacement.* SUNY Press, Albany, NY.

Skifter-Anderson, H. (1998) Gentrification or social renewal? Effects of public supported housing renewal in Denmark. *Scandinavian Housing and Planning Research* 15, 111–28.

Slater, T. (2002) Looking at the 'North American City' through the lens of gentrification discourse. *Urban Geography* 23, 131–53.

Slater, T. (2004a) North American gentrification? Revanchist and emancipatory perspectives explored. *Environment and Planning A* 36.7, 1191–213.

Slater, T. (2004b) Municipally-managed gentrification in South Parkdale, Toronto. *The Canadian Geographer* 48.3, 303–25.

Slater, T. (2005) Gentrification in Canada's cities: from social mix to social 'tectonics'. In R. Atkinson and G. Bridge (eds.), *Gentrification in a global context: the new urban colonialism.* Routledge, London.

Slater, T., W. Curran and L. Lees (2004) Gentrification research: new directions and critical scholarship. Guest editorial. *Environment and Planning A* 36.7, 1141–50.

Smith, N. (1986) Gentrification, the frontier and the restructuring of urban space. In N. Smith and P. Williams (eds.), *Gentrification of the city.* Unwin Hyman, London.

Smith, N. (1987a) Of yuppies and housing: gentrification, social restructuring and the urban dream. *Environment and Planning D: Society and Space* 5, 151–72.

Smith, N. (1987b) Gentrification and the rent-gap. *Annals of the Association of American Geographers* 77.3, 462–5.

Smith, N. (1992) Blind man's buff, or Hamnett's philosophical individualism in search of gentrification? *Transactions of the Institute of British Geographers*, NS 17, 110–15.

Smith, N. (1996) *The new urban frontier: gentrification and the revanchist city.* Routledge, London.

Smith, N. (2002) New globalism, new urbanism: gentrification as global urban strategy. *Antipode* 34, 427–50.

Smith, N. (2005) There's no such thing as a natural disaster. *Understanding Katrina: perspectives from the social sciences.* Social Science Research Council. http://understandingkatrina.ssrc.org/Smith/ [accessed 8 February 2006].

Smith, N. and J. DeFilippis (1999) The reassertion of economics: 1990s gentrification in the Lower East Side. *International Journal of Urban and Regional Research* 23, 638–53.

Smith, N. and P. Williams (eds.) (1986) *Gentrification of the city.* Allen and Unwin, London.

Sumka, H. (1979) Neighborhood revitalization and displacement: a review of the evidence. *Journal of the American Planning Association* 45, 480–7.

Tallon, A. and R. Bromley (2004) Exploring the attractions of city centre living: evidence and policy implications in British cities. *Geoforum* 35.6, 771–87.

Tickell, A. and J. Peck (2003) Making global rules: globalisation or neoliberalization? In J. Peck and H.W.C. Yeung (eds.), *Remaking the global economy.* Sage, London.

van Criekingen, M. (2006) Migration and the effects of gentrification: a Brussels perspective. Unpublished manuscript, Department of Human Geography. Universite Libre de Bruxelles, Belgium.

van Weesep, J. (1994) Gentrification as a research frontier. *Progress in Human Geography* 18, 74–83.

Wacquant, L. (2004) Critical thought as solvent of *doxa*. *Constellations* 11.1, 97–101.

Whyte, M. (2005) Less crime, busy streets are bad things? *The Toronto Star* 4 December.

Wyly, E. and D. Hammel (1999) Islands of decay in seas of renewal: urban policy and the resurgence of gentrification. *Housing Policy Debate* 10, 711–71.

Wyly, E. and D. Hammel (2000) Capital's metropolis: Chicago and the transformation of American housing policy. *Geografiska Annaler B* 82.4, 181–206.

Wyly, E. and D. Hammel (2001) Gentrification, housing policy, and the new context of urban redevelopment. In K. Fox-Gotham (ed.), *Critical perspectives on urban redevelopment*, Vol. 6, Elsevier Science, New York.

Zukin, S. (1982) *Loft living: culture and capital in urban change*. Rutgers University Press, New Brunswick, NJ.

Zukin, S. and E. Kosta (2004) Bourdieu Off-Broadway: managing distinction on a shopping block in the East Village. *City and Community* 3.2, 101–14.

40

"In the Face of Gentrification: Conclusion"

From *In the Face of Gentrification: Case Studies of Local Efforts to Mitigate Displacement* (2006)

Diane K. Levy, Jennifer Comey and Sandra Padilla

A range of approaches has been taken to address affordable housing needs in six diverse neighborhoods located across the country. The six neighborhoods represent the spectrum of gentrification and housing market pressures. Whether housing practitioners in these neighborhoods referred to housing market pressures and accompanying neighborhood change as revitalization or gentrification—as a positive or negative situation or a complicated mix of both—most agreed on the need to balance the strengthening housing market with affordable housing provisions so that lower-income residents are not displaced.

We draw from the case studies lessons related to the three types of strategies to reduce gentrification-related displacement: affordable housing production, affordable housing retention, and asset building. We also consider a number of cross-cutting issues important to strategy implementation: land availability; the role of city government; the role of community members; and the importance of economic development.

DISPLACEMENT MITIGATION STRATEGIES

not too late

Our findings begin with the fact that none of the practitioners believed it was too late to implement some type of affordable housing strategy. Even in later-stage neighborhoods, such as Central Area and Uptown, building or retaining affordable housing stock was still possible, though constrained. Figure 40.1 offers an overview of findings by strategy type and gentrification stage with regards to feasibility and implementation.[1]

Affordable housing production

Housing production is the key approach to addressing affordable housing needs in each of the six sites, regardless of the stage of the local housing market. The emphasis on production might be due in part to the relative ease of building new or rehabilitating existing housing units compared to retaining existing affordable housing. While production is common across the case study sites, the way in which projects are implemented is shaped by the local context. Housing production tends to focus less on incumbent residents than retention strategies. By focusing on increasing the affordable housing stock, production can mitigate exclusionary displacement, though it also benefits current residents who might move into new affordable rental or homeownership properties.

Two primary, and related, factors affecting housing production implementation are land availability and the stage of gentrification. As a neighborhood's housing market begins to gain strength, most of the units produced can be affordable because land costs are still relatively low and developable parcels are still relatively plentiful. In such a market environment, the motivation for housing development stems from neighborhood investment. Residents want to see their neighborhood improve while they, community based organizations and the city hope that initial investments lead to additional private investments for further revitalization. Under these conditions, it is feasible for nonprofit developers and niche for-profit developers to produce affordable housing. Their investment can serve as evidence to other builders that the financial risk is

	Stage of Gentrification		
	Early →	Middle →	Late
Affordable housing production strategies	Feasible Affordable housing	→	Constrained Mixed-income housing
Affordable housing retention strategies	Feasible Retain individual homes	→	Feasible Retain multi-unit properties
Asset-building strategies	Feasible Effective	→	Feasible Less effective

Figure 40.1 Housing strategy by stage of gentrification

sufficiently low and interest in the neighborhood is sufficiently high to make additional activity worthwhile. Bartlett Park and the Midtown areas in St. Petersburg are examples where land is available, new housing is affordable, and most people hope that additional investments will lead to both residential and commercial improvements.

In neighborhoods with strengthening or strong housing markets, high land prices constrain the number of new affordable units that can be built and the role of nonprofit developers in housing production. In such areas, nonprofit developers might partner with for-profit developers on mixed-income housing projects, leveraging the demand for market-rate housing and retail and commercial businesses to help finance affordable units. Community and city support for low-income housing can help motivate entities to build affordable housing. Inclusionary zoning regulations, for example, can encourage or require for-profit developers to include affordable units in their own projects. As we saw in Los Angeles's Figueroa Corridor, people anticipate a turn to the mixed-use and mixed-income models of development in the near future due to the increasing costs of housing and land. In Central Area of Seattle and in Chicago's Uptown, such development already is taking place.

Affordable housing retention

Most sites also employed strategies to retain existing affordable housing stock. In many instances, retention strategies focused on ensuring the continued affordability of housing units and the ability of current residents to remain in their homes and neighborhood—housing retention can mitigate secondary displacement of residents.

In neighborhoods beginning to experience increasing housing costs, retention efforts can strengthen the affordable housing stock through assisting residents with home improvements so that they can remain in their homes. The concern is not necessarily one of affordable housing supply. Such an approach tends to focus on already existing homeowners. Improvements help stabilize a neighborhood for current residents as well as send visual signals that investment is occurring, which in turn can attract additional investment. Early on, retention is often targeted to individual housing units or small blocks of units rather than larger-scale efforts. Until the housing market accelerates, there is not much concern with retaining large quantities of affordable housing stock—housing already in supply.

Affordable housing retention efforts often intensify once land costs increase and the available parcels diminish—and concern with the loss of affordable housing units becomes widespread. Retention strategies in stronger housing markets often target rental units. In Central Area, the CDC is looking into purchasing additional property-based Section 8 developments as they become eligible to opt out of the program, and as production opportunities wane due to high costs. Uptown offers a slightly different example of retention efforts. There, organizations anticipated future pressures on affordable housing and converted a number of privately owned affordable properties to nonprofit ownership before housing and development prices rose significantly.

Asset building

Asset building strategies, also used in each of the six sites, play a complementary role to production and retention approaches. The goal is to increase individuals' assets so that they have increased ability to address housing and other needs, making them less at the mercy of housing market changes. Individual development accounts (IDAs) and programs to increase homeownership are examples of such efforts. Alone, asset building efforts are unlikely to have a broad impact in a community, though certainly they are important for individual participants. In combination with other approaches, they can strengthen overall displacement mitigation efforts.

The implementation of asset-building approaches is not as affected by stage of gentrification as other strategies, production in particular. Programs related to asset building can be carried out regardless of land or property costs, although the outcome of such efforts can be greatly affected by the strength of the housing market. Whereas participants might be able to use IDA savings toward the purchase of a home in an area before prices increase, once prices are high, they are less likely to be able to do so.

CROSS-CUTTING LESSONS

The study sites differed from each other in many ways, but together they suggest a number of lessons that are important regardless of city size, housing market strength, or stage of gentrification.

Land availability is essential

The availability of developable land parcels is a factor for entities addressing affordable housing and displacement mitigation, regardless of the strength of the housing market. The availability and cost of developable sites will affect the choice of strategy— plentiful land at affordable prices makes housing production feasible; lack of land or high costs can encourage mixed-rate or mixed-use housing resulting in fewer affordable units or push organizations toward housing retention efforts.

People across the study sites spoke of the need to bank land early, before costs become prohibitive for affordable housing development. Purchasing parcels early at low cost can help control future development costs, ensuring affordable housing units for lower-income households. Effective land banking, however, requires foresight. Respondents from areas experiencing later stages of gentrification, such as practitioners in Uptown, spoke with regret of not purchasing land early. In some instances, people spoke of how hard it was beforehand to imagine their neighborhoods would ever experience such strong housing demand, such as in Atlanta's Reynoldstown. St. Petersburg's Bartlett Park is at a stage where the city and CDCs could bank land; it is available and costs have not increased dramatically. This site is also an example of how difficult it can be to convince other people of the need to bank something currently in supply. There is no guarantee that Bartlett Park will experience gentrification in the future. And there is little consensus among interested parties as to when, or if, attention to a possible future affordable housing pinch should occur. In places such as Bartlett Park in which there appears to be time to monitor land and housing cost trends, land banking can still take place in the near future if indicators suggest it should, and if support for such action can be garnered.

City Government involvement is crucial

The case studies suggest that local government involvement and leadership is vital to addressing affordable housing needs regardless of the stage of gentrification. Local government plays a key role in creating regulatory supports and removing barriers to housing development, providing project financing or technical support, and sending a message that affordable housing is an important component of the broader community. Attentive management of regulations and city programs can help create opportunities to affect neighborhood revitalization/gentrification and displacement, or hinder them. If a city does not proactively support the provision of affordable housing and become involved in efforts to manage gentrification forces, it will be that much more difficult for community organizations and developers to do so.

The case studies offer a number of examples. In St. Petersburg, the city was reviewing the zoning regulations and preparing to change them to better reflect local context and development needs. Without the zoning changes, developers in in-town neighborhoods would need to purchase two lots for one new house in order to meet zoning requirements that were established based upon suburban lot sizes. Changing the zoning regulations will allow new development without reducing the number of land parcels in Midtown's Bartlett Park and other city neighborhoods. Seattle's Department of Neighborhoods and Department of Housing were reviewing the Special Objective Area designation of Central Area, which was initially established to disperse additional affordable housing away from the neighborhood that already had an abundance of such housing. Now that housing costs have risen considerably in

Central Area, the city and community residents were discussing removing the designation so that it will be easier to build affordable units. By managing the SOA designation, it might be possible to affect the balance of affordable and market-rate housing production. Uptown provides another example of significant government involvement. Given the voluntary approach to inclusionary zoning established in the city, it is up to local aldermen to negotiate the inclusionary zoning requirements. To the advantage of Uptown's affordable housing community, its alderman is a strong proponent of inclusionary zoning.

Community involvement is crucial

Community involvement is crucial as well. It can help motivate city government and other organizations to support affordable housing initiatives. Community members can identify specific needs of a neighborhood and develop workable ideas. Once developments or programs move toward implementation, community members can assist or block any change.

The community played a pivotal role in a number of the case studies. Figueroa Corridor is a good example of strong community involvement in identifying and addressing local housing needs. Organizations active in the area have organized tenants and trained them on their rights in response to clear efforts to displace lower-income residents. Community involvement is not always in support of affordable housing and displacement mitigation efforts, of course. A pro-development organization in Uptown is against efforts that might slow the pace of investment in the area. Seattle offers an example of courting community support for its housing levies. The city is dependent upon community support for the levies—the levies are put up for vote. The city has marketed the levies prior to the elections. It also designed the first levy to be politically expedient by targeting funds to seniors. Based upon initial success, subsequent levies have expanded in scope to reach broader segments of the population in need of affordable housing.

It is interesting to note that while there is some level of organizational activity in each of the six neighborhoods, resident involvement in affordable housing activities was strong only in the three most gentrified communities. We are cautious in interpreting this finding, but it does suggest that residents are more likely to become involved once housing concerns are pressing. The challenge for community-based organizations is to promote

resident participation earlier so that people are involved with defining and addressing housing needs before options are limited and they feel powerless in the face of market forces.

Displacement is a housing and economic issue

Many respondents across the sites agreed that while affordable housing is needed, it is not sufficient by itself for reducing gentrification-related displacement. Employment and earnings also affect housing (and neighborhood) stability. In order for low-income residents of gentrifying neighborhoods to remain in place and benefit from neighborhood improvements, communities need to develop a holistic approach to mitigating displacement. In many of the neighborhoods in this study, business corridors experienced disinvestment similar to the residential communities. Changes to the housing and business sectors have been occurring reflexively—changes in one support changes in the other. Support for the development of existing businesses, so that they can weather change, and incentives for successful businesses to locate in the neighborhoods can create job opportunities for incumbent residents. Depending upon the wages offered, new jobs might in turn increase residents' ability to remain in their community.

Seattle offers two examples of economic development initiatives. Through the Chamber of Commerce's Urban Enterprise Center, employers are encouraged to offer jobs with decent salaries to former welfare recipients who receive job-readiness training. The program also supports the development of new businesses committed to hiring locally. The businesses receive technical assistance to take advantage of the changing market conditions. The CDC active in Central Area sets hiring targets for minority and women subcontractors for its development projects, and publishes the results in its newsletters.

WRAPPING UP

The term *gentrification* is laden with meaning, much of it negative in the eyes of people for whom it has become synonymous with displacement. Focusing on whether neighborhood investment, increasing land and housing values, and an influx of higher-income residents should be labeled *gentrification* or *revitalization* shifts focus away from what many respondents see as the key issue of concern—balancing the positive and negative changes that accompany increased neighborhood investment. Can ways be found to encourage invest-ment and residential stability at the same time? Are there strategies that might serve both goals? The case studies offer hope in this regard through their examples of community involvement—not to stop change from occurring but to help direct it. Nonprofit organizations and local governments can take advantage of the opportunities at hand to leverage additional affordable housing units from market-rate developments. But to strike a balance, involved parties need to take stock of changing con-ditions on a regular basis and act in a timely manner while it is possible to make adjustments. Starting late in the game in a context of cost limitations will only make it more difficult to make a difference. Attempt-ing to balance the forces at play in neighborhoods by necessity will be an ongoing process.

The one regret mentioned by respondents from areas in later stages of gentrification is that they did not act earlier, especially in relation to land acquisition. Considering displacement early on can help maintain neighborhood balance over time.

Interested parties can monitor changes occurring and plan courses of action rather than respond after the fact when options are constrained. Anticipating change might also reduce later community resis-tance if the people most affected by increasing costs are involved and know their concerns are being taken into consideration. It certainly increases the likelihood that the range of opportunities for future actions will be as broad as possible.

Note

1 The arrows in the chart pointing toward increas-ing degrees of gentrification should not be interpreted as suggesting neighborhood change occurs in one direction or along one path. For purposes of this study, we were looking at neigh-borhoods experiencing changes that at the time indicated increasing neighborhood investment and gentrification.

Plate 20 Gentrification and the Economic Crunch, the Lower East Side 1988. Graffiti that is relevant again 20 years later in the current economic downturn. Photography by Loretta Lees.

Sources of Readings

1 LONDON: ASPECTS OF CHANGE

Ruth Glass (1964) excerpt from *London: Aspects of Change*, London: McGibbon & Kee, pp. xviii–xix.

2 ALTERNATIVES TO ORTHODOXY: INVITATION TO A DEBATE

Neil Smith and Peter Williams (1986) excerpt from 'Alternatives to orthodoxy: invitation to a debate', in N. Smith and P. Williams (eds) *Gentrification of the City*, Boston: Allen and Unwin, pp. 1–3.

3 THE CHAOS AND COMPLEXITY OF GENTRIFICATION

Robert A. Beauregard (1986) 'The chaos and complexity of gentrification', in N. Smith and P. Williams (eds) *Gentrification of the City*, Boston: Allen and Unwin, pp. 35–55.

4 THE ORDER AND SIMPLICITY OF GENTRIFICATION – A POLITICAL CHALLENGE

Eric Clark (2005) 'The order and simplicity of gentrification – a political challenge', in R. Atkinson and G. Bridge (eds) *Gentrification in a Global Context: the new urban colonialism*, London: Routledge, pp. 256–264.

5 THE MATURE REVITALIZED NEIGHBORHOOD: EMERGING ISSUES IN GENTRIFICATION

Phillip Clay (1979) excerpt from 'The Mature Revitalized Neighborhood: Emerging Issues in Gentrification', in P. Clay *Neighborhood Renewal: middle-class resettlement and incumbent upgrading in American neighbourhoods*, D.C. Heath Publishers, pp. 57–60.

6 ISLANDS OF RENEWAL IN SEAS OF DECAY

Brian Berry (1985) 'Islands of Renewal in Seas of Decay', in P. Peterson (ed.) *The new urban reality*, Washington DC: The Brookings Institution, pp. 69–96.

7 THE DEMISE OF GENTRIFICATION? A COMMENTARY AND PROSPECTIVE VIEW

Larry S. Bourne (1993) 'The Demise of gentrification? A Commentary and Prospective View', *Urban Geography*, 14(1): 95–107.

8 THE CHANGING STATE OF GENTRIFICATION

Jason Hackworth and Neil Smith (2001) 'The Changing State of Gentrification', *Tijdschrift voor Economische en Sociale Geografie*, 92(4): 464–477.

9 TOWARD A THEORY OF GENTRIFICATION: A BACK TO THE CITY MOVEMENT BY CAPITAL, NOT PEOPLE

Neil Smith (1979) 'Toward a Theory of Gentrification: A Back to the City Movement by Capital, not People', *Journal of the American Planning Association*, 45(4): 538–548.

10A COMMENTARY: GENTRIFICATION AND THE RENT GAP

Neil Smith (1987) 'Commentary: Gentrification and the Rent Gap', *Annals of the Association of American Geographers*, 77(3): 462–465.

10B REPLY: THE RENT GAP REVISITED

David Ley (1987) 'Reply: The Rent Gap Revisited', *Annals of the Association of American Geographers*, 77(3): 465–468.

11 THE RENT GAP DEBUNKED

Steven C. Bourassa (1993) 'The Rent Gap Debunked', *Urban Studies*, 30(10): 1731–1744.

12 RE-ESTABLISHING THE RENT GAP: AN ALTERNATIVE VIEW OF CAPITALISED LAND RENT

Daniel J. Hammel (1999) 'Re-establishing the Rent Gap: An Alternative View of Capitalised Land Rent', *Urban Studies*, 36: 1283–1293.

13 GENTRIFICATION AND THE POLITICS OF THE NEW MIDDLE CLASS

David Ley (1994) 'Gentrification and the politics of the new middle class', *Environment and Planning D: Society and Space*, 12: 53–74.

14 CLASS DEFINITION AND THE ESTHETICS OF GENTRIFICATION: VICTORIANA IN MELBOURNE

Michael Jager (1986) 'Class definition and the esthetics of gentrification: Victoriana in Melbourne', *Gentrification of the City*, Boston, MA: Allen & Unwin, pp. 78–91.

15 'GENTRIFICATION' AND DESIRE

Jon Caulfield (1989) "Gentrification and desire", *Canadian Review of Sociology and Anthropology*, 26: 617–632.

16 'LIFE ON THE UPSLOPE': THE POSTMODERN LANDSCAPE OF GENTRIFICATION

Caroline A. Mills (1988) '"Life on the upslope": the postmodern landscape of gentrification', *Environment and Planning D: Society and Space*, 6: 169–189.

17 RETHINKING GENTRIFICATION: BEYOND THE UNEVEN DEVELOPMENT OF MARXIST URBAN THEORY

Damaris Rose (1984) 'Rethinking gentrification: beyond the uneven development of Marxist urban theory', *Environment and Planning D: Society and Space*, 2(1): 47–74.

18 GENTRIFICATION: CULTURE AND CAPITAL IN THE URBAN CORE

Sharon Zukin (1987) 'Gentrification: culture and capital in the urban core', *Annual Review of Sociology*, 13: 129–147.

19 THE BLIND MEN AND THE ELEPHANT: THE EXPLANATION OF GENTRIFICATION

Chris Hamnett (1991) 'The Blind Men and the Elephant: The Explanation of Gentrification', *Transactions of the Institute of British Geographers*, New Series, 16(2): 173–189.

20 ON BLINDNESS, CENTREPIECES AND COMPLEMENTARITY IN GENTRIFICATION THEORY

Eric Clark (1992) 'On Blindness, Centrepieces and Complementarity in Gentrification Theory', *Transactions of the Institute of British Geographers*, New Series, 17(3): 173–189.

21 GENDER DIVISIONS AND GENTRIFICATION: A CRITIQUE

Liz Bondi (1991) 'Gender Divisions and Gentrification: A Critique', *Transactions of the Institute of British Geographers*, New Series, 16(2): 190–198.

22 TOWARD AN ANALYSIS OF THE ROLE OF GAY COMMUNITIES IN THE URBAN RENAISSANCE

Mickey Lauria and Lawrence Knopp (1985) 'Towards an analysis of the role of gay communities in the urban renaissance', *Urban Geography*, 6(2): 152–169.

23 CAN YOU GO HOME AGAIN? BLACK GENTRIFICATION AND THE DILEMMA OF DIFFERENCE

Monique M. Taylor (1992) 'Can you go home again? Black gentrification and the dilemma of difference', *Berkeley Journal of Sociology*, pp. 101–127.

32 OTHER GEOGRAPHIES OF GENTRIFICATION

Martin Phillips (2004) 'Other geographies of gentrification', *Progress in Human Geography*, 28(1): 5–30.

33 THE CASE FOR GENTRIFICATION

William H. Whyte (1988) 'The Case for Gentrification', in W. Whyte, *City: Rediscovering the Center*, pp. 325–330. New York: Doubleday.

34 ISLANDS OF DECAY IN SEAS OF RENEWAL: HOUSING POLICY AND THE RESURGENCE OF GENTRIFICATION

Elvin K. Wyly and Daniel J. Hammel (1999) 'Islands of Decay in Seas of Renewal: Housing Policy and the Resurgence of Gentrification', *Housing Policy Debate*, 10(4): 711–771.

35 NEW GLOBALISM, NEW URBANISM: GENTRIFICATION AS GLOBAL URBAN STRATEGY

Neil Smith (2002) 'New Globalism, New Urbanism: Gentrification as Global Urban Strategy', *Antipode*, 34(3): 427–450.

36 GENTRIFICATION AS A GOVERNMENTAL STRATEGY: SOCIAL CONTROL AND SOCIAL COHESION IN HOOGVLIET, ROTTERDAM

Justus Uitermark, Jan Willem Duyvendak and Reinout Kleinhans (2007) 'Gentrification as a governmental strategy: social control and social cohesion in Hoogvliet, Rotterdam', *Environment and Planning A*, 39: 125–141.

37 THE RIGHT TO STAY PUT

Chester Hartman (1984) 'The Right to Stay Put' In: Charles Geisler and Frank Popper (eds), *Land Reform, American Style*, pp. 302–318. Totowa, NJ: Rowman & Allanheld.

38 THE RIGHT TO STAY PUT, REVISITED: GENTRIFICATION AND RESISTANCE TO DISPLACEMENT IN NEW YORK CITY

Kathe Newman and Elvin K. Wyly (2006) 'The Right to Stay Put, Revisited: Gentrification and Resistance to Displacement in New York City', *Urban Studies*, 43(1): 23–57.

39 THE EVICTION OF CRITICAL PERSPECTIVES FROM GENTRIFICATION RESEARCH

Tom Slater (2006) 'The Eviction of Critical Perspectives from Gentrification Research', *International Journal of Urban and Regional Research*, 30(4): 737–757.

40 IN THE FACE OF GENTRIFICATION

Diane K. Levy, Jennifer Comey and Sandra Padilla (2006) Conclusion from *In the Face of Gentrification: Case Studies of Local Efforts to Mitigate Displacement*, The Urban Institute, pp. 76–82.

INDEX